OXFORD

Nihon Kajo
Publishing

AN AGING WORLD

DILEMMAS AND CHALLENGES
FOR
LAW AND SOCIAL POLICY

with an Introduction by Peter Laslett

Edited by John Eekelaar and David Pearl

ISFL '88

AN AGING WORLD — DILEMMAS AND CHALLENGES FOR LAW AND SOCIAL POLICY

£39-50

Lof

OXFORD

Ni hon Kajo
Publishing

An Aging World

Dilemmas and Challenges
for Law and Social Policy

With an Introduction by
PETER LASLETT

edited by
JOHN M. EEKELAAR
Fellow of Pembroke College, Oxford, England
and
DAVID PEARL
Fellow of Fitzwillam College, Cambridge
England

CLARENDON PRESS · OXFORD
1989

An Aging World
Dilemmas and Challenges for Law and Social Policy
© 1989 Clarendon Press, Oxford (U.K.) and Nihon Kajo Publishing, Co., Ltd. (Japan)

ISBN 0-19-8254-091

This text is published under the joint imprint of Nihon Kajo Publishing, Co., Ltd. and Clarendon Press, Oxford. Distribution is implemented exclusively by the Clarendon Press.

ACKNOWLEDGEMENT

This volume is based on papers given at the Sixth World Conference of the International Society on Family Law. The Conference was held, under the patronage of H.I.H. Prince Takahito Mikasa, in Tokyo, Japan in April 1988. Many individuals and organizations encouraged, facilitated and assisted my efforts to coordinate this Conference. I wish to express my deepest appreciation for this support.

For their financial contribution to the Conference, I wish to thank the Science Council of Japan; the Japanese Ministry of Education; the Tokyo Metropolitan Government; the Life Insurance Association of Japan; the Marine and Fire Insurance Association of Japan, Inc.; the Trust Company Association of Japan; The Marubeni Foundation, Social Welfare Corporation; the Heart Foundation; the Kirin Memorial Foundation; the Fuji Memorial Foundation; the Egusa Foundation and the ninety private companies which provided such support. A significant portion of this financial assistance has been put toward the publication of the conference proceedings in both English and Japanese. The publication of the English version has been greatly facilitated by a generous grant for this purpose by the Commemorative Association for the Japan World Exposition.

In addition, I wish to extend my sincere thanks to Mr. John Eekelaar and Dr. David Pearl for their tremendous efforts in editing the conference papers. My only regret is that, due to limitations on the length of the text, only fifty-five papers could be included in this volume out of the eighty that were delivered by scholars and practitioners at the Conference.

February 1989

Ichiro Shimasu
Convenor
VIth World Conference
I.S.F.L.

Contents

VI

Introduction and Overview

by

Peter Laslett

The demographic scene — an overview

Peter LASLETT   University of Cambridge

There are several reasons why it is appropriate that an international meeting on family law and the elderly should have be been held in Tokyo. One is that the Japanese population is aging faster than that of any other country. There are now over thirteen million Japanese people above 65 years of age out of a total of 122 million, and their number is growing at an unprecedented rate. It is expected that there will be 20 million over 65 by the year 2000. The only population which seems likely to exceed the Japanese pace of aging, though in the early part of the next century, is also in Eastern Asia, the People's Republic of China with some ten times the number of people.

Nevertheless Japan is still relatively young among the developed, industrial countries. Slightly above Australia and the U.S.S.R., with a little more than 11% of people over 65, Japan is clearly below the U.S.A. and France at 13%, or England and Wales and Germany, which both have 15%. In 1964, however, there were no more than 6% of Japanese over 65, about equal to today's world average. Japan then is a newcomer to the body of elderly nations, and perhaps for that reason more surprised, perhaps more dismayed even than they are — or should I say we are? — to find the national society transformed by suddenly growing old.

There is another sense in which Japan is notable for the age of its citizens, since expectation of life at birth in that country is at the moment the highest in the world. As of 1984 Japanese males could expect to live for 75.54 years, and Japanese women for 80.18; along with Iceland, the smallest of the nation states, the first example of a national life expectation for one gender of over 80 years. The latest estimate is 80.93 for females and 76 years for males and females together. Moreover another East Asian neighbour, the community of Hong Kong, has joined Japan as its closest rival for length of life.

You may be surprised at this combination of figures. It looks strange that a population in which everyone lives for such a long, long time as in Japan, should have a smaller proportion of elderly people than Sweden where males have a life expectation of 73.8 years and women 79.9, very close to the figures for Japan and Hong Kong. Yet there are almost two thirds more people over 65 in Sweden than there are in Japan, 17% of the whole population as against 11% in Japan and 7 or 8% in Hong Kong. The fact is that there is a demographic trap here. It has been rare until recently for expectation of life to be the most important factor in determining how may older people there are in any population. The fertility record of the population in question has been much more influential in raising proportions of those in the higher age group. Japan, Sweden, and the countries of Europe, indeed all the developed countries, have seen their proportions get so big largely because their birth rates have been going down, until recently going down at very rapid rates. Hong Kong illustrates another factor in the aging process: it has a large immigrant population and immigrants tend to be young.

The importance of falling fertility in raising the proportion of old people is reasonable enough when you remember that as fewer and fewer babies are born, younger persons occupy less and less space in the population and older persons more and more. Nevertheless increasing life expectation does have an effect in causing proportions of the elderly to rise, especially if these increases occur before fertility, and after a long period of decrease, begins to level out at a low or very low rate. This has been the position in the 1970s and 1980s of all the countries which are classified as old, including Japan. Moreover it is important in itself that those in later life should have more years to go on living, since length of life in the later years is highly significant for the phenomenon which will concern me most in this overview of the demographic scene, that is the emergence during the last decade or two of what I shall call the Third Age, using the vocabulary which is now establishing itself for the discussion of aging.

My major task however is to provide family lawyers from all over the world with the bare demographic information which they need in order to take account of aging as a feature of family life. Since ours is a pre-eminently international society, this has to be done with international comparison in mind. Hence the necessity of presenting tables, and the first three sets of figures I have to show you illustrate the facts I have already mentioned. Let us look at them one by one and try to assess their interest for our present purposes.

Table 1 presents us with the ages of various continents and countries in terms of their proportions of elderly persons and spells out the differences between the developing and the developed areas. There are 5.8% of the people living on the globe who are over the age of 65, but the proportions in the developing countries are only just under a third of those in the developed ones, 4% as against 11.3%. Nevertheless there are already more elderly people in the Third World — 132 million compared with 128 million — and by the 2020s this discrepancy will have grown so much that there will be over twice as many. The general reason for these differences and changes is the much higher current fertility of developing countries. But fertility is now falling among them and mortality is falling too, often quite rapidly. The numbers of their elderly in relation to their populations are therefore bound to go up in the near future. Nevertheless the proportion of older people in the Third World in the 2020s will still be less than half of what we shall have in the developed countries.

What stands out in Table 1, then, is that developed societies at the present time are old societies, and undeveloped ones are young. This is evident in the lower panel, where Europe is far and away the oldest continent. The share of elderly people in European populations is larger by a quarter than that in North America, well over twice that in East Asia and four times that in Africa. As for individual countries, Sweden, West Germany along with Britain are the oldest listed in the lower panel of Table 1, and these are undoubtedly the oldest populations which have ever existed anywhere at any time in history. Whether it follows from all this that population aging inevitably accompanies economic development is not a question which we can discuss. It is clear however that a society can age without developing, and that developed societies can differ greatly from each other as to age.

Table 1. Proportions and numbers over age 65, present and expected future

	1980's	2000's	2020's
World	5.8% 259 million	6.6% 403 million	9.3% 760 million
Developed Countries	1.3% 128 million	13.0% 166 million	16.7% 230 million
Developing Countries	4.0% 132 million	4.9% 237 million	7.8% 530 million

Continents and countries, proportions over 65, 1985 and after

East Asia	5.8%	Japan	10%	France	13%
North America	10.6%	United States	12%	Sweden	17%
Europe	13.0%	Australia	10%	Poland	9%
South Asia	3.1%	United Kingdom	15%	Brazil	4%
Latin America	4.3%	USSR	10%	India	3%
Africa	3.0%	West Germany	15%	China	5%

Sources: G. Myers, in Handbook of Aging and the Social Sciences, ed. R.Binstock and E.Shanas, 1984 U.N. yearbooks and various

It can be forecast, nevertheless, that in the long term, over a century or a century and a half, all populations will be old populations, at least as old as contemporary Europe, and probably older, and this irrespective of degrees of development. In this sense, as was the case with industrialization itself, the developed world is undergoing a process of change which will sooner or later affect the whole globe. Bearing in mind the other conspicuous message of Table 1 which will become clearer as we proceed — that the aging of populations is a very recent, a sudden event — let us turn to our second table. Here two further major demographic patterns are evident, the relatively small numbers of the very old in the present group of elderly persons as a whole, and the preponderance of women among them, which gets more pronounced as the years go by.

It is quite evident that such things as those which we have been discussing must affect the family and so are important to family lawyers. Of course aging is only one of the developments with such a tendency, and goes along with the drastic and near universal fall in the numbers of children born to couples and

Table 2. Proportions over 55 by age groups, with gender ratios
With Gender ratios, males per 100 females   various years 1965-85

	55-9	60-4	65-9	70-4	75-9	80-4	85-
Japan (pop. 120,235,358)	4.8% (81)	3.8% (77)	3.4% (78)	2.6% (77)	1.7% (71)	0.9% (62)	0.5% (48)
United States (pop. 238,740,000)	5.1% (89)	4.4% (91)	3.9% (80)	2.9% (72)	2.1% (63)	1.3% (53)	1.0% (44)
Australia (pop. 15,378,646)	5.8% (100)	4.8% (92)	4.2% (86)	3.2% (79)	2.0% (69)	1.2% (61)	0.8% (37)
England & Wales (pop. 49,763,600)	5.5% (96)	5.8% (90)	4.3% (83)	4.3% (74)	3.2% (61)	1.9% (46)	1.2% (30)
West Germany (pop. 61,175,100)	5.8% (86)	5.5% (65)	3.4% (61)	4.6% (57)	3.5% (52)	2.0% (45)	1.1% (34)
France (pop. 55,061,000)	5.5% (93)	5.3% (87)	2.7% (81)	3.8% (71)	3.0% (61)	2.0% (50)	1.2% (34)
Sweden (pop. 8,350,366)	5.3% (96)	5.7% (94)	5.3% (90)	4.7% (83)	3.8% (74)	2.4% (60)	1.6% (47)
Poland (pop 36,913,515)	5.3% (84)	4.2% (77)	2.6% (70)	3.0% (65)	2.1% (58)	1.1% (46)	0.5% (36)
Brazil (pop. 135,564,000)	2.9% (97)	2.3% (96)	1.7% (94)	All over 70		2.6% (88)	
India (pop. 750,859,000)	2.9% (112)	2.3% (108)	1.7% (101)	All over 70		2.3% (100)	
China (pop. 1,003,913,927)	3.4% (107)	2.7% (100)	2.1% (92)	1.4% (81)	0.8% (68)	0.4% (57)	0.1% (45)

Source: *U.N. Demographic Yearbook,* 1985

present in their households, the rapid increase in divorce, in illegitimate children, in one-parent families, in cohabitation outside marriage and so on, all of which must likewise concern family lawyers and which may well have already been dealt with in earlier international gatherings of this kind. Japan has been touched by all these changes, but less so than the other industrial countries.

We know this, and we can discuss these things with some confidence in relation to Japan, because of a feature familiar to those who have any knowledge of the country; the facts have been recorded in considerable detail and, if the national census is anything to go by, with great accuracy. If we ask ourselves why Japan has been less affected by these changes, or less affected so far, the easiest answer is that the family is different in that country, with a different position in the social structure: perhaps the family is stronger, more traditional as many would say. It remains to be seen whether such a contrast will continue, or whether Japan, which is still early in the process of general familial change, will converge with Europe and America. The Japanese social structure, however, is very unlike the European, and the societies of East Asia and Asia as a whole have quite distinctive familial features. Accordingly, convergence between Japan and other Asian countries with Europe and North

America does not seem to me to be in any way inevitable. There is no need to emphasize the really significant point, which is that the figures we are surveying mean different things in very different social structural contexts. International, intercultural comparison, however necessary and valuable, is always superficial, always to some degree deceptive.

Aging is an ineluctable process nevertheless, and so are the two accompaniments of aging which are illustrated in Table 2. In the matter of the predominance of women, there are only eight Japanese men for every ten women between the ages of 55 and 59, only 7 between ages 75 to 79, and less than 5 after the age of 85. In Poland, France, Germany and my own country the feminization of the elderly begins later but is even more marked and over the latest ages two thirds or more of all those alive are women. There is an intriguing exception here in the countries of Southern Asia, where India has markedly more men than women in the 50s and 60s, and even after 85 the two genders are given as still equal in number. I say "given as" because there is some doubt as to the accuracy of these figures, women always being less likely to be properly registered. But the effect seems genuine and its causes the subject of debate: one of the outstanding examples of cultural differences affecting demographic phenomena. To appreciate the further weighty implications of Table 2, it has to be seen along with Table 3, and Table 4 as well. Proportions of the population at later ages have to be taken with expectation of life at those ages. Only thus can we appreciate why it is that the experts so often warn us that the "burden of the elderly" — as everyone calls it — is heavy now and will get heavier. Not only will their numbers in relation to the rest of the population continue to increase, but they will go on living longer into the time when their support is costliest in the means of their maintenance and in medical intervention.

This theme will no doubt come up many times in the course of the chapters in this book. It is my duty however to insist that only a fraction of the whole body of the elderly is dependent in any country. Nearly all of those in the Third Age are healthy and active, or potentially active, men and women. Many of them are highly productive, and very few of the elderly, or even of the old, have to be classified as being in the Fourth Age, that final stage of decrepitude and dependency which so often comes before death. It will be noticed that the numbers of the oldest old are relatively modest in Table 2.

In Sweden, with the highest proportion of the elderly and the most at later ages, those of 85 or over are scarcely 10% of all those over 65. The figure in the rest of Europe is between 7.5% and 9%: in Japan it is 5%. If we take those who are over 80, their share of all elderly comes to 23% for Sweden, 20% for Britain and France, 14% for Japan, 10% for China. But it is safe to predict that the proportion of the very old is due to grow. The crucial question, therefore, is how long people live and will live in the later age groups, and it is to these issues that we must now direct our attention. Future prospects, those which perhaps must concern us most as lawyers, sociologists or indeed as individuals, will have to be left to later chapter.

The conspicuous feature of Table 3 is how close together the current figures are. All the populations recorded are already long lived, or very long lived, in historical terms; the present average age of individuals and of populations, however measured, has no previous parallel in human experience. The competition between the nations as to which can attain the largest average number of years to live from birth has recently begun to lose some of its interest. In the mid 1980s only 2.6 years separated the highest, the Japanese, figure for expectation of life at birth for women from the lowest for an "advanced" country appearing in the list, England and Wales. This difference was a mere 3.3%, and it is safe to say that the value has become smaller since. The figure for Burma, the least developed country represented, was 79% of that for Japan, and survival at every one of the later ages recorded in the table was over three quarters as good as it was in Sweden, which had marginally the most favourable statistics for those of advanced years. Burma is not untypical of the developing world, and in these respects the differences between the developed nations themselves is marginal.

It is true, however, that Poland, the only eastern European society appearing in Table 3, is now somewhat concerned about a tendency for these figures to go down. The U.S.S.R. seems to be similarly placed, and perhaps other nations too, not all of them in eastern Europe. In fact, it is by no means safe to suppose that duration of life will show a continuing rise amongst seniors, or indeed at any stage. Infantile mortality has edged upwards recently in the United Kingdom, and AIDS might everywhere come to threaten the survival of younger persons on a potentially large scale. All such influences affect expectation of life at birth of course, and international competition to get to the top of the table might yet get keener once again, and perhaps a little gruesome.

Nevertheless, elderly people can now rely on continuing in a fairly healthy and active condition for appreciable periods of time in most countries. For males the figure is 20 to 22 years and for females 25 or 27 years at age 55, the birth anniversary which, with suitable qualifications, can be taken to mark the point at which the Third Age can be supposed to begin for most persons. It has been reckoned, in fact, that it will not be long before males at birth in a European country can expect to live a third of their lives after they have left employment, and females, who retire earlier, as much as half. As for the more advanced ages, Table 3 shows that estimates of remaining life lie between 13 and 15 years for men aged 65, and, for women, between 16 and 18. At age 75 the figures are 8 to 9 for men, 10.5 to 12 for women, and at 85, 4.5 to 6 for men and 5.5 to 6.5 for women. I have spelt out these statistics because they indicate a new, a very surprising situation, part of that sudden transformation which has been alluded to. How recently all this has happened can be judged from the next table and from my prize exhibit, Figure 1, setting out survival curves in England over the last 450 years.

Table 4 shows that life from birth has lengthened by 70% in England and Wales since 1891, though most of that growth occurred before the 1950s. Life expectation at later ages has risen by about the same percentage, but more of

Table 3. Expectation of life by gender, at birth and at ages after 55

	At birth		At 55		At 60		At 65		At 70		At 75		At 80		At 85	
	Male	Female	Male	Female	Male	Female	Male	Female	Male	Female	Male	Female	Male	Female	Male	Female
Japan (1984)	74.5	80.2	23.0	27.1	19.0	22.7	15.2	18.4	11.7	14.4	8.7	10.8	6.4	7.7	4.5	5.3
United States (1983)	71.0	78.3	21.4	26.7	17.8	22.6	14.5	18.8	11.5	15.2	9.0	11.9	6.9	9.0	5.1	6.6
Australia (1984)	72.5	79.1	21.8	26.8	17.9	22.5	14.4	18.5	11.3	14.7	8.7	11.3	6.5	8.3	4.8	5.9
England and Wales (1982-4)	71.6	77.6	20.5	25.4	16.7	21.3	13.3	17.4	10.4	13.8	7.9	10.6	6.0	7.9	4.7	5.9
W. Germany (1982-4)	70.8	77.5	20.6	–	16.8	21.1	13.4	17.1	10.3	13.3	7.8	9.9	5.8	7.2	4.4	5.1
France (1980-2)	70.4	78.4	21.1	26.6	17.4	22.3	14.1	18.2	11.0	14.2	8.3	10.7	6.1	7.7	4.4	5.4
Sweden (1984)	73.8	79.9	22.5	27.2	18.5	22.8	14.8	18.6	11.5	14.7	8.7	11.1	6.5	8.1	4.7	5.6
Poland (1984)	66.8	75.0	18.9	23.8	15.5	19.7	12.5	15.8	9.7	12.2	7.3	9.1	5.4	6.5	3.9	4.6
Venezuela (1975-80)	64.8	70.7	20.4	23.5	16.9	19.7	13.8	16.2	11.2	13.1	8.9	10.4	7.1	8.1	5.6	6.0
Pakistan (1976-78)	59.0	59.2	22.8	22.9	19.2	19.3	16.1	15.7	13.1	12.7	10.3	9.8	7.4	7.1	4.4	4.3
Burma (1978)	58.9	63.7	17.8	21.0	14.6	17.4	11.8	14.1	9.2	10.9	6.9	8.2	5.0	5.9	3.8	4.2

Source: U.N. Demographic Yearbook, 1985

Table 4. Expectation of life at later ages, United Kingdom, 1891-1984

	Males							Females						
	0	50	60	65	70	75	80	0	50	60	65	70	75	80
1891	41.9	17.5	11.9	9.5	7.3	5.6	3.9	45.7	19.3	13.0	10.4	8.0	6.1	4.3
1901	48.0	19.7	13.4	10.8	8.4	6.4	4.9	51.6	21.6	14.9	11.9	9.2	7.1	5.4
1911	49.4	20.2	13.7	10.9	8.4	6.5	4.9	53.4	22.4	15.4	12.3	9.5	7.3	5.5
1921	55.9	21.6	14.6	11.6	8.9	6.7	5.0	59.9	24.0	16.4	13.1	10.1	7.6	5.6
1931	58.4	21.6	14.4	11.3	8.6	6.4	4.8	62.4	24.1	16.4	13.0	10.0	7.4	5.4
1940	59.4	20.6	13.7	10.8	8.2	6.0	4.4	63.9	23.9	16.2	12.7	9.7	7.2	5.2
1951	66.2	22.2	14.8	11.7	9.0	6.7	4.8	71.2	26.2	17.9	14.2	10.9	8.0	5.8
1961	67.9	22.6	15.0	11.9	9.3	7.0	5.2	73.8	27.4	19.0	15.1	11.7	8.7	6.3
1971	68.8	23.0	15.3	12.1	9.5	7.3	5.5	75.0	28.3	19.8	16.0	12.5	9.4	6.9
1981	69.8	23.1	15.6	12.4	9.5	7.4	5.5	76.2	29.0	20.6	16.7	13.2	10.0	7.3
1984	71.5	24.6	16.6	13.2	10.3	7.8	5.9	77.4	29.6	21.0	17.2	13.6	10.4	7.6

Sources: S.H. Preston, N. Keyfitz, R. Schoen, Causes of Death: Life Tables of National Populations, New York, 1972, and Social Trends, 1988

the change has gone on since the 1950s and the process is continuing, for women at a quickening pace. With this evidence in front of us, we can understand why it is predicted that absolute numbers of elderly people, and especially the very old, will everywhere go on increasing for the rest of the century, and, for further reasons which I cannot go into, increasing more quickly throughout the first two decades of the next century. Meanwhile those in later life during these future decades — which means those in mid-life at the present time — will presumably go on living in most countries for even longer than their predecessors did.

So much then for the elements of the specifically demographic position in respect of aging as it is relevant to our discussions. Much has had to be omitted, and in fact much is so far lacking in the work of demographers themselves. Figures for expectation of life for instance, especially of the elderly, would be more illuminating for our purposes if they could be given as expectation of *healthy* life. This rather uncertain task has so far been carried out for only a few populations. One of them is France, where at the times of life which interest us, expectation of *healthy* life is estimated at about 90% of expectation of life itself, with the figures for men being rather better than those for women.

I should like now to touch upon a rather less familiar, somewhat technical subject, one which goes by the title, the rectangularization of the survival curve. I venture to introduce it only because two of the gravest of the issues about aging, the aging of populations as well as of individuals, depend upon it. These issues are the following:- whether there is a fixed human life span, and whether the Fourth Age, that of final dependency and death, is going to be abrupt and brief, or long and lingering. My exhibit as you will see, is entitled *Survival Curves for England for the Last 450 years*, that is, since the early 1540's.

A survival curve is the series of points made by proportions of an original birth cohort — here a thousand babies born in the same year — surviving to later ages. The effect which has to be appreciated is as follows. In earlier centuries, survival curves dropped catastrophically for the first year of life, representing the very high infantile mortality then normal, and after the first year of life described a flat, diagonal descent towards the final age group, in the late eighties. As history went on, there was little change in successive curves until the middle of the nineteenth century. Then the initial drop started to shorten and the survival curves began to fill out, to breast upwards and outwards. A tendency set in, it has been claimed, for the survival curve to approach the form of a right angle, to be rectangularized. If you look carefully you will see that a great deal of this swelling upwards and outwards has gone on since the 1940s: the process has been markedly speeding up during our own experience. These findings for England, the first society for which survival curves have been reconstructed for so far backwards in time, are no doubt representative of what has been happening in other of the now advanced societies, and in developing societies as well.

What those who have become known as the advocates of the theory of the

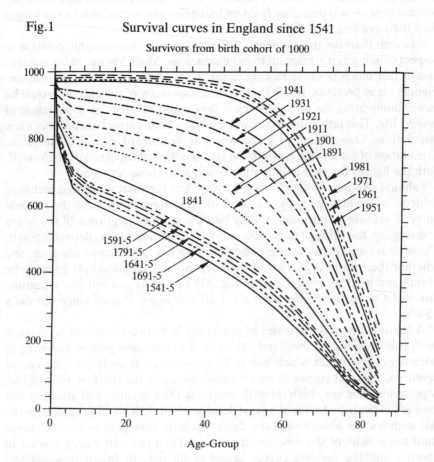

Fig.1   Survival curves in England since 1541

Survivors from birth cohort of 1000

Age-Group

Sources: Cambridge Group for the History of Social Structure, work of J.Oeppen Office of
the British Government Actuary, life tables

rectangularization of the survival curve take all this to mean is as follows. Rising standards of life and marked medical advance have been making it possible for everyone to go on living until closer towards the end of the fixed human life span and for more people to attain that span of years, realizable by only very few until our own time. They believe furthermore that final illness and death will be progressively confined to a few months on either side of the end of the fixed human life span. This phenomenon is referred to as the compression of morbidity, and implies that the Fourth Age will be mercifully short for all of us. Or for all of you, I ought to say, because I myself am already too far on in life to expect to see whether the rectangularization of the survival curve will ever be much more closely approached than it is now, if indeed it is going to be further approached at all.

For the trouble is that no one can yet be certain of the length of the fixed human life span, a concept which has to be distinguished from varying life expectation. Some experts have quoted numbers as high as 120 years or even 140 for the human life span: some even doubt if such a span can be established at all in view of our different relationship with the environment from that of other animals. There is, moreover, a disquieting amount of evidence countering the hypothesis which I have summarized, evidence which seems to show that the Fourth Age is not in fact getting shorter, that persons in their final sickness are not tending to drop off quickly at about the same age — 85 is often mentioned. The inferences which have been made from the tendency towards supposed rectangularization of the survival curve and from other evidence as well, are controversial, and becoming more so. Indeed, if you look intently at the figure, you will observe that the direction of the change in shape of succeeding English survival curves is not in fact towards the top right hand corner, but towards a point to the left of it along the top border of the figure. The underlying tendency scarcely seems to be 'rectangular' at all.

Perhaps the most persuasive reason why we should hesitate to accept the hypothesis of the compression of morbidity at the very end of life, is that it is just what we should all like to happen. My description has had to be incomplete of course, but I hope that these possibilities will appeal to family lawyers as of central importance to their interests. It makes an enormous difference whether grandmother or grandfather is going to be reasonably healthy and fairly independent up to the last month or two, or whether she is going to linger longer and longer, either bedridden at home, taking up much time and effort of the family and especially the wife, or in an expensive institution — a difference in terms of personal relations, of financial support, of hospital accommodation, of medical intervention and so on. It affects insurance arrangements, family budgets and national accounts as well.

We have still to run our fingers over some features of the life of the elderly which, if not all strictly demographic, are certainly included in the results published by demographers. How many of the elderly are widowed, is one of them: how many are divorced; how many live alone, and we must all be familiar with the fact that great and growing numbers of the old everywhere are solitary, though once again I shall have to leave the actual figures to later chapters in this volume. My final topic will be closest to our proper interests, the family relations of the elderly, that is to say, and kinship relations. This issue is usually presented as the prospect of an increasingly unfavourable relationship between the generations, more and more older people having to be supported by fewer and fewer younger ones, who may or may not be related to them.

Before I proceed, I should like to set out some of the details, economic as well as demographic, about the emergence of the Third Age into the 20th century. I shall not take the time to define the Third Age as a condition of life for individuals, how it is related to the First Age and the Second Age, not mentioned so far, or with the Fourth Age which has been mentioned once or twice. But one expression in Table 5 does need explanation if it is to be understood at all. The 3aI in the left hand bottom corner denotes the probability of a man at age 25 attaining the age of 70: it is simply the numbers out of 1000 born surviving to age 70 divided by the larger number surviving to age 25, and hence is always less than one. In demographic terms then the Third Age is present in a society when this probability is more then .5, meaning that a man aged 25 has more than even chances of attaining 70, taken here to be approximately the midpoint of the time he can expect to have after retirement. The figure for men alone is taken because of the near certainty that the figure for women will be greater. There is a further demographic qualification: at least 10% of the population of a country must be above 65 years. There must be in fact a substantial community of elderly people; they must have weight in the whole population of the nation. A yet further sign of its arrival in a country is the appearance there of the only institution which so far bears the title we have given to the active, participating elderly — that is to say a University of the Third Age.

Now there are many more countries than those listed in Table 5 which have male Third Age indicators greater than .5. China is amongst them and Sri Lanka. More will undoubtedly join them soon, as we have seen from the universally rising expectation of life at later ages. But few of the countries which are omitted from this table, which have the required value for the 3aI

Table 5. Countries qualified for the Third Age in demographic and in economic terms

U.S.A.	Finland
Switzerland	Australia
Sweden	Italy
Norway	France
Canada	Netherlands
Japan	Austria
Denmark	United Kingdom
West Germany	Belgium
	New Zealand

Demographic qualifications — – at least 10% above 65 – 3aI of at least .5	Economic qualifications — – approximate Gross National Product per head of at least $7,500

Source: Peter Laslett, "The Emergence of the Third Age", *Aging and Society*, 7, 1987, p. 151.

also have the second demographic qualification, that is over 10% of the population above the age of 65. Moreover it has been judged that none can yet afford to keep their elderly people at sufficient leisure, with sufficient material facilities, cultural and aesthetic facilities, to enable them to pursue the Third Age as it can be pursued within the nations on the list.

There are very rich countries like the Arab oil states which qualify economically but which likewise lack a large enough elderly community to qualify demographically. There is a still further possible condition for the existence of a Third Age, one which does not appear on the table and which affects the oil rich nations. There must be sufficient equality of distribution of wealth and income between classes and age groups for all elderly citizens of a country so as to enable them to pursue Third Age avocations. A rich elite amongst those in later life simply will not do. Perhaps if this criterion were applied to the chosen countries, the select list would shorten even further. I have some doubts about my own country in view of very recent developments. The concept of the emergence of the Third Age is based therefore on criteria which are entirely arbitrary — I have picked the qualifications out of the air, so to speak. The general theory of the Third Age is itself still incomplete and tentative, a suggestive hypothesis as of the present time and nothing more.

You may perhaps agree however that a community which has characteristics of this kind will typify the status, the policy, the outlook and the life style with which family lawyers will increasingly have to be concerned. The interests, the prospects and growing self confidence of elderly people cannot be properly grasped if they continue to be thought of as passive receivers, dependents, objects of welfare. We must leave the Third Age at this tantalising point and go on to look at the marital status of the older part of some of the world's populations.

The figures in this table are intended to bring out the remarkable extent of widowhood among the European elderly. There is an age in every population at which the widowed predominate over the married and it will be seen that, for the countries named, this age is remarkably constant among the men, and very late, about the middle of the 80s. For the women, however, the picture is very different. Widows constitute a majority of all women in the early 70s and, in some areas, even in the mid 60s. This is a noteworthy gender difference and the table demonstrates a pronounced tendency for the age at which widows become a majority to vary from country to country. This variation is cultural. It is due to the differing points in life at which people marry, to differing age gaps between spouses, and especially to differing rates of re-marriage, which is everywhere more difficult for women than for men.

When we remember that elderly women are much more numerous than elderly men, this table makes it clear how large a component widows are in the community we are studying. But widowhood is not the only unfavorable circumstance affecting elderly people. They may never have been married, and they may have been divorced. These possibilities are recorded in Table 8 for the United States of America where divorce is commonest. The incidence of

*Table 6. Age at which widowed persons constitute a majority of the ever
            married, European countries*

	Date	Widowers	Widows
Western Europe			
Austria	1982	85	68
England and Wales	1981	86	72
France	1982	86	72
Scotland	1981	84	70
West Germany	1982	85	67
Scandinavia			
Finland	1980	85	69
Iceland	1980	87	74
Sweden	1983	87	74
Central and eastern Europe			
Czechoslovakia	1980	84	69
East Germany	1981		68
Poland	1978		68

Source Wall, R.W., paper for a conference of the International Union for the Scientific Study
of Population, Berlin, 1984.

widowhood is again evident together with its tendency to increase markedly at
the later and latest ages: the contrast between men and women is transparently
clear. Hence the figures in the first column showing how much more likely it is
that an elderly man will have a resident spouse than an elderly woman. But
even in the divorce-prone United States, the proportion of divorced persons is
at present very low at the later ages. No doubt they have grown since the data
were collected, as they certainly will grow rapidly as younger generations move
into the later ages with their very much higher divorce rates.

As I have said, the final subject on which I should like to provide some
information is that of the numbers of kinsfolk elderly people are likely to have.
These calculations are recent in the study of aging, and I think it important that
all those interested should get to know about them. The estimates are the
outcome of simulating kinship numbers from demographic information, and
they need a little explanation. Since the number of relatives people will have at
any point in their lives evidently depends upon their ages and upon the birth,
marriage and death rates which prevail at the time, it is possible to calculate
these numbers from demographic information.

There are several methods of simulating kinship numbers, and the one used
here, computer micro-simulation using Monte Carlo probabilities, although
rather less reliable than others, has the advantage of yielding the whole
distribution of arrays of kin, for example how many people at a particular age
will have no child, one child, two children and so on, along with similar
numbers for parents, cousins, uncles, grandchildren, any type of kin at any
distance. The ease with which the *absence* of a particular type of relative can be
established makes this particular method valuable for the study of the family
life and the support systems of elderly people. It is clearly very useful to know

Table 7. *Marital Status Distribution of Elderly Population, By Age And Sex, USA 1980*

	Married, Spouse Present	Widowed	Separated or Divorced	Never Married	Married Spouse Absent	Total (Rounded)
MEN						
60-64	82.1	4.6	6.4	5.3	1.4	100.0
65-69	79.9	7.3	5.8	5.4	1.6	100.0
70-74	76.5	11.3	5.0	5.4	1.9	100.0
75-79	69.4	17.6	4.8	5.4	2.9	100.0
80-84	59.9	26.8	3.8	5.4	4.0	100.0
85+	41.2	43.4	2.9	5.9	6.7	100.0
WOMEN						
60-64	62.6	22.6	8.6	5.2	1.0	100.0
65-69	52.2	33.7	6.9	6.0	1.1	100.0
70-74	40.2	46.4	5.6	6.5	1.2	100.0
75-79	27.2	60.0	4.3	6.9	1.5	100.0
80-84	15.3	72.9	3.3	6.8	1.8	100.0
85+	6.4	81.8	2.4	7.6	1.9	100.0

Source: U.S. Census, 1980, public use sample, Table 45, reproduced by Sweet J.A. and Bumpass L.L., for a conference of the International Union for the Scientific Study of Population, Berlin, 1984.

that at age 66, on average, 38% of English women today (all the figures are for women) are likely to be without a daughter, and that this proportion is not likely to rise by more than a twentieth by the age of 88. It is also interesting to know that 100 women of age 66 can be expected to have 48 brothers and 55 sisters between them — about half a brother or sister to each person — but 379 cousins — about four to a person — and to see how drastically these figures fall at the latest ages. In this way we get some insight into why it is that the very oldest are so likely to be lacking in connections, so solitary in the world.

We know from the study of the residential position of the elderly, which is discussed in some of the chapters published in this volume, that a very high proportion live alone and that this tendency gets more pronounced as they pass from the 60s to the 70s to the 80s and to the 90s, when at last the propensity to live in institutions becomes quite common. The solitariness of the elderly varies however from continent and country to country. Japan and China have considerably fewer solitary elders than Europe, America and other areas. Unfortunately we can go no further here with topics of this kind.

There are, however, two preliminary inferences from micro-simulation studies which I ought to mention. First, that it would be wrong to take too alarmist a view of the kin prospects of the old. Kin numbers hold up surprisingly well as life goes by in contemporary societies: though fewer and fewer are being born, more and more of them survive to later ages. The numbers are small, however, and the problem of support so formidable that easy optimism is certainly not justifiable. This is particularly so for middle aged persons who may be liable for the support of longer and longer lived parents and even grandparents, as well as their own children and perhaps their grandchildren as

Table 8. Probable average numbers of close relatives for 100 elderly women: with proportions of individuals lacking such relatives: England, 1980s

	At age 44		At age 55		At age 66		At age 77		At age 88	
	Numbers per 100 women	Props. of individuals without	Numbers 100 women	Props. of individuals without	Numbers per 100 women	Props. of individuals without	Numbers per 100 women	Props. of individuals without	Numbers per 100 women	Props. of individuals without
Brothers	65	45%	–	–	48	57%	–	–	6	94%
Sisters	65	47%	–	–	55	54%	–	–	16	85%
First Cousins	484	4%	–	–	379	9%	–	–	115	9%
Sons	–	–	91	38%	91	38%	–	–	79	43%
Daughters	–	–	97	38%	79	43%	–	–	88	41%
Grandsons	–	–	–	–	156	34%	188	28%	191	28%
Granddaughters	–	–	–	–	147	36%	187	28%	187	28%

Probability of a woman at age 44 having
No brother or sister 17%
Either a brother or a sister 48%
Two brothers and/or sisters or both 18%
Three or more brothers and/or sisters 17%

Probability of a woman having descendants of any type
At age 77 .... 96%

well. The family, in the sense of a network of kin connections, is perpetually attenuating, getting narrower in its sideways spread but at the same time elongating over the generations.

The second result of simulation exercises concerns an extreme case, that of a country whose kinship bonding has always been of the first importance in social life and where the family has always, and still remains, the chief support of elderly people. I refer here to the People's Republic of China, whose kinship figures we have been studying and simulating in Cambridge, in cooperation with the demographers of Peking University in Beijing. We have found that a fall in fertility as drastic as that going forward in China could lead to a degree of kinship attenuation and of kinship isolation which could become catastrophic for the Chinese elderly and serious in its effects on Chinese society as a whole.

Part One

Demographic Background and Future Trends

Introduction

by David PEARL

This part is divided into two sections. The *first section* looks at the developed western world, and the *second section* looks in detail at Japan and China. Demography and History are important tools for the lawyers and the social administrators in the last decade of the present century, and planning policies for the aging population without regard to this information is a recipe for disaster. The introductory chapter to this book by Laslett (See Introduction) sets the scene in a powerful way for the discussion which takes place in the pages of this part of the book. Laslett identifies both a "third age" and a "fourth age", and the distinction is one which must be paramount in our minds. Paillat (Chapter 1) concentrates on the four identifiable factors which have contributed to the aging phenomenon in the western world: fertility, longevity, migration and nuptuality. It is all too apparent from Paillat that the "aging process" is now a significant demographic fact in all developed western countries; and policy makers ignore it at their peril. This applies both to "third age" and "fourth age."

But are these problems new? A detailed study of just one country, England, by Bonfield (Chapter 2) and Thomson (Chapter 3) brings home to us that the problems we face today have some echoes in the past. Bonfield concentrates on pre-industrial England. He asks three questions. First, were the elderly an identifiable legal group in pre-industrial England? Secondly, were the elderly more at risk of poverty than their younger neighbours? Thirdly, was the Poor Law calculated to address their needs? As Bonfield demonstrates, pre-industrial England was a society where the elderly were at greater risk of poverty than those under the age of 60. Some of the themes discussed by Bonfield are developed in his analysis of the later period. In short, the thesis presented by Bonfield and Thomson is that the "problem of old age" is not necessarily a product of industrial society (as is often perceived) but that most of the population, in England at any rate, had already become accustomed to retirement at around the age of 65, well before the dawning of the industrial era. A second theme emerging from these two chapters is that the generally accepted view of "the family" bearing the prime responsibility as carer requires considerable rethinking. The "community" in fact bore the major responsibility, and support for the aged through the family was a "short-term product of industrialization" (Thomson)

Section two looks at the challenges and strategies outlined by Laslett (See

Introduction) in two communities very different from the Western World, and very different from each other; China and Japan. Zeng Yi (Chapter 4) provides a fascinating account of Chinese strategies. He points to the birth control policy which still advocates one child per couple, but which acknowledges that there must be a degree of flexibility in the rural areas. Indeed, data shows that rural couples have more than one child. It is apparent therefore that the process of aging in urban areas will be much faster than in rural areas. However, there is a rural-urban migration which may well reduce the severity of the "population aging" in urban areas. Interestingly, Zeng Li suggests that this phenomenon may help to reduce the need for the State to replace the family in providing care for the elderly.

This theme — State care or family care — is a major component in the debate in Japan. Ogawa (Chapter 5) develops the debate in a seminal chapter using computer-based projections. He examines the impact of aging in the Japanese population on the total medical expenditure both at national and household levels. Programmes designed to support the elderly, both directly through the State and indirectly through family care, can only be developed once the economic and demographic processes are understood. Koizumi (Chapter 6) provides us with a very different perspective to the question, concentrating as he does on population-carrying capacity.

These chapters, written for the most part by demographers and historians, are of fundamental significance for lawyers, social administrators and others who will be required to react to the demographic data which is now available. The remaining chapters of this book explore the various responses which have been introduced or proposed.

Chapter 1

Recent and Predictible Population Trends in Developed Countries

Paul PAILLAT   National Foundation of Gerontology, France

Introduction

Whether a family be traditional or modern, contemporary families look like frail ships, shaken by a tempest. However they withstand in the middle of contrary undercurrents.

The family is subject to the influence of its environment and is modified by the action of three demographic key-factors:

a) natality/fertility

b) mortality/longevity

c) migration,

to which may be added a fourth factor, perhaps more sociological than demographic, namely marriage (nuptuality) and its counterpart, divorce.

I intend discussing these factors as they operate in developed countries, but this individual scrutiny should not overlook the fact that they interact one upon another. The so-called population explosion since the last war has been caused more by the fall of death rates than by any genetic frenzy. Whenever children die less, or less rapidly, the population to which they belong inflates until new generations, willing to curb their own fertility and able to do so, reach reproductive age, a process which lasts 50 years.

When and where fertility is better controlled, natality becomes a social phenomenon, meaning it is governed by fashion and is more sensitive to economic and political ups and downs.

As to migration, the role of the economy in determining its magnitude and fluctuations is well known. Peoples with low birth rates receive more foreigners than they send abroad their own citizens.

Discussion of Individual Demographic Factors

A. Fertility

By *fertility* we mean the frequency of births among a female population in the reproductive period of their life (15-45). In communities where contraception is not practised, the magnitude of fertility is partly determined by age-pattern (when there are many young women, there are many births) and partly by the death rate of women between birth and the reproductive age (15). In contrast, in communities where contraception is practised, the outcome of this behavior may be dramatic, since it is precisely these young women (*i.e.* the more fecund) who try their best not to have children or not too many children: contraception is much more efficient at age 25 than at age 40, because the proportion of deliveries after age 35 is declining rapidly in developed countries.

What is the picture in these countries, and particularly in Europe?

A generalized and sometimes spectacular decline of fertility since 1965, *i.e.* before the "oil crisis", is the common feature. Replacement of generations is no longer possible. Instead of 2.1 children per woman in reproductive age, the necessary level for replacement, taking into account death rate between 0 and 15 and childless couples, is 1.8 in France, 1.3 in Federal Republic of Germany, 1.2 in Italy, and 2.9 in Ireland. Such levels have never been so low in the statistical history of the concerned countries, and it is more striking since this process seems now to be stable. Very often, these low levels followed a sharp fall, as was the case in the Netherlands or in Quebec, formerly noted for their high fertility. In Japan, the trend was less rapid, but it started from a higher level than in Europe.

It is possible to express the fertility level by various indicators. Some may be

Table 1. Total Fertility Rate (TFR) in Some Developed Countries 1950-55 and 1980-85

	Europe							
	Northern	Western			Southern		Eastern	
	U.K.	France	FRG	Nether-lands	Italy	Spain	GDR	Poland
1950-55	2.19	2.73	2.09	3.06	2.32	2.35	2.30	3.63
1980-85	1.90	1.92	1.40	1.55	1.80	2.05	1.88	2.26

	USSR	USA	Canada	Japan
1950-55	2.82	3.45	3.71	2.77
1980-85	2.35	1.85	1.71	1.82

Source: World Population Prospects. Estimates and Projections, as Assessed in 1984, United Nations, 1986

of considerable interest to family law experts. For instance, if we generally use the *total fertility rate*(TFR)[1] which indicates the strength or weariness of fertility at a given date without any forecasting power, we can also compute the *parity-progression ratio* from birth order 0 to birth order *n*. This ratio produces the following question: how many women already having *n* children will have *n+1*, *n+2* ... and so on? In European countries, the striking evidence is the fact that this ratio drops after rank 2. The third child is more and more rare. The interval between two successive births is also an external indicator of couples' comportment; any interval much longer than the average proves birth control practice. When the birth order is higher (3 and over), the interval becomes longer. Incidentally, no statistical attention is given to the extension of multiple childbearings as a result of sterility treatment.

Every postponement of the first birth, mostly after age 30, results in a limitation of completed fertility. In developing countries it is necessary to wait until menopause before computing completed fertility, but there is no such need in developed countries, since there is practically no childbearing after age 40 (or even 35), with the exception of large families, often migrant ones.

The timing of childbearing plays a role which is well known to demographers. For instance, when young couples decide to postpone conception from year *t* to year *t+1* or *t+2*, one may draw a tentative conclusion in observing a higher birth rate during year *t+1* that fertility is on the rise, though it is only a shift in time. No population phenomenon can be estimated correctly over one or two years: we need a longer period.

According to the average age of mothers, the time difference between two successive generations is more or less large. Sociologists may wonder whether a narrow difference is good or bad (for instance, 20 years), but demographers know that narrow difference results in increasing the number of co-existing generations. Nowadays, unions start sooner but not necessarily births!

As a primary effect, a fertility decline reduces the size of families (nuclear type), and later does not allow the replacement of generations and thus provokes the *aging of population, i.e.* the increase of the proportion of old people in the total population. The importance of this process is obvious in developed countries.

A long-lasting fertility decline over generations reduces drastically the number of siblings; thus families, in an extended meaning, take on more and more the shape of a column instead of that of a pyramid.

B. Prospects

Experts are divided as to the future trend of fertility in developed countries. In the medium variant of their projections, UN demographers have assumed in 1984 some new rise in fertility, but many observers of the drop in countries formerly known for their natalist behavior, like the Netherlands, Italy or Spain, doubt this assumption to be valid. Perhaps UN demographers have paid too much credit to Easterlin's thesis on alternative cycles — a low fertility period being followed almost automatically by a higher fertility period — a thesis not shared by French experts.

What is noteworthy here is the fact that even a much higher fertility level (for instance, 2.4 instead of 1.8) would only slow down the aging process, without provoking any rejuvenation and would at the same time start a significant growth in the total population. It seems very unlikely today that future generations of European women will have more children. Stopping the decline would be a very positive step and a goal for a family policy, including for that purpose some pro-natalist features.

Table 2. France's Future Population, in ooo's, Under Three Fertility Assumptions, 1985, 2000, 2010, 2020

	Total	of which 60 +	%	85 +	%	Assumptions
1985	55 064	9 973	18.1	684	1.2	
2000-1	57 883	11 800	20.4	1 059	1.8	TFR 1 = 1.8
2	59 114	11 800	20.0	1 059	1.8	TFR 2 = 2.1
3	60 183	11 800	19.6	1 059	1.8	TFR 3 = 2.4
2010-1	58 766	13 256	22.6	1 171	2.0	
2	61 146	13 256	21.7	1 171	1.9	
2020-1	58 664	15 307	26.1	1 405	2.4	
2	62 589	15 307	24.5	1 405	2.2	
3	66 390	15 307	23.1	1 405	2.1	

Source: INSEE (National Institute for Statistics and Economic Studies): projections until 2040

A higher fertility level is so much the more needed that expected death rate decline after age 50 will start a supplementary aging process at the top of the "pyramid", another example of interdependence between factors.

No family-oriented policy will be successful if it does not take into account expectations of new female generations and it does not re-appraise role sharing between men and women in the households. Law, as such, cannot lag too long behind this transformation of post-industrial societies.

C. Mortality

For demographers *mortality* means the effect of death on a population or the shrinkage of the size of a given generation, caused by death.

It is impossible to study or discuss mortality without paying attention to sex and age. The main characteristics of the fall of death rates since 1945 is the fall in favour of the young, especially during their first year of life, as shown by the spectacular trend followed by infant mortality.

This specific fall explains progress made by the expectation of life at birth, also called 'mean length of life,' an indicator of the current intensity of death, because it is the average number of years a group of people is expected to live

Table 3. Infant Mortality Rate in Some Developed Countries, 1950-55, 1980-85 (deaths under age one for 1000 living births)

	U.K.	France	FRG	Italy	Spain	GDR	Poland
1950-55	28	45	48	60	62	58	95
1980-85	10	9	11	13	10	11	20

	USSR	USA	Japan
1950-55	75	28	51
1980-85	25	11	6

Source: UN, op.cit.

after a given age (whatever it is) if observed age specific death rates do not change. This indicator has no forecasting value; until today, actual recorded figures have always superseded computed ones. Thanks to this fall and its magnitude, the number of people reaching old or very old age has increased so much that belonging to the elder group is now a common feature in developed countries, as is shown by the following French figures:

Table 4. For 10.000 born alive, survivors at age 70:

	Men	Women	Difference
1952-56	4.817	6.220	1.403
1985	6.286	8.286	2.000
Gains:	1.469	2.066	597

A fundamental observation is that medical advances as well as economic and social progress have given to old age issues an importance, but they did not create the so-called "population aging", a common feature of every developed country around the world. The increase in the *proportion* of the elderly in the total population is the crucial demographic fact. Thus, there is a growing number of grandparents who, on average, are younger than their counterparts in the past.

If death rates after age 50 slow down more than between 20 and 50, as is the case in some countries such as the United States, Sweden and Japan, a part of the general aging process will be linked to the decline of mortality, but in fact it will be a new type of aging, leading to the increase of the number, and maybe of the proportion, of the great-grandparents.

Here we should point out that women are the main beneficiaries of this trend, but in countries such as France, Finland and interestingly the USSR, the cost of this benefit is high. Widowhood, and often loneliness, a social phenomenon, are their common lot, aggravated by the low level of their resources, especially when pensions are linked to past vocational life.

Mentioned figures are averages hiding differences. In fact, mortality varies widely according to marital status (married people live longer than non-married ones), and to social milieus. If we combine the different levels of fertility and mortality we observe wide contrasts in family types from one social group to another, contrasts made wider by internal migration; opening gaps between generations. Another criterion that must be considered when studying differential mortality is the type of settlement. Is it not paradoxical that expectation of life at birth is smaller in the countryside than in urban areas? Air pollution and stress are overcome by the quality and the density of medical and social services. But until when?

D. Migration

By *migration,* we mean a change of permanent residence from one part of the country to another (internal migration), or from one country to another (external migration). We will pay attention only to lasting migration, because they are the only ones which have an impact on families.

Internal migration has drained rural areas towards urban areas, or peripheric areas to the heart of industrial metropolis or economic and political capital cities. It had, and it still has, a negative effect on families and on family relationships, especially in areas of departure. Everywhere in Europe, at least when the national territory is wide, as in Japan, the departure of younger generations is followed by a concentration of aged and even very aged people to a point exceeding the local help resources in the medical, social and cultural domains because of the lack of younger people. This phenomenon has never been observed in the past with the same intensity, with the possible exception of limited accidental periods in Europe. In a geodemographic study of the French population we have noted the appearance, then the spreading, of aged areas becoming overaged and covering large parts of the territory: in these units the proportion of inhabitants aged 65 and over may often exceed 25%. At that level, a point of no-return is reached unless new activities come from outside and settle there. Is a 'too much aged area' appealing? This outstanding aging is not only caused by the decline of agriculture; it may be caused by the closure of manpower industries such as mining (this is the case of Wales or Western Virginia) or an obsolete textile industry.

Retired people from the cities, migrating into rural areas may provoke, after an euphoric period, new problems by the addition of this "imported" aging to the local one. Certain tourism-appealing areas are invaded by middle-class foreign retirees: for instance, this is the case on the European Mediterranean seaside.

In every case migration separates generations of the same family. As an example, we see that great-grandmothers live in the deep countryside, grandmothers in the heart of big cities, such as Paris, adult children and grandchildren in the suburbs, because economically available apartments are lacking in the city itself.

External migration and, more particularly, immigration of foreign workers has been a noted feature of Europe during years of strong economic growth when there was a shortage of local manpower, at least for some forms of occupation. In countries such as France and the United Kingdom, this migration has been supported by relationships inherited from colonial times. In contrast, Federal Republic of Germany, after absorbing millions of Eastern Germans, was compelled to import hundreds of thousands of Turks and Yugoslavs; France and Belgium received North African people who today make up the majority of foreign inhabitants. In fact, Islam has become the second religion in France.

For social reasons, some governments have helped wives and children of immigrants to join them and reconstitute families. Demographers observe that North African women have fewer children in France or in Spain than their sisters living in North Africa, a fact which illustrates the social characteristic of contemporary fertility and the pressure of social imitation. In psycho-sociological terms, the position and the future of foreign and mixed families raise extremely difficult issues. Recently in the total number of births in receiving countries, more than 10% were recorded in migrant or mixed families.

Table 5. Migration, a Population Factor in the Early 1980s

	Percent of migrants of total births	Percent of foreign of total population
Luxembourg	38.5	26.3
Switzerland	16.5	14.5
Belgium	15.5	8.9
F.R.G.	11.7	7.6
Sweden	10.2	5.1

Source: *Europe's Second Demographic Transition*, D.J. van de Kaa, Population Reference Bureau, 1987.

On the one hand, economic difficulties offer good arguments for slowing down immigration or even facilitating the return of former immigrants to their own countries, but on the other hand the spectacular population increase from Morocco to Egypt will result in serious political pressure during the 15 years to come.

E. Nuptiality

All over Europe nuptiality, *i.e.* the frequency of marriages among those not yet married, is declining, although some stabilization is observed, and even a slight increase as in Sweden. The current low level proves the existence of a new social model imported from Scandinavia, the so-called "consensual union" or "juvenile cohabitation". Often these unions are of a longevity which should be granted better legal recognition.

Consensual unions and, more generally, a greater freedom in sexual relationships were made possible by the adoption of modern types of contraception and more liberal access to abortion. Furthermore, more women today want to

Table 6. *First Marriages for 1000 Single, 1970, 1984*

	Sweden		England-Wales		France		FRG		GDR	
	M	F	M	F	M	F	M	F	M	F
1970	584	624	1009	1040	915	919	896	974	989	1025
1984	479	514	666	669	562	571	595	607	686	710

Source: D.J. van de Kaa, op.cit.

protect their independence, often obtained through a higher degree of education; some of them are very ready to have a child without willing to be part of a permanent couple with the child's father or with another companion. The so-called "single parent family" is developing; in Western Europe such families constitute 3 to 6% of the total number of all families. In the large majority of cases, women are the head of these families, and they are widowed or divorced. But in the Netherlands, 13% of single parents are women who have never married.

Family, in its traditional meaning, is less endangered by this new fashion, more acceptable to the young couples' parents than divorce, which is more frequent and recorded at a younger age than formerly. In France and Sweden the divorce index doubled between 1970 and 1984; it trebled in the Netherlands (34 divorces for 100 marriages) and the Danish index is 45 for 100 marriages, a record in Europe.

Combined Outcome from Concerned Factors

A. A developing new type of family: the 4-generation type

When and where probable life is over 70 years, meaning that more than the half of a given generation reaches that age, older generations survive longer than their former counterparts and are alive at the same time as younger generations instead of being substituted by them. Simultaneous existence of 4 and sometimes 5 generations is more and more frequent.

The theoretical demonstration is easy, but statistical evidence is lacking. However, the computation of the proportion of men and women aged 59 and 64, and aged 62 and 67, was made possible thanks to a French longitudinal survey covering two large samples (1,500 people each followed during 3 years). In direct line, 18 men aged 59 out of 100 belong to a 4-generation family (upwards): they have at least one parent, generally their mother; an adult child and a grand-child (in most cases, they have more); the same men at age 62 are less often in this position or the 4 generations are not the same: great-grand children have taken the place of the old forefather, but their needs and role are obviously not the same: this proportion is weaker among women of the sample but not necessarily in the population at large. At age 65, 8 men of the other sample out of 100 are also members of a 4-generation family, but there the substitution of the older members for the younger is more and more the rule. (In a sociological and juridical, more than demographic approach, the frequency of the phenomenon could be tabulated by taking into account not only the parents but also the parents-in-law: in this case, men are in a slightly better position because their parents-in-law are, on the average, younger than it appears for women, since in France, as in many Latin countries, men tend to marry younger women).

In every country where the probable life will exceed age 70 (mostly on the female side), a new development will take place: the simultaneous existence of two generations composed of retired people (60-65 as against 85 and over). If we observe the situation from the middle-step of the family, that of 40-year old woman, it is easy to understand the magnitude of role changes within this family. At one and the same time, this woman has to face coping with her mother (and even her grandmother), and meanwhile she is held responsible for her own daughter (or son) who is not yet economically independent. When laws, adopted at a time when such situations did not exist, do not include provisions for caring, they should be amended. Let us emphasize that concerned societies should, in their own interest, help families who spontaneously take care of older parents, rather than directly assuming this care, especially when the very old are dependent and frail. According to population projections, the number of French people aged 80 and over is going to double within 20 years; other European countries will follow the same path. Unfortunately, long life does not mean good health.

B. Decrease of siblings

There are very few studies conducted on siblings in the demographic literature, in spite of the fact that brothers and sisters often play a considerable role in families, on their own or because of their children (nephews and nieces).

Whenever the family climate is good, brothers and sisters provide services, may be members of small undertakings in farming, craftmanship or retail trade and also may be helpful in case of sorrow or grief. Less directly, when childless couples get older, they may consider their nephews and nieces as their "own" children, and this should be taken into consideration by laws governing inheritance.

The average number of siblings depends on the former fertility levels; at 50 or 60 years of age it depends also on differential mortality. In addition, even if lower classes have more children than upper classes, it is not likely that they have as many siblings when they reach the age of 50 as their contemporaries in the privileged groups who had less children. Statistical data is lacking here also, but in France, the longitudinal survey conducted by the National Foundation of Gerontology has provided the following information: 15% of the interviewed people aged 59 (born in 1922) were sole children, 7% had lost all siblings, so the average number of brothers and sisters is around 2 for the total sample, or 2.5 for those who have at least one brother or sister; the frequency of 4 brothers and/or sisters and more is 24%, but they constitute 42% of the total number of siblings in this sample. In the older sample (age 64, born in 1916), figures are slightly different, but in both cases, they are averages hiding regional and socio-economical differences which reflect differences in fertility and mortality.

With the arrival at old age of less numerous generations, the number of siblings cannot but decrease at a point where progressively adult children of very aged couples will take place within a column-shaped structure instead of the former pyramidal profile. Intergenerational relationships are likely to change, because very old people, instead of the help provided by 4 to 5 adult children, will rely only on that of 2 married children with 4 to 5 grandchildren (common model with 3 generations), or two married children, one of whom is retired, and 4 to 5 adult grandchildren, some of them with young children (model with 4 generations). In this new pattern, we have to point out again the scattered localization of various members of the family.

If the death-rate decline is generating more frequent 4-generation families, fertility decline is reducing the probability of a fifth generation family.

C. Other outcome of socio-demographic trend: incomplete families (single parent)

For many decades, the proportion of out-of wedlock births has been stable (around 8% in France), with quite different levels from one country to another (1.6% in Greece and 45% in Sweden).

In 1980, 80% of out-of-wedlock pregnancies (out-of-wedlocks births plus births within eight months of marriage) in Denmark and Sweden, resulted in out-of-wedlock births, to be compared with 61% in France, 50% in the Netherlands, 25% in Switzerland (according to a study made by a Swiss demographer, F. Hopflinger). In other words, having a child and getting married are more and more disassociated. When there is eventually a marriage, it is not necessarily with the child's (or children's) father, and therefore the number of children raised by their mother only is bound to increase, and if there is a man in the household he could be the husband or the companion but not necessarily the father.

Divorce is no longer combining with fertility as it was when, for instance, the new couple wanted to have a child to consecrate their union. Nowadays, it may be difficult for a sociologist to make typologies with so many possible cases. In the long run, what will become of these children born and raised in such a transient environment? Who knows if they will not wish a more stable family for their own children: when the world around is shapeless, a shelter is much praised. Let us remember that fertility started climbing in France during the black years, 1940-44, after a long tradition of low birth rates.

Concluding Remarks

Population trends in developed countries at the end of the XXth century can be summarized in the following way:

- A low fertility, much lower than the replacement level and including a generalized aging process, expressed on the one hand by an increase of the proportion of old people, and on the other hand by internal aging of the working age population;

- A lengthening of life after age 50, without anyone being able to state that quality of life after 80 will also improve.

This latter issue is worth paying attention to. Problems in very old age are not the same and cannot be solved the same way in a young population or in an aging one. 60-year-old "children" cannot provide as good a care for old dependent parents aged 85, as a 40-year-old child with a father or mother, aged 65 and in good health. The scattering of families all over the national territory is limiting exchanges of services between generations.

As long as an increasing number of men and women aged 60 to 69 enjoy good physical and mental health, it is wasteful to reduce their contribution to the welfare of the country and community. Technical skill may become obsolete, but vocational experience, handling of human relationships, job organization, reference and contacts networks are values which should not be cast aside. When it will be necessary to receive and integrate millions of people knocking at the doors of developed countries, when life will be more and more multiracial and multicultural, it will be extremely helpful to draw upon the experience of older generations, even if it is underadapted conditions. In history, young continents such as Northern America and the territory of the Soviet Union faced this challenge and survived: will an aged and divided Europe be able to do the same?

The weaker pressure on the employment market exerted by fewer young nationals, after a lower fertility period, is only a short-run advantage because of the multiplication of the elderly which calls for a complete reorganization of our societies.

We may conclude: population aging will be the socially central issue of the coming century, associated with disrupting population balance all over the world. Family experts and their legal advisers should not overlook a phenomenon which is to modify deeply relations within families as well as relations between families and society.

Notes

1. The TFR shows what should be the mean number of children per woman if age-specific fertility rates do not change.

References

U.N. Demographic Yearbooks and 1984 Projections
Europe's Second Demographic Transition, Dirk J. van de Kaa, Population Reference Bureau, March 1987
Transitions from Active Life to Retirement, a French longitudinal survey, National Foundation of Gerontology, Paris, 1988

Chapter 2

Was there a "third age" in the preindustrial English past? some evidence from the law

Lloyd BONFIELD   Tulane University Law School, USA

In his sketch of village and domestic life in pre-industrial England entitled *The World We Have Lost*, Peter Laslett stressed a particular demographic dimension of that society: its age structure. In evocative prose, he wrote that:[1]

> "... we must still imagine our ancestors right up to Victorian times in the perpetual presence of their young offspring ... In the pre-industrial world there were children everywhere; playing in the village street and fields when they were very small, hanging around the farmyards and getting in the way, until they had grown enough to be given child-sized jobs to do; thronging in the churches; forever clinging to the skirts of women in the house and wherever they went and above all crowding around the cottage fires..."

The prominence of children was not without ramifications. According to Laslett,[2]

> "The perpetual distraction of childish noise and talk must have affected everyone almost all of the time ... incessant interruptions to answer questions, quieten fears, rescue from danger or make peace between the quarreling"

Demographically, ours is a very different world. Children there no doubt are; but in late twentieth century Western Europe and North America a demographic transition has occurred that has resulted in the appearance of the elderly in large numbers.[3] The elderly today are perhaps as inescapable as were the children in the "world we have lost", remaining in the cities, but also populating the rural villages and market towns of modern Europe and America, and in the United States even creating their own villages, the retirement communities of Florida.

Just as the prevalence of children in the past greatly influenced the economy and the character of life in the manner suggested by Laslett's quote, or to speak more technically, just as the youthful age structure had an impact upon the modes of production and reproduction in pre-industrial society, the transition to an older age structure in modern, western society has had a range of profound social and economic ramifications. An important consequence of this demographic transition is that competition between the generations has ensued for economic resources, in particular, the largess of the welfare state. The elderly have formed lobbying groups to secure the survival of the programs of assistance that have been established in the twentieth century.[4] Concern, on the other hand, has been voiced that their share of the welfare pie may be excessive, particularly in light of political and economic ideologies current in some Western democracies.[5] As the cost of maintenance and medical assistance continues to outstrip inflation, as life expectancy continues to climb, as the numbers of the very old expand, those of the "fourth age", the debate is likely to sharpen.

But this chapter is about the past rather than the present. It seeks to elaborate in modest fashion upon the elderly as a social, economic, and most of all, a legal group in the pre-industrial English past. When it has been considered at all, the past has played rather an odd role in the current welfare debate. It can, and has been used, to legitimize a hoped for return to family responsibility for the maintenance of the elderly.[6] What better justification can there be for implementing social policy than an appeal to a glorious past? Yet the interpretation of England's past with regard to welfare has been questioned. In an important article, David Thomson has decried the factual and analytic shortcomings in the work of contemporary historians of social welfare.[7] In particular, he has argued that these historians have failed to see past the beginnings of the modern welfare state and have ignored the longer tradition of community support for the poor that has existed in England since at least the sixteenth century.

In part, the failure of historians of the modern welfare state to consider provision for the poor over time can be explained by the dearth of historical interest in the elderly. Indeed, we cannot even be certain that the use of the terms "elderly" or "aged" or the "third age" to describe those over sixty in the past is not anachronistic. The extent to which the elderly were historically a distinct social grouping is unclear. One way to determine this threshold question is to look to the law, and that is the intent of this chapter. Three issues regarding the elderly in the pre-industrial past will be explored here: first, were the elderly at law considered to be a group in the pre-industrial English past; second, were the elderly more at risk of poverty than their younger neighbours; and finally was the poor law calculated to address their needs? Explore rather than resolve these questions, because the author must concede that the chapter has no pretensions towards comprehensiveness. It will appear sketchy, evidence will be used selectively, in part due to the state of the art. The history of the elderly has yet to be written perhaps because historical interest has lain elsewhere, but also due to a dearth of evidence and its problematic quality.

I

With this caveat in mind, let us begin by considering exactly what the term "elderly" or "the third age" means in a legal sense in historical context. For we must recognize that these terms are primarily the jargon of the sociologist rather than the lawyer. In the contemporary west, old age is both a life cycle phase and a legal status. Here I use the term "legal status" to mean merely that some right and/or responsibility is defined at law as age-related and attaches to those who have reached a threshold age. A simple example of age-related legal status for the United States would be the eligibility for Medicare or Social Security retirement benefits that obtains at age 62 or 65.

However, the former term, "life-cycle phase", must be used by a legal historian with some trepidation, because modern sociologists and psychologists, under whose jurisdiction the concept is reposed, recognize a nearly infinite variety of developmental phases. Their predisposition to do so is not without historical precedent, even from lawyers. Francis Bacon, better known to us as Lord Chancellor than as gerontologist, recognized no less than 18 stages:[8]

> ... Conception, quickening in the wombe, Birth, sucking, weaning, feeding
> on Pap and Spoon-meat in Infancy, breeding of teeth at two years old, secret
> haire at twelve or fourteen, ability for generation, flowers, hayre on the
> knees, and under the armeholes, a budding beard, full growth, full strength
> and agility, grayness, Baldness, ceasing of flowers and of generative ability,
> inclining to Drinesse, a creature with three feets, Death."

Historians who have considered aging in the pre-industrial past, likewise seem to consider old age to be a distinct phase.[9] For example, Keith Thomas, in a seminal article on "Age & Authority" suggests that increasing years in early modern England brought with it recognition; pre-industrial society was imbued with what he calls the "gerontocratic ideal".[10]

A view of the distinctive status of old age in the past has not gone unchallenged. Roebuck suggests it was not until pension rights were established in the nineteenth century that old age was truly an age-related status.[11] But to what extent was the third age a status defined at law? To ask this question is not merely a lawyer's quibble; the fashioning of a legal status is persuasive evidence of the strength of society's recognition of a particular group as distinct. If the "third age" was a legal status, its denomination as such would be a more reliable index of society's conception of the elderly than the nebulous stages concocted by Bacon.

From the very preliminary research undertaken,it would appear, however, that law in the past, at least the common law, recognized no such legal status. It defined only two: minority and majority. The age of transition from minority to majority varied in the past[12] (and continues to do so in modern societies) depending upon the particular legal act involved. Once attained, majority conferred, as it does today, a range of political rights as well as discretion in civil matters, for example, the ability to enter into contracts (and to have contracts enforced against one) or to deal freely with property.[13]

Yet the majority-minority dichotomy may be too formalistic, even for early modern English common law. While the rights-based minority-majority structure was important in the past, one must not lose sight of the economic and social structure of that society. It would appear that in pre-modern England there were three life-cycle phases that had law-based aspects to their definition, rather than merely two. Childhood was the first. Then, as now, parents were legally responsible for the economic support of their children and the economic ramification of their conduct. Childhood, in most levels of society, lasted for fifteen years or thereabouts, until the individual left his or her home to enter the household of another as a servant or apprentice. This movement occasioned primarily an alteration in economic status, but some change in legal relationships likewise occurred. Economic support became the responsibility of the master who exacted labour in return for subsistence, and perhaps wages. Likewise, the responsibility for some aspects of the conduct of the servant or apprentice (or rather his or her misconduct) fell upon the shoulders of the master.[14] The length of this life-cycle phase varied depending upon the vocation. Service or apprenticeship could last for upwards of ten years, and might be passed with a single master or in a series of relationships.[15] It terminated, and a third and final stage, adulthood (for lack of a more precise legal term) began when a servant saved sufficient stake to form his own household, or the apprenticeship term ended and the apprentice found a slot as a journeyman in his particular trade. It was at that time when a status tantamount to our "majority" was effected.

To some extent, then, our present age-based distinction between minority and majority did not obtain in pre-industrial England. Full legal status with regard to property may have been attained at a particular age, but the tutelage of servanthood provided a transition period before full, independent economic and legal status. While one might consider university students to be the modern analogue, at least amongst the middle classes in America, differences are apparent. Students over the age of eighteen, who may be dependent economically on their parents for their tuition or lodging, have no legal or contractual right to support as would have been the case with apprentices and servants in past time, and modern day parents have no legal responsibility for the conduct of their student-children.

Having attained adulthood by moving out of service or apprenticeship, there was no further definite life-cycle stage, no "third age", at least at law. The lack of systematic retirement, as well as the operation of the system of social welfare, the early modern poor law (which I shall turn to shortly) does not suggest a society where age created a legal status; old age in itself did not entitle an individual to welfare payments as it does in modern, western society. While the elderly poor had long been considered amongst the deserving poor, the elderly were expected to work if they were physically able to do so. While the Elizabethan statute regulating labor, the Statute of Artificers, exempted men over 60 and women over 40 from being in compulsory agricultural service, the provisions in the vagrancy and poor laws, even Somerset's infamous act imposing slavery as a punishment for vagrancy, made no exception for the aged.[16] As we shall see, it was physical disability rather than age that qualified an individual for transfer payments from the community in pre-industrial England. Although it may have been recognized that the elderly had a predisposition towards incapacity, advanced age itself did not secure a right to welfare payments.

That age created no entitlement to poor relief in early modern England can be demonstrated by censuses of the poor. Because the Norwich census is the most informative of the late sixteenth century censuses, I shall refer to it in our discussion of the elderly.[17] The census takers in Norwich went into considerable detail regarding the physical and occupational status of the poor. The comprehensiveness of their inquiry clearly reveals that age alone, sometimes even coupled with illness, did not insure offers of poor relief. In Norwich, there were 248 households headed by individuals over the age of sixty who were considered poor. Fifty-seven percent of the households had members within who either worked casually or were considered able to work, and therefore did not receive poor relief. Those individuals who did receive poor relief did so because they were old *and* physically unable to work, not just because they were old.

The Norwich census, for example, describes Wylliam Townsynge, age 60, as "a diseased man that can nott work"; while his wife Margaret, age 64, "spyn white warpe".[18] The couple received no poor relief. Likewise, Maude House, age 60, "a widow that is a desolete thinge and beggethe" received no alms. She lived as a lodger in a house headed by a poor glover, Thomas Wylliams, as did one Thomas Stori and his wife Margaret, aged 75 and 60 respectively. According to the census takers, Stori "begeth" and his wife "spyn webbing". They were described as "veri poor," but received no payments.[19] Clearly, the elderly were expected to work, even Janis House a "widow of 85 years." who earned her subsistence by spinning wool.[20] While it is difficult to determine exactly why particular individuals were deemed entitled to community largess and others were excluded, particularly since some recipients (mostly women) did work, it is clear from the census that mere age was insufficient grounds by itself to allow an individual to poor relief.[21]

If provision for the poor and the text of poor laws did not for the most part distinguish the aged, we may consider other areas of law. A useful subject would be legal capacity. Having achieved majority at common law, discretion could only be limited by mental deterioration. Yet, the loss of discretion, in the past, does not appear to have been considered a function of age. For example, in discussing the descent of freehold land, Littleton, writing in the fifteenth century, and Coke, commenting upon the common law in the seventeenth century, both considered the issue of mental capacity.[22]

Neither raised the question of age as a factor in rendering a person *non compos mentis*. Rather, they focused on non-age-related mental states, lunacy and idiocy. Likewise, John Brydall in his lengthy treatise surveying the statute and common law of mental capacity published in 1700 did not even mention old age.[23] Indeed, none of the cases he abstracted seems to involve the elderly. Swinburne, in his *Briefe Treatise of Testaments and Last Wills*, did consider old age separately in his discussion of mental capacity. According to Swinburne, old age alone did not curtail testamentary capacity; he wrote:[24]

> "Olde age alone doth not deprive a man of authority and power of making testament, (for a man may freely make his testament how old so ever he be, for it is not the integrity of the body, but of the mind, that is requisite and testaments). Yet if a man in his olde age do become a very child again in his understanding, which thing doth happen to diverse persons, being as it were, worn away with extreme age, and deprived, not only of the use of reason but of sense also almost: such a person can no more make a testament than a child."

But how was this mental deterioration demonstrated? Significantly, Swinburne carried on in the same section to state the standard for determining age-related incapacity: if a man becomes "so forgetful that he hath forgotten his own name."[25] It is unclear as to whether this standard was adhered to literally, but if it was enforced in spirit if not in letter, it does suggest leniency when dealing with those whose mental powers were in decline.

This cursory glance at the legal commentators suggests that in past time old age was not a legal status. Age alone did not limit mental capacity to undertake legal acts. With regard to freedom of testation, the elderly could be disabled if they mentally returned to childhood, but the standard employed to limit was at best nebulous. Furthermore, there was no concept akin to the modern conservatorship in pre-industrial England, which if it could be routinely implemented, as in modern law, could serve to limit freedom of disposition in the third age. While guardianship was available and might be employed in cases where an elderly person became senile, it is clear from its nature that its thrust was not towards the old, but the idiot. At least as early as the reign of Edward II (1307-1327), the King claimed custody over the lands of "natural fools" holding the profits to his own use for the life of the incapacitated person. The writ *idiot inquirendo* established a procedure whereby a jury would be assembled to determine whether the individual was "sufficiently witted to dispose of his own lands with discretion or not".[26] If the jury found the person an idiot, they were to say first whether he had alientated land while so impaired, secondly whether he held other lands and in what tenure, and finally who was his next heir. Return was to be made to Chancery. The king would then take the land and person of the idiot into his hands, and presumably sell it as if it was the wardship of a minor. While reported cases touching the writ exist, there is practically no mention of the action being used against the elderly.[27] In short, this action was not a nascent form of conservatorship employed as at modern law to remove management of legal affairs from the elderly.

Here I am arguing not that old age brought with it no change in role, but rather that the transition had no basis at law. No doubt some individuals may have been cognizant of their own aging process. For example, Ralph Josselin, a seventeenth-century Essex clergyman, seems to have recognized that he was approaching a different phase. Towards the end of his life, Josselin's concerns moved away from his parishioners and contemporary political events to his family and his own health. He wrote in his diary: "Drought continues. the disorders of my family doleful. lord helpe mee with patience to weare out my dayes"; "much troubled with my legs and back with pains. it may bee god doth it to better my soul. that is my hope. and it may bee, yet revive my old age."[28] Still, he retained his position as vicar until his death. It is no doubt significant that retirement in past time was almost exclusively voluntary, and more common in vocations where physical labour was required. Josselin could continue as vicar, because canon law recognized no retirement age for clerics. Indeed, archbishops were appointed to vacant sees in their seventies.[29] Likewise there is no evidence to suggest that crown officers such as judges were removed, voluntarily or otherwise, at any particular age.

II

The argument thus far has been that old age in the pre-industrial past was not a legal status. Whether one would therefore wish to argue that, because law did not recognize advancing age as a determinant of legal status, as does modern society, old age was not as distinct a phase of the life-cycle as it is today depends upon the strength of one's views of law as an arbitrator of society and culture. Here I wish merely to suggest a fundamental divergence between our society's concept of the elderly and that which obtained in pre-industrial England: we are unable either directly or otherwise to find legal qualities for the definition of "aged". Further work must be undertaken before this definitional quibble of the third age in the past can be resolved, and I propose now to turn to a consideration of the relationship between age and poverty in premodern England.

To do so, we must first ascertain the proportion of the population that was elderly. In *The Population History of England 1541-1871*,[30] E. A. Wrigley & R.S. Schofield have produced an age structure for the English population from the aggregative analysis of parish registers in 404 English parishes, through a technique known as back-projection. Their data establish that the proportion of elderly, that is those over the age of 60, relative to the total population rose in the course of the mid-sixteenth to the end of the eighteenth century from roughly 7% of the population to slightly more than 9%. The movement in age structure was not linear; the quinquennia 1676-1680 witnessed the largest proportion of elderly, when 9.95% of the population was over age 60.[31] To place this figure in some context, the elderly today comprise approximately 16.5% of the population in the United States, 20.9% in the United Kingdom, and 14.25% in Japan.[32]

Thus, the elderly accounted for less than 10% of the population in early modern England, a smaller proportion than they comprise in modern, western society. We may now consider whether they were over represented amongst the poor. Before doing so, a word concerning evidence is required. It must be conceded that given the data available, such a calculation is problematic. In the first place, surviving early modern censuses of the poor were taken largely in towns: Norwich (1570)[33], Warwick (1587)[34], Ipswich (1597)[35] and Salisbury (1625)[36]. Though some urban parishes have been included in the Wrigley/ Schofield back projection, their data are primarily derived from the analysis of rural parishes; London, for example, was completely excluded, although some parishes in Ipswich and Norwich were included.[37] Here I am not arguing that the proportion of elderly derived by Wrigley and Schofield is therefore inaccurate (indeed it comports relatively well with Gregory King's own estimates in 1695).[38] Rather, if the elderly tended to live more in urban areas than in rural areas, then the composite figure for England might be too low a benchmark for the proportion of elderly in urban areas. There is, however, no reason to expect a wide variation in the distribution of elderly between urban and rural areas. Because historians do not live in a quantitative paradise, the Wrigley/Schofield figures are appropriate for comparison with the ages derived from the censuses to determine whether the elderly were over-represented amongst the poor.

Between 1571 and 1600, the percentage of elderly in the population as reconstructed by Wrigley and Schofield varied from 7.32% to 8.0%.[39] For the sake of comparison, let us assume that 8% of the population was elderly. In all four early modern English towns where censuses of the poor were undertaken, the percentage of elderly amongst the poor was considerably greater. In Norwich, 22% of the poor were over the age of 60[40]; in Ipswich, the figure was 14.3%[41]; in Warwick, around 18%[42]; and in Salisbury, 32%.[43]

The figures are even more striking when one counts households rather than persons. In the Ipswich census, there were 115 households in which the age of the head was known. Of that number, 42 or 36.5% of the poor households were headed by a person age 60 or above. Likewise in Norwich, 30% of the poor households were headed by an elderly person. It would therefore appear that age was related to poverty in pre-industrial England, at least in the towns.[44]

Moreover, the elderly poor were in greater need than their younger poor counterparts. In Salisbury, a census of the poor was carried out in 1625. Excluding apprentices, there were 222 individuals characterized as poor. Ages were given for all but 29 persons. Sixty-two individuals or 32% were over the age of 60. The aged poor in Salisbury were in dire straits; they were overwhelmingly (92%) characterized as "impotent." Only 5 of the 62 were sufficiently able to be set to do work. On the other hand, few of the younger poor were in such condition; the aged poor represented 85% (57 of 67) of the impotent poor. Likewise, the aged in Norwich were more in need than their younger counterparts. There were 248 households headed by individuals over the age of 60 who were considered by census takers as poor. Just over 41% received assistance, compared to about a quarter of all those included in the census.[45]

Yet the demographic data on the numbers of the elderly poor derived from the urban censuses which we have discussed must be placed in some economic context in order to confront the issue of exactly how great a burden the elderly poor placed on the community. We must bear in mind that the age-structure of pre-industrial England was more youthful than our own. Take, for example, Salisbury; as a proportion of Salisbury's population, reckoned at 6500, less than 1% were considered by the authorities to be aged poor.[46] By contrast, in Norwich, the elderly poor amounted to about 3% of the population. Those receiving transfer payments were even a smaller number; 102 households with 116 elderly individuals received poor relief in 1570.

It would, therefore, appear from the numbers receiving poor relief, that the burden which the elderly placed upon the community was not particularly significant, at least by modern standards. Proportions of elderly that society found in need were small, and moreover, the level of payment was also modest. Of the 102 households in receipt of poor relief headed by a person over the age of 60, 57 received 2d or less. A further 36 householders received 3d or 4d. Even the most generously provided household, that of William Hales and his wife Katherine who were "past work ...not hable to worke," received only 1s per week.[47] Estimations of the average wage for a labourer in the late sixteenth and early seventeenth century range from about £9 to about £10 5s per year.[48] Assuming the more modest figure of £9, Hales received slightly more than a quarter of a labourer's wage, while the average recipient was given about 5% of that wage.

III

The picture that emerges from our analysis of the early modern English urban censuses is that of a society in which the elderly were at a greater risk of poverty than those under the age of 60. Moreover, the elderly poor were more likely to be in dire need than younger counterparts. Yet, at least in Norwich, the level of need required to trigger poor relief appears to have been very great, and the amount of transfer payment was small, at least in comparison with what a wage earner could expect to make. How the poor made ends meet on such paltry sums must remain a mystery.

The censuses of the late sixteenth and early seventeenth centuries are particularly interesting to historians because they were taken at an hiatus in the history of poor relief, the period when an ecclesiastical-based system of welfare payments supplemented by voluntary contributions was yielding to a community scheme based upon mandatory contributions to what was to be called the "poor rate." It must be recognized that what was occurring was a transition. Although there is considerable controversy amongst historians regarding the generosity of monasteries to the poor, the religious orders did provide assistance in not insignificant amounts.[49] At the same time, prereformation Christian theology provided an impetus for bequests to the poor in wills as an aid to salvation. While the reformation did not result in a termination of the latter, the dissolution of the monasteries of course curbed that avenue of assistance. Although other sources of transfer payments to the poor, such as community aid or family contribution, are difficult to ascertain and may therefore be underestimated, the reformation has been seen as a crucial event in the history of provision for the poor in pre-industrial England because it diminished a major source of poor relief.[50]

Space does not permit a full consideration of the progression of the poor laws in sixteenth-century England, and given the relative proportion of elderly who were poor, one might argue that no discussion of the elderly in early modern England, even one as sketchy as this, should ignore development in legislation. With the formalization of the poor relief policy in the sixteenth century, our two issues, the elderly as a legally defined group and their susceptibility to poverty, may conjoin. Yet a glance at the statutes and a survey of their administration suggests that, in large measure, the aged poor were passive players in the ongoing drama of poor law legislation. Parliamentary involvement with the poor appears to have waxed and waned depending upon fears of disorder, be they real or imagined. While poor laws regularly recited concern for the aged and impotent poor, the timing and thrust of poor law legislation suggests that fears of uprising by the unemployed or underemployed able-bodied — the vagabond — not compassion for the needy, inspired parliamentary activity. So obsessed was parliament with the potential of the idle for disorder, that even slavery was turned to (albeit briefly and unsuccessfully) as a punishment for refusal to work.[51] Yet Somerset's vagrancy enactment of 1547 was not entirely out of character; the existing penalty for a second vagrancy offense was the gallows.[52] Let us now turn to the Tudor poor law to assess its concern for the elderly. We shall begin with a brief sketch of the socio-economic context of a century that witnessed a flurry of legislation dealing with the poor.[53]

The diminution and eventual termination of monastic contributions to the poor in the first half of the sixteenth century coincided temporally with an increase in the numbers of the needy. Like most historical phenomena, the increased number of poor can be attributed to a number of factors, some independent, others interlinked. Among the most significant causes of increasing poverty were three interlinked factors: the rise in population in England from approximately 2.5 million in the 1520s to just over 4 million by the early seventeenth century; a century of price inflation; and rising unemployment. Population increase was uneven from place to place, and the ability of individual local economies to absorb surplus labor varied. In some areas, landless individuals or even small landholders were forced to migrate to urban areas. This tendency greatly troubled government, because the movement of people, it was believed, led to unrest and disorder. A primary aim of the poor law was to compel individuals to remain where they were, and to have work made for them. By so doing, the migration of the vagabond would be controlled.

In addition to the increase in numbers, poverty was exacerbated by certain trends in agricultural production. Perhaps the most controversial in the minds of contemporaries was the enclosure of arable land and its conversion to pastural. This movement had a number of implications for employment. In the first place, pastural farming reduced the need for agricultural labour; and secondly, enclosure often extinguished common rights, such as access to wasteland for animals, the forest for firewood, the marshlands for fish. Common rights provided a means for the income of cottagers and labourers to be augmented, and their loss of common rights, coupled with the depression in the cloth industry in the latter part of the sixteenth century reduced by-employments through which those at the margin of subsistence were able to make ends meet.

The second agrarian factor in the increase in poverty was the movement in landholding which contemporaries called "engrossing." The rise in population and concommitant urbanization, particularly in London, created a demand for agricultural products, with resultant increases in prices for such commodities. Subsistence farmers were unable to profit from rising market prices, and found their income insufficient to purchase commodities which they did not produce. Unlike subsistence farmers, those farmers with sufficient land under the plough to farm for the market, be it freehold or copyhold or leasehold, could reap the benefits of rising prices. The economic squeeze on subsistence farmers in the last quarter of the sixteenth century, capped by a series of disastrous harvests in the 1590s, assisted the efforts of more prosperous farmers in acquiring the small holdings of their lesser neighbours leading to what has been termed "the disappearance of small landowners." While these individuals may have vanished as landholders, they appeared in rural parishes and the towns as candidates for poor relief.

It will be noted that our rudimentary discussion of trends in population and the economy in the latter half of the sixteenth century has largely ignored the elderly. To do so is not entirely inappropriate, because, with the exception of the depression in cloth making, environmental changes probably had little effect upon the elderly. As a proportion of the population, the numbers of elderly declined until after mid-century, when their numbers began to increase.[54] But the contents of poor law legislation strongly suggest that governmental concern was to suppress the increase in what contemporaries called vagabondage, an evil that was very much affected by demographic and economic change. That is not to say that the deserving poor were not mentioned, but what innovation and success that occurred was in the erection of an administrative structure to control movement of the poor. Still, it must be noted that after 1572, a compulsory poor rate was levied to support the poor in their parishes.[55] Because experimentation in provision for the poor occurred first in urban areas, it is to that context that we should turn. London will provide the example.

The initial focus of poor relief in London was upon the problem of episodic dearth.[56] Prior to 1520, the city reacted to poor harvests and high grain prices by public purchases to increase the supply. In 1520, the Common Council determined to establish a public granary and appropriated £1000 to be raised by craft guilds in proportion to their wealth. The movement to a permanent store is thought to have met with limited success as an ongoing institution, but its establishment suggests that the Aldermen were beginning to understand poverty as a continuous, rather than merely episodic, problem, and were prepared to turn to compulsory "taxation" to finance provision for the poor. At the same time, attention turned to the problem of vagrancy and begging. Four surveyors of the poor were appointed to license the deserving poor and to punish those who begged without license. Although the initial regulations did not render the city responsible for relieving the deserving poor, an ordinance of 1533 empowered the Aldermen to appoint persons to gather voluntary collections of alms and distribute them to the poor.

London's focus was similar to what was and what would continue to be the dual aspects of provision for the poor in pre-modern England. The problem of poverty was intertwined with that of vagrancy. It was believed that work was available for those who wanted it, and that the suppression of begging by the able-bodied would require them to take up employment, and diminish the problem of poverty. To establish a venue to enforce the labour of the able-bodied, the royal palace of Bridewell was granted to the city in 1552 for relief, employment and discipline of vagabonds.

Less attention seems to have been given over to the impotent poor. Although the dissolution of the monasteries removed a major source of both provision and shelter for the deserving poor, the city was slow to re-establish hospitals for the impotent poor. In 1544, Edward VI agreed to refound St. Bartholemew's hospital with an endowment of 500 marks if the Common Council would put forward a similar sum. After some delay, a plan of finance was arranged, and the foundation was confirmed by letters patent in 1547. Because voluntary collections were insufficient to support the hospital, the Common Council turned to compulsion. It was resolved that, in lieu of voluntary contributions, "the citizens and inhabitants of the said citie shall further contrybute and paye towards the sustentacon in maynteyning and fynding of the said poore personages the moitie or half deale of one whole fifteenth."[57] In addition to St. Bartholemew's, the hospitals of St. Thomas and Christ's were refounded.

The London system of licensing beggars, employing the vagabond and relieving the poor by a public contribution anticipated much of the national legislation of Elizabeth's reign culminating in the Poor Law of 1597 that remained in force into the nineteenth century. Whether the structure established in London was successful is unclear. Contemporary comment suggests that funds were not properly dealt with, begging continued and, in fact, arguably increased as the hospital attracted hoards of poor persons to the city. However, the action of the capital city was important because it gave royal officials an opportunity to test a particular system of poor relief. Indeed, other towns parroted London's provisions. Bristol, Canterbury and Norwich provided stocks of grain for their poor. Licensing of beggars occurred in Lincoln, Ipswich, Gloucester, Cambridge, Norwich and York. In Ipswich in the 1560s the poor were surveyed and licensed with a compulsory tax inaugurated and a municipal hospital erected. Cambridge adopted a similar system.[58]

Ultimately, however, the urban relief schemes had to be replaced by a national scheme. The increase in poverty was a national problem. Without a national system of compulsory payments to the poor rate, the towns were overwhelmed by the migration of the poor. While the substance of Elizabethan poor laws closely tracked earlier Tudor legislation, the enactment of a revised poor law in 1572 broke new ground in that it directed the collection of a compulsory parish poor rate.[59] In the act, Parliament continued to focus on the evils of idleness, and went to great length to define conduct that amounted to vagrancy.[60] Offenders were to be punished severely.[61] Although the act also recognized the need to provide for the impotent, Parliament did not define the needy with similar specificity, reposing instead discretion to select beneficiaries of poor relief in the Justices of the Peace.[62] Lists of the deserving poor were to be drawn up, and there were compulsory contributions to the relief of the poor in prescribed amounts.[63] "Overseers of the Poor" were to be appointed in each parish on a yearly basis in order to administer poor relief.[64] A wide variety of penalties obtained for dereliction of duty by appointed officials.[65]

Four years later, the Act of 1572 was amended, primarily to tidy up aspects of the scheme of administration. That the act endured for nearly a quarter century was due more to bountiful harvests than to the irradication of the root causes of poverty. Parliament's optimism, however, was illustrated by legislation of 1592[66] that relaxed the severe penalties attaching to vagrancy that had obtained since 1535: boring through the ear, imprisonment and whipping.

Hindsight would suggest that Parliament's action was premature. The following four years were ones of disastrous harvests with the price of grain in consequence rising by as much as 83%[67] Disorder, real and imagined, ensued.[68] When Parliament convened in the autumn of 1597, the first bill read dealt with the forestalling of grain. Immediately thereafter:[69]

> Mr. Finch shewing sundry great and horrible abuses committed by vagrant and Idle persons, offensive both to god and the world, and further shewing the extream miserable estate of the godly and honest sort of the poor Subjects of this Realm, moved for a Committee of this House be selected for redress thereof.

Finch's remarks set the tone for the session. No less than eleven bills concerning the poor were delivered to the committee for consideration.[70] After much debate, amendment and disagreement with the Lords[71] six bills emerged and received the Royal Assent: the first two deal primarily with the maintenance and improvement of husbandry[72]; the third was for the "Relief of the Poor"[73]; the fourth for "punishment of Rogues, Vagabondes and Sturdy Begghers",[74] the fifth, to encourage the building of hospitals and work houses[75]; and the sixth to better supervise charitable trusts.[76] Two private bills dealing with the poor were enacted; one established a hospital in Bristol[77]; the other a college for the poor in Kent.[78]

It has been suggested that the Poor Law of 1598 was not greatly innovative, and merely codified pre-existing law.[79] There was, in fact, little added generosity embodied within them. The act to encourage hospitals and poor houses did not provide funding, but merely allowed land to be settled by private individuals who so desired.[80] Three bills establishing hospitals in Warwick, York and Eastbridge, Kent were introduced but never received the Royal Assent.[81] A bill for the "maintenance of Hospitality, and for increase of all Victual and Flesh, whereby the Poor shall be much relieved" was rejected.[82] Likewise a bill to raise relief for the poor out of impropriated tithes was rejected.[83]

IV

Further legislation was enacted in 1601[84] setting the structure of poor relief that would endure for over two centuries. Contributions to the poor were to be raised through a compulsory parish poor rate and private philanthropy. But what of the aged poor? Our discussion of the poor law seems to have led us from them. Perhaps this is because its concern was reposed elsewhere. If the force which spurred Parliament to action was a fear of rebellion, then one might expect that the poor law addressed the young and able-bodied rather than the aged. After all, what danger to disorder did the elderly create? If the effectiveness of the Tudor poor law is judged by its paramount purpose, the suppression of disorder, Parliament's endeavors were rewarded. Few outbreaks of rioting occurred in the seventeenth century.

The poor laws's aspirations with respect to the aged were less ambitious, and the measure of its success less clear. The elderly presented less danger to order than the able-bodied unemployed, and unlike poor children, there was no future for which to prepare them. Perhaps this is why even private philanthropy did not single them out.[85] As Lord Keeper Wright noted in resolving a case of an answer entered by a guardian of a "superannuated person" in which withdrawal was sought, the answer should stand unlike a case of the guardian of a minor:[86]

> "because an infant improves and mends... and, therefore is to have a day to shew cause after he comes of age; but the other grows worse, and is to have no day."

Notes

1. 2nd ed. (London, 1971), 109
2. *Ibid.*

3. See the introduction to this volume by Peter Laslett, "The Demographic Scene: An Overview" for a survey.

4. For example,in the United States, the American Association of Retired Persons and the Gray Panthers.

5. See the chapter by David Thomson, "The Intergenerational Contract — under pressure from population aging" in this volume.

6. Members and the leader of The British Conservative Party have called for a return to an era where the family supported and cared for its weaker members in speeches too numerous to footnote.

7. David Thomson, "Welfare and the Historians" in L. Bonfield, R.M. Smith and K.Wrightson, eds., *The World We Have Gained: Histories of population and social structure* (Oxford, 1986), 355-78.

8. Francis Bacon, *The Historie of Life and Death* (London, 1638), 275.

9. For example, S.R. Smith, "Growing Old in Early Stuart England" *Albion*, 8, 125-41; K. Thomas, "Age and Authority in Early Modern England" (Proceedings of the British Academy, LXII, 1977) 205-48; Peter Laslett, *Family Life and Illicit Love in Earlier Generations* (Cambridge, 1977), ch 5.

10. Thomas, "Age and Authority", 211

11. Janet Roebuck, "When Does Old Age Begin?: The Evolution of the English Definition" *Journal of Social History*, 12 (1979), 416-428.

12. Thomas, "Age and Authority", 221-25.

13. Bromley and Lowe, "Family Law" 7th ed (1987).

14. Sir William Blackstone, *Commentaries on the Laws of England*, 4th ed. (London, 1770) vol i, 427-32. For example, the master was responsible for torts committed by his servant in course of his duties.

15. Ann Kausmaul, *Servants in Husbandry in early modern England* (Cambridge, 1981), chapter 3.

16. Statute of Artificers: 5 Eliz c. 4 (1562) sections 5 and 17; but see 27 Hen. VIII, c 25 (1536), and 14 Eliz c 5 (1574) where no age is mentioned in the definition of vagabond.

17. J.F.Pound, ed. *The Norwich Census of the Poor, 1570* (Norfolk Record Society, XL, 1970)

18. *Ibid.*, 50.

19. *Ibid.*

20. *Ibid.*, 56.

21. Indeed the "Orders of the Poor" drawn up in Norwich give no special treatment to the aged. "Sixe stripes with a whippe" was punishment for unlicensed begging. E.M. Leonard, *The Early History of English Poor Relief,* (Cambridge, 1900) Appendix III, 311.

22. E. Wambaugh, ed., *Littleton's Tenures in English* (Washington, D.C., 1903), Section 246b; Sir Edward Coke, *The First Part of the Institutes of the Laws of England* (London, 1628), Section 405.

23. John Brydall, *Non Compos Mentis: or, the Law Relating to Natural Fools, Mad-Folks, and Lunatick Persons* (London, 1700)

24. 2nd ed. (London, 1628), 73.

25. *Ibid.*

26. Brydall, *Non Compos Mentis*, 15.

27. At least in Brydall or Coke.

28. Alan Macfarlane, ed. *The Diary of Ralph Josselin,* 1616-83 (London, 1976)

592, 640.

29. Thomas, "Age & Authority", 212.

30. (London, 1981)

31. *Ibid.*, Table A3.1, 528-29.

32. Percentages derived from the "United Nations Demographic Yearbook, 1985".

33. Pound, ed. *Norwich Census.*

34. The surviving census for Warwick is of a single parish, St Mary's, and has been analyzed in A.L. Beier, "The Social Problems of an Elizabethan Country Town: Warwick, 1580-90" in Peter Clark, ed. *Country Towns in Pre-industrial England* (Leicester, 1981), 45-85.

35. John Webb, ed. *Poor Relief in Elizabethan Ipswich* (Suffolk Records Society, IX, 1966) reproduces the census of the poor in St. Clement's parish.

36. The Salisbury census is analyzed in Paul Slack, "Poverty & Politics in Salisbury, 1597-1966" in Peter Clark & Paul Slack, *Crisis and Order in English Towns 1500-1700* (London, 1972), 164-203.

37. Wrigley & Schofield, *Population History*, 38-40.

38. *Ibid.*, Table 7.10, 218.

39. *Ibid.*, Table A3.1, 528-29.

40. My own calculations derived from the census in Pound, ed. *Norwich Census.* See also, Appendix I, 95.

41. My own calculations derived from the census in Webb, ed., *Elizabethan Ipswich*, 122-140.

42. Beier, "Warwick", 58-61.

43. Slack, "Salisbury", Table 10, 167.

44. F.G.Emmison, "Poor Relief Accounts in Two Rural Parishes in Bedfordshire", *Economic History Review,* comes to the same conclusion, but with much inferior data.

45. Percentages on Salisbury derived from Slack; with regard to Norwich, from my own analysis of the Norwich census transcribed by Pound.

46. Slack, "Salisbury", 166.

47. Pound, ed., *Norwich Census,* 66.

48. Keith Wrightson, *English Society, 1580-1680* (London, 1982), 34.

49. W.K. Jordan, *Philanthropy in England 1480-1660* (London, 1959), 59, corrects the amount in the *Valor Ecclesiasticus* (L2700) to around £6,500 per annum.

50. *Ibid.*

51. 1 Edw. VI, c.3 (1547).

52. 27 Hen. VIII, c.25 (1536) was extended by 31 Hen. VIII, c.37 (1540). Arguably the statute lapsed.

53. For a more complete survey, see, Wrightson, *English Society,* ch. 5 and the references therein.

54. Wrigley & Schofield, Table A3.1, 528-29.

55. 14 Eliz. c.5 (1572)

56. This survey of London's response to the poor is derived from E.M. Leonard, *The Early History of Poor Relief* (Cambridge, 1900) 23-41.

57. From the Journals of the Common Council quoted in *Ibid.,* 29.

58. *Ibid.*, 40-46.

59. 14 Eliz c.5 (1572), section 16.

60. *Ibid.*, section 5.

61. *Ibid.*, section 2-4.

62. *Ibid.*, section 16.
63. *Ibid.*
64. *Ibid.*
65. *Ibid.*
66. 31 Eliz. C.10 (1592).
67. John Pound, *Poverty and Vagrancy in Tudor England* (London, 1986), 50.
68. John Walter, "A Rising of the People"? The Oxfordshire Rising of 1596", *Past and Present,* 107 (1985), 90-143.
69. Heywood Townshend, *Historical Collections: or an exact account of the proceedings of the four last parliaments of Queen Elizabeth* (London, 1680), 102.
70. Of the workload, Sir Simonds D'Ewes remarked, "being a thing scarce to be pattern'd that one & the same Committee had ... eleven Bills in agitation before them" *The Journals of all the Parliaments during the Reign of Queen Elizabeth*(London, 1682), 561.
71. According to the D'Ewes, *Journals,* 579-81, 590.
72. 39 Eliz c.1 (1598); 39 Eliz c.2 (1598)
73. 39 Eliz c.3 (1598)
74. 39 Eliz c.4 (1598)
75. 39 Eliz c.5 (1598)
76. 39 Eliz c.6 (1598)
77. 39 Eliz c.31 (1598)
78. 39 Eliz c.32 (1598)
79. Pound, *Poverty & Vagrancy,* 52.
80. 39 Eliz c.5 (1598)
81. The bills for the hospital at York was rejected, D'Ewes, *Journals,* 568, as was the one at Eastbridge, Townshend, *Historical Collections,* 122. The Warwick bill disappears from either Journal after its second reading. D'Ewes, *Journals,* 559, 567.
82. Townshends, *Historical Collections,* 124.
83. D'Ewes, *Journals,* 561.
84. 43 Eliz c.2 (1601)
85. Jordan, *Philanthropy,* 42, found 17% of charitable funds directed specifically to the poor.
86. *Leving v Claverly* (1704) Prec. Ch. 229.

Chapter 3

The Elderly in an Urban-Industrial Society: England, 1750 to the Present

David Thomson   Massey University, New Zealand

I want to pick up a number of themes raised by Lloyd Bonfield in his chapter on Early Modern England, and to look at the period from about 1750 through to the present. Until a decade or so ago, historians were confident that they knew the history of the law and the elderly in recent centuries, but now we are not nearly so sure. A good deal of rethinking of these issues is taking place, and I intend here to report upon these new developments in English history — I do not know that comparable new research and reinterpretative work is being carried out elsewhere.

In demographic terms, the society has undergone major changes and reversals of direction during the last 200 years. The switch from rural to urban residence and occupation was achieved during the nineteenth century for the most part, and this is perhaps the most obvious of the many developments. Less obvious, but highly important have been movements in the numbers of the aged — but we need to be careful here, for it is far too simple to talk simply of an 'aging of the population'.

During the first century of industrialisation, from around 1750 to about 1870, the population became very much more youthful than it had ever been before (Wrigley and Schofield, 1981). This phenomenon has been repeated in most societies as they have undergone industrialisation, and it came about as a result of three key factors. One was high fertility, which in English society, at least, appears to have risen sharply during the earliest stages of industrialisation. A second was declining infant mortality, although this occurred only to a slight degree until very late in the period, towards the end of the nineteenth century in England's case.

Meanwhile, adult mortality rates did not improve greatly, so that the length of life enjoyed by older persons was not very different in 1900 from what it had been a century earlier — the extension of adult life is a twentieth century development. The net effect was an extremely youthful society, in which only four to five percent of the total population was aged 65 years or more: in some of the major cities it was not more than one or two percent. It is from this unusual base that our present 'aging of the population' has proceeded.

The extension of health improvements to younger adults, and more recently still, to older ones, constitutes one of the two major demographic movements of the present century. The other, of course, is diminishing fertility, and together the two have produced the aging we discuss in the various chapters of this book. In the seventeenth and eighteenth centuries, eight to ten percent of the English population were elderly. The figure was just half that in the ineteenth century, and it stayed at that level till the century's end. It is now up to 15 percent, and will rise further in the next century, and the question for the historian is "how have the elderly fared in the centuries spanning these developments"?

The standard view has been that industrialisation and urbanisation were bad in their effects upon the elderly, since the former security and independence of the peasant farmer or small-town craftsman were lost in the shift to cash economies, factory production, and the new work disciplines imposed upon the labour force (Phillipson, 1982; Mitterauer and Siedel, 1982; Achenbaum, 1978; Graebner, 1980). According to this view, retirement emerged as an old age issue for the first time, as persons not fast enough or adaptable enough to meet the ever-changing requirements of industrial society were discarded as worthless and unemployable. The "problem of old age", in short, is a product of industrial society.

But the view now emerging from English research is that the change has been rather less dramatic. Most of the population had already become propertiless wage-labourers long before the appearance of full industrial capitalism, and retirement from the workforce at around age 65 seems to have been a recognised and accepted feature of life in rural economies which could not provide sufficient employment for all, except in a few short busy seasons of the year. Independent, self-employed traders or farmers were already a privileged minority before the arrival of the large factory — industrialisation may have hastened the final stages of this development, but it did not create a radically new situation for the elderly.

This brings us to the key question for social historians of old age. If the mass of the aged did not enjoy an independence gained through employment or property-holding, how then did they get by? In England by the early nineteenth century, there were nearly a million elderly persons, each of whom could expect to live 10 or more years past age 65 — how did the society cater to this? In societies which lacked state old-age pension schemes or secure institutions for saving, who cared for the aged? In particular, where did responsibility for the aged lie — with family and relatives, or the wider community?

Here again, some long-standing notions are now being challenged. The common understanding shared by sociologists, anthropologists, social historians, indeed everyone concerned with the study of past and present societies, has been that "families" bore prime responsibility for the elderly. That is, before the twentieth century and the rise of the modern welfare state, elderly persons looked to their younger relatives, both immediate and more distant

kin, for support, including financial assistance. The broad assumption amongst
scholars has been that, in most cases, an elder would live with a child or a
younger relative, or would live apart, but receiving help in some less-satisfac-
tory way. However, this view of the past and the changes wrought by industrialisation and urbanisation is not standing up to investigation.

The newer understanding is that the community or the "collectivity", rather
than the family, has for a very long time born a major responsibility for the aged
(Laslett, 1984; Smith, 1984; Thomson, 1986). This balance of past responsibilities may be demonstrated in several ways, and an excellent place to start is
with the legal history (Thomson, 1984b).

The balance of responsibilities in welfare matters between family and
community was laid out most clearly and importantly in the famous
Elizabethan Poor Law Act of 1601, which remained in force as the basis of
English welfare until 1948. This act stated that:

> ... the children of every poor, old, blind, lame and impotent person ... being
> of sufficient ability shall at their own charges relieve and maintain every such
> poor person ...

Historians have interpreted this to mean that prime responsibility lay with
relatives, but a number of qualifications should be noted. The first is that the
duty to assist the aged was laid down in a minor corner of a statute whose
purpose was to establish a public welfare institution in the Poor Law — that is,
to establish the antithesis of family responsibility. Second, the range of family
responsibilities was very limited: the elderly could look to children alone, not
to siblings nor nephews nor grandchildren nor in-laws nor any others. Third,
these responsibilities only came into force in certain limited circumstances —
when the parents were "destitute", rather than simply poor, and when the
children were judged by local magistrates to be "of sufficient ability" to do so.
The clause amounts to something very much less than a clear statement of the
duties of relatives.

Moreover, a study of the interpretations of the clause made by local
magistrates and the higher courts reveals that at least from 1700 the duties of
children to assist parents were being enforced in extremely few situations.
Aggrieved sons soon presented the courts with test-cases, and without exception the superior courts endorsed a very narrow interpretation of familial
obligations. Magistrates for their part demonstrated the greatest unwillingness
to entertain complaints against children, and the numbers of maintenance
orders recorded against sons was minute in most periods. In brief, the task of
providing for the elderly was seen even several centuries ago as a responsibility
of the whole community, and families were judged to play no special part in
this.

A second means of assessing where responsibility was lodged is the analysis
of Poor Law records. The 1601 Act — there had been earlier ones —
established the Poor Law as the prime bulwark against destitution for the
elderly and others, who could appeal to local Poor Law officials for assistance
from a fund financed by a local property rate (Thomson, 1981). Study of local

records shows that recourse to the Poor Law was the normal and accepted pattern in old age. The majority of all elderly men and women were maintained by the Poor Law, which granted them weekly pensions to be paid from around age 65 till death. These allowances, called "pensions" by all involved as a means of indicating their status, were much more generous, relative to the incomes of the non-aged, than have been state old age pensions in the twentieth century (Thomson, 1984a).

Interestingly, elderly persons who lived with their married or unmarried adult children received pensions just as did those who lived alone, and in many cases daughters who helped a parent with nursing and the like were paid a weekly allowance by the Poor Law for doing so — two excellent indications of the very limited view of family responsibilities held in that society. The notion that industrialisation weakened the position of the elderly, and that modern states have had to evolve new means of shouldering responsibilities formerly borne by families, is simply not consonant with the facts of English social history.

A range of other recent investigations emphasise still further the independence of the aged from their families, long before our own era. A sizeable minority of the elderly, perhaps a quarter, enjoyed private incomes, and so were free of dependence upon children — the dependence, in fact, flowed the other way. A few preserved independence through working into old age, though most retired from employment in their mid- to late-sixties. More received pensions for former military or civil service, and a few from private patrons. But for most of the "independent" — a favoured nineteenth century term — property and the income derived from it was the major source of income in old age.

Analyses of past living arrangements support the conclusion that the elderly were largely free of a dependence upon families before industrialisation and urbanisation. Large portions of the pre-industrial elderly lived apart from children, and this finding holds true even when children are seen to live in the near vicinity. Living alone in old age, or with an elderly spouse only, was not uncommon, and where the aged did live with younger relatives it was often because the aged controlled assets and hence were needed by the young, as much as it was a means of the young assisting the aged.

Scholars of the nineteenth and twentieth centuries, however, have found that the extended family of several generations was a much more common feature of new industrial and urban communities than it had been of older rural ones (Anderson, 1971). They observe, too, that kin, both immediate and more distant, were vitally important in the lives of populations adjusting to industrial society. In other words, support for the aged through the family appears to have been a short-term product of industrialisation and its breaking down of earlier community care.

The interpretation I have suggested which is emerging from recent research is one which emphasises a lack of change, where the position of the elderly in the past looks rather like the position today. The switch from elderly to youthful populations and back again to elderly ones does not appear to have made for major shifts in the circumstances of the old. However, I would not like to conclude this chapter without modifying this, for there has been change. There is in the evidence, for instance, the suggestion that youth-dominated societies are hard on the elderly, making little provision for them by contrast with times when the elderly are much more numerous — an interesting reversal of the usual assumption that a small population of the elderly will be treated generously, but that a heavy 'burden of dependence' will enforce a necessary hardness of policy.

More importantly still, the balance between community and family responsibility for the elderly is not one fixed for all time — it is dynamic, contentious, open to constant debate, and subject to continual shifting. Over a very long period, the balance may have favoured a heavy community commitment and a light familial one, but the locus of responsibility has moved between these two poles nevertheless (Thomson, 1986).

In the nineteenth century, for example, it moved steadily towards the family, as the society increasingly adopted arguments favouring minimal collective action and the highlighting of individual and family duty. Towards the end of the century this argument was pressed to an extreme degree: Poor Law assistance to the aged was cut to a fraction of its former levels, and the courts were employed as never before to force children to pay maintenance to their aged parents. The outcome may have been a triumph for ideology, but resulted in poverty for large numbers of the aged, and bitterness within families as the elderly and their children were forced into relationships of dependence which offended against the longer-standing values of the society.

From the end of the nineteenth century until the 1970s, the society was dominated by a reaction to the nineteenth century experience, and a new balance between family and community responsibility in welfare matters was sought which demanded little of children, and laid increasing obligations upon the collectivity. The proliferation of pension, superannuation, social security, health and other state programmes has been the feature of this era, but in the last decade a new phase has been entered. The emphasis once again is upon minimizing state activity, and expecting individuals and their families to do more to provide for old age.

The reasons for this latest swing are described variously as demographic — rising numbers of dependent elderly — or economic — national economies are not performing well enough to sustain generous support for the aged. Nevertheless, to this historian who has 'seen' it all happen before, the reasons seem to lie deeper, in a confusion as to the rights and duties of individuals and community which is inherent and inescapable in the mixed values of the society. The historian would suggest, too, that we prepare ourselves for a long and sustained programme to contract the activities of the state with regard to the aged, for the society has proven itself capable of this more than once before.

References

Achenbaum, A, 1978, *Old Age in the New Land*, Baltimore

Anderson, M, 1971, *Family Structure in Nineteenth Century Lancashire*, Cambridge.

Graebner, W, 1980, *A History of Retirement*, New Haven.

Laslett, P, 1984, 'The Significance of the Past in the Study of Aging', *Aging and Society*, 4,4: 379-90.

Phillipson, C, 1982. *Capitalism and the Construction of Old Age*. London.

Smith, R, 1984. 'The Structured Dependence of the Elderly in the Middle Ages and Thereafter', *Ageing and Society*, 4,4: 409-28.

Thomson, D, 1981. *Provision for the Elderly in England, 1834-1908*. Unpublished PhD thesis, University of Cambridge.

1984a. 'The Decline of Social Welfare: Falling State Support for the Elderlysince Early Victorian Times', Ageing and Society, 4,4: 451-82.

1984b. 'I am not my father's keeper. Families and the Elderly in Nineteenth Century England', Law and History Review, 2,2: 265-86.

1986. 'Welfare and the Historians', in L.Bonfield and others (eds). *The World We Have Gained. Oxford*.

Wrigley, E. and R Schofield. 1981, *The Population History Of England*, London.

Chapter 4

Population Policies in China: New challenge and Strategies[1]

Zeng Yi   The Institute of Population Research
Peking University, Beijing, China

A review of the population growth and population policies in China

China is a country with a total population of 1080 millions (SSB, 1987), more than one-fifth of the world population. Before 1949 (foundation of the People's Republic of China), China's population growth was characterized by a high birth rate, a high death rate and a low rate of natural increase. It was estimated that the birth rate in 1936 was about 38 per thousand, the death rate was 28 per thousand, and the natural growth rate was only around 10 per thousand. In the 109 years from 1840 to 1949, the average annual growth rate stood at only 2.5 per thousand (Qian, 1983, pp. 295). After 1949, the birth rates were fairly high (32-38 per thousand in the period of 1949-1957, see Figure 1). The death rates were remarkably reduced due to a more egalitarian distribution of food, and

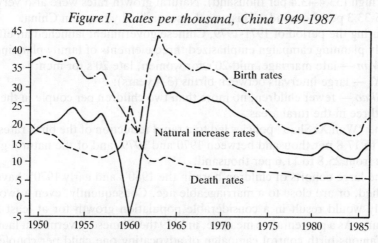

Figure 1. Rates per thousand, China 1949-1987

Source: State Statistical Bureau of China

universal, albeit rudimentary, medical care. Consequently, the natural growth rates were high (16-25 per thousand in the period of 1949-1957). This was the first baby boom in China. The results of the first census in 1953 spurred the Chinese government to launch the first birth planning campaign. Premier Zhou Enlai officially endorsed birth control in 1956. The government started to train birth planning personnel and launched a large-scale publicity campaign.

With the political movement against "rightists" in 1957 and the Great Leap Forward in 1958, the first birth planning phase came to an end. Some Chinese social scientists who warned against the potential economic problems of continued rapid population growth were criticized. Chief among them was Professor Ma Yinchu, who was removed from his position as president of Peking university and was not rehabilitated until 1978. Due to the damages done to the production capacity in industry and agriculture and to the declining living standards caused by the Great Leap Forward and the natural calamity in the three years that followed, the death rate increased remarkably during the years 1959-1961 (the death rate was as high as 25.4 per thousand in 1960) and the birth rates and the natural growth rates decreased substantially (the growth rate was as low as -4.57 per thousand in 1960).

The death rate fell to 10 per thousand in 1962 as normal conditions were restored. The post-crisis peak birth rate was very high (43.4 per thousand in 1963). The revival of the family planning programme took place in 1962. The State Council set up a birth planning campaign. Nationwide birth planning measures, promoting contraceptive use and late marriage, quickly followed. Just when this birth planning campaign might have started to bear fruit, the so-called Cultural Revolution, begun in 1966, disrupted the new programme. Red Guard activities shut down factories and distribution networks, so that supplies of contraceptives were cut off. Also, the administrative government controls on birth planning were lifted. The birth rates during the period of 1962-70 were very high (33.4-43.4 per thousand). Natural growth rates were also very high (25.5-33.3 per thousand). This was the second baby boom in China.

During the period of 1971-1979, Chinese government launched an efficient family planning campaign emphasized three elements of family planning:

- *Wan* — late marriage, mid-20's for women, late 20's for men;
- *Xi* — large intervals between births (3-4 years):
- *Shao* — fewer children, no more than two children per couple in the cities and three in the rural areas.

The "Wan Xi Shao" policies led to a rapid reduction of the birth rates from 33.4 to 17.8 per thousand between 1970 and 1979, and of the natural growth rates from 25.8 to 11.6 per thousand.

The large cohorts of children born in the 1960's and early 1970's have now reached, or are close to a marriageable age. Consequently, even a two-child family would result in a considerable population growth for at least half a century. As a preventative measure, in 1979 the Chinese government launched the famous birth control campaign of advocating one child per couple. The Chinese government regarded population control as something of strategic importance, and family planning as a basic policy (Qian, 1983).

Notwithstanding the widespread and successful family planning campaign, the birth rates in China have slightly risen from 1980 to 1982, mainly because of the large number of newlyweds which is attributed to the relaxation of the marriage-age restriction (i.e. the family planning policy of Wan, late marriage, in 1971-1979) by the New Marriage Law, which has been enforced since early 1981.

New Challenge

A. Recent raising in birth rates

The birth rates significantly increased up to over 20 per thousand in 1986 and 1987. The natural increase rates have increased from around 11 per thousand up to over 14 per thousand. The data of Total Fertility Rate which removes the effects of age structure also show the same trend (see Figure 1 and Figure 2). The reasons which may explain this unexpected rise in birth rates are as follows.

Figure 2. Total Fertility Rates, China, 1945-1987

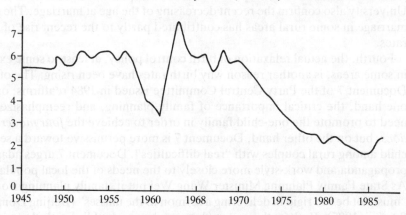

Source: 1945-1982: One-per-thousand national fertility survey
          1984-1986: Population Statistical Branch of State Statistical Bureau, Data
                     collection of the sampling survey of population changes (1984-1986).
          1987: unpublished estimate by a Chinese scholar

First, the young people who were born in China's second baby boom in the 1960s are reaching marriageable age, which has consequently resulted in a new baby boom.

Second, the large-scale economic reform, with emphasis on administrative decentralization, creates enforcement difficulties for the current family planning policy. One factor that may affect the birth rates is the responsibility system, which was introduced in the rural areas in 1979 and which has become increasingly popular in recent years. The responsibility system makes the household the unit of production, instead of, as before, the production team, which consists of about 25-50 households. The land is assigned to each household, and each household works independently for its own benefits. It seems that the new responsibility system to some extent has reinforced the economic value of children and the economic incentives of a large family. It seems also that the community and village level family planning workers cannot control things as efficiently as before, due to the administrative decentralization. Economic incentives and disincentives for family planning have become less powerful, because the peasants, who have recently had more money in their pockets due to the responsibility system, are not influenced by a system of rewards and penalties. The new policy, which enables peasants to move into small towns and cities, created an unexpected side-effect – those migrants escaped from the network of family planning in both their original and new localities.

Third, the administrative decentralization lessens the control over the age at marriage. For example, the In-Depth Sampling Fertility Surveys revealed that the average age at marriage in Shaanxi and Hebei decreased from around 22.5 in 1980 to 21.6 in 1984 (SSB, 1986). The small-scale social surveys in various parts of China, conducted by the Institute of Population Research of Peking University also confirm the recent decreasing of the age at marriage. The early marriage in some rural areas has contributed partly to the recent rise of birth rates.

Fourth, the actual relaxation of birth control policy, at least to some extent, in some areas, is another reason why birth rates have been rising. The official Document 7 of the Party Central Committee issued in 1984 reaffirms, on the one hand, the critical importance of family planning, and reemphasizes the need to promote the one-child family in order to achieve the *four modernizations*, but on the other hand, Document 7 is more permissive toward a second child among rural couples with "real difficulties". Document 7 urges adapting propaganda and work-style more closely to the needs of the local population. As State Family Planning Minister Wang Wei put it, family planning workers "must not be too rigid in delivering a sermon to the masses" (Beijing Domestic Service, 1985). Rather, they must "become bosom buddies with the masses" (visit them more often), "seek truth from facts" (discover the actual situation), and "avoid demanding uniformity in everything" (Dong and Wang, 1985, She and Shao, 1985, Bongaarts and Greenhalgh, 1985). Document 7 also upholds the principle of local discretion in devising regulations and setting targets in accordance with local conditions (Sun and Zhou, 1984, Bongaarts and Greenhalgh, 1985).

B. Forthcoming rapid population aging

Given the extraordinarily rapid decline of fertility in the 1970s and early 1980s and the maintenance of low fertility especially in urban areas, Chinese population has begun to age. It is predicted that China will have about 430 million people aged 60 and above in the year 2050, compared to just 77 million in 1982. The proportion of elderly is also determined by fertility levels in the forthcoming decades. Even under the scheme of two-children per family, the population aged 65 and above would be about 22 per cent in the middle of next century. China's urban areas will face the most extreme aging in the future; the Total Fertility Rate in China's cities dropped to 3.3 children per women in the second half of the 1960s and further fell to 1.4 in 1981 and has remained at this very low level since then. This will produce extreme aging of the population in China's urban areas unless urban fertility increase or many young rural people are allowed to migrate into the cities.

Proposed Strategies

Facing the forthcoming rapid population aging and difficulties in the implementation of family planning, should we give up the theory and practice of population control? The answer is obviously not. China's population density is three times the world average, four times that of the United States. China's farm land consists of 7 per cent of the world total, but it has to feed about 23 per cent of the world population. Many of China's important resources per capita are below the world average. For example, the territory per capita is only one-third of the world average; farm land one-third; pasture land one quarter; forest one-ninth and water one-fourth. Compared with those of the United States, they are even lower. Per capita farm land in China is only one-eighth of the US and forest only one-tenth. With China's present level of productivity and technology, excessive growth of population will surely increase the over-stretched pressure on the environment and resources. (Wu, 1985).

In order to achieve the national goal of modernization, China needs reform and an open-door policy. Administrative decentralization and previous central administration of family planning are in conflict with each other. Chinese government and people are actually facing a new challenge: how to respond to this new situation and how to improve our family planning program and population policy?

We realize that any sudden declaration of changes in current population policy in such a big country of about 1.1 billion population will create undesirable consequences. What we need is to gradually adjust and improve the population policy based on scientific research. To participate in this discussion, I propose to discuss some strategies for population control in China.

A. In the short run, to continue the current population policy, particularly focusing on reducing proportion of births of third and higher order. In the long run, to gradually and smoothly move to a two-child policy.

China's current birth control policy is to advocate one couple one child, with more permissiveness towards second birth in rural areas. The statistical figures and demographic data show that a big majority of rural couples are still having two or more children.

Table 1 gives the percentages of births of third and higher order among all births for the whole country, including both rural and urban areas. The figures for rural areas alone (not yet published for the years 1984-1986) are certainly higher than those for the whole country. These figures do not give information showing what proportion of women will eventually have three or more births, since they are period measures. A more deliberate demographic measurement that removes the effects of age structure shows even more acutely the tendency of births of high order. The life table analysis tells us that if a cohort of women followed the age-specific marriage rates and age-parity-specific fertility rates of Chinese women observed in 1981, the proportion of the hypothetical cohort members who would have borne three or more children would amount to 47.8 per cent!

Table 1. Percentages of births of order 3 and higher among all births, China

Year	1981	1984	1985	1986
Percentages	28.09	19.56	19.74	17.83

Sources: the figure for 1981 is from China's 1982 national one-per-thousand fertility survey; the figures for 1984, 1985 and 1986 are from: Population Statistical Branch of State Statistical Bureau, Data collection of the sampling survey of population changes (1984-1986).

The Total Fertility Rate was 2.6 children per woman in 1981. By eliminating all births of fourth and higher orders this figure would reduce to 2.38, and a further reduction of the proportion of women with three children from 26.7 per cent down to 14 per cent (i.e. the same as the proportion of women with one child) would bring Total Fertility Rate down to 2.0 children. (Zeng Yi, 1988). The Total Fertility Rate was 2.3 and 2.4 children per woman in 1986 and in 1987 respectively, compared with 2.6 children per woman in 1981, on which our life table analysis is based. Obviously, considerable scope exists for a further reduction of fertility, and we should focus on reducing the proportion of births of third and higher order.

Given the existing relatively high proportion of births of third and higher order, even under the campaign of promoting one child per couple, many scholars and officials realize that sudden relaxation of the birth control policy will create a sudden rush of births. The researchers and practitioners worry that as soon as the official policy opens up to universally permit two children, everyone will hurry to have another child, and no one will be willing to wait in case the policy changes again. Therefore, what I am proposing here is, first, to focus on reducing the births of third and higher order and on making particular efforts to the socio-economic approaches for changing people's attitudes toward high fertility (to be explored later). Second, the slogan could still be "To advocate one child per couple and to allow couples who fulfill certain conditions to have a second child with spacing". The conditions which make the couples entitled to have a second child should be gradually relaxed. At the same time, some areas in which socio-economic conditions and performance of family planning are better than the average can be chosen as the pilot testing areas to start the implementation of a two-child policy (some provinces have already started this kind of pilot testing). The experiences accumulated in these pilot testing areas can be used later on for the other areas. In other words, we should gradually permit more women to have a second child with spacing, so that the young women who wish to have two children will eventually have two children. This is actually a practical way of implementing a policy of two children with spacing which was proposed by some Chinese and foreign scholars. It was indicated that the proposed two-child with appropriate spacing could fulfill the dual goal of limiting the total population size and avoiding the drawbacks of one-child policy (Bongaarts and Greenhalgh, 1986). Of course, the path and speed of moving to two-child with spacing should be different from area to area, in accordance with the local conditions. For example, the proportion of women who will eventually have two children in urban areas may be expected to be much smaller than that in rural areas because many young couples in the cities do not wish to have more than one child.

B. To promote the changes in attitudes toward fertility in rural areas.

Numerous researchers, in many countries including China, demonstrate that there exists a negative relationship between levels of socio-economic development, education and people's desires number of children. In Western countries, socio-economic development and reduction of fertility occurred simultaneously. In China and many other developing countries, we cannot wait for socio-economic development to reduce fertility, simply because of the acute population pressure. Compared with other developing countries, the political and social structure of Chinese society is such that policy decisions can be quickly implemented. The local governments at various levels have been paying a lot of attention to birth control, but not many of them have been aware of the importance of promoting changes of attitudes toward fertility through socio-economic reform, because many cadres lack sociological and demographic knowledge of fertility attitudes. The proposed strategies for promoting low fertility attitudes mainly include three aspects:

(1). To pay more attention and to give more input to education.

China's 1982 census and many other data sources show that fertility decreases with the increase of women's education level (see Table 2). According to a 1982 nationwide one-per-thousand fertility survey, 37.2. per cent of women at childbearing ages were illiterate or semi-illiterate. The latest data of China's 1987 mini-census (sample size: one percent of the total population) show that 20.6 percent of total population of both sexes aged 12 and over are illiterate or semi-illiterate (SSB, 1987).

Table 2. Average number of children born to 50-year-old women by level of education, China, 1982

Education level	illiterate	primary school	middle school	high school	college
average no. children of born	5.86	4.80	3.74	2.85	2.05

Source: China's 1982 population census

Many cadres at various levels of government theoretically agree with the importance of education but practically pay little attention to it, because the outcome of investment in education is not immediately visible. With the responsibility system spread in rural China in recent years, some peasant families disrupted their children's schooling for their family farming or private enterprise. If we do not make strong efforts to alter this unfavorable trend, China will have many illiterate young boys and girls who will desire large families in the future. It will be very difficult to have family planning programs among those new illiterate or semi-illiterate young people. Therefore, we should allocate more investment into education and strictly implement the compulsory education law. Families which disrupt children's schooling should be under heavy economic penalties so that they could not get any benefits from their children's education discontinuance.

(2) To establish a system of private savings for old age care in rural areas.

Family support is traditionally an instrument for old age care in China. The state pension system currently operates only in urban areas. "Having sons for old age care" is still one of the main reasons why many peasants prefer to have a large family. The peasants' practical consideration is understandable: what could they do if they have neither at least one surviving son nor state pension when they get old? One idea that has had a wide airing is that China should develop a system of social insurance and social welfare and generally try to move from a family support system to a social support system. However, it is acknowledged that the costs of establishing such a system on the scale required by the rapid aging of the population is likely to be prohibitive for a country like China (Croll, 1988, p. 35). Therefore, we wish to seek an approach which can help peasants to reduce their reliance on children for old age care and, on the other hand, is feasible for implementation. Establishment of a system of private savings for old age care in rural areas may fulfill this dual-requirement. The private savings for old age care should be compulsory for all peasants through taxing or a "withholding system" of an appropriate proportion of peasants' incomes. The system of private savings is not only an instrument to help to solve the problems of rapid aging but also a powerful mechanism for promoting attitudes towards low fertility.

(3). To promote the living arrangement of a son-in-law who lives in the home of his wife's parents.

It is well-known that son preference is traditionally prevalent in China and other Asian countries. One major reason for peasants desiring more sons than daughters is that the elderly parents live with a married son and his wife, while their daughters marry into their husbands' families. Rural couples do not stop producing children until they bear at least one son. This is one of the major reasons why there are still so many births of order three or higher in China nowadays even under such a strong family planning framework. If we could alter the social tradition so that the living arrangement of a son-in-law who lives in the home of his wife's parents is considered as one of the normal ways of life, the families that have only daughter(s) will not wish to continue producing children until the birth of a son.

It is acknowledged that promoting the living arrangement of a son-in-law living in the home of his wife's parents is not easy but it is not impossible. This kind of living arrangement has been in existence in various parts of China for thousands of years. Recent data revealed that in some Chinese cities there are increasingly more and more parents who prefer to live with their daughter and son-in-law rather than their son and daughter-in-law because it could avoid the tension between daughter-in-law and mother-in-law.

Many socio-economic and/or political interventions can be considered for the purpose of promoting the living arrangement of a son-in-law who lives in the home of his wife's parents. For example, we may give rewards and priority of education, medical care, and housing to the families of only one or two daughters. The priority for loans and employment should be given to families in which a son-in-law lives with his wife and his wife's parents, and so on.

C. To utilize urbanization as an instrument for reducing the speed of population growth and problems of population aging.

According to China's 1982 census, 20.8 per cent of the total population lived in urban areas. This was much lower than the world average of about 37 percent and even lower than the average for other developing countries (not including

China itself) for about 32 percent in the same period.

Birth rates are much higher in rural areas than in towns and cities. In 1982, the total fertility rate for rural areas was 2.9 children per woman, compared with an urban rate of only 1.4 children per woman. With only 20.8 percent of the population living in urban areas, this implies a total fertility rate for the entire country of 2.6 children per woman. If the urban share were 50 percent, however, the national total fertility rate would be 2.1 children per woman. This simple calculation suggests that urbanization in China can have a major impact on fertility levels.

To respond to the new economic situation, the Chinese government obviously changed its previous policy of strictly controlling rural-urban migration. The official policy today is to restrict the expansion of big cities, to allow the development of medium-sized cities, and to actively promote the growth of towns. As a result of the new policy and the recent rapid economic development, it was estimated that the urban population in China increased at an annual growth rate of 4.4 percent between mid 1982 and the end of 1984 (Bei, 1986).

A study by the author and Vaupel (Zeng and Vaupel, 1987) provided calculations which may help us to better understand how urbanization may affect population growth and distribution of elderly population in China. We made two major scenarios with two sets of assumptions concerning fertility and rural-urban migration. The fertility assumptions for rural, town and city sectors

Figure 3. Total population size under two scanarics

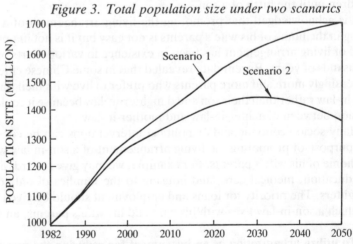

Note: Scenario 1: no rural-urban migration.
      Scenario 2: with rural-urban migration of standard age pattern.
Source: Zeng Yi and James W. Vaupel: Urbanization and population
        Growth in China, Paper presented at the International
        Conference or urbanization and urban problems, Tianjin,
        China, November, 1987.

are the same for both scenarios. One scenario assumes no urbanization or rural-urban migrants maintain their high fertility as in rural areas (we call it no urbanization scenario). Another scenario assumes the proportion of urban population will increase up to 40, 60 and 80 percent in the years 2000, 2020 and 2050 respectively and assumes the migrants will follow urban fertility norms after their residence change. The study shows that, with rural-urban migration under the above hypothetical conditions, there will be 28 million fewer Chinese in the year 2000 than if no migration occurred, 104 million fewer in 2020 and 333 million fewer in 2050 (see Figure 3).

As indicated before, the process of aging in urban areas will be much faster than that in rural areas due to the extremely low fertility in urban areas. The study indicates that the rural-urban migration (young people are most likely to migrate) will result in a comparatively younger population in urban areas. This may help economic growth and reduce the severity of population aging in urban areas. This may also help to reduce the need for the state to replace the family in providing care for the elderly.

In order to utilize urbanization as a powerful instrument for reducing the speed of population growth, two points should be emphasized. First, the strong family planning program should also cover the migrants. A special network of family planning should be established for the "flowing population" (i.e. those who travel between their urban working place and rural home) and the "temporary population in urban areas" (i.e. those who have actually moved into urban areas but have not yet received permanent urban residence). Good contraceptive services should be provided to all of the migrants. Second, with the development of an urban economy, the migrants should be encouraged and channeled to set up in urban areas through the approach of commercialization and private investment in housing and other community reconstruction. In the Chinese context, if a strong urban family planning program could cover the rural-urban migrants as well, the migrants who set up in urban areas will usually have to follow the urban low fertility norm, which will help to reduce the fertility level of China as a whole.

Conclusion

The efficient family planning program and the administrative control have been successful in reducing birth rates since the beginning of the 1970s in China. Given the rapid fertility decline and the recent economic and political reforms of administrative decentralization, new challenges are implied by the recent rise in birth rates and forthcoming rapid population aging.

More deliberate and fundamental socio-economic strategies should be considered. Any sudden relaxation of the birth control policy will create a sudden rush of births. What we need is to pay more attention and to give more input on socio-economic actions such as education, private savings systems for old age care, social innovation of living arrangements and living environment etc. With gradual changes in social atmosphere and people's attitudes toward fertility, the scheme of two children per couple with spacing should be gradually spread in accordance with local conditions so that young couples who wish to have two children will eventually have two children with appropriate spacing.

If an efficient family program including good contraceptive services could be provided to the numerous rural-urban migrants, China will be able to utilize ongoing urbanization as a powerful instrument to reduce the speed of population growth and the problems of population aging in urban areas.

Social-economic actions for population control purpose are known as the "beyond family planning approach" (see, for example, Krishnamurthy, 1987; Escap, 1987; Mason, 1986; Robinson 1975). Although it may sometimes not work very well in other developing countries, this approach is expected to work well in China, because the social and political structure in China is such that government intervention can be quickly implemented. The successful story of barefoot doctors in rural China, for example, supports this speculation. Imperative work for the students of Chinese population is to help government officials to be aware of the strategic importance of socio-economic actions for population control purposes.

Notes

1. The views presented in this paper do not imply the expression of any opinion of a government agency.

References

Bai Jianhua, 1986, "The situation of China's rural and urban population." *Renkou Yanjiu (Population Research)*, no. 2, 1986.

Banister J, 1987. "Implication of the aging of China's population." Paper presented at the "International Symposium on Family Structure and Population Aging", organized by the Institute of Population Research, Peking University, Oct. 1987, Beijing.

Bongaarts J. and S. Greenhalgh. 1985. "An alternative to the one-child policy in China". *Population and Development Review,* Vol. 11, No. 4, pp. 585-617.

Croll E. 1988, "Caring for China's elderly in 2050." *People,* Vol. 15, No. 1, pp. 34-35.

Dong Taituo and Wang Lingling. 1985. "National propaganda and education conference on birth control work stresses; propaganda work must adopt various forms to serve the masses." *Jihua Shengyu Ban (Birth Planning Page)*, 4 January 1985. in FBIS, China Report, Political, Sociological and

Military Affairs. No. 35 (15 April, 1985) pp. 60-61.

Krishnamurthy, J, 1987, "Population development integration – some questions and answers," *Labour and Population Activities in Asia and Pacific* No. 29, Sept. 1987. –

Mason, Andrew, et. al., 1986. "Population growth and economic development: lessons from selected Asian countries." *UNFPA: Policy Development Studies*, No. 10, New York: UNFPA.

Qian Xinzhong. 1983. "China's population policy: theory and methods." *Studies in Family Planning*. Vol. 14, No. 12.

Robinson, Warren C., (ed.), 1975, *Population and Development Planning*. New York: the Population Council.

She Mengren and Shao Boliang. 1985. "The practice of family planning is a choice made by Chinese people themselves." *People's Daily*, 15 July, 1985.

State Statistical Bureau (SSB). 1988. The major results of 1987 (1% population sampling survey).

Sun Yongsheng and Zhou Peiyan. 1984. "National population planning work progress viewed." *New China News*, 11 Oct. 1984.

United Nations, Economic Commission for Asia and the Pacific, Population Division, 1987. "Population and Development: Frameworks for Research and Planning." *Asia Population Studies Series*, No. 82, Bangkok: ESCAP.

Wu Cangping. 1985. "A preliminary inquiry into the strategy of China's population development." *Population Research*. No. 5, 1985. pp. 2-8.

Zeng Yi. 1988. "Changing demographic characteristics and family status of Chinese women." (forthcoming) in *Population Studies*.

Zeng Yi. 1986. "Changes in family structure in China: a simulation study." *Population and Development Review*. Vol 12. No. 4, pp. 675-703.

Zeng Yi and J. Vaupel. 1987. "Urbanization and population growth in China." Paper presented at the International Conference on urbanization and urban problems. Tianjing, Oct. 1987.

Chapter 5

Population Aging and Household Structural Change in Japan

Naohiro OGAWA

Population Research Institute,
Nihon University, Tokyo, Japan

Introduction

The story of Japan's postwar economic recovery and continued economic growth has been told many times. No less remarkable, however, was the unprecedented rapidity with which Japan moved through the final stages of her demographic transition. Subsequent to the postwar baby boom (1947-1949), Japan's fertility fell dramatically. During 1949–1959, the total fertility rate (TFR) decreased more than 50 percent, from 4.32 to 2.05 children per woman. Although there were only minor changes until the first oil crisis of 1973, TFR started to decline again to 1.72 in 1986. Moreover, mortality improved remarkably from the late 1940s to the mid-1960s. Female life expectancy at birth, for example, rose from 53.94 years in 1947 to 72.92 years in 1965. In 1986, it was 80.93 years, which is the highest in the contemporary world.

As a result of these pronounced demographic changes, the age structure of the Japanese population has been shifting to a marked extent. The index of aging (population aged 65 and over/population aged 0-14 x 100) was only 13.96 in 1950 and 19.06 in 1960, but increased to 29.53 in 1970 and 47.89 in 1985. In a virtually closed population such as the Japanese one, the aging of the population is induced solely by declines of fertility and mortality improvements (Martin and Ogawa, 1988). A projection-based analysis on these demographic changes in the index of aging shows that the fertility effect was approximately 10.5 times more dominant than the mortality effect over the period 1950–1970. it should be stressed, however, that the latter dominated the former during 1970–1985; mortality improvements contributed to the population aging process about 22 percent more than fertility reduction. This finding is consistent with the conclusion reached in one of the recent United Nations studies (1987) that the mortality effect on population aging becomes increasingly strong as the process of demographic transition and economic development proceeds. In view of the fact that Japan's population aging is expected to accelerate further at an unprecedented speed (Ogawa, 1982), the importance of the role played by mortality reduction in the age structural transformation is likely to be enhanced toward the end of this century.

In a developed country like Japan, the improvement of mortality implies an increase in the proportion of the aged population as well as an extension of life among the elderly (Ogawa, 1986). Because it is the case in virtually all populations that older age groups experience more illness and need considerably more health services than younger age groups, the decline of mortality among the elderly, *ceteris paribus,* calls for a greater amount of financial and manpower resources for the provision of health care for a country as a whole.

As documented by reviews of health programs and planning in world perspective (Maddox, 1982), there are vast inter-country differences in approaches to government intervention in the provision of health care. In Japan, social health insurance systems cover virtually every person in the country, whether through one of the six major schemes for employees and their dependents or through the livelihood protection system. These six different schemes have resulted from the fact that Japan's social insurance system has been largely formed and developed on the basis of occupational groups (Social Insurance Agency, 1986). Among the six medical insurance schemes, approximately 89 percent of the population is enrolled in the following three plans: (i) government-managed health insurance (GMHI), mainly for employees in medium and small-sized enterprises, (ii) association-managed health insurance (AMHI), for employees in large enterprises, and (iii) government-managed national health insurance (NHI), for persons who are not covered by any employees' insurance schemes. Over the period 1970-1985, the total medical expenditure increased by 2.7 times in real terms, and both population aging and medical technological progress account for a substantial part of this rapid rise in medical care costs. The proportion of the gross national product (GNP) allocated to medical care rose from 3.32 to 4.76 percent during the corresponding period.

In addition to the escalating cost of health care, the aging of the Japanese population is likely to demand a great deal of human resources to cope with a fast increase in the number of elderly patients who need intensive human care, including those suffering from senile dementia and those who are bedridden. Because the multi-generational family living arrangement has survived urbanization far better in Japan than in other developed countries (Petri, 1982; Ogawa and Hodge, 1983), a large proportion of these elderly patients is looked after at home rather than at institutional facilities. It should be emphasized, however, that as Japan's aging process advances over the next few decades, the number of these elderly patients is expected to increase at an alarming rate.

The principal objective of the present paper is to discuss the impact of the aging of the Japanese population upon (i) the future financial needs in the provision of health care services at the government level, (ii) the changing allocative pattern of such government health resources by type of household, and (iii) the manpower requirement in taking care of elderly patients at the familial level. In the next section, the method of projecting the total medical expenditure is discussed, together with a short description of a long-term macroeconomic-demographic modeling framework. In Section C, some of the principal projection results on both population and public medical expenditures derived from the long-term model are presented. Section D deals with a brief analysis on intertemporal changes in the allocation of the government medical expenditure among various household types. Section E discusses the estimated number of aged persons suffering from senile dementia and those who are bedridden, and the manpower requirements of these elderly patients at a familial level.

A Modeling Framework

A. NUPRI Long-term Macroeconomic-Demographic-Social Security Model

In the recent past, the Nihon University Population Research Institute (NUPRI) has prepared population projections as part of its modeling project funded by the Japan Medical Association. One of the main differences between the NUPRI population projections and other existing population projections, including those by the Ministry of Health and Welfare, is that the former are based upon both fertility and mortality endogenously determined within a macroeconomic-demographic-social security model, and the latter, upon these demographic factors exogenously given. One of the distinctive advantages of the NUPRI projections is that they clearly show various interrelationships among demographic, economic and social security related variables.

As illustrated in Figure 1, the NUPRI projections have been computed through the interaction of the following three submodels: the population submodel, the economic submodel, and the social security submodel. These three submodels are interdependent; the population submodel is first determined by a set of economic and social security variables with a one-year time lag, and then the variables in both economic and social security submodels are simultaneously determined, using the computed demographic variables. The NUPRI model is basically of the Keynesian demand-oriented nature, incorporating both price and wage adjustment mechanisms to solve the system for each year of simulation. The model contains approximately 800 variables, and most of the functional relationships in the three submodels have been estimated by OLS, using annual time-series data over the period 1965-1984.

In the population submodel, the fertility level for each year is estimated from a fertility model of the new home economics approach (Ogawa and Mason, 1986). Although the fertility model of the new home economics can be specified in various fashions, the equation adopted for the NUPRI projections

Figure 1. Interrelationship Among Three Submodels

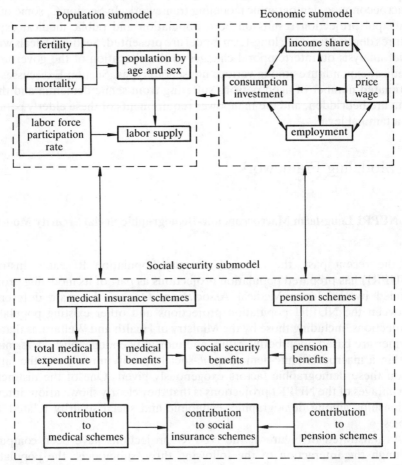

is a linear specification of the Butz-Ward type (Butz and Ward, 1979); TFR is estimated on the basis of husband's income, wife's market wage rate, and the fraction of the married female population currently employed.

Regarding mortality, the expectation of life at birth for each sex is computed as a function of the one-year lagged per capita total government medical expenditure measured in real terms. In this equation, the explanatory variable is expected to reflect, to a large extent, a level of medical technological progress. It is also important to note that, to keep predicted values within a reasonable range, the equation of life expectancy at birth for each sex has been estimated on the basis of a logistic curve with its ceiling imposed. The ceiling values for both sexes have been utilized directly from one of the hypothetical life tables compiled by synthesizing the best age-sex-specific mortality rate in the contemporary world (Kamagata and Hishinuma, 1982). The ceiling value for males is 78.12 years, and that for females, 83.58 years. Because a detailed framework of the model has been described elsewhere (Ogawa et al, 1986), no further explanation of the overall mechanism is necessary here.

B. Methodological Framework Used for Estimating the Costs of Medical Care

To quantify the effect of future changes in both size and structure of the Japanese population upon government medical expenditure, the following methodology has been adopted in the social security submodel of the NUPRI model. For each of the three major medical insurance schemes, the age-specific total medical cost is computed as the product of the four matrices shown as below:

$$\begin{pmatrix} \text{Population} \\ \text{by age and} \\ \text{sex} \end{pmatrix} \times \begin{pmatrix} \text{Age-sex-specific} \\ \text{probability of being} \\ \text{enrolled in the scheme} \end{pmatrix} \times \begin{pmatrix} \text{Age-specific medical care} \\ \text{cost per case} \end{pmatrix}$$

$$\times \begin{pmatrix} \text{Age-specific incidence of} \\ \text{receiving medical} \\ \text{treatment} \end{pmatrix} = \begin{pmatrix} \text{Age-specific total} \\ \text{medical care cost} \end{pmatrix}$$

The product of the first two matrices corresponds to the age-sex-specific number of those enrolled in the particular health insurance scheme. By multiplying this product by the third matrix, one can obtain the age-specific total number of medical cases (or patients) treated under the specific health insurance scheme. It should be noted, however, that due to data limitations, the multiplication has been done only on an age-specific basis rather than on an age-sex-specific basis. Then, the age-specific total medical care cost can be calculated by multiplying the age-specific total number of medical cases by the age-specific medical care cost per case. The total medical care expenditure for each health scheme can be obtained by adding the age-specific total medical care cost for all age groups.

The parameters for the first matrix are derived from the population submodel, while those for the other three matrices have been calculated from sampled data. In the case of the AMHI scheme, for instance, key demographic information on its enrollees is gathered by the AMHI administration on October 1 for each year on a 0.2 percent sample basis. Using the sample results for 1984, the age-sex-specific probability of being enrolled in this scheme has been computed for the second matrix. The AMHI administration also compiles data on the age-specific incidence of recourse to inpatient medical care, as well as the age-specific inpatient medical cost per case, through a 6.7 percent sample of all the medical claims submitted by hospitals and clinics during the month of September of each year. As regards outpatients, however, the data are gleaned through a 0.5 rather than 6.7 percent sample of the same information source. These sampled data on inpatients and outpatients gathered during one month have been blown up to a total membership size and adjusted to an annual basis.

Then, these inpatient and outpatient data have been combined together to calculate the parameters for the third and fourth matrices.

Although there are some differences in the timing of data collection from scheme to scheme, each scheme gathers the corresponding data, using comparable sampling methods. For this reason, we have applied a similar computational procedure to the data for the two other leading health insurance schemes in order to estimate the parameters for each matrix. The computed results are shown in Table 1,

One of the advantages of this computational method is that, because the four matrices on the left-hand side of the formula are all age-specific, the population growth effect as well as the age structure effect on medical care expenditure is directly captured.

Another advantage of this method is that it enables us to accurately identify some of the sources of a rise in medical expenditure. Note that except for the matrix for the population by age and sex, the parameters for the remaining three matrices on the left-hand side of the above formula have been derived from data for 1984. By multiplying these three matrices by the population actually observed in earlier years, one can project backward to ascertain the hypothetical age-specific total medical care cost for each of these years. Because a close examination of past data reveals that the parameters for the second and third matrices have been relatively stable, the difference between the hypothetical age-specific total medical care cost and the observed age-specific total medical care cost is attributable to (i) the price effect and (ii) the residual effect. Information on the time-series changes in the price for medical care services is available, so that the magnitude of the residual effect for each age group can be easily estimated. Roughly speaking, the computed residuals can be regarded as the cost-push effect due to the changing pattern of illness and medical technological advancement. In the NUPRI model, the age-specific residual effect for each health insurance scheme has been incorporated as a function of real GNP per capita, the price effect, as a function of nominal GNP; each of these equations has been estimated, employing annual data from the mid-1970s to 1984. To project these effects on total medical care expenditure over the simulation period, the levels of both real GNP per capita and nominal GNP are provided from the economic submodel.

Projected Results on Population and Public Medical Expenditures

Table 2 displays projected demographic results. Total population size, which is 121.05 million persons in 1985, continues to increase to 131.70 million persons in 2009. After reaching this peak, Japan's future population

Table 1. Estimated Parameters for Three Matrices for Three Major Health Insurance Schemes, Japan, 1984

| Age | Probability of Being Enrolled | | | | Incidence of Receiving Medical Treatment per 1,000 Persons | | Cost per Case (yen) | |
| | Insured | | Dependents | | | | | |
	Male	Female	Male	Female	Insured	Dependents	Insured	Dependent
				GMHI				
0- 4	0.0	0.0	0.2771	0.2726	0.0	707.20	0	6,864
5- 9	0.0	0.0	0.2598	0.2649	0.0	502.79	0	6,626
10-14	0.0	0.0	0.2546	0.2506	0.0	338.67	0	7,579
15-19	0.0570	0.0624	0.2188	0.2128	311.43	269.75	12,678	10,105
20-24	0.2127	0.2304	0.0876	0.1077	370.74	272.49	13,326	16,499
25-29	0.2931	0.1419	0.0134	0.1641	392.41	423.40	14,336	12,902
30-34	0.2885	0.1015	0.0039	0.1854	401.59	382.79	15,933	14,325
35-39	0.2714	0.1236	0.0010	0.1777	467.90	392.33	14,934	13,271
40-44	0.2565	0.1545	0.0016	0.1451	557.62	475.68	16,582	15,219
45-49	0.2488	0.1792	0.0031	0.1282	613.66	534.47	16,003	15,093
50-54	0.2194	0.1603	0.0035	0.1357	751.45	643.87	18,404	18,189
55-59	0.2696	0.1301	0.0109	0.1586	893.43	812.11	19,706	18,011
60-64	0.1638	0.0538	0.0175	0.1259	1,159.24	962.02	20,486	18,857
65-69	0.1060	0.0303	0.0470	0.1352	1,502.58	895.31	20,914	18,045
70+	0.0344	0.0091	0.0983	0.1517	1,525.57	1,057.57	27,995	35,171

AMHI

Age	Probability of Being Enrolled				Incidence of Receiving Medical Treatment per 1,000 Persons		Cost per Case (yen)	
	Insured		Dependents		Insured	Dependents	Insured	Dependent
	Male	Female	Male	Female				
0- 4	0.0	0.0	0.2830	0.2800	0.0	609.54	0	7,290
5- 9	0.0	0.0	0.2963	0.2821	0.0	574.99	0	7,152
10-14	0.0	0.0	0.2719	0.2715	0.0	364.34	0	7,853
15-19	0.0401	0.0628	0.2269	0.2236	258.08	281.16	13,232	10,424
20-24	0.2065	0.2470	0.0883	0.0917	369.14	293.43	13,224	15,427
25-29	0.2871	0.1153	0.0072	0.1645	363.85	505.43	15,077	13,869
30-34	0.2777	0.0633	0.0017	0.2370	347.31	410.90	14,773	13,351
35-39	0.2921	0.0582	0.0009	0.2290	377.82	427.80	14,965	12,926
40-44	0.2917	0.0603	0.0007	0.2103	429.09	395.62	16,528	14,448
45-49	0.2694	0.0628	0.0009	0.1565	547.63	561.15	17,219	15,937
50-54	0.2181	0.0576	0.0016	0.1289	695.00	738.64	18,462	16,671
55-59	0.1851	0.0436	0.0042	0.1031	843.90	713.80	19,531	17,405
60-64	0.0609	0.0132	0.0092	0.0665	1,549.80	1,023.06	20,961	18,670
65-69	0.0432	0.0057	0.0236	0.0982	1,374.78	777.32	21,010	19,363
70+	0.0111	0.0016	0.0572	0.1147	1,419.76	1,133.52	25,534	32,278

| Age | Probability of Being Enrolled | | | | | Incidence of Receiving Medical Treatment per 1,000 Persons | | Cost per Case (yen) | |
| | Insured | | Dependents | | NHI | | | | |
	Male	Female	Male	Female		Insured	Dependents	Insured	Dependent
0- 4	0.2872	0.2842				799.0		7,265	
5- 9	0.3101	0.3127				596.1		6,465	
10-14	0.3366	0.3541				367.9		7,153	
15-19	0.3501	0.3484				272.2		11,030	
20-24	0.2700	0.2398				293.8		14,567	
25-29	0.2564	0.2458				358.8		16,307	
30-34	0.2995	0.2907				350.7		15,952	
35-39	0.3237	0.3144				355.2		16,349	
40-44	0.3356	0.3319				380.1		17,833	
45-49	0.3702	0.3592				447.6		19,520	
50-54	0.3884	0.3998				545.3		19,264	
55-59	0.4289	0.5034				637.0		19,943	
60-64	0.6110	0.6431				731.5		19,509	
65-69	0.7432	0.6205				912.0		23,894	
70+	0.7332	0.5714				1,106.9		32,194	

is expected to decrease continuously to a level of 127.06 million persons by 2025. Throughout the projected period, TFR oscillates considerably; the lowest level is 1.701 for 1991, while the highest one is 1.826 for 2025. The male life expectancy at birth will asymptotically approach 78.12 years in 2022, and the female life expectancy at birth, 83.58 in 2021.

A few points of interest emerge with regard to age compositional changes shown in Table 2. In 1985, the proportion of the population at ages 0-14 is 21.51 percent, and the proportion of the elderly population aged 65 and over is 10.30 percent. Although the former shrinks continuously, the latter shows an upward trend throughout the projection period. It should be stressed that in the year 2003 the size of the latter exceeds that of the former.

Table 2. Projected Demographic Changes, 1985-2025

Year	Total population (million)	0-14 years old (%)	15-64 years old (%)	65+ years old (%)	$\frac{75+}{65+}$ (%)	Index of total dependency
1985	121.05	21.51	68.18	10.30	37.77	46.66
1990	123.84	18.50	69.63	11.87	39.66	43.62
1995	126.40	17.08	68.91	14.01	37.96	45.12
2000	129.25	17.05	66.74	16.21	38.22	49.84
2005	131.28	17.32	64.55	18.13	41.59	54.92
2010	131.64	16.94	62.83	20.22	43.98	59.14
2015	130.65	15.83	61.22	22.95	43.05	63.35
2020	128.94	14.96	60.95	24.10	45.52	64.09
2025	127.06	15.03	60.97	24.00	52.74	64.02

Secondly, at the present moment, those in the proportion of those aged 65 and over are considerably younger than most of the populations in the Western world, but the Japanese population is likely to become the world's most aged human population in the early part of the next century. More importantly, the Japanese population will reach the world's highest level of aging at an unprecedented rate, as revealed in Table 3. Japan's aged population arrived at a level of 10 percent in the year 1985, which was the latest among all the countries listed in Table 3. Despite this delayed onset in Japan, she is the first country in which the aged comprise more than 20 percent of the total population among the countries listed in this table. The length of time required to increase from 10 percent to 20 percent of the Japanese population is only 24 years. As compared with Finland, which will undergo the same demographic transformation at the second fastest speed among the eight countries selected for Table 3, the Japanese population will age at a tempo almost twice as fast.

Thirdly, the aging of the aged population deserves special attention. The proportion of those aged 75 and over in the aged population rises from 37.77 percent in 1985 to 38.22 percent in 2000, and even to 52.74 percent in 2025. These projected results indicate that the aging of the aged population is likely to accelerate substantially in the first quarter of the next century. This age compositional shift is prone to directly affect the pattern and level of demand

Table 3. International Comparison on the Speed of Population Aging

Country	Year in which the aged population reaches		Time required to increase from 10 to 20% (years)
	10%	20%	
Japan	1985	2009	24
Finland	1973	2021	48
Switzerland	1958	2012	54
Netherlands	1968	2020	52
Germany, Federal Republic of	1954	2010	56
Denmark	1956	2017	61
Luxembourg	1952	2022	70
Sweden	1929	2014	85

Source: United Nations, *World Population Prospects: Estimates and Projections as Assessed in 1984,* Population Studies, No. 98, New York, 1986. The data for Japan are based upon the NUPRI population projection.

for medical services, as will be discussed later.

Fourthly, the total dependency of the population is relatively low until the turn of the century. The index of total dependency decreases from 46.66 in 1985 to 43.71 in 1991, after which it rises slowly to 50.29 in 2000. In the next century, it is expected to increase almost continuously to 65.13 in 2018. In anticipation of these projected results, appropriate policies should be formulated to cope with negative effects of accelerating population aging before the end of this century.

Now, let us turn our attention to some of the projected results regarding government medical expenditure. A few important observations can be made from Table 4. First of all, although government medical expenditure is only 17.38 trillion yen in 1986, it is expected to rise monotonically to 44.56 trillion yen in 2000 and 113.63 trillion in 2025.

Secondly, the share of the medical expenditure for the population aged 65 and over grows very rapidly under all the three schemes, but its growth pattern differs considerably from scheme to scheme. The impact of population aging upon the medical care expenditure is the most pronounced in the case of NHI. This result reflects the fact that almost all the retired persons are enrolled in this scheme. Although the percent share of the medical care expenditure for the elderly is unlikely to exceed more than 50 percent in both the GMHI and AMHI schemes throughout the projected period, it is expected to reach a 50 percent level in the early 1990s under the NHI scheme. This result is in agreement with the other projected result (not shown here) that the NHI scheme is likely to encounter serious financial difficulties in the near future (Ogawa et al. 1986).

Table 4. Projected Medical Expenditure, 1986-2025

Year	Total medical expenditure (trillion yen)	Share of total medical expenditure in GNP (%)	Share of medical expenditure for those aged 65 and over (%)			
			GMHI	AMHI	NHI	Three schemes combined
1986	17.38	5.04	22.5	17.7	48.3	34.8
1990	21.32	5.25	24.2	19.5	49.8	36.7
1995	30.40	5.56	26.9	22.3	52.3	39.6
2000	44.56	5.81	29.5	25.1	55.0	42.7
2005	55.56	5.98	32.0	27.7	57.8	45.6
2010	66.55	6.07	34.8	30.3	60.5	48.7
2015	83.25	6.11	38.1	33.2	64.1	52.4
2020	98.64	6.13	39.7	34.9	66.0	54.2
2025	113.63	6.03	39.4	35.0	65.6	54.0

Thirdly, for the three health insurance schemes combined, the percent share of the medical care expenditure for the aged persons is 34.8 percent in 1986, but it grows to 42.7 percent in 2000, and to 54.2 percent in 2020. This result is consistent with the projected aging pattern; the proportion of those aged 65 and over rises continuously from 10.3 percent in 1985 to 24.1 percent in 2021 which is the peak year.

Fourthly, the share of GNP required rises gradually from 5.04 percent in 1986 to 5.81 percent in 2000, and to 6.13 percent in 2020. At this juncture, it seems interesting to compare these projected results with the levels being experienced in some of the industrialized countries. The share of GNP allocated to the medical expenditure was 7.83 percent for France in 1982, 7.64 percent for the Federal Republic of Germany in 1981, and 5.17 percent for England in 1983 (Health and Welfare Statistics Association, 1986). When compared with these statistics, the projected results indicate that Japan is likely to reach England's current level in the early 1990's, but is unlikely to rise to the levels being observed in France or the Federal Republic of Germany.

Apart from the above simulated results, the matrix-based approach yields several additional interesting numerical results. One of them is related to the pattern of age structural changes in the patients under each health insurance scheme, which can be estimated by multiplying the first three matrices. Because of the differentials in the age-specific incidence of sickness and in the age-specific probability of being enrolled in each scheme, the age structure of the patients tends to substantially differ not only with the schemes but also from what the conventional age structural indicators suggest.

Table 5 clearly illustrates this point. The conventional index of aging is only 50.46 in 1986, and increases to 95.15 in 2000. The value of this index exceeds 100 in the year 2003, and reaches the peak value (162.29) in the year 2021. In contrast, the comparable index of aging for the patients covered by the three principal health insurance schemes shows a considerably different pattern and level of aging. In 1986, the index of aging for the patients is 106.87, which corresponds to the value of the conventional index of aging in 2006. Although the peak values for both indices are recorded in 2021, the former is 2.1 times larger than the latter. It is also important to note that among the three schemes, NHI shows the highest value of the index of aging for the patients throughout the projected period.

Table 5. Comparison of Aging of Population with Aging of Patients, 1986-2025

| Year | Index of Aging | | | | |
	Population	GMHI	AMHI	NHI	Three schemes combined
1986	50.46	65.71	36.17	195.90	106.87
1990	64.19	82.78	45.62	246.30	134.40
1995	82.15	103.89	57.38	310.34	169.10
2000	95.15	117.38	65.44	356.03	193.19
2005	104.81	130.29	72.53	396.98	215.07
2010	119.43	152.48	84.09	461.87	250.62
2015	145.23	186.60	102.42	563.75	306.11
2020	161.40	230.07	114.62	625.77	338.75
2025	160.01	197.19	113.37	615.20	332.33

Allocative Pattern of Government Medical Expenditure by Type of Household: Linking to HOMES

In this section, we will analyze changes in the allocative pattern of the projected government medical expenditure among various types of households. Before proceeding to such analyses, let us first discuss the household projection package, HOMES. Most of the household projection models currently available provide information on the number of households and the age and sex of household heads. These models, however, do not treat the living arrangements of other members of the population in a comprehensive fashion. HOMES employs a unique methodology to determine the entire household membership in a way consistent with underlying mortality and fertility trends. The data requirements for HOMES are relatively modest. They consist of population projections that include age-specific fertility rates, and a recent census or large, representative survey that includes a household roster with the age, sex, and relationship to the household head of each household member. By using these data inputs, we are provided information on: (i) number of household, (ii) age and sex of the household head, (iii) households with single head, (iv) one-person households, (v) average household size, (vi) sex and age distribution of household members, (vii) number of children and grandchildren, and (viii) number of parents. If mortality among the elderly declines, for example, HOMES accounts for the impact on the number of households headed by elderly, the number of elderly living alone, and the number of persons living in

Table 6. Projected Number of Households and Average Household Size by Household Type, Japan, 1985-2025

Household type	Year								
	1985	1990	1995	2000	2005	2010	2015	2020	2025
Number of households (1,000s)									
Intact	27,574	28,881	30,038	31,093	31,642	31,559	31,090	30,523	29,825
Single-head male	367	406	441	468	494	517	535	544	541
Single-head female	1,880	2,003	2,089	2,139	2,172	2,202	2,218	2,202	2,142
One-person male	4,631	4,867	5,138	5,106	4,907	4,747	4,732	4,815	4,784
One-person female	3,710	4,079	4,433	4,628	4,756	4,861	4,978	5,045	4,974
Others	71	76	82	86	88	88	88	89	90
All households	38,233	40,312	42,220	43,520	44,060	43,975	43,641	43,217	42,356
Average household size (persons)									
Intact	3.81	3.71	3.63	3.60	3.60	3.62	3.63	3.64	3.66
Single-head male	2.50	2.33	2.17	2.04	1.93	1.88	1.85	1.82	1.80
Single-head female	2.53	2.42	2.29	2.20	2.15	2.14	2.12	2.10	2.09
All households	3.71	3.61	3.53	3.49	3.50	3.51	3.52	3.52	3.55

households headed by their offspring. Because a detailed description of this package is available elsewhere (Mason, 1987), no further discussion on the features of HOMES is necessary.

We have recently incorporated, by utilizing the tabulated results obtained from the 1985 Population Census of Japan, the HOMES package into the NUPRI long-term model, with a view to analyzing intertemporal changes in the relationship between the demand for government medical services and the pattern of household formation over the period 1985-2025. Table 6 presents the projected results with regard to the number of households and the average household size by household type. The following several remarks, made on the basis of this table, are noteworthy. First of all, the total number of households is expected to increase from 38.233 million in 1985 to 44.060 million in 2005. Although the mortality level is expected to continue to improve throughout the projection period, due to a sustained low fertility level, the total number of household start decreasing after 2005. In 2025, the total number of households is almost 4 percent less than that for the peak year.

Secondly, primarily because the predominant proportion of all the households combined belongs to the type of intact households (those with a head and wife present), these intertemporal changes in the total number of all the households are highly comparable to those of intact households. In 1985, the proportion of intact households in all the households combined is 72.12 percent, but it falls to 71.45 percent by 2000, and to 70.42 percent by 2025.

Thirdly, although the number of single-headed households (those in which the head's spouse is absent) is relatively small, its growth pattern is considerably different from that of intact households. It increases continuously up to the year 2010. Moreover, the majority of these households are headed by women; in 1985, for instance, 83.67 percent of the single-head households are headed by women, while it is 79.84 percent in 2025. In a universal marriage society like Japan, this sex differential reflects the difference in mortality between men and women.

Fourthly, the proportion of one-person households in all the households combined is substantially large, and grows gradually over time. It is 21.82 percent in 1985, and rises to 23.04 percent in 2025. More importantly, the number of one-person male households reaches its peak (5.138 million households) in 1995, while the number of one-person female households continues to increase until the year 2020. As is the case for the single-head households, this difference in the pattern of growth between the two sexes is attributable largely to sex differentials in mortality.

Fifthly, the average household size of all households combined falls from 3.71 persons in 1985 to 3.49 persons in 2000, but it grows gradually during the remaining projection period, thus being 3.55 persons in the final year of projection. A similar intertemporal change can be observed with respect to the average household size for the intact households. In contrast, the average household size for both single-head male and female households shrinks continuously over time; the former decreases from 2.50 persons in 1985 to 1.80

persons in 2025, while the latter, from 2.53 to 2.09 persons during the corresponding period.

The computed results based upon HOMES also show that the age composition of these various household types change considerably during the 40-year period. As can be seen through the inspection of Table 7, the proportion of those aged 65 and over is relatively low in 1985 regardless of household types, but rises rapidly with the passage of time. In the case of all the households combined, it increases from 8.91 percent in 1985 to 21.27 percent in 2025. Similarly, it grows from 9.65 to 22.76 percent in the case of the intact households, from 9.71 to 27.23 percent for the single-head male households, and from 7.85 to 20.65 percent among the single-head female households.

Table 7. *Projected Change in Age Composition of Total Number of Members by Household Type, 1985-2025*

(unit:%)

Household type	1985	Year 2000	2025
Intact			
0-14	23.66	18.94	16.79
15-64	66.69	65.58	60.45
65+	9.65	15.48	22.76
Single-head male			
0-14	15.87	10.60	9.32
15-64	74.72	72.69	63.35
65+	9.71	16.71	27.23
Single-head female			
0-14	19.99	15.09	13.75
15-64	72.16	71.31	65.60
65+	7.85	13.60	20.65
All households			
0-14	21.75	17.21	15.19
15-64	69.34	68.47	63.54
65+	8.91	14.32	21.27

The foregoing discussions based upon the projected results contained in Tables 6 and 7 indicate that the intertemporal growth pattern of the number of households, their average size, and their age composition differ pronouncedly by household type. No doubt, these inter-household differences affect the pattern of demand for government medical services. As presented in Table 8, for example, the aging of patients varies substantially among various household types. Throughout the projection period, the single-head male households show the highest level of aging; in 1985, 22.99 percent of the patients belonging to this household type are those aged 65 and over, and their number rises to almost 50 percent by the end of the projected period. In the case of the patients among the single-head female households, which show the lowest level

of aging during the period in question, the corresponding figure increases from
15.87 to 35.36 percent.

*Table 8. Projected Change in Age Composition of Patients and in Share of
Public Medical Expenditure for Those Aged 65 and Over, by Household
Type, 1985-2025*

Household type	1985	Year 2000	2025
Intact			
Patients aged 65+ (%)	19.47	28.47	38.97
Share of expenditure for 65+ (%)	33.06	42.24	53.33
Single-head male			
Patients aged 65+(%)	22.99	34.27	48.44
Share of expenditure for 65+ (%)	37.11	48.13	62.09
Single-head female			
Patients aged 65+ (%)	15.87	24.95	35.36
Share of expenditure for 65+ (%)	28.24	38.66	50.20
All households			
Patients aged 65+(%)	20.14	29.36	40.34
Share of expenditure for 65+ (%)	33.81	43.10	54.60

It is also interesting to observe in Table 8 that, although the share of
government medical expenditure allocated for those aged 65 and over is
expected to grow markedly irrespective of household types, the pattern of its
growth differs considerably among household types. For instance, the share for
elderly persons reaches 48 percent among single-head male households at the
turn of the century, as opposed to 39 percent for the female counterparts.
Furthermore, irrespective of household types, the share of government medical expenditure allotted for the elderly exceeds more than 50 percent in the
final year of the projected period.

In this section, we have found that there are considerable inter-temporal
differences in both size and structure among various types of households. We
have also observed that these differences in the formation of households over
time are likely to affect the allocative pattern of government medical expenditure among these different types of households. Primarily because of pronounced differences in the household composition of each public health
insurance scheme, these intertemporal changes in the allocative pattern of
public medical expenditure among various household types will undoubtedly
carry important implications in identifying some of the serious problem areas
existing in the current medical insurance system in Japan.

Family Support for the Bedridden Elderly or Those with Senile Dementia

The discussion developed in the previous sections indicates that Japan's unprecedented aging process will bring about the rapid growth of financial resources allocated for medical care services. In addition to financial resources, however, population aging in Japan is likely to require a great deal of human resources to cope with a fast increase in the number of the elderly patients who need intensive nursing, including those suffering from senile dementia and those who are bedridden.

Table 9. Age-Sex-Specific Probabilities of Elderly Persons Being Bedridden

Age	Male	Female
65-69	0.0245	0.0175
70-74	0.0397	0.0357
75-79	0.0582	0.0671
80 and over	0.1028	0.1389

Table 10. Age-Sex-Specific Probabilities of Suffering From Senile Dementia Among Elderly Persons Aged 65 and Over, in 1984, Japan

Age	Male	Female
65-69	0.016	0.010
70-74	0.036	0.026
75-79	0.037	0.056
80-84	0.085	0.161
85 and over	0.189	0.269

Source: Tokyo Metropolitan Government, *Survey on Living Conditions and Health*, 1980

To estimate the total number of these elderly patients, the age-sex-specific probabilities of suffering from senile dementia or who are bedridden have been computed for those aged 65 and over, by heavily drawing upon various sample survey results. The computed probabilities by age and sex for each type of patient are shown in Tables 9 and 10. As regards the case of the bedridden patients, the following three surveys undertaken by the Ministry of Health and Welfare in 1984 have been used: (i) the Basic Survey on Welfare Administration (a total sample of 88,000 households), (ii) the Survey on Social Welfare Facilities (all social welfare facilities covered), and (iii) the Patient Survey (a total of 5,282 hospitals and clinics). Note that in the NUPRI model, the patients are defined as being bedridden if they have been staying in bed at least six months, or if they have been admitted to the Special Welfare Nursing Homes. It should also be noted that, because these surveys have a relatively large sample size, the estimated probabilities can be considered highly reliable.

In the case of senile dementia, however, the computed probabilities are less reliable, primarily because the sample size of the survey is quite small. This survey, which is officially called "The Survey on Living Conditions and Health of the Elderly," was conducted by the Tokyo Metropolitan Government in 1980, covering a total of 5,000 Tokyo residents aged 65 and over. The response rate was 90 percent, and based upon this first round of survey results, intensive interviews were given by a group of five medical doctors to those first round respondents who had stated that they had some symptoms of senile dementia. To make final judgements, their families were also interviewed by the five doctors. At the end of the second round of the survey, a total of 198 persons were identified as those with senile dementia. Despite the limited coverage of the survey, we have used its results to compute the probabilities because there is no other information available at the present moment.

Given the assumption that the age-sex-specific pattern of the incidence of senile dementia and bedridden cases displayed in Tables 9 and 10 remain unchanged, the total number of the elderly patients have been projected over the period 1985-2020. The number of the bed-ridden patients among the population aged 65 and over grows by approximately three times over the 40-year period, i.e., from 657,000 in 1985 to 1,960,000 in 2025. Similar observations are applicable to the growth pattern of the aged population suffering from senile dementia. The total number of cases of senile dementia increases by 3.3 times during the corresponding period, namely, from 661,000 to 2,165,000.

Because of rapidly growing government medical expenditure and the unprecedent growth of the elderly population, increasing attention has recently been directed toward the role of families in supporting the health of their aged parents in Japan. One of the reasons for this shift in attention lies in the fact that unlike industrialized countries in the Western world, Japan enjoys a high percentage of extended families; 47.2 percent of the households were of the three-generation type. Another reason is the limited availability of institutional care. Primarily for these two reasons, the majority of the bedridden elderly or those with senile dementia are looked after at home in contemporary Japan.

From a policy point of view, it is interesting to compare the projected number of these elderly patients with that of those who are likely to be responsible for taking care of them. To accomplish this, we have obtained information on the age-sex distribution of care-givers at home for these aged patients from the following two sources: (i) The Survey on the Care of Bedridden Aged Persons (carried out by the National Social Welfare Council), and (ii) The Survey on Living Conditions and Health of the Elderly. One of the weaknesses of the former information source is the fact that, because it was conducted in 1977, information from this source is rather out-dated. Unlike the latter information source, however, the former survey was based upon a large sample, i.e., more than 174,000 sample cases. Moreover, in this survey, information was gathered by 160,000 social workers who had actually been serving with the sampled elderly patients. For this reason, the reliability of data collected in this survey can be considered extremely high.

Before discussing computed results, caution should be exercised with regard to the following two assumptions used. First, because both the surveys show that the overwhelming majority of the caregivers were non-working women, it has been assumed for the sake of simplicity that all of the elderly patients are taken care of by women outside the labour force. Second, the latter survey indicates that 21.1 percent of the elderly with senile dementia are bedridden, so that this percentage was used to avoid double counts. Based upon these two assumptions, the probability for non-working women having to take care of these patients has been computed over the period 1985-2025 for the following six age groups: 20-29, 30-39, 40-49, 50-59, 60-69, and 70 and over. The number of non-working women in each of these age groups has been estimated by multiplying the age-specific female population by $(1 - FLFPR)$, where FLFPR stands for the female labor force participation rate, for the corresponding age group. FLFPRs for the six age groups are estimated in the population sub-model of the NUPRI model, and their determinants differ considerably from age group to age group (Ogawa et al, 1986).

The calculated results are displayed in Figure 2. As can be seen by inspecting this graphical exposition, the probabilities rise over time for all the age groups. It should be stressed, however, that although the differences in the prob-abilities among these age groups are very small in the early years, they expand markedly over time; in 1985, for instance, the difference between those aged 20-29 and those aged 40-49 is only 0.0622, but increases to 0.2253 in 2025. Moreover, throughout the projection period, the former age group continu-ously shows the lowest probabilities, while the latter shows the highest. In the case of women in their 40s, approximately one out of every 15 women assumes the responsibility for taking care of one elderly patient in 1985, but one out of four women of this age group is likely to look after one patient in 2025. It is also interesting to note that the age group 30-39 undergoes the largest increase (4.52 times) in the probability in relative terms, i.e., from 0.0222 in 1985 to 0.1004 in 2025. On the other hand, the computed probabilities for the age group 70 and over grow only marginally from 0.0444 in 1985 to 0.0496 in 2025. These intertemporal differences in the pattern of an increase in the computed probabilities among the six age groups are attributable to changes in their labour force participation rates as well as in their cohort size.

The above computed results imply that the availability of institutional care as an alternative to home care should be urgently expanded to alleviate the heavy burden on middle-aged women taking care of elderly patients. It should be borne in mind, however, that the provision of such care at institutions gives rise to higher health care costs.

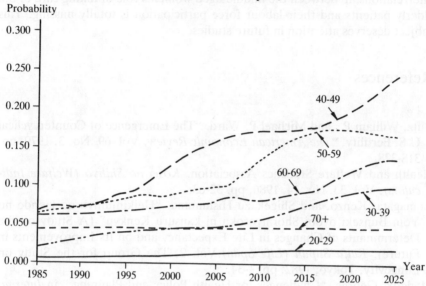

Figure 2. Age-Specific Probabilities for Non-Working Women Having to Take Care of Elderly Persons Suffering from Senile Dementia or Being Bedridden, Japan, 1985-2025

Conclusion

The present chapter has discussed, by utilizing a number of results generated from the NUPRI long-term macroeconomic-demographic-social security model with HOMES incorporated, the impact of the aging of the Japanese population upon total medical expenditure at both national and household levels and upon the manpower requirements of taking care of the elderly patients at the familial level.

Although the scope of material in this chapter is confined substantially to the Japanese context, her experience in providing health care for the elderly in her dynamic economic and demographic processes seems to be useful in formulating appropriate health programs for other countries, particularly developing ones undergoing rapid demographic changes. Furthermore, in the face of her fast economic development, Japan has retained some of the traditional cultural values, so that the Japanese model may be of relevance to policy makers in the developing region interested in combining the best of traditional and modern approaches in order to provide health services to the elderly. In addition, the methodologies employed in the present paper are highly applicable to most of the developing countries in Asia. One of the recent studies on the costs of health care in Thailand (Ogawa, Poapongsakorn, and Mason, 1987) is a salient example.

Although the effect of female labour force participation upon fertility has been fully incorporated in the current version of the NUPRI model, the interrelationship between the middle-aged women's role of taking care of the elderly patients and their labour force participation is totally missing. This subject deserves attention in future studies.

References

Butz, William P., and Michael P. Ward. "The Emergence of Countercyclical U.S. Fertility, "*The American Economic Review,* Vol. 69, No. 3, 1979, pp. 318-328.

Health and Welfare Statistics Association. *Kosei no Shihyo (Welfare Indicators),* Vol. 33, No. 14, 1986, pp. 52-63.

Kamagata, Kenzo, and Shigekazu Hishinuma. "Heikinjumyo no Hendo no Yoin Bunseki oyobi Shoraiyosoku ni kansuru Kenkyu" (A Study on the Determinants of Changes in Life Expectancy and on Its Improvements in Future), *Raifu Supan (Life Span),* Vol. 2, The Group for the Study on Longevity, Tokyo, 1982, pp. 1-34.

Maddox, George, "Challenges for Health Policy and Planning," in *International Perspectives on Aging: Population and Policy Challenges,* edited by R. Binstock, W.S.Chow, and J. Schulz, United Nations Fund for Population Activities Policy Development Studies No. 7, New York, 1982, pp. 127-158.

Martin, Linda G., and Naohiro Ogawa. "Cohort Size Effects on Employment and Relative Wages: the Case of Japan," in *Economics of Changing Age Distributions in Developed Countries,* edited by R.D.Lee, W.B.Arthur, and G. Rodgers, Oxford University Press, London, 1988.

Mason, Andrew. *HOMES: A Household Model for Economic and Social Studies,* Papers of the East-West Population Institute No. 106, Honolulu, 1987.

Ogawa, Naohiro. "Consequences of Mortality Change on Aging," *Consequences of Mortality Trends and Differentials,* United Nations Population Studies No. 95, Part III, Chapter 16, 1986, pp. 175-184.

Ogawa, Naohiro and Robert W. Hodge. "Fertility and the Locus of Family Control in Contemporary Japan," *Population Research Leads,* Series No. 14, United Nations ESCAP, Bangkok, Thailand, 1983.

Ogawa, Naohiro and Andrew Mason. "An Economic Analysis of Recent Fertility in Japan: An application of the Butz-Ward Model,*The Journal of Population Studies,* Population Association of Japan, Vol. 9, 1986, pp.5-14.

Ogawa, Naohiro, Nipon Poapongsakorn, and Andrew Mason. "Population Change and the Costs of Health Care in Thailand," paper prepared for the National Economic and Social Development Board of the Thai Government, and the Asian Development Bank, July 1987, 52 pp.

Ogawa, Naohiro et al. *Jinko Keizai Iryo Moderu ni Motozuku Choki Tembo: Feisu II (Long-term Prospects based upon the Population-Economic-Medical Model: Phase II),* Nihon University Population Research Institute, Tokyo, 1986.

Petri Peter A. "Income, Employment, and Retirement Policies," in *International Perspectives on Aging: Population and Policy Challenges,* edited by R. Binstock, W.S.Chow, and J.Schulz, United Nations Fund for Population Activities Policy Development Studies No. 7, New York, 1982, pp. 75-125.

Social Insurance Agency, Government of Japan. *Outline of Social Insurance in Japan, 1985,* Japan International Social Security Association, 1986.

United Nations. "Global Trends and Prospects of the Age Structure of Population: Different Paths to Aging," *Papers and Proceedings of the United Nations International Symposium on Population Structure and Development,* United Nations, New York, 1987.

Chapter 6

Aging and Population-Carrying Capacity

Akira KOIZUMI   Showa University School of Medicine
Tokyo, Japan

The concept of population-carrying capacity has been discussed mostly among ecologists. Howley[1] stated that the population-carrying capacity of the land is only partially determined by resources, climate, and other physical conditions, but it is also affected by the manner in which human population is organized to use the resources. Through their use of natural resources, human beings develop characteristic man-made environments. This is called human activities.

According to Boughey,[2] population density per square kilometer of land by culture type was 0.01 for midpleistocene hunter-gatherers, 0.05 for late-pleistocene hunter-gatherers, 10 for early agricultural communities and 20 for advanced agricultural communities.

Development of human activities, including advancement of science and technology, has widened the above-mentioned use of natural resources to a great extent. However, despite rapid development of human activities as a major component of population-carrying capacity, the population growth rate has been decreasing in industrialized nations due to declines in fertility. Accordingly, increase of population-carrying capacity of the land as expressed by population density has also become smaller than previously.

In spite of its size (as much as about one hundred and fourteen million), the population of Japan has been without any large international migration. Changes in population size are, therefore, due almost entirely to births and deaths. Annual changes in birth rate and death rate for 1900 through 1985 are shown in Fig. 1. The Birth rate has been higher than the death rate and the difference is shown as the natural increase rate. As shown in Fig. 1, the birth rate decreased after the peak of 36.2 in 1920 and the death rate also came downward after the peak of 27.3 in 1918.

Declines in mortality, and particularly in fertility, have brought a rapid transformation of age-distribution in the Japanese population. In 1955, percent age distribution of age 0-14 to total population was 33.4, and in 1985 it was 21.5. It is estimated that it will be 18.0 in 2000 and 16.4 in 2025. Percent age distribution of age 65 and above was 10.3 in 1985 and is estimated to be 16.3 in 2000 and 23.4 in 2025.

It is doubtless the that declines in fertility and mortality were attained by the development of human activities. Population-carrying capacity, particularly in terms of human activities, should therefore be understood as carrying capacity for population age structure rather than size of population. This new concept of population-carrying capacity or human activities can also be discussed from a strwy of social and economic aspects of medical care in relation to population aging.

Life expectancy at birth for Japanese females was reported in 1986 to be 80.93 years of age and that of males to be 75.23. These figures rank first among the countries of the world. However, it is only a recent phenomenon that Japanese life expectancy at birth has increased to such a high level. In 1971, life expectancy at birth was 75.58 for female and 70.17 for male. These figures marked the achievement of a long-cherished wish by the Japanese people for an average life expectancy for females of above 75 years and for males of above 70 years. In 1952, the life expectancy at birth of Japanese females exceeded 65 years of age, and in 1951 that of males reached the 60's.

In spite of the above-mentioned rapid growth of life expectancy in Japan, a mathematical model indicates that this rate has been lowering and will reach a plateau in the 21st Century[3] as shown in Fig. 2. The relationship between changes in life expectancy at birth and per capita national medical expenditure was also examined. Here, in order to remove the influence of long-term fluctuations on these figures, a correction was made using the consumer's price index published by the Bureau of Statistics at the Prime Minister's Office.

In Fig. 3, life expectancy at birth for each year is expressed as "y" in years and per capita national medical expenditure for the same year as "x" in yen. It is likely that life expectancy at birth is dependent on per capita national expenditure. However, there are two patterns as to the dependency. Therefore, curve fitting was tried by two equations; one by Equation A or "y — 37.66 + 6.92 x" corresponding to data from 1955 to 1975, and the other by Equation B or "y — -11.73 + 16.93 log x" corresponding to data from 1975 to 1985. Thus it can be explained that dependency of life expectancy on medical expenditure from 1955 to 1975 was higher than that from 1975 to 1985. In short, medical care pushed up life expectancy in the former period, whereas the effect of some other factors like health services, individual health promotion and so forth were also notable in the elevation of life expectancy in the later period.

As I have written elsewhere,[4,5] during the period of a rapid improvement in life expectancy at birth, nation-wide health surveys have shown an increase of sick people particularly among the elderly. It is assumed that there was a contribution of medical care to prolongation of life in that period. As shown in Fig. 3, quite recently some factors other than medical expenditure are likely to affect growth of life expectancy.

Life expectancy is an integration of age-specific death rates of a particular year. Therefore, growth of life expectancy means nothing but improvement of age-specific death rates. In general, this improvement was seen among younger age groups such as infants, children and young adults. From a cause-of-death point of view, this improvement reflects a reduction of deaths from infectious diseases, including tuberculosis. Quite recently, however, improvements have been seen among middle aged and even the elderly in relation to chronic degenerative conditions like cardiovascular diseases.

It is clear that both declines in fertility and mortality are the outcome of human activities and therefore of man-made origin. It is also clear that improvement of mortality or the growth of life expectancy is not our simple goal. Attention should be placed on healthier and more satisfactory longevity. This would also be attained by human activities in terms of population-carrying capacity.

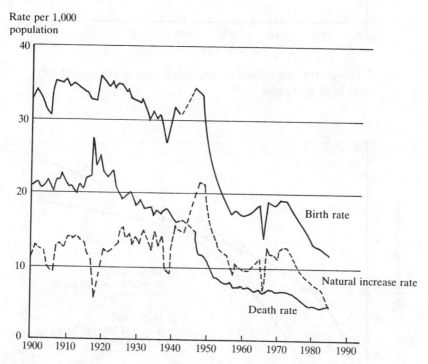

Rate per 1,000 population

Fig. 1 Annual changes in birth rate, death rate and natural increase rate, 1900-1985.

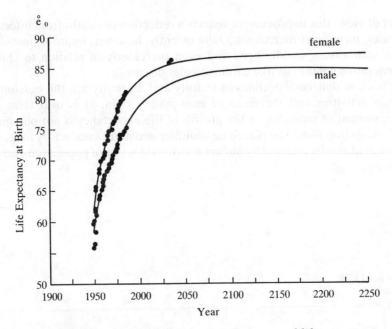

*Fig. 2 Gompertz curve fitted to annual change of life expectancy
at birth in Japan.*

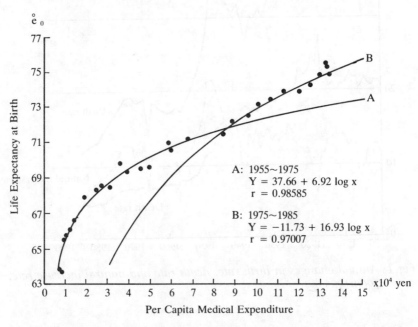

*Fig. 3 Relationship between life expectancy at birth and per capita medical
expenditure in Japan.*

Note: life expectancy is a weighted average of male and female.

Notes

1. Hawley, A.H.: *Human ecology — A theory of community structure*, Ronald Press, New York, 151, 1950.
2. Boughey, A.S.: *Man and the environment*, MacMillan, New York, 321, 1971.
3. Koizumi, A., Nishii, S., Sakai, N.: "Estimation of life expectancy by mathematical models," *Minzoku-Eisei (Japan Journal of Health and Human Ecology)*, 45: 184-188, 1979.
4. Koizumi, A.: "Health problems of the year 2000 and beyond," *Health Policy*, 4: 307-319, 1985.
5. Koizumi, A.: "Health Resources Aspects of Man Environment Systems": Suzuki, T. and Otsuka, R.(ed.); *Human Ecology of Health and Survival in Asia and the South Pacific,* 123-132, University of Tokyo Press, 1987.

Part Two

Family Support Systems

Introduction

by John EEKELAAR

This part is divided into three Sections. The common element running through them is the question of how resources are distributed across the generations: in this case, from the younger to the older. These chapters are primarily descriptive. Deeper issues of philosophy and ideology underlying the processes will be addressed in Part Three. *Section One* of Part Two exposes in detail how different societies, confronted with rapid social change, have adapted their institutions or created new ones in order to provide for human needs. *Section Two* primarily considers the contemporary position of the elderly in four different types of society within the context of their social relationships. *Section Three* examines the attempts made by various legal systems to impose a framework of legal obligations to control or guide the conduct of the primary social actors.

Rwezaura (Chapter 7) cites Simonds' provocative observation that, whereas nature appears to have implanted an instinct among animals to care for their young, protection of the old is not similarly ingrained, either among animals or humans. So socially constructed norms have to make good nature's deficiency, or else the old will perish. Rwezaura brilliantly demonstrates how conventions of "traditional" African societies which might have appeared obnoxious to external observers, such as the successive introduction of young wives into an older man's household, worked as a means of providing security for the man (and his earlier wives) as he grew old. A not dissimilar function was served by the Japanese custom of the adoption of majors (see Kato, Chapter 10). We may characterize such practices as the manipulation, by a society, through an ideology of deference to the elderly, of its human resources in such a way as to sustain its aging generation. And it is not simply a question of exploitation by the old. For, unlike the case of the animal kingdom, human society profits from the experience and wisdom of its older members. This theme of reciprocity between the generations is of great importance and will recur.

Yet, as Rwezaura shows, systems which propelled human resources to the benefit of the elderly began to break down with the introduction of a cash economy and the growing inclination among younger people towards personal autonomy. One consequence was an attempt by the elderly to re-assert traditional values. The new states have not yet provided sufficient alternatives to the loss of human resources. The remainder of this work will give prolonged examination to what these alternatives might be. But the interaction between inter-generational conflict and tensions between traditional values and newer ideologies can be readily understood.

Indonesia serves as an example of a state which is rapidly attempting to overcome its colonial past and provide security for its entire population. Yet the mechanisms of the modern state in making up for deficiencies in what Ihromi (Chapter 8) calls the "non-statutory social security system" will take many years to complete, if indeed they ever can be. The statutory social security system was introduced initially to cover those who directly served the state, in the army or in the civil service (although this extends to industrial workers in state-owned enterprises). There is a general public assistance programme for the indigent elderly, but this requires an elaborate application to be made to the Minister in each case. [The general problems of creating pension schemes adequate to the needs of the populations of third-world countries are discussed within the context of Tanzania by Wanitzek (Chapter 56)].

A remarkable case of a society in transition is described by Mladenovic (Chapter 9), that of Yugoslavia. Mladenovic observes how the socialist revolution by-passed the old: indeed, it could be perceived as a revolt against the previous generation: the domination of human resources by the then-elderly. Interestingly, Mladenovic found no appreciation of the privations of the elderly in the relevant political documents from the early days of the Russian and Yugoslav revolutions. Yet Mladenovic considers that industrialization and demographic change have been more significant than revolutionary ideology in bringing about a deterioration in the position of the elderly: the "atomization" of the family is shared by capitalist and socialist societies. Here again, state action is proving insufficient in replacing human resources with the currency of the state — money and social services. The problem is aggravated by the social variations within a still socially fragmented country. The conditions of the rural elderly are different from those in towns. Nevertheless, even within a changing and fragmented society, Mladenovic argues that a complete and coherent programme directed towards the elderly should be undertaken, and sets out the issues that need to be addressed. Most of these will receive detailed attention elsewhere in this work.

Section Two commences with data presented by Hoerl (Chapter 11), which is consistent with other empirical studies, on the place of the elderly within family networks in an urban industrial setting (Vienna). Elderly men are more likely to be married than women (and a spouse is the most significant provider of help), and a substantial minority have no kin at all. Nevertheless, those with children remain in frequent contact with them. (Mladenovic, in Chapter 9, provides similar data from an international study). Although financial help is quite rare, children frequently provide other forms of assistance. Some features of these relationships are of special importance. One is that old people are concerned about the *quality* of their relationships with their children: they do not wish to demand too much of them. Another is their *reciprocity*: they try to give something in return. But closeness with family members does not guarantee more happiness than contacts with friends. Ninomiya's Tokyo sample (Chapter 12) emphasizes the relatively low standard of living of the elderly. As in the Vienna study, the elderly's desire not to become dependent on their children comes across strongly.

Relative to their urban counterparts, the conditions of the elderly in non-industrialized countries seem to be harder. In Thailand, Sittitrai (Chapter 13) found that a high number had no spouse, even though as a result of the sampling technique, men may have been over-represented. The oldest received most of their support from children, although this does not seem to have provided them with obviously comfortable standards of living. In rural Zimbabwe, Hampson (Chapter 14) observes that the majority of elderly reported receiving no remittances from outside the household. The relatively large proportion of elderly with children provides a significant potential network of informal assistance, yet this appears to be weakening. Friends, rather than children, are the primary source of emotional support. Finally, within the exceptional society of South Africa, Burman (Chapter 15) reports how simplistic official belief that "the family" will provide for the black elderly is not sustained by the evidence. While much of the family dislocation can be attributed to, and is aggravated by, governmental policies, evidence from elsewhere indicates that social structural causes are also at work.

Should the law compel children to support their parents? This, in crude terms, is the issue addressed in *Section Three*. The law no doubt establishes (or reflects?) a system of normative behaviour, can create expectations and guide behaviour. So Mahmood (Chapter 16) shows how Islamic law equates the obligation to support the elderly to a religious duty, underwriting it by a system of succession whereby parents are among the primary heirs, and gives examples of its translation into modern civil codes.

Even in western countries, it has always been thought that, morally, children should support their indigent parents. But the way this has been translated into law has been varied — and extremely problematic. Gunn (Chapter 17) explains how this was achieved in England. The legal duty only arose when an elderly pauper was supported from parish funds. The enforcement of the obligation is essentially a revenue collecting exercise, exacted against relatives because it is thought that the primary duty of support falls (morally) on them rather than the community. Levy (Chapter 18) gives examples of how the state can indirectly attempt to enforce this obligation by reducing its assistance to the poor elderly where it considers the resources of family members could be used instead. That we are dealing with policies that cut across political ideologies is manifest when we consider the very similar provisions in Poland described by Stojanowska (Chapter 19).

Very clear parallels can be found to the laws found almost everywhere concerning child support. [For a comprehensive examination of these laws, see M.T. Meulders-Klein and J. Eekelaar (eds.) *Family, State and Individual Economic Security* (Story Scientia, 1988) 2 vols]. It is therefore easy to slip into a belief that they should be treated in the same way. But this may be a mistake.

It is arguable that a parent's obligation towards a child arises primarily from the parent's location as intercessor between the child and the wider community. The parent brings resources into the household and it is his social role to pass them on to the child. Hence it is, that the duty of support is usually owed to *any* child incorporated into the household, whether related by blood to the adult or not. The obligation thus primarily arises as a result of the structural relationship of parent and child to the community. This is not to argue that a biological parent may not owe duties to support children living elsewhere. But such a duty is secondary, and often subject to many qualifications.

At least where parents are living separately from their children, any obligation on the child to support the parent does not rest upon their structural relationship to society. It has therefore to be found elsewhere. That this is extremely hard to appears from the chapters by Levy and Stojanowska. We have do observed that social studies have revealed the importance of reciprocity in relationships between the elderly and their children, and the elderly's emphasis on the quality of these relationships. If there has been no reciprocity (the parent has long abandoned the child), imposition of the obligation seems inappropriate. If there has been reciprocity, the parent is unlikely to wish to mobilize the law against the child, which could destroy the value of the relationship. As Burman observes with respect to the norms of black South African society: "you just don't do things like that", a sentiment echoed by parents in America and Poland and perhaps everywhere. The reader may conclude that the grounds for enforcing the moral obligation by direct or indirect legal means are unsatisfactory. What is at stake is merely the wish to reduce the burden of certain public expenditures. Recourse against relatives (children) may be an ill-considered, and inefficient, way of satisfying the desire.

In this context, the concluding chapter of *Section Three* is of special interest. In it, Maeda (Chapter 20) explains that, although the Japanese Civil Code requires children to support and care for their parents, in Public Assistance Law a distinction is drawn between cases where the elderly parents live with children and where they do not. Only where they do, must the children keep them at the same standard of living as themselves and bear the cost of community services. Also it is only where a parent was living with the child when placed in a nursing home that the child must pay the fee. As Maeda notes, the policy of enforcement of the obligation by government is very lenient. Yet in Japan the majority of elderly live with their families, though this is decreasing, and the quality of such "home-care" is not always good, and often imposes considerable strains on the caregivers. While, therefore, the appropriateness of attempting (often unsuccessfully) to *compel* income transfers from children to aged parents may be questionable, there is no reason why those who care for parents within their home, and therefore establish a structure which requires them to provide for the parents, should not be supported by auxiliary services from the community to facilitate the discharge of their obligations. But, as we have seen, such co-residence is rare in the west and declining even in Japan.

Section One

Societies in Transition

Chapter 7

Changing Community Obligations to the Elderly in Contemporary Africa

B.A. RWEZAURA   University of Dar-es-Salaam, Tanzania

Introduction

Many writers on traditional African social systems have stressed the importance of age as a significant criterion for the attainment of authority, power, privilege, prestige and leadership in the community. In traditional Africa, the older the individual became, the higher were his chances for gaining upward mobility in the social hierarchy. Through a system of economic reciprocity, a person was able to use his wealth to attract additional dependents and thus to secure a greater degree of social security during old age.

The control maintained by elders over strategic resources, such as land, livestock, women and children, enabled them to ensure relative stability in junior/senior relations. Such stability was essential for the functioning of the traditional social order. Indigenous law and religion also played a supportive role.

Until the intervention of colonial rule in Africa, elders were relatively secure in their positions. However, changes associated with colonial occupation had far-reaching effects on junior/senior relations. Economic change, new forms of social and political control and new religions, all threatened the dominant position of the elders in many parts of Africa. Old age became a disability as well as an economic risk. As the household became increasingly dependent on the market for its basic needs, there was a corresponding decline in the system of economic reciprocity and a loosening of social cohesion. These changes, whose broad effects were felt beyond the junior/senior relations, challenged as well as undermined the entire traditional socio-economic system and demanded new solutions to problems of old-age security.

In their bid to retain their position, elders sought the assistance of the state to enforce traditional obligations. They made inflationary demands on their juniors in forms of high marriage payments, extortionate claims for seduction of unmarried daughters and adultery of wives. A study of some of the resultant conflicts which were mediated through state courts gives some idea of the degree to which socio-economic changes threatened the position of elders and also how the latter tried to minimize these adverse effects.

These economic hardships of the elderly are, unfortunately, not fully appreciated by the new states of Africa. It is often supposed, for example, that the local community in Africa still provides old-age security, when, in reality, its economic role has become attenuated. This chapter stresses that a timely recognition of these hardships is essential for African states to begin a process of creating an institutional framework for confronting the problem whose magnitude will certainly increase as we move into the twenty-first century.

The chapter is divided into four sections; the first examines briefly and generally the position of the elderly in traditional Africa and stresses especially their political and economic roles. Next, it looks at the social and economic transformation which followed the colonisation of Africa and its effect on the position of elders. In the third section are discussed the responses of the elders to these changes and the extent to which they have tried to retain their positions against opposing forces of change. In the concluding section, the paper argues that African states need to provide an alternative form of social security in the light of the diminishing economic security of the elderly in present day Africa.

The Elderly in Traditional Africa

Although the terms "elderly" and "traditional" can be controversial, especially among specialists, the use of these terms here is very general and approximate. It is recognized, for example, that a person's status as an elder in many African societies was dependent on certain social and political factors besides the mere accumulation of lived years. Even then, old-age and social status appear to be associated in defining the status of an elder in many traditional societies. For example, from the time of birth to maturity, old-age and timely demise, an individual went through a series of recognized stages, each higher than the previous one, until such a person reached formal retirement. Whether we wish to define the "elderly" to be a non-active person who has attained retirement age will depend upon the economic and social organization of that society. What is important in our understanding of the term "elderly" is to stress the essential characteristics of old age, such as physical frailty and mental dullness which accompany senility. These make the elderly wholly or partially dependent upon others to provide him/her with care and support for the remaining period of his/her life.

The term "traditional Africa" should also be specifically defined and so must its use in this chapter. By "traditional Africa" I refer to the approximate period before the integration of many African economic systems into a world economy. This integration occurred roughly at the end of the nineteenth century and was facilitated by colonial occupation of most Black Africa. The significance of this periodization lies in the massive transformation which followed the colonisation of Africa (Fitzpatrick 1979, Snyder 1981, Rwezaura 1985). Even then, whereas the term "traditional" refers to the above-mentioned period, it is not intended to draw a sharp divide between Africa's pre-colonial past and the colonial period. A degree of continuity, as well as co-existence of the past and present, is assumed. Hence, what in this chapter are described as the emerging economic and social relations during the post-colonial period are not unrelated to the pre-existing forms of economic and social organization. In other words, change in many cultures has sometimes tended to strengthen certain existing relations while at the same time undermining others (Rwezaura 1985).

There have also been innovative accommodations and adaptations. All these matters are significant in understanding the complexity of the process of change and the extant relations among people in modern Africa.

Elderhood as a Status Position

In many traditional African societies, an individual's social status rose in relation to his age. At the level of the family, a person's status was enhanced when he/she ceased to be a child and became initiated into adulthood. The new status gave an individual limited access to certain privileges originally not available to him or her. On marriage a young man's status rose once again, and he became a man, and this new status carried with it certain rights as well obligations (see generally Fortes & Evans Pritchard (Eds.), 1941).

For most women, procreation was considered important not only for the stability it brought to the marriage, but also for the honour it bestowed upon them in the eyes of their husband's lineages. From the position of mother, a married woman moved to that of mother-in-law when her own children were married, and thereafter she became grandmother to several grandchildren (Brown 1963: 58-60).

Among the Haya people of Tanzania, a son had a hut built for him by his father just before marriage and was allocated a banana garden with sufficient land for cultivation. All the marriage expenses were met by the father with the assistance of his kinsmen. For the Kuria of north-east Tanzania, a man must leave his father's homestead to establish his own place not later than the period when his first born son is circumcised. Malcolm Ruel has observed that when a Kuria initiate returns home from the bush, he must re-enter the homestead through the corral gateway of his own father and not that of his grandfather (Ruel 1958: 67). This rule no doubt was intended to assist the initiate's father to establish his own homestead and enable him to attain relative autonomy and thus begin preparing for his own elderhood.

Although many African societies had differing ways of marking an individual's ascent to a higher social status, the ultimate consequence of these procedures was to enhance the individual's chances as well as ability to gain power and authority over other people. Therefore, at the level of the family and neighbourhood, the head of the family was a highly respected individual. His accumulated wisdom and experience, his control over family property as well as ritual power, made him an undisputed leader of his extended family. His authority over his family was legitimated by custom, religion and different forms of social control, including public opinion. Within the wider community of the lineage and sub-clan, relations between elders and juniors were marked by similar respect for the elderly and a recognition of their authority over the juniors. It is in the acceptance of the status position of elders by juniors that one must look for the basis of the elders' economic and social security in traditional Africa. Some examples of the elders' sources of security are given below.

The Basis of Old-Age Security

It has been argued that, whereas all animals, including man, possess an instinctive drive to care for their dependent off-spring, unfortunately, they do not possess a similar instinct when it comes to the care of the elderly. Hence, Simonds has noted that respect for old age has resulted from imposed social discipline and not nature (1970).[2] In most cultures, children were trained from an early age to obey and respect their parents and other elder members of the community. There is a wealth of ethnographic data showing different ways in which the young have been taught to submit to the authority of the elders. Rattray (1956: 13), for example, noted in respect of the Ashanti of Ghana, that children were taught to honour and respect their elders and "to keep silent in their presence". Swazi children were trained "to regard the father as the legal and economic authority in the home. They were taught from infancy to obey the father's word and even married sons were never regarded as free from his control" (Kuper 1962: 96). Referring to Swazi traditions, Kuper noted that it was hard to convey the extent of the subservience of a Swazi son to his father:

> He works for him, consults him in all his negotiations, refers to him as 'his head', takes legal oaths 'by father'...[Even married sons] as long as they live in his homestead they are expected to hand over to him whatever they may earn, and he may, if he wishes, give them back a portion.

In societies where the age-grade system or generation classes were used to rank individuals and where initiation ceremonies were conducted to admit the youth into the lowest age-grade, respect for the elderly began hierarchically with members of the preceding circumcision set right up to the retiring age-grade (Spencer 1976; Ruel 1958; Baker 1935; Brantley 1978; Turnbull 1976; 51-61 and Gulliver 1956). Through this hierarchical system, an individual grew up knowing the importance of submitting to the authority of seniors and simultaneously learning to expect similar obedience from others below him.

Yet this education of the young generation ought to be seen mainly as a preparation for them to fit into an existing social and economic system which placed the elderly at the top, and thus enabled the elders to build up their old-age security. Perhaps the most significant source of security, which kept the juniors loyal to this system, was the elder's control over strategic as well as scarce resources, such as land, livestock, essential skills and ritual powers. The elders often used these resources in a manner which ensured that the economically active member of the community remained bound to them.

Within this order of things, kinship ties provided an institutional framework through which the elderly made legitimate claims upon labour power, property and the services of junior relatives, and also through which the latter made reciprocal demands on the elders. In other words, kinship ties in traditional Africa constituted an important criterion for the assignment of rights and obligations over property and other resources (Gluckman 1965: 74; Goody 1962; Gray & Gulliver 1964). As noted by Moore, rights to land among the Chagga of Kilimanjaro are handed from generation to generation in the patriline, and important ceremonies, beer parties and slaughtering feasts are organized on lineage basis. Thus, not only is an individual's life derived from his kin, but "one's livelihood comes from patrilineal kin" (1980: 30).

In West Africa, Bledsoe found that, because access to valued resources, such as land, livestock and labour, was traditionally gained through lineage affiliation, there were always many people who were eager to establish real or fictive kinship ties to gain these resources (1980: 58). But given the low technological level of development in these societies, the acquisition of land without having rights in people was not in itself socially advantageous. Emphasis was, therefore, placed on the expansion of one's lineage through marriage, procreation and the attraction of many dependents into ties of obligation.

Hence many ethnological studies on traditional Africa stress that the desire of most men was to establish beneficial kinship ties with a large number of people in order to attain political and economic power and to secure themselves during old age (Mair 1971: 82). Writing in 1935 about the Kuria people of Tanzania, Baker notes that, "it is the aim of every Mkuria to have as many wives as possible in order that he may beget a large number of sons who will increase his power in the clan .. and daughters who will, by their marriages, increase his herd of cattle" (1935: 62).

For the Kpelle of Liberia, Bledsoe argues that "political success rests not only on a person's ascribed position but also on his ability to create relationships of obligation and dependency with subordinates". However, Bledsoe cautions that, since such relationships take time to create and additional time to make use of, "political success is usually the reward of old age" (1980: 55).

One of the most widely known methods by which the elderly sought to achieve the foregoing objective was through marriage to younger mates. This practice is common among men in Africa and has been well documented (Simonds 1971: 177-216). Of the Lango people of Uganda, Driberg notes that "instances are not wanting in which a woman, on growing old, of her own instance presses her husband to marry a younger and more attractive wife ..." (1923: 155). The latter is expected to provide care and economic support to the elderly couple. According to Dundas, the aged Akamba of Kenya often married young women and Xhosa girls were said to be "literally dragged off" to be married to elderly men and households were listed in which the oldest wife was seventy and the youngest seventeen (Simonds 1970: 179-180).

Perhaps the best illustration of security in old-age through marriage is given by Holden who described the happy position of the Xhosa polygamist in a rather romantic way as follows:

> The man is then supported in Kaffir pomp and plenty; "he can eat, drink, and be merry", bask in the sun, sing and dance at pleasure, spear bucks, plot mischief, or make bargains for his daughters; to care and toil he can say farewell, and so go on to the end of life. As age advances he takes another "young wife" or concubine; and then another, to keep up "eternal youth"; for he is never supposed to grow old, so long as he can obtain a "youthful bride", she, by proxy, imparts her freshness to his withered frame and throws her bloom over his withered brow" (Holden 1963: 203-204).

Though life may not have been as rosy for all the elderly Xhosa and less still for most elders in other cultures, it cannot be denied nonetheless that even today, such forms of marriage continue to be looked upon as an investment for old age.[3]

In sum, what requires emphasis here is that old-age security in most pre-colonial African societies was embedded in their socio-economic system, and as we shall see in the next section, the economic and social transformation of these cultures affected, inter alia, the foundation of old-age security.

The Effects of Change on the Elderly

It has been argued by some writers that changes associated with colonial occupation of Africa greatly weakened the social and economic arrangements which formerly had guaranteed social security not only for the elderly but also for the entire community (Yeld 1966: 6; Moore 1978; Snyder 1981, Saul & Woods 1971: 103-104). The introduction of the monetary economy, new religions, new forms of social and political control and so on, weakened the dominant position of the elderly in many parts of Africa, thus leading to their loss of authority, political power and economic security, (Moore 1973; Snyder 1981).

Yet although this general assertion is in many respects supported by empirical evidence, there is also evidence suggesting the opposite tendency. Research has shown, for example, that in certain cases some elders have successfully used their traditional position effectively in order to accumulate more wealth than would have been possible in traditional times (Murray 1976; Yeld 1966; Rwezaura 1983, 1988). This amount of wealth has been acquired mainly by exploiting the new opportunities which the changing social and economic conditions create for the elderly. Therefore, there are elders in contemporary

Africa whose social security has been enhanced by change and others who have been marginalised by the same process. It is still true, nonetheless, that those who have lost their economic power constitute the majority of the elderly, and hence their condition calls for deeper consideration.

Writing about the elderly among the Chagga people of Tanzania, S.F. More notes that:

> Persons living in a swiftly altering world find that their social roles change as they perform them and each stage of growing older is a matter of arriving at something quite different from what it was for the age group just before (1978: 23).

But Moore adds that "some of that change is to advantage yet some has come to seem a total cheat" (1978: 23).

These wide-ranging consequences of change on the economic position of elders provide a useful clue to the central question of the dynamic relation between traditional forms of social security and the contemporary processes of economic and social change. It is my argument that change has created opportunities as well as constraints for elders. Change has also taken away the relative predictability of old-age security by altering the social and economic roles of the elderly. The consequence of this is that elders who consider that they are no longer assured of economic support from the wider family have adopted a defensive attitude, designed mainly to hedge themselves against the threat of destitution during old age.

In this sense, change has increased the elders' awareness of their relative positions in the community, while at the same time sharpening their sense of competition for the accumulation and retention of strategic resources. On the other hand, the younger who, as already noted, constitute the foundation of the elders' economic welfare, have utilized change to secure relative autonomy from ties of obligation to the elders.

Two sources from which elders have traditionally obtained their old-age security will be discussed. They include, first, the elder's control of nubile women and, secondly, their easy access to younger mates. I will show that the control by elders and their access to this group of women has declined and this has greatly undermined their essential sources of social security. Using statutory sources and court decisions, it can be seen how the elders' control over their juniors has also been undermined by the state as an agent of change and also how elders have fought back in an effort to retain their former position.

In this discussion, the concept of "wealth in people" (Bledsoe 1980; Schneider 1968; Mair 1953; Fallers 1964; Little 1951 and Gluckman 1941) has been used to illustrate the point that loss of rights in certain people leads to loss of wealth, prestige and authority. Bledsoe has argued, following previous writers on Africa (Goody 1971, Terray 1972), that "in any society the rights that people have in the services and persons of others are tremendously important." Referring to the Kpelle people of Liberia, Bledsoe notes that "men and the old have legal rights in women not only to reproduce and gain labour for supporting their immediate families but also to lure young men into ties of debt and obligation" (1980: 49).

Looking at marital strategy in Lesotho, Colin Murray has clearly demonstrated that the function of bridewealth in contemporary Basuto community is to
redistribute upwards, from the junior (active migrant) generation to the senior
(retired) generation, a proportion of the means of subsistence derived from
earnings in South Africa. Thus, by holding on to their nubile daughters, Basuto
elders are able to secure from their juniors substantial maintenance, instead of
relying merely on kinship morality (1977: 80).

But whereas most Basuto fathers can feel relieved that their control over
marriageable women will assure them of security in old age, researches in other
parts of Africa show a general loosening of parental control over their children.
It is argued below that the alteration in the pre-capitalist system of wealth in
people has adversely affected the economic security of the elderly.

The Concept of "Wealth in People" and its Modern Constraints

As noted already, the economic subordination of women and young men in
traditional Africa greatly assured their dependence on male elders. This
arrangement kept in check the strivings of these juniors to extricate themselves
from relations of dependence, until the moment arrived when they gained
relative autonomy while simultaneously increasing their rights in other people.
But forces of change, generated by colonial capitalism — as noted above — and
ecological factors, disrupted the scheme by enabling the junior to secure wealth
and social status outside the traditional sphere, and this provided a chance for
the juniors to disregard the authority of their seniors. Change also provided
new opportunities for women and children to free themselves from the control
of the elders by moving into urban centres or by selecting their own spouses
without too much interference from their parents. The colonial state and
Christian missions also created their own economic and cultural opportunities
for the juniors to free themselves from ties of obligation. This development
created tensions in the relations between juniors and seniors. Thus the system
of rights in people which seniors traditionally relied to gain their old-age
security came under heavy strain.

Writing about the increasing equality between men and women among the
Toro people of Uganda, Melvin Perlman (1985: 82-93) notes that, although
traditionally payment of bridewealth was a necessary condition to the legality
of marriage, yet, by the 1950s, bridewealth in Toro society, had radically
declined as a precondition for marriage, and many marriages had been
contracted without transfer of bridewealth. In a sample of 147 marriages
contracted between 1950-1960, Perlman found that over 82% involved no
payment of bridewealth.

The rapid fall of bridewealth transfers among the Toro has been linked by Perlman to the decimation of their livestock by the rinderpest epidemics which broke out at the turn of this century. The depletion of their livestock initially made it difficult for men to meet the costs of marriage. They offered to pay later though many did not. Such defaults gradually became tolerated and, as noted by Perlman, this made it easier for other men to follow suit, and the non-payment of bridewealth gradually became the custom among the lower classes, constituting the majority (1985: 87).

The decline in the institution of bridewealth among the Toro paved the way for relative acceptability, in later years, of a rule that fathers no longer had legal custody over their daughters after the age of 16 years. The effect of this rule, which was imposed by local administration courts, was to give greater freedom to daughters over 16 to select their own husbands without too much resistance from their fathers. As noted above, colonial courts were supportive of this law by refusing to apprehend eloping women, to award any damages or impose any fines against young men in cases of seduction or enticement of women aged 16 years and above. Thus, of 1,228 family cases heard by the Toro native courts between 1900 and 1960, only 3% were bridewealth cases and even the majority of these were for refund of bridewealth at the time of divorce rather than claims for the initial payment of bridewealth (1985: 87). Although colonial courts were not the only fora for the settlement of family disputes, this small percentage of bridewealth cases shows that non-payment of bridewealth was becoming accepted by many people.

Even though the decline of bridewealth as a condition for marriage in Toro society was sparked off initially by a natural cause, the rinderpest epidemic, other factors of change assisted its downfall and its importance was not revived even when the adverse effects of the rinderpest had long disappeared.[4] The consequence of this development was that, not only did fathers lose an important source of income, but they also lost control over their daughters. Young men who were expected to remain loyal to and supportive of their elders in anticipation of assistance at the time of marriage could now marry without parental help. Indeed, even in cases where bridewealth was transferred, a number of sons personally paid for their own marriages without their fathers' assistance. To this extent, fathers became dispensable as sources of wives, and this further undermined their power and authority over the young generation.

Reports of parents losing control over their daughters have been made by other researchers on Africa. Yeld's study among the Kiga of south-Western Uganda, in 1965, revealed similar trends. Yeld found that, although in traditional Kiga society the head of the household usually arranged and paid for his son's marriage, by the 1960s it was generally accepted by Kiga of all age groups that young persons of both sexes should be allowed free choice of a marriage partner (1966: 8). In a survey of 150 marriages, Yeld noted that 41 out of 50 marriages contracted by Kiga couples aged 50 years and above had been contracted without the brides ever selecting their husbands. The majority had not met their husbands before the wedding day. In the case of married women within the age group of 50 years and under, 68 out of 96 respondents stated that they had freely accepted marriage proposals without parental pressure. And in the case of spouses in the age group of 40 years or under, their marriages followed meetings between youngsters independent of any previous ties of relationship or friendship between their respective parents (1966: 8). Usually the young men and women who met at the local market, at Church services or Sunday school, soon fell in love and agreed to marry.

This freedom to select spouses among the younger Kiga must be related to the high number of elopements recorded by Yeld as well as extent to which the tradition of bridewealth payment was adhered to in these marriages. According to the Kiga data, Yeld found that among the reasons given for elopement by Kiga men were economic ones, that is, their inability to secure the necessary bridewealth. In such cases elopements provided an avenue to marry without paying for the wife.[5] Hence the freedom to select a spouse, the high rate of elopements and the failure of the husband and his agnatic family to meet his bridewealth obligation to the father-in-law, all combined to undermine the economic position of the elders in Kiga society.

Hence, although freedom to marry without paying bridewealth is cited here as a specific instance of the reduction in the elders' sources of power and economic support, it must be viewed in the broader context of social and economic change in which it occurred. For example, Yeld writes about how the 'pacification' of the Kiga facilitated freer mobility of people and goods leading to trade, wage employment and the inevitable dispersal of the extended family members to other parts of Uganda. On the other hand, the appointment of local chiefs as administrators and magistrates had the effect of undermining the authority of family heads. Such chiefs, being the appointees of the colonial government, were comparatively young, many were Christians and had some formal education. Change thus introduced a new group of 'elders' who competed with the traditional elites for power and prestige and set the pace for other juniors to challenge the authority of their seniors. As pointed out by Yeld.

> [t]he achievement of independence by the younger generation ... is fre-
> quently referred to in common conversation ... with the use of the verb
> "okwetegyeka" i.e. to become free. Fathers bemoan such freedom and the
> indiscipline of sons and their refusal to help their fathers in old age (p.6).

Francis Snyder makes a similar observation about new sources of power and wealth among the Banjal people of Senegal. He notes that

> [f]ormerly the accumulation and re-distribution of wealth and authority were
> reserved to elders, who controlled the access of their juniors to land and ritual
> office. Today adults are relatively poorer while new sources of wealth are
> open to youths outside the village ... By partially freeing youth from their
> dependence on elders and adults, migration has tended to legitimate new
> sources of power and authority"
> (1978: 241-242).

In 1974, two elderly Chagga told Moore how they remembered having been "slavishly obedient and deferential to their elders in youth, ever comforted by the thought that their turn to dominate could arrive with age". But they felt keenly disappointed that modernisation had now deprived them of privileges and the regard they expected (Moore 1974: 23).

In Zimbabwe, loss of elders' power over juniors appears also to have been at the root of the hot debate which followed the passing, in 1982, of the *Legal Age of Majority Act* (No. 15). The Act fixed the age of majority at 18 and expressly provided that it was to apply for the purposes of any law, including customary law. The consequence of this legislation, as later confirmed by the Supreme Court of Zimbabwe, was to free African women in Zimbabwe from the legal disadvantages of perpetual minority which they experienced under customary law. The ultimate effect of this legislation was that, after the passing of the Act, a father or guardian lost the right to recover any seduction damages in respect of his daughter, if at the time of the seduction she was eighteen years old or above. Similarly, the father lost a legal right to recover bridewealth if, after her 18th birthday, his daughter chose to be married without his consent. As the Supreme Court Justices put it in *Katekwe V.Muchabaiwa*,[6]

> "an African woman with majority status can if she so desires, allow her father to ask for *roora/lobola* (i.e. bridewealth) from the man who wants to marry her. She and she alone can make that choice".

Hence, whether she chooses to marry under the African Marriages Act (Cap. 238) or the Marriages Act (Cap. 37), she can still marry without the consent of her guardian (p. 16).

From the foregoing illustrations, it becomes apparent that economic and social change had the effect of reducing, if not in some cases completely taking away, the elders' control of the juniors, especially marriageable women. By giving juniors the freedom to travel, to belong to new religions, to gain European education, to work for wages outside the home, and so on, the freedom to break loose from relations of dependence was assured in advance (see also Chanock 1985: 36-37). Elders could no longer count on their juniors to provide for them during old age.

But this loss of control produced a counter-reaction. In an effort to protect themselves from the adverse effects of change, elders turned to customary law for support and adamantly held onto whatever resources they had. They also tried to enlist the support of the state in disputes with juniors and in other legal contexts. In the next section of this chapter, I consider some of the ways in which the elders tried to hedge themselves against the adverse effects of change.

The Elders' Response to Change

It has been argued that change altered relations between seniors and juniors, and, further, that for most seniors, the consequence of change was to diminish their right in their juniors. It has also been pointed out that, in certain specific fields, change created new opportunities for elders to gain economic advantage. In this context, therefore, an understanding of the elders' response to change must put into account the opportunities as well as constraints which resulted from this change. This way of viewing the situation also accommodates the idea that people's response to change is not simply a matter of reacting defensively to its adverse effects, but rather, and in more positive light, this form of response is powered by a creativity directed at minimizing the adverse effects while simultaneously exploiting any new opportunities which change creates. Under these conditions, although the system of rights in people is portrayed as having undergone massive alteration, it nonetheless still retains a subjective relevance and people's strategies to economic success continue to be mediated through the same system as if no change had taken place.

Some Specific Responses

No attempt is made here to present an exhaustive picture of the possible responses of elders to change. What is discussed is an illustrative range of actions which support the argument of this chapter and which are, hopefully, more commonly observable in many parts of contemporary Africa. They include the appearance during the colonial period of a defensive and rigid form of traditionalism which certain elders strove to use in order to retain their juniors' loyalty. Along with these neo-traditionalist claims on the juniors was the deliberate increase, to inflationary levels, of certain traditional payments such as bridewealth and compensation for wrongs. There was also, in some cases, creation of new compensable wrongs or the expansion of old ones.[7] Most of these conflicts and claims were mediated through the agency of the state, which sometimes supported and other times rejected such claims.

Martin Chanock's research in Malawi and Zambia shows the extent to which the loss of political and economic power by male elders during the colonial period gave rise to a strong neo-traditionalism that strove to reassert control over women and children. As Chanock puts it, "[t]he colonial system gave very few opportunities for Africans to make effective political demands but through customary law some were able to press for and to establish state recognition of certain vital social and economic aims (1987: 4, 1978: 80-91). Hence the establishment of "Local Courts" and indeed the operation of the entire system of Indirect Rule enabled the elders to create a defensive customary law whose major objective was to deal with what was seen as the disintegrative impact and structural change brought about by colonialism" (1978: 90, see also Hobsbawn & Ranger 1983).[8]

In post-independence Zimbabwe, the passing of the Legal Age of Majority Act 1982, as noted already, set in motion a series of neo-traditionalist efforts aimed at achieving a repeal of the Act. In an editorial comment, the Zimbabwe *Sunday Mail*(9-9-84) attacked the Act for having destroyed the people's culture and social norms (Nube 1983-4: 217). Even some Zimbabwean M.P.s who had passed the relevant Act retreated in the face of mounting neo-traditionalist pressure. After the decision of the Court of Appeal in *Katekwe V. Muchabaiwa*,[9] it became clear to most Zimbabweans that the effect of the Legal Age of Majority Act was to free women to marry or have liaisons with men without their parents' consent. In a public debate which followed the decision, the government was called upon to amend the Act in order to make bridewealth a legal condition to a valid marriage throughout Zimbabwe.

Some evidence of the impact of such pressure appeared in the speech of the Minister of Community Development and Women's Affairs, who declared that the Act would be amended to give back to parents control over their children, adding that "we want to retain our cultural values and we shall invite parents, elders, and traditional leaders to advise us on the necessary amendments needed to retain those social values we cherish" (Nube 1983/4: 217). The said Act has neither been repealed nor amended.[10]

From Kenya we have the recent case of S.M. Otieno which captured much local and international publicity.[11] The case brings out yet another instance of the forces of traditionalism. Although, on the face of it, the case concerned the determination of a conflict of burial rights between a widow and her children on the one hand, and the deceased husband's clan on the other, at the root of the dispute lay the fundamental questions of the control of resources between the male elders of the Luo clan and the widow and her children. As correctly put by Salim, the context in which the case was argued reflected "a struggle over inheritance right" between the parties (1987: 13). Judging from the public interest generated by the case and the manner in which interest groups used it to articulate their political demands, it is clear that the case was seized by traditionalists and used as a platform for making a stand against women and junior men who challenge their authority.

Commenting on the S.M. Otieno case, a prominent Kenyan journalist, Philip Ochieng, noted that the case brought out clearly the conflict between those who argue for the return to the traditional code of conduct and those who see tradition as a mirror of an economic and social system which is not only obsolete, but has sometimes been misused by men and elders to oppress and exploit women and junior men. Ochieng noted that elders daily pray for the return to the good old days "when young people had ... respect for age, seniority, and authority ... [and] when women knew their place and did not indulge in such a new fangled "nuisance" as women's liberation" (1987: 187).

But for some elders, the yearning for the return to the former times has gone beyond the mere wish, and as noted above, it has assumed many different forms, including opposition to progressive law reform. At another level, it has assumed the form of a hike in marriage payments. Studies dealing with the transformation of bridewealth have associated the big rise in bridewealth throughout Africa to the loss of economic security of the elders. For example, in areas where marriage payments were made in a series of instalments going beyond the date of marriage, social change provoked the insistence by prospective fathers-in-law of a lump-sum payment. One of the reasons for this was the elders' fear that their sons-in-law could not be relied upon to make voluntary contribution whenever occasion demanded. Yet the consequence of lumping together the payable bridewealth increased the economic burden on prospective suitors and made bridewealth appear to have gone up. This, in turn, provoked juniors' reaction in the form of elopements, premarital pregnancy or simple cohabitation without marriage.

But in other parts of Africa, bridewealth went up in real terms, and many poor households came to depend on it as a means of economic survival, while other families which were economically better off used it as a source of capital for their economic undertakings.[12] Its change from perishable, subsistence consumer items to hard cash made it possible for bridewealth to be used to acquire desired goods and services. On the whole, the procedure for payment, the manner of distribution and the consequences of failing to pay up assumed an individualistic character.

Some evidence of the deep conflict over bridewealth between elders and juniors is found in the large number of court cases which were brought by fathers to recover unpaid bridewealth. There were also corresponding cases dealing with claims for refund in cases of divorce.[13] As Baker noted concerning the Kuria of Tanzania, "it is rare to find a man who will return his daughters' bride-price except on the order of a Court" (1935: 113).

A similar trend reflecting the idea of elders trying to re-coup their lost economic security appears in claims based on the seduction of a daughter or on a wife's adultery. The high claims for a daughter's seduction which were brought in colonial courts and which continue to find their way into contemporary state courts are, at one level, an attempt by elders to control the daughters' strivings for autonomy, and, at another level, an effort to recover compensation for the loss or diminution of expected bridewealth. It should not be surprising, therefore, that a law which seeks to free daughters from the control of their parents will be resisted strongly.

Conclusion

In many industrialized countries of Europe and North America, the provision of care for the elderly is now accepted as the responsibility of the state.[14] This care is provided in different forms such as retirement benefits, insurance schemes, subsidised housing, medical care, tax-exemptions, etc. Although the function of the family in caring for the elderly has not been completely replaced in most of these countries, it has nonetheless been overshadowed by that of the state.

In the third-world countries, including those in Africa, whatever state arrangements exist for the economic support of the elderly, they are viewed as merely supplementary to the basic care provided by the family and community. Hence an examination of economic programs and development plans of most African states does not show special concern for the aged members of the community. In some African countries where labour laws, derived mostly from the former colonial power, make such provisions, pension schemes have been retained for the benefit of the retired work-force. Unfortunately, even in countries where such pensions exist, they are often heavily taxed and are thus inadequate to meet the recipient's basic needs. This is more so when one considers the ever rising inflation as well as the diminished ability of the pensioner to engage in other economic activities in order to supplement his/her pension benefits. It is no wonder that most public and private employees are afraid of retirement, and many, if given a chance, would be glad to stay on the job for as long as possible.

Whatever small benefits the state can offer to its retired work-force, the number of recipients is usually very small. It consists of a small percentage of the population while the majority is left without any form of state support. In their old age, when elders have become physically frail and intellectually dull, the burden of their up-keep seems to remain hanging in the balance.

The question, therefore, is upon whom should this responsibility fall. As argued above, the state in the third world does not consider this to be its obligation. Indeed its ability to offer such support is usually highly circumscribed by the weak resource base. There is a general belief that the extended family in Africa is intact and continues to provide for the elderly.[15] Yet, as this chapter has tried to show, whatever role the extended family still plays in providing for the aged, this role has undergone radical transformation.

I have not attempted a detailed description of how certain communities in contemporary Africa care for the elderly. My concern has been to discuss the transformation of the material basis on which most elders depend for their essential needs. It is possible that the case studies of specific African communities would show greater concern for the welfare of the elderly in those societies than this chapter has portrayed. Nonetheless, it is still largely accurate that economic transformation in Africa has adversely affected traditional arrangements for the care of the elderly. Hence, whatever happens in the next century, apart from state intervention, it is unlikely to strengthen the elders' economic security which they enjoyed in pre-colonial times. What may happen is that certain states will directly or otherwise underwrite some of the burden for the care of the elderly. And, perhaps more predictably, many elders who are today's youths will grow up to expect reduced support from the extended family, and, where possible, will try to make their own arrangements for old age. But, as is well recognised, the ability of most poor peasants in Africa to prepare for their old age security is largely constrained by wider economic forces which have been only touched upon.

Notes

* I would like to acknowledge with thanks the help of my colleagues Professors J.L. Kanywanyi and G.M. Fimbo who read through the paper and made very helpful comments.

1. In this chapter emphasis is placed on male elders who form the most dominant group in traditional Africa. Besides, the position of elderly women has been considered elsewhere (see Rwezaura 1985 & 1986).

2. Moore says of the Chagga that every son has to look after his father whether he likes him or not (1978: 38).

3. Referring to the differential sources of old-age security between Kiga men and women, Yeld argues that "since an ageing family head will have married younger wives who will be cultivating for him and who are likely to be favoured by him, a first or second wife cannot expect support from her husband in her old age but will turn to her adult sons" (1966: 4).

4. In Kuria society, where the effects of the rinderpest were comparable and where the payment of bridewealth was adversely affected, the end of the epidemic and subsequent rebuilding of herds led to the restoration of bridewealth to the pre-rinderpest levels, and, in some areas, to even higher levels (Rwezaura 1985: 71-73).

5. Similar trends have been reported in other parts of Africa. For example, Christian Missionaries interviewed in Mozambique by Welch *et al.,* said that there was a decline in the number of church marriages and that people were "turning more to traditional ceremonies or merely setting up joint homes without any formalities, and doing so not only in Mozambique but in all of Africa" (1985: 65). Snyder's research among the Banjal of Senegal also showed that many youths had contracted marriages with Non-Bajal men and women in disregard of the system of endogamy practised since pre-colonial times. He concluded that "these matrimonial changes reflect and contribute to a decline in the control of elders over youths [thus] undercutting the bases of gerontocratic authority within patrilineage and household" (1978: 243).

6. Supreme Court Civil Appeal No. 99/84 (Judgment No. S.C. 87/84).

7. Perlman's archival research in Toro, Uganda uncovered a range of sexual offences which were created by the King of Toro. From the draconian punishments prescribed for offenders one gets the impression that not only were these offences likely to be common at the time but also opportunity was availed by elders to gain compensation from the misdeeds of their wives. For example, Law No.2, March 26th, 1907 stipulated that
    "if any man commits adultery with another man's wife and there are witnesses, he will be fined Shs. 600/= or imprisonment for one year."
    The fine of Shs. 600/= was taken by the government and "the wife's husband [was] given another fine, being an addition" (No. 4 of 1907).

8. Similar reactions occurred in other parts of Africa. Among the Kuria of Tanzania, if a wife was guilty of adultery, she was either chastised or sent

home to her father "to get back one of the beasts paid as bride price" (Baker 1935: 111). According to Baker, the animal was taken by the husband as compensation, whilst the woman's lover "bragged of his success in his circle of friends". Yet in the 1930s and 1940s with the help of local administration courts, husbands began to claim adultery compensation directly from their wives, paramours. At first the amount was small i.e. one head of cattle, but by the end of the colonial period, the amount had trebled. In more recent years, this new customary law is asserted with much enthusiasm and rigidity, while the claimable number of cattle has continued to rise reaching beyond the figure of five head.

9. See note 6 supra.

10. More recently the Zimbabwe Supreme Court has decided that, according to the provisions of the *Legal Age of Majority Act,* women are equal to men in the application of customary law and therefore an adult daughter has a right to inherit her father's estate as "the nearest relative" in cases of intestate succession. In this case the dispute over the deceased's property was between a daughter and the deceased's brother, her uncle. See: IWRAW — The Women's Watch — Vol. 1, No. 3 (1987), pp. 2-3.

11. See for example an article in *The New York Times,* Saturday, May 16th, 1987 entitled: *"Court in Kenya Allows Tribe, Not Widow, to Bury Lawyer"* by Sheila Rule and *The Minneapolis Star and Tribune,* Sat. May 16th, 1987, with a caption: *"Widow Loses: Kenyan Court Upholds Tribal Burial Custom".*

12. For example, it is reported in the case of *Hamisi Gorogoro v. Asha Meragane,* 1977, LRT, n. 4 that after having received 32 head of cattle as bridewealth for his daughter's marriage, the father sold all the cattle and the cash realised was to open a shop.

13. This is particularly so in areas of high bridewealth and certainly my research in Tanzania confirms this position, see Rwezaura 1985.

14. This is also the case in socialist countries where their social security systems consist of a comprehensive package.

15. See, for example, the provisions of *Disabled Persons (Care and Maintenance) Act,* 1982, (Tanzania) which stipulates that relatives are obliged to contribute to the maintenance of disabled relatives by giving up to 33% of their incomes. If such relatives exist and are unwilling to provide such assistance, they may be compelled by the court to provide such assistance. In the absence of relatives, the Act requires local municipalities to provide support for disabled persons by establishing rehabilitation centres (ss. 14-19).

Bibliography

Ault, J.M. 1983, "State Power and the Regulation of Marriage in Colonial Zambia". *Theory & Society,* Vol. 12, No. 2 pp. 181-210.

Baker, E.C., 1935, *The Bakuria of North Mara Tarime, Tanganyika Territory.* Unpublished Manuscript.

Bledsoe, C., 1980, *Women and Marriage in Kpelle Society.* Stanford University Press, Stanford.

Brantley, C.; 1978, Gerontocratic Government: Age-Sets in Pre-Colonial Giriama". *Africa* 48

(3), pp. 248-264.

Brown, I.C., 1963, *Understanding Other Cultures*, Prentice-Hall Inc., Englewoods Cliffs, New Jersey.

Chanock, M., 1985, *Law, Custom and Social Order*, Cambridge University Press.

Clignet, R., 1970, *Many Wives, Many Powers, Authority and Power in Polygamous Families*, Northwestern University Press, Evanston.

Driberg, J.H., 1923, *The Lango*, T. Fisher Unwin Ltd., London.

Fallers, L.A., 1964, A "Social Stratification and Economic Processes in Africa", in: Herskovits, M.J. & Harwitz, M. (Eds.), *Economic Transformation in Africa*. Evanston, Illinois.

Fitzpatrick, P., 1979, *Law and State in Papua New Guinea*, Academic Press, London.

Fortes, M. & E.E. Evans-Pritchard (Eds.), 1941 *African Political Systems*. Oxford University Press.

Gluckmann, M., 1965, *Politics, Law and Ritual in Tribal Society*, Chicago.

——, 1941, *Economy of the Central Barotse Plain*, Rhodes-Livingstone Institute Papers, No. 7.

Goody, J., 1971, "Class and Marriage in Africa and Eurasia", *American Journal of Sociology*, 76, pp. 585-605.

——, 1962, *Death, Property and the Ancestors*, Tavistock, London.

Gray, R.F. & Gulliver, P.H. (Eds.), 1964, *The Family Estate in Africa: Studies in the Role of Property in Family Structures and Lineage Continuity*, Routledge & Kegan Paul, London.

Gulliver, P.H., 1963, "The Age-Set Organisation of the Jie Tribe",*Journal of the Royal Anthropological Institute* 83, pp. 147-168.

Holden, W.C., 1963, *The Past and Future of the Kaffir Races*, C. Struik, Africana Publisher, Cape Town.

Hobsbawn, E.J. & Ranger (Eds.) 1983, *The Invention of Tradition*, Cambridge University Press.

Kuper, H., 1962, "Kinship Among the Swazi", in Radcliffe-Brown, A.R. & Forde, P. (Eds.), *African Systems of Kinship and Marriage,*Oxford University Press

Little, K., 1951, *The Mende of Sierra Leone: A West African People in Transition*, London.

Mair, L., 1961, "Clientship in East Africa", *Cahiers d'Etudes Africaines* 11, pp. 315-325.

——, 1953, "African Marriage and social Change", in A. Philips (Ed), *Survey of African Marriage and Family Life*, London.

Moore, S.f., 1986, *Social Facts and Fabrications*, Cambridge University Press, Cambridge.

——, 1978, "Old-Age in a Life-Term Arena: the Chagga of Kilimanjaro in 1974", in: A. Simic (Eds.), *Life's Careers-Aging, Cultural Variations on Growing Old*, London, Sage Publications.

Murray, C., 1977, "High Bridewealth, Migrant Labour and the Position of Women In Lesotho", *Journal of African Law*, vol. 21, No.1, 1977

——, 1976, "Marital Strategy in Lesotho: The Re-distribution of Migrant Earnings". 35 *African Studies* 104.

Ncube, W., 1983/84, "The Decision in Katekwe v. Muchabaiwa: A Critique", *Zimbabwe Law Review*, Vol. 1 & 2.

Perlman, M.L., 1985, "Family Law and Social Change Among the Toro Of Uganda", *Journal of African Law*, Vol. 29, No. 1, pp. 82-93.

Radcliffe-Brown, A.R. Forde, D. (Eds.), 1962, *African Systems of Kinship and Marriage*, Oxford University Press, London.

Rattray, R.S., 1956, *Ashanti Law and Constitution*, Oxford University Press.

Ruel, M.J., 1958, *The Social Organisation of the Kuria*, Fieldwork Report, University of Nairobi Library.

Rwezaura, B.A., 1988, "The Changing Role of the Extended Family in Providing Economic Support for an Individual in Africa" in Meulders-Klein and Eekelaar (Eds.), *Family, State and Individual Economic Security* Story Scientia and Kluwer, Brussels.

——, 1985, *Traditional Family Law and Change in Tanzania*, Nomos, Baden-Baden.

——, 1983, *Traditionalism and Law Reform in Africa*, Lecture Series 17, Europa Institute, Saarbrucken.

Salim, A.I., 1987, "Conflict Between Common Law and Customary Law in Kenya: Some Reflections". Paper Presented at the Interdisciplinary Colloquium on Law, Society and National Identity in Africa, University of Bayreuth, West Germany, 9th-10th July, 1987.

Saul, J.S. & Woods, R., 1971, "African peasantries", in: Shanin, T. (Ed.), *Peasant and Peasant Societies,* Harmondsworth, Penguin Books, pp. 103-104.

Schneider, H.K., 1968, "People as Wealth in Turu Society", *Southwestern Journal of Anthropology* 24,pp. 375-395.

Simonds, L.W., 1970, *The Role of the Aged in Primitive Society,* Archon Books, Yale University Press.

Snyder, F.S., 1981, *Capitalism and Legal Change,* Academic Press, New York.

————, 1978, "Legal Innovation and Social Change in a Peasant Community: A Senegalese Village", in: *Africa* 48 (3), pp. 231-247.

Spencer, P., 1976, "Opposing Streams and the Gerontocratic Ladder: Two Models of Age Organisation in East Africa", in: *MAN* (N.S.), Vol. II, pp. 153-175.

Terray, E., 1972, *Marxism and "Primitive Societies". Two Studies.* New York.

Turnbull, C.M., 1976, *Man in Africa,* David & Charles, London.

Welch, G.H., Dagnino, F., Sachs, A.A., 1985, "Transforming the Foundations of Family Law in the Course of the Mozambique Revolution", in: *Journal of Southern African Studies,* Vol. 12, No.1 pp. 60-74.

Yeld, E.R., 1966, "Continuity and Change in Kiga Patterns of Marriage: An Analysis of Structural Change in Kiga Marriage in the 1930s and 1960s". Paper Presented at the University of East Africa Social Science Conference, December, 1966.

Chapter 8

Social Support Systems in Transition in Indonesia

Tapi Omas IHROMI   University of Indonesia

Introduction

In this chapter, the expression "social security system" is used to mean the system in a particular society through which people are protected against risks of partial or total loss of income from various causes such as death, sickness or accidents experienced by the main wage earner of a household.[1]

In many industrialized societies, social legislation has reached an advanced stage so that it encompasses matters such as Unemployment Insurance Law, Workmen's Accident Compensation Insurance Law, Child Welfare Law, National Pension Law and Law for the Welfare of the Aged.[2]

Regarding the need for passing such social security laws, most developing countries such as Indonesia face a big dilemma. Having undergone a colonial past during which their peoples were exploited, developing countries usually explicitly state in their constitutions that the achievement of social welfare for the entire population (including non-productive members) is the driving force for founding an independent nation. However, problems of economic under-development and overpopulation have prevented such countries from initiating adequate universal social insurance programs for the entire nation. In Indonesia, for example, the state social security system at present only covers that portion of the workforce and their dependents which is employed by the State, State-owned enterprises, the armed forces and modern sectors of industry and trade. This amounts to about 11.5% of the total workforce or about 20% the total population.[3] Thus the majority of the population, when faced by hazards of loss or insufficiency of income due to unforeseen events, has to resort to whatever means of social security is within its reach in order at least to ensure survival.

Those means are not covered in the statutory social security system and I would like to refer to these measures as "the non-statutory social security system." Some will probably prefer to call such measures "traditional means of social security" and others most probably prefer the expression "non-formal systems".[4] However, terms like "traditional" and "informal" do not entirely cover the means used by the people. Many of these means have indeed developed as part of the tradition existing within the network of kinship and neighbourhood relations which more or less entitles people to "claim" some assistance from kin and neighbours when they face problems, but in addition to these traditional means, new forms of assistance have developed, especially in urban communities. For this reason, I call these measures "the non-statutory social security system".[5]

The Statutory Social Security System

At present the statutory social security system in Indonesia covers three main categories of economically active people: Civil servants, the armed forces and industrial workers in the modern sector.

The social security programs covered are:
1. Old Age Savings (provident funds)
2. Death Insurance
3. Employment Injury Insurance
4. Pension Funds
5. Health Benefits.

A. Old Age Saving Funds

For civil servants, the program for Old Age Savings Funds is regulated by Government Regulation (Peraturan Pemerintah, P.P. 26, 1981). The existing program is compulsory in the sense that all civil servants are by law obliged to participate in this program. The program has been in existence since 1963, but some modifications changing its nature into a social insurance system for civil servants were introduced in the P.P. 26, 1981. Participants in this program have the following rights:

At retirement age (this is stipulated in the regulation of P.P. 32, 1979 as 55 for civil servants in general; for certain categories such as judges and professors, the retirement age is higher), the participant receives a lump sum which is calculated according to detailed criteria stipulated in the regulation. A sum comprising the total contribution paid by participant plus the accrued interest is also paid when the work is terminated prior to retirement age. When the cessation of work is caused by death of the participant, a lump sum, which is also calculated according to stipulations in the regulation, is also paid to the survivors of the deceased.

The program is referred to as Tabungan dan Asuransi Pegawai Negeri (abbreviated as TASPEN) , meaning Civil Servants Saving and Insurance Programs, and the management of the funds rests with a state-owned company PERUM TASPEN. In 1982, the status of this body was changed into that of a private corporation P.I.TASPEN. All the participants in the Old Saving funds have to contribute 3.25% of their salary monthly, which is subtracted automatically at the beginning of each calendar month. The TASPEN is subject to the control of the Ministry of Finance. For members of the armed forces there is a similar compulsory program of Old Age Savings Funds. From 1963 when the program of Old Age Savings Funds was introduced for the first time for civil servants, the program for the armed forces was combined with that of civil servants. However, due to the different characteristics of the retirement age and to other matters, in 1971 it was considered more appropriate to split the program. The management of the social insurance programs for the armed forces is the responsibility of a state-owned company, PERUM ASABRI, which is supervised by the Ministry of Defense. The Old Age Savings contribution of each participant of this program is 3.25% of income.

Industrial workers employed by state-owned companies, such as the state company operating electricity, are classified in the Indonesian system as civil servants. Contribution to Old Age Security Funds for these workers is of a similar nature as to that to the civil servants, i.e. compulsory, and the program is also administered by TASPEN.

For industrial workers employed by state-owned companies, a general regulation making the contribution for old age security funds compulsory was introduced in 1977 (Government Regulation, *Peraturan Pemerintah*: P.P. 33, 1977). The program is referred to as *Asuransi Sosial Tenaga Kerja* (ASTEK), meaning Social Insurance for Industrial Workers. For the Old Age Security Funds the workers have to pay a contribution of 1% of their wages and the company has to add 1.5% of the labourer's wages to the contribution. Each month these contributions have to be paid to the state-owned company ASTEK, which is entrusted with the management of the scheme. Every year ASTEK has to make a statement of account, indicating the total accumulation of the fund and the interest of each participant. ASTEK insurance is not yet universally compulsory for all workers and employers. According to P.P. 33, 1977, companies employing 25 workers and more, or which pay more than *Rupiahs* (Rp.) 1,000,000 in wages each month, are obliged to participate in the programs. For violators, a sanction of detention of three months maximum or a fine of Rp. 100,000 maximum is stipulated in Article 22 of P.P. 33, 1977.

B. Death Insurance

When participants (or their spouses or children) in TASPEN or ASABRI die, certain payments are made to survivors. Thus, in addition to the Old Age Savings benefit, the heir of a participant in these programs receives a death insurance payment. In the case of the death of a civil servant, or pensioner, the survivors will receive a sum equal to 150 percent of the latest monthly income. In the case of the death of the spouse, the payment equals 100 percent of the latest monthly income, and when children die (maximally up to three children) survivors will receive 50 percent of the latest monthly income. When participants of ASABRI or pensioners die, survivors will receive benefits six or seven and a half times the previous monthly income. Stipulations are found in the regulation on pensions, specifying that those in the lower ranks receive 7.5 times the monthly salary while the higher ranked persons will receive 6 times the monthly salary. Members of the armed forces also receive assistance for funeral costs amounting to between Rp. 40,000 and Rp. 90,000.

In the case of death of industrial workers, death benefits will be different for those who die as a result of an industrial accident and those who die due to other causes. Death insurance funds are paid based on the compulsory contribution of a half a percent of the worker's wage, which is the responsibility of the employer. This insurance entitles survivors to receive as much as Rp. 500,000. If the worker dies due to an industrial accident, survivors will also receive compensation, calculated according to principles set out in the Workmen's Compensation Act, and later regulated in Government Regulation P.P. 33, 1977.

C. Employment Injury Insurance

The Workmen's Compensation Act of 1947 was declared operative throughout the nation in 1951 (Act number 2, 1951). According to these Acts, employers of some 13 kinds of enterprises are obliged to pay compensation for industrial accidents, or for diseases contracted because of working relationships. The obligation to pay compensation is based on the principle of the employer's liability. There is no requirement for the worker to prove that the accident is not his fault. The 13 types of enterprises specified are enterprises which are considered to be risky or hazardous to the health of labourers, such as enterprises utilizing machines, all kinds of gas, chemicals and electric power. Each industrial accident in which workers are involved must be reported within 48 hours to the official assigned to Labour Force Supervision. The employer is liable to pay the worker the costs of medical care, and compensation for diseases contracted in relation to work, which cause total or partial disability.

When the accident leads to the death of the worker, compensation amounting to 60 percent of 48 months salary wages and Rp. 50,000 for funeral costs will be paid to the survivors (heir) of the worker. Prior to the formation of ASTEK (see previous section) as a state-owned company which is in charge of the management of contributions to the Worker's Accident Funds, compensation for industrial accidents was the responsibility of employers under legal stipulations only. No regulations requiring compulsory contributions were promulgated. Employers were free to initiate insurance programs, either by contracting with insurance companies, or initiating individual programs. In 1974, the program handled by *Dana Jaminan Sosial* (DJS), meaning Funds for Social Security, a foundation set up by the Ministry for Social Affairs in 1964 which managed, on a voluntary basis, health-related schemes such as medical care, maternity and death for the benefit of industrial workers, was expanded to include matters related to workmen's compensation. This became compulsory when ASTEK was founded in 1977. Now employers and workers are obliged to participate in the social security scheme administered by ASTEK, and programmes included are: Workmen's Compensation in the case of industrial accidents, Disability Insurance, Old Age and Survivor's Benefits (see: Old Age Security). ASTEK operates under the supervision of the Ministry of Manpower. The contribution for injury funds which employers have to pay ranges from 0.24% to 3.6% of total wages. The amount is decided according to the degree of hazard of a particular job. The maximum contribution of 3.6% of total wages has to be paid for the benefit of workers of ammunition-related plants and businesses.

D. Pension Funds

Stipulations about pension funds for civil servants and the armed forces are found in various regulations, of which the main are Act 6, 1966 and Act 11, 1969. In order to qualify as a pensioner and receive monthly payments, three requirements have to be met: the individual must have reached retirement age as stipulated by law, worked at least a certain period of time (specified in the law) and received official notification of being released from work in an honorable manner.

These requirements are formulated in line with the principles underlying the pension system, i.e. providing old age security and being a reward for services to the country over a long period of time. These stipulations accord with the existing system, whereby pension funds are entirely paid by the Government. The burden on the Government budget is considered to be increasing, because the monthly pensions are being paid over a relatively long period of time. Thus from 1975, participants in the pension scheme have had to pay a contribution now amounting to 4.75% of their income. Along with the Old Age Savings Funds contributions, these funds are administered by TASPEN. The monthly pensions are, however, still paid from the Government Budget. It is expected that soon the existing pension funds will be changed into a social insurance scheme and a pilot project is actually being operated in Bali. At present, civil servants may retire with monthly pension when they reach 50 and have served the government for at least 20 years. They must retire at 55. For certain officials, such as judges, retirement age is 60, and for full-time researchers working at an institute for research, university lecturers and professors, it is 65. Stipulations for retirement age of the armed forces is somewhat different. Higher ranked officers are entitled to retire at 48 and must do so at 55. Lower ranked officers may retire at 42, and must at 48. In order to qualify for pension, they must have served for at least 15 years.

The monthly amount received by pensioners, both of the civil servants and of the armed forces is calculated as follows: 2.5% of the basic salary for each year they have served. Such amount should not exceed 75% of the latest salary, and it is hoped that there will not be too drastic a change in the consumption pattern of pensioners when they receive 3/4 of what they have earned prior to retirement. When pensioners die, the widow or widower is entitled to a certain portion of the late spouse's pension.

E. Health Benefits

In 1968 the Government initiated a special fund, comprising compulsory contributions from civil servants and the armed forces for the purpose of financing medical care through such funds. Civil servants, members of the armed forces, pensioners and dependents are entitled to benefit from the program.

Unlike social insurance systems, this health benefit program does not provide income when participants are forced out of work due to sickness. The accumulated funds are utilized as a common reserve to meet the medical bills of those who become sick or need medical services. Thus, healthy people may contribute more in comparison to what they will ever spend, but those who are in poor health use more funds in comparison to what they have contributed.

The contribution which participants have to pay amounts to 2% of their income and that money is subtracted from their monthly salary. This program used to be managed by *Badan Penyelenggara Dana Pemeliharaan Kesehatan* (BPDPK), meaning the Agency for Health Maintenance Funds, an agency administered by the Ministry of Finance. In 1985, a state-owned company administered by the Ministry of Finance, namely the PERUM HUSADA BHAKTI, was set up to manage these funds.

The participants in the health benefit programs, and their dependents, have the following rights:
a. medical treatment, hospitalization and immunization
b. laboratory tests and other diagnostic tests
c. emergency treatment and other actions needed for health recovery
d. delivery of babies
e. medicine
f. medical equipment which physicians consider necessary for treatment
g. glasses, according to doctor's prescription
h. treatment by dentist, including the cost of protheses
i. family planning service.

Except for compensation for costs related to medical treatment of workers injured in industrial accidents, the programs administered by ASTEK do not cover health benefit schemes.

The previously mentioned DJS (Social Security Funds), however, administers programs covering matters such as health insurance, pregnancy, delivery and death insurance. The programs are handled on a voluntary basis and there were a number of enterprises, mostly in Jakarta and Surabaya, which participated in the schemes operated by DJS. The General Directorate of Marine Communications and the General Directorate of Labour Protection have issued a joint decision instructing employers to join the DJS programs for the benefit of all harbour workers in Indonesia.

As was pointed out previously, ASTEK does not operate health benefit programs. Because of the importance of health care, steps are being taken to expand the program to include health benefit schemes. A specific agency was set up, called *Badan Kerjasama Pemeliharaan Kesehatan Tenaga Kerja* (Agency for Cooperation in the Care of Conditions of Health of Industrial workers, BKPTK). The agency consists of representatives from the Ministry of Manpower, Ministry of Health and the state-owned company ASTEK. Thus this BKPTK handles matters related to health programs benefiting industrial workers.

F. Traffic Accident Insurance

A compulsory traffic accident insurance program was started in 1964. This program is handled by *P.T. Asuransi Kerugian Jasa Raharja*. The Ministry of Finance supervises this agency. Victims of a traffic accident are entitled to compensation for invalidity and medical care costs. Survivors receive compensation for relatives killed in traffic accidents.

G. Public Assistance Programs

I have pointed out at the beginning of this chapter that the realization of social justice for the entire population is a core idea in the constitution of the Indonesian State. It is indeed one of the five principles of the State Philosophy, *Pancasila*. But economic and population problems prevent the universal realization of statutory social security benefits for the entire population. Some public assistance programs do, however, exist and a few programs especially designed to serve old people will be mentioned here.

In Act 4, 1965, some principles were stipulated indicating that the State should initiate actions through which assistance for elderly citizens is provided. It is hoped that through such assistance elderly people can continue to lead a healthy life. It is also stated that the Ministry for Social Affairs is responsible for the supervision of non-governmental organizations which operate homes or other programs for the aged.

The principles in this Act were applied in a more detailed way in the decisions of the Minister for Social Affairs, such as Decision 3-1-50/107, 1971. Here it was stipulated that persons who are at least 55 and who are not capable of earning a living, or who do not possess the means to fulfill their daily needs, and who thus receive help from others, are entitled to make a request for public assistance. To this end a letter should be sent to the Minister for Social Affairs, accompanied by a declaration by local government personnel about the poor conditions of the old person. Furthermore, the close relatives should also declare that they have no objection to such a request by their parents (or other relative). If this person is considered eligible to receive public assistance, the Minister of Social Affairs will issue a decision stating the old aged status of the petitioner.

The issuance of such a decision implies that the elderly person will receive public assistance by being admitted to an old people's home operated by a government agency or a non-governmental organization or by being placed in a relative's house or at the residence of people who are willing to care for him or her. Food, living and medical care are thus secured through the admitted status of being old aged.

Some assistance is also provided in an indirect way through subsidies to all kinds of non-governmental organizations which operate programs providing social services to the public such as old people's home training centers for disabled persons.

The Non-statutory Social Security System

According to the census of 1980, the population of Indonesia was 146.776.473; 72.951.670 men and 73.824.805 women. The various programs for social security described earlier covered benefits for civil servants, members of the armed forces and industrial workers employed in the modern sector. Thus, about 80% of the population have no access to statutory social security systems. Some idea about the ways problems are solved will be obtained when we look closely at the way the people live.

Studies of families in distress show that kin help one another to overcome many of their problems. Even in urban areas, kin ties are still very strong, and people resort to a relative's willingness to help when misfortunes are experienced. Lower middle-class people in cities also rely very strongly on aid from neighbours, and sometimes receive more aid from neighbours than from relatives. The principle of reciprocity is at work here and one can observe that because a person participates actively in his community, which means helping persons in need and attending local rituals or festivities, he or she is then certain that in times of need he/she will receive help in return.

Thus good neighbours have the normative expectation that they will be helped when they need it, in accordance with experience, and this expectation is logical because he himself or she herself has acted in a similar way in the past. In urban centers, this principle of reciprocity is strengthened, because it is given a modern organizational framework. Associations administer contributions paid by members, which are used as a common fund for the benefit of families which experience misfortune.

The most common insurance for old age is reliance on the offspring. One can imagine that this may not encourage family planning, especially when there is no assurance yet that children will survive. With improvement in the general health care system it is hoped that the motivation for family planning will not be crushed by motives for securing care in old age by producing a large number of children. Investment in children's education is also strongly felt to be an insurance for old age and programs offering nurseries for the children of the needy are much appreciated.

Low salaried people working in government offices aspire for a better education for their children, and we can also observe that out of feelings of solidarity, higher ranked persons voluntarily collect funds to be donated towards the payment of tuition. Religious bodies also provide assistance to needy people. For many Muslims*, for example, the religious duty to pay *zakat* (social offering) is perceived as a command. The mosques collect this *zakat* and decide how it should be distributed to the poor. Christian and secular organizations also develop programs geared toward giving aid to the needy.

Rituals related to death can be very expensive, especially in some areas like the Toraja. Sometimes large sums of a family's reserves are spent on the funeral and related rituals. However, all the members of the extended family and the community assist in making the funeral into a respected occasion. Although such rites might seem to be wasteful or irrational, it provides the people concerned with emotional security and the satisfaction that the entire extended family pays respect to their parents and elders, and that such deeds will be rewarded. Blessings will be received in return. Deaths of neighbours and of relatives are indeed occasions which cause the network of relationships which link persons related through blood, or bound by friendship, into a "movement". All kinds of aid are provided for the family which experiences misfortune. Relatives and friends will come to the funeral and donate money in envelopes collected in covered baskets or a box. On the third and seventh evening, and on certain other evenings after the day a person dies, prayers are held in the house of the deceased. On such occasions, donations in kind are usually given by friends, neighbours and relatives.

This mechanism of mutual aid, or in the Indonesian term *gotong-royong*, still functions in rural and in urban areas, giving some security to people faced with problems. It is very common, for example, in modern offices in the urban areas to circulate lists where donations of fellow employees are noted down, and later handed over to the widow of a deceased. It was pointed out earlier that, in most cases, people who need help have to resort to siblings and other relatives or members of the extended family when they experience cessation of income or insufficiency of earnings. The feeling that relatives must help each other, that such duty is unavoidable, is still very strong. Such needy relatives may suddenly turn up at the residence of a sibling, a cousin or a member of his/her extended family to ask for support. He/she will stay there, until an opportunity to earn appears. In many cases, a better-off family may have poorer relatives living with them, doing odd jobs in the house and with a status somewhere between that of master and servant.

People from rural areas migrate to cities to improve their living conditions. People hardly ever migrate alone. They usually go to the city because a relative, or someone who was a neighbour in the village, has returned on a visit, and the new migrants accompany them back to the city. The ties between those who migrate and those who stay in the village remain strong. Migrants visit their village of origin at least once a year (usually during the festivities at the end of the fasting month) to pay respect to their elders, or to pay respect to the spirits of deceased ancestors. They visit parents, asking them forgiveness for any wrongdoing during the current year, cleaning the graves of ancestors and placing flowers on them. These duties are performed without question and are a source of emotional security. Suicide is very rare in Indonesia; perhaps it is because of such mechanisms.

In view of these traditions and the strong perception of all kinds of duties regarding friends, neighbours and relatives, a non-statutory social security system can be perceived which enables people to cope with problems to a certain degree. However, when needs reach a magnitude which is beyond the ability of the circle of friends, relatives and neighbours to satisfy, the system is no longer adequate. This is the case, for example, when the sick require expensive medical treatment. Relatives living in cities where public health centres are better equipped often give shelter to kin who are undergoing medical treatment. In fact, public health centres have been established in every district throughout the country, and these are highly subsidized so that little money is needed to gain access to them. But the medicine required is very expensive, and so are medical operations. Sometimes journalists discover that an operation cannot be performed, because the costs cannot be met by the extended family, and they write about it in newspapers. Many readers will then voluntarily raise funds. However, the number of such cases, is, of course, limited. Many more are not reached by voluntary philanthropy and it is hoped that as economic productivity rises, more revenue can be devoted to making social security schemes accessible to all sections of the population. The major problems, among others, are low economic productivity and poverty. In communities such as fishermen's villages, for example, earnings are very low.

During high seas seasons, when fishermen have to stay ashore, they have no earnings. Fishermen have to borrow money from their "bosses" so that their households can survive. When they later catch fish, the debts are repaid first and not much is left. Fishermen are, in most cases, constantly in debt to their "bosses". Because there is generally not much cash available in families of fishermen, not much material help can be offered to friends or relatives who need assistance.

Conclusions

Economic underdevelopment and population problems mean that, in Indonesia, there is not much surplus available for a universal statutory system of social security accessible to all sections of society. Only about 20 percent of the total population is covered by the statutory social security system. Even here, problems are encountered, such as the need to satisfy bureaucratic steps before benefits can be obtained and the ignorance of their eligibility by those who are meant to benefit from the programs. Attempts to overcome these problems should be made so that the schemes will prove truly beneficial for those who are meant to be served by them. About 80% of the people have to rely on non-statutory means of social security when they are faced with various kinds of financial difficutty. Observation of the conditions of life in rural as well as urban areas reveals that feelings of social solidarity, family solidarity, the unquestioned principles that relatives have to help each other, are still functioning as a social security mechanism among members of society at various levels.

Eventually, through the successive national development plans, conditions should be realized, which will enable Indonesia to introduce a universal and adequate system of social security. At present, however, great care should be taken so that existing traditional, non-formal or community measures do not decline. It is perhaps unavoidable that a process of individualization is underway and that the desire to enjoy consumption goods displayed at the market is overriding. Such matters will erode the forces which contribute towards achieving social security. Thus, it is of utmost importance that the vital function of the non-statutory social security system is recognized so that the right policy can be formulated and carried out.

With regard to the care of the elderly, one positive value, the moral obligation on the part of children to care for parents and elder relatives, is still very much alive. However, frequently poverty, especially in slums in the cities, prevents old people from receiving proper care. Poverty should be overcome so that adequate social security can be provided.

Notes

* About 90% of the population are Muslims.
1. Kertonegoro, 1987, p.7.
2. See, for example, the kinds of laws existing in Japan, offering universal social security schemes, in Yoshida Soeda, 1986.
3. See Esmara, 1986.
4. A symposium on social security systems in pluralistic societies was reported in Koning, 1987. and papers touched on terms like traditional and informal systems of social security.
5. See Koning, 1987.

Selected Bibliography

Dinas Sosial DKI Jakarta (Social Affairs Section, Jakarta Municipal Government), *Sekitar Masalah dan Penyelenggaraan Pelayanan Sosial Lanjut Usia* (On the problem of the implementation of services to the elderly), Jakarta,

1983.

Esmara, H. and Priyono Tjiptoheryanto. "The Social Security System in Indonesia", in *Asean Economic Bulletin* 3, 1986. pp. 53-67.

Evans, Jeremy (1987). "Old Age Security in Indonesia and Its Implications", in *Research Note International Population Dynamics Program,* No. 85. Canberra: Department of Demography, The Australian National University, 1988.

Kertonegoro, Sentanoe, *Jaminan Sosial: Prinsip dan Pelaksanaannya di Indonesia* (Social Security: Principles and Implementation in Indonesia). Jakarta: Mutiara, 1987.

Koning, Peter de, "Pluralism in Social Security: A Congress Report" *Newsletter XIII, Commission on Folklaw and Legal Pluralism.* International Union of Anthropological and Ethnological Sciences, February 1987, pp. 23-33.

Soeda, Yoshida, *Social Change and Social Security.* Paper submitted at International Conference on Social Welfare, Tokyo, November 1986.

Chapter 9

The Family and Old People in Yugoslavia and Some Other Socialist Countries

M. MLADENOVIC Faculty of Law, University of Yugoslavia
Belgrade

I

Old age is a part of life, but a vestibule of death as well. It at least has the value of life, and more than that — it provides hope for immortality. Offering this hope, all religions have made death easier. Materialistic philosophy and science have removed this hope from old people, but have offered, as a substitute, more justice and happiness in this world.

The loss of hope, the loss of religion, was described by Dostoyevsky with the power of genius in his novel *The Brothers Karamazov* in the famous scene of old Zosima's death. He was taken for a saint during his lifetime, and it was believed his body would be fragrant when his soul had departed for the Getsiman gardens. But sacrilege occurred: the cadaver began to stink of decay so suddenly and unnaturally that his disciples, losing faith in the divine character of the human being, revolted against God.

But this could also be interpreted as a revolt against the old man Zosima, against the rule of the old, against the sacred authority and cult of old age, against canons and dogmas, against a repressive civilization and hermetically closed society, and finally, against the pater familias, the patriarch as a symbol of divine and earthly power. If in old Zosima's fate, as well as in the clash of the son and father, Dimitriy and Fyodor Karamazov, Dostoyevsky had only announced the clash of two civilizations, then this Oedipus-like family drama was expanded in his *Evil Souls* and transformed into a social drama, anticipating the future socialist revolution. But he had also announced Stalinism (in the character of Stavrogyn and others) as it uglier face.

This introduction has been made for a purpose. It concerns the very complex and intricate message brought about by socialist revolutions and the countries of the so-called "real socialism". The basic idea is clear: abolition of class society and all its supports. This includes the abolition of the patriarchal family class structure. The revolution defended the "oppressed and humiliated", both in society and in the family. Engel's words are well known: "In a marriage of the bourgeoisie, the husband is a bourgeois and the wife a proletarian"; "Even the poorest proletarian has somebody at home who is even poorer than himself; it is the woman (wife)"[1] The following slogan was also popular: "All children are unhappy, some because they have nothing, and some because they have their families".[2]

It is for this reason that old people were not in the focus of the socialist revolution. Moreover, the revolution was directed against many of them. It was not only a class, but also a generational settlement of accounts. They are blamed for a long-standing lack of confidence in the family in socialist countries. The family used to be accused of being the last vestige of the exploitative society, a transmitter of social privileges, social power and class inequalities. It was therefore necessary *inter alia,* to free family members, deprived of their rights, from family tyranny. It is no accident that Marxism pushed only the "woman" and "child" issues into the forefront alongside the "class" issue. The question of old people went beyond ideological and strategic determinations of the revolutionary movements. When I sought relevant political documents relating to old people, dating from the early days of the Soviet and the Yugoslav revolutions, I found nothing worth mentioning. The most old people could expect was the protection of old proletarians, deprived of their rights, since they also shared the general fate of the working class.

But the socialist revolution was not needed to dethrone old people. They occupy a very favourable position only in traditional societies. There they have honorary positions, exert a certain power over all family members and enjoy great respect. The care for the old is viewed as a sacred duty of all family members. Their high status stems directly from certain institutionalized roles. It is thus a family model of a pre-industrial society. Most socialist revolutions encounter such types of family (an exception being the Central European socialist countries).

It seems that the position of old people has been more imperilled by changes in civilization than by ideological factors. It is hardly necessary to recall the extent to which industrialization and urbanization during the twentieth century have directly or indirectly influenced the transformation of the overall social structure, in general, and changes within the family in particular. The traditional extended family of rural society had fallen apart, and the new urban family could not reorganize as an extended family. A bigenerational, atomic, nuclear family became a dominant form, either as an isolated nuclear family or as a modified extended family. In all these cases, old people gradually leave the family nucleus, mainly in terms of space, but also, to a large extent, in terms of its content. At the very beginning, however, the position of old people did not seem to be dramatic, because they constituted a distinct demographic minority. Their drama took place a little later. This is so for all industrialized countries, socialist and capitalist, and increasingly so for developing countries.

II

The position of old people in Yugoslavia and in other socialist countries has to be assessed in the light of these general historical developments. However, it would be misleading to consider all socialist countries as being the same. In addition to sharing many ideological and cultural characteristics, there are also many differences between them resulting from diverse traditions. Yugoslavia is a typical example of these diversities vis-a-vis all other socialist countries. Differences may also be found within some compound socialist countries, like the Soviet Union and Yugoslavia. My focus will be principally on Yugoslavia. Some other socialist countries, especially the Soviet Union, will serve only as examples for comparison.

Yugoslavia is a small country. In 1921 it had only 12.5 million inhabitants and her present population is close to 24 million. Although small, it is replete with ethnic, religious, cultural and social diversity. Nineteenth and twentieth century life styles co-exist, together with traditional extended family groups and free informal unions. About 20 nationalities live there. Most are Slav, but there are others of non-Slav origin: Albanians, Hungarians, Romanians, and so on. There are three main religions: Orthodox, Catholic and Islam, as well as several dissident and other churches. Yugoslavia can be divided into the developed North and the less developed South, with the respective economic and cultural consequences. The political system is also complex. it is a federal state, consisting of six republics and two autonomous provinces within the SR of Serbia. Before 1974, the central authorities were relatively the strongest. In the post-1974 Constitution period, all federal units obtained very broad legislative, juridical and executive power. We can therefore say that there are eight legal systems in Yugoslavia, effective over many areas of the law including domestic relations and social law.

The 1974 Constitution proceeds on the basis of a doctrinaire concept of workers and communal self-management. An important decentralization and democratization of power was carried out. Principally, all power had to reside directly in the hands of the working class at the level of enterprises, and indirectly, via the elected delegates, from the community up to the Federal Parliament. The experiment had been inspired by great ideas, but in practice, the "ideal model" of self-management encountered numerous difficulties and the whole system moved to the current crisis. Steps are presently being taken to improve the system by carrying out constitutional reforms to enable it to respond to the requirements of a democratic society and a market economy.

Until the Second World War, Yugoslavia was basically an agricultural country. More than 80% of its population engaged in agricultural production. About 15% lived in cities. After the second World War, with the establishment of the socialist social order, came a rapid transformation into a modern industrial and urban society. According to the 1981 census, the agricultural population had dropped to only 19%. Indeed, the urban population did not increase at the same pace: in 1948 it was 20% and in 1981 - 46.5%. The rise was not even throughout the country, but it was strong everywhere. De-agragarianization and migrations were taking place from undeveloped to developed regions, from villages to cities and from Yugoslavia abroad. Many villages and regions became almost deserted, especially in the mountainous regions. Only old people remained there, those who could not adapt to changed conditions of the modern nomadic life. And more than one million young Yugoslavs found employment in European and even non-European countries.

Simultaneously, a very intensive process of family transformation was taking place. It particularly involved the following:

–the average number of family members dropped significantly. In 1948 it was 4.37 and in 1981, 3.62. However the differences between some regions remain large.

–the birth rate dropped sharply, particularly over the last thirty years. In 1955, 26.9 children were born per 1.000 inhabitants, and in 1986 only 15.4. Mortality fell only slightly in the some period: from 11.4 to 9.1. But population growth dropped drastically: from 15.6 in 1955 to 6.9 in 1986. Even simple biological replacement of the population has not been assured in some regions of Yugoslavia. However, Yugoslavia always produces paradoxical surprises. In the Autonomous Province of Kosovo, mainly inhabited by Albanians, the birth rate is one of the highest in the world: 37 per 1.000 inhabitants.

Structural atomization of the family has been accompanied by an important content atomization and dynamization of the family nucleus. First, the number of contracted marriages dropped: in 1948 there were 13 contracted matrimonies per 1.000 inhabitants, and in 1986 only 7.6. A fortunate aspect is that the number of divorces is low: about 1.4 divorces per 1.000 inhabitants. However, the number of divorces is not the only indicator of family disorganization.[3] Empirical research has shown that some families are only apparently well-integrated and others are really unhappy but have not fallen apart simply due to the pressures of traditional morality. The number of de facto permanently broken or severely disturbed families, which is not recorded in the statistics, is fairly large. A good indicator is the substantial number of single person households (about 14%) as well as the number of illegitimate births, which range from 6% up to as high as 18% in some regions. In addition to family problems, social pathology is increasing, as is reflected child neglect, juvenile delinquency, alcoholism, drug addiction, vagrancy, prostitution, rowdyism and the like.

Generally speaking, the Yugoslav family is passing through the historically recognized processes of structural and content atomization and of the strengthening of the bigenerational nucleus, by gradually rejecting the family members it can no longer support. But the very bigenerational standard is at the same time seriously undermined both externally and internally, so that it is also seized by family pathology. As to society's value-system, a dramatic clash has occurred between the traditional, inherited value-system based upon segregation and subordination of the family roles, on the one hand, and the new value system of socialist society which encourages emancipation of the woman and humanization of relations in the family, on the other. Although the outcome is certain, the family drama is not, for this reason, any easier for its participants nor for society as a whole. Nor has the legal system, which had proclaimed grand principles of equalization of men and women in all areas of social and political life and in all marital and family relations, been powerful enough to prevent the drama. Nor can the human provision of special care for children substantially change the situation until objective social realities have been surmounted.[4]

Hence the family in Yugoslav society is being substantially transformed. The following question, therefore, arises: what has happened to the old people? Are they still, to a greater or lesser extent, integrated into the system of family cooperation; are they close to the nuclear core; or have they been rejected from it and forced to spend their last days lonely and embittered? It is not easy to give a simple response. Yugoslav and world literature reveals opposing views. To obtain a more detailed picture, more information needs to be considered.

III

The first, and one of the most important facts, is that the demographic aging of the population, as a world phenomenon, has seriously affected Yugoslavia.[5]

This can be seen by comparing the number of persons aged over 60 in censuses covering the whole country. In 1921 it was 8.4%, in 1948, 8.7% and in 1981, 12.0%. For the years 2001 and 2020 the estimated percentages are 17.6 and 21.4, respectively. However, in the year 2000, when the percentage of persons over 60 will be 17.6, important differences will still exist between regions: their range will be from above 22% in Serbia up to 8% in Kosovo, and in 2021 from 26.5% in Serbia to 10% in Kosovo. At the same time important differences in the juvenile population will continue. In Serbia in 1981, the share of population younger than 19 was 27.5% and in Kosovo it was 51.3%. In 2021 it will be 24.6% and 34.6%, respectively.[6]

As elsewhere in the world, the aging of the Yugoslav population has very important implications for economic, social and health policies. This new environment requires a profound reorientation of the strategic long-term programmes of economic and social development. For socialist countries, including Yugoslavia, the old population represents a very serious issue of a class nature. Old people constitute the most endangered demographic and social group. They are the poorest, the least educated and the loneliest. Their return to the historical stage is mostly the return of the poor. The majority of them are remote from the centres of political power and decision-making. Research in Yugoslavia shows that only about 25% of people older than 65 have permanent sources of income in the form of pensions or permanent social aid. The pension provisions are unfortunately not all-inclusive and do not deal with people who lose their employment through various circumstances, and particularly, do not cover the elderly rural population.

Perhaps loneliness and feelings of desertion and rejection are the severest hardships affecting old people. A tragic feature of loneliness is that poverty and misery are generally linked with it. Some better-off people (except in some rural areas) are not so lonely because they make up for their old age with other comforts. They are generally not deserted by their children, relatives, or friends. On the other hand, where material provisions fail, elementary forms of human solidarity often cease as well. It is precisely this phenomenon which leads to a consideration of probably one of the main reasons for old people's alienation in the modern world: the family.

There are two hypotheses bearing on the relationship between the family and old people:

According to the first, the nuclear family has rejected its old members and they live their last days lonely and deserted. This view was dominant in Yugoslav sociological and gerontological literature up to the nineteen-fifties under the influence of Malinovsky, Barges, Muddock, and especially Parsons. Their theories of the nuclear, bigenerational family of industrial society assumed that in addition to the *orientation cycle* and *procreation cycle,* a third cycle of family life appears: the *isolation cycle* (partial or full), the so-called "third age", not only as a biological phenomenon, but as a style of life. This theory has many adherents, fewer among urban and more among rural sociologists and gerontologists. "Thus the law of evolution leads us to the modern family which provides a frame only for man's birth, but not necessarily for his death. It is not even the frame for his last years".[7] The conclusion is that all relatives from the traditional extended family in urban society remain outside the micronucleus, at the periphery of the family. They now form "secondary zones" with which links are relatively loose and disappear with time. These links will completely disappear in the future.

According to the second hypothesis, the family in urban society is not isolated from relatives who are formally outside the nuclear family. The number of parents who live permanently with their children is significant, even dominant, not only in rural but also in urban regions. Thus the allegation that links between parents and children break once the children establish their own families is erroneous. It is not true that a parent remains completely alone once widowed. The data compiled from a large number of empirical studies after 1950 [8] show that even after children leave the parent's house, links between parents and children continue and generally extend until the parents die. It is for this reason that one cannot talk about the *isolated nuclear family* as a dominant form. Such families certainly exist, but their number is relatively small. The *extended modified family* dominates, where parents do not live in the same space with their children, but economic and emotional links have not ceased between them. Finally, *three-generational families* are also common, both in villages and in cities (often out of necessity, but also for emotional reasons).

Although it might sound sophistic, I believe that both opinions are correct. To accept either as definitive would be a mistake. The problem is too complexs, because different historical stages are involved. There are two stages in the development of industrial society to which different rules apply. In the first, "primitive", stage the economic conditions relating to poverty are dominant. When the rural family of little property was stripped of power and its property expropriated, a surplus of people emerged in the family: relatives, parents, even children.[9] That is why the family radically breaks with these "surpluses", often brutally. It is no longer able to support them. This is the reason why many people became homeless overnight. Appeals to humanity, solidarity, respect were in vain. Thomas Malthus had this fact in mind when he wrote his famous accusation that the human dining table is not big enough to receive everybody. So, the uninvited must depart. Of all these events, the "rural exodus" is of special importance. It makes no essential difference whether it happens in a capitalist or a young socialist country. Neither was, in this first stage, prepared for the "migration of people". This process is underway today, but, in Yugoslavia, is coming to an end. Yugoslavia is thus still passing through the first stage of creating a modern industrial and urban society (with the exception of some developed parts of the country).

Therefore, in the first stage, a tendency towards structural, but also emotional, disintegration of the family is strongly pronounced. Only in the second, higher stage, which the industrial countries are presently experiencing, does tension subside while cohesion among relatives and solidarity become gradually reaffirmed. The network of relatives' interaction outside the family nucleus is expanding with a possible simultaneous further structural atomization of the family. The main reasons for this are improved social conditions, higher living standards and a better quality of life. This might seem, at first glance, improbable, but it was recently verified in a comprehensive international research project carried out in the United States, the United Kingdom, Denmark, Poland and Yugoslavia. The writer participated as Director of the Yugoslav section of the project.[10] The results were contained in a paper I gave to the world congress of Sociologists held in Uppsala, Sweden, in 1978. I will draw attention to a few basic conclusions from the paper.

First, it is very important to make a clear distinction between "living alone" and "being lonely". In the former case, persons who live alone (as singles or with a spouse) may be rejected from the family and feel lonely, but this is not necessarily so. Their real position is determined by analysing several elements: remoteness of the residence, intensity of interactions, i.e. frequency of contacts between old people and their relatives (personal encounters, telephone calls, letters, etc.), degree of their economic interdependence, quality (depth) of emotional ties between partners, children and other relatives, and so on. However, old people who live with their relatives may be in a worse position than those who live alone if they are emotionally deserted and rejected. Still, one would expect the majority of them to be successfully integrated into the three-generational family frameworks.

Our research showed that old people most frequently live alone in industrialized countries, but the majority of them do not feel lonely. Their spatial separation from relatives is not too great a handicap, because a system of intensive social and relative-related interactions is in place. On the other hand, in less developed countries (Poland and Yugoslavia), the majority of old people live with their children and relatives, but at the same time their emotional links are not significant. Old people feel unwanted, they live "beside" and not "with" their relatives; their death is expected as a relief for the family, and not as a misfortune. Naturally, this is neither a general nor a dominant rule, but its share in our research was rather high: 32% of old people (permanently or frequently) feel lonely in Yugoslavia; 20% in Poland, 9% in the United States, 7% in the United Kingdom, 4% in Denmark. Again, the largest percentage of old people who feel sporadically lonely is in Yugoslavia (34%), flowed by Poland (32%), the United States (30%), the United Kingdom (21%) and Denmark (13%).

Family structural atomization, unlike its emotional disorganization, does not reveal such drastic differences. Thus, 28% of old people live alone in Denmark, 22% in the UK; 22% in the USA, 17% in Poland and 15% in Yugoslavia. However the percentage without a single relative was the following: Denmark 1%, the U.K. 3%, the United States 1%, Poland 6% and Yugoslavia 10%. Such a situation in Poland and Yugoslavia is, *inter alia,* the result of massive destruction of the civil population during the past wars.

The data on old people who live alone, but who have children and relatives, is also interesting. The remoteness of the residence is one of the important indicators of contacts taking place between parents and children. In this respect, old people in industrial countries are again in a more favourable position. Thus 33% of old people live at ten or less minutes travelling distance in the USA; 32% in Denmark, 24% in the UK, 12% in Poland and 12% in Yugoslavia. A similar situation pertains regarding old people who live at 11-30 minutes travelling distance: 23% in Denmark, 16% in the UK and the USA and 8% in Poland and Yugoslavia.

Parents who lived separate from their children met at least one child on the same or a previous day. The percentages here were almost equal in all five countries. The exception was Poland (63%) while others oscillated from 53% (Denmark), 52% (the United States), 51%(Yugoslavia) and 47% (the United Kingdom). However, old people are in a more favourable position in industrial countries with respect to the encounters between parents and children at 2-7 day intervals: the UK 30%, Denmark 27%, the USA 26%, Yugoslavia 20%, Poland 13%. Finally, contacts in 8-30 day intervals are the highest in Yugoslavia (16%) and lowest in Poland and the United States (9%), while contacts in 30-day to 1-year intervals range from 10% in Poland and the United States to 9% in Yugoslavia, to 7% in the UK and 6% in Denmark. The number of parents who do not meet their children in periods over a year is relatively small and ranges from 4% in Poland and Yugoslavia to 2% in Denmark.

The data on interaction relationship via exchange of letters is interesting for

Yugoslavia. It shows that such a relationship is very infrequent. However, there are important differences in this respect between the urban and rural old generation. Old people in rural regions do not write because they cannot in 63% of such cases and in urban areas in 32%. Those who do not write because they have nobody to write to are 11% in villages and 10% in cities. Those not wanting to write amount to 5% in villages and 6% in cities. 21% of old people from rural areas write to their children; 52% from cities do so. Important differences are also found in terms of sex and category of those who do not write: village–males 49%, females 74%, city–males 22%, females 40%.

IV

This and other research has shown that the problem of the old population in Yugoslavia is becoming increasingly complex. It has especially deteriorated over the last few years due to the social and economic crisis which mostly affects old people and children.

Four groups of the elderly population may be distinguished:

–*Rural old people's households* are by far the most endangered, and the loneliest, often deprived of elementary forms of help. Health is bad, living conditions primitive and they have no hope that their situation can be essentially improved;

–*Poor old people's households* represent the proletarianized part of this population. The problem of the old is, in fact, the problem of *poor old people*. Many of them are social aid recipients, but the aid is often insufficient. A part of this population borders on the marginal groups, particularly if they have no relatives or belong to some ethnic groups (gypsies, for example);

–*Very old* (called old-old) people perhaps pose the greatest problems to the family and society. Old age is being increasingly divided into two cycles: the *"third age"* (from 60-80) and the *"fourth age"* (over 80). Due to insufficiently developed and organized home care and of other forms of medical protection, many families in Yugoslavia are exposed to great uncertainties.

–*Old females* are in a much worse position than males. First, they live, on average, eight years longer than males and therefore remain alone more frequently, widowed and often without the help of relatives. Those women rarely remarry, whereas a larger number of old males live with someone in the family, a relative and/or a spouse. Moreover, generational transmission by a male is more important than by a female. Research frequently indicates the importance of "women clans" in inter-generational relations. Relations between mother and daughter are more intimate than those between mother and son. It is, therefore, less favourable for an old woman if she only has sons.

A specific issue which for some time divided theoreticians and practitioners concerned the forms of care for old people: whether to construct homes or to give preference to enhancing the ability of the nuclear family to undertake care for its old members. For a time, the preference in Yugoslavia was to construct homes for old people and it was even proposed that entire settlements for the old should be built. These ideas are now almost completely abandoned, which means that children do not get rid of their parents by sending them to homes for the aged. The need for such homes cannot be denied, but homes for the aged must become the last resort in cases where old people have no relatives or when, for whatever reason, private family accommodation cannot be assured. Gerontologists and social politicians are presently thinking in this direction. Combined homes, in which several generations would live simultaneously, are also being considered.

V

As regards relations between the family and the aged, processes similar to those in Yugoslavia are found in other socialist countries. The Soviet family is basically bigenerational, but there are great regional variations. Thus the share of the multi-member family (with five or more children) in the Russian SSR is, in the worker-employee family, 0.4%; the kolkhoz family 2.4%; in the Tadzhik SSR, the worker-employees family, 19.3%: the kolkhoz family, 35.8%. Still, for the whole USSR territory, the average number of members per family household is 3.5 which indicates an important structural atomization of the Soviet urban family.[11] In 1986 the urban population formed 65.6% and the rural 34.4% of the total. However, the proportionate share of worker-employee families is much higher than that of urban (87.6%). A specific feature is that the citizen in the Soviet Union is mostly a "family being": in 1979 in urban areas 872 per 1000 inhabitants lived in the family, and 128 as singles, while in the rural area 913 inhabitants per 1000 lived in the family, and only 87 as singles.[12] It is interesting that individual farmers' households no longer exist. The asymmetry in the number of men and women is also important for demographic policy: 47% men against 53% women. Birth rate and population growth are permanently declining: in 1940, the number of births per 1000 inhabitants was 31.2 and in 1985 19.5. Over the same years the ratio of deceased was 18.0 and 10,0 respectively. The growth of population in 1940 was 13.2 and in 1985, 8.8.[13]

Such demographic movements have led to a substantial increase in the population over the age of 60. Thus, in the early nineteen-eighties their share was 13% of the total population, and it is expected to be 17% in 2000. In the Baltic Republics, the aged population has already reached 18%, and in the Central Asian republics the percentage ranges from 7 to 10. Although most old people traditionally live with their children, there is an increasing number who live separated from them. The largest proportion of these are old women. Of 1000 men over 60, only 58 live separated from the family, while 246 of such women do so. Also, the number of old people who live with children or relatives is much larger in the villages than in the cities (90% to 66%).[14]

The population of Czechoslovakia is a little older than the Soviet. According to 1980 figures, the proportion of persons over 60 was 15.37%. This is envisaged to rise to 16.8% in 1990 and to decline insignificantly (16.1%) by the year 2000. In a period of only thirty years (1950-1980) their number increased by 67%. It is characteristic that the number of persons over 80 is rapidly growing so their estimated share in the population is envisaged to be 13.4%. Women form the larger proportion of old people. In 1980 their share in the total population was 51.3%; but it was 59.1% of the group over 60 and 69.2% of those over 80. Hungary[16] has an even older population. In 1980 the proportion of persons over 60 was 17.1%. Demographic forecasts indicate an increasing number of these persons up to the year 2000. It is expected that every fifth inhabitant of Bulgaria will be above 60 in the year 2000.

The socialist countries of Europe are passing through a rather dramatic stage of family atomization.[18] As in Yugoslavia, two phenomena are widespread: a relative decline in the marriage rate and a considerable rise in divorce. Thus in Czechoslovakia the number of marriages in 1950 was 10.8% per 1000 inhabitants; in 1982 it was 7.6%; in the Soviet Union it fell from 11.5 to 10.3 over the same years; in Hungary from 7.7 to 7.1; and in Bulgaria from 10.7 to 7.8. The number of divorces in most of these countries is among the highest in the world. In the Soviet Union there were 0,4 divorces per 1000 inhabitants in 1950 and in 1982 — 3.3; in Czechoslovakia the rate rose from 1.1 to 2.2, in Hungary from 1.2 to 3.0 and in Bulgaria from 0.8 to 1.4.

Those data show that old people frequently cannot seek support from their children. It is no longer a question of extreme ideology, as in the early days of the revolution. Quite to the contrary, the programmes of all socialist countries presently underline the family as the most important basis of the social and emotional safety of the aged. It is especially underscored that old people should remain in the flat in which they have been living and that support and assistance must be provided to their children to allow them to continue to care for their parents. But it must be recognized that many children, and particularly other relatives, will no longer be in a position to meet this obligation. Some children have hardly ever lived with one parent. Their obligations are owed more strongly to a stepfather or stepmother who raised them rather than a father or mother who left them. Some parents have not met even the minimum obligations towards their children. All these new circumstances have been receiving increasing consideration in family legislation. Overall social strategy should, therefore, take into account all the changes taking place in the structure of the population and those which will take place by the end of the present and early in the next century. Forecasts are that changes will be even more profound and more versatile.

VI

The final issue in connection with old people may be formulated in the following manner: Has the normative-legal system in socialist countries been slow in formulating the legal and social care for the old?

The response could be that it has, but not more, or at least not much more, than, in most of the industrial countries of the West. A certain delay may be seen from the following facts:

First, a codified legal system of the elderly does not exist in any socialist country, either within Family Law or as an autonomous legal matter.

Second, the constitutions of some of these countries do not make specific reference to old people, and only slight, but insufficient progress has been made in some others. For example, in addition to the already traditional obligations of parents to support their underage and incapable children, the 1974 Constitution of Yugoslavia contains a supplement regarding the obligation of children to take care of their parents who need help (art.190, para. 3, word 2). The same provision has been in the constitution of the USSR since 1977(art. 66). Indeed, the Soviet Constitution also envisages an obligation of the state to help "large families", but in this context it is families with a large number of children which is meant rather than old people(art. 53).

Third, even family legislation has not yet sufficiently appreciated the urgent need to reconsider a global approach to the regulation of the status of old people. However, the largest (though not spectacular) improvements have been made here. First, Yugoslav law has introduced a number of new features. It has further elaborated a constitutional provision on the obligation of children vis-a-vis old parents. However, the children may be exempted from this obligation if a parent had been deprived of parental rights and did not support the child although his means allowed him to do so, or if the Court should find that, in all circumstances of the case, this would cause obvious injustice to the child (the Law of the SR of Serbia, art. 302, papa. 2). A similar provision is also contained in some other federal laws of Yugoslavia. Soviet law has accepted the same solution in a slightly different way (art. 20 of the Bases of Legislation on Marriage and Family of the USSR). The laws of other socialist countries do not contain such provisions. The law of Czechoslovakia however, contains a provision on the special obligations of children vis-a-vis parents, but not the possibility of exempting children from them (para 87).

Yugoslav law also contains a provision by which an organ of guardianship may, in the name of an old and self-supporting person, in accord with his proposal or under his proper initiative, initiate and pursue proceedings to enforce his right to support by relatives who are bound by law to support him. If this person opposes this, the organ of guardianship is not authorized to initiate the proceedings in his name (art. 314 of the Family Code of Serbia). However, children and relatives who are bound to take care of aged persons receive help from the social community if they ensure the material and social position of the aged people (art 8, para. 2 of the Law of Serbia). However, the care for the aged is fully undertaken by the social community when children are unable to provide it and there are no relatives who are bound by law to render the necessary help (art. 8, para 2.). This last provision is not contained in any other federal law either in Yugoslavia or in any other law of the socialist countries. But Soviet law contains a general provision that: "Citizens are entitled to support in the case of old age, illness, full or partial incapability or the loss of persons who support them" (art. 14 of the Constitution of the Belorussian SSR).

The law should have regard to the support given by a step-child to a step-parent. This legal link will become increasingly important. There is an explicit reference to this issue in some laws (Yugoslavia, Poland, Hungary). The Family Code of the German Democratic Republic, in particular, sets out the obligations of grandchildren vis-a-vis grandfathers and grandmothers, and vice versa (art. 81).

Many of these norms would remain mere aspirations were they not transformed, through other legal provisions, and particularly measures of social policy, old age pensions and disability insurance policy, into a complete system of social care for the old. Important efforts have been made recently in this regard in all socialist countries, but with variable results in practice. This activity has particularly strengthened after the adoption of the *"Vienna International Action Plan on Aging"* of the World Aging Assembly held in Vienna in 1982. The Yugoslav Government adopted an ACTION PLAN in 1984, and the Programmes of Social Care for Old Persons for the Period up to 1990 were prepared on this basis by all federal units. In addition to possible similar programmes, other socialist countries have introduced certain measures into their socio-economic development programmes, as well as into their political programmes adopted at Party Congresses (Communist, Workers, etc.).

The underlying idea of all the documents could be expressed as follows: *"It is a natural human need and an inalienable right to live during old age in the desired social and family environment. The social community, therefore, strives to create appropriate conditions for the aged so that they may spend their old age in their own apartments and/or with their family members and relatives"* (para. 10 of the Action Plan of Yugoslavia). A similar idea is also incorporated in the Soviet documents and those of other socialist countries.

I will cite as examples the ideas of the *Programme of Social Care for Old Persons of the SR of Serbia*. After determining the general social strategy in the area of aging and old age, the programme sets out the *fields* where it will be applied. They are: space planning, housing policy, education and culture, pension and disability insurance, health protection, family and relative-related solidarity and protection, tax policy, science and research work, and other fields as needed.

The family has a special role in this system. The family has to be allowed to realise its social-protective function vis-a-vis aged members as fully as possible. For this reason the appropriate social benefits shall be assured for the family:

–provision of multiple links with society and with social solidarity system

–insistence on the legal and moral obligation of relatives, initiation of actions of a moral-educational nature and the enforcement of legal obligations and responsibilities

–provision of benefits in terms of solving issues concerning housing, health protection, tax incentives, employment, home medical treatment and care, home services, recreation, farmers household related help and other issues for the family with old members

–provision of social work, legal assistance and of other technical services,

–development of solidarity with neighbours and of activities of humanitarian organizations in providing services to families who care for old persons, as well as of voluntary citizens' activities within the local communities aimed at protecting old persons

–encouragement of the establishment of alimony funds from which alimony for the aged would be paid in the cases when their relatives are not able to do this (these funds are envisaged in the Family Code of Serbia — art 24, and in the Law on Alimony Funds of the PR of Poland).

The Programme envisages and/or proposes amendments to a number of legal provisions and gives instructions to all specialist and other organs which are to undertake obligations towards old people and families of old people. Particularly underlined are the obligations of Social Work Centers in terms of their increased supervision over implementation of the legal and moral obligations of relatives. Initiation of proceedings aimed at depriving relatives, who have neglected their obligation to support and care for old people, of their inheritance rights is insisted upon, as well as the collection of costs arising from the already paid alimony in all cases where such grounds exist.

This and all other documents in connection with old people have been inspired by humanitarian ideals. In this respect the socialist countries have both an historical and an ideological mission. It depends only on them to what extent these ideas will be converted into reality. Even when God was creating this world He wanted it to be the best of all possible worlds. We are rightly asking: Is it the best?

Notes

1. F. Engels, *Poreklo porodice, privatnog vlasništva i države (The Origin of the Family, Private Property and the State)*, edition, Beograd, 1956.
2. Renouveau des idées sur la famille, Travaux et Documents, Cahier No 18, Paris, 1954.
3. Statistički godišnjak 1986 *Statistics Yearbook*, 1986, Beograd, 1987.
4. M.Mladenović, *Osnovi sociologije porodice (Elements of Family Sociology)*, Beograd, ed.V.,1987.

5. Izazovi starosti — *Zbirka dokumenata UN (Challenges of Old Age - The UN Anthology of Documents)*. Beograd, 1984. p.51-55
6. D.Breznik, *Fertilitet stanovništva Jugoslavije i demografski aspekti planiranja porodice (The Fertility of the Yugoslav Population and the Demographic Aspects of Family Planning)* Beograd, Socijalna politika, 11-12, 1987. p.169-180.
7. M.Živković, *Koreni, konstituisanje i tekovine gerontologije (The Roots, Constitution and Issues of Gerontology)*, Beograd, Gerontološki zbornik, 1973.p.1-33.
8. M.Mladenović, *Socijalna politika i Borodica (Social Policy and the Family)*, Beograd, 1980, ed.II.
9. M.Živković, *Osnovne karakteristike stare populacije relevantne za dalji razvoj socijalne politike (The Basic Characteristics of Old Urban Population Relevant for Further Development of Social Policy)*, Beograd, 1973.
10. M.Mladenović, "Status of Old People Within the Conditions of Family Transformation in Yugoslavia," Paper for the 9th World Congress of Sociology, Uppsala, 1978.
11. Vasìeva, Je.K., *Seǹja v socialističkom obščestve (The Family in Socialist Society)*, Moskva, 1985.
12. *SSSR v cifrah v 1985 godu (USSR in Figures in 1985)*, Moskva, 1986.
13. M.Mladenović, *Porodica u Sovjetskom Savezu i drugim socijalističkim zemljama (The Family in the USSR and in Other Socialists Countries)*, Beograd, Sociologija, N° 3, 1987, p.339-365.
14. *Izazovi starosti — zbirka dokumenata UN (Challenges of Old Age - The UN Anthology of Documents)*, Beograd, 1984, p.540
15. ibid.,p.525
16. ibid.,p.464
17. ibid.,p.516
18. M.Mladenovič, *Razvod braka u socijalističkim zemljama (Divorce in Socialists Countries)*, Beograd, Gledišta, n° 9-10, 1987,p.48-83.

Chapter 10

The Adoption of Majors in Japan

by Ichiro KATO

Chancellor of the Seijo Gakuen,
Professor Emeritus of The University
of Tokyo, Japan

Adoption of Majors in Japan

In Japan, close to two thirds of adoptions are accounted for by adoption of majors (aged 20 or over). Before considering the relevance of this phenomenon to the law relating to the elderly, I would like to briefly review the mechanism of the adoption system of Japan and related statistics.

A. The Mechanism of Adoption

Before the war, the courts had no role in the adoption of a child. It had long been the rule of the old Civil Code (enacted in 1898) that registration in the relevant register of an agreement of adoption, duly executed jointly by an adopter and an adoptee, legally constitutes an adoption. In the case of a child aged less than 15, his or her parents can sign the agreement on behalf of the child, and in the case of a child between 15 and 20, he or she can sign the agreement with the consent of his or her parents. On the other hand, any person who has reached 20 is competent to sign an agreement of adoption on his or her own behalf as an adoptee.

Under this system, however, there was a danger that the parents of a child might be tempted to sell the child under the guise of an adoption in order to reduce the mouths to feed or simply for monetary gain. Indeed, many cases of human traffic disguised as an adoption had been reported before the war, involving the sale of children for the purpose of training them as entertainers (in the case of female children) or as laborers (in the case of male children). It might be mentioned in passing, however, that human traffic is possible without going through the formality of adoption.

After the war, the Family Law in the Civil Code underwent a sweeping amendment in 1947, under which it has become mandatory for any person proposing to adopt a minor to obtain the leave of the family court (Article 798 of the Civil Code). This article is designed to protect the well-being of the minors involved in adoptions. However, when a person proposes to adopt any of the lineal descendants of his own or of his spouse, such a person exceptionally is not required to seek the leave of the family court (the proviso to Article

798), the reason being that the well-being of such a child is not normally threatened. Examples are the adoption of a child of the other spouse or of his or her grandchild.

By contrast, the adoption of a major, properly evidenced by the registration of an adoption agreement, duly executed by the adopter and the adoptee, is automatically sanctioned as it was before the war since such adoption poses no danger of abuse. In addition, the 1987 amendment to the Adoption Law (Articles 817-2 through 817-11, inclusive, of the Civil Code) has instituted a special adoption which makes the adoption of a minor under 6 subject to the leave of the family court upon application by an adopter. The provision is directed at putting on adopted minor in an almost identical position to that of a natural child of the adopter in terms of extinction of kinship with the real parents, prohibition, in principle, of the dissolution of the adoptive relation, and way of entry in the family register.

B. Statistics of Adoption

Under the adoption system of Japan, adopted children may largely be divided into the following three groups (B, C, D) in terms of the requirement to obtain leave of the family court.

Total adoptions	A
Adoptions of minors:	
Those subject to the leave of the family court	B
Those not subject to the leave of the family court	C
Adoptions of majors	D

According to the 1986 statistics, which are the latest available, A stood at 91,732 and B at 3,297. Accordingly, 88,435 (A-B) represents the total number of C+D. As no statistical breakdown of C and D is available, we can only surmise the figures on the basis of the data generated by surveys covering only part of the areas. The findings of these surveys made public so far are summarized as follows (Table 1):

Table 1. Adoptions

Year/Period	Source	Ratio of the Adoption of Majors to Total Adoptions (%)
1955	Sample survey (cities) by the Ministry of Justice	45.7
Nov/56-Jan/57	ditto	52.2
Apr/57-Mar/58	Survey of Okayama City by Prof. Masanori Yamamoto	58.6
Oct/82	Sample Survey by the Ministry of Justice	66.8
Breakdown	Large urban centers (with a population of 500,000 people or more)	45.7
	Cities (with a population of fewer than 500,000 people)	67.0
	Towns and villages	78.3

Although these findings are based on sample surveys, they serve to show a sharp increase in the ratio of adoptions of majors to the total number of adoptions from 45.7% in 1955 to 66.8% in 1982. They also underscore the trend that the ratio of adoptions of majors is larger in rural communities than in large urban centers: 45.7% in large urban centers, 67.0% in small- and medium-size cities, and 78.3% in rural towns and villages.

Since 1955, 90,000 to 100,000 cases of adoption have been registered each year. Of these, 50,000 to 60,000 cases (the latter being in 1986) were accounted for by adoptions of majors, suggesting that while they have been on the rise in recent years, the increase was not significantly large. Meanwhile, the number of adoptions of minors sanctioned by the family court has been decreasing markedly, from about 40,000 cases in 1955 to 2,557 cases in 1986. By contrast, the number of adoptions of minors not subject to the leave of the family court, that is, adoptions of lineal descendants of the adopters or their spouses, has been increasing gradually during the same period according to sample surveys, from 19-23% (20% on average or about 20,000 cases a year) of total adoptions in 1950 to 30% (about 27,500 cases) in 1986.

The sharp decrease in the number of adoptions of minors subject to the leave of the family court is largely blamed on the decreased supply of adoptable children. Before the war, about four children to a family had been the norm. Today, their number has decreased to an average of 2.2 children. On the other side, illegitimate children are a potential source for adoption. In Japan, however, the number of illegitimate children is extremely small. They numbered about 100,000 (or 3.9% of total births) in 1947 and 13,398 (1.0%) in 1987.

Meanwhile, the number of adoptions of lineal descendants of the adopter or his spouse has increased. This is attributable to the facts that the number of divorces (and accordingly, the number of remarrying divorcees) has increased in recent years, leading to an increase in the number of adoptions of children born in a previous marriage and that the number of cases where persons adopt the children of their spouse or their own grandchildren for the purpose of reducing their inheritance tax liabilities has also increased.

The Role of the Adoption of Majors and Its Functions

A. The Role of the Adoption of Majors

As noted earlier, the number of adoptions of majors registered each year is estimated at about 60,000, accounting for two thirds of the total adoptions of about 90,000. Their number has tended to increase but it has not gone significantly beyond the annual range of 50,000 to 60,000 in the past thirty years.

What are the motives prompting people to adopt majors? First is the age-old practice of taking a son-in-law into the family. When a family has a daughter but no son, it customarily adopts a man as husband for the daughter to have him succeed to the family business and estate. In prewar years, the Civil Code contained provisions which combined marriage and adoption. After the war, however, they were repealed on the grounds that the combination of marriage and adoption as a single act was a vestige of the ancient family system which had outlived its relevance to changes in values and the family institution. Under the modern system, therefore, marriage and adoption are effected separately, but that has not really changed anything in practice. The practice of adopting a son-in-law into the family is mostly followed by farming households and proprietors of small- and medium-size businesses who wish to have the son-in-law succeed to their family business.

According to a sample survey conducted by the Ministry of Justice, sons-in-law adopted into the family accounted for 15-20% of adoptions in 1955-57. If that was the case, adoptions of sons-in-law would have constituted 30-40% of the total adoptions of majors in those years and 20-30% of them today. However, given the fact that the child population has decreased over the years, and as many independent-minded men are too proud to be adopted into the family of their wife, the actual ratio might be much smaller. (There is a saying that "if you have a handful of rice bran, don't demean yourself by becoming an adopted husband.")

In addition, those who do not have an heir tend to adopt a major due to their need to have him succeed to their family business or estate. Many adopt a minor for the same purpose, but one drawback of adopting a minor is the burden of looking after him until he reaches adulthood, whereas the adoption of a major obviates that problem.

Why do people need an heir? In the first place, they want to have someone who can inherit the family name and continue the family line. As a daughter is customarily married off to a husband and will identify herself by her husband's family name, the family name of her parents will come to an end unless her husband agrees to take her family name or be adopted into her parents' family. When they have no alternative, many city dwellers are more receptive than their rural counterparts to the idea of letting their family name disappear after their death or of adopting a son of their daughter, if any, as their son.

The second reason for adopting an heir is the succession of the family estate. In the absence of legitimate children, a person's estate will pass to his spouse, his brothers and sisters or their children. In that case as his brothers and sisters have no legal reserve portion in his estate, he is free to bequeath it to others. However, people prefer to have an adopted son succeed to the estate as a member of the family.

The third reason for people wanting an heir is the need to have someone to look after them in their last years . What they need and wish for is not mere economic support. They want compassionate caring with filial warmth.

Of the three reasons outlined in the foregoing, the succession to the family name and the inheritance of family estate are two sides of the same coin. Initiation of an adoption is more often than not influenced by pecuniary considerations, that is, the inheritance of the family estate. And the third reason, the need for caring for the adopter in his old age, can actually be satisfied in exchange for the inheritance of an estate. Put bluntly, the adoption of a major is often achieved when the needs of the adopter and the adoptee coincide. The adopter says in effect that "I will bequeath my property to you, and I want you to look after me until I die," and the adoptee agrees that "if you leave your property to me, I will take good care of you the rest of your life as you wish."

A survey conducted in 1982 shows that adoptees in their twenties accounted for 58.5% of adopted majors, those in their thirties 25.8%, those in their forties 8.7%, those in their fifties 5.4%, those in their sixties 1.3% and those in their seventies 0.2%. It is natural that an overwhelming majority of adopted majors should be in their twenties and thirties. One wonders what are the motives behind adopting majors in their fifties and older. While the Civil Code prohibits the adoption of older persons and ascendants (uncles and aunts even if they are younger than the adopter), any younger person even if he is only one day junior to the adopter can be adopted.

In Japan, it is customary to select a major for adoption from among relatives and seldom from among the totally unknown or unrelated. Most commonly, nephews are adopted, but there are farming households and proprietors of small- and medium-size businesses which adopt a younger brother of the adopter to have him succeed to a farming or family business.

A great majority of adopted majors are males. According to the 1982 survey, adopted minors were more or less equally males and females, while males accounted for 80% of adopted majors. This suggests that people consider that adopted male majors are better equipped to inherit the family name, look after their adopting parents and manage inherited property.

B. Merits and Demerits of the System of Adopting Majors

The child adoption system is primarily intended for the protection and caring of minors, and the adoption of majors is something extraneous to the system because it is not motivated by compassion for the child but by the archaic values attached to the family name and family property.

From this perspective, when the archaic family system was abolished in 1947 by virtue of a sweeping amendment to the Family Law and an individualistic one was enacted, there had emerged a body of opinion calling for the abolition of the archaic system of adoption of majors. However, the system survived the amendment and has since been utilized as it had been before. In the ensuing years, opposition to the system has receded and the argument in favor of leaving the system intact has gradually prevailed.

In light of the ideal underlying the contemporary child adoption system, adoption of majors may seen repugnant. However, when viewed as a support-cum-inheritance agreement which entitles the adoptee to an estate in exchange for an obligation to take care of the adopter for the rest of his life, the system is not without merits. As long as the agreement is entered into by and between two adults of their own volition, third parties have no cause to object, or to call for the abolition of the system, provided that it is not obviously abused.

Let us take a look at the picture from an opposite angle. After the war, the life span of Japanese people has lengthened markedly, posing serious problems of caring the aged. On the other hand, the birth rate has declined just as rapidly, and the number of children per family fell to 2.2. Some have no children at all, while others have normally one or two sometimes three, rarely four or more, children. If the parents are blessed with a child (particularly, a male child), they can rely on the child for support and caring, but those without any child need an adopted child to look after them when they grow old.

When a couple have no child born of their wedlock after they reach 40, they will start looking for someone among their relatives to adopt. However, given the decreasing number of children, their choice is rather limited and they may end up adopting a nephew where feasible. If the candidate selected for adoption has the same family name as the adopter, so much the better, as the adopted major need not change his family name.

In the absence of a system for adopting majors, the parties will have to sign an agreement of support and caring in exchange for a will signed by the older party. (It is to be remembered that, unlike in West Germany, there is no system of inheritance agreement (*Erbvertrag*) in Japan.) As the older party can revoke his will any time, there is no guarantee that the agreement of support and caring cannot be separated from the inheritance agreement. If there were no system of adopting majors, a new system would have to be created combining the two into one in order to assure the inseparability of the agreement and inheritance. In this respect, the system of adopting majors obviates the troublesome necessity of writing an agreement and a will separately. And it is for this purpose that the system of adopting majors has long been utilized widely by the public in Japan.

Section Two

Economic and Social Circumstances
of the Elderly

Chapter 11

Family, Society, and the Elderly: The Vienna Case

by Josef HOERL   Institute of Sociology, University
of Vienna and Ludwig Boltzmann Institute
for Social Gerontology and
Life Span Research.*

The "Family": Some Introductory Remarks on Concepts and Approaches

It is increasingly evident that the vision of the family as a discrete social form is outworn (Gubrium 1987). By using what we think is a *general* notion, namely "family", we risk beginning all our comparative thinking from the point of view of *one* specific historical type of the "reproductive constellation" and consider this as the measuring stick for a universal pattern.

I agree with Yamane (1983, 77f.) that recently "various styles of life (...) have appeared in a far more permissive situation than ever. (...) It seems to me that the present situation demands that we reconsider the meaning of the family more flexibly. We can no longer rigidly hold to traditional views of the family as being only a living unit group. Thus considered, the new emerging phenomena should be interpreted as the manifestation of criticism against the traditional ways and ideas about the family, and we should not regard them as signs of crisis of the family institution, but as trials given to the family institution. (...) the family will continue along with man in the future; because (...) the family as an institution is an existence closely associated with human nature."

By adopting this view I give precedence to understanding over terminology, but there are many ways of understanding families. Morgan (1975, 206f.) provides some poignant examples: "My family may be an imperfect but deliberately willed attempt to conform to some ideal of 'the Christian home' or it may be a series of traps, a thing out of control, threatening and stifling. I may wear my family lightly, ready to put it aside should the opportunity or occasion arise, or it may be an ever present cross to bear. (...) Thus the picture of the kinship universe is one of increasing fuzziness at the edges and more definite, but still flexible, notions of duty, reciprocity, closeness (with the possibilities of conflict) nearer the centre."

The danger in defining the family inadequately is twofold: we may shut our eyes to the diversity of definitions, understandings and evaluations of family life and we may extrapolate an arbitrary selection of existing emotional and social structures into the future.

We may do that and overlook that *no* type of "family" effective at present will possibly operate thirty or fifty years from now. A good example is the perennial debate on the existence of the so called isolated nuclear family (Parsons 1944). There is an obvious lack of absolute criteria for the concept of "isolation". This difficulty cannot be eliminated. Consequently, the once heated discussion has considerably slowed down and "concern has shifted from the question of whether the nuclear family is isolated to the conditions under which it is more or less isolated; from the question of if kinship is important to when it is important; and from the search for appropriate descriptive labels to a search for causes and consequences." (Lee 1980, 931).

While it is true on the one hand — and will be shown empirically later in this chapter — that older people usually are not socially isolated from their kin in terms of contact frequencies, on the other hand there is a danger of overestimating the role of kin relationships in the lives of the elderly. For instance, empirical research shows that many families develop a severe if often concealed crisis when they reach their limitations in providing care needed by the dependent relative (Brody 1977).

There are two further reasons which can be identified as limiting even more the ability of families to bear the burden of support and caregiving for their dependent members alone in the future. Demographic projections leave little doubt that as a result of low fertility rates, the increased lifespan of men and women and changes in patterns of other social behaviour:

(a) the number and proportion of dependent, i.e. primarily very old, disabled and chronically ill people in the population will continue to increase (Hoover & Siegel 1986); but also the estimated prevalence of severe mental handicap will continue to rise (Moroney 1978);

(b) we will have to expect decreasing *family sizes,* i.e. the pool of available family caregivers will shrink; at the same time as the older generation increases in age, there is an increased likelihood of more *generations* within the family;

(c) divorce rates and "incomplete family forms" will continue to increase, with consequential complication of the generational structure of older persons, e.g. "the grandparent may not know how to continue a relationship with the ex-grandson-in-law because there are few societal norms defining this relationship." (Brubaker 1985, 65).

As "family care" is a euphemism for care by female kin — women still perform most of the help, assistance, support or tending that care comprises -, it is not unreasonable to expect sooner or later a social change in this field of special unequal division of labour (Finch & Groves 1980). In particular, women will certainly continue to enter the labour market in increasing numbers and try to remain there even during the years of child rearing. Thus it is highly doubtful that tomorrow's daughters will be "ideologically" ready and willing to continue today's pattern of caregiving and it is even less clear that tomorrow's sons will take their share of caregiving responsibility.

To perceive phenomena such as low fertility rates, increased divorce rates or paid employment of women as the origins of social "problems" may be a biased view; nevertheless, these phenomena cause problems for others, particularly for children and for the dependent elderly. Thus we are forced to rate the future family's ability to manage support problems rather cautiously.

Despite this, the fiscal crisis of the welfare state and a certain conservative backlash in ideology have led some policy-makers to recommend a strengthening of family solidarity and even a more or less pronounced "re-privatisation" of support tasks. But "...what is meant by saying that families need to be strengthened...? Such statements must be based on some notion of strength and weakness that goes beyond rhetoric, if they are to be useful for policy." (Moroney 1986, 31).

There is no solution in a policy based on encouraging even more informal support by the kinship system, in the first place because "... as far as the family is concerned, its full potential is already being utilised. There is no evidence of a significant pool of potential family carers" (Walder 1985, 51) but also because irreversible social changes have already occurred. Some of these developments have been mentioned above.

The rapid expansion of bureaucratic social services is symptomatic of these changes. This development towards increased utilisation of formal sources of support does not mean that family and kinship are becoming unimportant or suppliers only of affection. But we should be warned against over-idealising and overburdening family support networks with expectations which cannot be fulfilled (cf. also Rosemary 1977).

We face a situation of structural changes and transitions which creates a special dilemma for individual family members. This dilemma is poignantly summarised by Streib (1977, 213): "On the one hand, in keeping with traditional family norms and expectations, they may wish to assist older family members. However, in a modern society, there are also services available through formal organizations. If the family members avail themselves of these services, they sometimes feel they are neglecting their family obligations. There is also a dilemma when they decide whether they are entitled to receive such services even though they might be able to meet the needs of their older family members by heroic means and economic sacrifice (...) The dilemma is sharpened if the family realises that neighbors and other citizens are receiving help for their aged parents."

Intimacy and Privacy as Features of Family Life

By examining the historical roots of changes in family support obligations (cf. Hoerl & Rosenmayr 1986) one can conclude that since the beginning of the nineteenth century the quest for *privacy* as an important sector and ingredient of human life was underlined and supported. Perhaps equally powerfully, the separation of dwelling and place of work played an important part in this development of the private sphere. "Intimacy at a distance" (Rosenmayr 1958, 1985) reflected and reflects the wish to be "somehow" *close* — for practical and emotional reasons for support on both sides — and yet — also on both sides — to remain *separate,* for reasons of autonomy and in order to "domesticate" dependencies.

Analysing processes of de-institutionalisation of the family, Schulz (1983) emphasises "partial relationships" within the family, which lead to the breaking up of the "total role" of mother, father, etc. This and the appearance of new alternative patterns of sex life, communal forms of living, and so on, bring about increasing degrees of freedom in the self-definition of the family as a group. Gubrium (1987, 24) puts it clearly: "... a family is not so much a self-contained entity as it is a way to frame and represent social relations, gaining meaning from usage and application..."

Therefore, family interaction (including help) will, in the future, probably be determined more by the wider scope and growing weight of self-definition of each individual family as a group. An individualistic mentality will impact more directly upon *behaviour* patterns. Ideological and life-style pluralism will work in this direction.

With regard to intimacy, there is a tendency to demand more and more consideration for the individual case. We could almost say that we have a family "à la carte" (Rosenmayr 1983); i.e. each member of the family demands his own view and idea of the family, and each family, so far as it develops traits of a common consciousness, also demands to be an individual creation. This will have an impact on the degree and type of integration which these new forms can offer and will be willing to offer to *old people* who are in some way "relatives."

This is particularly important in view of a self-conscious definition of filial obligation. Calculated risks of mutual exposure are increasingly forming part of the basic assumptions of inter-individual relations. Obligation becomes self-defined and thus precarious.

The system of a family à la carte requires, of course, special agreements to establish who is, at a certain moment, for a certain period, responsible for what, and what liberties he has. The bond of solidarity must constantly be renewed and re-established. This is already bringing about important problems with regard to the functional and emotional needs of the elderly, and these questions of coordination and assignation will certainly increase (cf. Rosenmayr & Rosenmayr 1983).

Empirical Results on Type, Frequency, and Nature of Elderly's Kin Interactions and Their Views on Some Social Issues

The following results on the type, frequency, and nature of kin interactions confirm evidence of previous research from Austria and other industrialised societies (cf. Hoerl & Rosenmayr 1982, Horowitz 1985, Shanas 1979) that the elderly are part of family networks. On the other hand — as we shall see — some empirical findings stimulate doubts as to the *future* quality of intergenerational relationships which were discussed in the introductory section of this chapter.

These empirical findings are from a representative sample (n=274) conducted in 1983 comprising interviews with non-institutionalised elderly people (aged sixty and over) in an old residential section of Vienna called Rudolfsheim-Fuenfhaus. This district is characterized by a high proportion (26 %) of elderly inhabitants. The findings reported here are part of a broader comparative investigation of the elderly's living conditions in Tokyo and Vienna.

The formerly held belief that the elderly were neglected and isolated finds no basis in the empirical data: over half are married; over two-thirds have at least one living child, and over four-fifths of these have one living within one hour's travel time away. Over three-fourths of the elderly see a child at least once a week; and over one-third do so almost daily. Three-fifths share a household with a spouse (or another family member); almost two-thirds have siblings. Moreover, interaction and assistance flows both ways between the elderly and their kin.

A. Differences According to Age, Sex and Marital Status

Family-status patterns vary considerably with regard to the different sex and age categories. About three-fourths of the men are married in each age category. For women the percentage is 64% of the young-old and this drops to 23% in the over 70 age category. Compared to rural parts of Austria or other countries, the proportion of childless elderly people is extremely high in Vienna: in our sample 31% are childless. Among those with children, 17% of the children in the closest proximity live more than one hour travel time away. One-fifth of the elderly are neither married nor have children. One can rightfully say that there exists a substantial minority without available kin. Being unmarried *and* childless is the most important "demographic risk factor" for getting no informal help.

The husband-wife relationship is enormously important, especially where nursing is necessary in case of illness. Men are in a more favorable socio-demographic position. The proportion of married men surpasses by far the proportion of married women; similarly, the proportion of men sharing a household with another family member is higher than among women. The disadvantageous position of women in view of the composition of the household can be demonstrated most clearly by comparing one-person households with larger ones. Only a minority of all older men live alone (19%) but a majority of the women do: 59% of those 65-70 years old and 68% of the women over 70. It can be shown that people in one-person households have their nursing needs least adequately taken care of.

B. Contact Patterns with Children and Siblings

The old stereotype of the elderly as people who are cut off from contacts with their children is certainly wrong. 83% of all elderly with children, can reach them within one hour and 58% within half an hour; 19% live with a child in the same household or in the same block.

There is a clear preference for living *near* but not *with* an adult child, even among the widowed or those needing more help with household tasks. A total of 66% is strictly opposed to the idea of sharing a household with an adult child; joint living seems to be more readily accepted only in case of a deteriorated health status, but even then it is by no means generally regarded as desirable.

This result gives further support to the expression introduced earlier in this chapter, "intimacy at a distance" (Rosenmayr 1958, 1985), as characteristic of intergenerational relationships in Western societies. Obviously, intergenerational households are regarded as a *potential* source of conflict. One should not forget, however, that this preference for privacy creates a kind of vulnerability for older family members if they should eventually reach a state where they need constant care and attention rather than occasional visiting.

The frequency of contact depends to a great extent on the distance between parents and child. People having a child in the same block (not the same household!) are visited daily more frequently (81%) than those living within half an hour's driving or walking distance (38%). Contact between siblings is not so frequent: a quarter see a sibling at least once a week; among the childless, elderly contacts with siblings are more frequent.

C. Patterns of Help and Assistance

Extensive aid and social support within the family system can also be documented. Analysing five tasks of daily living (cooking, laundry, cleaning, shopping, and transportation) less than one-third do not receive any assistance; among married persons this percentage is even smaller (14%). The desire for more help with daily tasks is expressed by only 10%, slightly more often by childless (13%) and widowed (14%) persons.

Looking at financial exchange processes between the generations, 65% of the elderly parents pass on income benefits to their children and grandchildren; not much financial support by family members benefits the elderly; only 9% of the elderly receive some kind of financial aid. This example shows that older people give benefits and services as well as receive services. As a general rule, it would seem that parents continue to give to their children one way or another in a kind of balanced exchange which Aldous (1987, 231) characterises as follows: "... each generation contributes its surplus resources to alleviate deficits in the other generation's living economy."

The closer a child lives to an old person, the more likely it is that there will not only be frequent contact but also help with household tasks. For example, Lang and Brody's (1983, 197) study also found that the " (...) living arrangement proved to be the most salient explanatory characteristic for the amount of help provided (...)"

Such findings might border on the trivial, except that geographical distance from kin may interact with a variety of other factors. One has to bear in mind that proximity implies at least two elements: it is an expression of social closeness, and it exerts a certain pressure by the increased visibility of needs, which in turn increases the probability that help will be given. Proximity, so to speak, enforces aid. Cicirelli (1983) argues on the grounds of the life-span attachment theory that " (...) other things being equal, the adult child who is more attached to the parent will have greater residential proximity than a less attached child in the same situation."

D. Nursing Patterns

What are the chances of being nursed at home? This problem was investigated for (a) short-term care, i.e. illness no longer than 1 week, (b) medium-term care, i.e. in case of illness of 3-4 weeks, (c) long-term care. Old people were *not* asked to give information on present *actual* support but were asked to evaluate their general position.

First of all, it is easy to recognise that the majority of the elderly expect care from *informal* sources (i.e. spouse, children, friends, neighbors) in cases of short-term illness. In case of illness no longer than 1 week, only 26% and in case of illness up to one month, 45% do not expect aid from informal sources.

This picture changes completely, however, with long-term care. For long-term nursing care, a majority of 74% expects either help from *formal sources only* (i.e. social service, hospital or nursing home) or no help at all.

Again, these expectations vary considerably according to marital status; married people expect much more informal help even in case of long-term care (mainly provided by the spouse, of course) than single, widowed or divorced people. This significant difference according to marital status can be found not only for married men (who "traditionally" expect to be cared for by their wives) but to some (limited) extent also for married women: 12% of unmarried women as against 25% of married women expect to receive long-term care from informal sources if occasion arises. The role of husbands as care providers seems hitherto to have been underestimated; at least in our study, husbands are expected to take their share of responsibility.

Having children (i.e. a daughter or daughter-in-law) is also a factor which contributes to a more optimistic view by the elderly when evaluating their chances for informal help in the case of long-term care. Among the unmarried, *childless* elderly, only 6% expect help from informal sources, whereas among the unmarried elderly *having* children, 19% expect informal help. In case of medium-term and short-term care these differences are similar.

E. Conclusions from the Results on Assistance Patterns

The differences between older persons with and without family are striking. Obviously, older people are more likely to expect to be supported by an informal caregiver if there is one available. Spouses come first, and children come second. Results, especially as regards long-term care, indicate that the elderly are reluctant to "overstrain" family nursing resources. There appears to be a pronounced tendency by the elderly (cf. also Hoerl and Rosenmayr 1986) to deny filial obligations toward old parents in case of long-term care. Perhaps the attitude that they should not burden anyone, even their own children, with their more severe personal difficulties reflects a fear that this might precipitate other problems.

Other research on intergenerational relationships (Bengtson and Kuypers 1971, Knipscheer and Bevers 1985) indicates that elderly parents are more concerned with maintaining good relations than are their children. The younger family members have a vested interest in establishing their independence from their parents, differentiating themselves from the older generations, and thus emphasise the ways in which they are different from their parents. The old, on the other hand, have a "developmental stake" in the continuation of their family lineage and values. For this reason older parents overemphasise what they have in common with their children and overlook or minimise disagreements and differences. Consequently, the elderly will avoid demands which may strain intergenerational relationships.

The caregiver role is ordinarily expected to be taken by only *one* person, usually a close family member. Only exceptionally are additional family members (or friends and neighbours) involved in any substantial form of caregiving. Even less frequently can one find cooperation between informal caregivers and social services. The selection of this primary caregiver follows a hierarchical pattern (cf. Cantor 1979, Dono et al. 1979). Older people turn to their spouse for aid, but when there is no marital partner or she/he cannot supply the necessary aid, they turn to their children. If there is no spouse and if there are no children, these people turn to other relatives or friends or neighbours.

I must add that according to our data, *full* substitution does not by any means occur. Spouses are not only the first choice but also provide the most extensive and comprehensive care. Involvement is less for children and least for friends and neighbours. This can be demonstrated by comparing the nursing expected to be given by spouses, daughters and sons. 89% of those married expect that a their spouse will take over some kind of nursing care. On the other hand, only 37% of the elderly with daughters expect that the daughter will take over some kind of nursing care. For those with sons, this drops to 19%.

A spouse clearly occupies the highest level of expectation as a family caregiver while daughters are estimated as less and sons as the least willing and able to meet the old parents' needs. For example, Lopata (1973) found that nearly half of the widows she studied, reported that they provided care for their husbands before their deaths. This care was provided in the home and most had been caregivers for more than a year. As a result of this situation, role overload is frequently found in many wives. Fengler and Goodrich (1979) referred to the caregiving wives in their study as the "hidden patients", because they were worried, frustrated, saddened, resigned, and impatient with their husbands' health conditions.

F. Friendship Roles vs. Family Roles

The factual and symbolic importance of the family in the life of the elderly has been shown extensively. On the other hand it can be argued that the *quality of life and life satisfaction* depend more heavily on the performance of extra-familial roles as friend, neighbour, club member, volunteer in welfare activities, and such like, at least until the older persons are healthy and no longer need to be cared for. For example, Lehr (1982) could demonstrate that family-centred elderly women show a much greater propensity for depression than women who perform non-family roles and tasks. Arling (1976) found that contacts with friends were more important than contacts with grown children in predicting the morale of the elderly. Tobin and Kulys' (1980) findings suggest that the firmest affectionate (not instrumental) support relationship was among friends.

If we analyse social life feelings within our sample of elderly people we can draw similar conclusions. Higher life satisfaction, a lower degree of loneliness and a more positive retrospective view of life are significantly associated with a high number of friends. Having children or not, however, does *not* make a difference regarding these life feelings. This is true for all age groups, but the correlation is strongest among the young-olds.

G. The Role of Social Services

As has been mentioned above, the social service sector has experienced tremendous growth since the beginning of the sixties. *Knowledge* of open care services among the elderly is almost universal: 98% know of the existence of the two most widespread social services: 'home help' and 'meals on wheels'. Yet, still only a small minority of the elderly people (less than 4% in the sample) actually *receives* regular assistance from home help. Further, 23% expressed interest in receiving home help and 11% expressed interest in receiving meals on wheels in the future.

There is some evidence that having a family available reduces the probability of current use or interest in future use of formal services in the community.

84% of the married couples neither use nor are interested in using social services, compared to 64% of those who are unmarried. The same is true whether they have children or not: 79% of elderly who have children neither use nor are interested in services, compared to 64% of the childless elderly.

The reluctance to use formal support does not prevent *attitudinal* acceptance of services. The same is true for acceptance of residential homes for the elderly which is rather high: 16% of all of the elderly have already registered for admission and a further 31% intend to do so in the future. Of course, such declarations of intent should not be confounded with actual behaviour in the future, since it may only be a precautionary measure. Nevertheless, one may conclude that there is *basically* a positive attitude towards residential institutions. On the other hand, as reported earlier, there is no intention at all by the vast majority of sharing a household with adult children.

There are marked differences according to availability of kin with regard to prospective plans for relocation into a residential home. Among the widowed, 28% have already registered for admission, but only 10% of the married. 24% of the childless have already registered, but only 13% of those with children. These significant differences between those with and those without kin remain stable throughout all age groups.

H. Significance of Different Areas of Life

The most important area of concern for the future is health. 40% indicate definite health worries whereas only 6% expect any monetary problems. This optimistic outlook with regard to income may be attributed first to the social security system which guarantees everyone beyond retirement age a minimum pension, and second (possibly even more important) to the elderly's low level of aspiration. Today's elderly experienced the social and economic crises during the thirties and forties and usually were socialised to a life style of moderation and contentedness. The *objective* financial situation seems to be not so favourable, however, since 19% declare themselves not to be in a position to spend any extra money, such as for holidays or hobbies.

Regarding other areas of concern, war fears are expressed by 27% and worries about environmental pollution by 20%. No worries at all are reported by 30%.

Respondents were also asked to rank in order six different sectors of life (paid work, leisure, family, friends, help for others, commitment for general societal purposes) according to the importance in which they held them. The overall impression obtained is that most elderly support an ideology of privacy and individualism preferring family, friendship and leisure relationships.

The 'family' was considered by far the most important sector. It was ranked first by 72% and second by a further 13%. Next are 'friends', who were named by 10% as the most important and by 38% as second most important life sector. Least important was 'paid work' which was assigned sixth (and lowest) rank by 58% of the elderly.

Two conclusions can be drawn from these findings on the significance of areas of life:

(1) In public opinion it is often taken for granted that older people are alienated from their families. Data suggest, however, that the family still plays the major role in the life of older people; the centrality of family relationships and the strong ties between parents and their adult children were already indicated earlier by the proximity of kin and patterns of contact. As we have also seen, there are comparatively few claims on the children for more intense help and nursing aid because older people do not want to interfere too directly with the lives of their adult children for the sake of good and harmonious relationships.

(2) Since factual retirement age in Austria is rather low, there is usually not a legal obligation, personal desire or economic necessity to work beyond the age of sixty. Therefore, in our sample only 2% are still active members of the labour force and 6% earn some extra money to supplement their pension. Furthermore, 61% indicate that they retired without any regret whatsoever. It is unsurprising, therefore, that paid work is rated very low as a life interest.

I. The Elderly's Evaluation of Societal Trends

The problem of altruistic behaviour and solidarity in modern society is evaluated in a rather pessimistic fashion by a majority of the respondents. No less than 79% of the elderly agree with the assumption that the general willingness of people to help each other is weaker now than it was when they were young. A related finding concerns the existence of the so-called "generation gap" between young and old members of society. 57% of the elderly agree with the assumption that the generation gap is wider now than it was in former times; 18% say it remains the same, 19% consider the gap is narrower, and 6% think that a comparison makes no sense at all. Since there is no empirical evidence from that era, it is difficult to know what the true situation was at that time. Nevertheless, a certain feeling of social alienation definitely seems to prevail among older people today.

There is a rather strong negative stereotype of youth among the elderly. This can be shown by analysing the answers to the question: where do older people find the closest help and understanding? (multiple positive responses were possible):

'Own children' .... 56% positive votes
'Social services' .... 53% positive votes
'Other older people' .... 49% positive votes
'Pensioners' organizations' .... 39% positive votes
'Church' .... 33% positive votes
'Youth' .... 20% positive votes

Youth' is ranked in the last position; one possible explanation for the assumed lack of intergenerational understanding in society may be that older people try to counteract the low esteem in which they are held by society. They do so by disparaging the young generation because this is another group with an insecure social status.

It should be noted, however, that most elderly do *not* criticise their *own* children as lacking in help and understanding. The perceived generation gap occurs only in society as a whole, not within the person's own family. This result is in accordance with other studies which show that family members think there is a generation gap in society as a whole but rarely perceive one in their own families (Atchley and Miller 1980).

Summary and Conclusions

On the one hand, cross-sectional empirical data from Vienna confirm the unbroken centrality of family relationships indicated by proximity of kin, patterns of contact and affective relationship. On the other hand, several social and demographic trends have been identified as probably limiting the future ability and willingness of families to support their frail and dependent old relatives.

The sociological prediction is that attitudes and life practices will change in a direction of a more *self-conscious attitude of give and take* and of a greater resistance against being engaged in long-term activities with no definition of how long they should last, as far as assistance is concerned. There will be more immediate reflection of society within the family as a kin support and exchange group. There will also be more selectiveness in the care and kinship group. Rosenmayr (1983) calls *singularisation* a social status which does not have to be solitude and does not have to be despair, but is a certain *status of separateness,* which may be amply illustrated from demographic and sociological studies.

Contracts in this precarious society tend to be contracts of a time-limited nature. The *unlimited* aspect of cooperation was part of the classical traditional family solidarity. Today, however, for example, the issue of long-term care is much more complex and Viennese empirical results also indicate that "feelings of obligation may not be sufficient to encourage continual care of an older person." (Brubaker 1985, 122).

Finally, relations between the elderly and their families in our industrialised societies can only be understood and analysed when taking into consideration the *intervention of the state,* that is, the massive expansion of formal services, especially over the last three decades.

The family and the state (represented in this case by social bureaucracies) cannot live without each other, but their goals and communications may not agree (Sussman 1977). Speed of adaptation, flexibility in meeting non-uniform events, and application of "non-technical knowledge" (Litwak 1985), (that is, knowledge learned through everyday socialisation) are the primary group's special strengths in the informal/formal complex. Formal organizations cannot emulate such an environment with any consistency. Each expert working there has a specific job to do, normally under severe time restrictions. Frequently, organization members try to modify official rules, but the bureaucratic environment will allow the development of intimacy, love and solidarity only within rather strictly defined limits. Hence, "to the extent that an older person can rely only on the formal organization or only on family resources, or to the extent that the two structures work at cross purposes, to that extent will some of the older person's needs remain unmet." (Horowitz 1985, 200). Consequently, some kind of *shared responsibility* should be realised. This is only feasible, however, when we have acquired more knowledge of family psychodynamics to allow new structural approaches to develop (Tobin 1987) regarding the complementary roles of family and social services.

* The research mentioned was supported by the "Association of the Study of Welfare Policy in the Family" (Tokyo)

References

ALDOUS, J. (1987), New views on the family life of the elderly and the near-elderly, in: *Journal of Marriage and the Family*, 49,227-234.

ARLING, G. (1976), The elderly widow and her family, neighbors, and friends, in: *Journal of Marriage and the Family*, 38,757-768.

ATCHLEY, R.C. & MILLER, S.J. (1980), Older people and their families, in: *Annual Review of Gerontology & Geriatrics*, 1,337-369.

BENGTSON, V.L. & KUYPERS, J.A. (1971), Generational differences and the developmental stake, in: *Aging and Human Development*, 2,249-260.

BRODY, E.M. (1977), *Long-term Care of Older People: A Practical Guide*, New York: Human Sciences Press.

BRUBAKER, T.H. (1985), *Later Life Families*, Beverly Hills: Sage.

CANTOR, M. (1979), Neighbors and friends: An overlooked resource in the informal support system, in: *Research on Aging*,1,434-463.

CICIRELLI, V.G. (1983), Adult children and their elderly parents, in: T.H. Brubaker (ed.), *Family Relationships in Later Life*, Bevery Hills: Sage, 31-46.

DONO, J.E., FALBE, C.M., KAIL, B.L., LITWAK, E., SHERMAN, R.H., & SIEGEL, D. (1979), Primary groups in old age, in: *Research on Aging*, 1,403-444.

FENGLER, A.P. & GOODRICH, N. (1979), Wives of elderly disabled men: the hidden patients, in: *Gerontologist*, 19,175-183.

FINCH, J. & GROVES, D. (eds.), (1983), *A Labour of Love: Women, Work and Caring*, London: Routledge & Kegan Paul.

GUBRIUM, J.F. (1987), Organizational embeddedness and family life, in: T.H. Brubaker (ed.), *Aging, Health, and the Family*, Newbury Park: Sage, 23-41.

HOERL, J. & ROSENMAYR, L. (1982), Assistance to the elderly as a common task of the family and social service organizations, in: *Archives of Gerontology and Geriatrics*, 1,75-95.

HOERL, J. & ROSENMAYR, L. (1986), Notes on the 'post-family family', Paper prepared for the IIASA conference, Sopron, Hungary, September 3-5.

HOROWITZ, A. (1985), Family caregiving to the frail elderly, in: *Annual Review of Gerontology and Geriatrics*, 50194-246.

HOOVER, S.L. & SIEGEL, J.S. (1986), International demographic trends and perspectives on aging, in: *Journal of Cross-Cultural Gerontology*, 1, 5-30.

KNIPSCHEER, K. & BEVERS, A. (1985), Older parents and their middle-aged children: Symmetry or asymmetry in their relationship, in: *Canadian Journal on Aging*, 4,145-158.

LANG, A.M. & BRODY, E.M. (1983), Characteristics of middle-aged daughters and help to their elderly mothers, in: *Journal of Marriage and the Family*, 45,193-202.

LEE, G.R. (1980), Kinship in the seventies: A decade review of research and theory, in: *Journal of Marriage and the Family*, 42,923-934.

LEHR, U.M. (1982), Depression und "Lebensqualitei" im Alter-Korrelate negativer und positiver Gestimmtheit, in: *Zeit-schrift fuer Gerontologie*, 15,241-249.

LITWAK, E. (1985), *Helping the Elderly: The Complementary Roles of Informal Networks and Formal Systems*, New York: Guilford.

LOPATA, H.Z. (1973), *Widowhood in an American City*, Cambridge, MA: Schenkman.

MORGAN, D.H.J. (1975), *Social Theory and the Family*, London: Routledge & Kegan Paul.

MORONEY, R.M. (1978), *The Family and the State: Considerations for Social Policy*, London: Longman.

MORONEY, R.M. (1986), *Shared Responsibility: Families and Social Policy*, New York: Aldine.

PARSONS, T. (1944), The social structure of the family, in: R.N. Anshen (ed.), *The Family: its Function and Destiny*, New York: Harper & Brothers, 173-201.

ROSENMAYR, L. (1958), Der alte Mensch in der sozialen Umwelt von heute, in; *Koelner Zeitschrift fuer Soziologie und Sozialpsychologie*, 10, 642-657.

ROSENMAYR, L. (1977), The family — A source of hope for the elderly?, in: E. Shanas & M.B.Sussman (eds.), *Family, Bureaucracy, and the Elderly*. Durham, NC: Duke University Press, 132-157.

ROSENMAYR, L. (1983), *Die spaete Freiheit*, Berlin: Severin & Siedler.

ROSENMAYR, L. (1985), Changing values and positions of aging in Western culture, in: J.E. Birren & K.W. Schaie (eds.), *Handbook of the Psychology of Aging*, New York: Van Nostrand Reinhold.

ROSENMAYR, L. & ROSENMAYR, H. (1983), Gesellschaft, Familie, Alternsprozess, in: H. & H. Reimann (eds.), *Das Alter*, Stuttgart: Enke, 45-70.

SCHULZ, W. (1983), Von der Institution "Familie" zu den Teilbeziehungen zwischen Mann, Frau und Kind, in: *Soziale Welt*, 4,401-419.

SHANAS, E. (1979), Social myth as hypothesis: The case of the family relations of old people, in: *Gerontologist*, 19,3-9.

STREIB, G.F. (1977), Bureaucracies and families: Common themes and directions for further study, in: E. Shanas & M.B. Sussman (eds.), *Family, Bureaucracy, and the Elderly*. Durham, NC: Duke University Press, 204-214.

SUSSMAN, M.B. (1977), *Family, Bureaucracy, and the Elderly*. Durham, NC: Duke University Press, 2-20.

TOBIN, S.S. (1987), A structural approach to families, in: T.H. Brubaker (eds.), *Aging, Health, and the Family*, Newbury Park: Sage, 42-57.

TOBIN, S.S. & KULYS, R. (1980), The family and services, in: *Annual Review of*

Gerontology & Geriatrics, 1,370-38oj-399.

WALKER, A. (1985), From welfare state to caring society?: The promise of informal support networks, in: J.A. Yoder, J.M.L. Jonker, & R.A.B. Leaper (eds.), *Support Networks in a Caring community,* Dordrecht: Martinus Nijhoff, 41-58.

YAMANE, T. (1983), Sex and the family: The nature of the family as a human institution, *Komazawa Journal of Sociology,* 15,69-78.

Chapter 12

Welfare and Support for the Elderly in the Community

— from a survey in Sumida-ku, Tokyo, Japan —

Takatomi Ninomiya

Faculty of Economics,
Oita University, Japan

Introduction

The Association for the Study of Welfare Policy for the Family has conducted a comparative study of Tokyo and Vienna from 1983 to 1985. This chapter does not present the results of the entire study, which is still in progress, but introduces information from one part of the study which deals with the actual conditions of the elderly in modern Japan and points to some problems of Japan's welfare policy for the elderly. The first part deals with the outline of the survey; the second concerns the results of the analysis, and the last is a brief summary of the study.

Outline of the survey

We carried out the survey* to determine what kind of social conditions are necessary for self-support for the elderly from the standpoint of solidarity of the family and community, and the role of institutions and policies as a whole.

On selecting the area for the survey, we thought it necessary to understand how individual lives had, over a long period of time, been effected by the changes in the community, and how the actual conditions of the elderly have been influenced by administrative policies. Sumida-ku (Sumida-ward) was selected for this survey because it has a high proportion of elderly people, lies close to the center of the metropolis, and still retains an old town (Shitamachi) atmosphere.

Sumida-ku is situated between the Sumidagawa River and the Arakawa River in the northeastern part of the Tokyo metropolitan area. It covers an area of about 14 square kilometers and comprises about 230,000 residents (1984). For the survey area, we chose the following three blocks, Kyojima, Oshiage, and Bunka, which lie in the center of the ward. Many old tenement houses remain, having been saved from the damage of the Kanto Earthquake (1923) and World War II (1945). Also, many city apartments built for lower income residents in the 1960s are intact. This area is home to 35,687 people (17,627 men and 17,960 women), and the number of residents 65 years and over was 11.7 percent in 1984.

As informants, we chose single senior citizens and senior citizen couples aged between 60 and 74, living independently. The primary reason for the choice is that this generation will be faced with the problems of help and support in the near future, though they live independently now. The secondary reason is that it is appropriate to examine this generation in order to get a short-term view of the future of Japanese society, because households of elderly singles and couples are gradually increasing along with the trend toward nuclear families. We conducted the survey by way of interviews with a questionnaire for 159 single households chosen from 974, and 147 couple households chosen from 644 (87 men and 219 women). Both groups were chosen at random. This comprises 23 percent and 15 percent of the aged households, respectively.

The survey area has been an industrial area where Japan's once-modern industries such as chemicals and spinning have flourished since the early Meiji period (1890s). Due to a lack of modernization during a period of rapid economic growth in the 1960s, many factories moved out of the area. The decline of industry in the area caused a decline in population from 1963 when the number had reached a peak of 326,234. The young generation left as jobs became scarce, and this heightened the proportion of the aged. There remain many small-scale manufacturing industries in the area, together with wholesaling and retailing, and the majority of the elderly have been employed in such work from their youth. Even today, the employment rate of the aged is high: for 65 and over, it is 41 percent. Those people work in small factories, petty retail stores, or in their homes.

The Living conditions of the elderly[1]

We investigated the living conditions of the elderly from various aspects such as income, occupation, health, housing, social relations, family relations, and interest in public welfare services. We noted that, in most of these aspects, remarkable differences in living conditions were found according to income level. All the informants are therefore, divided into four classes according to their income level. The characteristics of each class can be clearly adduced by classifying them in such a way.

Analysing the classes, we considered the following information: it has been established that a single household requires at least 100,000 yen month, and a couple household 150,000 yen to live normally in this area. Thus the base level of income was set at these incomes. Three classes were established above this lowest class according to the increase in income. For every 50,000 yen (single) and 100,000 yen (couple), a higher class was established. According to the results of the survey, 59 percent of single households have incomes less than 100,000 yen a month. Eighty-seven percent of the single households (139 persons) are women, and 61 percent of them earn less than 100,000 yen a month. As for couple households, 32 percent of them have monthly incomes of less than 150,000 yen.

I will now summarize the results of the analysis: First, as to economic self-support, the elderly subsist on low pensions supplemented by low earnings. Though their standard of living was low, the number who depended on the Livelihood Protection Law or civil laws concerned with family support was extremely small. The main resources of the elderly are pensions (44%), wages (23%), earnings from business (17%), and livelihood assistance (8%). Eighty-three percent of the informants received pensions: 47 percent had a national annuity, and 33 percent a welfare annuity. On average, the former received approximately 26,000 yen a month and the latter 120,000 yen. Therefore those who received a national annuity were forced to work to maintain their livelihood. Eligibility for national annuity is determined by type of employment. Many of the workers belonging to the lowest class engaged in simple work such as selling, or semi-skilled work, and they were not qualified to receive a welfare annuity.

As to health, 30 percent of the interviewees had not consulted a doctor in six months, 18 percent received medical treatment occasionally, 49 percent regularly, and 3 percent were hospitalized. Especially in the lower class, the percentage of those who were conscious of their poor health was high: about 60 percent. Regarding housing, 45% of respondents lived in their own houses, 20% in public housing, 20% in rented houses and 13% in apartment houses. Average floor space was about 33 square meters, about average for Tokyo. Forty-five percent of them had baths, and 90 percent had indoor toilets.

As for social relationships, they had generally established close rapport with neighbours and friends, because 42 percent of them had lived in the same place for more than 30 years, although 97 percent had been born outside the survey area. Those in the higher class were generally long-term residents, but those in the lower class were divided into two groups: those who had lived there more than 30 years (30%) and less than 5 years (22%). This is because there are long-term residents who have continuously worked in the lower levels of society, as well as short-term, lower-income residents.

The elderly had many friends, both within and beyond the neighbourhood, and their frequency of contact was high. Those in the highest class had many friends, although not always among their neighbours. Those in the highest class who had many friends ran businesses at home, while those with few friends had only their acquaintances from former workplaces. The middle class exhibited good relations with their neighbours. This is because they spent their life working at home. And it is the people in these classes who support the downtown (shitamachi) concept. Persons in the low class have few friends.

As for family relationships, 75 percent of all the informants had children, most of them two or three; and in the low class they had at least two. Forty-five percent of the elderly who had children talked to them over the telephone and were visited at least once a week. However the percentage of children who visited almost everyday was very low: 5 percent in single households and 15 percent in couple households. The percentage of both who talked over the phone and visited was low in the lowest class (about 35%). Moreover, 46 percent of sons and daughters who made frequent contact with their parent(s) lived within 30 minutes travel, 20 percent within an hour and 33 percent more than an hour. In the lowest class, 44 percent of the children lived a distance of more than an hour away, but in the highest class, 68 percent were within half an hour.

Only a quarter of the elderly expected their children to live with them in the future. And, less than a quarter of them planned to utilize old people's homes. Therefore the majority seemed to recognize that they had to maintain their present situation. As to the elderly who had children, 35 percent planned to live with their children, 40 percent planned not to do this, and 25 percent had not yet decided. Most of the elderly who planned to live with their children were going to move into their children's houses, especially those in the lowest class where the percentage was 70. Only in the highest class were the children going to move into their parent's houses (60%). In both the lowest and the highest classes there were more people who had no plans to live with their children than those who did. Each class had different reasons, however. In the highest class, the reason was that most of them had no desire to depend on their children in the future, and were confident of their ability to live independently. On the other hand, in the lowest class the reason was that their houses were too small or the children did not have the financial means or the desire to live with them. Only 6 parents accepted monthly allowances from their children as a primary source of funds, while only 20 accepted them as a secondary source.

As for interest in social welfare services, 23 percent of the informants planned to use old people's homes in future; 80 percent of them wished to use the public homes for the poor. As for information on public welfare services, 90 percent knew about fee tickets for public baths and mass transportation discounts, and more than 80 percent utilized them. Counselling services and the Friendly Visit Program for single households were known to only 44 percent and 30 percent respectively. This is a problem in the low class where the figures were 40 percent and 20 percent, because such services are regarded as necessary in this class. Regarding services for the bedridden, bathing or body cleaning services are known to 73 percent, homehelper to 70 percent, shortstay to only 32 percent, and public thanks for family caregiver[2] to only 25 percent.

In present-day Japan, according to the statistics on monthly incomes of the aged, a single household receives 120,000 yen a month, and a couple household

280,000 yen, on average[3]. About 60 percent of the households surveyed received less than this average. Therefore, it can be said that the data received here showed the low standard of living of the middle class elderly as a whole.

Conclusion

The proportion of the aged in the total population has been well over 10 percent since about 1980. As a result, the Japanese government has reconsidered its traditional policies for dealing with the elderly which were formulated mainly for the purpose of helping the poor. The government attaches importance to the self-support and independence of the elderly, and to the contribution of the family and community. It also promotes policies to make good use of the private sector.

The goal of helping the elderly to become self-supporting means to provide conditions in society that allow them to live with dignity until death. The government places great expectations on the Japanese traditional way of life; that is, two or three generations living together, with the younger generation taking care of the older generation. We believe this to be wishful thinking, because the traditional family structure is rapidly declining. For example, the percentage of three-generation households with elderly over 60 has declined from 55 percent in 1970 to 41 percent in 1985, and is expected to decline further.[4]

Commercial welfare services for the elderly continue to grow, but only those with sufficient funds are at present able to enjoy these expensive services. Though it is unavoidable that the elderly pay for the services to some extent, the costs of the services should be such that they do not exceed the limited budgets of the average elderly. Added to this are problems of responsibility which must be borne by local and national government. The central government is, however, gradually transferring authority for social welfare to local public entities. These local organizations will be burdened with difficult tasks because the central government is reducing the rate of financial support.[5]

From our survey in Sumida, we regard the present condition for self-support and self-help of the elderly below the middle class level to be insufficient. We find especially that the lower the class, the worse the conditions become. Moreover, the worse the conditions are, the more the necessity of help arises. Those who belong to the lower class are isolated in society. They lack information about public services. They need help from family, friends, neighbours, and the government. It is impossible to expect adequate help for the elderly given the present situation.

Having considered the actual conditions of the elderly and present welfare policy, we conclude that the following steps are necessary to improve the situation:

1) It is necessary to provide employment opportunities for the elderly, giving

priority to those most in need. It is also necessary to establish an adequate pension level in order to secure individual self-support.

2) It is necessary to activate mutual support systems which can provide the aged with sufficient resources and information to maintain or expand their social relationships. Also social systems should be organized which can replace family and relatives as total support systems.

3) Living conditions of aged single women are extremely difficult. It is very hard for them to obtain services from commercial sources. It is clear that welfare services must be better funded. But those services should also be made easier to use.

4) As for the administration of welfare policies, local governments must understand the welfare needs of each individual and establish an administrative system to meet those needs from a total perspective.

Notes

* This survey was conducted by the Association for the Study of Welfare Policy for the Family.

Members of the Association for the Study of Welfare Policy for the Family: Soichi NASU, President (Shukutoku Uni.), Seiichi YODA (Tokyo Deizai Uni.), Nobuyoshi TOSHITANI (Tokyo Uni.), Hiroshi OIKAWA (Meijigakuin Uni.), Kenichi KAWAI (Meiji Uni.), Hiroaki SHIMIZU (Institute of Population Problems) Michiko NAOI (Tokyo Metropolitan Institute of Gerontology), Takatomi NINOMIYA (Oita Uni.), Shunichi FUEKI (Welfare Uni. of Japan), Yataro YOSHINAGA (Kumamoto Uni.), Kazumichi YAMASHITA (Ashiya Un9.), Kunio SUE (Tokyo Keizai Uni.), Yoko NODA (Bunkyo Uni.), Akio SHIMOYAMA (Shukutoku Uni.)

1. For the details of this analysis, see The Association of the Study of Welfare Policy for the Family: Support and Welfare for the Elderly in Aging Society ①③" The Journal of Tokyo Keizai University, No.150153, 1987.
2. The "public thanks for family caregiver" consists of four services which are worth 25 thousand yen each: invitation to use the Sumida-ward vacation resort located at Izu highland and three coupon tickets for meals, massage and travel.
3. *Handbook of Statistics* by Districts on Aging Society, p.334,336, 1987.
4. Humio MIURA: *Illustrated White Book of The Aged*1987, p.53, 1987.
5. The Economic Welfare Bureau of Economic Planning Agency (ed.): Composition of the Aged Society, 1986. The Study Group of New Welfare Policy (ed.): Why Is Health and Welfare the Question at Issue Now?,1987. Nobuyoshi TOSHITANI: *Family and State* 1987 (Useful for understanding Japanese family policy).

Table 1. Welfare and Support for the Elderly in the Community
— from a survey in Sumida-ku
Takatomi NINOMIYA (Oita University, Japan)

Class	Household	Level of Income (thousand yen/ month)	Main Resources (most important ◎, next ○)			
			business	wages	annuity	livelihood assistance
I top (69)	single (15) couple (54)	200 or more 300 or more	◎	○		
II upper middle (64)	single (21) couple (43)	150 up to 200 250 up to 300	○	◎		
III lower middle (69)	single (30) couple (39)	100 up to 150 150 up to 250		○	◎	
IV bottom (101)	single (93) couple (8)	less than 100 less than 150			○	○

(total303)

*income from business

	Kind of Annuity	Longest Type of Job Held (the longest ◎, next ○)					health
		self employed business	office work	skilled work	unskilled work	selling & services	
I 69	welfare annuity	◎	○	○			good
II 64	welfare annuity	◎		○		○	not bad
III 69	welfare annuity national annuity	○		◎	○		not bad
IV 101	national annuity			◎	○	◎	bad

Residence / Social Relations

	house	space	bath	toilet	period	neighbourhood friends	friends
I 69	one's own house	80m²	yes	yes	over 20 years	many (a few)	many
II 64	one's own house	70m²	yes	yes	20 to 30 years	many	many
III 69	municipal rented tenement	50m²	no	yes	20 to 30 years	many	many
IV 101	apartment	30m²	no	no	less than 5 years over 30 years	a few	a few

Family Relations / Joint Living in Future

	Number of children	contact with sons/ daughters	distance from children (time)	to live together	If YES/Which party will move?
I 69	2~3	frequent	within 30 minutes	no	children
II 64	2~3	frequent	about 1 hour	yes	parent (s)
III 69	3~4	occasional	about 1 hour	yes	parent (s)
IV 101	0~2	rare	more than 1 hour	no	parent (s)

Reason Given in case of Living Separately in Future / Public Services

	Children don't want	space problem	utilize old people's home	information
I 69	yes	no	no	well known
II 64	no	yes	no	well known
III 69	no	yes	no	known
IV 101	no	yes	yes	not well known

Chapter 13

Social Support Systems for the Elderly in Rural North Thailand

Werasit SITTITRAI

Social Research Institute,
Institute of Population Studies;
Chulalongkorn University;
Bangkok, Thailand

Introduction

This project is a collaboration between the Institute of Population Studies and the Social Research Institute of Chulalongkorn University as part of the United Nations University's Project on Poverty and Welfare Resource Allocation: Social Support Systems in Transition which is coordinated by Dr. Akiko Hashimoto. The two principal investigators on this project, Social Support Systems of the Elderly in Rural Northern Thailand, are Dr. Werasit Sittitrai and Dr. Surichai Wan'Gaeo. The project consultants include Dr. Amara Pongsapich and Dr. John Knodel. The fieldwork was done in mid-1987 in Mae Chan District of Chiangrai Province, which was randomly selected from areas in the northern region of Thailand. The province is 800 kilometres from Bangkok and the district is approximately 28 kilometres from the provincial center. The total number of elderly interviewed was 309 in 11 villages. The selection was done such that one of the elderly in every household in the villages was interviewed.

The Country Profile

Change occurring in this century has been rapid and drastic. At the beginning of the century there were major political, legal, and administrative changes, e.g., in the 1930s from monarchy to democratic parliamentary government. The Great Depression in the 1930s and the World Wars caused some disruption to the economy and difficulties in the lives of the people. After World War II, and especially during the 1950s, there was noticeable foreign assistance and influence, particularly from the United States and the World Bank, in promoting modernization and public health improvement. Large amounts of military aid followed the government's adoption of the U.S. Anti-Communist policy. But, it was not until the early 1960s that family planning programs were introduced through the efforts of a private hospital. Briefly, the significant phenomena during the period between 1920 and 1970 were rapid population growth, the expansion of government bureaucratic administration and modernization programs, the influence of foreign governments and international agencies in the direction of the country's development efforts, centralized monetization, and commercialization and the expansion of trade in both internal and international markets. Population increased rapidly throughout this period. The decades of the 1970s and 1980s were marked by drastic reduction in the population growth through fertility decline primarily effected by the government's efforts, intensive commercial production of agriculture and trade, and rapid westernization and urbanization of culture.

The total fertility rate declined from 6.3 in the early 1960s to around 4.5 in 1975. The decline began earlier and was more drastic in the North (Knodel, et al. 1987: table 4.1). The fertility decline occurred in both rural and urban areas, but although fertility rates were higher in rural areas, the rate of decline was more rapid than in urban areas. The total population of the country was 26.2 million in 1960 and 44.8 million in 1980, (National Census), and the growth rate has continued to drop since 1970. In 1980, Bangkok had about 5 million people and Chiangmai, the second largest city, had only 100,000. Urban (municipality and Bangkok) population accounted for only 17 percent of the total population (National Census).

The economic development of Thailand is characterized by agricultural growth and diversification, export promotion, expansion of private enterprise, and the encouragement of foreign investment (Sittitrai 1988: 399-400). The GNP growth was 8 percent per annum between 1958 and 1966. Since 1960, as the World Bank puts it, the rate of growth has been impressive and is matched by few developing countries. The GNP grew at the rate of 6.8 percent during the period 1970-1977. However, the total debt outstanding of the country increased steadily through the 1970s and 1980s.

The status and roles of women in the family, economic activities, and cultural practices have been recognized traditionally, while not being exactly equal to those of men. However, concomitant with socioeconomic and cultural changes during the 1970s and 1980s, women's status and roles became more and more equal to those of men. In some areas, for example in the North, women have more significance in the family structure and network than men, e.g., their role in matrilineage which is dominant. There are some variations in the role and authority of women in family economic affairs. Thailand never had the strong Confucian influence resulting in male supremacy as in Korea, although a preference for sons might have been dominant in the distant past or among the Chinese. According to recent data there is currently no strong preference for children of either sex among the population of Thailand; there is, however, a strong preference now for small family size. Newly married couples in the 1980s (and their parents) prefer one or two children only. The contraceptive prevalence rate is approximately 65-67 percent. Spouse selection has always been the child's decision with possibly a slightly stronger influence in the past of the parents' and other family members' opinions. Parents are permissive about dating and courtship, as well as marriage. In the past, there seemed already to be a certain liberality in ideas and practices concerning divorce, remarriage, and mistress-ship, and now there seems to be even more liberal thinking in these matters. Between 1960 and 1978 most divorces occurred when couples were between 27 and 31. Also, according to the National Economic and Social Development Board (1981), the number of divorced couples increased from 17,608 in 1977 to 27,236 in 1981, an increase of 55 percent.

Various traditional cultural practices still bring family members together several times a year so that they maintain close ties and continue visitation or reunions, e.g., Song Kran (Thai traditional New Year), and some other sweet-making festivals. At the same time, education, land scarcity, occupation, and post-nuptial residence tend to increase the geographical dispersal of family members. The trend is toward more permanent dispersal than was the case in the past when it would be more temporary and periodical or seasonal.

Division of labor between husband and wife or men and women exists, but is not always clear-cut or strict. Women take care of household chores, but there is some flexibility depending on situation and/or necessity, and everyone has to help. In the 1980s, household earning became important, and it was found that the husband and wife are willing to take turns caring for young children while the other goes out to earn wages. In the North, women can be hired for some, but not all, of the agricultural tasks and their wages are lower than those of men. However, in some places in the Central region, women are hired to do everything in the sugar cane fields that men are, and their wages are the same.

Almost the entire population of Thailand is Buddhist. According to the 1980 census, Buddhists accounted for 95.5 percent, while Muslims were 3.8 percent, and Christians 0.5 percent. There was some regional variation, particularly in the South, where 24.6 percent of the population is Muslim (primarily in the four southern border provinces), while Bangkok had 4 percent and there was no more than 1.5 percent in other areas. The dominant sect of Buddhism is Theravada, although, in reality, the belief and practices are intertwined with those of Hinduism and animism. The influence and significance of Buddhism are seen in the socio-economic and political history of Thailand. For example, in rural areas local Buddhist monks and temples were the primary source of literacy education, and they played a crucial role as community activity organizers, religious leaders, and physical and psychological welfare providers. In the present time, the government formal educational system has replaced the role of the monks and temples in education. However, many monks still perform tutoring for the temple boys, and monkhood and monk schools are still a significant avenue for village boys to obtain a formal education.

Not only has the fertility rate reduced, but life expectancy has increased.

These factors contribute to the increase in the number and proportion of the elderly. The elderly population (aged 60 and over) has increased from 1.2 million (4.6 percent of total population) in 1960 to 2.4 million (5.5 percent) in 1980 and is projected to grow to 5.3 million (7.7 percent, on the assumption of low fertility) in 2005 (Chayovan 1985: 3,20). From existing data and literature, the elderly still hold significant status and roles in the family and society, but socio-economic changes have undermined some aspects of their influence, e.g., as community leaders or as experts in household occupational skills. Most elderly live with their families and have support from spouse and children, but it is not clear what the quality of that support is (Sittitrai 1985: 31-35). Existing data are still vague in depicting family structure in relation to old people (Stittitrai 1985: 26). According to the 1980 census, a little over half of the elderly were recorded as household heads. Of these household heads, 52.5 percent were heading extended family households and 47.5 percent were heading nuclear family or unrelated individual households.

Most of the problems cited by the elderly concerned health and financial difficulties or discontent with the people with whom they lived (Sittitarai 1985: 29, 35; Chayovan 1985: 35-40).

Findings

The sample population of 309 elderly persons (aged 60 and above) was more male than female (52.4 percent vs. 47.6 percent). These proportions are different from the provincial proportion of 48.3 percent elderly men shown by the 1980 census. This may be a result of the sampling technique of selecting a man and woman alternately in each house-hold. Over half of the sample (66 percent) were 60-69 years of age, and the rest were age 70 or above. Only 48 percent of them were currently married (living with a spouse). The rest were either single, divorced, widowed, or separated. This indicates that only half of the sample could receive support from their spouse. The majority of them were illiterate (75 percent). The vulnerability of the majority of the elderly was also revealed by the data showing that the large majority of them had health problems, physical difficulties, and showed signs of chronic undernutrition.

In addition, these findings agree with results from previous studies in that the majority of the elderly were facing economic and physical or health difficulties. The cases of those with health problems, undernutrition, and physical difficulty were found to be higher among the older, the women, those who were not working, and the poor. This was also true for the conditions described as "can't sleep well", "depressed", "loss of memory", and "loneliness". These conditions were found with much higher proportions among the single/divorced/widowed than among the currently married couples. Accordingly, positive responses to: "help with neighbors (give and receive)", "having someone you feel close to", "having respect from others", and "receiving help in the household" were found in lower proportions among the older, poorer, not working, or single/divorced/widowed/separated individuals.

The primary source of livelihood of these elderly was found to differ from the widespread belief that the children are the primary support providers for virtually all elderly. It was found in this study that only 57 percent of the elderly had their children as their primary source of livelihood. When examining age and its correlation with livelihood, it was found, as might be expected, that earnings from work were the primary source of livelihood for the younger elderly (e.g., 60-64), while children's support was more predominant for the older elderly (e.g., 80 and above).

Examining the social networks of closeness and support, both quantitative data and qualitative information showed that these were experienced to the greatest degree from a spouse, then from children, close relatives, and finally close friends, in that order. For example, the elderly had more close relatives than close friends, and they indicated that closeness and support were provided more often by close relatives than close friends. Spouses would be the first they would turn to for support and comfort. Formal sources of support, such as the government, were minimal, occasional, and often unreliable, with the exception of government health services, which were somewhat more substantial and reliable than other aspects.

There were seven "layers" of support on which the elderly could depend. However, it should be noted that the quality and extent of support depended on many factors, including individual personalities. It was also true that not every layer would provide every aspect of support. These "layers" were:

1. Spouse
2. Children
3. Grandchildren
4. Neighbors, friends
5. Temple
6. Community
7. Government, non-government agencies, private charity

Changes in society can have impacts on the support systems for the elderly in many ways; many aspects of the systems of support can be undermined. Change can create conditions (socio-economic, cultural, legal, and even physical) resulting in more or in less need for support. New support systems may be introduced and old support systems can be revived. Some systems will survive the changes, the old forms appearing in new contexts. Change can be both beneficial and disruptive to the elderly and their support systems. For example, modern laws and legal procedures led to the disappearance of the role of the elderly as conflict arbitrators in village communities. This caused a significant reduction in their status and authority. On the other hand, many of the elderly sought new means to secure the support and attention of their children. One of the means was to use the modern legal inheritance laws and legalized written wills to make sure that each child would receive a share of the property as willed by the elderly in proportion to the amount of care provided.

Positive approaches to be recommended are:
1. Direct help, such as introducing new welfare schemes and helping to strengthen locally initiated welfare schemes.
2. Indirect help, such as creating conditions favorable to support systems and encouraging traditional values and practices of paying respect to the elderly and of the local community supporting its elderly.

Table 1. Basic Characteristics

	Number	Percent
Age		
60-64	105	34.0
65-69	68	22.0
70-74	62	20.1
75-79	36	11.7
80-84	38	12.2
Total	309	100.0
Sex		
Male	162	52.4
Female	147	47.6
Marital Status		
Currently married	148	47.9
Widowed	150	48.5
Single, divorced, separated	11	3.6
Education		
No education	256	82.8
Primary	51	16.5
Others	2	0.6
Literacy		
Literate or semiliterate	77	24.9
Illiterate	232	75.1

Table 2. Social Networks

	Number	Percent
Number of Children		
None	15	4.9
1-2	48	15.5
3-4	85	27.5
5-6	83	26.9
7-8	59	19.1
9 or more	19	6.1
Total	309	100.0
Siblings		
None	85	27.5
1-2	131	42.4
3-4	71	23.0
5 or more	22	7.2
Close Relatives		
None	147	47.6
1-2	132	42.7
3-4	22	7.1
5 or more	8	2.6
Close Friends		
None	198	64.1
1-2	98	31.7
3 or more	13	4.2

Table 3. Income

	Number	Percent
Personal Income Per Month		
Rich (1,250-5,908)	17	5.6
Better-off (500-1,242)	38	12.6
Moderate (167-475)	62	20.5
Poor (50-166)	52	17.2
Very Poor (0,8-44)	133	44.0
Total	302	100.0
Household Income Per Month		
Rich (4,475-38,000)	22	7.1
Better-off (2,500-4,150)	28	9.1
Moderate (842-2,469)	141	45.8
Poor (545-833)	46	14.9
Very Poor (0,15-541)	71	23.1
Total	308	100.0

		Number	Percent
Table 4	Work		
	Working	144	46.6
	Not working	165	53.4
	Total	309	100.0
Table 5	Employment		
	Agriculture	103	33.3
	Labor	27	8.7
	Private Service	14	4.5
	Not working	165	53.4
Table 6	Primary Source of Livelihood		
	Work	88	28.5
	Pension, rent, savings	21	6.8
	Children's support	175	56.6
	Others	25	8.1
Table 7	Health Condition at the Present		
	Very Good	19	6.1
	Good	88	28.5
	Moderate	115	37.2
	Poor	75	24.3
	Very Poor	12	3.9
	Total	309	100.0
Table 8	Having Health Problems		
	Yes	253	81.9
	No	56	18.1
Table 9	Sleeping Problems		
	Everyday or almost everyday	56	18.2
	1-2 times/week	55	17.9
	Once a month or less	33	10.7
	No problem	163	53.1
	Total	307	100.0

		Number	Percent
Table 10	Unhappy/Depressed		
	More than last year	80	25.9
	Equal	31	10.0
	Less	17	5.5
	No problem	181	58.6
Table 11	Loss of Memory		
	More than 5-10 years ago	105	34.0
	Equal	13	4.2
	Less than	2	0.6
	No problem	189	61.2
Table 12	Loneliness		
	Often	52	16.9
	Sometimes	99	32.1
	Rarely	51	16.6
	Never	106	34.4
	Total	308	100.0
Table 13	Chronic Undernourishment		
	Yes	233	75.4
	No	76	24.6
	Total	309	100.0
Table 14	Obesity		
	Yes	5	1.6
	No	304	98.4
	Total	309	100.0

References

Knodel, John, et al., *Thailand's Reproductive Revolution,* University of Wisconsin Press, 1987.

Sittitrai, Werasit, *Rural Transformation in Northern Thailand,* PhD dissertation, Department of Political Science, University of Hawaii, 1988.

Sittitrai, Werasit, "Existing Family Structure" and "Employment and Financial Support of the Aged" in Institute of Population Studies, Chulalongkorn University and Population and Manpower Planning Division, NESDB, *The Thai Elderly Population,* 1985: 24-35.

Chayovan, Napaporn, "Overview of Demographic Trends", and "Health Status" in Institute of Population Studies, Chulalongkorn University and Population and Manpower Planning division, NESDB, The *Thai Elderly Population,* 1985: 3-23, 36-40.

Chapter 14

Social Support for Rural Elderly in Zimbabwe: The Transition

Joseph HAMPSON   University of Zimbabwe

Introduction

There is an almost inverse correlation between the strength of belief in the effectiveness of support and caring functions of the African extended family, on the one hand, and a solid data and observational base on the other. In other words, little is known objectively about the functioning of the African extended family with regard to welfare, and most work in this field has been an analysis of assumptions rather than testing of hypotheses. The fairly universal phenomenon of urban destitute elderly throughout Africa is explained in terms of the 'breakdown' of the extended family support networks in the face of encroaching modernisation and urbanisation, and the unspoken corollary that rural elderly (because they are not so far 'advanced' in this modernisation process) are still members of a strong and effective support system based on family and kin is assumed without argument. The present chapter reports on various studies that are relevant to this issue and then tries to move the analysis beyond the level of assumption.

Social Support: Theory

Initially there is need for some orientation with respect to the foundations of social support theory. Caplan and Kililea (1976) produced a milestone in analysis of support systems. In looking at the family, they proposed three characteristics of the 'significant others' who constitute a person's network of support systems: the significant other must "1) help the individual mobilise his psychological resources and master his emotional burdens, 2) share his tasks, 3) provide him with extra supplies of money, materials, tools, skills and cognitive guidance to improve his handling of his situation" (1976: 20). Although Caplan and Kililea were referring to the support systems found in a family and being provided by a 'significant other', they created a useful distinction between emotional support, support in tasks or activities of daily living, and material support, and this distinction applies for all support systems. The authors conclude that the support systems of the family can have nine dimensions. These are as the collector and disseminator of information about the world; as a feedback guidance system; as a source of ideology; as guide mediator in problem solving; as a source of practical service and concrete aid; as a haven for rest and recuperation; as a reference and control group; as source and validation of personal identity; as contributor to emotional mastery. Within healthy families Caplan and Kililea further point out that the supportive operations have to be mutual and reciprocal in terms of need satisfaction.

A further variation on the nominal definition of 'social support' was provided by Garbino (1986: 33) . He said the "social support network meant a set of interconnected relationships among a group of people that provides enduring patterns of nurturance (in any or all forms) and provides contigent reinforcement for efforts to cope with life on a day-to-day basis". However, network analysis, helpful though it may be occasionally, is eschewed from our nominal and operational definitions of social support so that the dynamic elements of a *process* of support can be analysed better. The focus on *systems* means that a systems approach to the question of support can be pursued. Within this chapter, and based on a cross-national study of elderly by UN University,[1] then, social support systems will be used to mean:

> 'formal and informal social mechanisms whereby individuals requiring financial, physical and emotional help for maintenance of dignified existence are given assistance.'

It is to be noted that these mechanisms can be of the formal type (state support and community organisations' support) and informal (other individuals, family, neighbours, and extra-familial network). Here we use "social network support" to mean "the range of support systems or systems of exchange that is non-institutionalised and informally organised by neighbourhood networks or extra-familial networks." Thus, "network" is used in a narrow sense to describe that type of informal social support lying outside the family.

Social Support: Rural Elderly

Without genuine longitudinal studies, it is difficult to be very specific and definitive about the changing nature of support systems available to elderly rural Zimbabweans, but there are indications of (1) growing economic differentiation and pauperisation, (2) very rudimentary welfare services with indifferent field staff (3) stronger informal support systems available to poorer elderly, (4) some elderly being more vulnerable and insecure in terms of social security systems provision.

A. Economic Differentiation

In a small survey of 300 elderly in some 245 households from three districts of Zimbabwe, 54 per cent of the sample households had no cattle. Those without cattle have to hire draught power from those who have, usually at high rates equivalent to at least the cost of tractor hire, but less efficient than tractor power because available draught beasts are undernourished at the beginning of the ploughing season when their efficiency is needed most. Lack of livestock also means that the households lack their own form of transport (a scotch-cart) so that agricultural, building and household activities like the carrying of firewood are all severely restricted and done by hand. A household without cattle also suffer from an absence of available manure, and any fertiliser used has to be bought and transported at very high cost. (Hampson 1985: 53).

Another study by Jackson *et al* (1987) shows that crop and livestock incomes, remittances, off-farm and on-farm wage income, and self-employed income all varied greatly in a Zimbabwean sample. For example, in a representative household sample across all agro-ecological areas of the country, Jackson pointed out that some 62 per cent of households received no remittances, the mean remittance was $348.20, but that the top 10 per cent of households enumerated had approximately $1,000 per household remitted to them. For total income the top 10 per cent of rural households had incomes in the range of $1,467 to $5,394 and controlled 41.7 per cent of all measured income. The bottom 25 per cent had incomes of $225 or less and controlled 4.3 per cent of all measured income. An important finding, from the perspective of household viability and quality of life, is that it would seem that "in Zimbabwe it is diversification and the versatility of household labour which appears to raise income... the transition into the non-subsistence activities is a central aspect of the escape from rural poverty" (1986: 63).

Economic differentiation was also a feature of the UN University study in Zimbabwe. In a representative community, case study and questionnaire material demonstrated a very wide range of income from cash crops, a range in ownership of livestock, and a majority of elderly reporting no remittances from outside the household (even when they had employed sons). The evidence of pauperisation was present, too, with extremely low crop yields and no other source of income.

B. Welfare Services

The main form of formal support at the time of the UN University study (1987) was that of drought relief. Unfortunately the study showed that the delivery of services was very uneven, poorly organised, and discriminatory. It was uneven, because parts of the areas were very remote and almost inaccessible by vehicle, and in these areas small communities received no drought relief. The system was poorly organised because the maize meal was delivered at irregular intervals. Because there was only a standard amount of maize meal given, the recipients from big families suffered whilst others from small families had more than their needs. Sometimes the officers distributing the drought relief food would give to first comers, without checking on eligibility, and when elderly arrived later, they were told that distribution was finished and maize meal had run out. Amongst the elderly, further discrimination existed, for elderly men were more likely to be given than elderly women. The other form of official support is that of public assistance, but this has been of no relevance to the lives of elderly in Mangwende (the UN research area): less than one per cent receive such assistance.

C. Informal Support

Indigenous systems of support and welfare have been but rarely analysed. Gerdes (1975) used the example of Ethiopia to discuss ways in which different indigenous schemes of social security could be adapted to modern nation-state requirements. The devastating effects of drought in sub-Saharan Africa have focused attention on indigenous coping mechanisms and responses. Fleuret (1986) discussed the systems of exchange, risk insurance, and social organisation that are mobilised in the face of drought in sub-Saharan Africa. The relational and kinship networks often cross ecological, cultural and socioeconomic boundaries, and transfer flows of goods, livestock, food and even labour (in the form of children) can be a source of support in time of crisis.

Within Zimbabwe, a number of indigenous systems for agricultural and other labour can be termed 'social network support' and are potentially available to the elderly.

Zunde: is the work provided for a chief or headman in his fields. There are two motives for such work: one is homage, the other is that, in exchange for work in his fields, the subjects have a right to call upon some of the harvests in times of drought.

Nhimbe: is a beer party for labour, which tends to be restricted to members of the same village. This is because the work is done on a rotational basis, during times of high labour demand (ploughing, wedding and harvesting). The hosts are expected to provide beer.

Jangano: is a mutual and reciprocal work party, with a smaller and more closed membership than *nhimbe,* where the work provided is for the benefit of the whole group and where each member in turn is given access to the group's labour power. The hosts' obligation only extends to providing food.

Jakwara: is the least formal system of access to labour whereby the hosts brew beer and offer an open invitation to assist in harvesting. Here there is no obligation to reciprocate, and anyone, even a passer-by can be involved.

The UN University study shows evidence that, although the classic forms of indigenous support through labour are no longer common, nevertheless certain variations are used in times of crisis. Thus in an emergency these systems can be reactivated.

The support provided by the family is the most central type of informal support system available to elderly Zimbabweans, and principally the family means children. In a sample of elderly in three areas of the country, only two per cent of the elderly said they had no children, and only 30 per cent reported living in a household apart from any of their children. Shona society is patrilineal and sons and daughters would grow up in the extended family which included grandparents, parents, brothers, sisters, uncles and their children. All the children would respect or 'fear' (the Shona word *kutya* is equivalent to both meanings) their father, and, by extension, all elderly relatives. As the extended family grew unwieldly and as the head of the family died off, younger brothers of the deceased could move to form their own family unit. However, when a man died, his responsibilities for the family were taken over by a surviving brother or cousin, and this brother would look after the widow in old age, and would be known as *baba* or father to his deceased brother's children. The deceased's eldest brother would not only take over the property of the deceased, but could acquire marital rights over the widow if she was in agreement, otherwise the widow could return to her own family. All younger members of the extended family would thus honour their elderly relatives, and would be expected to visit them frequently, and invite their help and assistance on matters that arose from day to day. Elderly female relatives had a particularly important role to play in socialising Shona girls, and in marriage procedures would be the ones who handed over the bride to the husband.

The relationship between elderly parents and their children is strengthened by the very common practice of young boys and girls staying with their grandparents for an extended period of time. In his study, Gelfand, (1979) reports that most children are sent between the ages of three and six, and for a period of two to three years. Most children seem to stay with the maternal grandmother, and in some cases the child's mother would also be staying with the grandmother. The data gathered for the UN University study, however, seems to indicate that in Zimbabwe this practice is decreasing. A number of factors can be adduced to explain the trend: universal education means children become less able to stay with grandparents, and one result of urbanisation is that mothers are less willing to leave relatively better health facilities for bearing children so as to be with their rural parents for the birth of their children.

Our case study material gathered so far shows that the cultural ideal of close care for elderly parents by children may exist, but there are significant exceptions. For instance, an elderly woman says that although her children help her with the occasional gift, "A gift is just a gift, and you can't rely on it". A more world-weary note was struck by one elderly man, "To have them or not have them makes no difference, so why should I bother myself thinking about them." Yet in general the number of living children has a positive influence on the extent to which elderly Zimbabweans perceive the existence of emotional, emergency, and material support and of support for activities of daily living. This conclusion is not unique to Zimbabwe. For example, in a study of rural households in Botswana, Chervichovsky *et al* (1985) conclude that "there is a strong positive correlation (between the three variables of number of living children, household income, and transfer income) ... including the likelihood that the welfare of the elderly is closely related to the number of children living" (1985: 190).

For elderly women one crucially important variable in perceived support is the extent to which they have been able to maintain contact with their 'home' area. This acts as a form of support insurance so that in the case of divorce or bereavement the widow will have contacts with her original family that can be reactivated. Of course distance is a significant intervention variable, for if the siblings and parents' homes are far away, there is less likelihood that the elderly have maintained contact.

Within Shona society the *sahwira* or funeral friend is a very significant relationship between two individuals (and, by extension, between two families) , and is used not only to mobilise emotional support, but also material and emergency support. The *sahwira* is the one with whom the sanctions governing acceptable language and behaviour fall away, and even in a funeral setting the *sahwira* is allowed to make jokes about the dead partner in a way that would not be permitted to anyone else.

When asked about emotional support, 74 per cent of the sample of elderly in the UN University study reported being given emotional support when needed, 2 per cent said they did not need such support, and 24 per cent said they were not offered such support. Of the group of elderly who did not receive such support, only 16 per cent said the first helper came from their children, whereas 27 per cent reported a peer friend or *sahwira* as such a supporter; whereas some 38 per cent reported a son or daughter as being the second helper. In addition, there seems to be clear reciprocity in emotional support, for elderly report that when they themselves offer emotional support (and only 63 per cent said they did, while 4 per cent said it was not needed), the recipients were children for 16 per cent and peer friend or *sahwira* for 29 per cent, and 11 per cent offered such support to their neighbours.

Neighbourhood support seems to be important for rural elderly in times of emergency, like drought. Respondents in the UN University study report how neighbours will make a collection of mealie-meal to provide assistance to a particularly destitute member of a village. The neighbourhood network is now formalised into the local government and party structure of VIDCO (Village Development Committee) and WADCO (Ward Development Committee), and, at that level, initiatives are also taken to assist elderly with emergency support.

In terms of financial support, some 38 per cent report not receiving financial assistance, mainly from a son (36 per cent for the group) or daughter (10 per cent). Only 27 per cent of the sample of elderly report offering financial assistance to others: the most likely recipients are neighbours (19 per cent), and peer friends or sahwira (30 per cent), while children are much less likely (17 per cent of the recipients.)

In daily tasks, the network of support is very unsymmetrical. Some 36 per cent of the sample give help and support with daily tasks, and 72 per cent are recipients of such support. Here the pattern of support given to the elderly clearly lies with close family members: *son-in-law* (30 per cent) or *daughter-in-law* (15 per cent) or children (19 per cent), whereas *sahwira,* neighbour, peer friend and spouse are less common (7, 8, 5, and 5 per cent respectively). Daily support is reciprocated in only 36 per cent of cases, and the likely recipients are not family so much as neighbour (20 per cent) peer friend (19 per cent) and *sahwira* (16 per cent).

These findings confirm the suspicion by other researchers that, for example, food sharing is not a significant traditional support or coping mechanism. For example Cheater and Bourdillon (1982) argue that its significance is perhaps symbolic rather than material. Presenting data from interviews with elderly during the 1982 drought they say (1982: 20):

> The normal pattern of sharing in rural Zimbabwe, where it occurs at all, takes the form of individualised exchange between related households rather than some form of collection and redistribution from communal store houses. A majority of respondents who suggested (sharing) as a collective response were women... Since women are integrally involved in the preparation of food, and presumably are accustomed to lending small items of food to their fellow housewives in normal times, it is possible that this... is a sex-differentiated view of coping mechanisms at the collective level... What is clear, is that sharing is no longer a viable response to drought, if it ever was, even in the view of our elderly Zimbabwean respondent.

In times of stress, elderly have also resorted to strategies of invoking the informal support systems through 'borrowing' food, of visiting relatives during meal-times (the Shona expression *kukwata* describes such activity), and of gleaning food grain from other fields after harvests. Theft of food is also reported within the community, although the identity of the 'thieves' could not be ascertained.

D. Vulnerable Groups

The UN University data is currently being analysed, but tentative indications, supported from other studies, are that the following groups are ill-served by formal support systems, and that even the informal support systems cannot meet even their basic needs:
- elderly on their own with no children nearby;
- elderly widows who have elected to return to their 'home' area;
- elderly farmers who have neither livestock nor agricultural implements;
- elderly who suffer from serious emotional and psychosomatic illness but who lack an emotional support network.

Discussion and Conclusion

Because the UN data still remains to be analysed, the following discussion can only at this stage be preliminary and tentative. However, it does seem that, in line with other rural household studies within the country, there is a considerable degree of poverty and destitution. In spite of Zimbabwe's food self-sufficiency and even its exportation of maize and cattle, many experience hunger and have no livestock. It would seem that the socioeconomic forces underlying rural social differentiation are perhaps more significant than the forces responsible for the division between rural and urban development, and further that the unit of analysis of household hides gender and age differences within households. The study of elderly within households points up these two issues of rural inequality and household inequalities with considerable sharpness. Within a food exporting country, elderly rural farmers are hungry; within a society that values and respects the elderly, a significant proportion feel marginalised and bereft of support. For some who contributed over the years to the support of children and others within the extended family, their expectations of reciprocal support later in life have not been met.

Informal support systems are much more effective than formal systems in Zimbabwe in identifying, and in some cases meeting social support needs, but are severely hampered by the poorly resourced community base when the system is neighbourhood and family support. Daughters-in-law play an important role in daily care and even emotional support of elderly parents, although there are many cultural and ritual behaviours in interaction that are prescribed. Like women in most other cultures (Brody, 1981) , Zimbabwean women are in the main responsible for care of elderly parents, but the difference lies in the fact that, if unmarried, the chances are very high that such daughters will be caring for their own parents; if married, they will be caring for their husbands' parents. Kin support can cut across the economic and social differentiation of the community (and indeed of the country) but evidence seems to indicate that the actual content of support is variable, irregular, and tends to reinforce rather than lessen inequalities. Tribe (1976) has speculated on likely reasons for this. Higher-income members of a household or family are likely to have a large number of demands put on them by others, while they themselves are likely to find that the family cannot provide significant economic support for them as compared with their anticipated consumption levels (1976: 190). Thus the inequality within households and families and any kin is likely to reduce the potential for economic reciprocity, and indeed for other types of reciprocity as well.

The current formal systems of support and welfare provided by government (drought relief and public assistance) do not meet the needs of elderly. A number of reasons account for this state of affairs: (a) they are not targeted specifically at the elderly, and hence lack the concern that could alert responsive programme structures to the existence of unmet need, (b) programmes are underfunded (for example, the public assistance programme has around a $300,000 monthly expenditure for about 29,000 recipients) and the manpower lack training, and (c) political and other considerations interfere with the work of welfare.

The current situation in Zimbabwe generates a number of policy requirements. The first is that there needs to be both a programme of developing *preventive* policies (aimed at restoring and maintaining effective indigenous systems of support) alongside a programme of developing *remedial* policies (that relieve destitution and the serious effects of pauperisation) if effective social support for elderly is to be maintained.

In regard to preventive policies, it seems necessary to make a detailed study of how indigenous and informal social support systems in Zimbabwe can be modified so as to be replicable and so integrate within an effective national programme. Obviously some form of villagisation in welfare services is required. This will ensure more accurate identification of those elderly in need, a faster response to deal with acute problems, and a more caring and less impersonal form of assistance. Integrated within the present VIDCO and WADCO structures, it should be possible to provide such welfare services within a framework of social development programmes. Such integration of indigenous and state welfare systems parallels developments in developed countries seeking to find ways of integrating formal and informal social care (Whittaker, 1986; Garbino, 1986; Hoch & Hemmens, 1987).

Within the ambit of 'remedial' programmes, it needs to be borne in mind that the needs of rural elderly have not been sufficiently analysed until now. Their health status and health needs remain a cause for speculation, yet we know that elderly death rates are disproportionately higher in famine times than in normal times. The differential effects of drought on elderly and young, male and female, must be studied and action taken accordingly. 'Remedial' programmes are needed, then, in health, but are also required for agricultural, educational and welfare sectors. Elderly household heads who lack draught power and who lack a source of remittance outside the household are likely to be disadvantaged compared to younger household heads in the same position, because the latter have more likelihood of having off-farm employment or informal sector activity. Such elderly would need a more interventionist programme where financial and material support is provided.

Note

1. "Social Support Systems in Transition" is a cross-national study of elderly in seven countries (India, Thailand, Zimbabwe, Egypt, Brazil, South Korea and Singapore) coordinated by Akiko Hashimoto of UN University, Tokyo. This chapter reports on preliminary results from data gathered in Zimbabwe.
    Country reports and a comparative study are being compiled.

Bibliography

Brody, E. 1981. "Women in the Middle and Family Help to Other People". *Gerontologist*. XXI, No. 5. 471-480.

Caplan, G. and Kililea, M. 1976. *Support Systems and Mutual Help: Multidisciplinary Explorations*. Grane and Straton. New York.

Cheater, A. and Bourdillon, M. 1982. "Drought in Southern Zimbabwe: 1982". Hlekweni Training Centre. Bulawayo: Mimeo.

Chervichovsky, D. *et al* 1985. "The Household Economy of Rural Botswana: an African Case." World Bank Staff Working Paper. Washington.

Flueret, A. 1986. "Indigenous Responses to Drought in Sub-Saharan Africa." *Disasters*. X, 224-229.

Garbino, J. 1986. "Where Does Social Support Fit Into Optimising Human Development and Preventing Dysfunction?" *British Journal of Social Work*. XVI, 23-37.

Gelfand, M. 1979. *Growing Up in Shona Society*. Mambo Press. Gweru.

Gerdes, V. 1975. "Precursors of Modern Social Security in Indigenous African Institutions." *Journal of Modern African Studies*. XIII, No. 2. 209-228.

Gottlieb, B. 1981. *Social Networks and Social Support*. Sage. Beverly Hills.

Hampson, J. 1985. "Elderly People and Social Welfare in Zimbabwe." *Ageing and Society*. 5. 39-67.

Hoch, C. and Hemmens, G. 1987. "Linking Informal and Formal Help: Conflicting along the Continuum of Care." *Social Service Review*. LXI, 432-446.

Jackson, J. *et al.* 1987. *Rural Development Policies and Food Security in Zimbabwe*. Part II, ILO. Geneva.

Tribe. M. 1976. "The Household Economy and Social Security Policy, with particular reference to Africa south of the Sahara." *International Journal of Social Economics*. 3 (3). 179-197.

Whittaker, J. 1986. "Integrating Formal and Informal Social Care: a Conceptual Framework." *British Journal of Social Work*. XVI, 39-62.

Chapter 15

Law Versus Reality: The Interaction of Community Obligations to and by the Black Elderly in South Africa*

Sandra BURMAN

Research Fellow,
Queen Elizabeth House,
University of Oxford, UK

Introduction

In South African law, provision for support of the elderly is ostensibly modelled on First World systems, providing welfare payments for the aged where private pensions are absent or insufficient, and backed up with private law duties of support. State pensions are officially available to all those over a given age who are resident in South Africa and who pass the means test. In addition, according to the Roman-Dutch civil law of the country and customary law (which applies to those who who are classified as Black[1] and who invoke customary law in appropriate cases), there is a legal obligation on a range of family members, in a stipulated order, to provide for another member of the family in time of need. Yet research literature and fieldwork[2] show that the position of the elderly, and particularly those classified as Black, is in reality frequently very different from that which a simple statement of the law would lead one to expect. This chapter is an examination of the divergence between law and reality for even that section of the Black elderly for whom better provision is made: those in the urban areas. However, the mechanisms involved are complex and, in the limited space here, it is not possible to do more than present an overview. After an outline of the welfare and legal provisions, the salient points revealed by research are briefly discussed, and the chapter concludes with some suggested alternatives. While much of the data reveal the grassroots effects of apartheid for the aged, some may have a wider application to African or Third World countries in general.

Legal Provision for Support of the Elderly

In South Africa social pensions for those classified as White, Coloured, and Asian are officially administered by one government department, but provisions for each group are controlled by the three separate Houses in Parliament for Whites, Coloureds, and Asians. Pensions for those classified as Black within what the South African government defines as the Republic of South Africa are controlled by the four separate provinces except within the territories of the six non-independent 'homelands' whose administrations control pensions there. In the four 'independent homelands', in the rest of South Africa, pensions are administered by the governments of each, which have their own state pension systems, giving lower pensions than South Africa from budgets supplied by the Republic. Movement by Blacks from an urban to a rural area may therefore require transfer of pension payments to another administration, or even loss of a South African pension and a totally new application to another government. Citizens of an 'independent homeland' who cannot prove that they have been resident in South Africa for the preceding five years do not qualify for a South African pension.[4]

The South African state pension scheme is non-contributory, paid from central funds. A state pension is a legal right, provided the person is eligible. The amounts of pensions, and to some extent the conditions, differ between population groups. Table 1 shows the main differences.

In calculating income, the combined income of a married couple is halved when the means test is applied — except where an applicant is blind. (Half and that total is then halved.) Where an applicant has more than one wife, according to custom, the Department divides the joint income of all spouses by the number of spouses (husband and wives included), provided the applicant supports his wives. In the most recent annual increases at the time of writing (which gave the above figures), amounts were increased by exactly the same number of rands for each population group, resulting in a higher proportional increase for people starting on a lower base. The gap is thus being narrowed, albeit very slowly.[5] However, the benefits payable to social pensioners are in no way connected to either final wages or a national average wage. The effect of this can be seen when viewing table 1 in the light of the authoritative poverty subsistence tables which the University of Port Elizabeth's Institute for Planning Research regularly publishes for each population group. It estimated that in September 1987 a Black household of two adults in Cape Town would need a *minimum* of R 126.30 for basic requirements, before paying for such necessities as rent and transport.

Where pension provision is absent or inadequate, it may be possible to obtain support through use of the law. According to the civil law of the country, a duty of support exists between a range of people in a pre-determined order, always assuming that the person claiming support is unable to support her- or himself and that the person from whom support is claimed is able to support the claimant. Both these requirements are concerned with questions of fact to be determined by the court in each case. Relationships to which, if the other requirements are satisfied, the law attaches a duty of support are: husband and wife; parent and child; grandparent (or further ascendant) and grandchild (or further descendant) ; and collaterals related in the second degree, i.e. brothers and sisters and including half-brothers and sisters. Duties of support are generally reciprocal: they may arise in either direction, depending on the circumstances.[6] A notable exception is the illegitimate child, who, though entitled to support from his father, owes him no corresponding duty. There is

Table 1. Pensions: a Comparison of the Main Conditions and Amounts in 1987-8 for each Population Group

Conditions/Amounts	White	Col./Indian	Black
Age at which payable	men — 65 women — 60	men — 65 women — 60	men — 65 women — 60
Maximum pension	R218 pm	R167 pm	R117 pm (paid every 2 months as R 234)[1]
Maximum income + maximum assets to qualify for maximum pension	R90 pm + R10 000	R45 pm + R5 000	R22.50 pm OR R2 500 if no income[2]
If no income, maximum assets to qualify for minimum pension	R42 000	R28 000	R19 100
Maximum income to qualify for minimum pension	R218 pm	R147 pm[3]	R83 pm
Attendant's allowance[4]	R26 pm	R18 pm	R16 pm
Age at which income no longer assessed, if working	men:over 70 women: over 65	men: over 70 women: over 65	men: over 70 women: over 65

Notes:
1. In August 1987, in response to pressure from community organizations, it was announced that the payment of Black social pensions on a monthly basis would be phased in during the next three financial years.
2. Whites and Coloured/Asian figures represent maximum assets where there is also income. This figure was not provided for Blacks.
3. R142 for those classified as Indians.
4. Payable to those who require one, and to all those over 85; for the latter, payment is automatic for all groups except Blacks, who have to apply for it.
Sources: Compiled from South African National Council for the Aged Information Centre Fact Sheets for each population group (October 1987).

some debate as to whether the illegitimate child's paternal grandfather can be held liable in any case.[7] Between relatives by affinity there is no duty of support: thus there is no duty to maintain indigent parents-in-law. Similarly, a step-parent cannot claim support from a step-child.

The right to claim support from a deceased estate is more limited than from living relatives. It can be claimed only from the estates of a mother and father, if the estate is adequate, but not from that of a spouse. As a result of 19th

century legislation which abolished the 'legitimate portion' and judicial decisions which have resulted in complete freedom of testation, 'a destitute
surviving wife, husband or major child who has been cut off by the testator in
his will has no legal remedy unless he or she can show that the testator was
insane at the time of making the will'.[8]

An alternative source of a right to support may be found in customary law
where both parties are classified as Black and have a claim under a relationship
recognized under customary law. Between spouses the right is not symmetri-
cal, since a wife in a customary union is regarded as a minor under the
guardianship of her husband (except in the few areas where this has been
changed by regulation) , and cannot, with a few trivial exceptions, own any
property. Her husband has an obligation to house, feed and clothe her in a
manner commensurate with his means, but a wife has no right of action against
her husband for the enforcement of his duties towards her. She may, however,
leave him and return to her former guardian's homestead, and the latter is
obliged to support her until he has prevailed upon the husband to remedy his
fault. In the case of a customary law widow, if she is willing to remain at the
homestead of her husband's heir, or at a place agreed with him, and to continue
to perform the domestic duties of a wife, she has a claim for support.[10] This heir
would probably be her husband's son (though not necessarily hers, as customary law marriages are at least potentially polygamous) or his brother or father
where he had no son. Thus, she may in customary law have a claim for support
from her father- or brother-in-law, or step-son, none of which claims exist in
civil law. The price, however, is loss of her freedom of movement. It is not clear
whether her right to support exists where she insists on leaving the homestead
or refuses to return to it, against the wishes of the heir.[11]

It can therefore be seen that even those receiving pensions will quite possibly
have a *prima facie* claim on a relative if they are in need despite their pensions.
Given the prevalence of large families among· those classified as Black,
compared with other population groups, proportionately fewer elderly Black
people are likely to be so bereft of relatives that there is nobody on whom they
theoretically have a claim under one system of law or the other, though there
may be a price to pay for such support. But the question must be asked how well
these welfare and other legal 'safety nets' actually operate to prevent the
elderly going in need.

Pension Claims in Practice

My fieldwork undertaken in the Cape over the past seven years bears out the
findings of an in-depth 1983 report of the Human Awareness Programme (a
Johannesburg education and research centre) on Black pensions in the public
and private sector: that many Blacks who qualify for pensions do not receive
them, either because they have not claimed them or have been unable to prove

their qualification.[12] According to the 1983 report, in 1982, Black social old age pensioners constituted 1.5% of the Black population, which was under-represented in terms of the total numbers of the various population groups in South Africa. Six per cent of White South Africans were receiving state pensions but the number of people over the age of 60 according to the 1980 census were: Black-814,480; White-515,840; Coloured-129,000; Asian-36,680. (This reflected the higher life-expectancy of Whites.) Even given the differ-ential means tests, far more Blacks than Whites qualify in terms of income for pensions, partly because of the unsatisfactory way in which private pension funds operate in the economic conditions of an apartheid society, although none is racially discriminatory *per se*.[13]

Applications for a social old age pension must be made to a magistrate or a pensions officer. Proof of age, citizenship and indigence must be furnished. The application has to be approved either in Pretoria or the capitals of the 'homelands'. Once it is approved, the pension arrives to be collected at the office of application every two months. Although nothing in the Social Pen-sions Act or its regulations provides for the fixing of certain dates on which applications may be made, the Black Sash (a civil rights women's organization which runs legal advice offices throughout the country) has in the past reported that some pension offices are fixing dates on which applications can be made — in some cases as few as two per year only, which has particularly serious implications in scattered rural areas.[14] Moreover, there is inadequate staff in some areas, particularly rural areas where one magistrate cannot hope to cover the district.[15] Illiteracy and failure to register births both contribute to many being without birth certificates and therefore having difficulty in proving that they have reached the qualifying age, a problem which results in some clerks turning away applicants aged 80 or more on the grounds that they are 'too young'.[16] Although the time taken to process an application should be no longer than two months, the wait from application to receipt of pension can be as long as 2-2½ years.[17] The handover of pensions administration to 'homeland' administrations has increased the delays, irregularities, corruption and confu-sion.[18] (There is evidence that these features are even worse for people in the 'independent homelands'.[19]) However, pensioners are rarely refunded for delays in the processing of applications.[20]

Where pensions *are* granted, collection has long been an arduous exercise. Pensions have been payable only every second month, in arrears, only to the pensioner, and on such dates and at such places as the pension officer may determine. Pensioners, at the time so writing usually first collect their pension card from the officer, then put a thumb print to a receipt, and then receive their money. (Other population groups may have their pensions paid into banks or post office, and in 1987 the government announced it would in due course be making this facility available to Blacks too.) Because of the large numbers and uncertainty that the pension will indeed arrive, pensioners often queue all night outside the pay-out point, despite heavy rains or below-freezing temperatures in highveld winters.[21] Recently, for example, the crush was so great at one pay-out point in Soweto where several thousand pensioners were waiting, that a pensioner was crushed to death and several others injured in the stampede caused by official (but bribed) 'marshalls' assisting latecomers to go to the top of the line.[22] In some areas the facilities at the pay-out points are totally inadequate. During field work in Cape Town, queues were witnessed where lack of seating forced old people to *stand* for hours outside, irrespective of the weather, and in damp and draughty corridors; and these conditions are common.[23] At the end of the queue, there may be no payment. The paymaster may work there for only a few hours; the money may run out after the banks close, so that pensioners have to go to another pay-out venue or return on another occasion; or their money may simply not be there.[24] The current practice of signing a receipt (with a thumbprint) *before* receiving the money sometimes results in those who then complain that the money handed to them is short of the full amount being told that they have already signed for it.[25] It is true that there are provisions in the regulations[26] for an appeal to the district pension officer, but this needs to be in writing. Further, given the deference to authority in an apartheid society, these appeal provisions do not necessarily work as they should unless assistance and support is available.[27]

Where pensions *are* obtained, it must be asked how adequate they are. As demonstrated above, they can prevent abject want if the pensioner does not have responsibilities for anyone else, few transport or other expenses, and pays only a low rent. However, in urban areas a particular problem is the chronic shortage of housing, resulting in high rents on sub-leases which eat up much of a pension. (A very high proportion of Black housing is provided by the local authorities for low rents, but it is common for the tenant then to sub-let rooms.) Despite some limited rent exemption schemes for pensioners, many old people have recently been among those evicted as local authorities moved to recover long-standing rent debts.[28] Moreover, as will be shown below, over two-thirds of pensioners in our survey had some financial responsibility for descendants. However, given the greater facilities available in urban areas, in practice urban pensioners receive more benefits than their rural counterparts in most other respects, even where benefits are ostensibly available throughout South Africa. In some centres they receive free or reduced rate bus transport to pension pay-out points, and pensioners receive 40% fare reductions on South African railways once their applications (involving payment of a small sum) have been accepted. At least two large supermarket chains offer small discounts to pensioners on one or two days per week. Pensioners may receive free attention and medicine at all Provincial and day hospitals, and free or subsidized hearing aids, spectacles and false teeth. (Wheelchairs are available but pensioners have to contribute something.) Free legal aid is available to pensioners and TV and radio licences are reduced for them, as and dog licences for one dog on certain conditions. Most importantly for a partially illiterate population, in urban areas there are far more social workers available to assist with advice and the necessary applications, as well as the very limited supply of emergency food parcels. There are also more charities available from which similar emergency food may be obtained, and 'lunch clubs for pensioners', which, for a nominal membership fee, supply lunches in some centres on a limited basis. Old-age homes for Blacks are very scarce even in urban areas — for example, there are only two 'transit camps' in Cape Town, with some 70 places, although by September 1986 the Black population of the Greater Cape Town area was estimated to be some 620 000 and is growing rapidly.[29] But there are even fewer old age home places per head of population outside the cities.

In rural areas, difficulties are considerable increased, not only by the dearth of the above-mentioned facilities, but also because of the effects of the big distances involved. Thus food prices in rural trading stores are higher than in towns, and transport costs to and from pension pay-out points in the rural areas are very high. Some pensioners are forced to leave their homes two or three days before pay-out day in order to be first in line.[30] In addition, apartheid measures have particularly disadvantaged rural areas. Subsistence farming is becoming increasingly difficult because of the poor land, little water, and lack of fencing in the 'homelands', to which many additional people have also been removed. One third of the people in the 'homelands' have no access to land at all. This, together with the effects of influx control (or, more lately, 'orderly urbanization'), resettlement, and migrant labour policies, have resulted in large numbers of old people, women, and children often depending for survival solely on pensions and migrant labour remittances. Yet there is evidence that the obstacles to applying for old age pensions are so great, particularly in resettlement areas, that many become apathetic and hopeless.[31]

The Duty of Support For the Elderly in Practice

Where pensions are not obtained or prove inadequate to needs, the family is the remaining 'safety net' provided by the law. During fieldwork it was found that there was often a tendency for officials to believe that Black families remain so close-knit, even after more than a century of urbanization and 40 years of apartheid, that 'the family will provide' if all else fails. Research did not bear this out. Interviews with social workers, religious leaders, pensioners, and their offspring of working age all produced unanimity on the low number of children who supported their aged parents. In our survey of 98 people of pensionable age in Cape Town, only 32 reported receiving support in cash or kind — including rent — from their direct descendants (a further 2 received help from other family members, in the form of rent, and 2 were paid for rent or childcare only by non-relatives), while 62 appeared to receive no support at all, apart from pensions. A third of those receiving assistance claimed to receive it only sporadically, though several of these said that the son or daughter helped when they got money themselves.[32] There is a shortage of figures in reported research but recent work by Professor Maqashalala in the Ciskei on support systems among a statistically random sample of 100 rural Black widows (nearly all of whom were over 60) showed that, although 80% had no available income from savings, insurance, or work, their families were far from the first on the list of people to whom they could turn in practice for support: 'in decreasing frequency widows received help from neighbours, friends, sons, daughters, other relatives, parents and employers.[33]

Nonetheless, interviews with commissioners, magistrates, legal aid and maintenance officials, and social workers revealed that legal cases brought by the elderly for support from their families were virtually unknown. No reports could be found on support cases brought by the elderly under customary law, and interviews, which were all conducted in urban areas, revealed none. It seemed unlikely that, in civil cases at least, this total absence of cases was due to the expense involved; this is minimal under the Maintenance Act 23 of 1963, which is used extensively by parents of all population groups claiming child maintenance from the children's fathers, and has largely superseded the Supreme Court's jurisdiction to make a maintenance order. Nor, given the large number of child maintenance cases, would the explanation appear to lie in a belief that relatives are too poor to pay, although this no doubt plays a role. (A very high proportion of most households in the survey appeared to contain a number of unemployed people of working age.) Rather, the complete non-use of the law for obtaining support in this way would seem to stem from attitudes among the Black population. This was corroborated by social workers, who reported that elderly parents never sued for their own support because it was completely contrary to the norms of Black society for parents to bring a legal case against their own children: 'you just don't do things like that'. In the light of the total absence of cases brought by the elderly for their own support against other members of their families too, it would seem that the same ethic applies to all family members. Whatever the provisions of the civil law, it appears at present to be so out of step with the sentiments of at least one section of the South African public as to be irrelevant as a source of support.

The Duty of Support By the Elderly in Practice

However, while children of the elderly would often seem on the evidence not to feel obliged to, or be forced to, honour family obligations to their aged parents, the same does not apply in reverse. Social workers reported that, given the dire shortage of housing for Blacks, elderly people frequently made great sacrifices to protect their children from losing their accommodation. Where the house lease was in the pensioner's name, it was not uncommon for them to refuse to move to sheltered accommodation where it was available, despite maltreatment or neglect from their children who did not qualify for housing in their own right.

Even where such considerations did not apply, the lack of old age homes, the difficulty of paying rent from a pension, and the housing situation resulted in most old people in urban areas living with their children. In our Cape Town sample of 98 people of pensionable age, 70 lived in their own houses, 15 in their children's, 5 in old-age accommodation (an unusually high figure resulting from the nature of the sample), and 10 with other relatives, friends, or as lodgers. Nobody in a house lived alone. From our slightly incomplete information on the number of occupants per house,[34] we obtained an average of 7.3 people per house, including any backyard shed (probably an underestimate) , with the highest number in one house being 22, although no house was bigger than four rooms, including the kitchen. Interviews with pensioners, their children, and social workers all showed that very often the children live on their elders' pensions, since wages are low and employment uncertain. As a result of their composition, 19 households were definitely in receipt of more than one social pension (including 4 disability grants) . The pension is incorporated into the family income — sometimes forcibly as the pensioner emerges from the pay-out point to where the family is waiting, despite efforts by social workers to intervene. Social workers told of instances where aged and confused grandmothers or great-grandmothers were left filthy, virtually ignored and half-starved in a corner of the family house from pay-out day to pay-out day. However, the dependence of the family on their pensions at least ensures a roof over their heads, a modicum of food, and, for those with more dutiful children or in a better situation to assert themselves, incorporation into a family structure and even some power within it.

The provision of housing and contribution of their pensions are not the only ways the elderly provide support to their families. There are in South Africa a high number of single-parent families, resulting largely from illegitimacy and divorce. Statistics are not collected for customary law divorces, and both divorce and illegitimacy figures are far from reliable for most groups.[35] However, interviews and other fieldwork indicate that in Cape Town, the second-largest city in South Africa, the probability is that among Blacks over 50% of marriages (by either civil or customary law) will end in permanent separation or divorce. An indication of the size of the illegitimacy phenomenon is vouchsafed by the national census figure for illegitimacy among Blacks in 1980, which was 43%, and the 1986 figure for Cape Town, which was 66.2%.[36] A common pattern in lower-income groups in South Africa is for single-parent families to take the children to live with relatives, most commonly the children's grandparent (s) . This is a result both of childcare problems, given the dearth of crèches, and also the legal prohibition on parents who are not classified as White having their children with them at their 'live in' domestic work in areas set aside for Whites. Shortage of accommodation and high unemployment among unskilled workers conspire to force many single mother to take 'live in' jobs. Unless they are able to pay their parents the full cost of bringing up a child, it is frequently the case that the only other source of funds for this purpose is the grandparents' pensions.

Two further causes of grandparents finding themselves bringing up their grandchildren are direct consequence of customary law practices. Customary law dictates that transfer of a child from the mother's to the father's family is governed by the undertaking to pay bridewealth (and, strictly speaking, its actual payment). Since no bridewealth is paid unless there is a marriage, an illegitimate child remains legally, and usually in fact, with the mother's family, unless she subsequently marries the child's father. Where she marries some other man, the child does not usually accompany her to her married home. Her new husband has no obligation in either civil or customary law to support the child and will now have a new family of his own to support, as well as any earlier legitimate or illegitimate children he may have for whom a maintenance order exists. He is therefore most unlikely to contribute to the upkeep of his wife's illegitimate child or, so research shows, to allow her to do so, as his payment of bridewealth to her family tends to lead to resentment of any further outflow of family money to them.

Second — though a matter more of custom than law — in certain areas, such as Pondoland in the Transkei, it was common to send the eldest grandson and granddaughter to his or her paternal grandparents to be of (unremunerated) assistance and 'learn how to behave', since it was felt discipline would be better there than at home. This arrangement was always very flexible, depending on such factors as the mother's age as well, but established a pattern of childhood. Research in Xhosa-speaking areas has shown that schooling and employment opportunities, migrant labour and urban school riots have also increased the number of children living for part of their lives with relatives, frequently grandparents.[37]

Although there is much mention in the literature of the high number of grandparents bringing up their grandchildren, there is a shortage of figures and none could be found on the number who were of pensionable age, quite apart from what income they were receiving or its sources. (Since girls in the townships are frequently mothers by the age of 16, the mere fact of being a grandmother, or even a great-grandmother, does not guarantee that the person in question is of pensionable age.) Our Cape Town survey showed that just under a fifth of the parents of the children under the age of 21 enumerated in the survey did not live in the house, although their children did. In such cases grandparents obviously played a major role in raising the children. But in addition, all but 17 of the interviewees claimed to be looking after their grandchildren or great-grandchildren (and, in one care, the interviewee's own child). Several cared for six or more (often cousins as well as siblings), though in a few cases the ages of the grandchildren made it seem unlikely that much care was in fact required. Sometimes they cared for other children at the same time. In addition, three women were caring only for children who were not their descendants: two for children of more distant relatives, and another for a child abandoned with the interviewee when she was acting as a childminder. Thus a total of 83% claimed to be providing childcare services, and it is likely that almost all were indeed doing so. Their value to the household was thereby no doubt greatly increased, especially as only 31 of the 70 who appeared to be either wholly or partially supporting the children claimed to receive any assistance in return from the children's parents. Medical sources have pointed out that malnutrition among black pensioners in compounded by the number of dependents they often have. 'A grandmother would rather starve herself than see her grandchildren die'.[38]

Remedies?

The current position of the elderly in the Black community has much that is obviously undesirable about it. The private law remedies available are based on assumptions about norms in the society that do not pertain, and there is no point in improving the private law provisions if, as seems evident, its potential beneficiaries are not prepared to use them. Resort must therefore be had to improving the legal provisions which govern the working of private pension schemes (which is outside the scope of this paper) and the welfare system.

The current inequitable racial differentiation of pensions is a direct reflection of the maldistribution of power within South Africa's apartheid society, and is unlikely to change radically in the near future. However, various training and administrative measures could be instituted immediately, as recommended by the Black Sash and the 1983 report, to improve the application and pay-out procedure, to link the means test to the number of dependents, to improve back pay provisions, and to enable Black pensions to be paid into bank and post office accounts.

In the longer term, however, more radical solutions must be found. Assuming that equality of pensions for all groups in the society becomes the goal, some formula will have to be found, in the short-term at least, to cope with the great disparities in rents between areas at present set aside for different population groups. The much more fundamental problem, however, is that the country cannot afford to raise everyone to the current level of White pensions and, if the economy is not allowed to grow in the period before political equality is achieved, may not be able to maintain even the current lowest level of pension once everyone qualified is able to obtain one.[39] It would therefore seem that solutions other than First World welfare models must be sought. However, it is evident that trying to turn the clock back to a society in which the family provided support cannot work in a country which has undergone as extensive a disintegration of the family as has occurred in South Africa. In such a situation there is much to be said for supplementing very low pensions with the provision of services for the aged on a large enough scale to reap the benefits of economies of scale. However, the disadvantages of extracting old people from virtually all family structure, as tends to occur when they are placed in old age homes, are well documented. At present, where family affection or duty fail, the elderly usually retain a place in the family unit — in urban areas at least — by dint of their usefulness as sources of housing income and childcare. It would seem, therefore, that solutions should be sought which maintain this situation while simultaneously easing the concomitant disadvantages for the aged.

Some cash payments will have to remain, and should be supplemented *appropriately*. Since all the evidence in South Africa is that the private maintenance system does not work, [40] it should be abolished and the money thereby saved diverted towards child allowances payable to the person with whom the child lives and available on more generous conditions.[41] This fund should, ideally, be supplemented by a tax on parents with whom the child is not living. There are, of course, problems of proof and inflexibility with this system — in Black communities at the moment many children are moved between relatives frequently — but it would be a far more equitable arrangement than at present pertains and the solution of the technical problems could no doubt be sorted out in practice. While this may indeed result in an increase in deliberate unemployment, a choice between subsidizing the lazy or penalizing the children and elderly seems inevitable.

In addition, in urban or more densely populated rural areas, social workers could be employed to help grandmothers to organize communal childcare units, staffed mainly by the elderly, which would nonetheless relieve them individually of many of the more onerous aspects of the work and would benefit from economies of scale. (This has in fact begun in Cape Town on a small scale.) For those too old or infirm to work, more communal meals clubs, supervised (rather than staffed) by community workers and staffed by the more able elderly, would again reap the benefits of scale while supplementing pensions with small payments. Similarly, family care of the bedridden or confused aged could be supervised by community workers, who would then authorize weekly payments to the family from the old person's banked pension, thus ensuring at least a modicum of care for those elderly in need of it. Meals-on-wheels services could again be at least partially staffed by the elderly, and community workers distribute the food to ensure that the recipient indeed got the meal. (Meals-on-wheels are currently not provided by the state but, in a few places, by overworked charities.) This would relieve the family of some of the work involved in caring for the aged. While these measures would obviously require a considerable increase in community workers, with the concomitant wage bill, the term is used to denote those who do not receive the full training or pay of qualified social workers.

These tentative suggestions are far from ideal; there are no doubt many other and better possibilities. However, what is essential is that a post-apartheid South Africa, in common with other Third World countries, recognizes the need for rethinking First World models of assistance to the aged and adopts creative solutions more in tune with local conditions.

Notes

* I am indebted to Ms Florence Mphahlele and Ms Zorina Basavah for research assistance with much of the data in this study, and to Dr K Hughes for helpful criticism of an earlier draft. The research, as part of a larger study, was sponsored by the British Academy, Lady Margaret Hall, Oxford, the Nuffield Foundation, the Economic and Social Research Council, the Human Sciences Research Council, the Anglo-American and De Beer's Chairman's Fund, and the Harry Oppenheimer Institute for African Studies, University of Cape Town. Funding from the Sasakawa Fund, Oxford, and The British Academy made possible the Presentation of a paper at the 6th World Conference of the International Society on Family Law.

1. Under the system of 'race' classification set up by the Population Registration Act 30 of 1950, there are 22 categories, which are generally collected under the broad heading of 'White', 'Coloured', and 'Black', with 'Asian' as a sub-category of 'Coloured'. The terminology is colonial in origin but current usage has uniquely South African governmental overtones. Broadly, 'Whites' are those supposedly of European descent, 'Blacks' of African descent, 'Asians' of Asian descent (largely from the Indian sub-continent and some from China but excluding those considered of Malay descent), and 'Coloured' embraces all other groups, including the (largely Muslim) descendants of Indonesians and Indians brought to South Africa by the original Dutch colonists and known as 'Malays'. Since the terms are used in all official data and literature discussed throughout this chapter, the need for clarity has obliged me to use the same terminology. Similarly for such phrases as 'population groups'.

2. The fieldwork data referred to were collected during the course of a larger study on the maintenance of children, which included a pilot survey in Cape Town of 100 members of the Nyanga and Guguletu lunch clubs for Black pensioners and the disabled. At the clubs, most members were women and only these were interviewed, as our focus was on childcare. Two of the interviews were subsequently eliminated as the interviewees were disabled but not of pensionable age. The other fieldwork sources of data most relevant to this were lengthy interviews conducted with a number of divorcees, social workers, lawyers, Black Sash Advice Office workers, and officials of all population groups in Cape Town, Grahamstown, and King William's Town, with some additional interviews in Johannesburg and Durban. However, given the sensitive nature of the information being asked, most interviews were granted only on condition that the informants were not identified. Most of the statements below for which newspapers and report sources are cited as examples were also corroborated during fieldwork.

3. 'Homelands' is the euphemism for areas now set aside for Blacks. They have two different types of legal status: non-independent and independent. The former are local administrative regions within the Republic of South Africa. 'Independent homelands' have been proclaimed as independent countries by the South African government but have not been recognized as such by any other country.

4. This information was supplied by the Cape Provincial Administration, which administers Black pensions. The current SANCA fact sheet appears to contradict this but is unclear.

5. *SAIRR Quarterly Countdown*, No. 5, 1st Quarter 1987, p. 36.

6. PQR Boberg, *The Law of Persons and the Family* (Juta, Cape Town, 1977) pp. 249-50, 276

7. Boberg, p. 341

8. Boberg, p. 279-85; HR Hahlo, 'Maintenance Out of a Deceased Estate: An Epitaph' (1964) 81 *South African Law Journal* 1 at 2. At the time of writing reform of this affect of the law was under investigation by the Law Commission.

9. JC Bekker and JJJ Coertze, *Seymour's Customary Law in Southern Africa,* Fourth Edition (Juta, Cape Town, 1982) p. 140

10. Bekker and Coertze, p. 215

11. TW Bennett, 'Maintenance of Minor Children: A Problem of Adapting Customary Law to meet Social Change (1980) *Acta Juridica* 115; C Dlamini, 'Maintenance of Minor Children: The Role of the Courts in Updating Customary Law to meet Socio-Economic Changes' *South African Law Journal* 101 (1984) 346

12. Human Awareness Programme, *Pensions: An Assessment. State Pension Scheme and Private Pension Funds — How they affect black people in South Africa.* Special Report, No. 4 (June 1983). I am indebted to this report for much information in this section.

13. See e.g. *ibid*, pp. 29-33

14. e.g. Memorandum on the administration of African pensions in some areas of Natal as experienced by the Natal Coastal Region of the Black Sash, 1980.

15. Black Sash Report, 1976

16. e.g. *Sunday Express,* 26 June 1983

17. e.g. *Sowetan,* 15 April 1982

18. e.g. *Cape Times,* 11 May 1981; Human Awareness Programme, *Report,* pp. 16-17

19. e.g. RJ Haines *et al.,* 'The Silence of poverty: Networks of control in rural Transkei', Carnegie Conference Paper No. 48, Second Carnegie Inquiry into Poverty and Development in Southern Africa, Cape Town, 13-19 April 1984

20. Black Sash Memorandum, 1980

21. e.g. *Sowetan,* 7 July 1982

22. *Star,* 11 September 1987

23. e.g. Letter to Dr P Koornhof from the Grahamstown Advice Office, 12 December 1979; Black Sash Memorandum, 1980

24. e.g. Black Sash Memorandum, 1980; *Cape Times,* 16 March 1981

25. e.g. Black Sash Advice Office Report, 13 June 1980

26. Regulations proclaimed in terms of Article 17 (1) of the Social Pensions Act, 37 of 1973

27. e.g. Black Sash Pensions Report, East London, 5 May 1980, but cf. e.g. Black Sash Johannesburg Advice Office Report, 1980

28. e.g. *Cape Times,* 11 May 1981; *Sowetan,* 5 October 1982; *Weekly Mail,* 24 July 1987

29. *Cape Times,* 24 June 1987, quoting the Minister of Constitutional Development and Planning in Parliament on 23 June 1987

30. *Sowetan,* 25 August 1982

31. e.g. Report on Winterveld Resettlement Area, *Sash,* May 1982

32. It was evident that total reliance could not be placed on either these figures or those on children below, since conflicting motives for not telling the truth were revealed during interview, e.g. a desire to boast of dutiful children; a hope of more help if greater need were evident; or a fear that pensions might be stopped if other sources of income were revealed.

33. T Maqashalala, 'Support Systems among African Widows', paper presented at a

seminar at the School of Social Work, University of Cape Town, 16 October 1986, p. 10

34. Some living in backyard sheds could not detail the full number living in the main house, and *vice versa* where the interviewee lived in the house. (Some 18% of the Black population lives in small sheds in backyards; *Argus,* 8 August 1987)

35. C Simkins, 'Household Composition and Structure in South Africa' in *Growing up in a Divided Society: The Contexts of Childhood in South Africa,* eds. S Burman and P Reynolds (Ravan, Johannesburg, 1986); S Burman and R Fuchs, 'When Families Split: Custody on Divorce in South Africa' in *ibid.*

36. C Simkins, 'Household Composition and Structure in South Africa' in *ibid; Annual Report of the Medical Officer of Health, City of Cape Town, 1986,* Table III.13.

37. Personal communication, Professor Monica Wilson, 7 May 1982; Cape Town research interviews

38. e.g. *Cape Times,* 11 May 1981

39. DW Williams *et al.,* 'The Realities of Social Security in South Africa', Paper for the Actuarial Society of South Africa, 1987.

40. S Burman, 'Marriage Break-up in South Africa: Holding Want at Bay?', *International Journal of Law and the Family* 1 (1987) 206-247

41. Child allowances for Black children are currently low, available only for four children per family, and very difficult to obtain: the father must either be proved to be untraceable, disabled, or in prison, and the mother must usually be employed and also faces a stringent means test. See *ibid.*

Chapter 16

Law and the Elderly in the Islamic Tradition

Tahir Mahmood

Department of Islamic and comparative Law, Indian Institute of Islamic Studies, New Delhi, India

In the Islamic tradition the position of the elderly is dealt with by imposing multifarious moral, social, legal and financial obligations on the young for the benefit of the elderly. The liabilities of individuals in this regard are sought to be based on kinship or some other family relationship. Remedies are provided for the enforcement of this liability of the individual through various forms of social control exercisable by society and the state.

The two foundational sources of Islamic law and sociology — the Qur'an and the Sunnah — are replete with precepts meant to afford all possible physical, mental and emotional comfort to the elderly through the medium of family obligations. Before examining these precepts we should first examine the structure of the Muslim family.

Islam does not prescribe any specific organizational family type. Traditionally, however, the Muslim family structure has been, and remains, closer to the extended than to the nuclear type. The Muslim family is basically different from the traditional joint family or coparcenary of India, the foundation of which is joint ownership of property categorized as "ancestral" in contradistinction to "self-acquired". Unity of residence is, also, not a basic characteristic of the Muslim family. Members of a Muslim family may or may not occupy a common residential unit. Residence may be shared by all members, or some or all of them may be living separately and independently. In all these cases family ties remain intact and family obligations must be discharged by all members. A Muslim family primarily includes the self, the spouse and the immediate ascendants and descendants — the position of none of these constituents being inferior to any other. Besides these immediate constituents, there may in a family be other positions occupied by agnates, cognates, enates or collaterals. So the extended family of Islam may be a conglomeration of individuals or nuclear families all living under the same roof or in separate dwelling units, but bound in either situation by the bond of mutual rights and obligations commanded by religion.

Under the scheme of intergenerational roles, prescribed by Islam for the family structure which it recognizes and promotes, the elderly have indeed a place of honour. Their security, protection and comfort are guaranteed by the behavioural norms and obligations to which younger members of the family are subjected. Before examining the details of these norms and obligations, we shall review the dictates of the Holy Qur'an and the Prophet's Sunnah which deal directly with this subject.

The Qur'an and the Elderly

The Qur'anic model of the elderly is that the family consists of parents, whose rights the Holy Book seeks assertively to enforce. Remarkably, numerous exhortations demanding a strict adherence to the most fundamental tenet of Islamic religion, viz. monotheism, are followed in the Qur'an in quick succession by rather stern warnings and directives that one must be extremely respectful, dutiful and helpful, materially and otherwise, to one's father and mother — particularly if either of them is in old age. The verses that are clearest on the subject so address the man:

> "Thy Lord decrees that ye worship none but him,
> And be nice to thy parents,
> If either or both of them become aged in thy lifetime,
> Say not a word of disrespect to them nor revile them;
> And speak to them kind words;
> Behave with them with utmost humility
> And seek for them thy Lord's protection,
> As they sought it for thee"
>
> (XVII: 23-24)

Another significant verse proclaims:

> "God warns ye in respect of thy parents;
> In travail upon travail did thy mother bear ye;
> And gave ye suck for two years —
> You must, then, obey God and thy parents;
> And God's law is decisive".
>
> (XXXI: 14)

Nearly a dozen other verse found in different chapters of the Qur'an repeat in varying terminology the message of the verses quoted here. In a nutshell, these enjoin that, since Islam would in no case compromise its basic tenet of the unshared and exclusive right of one Supreme God to be worshipped, old parents cannot be recommended as objects of worship; but they are virtually placed immediately next to God. And only a believer can understand what worldly privileges and rights can and should be enjoyed by one whom the Qur'an places next to God. The placing of parents on such a high pedestal under the Qur'anic exhortations is aimed at providing a firm scriptural foundation for the formulation of detailed socio-legal principles in order to secure for the parents all possible material and emotional comfort that the children can afford to provide.

As stated above, old parents constitute only a model in the Qur'anic plan of protection for the elderly; rights of other elderly relatives and aged members of the family are to be determined in accordance with this model. Exponents of the Holy Book have established, with the help of internal aids to construction available within the scripture, that grandparents and other elderly ancestors and collaterals, having no children of their own to fulfill their Qur'anic rights and privileges, would stand in the place of parents for their grandchildren, grandnephews and grandnieces. All these are, in the terminology of the Qur'an, *dhawi'l qurba* (kith and kin) the old and the needy among whom are declared by the Holy Book to be the most rightful recipients of all possible help from their affluent relatives.

On the structure of its concept of the family, the Qur'an thus erects a system of material and moral protection for the elderly. Notably, the Holy Book makes it absolutely clear that a person who gives any kind of material or emotional support to an elderly relative is in no sense doing him a favour; he is only discharging his own sacred obligation and thereby acquitting himself well in the sight of God.

The Sunnah and the Elderly

The dictates of the Qur'an relating to the protection of parents and other elderly relatives were explained, illustrated and demonstrated by the personal action of the Prophet of Islam. In an awe-inspiring exhortation he said:

"Curse be on him who finds either of
his parents in old age and does not
attain eternal bliss by serving them well."

On another occasion in a metaphoric warning he declared:

"None else but parents are
their children's heaven or hell"

To this stern warning he once added that:

"Punishment for every sin can be deferred
to the eternal life but not for that of
neglecting one's parents; for this sin
One must suffer in one's worldly life".

Notably, between the parents, the Prophet gave preference to the mother, saying that her rights were thrice as much as those of the father, and declaring, again metaphorically, that for every person paradise lay at the feet of his or her mother.

Besides the parents, the Prophet spoke of the rights of grandparents, aunts and elder brothers whom he equated with parents, mother and father respectively, thereby attracting to the benefit of those relatives the application of the clear Qur'anic obligations of individuals relating to the well-being of their parents. He also strongly asserted that one must do everything possible for the friends, companions and associates of one's parents after the parent's death. As regards neighbours, in a meaningful exhortation he told his followers that the aged and the infirm among the neighbours had every right short of succession to property.

The Elderly in the Classical Islamic Law and Sociology

These precepts of the Qur'an and the traditions of the Prophet were developed by the early doctors of Islamic law and sociology into detailed legal rules aimed at procuring all necessary material and emotional comforts for the elderly. The socio-legal doctrines evolved by them for this purpose were multifarious, and they directly and indirectly protected the interests of the aged. We proceed briefly to explain some of these doctrines.

The foremost pro-elderly doctrine of Islamic law is the doctrine of absolute ownership of property. The rule of right by birth in ancestoral property, which has been the cornerstone of some other societies, never had any recognition in Islam. In Islamic law, every owner of property, man or woman, is the absolute owner of his or her property; during his or her life-time, his spouse, children or any other relative have no rights in it whatsoever. Till their last breath the aging and the aged enjoy full and exclusive rights in their property; in no way can their enjoyment of their property be hampered by any present relative or would-be heir. The concepts of 'spes successionis' and 'heir-apparent' are wholly foreign to Islam.

Under the law of inheritance, both parents of the praepositus are among the primary heirs. They cannot be excluded either by each other or by any other heir. Under the major schools of Islamic law, in the absence of the mother, a maternal grandmother how high so ever, and in the absence of both parents, a paternal grandmother, how high soever, became the heirs. When the father has predeceased his child, the latter's grandfather, how high soever, will be among its heirs. All these ancestors, notably, inherit as primary heirs. In the absence of certain primary heirs, ancestors by distant relationship, such as the mother's grandfather, father's mother's father, uncles, aunts, grand-uncles and grand-aunts and higher collateral relations may also inherit as remote heirs. The Islamic law of inheritance, thus, remarkably takes care of many an aged relative of the praepositus and gives them shares in the property of the deceased, even at the cost of its excessive fragmentation.

As regards maintenance, books of classical Islamic law lay down the following rules relating to parents who may be aged, infirm or otherwise indigent:
(1) the father is to be maintained by his children, both male and female, where he is ready, and the latter are able to provide maintenance (both the son and the daughter, whether married or unmarried, must maintain him, their responsibility being joint and equal) .
(2) the mother is to be maintained by her sons and daughters, jointly and

equally, irrespective of whether she has capacity to earn;
(3) if children cannot provide separate maintenance for their parents, they are required to take the parents to live with them;
(4) as between parents, if a child can maintain only one of them, major variants of Islamic law give priority to the needs of the mother while the rest provide that what the child can provide is to be divided between both parents if both are needy;
(5) so long as a person has a child, male or female, capable of earning and providing maintenance, the entire liability to maintain that person is on the child; no other relation can be asked by the child to share the liability.

Paternal and maternal grandparents, how highsoever, are to be maintained, if they have no nearer descendants to provide maintenance for them. Notably, there is no order of priority in this respect between maternal and paternal ancestors — both categories have equal rights. In addition to these near relatives, a person may also be required to maintain a remotely related member of the family should the circumstances so demand. Among those who may be so entitled to maintenance may be a stepmother, a sister, an aunt, an uncle, a grandaunt and a granduncle. No old person will, however, be left without financial and emotional support, which must come from one or other of his or her family, which Islam indeed treats largely as an extended family for the purposes of maintenance. And maintenance for this purpose would include food, clothing, residence, other day-to-day needs, respect and personal help if required.

It is noteworthy that the 'family' in Islam is not necessarily a religious unit. Rights of maintenance and privileges of emotional support would, therefore, be available to the parents, grandparents and other elderly members of the family, irrespective of whether any of them is or is not a follower of Islam. Religious uniformity is not a condition in Islamic law for the enforcement of rules of maintenance. And the principle holds for both ascribed blood ties and acquired relationships.

As regards acquired relationships, Islam (as is well known) does not recognize the fictitious relationship of adoption. The philosophy of non-recognition of adoption seems to be based on multifarious considerations, one of which is that natural parents should not be deprived of their children who could be an asset for them in old age. The socio-legal policy of Islam to treat children as the foremost source of material and emotional comfort for the elderly comes into conflict with the ideology of adoption. At the same time, however, an issueless person may want to adopt a child an a security for old age. To reconcile these conflicting situations, adoption of children of unknown parentage has now been legalized in some Muslim countries such a Somalia, Tunisia and Turkey.

While adoption is not recognized in Islam, some peculiar acquired relationships recognized by Islamic law, which attract our attention in the context of legal arrangements to assist the elderly are fosterage (rada'ah) , "acknowledged kinship" [nasab-i igravi] and "successorship by contract" (wala) . A person who has been raised during his infancy by a woman other than his natural mother acquires a foster-relationship with her and her immediate relatives. And a foster mother or another relative by fosterage may have to be maintained by him or her if they are aged and infirm. As regards "acknowledged kinship", a person of unknown descent may be accepted by someone as his "kinsman" indirectly or remotely related to him. Such a person will be entitled to the acknowledged person's estate if he has no other heir. Similarly, without formally acknowledging any form of kinship, one may enter into a "treaty of guardianship" (mu'ahada-i wala) with another person on mutually agreed terms. Such a contractual "ward" may agree to discharge various kinds of liabilities for the promisee and, in consideration of that, get a share in his property after his death. All these acquired relationships may indeed be of great help to the aged in special circumstances.

In Islamic context, family rights and obligations are not always private affairs of no concern to the rest of the society. Basically these are, of course, assigned to family members and are to be administered on a domestic level. But in the case of serious non-compliance with the law, religion commands society, represented by custodians of legal and judicial authority, to take necessary action. All the aforestated family obligations towards the elderly, relating to maintenance, are therefore, enforceable by the state where Islamic law is operative. A delinquent son, daughter, or other descendant or collateral who neglects to provide reasonable comforts of life to a parent or other elderly relative, may be forced by the state to discharge his or her obligation. Where an aged person has no relative near or distant to take care of him, the machinery of society or the state must move to help him. The Islamic institutions of 'waqf' (religious trusts), 'zakat' (religious tax), 'bait-al-mal' (state exchequer) and 'sadaqa' (charity) assume special significance in such cases. And the concept of 'charity' in Islam is typical of Islam's attitudes to 'dhawi'l-qubra', viz., relatives. Here charity literally 'begins at home' and so 'waqfs' by way of settlement on one's family are valued. For the beneficiaries, interest in such a waqf may be much more secure in old age than a possible help from a public waqf or other resources of the state.

Law and the Elderly in Modern Muslim States

We have detailed the rules of the classical Islamic law and sociology relating to protection of and security for the elderly. We now proceed to examine the relevant provisions of the legal codes enacted in modern Muslim states in order to see how far these rules have been retained, improved upon, supplemented or replaced by alternatives, in the contemporary world of Islam.

The Iraqi Code of Personal Status 1959, while enforcing maintenance rights of parents and relatives, enacts a number of safeguards. The following text of the Code is noteworthy:

Art. 61:   Maintenance of poor parents, even if they are capable of earning, is binding on well-off children, old or young, provided that it doesn't so appear that the father is unreasonably insisting on sitting idle.

Art. 62:   Maintenance of every indigent person is binding on those of his or her legal heirs among the relatives who are affluent, in the proportion of their presumptive shares in his or her estate.

In Jordan, the new Code of Personal Status 1976 provides:

Art. 172:   (i) Affluent children, both male and female, shall be bound to provide maintenance to their parents if they are indigent — even though they may have capacity to earn.
                    (ii) If a child is indigent but has capacity to earn, he must work and provide maintenance to his indigent parents. If a son is working but does not earn in excess of his own and his wife's and children's requirements, he must keep his parents. with him and feed them as well as his family.

Art. 173:   Maintenance of indigent minors, as also of all elderly people who are incapable of earning due to physical or mental infirmity, is required of those of their relatives who under the law of inheritance would be their heirs, in proportion to their presumptive shares. If such an heir is indigent, the liability will pass on to relatives who will be the heirs next; and the latter can recover the expenditure so incurred from the former when his position improves. Evidence of affluence shall supersede that of indigence.

In South Yemen, the Family Law of 1974 provides:

Art. 24:   Affluent children, both male and female, shall provide maintenance to their parents who are indigent or have retired employment, provided that they do not seem to be unnecessarily sitting idle.

The Syrian Code of Personal Status 1953 (as amended in 1975) lays down the following law:

Art. 158:   All affluent children, male or female, young or adult, must provide maintenance for their indigent parents, even if they are capable of earning, provided that it does not appear that the father is unreasonably insisting on sitting idle.

In Tunisia, the 1956 Code of Personal Status (as amended extensively in 1980) says:

Art. 44:   Maintenance of parents and grandparents is required of well-off children and grandchildren.

Art. 45:   In the case of plurality of children, such maintenance shall be binding in accordance with their financial condition and not according to age or rights of inheritance.

The Algerian Family Code of 1984, which replaced in that country all contrary rules of Franco-Algerian law, declares:

Art. 77:   Descendants shall maintain their ascendants, and vice versa in the order of the right to succession.

In North Yemen, the Family Law of 1978 enacts the following:

Art. 152:   Maintenance of an indigent father and grandfather, how highsoever, and of such a mother and grandmother, how highsoever — even though they have capacity to earn — is binding on affluent children and other nearest descendants how lowsoever — male or female, young or grown up — and within a single generation of descendants such ability will be shared equally. Maintenance of the mother has priority over that of the father and of the father over that of other relatives.

Art. 153:   Maintenance of an indigent stepmother is obligatory for affluent
                   stepchildren.
Art. 155:   Maintenance of an aged or otherwise indigent person who cannot earn is
                   binding on those of his affluent relatives who would be his heirs, in
                   proportion to their shares.

In Kuwait the Code of Personal Status 1984 says:

Art. 201:   Affluent children, both male and female, shall provide maintenance to
                   their indigent parents and grandparents even if they are of a different
                   religion and although they may be capable of earning. In case of plurality
                   of children the obligation shall be discharged in accordance with their
                   respective affluence.

In several Muslim countries, executory legislation, of civil or penal nature, provides rules for the enforcement of the rights of the elderly to receive maintenance from their affluent relatives. In Egypt, for instance, under the provisions of the Maintenance Orders Enforcement Law of 1976:

(i)   all suits relating to maintenance of parents and other shall be expeditiously decided and
      the decrees passed speedily executed;
(ii) the Nasir Social Bank shall pay the maintenance amount decreed to parents, etc., out of
      the payer's account in the Bank; and
(iii) a person ordered to pay maintenance to a parent, etc., must deposit in the Bank the
      amount decreed within the first week of every month and the Bank shall pay it to the
      claimant.

In Libya Article 398-A of the Penal code of 1953 penalizes a person who fails to comply with a court order to provide maintenance for his ascendants, etc., despite having the capacity to do so. The punishment is one year's imprisonment.

The Penal Code of the Sultanate of Oman, in force since 1974, similarly provides:

Art. 212B: A person who has been ordered by the court to pay monthly maintenance
                   to any of his ascendants, or to any other person whom he is legally bound
                   to maintain, and does not pay any of the instalments for two months shall
                   be punishable with imprisonment for one to six months and a fine
                   equivalent to the amount which he fails to pay.

In Pakistan and Bangladesh, under section 488 of the Criminal Procedure Code 1898 a person can seek a maintenance order against any of his or her children. This provision is of a substantive nature and provides relief against vagrancy.

As regards inheritance rights of parents, grandparents and higher ancestors, the classical Islamic law which treats them as primary heirs of the praepositus taking fixed fractional shares remains in force under the modern family codes of Algeria, Egypt, Iraq, Kuwait, Morocco, Syria, Tunisia, North Yemen, Somalia and Tunisia. In some of these countries (Algeria, Egypt, North Yemen, Syria, Tunisia) and in the Sudan, the grandfather has now been made a co-heir with the brothers and sisters of the deceased (whereas in the classical law of certain countries he was to exclude them altogether) . In many other Islamic countries, including Pakistan, the classical uncodified law on the subject still applies without any change.

The Islamic legal rules for the custody of minors are also extremely significant in the context of the emotional solace of the elderly. Under these rules, the mother of the minor child, male or female, has a preferential right to its custody. In the absence of the mother this right passes to the maternal grandmother, how highsoever, paternal grandmother, how highsoever, sister, maternal aunt and paternal aunt — in that order. Most of those Islamic countries where the family law has been codified have introduced no changes in these rules and aged females continue to benefit from them.

In the legal framework of the Muslim countries, despite its reform and modernization in many of them, the elderly have to face far fewer problems than their counterparts in the western societies, where intergenerational estrangement often creates havoc for the elderly. The influence of foreign culture which swept most parts of the Muslim world during colonial rule by western powers and the impact of industrialization and urbanization has in recent times eroded some of the Islamic traditions aimed at securing the welfare of the elderly. Legal and judicial means are to be evolved to remedy such situations.

Chapter 17

The Development of Laws Relating to Filial Support in Australia

Peter A. Gunn   Department of Sociology,
                                 University of Tasmania, Australia

Introduction

Of recent years, much has been made of the impact of modernisation processes on the status of the aged (Burgess, 1960; Goode, 1963; Nimkoff, 1962; Palmore and Whittington, 1971; Palmore and Manton, 1974; Cowgill and Holmes, 1972; Cowgill, 1974). The changes are seen by some as profound (Parsons, 1942; Nimkoff, 1962), and involve the erosion of familial, and particularly filial, ties.

In modern societies the division of responsibility for the care of aged people is shared. Garrett (1979-80:793) has suggested that at present '...four methods are used for the support of the non-working aged in the United States; social insurance, public assistance, family responsibility, and personal assets'. While the relative emphasis on each of these components may vary from nation to nation, the same fundamental structure may be observed in many countries. Filial responsibility laws do not stand therefore in isolation, and they are controversial precisely because the issues raised by them bear directly upon the way responsibilities are divided between the public and private spheres.

Viewed from this perspective, the exercise of legal sanctions which regulate the behaviour of adult children toward their aged parents can be seen to tap either or both of two motivational bases: it may be directed toward the further strengthening or reassertion of filial bonds in a climate in which it is believed they are being eroded, or it may serve as a hedge against the growth of public debt brought about by the rise in financial dependency among aged people.

In the main, the first of these views is reflected in the analyses offered by modernisation theorists. This tradition, owing much to Parsons (1942) but spelt out by Goode (1963), suggests that in the modern world, widespread ideological shifts occurred which favoured the conjugal family ideal. Independently, in the development of industrial societies, geographical mobility has been rewarded, social mobility encouraged, dependence on the kin network reduced through an emphasis on achievement rather than ascription as the basis for advancement, and nepotism rendered ineffectual by specialisation (Goode, 1963: 369-370).

As the elements of the industrial system were put into place the resulting relations made the realisation of the conjugal family ideal possible. In the changing climate where the web of kinship did not have the same utility in the struggle for advancement, familial, and particularly filial, relations, were weakened progressively. By extension the state is asked to bear the burden once borne by the familial system and it responds with the assertion of filial responsibility.

A second tradition has grown out of the pioneering work of Leo Simmons (1945). Rendered all the more interesting by its cross-cultural perspectives and for its attention to non-industrial as well as industrial societies, this tradition asserts that the status of the elderly in any social system is dependent upon the relative costs and contributions which aged people collectively represent in the context of scarcity or abundance in the wider economy (Amoss and Harrell, 1981). Esteem for elders flows when contributions outweigh costs. Conversely when costs outweigh contributions filialism necessarily becomes attenuated, and the state is under pressure to incorporate care of the aged into the public domain.

A third and not unrelated tradition focuses on the distribution of social power and on the manner in which the modernising process has transformed the status relationships which once existed in traditional societies. When elders no longer command the resources necessary to the status placement of their children, they are no longer in a position to dictate the terms under which their aging years will be spent (Salaff, 1981).

The weakness of these arguments, which couple modernisation with a need to reassert filial piety, is that they assume tacitly that the burden of care is constant in the main, while the willingness of families to support their elderly members is diminishing. By default, the state is left with an expanded role.

Yet there is a much stronger case that can be argued, namely that changing demographic, economic and social regimes, such as those which have been experienced in the countries of western Europe and North America, as well as Australasia and some of the more developed countries in the Pacific, have created a rising burden of care, which the familial system, however strong it may be, is ill-equipped to meet.

Such arguments have been advanced by Spengler in his analysis of shifts in the responsibility for the aged in America. He argues that during the 1930s, public provisions for aged people replaced the filial responsibility which had previously been enshrined in the laws of many of the American states (Rheinstein, 1960, 1965), as a result of changes in national demographic and economic regimes in an altered climate of public opinion (Spengler, 1969:368-374).

The economic and demographic changes included the massive unemployment of the great depression, the demographic aging of the population, the growth of poverty attributable to increased urbanisation, the identification of aged households as being especially vulnerable to poverty, the appreciation that inflation has eroded lifetime earnings, and the rise in per capita income which affected the capacity of the nation to pay.

At the same time, a 'politically and economically oriented poverty ideology' emerged from the secular transformation of the religious obligation to be charitable, to be coupled with a new philosophy of public spending associated with the rise of Keynesianism (Spengler, 1969:368).

In the Australian case, both elements alluded to by Spengler have been used to account for the rise of public welfare provisions. Some, like Kewley (1973), have drawn attention to a new 'collectivism' evident in the ideological climate, usually associated with the emergent 'nationalism' of the 1880s and 1890s. Conversely, Cairns (1976) and Roe (1976) both argue that although there was a new measure of unity around the turn of the century about the need to assist the elderly, the important determinants and impediments were not ideological so much as demographic and economic.

The controversy over filial piety becomes particularly acute when, in the face of a rising burden of care, the belief prevails that the expansion of state responsibility for dependent groups, including the aged, can only be at the cost of continued national economic growth. As nations face both difficult financial times and new demographic regimes, past attempts to exact filial piety by norms of law can provide useful lessons which guide the development of public policy.

The right to relief

In none of the Australian colonies in the nineteenth century, nor in New Zealand, was there the expectation that the Government would, as a right, provide for the needs of any aged people who fell upon hard times. Yet destitution was not unknown and institutions arose in the colonies for its management which bore a striking resemblance to those of England.

In England, the main parameters of the charitable order became evident with the Elizabethan Statute of Charitable Use of 1601, which outlined the groups most likely to experience poverty and thereby gave some shape to the institutional response. The Statute was directed toward:

> 'The relief of aged, impotent and poor people; the maintenance of the sick and maimed soldiers and mariners; ...the education and preferment of orphans; the ...maintenance of houses of correction; ...supportation, and help of ...persons decayed.' (Kennedy, 1982: 2)

Combined with the Poor Law of 1597, and particularly its revisions and expansions in the Statute of 1601, institutions emerged which met in part the new order created by the closure of the monasteries and the reduction of the charitable arm of the church on the one hand, and on the other, the new forms of poverty created by the progress of the enclosure movement. The needs of paupers were met, after 1601, out of a parish fund which was accumulated by means of an annual tax on property, known as the Poor Rate. Residents in the Parish who were designated paupers had a right to charitable relief under the Poor Law. At the inception of the scheme, the relief was provided in both indoor and outdoor forms. In English common law there was no duty for an adult child to provide for the needs of an indigent parent, save for the right which might arise from breach of contract (Garrett, 1979-80: 794). Under the Act of 1601, the aged poor could not claim against their adult children — the claim was against the Parish.

In addition to the rights given to the indigent under the Poor Law, rights were also given to Parishes. Thomson (1980) notes that the Act of 1601 gave to Poor Law officials the power to take to court the near relatives of those aged people who were in receipt of assistance, who were of sufficient means, and attempt to recover from them all or part of the cost of the aid which was being provided to their parents. The extent of consanguinity recognised in the Act of 1597 was expanded in the revisions of 1601 to include:

'The father and grandfather, mother and grandmother, and children of every poor, old, blind, lame and impotent person being of sufficient ability, shall at their own charges, relieve and maintain every such poor person, in that manner, and according to that rate, as by the justices of that county where such sufficient persons dwell, in their Sessions shall be assessed...'

There was much regional variation in the operation of the old Poor Law (Marshall, 1968). The filial responsibility provisions were little used until the rise of the successive demographic and economic crises which prompted the Commission of Enquiry of 1832 and eventually the Poor Law (Amendment) Act of 1834 (Thomson, 1980:129). Under pressure from the Poor Law Commissioners, Parish Poor Law officials, often reluctantly, applied more stringently the workhouse test, gave new expression to the principle of less eligibility, and began some actions against the kin of aged paupers — all measures designed to hold down the number of applications for, and the cost of providing, public relief.

The situation in New Zealand in the nineteenth century may be contrasted with that which prevailed in England. In New Zealand, paupers had no claim on the Parish. However, after the passage of the Destitute Persons Ordinance of 1846, they did have the right to claim support from their kin. The consanguines recognised in the Act included:

'The father and grandfather, mother and grandmother, and the children of every destitute person not able to support himself by his own labour, [such kin] shall, being of sufficient ability, be liable to support every such destitute person.'

In nineteenth century Australia, the destitute, including indigent aged people, had neither the right to apply to the parish for relief nor the right to claim support from close categories of kin. For the whole of the nineteenth century relief from hardship was dependent upon charity.

The Charity System in Australia

The observation that there were no rights to relief in the Australian colonies should not obscure the operation of numerous institutions which served to protect the worst cases against the vagaries of old age in a new land.

In the Australian colonies of the nineteenth century the charity system which met the needs of the aged and infirm paupers included, in addition to the operation of charitable organisations, which provided both indoor and outdoor relief, the hospitals for the aged sick which were often begun by private philanthropy but funded almost solely by the government, the asylums which were all in government hands, and the gaols of the various colonies. For destitution meant recourse to private charities for many, and for some the asylum or the gaol. Because control of welfare lay with the private charities, the system of relief for the destitute was characterised by discretionary rather than statutory payments.

In the main, in New South Wales, destitution was alleviated through charitable societies. Amongst the earliest was the Benevolent Society of New South Wales, which was established in 1818. This Society, like others which followed, was ostensibly funded from private contributions, but the largest donor was the British (and later the Colonial) government. From the beginning, the demand for relief exceeded the voluntary contributions which leading citizens made to the Society and colonial governors agreed to make up the deficit, often more than half, and sometimes three quarters of the Society's revenue. As the century progressed, other societies, notably the Hawkesbury Benevolent Society, as well as hospitals and asylums, met the needs of the destitute, including the aged poor.

After 1862, the role of the Government in New South Wales expanded when it took over the control of the Asylum for the Aged and the Infirm, while continuing to delegate to the Benevolent Society the responsibility of providing care to lying-in women, sick and destitute children, and outdoor relief.

The cost of this care was considerable in the fledgling society. While in 1851 Governor La Trobe assigned £19 in unclaimed poundage to the Benevolent Society, the amount of support had grown to £100 in 1856, coupled with a commitment to make annual payments. By 1887 the demand on the Government purse had grown substantially, with the annual contribution rising to £3,000 or three quarters of the Society's budget.

In July 1834, so much of the English Lunacy Laws of 11 Geo and 1 Wm IV, C.65 as related to idiots and persons of unsound mind or their estates had been brought into the laws of New South Wales (and consequently Victoria) via 5 Wm IV No. 8. This Act subsequently was amended by 7 Vic No. 14 on 12th December, 1843, which act became the Principal Act. Section 12 of that Act provided that:

> '...no insane person being a convict confined in the said asylum shall be supported out of any funds of the colony whether local or general...'

Additionally, Section 13 permitted the superintendent of an asylum to arrange with 'any relative guardian or friend' to defray the expense of his or her maintenance in the asylum and to reimburse himself or herself out of the funds or property of the lunatic or idiot.

In the light of this dependence upon limited and uncertain sources of funding it is of little wonder then that in S.147 of the Lunacy Act of 1878 (42 Vic No. 7) the New South Wales government provided that any two justices, upon application from the Master in Lunacy that any patient had not an estate sufficient for his own maintenance or whose estate had been exhausted on his own care, might for purposes of supplementation:

'...make an application in writing to the father of such patient or if the father be dead to his mother or if such patient be a married woman to her husband or to one or more of his or her children being of the age of twenty-one years or upwards...for the payment of a reasonable sum...for or towards the maintenance, clothing, medicine and care of such patient.'

Due to common origins, the system of benevolence in Victoria was little different from that of New South Wales. Here too, relief was dispensed through the benevolent societies, the largest of which was the Melbourne Ladies Benevolent Society established in 1851 (Kennedy, 1974: 256), and again the colonial government was the largest subscriber to the society's funds. As in New South Wales, the Victorian government after the middle of the century ran insane and inebriate asylums and hospitals for the sick and infirm. Together with the gaols of the colony, these asylums became repositories for aged and infirm paupers and lunatics, although for most of the century the aged do not appear to have been in the majority.

Over the course of the century, the Benevolent Societies of New South Wales and Victoria provided both indoor and outdoor relief, with the balance being dictated by the availability of funds. In neither colony did the aged poor have a right to relief, outdoor or indoor, nor was it a privilege of great note for, as attested by the numerous Commissions of Inquiry which were carried out, conditions became worse as the century progressed and societies commonly tested the deserving nature of applicants by offering 'the asylum'.

By 1870, the cost of supporting the benevolent, insane and penal institutions had become sufficiently acute for the Victorian government to establish a Royal Commission into the Conditions and Management of the Charitable Institutions of the colony. The Commissioners reported that:

'...the want of some effectual means of making children liable for the relief of their parents, and parents for their children (adults it may be) and grandchildren, is very much felt in the benevolent asylums.'

Clearly the Commissioners were aware of the Poor Law precedents but were most reluctant to establish a tax on property by which any poor law would be funded. They noted (1871:xvi):

'As regards the levying of a poor-rate, we are of the opinion that it is inadvisable. A poor-rate necessarily involves a law of settlement and a right to relief, followed, it may be, by a workhouse test, either of which must be a

source of incalculable misfortune to a community. In this respect we agree
with the Commissioners of 1862, with whom it was a fundamental principle
that the Constitutions of both hospitals and asylums as charities, should be
maintained. It is also, at present, impractical to devolve the whole cost of the
Charities upon the rates...'

Having need of finance they recommended (1871:xviii) that the government
impose a levy of one-tenth of one shilling in the pound of rateable value of all
properties upon all municipalities to come into force after July 1872, and to
reduce subsidies to benevolent societies from £1 raised through private subscriptions. The Royal Commission's recommendations went unheeded —
perhaps because of the infancy of the system of municipalities.

In the colony of South Australia, the provision of relief came more closely
under the control of the government through the operation of the Destitute
Poor Department. Although its origins lay in private philanthropy its heavy
dependence on the government for finance reduced its autonomy.

Receipt of indoor relief required proof of destitution (Dickey, 1981:190),
including the demonstration that familial support was absent. The provisions of
the Destitute Persons Relief Act (No.11 of 1842-3) required that grandparents,
parents and children care for each other and the consanguinity recognised in
the Act followed the Poor Law precedent.

Of its origins Dickey says (1981:90):

'When first enacted as 6 Vic 11 by Govenor George Gray in 1842, it had been
unique in applying that single element in English Poor Law to an Australian
colony. Its original intent had been to protect the Government from applicants who had close relatives with resources available to assist.'

The similarity with the English Poor Law ended with the right of the officials
of the Destitute Board to attempt to recoup all or a portion of the cost of indoor
relief. The poor in South Australia had no right to relief by the State as
provided in the English Poor Law nor could they start a maintenance action
against their kin as provided by law in New Zealand.

Similar provisions were enacted in Western Australia with the passing of the
Destitute Persons Relief Ordinance in 1845 (9 Vic No. 2), although the focus of
the legislation, as with most of the maintenance legislation enacted in the
various colonies, was upon the recovery of assistance given to deserted wives
and children.

In Tasmania, like South Australia, the control of welfare lay primarily with
the government. From the earliest days of the colony, private benevolence was
in evidence, and charitable societies were established in the major centres,
providing both indoor and outdoor relief in cash or kind, depending upon the
character of the applicants, but the financial dependence of these private
charities on the government was substantial.

Imperial Dependents comprised the majority who sought assistance — the
casualties of the system of penal transportation who, in the years after their
servitude ended, found it difficult to sustain their independence. The degree to
which the charitable burden was expanded by the presence of these former

convicts was revealed to members of the Royal Commission on the Charitable Institutions of Tasmania which heard that in 1887 some 82% of the residents of the New Town Charitable Institution were free by servitude, 15% had come free to the colony while only 3% were native born. The Commissioners took the view that the extreme age of some of these inmates would soon lead to a reduction in the burden of care.

In 1862 the Tasmanian government enacted the Indigent Persons Act (26 Vic No.3) to allow the recovery from recipients who were of means, of all or portion of the cost of their care in the institutions, gaols or asylums of the colony. The provisions of this act were strengthened to allow for the recovery of maintenance from close kin by the passing of the Public Charities Act (37 Vic No.15) in 1873, and again in the Charitable Institutions Act of 1888 (52 Vic. No.8) with further revisions concerning the responsibility of kin being enacted in the Public Welfare Institutions Act of 1935 (26 Geo. No. 15).

In 1885 in Queensland, provisions were enacted, similar to those in force in South Australia and Tasmania for the recovery from relatives of relief paid to inmates in charitable institutions, with the passage of the Charitable Institutions Management Act.

The relevant clauses of the Act are:

§8 The relatives of an inmate hereinafter mentioned shall, if they are of sufficient means, be liable to defray the cost of such inmate's maintenance in an institution.

§9 If any relative of an inmate refuses to pay on demand any sum of money which is demanded of him by the curator, then any Justice of the Peace may, on the complaint of the Curator, or any person authorised by him in that behalf, issue his summons to the relative named in such complaint, requiring him to appear before any two justices at a certain time and place to be therein named to show cause as to why he should not pay such money.

§10 Any two Justices of the Peace may hear and determine any such complaint in a summary way, and make such order therein as they think fit.

§11 The relatives of an inmate shall be held liable for his maintenance in the order and according to the priority hereinafter enumerated:
(1) Husband or wife;
(2) Father or mother;
(3) Children of the age of 21 years.

Additional clauses allow for the apportionment of costs between relatives (§12), the duration of the order (§13) and the right of relatives to apply for a variation or discharging of the order (§14).

The Pressure for Change

In March 1890, a Royal Commission on Charitable Institutions began in Victoria. Its terms of reference included consideration of:

> ...the manner of making persons contribute toward the support of indigent relations who are burdens on Charitable Institutions, and the best means of recovering the moneys due to such institutions (1890:1).

What was different about the Victorian consideration of relative responsibility laws was not the manner in which the problem was cast but in the vastly different economic and demographic environment which now prevailed, for the Australian colonies were by this time in the grip of a profound depression.

For thirty years after mid-century the Australian economy had boomed. Gold and high commodity prices for wool and wheat gave rise to rapid capital formation, low unemployment and high wages. For some years, particularly in the decade of the 1870s, high rates of private capital formation led to building speculation and to the rapid growth of the major cities. Public capital formation was forced to rise to provide the infrastructure of roads, communications and other services required by this rapid urbanisation. In the main, this capital was raised on overseas markets.

In the decade of the 1880s, commodity prices declined sharply, causing a severe contraction in private investment. Public investment in capital formation could not be sustained, because of a decline in the inflow of foreign capital in response to the weaker economy. Robbed of employment-creating funds, the country lapsed into a depression in 1888 which was to peak in 1895.

Whereas in previous years private and public moneys had been combined to meet the demand for charity in each of the colonies, now private subscriptions for charitable purposes dwindled alarmingly, and more seriously, governments found themselves unable to sustain their customary expenditure on relief.

Commensurately, impoverishment and demographic change combined to increase the demand for assistance. Numerically, the population which was aged 65 and over grew only slowly — from 11,600 in 1861 to 153,000 by the turn of the century. Over the same period the proportion aged grew from 1% to 4% of the population, which level was modest by the European of standards of the day.

Prior to the late 1880s, the buoyancy of the economy had permitted the survival of an ineffectural system of charitable relief, based on indoor and outdoor relief by charitable societies, using private and public funds, on hospitals and infirm asylums funded by governments, and on gaols. The depression, coupled with the aging of the population, dramatically raised the level of demand and placed the charitable institutions under such strains that many did not survive.

The New South Wales statistician, Coghlan (1894:969) noted at this time that:

> 'It is very probable that the most immediate effect of depressed times is to

send the asylums a number of harmless but demented persons, who in more
prosperous days are supported by their relatives.'

Making matters worse, the *per capita* costs of providing welfare services,
particularly to those in hospitals for the aged and infirm, had begun to rise late
in the nineteenth century and were to rise even more sharply in the first decade
of the twentieth.

With the decline in both private subscriptions and government support, and
the rise of mass unemployment, Kennedy (1974:265) suggests that the Melbourne Ladies Benevolent Society by 1982, like others:

'remained an increasingly feeble weapon to wield against Melbourne's
deepening problem of poverty: understaffed, haphazardly and inadequately
financed, inefficiently managed, confused in purpose, and basically and
radically incomprehending.'

The Old Age Pension Movement

The spread of poverty during the depression of the 1890s created a new class
of dependents in society — people who could only be thought of as 'deserving'.
As Dickey notes (1966:21):

'Poverty had struck the most skilled and respectable of artisans, the most
careful and improving of men had gone down through no fault of their own.'

The deserving nature of this group dictated that indoor relief was less
appropriate than some revised system of outdoor assistance. In both Victoria
and New South Wales, pressure mounted to debate the utility of a scheme of
old age pensions. As early as 1895 J.C.Neild and the Reverend F.B.Boyce
spoke publicly in favour of pensions, and in September of that year the matter
was debated in the New South Wales Legislative Assembly. It was Neild's hope
that pensions would lead to an emptying of the Asylums of the Aged and Infirm
by replacing indoor, with a form of outdoor relief. In April 1896, a 'League for
Providing Pensions for Old Age' was commenced, and in July of the same year
in the Legislative Assembly a Select Committee on Old-Age Pensions was
established.

Soon after, in early 1887, Victoria moved to establish a Royal Commission
on Old-Age Pensions. Later, in August, a Select Committee, subsequently to
be replaced by a Royal Commission, was appointed in South Australia to
inquire into the Aged Poor.

It is evident that these commissions of Inquiry were well aware of English,
Continental and Trans-Tasman developments — not the least of which
influences were the Maintenance of Parents Act of 1890, passed in the English
Parliament, and the Destitute Persons Act (No.44 of 1877), passed in the
Dominion of New Zealand, which Acts provided for the recovery of the costs
of indoor relief from kin who were of sufficient means.

What was also of significance was the perception that elsewhere there was growing acceptance of the principle of governmental involvement in the provision of pensions. The South Australian Commission reported inter alia:

'It will thus be seen that the provision of some scheme of pensions for the aged in lieu of the present system of poor relief is regarded in several countries as being within the bounds of practical politics.'

New Zealand led in the introduction of old-age pensions in Australasia with a scheme which came into force on 1st April 1898. The Australian States competed to enact similar legislation with the Victorian scheme coming into force on 18th January, 1901 and the scheme in New South Wales on the 1st August the same year. Somewhat later, Queensland enacted similar legislation but the schemes in all three states were superseded by the Commonwealth Scheme, which began to provide payments from 1st July, 1909.

All these acts were to be universal schemes for the payment of age-related benefits. Gone was the discretionary system of charitable payments via the Benevolent Societies which characterised the nineteenth century welfare system. None relied on specific revenue raising measures but all were funded from general revenue. All were hedged about with exclusions to limit the total cost of the schemes.

Strikingly the traditions of the nineteenth century were not fully eroded. The Victorian Act made it possible to defray part of the cost of the payment of age-related pensions by requiring close categories of kin to contribute if they were of sufficient means. Section 8 (m) of the Act in Victoria required applicants for the pension to demonstrate that:

'the husband, wife, father, mother or children of the claimant or all of them are unable to provide or maintain the claimant.'

In 1901 when the Bill was passed into law, Victoria had not fully emerged from the depression. Clearly the persistence of this type of provision in the Old-Age Pensions Act was that it served to hold down the cost of the scheme rather than bolstering a weakened familialism. What is more, with the passage of the old-age pension legislation, the nineteenth century discretionary schemes were put aside. Now a statutory right to assistance existed where none had previously.

When depression again affected Australia, this time from 1929 to 1932, filial responsibility was again canvassed as a mechanism for holding down the cost of providing old-age pensions. The depression left many older Australians experiencing great hardship, and the number of applicants for pensions rose sharply. In the Financial Emergency Act of 1932, the near relatives of pensioners again became liable to contribute toward their support. By the time administrative arrangements were in place for the implementation of the Act, much time had passed and no action had been taken as late as April 1934. In June of the same year the Government decided to repeal the Act and proceeded to do so in March 1935.

Broadly, then, relative responsibility laws in Australia have taken two main forms. The first was the predominantly nineteenth century pattern in which close categories of kin were required to provide financial support for the care and maintenance of their indigent aged relatives, while the second sought to recoup all or part of the cost of old-age pensions from the kin of recipients if they were of sufficient means. The question remains as to whether these measures were effective in controlling the cost of a growing welfare system.

The question of effectiveness

In the 1898 Victorian Royal Commission on Old Age Pensions, representatives from the major institutions for the aged and infirm at Melbourne, Ballarat, Bendigo, Castlemaine, Ovens, Geelong, Ararat and the Immigrants' Home were questioned about the presence in their institutions of inmates who had relatives who could assist them. Most answered the question in the affirmative, but when pressed to provide the percentage of cases for whom this was so either could not say, thought it very small, thought it about three percent, or about five percent or found it impossible to say. Representatives from a further seven institutions in country districts reported in substantially the same way. When asked whether relatives contributed to the care of inmates, almost all reported that contributions were slight. Whatever the powers that lay with the institutions, it is clear that they were not being exercised in a manner which raised much additional revenue.

In the case of the Victorian pension scheme which allowed for the cost of pensions to be defrayed by contributions from close categories of kin, the Hansard record for the year 1907 records that while the amount spent on old age pensions was £250,000, the sum which was recovered from relatives amounted to only £4,000. What made it worse was that it was not an easy system to administer. Each case had to be heard individually, and the sittings in the initial months of the scheme absorbed many weeks. Neither was it possible to keep track of people whose circumstances had changed, nor to ascertain whether declarations as to the availability of kin were made honestly. Issues of compulsion arose concerning wives with parents to support who were not granted the means to do so by their husbands. Pride and a sense of independence, together with a distaste for bringing one's children before a magistrate stood between some old people and the old-age pension which was their entitlement. In sum, the Act was met with a good deal of hostility.

In the case of the Financial Emergency Act of 1932 all attempts to specify clear administrative guidelines as to who was liable for the provision of support were so ineffectual that by the close of the scheme it had been possible to raise only £2,486.

Conclusion

The purpose of this chapter has been to demonstrate how the growing number of aged people in Australia were, in the boom years in the third quarter of the nineteenth century, absorbed into a charity system based on the absence of any right to relief, how this system became attenuated by economic and demographic change to the point where it eventually failed despite the attempts to recoup part of its cost from the close kin of those receiving assistance, and how filial responsibility laws were used as a hedge, even in the present century, until sufficient resources for the realisation of welfare ideals became available.

The general lesson to be learned is that the assertion that families bear the prime responsibility for the care and maintenance of their aged members, in spite of the rising burden of care, is likely to be heard loudest when the view prevails that any expansion of state responsibility in the welfare field could only be at the cost of national economic development. However true that belief, the Australian experience suggests that the value to general revenue of relative responsibility schemes is likely to be minimal.

References

Amoss, P.T. and S.Harrell, 1981, *Other Ways of Growing Old*. Stanford, Calif.:Stanford University Press.

Burgess, E.W., 1960, 'Family Structure and Relationships.' in Burgess, E.W. (ed) *Aging in Western Societies*. Chicago: University of Chicago Press.

Cairns, J., 1976, 'Working Class Foundations of the Welfare State.' in Roe, J. *Social Policy in Australia*. Sydney: Cassell, Australia.

Coghlan, T.A., 1891, *Wealth and Progress in New South Wales*. Sydney: New South Wales Government Printer. (See also vols. 1893, 1894) .

Cowgill, D., 1974, 'The Aging of Populations and Societies.' *Annals of the American Academy of Political and Social Science*, 415: 1-18.

Cowgill, D. and L. Holmes (eds), 1972, *Aging and Modernisation*. New York: Appleton Century Crofts.

Dickey, B., 1966, 'Charity in New South Wales, 1850-1914: Outdoor Relief to the Aged and Destitute.' *Royal Australian Historical Society Journal*, 52 (1) : 9-32.

Dickey, B., 1981, 'Dependence in South Australia, 1888: The Destitute Board and its Clients.' *Australia 1888*, 8 (Sept.): 88-96.

Garrett, W.W., 1979-80 'Filial Responsibility Laws.' *Journal of Family Law*, 18 (4): 793-818.

Goode, W.J., 1963, *World Revolution and Family Patterns*. New York: The Free Press.

Kennedy, R.E.W., 1974, 'Poor Relief in Melbourne: The Benevolent Society's Contribution 1845-1893.' *Royal Australian Historical Society Journal*, 60 (Dec) : 256-266.

Kennedy, R.E.W., 1982, *Australian Welfare History*. South Melbourne: Macmillan.

Kewley, T.H., 1973, *Social Security in Australia, 1900-72*. Sydney: Sydney University

Press.

Marshall, J.D., 1968, *The Old Poor Law, 1795-1834*. London: Macmillan.

Nimkoff, N.F., 1962, 'Changing Family Relationships of Older People in the United States During the Past Fifty Years.' in Tibbits, C. and W. Donahue (eds) *Social and Psychological Aspects of Aging*. New York.

Palmore E.B. and K.Manton, 1974, 'Modernisation and the Status of the Aged: International Correlations.' *Journal of Gerontology*, 29:205-210.

Palmore, E.B. and F.Whittington, 1971, 'Trends in the Relative Status of the Aged.' *Social Forces*, 50 (Sept) : 84 — 91.

Parsons, T., 1942, 'Age and Sex in the Social Structure.' *American Sociological Review* 7: 604 — 616.

Roe, J., 1976, *Social Policy in Australia*. Sydney: Cassell, Australia.

Rheinstein, M, 1960, 'Duty of Children to Support Parents.' in Burgess, E.W. (eds) *Aging in Western societies*. Chicago: University of Chicago Press.

Rheinstein, M., 1965, 'Motivation of Intergenerational Behavior by Norms of Law.' in Shanas, E. and G. Streib. *Social Structure and the Family: Generational Relations*. Englewood Cliffs, N.J.: Prentice Hall.

Salaff, J. W., 1981, *Working Daughters of Hong Kong: Filial Piety or Power in the Family?* New York: Cambridge University Press.

Simmons, L., 1970, *The Role of the Aged in Primitive society*, Archon Books.

Thomson, D.W. 1980, *Provision for the Elderly in England, 1830 — 1908*, Unpublished PhD. Thesis, University of Cambridge.

Victoria., 1871, Royal Commission to Inquire into the Conditions and Management of the Charitable Institutions of the Colony, *Report*. v.Pp. 1871, v.2, no.1.

Victoria., 1890-6, Royal Commission on Charitable Institutions, *Report*. V.Pp., 1890, v.4, No. 203; 1891, v.6, No.210; 1892-3, v.4, No.60; 1895-6, v.3, No.48.

Section Three

The Legalisation of Family Support

Chapter 18

Supporting the Aged: The Problem of Family Responsibility

Robert J. Levy   University of Minnesota, USA

Following the precedent set four hundred years ago in the "Elizabethan Poor Law,"[1] most states of the United States enacted some form of financial support program for the dependent aged.[2] The state programs were regularized and made much more uniform in 1935 when the Social Security Act[3] made the federal government the dominant financial and administrative partner in the operation of these "cooperative" welfare endeavors. The same statute enacted the completely federal "insurance" scheme now officially described as the "Old Age, Survivors, Disability Health Insurance" program[4] and always known popularly as "Social Security.[5]

This is not the place to review the ancient English and American tradition of "relief" and the "relative responsibility" policies which have been its constant companion; the history has been traced frequently and well by others.[6] It is clear that continuing expansion and enrichment of welfare programs is the common experience of industrialized societies. Yet governmentally financed welfare programs have customarily included provisions designed to recover at least some of the expenditures from persons related biologically and/or familially to the welfare benefit recipient. Even as governments have recognized their responsibility to protect old people from the consequences of abject poverty, they have also followed the Elizabethan Poor Law's original initiative to share that financial responsibility with close relatives of aged fund recipients. Which "responsible relatives" are required to support their aged kin, the nature of the financial partnership to be established between the government and the responsible relative, the nature and scope of the "defenses" to support liability which the financially responsible relative may claim — these and many other issues have been variously resolved from state to state and from time to time. But the basic policy has been observed uniformly: parents are required to support those children and children are required to support those parents, who are recipients of government financial aid.

I

Methods of Enforcing Family Support Obligations

We can begin by describing the various ways that "family" or "relative" "responsibility" for the support of indigent persons can be "enforced."

A. Direct Enforcement

It is possible to find in recent American judicial reports cases in which an indigent person has tried to obtain support directly from a relative made liable by a state statute of apparently universal application.[7] Indeed, one can even find cases in which the support obligation has been enforced by use of the criminal sanction. In *State v. Kelly,*[8] for example, a son was convicted of failing to support his 72 year old, "infirm and semi-invalid" mother. The court held that the mother fit the statutory description of a person "who is destitute of means of subsistence and unable either by reason of old age, infirmity, or illness" to support herself. Mrs. Kelly was receiving a small old age insurance benefit under a federal statute, but lived with her daughter and son-in-law and received direct payments from the couple for "hospitalization insurance, doctor and medicine" bills as well. The court held that the term "destitute of means of subsistence" in the statute did not exclude aged persons who were being supported by the defendant's sibling.[9] Behind the arid statutory analyses in opinions like *Kelly,* of course, lurk human and family tragedies whose dimensions are difficult to determine. Yet despite the cases imposing a direct relative support responsibility, a search of the appellate cases suggests that direct enforcement, whether accomplished by civil or criminal process, is commonly limited to the fathers of young children.[10]

B. Indirect Enforcement

Expansion of government responsibility for the poor has led to great increases in indirect enforcement of such relative support obligations by means of welfare benefit denials and benefit diminutions. Consider the only noncontroversial family responsibility program, compelling support for dependent children from their fathers. Suppose that a statute provides income supplement to poor children and their mothers. (In the United States the program is Aid to Families with Dependent Children, or "AFDC.") The federal statute (or its accompanying regulations, perhaps, or a state law which is required by the federal statute) may demand that both the mother and the father contribute to the child's support. The resulting "family responsibility" can be "enforced" indirectly in the administrative process of benefit determination. If the child's father earns more than the welfare program's eligibility minimum, the child will receive no benefit; actual income flow to the child may not be guaranteed, but *part* of the purpose of the support requirement, to limit the expenditure of government tax dollars, is nonetheless served. The result is the same if the child is eligible for a benefit whose size is determined by the child's "need": when the child's benefit is decreased in accordance with a parent's income, family responsibility is "enforced", government expenditures are saved, even if the child's income flow is not necessarily increased.[11]

Indirect Enforcement: The "Needs" Test

So long as welfare programs are based on delivering subsistence income to recipients, on a "needs test," some form of relative responsibility is inevitable: unlike "social insurance" programs which guarantee benefits to all members of the covered class, welfare benefits are designed for and limited to the needy - that is, those whose current income is insufficient to cover current expenses. And if the government must determine the recipient's "needs," it must take account of "resources" (whether income or assets) of the recipient which could be used to reduce the recipient's benefit.[12] Moreover, so long as the government must and will look to the recipient's resources, it is not unnatural (although neither is it inevitable) that the government will look as well to the resources of those persons whose familial relationship is sufficiently close to the recipient that it seems natural or appropriate that they would help the recipient if the government benefit were not available.

A. Resources of the Welfare Recipient

These features of welfare programs based (let me re-emphasize) on "need" have produced a host of complex and difficult issues for welfare administrators even when the issues are limited to the resources of the recipient himself or herself. A few examples should suffice.[13] Should an aged person be deemed eligible for welfare despite the fact that she has an unencumbered residence which, if sold, would provide her ample support for a limited or substantial period? The issue is one of determining *which* assets an applicant for welfare must "spend down" to the welfare eligibility level.[14]

Or suppose that an applicant for old age assistance has transferred his home to his children before entering a nursing home, thus assuring his poverty and entitlement to welfare benefits. To what extent should the asset transfer be deemed fraudulent and therefore ignored in determining the applicant's eligibility? This issue alone produced a flood of state court litigation during a period when most state rules differed with the prevailing federal mandate.[15] It then occasioned a complex amendment to the federal statute permitting (and another, subsequently, requiring) the states to ignore such transfers. The amendment no doubt became politically acceptable (perhaps essential?) when it became clear to the congress that many state and federal tax dollars were being expended allowing families to strip their aged parents of funds before placing them in government supported nursing homes.[16] The federal statute was followed by a round of federal court suits brought by legal service lawyers for the aged poor, attacking the constitutionality of the federal statute.[17]

It is a short step from direct determinations of a welfare applicant's available resources to the administrative task of arranging continuing determinations of recipient eligibility. Suppose that a recipient's resources suddenly increase — because of a worker's compensation or a volunteer fireman's award, the legislative responses to this problem, as well as the judicial interpretations of resulting ambiguous statutes, have varied with the condition of the economy and the community's toleration of welfare expenditures. One form of "recoupment" was standard for many years — the imposition upon the estates of aged recipients of an obligation to reimburse the government for welfare benefits.[19] The reimbursement obligation was often imposed by way of a lien on the estate of the recipient.[20] The requirement has produced even more complex legal issues. For example, when a recipient dies owning a joint estate with his wife in a residence, may the state impose a reimbursement obligation on the residence despite the fact that under state law a joint estate passes automatically at the death of one joint owner to the other?[21] The Constitutionality of the reimbursement obligation was affirmed in *Snell v. Wyman*[22] even during one of those occasional periods of "welfare liberalism" in the United States. The "Medicaid" program, enacted during the same period, barred the states from establishing liens against the estates of recipients prior to their deaths and from claiming reimbursement for benefits except from the estates of recipients or their spouses.[23] As the Boren-Long amendment indicates,[24] however, the trend toward protecting relatives from liability for the aged (if it was in fact a trend) was short-lived.[25]

B. Resources of the Recipient's Spouse

It is another easy, but by no means inevitable, step from determining continuing eligibility and insisting on "recoupment" to a requirement that a recipient's family expend its "available resources" on the recipient. The justification for making some classes of relatives liable is obvious. Few disagree with the proposition that fathers who are absent from the home should support their children to the extent of their ability, whether or not the government provides the children's mother with supplementary support; under these circumstances, using the welfare administrative structure as an enforcement aid reinforces a community and moral norm even as it saves tax dollars.[26] Community consensus may not be as clear for the liability of other relatives — but their responsibility flows inevitably from the needs and resources principles of welfare administration based on "need." Consider the income and resources of spouses of recipients. Should a wife be permitted to profit from governmental welfare largess while married to a man whose income or resources are such that he is not also entitled to welfare? Even a very strong state commitment to spousal financial independence[27] would not persuade most state legislators that spouses are completely separate actors when welfare benefits are at stake. Indeed, in an important sense, this problem of financial responsibility seems akin to the problem of aged parents who give their assets away to family before seeking government welfare aid — a situation which led, eventually, to the Boren-Long Amendment and federally mandated imposition on the aged of responsibility for their "phantom assets."[28]

C. Resources of Children and Other Relatives

It is a much more substantial stride from notions of spousal responsibility in welfare administration to requiring that a larger group of relatives help the government pay for the dependent aged. Although some state statutes (once again following the precedent set in the Elizabethan Poor Law) have imposed liability on siblings and grandchildren,[29] the most common class held liable for support of the aged is children. Yet attributing to parents the income and resources of their children, closely related though they may be, causes problems in defining the proper scope of liability.

1. Which Children Should be Liable?

Should a child who offers to support her aged and poor parents by providing them with housing in her own home be exempt from direct financial contribution if the government provides cash benefits? The answer obviously depends upon the specific language of the statute as well as on the policy the court determines the welfare program was designed to promote — but judicial attitudes toward filial support for parents will obviously also play a role.[30]

Of this there can be no doubt: imposing support responsibility on children entails finding solutions to agonizingly difficult legal issues in embarrassing, sometimes even tragic, factual contexts. In some states, for example, a child who was abandoned by his parent is not required to support that parent.[31] In *Lasher v. Decker,*[32] an application by the local welfare commissioner to obtain support from the adult child of an old age assistance recipient, the trial judge interpreted ambiguous statutory language to permit refusal to order support when the parent had abandoned the child during his infancy.[33] But judicial interpretation of ambiguous legislative language cannot always carry the day. In *Mitchell v. Public Welfare Division,*[34] the recipient's son was resisting a support action, because during his minority his mother had "deserted or abandoned" him, a defense specifically provided by the relative responsibility statute. The trial judge's imposition of liability was affirmed. When the defendant was born, during the Great Depression and in another state, his father was married to and living with another woman — and his mother left him with his stepmother when he was a year old because she could not afford to care for him; but the mother moved in with the family when her son was four and lived there until the defendant went into the army twenty years later. The son later brought his mother to Oregon to live near him — but did not want to contribute to her welfare benefits. The court quoted the mother's testimony concerning her initial departure from the defendant:

> I wasn't able to take care of him, carry about the place and work.
> . . .I didn't just give him away, but I just left him.
> No, I didn't have money to. . .
> Nothing but a birthday gift or Christmas package or something like that.
> . . .I did see him every once in a while.

The court found that since the mother's work on the farm, "small as it might have been, contributed to the food raised for all of the farm's occupants,"[35] the mother had neither "deserted" nor "abandoned" the defendant and he was therefore liable to the government for a share of her welfare benefits.[36] It is not obvious how these issues should be handled legislatively or in practice: it seems unfair to impose support liability on a child for one who has mistreated that child in the past; but the standard defenses are inevitably vague, and the marginal cases present an unpleasant and unedifying spectacle — especially those in which an ungrateful child (or one who simply wants to share support for his parent with the government "as other taxpayers do") tries to take legal advantage of actual or perceived ancient parental neglects. A statute proposed for New York by a private social welfare research commission indicates some of the difficulties:

> No relative of a recipient of, or applicant for, public assistance and care, who would otherwise be legally responsible for the support of such recipient or applicant shall be liable for such support if the recipient or applicant shall have been found by a court of competent jurisdiction, whether civil or criminal, to have committed an act equivalent to any of the violations of law set forth below (or their equivalents in any other jurisdiction), according to the terms of which the relative was a victim or subject of such violation (The sections referred to . . .are those of the New York Penal Law) : Abandonment; Abduction; Assault; Bigamy; Carnal Abuse of a Child; Compelling Woman to Marry; Compelling Prostitution by Wife; Endangering Life or Health of Child; Incest; Kidnapping; Maiming; Non-support of Child; Prostitution; Rape; Robbery; Sodomy.
>
> Provided, however, that the above protection against liability shall not apply to any relative of full age and legal capacity who, by his or her conduct subsequent to the commission of the violation of law by the recipient or applicant, has voluntarily forgiven the recipient or applicant for the commission of the violation of law.[37]

The specification of offenses and the requirement of a judicial finding certainly provides greater certainty than the traditional statutes. But societal ambivalence about these issues reappears in the "condonation" provision; and that provision, however logical, will reintroduce just the unpleasantness that cases like *Mitchell* have always encouraged.

But are aesthetic considerations relevant? If relative responsibility is seen simply as a direct tax measure, as a convenient means of saving government revenues by imposing upon a narrower (but by no means an arbitrarily chosen) class than taxpayers generally, a true public policy dilemma can be avoided. It may still be unfair to impose support on children who were once abandoned or maltreated by their parents, but tax policy, like life itself, is not always fair.

Even if there is no dispute about the general policy of imposing liability on children, difficult doctrinal and administrative judgments must be faced. Should the liability of sons with working wives be the same as the liability of working daughters with working husbands? In *Page v. Welfare Commissioner*,[38] the Connecticut relative responsibility statute was held to violate the Equal Protection Clause:

> The plaintiff's mother was, in 1973, a recipient of public assistance. . . The commissioner's financial investigation revealed that the plaintiff was married, living with her husband, and the mother of four minor children. Both the plaintiff and her husband were employed, with gross monthly incomes of $481 and $649.50, respectively. In determining the amount of the plaintiff's monthly contribution to the support of her mother, the commissioner allowed her an exemption of $325, which was then the exemption for a single person living outside the home of the public assistance recipient. No exemption was allowed the plaintiff for her four children. The support contribution was computed by taking one-half of the difference between her gross monthly income and the exemption allowed.[39]

Because the statute as interpreted by the commissioner allowed working male children of welfare recipients an exemption for their minor children while denying such an exemption to married working females, the court held that the statute discriminated unconstitutionally against women:

> The regulations here in question clearly differentiate between working married mothers and working married fathers. The earnings of the latter are granted significantly greater exemptions in the financial determination of ability to contribute to the support of a needy parent than are the earnings of the former. As a result of this distinction, working mothers married to working husbands are able to contribute only a disproportionately small share to the support of their immediate household. The benefits which flow to the immediate household of a working parent who is also liable for the support of his or her disabled parent, therefore, depends upon the sex of the working parent. This is precisely the situation which the Supreme Court ruled unconstitutional [in an earlier case].[40]

2. Administrative Problems

If children are to be liable, the legislature must make difficult choices about the amount of their liability. The alternative, of course, is to leave local welfare administrators and prosecuting attorneys discretion to make their own choices.[41] Some picture of the complexities can be gathered from the matrix developed by California welfare officials to guide the discretion of local officials in administering filial responsibility provisions:

THE RELATIVES' CONTRIBUTION SCALE OF THE WELFARE AND INSTITUTIONS CODE SECTION 12101, AS AMENDED BY THE DEPARTMENT OF SOCIAL WELFARE RELATIVES' CONTRIBUTION SCALE

Column A: If relative is 60 years old or older and gross monthly income is:

Column B: If relative is under 60 years old and gross monthly income is:

Column C: Then net monthly income is:

Column D: Maximum required monthly contribution if number of persons dependent upon income is:

A	B	C	1	2	3	4	5	6 or more
S 0. -1001.99	S 0. - 667.99	S 500 or under	S 0	S 0	S 0	S 0	S 0	S 0
1002.00-1051.99	668.00- 701.33	501- 525	20	10	0	0	0	0
1052.00-1101.99	701.34- 734.66	526- 550	25	15	0	0	0	0
1102.00-1151.99	734.67- 767.99	551- 575	30	20	0	0	0	0
1152.00-1201.99	768.00- 801.33	576- 600	35	25	2	0	0	0
1202.00-1251.99	801.34- 834.66	601- 625	40	30	10	0	0	0
1252.00-1301.99	834.67- 867.99	626- 650	45	35	15	5	0	0
1302.00-1351.99	868.00- 901.33	651- 675	50	40	20	5	0	0
1352.00-1401.99	901.34- 934.66	676- 700	55	45	25	10	5	0
1402.00-1451.99	934.67- 967.99	701- 725	60	50	30	15	5	0
1452.00-1501.99	968.00-1,001.33	726- 750	65	55	35	20	10	5
1502.00-1551.99	1,001.34-1,034.66	751- 775	70	60	40	25	15	10
1552.00-1601.99	1,034.67-1,067.99	776- 800	75	65	45	30	20	15
1602.00-1651.99	1,068.00-1,101.33	801- 825	80	70	50	35	25	20
1652.00-1701.99	1,101.34-1,134.66	826- 850	85	75	55	40	30	25
1702.00-1751.99	1,134.67-1,167.99	851- 875	90	80	60	45	35	30
1752.00-1801.99	1,168.00-1,201.33	876- 900	95	85	65	50	40	35
1802.00-1851.99	1,201.34-1,234.66	901- 925	100	90	70	55	45	40
1852.00-1901.99	1,234.67-1,267.99	926- 950	105	95	75	60	50	45
1902.00-1951.99	1,268.00-1,301.33	951- 975	110	100	80	65	55	50
1952.00-2001.99	1,301.34-1,334.66	975-1,000	115	105	85	70	60	55
2002.00-2051.99	1,334.67-1,367.99	1,001-1,025	125	115	95	80	70	65
2052.00-2101.99	1,368.00-1,401.33	1,024-1,050	135	125	105	90	80	75
2102.00-2151.99	1,401.34-1,434.66	1,051-1,075	145	135	115	100	90	85
2152.00-2201.99	1,434.67-1,467.99	1,076-1,100	155	145	125	110	100	95
2202.00-2251.99	1,468.00-1,501.33	1,101-1,125	165	155	135	120	110	105
2252.00-2301.99	1,501.34-1,534.66	1,126-1,150	175	165	145	130	120	115

Or consider the impact of the Boren-Long amendment's effort to deny welfare benefits to those whose spouses have assets sufficient to support them. The federal and state statutes and the controlling federal and state regulations are too long and complex to report here.[43] But consider *Manfredi v. Maher,*[44] one of a series of federal cases brought to test the constitutionality of the Boren-Long amendment's provision for interspousal income attributions in determining eligibility for Social Security Act Title XIX (Medicaid) benefits where one of the spouses is confined for a long term at a nursing or convalescent home. Notice how complex the administration of even spousal resources provision can become; and notice as well the evasive efforts such a provision can produce:

> Arthur O. Guertin is a retired person in his seventies. His wife, Lucy Guertin, 66, resides at the Hamilton Pavilion nursing home, . . ., having entered that institution on May 14, 1974. Authur Guertin has exhausted his savings and borrowed against his insurance policies to support his wife in the home. After these resources were used up, Lucy Guertin applied for and began to receive Medicaid benefits.
>
> Arthur Guertin's total current income consists of a state pension of $179.62 per month, plus $271.90 in Social Security old age benefits. Of the $451.52 per month thus received, Authur Guertin must contribute $229.52, or somewhat more than half of the total amount, toward his wife's support in the nursing home. Should he refuse to make such contributions, Lucy Guertin would be denied Medicaid assistance, with the result that she would ultimately be forced to leave the home. After making the contributions required by the state, Authur Guertin is left with $222 per month out of which he must meet all personal and household expenses.
>
> The impact of this financial privation upon Arthur Guertin's life style has been pronounced. Guertin testified before the Court that he has been obliged in recent months to subsist on the equivalent of one and one-half meals per day (coffee and toast in the morning, a "light lunch" during the evening, and sometimes a sandwich at noon). He has been unable to afford the cost of a low-salt diet, and a doctor has ascribed a recent illness to the plaintiff's failure to maintain such a diet. In order to conserve on energy costs, Guertin reportedly restricts himself to one bath a week, and uses a single 60-watt bulb for illumination in the evenings when needed, but he also sits in the dark for long hours with no lighting at all. Despite these measures, Guertin is unable to meet utility payments. Indeed, his various expenses are such as to leave him perpetually in debt, dependent on such help as he occasionally receives from relatives. It has been suggested to Guertin that he could solve his financial problem by divorcing his wife, but he refuses to do so, and thereby continues to be subject to the state's income attribution rule.[45]

Or consider the situation of one of the plaintiffs in another "spend down" case, *Norman v. St. Clair*[46]:

> At the time of the suit, 79-year-old Troy Norman was institutionalized in a skilled nursing home in Mississippi. According to affidavit testimony, Mr. Norman's health was such that he could not receive the proper nursing care from his wife at home. He received a monthly Social Security disability check

for $160.50. He had no other source of income and was eligible for Medicaid.

Troy Norman's wife, Nonnie Mae, lived in the community with their 14-year-old son Thomas. . . . Mrs. Norman had a monthly employment income of $298.26 (excluding taxes, social security, and employment-related expenses) and received monthly social security checks for $47.90. Their son Thomas also received a social security check of $47.90. Mrs. Norman was not eligible for Medicaid. Application of the state's calculation of Medicaid eligibility and Medicaid income yields the following:

Net monthly income of ineligible spouse	$346.16
Less standard allowance for spouse's needs	78.00
	268.16
Less allowance for minor child ($65.00-$47.90)	17.10
Deemed Income	$251.06

The deemed income from Mrs. Norman is added to Mr. Norman's income (minus the $7.50 disregard) producing a total income available to Mr. Norman of $404.06. Since this is less than $450, Mr. Norman is eligible for Medicaid.

To determine how much of his medical expenses Mr. Norman must pay himself, the state calculates as follows:

Net monthly income of Mr. Norman	$153.00
Net monthly income of Mrs. Norman	346.16
Total net monthly income of both	499.16
Less allowance for Mr. Norman	– 34.00
	465.16
Less allowance for Mrs. Norman	– 140.00
	325.16
Less allowance for unmet needs of Thomas ($65.00-47.90)	– 17.10
Equals "Medicaid Income" to be paid by Normans to nursing home	$308.60

The state's allowance of $140.00 for Mrs. Norman's living expenses is a uniform amount which does not vary.

As these figures suggest, $189.06 of Mrs. Norman's income is deemed available to Mr. Norman to be used in paying his nursing home medical expenses. . . .

My purpose in providing such detail of these sad chronicles is not to bias consideration of the wisdom of relative responsibility provisions, but simply to emphasize that the policy calculus must include an estimate of the administrative cost of creating as well as enforcing relative responsibility.

II

It seems clear to me that a rational public policy decision as to the wisdom of enacting or maintaining legislation requiring adult children to support their aged parents requires careful weighing of a number of broad considerations. Those considerations are quite different from each other and are difficult to quantify or to compare. I will address each of the relevant considerations in a summary fashion.

The "Moral" Issue

No relative responsibility program would last without some community consensus as to its fairness. The ancient lineage of relative responsibility laws suggests that there is a consensus that adult children should support their aged parents. Thus, commentators have spoken" of 'strengthening family bonds,' the 'obvious fairness' of such a requirement, or the 'moral responsibility' involved" in defending filial support programs.[47] Judges often appear convinced that such provisions are just:

> It seems eminently clear that the selection of the adult children is rational on the ground that the parents, who are now in need, supported and cared for their children during their minority and that such children should in turn now support heir parents to the extent to which they are capable. Since these children received special benefits from the class of "parents in need," it is entirely rational that the children bear a special burden with respect to that class.[48]

> But in recent years social welfare theorists, as well as moral philosophers and legal commentators, have claimed that the consensus is changing. The 1961 White House Conference on Aging (whose conferees did not necessarily represent a spectrum of interest and attitudes on such issues) concluded that laws and practices which enforce or assume support from adult children, and in many places with little or no regard for the needs and responsibilities of adult children and their young, weaken family relationships and family responsibility, and are destructive to older persons and the families of their adult children. Such requirements should be removed from State laws and practice.[49]

Most arguments against filial support laws begin with a description of demographic changes which are thought to drive ethical values: the number of aged persons in the population is growing rapidly and aged people are living ever longer; the imposition on their children of a support obligation, therefore, has become and will continue to be a more onerous burden than it was in the past:

> filial obligations were far less likely to be called upon at the turn of the century, they were likely to be burdensome over a much shorter period of time, and they were more likely to be shared by a greater number of children per aged parent.[50]

Moreover, there is respectable opinion arguing against relative responsibility because it impacts most harshly on the poor and helps to insure that dependence will pass from generation to generation:

> [A]lmost all observers agree that the social effects of the challenged relative responsibility provisions are harsh and self-defeating. "[A] large body of social work opinion [has long maintained] that liability of relatives creates

and increases family dissension and controversy, weakens and destroys
family ties at the very time and in the very circumstances when they are most
needed, imposes an undue burden upon the poor. . . and is therefore socially
undesirable, financially unproductive, and administratively unfeasible.". . . .
As Justice Friedman, writing for the Court of Appeal in the instant case,
observed, "[The challenged provisions] strike most aggressively and harshly
at adult children occupying the lower end of the income scale. the enforced
shift of subsistence funds from one generation to the other distributes
economic desolation between the generations. It injects guilt and shame into
elderly citizens who have made their contributions to society and have
become dependent through life's vicissitudes.[51]

And the widespread rejection, in the literature if not the cases, of the policy
underpinnings of the Boren-Long amendment suggest a stirring of the intellectuals to support nonreimbursable government welfare expenditures.[52]
Moreover, in recent decades there has been some retreat from adult child-
relative responsibility provisions.[53] Yet no matter how exquisitely the
philosophers analyze the issues, the "moral" consideration may best be captured by the emotional expressions of those parents who object to impositions
on their children. Consider the arguments of Jennie Baxter, a 75 year old
Californian receiving old age welfare benefits who opposed the subsequently
abolished California relative responsibility program:

No one is born into this world with a debt to their parents for their birth and
contributions until their maturity. That is the parent's contribution to life and
society. When the child reaches maturity, he starts a new separate unit and in
turn makes his contribution to life and society as did his parents, carrying on
the generation cycle through eternity. The children should not be saddled
with unjust demands that keep them at or near the poverty level with no hope
to escape it, just because a parent still breathes. And aged parents should not
have to live their remaining lives facing the heartbreaking experience of being
such a burden to their children. Many would prefer death but are afraid of
retribution for taking their own lives. Their grief — a living death.[54]

But if the moral consensus is changing, what explains the subtle shift toward
more relative responsibility provisions, a trend recognized even by opponents
of such programs?[55] And there can be no doubt as to the powerful support for
new initiatives compelling parents to support their children.[56] Wisconsin even
passed a statute requiring support of a dependent child by the child's grandparents if the parent of the child is also dependent.[57] It is doubtful that the moral
consensus in the United States favoring support of parents by their adult
children has disappeared.

The Administrative Issues

A fair assessment of "relative responsibility" cannot be accomplished without evaluating the administrative problems such a program would entail. A homely example should suffice to illustrate the point. If it costs more to identify, find and "prosecute" responsible relatives than could be collected from them, establishing or retaining such a program would undermine the tax saving purposes it supposedly serves. Some people would urge that the program be retained in any event because it asserts and reinforces a moral norm. But legislatures which have eschewed all concern with efficiency in the pursuit of morality have often found their policy efforts defeated.[58]

To devise the complex reimbursement formulas many states have adopted[59] requires personnel time and money; finding "responsible relatives" and obtaining money from them requires even more. And if the responsibility provisions contain discretionary exceptions, such as those for abandoned or maltreated children described earlier,[60] the costs of administration and enforcement will inevitably be even higher. There is no need to reemphasize the administrative difficulties and costs produced by the very complexity of the statutes and their policies. On the other side of the ledger, very little is known, nationally or for any state, as to the real return which might be realized from a fully enforced relative responsibility provision. One study in California, more than thirty years ago, discovered that although county officials believed by more than two to one that the programs cost more to administer than they produce in revenue, at least one county director who gave figures reported almost $6 collected for every dollar spent.[61] More recently, Baldus reported that in 1969 reimbursement provisions returned approximately .7 of one percent of welfare transfers in that year. National gross savings, including savings from deterred applications, were estimated to be between $80 and $90 million and the administrative cost of collection was approximately thirty percent.[62]

Even if more complete national or state collection figures were available, the cost-benefit ratio question might not be answerable because of the tradition of discretionary administration of relative responsibility. No one seems to doubt that local welfare officials as well as prosecutors in fact fail to insist on support in some cases. One study concluded:

> Despite a great deal of talk about "making responsible relatives live up to the law," [relatively few counties bring suit]. Boards of supervisors are generally willing, after the registered form letter has failed to produce results, to have the county attorney write an official warning threatening a suit, but, all being elective officials, neither he nor the supervisors have any stomach for forcing people to support their aged relatives against their will. As politicians, they figure — and no doubt correctly — that they would lose more votes than they would gain through such proceedings. In the last analysis it would seem that the vigor and, to some degree, the success with which this provision is administered depend heavily on the attitude of the board of supervisors. . . .[63]

The same study reported that some prosecutors refused to seek funds from those adult children who claimed that their parents had not provided them support as children, despite the absence in the statute of an "abandonment" or "nonsupport" exception. Moreover,

> One director told of a professional man whose income was [at the top of the payment scale matrix]. But he is reported to have told the district attorney that if he made him pay he would force [the prosecutor] to press charges against all the others who had been notified of obligations but had not paid. The district attorney could not face the prospect of making so many political enemies, so nothing more was done. . . . [64]

No proper cost-benefit analysis can be undertaken if we simply do not know the amounts which should be placed on either side of the equation.

But discretionary administration is not conceived by welfare administrators as an evil to be eliminated or at least controlled. Rather, social welfare theorists see much discretion as a virtue. Public welfare programs are seen as social service "providing preventive, rehabilitative and family strengthening services (and not merely a 'dole')" through the services of professional social workers who view relative responsibility not in "a narrow economic sense" but "in its broadest social and psychological context."[65] The most recent policy study recommended clear and fair rules which leave a discretionary "residue of manageable size." The exercise of discretion presupposes, the study claimed, deployment of an adequate number of "professionally qualified and experienced social workers" supervised by "adequate and professionally qualified supervisory personnel in key welfare center positions."[66] The scope of discretion and reasons for providing for it were described with specificity:

> [The view that the public welfare program is a social service agency] introduces considerations which cannot be measured in dollars and cents, may never be expressed in such terms and, in fact, may have to be ignored insofar as the legally responsible relative is concerned. . . .
>
> Likewise, the gift of the adult to his aged parents, expressed by regular visiting and interchange, a continuing affectionate contact, the meeting of extra needs not regularly included in the Department of Welfare budget, has a meaning far greater to the maintenance of strong family ties and a sense of responsibility of family members for each other than the insistence by the Department, under the law, for a specific amount of support.
>
> Enforcement may easily result in lessening rather than strengthening significant family relationships.
>
> On the other hand a professional evaluation of family relationships may lead to the conclusion that a non-supporting relative, financially able to contribute, should be helped to see the psychological meaning and value to the economically dependent relative and to himself that a financial commitment would symbolize. . . .
>
> The use of discretion, therefore, would make it possible for the professional worker to move either way, to recommend waiver of the support requirement or to help the relative see the social and psychological values that in some instances money payments can represent.

The exercise of professional discretion, as it pertains to familial responsibility, is a subtle, complex matter, This is so because it requires placing in the fore and not the background the social and psychological considerations which need to be evaluated by a professional social worker. Yet it is the proper estimate and balance of all these factors which determine whether family life is strengthened or weakened by legal insistence upon support.

The freedom to use professional discretion, properly exercised, could well result in a major advance in reducing the cycle of dependency because the emphasis would be placed on social, not merely economic, values. If family ties are being or have been continuously and badly weakened over a long period of time, moral obligations tend to fade into non-existence. Even a sincere attempt at legal enforcement is then not only economically costly and socially destructive but often becomes a mockery and a farce. But. . . when money can be used to restore poor relationships to healthy ones or to maintain good ones, the professional worker with discretionary powers can use social work skills to help the responsible relative understand and achieve this.

When responsibility for economic support is not voluntary and resort to the law seems necessary, it suggests the possibility that some breakdown in family relationships has already taken place or that superior value is placed by the responsible relatives, and often by the applicant for assistance himself, on the long-term inspirations and goals of the responsible relative for his own family. Therefore, such cases require the judgment of qualified social workers in public welfare programs.[67]

No more persuasive paean to professional discretion could be devised. But such commendation ignores the extent to which professional discretion built into public programs — in the schools, in juvenile courts, in mental institutions, in prisons, has both failed and either delayed or obstructed desperately needed social reform. The movement toward "determinate sentencing" is the most notorious, but by no means the only, contemporaneous effort to escape the tyranny of professional discretion.[68] Because of "the lower status professionals accord to public agency employment (impeding the employment of highly qualified professionals) and the civil service protection afforded public employees (impeding elimination of professionals who perform poorly) ,"[69] there is no reason to believe that discretion will be exercised any more wisely in public welfare-relative responsibility administration than it has been in other fields where administrators have some power to coerce clients. In fact, anecdotal evidence, some of it reported above,[70] suggests that in this field of endeavor, as in others, studies of official discretion will turn up a significant number of abuses. Indeed, the federal government itself has turned away from professional social worker management of public welfare caseloads.[71] (On the other hand, if efforts to achieve uniformity are of the kind indicated in the *Manfredi* and *Norman* cases,[72] where collections are placed at a level which can be attained only at great personal expense for many families and with a substantial inducement to relative evasion, evasion through administrative discretion may be both inevitable and healthy).

Of Deterrence and Individual Dignity

The progression of federal policy — from Medicaid's 1965 prohibition of relative responsibility[73] to the 1980 Boren-Long amendment's authorization of state plans containing "transfer of assets" punishments,[74] to the permission given in the 1982 Tax, Equity and Fiscal Responsibility Act for state plan provisions imposing eligibility sanctions for pre-application transfers of family homes[75] — suggests an unpleasant possibility. It may well be that as the expense of welfare programs increases, legislators (and perhaps the public as well) will demand greater financial accountability from recipients and a wider net for catching alternative resources — simply to save money. No doubt responses to current fiscal exigencies play a role in such developments; and it is also likely that these changes have something of a tidal quality.[76] But at bottom a social norm may be lurking: government subsidy of the poor cannot be too large nor too generous — and relative responsibility enforcement is seen as a way of avoiding both evils.[77]

It certainly seems clear that relative responsibility provisions have not been designed (and may not be operated) exclusively to raise money. Rather, they operate at least in part to deter increasing welfare roles. Some of the cases[78] and many of the commentators[79] recognize the matter explicitly. But little is known empirically about the deterrent efficacy of relative responsibility. The usual illustration, the experience in Maine during 1948, is not altogether clear. When the State revived its relative responsibility law by requiring all children of assistance recipients to submit detailed financial data, more than 2,000 cases were closed.[80] Detractors of relative responsibility point out that 40 percent of these closings were due to a failure by children to submit financial statements.[81] In one sense, of course, this deterrent success is exactly what we want to accomplish: the costs of relative responsibility enforcement are minimized and the largest possible tax saving has been accomplished because no welfare payment at all, rather than a welfare payment reduced by the relative's reimbursement, is paid. But neither defenders nor detractors of relative responsibility can claim victory here. We do not know what group of applicants, otherwise eligible, has been deterred from applying for benefits. If poor aged parents whose children are also poor but proud have not applied, we have saved tax dollars but only at what many would consider too substantial a cost to the aged poor *and* their poor adult children. But suppose the relative responsibility program has instead deterred from applying those poor aged parents whose adult children can afford to support them but are unwilling to do so because of the availability of an alternative source of support, government welfare benefits? In the second case, our deterrent policy has singled out just the group whose behavior we wanted to affect. In the absence of much more reliable information than we have had in the past, is it safe to make any assumptions about targeted groups? The most realistic assumption is that some of both groups will be affected. And yet, considering the size of welfare benefits in most states, even today,[82] and relying (in a different fashion, for this purpose) on the belief that there is a national consensus that adult children should support their aged and dependent parents, doesn't it seem likely that a deterrent policy might affect a larger portion of "false positives," of parents of poor but proud children, rather than parents of wealthy but crass children?[83]

The deterrence rationale justifies intrusive investigations by welfare personnel of all families in order to deny or diminish subsistence funds to that small proportion of the welfare applicant and recipient population who are getting a "free ride" — that is, those who are living on government largesse when they could be living on the largesse of their children. Phrasing the matter in this fashion makes it difficult to ignore the unresolved issues of welfare applicant and recipient dignity: to prevent "cheating" by a few we are imposing on all the indignity of an investigation of their children's resources. (Investigation of the resources of relatives may not occur until after the applicant has been declared eligible — but that administrative refinement postpones but does not change the essential nature of the indignity.) Can such intrusive governmental forays be justified? They are certainly a familiar aspect of the American tradition.[84] This tradition has had vocal opponents — and their voices have been heard: the "categorical assistances" were combined into "SSI," a substantially less fully investigated, less socially stigmatized, program;[85] eligibility investigations have become the responsibility of payment analysts, instructed to take the word of applicants, rather than social workers trained to investigate fully and given a writ which runs to every aspect of a recipient's life;[86] critics of past and present welfare administration are beginning to formulate proposals for structural change which offer some hope that a truly humanitarian welfare system may eventually evolve.[87]

Despite some changes in the system, in the United States "welfare" has never been seen as an "insurance" program; unlike "Social Security," welfare recipients, "on the dole," are seen as less deserving because they have not earned the stipend.[88] The "needs" test, then, and the relative responsibility notion it engenders, serve multiple functions: by discouraging applications and demeaning even "qualified" applicants and their families, the policy saves welfare expenditures even as it reinforces the norm about welfare recipients.[89] We have exhibited a stubborn commitment to distinguishing "earned" from "unearned" old age benefits — even if a very large group of recipients of "earned" benefits have not in fact earned them and the rest have been fooled into believing that their premium payments are used only to pay for their own future benefits.[90] But it is wise to try to diminish the psychological gap between earned and unearned benefits? The "insurance myth" may provide vital underpinning for continuing public support for the taxes which pay for "Social Security." It is also essential to insist upon relative responsibility, as on other aspects of "needs"-related welfare administration, as a continuing symbol of and as a way of perpetuating the "undeservingness" of those who are "on the dole"? Such questions cannot be avoided, in the end, if relative responsibility issues are to be laid to rest once and for all.

III

American society has changed in a variety of ways since the 1960s and 1970s when egalitarian sentiments were politically popular and legal advocacy for the poor (in the courts and the legislatures) was helping to decrease "the great arbitrariness and chaos of the welfare mess."[91] Support for welfare liberality has declined, even among liberals, as concern for the budget deficit has grown. It is clear, of course, that we will not have to worry about relative responsibility when our society's wealth has been spread among the population sufficiently so that all adult children have sufficient resources to support their parents as well as their own spouses and children — *and* if at that time all adult children recognize the moral obligation to support parents which is thought to be the societal consensus. Perhaps by then (simultaneously, perhaps?) the poor but "undeserving" aged will all have been incorporated into the supposed insurance scheme of OASDHI, completing the great expansion of coverage accomplished two decades ago[92] — and because insurance recipients' children need not repay their parents' monthly stipends, we won't have to debate the nature of the moral consensus. But, sad to say, *those* millennia appear to be more than twelve years away at this writing. Until then, we will continue to struggle — with our aged poor and with our societal and personal ambivalence about their children's responsibility.

Appendix

42 U.S.C. §. 1396p:

(c) Denial of medical assistance; period of eligibility; exceptions

(1) Notwithstanding any other provision of this subchapter, an individual who would otherwise be eligible for medical assistance under the State plan approved under this subchapter may be denied such assistance if such individual would not be eligible for such medical assistance but for the fact that he disposed of resources for less than fair market value. If the State plan provides for the denial of such assistance by reason of such disposal or resources, the State plan shall specify a procedure for implementing such denial which, except as provided in paragraph (2), is not more restrictive than the procedure specified in section 1382b (c) of this title, and which may provide for a waiver of denial of such assistance in any instance where the State determines that such denial would work an undue hardship.

(2) (A) In any case where the compensated value of disposed of resources exceeds $12,000, the State plan may provide for a period of ineligibility which exceeds 24 months. If a State plan provides for a period of ineligibility exceeding 24 months, such plan shall provide for the period of ineligibility to bear a reasonable relationship to such uncompensated value.

(B) (i) In the case of any individual who is an inpatient in a skilled nursing facility, intermediate care facility, or other medical institution, if such individual is required, as a condition of receiving services in such institution under the State plan, to spend for costs of medical care all but a minimal amount of his income required for personal needs, and, who, at any time during or after the 24-month period immediately prior to application for medical assistance under the State plan, disposed of a home for less than fair market value, the State plan (subject to clause (iii)) may provide for a period of ineligibility for medical assistance in accordance with clause (ii).

(ii) If the State plan provides for a period of ineligibility under clause (i), such plan —

(I) shall provide that such individual shall be ineligible for all medical assistance for a period of 24 months after the date on which he disposed of such home, except that, in the case where the uncompensated value of the home is less than the average amount payable under the State plan as medical assistance for 24 months of care in a skilled nursing facility, the period of ineligibility shall be such shorter time as bears a reasonable relationship (based upon the average amount payable under the State plan as medical assistance for care in a skilled nursing facility) to the uncompensated value of the home, and

(II) may provide (at the option of the State) that, in the case where the uncompensated value of the home is more than the average amount payable under the State plan as medical assistance for 24 months or care in a skilled nursing facility, such individual shall be ineligible for all medical assistance for a period in excess of 24 months after the date on which he disposed of such home which bears a reasonable relationship (based upon the average amount payable under the state plan as medical assistance for care in a skilled nursing facility) to the uncompensated value of the home.

      (iii) An individual shall not be ineligiblic for medical assistance by reason of clause (ii) i f:

      (I)   a satisfactory showing is made to the State (inaccordance with any regulations promulgated by the Secretary) that the individual can reasonably be expected to be discharged from the medical institution and to return to that home,

      (II)   title to such home was transferred to the individual's spouse or child who is under age 21, or (with respect to States eligible to participate in the State program established under subchapter XVI of this chapter) is blind or permanently and totally disabled, or (with respect to States which are not eligible to participate in such program) is blind or disabled as defined in section 1382c of this title,

      (III) a satisfactory showing is made to the State (in accordance with any regulations promulgated by the Secretary) that the individual intended to dispose of the home either at fair market value, or for other valuable consideration, or

      (IV) the State determines that denial of eligibility would work an undue hardship.

  (3) In any case where an individual is ineligible for medical assistance under the State plan solely because of the applicability to such individual of the provisions of section 1382b (c) of this title, the State plan may provide for the eligibility of such individual for medical assistance under the plan if such individual would be so eligible if the State plan requirements with respect to disposal of resources applicable under paragraphs (1) and (2) of this subsection were applied in lieu of the provisions of section 1382b (c) of this title.

Notes

1. For a general discussion, see tenBroek, California's Dual System of Family Law: it's Origin, Development and Present Status, 16 *Stan. L. Rev.* 257 (1964) .
2. Lopes, Filial Support and Family Solidarity, 6 *Pac. L.J.* 511 (1975).
3. See 42 U.S.C. §301 (1935).
4. The program was amended to include medical and hospital benefits ("Medicare") in 1965. See Pub. Law 89-97 (July 30, 1965) , codified in 42 U.S.C. §1395, 1396 (1982).
5. The OASDHI program does not provide actuarially based insurance benefits based on invested premiums, of course, because younger workers (and in the medical provisions, government funds) subvent payments to retired workers and their survivors. Perhaps the description indicated that distinguishing "insurance" from the "categorical" "welfare" programs which provide subsistence to the poor

provides an important but symbolic support for public acceptance for an additional tax on workers. See note 91 infra and accompanying text.

6. See generally Riesenfeld, The Formative Era of American Public Assistance Law, 43 *Calif. L. Rev.* 175(1955): tenBroek, supra note 1; Lopes, supra note 2.

7. See, *e.g.*, *Pickett v. Pickett*, 251 N.E.2d 684 (Ind. App. 1969) (civil suit by divorced mother against son for support after death of former husband; son had received $238,000 from father's estate plus a house which he transferred to his mother-in-law; mother brought suit for support after being evicted from the house transferred to mother-in-law; support award affirmed).

8. 2 Ohio App.2d 174, 207 N.E.2d 387 (1965).

9. For a similar holding under the same statute, see *Beutel v. State*, 36 Ohio App. 73, 172 N.E. 838 (1930).

10. For some of the difficulties with any kind of enforcement of support against fathers in the United States, see Chambers, *Making Fathers Pay* (1979).

11. Given impetus by a recent federal statute, parental support of children has become a favored policy in the United States; and a variety of direct enforcement techniques have been adopted and are being used with greater frequency. See generally United States Senate Finance Committee, Report No. 98-387, to Accompany H.R. 4325, Child Support Enforcement Amendments of 1984, 98 Stat. 1305 (April 9, 1984).

12. The Social Security Act required "state plans" to "take into consideration any other income and resources" of an applicant for public assistance. See generally Levy, Lewis and Martin, *Social Welfare and the Individual* 68-85 (1971) . See also notes 14-29 infra and accompanying text.

13. The most complex issues require courts to determine the extent to which state-created private law doctrines determine rights and responsibilities under welfare programs created by the federal government. The issues are similar to those which commonly arose under the Internal Revenue Code before the United States Congress began to provide specific federal definitions of common property concepts Similar problems are sometimes created in the "insurance" provisions of the Social Security Act. See, e.g., *Capitano v. Secretary of Health and Human Services*, 732 F.2d 1066 (2d Cir. 1984).

14. *Dep't of Social Services v. Barbara M.*, 474 N.Y.S.2d 195 (Fam. Ct. 1984) ; *Lee v. State Dep't of Pub. Health & Welfare*, 480 S.W.F.2d 305, 309 (1972); *Matter of Welfare of C.S.H.* 408 N.W.2d 225, 227 (1987); *DeJesus v. Perales*, 770 2d 316 (1985).

15. E.g., *Haight v. Kandiyohi County Welfare Board*, 291 Minn. 538, 191, N.W.2d 559, (1971); *Downer v. Dep't of Human Resources*, 705 P.2d 144 (1985).

16. See 42 U.S.C. §1396p (1982). The Appendix contains copy of subsection (c) of the amendment as quoted in *Lewis v. Hegstron*, 767 F.2d 1371, 1374 n.2 (9th Cir. 1985) (Oregon's administrative rule defining a period of ineligibility for benefits for Medicaid applicants who have transferred their homes for less than fair market value within two years of application does not conflict with Social Security Act's federal standards). See also note 43 infra and accompanying text.

17. *Schweiker v. Gray Panthers*, 453 U.S. 34 (1981); *Randall v. Lukhard*, 709 F.2d 257 (4th Cir. 1983) ; *Synesael v. Ling*, 691 F.2d 1213 (7th Cir. 1982); *Fabula v. Buck*, 598 F.2d 869 (4th Cir. 1979). See also Note, The Asset Transfer Dilemma: Disposal of Resources and Qualification for Medicaid Assistance, 36 *Drake L. Rev.* 369 (1986-87); Note, To Deem or Not to Deem: Evaluating and Attributing Available Spousal Income to an Institutionalized Medicaid Applicant, 67 *Va. L. Rev.* 767 (1981).

18. See note 22 infra.
19. Levy, Lewis & Martin, *Social Welfare and the Individual* 129 (1971); *Estate of Hinds v. State.* 390 N.E.2d 172, (1979). For an impressive empirical study and brilliant examination of reimbursement policies, as well as an analysis of the problems which parallels the approach adopted in this paper, see Baldus, Welfare as a Loan: An Empirical Study of the Recovery of Public Assistance Payments in the United States, 25 *Stan. L. Rev.* 127 (1973).
20. See *State Board of Social Welfare v. Teeters,* 258 Iowa 1113, 141 N.W.2d 581 (1966); *Thomas v. State,* 241 Iowa 1072, 44 N.W.2d 410 (1950); *Goff v. Yauman,* 237 Wis. 643, 298 N.W. 179 (1941) .
21. See *Application of Gau,* 230 Minn. 235, 41 N.W.2d 444 (1950).
22. 281 F. Supp. 853 (S.D.N.Y.), aff'd mem. 393 U.S. 323 (1969).
23. 42 U.S.C. §302 (a) (ll) (E) (1969).
24. See note 16 supra and the Appendix infra.
25. See also note 55 infra and accompanying text.
26. The statement is true so long as the enforcement effort does not cost more administratively than it returns in collections from absent fathers. For some indication that a cost-benefit analysis which includes non-monetary costs of enforcement is appropriate in determining issues of relative responsibility, see note 58 infra and accompanying text.
27. Bruch, Management Powers and Duties Under California's Community Property Laws: Recommendations for Reform, *34 Hastings L.J.* 229 (1982).
28. See note 14 supra and accompanying text.
29. See, e.g., Ill Rev. Stat. ch. 23 §3-1.2 (Smith-Hurd 1967), Iowa Stat. Ann. §249.6 (1969). Both statutes are cited in Levy, Lewis & Martin, op. cit. supra note 20, at 125. The Iowa statute has been repealed. See generally tenBroed, California's Dual System of Family Law;: It's Origin, Development and Present Status, 16 *Stan. L. Rev.* 257, 258 (1964).
30. See, e.g., *Los Angeles County v La Fuente,* 119 P.2d 772 (Cal. Ct. App. 1942) (daughter's offer to house her parents with her family no defense to suit by welfare department for contribution where statute authorized suit against "spouse or adult child pecuniarily able to support" aged person and purpose of Old Age Security Act was to leave considerable freedom of action to those receiving aid). But see *Nichols v. Social Security Commission,* 349 Mo. 1148, 164 S.W.2d 278 (1942) (applicant living with child denied eligibility because legislature had recently amended statute to make ineligible a person with income or resources sufficient to provide reasonable subsistence "whether such income or resources is received from some other person or persons"; Commission cautioned to investigate carefully financial ability of such children lest dutiful children be penalized while children who lack "pride of family and filial affection" profit from refusing to support their parents).
31. See Mandelker, Family Responsibility Under the American Poor Laws, 54 *Mich. L. Rev.* 497, 517-518 (1956). For some indication that exceptions similar to this one are not unique, see 45 C.F.R. §232.12 (b) (2) (1979) (Social Security Act's requirement that mother "cooperate" with law enforcement authorities to establish father's paternity is subject to a "good cause" exception where establishing the child's paternity would result in the likelihood of physical harm to the mother or to her child, where the baby was conceived as a consequence of forcible rape or incest, or where the mother is considering placing the child for permanent adoption). See also *Case County Welfare Department v. Wittner.* 309 N.w.2d 320 (Minn. 1981)

(county welfare boards have right to appeal state public welfare department's decision that mother need not identify alleged father) .

32. 43 Misc.2d 211, 250 N.Y.S.2d 615 (Family Ct. 1964).

33. The statute, N.Y. Fam. Ct. Act §415, read: "In its discretion, the court may require any such person [an adult child] to contribute. . ." for an instance of the creation of an abandonment exception by California administrators, see Bond, Baber, *Our Needy Aged* 319 (1954): One county director reported that district attorney refused to prosecute children who claimed that the parent-recipient would not support them as children — although the California statute contains no 'abandonment' exception."

34. 528 P.2d 1371 (Ore. App. 1974)

35. Id. at 1372.

36. For a sample of the kinds of unpleasant factual squabbles about ancient family history to which such defenses can lead, see, e.g., *Cheathan v. Juras,* 501 P.2d 988 (Ore. App. 1972) (son liable for mother's nursing home care despite fact that she had placed him and his belongings in the street and placed younger brother for adoption because mother's medical record indicated she was mentally ill and not responsible for her actions due to a case of progressive Multiple Sclerosis) ; *Drugg v. Juras,* 501 P.2d 1313, 1315 (Ore. app. 1971) (relative responsibility proceeding reversed for findings of fact as to whether parents had been responsible for son's dependency as a child, a defense to liability; son was oldest of six children and compelled to work and to give his earnings to drunken father; son left home and took full-time work at eleven years of age; younger sister corroborated son's testimony, reporting that "his father gambled away much of the family's meager income, the family was hungry much of the time, the [son] had inadequate patched clothing, and as a result of these thing he (as well as she) was the object of ridicule at school to the extent that he was ashamed and truant"); *Denny v. Public Welfare division,* 483 P.2d 463 (Ore. App. 1971) (son liable for welfare benefits to mother despite statutory exemption for child whose parent "without good cause, was responsible for the child's being 'dependent'"; although mother had laced defendant in foster homes only to enable her to try to earn a living) .

37. See Community Service Society of New York, *Familial Responsibility and Public Welfare: Issues and Recommendations* 15 (1964).

38. 170 Conn. 258, 365 A.2d 1118 (1976).

39. Id. at 1121, 365 A.2d at 1121.

40. Id. at 1124, 365 A.2d 1124. The Connecticut Supreme Court's sex discrimination — equal protection analysis might be explained in part by the Court's opposition to the very notion of a family responsibility scheme.

41. As to the problems of discretion, see the text following note 62 infra.

42. This matrix is reported in *Swoap v. Superior Court of Sacramento County,* lll Cal. Rptr. 136, 148, 516 P.2d 840, 854 (1973) . The statute read in part (id. at 139, 516 P.2d at 843 n.3): "For purposes of this chapter, income of an adult child is defined as the sum of the income constituting the separate property of the adult child, the income (excluding earnings) which is community property subject to the direction and control of the adult child, and the earnings of the adult child but not of his or her spouse. In computing net income, a flat 25-percent allowance shall be permitted for the cost of personal income taxes, disability insurance taxes and social security taxes, expenses necessary to produce the income, including the cost of transportation to and from work, meals eaten at work, and union dues, and the cost of tools,

equipment and uniforms. . . ."

43. Consider the remarks of Judge Friendly in *DeJesus v. Perales,* 770 F.2d 316, 321 (2d Cir. 1985) (upholding as consistent with the Social Security Act a New York regulation that requires an applicant to "spend down" his resources to qualify for Medicaid) : "This appeal requires the interpretation of a statute of unparalled complexity. . . . The Supreme Court has characterized the Social Security Act as 'among the most intricate ever drafted by congress' and has quoted our observation. . . that the Act is 'almost unintelligible to the uninitiated.'"

Appendix A contains the text of 42 U.S.C. §1396p (c) (1982), as quoted in *Lewis v. Hegstrom,* 767 F.2d 1371 (9th Cir. 1985), a case which held that Oregon's administrative rule defining a period of ineligibility for benefits for Medicaid applicants who have transferred their homes for less than fair market value within two years of application does not conflict with the Social Security Act.

44. 435 F. Supp. 1106 (D. conn. 1977) (regulation requiring interspousal income attribution in determining eligibility for Medicaid benefits violates Social Security Act).

45. It is not clear that a dissolution of marriage will always be allowed in cases of this type. *In re Bennington, Cause No. 576-260* (Super. Ct., Lake County, Ind. May 26, 1976), the court ordered further hearings on an attempted marriage dissolution by a couple faced with a state welfare regulation of the type promulgated in Connecticut, stating that "should [the state's] regulations be valued it is not clear that the parties should be permitted to circumvent [them] by going through a dissolution." Slip op. at 3. [court's footnote.]

46. 610 F.2d 1228, 1233-34 (5th Cir. 1980).

47. See Lopes, Filial Support and Family solidarity, 6 *Pac. L.J.* 508, 525 (1975), quoting other commentators. See also Community Service Society of New York, supra note 38; Bond, Baber, *Our Needy Aged 316 (1954).*

48. See *Swoap v. Superior Court of Sacramento county,* lll Cal. Rptr. 136, 147, 516 P.2d 840, 851 (1973) (majority opinion). The Court added in a footnote that the rational is supported by the inclusion of an "abandonment" exception. Ibid.

49. Report of the White House Conference on Aging, *The Nation and its Older People* 173 (1961). See also Community Service Society of New York, supra note 38, at 6, listing a variety of union, professional and political groups favoring the elimination of relative responsibility in the Medical Assistance to the Aged program.

50. Daniels, *Family Responsibility Initiatives and Justice Between Age Groups, Law Medicine and Health Care* 153, 154 (September, 1985). Professor Daniels, a philosopher, constructs a strong case against a moral obligation on the part of children.

51. *Swoap v. superior court of Sacramento county,* lll Cal. Rptr. 136, 160, 516 P.2d 840,864 (1973) (dissenting opinion) . See also Baldus, supra note 19.

52. See Daniels, supra note 50; Lopes, supra note 47; Note, Relative Responsibility Extended: Requirement of Adult Children to pay for Their Indigent Parents' Medical Needs, 21 *Fam. L.Q.* (1988) ; Patrick, Honor Thy Father and Mother: Paying the Medical Bills of Elderly Parents, 19 *U. Rich. L. Rev.* 69 (1984) ; Note, To Deem or Not to Deem: Evaluating and Attributing Available Spousal Income to an Institutionalized Medicaid Applicant, 67 *U. Va. L. Rev.* 767 (1981) ; Acofrod, Reducing Medicaid Expenditures Through Family Responsibility: Critique of a Recent Proposal, 5 *Am.J. Law & Med.* 59 (1979-80) ; Note, Pennsylvania's Family Responsibility Statute — Corruption of Blood and Denial of Equal Protection, 77

Dick. L. Rev. 331 (1972) ; Van Houtte and Breda, Maintenance of the Aged by Their Adult Children: The Family as a Residual Agency in the solution of Poverty in Belgium, 12 *Law & Soc, Rev.* 645 (1978) . But see Garrett, Filial Responsibility Laws, 18 *J. Family L.* 793 (1979) .

53. See Cal. Stats. 1975, c. 1136, p.2811, §1. See Calif. Welf. & Inst. Code §12350. Cf. Estate of Hinds, 390 N.E.2d 172 (Ind. App. 1979) (statute terminated support liability of adult children of parent for adult child institutionalized for a continuous period of more than twelve months) . Cf. Baldus, supra note 19, at 216: "After the enactment of the social Security Act in 1935, recovery was adopted in OAA and AB programs throughout the country. However, a repeal trend began in the South in the late 1930's and spread to the southwestern and Border States in the 1940s and 1950s."

54. See note 51 supra.

55. See Daniels, supra note 50, reporting new initiatives in three different states. See also the description of the Boren-Long amendment, notes 16-17 supra. See also Ackford, supra note 52, describing a Massachusetts Welfare Department initiative to impose responsibility on adult children with taxable incomes over $20,000 per year to contribute to the cost of nursing home care for their parents receiving Medicaid. Massachusetts had repealed its family responsibility law when the original Medicaid statute circumscribed the states' ability to collect from parents and children. See note 23 supra. The Department's proposal, which antedated Boren-Long, was submitted to the Department of Health, Education and Welfare pursuant to a Social Security Act provision allowing formal waivers of the federal requirements of the Act.

56. See note ll supra.

57. See Wis. Stat. Ann. §49.90 (1) (a) (2) (1985) .

58. See, e.g., Skolnick, *Justice Without Trial: Law Enforcement in Democratic Society* (1966) . But see the text following note 83 infra.

59. See the matrix once adopted in California, note 42 supra. Other states have similar schemes.

60. See notes 29-37 supra and accompanying text.

61. Bond, Baber, *Our Needy Aged* 201 (1954) . Yet the numbers were quite small, experience in one county may not be generalizable and there was no check on the accuracy of the figures reported. See also Community Service Society of New York, supra note 37, at 9, reporting that although a prior study of New York had found a similar 7 to 1 return ratio, collections from relatives had been lumped with recipient reimbursements and the cost figures had ignored expenditures required to establish existence of relatives and their ability to contribute. Chambers, op. cit. supra note 10, reported data that suggested that criminal enforcement of fathers who do not support their children may improve performance generally.

62. Baldus, supra note 19, at 133-36. Although reimbursement return for OAA, the welfare program for the aged, was considerably higher than for other programs, reimbursement amounts declined precipitously in states which did not employ post-death estate lines. Id. at 190. Since decedents' homes are easier to find than relatives, and lined estates are easier to collect money from than unwilling children, it seems likely that collections from relative responsibility laws would produce less return than would reimbursement laws. Baldus reports that federal cost analyses and welfare officials agree. Id. at 197 n.261. See also id. at 196-98 (crescribing how little is known about inreimbursement collection costs) .

63. Bond, Baber, supra note 61, at 201.
64. Id. at 319.
65. Community Service Society of New York, supra note 37, at 27.
66. Id. at 26.
67. Id. at 28-29.
68. See, e.g., Feld, Criminalizing Juvenile Justice: Rules of Procedure for the Juvenile Court, 69 *Minn. L. Rev.* 141 (1984) .
69. Levy, Custody Investigations in Divorce Cases, 1985 *Amer. Bar Found. Res. J.* 713, 719.
70. See notes 64 and 65 supra and accompanying text. Cf. Handler, Controlling Official Behavior in Welfare Administration, 54 *Calif. L. Rev.* 479, 493-95 (1966) (social worker discretion in determinations of which mothers were to work and what they had to do) . But see Handler, Discretion in Social Welfare: The Uneasy Position in the Rule of Law, 92 *Yale L.J.* 1270 (1983) (recommending a return to structured discretion) .
71. The former categorical assistance programs are now merged in the federally financed (although the states can supplement federal payments) and administered program known as "Supplementary Security Income" (or "SSI") . See Social Security Amendments of 1972, Pub. L. No. 92-603, §301. Even the AFDC program, still segregated because, it seems, its recipients are less worthy, is now administered mechanically rather than by professional clinicians.
72. See notes 44-46 supra and accompanying text.
73. See Conf. Rept. No. 682, July 26, 1965, to accompany H.R. 6675 (Social Security Amendments of 1965) , 105 Cong. & Admin. Code, 89th Cong., 1st Sess. 2147 (1965) .
74. See note 16 supra.
75. The later events in the story are told in *Lewis v. Hegstrom,* 767 F.2d 1371 (9th Cir. 1985) .
76. For a description of the legislative trends toward and away from repeal of lien and reimbursement provisions, see Baldus, supra note 19, at 176-77. Baldus also reports reimbursement legislation variations from region to region based upon political, economic and property value considerations. Id. at 135. Yet "trends" are fairly gross phenomena. One example should suffice. The years of the Reagan Administration have obviously not produced liberalizations of welfare. But see "Expanded Right to Medicaid Shatters the Link to Welfare," *N.Y. Times,* March 6, 1988, p. 1, col. 5 (describing expansions achieved in coverage during last eight years by provisions "hidden" in comprehensive budget reconciliation bills) .
77. That judges are subject to these tidal changes is indicated by the California courts' adventure with the Constitutional invalidation of relative responsibility provisions. The story is told in a majority opinion which backs away from the precipice, validating the adult child responsibility statute. See *Swoap v. Superior Court of Sacramento County,* note 48 supra.
78. See, e.g., *Lewis v. Hegstrom,* note 75 supra, at 1378: "We believe that in enacting section 1396p (c) (2) (B) , Congress sought to reduce budget outlays and to create a strong disincentive to the transfer of homes for less than fair market value. . . By pegging the period of ineligibility to the average amount the state actually pays for medical services to Medicaid recipients, government moneys are spread the furthest. A longer ineligibility period results through such a computation; a longer ineligibility period creates a stronger disincentive to the transfer of a home for less

than fair market value."
79. See e.g., Lopes, Filial Support and Family Solidarity, 6 *Pack L.J.* 508, 522 (1975) : "By far the most important cost saving aspect of filial support laws lies in their inhibitory effect on applications for public assistance." Baldus, supra note 20, at 155-56, found a statistically significant relationship between reimbursement and relative responsibility policies and the percentage of old age assistance recipients receiving support from one or more adult children. See also id. at 176-77 (significant negative relationship between home ownership and OAA explained by deterrent effect of reimbursement law) . The budgetary savings produced indirectly by the deterrent effect of reimbursement provisions is analyzed separately. Id. at 198.
80. See Stevens and Springer, Maine Revives Responsibility of Relatives, 6 *Pub. Welf.* 122 (1948) , reported in Lopes, supra note 79 at 527.
81. Id. at 527.
82. Consider the amounts at stake in the *Norman* and *Manfredi* cases, quoted in the text accompanying notes 44-46 supra.
83. In addition, Baldus, supra note 19, at 156-57, provides data strongly suggesting that adult children who support their "deterred" aged parents do not provide as much support as a welfare grant would. Cf. id. at 163 (following passage of Washington statute limiting estate reimbursement liability if heirs prove their inability to support welfare recipient during lifetime, reimbursement collections declined substantially) . Baldus' interrupted times series, regression analysis of relative responsibility laws led him to conclude that such laws have a "slight" deterrent effect. Id. at 201-02.
84. See *Wyman v. James,* 400 U.S. 309, 319 (1971) (welfare department caseworker does not need search warrant to insist upon home visit with AFDC recipient; "one who dispenses purely private charity naturally has an interest in and expects to know how his charitable funds are utilized and put to work. The public, when it is the provider, rightly expects the same.") See Burt, Forcing Protection on Children and Their Parents: The Impact of Wyman v. James, 69 *Mich. L. Rev.* 1259 (1971) .
85. See Liebman, The Definition of Disability in Social Security and Supplemental Security Income: Drawing the Bounds of Social Welfare Estates, 89 *Harv. L. Rev.* 833 (1976) . The AFDC program was not included in the merger. The decision was not surprising since AFDC recipients, no better off financially than those of other programs, were deemed less deserving. Id. at 865-66.
86. For a description of the routinization and bureaucratization of welfare, see Simon, Legality, Bureaucracy, and Class in the Welfare, System, 92 *Yale L. J.* 1198 (1983) . Handler, supra note 70, suggests that, on balance, such changes have not significantly improved the welfare system for poor people.
87. See, e.g., Handler, supra note 70, at 1280-86; Liebman, supra note 85, at 833.
88. See, e.g., Baldus, supra note 19, at 220-21, citing Segalman, The Protestant Ethic and Social Welfare, 24 *J. Social Issues,* Jan. 1968, at 125, 128: "The dominant influence over welfare policy in the North has been the Protestant or middle class ethic, which sees the improvidence, idleness, and immorality of poor persons as the cause of their poverty." See also Handler, supra note 70, at 1271-72; Liebman, supra note 86, at 864-67.
89. Although some welfare administrators claim that reimbursement schemes help welfare recipients overcome their sense of inadequacy, Baldus, supra note 19, at 161, the National Welfare Rights Organization, the leading American advocacy organization for welfare recipients during the 1960s, claimed that recovery adds to

the stigma of welfare: "Welfare keeps us in a humiliated state of deprivation. To demand repayment compounds the humiliation and is a scandal." Ibid. See also Liebman, supra note 86, at 866: "Indeed, an important determinant of Social Security policy has been a widely held belief that recipients' feelings of entitlement and legitimacy depend on exclusion of the undeserving." See also note 91 infra. See generally Law, Women, Work, Welfare, and the Preservation of Patriarchy, 131 *U. Pa. L. Rev.* 1249 (1983) .

90. See Cohen, The Development of the Social Security Act of 1935: Reflections Some Fifty Years Later, 68 *Minn. L. Rev.* 379 (1983) . The authors of the Social Security Act apparently began to use "insurance" and "contributions" language only after the Supreme Court upheld the Constitutionality of the Act. "The emphasis on 'insurance' and 'contributions' terminology created a sharp distinction in the public mind between 'welfare' and 'social security.' This distinction was maintained until 1965." Id. at 398. Of course, there were many, like Milton Friedman, who objected to the insurance terminology: "The very name — old age and survivors insurance — is a blatant attempt to mislead the public into identifying a compulsory tax and benefit system with private, voluntary, and individual purchase of individually assured benefits." Cohen and Friedman, *Social Security: Universal or Selective?* 27 (1972) .

91. Handler, supra note 70, at 1273. For some idea of the methods of legal advocacy and how successful they sometimes were, see Note, To Deem or Not to Deem: Evaluating and Attributing Available Spousal Income to an Institutionalized Medicaid Applicant, 67 *Va. L. Rev.* 767, 775 n.47 (1981) (listing all federal court cases brought to attack the validity of state Medicaid family responsibility provisions; twelve of thirteen suits successful prior to Supreme Court decision) . See also Simon, supra note 87, at 1199: "For better or worse (and I don't intend to argue it has been only for worse) the welfare system has been transformed in the past two decades. Lawyers and legal ideas have played a central role in this transformation."

92. See Old Age Survivors and Disability Insurance Amendments of 1965, P.L. 89-97, 79 Stat. 286, July 30, 1965, 42 U.S.C. §401 et seq. (1982) .

Chapter 19

Support Payments by Children to their Parents and Welfare Provisions in Poland

Wanda Stojanowska

Assistant Professor,
Instytut Prawa Sadowego,
Warsaw, Poland

Introduction

The purpose of the legal institution generally referred to as the maintenance obligation, is to secure a means of support for people who are unable to meet their justifiable needs from their own resources. The maintenance obligation is not so much designed to safeguard particular property rights as to secure support for people entitled to it by legal means. The maintenance duty which exists between close relatives provides a legal sanction for the moral obligation to assist those of our kin who cannot support themselves, and who are related to us by blood, adoption or affinity.

The maintenance obligation relieves the burden on public funds which, in its absence, would have to provide for people unable to maintain themselves.

The provisions relating to the maintenance obligation within the Polish legal system are to be found in the Family and Welfare Code which has been in force since 1 January 1965 (sections 128 — 144)[1].

The following discussion concerns the maintenance obligation of children toward their parents who are unable to support themselves, and the ways in which the parents can vindicate different claims before courts. In order to acquire a better understanding of the nature of this obligation, the issues will be discussed with reference to general maintenance provisions and other types of maintenance obligation.

The financial means of children under a maintenance obligation are not always sufficient to cover the full cost of supporting their parents. In such cases, the parents receive assistance from the State, in the form of supplementary benefits, if they are not entitled to disability or old-age pensions sufficient to provide them with support. Thus, it becomes necessary to relate these issues to the maintenance duty. The common thread that runs through these two classes of issues is the controversial problem within Polish law as to whether the provisions of the Polish Family and Welfare Code recognize the concept of the "unworthiness" of the parent eligible for maintenance, taking into account his past conduct, (such as a failure to provide maintenance for children), given the lack of clearly defined legal norms in this respect. The adoption of this concept would mean that the burden of supporting such parents would be shifted onto the State. Social security for people unable to support themselves because of old age or sickness is provided for by the section 70 of the Constitution of the Polish Peoples' Republic.

The problem of old peoples' welfare has received special attention, especially in non-legal publications. Better legal, organizational, and psychosocial solutions are sought for the elderly. However, the implementation of these new forms of care is hindered by many difficulties and obstacles, not necessarily merely financial. Large sums of money are expended on social care, but the organizational methods and functioning of the social care system remain inadequate. This is partially due to prevalent attitudes towards old people. It has been pointed out, for instance, that public attention has been focused on children's welfare, as exemplified by the adoption of the Declaration of Children's Rights by the U.N. in 1959, whilst the problems of old age go largely unnoticed. Consideration has even been given to passing an act in the form of a "Bill of Old Persons' Rights", which would safeguard their interests in the same way as certain other acts secure the interests of people working in professions requiring special protection.[2] Old people living with families are often exploited and overburdened with house-keeping duties; those living apart from their families fail to take proceedings to obtain the support due to them from their children, and consequently suffer hardship before being assisted by the State through social security services. Fortunately, this happens to only a small group of people.

There are almost alarmist references in the literature to the emergence of negative attitudes towards elderly people even within the closest family, with the situation being very tellingly described as "children first, old people last". Different social demographic groups, it is said, have been affected by the social-economic crisis to a different degree, with the old generation being the worst hit.[3] There is a dearth of representative scientific studies on the functioning of provisions which govern the maintenance obligation between children and their parents. The only source of empirical data is the unpublished analysis of 477 court cases in which a valid judgment was passed in the first half of 1980. This analysis was conducted by the Family and Minors Department of the Justice Ministry.[4] Some knowledge about the functioning of the maintenance obligation in court practice is provided from a survey carried out by the author for this publication. The survey was based on 75 court cases related to this problem.[5]

Although the number of cases was relatively small and does not constitute a representative sample, in view of the overall small number of maintenance claims made by parents against children in any given year in Poland (in 1986 out of 121,235 maintenance claims there were only 1549 such cases), they may be regarded as providing some grounds for generalizations about and insight into the issue.

The maintenance obligation and the maintenance fund in Poland — basic facts

The duty of maintenance is provided for in the Constitution. Section 79 of the third statute proclaims: "The Polish Peoples' Republic safeguards the implementation of maintenance rights and duties." This implementation is carried out not only in accordance with the provisions of the Family and Welfare Code, but also through penal law which provides legal sanctions in cases of avoidance of the maintenance duty.[6]

The provisions of the Family and Welfare Code specify clearly the order in which the maintenance obligation arises with regard to different categories of persons under the duty. The obligation of one party to marriage to provide the means of support to his partner after the marriage is dissolved or annulled takes precedence over the obligations of that person's relatives (art. 60, 61, 21, 130 of the Family and Welfare Code). With regard to the maintenance obligation of relatives, priority is given to that of descendants (children, grandchildren) in relation to that of ascendants (parents, grandparents); second in order is the obligation of ascendants to descendants, and lastly, that which exists between siblings. This legislative solution with regard to linear relatives is based on the assumption that the discharge of the maintenance duty is likely to be easier for the children of the person entitled than for their parents, who most often would be of very advanced age and consequently incapable of earning wages. Persons related to the entitled person in the same line (e.g. several children) are bound to pay maintenance in the same order, contributing in proportion to their income from earnings and capital.

Insofar as the maintenance obligation of children towards parents is concerned, the order mentioned above is in practice of no particular significance, taken in relation to the obligation of one divorced spouse towards the other. This is shown by our own studies. The financial obligation of divorced spouses are very limited. Hence maintenance from one parent in favor of the other does not suffice to meet the justifiable needs of the entitled party, and by the same token, does not eliminate the necessity of claiming maintenance from the children.

One of the most important problems of the maintenance obligation concerns the prerequisites for its existence. The prerequisites are governed by different rules, according to the persons between whom the obligation exists. Basically, the existence of the maintenance obligation depends on two factors; the needs of the person entitled and means of the person obliged. The first is formulated differently depending on whether it concerns the maintenance duty of parents towards children, or the duty towards other relatives. Parents are under an obligation to maintain their child, that is to provide for its upkeep and upbringing, if it is unable to meet the costs out of its own resources. In the case of all other maintenance obligations, including the obligation of children towards parents, the prerequisite is that the entitled person should be in distress. The term "distress" is not easy to define. It is assumed that a person is said to be in distress if that person is unable to obtain unaided (that is, either as income from earnings or investments) sufficient means to cover his justifiable and necessary needs. It is equally difficult to define justifiable and necessary needs. These needs are determined within the context of the specific circumstances of the person entitled, such as his age, his health and place of residence. One of the characteristic features of the maintenance obligation as legislated in the legal systems of socialist countries, is the rule that in the case of a conflict of interests between the person under the obligation and the one who is entitled, preference is given to the interests of the entitled person.[7]

The second prerequisite for the existence of the maintenance obligation between linear relatives is that the debtor must have some, if only limited, capital or wage earning capacity, that is, some financial means enabling him to meet, at least partially, the justifiable needs of the entitled person.

One of the methods by which section 79 of the third statute of the Constitution is implemented is through the maintenance fund set up by the Act of 18th July, 1974[8], the object of which is to provide better care for children and other people who suffer hardship because orders for the maintenance due to them cannot be enforced. This category of people includes, among others, parents who have been awarded maintenance by courts from their children. The payments from the maintenance fund are made by the Social Security Office. Periodic studies conducted by that office reveal that over the last ten years there has been a steady decrease in the number of parents[9] who claim payments from the fund on account of maintenance legally ordered from their children. This may be due to the fact that the numbers of such proceedings before courts decrease every year.

The setting up of the fund has increased the responsibility of family members with regard to the fulfillment of their maintenance duties, since the State, in making payments from the funds, has assumed the enforcement of maintenance due from persons under the obligation. In this way, the enforcement of the maintenance obligation has ceased to be a private matter between the parties. It is especially important for parents, who, because of old age and certain psychological inhibitions, find it difficult to exact their dues from their children. It is also important for them that there is a statutory right to draw financial provision from the maintenance fund after the death of the person under the obligation, before a permanent social security allowance can be arranged.

The problem of the "unworthiness" of the claimant

It appears from both the studies conducted in 1980 and from our own survey that it is not uncommon for children to explain their unwillingness to provide for their parents on their own accord, by reference to instances of their parents' past dishonourable behaviour towards them. For instance, in one of the cases from our survey, the following testimony given by the claimant's son was recorded in court minutes: "I am a son of an unmarried mother. It was never established who my father was. My mother put me into a community home and never took an interest in me. She was an alcoholic and lived with different men. She has not earned the right to any kind of pension because she was fired from every job she had. I do not feel I have an obligation to provide her with maintenance." In the end, the son made an agreement in court with his mother to pay her a small amount of money. The mother, convinced by her son's arguments, agreed to a reduction in the amount claimed. The son was instructed by the court that there is no provision in Polish law exempting children from maintenance obligation towards parents who had in the past behaved dishonourably towards them. This induced the son to make the agreement.

In fact, there is no clear provision in Polish law to the effect that "unworthiness" is a ground for losing the right to maintenance. The Supreme Court has not applied to such situations the fifth statute of the civil code, which introduces the concept of "community life" as the basis for ascertaining whether the claimant has or has not abused his legal rights. The concept of abuse of the law can be applied to the realization of almost all individual rights, including legal relations within the family. But as far as the maintenance obligation is concerned, the prevalent view is that this duty should be enforced irrespective of the past attitude and behaviour of the claimant.

The Supreme Court, in a decision of 1974[10], did not rule out the possibility of applying statute 5 of the civil code in principle, but held that this would have to be limited to very exceptional cases. It did not, however, delineate the criteria by which a case may be judged to be exceptional, with the result that, in practice, courts do not apply statute 5 of the civil code, so they do not assess the worthiness of the claimant in terms of community life principles. More recently, many legal authorities have favoured applying this rule. But, as yet, the possibility of admitting a charge of unworthiness of the claimant in maintenance proceedings has been categorically rejected.[11] Recently T. Smyczyński has supported the view that a claimant can be refused maintenance on the basis of statute 5 of the civil code if he was guilty of past reprehensible behaviour, and that this is not confined to exceptional cases. The author argues that it is difficult to expect the wronged person to give help to someone who has done him moral injustice, and that it is immoral to demand such help. He refers to statute 5 of the civil code and expresses the opinion that this rule can provide a safeguard against unjust decisions in maintenance cases. He maintains, among other things, that the argument that taking into account "unworthiness" of the claimant would, supposedly, put a burden on the social security fund, is unconvincing, since these would be rare cases, which would generally arouse moral disapproval. The author is of the opinion that to pass over moral judgements in maintenance cases is undesirable, and can negatively affect legal and moral consciousness of citizens, weakening their motivation in discharging family duties.[12]

It is difficult not to agree with Smyczyński. His views are also supported by the results of the 1980 studies. About 4% of the children in the cases studied, justified their refusal to pay maintenance on the basis of their parents' past misconduct towards them. Their grievances mainly concerned desertion of the family and failure to take an interest in its welfare during their childhood. References were made to other instances of the claimant's misbehaviour, for instance, alcoholism and cohabitation.

The legislative solutions in other countries seem to suggest that it might be desirable to adopt regulations which provide for children's refusal to maintain parents who had behaved dishonourably. Such solutions are to be found in all socialist countries, with the exception of Romania, and also in the legal systems of France, Austria, Switzerland and Sweden. There are two solutions to the problem under discussion. One is to formulate a general rule for refusing to enforce a maintenance claim if it offends moral principles (as in Czéchoslova-kian and Hungarian law), or to outline circumstances under which mainte-nance claims should be refused. Such circumstances could include cases where the entitled person is guilty against a person under obligation to provide maintenance, or against his spouse or relatives; also, when the claimant brought his distress upon himself (as in the law of East Germany and Bulgaria). The second solution is to list the circumstances when, and family members with regard to whom, it is permissible to refuse maintenance (as in Soviet law). Parents' failure to provide their children with proper maintenance and school-ing is the most typical circumstance which justifies the refusal to pay mainte-nance.[13]

Parents' enforcement of maintenance claims from children in court practice

As was mentioned at the outset of this chapter, the number of maintenance proceedings by parents against children is small, relative to the total number of maintenance cases in Poland every year. It oscillates between one and two per cent. It is a very small number indeed, and it seems there are many more parents who are entitled but do not enforce their claims. This is a speculative statement since no representative studies of this problem have yet been conducted.

Table 1 shows maintenance proceedings taken by parents against children in the courts over the past five years, in comparison with the total number of cases covering all types of maintenance obligation.

Table 1

Year	Number of maintenance proceedings of parents against children		Total number of all maintenance proceedings
	Total	cases lodged for the first time	
1982	2291	1215	103 460
1983	2100	2093	116 592
1984	1712	1040	115 381
1985	1583	901	112 853
1986	1549	830	121 235

Table 1, compiled on the basis of court statistics, reveals a decrease in the number of relevant cases, with a simultaneous increase in the total number of all other maintenance cases.

The 1980 study and our own research show that parents are more inclined to turn to social security than to claim maintenance from their children before the courts. Of the total number of 477 cases studied which were examined by courts in the first half of 1980 in the whole country, only in 193 cases (40.4%) was the litigation initiated by the interested party; 145 cases (30.4%) by the mother, 39 cases (8.2%) by the father, 9 cases (1.9%) by the mother and father jointly. In 238 cases (49.9%) the claim was lodged by the Polish Welfare Committee; the prosecutor initiated proceedings in only 26 cases (5.5%), and the Polish Women's League in 20 cases (4.2%). Out of the 477 cases studied, 419 were lodged for the first time, and in 58 cases the application was for an increase in a previously awarded payment.

It should be mentioned that an important means of overcoming parents' reticence in lodging maintenance claims against their children is the possibility that application may be made on behalf of the parents by the prosecutor and social organizations listed in the regulations.[14] The 1980 study shows that parents find it embarrassing and painful to have to initiate court proceedings to obtain maintenance from their children. This reluctance is usually only overcome when the parents find themselves living in poverty, totally unable to take care of themselves and dependent on others for help. This usually arises when the parents are over 75 or have lost the support of a spouse who died. Of the total number of claimants in the 477 studied cases (494 persons) 52.4% were over 75 years of age, and 18.6% were between 71-75. Most of them were widows or widowers (69.0%). The majority of the entitled people were unemployed (39.9%), among them 30 fathers and 167 mothers. The second largest group were farmers (30.0%). 34.2% (166 mothers and 3 fathers) drew social security benefits. 26.7% persons (25 fathers, 107 mothers) had no means of support whatsoever. 11.9% persons (23 fathers and 35 mothers) received disability or old age pensions. 7.9% persons (7 fathers and 14 mothers) received partial support from their children. Ten mothers (2.0%) lived off alimony ordered from the husband, and 3.2% persons (2 fathers and 14 mothers), from maintenance ordered from children. Other sources of support were almost entirely absent (2 persons were supported by people with whom they cohabited).

In the 477 cases studied, the courts usually ordered the maintenance to be paid. The claims were dismissed only in 14.3% of cases. In 5% of cases the maintenance ordered was above the sum claimed. The Polish law of civil procedure provides for such an outcome in maintenance cases. 15.3% of cases ended in agreement. In 27.3% of cases the claims were recognized in full, and in 37.7% partially. Only in 4.5% of cases was an appeal brought, in 9 cases by the plaintiff and in 12 by the defendant.

It is significant that of a total of 1549 maintenance cases brought by parents against children, examined by courts in Poland in 1986, 830 were first-time claims. The rest concerned claims for an increase in the maintenance already awarded. From the total 1549 cases, in 431 (27.8%) the claim was recognized in full, in 504 cases (32.5%) partially, in 27 cases (1.7%) the court ordered maintenance above the claimed amount, and in 499 cases (28.9%) the parties entered into an agreement.

It should also be noticed that the maintenance ordered from children in favor of their parents is generally lower than that ordered from parents in favor of children. It seems that the reason for this lies in the fact that many parents have some private income. Moreover their needs are smaller, usually being limited to matters of sustenance, whereas provision has to be made for children's education.

The 1980 study provided some interesting information concerning reasons given by defendants for failing to pay maintenance. The following reasons were given:

1. 65 defendants (5.3%) did not consider their parents to be in distress. 11 defendants thought their parent could work and support himself and 12 considered the parent's pension to be sufficient.
2. 9 defendants (0.7%) alleged they had no income from earnings or capital assets. They were mentally handicapped and penal institution inmates.
3. 311 defendants (25.3%) justified their refusal to provide for their parents by saying that their own financial and family situation was difficult.
4. 141 defendants (11.5%) applied for the dismissal of the claim alleging that:
   – they lived with the parents /claimant/ and partially supported him (14 defendants) .
   – they provided partial means of support in kind (31 defendants) .
   – they voluntarily supported their parents as much as they could and anything above it would be beyond their means (64 defendants) .
   – they wanted their mother to live with them and in this way maintain her (12 defendants) .
5. 151 defendants (12.3%) considered themselves to be under no duty to

provide their parent with maintenance, alleging that:
– their parents should be supported by social security (8 defendants) ,
– the mother should be supported by the son she used to work for, and whose children she raised (7 defendants),
– parents should only be supported by the child which took over the farm (15 defendants) ,
– the parent gave over the farm to the State (25 defendants) ,
– he already supports his mother-in-law (1 defendant) .

6. 14 defendants (1.1%) claimed that their refusal to pay maintenance was justified in view of their parents' past reprehesible behaviour towards them, alleging that:
– the parent deserted the family and broke off all contacts for many years (11 defendants) ,
– the father neglected the child in childhood (1 defendant) ,
– the mother abandoned the child in childhood (1 defendant) ,
– the mother sold her farm and gave nothing to the daughter (1 defendant) .

7. 34 defendants (8.8%) believed they had no obligation to pay maintenance in view of the way the entitled person misbehaved in other ways, alleging that:
– the parent was an alcoholic (29 defendants) ,
– the parent lived in concubinage (5 defendants) .

8. 505 defendants (41.1%) could not sensibly explain why they did not support their parents (e.g., 13 defendants justified themselves by saying their parents did not demand maintenance payments).

It should be stressed that none of the defendants argued that it was the husband who is primarily responsible for the mother's maintenance. This was almost certainly due to ignorance of the legal provisions.

Another set of data, revealed by the 1980 study, deserves to be mentioned. It appears that while the proportion of claimants living in towns and villages was more or less the same, over two-thirds of the defendants were city dwellers. It should be remembered that social networks in rural communities are closer than in towns.

It was stated earlier that parents are very reluctant to enforce their mainte-nance claims before courts. In one of the cases studied, an application for a maintenance order was issued by the prosecutor on behalf of an entitled father. During the proceedings, the father expressed his surprise and displeasure at his children being summoned before the court. He wanted to know why the prosecutor made the application, and was told that it resulted from an allowance granted him by the Polish Welfare Committee in response to an application he had made. The father admitted making the application because of temporary financial difficulties, but said he was now working under a domestic system, earning enough to support himself, and therefore did not want any financial help from his children. It appeared however from the evidence in the files of his case that he did in fact need financial assistance from his children, but was unwilling to have it enforced by a court order. In several other cases the parents refused to consent to the proceedings being continued against their children, without giving reasons for their objections. In such cases, the parents made a choice as to the source of their provision, voluntarily waiving their right to claim maintenance from their children, and in so doing, shifting this responsibility onto the State. There have been no studies so far which estimate the magnitude of this phenomenon.

There are cases of fictitious lawsuits in which parents demand very small maintenance payments from their children, which bear no relation to the defendant's real resources, in order to be able subsequently to apply for supplementary benefits. Recently, in several such cases, the Minister of Justice appealed against the final decision. Such (fortunately infrequent) fictitious claims are deterred by the rule already referred to, according to which maintenance can be ordered in excess of the claimant's demand.

An effective means of preventing such fictitious litigation, as well as safe-guarding impoverished parents who do not want to obtain maintenance from children through the courts, is provided by section 140 of the Family and Welfare Code, subsection 1 of which states: "A person who provides another person with maintenance or education without obligation or who is obliged because securing maintenance from a person under the same or more direct obligation would have been either impossible or very difficult for the claimant, may demand repayment from the person who should have provided that maintenance".

However, there are few court cases in which so-called retrospective claims are made on the basis of this provision. Only exceptionally does the State take proceedings against children to recover sums paid for the maintenance of their parents.

Welfare provisions for parents

Social care has for a long time been an integral part of the social welfare system, and, in view of its philanthropic and charitable character, is referred to as social assistance. The fundamental principles of the social care system and the services it provides are contained in statute 70 of the constitution which proclaims: "1. The citizens of the Polish Peoples' Republic have the right to medical care and assistance when sick or incapacitated for work. 2. The full realization of this right is achieved through development of social insurance against sickness, old age and disablement for work, as well as through development of various forms of social care...".

An Act of 23rd August, 1923[15] covers the basic form of social assistance in Poland but this has become outdated. The range of provisions under the Constitution is much wider than that contained in the Social Assistance Act of 1923. The organization of social assistance services is mostly informal in character, since there does not exist a right to those services in the sense of a legal claim, and the range and administration of the services depends on the assessment of welfare bodies — hence, a proper organizational framework of social assistance is of crucial importance.[16]

Presently, a draft for a new Act to replace the Act of 1923 is under discussion. The Act has become obsolete because in reality social assistance functions in Poland under many legal regulations of a lower legal status than the Act. The new Act is to cover, among other things, the provisions contained in those regulations, sanctioning and extending the current humanitarian practice whereby social workers employed by the social assistance agencies monitor the living conditions of old people who are without an income from disability or old-age pension. In this way, the help given to old people who require such assistance does not have to be elicited by the interested parties, but follows from regular, periodical checks on old people's living conditions. According to the draft, the new Act is to regulate in a more precise way than previously the provisions and the mode of granting benefits to people who require financial assistance from the State.

Under the present legal system, social assistance takes various forms. The benefits it covers are: (1) financial, (2) in kind, (3) in the form of services, (4) institutional. The financial benefits are permanent, periodical, or one-time lump sum payments awarded depending on the circumstances of the person concerned. The benefits in kind and services consist in providing old people, especially the disabled, with food, clothing and fuel, and in performing necessary services such as cooking, washing, and taking care of a sick person. The services within the institutional system consist in providing care in different kinds of nursing homes for old people who are unable to live by themselves.[17]

Payment must be made to stay in a nursing home. Persons drawing disability or old-age pensions pay an amount not exceeding 75% of their income. The charge for people without disability or old-age pension is paid for by members of the family who are under the maintenance obligation or, if the person has no family, by the State. Nursing homes are an integral part of the social assistance system.

Social assistance is given on the basis of an environmental inquiry which determines the need for help to be provided by the State or other social organization. The welfare system assists people who are incapable of working due to old age and who are unable to support themselves because they are not eligible for old age or disability pensions or who do not have a family capable of paying maintenance, or if they have only partial means of support (such as a maintenance provision, family help) which amounts to less than 80% of the lowest old-age pension, or 100% for people classified as first-degree invalids. Permanent benefits fall within these limits. Periodic benefits are granted for a six month period with the possibility of extending the payment to ten months in one year. One-time benefits (financial or in kind) are awarded to meet specific, basic requirements with regard to, for example, clothing, sheets and domestic appliances.

Environmental health and social care is performed by the district physician, environmental nurse and social worker. This is because frequently there is an overlap between the health and social needs of elderly people. Social workers constitute one of the basic links in the organization of social care.

It should also be mentioned that in 1960, the Ministry of Health and Social Welfare was set up in Poland, in place of the Ministry of Health. In this way health care and social assistance have been integrated. Formerly, social assistance fell under the remit of the Ministry of Employment and Social Welfare.

Conclusions

The maintenance obligation of children toward their parents, described here, both from the point of view of legal theory and court practice, together with the problem of social security provisions, poses certain questions and leads to reflection on the causes of certain phenomena. Since the issues under discussion have not been subject of a representative study, the conclusions must be more in the nature of hypotheses than of definite assertions.

The number of relevant cases seems to be small in relation to the total number of maintenance cases dealt with by courts, and in view of the observed reluctance of parents to enforce their maintenance claim against their children through courts. It should be remembered, however, that where the person under the obligation fails to fulfill his maintenance duty, it is deliberate. In families which function normally, where there is no animosity between parents and children, it is natural for children to provide financial relief for parents who do not have a source of income. The relatively high proportion of cases, covered by the survey presented in this paper, in which the defendants charged their parents with being "unworthy" of the claimed maintenance, seems to confirm that view. The parents against whom the charge of "unworthiness" was laid, did not have any qualms of conscience, and categorically demanded maintenance from their children. Another, quite numerous group consisted of defendants who justified their failure to provide for their parents by saying that they were not aware that they were under such an obligation, or who simply could not furnish a sensible explanation. It is difficult not to condemn such an attitude. It means that in the majority of maintenance cases initiated by parents against children, at least one of the parties does not command respect on moral grounds. This perception is widespread. It is therefore hardly surprising that parents avoid taking proceedings against their children. They choose other ways of seeking help, turning, most often, to state social assistance organizations.

As for the problem of the "unworthiness" of parents, it must be considered right to allow the objection to be raised in view of the arguments considered earlier.

Parents' reluctance to enforce their maintenance claims in relation to their children is also explicable in terms of the general economic situation of the country. The crisis is felt, to some extent, by all citizens. Parents, aware that the financial resources of their children are hardly sufficient to cover their own needs, turn for assistance to the State so as not to put an additional burden on their children. This hypothesis is substantiated by the fact that the State finds it difficult to recover from children the sums expended on the maintenance of their parents. Over one quarter of the defendants in the cases studied explained their evasiveness in fulfilling their maintenance duties as being due to their poor financial situation.

These observations are not very revealing, since it is obvious that court actions against children to enforce their maintenance claims are a manifestation of a certain family pathology, and the parents' reluctance to undertake such proceedings is from the psychological point of view quite normal and laudable.

It should be stressed that there are relatively few people in Poland who are entitled to claim maintenance from their children, that is, people who live in distress, which, as was previously stated, is the basic condition for the existence of the maintenance obligation. This assertion is confirmed by the regulations relating to disability and old age pensions. Between the World Wars the social insurance system covered 15% of the population; in 1970 it reached 75%, and in 1980 — 100%. It is one of the greatest achievements of the socialist system. In 1972 members of agricultural co-operatives became eligible for the full range of benefits, on a par with other employees. In 1974 the rights were extended to free-lance artists and in 1976 to persons working for state-owned enterprises under the domestic system. In 1978 individual farmers became eligible for old-age pensions. The gradual extension of pension rights to different groups of employees led to an excessive diversification of disability and old-age schemes. In 1980 there were fifteen such schemes, which made it difficult to implement a specific social insurance policy. The Employees and their Families Pension Act of 14 December, 1982[18] has regularized the previous system of benefits.

Disability and old-age pension payments constitute a significant portion of the State's expenditure on social welfare. Compared to other European states, especially socialist countries, this share is smaller in Poland. This is because the process of population aging is less advanced (there are fewer elderly people), and the retirement age is set higher (people become eligible for pensions later). Poland is among the countries whose expenditure on pensions in proportionally small (44.5%), in comparison with DDR (53.6%), Bulgaria, Hungary and the USSR where it amounts to 50%. The number of disability and old-age pensions is growing in Poland. Between 1960 and 1980, the number had grown by 80-300%. Pensions amount to 30 — 57% of the average national wage. These are supplemented by other social benefits and allowances, such as rent allowances, free drugs and cheap fares.[19]

On the basis of the above considerations, it may be said, that the maintenance obligation of children towards parents does not play a major role in the system of securing decent living conditions for elderly people. However, the problems that have already come to light should not be disregarded, nor should we ignore the fact that crucial evidence is missing because no representative studies have been carried out.

Attention should be paid to the fact that for elderly people, besides having secure maintenance, it is equally important to be "noticed", to be able to fulfill their psychological and intellectual needs[20]. The shortcomings in the case of the elderly observed at the beginning of this chapter are mainly in this area. Such "services" cannot be ordered by a court, and no enforcement agency can exact these from children. It seems we might do well to consider ways of shaping people's attitudes from early childhood, so that humanitarian attitudes towards elderly people become widespread. As such, it is therefore a task for the education system. I am not sure whether passing special acts, such as "Bills of Rights of the Elderly", or the adoption by the UN of a declaration along the lines of "The Rights of Children" would bring positive results and improve the lot of elderly people. Such steps, however, might be considered, and should they be rejected, we may try to find other ways in which the law can assist the elderly, and possibly, areas in which legal adjustments should be made.

Notes

1. see Gwiazdomorski, J., *The System of Family and Welfare Law, Part* I; (Polish Academy of Sciences Publications, 1985) pp. 995-996.
2. see for example Frackiewicz. L., *The Bill of Rights of Elderly People,* (Trade Union Publishers, 1985) pp.3-6.
3. Frackiewicz, L. *op. cit.* pp.7 and 138.
4. This analysis was carried out by Judge A. Hofmańska, employed in that Department. In further references in this chapter I shall use the term "the 1980 study" when presenting results of that analysis.
5. Considering the small number of court files studied I shall use the results of the survey only as an illustration without giving numerical data, and shall refer to it as "our survey" to distinguish it from the analysis carried out by the Ministry of Justice.
6. see Gwiazdomorski, J., *op. cit.* p.1003.
7. see Gwiazdomorski, J., *op. cit.* p.1015-1017.
8. Dziennik Ustaw no 27 section 137. See also Stojanowska, W., Alimony Funds., *Annual Survey on Family Law,* 1983-1984, vol.8, produced by the International Society of Family Law, 1985, pp. 120-121.
9. Unpublished information concerning statistical studies on the maintenance fund, carried out by ZUS in Warsaw.
10. see Resolution of the Supreme Court of 7th August, 1974. Orzecznictwo Sadu Najwyzszego, section 160.
11. see Gwiazdomorski, J., *op. cit.* pp. 1025-1027 and the included bibliography.
12. see Smyczyński, T., *Roszczenia alimentacyjne a zasady wspólzycia spolecznego (Maintenance Claims and Community Life Law)* "Studia Prawnicze", 1983, zeszyt 1 /75/ pp. 86-90.

13. *op. cit.* pp. 70-71.
14. The list of these organizations is included in the instruction issued by the Ministry of Justice on 18th July, 1965 /Dz. U. Nr 37, poz. 213/. In maintenance cases, applications can be made by among others: Trade Unions, Polish Women's League, Polish Welfare Committee, Social Anti-Alcohol Committee, Polish Society of the Deaf, Polish Society of the Blind, Polish Disabled Soldiers Association, the United Union of Pensioners and Handicapped Persons.
15. Dziennik Ustaw nr 92, section 726.
16. see Frackiewicz, L., *op. cit.* pp. 72-73.
17. *op. cit.*
18. Dziennik Ustaw, nr 40, section 247.
19. see Frackiewicz, L., *op. cit.* pp. 82-83
20. The family plays an important role in the life of elderly people, even if not living with their children. Sharing accommodation with their children, which is uncommon in highly developed industrial societies, is not the most important feature of the relationship between elderly people and their adult children. What counts is the emotional bond between them: see Rembowski, J., *Psychologiczne problemy starzenia sie czlowieka (Psychological Problems of Aging)* , PWN, Warszawa — Poznań, 1984, p. 13.

Chapter 20

Decline of Family Care and The Development of Public Services — a sociological analysis of the Japanese experience —

Daisaku MAEDA   Department of Sociology,
          Tokyo Metropolitan Institute of Gerontology
                                                  Japan

The Elderly and the Family in Developed Countries

Many people in developing countries tend to think that in developed countries the elderly are abandoned by their children and live a solitary and miserable life. This is not true. The American social gerontologist, Elaine Brody, describes the social network of the elderly in the United States as follows:

'While family structure and composition have no doubt undergone profound changes, the theory of the isolated nuclear family has been discredited. ... Studies and the observations of practitioners have ... shown that despite the greatly increased number of old people, personal ties between the generations continue to be strong and viable; families continue to behave responsibly in helping their aged; and when they are unable to do so, a constellation of personal, social and economic forces may be at work. Thus, the collective social and cultural rejection of the aged has not been acted out on the individual or family level.'
(Brody, E 1988)

Regarding aging parent and adult child exchange relationships, Barry D. McPherson summarizes the situation in developed countries as follows:

'Recent demographic changes such as decreased family size, childless marriages, and fewer single adult daughters, combined with an increasing number of middle-aged women in the labor force, have led to a decrease in the availability and opportunity of children to care directly for aging parents. As a result, more social and health care support services are provided by the private and government sectors. Nevertheless, in most societies the family is the first and major resource for the elderly, of whom less than 10 percent are ever institutionalized. ...' (McPherson, B.D., 1983)

Traditional Family Care Still Functioning in Japan

A. Legal Aspects

What Brody and McPherson described is true of Japan. Furthermore, Japan preserves the traditional family care of the elderly much more strongly than other industrialized countries. This is mainly due to the fact that her industrialization started much later than in Western European or North American countries. Thus, even today the Japanese Civil Code stipulates, in the well-known article 877, that those who are in a lineal relation, as well as siblings, are responsible to support and care for each other.

It should be noted, however, that even in the actual administration of Public Assistance Law, which is the strictest among various laws with regard to the enforcement of the mutual responsibility to support and care *for each other* among relatives, the responsibility of children toward their aging parents is regarded to be *relative* in contrast with the *absolute* responsibility of parents toward their young children. This means that children who become independent from their parents only need to support and/or care for their aging parents if they have sufficient financial and social capability after having secured a decent life for their own families. However, when one lives with one's parents in the same household, one is required to secure the same level of living for one's aging parents as one's own level.

In the administration of the Law for the Welfare of Elderly Persons, the responsibility of children toward their aging parents is defined still more narrowly than it is in respect of public assistance. The current regulation of the Ministry of Health and Welfare concerning charges for public community services, that is, day care, respite care, and home-help service, only requires a child who is actually living with his/her aging parents in the same household to bear the financial responsibility. That is, the regulation requires that the household as a whole should be responsible for paying the fee. Thus, a child who lives separately is not required to bear the financial responsibility, however well-off he/she is. The cost of the public community services is quite reasonable. For example, the charge for respite care service is only about 1,000 yen a day which is designed to be roughly equivalent to the cost of three meals.

In the case of charges for institutional care in nursing homes and ordinary homes for the aged, *only the child who had been living with aging parents when the official decision of placement was made* is required to pay the fee. In addition, the sum imposed on such a child is not as great as it is under public assistance law. Generally speaking, the financial burden resulting from the admission into an institution established under the Law for the Welfare of Elderly Persons is much lighter than that which arises from the support and care of aging parents at home. Of course, home care imposes physical and psychological burdens as well.

It should also be stressed that both financial responsibility and responsibility to care for aging parents is now defined very narrowly in the actual administration of the Law for the Welfare of Elderly Persons. That is, when aging parents become seriously impaired and require help in their daily living, but a daughter or a son's wife living with them is working outside the home, they are not required to leave their employment in order to care for an aging parent, even if the family is well-off and the wife's income is not indispensable. The family can ask the government to provide the necessary care for their aging parents in a nursing home. What they are required to do is only to pay a fee, according to the regulation mentioned above. However, some middle-aged women still leave professional jobs such as school-teaching in order to care for their mother or mother-in-law. This means that, in spite of the modernized administrative regulation of the law, such social pressure, deeply rooted in the traditional mores, that children should care for impaired aging parents in their own homes, still exerts a strong influence in Japan.

Thus, it is now clear that though our Civil Code stipulates the responsibility of children toward aging parents, in the actual administration of public services, the legal responsibility of children is limited. The government does not compel children to live with impaired aging parents in order to care for them. When children place them in an institution, the government collects a fee the amount of which is usually significantly smaller than the amount necessary to support and care for the aged in their own homes. Only an extremely well-off family whose yearly income is over 18.5 million yen (about U.S. $140,000) is required to pay the full cost. The number of such families is very small. At present, only about one out of 1,000 families who place their aging parents in nursing homes is paying the full fee.

I should here refer to two more examples of the changing government policy regarding children's responsibility towards aging parents, both financial and in terms of actual caregiving. In Japan, there are a number of Keihi Rōjin Homes, which can be translated literally as a home for the aged which charges a moderate fee. This type of home is designed to serve elderly persons whose income is higher than the ceiling for admission into an ordinary home for the aged. The residents in these homes are required to pay only such direct living expenses as meals, heating, electricity, and so forth. If their income is not sufficient to meet the full amount of these expenses, the government provides financial assistance to meet the shortage. In addition, the government subsidizes all the indirect costs, such as wages of the employees of the home, expenses for construction and repair of buildings, and so on. In the case of this type of home, which is designed to serve those whose income is higher than the maximum for an ordinary home for the aged, the children are not required to pay anything, even though a substantial amount of running and construction expenses are subsidized by the government. On the other hand, as mentioned above, children who place their parents in ordinary homes for the aged which are designed to serve comparatively less well-off older persons are requested to pay the fee according to the fee scale.

The second example is the "Health Care Facility for the Elderly" which is designed to serve elderly persons who are seriously impaired or suffer from a serious chronic disease and are unable to live in the community. The amount and level of care services required by patients of this facility is thought to be about the same as those of a Nursing Home. For this, the government pays all the costs of medical and nursing services in accordance with the Law for Health and Medical Services for Elderly Persons. The patients are required to pay the rest of the cost, that is, of meals, clothes, and other items for which patients would need to pay if they lived in their own homes. In the case of this facility, even spouses who should bear an *absolute* responsibility to provide support and care are not requested to pay anything more, even if they very rich. Many people believe that, in light of our rapidly maturing public pension programs, this facility will soon become the mainstream of our institutional care service system for the elderly.

In conclusion, the point made here is that, despite the stipulation in the civil code, the present policy of the government is very lenient with regard to the enforcement of the legal responsibility of children to support and care for their aging parents, that it will become more even more lenient, and eventually the responsibility of children towards aging parents will become a moral rather than a legal one.

B. Social Aspects

In this section, I want to describe the social aspects of traditional Japanese family care of the elderly.

As Brody and McPherson pointed out, even in the industrialized countries of Western Europe and North America, the proportion of the elderly who are institutionalized is very small. In Japan, it is only about 1.7 percent. In other words, even in these countries the overwhelming majority of the elderly live in the community with the support of relatives, friends, and neighbors. There is, however, a conspicuous difference between western countries and Japan. In western countries, when seriously impaired older persons live in the community, in almost all cases they are cared for by a spouse. In many cases a grown child living nearby helps them. It is very rare, however for a child to move into the parent's home or take him into her own home to care for him when a spouse cannot provide the necessary care. Instead, such older persons usually move into an institution.

In Japan, on the contrary, the majority of seriously impaired older persons are cared for living together with their children. Needless to say, a spouse plays an important role, when possible, but the existence of a middle-aged caregiver living with them makes it possible for the most seriously impaired persons to continue to live in the community. A recent nationwide study estimated the proportion of the bedridden (those who had been in such a condition for more than 6 months) in the population aged 60 and over in 1984 at 2.7 percent

Figure 1. Proportion of Bedridden Old People by Places of Living

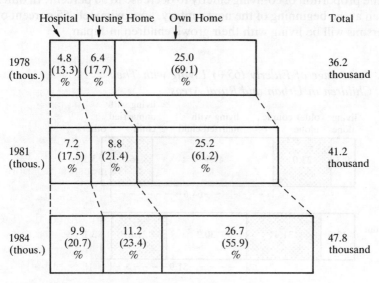

Source: Ministry of Heath and Welfare, 1985-b

(Ministry of Health and Welfare, 1985-a). As shown in Figure 1, of all the bedridden elderly, 56 percent were cared for by their spouse, child, or other relative in their own homes. The proportion of the bedridden elderly institutionalized in nursing homes was only 23 percent, and the remaining 21 percent were hospitalized.

Another important difference is the very high proportion of elderly persons living with children in Japan. According to the latest National Census of 1985, 63.4 percent of the Japanese elderly over 65 live with their grown children. As shown in Figure 2, this traditional pattern of living arrangement and family care for aged parents is still fairly well preserved, even in the completely industrialized and urbanized metropolitan areas of Japan, where the influence of western culture is felt much more strongly than in other areas. That is, even in such areas, still more than 50 percent of the elderly over 65 live with their grown children. The same figure shows that this proportion is significantly higher in less industrialized areas. Especially in rural areas, more than 70 percent of the elderly over 65 live with their adult children.

It should be noted, however, that the proportion of the elderly living with their adult children has been decreasing very rapidly over the last thirty years, parallel with the industrialization and urbanization of Japanese society. As shown in Table 1, it has been decreasing at the rate of 0.9 percent a year over the last fifteen years. In addition, it seems that the rate of decrease has been accelerated in recent years, as shown in the same Table. But, it should be noted that even if this accelerated rate continues, it will take more than twenty-two years for the proportion of co-living elderly to decrease to 50 percent. In other words, even at the beginning of the next century, approximately 55 percent of elderly persons will be living with their grown children in Japan.

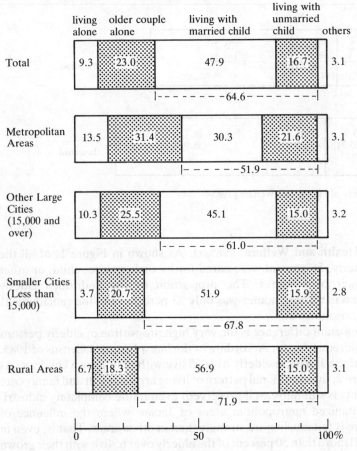

Figure 2. *Percentage of Elderly (65+) Living with Their Children in Urban and Rural Areas*

	living alone	older couple alone	living with married child	living with unmarried child	others
Total	9.3	23.0	47.9	16.7	3.1
			------- -64.6- ------		
Metropolitan Areas	13.5	31.4	30.3	21.6	3.1
			------ -51.9- -----		
Other Large Cities (15,000 and over)	10.3	25.5	45.1	15.0	3.2
			------- -61.0- ------		
Smaller Cities (Less than 15,000)	3.7	20.7	51.9	15.9	2.8
			------ - -67.8 -----		
Rural Areas	6.7	18.3	56.9	15.0	3.1
			------ - -71.9 -------		

0   50   100%

Source: Ministry of Health and Welfare, 1985-a

Table 1. Decrease in Percentage of Persons 65 Years of Age and Above Living with their Children

Year	Living with Children	Aged Couple Only	Living Alone	Others	Total	Decreasing Rate of "Living with Children" per year
1970	76.9	12.1	5.5	5.5	100.0	0.88 ⎫
1975	72.5	15.7	6.9	4.9	100.0	0.76 ⎬ 0.9
1980	68.7	18.9	8.2	4.3	100.0	1.06 ⎭
1985	63.4	21.5	9.6	5.5	100.0	

Note. Persons living in institutions were excluded.
Source: Statistics Bureau, General Executive Office, National Census, 1970, 1975, 1980, 1985

This estimate is made solely by extending the recent statistical trend into the future. But there is another factor which reinforces the prediction. In 1981, the Section on Aging (Rojin Taisaku Shitsu) of the General Executive Office of the National Government carried out a nationwide survey of the opinion of middle-aged persons about life after retirement and the care to be given. According to this survey, as shown in Table 2, 58 percent of married men and women aged between 30-49 think that one of the children's families should live with aging parents. When they were further asked what they thought about the living arrangement of aging parents if one of them gets frail or dies, more than 83 percent answered that one of the children's families should live with the surviving parent.

This implies that unless the attitude of the present middle-aged generation changes significantly, which is most unlikely, at least in the next thirty-five years, the living arrangements of Japanese elderly person will not change much so as to become similar to that of Western developed countries.

Table 2. Opinions of Middle-Aged Persons about Life after Retirement and the Care to be Given
Age 30-49

acconditions of parents	Opinions on living arrangements of aging parents				
	son's family should live together	daughter's family should live together	(sub-total)	married child should live separate from parents	D.K.,N.A.
in general	45.9%	12.3%	(58.2%)	30.4%	11.4%
when one of the aging parents gets frail	62.1%	21.4%	(83.5%)	6.6%	9.9%
when one of the aging parents died	63.2%	20.5%	(83.7%)	5.0%	11.3%

Source: Section on Aging, General Executive Office, 1981
Notes: National representative sample (1,259) of middle-aged married men and women aged 30-49

Attitude of Middle-Aged Japanese Persons on Family Care of the Bedridden Elderly

In the previous part of this chapter, I stressed that, unlike western countries, in Japan the majority of bedridden older person are cared for by their spouse and children in their own homes. Some Westerners have attributed this to the limited amount of nursing-home beds available. The shortage of beds in institutions, however, seems to be only a minor reason why the majority of Japanese old people are cared for by their families.

The recent nationwide survey of the opinions of middle-aged married persons cited above *(Section on Aging, General Executive Office, 1981)* also studied children's plans for the care of their parents when the parents become bedridden. According to the survey, slightly more than 80 percent answered that the child or the child's spouse would care for an aged parent, and approximately 10 percent answered that the parent's spouse should provide care. Less than 3 percent answered that they were planning to depend upon resources other than family members, such as a paid housekeeper, public home help services and nursing homes (Table 3). Thus, it is clear that, in Japan, the overwhelming majority of middle-aged persons still firmly believe that care of bedridden older parents is the responsibility of their children.

Table 3. Children's Plans for the Care of Their Parents When Parents Become Bedridden

Planned Source of Care	For Husband's Parents N=1,1017	For Wife' Parents N=1,079
Parent's spouse	11.1%	8.9%
Respondent himself/herself	24.4	10.0
Respondent's spouse	18.9	6.8
Brother	13.8	18.8
Brother's spouse	16.9 81.7%	31.4 83%
Sister	2.0	7.3
All brothers and sisters	5.8	8.7
Other family members or relatives	0.6%	0.7
Sub-total	93.4%	92.6%
Other resources (paid housekeepers, public homehelpers, nursing homes, etc.)	2.9%	1.7%
Don't know	3.7%	5.7%

Source: Section on Aging, General Executive Office, 1931

However, there is a great gap between attitudes and facts, As shown in Figure 1, in Japan almost half of bedridden old people are hospitalized or institutionalized. Even if we admit that a number of those bedridden old people do not have children, or are too seriously impaired to be cared for by the families, or do not have a caregiver who is able to care for them, this gap between attitudes and reality means that many middle-aged persons do not provide care for other reasons. For example, they might choose to continue a career rather than sacrifice it, or a bedridden older person might prefer to enter a hospital or nursing home rather than be cared for by his or her children, for fear of being too much of a burden, or children might not wish to provide the care because relationships have become difficult.

Change in the Roles Played by Children

Reference was made to the gap between attitudes and behavior of middle-aged Japanese persons in relation to the care of bedridden parents. However, the avoidance of a culturally expected role is made possible by the development of formal support and care services. A similar phenomenon can be observed in other aspects of relations between the elderly and their adult children. Comparing two nationwide studies on the care of older parents carried out in 1974 and in 1983 (*Section on Aging,* 1974, and 1983), the proportion of children (married middle-aged male children) providing economic support to their aging parents is shown to decline:

	1974	1983
children aged 35-39	41%	36%
children aged 40-44	42%	40%
children aged 45-49	48%	42%

To the question why they do not provide financial support for aging parents (in the 1983 survey), 54 percent of those who were not doing so answered that their parents were well-off and did not need such support. During the course the nine years, Japan's economy expanded greatly, and the income of these middle-aged men had improved substantially. Therefore, the reduced proportion of economic support to aging parents reflects the greater financial independence of the elderly brought about by the development of public pension programs.

The importance of the role of adult children in health care has also greatly changed. As shown in Figure 1, in 1978, 69 percent of bedridden old people were cared for in their own homes (*Ministry of Health and Welfare,* 1985-a) . The same survey conducted only six years later, showed that this proportion fell to 56 percent.

Causes of Decline in the Family Role in the Care of Aging Parents

As pointed out several times in this chapter, the pattern of traditional family care of the elderly is still well maintained in Japan. But it is also true that there has been a significant decline in such family care over the past several decades.

At least four factors should be considered as causes of this decline in the context of social situations in Japan:

1) change in the socio-economic structure of Japanese society as a result of the second industrial revolution;
2) demographic changes;
3) decreased capability of families to care for their aging parents, and
4) development of formal support and care services.

First, we will consider the impact of the second industrial revolution.

A. Impact of the second industrial revolution

Japan has been experiencing a second industrial revolution since 1955. At that time, the proportion of the population which was engaged in agriculture was approximately 41 percent. This proportion decreased to approximately 9 percent in 1985 *(Statistics Bureau, General Executive Office, 1955, 1958)* . This reduction of the agricultural population had a profound impact on the socio-economic structure of Japanese society. In Japan, and also in other East-Asian countries, when the head of a household is engaged in agriculture, all the adult members of the household, including the elderly, also work together in agricultural production to help the head of the household. In other words, all the household members of East-Asian farmers produce and consume collectively. In a society where this type of household is predominant, it is quite natural and, convenient for all, family members to live together in the same household.

In industrialized societies, where an older and younger generation are both engaged in secondary or tertiary industry, the two generations generally have separate incomes. In addition, because of the different life-styles of the two generations, caused by different occupations, in many cases it is more natural, and, above all, more convenient, for the two generations to live separately.

Secondly, industrialization has brought about much higher geographical mobility of working populations. In industrialized societies, people change their jobs much more frequently than before. Even when they remain in the same firm, most employees are frequently forced to move to other industrial areas for various reasons. In such cases, aging parents tend to prefer to remain at the original residence rather than to move to an unknown place with the child's family in order to continue to live together.

Thirdly, in our industrialized areas, housing for workers is, generally speaking, not large enough for two generations to live together.

Last, but not least, the awakening of a sense of selfhood among the general public aroused by higher education, higher living standards, and the influence of western industrialized countries has also played a very important role with regard to the change in living arrangements of the elderly in Japan. That is, an increasing number of both the older and younger generations prefer to live separately from each other for the sake of personal independence and freedom.

All in all, Japanese society is now in a state of conflict with regard to the family care of elderly parents, where the impact of traditional culture and that of industrialization and modernization co-exist.

B. Impact of demographic changes

One feature of Japan's recent demographic changes is an increase in the number of unmarried and/or childless old people, together with an increase in the total size of the aged population. Moreover, because of improvements in the general standard of living, as well as in medicine, the number of very old persons, 80 years or above, has increased significantly, as shown in Table 4. The more advanced age of dependent older parents means that the age of their caregiving children is also higher. In many cases, children themselves are already old and their own health is not good enough to provide needed care.

Table 4. Index of Increase in Number of Older Persons, 1950-2020

Age	1950	1975	2000	2020
60-69	100	190	360	371
70-79	100	214	499	765
80+	100	323	1193	2398

Source: 1. Statistics Bureau, General Executive Office, National Census, 1950, 1975
              2. Institute of Population Problems, Ministry of Health and Welfare, 1986

C. Decreased capability of families to care for aged parents

Several social factors have contributed to the decreased capability of families to care for aging parents. First, a great migration of the younger generation from rural to urban areas has occurred. On the urban side, the development of industry brought about dispersion of industrial areas. Thus, persons who were born and raised in urban locations often find it difficult to obtain employment in the urban area where their older parents live. As a result, in urban as well as in rural areas, the proportion of old people living alone or only with their spouse has increased.

Another social factor is the growing number of working women. Many of the married, middle-aged women who were once the most dependable caregivers of dependent older parents are now working outside their homes.

Finally, the number of children in Japan has decreased rapidly since 1950. As a result, persons with fewer children are now gradually entering the aged population. Obviously, when old people have fewer children, their chances of depending on them are reduced. This factor will make the need for services for old people, both community and institutional, more acute in the near future.

D. Development of formal support and care services

Theoretically speaking, formal support and care services were developed to cope with the various problems the elderly and their families are facing in the industrialized society of present-day Japan. However, as economists frequently point out, supply arouses demand. Although the development of various forms of formal support and care services in recent years has made it possible for people to depend upon them with regard to the care of their aging parents, it should be stressed that the original aim of the development of formal support and care services was to solve or at least alleviate the problems of the elderly and their caring families. The present situation of our formal support and care services will be discussed in this section.

Difficulties of Families Caring for Impaired Aging Parents

The impact of the demographic and social changes described above has been so marked that the recent development of formal support and care services could not fully meet the expanding needs of the elderly and their families. Thus, the impaired elderly are frequently cared for by families with insufficient capability to provide the care needed. In these cases, the quality of care is very poor, and, at the same time, the sacrifice of the caring family is very great. Without a doubt, institutional care should be provided in some cases. In other cases support from outside sources can effectively complement the function of the family and, as a result, the level of care will become adequate and the family's burden will become lighter and more bearable.

To effectively plan and implement social services for the impaired elderly, it is vitally important to know who is actually caring for them, and under what conditions. Recently a number of such studies have been conducted in Japan. The results of two of these investigations deserve special attention.

The question of who is caring for bedridden older people is answered in Table 5, which describes caregivers in relation to the gender of the bedridden elderly. As seen in the Table, 61 percent of bedridden older men are cared for by their wives, and 22 percent are cared for by their son's wives. On the other hand, 50 percent of bedridden older women are cared for by their son's wives, and 28 percent are cared for by their own children. These figures reveal several very serious problems. First, the average age of the caregiver is high. About one fourth of the caregivers for bedridden old people are aged 60 and over, including 3 percent who are aged 80 and over. Second, the majority of caregivers are son's wives or married daughters, who are generally at the prime stage of life and are busy with many duties, such as work and the care of their own children. Third, in some cases, the bedridden elderly are cared for by unmarried sons or daughters who are usually also working full-time. It is often very difficult for these caregivers to have the opportunity to marry, and because of the social pressure dictating that children should take care of their aged parents, they seldom place their parents in institutions.

Table 5. Caretakers of Bedridden Older Persons

Caretaker	Bedridden	
	Males	Females
	%	%
Spouse	61.0	11.4
Children (including both sexes)	10.8	27.7
Son's wife	21.7	50.4
Grandchildren (including both sexes)	0.8	2.7
Others, unknown	5.7	7.8

Source: National Council of Social Welfare, 1979

Further evidence of the difficult conditions experienced by Japanese caregivers can be seen in Table 6, derived from a study conducted in Tokyo by the Sociology Department of the Tokyo Metropolitan Institute of Gerontology in 1981. This Table describes the care of physically impaired old people living in the community in terms of the degree of difficulty experienced by caregiving families. As can be seen in the bottom line of the Table, well over two-thirds of the impaired elderly are cared for by families whose degree of difficulty in caregiving is very serious. Even among the most seriously impaired older persons who are completely bedridden and/or totally incontinent, more than half are cared for by families who experience very serious difficulty in doing so.

From the viewpoint of ascertaining the unmet needs of the impaired elderly and their families, the most seriously impaired older persons cared for in a family which has greatest difficulty in providing the care require special attention. As shown in Table 6, these cases account for 6.8 per thousand of the population over 65 living in the community. It is quite clear that these persons should be institutionalized as soon as possible for their own well-being as well as that of their caregivers. As this study was conducted seven years ago, the proportion might now be slightly smaller, owing to the development of the institutional services mentioned earlier. However, as the availability of nursing homes is still seriously inadequate in large metropolitan areas, it is certain that there are still many such families which have been awaiting admission into nursing homes for a long period. In many of these families, both the impaired elderly and their caregivers do not desire institutionalization because they think that care for aging parents should be provided by the children (including the son's wife) in their own home.

In Table 6 the proportion of families whose degree of difficulty in caregiving

Table 6. *Prevalence Rate of Impaired Older Persons by Degree of Physical Impairment and by Degree of Difficulty of Caring families*

Degree of Impairment	Degree of Difficulty of Caring Families					Totals
	Very Difficult	Slightly difficult	No difficulty	Unable to care or not caring	Degree of difficulty not known	
Most seriously impaired	6.8	2.6		—	0.2	9.6
Seriously impaired	16.8	2.8		1.4	—	21.0
Moderately impaired	20.5	8.1	0.2	7.2	—	35.9
Slightly impaired	5.4	1.2	0.2	6.5	0.2	13.5
Totals	49.5	14.7	0.4	15.1	0.4	80.0

Note: The number in each cell indicates the prevalence rate of the category per 1,000 persons aged 65+.
Source: Tokyo Metropolitan Institute of Gerontology, Sociology Department, 1983

is very serious accounted for more than 60 percent of all families caring for the impaired elderly. If one takes into consideration those families for whom caregiving conditions were slightly difficult, almost four-fifths of the caregiving families reported some difficulty.

Not all of these families need external care services immediately. It is quite likely, however, that most of the families caring for the most seriously impaired older persons will need some form of outside support in hte near future. Because community services to support these families are not very well developed, the hardships that they experience are often very grave. The term "family care" has a beautiful and noble connotation, but, in many cases, it is accompanied by the painful sacrifice of the caregivers, and the quality of care is frequently poor.

Table 6 shows the results of an objective measurement of the needs of the impaired elderly and their families. The same survey also studied the subjective needs in these cases and found that the number of respondents who expressed needs subjectively was much smaller than the number of cases diagnosed objectively as having needs. For example, the study showed that less than half of the families who were judged as needing home help services stated that they wanted that service. However, these implicit needs will no doubt become more and more explicit as the number of impaired older persons increases and as our society continues to change. The rising number of married middle-aged women anticipated to enter the labor force in the future is likely to be especially important in the shift from implicit to explicit needs.

Thus it is urgently necessary that we develop various types of institutional and community care services for the impaired elderly and their families as well as support and encouragement programs for those families.

Development of public services for the impaired elderly

In order to cope with the problems of the impaired elderly and their caregiving families, Japan has been developing various kinds of national services, ranging from institutional care to tax deduction or tax exemption programs. The national programs are all administered by local governments with subsidies from the national government. In addition to these programs, a number of local governments have established their own programs, although, generally speaking, the effects of local programs are limited when compared with those of the nationally supported programs.

A. Development of institutional care

Since 1970, the total number of beds in all kinds of institutions for the aged (including those for ambulant but frail elderly) has more than doubled, from 75,400 to 205,600 in 1985. But, due to the very rapid expansion of the population of the elderly as a whole, the increase in the proportion of institutionalized elderly was less conspicuous, from 1.02 percent to 1.65 percent, which is still remarkably small, compared with other developed countries.

1. Home-help services

In 1970, the number of home helpers throughout Japan was 6,100 (full-time). By 1987, the number had increased approximately four times, to 23,500. Over these seventeen years, the ratio of the number of home helpers to persons over 65 had increased from one per 1,210 to one per 530.

2. Provision of special equipment for bedridden older persons

This equipment includes special beds and bath-tubs, hot water heaters, mattresses, and so forth.

3. Short-term stay services

Short-term stay services for the bedridden elderly are fairly well-developed in Japan. In 1987, the national government assigned a subsidy for local governments to serve approximately 41,000 bedridden older persons throughout Japan. They can stay for a week in a nursing home for any reason, including giving respite to a caregiver. The length of stay can be extended when necessary.

4. Day-care services

In 1986, the national government announced as a long-term goal the development of a comprehensive, long-term, social security and health and social service programs for the aging society. In this announcement, the national government revealed that the goal for the development of day-care services is to establish 3,000 day-care centers throughout Japan in the near future. The government further said that in the long run, approximately 10,000 such centers should be established, including small-scale branch centers. In 1987, approximately 500 centers were established, including those not supported by the national subsidy.

Day-care services are expected to provide rehabilitation and reactivation services, and thereby enable elderly persons to become independent, or at least less dependent, in their daily living, which will alleviate the pressures on caregivers.

5. *Loans to caregivers who build or remodel their homes*

This program is provided for caregivers who build or remodel a house with an independent room for older parents, or add such a room to an existing home.

6. *Tax deduction or exemption*

Income tax credit is given to all taxpayers, regardless of income, who are supporting older persons over 70 whose income is below a certain level. When the old person is the taxpayer's or the spouse's parent and lives in the same household as the taxpayers, and when the degree of impairment is very serious, the deductible amount is further increased. Similar credits are also given for local taxes. The amount that is deductible, however, is rather small when compared to the amount actually needed to support an old person in the home. Therefore, this program should be regarded as a means of encouraging family caretaking rather than as real support.

Conclusions

The family is, and will continue to be, the most important source of support for the elderly in Japan. In the future, however, the relative importance of the role of family will inevitably decrease because (1) the proportion and real number of frail and impaired older people who are no longer independent in their daily living will greatly increase and (2) the capability of families to care for older parents will decrease due to demographic changes, industrialization, and urbanization. Therefore, various social services for the frail and impaired elderly and support services for the families who care for them will undoubtedly need to be expanded.

References

Brody, Elaine, "Aging", in *Encyclopedia of Social Work,* 17th edition, Vol. I. National Association of Social Workers, 1977

Institute of Population Problems, Ministry of Health and Welfare, *Estimated Future Population of Japan,* Tokyo, 1986

McPherson, Barry D., *Aging as a Social Process* (p.136), Butterworths, Toronto, 1983

Ministry of Health and Welfare, *Kōsei Gyōsei Kiso Chōsa Hōkoku: Shōwa 60-nenban* (The Report of the Fundamental Survey for the Health and Welfare Administration, 1985 edition), Tokyo, 1985-a

Ministry of Health and Welfare, *Kōsei Hakusho: Shōwa 60-nenban* (White Paper on Health and Welfare Administration, 1985 edition, p.45), Tokyo, 1985-b

National Council of Social Welfare, *Rōjin Kaigo Chōsa Hōkokusho* (Report of the National Survey on Caretakers of the Elderly), Tokyo, 1979

Section of Aging (Rōjin Taisakushitsu), General Executive Office, *Rōgono Seikatsuto Kaigoni Kansuru Chōsa* (Survey of Opinions about Life After Retirement and the Care to be Given), Tokyo, 1981

Section of Aging (Rojin Taisakushitsu), General Executive Office, *Rōjinno fuyōni AGE Kansuru Chōsa* (Survey on the Support and Care of Aged Parents), Tokyo, 1974, 1983

Statistics Bureau, General Executive Office, *Kokusei Chōsa* (National Census), Tokyo, 1950, 1955, 1970, 1975, 1980, 1985

Tokyo Metropolitan Institute of Gerontology (Sociology Department), *Zaitaku Shōgai Rōinto Sono Kazokuno Seikatsu Jittai, Oyobi Shakaifukushi Need-ni Kansuru Chōsa Kenkyū (3) — Tōkyōno shitamachino Baai* (Study on the Needs of Impaired Old People and their Families (3) — in the case of the older sections of Tokyo), 1983

Part Three

Contemporary Problems Of Legal

And Social Policy

Introduction

by John EEKELAAR

We have considered already, in Part Two, the role the law might play in forcibly moving private resources between family members. This remains a significant option with regard to the legal input into social policy towards the elderly. But it is far from the only, or the most important, one. Levine (Chapter 21) sets out the many contexts in which law may be operationalized in this area. He observes that many of its goals may be achieved by alternative means, such as discretion and custom. Law is not necessarily better. Yet, in some societies at least, the institutional values of the law may have a particularly significant role to play. These values have to do with the uniform application of constitutional principles; the establishment of rights and impartial supervision over the discharge of public responsibilities.

London (Chapter 22) provides an excellent example of how legal values can be mobilized at a constitutional level to combat one feature of what is often referred to as "ageism", mandatory retirement, in his powerful analysis of the Canadian provisions, in particular, that of the Canadian Charter of Rights and Freedoms which, from 17 April 1985, gave every individual a "right to equal protection and equal benefit of the law" without discrimination on the basis of age. Henceforth, any such discrimination is lawful only if this "can reasonably be justified in a free and democratic society". Much, then, will turn on whether mandatory retirement can be so justified.

The arguments are fully canvassed by London, and need to be considered further in the light of the ensuing chapters by Guillemard (Chapter 23) and Thomson (Chapter 24). Yet one preliminary point should be considered. If *any* measure which discriminated on the ground of age is viewed as "ageism", and accordingly indistinguishable from "racism", or "sexism", it would be difficult *ever* to justify it in a "free and democratic society". But can it be so considered? Is a law which prohibits *any* child, no matter how gifted, from receiving public education until age six to be placed in the same bracket as a law which allows children of one race to begin school at six and of another at ten? It must surely matter that in one case the criterion applies potentially to all members of society, whereas in the other some members are disadvantaged on the bases of characteristics unique to themselves which they cannot alter. The point is not that universal age restrictions on entering or leaving education or employment are necessarily acceptable, but that their repugnancy needs to be established (if at all) by more elaborate argumentation than re-iteration of the rhetoric associated with racial or sexual discrimination.

Guillemard (Chapter 23) argues that mandatory retirement constructs a social definition of old-age as being the stage when an individual is banned from the labour market. Indeed, that retirement policy has operated as a function of employment policy is well established. The European drive towards lower retirement ages during the late 1970s and early 1980s was a clear attempt to cope with unemployment and, in Guillemard's view, has threatened earlier policies aimed at integrating the elderly within their community. But how do the arguments of London and Guillemard stand beside the thesis expounded by Thomson (Chapter 24)? Here is a different perception of the inter-generational conflict. In this view, not only is the full weight of the demographic shift to older societies being borne by the younger generation, the older generation has also captured the political process and is imposing on its successors burdens far in excess of those it suffered in its youth. Thomson selects a variety of indicators to establish the claim that the modern old (and soon-to-be old) are benefitting at the expense of youth: the elderly are no longer the most impoverished sector; social security expenditure on the elderly has grown while benefits to the young have declined; the elderly live longer, while infant mortality has risen; education and employment provision for the young has deteriorated; the old benefit from capital savings and high interest rates, and lowering of high marginal tax rates has aided older rather than younger earners.

Many more features of contemporary policy could be cited to support Thomson's case. Yet many will want to broaden the perspective. The arguments run counter to that of those who see expansion of mandatory retirement as forcing the old out of work in favour of the young. But perhaps the "Thomsonian" thesis would view the attack on mandatory retirement as yet another strategy of the older generation to consolidate its economic superiority over young people who have heavier commitments and are struggling for higher incomes. Again, even if the economic position of pensioners has improved, and OECD data cited by Holtzmann (chapter 51) support this, the improvement is only relative to other 'disadvantaged' groups, and in many societies they are over-represented among the poor. [For a British discussion, see Alan Walker, "Pensions and the Production of Poverty in Old Age" in Chris Phillipson and Alan Walker (eds) *Ageing and Social Policy* (Gower, 1986), ch. 10. In Britain in 1985, the poorest household was that of a lone parent with a child; this was followed, in order of increasing wealth, by that of a retired adult, of two retired adults, of two adults with two children, of two adults and one child, of one adult (not retired) and, best-off of all, two adults (not retired): information supplied by the *Family Policy Studies Centre*]. Fundamentally, however, it must be for the reader to decide how far the economic policies of many contemporary industrialized societies, which have sought to boost private wealth at the expense of public service provision, can be characterized in terms of "generational politics" rather than the more orthodox perceptions of free enterprise v. social planning, monetarism v. Keynesianism, rich v. poor, capitalism v. socialism. Also, it seems that the "Thomsonian" thesis is of relevance only to the industrialized world. The problems of the developing world are, as we have seen, of a different order.

Gec-Korosec's description (Chapter 25) of labour and education law in

Yugoslavia, so far as it pertains to the elderly, is of interest within the context of the debate on mandatory retirement. Despite the generalization that maximum ages may not be fixed as a qualification for employment, it is evident that this is heavily qualified by the demands of employment policy. Thus the employee must normally retire when the pension requirements are fulfilled *unless no suitable replacement can be found.* However, retirement at a stated age will usually only be required if the employee has, additionally, worked sufficient years to qualify for full pension (a possible approach referred to by London), introducing an equity into mandatory retirement which an age limit alone overlooks. Gec-Korosec's account of educational opportunities for the elderly is also of importance, since it is an area of law and policy to which insufficient attention is usually given.

The remaining chapters in this part deal with a variety of issues in which legal policy can play an important part. Graycar (Chapter 26) emphasizes the usefulness (perhaps necessity) of establishing that the elderly have *rights.* This avoids the pitfalls of characterizing the elderly as a problem, a group apart from society *to* which things need to be done.Instead, it focusses on each old person as an individual in his or her own right with legitimate claims against society. He examines the role of the Commissioner for Ageing in South Australia (an office which he holds) in furthering the rights of the elderly. This involves a consideration of various sets of more general legislation which are of relevance to the elderly, such as laws concerning equal opportunities, legal services, mental health, residential tenancies and mode of death. Legal protection of their conditions of accommodation, whether private or in nursing homes, is given particular attention. This theme is further explored by Frost (Chapter 27), who describes the Danish policy which culminated in a total prohibition on the construction of new residential homes for old people. But provision of care for old people, whether in their own homes or in residential accommodation, raises issues of supervision over the providers and self-determination by the receivers, both of which are crucial in the articulation of any policy which claims to recognize that the elderly have rights.

Bainham (Chapter 28), examines English legal doctrines relating to the acquisition of rights in private dwellings, and finds that the law has been so obsessed with the model of the nuclear family that it has totally failed to take into account the legitimate aspirations of the elderly to fashion their living arrangements according to their requirements. The chapter illustrates the fine balance that must be drawn between marking off the elderly as a "different" population from the whole, with the attendant risks of its marginalization and even discrimination, and an approach which could be so integrationist as to fail to adapt provisions designed for persons experiencing one stage of the life-cycle to those in quite a different position. Lund-Andersen and Munck (Chapter 29) continue the consideration given by Bainham to cohabitees, but broaden it to include an examination of the impact of a wide range of Danish legal provisions on elderly cohabitees. The position is revealed as being confused and contradictory, something likely to be repeated by a similar examination of most legal systems. The Committee on Marriage wished to continue to promote marriage, even, it seems, for the elderly (themselves perhaps the survivors of earlier marriages). But a method of doing this consistently with the wish to protect the "weaker" party in cohabitation and to introduce the principle that social benefits should be provided on an individual, rather than "family" (or "status") basis, has not yet been found.

This Part concludes with a look at how the interests of the elderly are relevant to law and policy relating to consumers. And if Reyes's description (Chapter 30) of the current position in the Philippines leads to the conclusion that much remains to be done in this area in that country, the reader may ask how far these issues have been addressed, if at all, in his or her own jurisdiction. Finally, Coleman (Chapter 31) describes the various initiatives which have been made in the United States to make legal services available to the elderly. Legal service provision differs greatly from country to country, and the American legal structure has its unique features. But any viewpoint which maintains that legal ideas or institutions have any role to play in the implementation of a policy towards the elderly must pay close attention to the way legal services are made available to the elderly in the community.

Chapter 21

The Role of the Law

Martin Lyon Levine[1]   University of Southern California,
                                                 Los Angeles, USA

Is law important?

My thesis is that law, suitably understood, has important functions for aging. "Elderlaw" or "aging and law" encompasses a broad scope of important legal topics. Law is important on two levels: to legal problems of an aging society, and to legal concerns of older individuals. It thus has roles as a means for planning by society as a whole, and as a system of administration that protects individual expectations and claims. In my discussion I will mention three perspectives on law, and recommend one as most useful to those concerned with problems of the elderly. I will also outline eight specific roles of the law important to older individuals and an aging society.

Alternatives to law. "Law," however, is not the only way to fulfill these roles. It is a social decision, contingent on certain cultural and historical facts, to use law in this way. These roles of the law are not inherently natural nor do they follow from the very definition of law. Where Americans have used law, for example, other societies may have used other social institutions. Examples of alternatives to law include the use of political discretion or customary practices.

Ethics and policy. In law, the most interesting and hardest questions are normative: what should legal decisionmakers do? For this reason, policy and ethical issues for the elderly intersect the legal issues. Lawyers interested in this subject therefore have reason to fashion a dialog with colleagues in the fields of ethics and of social policy, and those scholars may be surprised that lawyers share interests with them.

Comparative approach. Because law could be used in many different roles, lawyers from different countries will find much of value by talking with one another about the experiences of their own nations. Social experimentation is difficult to do but using the experience of other countries provides an alternative,what scientists call a quasi-experiment.

What may be most interesting is to find that things we take for granted as self-evident are regarded in another nation as controversial or wrong, while the other nation may have taken as given things we have never even considered.

The problems to be faced

Law's role for the elderly on the two levels I have mentioned deals with two sets of problems. The micro-level problems are those of older individuals (what can be called "a legal context for aging", or the influence of law on the task of seeking a successful old age). The macro-level problems are the issues of an aging society.

Micro level. The individual now faces a usual life course including a period of productivity longer than in traditional times. This is typically followed by a period of old age also far longer than ever before, often without employment, without the security of a family support system, and with substantial needs — particularly income maintenance, health, housing, long-term care, and protective services.

Macro level. Our aging societies also face new demographic realities without precedent in world history. There are not only large numbers of elderly, but also numbers of the very old, and a large fraction of the population who are elderly.

Scope

The scope of subjects in which the law plays an important role for the elderly is very broad.

A. Content

The content of the subject " aging and law" includes many diverse topics that can be grouped in five areas (Levine, 1986).

The legal system. Lawyers can be excused for thinking of legal services first. Laws in some countries guarantee to older persons, either together with other citizens or as a special right, the right to free or reduced-rate legal services. In some nations, the elderly person's claim to government benefits is treated as a legal right, enforceable through the courts. Old age may be treated as a legal status, like childhood, entailing either disabilities or entitlements; or a civil rights approach invoking "age discrimination" may command that decisions be age-neutral.

Income maintenance. In many nations, public pension and social insurance programs help maintain an adequate replacement ratio for retired elderly. The provision of services and redistribution of goods is one of the major categories of law's primary functions (Raz, 1973) and the elderly are among the most important beneficiaries of this function.

Laws can also help the elderly by protecting benefits promised under private pension regimes. In the USA, prohibitions of mandatory retirement and of other age discrimination in employment provide a legal framework so that the elderly can continue to earn. Our legal systems have no "mandatory retirement rule" for ownership, thus protecting the individual's wealth as she enters old age.

Health and mental health. Laws can be used to establish programs to provide services, or reimbursement for expenses, to meet the health and mental health needs of the elderly. In some nations, provisions based on age provide the elderly with significantly more benefits than younger persons. In other countries, old age may be treated as a disqualification for expensive medical procedures. Especially important are provisions for long-term care in institutions, and for alternatives to institutionalization — both subsidization of costs, and protection of individual rights.

The vulnerable elder. Traditional concerns of lawyers are the laws concerning protective services, including formal guardianship and conservatorship, for the elderly. Special rules can provide for the elderly person to exercise autonomy over health care and life-and-death decisions, through laws on informed consent for medical treatment, living wills, and durable powers of attorney for health care. Or the best interests of the older person can be sought through rules recognizing the decision-making authority of doctors or family.

Other rights. Other programs, laws and rights may exist which deal with people differently because of their old age, or which (though age-neutral on their face) impact differentially on the elderly, such as: housing provisions, rights of grandparents, transportation programs, nutrition programs, and so on.

B. Themes

Several basic themes underlie these legal provisions: (1) helping the individual elder preserve her autonomy of control over her own life, (2) developing governmental programs to substitute for the traditional patterns of family support, (3) meeting the special needs of the elderly and (4) allowing the elder a position of equality in society without age discrimination. I explore the last theme in my book *Age Discrimination and the Mandatory Retirement Controversy* (Levine, 1988a).

Form. For all the content areas, modern law usually has proceeded by statute rather than by judicial innovation, by setting up new governmental programs more often than by recognizing new causes of action, and by providing methods of satisfying claims that may not always rise to the level of legal rights.

Three Perspectives

In considering legal problems of an elderly society and older individuals, lawyers from different legal traditions may use quite different perspectives. I want to differentiate three different points of view on the role of the law, while recognizing that, to those who have been following current debates among legal scholars, the perspectives I have defined here may seem remarkably old-fashioned.

A. Perspective A

Doctrinal. In many countries "law" may be defined as a body of doctrine, studied in classical terms. Legal doctrine can be seen as a set of definitions and axioms, from which detailed propositions can be demonstrated. Many legal scholars in many nations take an approach within the range that may be called classical, formalist, doctrinal, or conceptual. The method of thought may be deductive, reasoning from principles to specific cases, or inductive, reasoning from specific cases to principles. In either case, scholars can analyze the terms of a legal code, or of judicial opinions, trying to bring order to them. The law relevant to the elderly would then be seen as certain traditional doctrines or as innovations in doctrine.

Autonomous. Law, conceived as a set of doctrines, is often seen as relatively autonomous. Legal changes important to the elderly might be generated by development concepts and preferences already manifest in existing law.

Unimportant. Law, as conceived in this first perspective, is a rather minor player in a world where important decisions are made through other social institutions, and in another vocabulary. Depending on the society, the key social institutions may be business, government, politics, party or family. From this perspective, it is unusual and awkward to talk about important issues by using legal concepts, because courts and lawyers cannot be expected to have any really important role to play in most matters of great significance to the society, such as responding to demographic aging. A dichotomy may be drawn between maximalism and minimalism, law as social engineering or as legal craftsmanship, and lawyers as high priests in a world of norms and principles or as trouble-shooters in case of conflict (Feldbrugge, 1968).

While the several points in perspective A are not logically one, they are often held together: law is viewed as an autonomous body of thought, but it is accepted that major decisions are made outside the law, and that courts and judges play a peripheral and not a central role in society's decisions.

B. Perspective B

Important but Dependent. A second perspective assumes that other social institutions are the dominant ones in society — perhaps business or government. But in this perspective, courts and the law are nevertheless expected to play an important role, which is still a subservient one. For example, a government which makes all major decisions through its internal political processes might nevertheless be accustomed to carrying out its will through courts and codes of law.

A Facade of Doctrine. From this perspective, any pretensions to autonomy by courts or scholars is a facade, a mystification, concealing the true bases of decision that underlie them. The web of doctrine in Elderlaw, in this perspective, is part of that facade.

C. Perspective C

Important and Interactive. I think that law does have a role, and an important one. It is a perspective borrowed from European intellectuals to see law as more than a system of doctrine, but also as a set of social institutions and cultural ideals. The institutions of law (including the legal profession and the courts) are influenced by other important social institutions (businesses, unions, political forces, and churches) but also influence them; the arrow of social causation goes both ways.

Law as a tool. Law's role for the elderly can be seen within this third perspective, in an idea borrowed from the Europeans, in terms of law as means to an end. Social actors (lobbyists for the elderly, lawyers, governments) make use of legal concepts and the legal system to achieve desirable social consequences. Even the use of legal rights can be evaluated, within this perspective, in consequentialist rather than deontological terms. Law is different from other cultural ideas and social institutions, but like them is can be used as a tool.

Koopmans (1986) differentiates two stages in the role of the law, both in legal practice (what people actually do with the law) and in legal theories. The first stage is characterized by a strong belief in institutions. The second is an instrumental conception of the law, in which law is seen as a means to certain ends. The first stage is a discovery of the importance of law and legal institutions; in the second one discovers how many interesting things you can do with law. This second stage argues that it is characteristic of the law to serve the policy ends or goals of the community (Lasswell & McDougal, 1967; McDougal, 1966).

Eight roles

Law's roles for both individual and social problems is important, but in saying this, I use the term "law" as a shorthand for various cultural ideas and social institutions — including at least eight facets: the roles of government, legislation, the idea of rights, the rule of law, courts, and lawyers.

Society is increasingly using government agencies, rather than the family or factory or other social institution, as mechanisms through which to provide and pay for services and goods needed by older persons.

Law can provide orientation as well as regulation (Kulcsar, 1983), for example through statements of national policy or ideal goals, expressed by the legislature of the courts. Examples include the U.S. Older Americans Act and expressions of opinion by superior courts.

Legislation is a way for society consciously to alter social arrangements to meet new demographic realities. In legislation, one need not attempt to deduce all specific decisions from a few general principles or concepts. It is understood that the lawmaker must make choices, and that law-making is a trial and error affair, where compromises must be made because of political opposition, administrative concerns, and the budget. In legislation, also, one need not struggle to find legitimacy for changes in the law; whether arguments for government legitimacy are democratic or non-democratic, legislatures or their equivalents are accepted as generators of new law.

The idea of legal rights provides concrete embodiment of moral claims, so as to protect older persons' entitlements and expectations created by statute or custom. The idea of rights supports the individual's claim.

Contrast the idea of legal rights with an idea of non-rights. There are governments that set up extensive programs for the elderly providing that, under certain conditions, older persons are to receive a pension, or medical services, or transportation. One might say that any individual older person in such a country has an expectation she will receive those benefits. Nevertheless, in such a country, a low-level administrative official, or a policy-making high official, may have discretion to deny that expectation. The denial may be because of budgetary reasons, or changed priorities, or administrative difficulties, or frankly political considerations, or for any of the host of reasons that (let us assume) would have been legitimate in setting up the program to begin with. Within a regime of legal rights, however, once the specific expectations are created by law, they are considered valid without any need for the type of balancing of competing claims that went into creating the law initially.

The concept of the rule of law — if it is any different from the idea of legal rights itself — is a particular idea about rights. A nineteenth century British idea, this concept implies that government will be administered through rules, and that they will be obeyed by officials as well as by citizens. The rules are to be administered equally — and the principle of equality suggests that extraneous considerations will not be allowed to dilute the application of the substantive rule. And the rule will be administered fairly — the principles of fairness suggest an attention to accurate facts, and to procedures likely to yield accurate facts.

The ability to appeal for court enforcement of rights can give the elderly access to justice, so that the promised rights become real. To say that someone has a "legal right" then means that she can go to court and secure a court order to secure those rights, or to compensate for their denial. A court is a kind of institution where anyone, no matter how poor or insignificant, can challenge the great and powerful, and can base the challenge on the norm — on what is supposed to be. Law provides the individual with access to institutions of authority.

We can imagine some other social institution other than a court that could play such a role — a powerful individual, a labor union, a company, a political party. If any institution plays such a role in a society we can say that abstract rights have become institutional ones. When courts are the institution to enforce rights, than we expect certain additional virtues, such as that the institution will be open to all persons, and that decision will be made according to rules.

Law can also provide a means for mobilization (Zemans, 1983). A lawsuit can be a focus for political activity and legal norms can stimulate political organizing.

Private lawyers or subsidized legal services programs for the elderly are means to make effective the access to courts.

Lawyers are not always be required. If a country has such an efficient court system that lawyers are not needed, so much the better. Or if specialized personnel exist to help claimants, but instead of being called lawyers are called paralegals, or court clerks, or ombudsmen, it makes little difference. But in a world where the individual is often helpless in the face of a vast bureaucracy, and where the elderly are particularly required to deal with bureaucracies for their basic needs, providing lawyers for the elderly who need them is a great force for equality. It provides a sword and a shield in the fight against bureaucracy.

Conclusion

Gerontology for lawyers. Because law has roles for the elderly of the kind I have mentioned, gerontologists and lawyers are beginning to forge ties with one another. And more lawyers are realizing the importance of legal problems of the elderly.

Law for gerontologists. Gerontologists who have long studied social policy issues are beginning to realize that lawyers may have something to say on those topics. (Levine & Berhman, 1988).

New networks for interaction. Because the world needs some way for gerontologists and lawyers to talk to each other on these topics, the International Federation of the Aging, with the World Health Organization, has formed EAGLE, the exchange on gerontology and law topics whose formal name is the International Society on Aging, Law and Ethics.

Note

1. UPS Foundation Professor of Law, Gerontology, Psychiatry and the Behavioral Sciences, University of Southern California, (Los Angeles 90089-0071 USA) President, International Society on Aging, Law and Ethics, (London); Honorary President, National Senior Citizens Law Center (Washington DC and Los Angeles); and past Chairman, Association of American Law Schools Section on Aging and Law (Washington DC). The studies underlying this paper were supported by the generosity of the UPS Foundation, the philanthropic arm of the United Parcel Service.

References

F.J.M. Feldbrugge, *Tussen theologie medicijnen; rechts als regels en recht als proces*, Inaugural address at Leiden (1968), quoted in T. Koopmans, *The Role of Law in the Next Stage of European Integration*, 35 ICLQ 925-931, (1986)

T. Koopmans, *The Role of Law in the Next Stage of European Integration*, 35 ICLQ 925-931 (1986)

Kalman Kulcsar, "Social and Historical Variations and Possibilities in the Role of Law Making," *International Journal of the Sociology of Law 11* (1983): 277.

Harold Lasswell & Myres McDougal, **"Jurisprudence** in a Policy Oriented Perspective," *Florida Law Review* (1967) 19 486.

Martin L. Levine, *Age Discrimination and the Mandatory Retirement Controversy*. London & Baltimore: The Johns Hopkins University Press, 1988. (a)

Martin L.Levine, *Elderlaw: Legal, Ethical and Policy Issues of Older Individuals and an Aging Society*. Washington, D.C.: Legal Services Corporation, 1988. (b)

Martin L. Levine & Simon Bergman, *Justice for the Elderly: International Variations*. Jerusalem: Brookdale Institute of Gerontology, 1988.

Myres McDougal, "Jurisprudence for a Free Society", *Georgia Law Review* 1 (1966): 1

Fabian M. McKinnon, "The Role of International Law in Inter-state Conflict: Nine Aspects, *"Co-existence* 20 (1983): 27

Joseph Raz, "On the Functions of Law," in *Oxford Essays in Jurisprudence, second series*, ed. A.W.B. Simpson. Oxford: Clarendon Press, 1973.

Frances Kahn Zemans, "Legal Mobilization: The Neglected Role of Law in the Political System," *American Political Science Review* 77 (1983): 690.

Chapter 22

The Canadian Experience in Mandatory Retirement: A Human Rights Perspective

Jack R. LONDON

Faculty of Law,
University of Manitoba, Canada

Introduction[1]

The subject matter of this chapter is the Canadian experience in mandatory retirement. More precisely, it deals with the current debate surrounding, and progress being made in effecting, the abolition of mandatory retirement in the Canadian workplace, and the human rights therein involved.

Inevitably, any attempt to describe rules, policies or practices in Canada meets head on in collision with the reality of the Canadian political structure. Canada is a confederal state. By virtue of its Constitution[2], legislative authority and jurisdiction is divided between parliament, that is, the federal government, and the legislatures of ten provinces, each of which has legislative authority within its constitutional allocation and its own geographical boundaries. Two territories, Yukon and the Northwest Territories share some equivalence of provincial legislative power in their respective geographic boundaries, but are really subject to federal control. In each case, the governments carry out their constitutional jurisdiction and function through bureaucracies which are organized and subdivided through Executive Ministries. Parliament and the Executive regulate employment within the federal bureaucracy and in federally regulated industries like banking and transport. Each of the Legislatures and Provincial Executives regulate employment within their territory. Local and municipal governments are creatures of the provinces and subject to their respective provincial legislative jurisdiction. For the most part, the better view is that undertakings of the federal government, are subject to provincial laws of general application.[3]

The most important exception to this rule, for present purposes, relates to the laws regulating employment practices. Employees within the federal Civil Service as well as those in federally-regulated industries, will be subject to federal statutes and standards of employment and federal human rights legislation, wherever the employment or employee may be resident. Provincial laws will not be applicable. Conversely, employees in the private sector, as well as those employed by provincial governments or in industries regulated by provincial governments, will be subject to provincial employment and human rights laws in the province of residence, employment or undertaking.

Thus, it is important to recognize, at the outset, that, in Canada, persons performing otherwise identical work as employees may have quite different rights and standards applicable to their employment, which rights will vary on the basis of:

1) whether or not the employee is subject to legislation of the parliament of Canada or that of one of the provinces or territories; and

2) the peculiar and particular regime of the proper law of the province or territory of employment each of which differs from that of the others.

Moreover, subject to the overriding principles of the Canadian Charter of Rights and Freedoms,[4] there is no accepted test which gives predominance to federal, over provincial, legislative regimes in the area of employment and human rights law. Needless to say, significant differences also are prevalent in the regimes of the federal and provincial governments.

Prior to April 17, 1982, the day on which the Constitution Act, 1982 was proclaimed in force in Canada, the right of the federal and provincial governments to promulgate employment and human rights laws and standards in their respective legislative jurisdictions was virtually unfettered. To that time, Canada had a limited system of judicial review which essentially restricted Canadian courts to acting as arbitrators of jurisdictional squabbles between the levels of government. To all intents and purposes it can be said that judicial review involving resolution of the fundamental rights of groups or individuals in conflict with state power was virtually non-existent in Canada.[5] The Constitution Act of 1867,[6] which allocated legislative and functional powers between the federal and provincial governments, did address some issues of values, essentially based on notions like the "rule of law," but the ramifications and effects were rather sterile and certainly infrequent.

However, with the entrenchment of the Canadian Charter of Rights and Freedoms in the Constitution Act as of April 17, 1982, the Canadian Constitution for the first time formally addressed and protected a number of values, including, for example, the fundamental freedoms of expression, religious belief, association, and mobility within Canada, protections related to the criminal justice system and many others. One of those protected values is that of "equality" and the right of individuals to live and work free of a number of proscribed grounds of discrimination, including discrimination based on age.[7] The Charter thereby clearly extended to Canadian judges the power to review legislation and governmental action on the basis of its congruence with the values protected in the Charter, i.e., true judicial review. And the Canadian courts, more or less, have accepted the invitation to become partners, if junior partners, with the legislative and executive branches of government in determining the "rights" of Canadians. Thus, as will be seen more fully later, the right of an employer to retire an employee compulsorily at a certain age is dependent, in Canada, not only on the applicable law of the jurisdiction, as earlier mentioned, but also on the question of whether or not that law itself can withstand judicial scrutiny under the Charter of Rights and Freedoms, particularly section 15 thereof. In that regard, the development of Canadian law is, as yet, embryonic.

Overall, one might describe the Canadian landscape on the issue of mandatory retirement as a patchwork quilt, uniquely consistent with the Canadian tradition, indeed fetish, for ambiguity in its value orientation and schizophrenic in its treatment of its citizen's rights.

Within that general opening context, the Canadian experience with mandatory retirement will be addressed as follows:

1. The Human, Social and Economic Issues Involved;
2. Legislative and Judicial patterns;
3. The Impact of the Canadian Charter of Rights and Freedoms.

The Human, Social and Economic Issues Involved

The inconsistent mosaic earlier described is perhaps understandable. Notwithstanding significant advances in social welfare programmes in Canada, for most people the characteristics of their employment are the major determinants of their standard and quality of living. In a very real sense, for most Canadians, the jobs are their capital and their capital is their security. This capital is measured both by its flow of income, in the form of wages or other compensation, and by its longevity, represented by the timing of termination through dismissal or retirement. Equally important are factors such as posttermination capital rights; in particular, pension rights. There are also a number of inherent psychological issues, including job satisfaction, working conditions and access to benefit plans.

One's self perception is inextricably wound up with the work one accomplishes. Those who are unable to access jobs feel understandably diminished and angry. Those feelings are echoed in the minds of some who are forced to leave because of age related retirement policy, though, overwhelmingly, it is a matter of public knowledge that most workers look forward to retirement years with great anticipation.

Until recently, we had become quite easy with the selection of age sixty-five as a "normal" retirement age. The notion followed on the development of social security programs in many parts of the industrialized world. In 1889 Otto Von Bismarck, then Chancellor of Germany, initiated social security programs for Germany. Since 1916, those programs set 65 as the age when people would begin receiving social security and pension benefits.[8] As a result, age 65 came also to mean the time of mandatory retirement for many working people.

In the United Kingdom, paragraph 64(1)(b) of the Employment Protection (Consolidation) Act, 1978, c.44 (U.K.) as amended, excepts from the provisions of the Act which prohibit unfair dismissal, the dismissal of an employee upon attaining the "normal retiring age" for the position, or age 65. In the United States mandatory retirement at age 65 became the prevailing practice in the decades following the enactment of the Social Security Act in 1935.[9]

In 1967 in the United States, the Age Discrimination in Employment Act[10] protected persons age 40 through age 65 against age discrimination. However, by the mid-seventies the issue had become one of civil rights with the increasingly prevalent view being that mandatory retirement at a specific age was offensive. On April 6, 1978, the Age Discrimination in Employment Act of 1967 was amended[11] to extend protection against age discrimination for most non-federal workers up to age 70. It also eliminated the upper age limit for most federal employees. Tenured employees at institutions of higher education were excepted from that protection until July 1, 1982. In 1986, the Age Discrimination in Employment Amendments[12] removed the age seventy limit completely, once again providing a 7-Year exemption with regard to tenured faculty members of colleges and universities.

It is important to note that throughout the American and Canadian experience, university professors have been identified, along with judges, senior executive management, employees in jobs involving public safety, and a number of public service occupations, as being particularly problematic when abolishing compulsory retirement. Sometimes the focus is appropriate. Sometimes it is simply a guise to relieve administrative inconvenience.

In Canada, as will be described more fully hereafter, the trend since the early 1970s, both constitutionally and in the legislative programs of several provinces and the federal government, has been to diminish or abolish the practice of mandatory retirement which had previously been considered normal in Canada at age 65.

These changes in law and policy have generated much debate in all jurisdictions, whether legislatively active or passive. A review of the literature, as well as the legislative and judicial proceedings, discloses a number of arguments which repeat frequently on both sides of the issue, regardless of the jurisdiction in which it is addressed or, indeed, whether or not the forum is legislative or judicial.

The arguments said to favour a policy of non-consensual, mandatory retirement at a given age, say 65, are as follows:
1. A universal mandatory retirement scheme promises more rapid upward mobility for individuals within an employment system;
2. It allows for the more frequent entry of younger employees into the system, thereby reducing the incidence of chronic youth unemployment;
3. In many sectors, notably in universities and industries dependent on research and development, compulsory retirement prevents staleness and promotes renewal and progress;
4. It honours the fundamental principle of freedom of contract, consistently argued both by management and labour, both of which institutions often do not regard mandatory retirement as age discrimination or an infringement of

rights. In this context, a mandatory retirement age is simply one of the plethora of benefits and obligations which need to be bargained in an employment contract, particularly where bargaining is collective;

5. The abolition of mandatory retirement has an adverse impact on pension rights and plans because pension benefits are dependent on definition of "normal retirement age" for proper actuarial determination. At the very least, significant changes would be required to entitlement. Perhaps, more importantly, it is argued that the right to retire on pension has been a long hard-fought-for benefit in the collective bargaining process which is put at risk, at least symbolically, with the notion that retirement on pension is not an "expected" benefit, but rather one of individual choice.

Indeed, it might be argued that the movement towards abolition of mandatory retirement is a rather insidious attempt by conservative forces to ensure that workers are conditioned to expect to remain in employment even after age 65. The passing of the baby boom generation, it is frequently predicted, will result in a labour shortage, requiring more workers. Older workers will be a source of supply. Moreover, conditioning older people to work longer will relieve younger people of the obligation to support them through heavier pension contributions and the high tax rates required to pay for expensive social security benefits.

In this view, since there will be an increased cohort of older people resulting from the baby boom years and fewer younger people to support them, the burden on those younger people would be alleviated if we reduced the magnitude of pension and social welfare benefits and therefore the cost to be borne by the younger workers and taxpayers;

6. Older people, through the provision of massive social security benefits, both public and private, including pension benefits, health care assistance, tax benefits and geriatric social services, are already benefitted disproportionately to their entitlement and need in the society. The abolition of mandatory retirement, it is argued, therefore cannot be justified on the basis that it is "age discrimination" since rather than being discriminated against, all things considered, the elders of our communities are actually treated more beneficially than are younger people;

7. Since disease, illness and disability increase with age, the cost of employee benefit plans such as short and long term disability insurance, health and dental care insurance, life insurance, accident insurance and sick leave benefits will be greatly increased either at the expense of the employer, and hence the productivity of the economy, or of other younger workers;

8. The certainty of mandatory retirement encourages planning by individuals for their retirement years. The absence of it may lead to more chaotic and dysfunctional retirement proceedings on the part of those who will procrastinate on the assumption of continued employment;

9. Promotion and seniority systems will be adversely affected to the fiscal and psychological disadvantage of younger workers and those with less seniority;

10. Particularly in institutions or industries with fixed budgets and/or fixed

worker complements with tenure, the absence of mandatory retirement will have the effect of continuing to appropriate large, and larger, shares of salary budgets in favour of more expensive, older employees. The theory, and fact, here is that generally our compensation systems work on a deferred model. We defer compensation in two ways. We extract a portion of earnings in early years in order to fund pension benefits in later years. Moreover, we do not reward productivity in employment appropriately throughout a working career, rather paying lower wages early in a work position and higher wages later. Thus, the salary of an older worker, who may or may not be more productive than a younger worker, is almost inevitably greater than of the younger worker. The abolition of mandatory retirement, to the extent that older workers remain employed, inhibits, or prohibits, redistribution of the salary lines of older workers in favour of other institutional purposes or in favour of less expensive junior workers, thereby decreasing expansion of the workforce. This problem is particularly acute, it is argued, at universities and in the bureaucracies which have tenure of special job security;

11. A policy of mandatory retirement relieves management of the need to test the "productivity" of those nearing the end of their careers, sometimes called the "coasting period." The abolition of mandatory retirement would lead to an increase in the evaluation and monitoring of employees, and increased incidence of dismissal for cause, with consequent increase in grievance and litigious procedures contesting those decisions. Both financially, psychologically and productively, the costs are significant. Moreover, in some jobs, teaching for example, the measurement of performance or productivity is so difficult and abstract a venture that it cannot be done effectively, requiring a more arbitrary system of definition such as that of fixed compulsory retirement age. This argument completely ignores the fact that we do already monitor and evaluate, even in the teaching profession;

12. In that context, generally, the phenomenon of mandatory retirement preserves the dignity of an older worker who has slowed down, or is less competent, in that, under a mandatory, universal scheme, the individual is simply "retired," not for any personal reasons, but because of general policy considerations which do not involve any negative stigmatization of the individual's performance or personhood.

The arguments favouring mandatory retirement are significant and not unpersuasive, though the spectre of harm is somewhat exaggerated given the existing data in Canada and the United States.

However, the arguments against mandatory retirement and in favour of schemes of voluntary employment which allow an individual to choose to retire at a "normal retirement age," or earlier, on pension, or to continue working, are more highly persuasive. Even in the event that the spectre of some systemic dysfunction resulting from abolition was real, basic notions and principles of fair and equal treatment of the working population and equality of opportunity, at any age, argue heavily in favour of voluntary rather than mandatory retirement schemes. These arguments are as follows:

1. Foremost, mandatory retirements on the basic of age alone ought to be rejected because denial of opportunity of any kind, when grounded in stereotypical assumptions, is inherently and distinctly unlovely, perhaps even evil. Each of us has the right to be assessed for who and what we are, not what we are assumed to be. Any narrowing of the vision of equality of opportunity in employment,and of respect for the individual employee, ought not to be countenanced by the legal system nor by the policies of any institution. Because mandatory retirement assumes that older workers either are less competent or less entitled than younger workers to the opportunity of employment, it offends basic notions of human and civil rights and liberty. It is no answer to argue that age discrimination, which is the basis of mandatory retirement, is not like other forms of discrimination since, if one lives, everyone reaches the age of retirement and is then equally treated with all others. There is involved, nevertheless, a denial of opportunity and fulfillment in one's work. More importantly, there is inherent, in that notion, an assumption that all persons reaching the defined age of normal retirement will have had equal access to, and an equal term of, employment in the years preceding employment as well as having derived equal income therefrom. That obviously is inaccurate. People are able to access employment, and remain in employment, at quite different times and rates. The attainment of a certain age is therefore merely a very arbitrary, and unsatisfactory measure of historical opportunity. If mandatory retirement has value in the society, it should be based not on an arbitrary fixed age but rather on the concept of retirement after having been in employment for a certain aggregate of years, consecutive or not, or having achieved a certain income in aggregate over time;
2. Absent a general rule in the community that all persons employed or self-employed must cease gainful endeavour at the magic age, mandatory retirement imposes a burden on workers not also imposed on others, which is inherently unreasonable;
3. Our society and community generally accord higher status and respect to people who are gainfully employed than to those who are not. Those who are employed are often characterized as more "worthwhile" than those who are not. Neither law or policy ought to prescribe that an individual must suffer loss of self esteem and/or a diminution of community respect, even though competent, simply because of having reached a certain age. Indeed, the psychological difficulties of adjustment to the retirement period may lead to increased physical and medical disability;
4. Two of the basic justifications for mandatory retirement plans usually are argued to be those of "efficiency" and "safety." However, the importance of those factors is already accounted for in the existing anti-discrimination legislation in Canada through the provisions of exception for bona fide occupational qualifications and requirements, ie. if age is a relevant and reasonable factor, the means to ensure its being factored into employment decisions is protected in current legislation. If there are exceptional problems in particular environments, say in executive management ranks, for example, it

is more appropriate to deal with those matters as exceptions to a general rule prohibiting mandatory retirement. Public safety concerns would be addressed in the same way;[13]

5. The argument that the legislated abolition of mandatory retirement constitutes a denial of freedom of contract, a point of opposition taken frequently both by management and labour groups, is a misplaced objection. The days of laissez-faire economics and the sanctity of contract are long since passed. We, as a community, subject freedom of contract to limitations in many ways. One need think only of consumer protection legislation, restrictions on alienation of property and the entire regulatory mechanism of government as examples. Even closer to the point, current human rights legislation, not to mention constitutional protections, prohibit freedom of contract which involves discriminatory activity or effect. The real issue, then, is whether one accepts "ageism" as discriminatory behaviour in the same sense as racism or sexism or discrimination on the basis of ethic origin. As the baby boom ages, and as technology advances life expectancies, our consciousness is more and more raised to appreciate the equivalence of ageism as discrimination on a par with other earlier identified practices. Indeed, as will be seen hereinafter, the Canadian Charter of Rights and Freedoms, in subsection 15(1), does not differentiate between discrimination based on age and that in the other proscribed categories;

6. Experience both in the United States and in Canadian jurisdictions which have abolished mandatory retirement or extended it to older ages seems to indicate, though the evidence is fragile, that very few if any problems have actually arisen in the marketplace;[14]

7. The arguments of significant adverse impact on pension and benefit plans arising from the abolition of mandatory retirement are highly exaggerated. There is no evidence that the actuarial basis of pension plans will be adversely impacted by the abolition of mandatory retirement so long as employees are entitled to no further accrual of benefits after a "normal retirement date," particularly where there is an actuarial adjustment which merely pro-rates payments to expected life span. In the case of benefit plans, where costs do increase unusually with age, a decision must be made on continuation of those benefits for older employees. Though the preference would be to continue such plans, in the event that the costs were very significant, that particular plan or fringe benefit could legitimately be discontinued after the "normal retirement age," or, the employee might share in its increased cost;

8. As was earlier indicated,[15] employment productivity is not rewarded evenly throughout the life of a job. For the most part we employ a deferred compensation system wherein higher earnings accrue, as do pension benefits, later in a career whether or no productivity has remained constant throughout. Thus, the argument is sometimes made that the employee is underpaid in earlier years and overpaid in later years, and that an employee choosing to remain on the job after normal retirement age will receive wages increasingly in excess of productivity, soon receiving more in lifetime income than was produced in

career value. The subsidization would come from other employees or the employer. But the theory is only partially accurate. Both inflation and the variations in pension entitlements argue the other way.

Most employees do not have pension rights other than those available under social security systems, in Canada, the Old Age Security Pension and the Canada Pension Plan. In the Canada Pension Plan, only those who have worked and contributed are eligible (though spouses may earn a reduced benefit on the death of the worker). Even amongst those who are covered by personal pension plans, (generally those who are subject to collective bargaining), vesting rights, portability and variation in definition of years of service all have an effect on the benefits of many workers. Moreover, most pension plans, and pension benefits, are not indexed so that inflation eats away at pension value. Thus, for many, if not most, workers, working past retirement may constitute an economic necessity in order to survive with dignity in retirement years;

9. Mandatory retirement, with few exceptions, works to the extreme disadvantage of those most vulnerable in our society, ie. those in low paying jobs and those underrepresented in the work force. Women are particularly adversely affected by mandatory retirement schemes.[16] The disadvantaged position of women, and other underrepresented groups, results from three phenomena. First, it is notorious that women have more difficulty than men accessing employment of any kind. Secondly, women are paid on average less than men even for work of equal value, which means that their pension benefits are inevitably lower than those of men since pension benefits are dependent on the level of earnings during employment. Thirdly, and similarly, because women delay and defer employment for purposes of child care, their ability to access quality jobs and to be entitled to pensions equivalent to men is substantially disaffected.

For that reason, in its brief to the Ianni Commission, L.E.A.F.[17] said: "In L.E.A.F.'s view, mandatory retirement is another example of adverse effect discrimination against women. Because of the special characteristics of women as employees, including their relatively low wages and shorter work histories, and their low levels of pension benefits, a mandatory retirement policy has a disproportionate and discriminatory adverse effect upon women."

10. The issue of increased productivity monitoring and evaluation systems as necessary replacements for mandatory retirement also does not bear close scrutiny. Nor does the notion that employees in their later years should be "carried" even though not productive. The arguments make several assumptions which are neither demonstrable nor acceptable. First is that age and incompetence tend to be related. Yet the vast majority of employers who have relied on the age/incompetence correlation in arguing retirement cases, have failed.[18] The medical and commonsensical evidence, so far at least, has not been supportive. Moreover, there is an incorrect assumption that senior employees presently escape job evaluation (they don't) and that employees tend to continue to work in jobs in which they offer unsatisfactory perfor-

mance. Moreover, the assumption seems to be made that retiring all workers is preferable to seeking proper job action against the few who are not competent. These are classic discriminatory assumptions;

11. One of the most frequently made arguments in favour of mandatory retirement policies is that its absence stultifies institutions, prevents renewal of spirit and personnel and affects young potential workers unfairly and disproportionately.[19]

Once again, the evidence in support of these contentions, tenured environments perhaps excepted, is at best tenuous. First, as will be dealt with more fully later, the incidence of over-holding after a normal retirement age is low, and tends to stabilize after a short period of time.[20] Secondly, even if it were true that the abolition of mandatory retirement increased unemployment amongst the young, or prevented renewal, there is no reason to accept the notion that the burden of solving those problems ought to be placed on otherwise competent and willing older workers. That is classic discrimination; the singling out of one group based on stereotypical characteristics in order to solve a problem not of their making. If it is the objective of the economy to ensure work for all those who seek it, the appropriate response as earlier indicated, is to limit employment to a certain number of years, or income, whenever accumulated, rather than by imposing mandatory retirement that is age based.

In any event, the evidence is at best ambiguous, and, more realistically, uncompelling, that the opening of jobs at the senior level inevitably implies increased access at junior levels. While that may be true at institutions like universities, it is unlikely to be true in other institutions or industries where complex variables impact on the decision on replacement. Consider, first, the growing phenomenon of replacing human jobs with technology. Second, there is the ever increasing practice of meeting budget restrictions and deficiencies by reductions in gross employee complements, very often through the attrition of older, retiring workers. On the other hand in an economy with increased consumer demand, new jobs for young workers would be opened simply because of the requirement for labour force growth to service the increased demand;

12. In fact, it is likely that the abolition of mandatory retirement would have limited impact, perhaps even only symbolic, on the Canadian federal and provincial economies, certain specific institutions, like universities, perhaps excepted. A concise review of the somewhat impressionistic and unreliable evidence that exists on impact, was provided in the evidence in the *Connell* case.[21] In his report to the Court, Professor Riddell said:

"In assessing the impact on the labour market of abolishing mandatory retirement, one of the important factors to consider is the number of individuals likely to be affected by such a change. Evidence from a Conference Board of Canada Survey (of 222 employers with 1.4 million employees) indicates that '...for the economy as a whole, approximately 54 percent of the employees work for employers with private pensions and are therefore affected by mandatory retirement policies. However, the Conference Board Study also reveals that of employees already 55 years of age, over 70 percent will probably leave the employer before age 65 due to early retirement (50%), death (15%), and layoff (6%). Consequently, only a very small fraction of the labour force (about one-fifth of 1%) is likely to be actually constrained by mandatory retirement in any given year (D. Dunlop, Mandatory Retirement Policy, Conference Board of Canada, 1980, p.7) Other studies have also estimated small impacts from abolishing mandatory retirement. A study of the Economic Council of Canada (C. Kapsalis, Pensions and the Work Decision, 1979) produced an estimate of 0.3% and one by the Ontario Ministry of Labour (Ontario Ministry of Labour, Internal Memorandum, 1985) produced an estimate of 0.45. The small magnitude of effects estimated in these Canadian studies is consistent with the U.S. evidence regarding the impact of the 1979 Age Discrimination and Employment Act which raised mandatory retirement age from 65 years to 70 years. A study carried out by the Urban Institute for the U.S. Department of Labour estimated that this Act increased the U.S. labour force by 0.2%."[22]

Large-scale impact is therefore unlikely.[23] In fact, in evidence recently presented to Board of Inquiry in Alberta under the Individual's Rights Protection Act,[24] Dr. Frank Reid, Associate Professor in the Department of Economics For Industrial Relations (University of Toronto), indicated that though there initially is a reduction in the flow of new hires if mandatory retirement is eliminated, the flow of replacement returns to its initial level in either five or ten years. In other words, within a relatively short period of time an equilibrium position is reached as the newly liberated older workers themselves begin to retire[25];

13. Mandatory retirement eliminates the experience and valuable insight of older workers, particularly in university and pedagogical systems, to the detriment of students and younger colleagues;

14. The elimination of mandatory retirement provides impetus to management to produce more beneficial and flexible incentives and programs to induce earlier, rather than later, voluntary retirement. Programs which induce voluntary retirement are to be preferred to those which do so on a compulsory basis. Moreover, the evidence is quite clear that, with few exceptions, employees in most jobs prefer to retire earlier rather than later and are doing so in ever increasing numbers.[26] Early retirements also allow for renewal to take place.

Therefore, it is suggested that as a matter of policy and law, individual choice in the retirement decision is preferable to an arbitrary, mandatory retirement scheme which implicitly denies an individual's capacity and desire.[27] In those job functions or institutional settings in which the absence of mandatory retirement impacts extraordinarily, problems can be relieved by specified exceptions and exemptions, though the onus should be on those seeking exception and the standard to be met must be difficult.

Indeed, that has been the tone, if not the absolute conclusion, of the three most prominent Task Forces and Commissions of Inquiry which, in this decade, have examined the issue of the abolition of mandatory retirement both at the provincial and federal levels.[28] Of course, the long and short term effects of abolition need to be examined and reexamined periodically as the country gains more experience on real effects.

In sum, economic security is a primary drive and of signal importance to Canadians because it promises independence and flexibility in life. Thus, the general trend can be said to be moving in favour of the abolition of universal mandatory retirement schemes. In the words of the Canadian Non-Governmental Organization's Report prepared for the World Assembly on Aging, held in 1982:

> "Compulsory retirement, for the most part at 65, is a developmental issue; it is one of the major obstacles to improving the status of the elderly. Retirement has the implication of value terminated....The widespread opinion of our participants in the discussions was that compulsory retirement must be replaced by a forum which provides a number of options and has the appropriate linkages with pension plans."[29]

Legislative and Judicial Patterns[30]

As was indicated at the outset, Canada presents a difficult, complex and often confused legal mosaic. Constitutional issues aside, the current landscape on the lawfulness of mandatory retirement varies significantly with region, age, and nature of employment.

Statutory treatment

The purpose of this part is to review the different statutory treatments accorded the retirement rights and obligations of Canadian workers. Given the limited focus of this discussion, reference to pension and insurance plans which, of course, also have significant effect, will be omitted.

When the Canadian Bill of Rights[31] was proclaimed in 1960, many Canadian jurisdictions had statutes prohibiting discriminatory practices on enumerated grounds. In 1960, age was not included as a proscribed ground in any of the provincial statutes and it was not identified in the Canadian Bill of Rights as one of the fundamental freedoms enjoyed by Canadians. As of 1960, race, national origin, colour, religion and sex were proscribed grounds of discriminatory treatment. Ageism had not yet been addressed. Indeed the word, let alone the concept, was not yet known.

In the years since 1960, tremendous changes have occurred, though it is to be noted that age discrimination continues to be permitted in many parts of Canada in certain non-employment areas including, for example, housing and public services.[32]

However, discrimination in employment is prohibited in all Canadian jurisdictions, including the federal jurisdiction, except in Yukon. Similarly, age is a proscribed ground of discrimination in all parts of Canada other than in Yukon. But, there the similarity of treatment ends. The prohibition against age discrimination in employment is restricted to those below the age of 65 in the provinces of British Columbia, Saskatchewan, Ontario, Nova Scotia, Prince Edward Island, and Newfoundland. Conversely, New Brunswick, Quebec, Manitoba and Alberta prohibit age discrimination in employment, including mandatory retirement, below and beyond the age of 65. The Canadian Human Rights Act, which applies to the federal Crown as employer, as well as to employers and employees operating in federally regulated undertakings, such as banks and airlines, does not prescribe an upper age limit beyond which mandatory retirement is permitted. However, the benefits historically have been illusory since the Act[33] does not prohibit termination that is a result of an individual having reached the "normal age of retirement" for individuals working in similar positions. Moreover, the Act provides that it is not a discriminatory practice if employment is terminated because an individual has reached the maximum age that applies to that employment by law.[34] Since mandatory retirement in the public sector normally has its basis in law of one kind or another, the Act generally has had no application to the public sector rules. Thirdly, it is not age discrimination to retire someone in accordance with any superannuation fund or plan established by Act of Parliament before March 1, 1978.[35]

Therefore, in effect, until recently the Canadian Human Rights Act did not affect mandatory retirement in the public sector in more than a limited way because of the exceptions to the prohibition on age discrimination in employment that permits forced retirement at a "normal age." Reform had been promised in *Toward Equality*.[36] To date, the major change implemented has been to remove the previous provisions of the Public Service Superannuation Regulations (P.S.S.A) which permitted mandatory retirement in the federal public service. Thus, mandatory retirement has been banned for direct employees of the federal government as well as federally appointed boards, commissions and corporations. But the Act itself has not been amended, to the continued detriment of many workers in the federal sphere.

At the other end of the scale, the provincial age of majority is the minimum age at which protection is granted in Saskatchewan, Ontario, New Brunswick, Prince Edward Island, Alberta and Newfoundland. In British Columbia and Nova Scotia age 40 or 45 is the minimum age of protection. The federal legislation, and that in Manitoba, Quebec and the Northwest Territories does not define age at all. However, discrimination in employment under the age of majority is generally tolerated.

The complexity and inconsistency of result for Canadian workers is clearly evident. Some workers are protected between the age of minority, usually 18, and age 65. But beyond that there is no protection. Some Canadian workers are protected against mandatory retirement at all ages. Others, notably in the federal sphere, are protected at all ages unless it is otherwise normal for them to be retired. Workers in Yukon have no protection at all.

In New Brunswick and Newfoundland, an employee may be terminated so long as the employee is a member of a bona fide retirement or pension plan. Canadian judges of Superior courts are forced to retire at age 75 pursuant to the provisions of The Canada Act (1982).[37] Provincial judges on the other hand are subject to the various provincial codes and therefore to earlier retirement. Members of the Canadian Armed Forces and the Royal Canadian Mounted Police are retired based on age and rank before age 65.

Two other general forms of exception, permitting age discrimination and, therefore, mandatory retirement, regardless of age, are also prevalent. In many of the anti-discrimination statutes certain limitations or preferences in employment based on age are permitted in the case of exclusively social, charitable, religious, or educational organizations, not operated for profit.[38]

The other important exception is the almost universal provision in anti-discrimination statutes which permits discrimination, including mandatory retirement, on the basic of bona fide occupational qualifications or requirements. The significance of the differences in terminology in the several statutes, though important, will not here be addressed. The actual wording of the exception varies from jurisdiction to jurisdiction, as does the interpretation of its significance. In Manitoba, the jurisdiction in which amendments to the Human Rights Code have most recently been promulgated,[39] subsection 14(1) reads as follows:

"No person shall discriminate with respect to any aspect of an employment or occupation, unless the discrimination is based upon bona fide and reasonable requirements or qualifications for the employment or occupation."

Some jurisdictions legislatively define the exemption overbroadly. For example, subsection 14(8) of the Manitoba Code stipulates that age and other characteristics are bona fide and reasonable requirements or qualifications, justifying discrimination, when a person is chosen to provide personal services in a private residence, so long as the employer discriminates for the "bona fide purpose of fostering or maintaining a desired environment within the residence..." "Personal services" are defined in subsection 14(9) to mean "work of a domestic, custodial, companionship, personal care, childcare, or educational nature, or other work within the residence that involves frequent contact or communication with persons who live in the residence."

The Manitoba Code, like most others, also provides for the promulgation of regulations effectively allowing for discrimination in benefit plans, and certain insurance plans, though not compulsory retirement.[40]

More important, however, than the stipulated extension of the bona fide occupational requirement or qualification exception in the Manitoba legislation to personal services, is its utility, there and elsewhere, as a generic exception permitting age discrimination and, hence, mandatory retirement.

The concept (hereinafter referred to as B.F.O.Q.) has its origin in Title 7 of the U.S. Civil Rights Act, 1964, which dealt with discrimination in employment on grounds other than age. When that federal legislation was supplemented in 1967 by the Age Discrimination and Employment Act,[41] the B.F.O.Q. exception was carried forward as an appropriate limitation on the prohibition against age discrimination in employment decisions. Its definition, the limited legislative articulation aside, has essentially been the result of judicial decisions and it is therefore with those decisions that the exploration of judicial intervention in mandatory retirement cases begins.

Case Law Highlights

The leading decision in Canada on what constitutes a legitimate B.F.O.Q. is that of the Supreme Court of Canada in *The Ontario Human Rights Commission, et. al.* v. *The Borough of Etobicoke.*[42] The case involved the legality of the mandatory retirement, at age 60, of firemen employed by Etobicoke, that retirement having been mandated by a clause in the collective agreement. McIntyre J., for a unanimous court, approbated what was common ground between the parties, ie. that compulsory retirement at age 60 constituted a refusal to employ or continue to employ the complainants and therefore was a form of discrimination prohibited by section 4 of the Ontario Human Rights Code. He observed that, under the Code, non-discrimination is the rule of general application, and discrimination, where permitted by way of the bona fide occupational provision, is the exception. The burden of proof of the existence of prerequisite circumstances for the application of that exception, he said, is on the employer. Moreover, he said (P. 208):

> "To be a bona fide occupational qualification and requirement, a limitation, such as mandatory retirement at a fixed age, must be imposed honestly, in good faith, and in the sincerely held belief that such limitation is imposed in the interests of the adequate performance of the work involved with all reasonable dispatch, safety and economy, and not for ulterior or extraneous reasons aimed at objectives which could defeat the Code. In addition it must be related in an objective sense to the performance of the employment concerned, in that it is reasonably necessary to assure the efficient and economic performance of the job without endangering the employee, his fellow employees and the general public."

Having established both subjective and objective prerequisites, he went on to say (P. 209):

> "We all age chronologically at the same rate, but aging in what has been

termed the functional sense proceeds at widely varying rates and is largely unpredictable. In cases where concern for the employee's capacity is largely economic, that is where the employer's concern is one of productivity, and the circumstances of employment require no special skills that may diminish significantly with aging, or involve any unusual dangers to employees or the public that may be compounded by aging, it may be difficult, if not impossible, to demonstrate that a mandatory retirement at a fixed age, without regard to individual capacity, may be validly imposed under the code. In such employment, as capacity fails, and as such failure becomes evident, individuals may be discharged or retired for cause."

The Court went on to indicate that the evidence adduced cannot be "impressionistic" and that, more likely than not, it requires some scientific or statistical basis. Lastly, the Court clearly indicated that the protections of the Ontario Human Rights Code, having been enacted by the legislature for the benefit of the community at large, and of its individual members, clearly fell within "that category of enactment which may not be waived or varied by private contract"[43] even by a collective agreement.

Subsequent decisions in lower courts have indicated two trends. The first is that the B.F.O.Q. exemption will be rather strictly construed and available in relatively narrow circumstances.[44] Nearly all the cases in which it has been successfully invoked involve safety considerations, most commonly the safety of the public.[45] However, even then the Courts are strict. Very recently, in a Charter case to which further reference will be made,[46] the British Columbia Court of Appeal did not imply into section 15(1) of the Charter a B.F.O.Q. exception in the case of physicians' hospital privileges after age 65. Clearly, the cases have indicated the difficulty that employers face in bringing convincing evidence on the effect of aging on job performance.[47]

The issue of B.F.O.Q. aside, both Court decisions and those of Adjudicators and Boards of Inquiry under the various human rights codes have been influential in, and tended to be accepting of, the abolition of mandatory retirement. Within the statutory framework of the relevant legislation, ie., subject to the particular definition of protected ages and the exceptions thereto earlier referred to, Canadian human rights adjudicators and judges have tended to give very liberal, progressive and farreaching interpretations to the anti-age discrimination provisions of Canadian human rights legislation.[48]

The most significant jurisprudence has resulted from decisions under the human rights legislation in the province of Manitoba,[49] which does not define an upper limit of age beyond which discrimination is permitted. Therefore, a short review of that province's decisional history is instructive.

In *Flyer Industries* V. *Derksen*,[50] the Adjudicator, in interpreting specific provisions of the Manitoba Human Rights legislation interpreted the intent of the legislation in these terms:

"I do not believe that the legislature intended that an individual could be denied employment or the continuation of employment simply because he or she has reached a particular age, any more than it intended that someone who is just slightly of the wrong race, nationality, religion or colour, could be denied that equality of employment opportunity so long as all persons of that race, nationality, religion or colour were similarly denied."

"The adjudicator held, effectively, that provisions of a collective agreement requiring mandatory retirement at age 65 were void because of the protections against age discrimination contained in the Manitoba Human Rights Act.[51]

In *McIntyre v. The University of Manitoba*[52] the Manitoba Court of Appeal dealt with the case of a member of the academic staff of the University of Manitoba who was forced to retire at the age of 65 pursuant to a collective agreement between the University and its Faculty Association which incorporated the mandatory retirement provision of the University's pension plan. The Court held the retirement to be illegal. Huband, J.A., writing for the majority of three of the five judges, dismissed the University's argument and in so doing said[53]:

"The Act was intended to protect the public at large from discrimination, not just on the basis of age, but on the basis of other characteristics well. Where there is a term in a contract, including a collective agreement, which collides with a statute which is intended to protect the public, the contract, or the specific term thereof is to that extent invalid."

Moreover, he added[54]:

"What is obvious is that, in passing legislation without any limitation by way of definition of the word 'age,' the Manitoba Legislature intended to prohibit discrimination in employment against its adult citizens of whatever age."

In *Newport v. Manitoba*,[55] the Manitoba Court of Appeal considered the case of Aubrey Newport, a Manitoba civil servant whose employment was governed by the Civil Service Act[56] and the Civil Service Superannuation Act[57] which, in combination, provided that all provincial government employees must retire at age 65. The unanimous Court of Appeal held that the Human Rights Act, even though the more general of the statutes, was paramount and prevailed over the more specific requirements of compulsory retirement for a civil servant at age 65 under the other earlier legislation. In a companion case, *Parkinson v. Health Sciences Centre*[58], the Manitoba Court of Appeal faced the issue of a neurosurgeon who, pursuant to the hospital's by-laws, was required at age 65 to retire, entailing the loss of admission and treatment privileges. The majority of the court declared that the hospital by-law contravened the Human Rights Act. In so doing the majority disagreed with Hall J.A who was unhappy with the result, observing[59]:

"A further observation is in order. One is constrained to say that what is in need of amendment is not the by-law of the Health Sciences Centre but rather the Provisions of the Human Rights Act. The rights created in that statute should not be asserted in general and absolute terms. In the context of the present case, the rights of non-discrimination of medical staff must be consonant with the rights of patients, and the governing body of the Health Sciences Centre should be given authority to ensure, in a practical way, continuity of quality medical care. Some objective test of age is required, otherwise equality of opportunity based upon bona fide qualifications becomes the risk of the patient. Are patients at risk until medical staff decide that one of their members has demonstrated a lack of continuing qualification? In my opinion, the answer to that question is 'no,' and thus the need arises for amending legislation that permits age discrimination in the case of those afforded hospital privileges at the Health Sciences Centre."

The Manitoba Legislature significantly revamped and expanded that legislation in 1987.[60] It did not heed the call of Mr. Justice Hall to define an exception, even in the case of neurosurgeons.

Lastly, in a case originating in Manitoba, the Supreme Court of Canada set what is perhaps the high water mark for human rights legislation and anti-age discrimination cases in Canada. In *Winnipeg School Division No. 1* v. *Craton*,[61] the Supreme Court of Canada faced the mandatory retirement of a teacher whose employment had been terminated upon turning 65 pursuant to the collective bargaining agreement between the school division and the teachers' society. The collective agreement was entered into pursuant to provincial legislation[62] which empowered a school board to a fix a compulsory retirement age for teachers which, in the terms of the legislation, "shall not be less than 65 years of age." The collective bargaining agreement set 65 years of age as the retirement age.

Craton argued that there was a clear conflict between section 50 of the Public Schools Act and subsection 6(1) of the Human Rights Act which prohibited age discrimination in employment. Section 50 of the Public Schools Act had been passed in 1980, but was to the same effect as a similar provision originally enacted in 1964. Nevertheless, the re-enactment of the specific provision allowing for early retirement at the age of 65 followed in time the promulgation of the prohibition contained in subsection 6(1) of the Human Rights Act passed in 1974. The employer contended that the Public Schools Act of 1980 was not a mere re-enactment and consolidation of the earlier statute, but was actually specific legislation designed to reaffirm the right of the board to create a mandatory retirement age for school teachers, despite the provision of the Human Rights Act.

The Supreme Court decided, inter alia, that the Human Rights legislation prevailed and the statutory entitlement of the School Board to set a mandatory retirement age was void. In doing so the Court held[63]:

"Human rights legislation is of special nature and declares public policy regarding matters of general concern. It is not constitutional in nature in the sense that it may not be altered, amended, or repealed by the legislature. It is, however, of such nature that it may not be altered, amended, or repealed, nor may exceptions be created to its provisions, save by clear legislative pronouncement. To adopt and apply any theory of implied repeal by later statutory enactment to legislation of this kind would be to rob it of its special nature and give scant protection to the rights it proclaims. In this case it cannot be said that s.50 of the 1980 Consolidation is of sufficiently express indication of a legislative intent to create an exception to the provisions of s.6(1) of the Human Rights Act."

In each of these cases, the courts relied on the Manitoba Human Rights Act which did not, and does not, define protection against age discrimination in employment to be limited to a certain age. In jurisdictions like Manitoba, human rights legislation has been sufficient, therefore, to effectively abolish mandatory retirement, subject to the special exceptions individual to the respective legislative jurisdictions. However, as was earlier indicated, the larger number of Canadian jurisdictions continue to limit the proscription against age discrimination in employment to persons under the age of 65. In those jurisdictions, mandatory retirement continues as a viable institution. It is at this point, in those provinces and jurisdictions, that the Canadian Charter of Rights and Freedoms becomes most relevant. *Craton* elevated human rights legislation to near, but not quite, constitutional status. It is therefore to the Charter that we now turn.

The Impact of the Canadian Charter of Rights and Freedoms

Subsection 52(1) of the Constitution Act,1982 provides:

"The Constitution of Canada is the supreme law of Canada and any law that is inconsistent with the provisions of the Constitution is, to the extent of the inconsistency, of no force or effect."

The Canadian Charter of Rights and Freedoms is entrenched in the Constitution and therefore is the supreme law of Canada in accordance with subsection 52(1). Its application is determined, by virtue of subsection 32(1) as follows:
"This Charter applies

(a) to the Parliament and Government of Canada in respect of all matters within the authority of Parliament including all matters relating to the Yukon

Territory and Northwest Territory; and

(b) to the legislature and government of each province in respect of all matters within the authority of the legislature of each province."

However, in peculiar Canadian fashion, section 33 provides as follows:

"(1) Parliament or the legislature of a province may expressly declare in an Act of Parliament or of the legislature, as the case may be, that the Act or a provision thereof shall operate notwithstanding a provision included in section 2 or sections 7 to 15 of this Charter.

(2) An Act or a provision of an Act in respect of which a declaration made under this section is in effect shall have such operation as it would have but for the provision of this Charter referred to in the declaration.

(3) A declaration made under subsection (1) shall cease to have effect five years after it comes into force or on such earlier date ad may be specified in the declaration."

The purpose of section 33 of the Charter obviously is to preserve a significant residue of the doctrine of parliamentary supremacy. Section 33 effectively allows Parliament or the legislatures to pass laws notwithstanding their offensiveness to certain provisions of the Charter, and further provides that such opting out provisions may be declared for successive and infinite five year periods.[64] The power has already been employed, though very infrequently.[65] Moreover, recently, calls have been heard from the president of the University of British Columbia to employ section 33 to end what he perceives as an intolerable situation with regard to the effect of the *Connell* decision[66] which ends mandatory retirement in most circumstances in that province.[67]

It is to be noted that section 15 of the Charter is a potential subject for the legislative override under section 33 since it is there mentioned.

Section 15 of the Charter, the so-called "equality" section, was given a delayed implementation date, coming into force only on April 17, 1985, in order to allow governments time to review and amend their laws. It provides as follows:

"15(1) Every individual is equal before and under the law and has the right to the equal protection and equal benefit of the law without discrimination and, in particular, without discrimination based on race, national or ethnic origin, colour, religion, sex, age, or mental or physical disability.

(2) Subsection (1) does not preclude any law, program, or activity that has as its object amelioration of conditions of disadvantaged individuals or groups including those that are disadvantaged because of race, national or ethnic origin, colour, sex, age, or mental or physical disability."

The overriding charging section of the Charter, section 1, provides as follows:

"The Canadian Charter of Rights and Freedoms guarantees the rights and
freedoms set out in it subject only to such reasonable limits prescribed by law
as can be demonstrably justified in a free and democratic society."

Thus, the right against discrimination on the basis of age, on which
challenges to mandatory retirement inevitably will be based, is not absolute.
The protections of section 15 are subject to the political realities of opting out
legislation under section 33 as well as to the limitations prescribed in section 1
of the Charter, ie. to judicial determination that offensive legislation constitutes a reasonable limit prescribed by law demonstrably justified in a free and
democratic society.

It is to be observed about section 15 that its breadth is much more sweeping
than that of the equal protection clause of the U.S. Constitution;[68] that its force
is expressed in its opening words which include the right to the equal protection
and equal benefit of the law without discrimination; and that the particulariza-
tion of proscribed grounds of discrimination does not on the face of the section
admit of exception for such matters as bona fide occupational qualifications or
requirements.

Moreover, it is to be observed that by virtue of the limited formulation of
section 32, Charter protections do not extend to regulate directly actors,
actions and agreements in the private sector.[69] The private sector will therefore
continue to be regulated primarily, perhaps exclusively, by the provincial and
federal human rights codes to which earlier extensive reference was made. The
Supreme Court of Canada has begun the task, perhaps infinite in time, of
determining the exact nature of the connection required between government,
as such, and an actor, entity or action so as to bring him/her/it within the reach
of the charter, ie., within the defined limits of "government." Essentially the
questions are when and whether a sufficient connection exists so as to include a
person, practice or entity within the definition of section 33?

The intricacies of that debate, though fascinating, cannot adequately be
detailed here. Suffice it to assume that the charter protections of section 15 will
be accorded directly to civil servants at both levels of government; likely to
employees of municipalities and other local boards; school boards; crown
corporations and agencies; public hospitals; the Armed Forces and the police.
The provisions will not apply to entities which simply derive all or substantial
portion of their funding from government sources.[70] Some further control or
connection is required. Universities in Ontario and British Columbia have
been held not to constitute "government" in the sense of the sense of the
Charter.[71] On the other hand the Vancouver General hospital was held to be
government in nature, though not itself part of the legislative, executive or
administrative branches of government, because of the extensive control
exercised by the government over the operation of the hospital generally, and
the formulation of its retirement policy in particular.[72]

Moreover, it is as yet unclear when a policy or practice of a governmental
agency, not recorded in statute or regulation, will constitute a "law" within the

meaning of that term in section 15. In a recent decision involving the Essex County Separate School Board, a three-member Ontario Divisional Court Bench split on the issue. Two members of the court held that no "law," in the relevant sense was involved in the Board's policy of retiring employees at the age of 65 and that the Charter was not intended to affect private matters such as employment relationships even if the employer was a public body subject to the Charter. The third judge thought that the policy was a "law" which could be tested against the Charter.[73] With respect, it is unlikely that the position of the Ontario Divisional Court will be upheld on appeal because to do so would permit the easy avoidance of Charter requirements simply by converting discriminatory rules of statute or regulation into practices. Indeed, the recent decision of the British Columbia Court of Appeal in *Connell* seems to make that point.[74]

There are, therefore, two ways in which the provisions of section 15 can be made applicable to prohibit mandatory retirement. The first, is by direct application to the statutes, regulations or practices of government in relation to their own employees. The second, and more profound method of application is by using section 15 of the Charter,[75] in effect, to amend the human rights codes themselves through the voiding of offensive provisions. In such a case, the lawfulness of mandatory retirement at any age in employment in both the public and private sectors would be affected.

Where the relevant legislation does not set an outside limit on protected age, resort to the provisions of section 15 of the charter is unnecessary, since the code itself accomplishes the task. In such cases, only exceptional rules within the legislation, like bona fide occupational qualifications or requirements exceptions, may conceivably require challenges under section 15 of the Charter, if that be desirable.[76]

However, in those provinces, and federally, where the antidiscrimination legislation perscribes a maximum age, normally 65, beyond which discrimination is allowed, the equality provisions of section 15 of the Charter may have quite significant utility in striking down the limitation, while preserving the proscribed ground of discrimination.[77] Indeed, Canada is poised on the brink of major determination by the Supreme Court of Canada of the implications of section 15 on the constitutional validity of legislation limiting the maximum age for protection under human rights statutes. The drama has developed because of very conflicting recent decisions by two significant Courts of Appeal in Canada, in British Columbia and Ontario. Because of their central importance, we now turn to examine those cases in some detail.

The issues were identical in *McKinney* v. *The University of Guelph et al.* (Ont. C.A.)[78] and *Connell and Harrison* v. *The University of British Columbia* (B.C.C.A).[79] Briefly put, the appellants, who in each of the cases were either faculty or librarians employed by universities, challenged the right of the university to mandatorily retire them at age 65. The impeached policies were in some cases contractual, and in one case, sanctioned by a formal resolution of the Board of Governors. Nothing turned on the form of imposition.

In all cases the Universities alleged no grounds other than the attaining of the age of 65 years as justifying termination or retirement. In both provinces the relevant legislation proscribed, ie. prohibited, discrimination in employment on the basis of age for persons under 65 years of age, but impliedly sanctioned discriminatory action against those 65 years of age or more.

A number of important and interesting issues were addressed by both courts, including, in the Ontario case, the utility of social science material as evidence in analysis of section 1 of the Charter (held to be useful but with caution). The most important issue faced by the Courts, however, was whether the provisions of the respective human rights codes, limiting antidiscrimination protection to those under the age of 65, offended subsection 15(1) of the Charter and to that extent were of no force and effect. The appellants, in effect, sought declarations that the limitation provisions of the human rights codes failed to grant them equality before and under the law and, in particular, the equal protection and equal benefit of the law without discrimination based on age.

Both the British Columbia Court of Appeal and the Ontario Court of Appeal concluded that none of the universities there involved had sufficient connection with government to be included in the scope of that term as used in section 32 of the Charter.[80] Government simply did not have the requisite involvement and control. Thus the provisions of section 15 of the Charter did not directly apply to void the mandatory retirement policies and agreements of the universities, which, for all intents and purposes, were considered private institutions.

Both the Ontario Court of Appeal and the British Columbia Court of Appeal further were in agreement that the mandatory retirement policies of the universities offended the equality guarantees of section 15 of the Charter.

In *Connell*, the British Columbia Court of Appeal faced the B.C. *Human Rights Act* which provided as follows:

> "8(1) No person or anyone acting on his behalf shall
> (a) refuse to employ or refuse to continue to employ a person, or
> (b) discriminate against a person with respect to employment or any term or condition of employment,
>   because of the race, colour,....or age of that person...."
> "(3) Subsection (1) does not apply
> (a) as it relates to age, to any bona fide scheme based on seniority, or
> (b) as it relates to marital status, physical or mental disability, sex or age, to the operation of any bona fide retirement,superannuation or pension plan or to a bona fide group or employee insurance plan.
>   (4) Subsections (1) and (2) do not apply with respect to a refusal, limitation, specification or preference based on a bona fide occupational requirement."
> "1. In this Act "age" means an age of 45 years or more, and less than 65 years;..."

On the Section 15 issue the Court said:

> "We are of the opinion that the evidence, considered as a whole, does not

support the conclusion that employment-related discrimination against those over age 65 in the guise of mandatory retirement schemes is fair and reasonable. On the contrary, the plaintiffs have, in our view, discharged the burden upon them of showing that exclusion of those over 65 from protection against having their employment terminated is unfair and unreasonable. In these circumstances, discrimination under s.15(1) of the Charter is established."[81]

In the *McKinney* decision, the Ontario Court of Appeal, ruling on the implication of section 15, said:

"In the present case there can be no doubt that s.9(a) [of the Ontario Human Rights Code] has a prejudicial and adverse impact on University staff over the age of 65 in comparison with others under that age. Because of these easily observable prejudicial effects, the section discriminates against staff over the age of 65 and denies the equal treatment to which they are entitled under s.15(1). The finding that s.9(a) discriminates contrary to s.15(1) is readily distinguishable from the question whether it can be justified as a reasonable limit on s. 15(1) rights under section 1."[82]

The reference in the quotation is to section 9(a) of the Ontario Human Rights Code which provides:

"Age' means an age that is eighteen years or more, except in subsection 4(1) where 'age' means an age that is eighteen years or more and less than 65 years;"

Subsection 4(1) of the Code stipulated:

"Every person has a right to equal treatment with respect to employment without discrimination because of race, ancestry....age...or handicap."

Subsection 4(1) of the Ontario Human Rights Code therefore proscribed discrimination, inter alia, on the basis of age, but only to age 65. In coming to its conclusion on ss.15(1), the Court seemed prepared to accept a broad definition of "discrimination" as including differentiations which were "invidious," "unfair," "irrational," "adverse," or "prejudicial."[83] Moreover, and contrary to the constitutional history of the United States, the Court was clear to point out that the standards of review for the various enumerated forms of discrimination in section 15(1) do not differ according to the ground involved. In so doing, the Court inherently and explicitly rejected the three-tiered test sometimes employed by the American courts. Howland C.J.O., writing for the majority of four of five members of the Court, said:

"The American approach must be regarded as a product of the peculiar history of the 'equal protection' clause. In comparison to the principled and consistent standard of review called for by s.1 of the Charter, the equal protection clause is conceptually unclear and problematic in application. The restiveness felt by justices of the United States Supreme Court in dealing with it is warning enough that it should not be adopted by Canadian courts unless such adoption is clearly mandated by s.15. In our opinion, it is not, and, for this reason, we must with respect disapprove of that part of Justice Gray's judgment which applies a lesser standard of review to legislation involving age-based discrimination than to other types of discrimination. The application of standards of review under s.1 to legislation which prima facie infringes equality rights under s.15 is primarily an evidentiary and forensic problem. Each case is different and it is to be expected that the justification of discriminatory legislation will be more difficult in some cases than in others. This does not mean that different standards of proof apply to different categories of cases. It means, simply, that meeting the onus of establishing s.1 limitations on s.15 rights requires careful factual analysis in every case."[84]

But the Ontario and British Columbia Courts disagreed sharply on the central issue of whether or not the infringement inherent in the restrictive definitions of age in the respective human rights codes was constitutionally permissible as a "reasonable limit" prescribed by law demonstrably justified in a free and democratic society under section 1 of the Charter. The evidence presented to the *Connell* court, which cut both ways on the issue of whether competence decreases with age and on the question of adverse social, economic and institutional impact, was similar to, and in some respects identical to, the evidence considered by the Ontario Court of Appeal in *McKinney*.

However, the evidence in *McKinney* appears to have been more substantial. So was the detailed reasoning of the Court. In both cases it would be fair to characterize the response of the Court to the evidence as mixed. In *McKinney*, however, the Court accepted the reasonableness of the limit imposed by capping age discrimination at age 65. In *Connell* the British Columbia Court of Appeal did not. Of course, the question of the reasonableness of mandatory retirement is the central issue not only in the judicial debate, but more broadly in the community. The Charter debate is therefore a litmus test of social policy.

The test of "reasonableness" in section 1 of the Charter had earlier been enunciated by the Supreme Court of Canada in *R. v. Oakes*.[85] In *Oakes*, the Court established that the onus of proving that a limit on a right or freedom guaranteed by the Charter is reasonable and demonstrably justified in a free and democratic society rests on the party seeking to uphold the limitation, usually the government. Secondly, the Court set the standard of proof under section 1 as the civil standard, namely, proof by a preponderance of probabilities.

At pages 138-39 of the *Oakes* decision Dickson, C.J.C. defined the tests of "reasonableness" under section 1 as follows:

"To establish that a limit is reasonable and demonstrably justified in a free and democratic society, two central criteria must be satisfied. First, the objective, which the measures responsible for a limit on a Charter right or freedom are designed to serve, must be 'of sufficient importance to warrant overriding a constitutionally protected right or freedom...' It is necessary, at a minimum, that an objective relate to concerns which are pressing and substantial in a free and democratic society before it can be characterized as sufficiently important. Second, once a sufficiently significant objective is recognized, then the party invoking section 1 must show that the means chosen are reasonable and demonstrably justified. This involves 'a form of proportionality test.' Although the nature of the proportionality test will vary depending on the circumstances, in each case courts will be required to balance the interests of society with those of individuals and groups. There are, in my view, three important components of a proportionality test. First, the measures adopted must be carefully designed to achieve the objective in question. They must not be arbitrary, unfair, or based on irrational consider-ations. In short, they must be rationally connected to the objective. Second, the means, even if rationally connected to the objective in this first sense, should impair 'as little as possible' the right or freedom in question. Third, there must be a proportionality between the *effects* of the measures which are responsible for limiting the Charter right or freedom, and the objective which has been identified as of 'sufficient importance.'" (citations have been omitted)

In *Connell* the British Columbia Court of Appeal found that the means chosen by the British Columbia Legislature to further its objectives were neither reasonable nor demonstrably justified. The Court denied a rational connection between any of the objectives cited by the University and denial of protection against employment-related discrimination to persons over the age of 65.[86] It found the means adopted by the legislature in limiting employment-related age discrimination to persons between the age of 45 and 65 unjustifiably eliminate the right of the worker who is over the age of 65 not to suffer discrimination in employment. Thirdly, the definition of age in the Act failed the proportionality test because the limitation there in question, denial of protection to persons over 65, had not been shown to advance the objective of protecting older workers against employment-related discrimination.
In the words of the Court:

"This leaves the respondents with only the suggestion of administrative convenience to support mandatory retirement at age 65, and administrative convenience cannot justify overriding rights guaranteed by the Charter. ....."[87]

Finally, the Court referred to the just decided decision of the Ontario Court of Appeal in *McKinney*. The Court said:

"We are aware of the different conclusion reached by the Ontario Court of

Appeal in *McKinney* .... The court, Blair J.A dissenting was of the opinion
that the need to preserve pension plans and to permit renewal of the work
force by employment of younger persons raised concerns sufficiently pressing
and substantial to warrant permitting the infringement of the plaintiff's
constitutional rights.
> The evidence before us does not support that conclusion. ....."[88]

Indeed the Ontario Court of Appeal had the month earlier, come to a
contrary conclusion in *McKinney*. In that case the Ontario Court found that the
predominant concerns of the age limitation were:

> "1. The need to provide for a compromise between an uncontrolled right to
> work regardless of age as against a right to work to a specific date, 65 years of
> age or over, established by a pension plan, university policy or a negotiated
> agreement, which would, at the same time, preserve pension rights; and
> 2. The need to make provision for renewal of the work force by employment
> of younger persons."[89]

The Court took pains to point out that its decision applied only to mandatory
retirement respecting members of the teaching staff of universities and university librarians and that it was accordingly considering only evidence particular
and pertinent to universities.[90] Tenure loomed large as a factor. Interpreting
the evidence before it, the Court found the objectives of the legislation not to
be trivial, but rather pressing and substantial and warranting overriding a
constitutionally protected right.[91] It found that there was a clear rational
connection between the measures adopted and their objectives on the basis
that mandatory retirement policies are "an integral part of a complex set of
rules that govern the work place."[92] Howland, C.J.O. went on:

> "To abolish mandatory retirement would have repercussions on a number of
> aspects of the personnel system. The present policies of the universities
> preserve the system of tenure. They avoid the problems of a stricter appraisal
> of faculty which would be necessary if there were not a finite date of
> termination. They also maintain the existing pension plans which are based
> on an accepted retirement age. As Peter Hirst, a pension actuary stated, the
> pension plans would have to be reviewed if mandatory retirement were
> abolished. Some administrative costs would be involved, even though their
> financial stability, and the financial security which they provide should not be
> affected. ...Renewal is more readily accomplished by a retirement policy
> which is mandatory at a definite date."[93]

On the issue of whether the statutory limitation impaired the right to
freedom from discrimination on the basis of age as little as possible, the
majority, without asserting a correlation between age and a decline in cognitive
functions, thought it reasonable to use 65 as a benchmark for retirement rather
than leaving the matter to individual choice and the possible alternative of

dismissal for cause. Howland, C.J.O., for the majority, said:

> "... Legislation does not have to be tuned with great precision to withstand
> judicial scrutiny, and it is not our role to consider how the legislation might
> have been made more precise."[94]

On the issue of the proportionality between the effects of the measures in the legislation and the legislative objectives, the Court accepted that it was proportional, saying:

> "Overall, we consider that the effects of the measures imposed by the
> retirement policies of the universities are not out of proportion to the
> objectives of s.9(a). The problem which led the United States to make a
> special exemption for tenured faculty members does have its counterpart in
> Ontario and this problem will continue for some time to come. It is not
> unreasonable for the legislature to proceed slowly in changing the age for
> mandatory retirement."[95]

Blair, J.A. dissented, holding, inter alia, that with reference to the age restrictions contained in section 9(a) of the Ontario Human Rights Code:

> "Its objective, at least so far as university faculty are concerned, is of
> sufficient importance to justify overriding the appellant's Charter right and
> the means adopted are rationally connected with that objective. Section 9(a),
> in my opinion, does not satisfy the third requirement of the *Oakes* test that the
> measure should impair 'as little as possible' the right or freedom in question.
> Section 9(a) does not merely limit or restrict the appellant's Charter right
> under s.15(1). It eliminates it because, under the Code, no protection against
> age discrimination in employment is provided after the age of 65. The absence
> of any qualification to the complete denial of the Charter right, to which I
> referred above, results in the failure of s.9(a) to meet the *Oakes* test."[96]

He went on to conclude:

> "While the conclusion which I have reached would be limited, on the facts of
> this case, to a declaration that the appellants, who are tenured university
> staff, are not subject to compulsory retirement at the age of 65, it also has
> wider ramifications because it is based on two findings that could apply to all
> employees in Ontario. The first is that s.9(a) of the Code is inconsistent with
> s.15(1) of the Charter because it denies protection against age discrimination
> in employment of persons over 65. The second is that there are no standards
> in s.9(a) or elsewhere in the Code upon which a justification of this denial
> could be based under s.1 of the Charter."[97]

The decisions in *McKinney* and *Connell* are irreconcilable. The decisions of the British Columbia Court of Appeal in *Stoffman* v. *Vancouver General Hospital*[98] and *Douglas/Kwantlen Faculty Association* v. *Douglas College*,[99] delivered concurrently, come to the same conclusion as *Connell*. In the former case the British Columbia Court of Appeal used s.15 of the Charter to strike down the mandatory retirement at age 65 of a physician's privileges in a hospital. In the latter case the Court struck down the mandatory retirement provisions of a collective agreement which required professors at Douglas College to retire at age 65. In both cases the court found sufficient government control to employ the Charter directly in striking down the offending provisions of the particular collective agreement and hospital rule.

At best, therefore, the implications of the Charter of Rights and Freedoms, though clear in the individual provinces of decision, are most unclear in terms of the whole of Canada. One must await the decision of the Supreme Court of Canada which will be required to reconcile the inconsistent rulings.

That reconciliation, when it comes, may finally determine the legal position of mandatory retirement throughout Canada. In the event that the Court follows the lead of the British Columbia Court of Appeal, only two routes will be left open for those legislatures which seek to permit mandatory retirement.

First, all reference to protection against age discrimination in employment at any age could be withdrawn from a particular human rights code completely. In that event, age discrimination would not be a proscribed ground of discriminatory treatment at any age so that the argument, essential to a challenge under section15(1) of the Charter, of inequality of treatment by or under the law, would be eliminated. In other words, it is unlikely that section 15(1) grants power to the judiciary to read into human rights legislation a ground of proscribed discrimination.[100] It simply ensures that the legal proscription, when offered, is applied evenly, equitably and fairly within the group which is protected.[101]

Secondly, it is open to Parliament and/or the legislatures to employ the powers granted in section 33 of the Charter specifically to override the benefit of section 15(1) impact on human rights legislation, by use of the non obstante clause.

Neither action is probable. More likely, the Supreme Court, when it resolves the conflicting appellate court decisions, will define the "reasonableness" of mandatory retirement policy in Canada. Until that happens, Canada will continue to experience a confused, schizophrenic and rationally indefensible policy on mandatory retirement. Until an authoritative Supreme Court decision is forthcoming, the dichotomous constitutional decisions of the Canadian appellate courts will continue accurately to mirror the image of an inconsistent political landscape.

Notes

1. See, as well, the author's published notes for an address at a Symposium — "The University of Toronto Through the 80's — Where Should We Go and How Can We Get There?" published under the title *"Mandatory Retirement"* in *Who's Who in Canadian Law*, 4th ed., 1985-86; Trans-Canada Press.
2. The Constitution Act of 1982.
3. See, Hogg, *Constitutional Law of Canada*, Second Edition, Carswell, 1985.
4. Part I, The Constitution Act, 1982, which is Schedule B of the Canada Act 1982, c.11 (U.K.).
5. Unless sanctioned in particular cases by a specific statutory provision.
6. Then referred to as The British North America Act, 1867, (U.K.).
7. Section 15.
8. *McKinney*, et al. v. *The University of Guelph*, et al., [1988] 24 O.A.C., 241 at p.285 (Ont. C.A.).
9. 1949 Stat. 620.
10. 1967,29 U.S.C. Para. 621 et seq.
11. By Public Law 95-256.
12. 1986, Public Law 99-952.
13. This will be discussed later when the discussion turns to bona fide occupational qualifications and requirements.
14. See Part 2 of the *Report of the Ontario Task Force on Mandatory Retirement: Fairness and Flexibility in Retiring from Work*, December 1987, Chaired by Ron W. Ianni and prepared for the Ontario Minister of Labour, (The Ianni Commission), as yet unpublished, which surveys the experience in Manitoba, New Brunswick, Quebec, the Federal Government and the United States, with particular reference to New York State, California, and Michigan. The several reports therein contained come overall to the conclusion of minimal, if any, impact except in particular industries or undertakings, such as universities. In fact, the Ianni Commission concluded that the issue of whether to ban mandatory retirement may well have a greater symbolic rather than practical reality for the people of Ontario. As the Report says:
   "Experience outside Ontario suggests that the prohibition of mandatory retirement is common both in legislation and in judicial decisions. It has generally not been disruptive so far because there has been a strong trend towards earlier rather than later retirement. There is some fear that changed economic conditions might reverse the trend and encourage delayed retirements, with possibly harmful results. Moreover, in most cases the elimination of mandatory retirement has happened so recently that long term effects may not yet be discernible.
   However, as in Ontario, the question whether mandatory retirement should be allowed is generally a very small issue, entirely overshadowed by concerns about retirement income security and pension plan equity." See, also, note 28.
15. Page 333, Point 10.
16. The converse is true in workplaces which have limited tenured jobs, like universities, in which women have been unrepresented. If the men overhold their tenured positions the inherent systemic discrimination necessarily continues since no places become available for women to access. The same point is accurate, as will be seen

infra, on the whole question of renewal within closed systems like universities.

17. Women's Legal Education and Action Fund, at page 335.
18. eg. *Greyhound* v. *McCreary and Can. Human Rights*, Commission (1987) 78 N.R. 192 (F.C.A.). and *Etobicoke*, infra, note 42.
19. See the reasoning of the Ontario Court of Appeal in *McKinney*, supra, note 8.
20. The Ianni Commission estimated that only 25,000 to 50,000 persons would stay on after normal retirement age in a matured system if Ontario banned mandatory retirement; ie., less than 1% of the *total* provincial labour force.
21. *Connell and Harrison* v. *University of British Columbia*, [1988] 21 B.C.L.R. (2d) 145 (B.C.C.A.).
22. Page 159.
23. That was also the conclusion of the *Rothstein Commission* (Manitoba, 1982) see, infra, fn.28.
24. *Dickason* v. *The Governors of the University of Alberta*, January, 1988, vol. 9, Canadian Human Rights Reporter, Paras. 34905-34969.
25. Note in particular the evidence presented at para. 34943.
26. Ianni Commission.
27. For an unhappy commentator, see, Flanagan, Thomas "Policy-making by Exegesis: The Abolition of Mandatory Retirement in Manitoba," Canadian Public Policy, XI:1:40-53, 1985.
28. See *Report of the Commission on Compulsory Retirement (Manitoba)*, Marshall E. Rothstein, Q.C., Commissioner, February, 1982; *Equality for All: Report of the Parliamentary Committee on Equality Rights*, J. Patrick Boyer, M.P., Chairman, Government of Canada, October, 1985, pp. 17-24; *Toward Equality: The Response to the Report of the Parliamentary Committee on Equality Rights*, Government of Canada, 1986, pp. 9-11; *Report of the Ontario Task Force on Mandatory Retirement: Fairness and Flexibility in Retiring from Work* (Ontario), Ron W. Ianni, Chairman, Draft Report made available December 1987 (referred to herein as the Ianni Commission). The Ianni Report, together with the schedules and appendices thereto attached, contains the most recent surveys and data base regarding the incidence and effect of mandatory retirement in Canada. The author is grateful to the Chairman for having made available a copy of the draft report which is as yet unpublished and for permission to report its overall conclusions. The Commission found the existence of mandatory retirement does not represent a burning social issue for most people in Ontario and that mandatory retirement has become largely symbolic as an issue. For that reason the members of the Task Force were divided on whether the government should take action to ban it. The Chairman of the Task Force supported a formal ban. The two other members of the Task Force believed that there should be no formal government action for abolition because it is unnecessary and not widely demanded and because not enough time has passed to allow a recent evaluation of the experiences of jurisdictions that have imposed bans. They would suggest instead other initiatives which could and should be taken to ensure grater flexibility in retirement and to allow individuals, in appropriate circumstances, to carry on beyond age 65.
29. Government of Canada, National Advisory Council on Aging, *Moving Ahead With Aging in Canada* (October, 1983), p. 20.
30. For a comprehensive review of age discrimination and mandatory retirement issues in Canada, see *Passage to Retirement: Age Discrimination and the Charter*, M. Elizabeth Atcheson and Lynne Sullivan, Chap. 5 in Bayefsky and Eberts, *Equality*

Rights and the Canadian Charter of Rights and Freedoms (1985).

31. R.S.C. 1970, App. III.
32. for the details see, *Atcheson* and *Sullivan*, supra fn. 30, at page 240 and following.
33. Section 14(c).
34. Section 14(b).
35. Section 48(1).
36. Supra, n. 28.
37. Subsection 92(2).
38. See for example subsection 4(7) of the Ontario Human Rights Code, R.S.O. 1980 c.340.
39. C.C.S.M. H.175, c.45, 1987.
40. Ss. 14(7).
41. Supra, fn. 10.
42. (1982) 1 S.C.R. 202.
43. P. 214.
44. See, *Winnipeg* v. *Ogelski* [1986] 6 W.W.R. 289; *Finlayson* v. *Winnipeg Police Department*, (1983), 3 W.W.R. 117 (Man.C.A.); *Greyhound* v. *McCreary*, et al., supra, note 18, and *Voyageur Colonial* v. *Can. Human Rights Comm.* (1980), 1 C.H.R.R. D/239.
45. *Air Canada* v. *Carson*, et al., [1985] 1 F.C. 209 (F.C.A.); but see *Parkinson*, infra, note 58. Also, see *Campbell* v. *Air Can.* (1981), 2 C.H.R.R. D/602; *Stevenson* v. *Air Can* (1982), 3 C.H.R.R. D/021; *Air Can* v. *Stevenson* (1982), 3 C.H.R.R. D/1025; *Chambers* v. *C.P.Air* (1982), 3 C.H.R.R. D/1029; *Lamont* v. *Air Can* (1982), 3 C.H.R.R. D/1128.
46. Stoffman, infra, n. 72.
47. See cases cited in notes 44 and 45.
48. See case cited in n. 18.
49. Supra, n. 39.
50. Unreported decision of an Adjudication under the Manitoba Human Rights Act, by Professor Jack R. London delivered June 2, 1977, extensively referred to, inter alia, in *McIntyre*, infra, fn. 52.
51. The provisions of the Code then were somewhat different than at present. See *McIntyre*, infra, fn. 52.
52. [1981] 1 W.W.R. 696.
53. P. 702.
54. P. 710.
55. [1982] 2 W.W.R. 254.
56. R.S.M. 1970, c.C110.
57. R.S.M. 1970, c.120.
58. [1982] 2 W.W.R. 102; leave to appeal to S.C.C. refused 18 Man. R. (2d) 31.
59. P. 113.
60. The Manitoba Human Rights Code, C.C.S.M. H175, c.45.
61. [1985] 6 W.W.R. 166.
62. The Public Schools Act, 1980 (Manitoba), c.33, s.50.
63. P. 172.
64. Ss. 33(4) and (5).
65. e.g. Section 92, Charter of Human Rights and Freedoms R.S.Q. c.12.
66. Supra, n.21.
67. "Retirement ruling a threat to Universities, UBC head says," *The Globe and Mail*,

Wednesday, March 23, 1988, Page A4.

68. The fifth and fourteenth Amendments.
69. *Retail, Wholesale and Department Store Union, Local 580* v. *Dolphin Delivery,* [1986] 2 S.C.R. 573.
70. *Blainey* v. *Ont. Hockey Assoc.* (1986) 14 O.A.C. 194 (Ont. C.A.).
71. *McKinney* and *Connell*, supra, n.n. 8 and 21, respectively.
72. *Stoffman* v. *Vancouver General Hospital* (B.C.C.A.) [1988] 21 B.C.L.R. 165. To similar effect see *Douglas/Kwantlen Faculty Association* v. *Douglas College* [1988] 21 B.C.L.R. 175.
73. *Ontario English Catholic Teacher Association* v. *Essex County Roman Catholic Separate School Board* [1987] 58 O.R. (2d) 545.
74. Supra, n. 8, at P. 150.
75. Or section 7.
76. Eg., an over-broad set of exceptions.
77. See, *Blainey* v. *O.H.A.*, supra, n. 70, in which the Ontario C.A. effectively used s.15(1) to excise from the Ontario Code a qualification on a statutory right to equal gender treatment, a qualification which permitted gender segregation in athletic activities.
78. Supra n. 8. Several Ontario universities were Respondents.
79. Supra n. 21.
80. To the contrary conclusion, see *Douglas/Kwantlen Faculty Association* v. *Douglas College*, supra n. 12 wherein the British Columbia Court of Appeal came to the contrary conclusion based on the peculiarities of the control of the government of British Columbia in the affairs of that institution.
81. Page 160.
82. Page 271.
83. Page 271.
84. Page 276.
85. [1986] 1 S.C.R. 103.
86. Pages 156, 157 and 162.
87. Page 163.
88. Page 163.
89. Page 281.
90. Pages 281 and 289.
91. Page 284.
92. Page 284.
93. Page 284.
94. Page 288.
95. Page 288.
96. Page 298.
97. Page 299.
98. Supra, n. 72.
99. Supra, n. 72.
100. The point is not absolutely established. But see *Hunter et al.* v. *Southam Inc.*, [1984] 2 S.C.R. 145, particularly the oft-quoted passage of Dickson, J. as he then was, at pp. 168-169 where he said" ....while the courts are guardians of the Constitution and of individuals' rights under it, it is the legislature's responsibility to enact legislation that embodies appropriate safeguards to comply with the Constitution's requirements. It should not fall to the courts to fill in the details that will render legislative lacunae

constitutional."

The principle was confirmed in *R.* v. *Oakes*, *supra*, note and again in *McKinney*. However, there are as yet no authoritative cases on the effect of section 15(1) on legislation which is deficient in doing equal treatment between various groups or classes of people in the community.

101. Of course ss. 15(1) would still prohibit mandatory retirement in those cases where the Charter applied *directly* to the workers, eg., government employees.

Chapter 23

Old Age Policies in Developed Western Countries and their Implications for the Status of the Elderly

Anne-Marie GUILLEMARD*

Centre for the Study
of Social Movements,
University Panthéon-Sorbonne,
Paris, France

For sociologists, (public old-age policies) cannot be analyzed without also examining the successive social constructions, which they imply, of the realities of old age. Since public policy has increasingly assumed responsibility for managing old age, it has become a key factor in setting the limits of age-classes and redefining the social contents of stages of the life-cycle. My interpretation of these developments will attempt to associate changes in public old-age policies both with the changing images, or representations, of old age and with changes in the social status of the elderly. In this way, each period of the development of old-age policy can be related to a particular way of constructing old-age, to the social significance and meaning of growing old.

A rapid, schematic assessment of the old-age policies applied in industrialized Western nations might lead us to think that these societies have gradually, over the decades, improved their way of managing old-age problems. After proposing segregative solutions that assigned a marginal status to the elderly, these societies have sought new means of integrating them. Pension systems have been extended and reformed so as to raise considerably the living standards of the retired; they are no longer the "economically underprivileged", the poor, as they used to be during the 1950s and 1960s. In addition, facilities have been set up, and services provided in order to help the elderly to remain in their environment and continue living at home. Social progress seems to be under way, slowly but surely. However my research on trends in old-age policies, particularly from 1945 to 1985, leads me to be more pessimistic.[1] An examination of recent history shows that economic factors have caused that social policy to disintegrate.

In effect, measures intended to manage unemployment and reduce joblessness have taken root in old-age policy. Schemes for early withdrawal from the labour force are evidence that the needs of the production system have become a priority imposed on social policy in general, and old-age policy in particular. Although old-age policies have managed considerable transfers from the economy toward the elderly, they have not kept these persons from being turned into cared-for dependents, instead of being treated as fully-fledged citizens who participate in society.

The current crisis of old-age policies—which could eventually threaten pension systems—is not only connected with the simple arithmetic of the changing proportion of the active to the inactive population and the decrease in labour-force participation as a result of the slow-down of economic growth and the rise of unemployment. This crisis seems rather to be a product of confusion about the meaning of old age, as public policies have gone adrift, tossed back and forth among various objectives. At bottom, this crisis is related to the cultural model of how the life cycle is organized.

In our societies, which are aging and will continue to do so, it is unsettling that old age is not considered to be a special experience and that the elderly merely represent a superfluous, redundant work force. The sudden expansion of early withdrawal schemes is deeply disturbing. On the pretext of solving unemployment, the opportunity has been lost of adapting to an aging world, an adaptation that calls for a positive definition of the relations between old age and society. The present situation is paradoxical in that our societies, though ineluctably destined to age, define a set of persons as being occupationally old, and hence fit to be banished from the labour force and from society, and, furthermore, have been lowering the age limit forcing people into this set.

I would like to use the history of old-age policies to illustrate these remarks. From the perspective taken here, these policies form part of a complex of public interventions which shape the relationship between old age and society. This implies a global approach to understanding how old age has been managed, which takes into account retirement policies, social service policies and employment policies aimed at the elderly.

Three phases can be discerned in the way developed Western countries have managed old age. Each phase has produced a dominant social image of old age and of the status of the elderly and their rights and obligations.

The First Period: Setting Up Pensions Funds

Prior to the 1960s and 1970s, the problems of the elderly were seen, first of all, as being financial. They concerned living standards and economic transfers. Retirement pension systems were drawn up in order to create a solidarity between generations that would cover the risks of old age. The development of the right to retirement meant that old age became a period of rest following a life of work. Outside these pension systems, a policy of assistance, or poor-relief (almshouses, old-age homes, allowances in cash or in kind) was pursued to help those who where not thus insured.

Pensions have undeniably raised the living standards of the elderly, but they have had some less positive effects. They treated problems mainly as matter of money, to be dealt with by welfare transfers from the economy. Demands were calculated in financial terms even though they were much more complicated. For instance, the constantly reiterated demands of labour that pensions should be raised and the retirement age lowered were grounded in complex aspirations having to do with, on one hand, modifying working conditions and, on the other, limiting the sense of alienation caused by working. Pensions have been mechanically increased without adequately satisfying such aspirations. A system of economic transfers, of redistribution, has been set up without sufficient concern for the social integration of retired people.

The Second Period: Social Programs for Integrating the Elderly

During the second period, attention was paid not only to making up for lost income and maintaining living standards, but also to the life-style of the elderly. Concern was focused on the "segregation" and "marginality" of this group. Measures were adopted with the aim of integrating the elderly. Beginning in the 1960s in France and in 1965 in the United States with the passage of the Older Americans Act, this new policy took shape around programs for setting up facilities and providing localized services in order to help the elderly to continue to live normally in society.

During this period, pensions were no longer taken to be the ultimate end of old-age policy; they were but one of the means necessary for integrating the elderly and preventing them from becoming social outcasts. Attempts were made to enhance the social status of this age-group; phrases such as "senior citizen" or, in French, "Third Age" were coined. These new labels reflected the efforts being made to consider old age not as the end of life, a time of relegation, but a third stage in the life-course, a stage corresponding to a particular way of living and being integrated in society. A new citizenship was extended to the elderly, who, besides having a social right to rest after a life of work, thus obtained a civil right to be socially integrated in accordance with their position on the age-scale.

Evaluations of these integrative social policies[2] have shown that the results have not always corresponded with the intentions. In particular, increasing the services provided to senior citizens has often retained, or even enhanced, their dependency. Despite its limits, this second period of old-age policy is important because old age was recognized as a particular experience, a phase of life entitling persons to full social integration.

The Third Period: The Impact of Measures For Disengaging Aging Workers From Employment

In the late 1970s, growing concern about unemployment suddenly brought about a breakdown in the system of old-age protection. Western nations began to adopt measures for the early withdrawal of aging employees from the labour force, sometimes as early as age 55. The labour force participation rate of the 55-64 age-group fell, from 1970 to 1985, as follows (OECD):

> United States: from 81% to 59%;
> France: from 75% to 50%;
> West Germany: from 82% to 57%;
> Netherlands: from 81% to 54%; and
> United Kingdom: from 91% to 66%.

As a result of this massive stimulus to withdraw from the labour force, the system of social protection was financially unbalanced. Depending on the country, various subsystems were used to manage, even facilitate, early withdrawals: unemployment compensation, disability insurance, private pension funds and, exceptionally, public pension funds. Whatever the means used, the age for withdrawing from the labour force was lowered, thus increasing the number of "inactive" persons living on welfare transfers. Thus was precipitated the financial crisis which, as a result of both the slow-down of economic growth and the aging of the population structure, had been looming over the whole system of social protection.

Apart from its financial consequences, this policy has had serious social and cultural effects. Early withdrawal schemes — designed mainly to manage the problem of unemployment — have considerably worsened the situation of persons at the upper end of the age-scale: they are precipitated much earlier and more suddenly from the labour force. These schemes directly contradict the policies of integration which were being applied in various countries because they are based on a tacit acceptance of age-discrimination in the labour force. The aging worker's right to a job has been restricted; this becomes obvious when we observe that the retirement system no longer determines the conditions of early withdrawals, or of "pre-retirement". In most countries, public pension funds are founded on the principle of separating the right to a job and the right to a pension. Because unemployment or disability insurance — not the retirement system — mainly regulate these definitive, early withdrawals from the labour force, new principles have been introduced which make the right to receive welfare transfers conditional on cessation of employment. Therefore, the last phase of life is redefined as a period when it is unjustified or, we might say, illegal to work. The policy of removing aging workers from employment has led to denying that older persons have a right to a job.

Under these conditions, since employees are divided into two groups according to age, how is it possible to fight against segregation "downstream" when it has been practised earlier "upstream"? The policy of making aging workers unemployed tears the policy of integrating the elderly, and it compromises any effort to define the status of the elderly other than in terms of the exigencies of the labour market. Since people are "growing old" at a younger age, due to early withdrawal schemes, old-age has come to mean "non-work".

There is no other social content in it. To become old means, inevitably, being forced out of the world of reciprocity and into a world of "unproductive" persons where one's livelihood is granted, not earned.

Most developed countries seem to have adopted an absurd strategy for handling the problems that will inevitably arise as their population structures age. They have turned their backs on the future. They have deprived old age of social meaning, even though this phase of life is our future; for soon it will cover as much as a third of the life-span and include as many as a quarter of the population.

* Translated by Noal Mellot, CNRS, Paris.

Notes

1. Anne-Marie Guillemard, Le declin du social. *Formation et crise des politiques de la vieillesse*, Presses Universitaires de France, Paris, 1986.
2. Carroll Estes, *The Aging Enterprise*, Jossey Bass, San Francisco 1979; and Anne-Marie Guillemard, *La vieillesse et l'Etat*, Presses Universitaires de France, Paris, 1980.

Chapter 24

The Intergenerational Contract — Under Pressure From Population Aging

David Thomson

Department of History,
Massey University,
Palmerston North, New zealand

Introduction

The phenomenon of population aging, of rising numbers of the elderly and shrinking proportions of the young, is now well recognised by demographers, by social analysts in many fields, and increasingly by a wider public. In a number of European nations the aging trend has been apparent for more than a century now, but in much of the world, including Japan, it is a development of the last few decades only. During the next 40 or 50 years the world population will undergo a rapid aging, so that by 2030 or 2040 around one in every five people will be elderly compared with one in twenty or twenty-five in the earlier part of this century. The fact that this move is occurring across the greatest variety of communities at about the same moment in time makes it possible to talk of this shift, this historic transition from youthful to elderly populations within the span of a single lifetime, as one of the decisive landmarks in human existence.

Yet while the scale of the change is now being comprehended in at least some of its dimensions, its significance and implications have still to attract our thoughtful attention. It is high time that they did so, and to this short contribution to the task, I bring the perspective of an historian of welfare and the elderly in western societies (Thomson, 1984a; 1984b;1986). I bring, too, an intention to be provocative, for I want to nudge the current debate about aging and the elderly out of its familiar and now comfortable paths, in some newer and perhaps more controversial directions. The dominant view is still that the aged are poor, powerless, and most of all "childish", by which I mean that they are absolved of all responsibility for the world and their position in it. They are, in short, to have things done to them and for them, but are not part of the active, decision-making, obligation-bearing adult world.

This view I want to challenge. Rising populations of the elderly in modern societies are affecting the life-chances, the expectations and the material circumstances of all persons, infants just as much as octogenarians. The growth is producing shifts of power and resources between age-groups at the end of the twentieth century which will call into question some of our most cherished beliefs about the bonds that link one generation to another. Aging, I want to suggest, is affecting long-standing contracts between the generations, in ways which are yet unclear, but which are likely to be profound. To talk of aging as meaning more elderly people, more need for state pensions or home help services or hip replacement operations, is to miss the significance of what is taking place. The aging of populations is reshaping the terms of modern life for every citizen at all of the stages of his or her life, and not just the last.

My claim that aging has still to engage our serious attention may at first seem dubious, even silly or churlish. A great deal of thought is now being directed towards the support requirements of aging populations, using the term support here to mean a variety of needs — financial, medical, emotional or familial. However, to think of aging thus is to comprehend the new realities in a very narrow way. In large part, this derives from our focus upon demographic aging, just one aspect of the contemporary process of aging. This concentration upon the numbers of one age or another, on sex or marital status or health group or another, is readily understandable, if unfortunate, for demographic aging is undeniably important, easily identifiable, and above all reassuringly measurable. But it is only one form of aging.

Of the other manifestations of aging in the late twentieth century, I want to isolate here "political aging", what we might also call "the aging of the modern welfare state", as the most significant of all. Across a range of nations, there has become apparent to the historian a marked tendency in recent years for the priorities of the community and its institutions to "age", that is to move towards the interests of older rather than younger persons, and to do so at a pace that bears little or no relation to demographic changes. The aging of the electorate has in the last 20 years resulted in a marked and hastening shift in the community's interests, investment policies and spending priorities in such obvious realms as social security and health, but also in education, housing, taxation, investment, employment and financial decision-making.

Such a move, we might all want to argue, is a good thing. For too long the elderly have had a poor deal, receiving insufficient attention, being left to live in impoverished or undignified or deprived circumstances. Yet while there is much to sympathise with in that reaction, it has to be borne in mind that a redirection of interest in state policy such as we are now witnessing has profound implications for the intergenerational contracts which bind the successive members of a society. My concern is that, if societies do not think carefully about this, if we do not recognise that aging is affecting relationships between people of all ages, and that the elderly themselves are going to be called upon increasingly to bear some of the consequences of these changes as they are not now doing, then the compact between the generations is in danger of collapse at the end of the twentieth century, with unhappy consequences for all.

The Contract Between Generations

Terms such as "intergenerational contract" and "the compact between generations" will be employed throughout this chapter. In using them, I refer neither to private legal contracts such as wills or trusts, nor to statutory obligations and duties that may lie upon one generation or another. These do of course exist in all societies. In modern nations, for example, parents bear legal obligations towards minor children, though we are seeing these enforced with decreasing vigour.

Fewer legal codes now incorporate reverse obligations, between adult children and aging parents, although if we turn our gaze back a little in time the position is different. Britain's welfare statutes, for instance, included until 1984 the requirement that children assist destitute parents. New Zealand's Maintenance of Destitute Persons laws laid a comparable requirement upon adult children, until they disappeared from the statute books in the 1950s: in the federations of North America and Australia, where welfare provision remains largely a preserve of the states, the removal of legal ties between children and their elderly parents has proceeded in slow and piecemeal fashion, and a number of states still retain these provisions. The nations of continental Europe furnish many further examples of each of these histories.

But while a legal intergenerational contract of a familial nature between adults and the elderly still survives in a number of nations, or did so until comparatively recent times, in most others, it is not evident that these obligations have been enforced widely, or indeed even observed voluntarily between family members. The research work of myself and others on England, for example, reveals that from the early eighteenth century, if not for longer, the legal obligations of adult children towards aged parents were interpreted by the high courts in the most restricted of manners, so that they were deemed actionable in very few circumstances indeed (Smith, 1984; Laslett, 1987; Thomson, 1984b).

Moreover, magistrates throughout the country demonstrated the greatest reluctance — in most but not quite all eras — to take any action whatsoever in connection with cases involving impoverished parents and children who would offer them no assistance. Quite simply, requiring children to support parents through statutory procedures was an offence against the traditions and values of English society. At the same time the magistrates and higher courts harboured no qualms about insisting upon the duties of parents towards minor children — an interesting confirmation of Caldwell's belief that western societies are marked by the flow of resources and responsibilities from older to younger relatives, a flow which is not counterbalanced by transfers later in life between younger and older relatives (Caldwell, 1982). The situation in other countries remains unexplored to my knowledge, but I would want to see strong evidence to convince me that the legal intergenerational contract between adults and the elderly has been of significance in recent history.

Much more important than statutory requirements, have been the implicit, unwritten, indeed largely unspoken compacts between successive generations, compacts which have perhaps been all the more powerful for being little explored and articulated. By implicit compact I mean the values, the habits, the conventions of behaviour which give one generation an expectation of certain actions on the part of another. The legal compact between generations may have afforded the elderly scant comfort or protection, but the implicit one makes up for this by imposing obligations to assist upon successors. Such understandings are not confined to families: they bind all of the members of all generations, and so operate in the "collective welfare societies" of the European tradition just as much as they do in the "familial welfare societies" of Asia and elsewhere.

It is these understandings, these inchoate senses of obligation to behave in certain ways toward the elderly, which are coming under enormous pressure from the aging of our populations, and that forms my theme. But how useful, it might be wondered, is it to talk as though there was one understanding between generations, one shared notion of implicit contract, when we are analysing an aging process which affects a great range of societies of a decidedly varied nature? For on the face of it, the compacts between generations range greatly from one community to another. A 40 year old man — or woman — from London or Sydney, removed suddenly into a family in Tokyo or Beijing, would experience the greatest of confusion and anguish as he found himself expected to share his resources, his time, his decisions and more with the elderly and with children in ways and to degrees that were utterly foreign to him. Even so, at a deeper level, all societies with their very different intergenerational contracts will share a common experience of tension as they age, and for this reason it makes sense to talk of the one intergenerational contract, rather than of the many.

Population aging of the scale and pace to be witnessed now and in the coming few decades will produce generations of inconsistent size and life expectancy. A further consequence is that the demands for a share of resource flows will vary markedly as these alternatively swollen and shrunken generations or cohorts pass through the various phases of life. Generations, as they age, will face greater and lesser demands for support from others, and will in turn exert inconsistent requirements for assistance from those who preceed them and those who follow. It is this inconsistency — which may well be heightened, as it is in the present, by a rising expectation of what each elderly person deserves in the way of resources — that strikes at the spirit of reciprocity. And reciprocity is and has to be the fundamental principle which underlies all intergenerational contracts, no matter what their particular nature in this or that society, no matter whether they are legislated and articulated or unwritten and unspoken, whether they are contracts for flows towards or away from generations in particular phases of life.

A belief in and an expectation of reciprocity is critical to all intergenerational contracts, regardless of their particular forms. At any one moment a major portion of all persons are net losers from intergenerational resource transfers. That is, they would individually be better off today if there was no requirement that they share their resources with others older or younger than themselves. However, they submit to a redistribution of their incomes and wealth, through family exchanges, taxation, investment in superannuation schemes and the like, in the belief that this will benefit both those in need of help now, and, crucially, themselves in future, since it will obligate others to do the same for them in time. I cannot accept that humans indulge in resource distribution simply out of a selfless altruism, without an expectation of a repayment later in life, or in some recognition of a duty to repay a debt for prior benefits. It is this vital sense of reciprocity, this sense that "my time will come", which makes high levels of taxation acceptable amongst the adult populations of western societies, or makes tolerable the demands, the directives and the manipulations reported of the elderly in communities of the familial welfare model.

This assumption of reciprocity, of consistent behaviour over long periods of time so that the sacrifices of today will be rewarded in like manner and at an appropriate level at some time to come, is being challenged by population aging. Reciprocity presupposes a number of things, including a stable population state, and an unchanging array of benefits and contributions, so that each participant in an intergenerational compact can be confident that "in my turn, I will be treated in like manner, with those who follow me making their surplus resources available to me, just as I have shared mine with others who have gone in need before me".

This critical confidence is proving unfounded however. The historian of welfare must be struck by the inconsistency of benefits and contributions during the last century, just as he or she must by the non-stable state of population size and composition. Closer to the present, the historian is struck too by the fact that our aging populations are beginning to behave in ways quite antithetical to notions of consistency and reciprocity - they are acting to accelerate growing discrepancies between the gains and losses accruing to successive generations through the operation of the intergenerational contracts. The result will be — indeed, it already is — serious undermining of vital notions on the advantages of pooling and sharing resources and risks, of having an intergenerational contract at all.

Demographic Aging

To put it another way, we might say that the implicit intergenerational contract of reciprocity is under assault from aging in at least two distinct though not unrelated ways. The first attack comes from what we can call demographic aging, meaning that complex of developments including increased longevity and declining birthrates which produce a marked increase in the size of the elderly component of a population. Our existing measures of demographic aging concentrate upon aging at the impersonal level of regional or national populations, and for this reason fail to address the question of what these changes in length of life or birth numbers mean to the experiences of individuals.

More specifically, they fail to reveal the experiences of successive cohorts as they live through the transition of the later twentieth century from youthful to elderly populations. Since the experiences accumulated over a lifetime by cohorts as they age — "cohort-specific experiences" we might call them — are not the focus of current studies or theories on social processes, we will need to speculate about them here. For they cannot be ignored: the sense of reciprocity, of like treatment for like behaviour, is a function of individual actors' experiences across time, of the memories and expectations they will build up, and not of figures which detail portions of the population in this or that category at one moment in time.

What might these experiences of successive cohorts look like, we can wonder, to those living through them, and why do they endanger the notion of intergenerational contract? Let us consider two very simple examples by way of illustration: the details would, of course, vary, depending upon the particular society in question, but the essentials of the illustration will be evident even if we ignore this caveat. A young adult of 1900 could have expected, given the demographic facts of that time, to have to invest very little in support of the aged, regardless of whether the elderly were deemed to be a family or a collective responsibility, and irrespective of whether the aged were treated generously or poorly. Our young adult could have assumed that only one parent might survive to age 65; that there would be no grandparents alive at that stage; that the one parent would not live many years into old age; and that there would be a number of brothers and sisters alive with whom to share the responsibility of providing for the aged. If we accept that the parent would live 10 years past age 65 — about the expectation of life of an elderly Briton in 1900 — then the 10 "dependant-years" of the elder would mean no more than two or three or four dependant-years per surviving child.

Between 1900 and 1980 the agedness of the British and a number of other populations doubled, according to our conventional demographic measures of aging, and a trebling will have occurred by the third or fourth decade of the next century. But these figures fail to indicate the realities facing successive generations. The young adult of 1980, for instance, could expect that both parents would live to reach old age; that a grandparent would still be alive at that stage, and so in need of support also; that the parents would live a further 15 or 20 years apiece into old age; and that there would at most be one sibling with whom to share this responsibility.

In terms of supporting the dependant-years of the elderly, the young of the late twentieth-century face responsibilities that are five to ten times greater than those of earlier this century — not the doubling as indicated by conventional measures. The young of early in the next century, that is the infants of today, face duties towards the aged which will be ten to twenty times those faced by people like themselves but living just a century before them. The experiences of society and individual are vastly different. Nor have I chosen an extreme illustration here. By drawing my figures from Britain, I have focused upon a country where the change in relations between the generations is occurring more slowly than in most other parts of the world: in Japan the shift is occurring much more swiftly than this.

Such illustrations are of course highly contentious, because of their simplicity amongst other things. Yet despite the obvious failings, the example does bring into focus a perspective not apparent in current measures of aging or in our debates upon aging. What might appear at one level to be a consistent intergenerational agreement appears anything but that when seen through the eyes of successive generations or cohorts. Suppose, for instance, that in the Britain of our illustration, it had been decided that each elderly person should have an annual income equivalent to exactly one-half of that of each non-elderly adult. This policy, if held to across the century, might represent consistency from the viewpoint of the aged person, but something very inconsistent indeed seen from the vantage-point of individuals accumulating a lifetime of experience. Those who were young by the end of the century would be handing over portions of their resources to the aged on a scale quite inconceivable to those who had been young before them. It is by no means clear how a sense of reciprocity, of comparable benefit for comparable sacrifice, can survive such manifest inconsistency.

To phrase it another way, we might observe that the intergenerational compact assumes a demographic stability, a persisting balance between the numbers of young, old, and those in between. Across much of human history this assumption of stability, of no overall growth or decline in the size of successive generations, would indeed have been a reasonable one to make. Individual families and communities would face dramatic imbalances, as disease or famine decimated a cohort or two, but the aberrations would have been essentially random, directionless, local and self-righting.

Rapid population growth, followed by the halting of growth, has shattered this pattern. But until recently successive generations benefited greatly from this break with the past — with few short-lived exceptions, modern populations have been ones in which subsequent generations were larger than those that preceeded them. Each generation cared for a small number of the elderly, and became in turn the responsibility of a larger group of the young. The result was a small flow of resources from the young to the old, as population growth kept each generation from facing the real costs of its own old age. The whole experience encouraged the expansion of welfare provisions for the aged, and the belief that there was no limit to what the aged might be promised or offered.

At the end of the twentieth century, a very different situation pertains. No-growth, and the birth of cohorts which are significantly smaller than those preceeding them, mean that the compact between generations is being altered radically. Those born today face sharing their resources with the aged on a scale which is without precedent — it is being expected that they will provide flows of wealth towards the aged which others before them have not done, and, more particularly, that they will provide this flow to elderly persons who in their time had done very little for the aged who went before them.

An apparent consistency of compact — that the aged deserve a certain income relative to that of the non-aged — will produce such a grossly inconsistent outcome, from the viewpoint of those who come later, that they cannot be counted on to play the hand dealt to them by history. The question we have been debating in the 1970s and 1980s has been "can the coming generations afford to sustain the elderly in the manner which they have come to expect?". The issue for the 1990s and beyond will not be "can they", but "will they" and even more bluntly "why should they feel bound to do so?". Are they bound to honour an intergenerational contract which, under the guise of consistency and reciprocity, produces extremely iniquitous and irresponsible results? For this is the true issue and the real challenge facing aging populations.

Political Aging

I noted previously that at least two types of aging could be identified, that both go to the heart of the question of reciprocity, and that demographic aging was the better-recognised of the two because it is the more readily measureable. We pursued our illustration of the effects of demographic aging after making the assumption that no other aging is occurring, and that the demands of the aged for a share of resources remained at a consistent one-half of the income of a non-aged person. However, this last has been far from the reality in aging societies in recent decades.

The second aging, that which I shall call "political aging", is a development of growing importance in the 1970s and 1980s. By "political aging" I do not have in mind the years of political leaders or the led, although there may well be a connection between these and the real " political aging". Nor do I intend to discuss a possible loss of vigour or enterprise which some observers claim to note as an inevitable adjunct of demographic aging. What I want to highlight is a decisive turn in policies and priorities, away from the child- and young-adult-centred programmes of the 1930-70 era, and towards the interests and concerns of the aged and soon-to-be-elderly. This "aging of the Welfare State" is apparent in Europe, in North America and in Australasia: it remains an open question whether a comparable aging of priorities is taking place in societies with less developed collective welfare provisions, where families bear more direct responsibility for the aged — but I suspect very strongly that it is.

To demonstrate this reshaping of modern societies in the aging interests of their populations is an enormous task that goes well beyond the scope of this chapter, and some illustrations alone must suffice to indicate the nature of the process. All of my examples are drawn from the European, North American and Australasian cases known best to me.

A first indication of the shift towards the concerns of the aged and soon-to-be-elderly comes from studies of poverty. Surveys of the poor break in two around 1970. Those made prior to that date had, without exception, emphasised the presence of large numbers of the elderly amongst the poorest of a number of countries. At the same time they had recorded the progressive removal of children and young adults from the ranks of the poor, as a result of improved earnings, growing family allowances, tax relief for young families and the like. But since the early 1970s a reverse pattern has set in. Reports from the United States, Britain and elsewhere have been cataloguing yearly rises in the numbers of the young inhabiting the lowest ranks of the income ladder, and the hastening removal of the elderly from amongst the impoverished (Easterlin, 1987; Fiegehen 1986; Field, 1980; Harrington, 1984; Lister, 1982; Preston, 1984). Others, who have not used such figures and who have not set out to make the same point, nevertheless confirm it in an indirect way — by discussing poverty without mentioning the aged. In a recent book surveying poverty in my own country, for example, the authors make a very telling point, quite unwittingly and without realising it, when they devoted just one, short and halfhearted paragraph to the elderly (Waldegrave and Coventry, 1987).

A second hint of this realignment of interests comes from figures of government spending. In a number of spheres, but most obviously in health and social security, the downgrading of the concerns of the young and the highlighting of those of the aging is very evident. Everywhere — I am aware of no exceptions — expenditure upon universal child or family benefits is declining as a proportion of national income or government expenditure, while comparable expenditures upon universal benefits to the aged are mounting (OECD, annual; Nordic Council, annual). In New Zealand, to give but a single instance of the trend, the value of the child benefit has multiplied just four times in the last 30 years in unadjusted dollar value, and there is now talk of doing away with it altogether. Over the same period, prices have risen eight times, wages nine times, and the universal pension given to each aged person sixteen times (twelve times in after-tax value). Almost all of the change has occurred since 1970, and not surprisingly the percentage of national income devoted to one type of benefit has halved, while the other has doubled, although no demographic shift in the balance of old and young has taken place on this scale (Thomson, 1988).

A further indication of this historic reversal comes from mortality statistics. Health specialists, demographers and others have long treated measures of death rates as useful indicators of the resources available to groups within a society, for in general there is a good correlation between low mortality rates and the presence of substantial resources in the forms of income or services. During the last decade a little-discussed divergence has become apparent in these statistics — while the mortality rates amongst infants have been deteriorating, those amongst older persons have been improving rapidly. In the United States, for example, the chances have been rising in the last decade that a child will die early in life, in contravention of a century-long pattern of improvement, and in the last year, the British government has had to admit that after a number of years in which infant death rates did not improve, they have now begun to worsen (Preston, 1984).

Meanwhile, expectation of life has been extended for adults, and the rate of improvement has been greater the older the adult. Nor do we at present know the full extent of the divergence, for while conventional measures suggest a substantial extension of lifechances in the later years, a number of recent studies indicate that the improving longevity of the aged is in fact much greater than had been suspected or measured hitherto. Unless we are going to abandon the belief that mortality trends reflect the disposition of resources in modern societies, then we are left with the strong suggestion of a substantial redistribution of resources in favour of the older members of the community.

Other studies suggest further evidence of this swing in fortunes. In the United States and a number of other countries, a major controversy surrounds the fall in educational standards: regardless of whether the fall is absolute or relative only, the whole is indicative of a declining investment in education which parallels the fall in child health standards. We might point, too, to the mounting concern with youth crime rates or unemployment, or to a more recent concern — the growth in youth suicides and psychiatric committals, while those amongst older persons decline — as further evidence of a fundamental change in the disposition of resources in societies increasingly unfavourable to the young. Survey reports of the cynicism and disinterest which youth show towards politics and the state, by comparison with the high levels of involvement and expectation of older persons, fit the wider pattern.

Analyses of personal and household incomes and expenditures reinforce this suspicion. A number of recent US reports indicate a rise in the 1970s and 1980s in the resources and consumption of older persons, relative to those of younger ones. By 1985 the President's Economic Advisors were noting that the average aged person now received and spent as much as did the average non-aged one, and that the time had come to stop thinking of the elderly as poor (Council of Economic Advisers, 1985).

My own investigations of British, Canadian, Australian and New Zealand data point to similar conclusions. By the mid-1980s, for example, the New Zealand elderly on average spent as much or more than did persons in their 20s and 30s: if we extract housing spending from the totals, since almost all of the elderly owned their own homes and so faced few costs, the aged were spending considerably more than were others. Moreover, the New Zealand elderly at the same time appeared to be saving growing amounts of income, while saving amongst the young was shrinking (NZ, Household Sample Survey, annual; Thomson, 1988b). Similar trends are apparent in Britain (Fiegehen, 1986; UK, Department of Employment, annual).

In thinking about the significance of this redistribution of income towards the aged it is important to keep a number of points in mind. A range of changes apparent in the last twenty years might have led us to expect that the aged would have become poorer than others. Those past age 60, for example, have been retiring from the paid workforce earlier and in much greater numbers, and it might have been expected that this loss of income would leave them poorer than others. Meanwhile younger persons—women that is — have been taking on growing amounts of employment, and thus exerting additional new claims for a share of the society's resources. Moreover, the young have for twenty years now been reducing their fertility, and so shrinking the numbers of children with whom they must share their resources. Given that the numbers of children are taken into account in these analyses of income available to agegroups, a fall in fertility should have produced a corresponding boost in the average incomes and expenditures available amongst young adults.

Further, these societies in recent years have been failing to invest in the future, in ways other than not reproducing "human capital". Capital formation, or investment in lasting structures which will enrich the future, has now fallen to its lowest levels for many decades (OECD, annual). Non-investment in the future may have many benefits for the middle-aged and elderly — more is available for consumption now — and few penalties since they will not be present in the future, but the consequences are rather more serious for the young. It might have been expected that those who will bear the long-term cost would be the ones enjoying the short-term benefits. It might have been expected, too, that the massive deficits now being amassed by governments, and in many cases whole societies, would be done to benefit those who will pay in later years for this short-sightedness.

But such expectations are confounded by the results. Despite assuming future costs and penalties in order to sustain consumption today, the young appear not to be enjoying the immediate fruits of current policies. That is to say, the young have "fought back" against the flow of resources to the aged, by adapting their behaviour and incurring long-term costs, but have still failed to halt, let alone reverse the movement of income in favour of older persons. The surveys which show a small movement of income towards the aged are very much more significant than they might at first seem.

The process by which this redesigning of the modern state is taking place is complex, and differs from one country to another. In each case it is an accumulating — and accelerating — outcome of a myriad of seemingly unrelated economic and political decisions, few of which have an ostensible intent to redistribute life-chances in favour of certain generations, but which are nevertheless part of larger movement working to that end. In a study of the process in New Zealand, I have pinpointed the following processes as significant in this redistribution, and I believe that each has its counterparts in other societies, though in varying mixes and to differing degrees (Thomson, 1988b).

In the realm of social security policy, for instance, some recent moves have quite openly and clearly been designed to advantage certain age groups, while other changes to the same end have been less deliberate. In the last twenty years all assets-testing for age benefits has been ended, though this is not true of other benefits; incomes-testing for universal age benefits has also disappeared, which means that all elderly persons, regardless of income or wealth or employment, now receive the same universal state pension (which is subject to income taxation); the age for entitlement to this benefit has been lowered to 60 for both men and women; all pensions have become payable out of general taxation, and there is no attempt to maintain a social security fund or to record what contributions individuals might make; the level of payment has been raised and fixed in a new relationship with after-tax earnings of the non-elderly; and the age benefit has been indexed, as other social security payments have not, to both wage and price movements, whichever in a year proves more favourable to the aged. During the same twenty years, social security benefits to the non-elderly have slipped in value relative to earnings in a number of instances, most noticeably in the case of the universal child benefit.

Changes in housing policies have been of central significance in the redesign process. In the period from the later 1930s to the early 1970s the state made massive investments in housing, both through building and letting low-rental accommodation, and through giving low-cost loans to homebuyers. Almost all of the benefits went to young adults. But since the mid-1970s such investing by the state has all but ceased, so that by the mid-1980s assistance with housing for young families was at around one-tenth of its former levels, when measured as a fraction of national income.

The removal of income taxation exemptions has been another change of great importance. Basic rates of income tax on average incomes have more than doubled during the past 30 years, so that those who made most of their contributions to this reciprocal welfare system some time ago made very much smaller contributions than do those who follow them. But more striking still has been the elimination of certain types of income tax reliefs. In New Zealand, as in many countries, dependants and spouses who did not have their own earnings used to bring substantial taxation reliefs to a young family. A family of three children in the 1950s or 1960s, for example, paid no income tax at all if it had average or lower income, because of the deductions allowed to it. The cash benefits received at the same time gave, in effect, a substantial "negative" income tax during the years when the present middle-aged and elderly were making a major part of their "contribution" to the reciprocal welfare arrangements.

Since the early 1970s, taxation exemptions for children and non-earning spouses have been whittled away, and in the mid-1980s they have ceased to exist at all. One result of this is that much more of the total income tax bill of the country is now paid by younger adults. The recent lowering of high marginal tax rates works to a similar inequitable end, since most high incomes are earned by older persons, that is, by the now-aging young adults of the 1940s, 50s and 60s. The very recent elimination of all income tax relief on contributions to superannuation schemes, after such relief had been in place for several decades, is but one more example of a larger process of altering the terms of the intergenerational contract for those who come later.

The control of employment has been another critical factor here. In the

1940s, 50s and 60s, the society had little in the way of employment policies — there were more jobs available than workers, and the need to ration jobs was minimal. Immigration rates, however, were controlled so as to maintain the "overfull employment" and so boost earnings. But following the international economic downturn of the early 1970s "rationing" became necessary, and it is evident that the society decided in effect that the employment experiences of the aging were to be protected, at the expense, if necessary, of those who followed them.

Youth unemployment became a standard feature of most modern economies, while the earnings of those young who had jobs fell relative to those of older workers. Redundancy agreements, job protections, "tenure", policies of shrinking staffs by non-replacement rather than dismissal, and the altering of service conditions by the substitution of short-term contracts for 'lifetime employment" or by altering the terms of membership of superannuation schemes, have been just some of the means by which the society signals its new priorities — that if there is a shortage of employment available, it is to be rationed so that the earnings and employment benefits of older persons are secured before those of younger ones.

The changing of contributions to health and occupational pension schemes reflect the same message: the rate of payment for younger workers who belong to such schemes in many countries are now considerably higher than were the rates for young people in earlier years, although rates of benefit are not adjusted to reflect this. The linkage between contribution and benefit has been broken quite deliberately in the interests of moving income between generations.

The maintenance of high interest rate structures in the 1980s has been one more powerful means of shifting resources towards older persons. For the last twenty years interest rates have been rising, and this always carries with it the potential to shift income from primarily youthful borrowers to older lenders. This shift didn't happen until the 1980s, for the society also ran high inflation rates, but in recent years a wide gap of real return has opened between price inflation and interest earnings.

Furthermore, the terms upon which money is lent have now been amended, in New Zealand as elsewhere — until the late 1970s both legal restraints and public opinion determined that lending was carried out on terms essentially favourable to borrowers. In particular, interest rates were not adjusted after the mortgage was granted, so that the borrower enjoyed the gift of inflation-reduced repayments and of untaxed capital gains. But in the 1970s and increasingly in the 1980s, this consensus of opinion has gone, along with the legal restraints which bolstered it, and lenders now alter mortgage terms at will to ensure continuing high rates of real return. The perhaps unintended message is once again clear — that older persons are not prepared as they age to pass on the benefits they themselves had formerly enjoyed, but instead expect high real returns on their savings.

Other examples of the shift in emphasis in social and economic policy come from the new programmes to charge for public services. In the last decade individuals and their families have faced increased charges upon services which were formerly free or near-free to the user — for education for instance, or for a range of medical treatments. The intention now is to make the 'user pay' so as to encourage 'efficient and responsible' public services — and to ease budget deficits. An effect, however, is to widen the gulf between what living in the modern welfare state has meant to those who experienced its low-cost and high-benefit earlier years, and those who have not.

In a broader sense, what we are witnessing is an adjustment to the real costs of operating a modern welfare state. From the 1940s through to the 1970s the populations of these states were shielded from the full cost of what they were awarding themselves as they expanded their welfare states, through a combination of rapid economic growth, peculiar demographic circumstances, a careful shaping of the range of benefits paid out, and massive deficit financing. Central to the process of expansion was the acceptance of what we might call 'retrospective awards', meaning that people who had spent ten or twenty or thirty years of adult life making the small contributions appropriate to a low level of public services, pensions and the like, found themselves being awarded much larger benefits later in life which should, in terms of equity, have been preceeded by larger contributions — and which entailed greater contributions from those who followed.

It is perhaps little wonder that expansion has seemed such an excellent idea to the older members of the present welfare states, but from the 1970s a young adult population has emerged which faces spending the whole of its adult life paying the high 'true' rate of contribution. It faces, too, the prospect of 'retrospective diminution' of its welfare state benefits — for in all modern societies there is apparent now a recognition that the process of expansion cannot be sustained, and more, that demographics will force an inevitable cutback.

The talk is now of raising pension entitlement ages in future, of doing away with universal pension schemes, of reintroducing assets and means-testing, of expecting people to provide for their own old age. In short, no intention is evident to maintain the existing rate of benefit, let alone of expanding it, once the present aged and soon-to-be-elderly have made their claims. A connection between level of benefit and level of contribution over time is not assumed to figure in the operation of intergeneration contracts. The concept of collective social security organised through the institutions of the modern welfare state seemed an excellent one when the full costs of this were avoided or ignored, but it is not clear that populations will prove irrevocably attached to the notion as their lifetime contributions mount and their benefits dwindle.

All of the above has the most serious of implications for intergenerational contracts — and having studied the situation in a number of countries, I see little reason to think that my New Zealand example is alone or unique. Some of the processes by which 'political aging' is taking place have been indicated, along with a few of the consequences. The full extent of the redistribution of fortunes or life-chances between generations cannot yet be known, in part because our statistics on these issues are very poor, but more because much of the change has been 'absorbed' by younger persons who have responded by adapting their lives in a variety of ways — by marrying later or not at all, by having fewer or no children, by not investing, by taking on additional employment, by accepting older or smaller or cheaper homes and the like. The measureable shift in economic resources between age groups is a residual, being that portion of the full change which the ill-favoured have not been able to deflect or divert into the future.

Some idea of the possible scale and pace of the underlying change in fortunes can be gained from modelling exercises, that is from attempts to assess the circumstances individuals would be in today, if they had not modified their behaviour but instead continued to act as those who went before them had done. One such piece of research which I have undertaken in New Zealand was designed to assess changes in housing cost, since these costs are affected by a wide range of the 'political aging' effects outlined above. The exercise explored the question 'what portion of after-tax income would identical young families have to devote to mortgage repayments on identical first homes, at various dates during the last thirty years?'

The finding was that young families in the mid-1980s now must devote three times as great a portion of their income to the same simple purchase as did families of identical characteristics in the 1950s or 1960s — and that was after making a very conservative set of assumptions about the changes. We do not find, of course, that young adults are now paying these trebled costs, except in those few instances where individuals persist in trying to behave as their parents had done — most have responded by securing other forms of housing, by delaying children, by sending the mother back into the workforce and so on.

A second way of highlighting the changes is to explore the experiences which individuals might accumulate, if they were alike in every characteristic bar the accident of being born twenty or thirty years apart. I have attempted this for men and women born in New Zealand in 1930 and 1960, and found that by age 40, the net level of contribution and benefit from social welfare, health, education and taxation programmes was at least five times greater for those born in 1930 than for those born thirty years later. Beyond age 40, the divergence in experiences look set to be even greater, in view of present talk of dismantling age benefits after the year 2000 or 2010 when the numbers of the aged will increase very rapidly.

'Political aging', it needs to be emphasised, is compounding an underlying demographic aging in at least two ways. A shift in life-chances is the result of the substituting since the early 1970s of an elder-centred for a youth-centred state. But just as importantly — and perhaps even more troublingly for the principle of reciprocity — certain persistent generations of "winners" and "losers" are emerging. The first "welfare generation", the prime beneficiaries of the early youth-state, have succeeded in having the state amended as they age so as to keep themselves at the point of benefit, and others at the point of contribution. That is, the first welfare generation of the modern welfare era looks set to remain the only welfare generation. How and why they have succeeded in this is an issue too large to tackle here, and it is somewhat tangential to our theme of reciprocity and intergenerational contract. But the effect is to produce what may well become the most divisive of social issues at the end of the present century. Reciprocity and the intergenerational contract, I believe, cannot stand this type of abuse.

Comment — The Questions for the 1990s

This contribution I suspect, will strike some as extremist, and unconvincing when the arguments are presented so briefly. Others may find it offensive, one is not supposed to speak in these tones about one's elders. Many will be tempted to insist that this process of aging is not apparent in their particular portion of the globe, an issue I will be addressing elsewhere. However, I risk these censures because I want us all to appreciate the importance of thinking about aging as a process which is having profound effects throughout our societies. In particular, I want to draw attention to the fact that the compact which binds successive generations in any society is being assaulted by both demographic and political aging — so severely assaulted that its survival in any recognisable form cannot be assumed.

Extremely awkward and perhaps distressing questions will have to be addressed, such as "what responsibility does a succeeding generation bear towards its predecessors, when demography makes their prospects of contribution and benefit from the welfare compact so very unequal, and when the later generation and its difficulties are the product of decisions made by the former, not by themselves"? Another might be "is a generation bound to honour the obligations passed on to it by a predecessor, when the earlier group acted irresponsibly or selfishly or inconsistently in defining those obligations"?

A third is "can or should the aged and soon-to-be-elderly be shielded from the consequences of their former and current behaviour — are they absolved by age alone from responsibility for the world they helped to shape and bequeath to others, and in which they now form such a major presence and influence?" And how are we to respond to the standard defenses of the aging — that "we paid for all this through our taxes earlier in life", or simply that "pensions are an inalienable right"? Such unsettling issues go to the heart of our welfare arrangements, in collective just as much as familial welfare systems, and to note that reciprocity in intergenerational contracts used to be achieved will be of little avail in the debates at the end of the twentieth century.

References

ABS, various. *Household Expenditure Survey*. Canberra.

Burbidge, J. 1987. *Social Security in Canada: An Economic Appraisal*. Canadian Tax Foundation Paper No 79. Toronto.

Clark, R. and others. 1984. *Inflation and the Economic Well-being of the Elderly*. Baltimore.

Committee on the Economic and Financial Problems of Provision for Old Age (Phillips Committee), 1954. *Report*. London.

Council of Economic Advisers to the US President, 1985. Annual Economic Report of the President, Transmitted to the Congress, February 1985. Washington.

Coward, L. 1974. *Mercer Handbook of Canadian Pension and Welfare Plans*. Toronto.

Creedy, J. 1982. *State Pensions in Britain*. Occasional Paper XXXIII of NIESR. Cambridge.

CSO, annual. Annual Abstract of Statistics. London.

—— annual. *Social Trends*. London.

Diamond, P. 1977. "A framework for social security analysis", *Journal of Public Economics*. 8:275-98.

Easterlin, R. 1980. *Birth and Fortune*. New York.

—— 1987. "The new age structure of poverty in America: permanent or transient?", *Population and Development Review*. 13, No 2: 195-208.

Eichengreen, B. 1987. *Juvenile Unemployment in Interwar Britain: The Emergence of a Problem*. CEPR Discussion Paper No 194. London.

Ermisch, J. 1983. The Political Economy of Demographic Change. London.

—— and H. Joshi. *Demographic Change, Economic Growth and Social Welfare in Europe*. CEPR Discussion Paper No.179.London.

Estes, C. and others, (eds). 1983. *Fiscal Austerity and Aging*. Beverly Hills.

Fiegehen, C. 1986. "Income after retirement", *Social Trends* 16. London.

Field, F. 1980. *Fair Shares for Families*. Study Committee on the Family, Occasional Paper No 3. London.

Flora, P. and others. 1986. *State, Economy and Society in Western Europe, 1815-1975*. London.

—— and A Heidenheimer (eds). 1983. *The Development of Welfare States in Europe and America*. New Brunswick.

Graycar, A. 1979. *Welfare Politics in Australia*. Melbourne.

Guest, D. 1985. *The Emergence of Social Security in Canada*. Vancouver.

Harrington, M. 1984. *The New American Poverty*. New York.

Health and Welfare Canada, 1986. *Overview: The Income Security Programmes of Health and Welfare Canada*. Ottawa.

Hugo, G. 1986a. *Population Ageing in Australia*. Papers of the East-West Population Institute, No 98. Honolulu.

—— 1986b. *Australia's Changing Population*. Melbourne.

Ismael, J. (ed). 1985. Canadian Social Security Policy. Kingston.

—— 1987. *The Canadian Welfare State: Evolution and Transition*. Regina.

Jones, M. 1983. *The Australian Welfare State*. Sydney.

Katz, M. 1983. *Poverty and Policy in American History*. New York.

Kutza, E. 1981. *The Benefits of Old Age*. Chicago.

Leman, C. 1980. *The Collapse of Welfare Reform: Political Institutions, Policy and the Poor in Canada and the United States*. Boston.

Lerner, A. 1959. "Consumption-loan interest and money", *Journal of Political Economy*. 67:512-18.

Levy, f. 1987. *Dollars and Dreams: The Changing American Income Distribution*. New York.

Lister, R. 1982. "Income maintenance for families with children", in *Families in Britain*, ed. R. Rapoport. London.

Mendelsohn, R. 1979. *The Condition of the People: Social Welfare in Australia*. Sydney.

—— 1983. Australian Social Security Finance. Sydney.

NZ Department of Statistics, annual. *National Income and Expenditure*. Wellington. —— annual. *Household Sample Survey*. Wellington.

—— five yearly. *Census of Population and Dwellings*. Wellington.

New Zealand Planning Council, 1979. *The Welfare State*. Paper No 12. Wellington.

Nordic Council, annual. *Yearbook of Nordic Statistics*.

Parsons, D. 1984. "On the economics of intergenerational control", *Population and Development Review*. 10, No 1: 41-54.

OECD, annual. *National Accounts*. Paris.

Patterson, J. 1981. *America's Struggle Against Poverty*. Cambridge, Mass.

Preston, S. 1981. "Children and the Elderly: Diverging Paths for America's Dependents", *Demography* 21, No 1: 435-57.

Ross, D. 1981. *The Working Poor: Wage Earners and the Failure of Income Security Policies*. Toronto.

Samuelson, P. 1958. "An exact consumption-loan model of interest with or without the social contrivance of money", *Journal of Political Economy*. 66, No 6: 467-82.

Scott, P. and P. Johnson. 1988. *The Economic Consequences of Population Ageing in Advanced Societies*. Background Paper to the Conference on Work, Retirement, and Intergenerational Equity, 19-21 July 1988,Cambridge.

Scotton,R. and H. Ferber. (eds). 1978. *Public Expenditures and Social Policy in Australia*. Melbourne.

Sikora, R. and B. Barry. (eds). 1978. *Obligations to Future Generations*. Philadelphia.

Thomson, D. 1984a. 'The Decline of Social Welfare: Falling State Support for the Elderly Since Early Victorian Times', *Ageing and Society*, 4, 4:451-82.

—— 1984b. 'I am not my father's keeper: Families and the Elderly in Nineteenth Century England', *Law and History Review*, 2,2: 265-86.

—— 1986. 'Welfare and the Historians', in L. Bonfield and other (eds)., *The World We Have Gained*. Oxford.

—— 1986. "The Overpaid Elderly?" *New Society*, 7 March:3-4.

—— and B. Macdonald, 1987. "Mortgage relief, farm finance, and rural depression in New Zealand in the 1930s", *New Zealand Journal of History*. 21, No 2: 228-50.

—— 1988a. "The intergenerational contract — under pressure from population ageing", Paper to the Sixth World Conference of the International Society on Family Law, Tokyo, 1-11 April 1988. Publication forthcoming.

—— 1988b. Selfish Generations: *The Ageing of the Welfare State*. Wellington. Publication due late 1988.

Thurow, L. 1980. *The Zero-Sum Society*. New York.

UK Department of Employment, annual *Family Expenditure Survey*. London.

US Bureau of the Census, annual. *Current Population Reports*. Washington.

Waldegrave, C and P. Coventry. 1987. *Poor New Zealand*. Wellington.

Wilding. P. (ed). 1986. In *Defence of the Welfare State*. Manchester.
Wilensky, H. 1975. *The Welfare State and Equality*. Berkeley.
Wilson, T. (ed). 1974. *Pensions, Inflation and Growth. London*.
Wroe, D. 1973. "The Elderly", *Social Trends* 3. London.
Wynne, E. 1980. *Social Security: A Reciprocity System under Pressure*. Boulder, Col.

Chapter 25

The Elderly in Labour and Education Law in Yugoslavia

M. GEČ-KOROŠEC   School of Law,
University of Maribor, Yugoslavia

Introduction

In the Constitution of the Socialist Federal Republic of Yugoslavia of 1974,[1] the chapter on The Freedoms, Rights and Duties of Man and the Citizens spells out, in more detail, the right to work, the freedom to work and the rights connected with work. According to the Constitution, the right to work is, therefore, guaranteed and the rights acquired on account of labour are inalienable.[2] The freedom to work is guaranteed, which means that everyone should be free to choose his or her occupation and every citizen should have access, on equal terms, to every job and every function in society.[3] The Constitution also states that working people have the right to such working conditions as ensure their physical and moral integrity as well as safety at work.[4]

The Constitution also defines cultural-educational rights according to which all citizens are entitled, under equal conditions specified by statute, to acquire knowledge and vocational education at all levels of education, free schools and other institutions of education.[5] The Constitution also specifies freedom of scientific and artistic creation which is, in essence, freedom of thought and choice.[6]

The Constitution of the Socialist Federal Republic of Yugoslavia of 1974 also defines in detail, the respective competence of the Federation, its six Socialist Republics[7] and the two Socialist Autonomous provinces.[8] The Federation may only regulate basic rights of workers in associated labour while the Republics and Autonomous Provinces may regulate, in more detail, labour relations concerning specific situations in the individual Republic and in the Autonomous Provinces. Education is also within the competence of all Republics and Autonomous Provinces of which the fundamental social objective is to create a free, responsible, creative and multi-faceted personality in a socialist self-management society. Vocational education ensures that education is a permanent process, enabling people to develop their abilities and to acquire knowledge throughout their life.

In the SFRY, eight laws regulate labour relationships[9] and others regulate vocational education in individual Republics and Autonomous Provinces.[10] Here we will focus on those regulations relevant to the employment and education of the elderly, with special emphasis on the Socialist Republic of Slovenia. The differences between the individual Republics and Autonomous Provinces and legal opinions will be considered.

The Position of the Elderly in Labour Law

A. Establishment of a Labour Relationship

1. General

Apart from the provision on freedom to work which is developed in more detail by the Federal Associated Labour Act[11] and by the individual laws of Republics and Provinces on the establishment of labour relationships, there is a rule in Yugoslav law which states that a labour relationship may be established by any person who meets the eligibility requirements determined by workers in a basic organization of associated labour according to the needs of the labour process and in conformity with self-management enactments and law.[12] A labour relationship may, therefore, be established according to and under the conditions regulated by Law and other enactments.

2. General requirements for the establishment of a labour relationship

To establish a labour relationship, the worker who wishes to be employed must meet general requirements prescribed by Law. Two general requirements are well established under the present Law on labour relationships.[13]

aa) a minimum age of fifteen is specified for ordinary jobs, although in individual and special cases the age can be varied. A higher minimum age can be specified by special regulation for more demanding jobs.[14]

bb) the general condition of health of the worker must be proved by a compulsory health certificate. Special attention is paid to the capacity of a disabled person who is looking for employment. The present Law on labour relationships of the Socialist Republic of Slovenia, for example, states that any disabled person, who with rehabilitation or retraining is capable of performing specific jobs is considered generally healthy. But the present Law on labour relationships of the SR of Slovenia does not state the mode according to which the state of general health is established, but uses the provisions of other Republics (Croatia, for example, in its Law on Labour relationships[15]).

As regards age, it should be observed that the Law generally specifies only a minimum age and that it is impossible to fix a maximum age for the establishment of a labour relationship.[16] In practice, this means that employment should not be refused to a person of any age if he proves by medical certificate that he is healthy and capable of carrying out specific jobs provided that he has not yet served the number of years required to qualify for the old-age pension, and meets any special requirements for the establishment of a labour relationship. Thus any person who has not accumulated the years required to qualify for the old age pension (40 years for men and 35 for women)[17] and who proves he is in good health, can apply for the job regardless of age.

These two general requirements are of crucial importance for establishment of labour relationships. Without them the relationship will be considered null and does not attract the legal consequences which follow from the mutual relations of workers in associated labour.[18]

3. Specific requirements for establishment of a labour relationship

By "specific requirements for the establishment of a labour relationship", we understand the requirements a worker must meet to perform those jobs to be carried out in the basic organization of associated labour. Besides the two general requirements, a worker must also meet specific requirements determined according to the specific labour processes to be carried out by a worker or according to the specific working conditions. Specific requirements for establishment of a labour relationship are not, as are both general requirements, of crucial significance for the existence and duration of a labour relationship. They are restricted only to the performance of specific jobs in a basic organization of associated labour. Such requirements are specified by self-management general enactments on labour relationships as a condition for the performance of specific jobs. The most common specific requirements are the following: required professional education, professional examination, specified practical experience, specified characteristics and related upper age-limits for the safety of elderly workers in heavy work and in work which is harmful to health and life.[19]

An upper age limit as a special requirement for establishment of a labour relationship can be stipulated by the self-management general enactment of the organization of associated labour or can be specified by Law for specific jobs or tasks. Examples are:
- the law on vocational education in the SR of Slovenia which in Article 193 specifies that the labour relationship is terminated for university teachers and scientific workers who meet the prescribed requirements for retirement and reach 70;
- the law on the fundamentals of the social self-protection system;
- the law on air-navigation of 1986 specifies in Article 157 that the tasks of the captain of a plane shall not be discharged by a person who has reached 60;
- the law on the internal affairs of the SR of Slovenia of 1980 specifies in Article 85 that a person, who wishes for the first time to enter the labour relationship of a policeman, shall meet special requirements and not be older than 27;

- the law on carrying out the internal affairs within the competence of the Federal Administration Organs of 1985 states in Article 40 that a worker carrying out special duties in the Federal Secretariat of Internal Affairs can, on account of the specific conditions and character of the employment, exceptionally terminate the labour relationship with the rights to the old-age pension before fulfilling the general requirements for the old-age pension, if he has worked for twenty years, of which at least ten years should be in activities where the working time is counted as double. These persons enjoy special benefits in the determination of their pension.

These provisions are designed only as security provisions and not to be discriminatory concerning age.

Elderly persons who have not yet accumulated a sufficient number of years for retirement and meet general health requirements and any specific requirements for the establishment of a labour relationship can be employed regardless of their age. Other provisions of the Law on labour relationships also apply to these persons. They concern applications in response to job advertisments or public competition of a basic organization, the procedure for selection of candidates, trial work periods, obligation of a written agreement with the self-management general enactments and the provisions in the work-book.

4. The practice of the Courts

It should be specially pointed out that in 1978, the Constitutional Court of Yugoslavia enacted the provision according to which every citizen is entitled to freedom to work throughout the SFR of Yugoslavia on equal terms valid in the place of employment.[20] A provision passed by the Associated Labour Court of Slovenia stated that a worker cannot establish a labour relationship for an indefinite period unless he meets all the general and specific requirements specified by the self-management enactment of labour relationships as a condition for the performance of specific tasks.[21]

In relation to the upper age limit, the Constitutional Court of the Autonomous Province of Vojvodina[22] has stressed that a provision of a basic organization of associated labour, according to which the candidate for the job of a watchman could not be over 50 was contrary to the present Law on the fundamentals of the social protection system. That law specifies that activities involving safety at work may not be undertaken by a person over 60.

In the Constitutional Court of Yugoslavia a woman worker initiated the procedure for the assessment of the constitutionality of a provision placing women workers in position of inequality vis-a-vis men. The provision states that the worker terminated the labour relationship by force of law in Federal Administration Bodies after 40 years' service and attainment of age 60, when a female worker completes 35 years' service and reaches the age of 55, or a male worker reaches 65 years and a female reaches 60 years and they have both completed 15 years' service. The Court was of the opinion that the constitutional principle on the equality of both sexes had been violated[23] and for this reason a law, amending the provision by permitting a woman to demand in writing that she should continue in work until the upper limit of the retirement period and age prescribed for men, was adopted.

5. *Temporary and occasional work*

Labour legislation of the individual Republics and Autonomous Provinces also regulated, in more detail, temporary and occasional work. Temporary work is considered as work which, in a basic organization of associated labour, occurs occasionally, and there is no need to establish a labour relationship with a new worker. Occasional work is that which lasts for a short, defined period and therefore does not require the establishment of a labour relationship. In both cases there is, according to Law, a time limit of 60 days in a calendar year.

For temporary and occasional jobs, a contract of employment between the worker and the basic organization of an associated labour must be signed. The contract must specify, in particular, the following obligations and rights: the obligation to perform the agreed work, the right to payment and the right to insurance in case of an accident at work or illness caused by it.

Unemployed or partly employed people have priority in obtaining such work; other people can be employed in such jobs only if a competent employment agency establishes that there are no unemployed or partly employed persons who meet the relevant requirements. The law does not specially define the categories of unemployment or partial employment. *Partly employed persons* can be held to be those who work less than half of the full-time working period, or those who work under a contract with similar obligations, responsibilities and rights as the workers who are in a labour relationship but who are themselves not in a labour relationship. *Unemployed persons* can be considered those who are not in a labour relationship or who work under a contract and without the obligation, responsibilities and rights required for the work of employed persons.[24]

Basic organizations of associated labour must retain records about working under contract and the number of hours performed by these workers. They must send the data once a year to the employment agency. If this agency establishes the existence of unemployed or partly employed workers with the relevant qualifications, then it informs the basic organization of associated labour about them. It is known that, in practice, work contracts for temporary or occasional jobs are, in particular, signed by elderly people who are already retired and receiving lower pensions.

B. Termination of the labour relationship

1. *General*

The modes of termination of the labour relationship vary within the Yugoslav legal system. They are classified mainly into three groups:

(1) termination of the labour relationship at the worker's request
(2) termination of the labour relationship at the request of other workers
(3) termination of the labour relationship by force of law.

2. *Termination of the labour relationship through eligibility for old-age pension, and the possibility of further employment*

In the Socialist Republic of Slovenia, the termination of the labour relationship at the request of other workers includes the situation in which a worker meets the eligibility requirements for an old-age pension and the competent body of the basic organization does not wish him to continue work.[25]

According to the present Law on labour relationships of the SR of Slovenia, a worker's labour relationship must be terminated if he fulfils the eligibility requirements for an full old-age pension, unless the competent body agrees that he can continue to work. The accord can be given if it is established that no candidate who meets the eligibility requirements has applied for the job. Advertisement or public competition for the job must occur at least three months before the worker is due to retire. The advertisement or public competition is to be repeated every year until a person meeting the public competition requirements applies for the job. These regulations allow elderly people who have met the eligibility requirements for a regular old-age pension to continue working, though the Law gives preference to those seeking work.[26]

Other Republics and the two Autonomous Provinces regulate the possibility of elderly people continuing to work in different ways. The Socialist Republic of Serbia enacts that a worker's labour relationship shall be terminated by force of law if he has worked 40 years or reached the age of 65 and worked at least 15 years. But the Law also recognizes the need for personnel. In such a case, the self-management general enactment can define jobs to be carried out by the worker after he has worked for 40 years, but only until he reaches 60 if, after public competition or advertisement, no person with the necessary qualifications has applied for the job.[27]

The Autonomous Province of Vojvodina provides that a man's labour relationship shall be terminated by force of law if he has worked 40 years and if a woman has worked 35 years. Also, a man must retire at 65 if he has worked 30 years and a woman at 60 if she has worked for 25 years. There is an exception: a worker, who is eligible for an old-age pension can remain in employment for a maximum of three more years while the job is advertised every 12 months to enable a new candidate to apply for it.[28] In the SR of Bosnia and Herzegovina, a male worker's employment is terminated by force of law if he has worked for 40 years and a female worker if she has worked for 35 years, or when a man reaches 65 or a woman reaches 60 and they have both worked for 25 years. A woman worker can, on the basis of a written statement, remain in employment until she has worked for 40 years or until she has reached 65 and has worked for 25 years. Exceptionally, and by a decision of the competent body of a basic organization, which must be in conformity with the self-management general act or with the social compact on the performance of personnel policy, it can be determined that a worker's labour relationship is not terminated even though he or she is eligible for an old-age pension.[29]

The Socialist Republic of Montenegro merely stipulated that a worker's labour relationship shall be terminated by force of law if the worker has worked for 40 years, or has reached 65 and has worked for 20 years. This Republic does not therefore envisage the possibility of further employment of the elderly who are eligible to receive old-age pensions.[30]

The best provision is that of the SR of Bosnia and Herzegovina, as it provides further employment specified by the self-management general enactment of the basic organization or by the social compact on the implementation of personnel policy. The solution in the present Law on labour relationships in the SR of Slovenia is also very advantageous, as a worker can continue after qualifying for a full old-age pension, if the competent body agrees after an annual unsuccessful advertisement of the job. This is not restricted to three years, as it is in the Autonomous Province of Vojvodina.

The Position of the Elderly in Education Law

A. General

All the Republics and both Autonomous Provinces have introduced vocational education. Adult education, and thus the education of the elderly, is defined as part of the unified social education system in Yugoslav socialist society. It is recognized that the acquisition of new knowledge must occur throughout the entire life cycle, and not only the repetition and completion of existing knowledge. This is particularly important for the elderly. In the year 2,000 people over 60 will form 16% of the entire Yugoslav population, 4% higher than the number of children between 7 and 14. For this reason, it is already necessary to think about the needs of this population who, during the last 20 years of life, will not merely be waiting to die but will still wish to be socially useful and physically and spiritually active.[32] For this reason, the system of vocational education provides various forms of adult education and education for the elderly.

B. Educational schemes for the elderly

The system of the vocational education provides various types of education for the elderly; apart from the classical school method, it also offers shorter types of formal and non-formal education as well as self-study. In the system of vocational education, the elderly are treated in the same way as other partici-pants in education. These are working people and others who are involved in organized education in order to acquire and complete their professional education or receive "on-the job training".

The forms of the education available to the elderly are mainly the following: on-the-job training, work-and-study schemes, self-study and full-time study schemes.

On-the-job-training is education for people who are in the midst of a course of education, acquiring or completing their professional education, either in a labour relationship or while partly carrying out their labour obligations.

Work-and-study schemes are designed for workers sent by their organizations of associated labour to acquire or complete their professional education or for workers who have acquired the necessary practical experience in their work.

On-the-job-training and the *work-and-study scheme* have special features:[34]

1. Special rights and obligations of workers involved in on- the-job-training and in the work-and-study scheme.

Conditions related to and the mode of exercising the rights and obligations connected with on-the-job training and work-and-study schemes are regulated by the self-management general enactments of the basic organizations of associated labour. These enactments determine, in particular, the cases and the scope of workers rights of absence from work for training, the right to substitute income owing to their absence from work during training and their obligations after training.

The workers' rights and obligations are stipulated by contract and signed between a worker and a basic organization of associated labour. The law does not lay down any upper age limit for workers who wish to take advantage of the schemes, so a worker can begin training regardless of his or her age.

2. Adaptation of individual educational programmes for participants with previous work and life experience

When workers with previous knowledge accept training, the educational institution prepares an educational programme which takes into account the participants' present knowledge.

3. Adaptation of the educational organization for participants in on-the-job-training

The educational organization (institution) coordinates educational work with the participants in on-the-job-training and thus considers their labour obligations and other relevant circumstances such as: working conditions, distance from work and practical experience. Within the framework of such coordination, the institution devises appropriate organizational forms of educational work, in agreement with the participants.

Self-study also plays a very important part in the system of vocational education. In conformity with the principle of knowledge equivalence acquired by organized training and knowledge acquired by self-study, the law specifies that every citizen is entitled to test his or her knowledge acquired by self-study.[34] Such an examination can comprise one or more subjects, together with other components of the syllabus over one or more years or the content of the syllabus as a whole. Thus the Law requires educational institutions to determine the conditions, methods and terms of examinations for knowledge acquired through self-study. It must publish these at least three times a year.

The present Law does not specify an upper age limit for testing knowledge acquired through self-study and this form of education can be used by all citizens regardless of their age . All workers, working people and citizens have free access to these forms of vocational education under equal conditions specified by law. As resources are limited, the law specifies that the participants shall contribute to the payment of individual services necessary for carrying out the educational programmes. The contribution can be determined by educational organizations according to criteria set out between the users and performers of programmes. This is specified by the self-management agreement on the fundamentals of the plan. Citizens are entitled to free examinations when they take them for the first time. If they have to repeat them in the same subjects, the participants are obliged to contribute to their cost.

It should be pointed out that the elderly also have the possibility of *full-time education*, especially at two-year post-secondary schools or at higher schools and faculties. There are well-known cases when retired persons begin as full-time students at two-year post-secondary schools or at faculties in order to fulfil the ambitions of their youth. Neither the law nor educational organizations, as a rule, refuse full-time education to the elderly because of their age.

C. Education of the elderly in practice

Education of adults as well as of the elderly has, nowadays, become an increasingly important social activity and is an integral part of a general social plan for education. This education should be carefully planned and not only provide for special skills. On-the-job-training and the work-and-study schemes have become a very important component of vocational education. Part-time students constituted from one-third to one-half of all the graduates who have recently graduated in the SR of Slovenia at two-year post-secondary schools and at faculties. In the academic year 1980/81 the number of part-time graduates reached its peak; there were 1708 part-time graduates which amounts, in comparison with the total number of all graduates (4786), to 35,7%,[35] but recently the number of part-time students has decreased and the number of full-time students increased.

In the academic year 1987/86, 28.041 full time students were enrolled at both universities of the SR of Slovenia (Ljubljana and Maribor). There were 7.102 part-time students and 181 students on the work-and-study scheme. To improve the quality of on-the-job training and of the work-and-study scheme, better and more carefully planned conditions should be procured. This will be cheaper than extending full time study. If the conditions for part-time study are improved, Yugoslavia can reach the present level of education in developed countries by the year 2,000. Within the Slovene Pedagogical Society — the section on education for the "third age", there is a special programme of adult education. The average age of the participants is 60 years, and they are all retired. They meet, generally, twice a week for two periods in various groups. They are involved in painting, ceramics, literature, philosophy, journalism, foreign languages, computer science, music, history etc. We refer to it as the University of the Third Age. The teachers are mostly retired professors and other intellectuals. This form of education has already been organized in many towns of the SR of Slovenia. The strongest centre is in Ljubljana with approximately 600 participants. The education is partly financed by the participants themselves and partly by funds generated through seminars in which lecturers are trained to teach the elderly. Adult education is carried out in various circles, study-groups and seminars. At the end of the seminar the participants receive a certificate of attendance.[36]

Conclusions

This chapter shows that much attention has been devoted to the elderly in our socialist self-management society. The elderly can establish a labour relationship after they are eligible for old-age pension. This is regulated variously in individual Republics and the two Autonomous Provinces in accordance with employment opportunities in various fields. As the number of the unemployed has recently increased in the SFRY, the opportunities for employment of the elderly have also diminished. Amendments to the present legislation are in preparation.

The elderly have many opportunities to be involved in the educational process regardless of their age. Much is being done to raise the quality of adult education to match that given to young people. This can be achieved by the application of appropriate criteria and by the procedure of knowledge verification.

Notes

1. The Constitution of the Socialist Federal Republic of Yugoslavia, published in the *Official Gazette of the SFRY*, No. 9/1974.
2. See 1st and 2nd paragraph of Art. 159 of the Constitution of the SFRY of 1974.
3. Art. 160 of the Constitution of the SFRY of 1974, compare: M. Strobl, I. Kristan, C. Ribičič, *The Constitutional Law of the SFR of Yugoslavia*, 4th altered and completed publication, Ljubljana, 1986, pp.106-110.

4. Art. 161 of the Constitution of the SFRY of 1974.
5. See 3rd section of Art. 165 of the Constitution of the SFRY of 1974;
6. See 2nd section of Art. 165 of the Constitution of the SFRY of 1974; compare: M. Strobei, I. Kristan, C. Ribičič (ibid.3) p. 132-135.
7. The Socialist Federal Republic of Yugoslavia consists of the Socialist Republic of Bosnia and Herzegovina, The Socialist Republic of Croatia, The Socialist Republic of Macedonia, the Socialist Republic of Montenegro, the Socialist Republic of Slovenia and the Socialist Republic of Serbia.
8. The SFRY also consists of the Socialist Autonomous Province of Kosovo and the Socialist Autonomous Province of Vojvodina, which are constituent parts of the Socialist Republic of Serbia.
9. Law on labour relationships of the SR of Bosnia-Herzegovina, published in the *Official Gazette of the SR of Bosnia and Herzegovina*, No. 4/1984, 40/1984 and 9/1986; Law on labour relationships of the Socialist Republic of Montenegro, published in the *Official Gazette of the SR Montenegro*, No. 27/1985. Law on labour relationships of workers in associated labour of the SR of Croatia, published in *Narodne novine SR of Croatia*, No. 40/1982; Law on labour relationships of the SR of Macedonia, published in *Official Gazette of SR of Macedonia*, No. 45/1977, 3/1983, 3/1985 and 42/1985. Law on labour relationships in the SR of Slovenia, published in the *Official Gazette of the SR of Slovenia*, No. 24/1983, 5/1986 and 47/1986; Law on labour relationships of the SR of Serbia, published in *Official Gazette of the SR of Serbia*, No. 37/1986; Law on labour relationships of the SAP of Kosovo, published in *Official Gazette SAP Vojvodina*, No. 32/1981.
10. Laws regulating the vocational education:
Law on higher school education of the SR Bosnia Herzegovina, published in the *Official Gazette of the SR Bosnia and Herzegovina*, No. 11/1985; Law on higher school education of the SR of Montenegro published in *Official Gazette of the SR of Montenegro*, No. 14/1985, 16/1985, 3/1986; Law on vocational education of the SR of Croatia, published in *Narodne novine, the SR of Croatia*, No. 20/1982, 28/1983, 12/1985, 19/1986, and 32/1986; Law on vocation education of the SR of Macedonia, published in *Official Gazette SR Macedonia*, No. 16/1985, 2/1986 and 29/1986; Law on vocational education of the SR of Serbia, published in *Official Gazette SRS*, No. 14/1986; Law on the post-secondary education of workers in the AP of Kosovo, published in *Official Gazette SAP Kosovo*, No. 21/1975 and 37/1981; Law on higher school education of the SAP of Kosovo, published in *Official Gazette SAP Kosovo*, No. 43/1974, 28/1979, 22/1982. Law on education of the AP Vojvodina, published in *Official Gazette SAP Vojvodina*, No. 15/1983, 19/1983, 20/1985.
11. Compare Art. 167 of The Associated Labour Act, published in *Official Gazette of the SFRY*, No. 53/1976.
12. See M. Novak, *Delovno pravo (labour law)(special part)*, Ljubljana, 1987, p. 17.
13. See, for example, 2nd section of Art. 18 of the Law on labour relationship of the SR of Slovenia (ibid. 9); to cite: The Law on labour relationship.
14. See also Law on labour relationships, with comments and judicial practice, Ljubljana, 1982. p. 57.
15. Law on labour relationships of the SR Croatia (ibid. 9), see Art. 2 and 4 and 1st paragraph of Art. 6.
16. See M. Novak (ibid. 12), p. 19.
17. Article 19 of Law on retirement and disabled insurance of the SR Slovenia, published in *Official Gazette of the SRS*, No. 27/1983.

18. M. Novak (ibid. 12), p. 20, different opinions by A. Baltić and M. Despotović: *Osnovi radnog prava Jugoslavije (Fundamentals of labour law)*, Belgrade, 1979, p.p. 37, 38; the authors point out that in the so-called "factual law labour relationship" a worker may exercise rights and fulfil the obligations stemming from a labour relationship.
19. See A. Baltić, M. Despotović (ibid. 18), p.p. 163-165.
20. The Constitutional Court of Yugoslavia (USJ), No. U 348/75 of 27.4. 1978, Provisions and opinion of the Constitutional Court of Yugoslavia 1978, Belgrade 1979 p.p. 126, 127.
21. Provisions of the associated labour court of the SR Slovenia, No. Sp. 107/81 of 24. 4. 1981 *Gospodarski vestnik (Economic Gazette)*, No. 10 (12. 3. 1982), No. 49.
22. Provision No. U 103/78 of 5. 10. 1978 published R/SAPV, 6/79, B 1/79, p. 10.
23. Provisions of the Constitutional court of Yugoslavia, No. U 200/80 of 2. 6. 1982; see Z. Crnić, Z. Momčinović, Prestanak radnog odnos Zaščita prava radnika (Termination of the labour relationship-Protection of workers' rights), Zagreb, 1983, p. 81.
24. See Law on labour relationships with comments and judicial practice (ibid. 14), p. 732; M. Novak (ibid. 12), p. 143, ibid. 281.
25. See A. Radovan, *Prenehanje delovnega razmerja, Delovna razmerja v teoriji in praksi (Termination of labour relationship, Labour relationships in theory and practice)*, Ljubljana, 1980, p.p. 439-461; M. Novak (ibid. 12) , p. 110.
26. See Art. 173 of Law on labour relationships of the SR of Slovenia (ibid. 9).
27. See Art. 130 of Law on labour relationships of the SR of Serbia (ibid. 9); compare A. Baltić, M. Despotović(ibid. 18), p. 293.
28. See Art. 120 of Law on labour relationships of the AP Vojvodina (ibid. 9).
29. See Art. 99 of Law on labour relationships of the SR of Bosnia and Herzegovina (ibid. 9).
30. See Art. 125 of Law on labour relationships of the SR of Montenegro (ibid. 9).
31. See Art. 120 of Law on labour relationships of the AP of Kosovo (ibid. 9).
32. See Adult Education in the Long-Term Development of the SR of Slovenia, Aktualna tema (Current Topic), Ljubljana, 1985, p.82 ibid. 2.
33. See Vocational Education (Law with comments and executive regulations) 2nd altered and competed issue, Ljubljana 1983, p.p. 54, 55.
34. Compare for example, Art. 105 of Law on the vocational education of the SR of Slovenia.
35. Compare Adult Education in the Long-Term Development of the SR of Slovenia (ibid. 33), p. 34, 35.
36. Data are provided by the Home of the elderly "Draksler-Marjana", Ljubljana-Šiška, where this form of education is carried out.

Chapter 26

Protecting the Legal Rights of Older People: State Government Initiatives in Australia

Adam GRAYCAR   Commissioner for the Ageing,
                                  Adelaide, South Australia

The Context of rights

Recent decades have seen social, industrial, demographic and technological change of a magnitude not envisaged or experienced ever before. Social change, especially changing family relationships and general community behaviour has created a tension about norms of interaction and reciprocity. Increasing industrialisation has not automatically benefitted all the people in the community. Industrial progress has not eliminated poverty, it has not ensured that all people are adequately housed, adequately serviced with health care, have adequate access to the employment market, or receive adequate incomes.

Demographic change has meant that we are witnessing higher proportions of elderly people in all societies, greater life expectancy at birth and at all advanced ages, substantial drops in age specific mortality rates higher ages, high rates of chronicity, a surplus of women at higher age groups, most of whom have no spouse, and overall a very diffuse elderly population, spread across thirty or forty years of life, differentiated by age, sex, class, ethnicity, spatial location, and health status.

Technological and scientific change has given people more years in which to live, yet it has also given them more years in which to die. This places an enormous strain on our service delivery institutions and on our community integrative systems. While life expectancies have increased, the associated dependencies are more chronic than transitional, and families are less technically and emotionally able to provide the support required.

Our society is very skilled at developing solutions to technical issues. We can land people on the moon, explore outer space, communicate or travel anywhere. We are skilled in coping with problems with no human ingredient at all. We can keep people alive for twenty to twenty-five years beyond retirement yet we cannot ensure that they can live those years in dignity. We cannot always guarantee their rights in a society in which social and technological change moves more quickly than legal change.

Every aspect of the lives of elderly people is affected by change and its social ramifications, from increased consumer activity, through electronic banking, travel and entertainment, changing family structure, to systems and processes of care and support for frail elderly people. Protection of the rights of elderly people has not always kept pace with the changes. While social and technological change is essentially unregulated, responses by governments are heavily circumscribed.

Rights of elderly people can be examined under two general headings — rights which they share with all other citizens, such as common law rights and consumer rights, and rights which arise because of their special vulnerabilities, particularly when one leaves one's long standing place of residence and moves into new form of accommodation, accommodation which is occupied solely because of vulnerability, whether physical, social or economic.

Very often stereotypes about elderly people confuse issues about rights. It is important to remember that most older people in most industrialised countries at least, are not sick, are not disabled, are not desperately poor, are reasonably well housed and like the locations they live in. There are, however, significant numbers that do have difficulties in many areas. Governments and the general community must discard the totally inappropriate stereotype that older people *are* problems, and concentrate instead, on the problems they *have*. To do so requires good policy analysis, strong community responsiveness and very importantly, the elimination or unrealistic, patronising and unhelpful stereotypes.

Respect for and accommodation of the rights of elderly people involves the conflict between citizen and group demands for inclusion in the face of institutional and group policies which promote exclusion. Many elderly people find themselves in situations of actual and potential exclusion from a broad range of social allocations, and societal respect.

Individuals and groups make claims for well being on the state, their families, employers, and on their communities. The future well-being of the elderly population depends on how these claims are presented, and on the capacity and willingness to respond, by those upon whom the claims are made.

Claims are made mostly for an adequate income, for appropriate living arrangements, and for high quality services. Such claims impact upon the whole question of moral responsibilities of political systems to address the broader human rights issue, the protection of individuals and their property, those indefinable rights of independence and dignity. While a Bill of Rights may offer appropriate protections, Australia has no such Bill.

Which claims then should governments address within the concept of the elderly person's rights to independence and dignity? Claims for income, accommodation and services, as well as for information and inclusion form the basis of the need system.

There are four major delivery systems which can act on these needs or claims; the statutory system, the commercial system, the voluntary system, and the informal system. Politically and socially we have not been able to determine authoratitively how these should relate to elderly people. Finding a moral and financial response to these claims by older people recognises that these claims are rights. It is the responsibility of our statutory systems to codify and protect these rights. The rights in question may be by-products of social, industrial, demographic or technological change, and the active pursuit of the protection of rights reflects the dominant ideology in a society and the willingness and capacity of the authorities to respond to claims and interest group activities.

The elderly population to which we must respond involves some definitional difficulties. When is one old? At age 65, a convenient historical benchmark, most people are physically healthy and mentally alert. To them, the criterion of "old age" is their exit from the paid labour force. However, in all industrial societies, we have seen earlier and earlier retirement, and thus for many it is a socio-economic rather than a biological criterion which labels them as " aged".

Increasing numbers of our over-65s, however, are over 75, and more likely, especially at the top end of the age spectrum, to need more than average levels of support from the community. In addition to economic and social dependencies, physical limitations and disabilities become part of the lives of many people.

In essence, we have and will continue to have, two older populations, each defined as old with very different and incompatible definitions. One population is deemed too old for the paid labour force, and one deemed too old to participate physically and emotionally in mainstream society. We are facing two explosions — an explosion of perceived uselessness and an explosion of care. We are thus looking to protect rights that arise from quite different contexts.

There is no doubt that many elderly people are vulnerable. There are physical vulnerabilities, and evidence for these can be found in epidemiological and chronicity data. The most notable are increasing incidence of dementia, immobility and incontinence, and their multifarious ramifications. Many elderly people are also financially vulnerable. In general, retirement incomes are insufficient to maintain pre-retirement lifestyles, and the ramifications of economic vulnerability have numerous social consequences. These are addressed through housing and accommodation policies, transport policies, taxation policies, health care financing, just to mention a few of the areas in which the State tries to develop a protective or compensatory infrastructure. The State clearly acknowledges the vulnerabilities and responds in accordance with moral willingness and financial capacity. The extent that legal rights of elderly people are codified and protected reflects the perception of legitimacy of the claims made by those people.

This chapter examines *State* government initiatives in protecting the legal rights of elderly people. This of course immediately raises the spectre of federalism. Federalism, essentially a means of controlling power by dividing it, creates two (or more) spheres of jurisdiction. In Australia, responsibility for community well-being is caught up in the politics of federalism which sees shifts, over time, in the balance between control and decision-making at the centre, and control and decision-making in the States. The Federal Government in Australia collects about 80 per cent of taxation revenue. Approximately one-third of Federal revenues go to the States according to complex formulae tempered both by rational measurement methods and political pragmatism. The States raise revenue through a variety of taxes and charges.

The Constitution gives the Federal Government powers in income maintenance (pensions and retirement income), and the power over resources has meant that the Federal Government has assumed responsibility for nursing homes and most residential care for elderly people.

The State Governments, however, have a wide range of responsibilities in the human services, and have complex legal structures and thus are in a position, both legally and politically, to address the rights of elderly people, or any other group of people.

The Federal Government has established a Human Rights and Equal Opportunity Commission, and is a signatory to various international human rights conventions. In areas in which it provides services, it has various appeals mechanisms or tribunals should there be a dispute, for example, over pension matters or immigration of an elderly relative, etc.

The States, on the other hand, have a plethora of arrangements, some legal, some quasi-legal and some embedded within the general human service structures to protect the rights of elderly people. There are arrangements which work well, and others which could be improved. There is a difficulty, however, in responding to our very diverse elderly population, however defined.

State Government Measures

All Australian States provide similar services to their elderly population, although the responsibility for service provision differs from State to State. Not all States however, address the same range of rights for elderly people. In developing a State government perspective one can draw up a catalogue of services for older people — legal services through the public Trustee and the Guardianship Board; domiciliary services such as home help, occupational therapy and paramedical support; home nursing; educational services for older people; recreational services sponsored by the State Government; Meals on Wheels; psychogeriatric services through the mental health system; acute hospital care; dental care; and eye care; home assistance services (in conjunction with Local Government); housing services through the Housing Trust, to name the major ones. Some of these have components of Federal funding. In addition, the State Government provides a wide range of concessions to elderly people, most notably both public transport and concessions for vehicle registrations and licences, electricity and water concessions, and concessions for local government rates.

The State Government funds the financial deficits to State public hospitals which provide a range of services for the aged in addition to general hospital services. These include free diagnostic services, paramedical services, dental care and "long stay" beds especially in recognised country hospitals. State Governments provide continuous nursing care for aged persons in their nursing homes and hospitals. Some of these facilities also contain day centres for the aged which provide extended care services, for example occupational therapy and social activities such as handicrafts, films and excursions.

The South Australian (State) Department for Community Welfare provides a number of services for the aged, including provision of information, counselling and recreational activities, visiting and socialisation services, and provides funds for non-government welfare organisations to provide other services. The Department also has a role in providing emergency financial assistance to aged persons. In conjunction with the Federal Government, the State Government funds senior citizens' centres and funds a range of domiciliary services. It could thus be argued that, by providing a range of community, health and social services, the State Governments are contributing to the rights of elderly people to participate as fully as possible in society, and therefore are contributing to inclusion, rather than fostering exclusion. This of course is a very general proposition and may stretch comprehension of the notion of rights.

There are, in addition to general participatory and inclusionary State activities, some specific mechanisms addressed to protecting the rights of elderly and other vulnerable people. The following illustrations relate specifically to South Australia.

The *Commissioner for the Ageing Act (1984)* contains measures for advocacy for elderly people. The Act has objectives oriented to the enhancement of the quality of life of elderly people and the reciprocal enrichment of the community in which elderly people live. The Act requires the Commissioner to provide policy advice relating to programmes and services for the aging, and in so doing to monitor practices of all levels of government, gather data and undertake research, and consult widely. In a nutshell, the Commissioner protects and furthers the rights of elderly people by providing policy advice, co-ordinating governmental activities and acting as an advocate for elderly people and their organisations.

The Commissioner for the Ageing Act is the only legislation of its type in Australia. The Government of South Australia has recognised the vulnerabilities of certain categories of people and moved to protect their rights within the policy arena. In addition to the Commissioner for the Ageing, South Australia is the only State with a Childrens' Interests Bureau, which looks after the rights of children. It also has special offices dealing with people with disabilities, Aboriginal people, people from non-English speaking backgrounds, women and youth.

The *Equal Opportunity Act (1984)* makes unlawful discrimination on the grounds of sex, marital status, sexuality, pregnancy, physical impairment and race, in the areas of employment, provision of goods and services, accommodation, sale of land, education, clubs and associations, and advertising. The Office of the Commissioner for Equal Opportunity, which administers this act and Federal equal opportunity legislation in South Australia provides a broad range of services, including policy and legal advice, community education, publicity and promotion of equal opportunity principles and practices, and investigation and conciliation of complaints. South Australian equal opportunity legislation does not at present provide protection where there is discrimination on the basis of age. (Nor is this the case anywhere in Australia).

The South Australian Government *Legal Services Commission* provides or arranges for the provision of a range of legal services to low income people, many of whom are elderly. Assistance is subject to the Commission's guidelines covering the ability to pay and the merit of the case, and is given for criminal, civil and family law matters.

The *Guardianship Board*, established under the Mental Health Act (1976-9), assists persons suffering from mental illness or mental handicap by acting as their guardian and ensuring the proper management of their affairs. This only occurs, if through either of these disabilities, a person is considered unable to look after his or her own health and safety or is incapable of managing his or her own affairs, or, in the case of mental handicap, if it is neccessary for the protection of others. The Board is then able to act as that person's guardian and make specific directions relating to medical or psychiatric treatment, medical or dental procedures, institutional custody and financial and property administration.

61% of applications to the Board were for people over 50, and 36% were for those over 70. To enable people to make some provision against possible future difficulties in financial management, which may result from, for example, a dementing illness or a stroke, an enduring power of attorney can be made. This enables a person to nominate a donee while still able to make an informed consent.

Both the Federal and State Governments have *Ombudsmen* who are officials who investigate complaints about administrative actions of State and Commonwealth Government departments and authorities, and Local Government Councils. If a person is aggrieved by an administrative action or omission, the Ombudsman system provides a simple and informal means of having it brought to notice and investigated. If an Ombudsman considers that an action is wrong, he or she can recommend that it be put right. A person may complain to the State Ombudsman about any decision, act, omission, proposal or recommendation relating to administration by any State Government department or authority set up by Act of Parliament, or by any Local Government Council or its officers. This includes any State provided service for elderly people.

The Ombudsman cannot investigate judicial matters, matters in which a person has the right of appeal or legal remedy — (unless the Ombudsman considers it is not reasonable for that person to resort to such actions), actions of private persons, businesses or companies, or police actions. The Ombudsman Act (1972) therefore does not attempt to protect a wide range of the rights of elderly people, but it does cover significant ground.

The *Natural Death Act (1983)* also enables a person to direct his or her intent that extraordinary life prolonging procedures are not to be undertaken in the event of a terminal illness. Terminal illness is described as any illness, injury or degeneration of mental or physical faculties.

The *Residential Tenancies Act (1978)* applies to all residential tenancies; that is to landlord/tenant relationships. Rights and obligations of all parties are defined and disputes are heard by a Residential Tenancies Tribunal. This Act provides protection for elderly tenants faced with excessive rental increases, possible evictions or other tenancy matters. This system of course applies to all age groups. Retirement Villages are by definition excluded from the Residential Tenancies Act and in 1987 a Retirement Villages Act was proclaimed to establish the more specialised requirements of this form of accommodation. This Act establishes security of tenure provisions, minimum information to be given to prospective leasees, and a disputes mechanism. Formal disputes are heard by the Residential Tenancies Tribunal.

Protecting Rights in Special Accommodation

All the above-mentioned provisions (except the Commissioner for the Ageing Act) relate to the community as a whole and are not exclusively for elderly people. Elderly people, however, are among those who stand to benefit and have their rights protected and enhanced. Many, of course, have special needs. Most elderly people in Australia (over 93%) live in private residences. However, actual and perceived vulnerabilities create a situation where some elderly people move to special accommodation. Two such forms of accommodation, Retirement Villages and Nursing Homes, cater to very different types of elderly people. In both of these accommodation arrangements the rights of elderly people can be at risk, and in both of these situations, the State Government has taken firm initiatives to protect the rights of residents.

A. Retirement Villages

In recent years, Australia has seen a growth in retirement villages. These are complexes of anywhere from twenty to several hundred high quality independent apartments or small houses, all occupied by retired people. The resident pays a premium of up to $A100,000(four to five times the annual income of the average worker), and in the past there was no method of protecting the investment or the rights of these residents. Many of the older people who invest in such villages do so in the belief that they are buying the house or apartment.

In fact many do not appreciate the only entitlement that they have is of a licence to occupy a particular unit in the village and to use certain community facilities. The licence to occupy the unit can be revoked and this can cause hardship for the resident.

The Retirement Villages Act was proclaimed in 1987 and the main objectives of the Act are to increase security of tenure provisions for both the village and the resident, to increase prospective residents' awareness of the issues when considering a contract and to provide mechanisms for the resolution of disputes. The Act requires that prospective residents be given information which alerts them to protections available under the Act. A "Plain English" version of the Act has been prepared and there is a legal obligation on the owners to give this information to clients before a contract is completed. A copy of the village's rules must also be included. This provides residents with information which assists them in their decision-making at the time of their purchase and which can be used for future reference if the need arises. Increasing consumer awareness of rights and responsibilities at the point of decision-making is a necessary and valuable community service. Dispute resolution has been addressed in a number of ways. Internal disputes, such as between residents, and between residents and management over day-to-day management decisions have been designated as remaining 'in house' and the method of resolution has been left to the organisation and the residents. A key feature of the Act is the provision which establishes individual security of tenure. Contracts usually contain a provision that the owner (or the resident) can give notice to leave. Because there was no definition of 'necessary grounds' for terminating residents, it was felt that more stringent procedures should be instigated to protect both parties. For the resident in particular, this is especially necessary, as it is this person's housing security as well as financial interest which is often at stake. The Act therefore supports a resident's right of occupation that will continue until death or by agreement to terminate. If a resident is asked to leave and does not want to, the right of occupation can only be terminated if the owner convinces the Residential Tenancies Tribunal that a serious breach of the contract or of the residence rules has occurred, or that the resident is not mentally or physically capable of remaining at the village. In the latter situation, formal and appropriate assessments would be required.

Other statutory rights include an obligation on the administering authority to hold an annual residents' meeting within four months of the end of each financial year. At the meeting, accounts must be presented which show income and maintenance charges for the previous year, how these were allocated and estimates of income and maintenance charges for the following year. This will then provide important information to the residents for their own budgetary planning as well as providing information on the financial situation of the village. Increases in maintenance charges have been an important concern to residents and this provision affords them the opportunity to know how to comment and how to plan.

B. Nursing Homes

Increasing longevity and chronicity at higher ages gives us a potential for virtually unlimited growth in the number of nursing home beds. Policies have been implemented in Australia to ensure that admission to a nursing home is available only to those who are unable to live independently and who have been assessed by a multidisciplinary Geriatric Assessment Team as requiring professional nursing care on an ongoing basis.

Given the high rate of dementia, incontinence and immobility among nursing home residents, it is important to recognise that nursing home residents are among the most powerless, most isolated and most dispossessed in our society. Many of these people are unable to organise and lobby on their own behalf. Considerable attention (described below) has been paid to ensuring that their rights are maintained, that the services they receive are appropriate, and are geared towards enhancing and maximising their life chances.

Policy considerations have to take account of philosophical issues, especially of what is expected of our nursing home system. In simplistic terms a continuum can be drawn from basic custodial care to holistic care. A custodial level of care makes no attempt to maintain function, either physical or psychological. It aims to keep patients safe, comfortable, fed, clean and supervised. It equates with what has been called "Minimal Warehousing". A holistic level of care supports quality-of-life-related programs aimed at keeping the physical, social and mental capacity of each individual to a maximum. A holistic approach to care focuses on the positive aspects of life, on a state of high resident satisfaction. Any choice involves a philosophical stance on what is desirable for our older poppulation and ideally a commitment to back that stance with tangible resources. As well as providing tangible resources there needs to be some substantive product that describes, demonstrates and codifies residents' rights in this situation. Many residential institutions have a code of practice or a code of rights. What should be included in such a code? There should be statements which address personal and social issues, physical environment, and staff management issues. The Center for Policy on Ageing in England has developed a comprehensive Code of Practice for Residential Care which includes some of the following:

- Residents should have a signed agreement which states the terms and conditions under which the accommodation is offered. This reinforces the fact that the resident is buying a service and is entitled to rights and protections as in any other such exchange.
- Residents should be able to see their visitors, wash, dress and use the toilet in private.
- The staff and management of the home should not become involved in the residents' financial affairs.
- Medical treatment should not occur without a resident's or guardian's valid consent.
- Residents who are able to look after their own medication should be

encouraged to do so.
- Medication should not be administered as a means of social control.
- All homes should have a complaints procedure.

The Australian Federal Government has recently prepared a booklet entitled *Living in A Nursing Home — Outcome Standards for Australian Nursing Homes*. In this booklet there are seven objectives and each of the objectives has attached to it a set of measurable outcome standards which are not dissimilar to a code of practice.

The objectives are categorised under:
1. Health Care
2. Social Independence
3. Freedom of Choice
4. Homelike Environment
5. Privacy and Dignity
6. Variety of Experience
7. Safety

To take one example, under Social Independence, the sub-objectives include freedom to maintain friendships, freedom to manage financial affairs; freedom to come and go; freedom to practice religious or cultural customs; freedom to maintain obligations as citizens. The appropriate Outcome Standards propose that residents be enabled and encouraged to have Visitors of their choice and to maintain personal contacts; that residents be enabled and encouraged to maintain control of their financial affairs; that residents have freedom of movement within and from the nursing home, and that they be restricted only for safety reasons; that provision is made for residents with differing religious, personal and cultural customs and so on. All of these proposed outcomes involve freedoms and personal values which we would never question as applying to people living in their own homes. Institutional living has such an enormous impact on a resident's life that structures must be created to ensure that their rights are recognised. While admission to a nursing home diminishes the activities of residents, efforts should be made to ensure that residents' rights are not diminished accordingly. In reality, rights are restricted by impairment and disability, but certainly impairment and disability should never be used as an argument for restricting rights.

One area in protecting rights is the development of an unequivocal and coherent policy on the role of professionals in nursing homes. There clearly needs to be a policy on the role of medical practitioners in nursing homes, and on the activities of nurses, social workers, physiotherapists, etc, particularly as there is potential for conflict between their responsibilities and the rights of residents. Work in this area is only just now beginning.

A charter of rights is essential for all residential facilities. It should be mandatory on admission for senior staff to spend time with the resident and her or his family to go through with them the charter of rights, explaining the rights and the obligations. My Office is presently developing such a standard or uniform charter of realistic rights and obligations. A code of rights is an empty vessel if there are no means by which those rights can be respected and enforced. Nursing Homes should be expected to develop procedures for dealing with complaints about breaches of rights.

For complaints which cannot to be resolved within the institution, in 1988 the State Government took the initiative of establishing a joint State/Federal complaints mechanism in my Office. We hypothesized that many complaints and unresolved problems are of an idiosyncratic rather than a policy nature. Consequently it was argued that mediating procedure rather than a formal and legalistic mechanism would suffice. It is hoped that the overwhelming majority of cases can be mediated or conciliated, and only in rare and exceptional circumstances would there be a need for a legalistic solution.

While the complaints mechanism has no power to invoke direct sanctions it has two avenues to pursue should mediation or conciliation not be satisfactory. First, in an advocacy capacity it can encourage a disaffected party to seek a common law solution, and facilitate that process. Second, as nursing homes in Australia depend on continuing government subsidies and on government approval for admissions, failure satisfactorily to resolve disputes could involve governments using their funding and admitting powers as sanctions.

The Federal Government has taken significant initiatives in the codification and protection of rights of nursing home residents. Not only has the Federal Government developed the outcome standards mentioned above (*Living in a Nursing Home — Outcome Standards....*), they have hired teams of inspectors to visit all nursing homes to ensure that the outcome standards are being met and that the residents' rights are protected.

While one can establish inspection systems and complaints procedures, and develop charters of residents' rights entailing rights and obligations, as well as dispute resolution procedures and advocacy systems, it is imperative that an important protection of rights will involve the provision of appropriate staffing levels to provide the care that is required. It was earlier suggested that there was a continuum of care which ranged from custodial to holistic care. If there were insufficient or inappropriately trained staff then all that could be expected, it is argued, would be a level of custodial care. All nursing home residents, by virtue of their dependency and vulnerability, and by virtue of legislatively enshrined regulations have a right to holistic care as described above in the enumerated outcome standards. To take the argument to its logical conclusion, the rights of residents are being infringed and limited if the staff provided are insufficient in quality or quantity.

We have yet to resolve whether any potential failure to meet outcome standards is an example of infringement of rights or discrimination against vulnerable elderly people.

Discrimination

It was pointed out above that although Australia has equal opportunity legislation, discrimination on the basis of age does not fall within the purview of any of that legislation. While the United Nations has recommended that countries consider the question of age discrimination and while countries such as the U.S.A. and Canada have passed legislation, there is no federal legislation relating to age discrimination in Australia, and State Governments are only now starting to consider the issue.

The Government of South Australia has an Age Discrimination Task Force which includes the Commissioner for Equal Opportunity and the Commissioner for the Ageing. The Commissioner for the Ageing Act (1984) lists among the functions of the Commissioner "to assess the incidence of discrimination against the ageing in employment, and to promote action to overcome such discrimination" The Age Discrimination Task Force is presently half-way through a twelve month exercise in which its brief is to monitor age discrimination in the areas of employment, finance, advertising and accommodation. The exercise is intended to make an assessment of the extent of age discrimination practices and following this, a determination of the need for governmental action, legislative or otherwise. The Task Force has already found evidence of discrimination in personnel practices involving older workers. Strictly speaking these are not "elderly" people, but older workers are being treated unfairly both as employees and potential employees.

Age discrimination can be seen as a denial of equal opportunity arising from incorrect assumptions made about a person's abilities and needs on the basis of their chronological age. It is the receipt by a person of *less favourable treatment* than that accorded a person in a more favoured age bracket in the same or similar circumstances. Whether the discrimination is intentional or unintentional, it is denial of equality of opportunity. When examined on an individual basis many age restrictions can be seen to be erratic and unreasonable. They reveal incorrect assumptions regarding a person's experience, health, maturity, status or finances. Numerous reports have analysed and dissected judgements and behaviours based on such incorrect assumptions and arbitrary determinations. Yet no State Government in Australia has made an unequivocal political commitment to the introduction of appropriate legislation.

While principles can be espoused about excluding people from jobs, goods, services or provision of credit on the basis of age, there is an area of contention relating to whether insufficiency or diminution of access constitutes a ground for discrimination. If a nursing home is funded at a level which allows only custodial care, are the residents who deserve more, being discriminated against? Many countries have seen cuts in their public health care systems. As most users of public general hospitals in Australia are elderly people, does this fiscal austerity constitute discrimination against older people? Some would argue yes, but I would argue no. One could not bring an action against any individual alleging age discrimination in this type of situation. Where there would be grounds, if the legislation were introduced, would be in employment practices, training practices, forced retirement, denial of credit facilities, unequal payments for similar services (charging older people more for motor vehicle insurance is one practice that has come to our notice).

Conclusion

This chapter has attempted to identify certain principles and practices, note that claims are made by elderly people and show that many of these claims are translated into rights. The response to the claims gets tied up in an overall societal response to choices between conflicting political objectives and goals, and how they are formulated, especially about the perennial disagreements about the permissable degree of income and resource inequality. The search for a consensus which ensures the protection of the weak, the vulnerable and the disadvantaged, must begin with an understanding of social structure and political life, for these are the determinants of our social structures.

There are both ideological and structural responses to the choices. The ideological relate to the degree of legitimacy of the claims. The structural relate to whether the claim should be met through the public or private sector, and if the former (especially in a federal system), by what level of government.

The limitations on a State Government have been identified and the chapter showed areas in which initiatives have successfully been undertaken by a State Government and one important area, age discrimination, in which there is still a great deal to be done.

Chapter 27

The Law as an Instrument for Democracy and Welfare in Danish Elder Policy

Lis FROST   University of Aarhus, Denmark

Introduction

The purpose of this chapter is to point out some characteristics of the law relating to the elderly in Denmark. I will discuss in particular the rules concerning the public discharge of care for the elderly in their own home or in special housing, e.g. an old people's home. The "philosophical" basis for dealing with care is that it is fundamental to the human condition that every human being depends on other human beings. Society's ability to provide care is therefore an indication as to its moral status. Furthermore, the very question of care for the elderly has been placed on top of the political agenda in the 1980s.

Instead of dealing with a multitude of rules, I will attempt to place the regulation of conditions for the elderly in a (post) modern landscape in which democracy and welfare are the most noble (ornamental) plants.

It is usual to see modern developments in terms of a change in the character of the state. According to this view, the transition from a state of law to a welfare state, and the distinction between the legislation of the state of law and legislation of the welfare state are decisive. I do accept this distinction, but see the concepts as representing steps along a greater and older path: the realisation of human rights. Naturally, this project cannot be dated very precisely, but the political agenda was evident with the publications of Locke's *Two Treatises of Government*, 1690 and Rosseau's *Le Contrat Social*, 1762. The leading idea was the concept of the universal human being in possession of certain fundamental rights; that is to say, liberty and equality. Since then there has been a constant discourse about implementation of this project of human rights, the law being seen as its instrument, more or less in step with material developments, and the project becomes increasingly extensive each time the "text" is read.

At first the idea of rights was confined to securing political rights in a narrow sense: democracy, freedom of speech, freedom of assembly and so on. In the nineteenth and especially, the twentieth centuries these formal rights were expanded as result of economic and social demands such as the right to food, education, and medical care. This idea of (human) rights has spread to all areas of society, but at different times, both as ideology and as (tentatively) practised policy. Firstly, the male bourgeoisie gained political rights; secondly, the working class men gained political and social rights — partly because of the Labour movement — and finally, women gained political rights around the turn of the century and economic rights especially from the middle of 1970, partly because of the Womens' movement. Although the project has not yet been fulfilled, the bourgeoisie, the workers, and women have produced their movements to plead their cause at "the right moment". It has been otherwise for the elderly. For them, equality, and self-determination have been notably absent.

The elderly on the agenda

On March 20th 1979 the Danish Minister of Social Affairs appointed a Commission with the task of examining and evaluating the conditions of life of the elderly. The Commission was to make recommendations to improve them. There were three reasons for the setting up of the Commission:
(*a*) It was thought that changes in the patterns of family, work, shopping, transportation and so on had caused a deterioration in the elderly's way of life and (*b*) that this had led to an increased consumption of and demand for public services. (*c*) The elderly were and are a growing proportion of the population.

The thrust of the recommendations was to improve the opportunities for the elderly to lead their own lives and to remain in their own homes as long as possible.

The Commission published three reports in 1980-1982[1]. The government has based its policy for elderly people on these reports and this has resulted in several legal changes over the last five years.

It is the case that the proportion of elderly in the population has been increasing quite rapidly in recent years. This is partly due to changes in the (legal) definition of the term "elderly", and partly due to demographic changes deriving from longer duration of life and changed birth-rates[2].
The total population; by sex:

	Total	Women %	Men %
1977	5,079,879	50,53	49,4
1987	5,124,794	50,71	49,29

The population over the age of 60; by sex:

	Total	Women %	Men %
1977	961,735	55,80	49,20
1987	1,044,562	57,0	43,0

The percentage of the population over the age of 60; by sex:

	Total	Women	Men
1977	18,93	20,90	16,92
1987	20,38	22,91	17,78

The further up the age scale one goes, the clearer it becomes that the group of elderly is increasing. It is also noticeable that the shortfall of men is highest in the oldest groups. The last point is an important explanation (although it is not the only one) of the fact that the number of widows is much higher than the number of widowers:

	Widows	Widowers
1977	250,185	70,040
1987	282,906	75,060

Married women can expect to become widows, while husbands can expect not to be the survivor.

It is also true that the consumption of public resources increased heavily through the 1960s and the 1970s. In 1970 the total budget for social and health measures (excluding hospitals) was a little more than 7 billions D.KR. In 1980 the figures had increased to approximately 32 1/2 billion D.KR., an average of 16, 8% per year.

Finally, no one can doubt that the daily life of elderly people in 1988 is very different from that of their parents. In my view, the most important explanation is to be found in the changes in the systems of (self-) support, which have especially taken place over this century; that is to say the reliance on wage labour, as the dominant source of support[3].

When life is structured around wage labour, movement out of it creates a risk of poverty, not only in an economic sense but also in a social sense. The more people rely on wage labour, the weaker becomes the sense of personal obligation. The inner circle breaks down, and an unsatisfied need for care arises. The need exists for everyone, but it is most visible with small children, the sick, and the elderly. One of the most decisive factors in this century has been the integration of women into the registered and paid labour force.

When the conditions for generating private care-ethics disappear, the problem can be "solved" either through public sources or by purchasing services in the market. Up to now it has been seen as a public duty to make sources available. This has mainly been done by an enormous growth in the female labour force, and this again has weakened the ethics of caring.

Care as a part of maintenance law

Legally care can be seen as a part of maintenance law in the way this conception has been generated by women's law in Scandinavia[4]: Here a distinction is drawn between *money*-maintenance — such as wages, unemployment relief, pension, and social benefit — on one hand, and maintenance in *kind* and *care* — such as housing, clothing, food, and care — on the other.

The main basis of the *primary* maintenance-system is private law, as in marriage contracts and wage labour contracts. During this century, wage labour has become the major source of maintenance, ideologically, economically, and legally, and today more than 70% of the population between the age of 15 and 74 is in the labour force. In 1985 there were 45,6% women and 54,4% men. The frequency of work is 65,2% for women and 78,4% for men. The dominance of wage labour also means that money-maintenance becomes more important than maintenance in kind and care. Maintenance in kind and care is reduced to a form of consumer goods, to which wage labour provides access.

If the primary maintenance system fails, the welfare state enters with *subsidiary* sources of maintenance. It can be money — pensions, social benefits and so on — but it can also be in kind and care, such as by performance of labour in the home or in an institution. The state also attempts to restore people to the primary source of maintenance; that is, wage labour. This is expressed by schemes of re-education, retraining, job-creation and job-offers.

Legally a person becomes old when through age she is no longer expected to acquire money-maintenance — and thereby the basis for consumption in kind and care — from the group of primary maintenance-sources. Because wage labour is the fundamental structure, retirement from the labour market defines when a person is old. The growth of unemployment is one important reason why the watershed "natural" retirement with a right to public support has been altered. Formerly the age limit was 67 for men and 62 for women, and the pension was not dependent on former wage labour. From 1979 it has been possible to receive a pension, although a reduced one, at 60. This type of public support is only available for persons retiring from the labour market. (In 1984, the distinction between men and women was repealed on account of the policy of equality between men and women. Women's entitlement to a pension at 62 *independently* of wage labour was thus removed, and the rule for men became the standard. This has especially affected full-time-housewives. They cannot receive public support intended for people over 60 because this support is reserved for people who have been in the labour market. They can only receive the pension for people over 67, and thus they have lost five years' pension).

Public care-giving

A. Planning of care for the elderly

During the 1960s and the 1970s, women who were at the age of "high capacity for work" were liberated from unpaid housework and nursing for family, neighbours and friends to paid housework and nursing for strangers. For elderly people this meant a strong movement from private to public care, because their wage-earning family could no longer care for them. This caused an expansion in public budgets and also in public duties, and the need for a comprehensive review over and a more efficient direction of welfare policy became overwhelming. The answer to these problems was found partly in decentralization and partly in a (local) duty to plan for the future[5].

The duty to undertake planning can be found in Act No. 227 of May 27th, 1970, regarding the administration of social and certain health measures and a Circular of November 14th, 1983 from the Minister of Social Affairs. According to these, the local council, in co-operation with the county council, are obliged to draw up plans for a period of twelve years and to keep them under review. The plans are sent to the Minister of Social Affairs, who controls and confirms their legality. The rules can be characterized as framework law, whose purpose is to set up the guidelines within which local politicians have to negotiate. They do not lay down matters of substance. The purpose of using local planning is to create a flexible system. Yet in practice, the state is not interested in flexibility. The state is first and foremost concerned with assuring that financial considerations are given priority. The local authorities make returns to the Ministry of Social Affairs, which thus ensures that they consider the " correct" questions. These questions are: What needs are covered today, what changes can be expected, what needs will the local council be able to — and wish to — fulfill in the future, and what its proposals are. Furthermore, the Ministry gives instructions for calculating the costs of the measures. In this way a certain rationalization in political decisions is secured[6]. Unlike the traditional mandatory norms, which can be characterized as intermediaries of culture (bound by tradition and power-relations), the planning rules can be characterized as intermediaries of control over local decisions to ensure they are based on economic-rational criteria as a foundation for concrete policy implementation[7].

From the standpoint of rights and democracy, this form of legal regulation must clearly be criticized. It seems democratic that plans are made and negotiated on a local level, and self-administration was used as an argument during the debate about the passing of the planning law, but the process does not guarantee that the elderly have any influence over what actually takes place in the local area. First, there is no obligation to submit the plan to those who are affected. Second, the plans when passed do not give citizens any legal claims. The basis for the plans is found in the Social Assistance Act, which contains rules that direct the local council to take care of the elderly through home-help arrangements, old peoples' homes, day-centers and so on. But even these rules do not create legal claims for citizens[8].

Also from the perspective of administration it has become apparent that the laws are deficient. They have not led to the expected rationalization and efficiency. From 1972 to 1979, the number of places in institutions for elderly increased by 50%, and still there were not enough places to meet the growing demand. Since 1980, the Minister of Social Affairs has sent out a number of circulars with appeals for reducing public budgets and for reorganizing policy towards the elderly[9]. The slogan "right to a place in an old peoples' home whenever needed" has been turned into "right to stay in one's own home as long as possible", implying a slowdown in activity, staff-expansion and so on. However, the appeals penetrated slowly, and the new signals culminated in the summer of 1987, when an Act totally banning the building of new old peoples' homes was passed[10].

The political goal for the future is that as few people as possible should receive public care in old peoples' home and that the necessary aid shall be given to the elderly in their own home. This aid can be given through special arrangements for calling in professional assistance, for eating in canteens, for delivery of food, and for home-help. The ministry has especially stressed an improvement of home-help facilities.

Home-help started during World War II as an unemployment initiative and was meant as an aid for sick housewives and women in childbirth. Gradually the arrangement was extended to the elderly, with the possibility of state subsidy, and in 1968 a Bill was passed which established proper help for pensioners. In 1976 the differentiation between housewives and pensioners was dropped, but in reality the separation was continued through a new distinction between temporary and continuing home-help. Continuing home-help is now a predominant part of public care for the elderly, and from 1 January 1989 it is provided as a free service without regard to the economic situation of the recipient.

The consumption of home-help has greatly increased, from 16,180 full-time jobs in 1976 to over 20,224 in 1980 to 25,531 in 1986. (The number is misleading as regards the number of persons working as home-helpers. Most home-helpers are women working part-time, and thus there are more women working in this sector than the figures show). The planned expansion in home-help keeps pace with increasing demand following the demographic changes. All the same it is obvious that home-help has become the flexible link in public care for the elderly. It is easier to expand the staff of home-helpers than to build a whole institution, and it is also much cheaper. Women's traditional qualifications as caregivers are useful for employers. They lead to low education and to low wages — as in other traditional areas of female employment[11].

B. Exercise of care for the elderly

How does democracy and care operate within old peoples' homes and the organisation of home-help?

As in the case of other welfare laws, the state is seen as a friend and helper. The assumption is that the state and the subject have common interests, and that it is therefore unnecessary to pay attention to any rule of law. This is apparent in decisions concerning the provision of home-help or a place in an old peoples' home.

The goal is to provide care and practical help. But it is the professionals — doctors, social workers and so on — who decide whether there is a need at all, and if there is, its extent and how it is to be met. The services are discretionary with little opportunity for complaint or influence over the nature of the care[12].

Regarding *home-help*, the decision whether to provide it is made by the Social Welfare Committee without recourse to administrative review. The home-helper's task is to "do the housework and to assist with personal needs—", (cf. Circular of October 10th, 1980 concerning practical assistance in the home under the Social Assistance Act). Thus, the home-helper intrudes upon the most intimate aspects of daily life. Nevertheless, the elderly person has no right to decide who is going to do the job and how it is going to be carried out. The home-helper is employed and paid by the local council, which has full authority of an employer even when the recipient is paying a contribution to the local council for receiving the aid. Local authorities are obliged to supervise the work, and of course the unsatisfied user can complain to the authorities. It is also possible to discuss problems quite informally with the home-helper herself, but the point is that the elderly person has no legal competence to make claims and decisions.

As to *residence in an old peoples' home*, issues of self-determination and democracy are pushed to extremes, because the home, in principle, has to cover all the needs of the inmates. In this case, too, the Social Welfare Committee makes the decision to grant a place, partly on the basis of medical opinion. The decision is subject to administrative recourse to a county authority. The local administration makes the final decision as to which home the elderly person can be admitted. According to a circular, local authorities must have regard to requests put forward by the person concerned. This does not always happen and in September 1987 the Minister of Social Affairs found it necessary to underline the principle[13]. If the elderly person cohabits with another person, whether a spouse or not, it cannot be assumed that the other will be admitted to the home, unless he or she has an independent need for residence in the old peoples' home.

Decisions touching on daily life in the home are largely delegated to the staff in the home or to local authorities. If possible, daily management should take place in collaboration with a residence board. The idea is that the board should deal with questions concerning everyday activities in the home. Nevertheless, boards have been established in only 60% of old peoples' homes, and there are no rules for their composition. A board could for instance, be dominated by staff and relatives of the residents. The board has no legal competence to make decisions.

The elderly are charged for their residence in an old peoples' home in a special way. For the typical elderly person, whose pension is the main basis of economic support, the local authority withholds the total amount as partial payment of the costs for a place in the home. The authority only pays out pocket money to the elderly person, and as she is supposed to have most of her needs fulfilled at the home, she only receives a very small sum (at present 610 D.KR. a month).

C. The crisis in elder-policy, the crisis of law

The problems described above can also be represented in phrases like: The elder-generation is excluded from the project of human rights; elder-policy is a manifestation of encirclement by the state, of deprivation of control over one's life; the system is strangling the "Lebenswelt" it is meant to preserve.

This means that the system can no longer be legally justified. The law is in difficulty because it can no longer recreate and procure the idea of democracy, and it can hardly reproduce an ethics of care because utilitarianism is to a great extent at its centre.

Previously, the state's policy has tended to "solve" the problems of a lack of democracy and welfare/care by giving the elderly better opportunities to adapt themselves to the system — as wage labourers and consumers. Wage labour is closely connected with money-support, which has not been discussed in this chapter. It should, however, be mentioned that an Act on part-time pension has been passed to make the transition from wage labour to life as a pensioner smoother. It is obvious that this remedy offers only limited possibilities.

There have been other initiatives attempting to treat the elderly like consumers. For instance a rule has been enacted (The Social Assistance Act § 85 a), which gives the local councils authority to pay the whole pension to individuals resident in an old peoples' home. The pensioners then have to buy — and to choose — services available in the home. They may be services such as food, cleaning, washing, hairdressing, china painting. The rule comes into force on 1 January 1989.

Recently, a new Act on establishment of housing for the elderly and handicapped people has also been passed.[14] The Act should partly be seen in connection with the ban on building new old peoples' homes. The idea is to make it possible for the elderly to rent a flat or a house on their own, such as in an elderly-center, where she can find facilities similar to those in an old peoples' home. Here we can also see the principle that the elderly can choose whether she wants to dine at the restaurant or in her home, send her clothes to the laundry or wash them herself and so on.

This can be seen as a development towards a self-regulating system, where the purpose is to secure and strengthen the starting point: the right to stay in your own home. This will probably also mean that the rules of public care will become more characterized by the marks of private law with agreement as the underlying principle.

Before my concluding remarks I should refer to another trend which I find more provocative and inspiring. Since 1983 it has been possible to make experiments inside public institutions under the provisions of the Social Assistance Act. The local council takes the initiative, and the Ministry of Social Affairs confirms the experiment for a period. A number of experiments have occurred in relation to old peoples' homes. For instance, there are experiments where the old people are involved in the work in the home — cleaning, cooking, gardening and so on. This type of experiment has aroused much debate. The critics fear that the experiments lead to exploitation of pensioners as unpaid workers, and that the purpose is to camouflage budget reductions. The staff and their unions have been especially negative because they fear for their jobs in a period of unemployment. I doubt whether this is the problem *in the long run*. Perhaps a more relevant assessment would focus on the low appreciation of different kinds of social work. In Sweden for instance it is difficult to recruit nurses, and some hospitals advertize in Danish newspapers to attract Danish nurses to Sweden. (But this is another question). The elderly have been much more positive, because in this way they work for the other residents as well as for themselves.

Concluding remarks

Even though Danish elder-policy is characterized by economic considerations, which is probably unavoidable, legal policy-makers use phrases like "Old people should not feel unwanted" and "We need the elderly and their experience". Most of the policy pursued indicates however, that the elder-generation is seen more in terms of finding remedies than as positive goal. Crudely, the elderly are considered as being on the margins of society, useful only when they can strengthen its centre. They are used in job creation for younger people and as consumers in the market. If a real care-ethics is sought it will be necessary to place relations between people, reciprocity and responsibility in the centre[15]. Apart from the experiments mentioned earlier which are positive *in this respect*, reference should be made to a proposal now before the Danish Parliament[16]. The proposal gives men and women the right to paid leave from work to nurse seriously ill or dying persons in their home. Contrary to the dominant schemes which are economically motivated, this is centred on people. Such proposals have been rejected in the past, partly because it was thought they would exclude women from the labour market and that some sick people prefer professional care. Such problems must be taken seriously. But it is also important not to overstate them. For instance, the very idea of women going back to the kitchen is impossible to entertain, at least in Denmark.

Women in the labour market are an economic necessity. They have come to stay. A much bigger problem is that women hold such a poor position in the labour market. This should be taken very seriously. Problems should not, therefore, be ignored. But the elderly must be seen in the light of a positive policy, not simply as a problem that needs a solution.

Notes

1. Ældrekommissionens 1. delrapport, maj 1980: "Aldersforandringer — ældrepolitikkens forudsæninger" ("Changes in Age-Premises of the Elder Policy"). 2. delrapport, april 1981: "De ældres vilkår" ("The Conditions of the Elderly"). Ældredommissionens 3. og afsluttende delrapport, maj 1982: "Sammenhæng i ældrepolitikken" ("Coherence in the Elder Policy").
2. The figures in this chapter are based on "Levevilkår i Danmark", Statistisk oversigt 1984 ("Conditions of Life in Denmark"). "Statistisk tigrsoversigt 1987" ("Statistical Ten-Year Outline 1987").
3. Anna Christensen: "Lönearbetet som Samhällsform och ideologi" in Sociale Värderingesförändringar, fyra essäer, Stockholm 1983 ("Wage-labour as Social Structure and Ideology").
4. Tove Stang Dahl: "Kvinners rett til Penger" in T.S.Dahl (editor) Kvinnerett II, p. 11-30, Oslo 1985. See also Tove Stang Dahl: "An Introduction to Feminist Jurisprudence", Oslo 1987.
5. Kirsten Ketscher: "Om planlægningsbegrebet som retsform" in Retfærd no. 12, p.1-9, 1979 ("On the Concept of Planning as Legal Structure"). Kirsten Ketscher: "Pas På hinanden eller pas dig selv" in Retfærd no. 24, p.30-41, 1983 ("Take Care of One Another or Mind Your Own Business")
6. "Almindelig vejledning om udbygningsplaner på sociale og sundhedsmæssige områder", Sept. 1977 ("General Guidance on Plans for Development in the Areas of Social Security and Health Services"). Lis Frost m. fl.: "Sundhedsplanlægnong specielt i relation til kvindeinteresser" in Kvinder of Offentlig planlægning, semi-narrapport p.30-49, 1981 ("Health Planning especially in relation to Womens' Interests").
7. Anna Christensen: "Kvinnorätten och lagpositivismen" in Retfærd no. 33, p. 88-96, 1986 ("Women's Law and Jurisprudential Positivism"). HåKan Hydén: "Till Kritikken av den offentliga rätten" in Retfærd nr. 30, p. 7-21, 1985 ("Towards a Criticism of Public Law").
8. The Social Assistance Act (bistandsloven) §se 50,74 and 79.
9. See for instance Socialstyrelsens vejledning af august 1980 om bedre ressourcean-vendelse i ældreseltoren (Guidance of August 1980 from the Social Administration regarding better Application of Resources on the Elder Sector) and Socialminis-teriets vejledning nr. 83 af 30.6.1983 om stop for nyetablering af daginstitutionerfor børn of af plejehjem for ældre samt begrænsning af ressourceforbruget i øvrigt (Guidance no. 83 of June the 30th 1983 from the Ministry of Social Affairs regarding ban on Establishment of New Kindergartens and Old Peoples Homes Plus Restric-tion of Use of Resources in General).
10. Socialministeriets skrivelse af 3.6.1987 vedr. stop for opførelse af plejehjem of

beskyttede boliger efter bil. d. 1.1.1988 (Letter of June the 3rd 1987 from the Minister of Social Affairs regarding ban on building of Old Peoples Homes and Protective Housing in accordance with the Social Assistance Act).

11. Socialministeriets cirkulære af 8.10.1981 om uddannelse af hjemmehjælpere med flere (Circular of October the 8th 1981 from the Ministry of Social Affairs regarding Training of Home-helpers and Others). Socialstyrelsens cirkulæreskrivelse nr. 2 af 29.1.1988 om administrative retningslinjer for kurser for hjemmehjælpere (Letter no. 2 of January the 29th 1988 from the Social Administration regarding Administrative Guidance on Courses for Home-helpers). Birgitte Liebach: "Lavindkomstproblemer blandt kvindelige servicearbejdere", arbejdsnotat nr. 13 (1979?) ("Low Income Problems among Female Service-Workers"). Redegørelserne '85, '86 og '87 om social — og sundhedsplanlægning, Socialstyrelsen (Accounts '85, '86 and '87 regarding Social and Health Planning).

12. Bistandslovens kap. 12 og kap. 16 (The Social Assistance Act Chapter 12 and Chapter 16) In. min. og soc. min. og skrivelse af 9.9 1983 om plejepatienters sygehusophold (Letter of September the 9th 1983 from the Ministries of Home Affairs and Social Affairs regarding Stay in Hospitals for Patients who need nursing). Socialministeriets cirkulære af 22nd december 1986 om institutioner under Kommunerne (Circular of December the a and 1986 from the Ministry of Social Affairs regarding Institutions under the Local Authorities).

13. Socialministeriets henstilling af 16.9.1987 om samarbejde mellem kommuner ved plejehjemsophold (Appeal of September the 16th 1987 from the Minister of Social Affairs of Cooperation between the Local Authorities in Case of Residence of Old Peoples Homes).

14. Lov nr. 378 af 10.6.1987 om boliger for ældre og personer med handicap (Act no. 378 of June the 10th 1987 regarding Housing for the Elderly and Handicapped Persons).

15. Lis Frost: "Retfærdighed. Om Rawls og Habermas, og om Kvinderetten som et utopisk project" in Retfærd no. 40 p. 6-21 ("Justice. About Rawls and Habermas and about Women's Law as an Utopian Project"). Merry Scheel: "Nel Noddings omsorgsetik. Et alternaativ til pligtetik og nyttemoral" in Philosophia vol. 16, no. 1-2, p. 20-46, 1987 ("Nel Noddings' Ethics of Care. An Alternative to the Ethics of Obligation and to Utilitarianism").

16. The Bill was passed on April the 14th 1988. See the Act of Free Municipalities § 36 a.

Chapter 28

Shared Living Among the Elderly: A Legal Problem in Search of a Home*

Andrew BAINHAM   University of East Anglia, England

Introduction

Considerable importance is attached to care of the elderly in the community and to promotion of their independence. It is considered a desirable objective that elderly people should remain in their own homes for as long as possible and that institutional care should be avoided unless this is clearly necessary. On a more theoretical level it is now widely argued that the concept of dependency of the elderly has been socially manufactured. It is said that social service provision has been delivered in ways which have restricted the freedom and individuality of older people and that this has created an artificial dependency.[1] Social scientists now advocate a change of policy direction and contend that new ways should be found of fostering independence and self-help among the elderly.[2]

This article is concerned with the potential benefits and risks of home-sharing between unrelated elderly people, particularly those arrangements which are entered into for reasons of companionship or mutual support. There are, it is suggested, several reasons why this subject merits attention at the present time. First, a sharing arrangement may be one way of enabling some elderly people to remain in the community who might otherwise require institutional care. An older person who is unable to cope with living alone may be able to maintain a semi-independent lifestyle through interdependence with another elderly person. Secondly, sharing a home is the type of arrangement which may offer the opportunity for mutuality and reciprocity in social relations. This is thought to be an important factor in preserving morale and life satisfaction in elderly people. Thirdly, there is increasing awareness that the traditional importance accorded to the supportive role of the family has been exaggerated and that the value of contact with friends and age-related peers may have been underrated. Finally, English law contains many instances of home-sharing arrangements involving the elderly. Some of the decided cases provide an insight into the legal characterisation of this kind of arrangement. It will be contended that these cases demonstrate that English law is not presently geared to the form of residential companionship arrangement between older people which is the subject of this discussion. They display a preoccupation with relationships which at least have the appearance of heterosexual unions and show that various forms of relief which might be sought by elderly companions are restricted to those who are, or have been, living in formal marriage or in 'marriage-like' relationships. In short, English law has, for some purposes, made provision for the social needs of those who live together in the state of marriage or cohabitation.[3] At the same time there has been a reluctance to acknowledge that similar needs can exist in those relationships which fall outside this dual classification.

This approach, it will be argued, is bound to create legal problems for elderly people who decide to co-reside for reasons of companionship, support or mutual convenience. They cannot be properly characterised as living together as husband and wife even where they are of the opposite sex. *A fortiori*, they cannot where they are of the same sex. Moreover, the phenomenon of elderly single-sex companions is likely to become an increasing problem in most societies given the demographic changes which have led to the 'feminisation of old age'.[4] Increasingly, it may become necessary for the law to take account of the claims of two elderly women who have chosen to share a home.

A case can be made for saying that these elderly companions have needs in common with marriage partners and cohabitants, particularly regarding security in the home and financial security. Yet, legal developments relating to marriage partners and cohabitants illustrate that conceptual reasoning rooted in one context, when applied to a different social category, can produce unintended or incongruous results.

Before considering some of the legal difficulties surrounding shared living it is appropriate to consider some of the social advantages available to those elderly people who might contemplate home sharing.

Social Benefits of Sharing

The most immediate potential benefit of shared living would seem to be prevention of social isolation and loneliness. The correlation between living alone and subjective feelings of loneliness is well documented. Shanas et at found that the single most important determinant of old people's feelings of loneliness was sleeping in a structurally separate dwelling alone.[5] Fengler, Danigelis and Little reported a higher level of life satisfaction among elderly people living together than among those living alone.[6] They also offered the tentative view that friendship-based, co-residential living was associated with an even higher level of life satisfaction than that which was kinship-based.[7]

The importance of friendship in maintaining the morale of the elderly is a central theme of the work of the American writer, Zena Blau.[8] Her concern has

been with the adverse consequences of major social role exits, arising particularly on retirement and bereavement. It is her view that extensive social
interaction with age peers can constitute an effective substitute for marital or
occupational roles.[9] But perhaps her most significant conclusion is that meaningful associations with other elderly people are *more* effective in this respect
than are relationships with adult children. This view casts doubt on a social
policy which attaches primary importance to the intergenerational support
network.

The basis of Blau's thesis is that family support for the elderly derives from
obligation and, consequently, lacks the voluntary quality which is a characteristic of friendship. In her words, 'because friendship rests on mutual choice and
mutual need and involves a voluntary exchange of sociability between equals it
sustains a person's sense of usefulness and self-esteem more effectively than
filial relationships'. In contrast, 'children and parents, by definition, cannot be
equals or contemporaries'.[10]

The dilemma for older people, as noted by Blau, is how to preserve
independence from their adult family by maintaining separate households,
while confronting the problem of loneliness which living alone might engender.
One possible answer to this quandary is for them to seek relative independence
through *interdependence* by sharing their homes with unrelated people who can
share their needs, interests and attitudes.

In addition to mutual support and companionship, home sharing can have
economic advantages both for the elderly people concerned and for the state. It
enables a pooling of resources, housing costs and household expenses. In short,
two can live more cheaply than one. This is no small consideration given the
large numbers of older people in England living in poverty or on the margins of
poverty.[11] The state may benefit from sharing arrangements since it can be
saved the high cost of residential care which might otherwise result from the
institutionalisation of elderly individuals unable to remain in the community
alone. Social services departments might also be relieved of some of the burden
of social work support where elderly sharers are able to assist one another with
household tasks.

Organisational Assistance

The range of existing schemes for home sharing in the United States and
Britain was the subject of a study by Sheila Peace.[12] She considered the
available alternatives and made an evaluation of each. Broadly, the types of
arrangement include sharing private homes in the community, group housing,
family placement programmes and small group living within institutional
settings. What all of these arrangements have in common is that they can be a
preferred option for some older people who, for reasons of health or social
isolation, no longer can or wish to live alone, but who do not require the more

intensive levels of care provided in a large institution. This article is primarily concerned with private home sharing, but family placement programmes are organisationally significant since they are mainly sponsored by public agencies as a community-based alternative to residential care.[13] A number of social services departments in Britain have schemes under which older persons are placed as 'paying guests' in a private family or in family-like settings with unrelated persons. The intention is to improve their quality of life while enabling them to preserve a semi-independent life style. Social services play an important role in identifying and assessing the needs of people for whom this type of arrangement might be appropriate, finding the right placement for individuals and in monitoring and following up the success of the arrangement.

These schemes contrast with the relative informality of private home-sharing arrangements.[14] These tend not to involve the participation of public agencies, although in the United States there has been a significant growth in private, largely non-profit making, agencies specialising in such arrangements. The common characteristic of these arrangements is that two unrelated individuals share a single family home which is owned or rented by one of them. Arrangements can range from basic board and lodging to a fully communal arrangement involving the provision of companionship and a sharing of financial costs and household tasks. The agency acts as an intermediary in introducing prospective sharers and counselling them in what sharing involves. It may also assist with the drawing up of a written agreement dealing with such matters as rent, financial arrangements, areas of the home to be shared, responsibility for maintenance costs and domestic duties.

Perhaps the most important function of the agency is to ascertain the expectations of individual clients and to endeavour to produce a successful match based on expressed preferences, needs and interests and a professional assessment of the respective personalities.[15]

In Britain there is a private market in housekeeping, home help and companionship services for the elderly.[16] Involvement appears, however, to be largely limited to profit-making agencies.[17] It may be that greater consideration needs to be given to the professional organisation of such services. One possibility would be to extend the existing family placement schemes co-ordinated by social services. It is suggested that for some elderly people, sharing a home presently occupied by one of them may be of greater social benefit than placement in an intergenerational family setting. However successful family placements may be in creating the ambience of family life, they may lack the mutuality and reciprocity of support which can exist between sharers of comparable age and life situation. Community-based services, such as the elderly persons support units pioneered by Sheffield City Council in 1984, may offer a relatively less organised opportunity for the introduction of potential home sharers with professional assistance.[18]

Some Legal Difficulties in Sharing Arrangements

None of the supposed advantages of home sharing means that individual sharing arrangements will necessarily work out. The sharing process is fraught with potential pitfalls. Someone who decides to move into the home of another elderly person may well be giving up the security of existing accommodation. He or she may be placed in a vulnerable housing situation in the event of the death of the chosen companion or disagreement between them. The supposed financial advantages of sharing may also prove to be illusory if the state withdraws or reduces social security benefits on the basis that the two individuals are 'cohabiting'. Careful consideration therefore needs to be given to finding ways of providing legal security for those who decide to embark on home sharing.

A. Security in the Home

The right to remain in the home is likely to become an issue either on the death of one of the sharers or in the event of a breakdown in their relationship. Death is a reasonably proximate contingency for older people and should it materialise within a short time of the commencement of a sharing arrangement, the survivor may be threatened with eviction. Where the home was rented by the deceased under a protected tenancy, someone living with him at the time of death may, in certain circumstances, succeed to the tenancy. But in the case of both public and private tenancies the survivor must have resided with the deceased at the property in question for a prescribed statutory period.[19] In *South Northamptonshire District Council* v *Power*, an elderly man moved in to live with a widow on the death of her husband. This home was owned by the widow and it was not disputed that the couple were living there as husband and wife. Sometime later, the widow was granted a tenancy of senior citizens' accommodation by the local authority. The male cohabitant, unknown to the council, continued to live with her in this accommodation. 9 months later the widow died and the issue was whether the man could succeed to the tenancy. The couple had lived together as members of a family for a period exceeding the statutory 12 month requirement,[21] but they had done so for less than this period in the council property which was the subject of the proceedings. The Court of Appeal held that the council was entitled to possession. The Court interpreted the legislation to mean that the requirement of 12 months' residence referred to residence at the property which was the subject of the application.

This case clearly illustrates that an elderly person who moves in with a tenant who then dies within a short time of the move will not have security in the home. More particularly it reveals the dangers to long-standing sharers of a death occurring soon after a change of home.

Where the statutory period of residence is satisfied, succession to the tenancy by an unrelated individual will turn on whether the survivor can demonstrate that he was a member of the deceased's family. Family membership is not defined in the legislation governing private tenancies and it has been left to the courts to consider whether in individual cases the necessary familial link was established. In so doing, they have purported to ask themselves how the ordinary man would regard the relationship. A closer examination of the decisions indicates, however, that an unrelated individual is unlikely to qualify unless his relationship with the deceased can be characterised as quasi-marital. Thus, a long-standing platonic relationship between an elderly childless widow and a much younger man, although similar in nature to that of aunt and nephew, was held by the House of Lords not to mount to a familial relationship.[22] On the other hand, it now seems to be accepted that two unmarried adults cohabiting in a relationship analogous to that of husband and wife will be regarded as family members for these purposes.[23] The determining factors will be the apparent permanence and stability of the relationship and whether the partners regarded themselves or held themselves out as husband and wife.[24] It would appear, however, that the adoption of an independent lifestyle or an unwillingness to conform to the traditional social roles of married couples could be fatal to the success of the application.[25]

The latest reported decision on the transmission of private tenancies is particularly relevant to the situation of elderly companions. In *Sefton Holdings Ltd* v *Cairns*[26] the defendant, an elderly spinster, claimed the right to remain in the home in which she had been living with a family for almost 50 years. Having lost both her parents and her boyfriend, who had been killed in the Second World War, she was taken in at the age of 23 by the original tenant and his wife at the request of their daughter. She was treated by the couple as their daughter, and the two younger women regarded themselves as sisters. When the tenant died in 1965, his daughter succeeded to the tenancy. She then died in 1986, and the question was whether a second transmission could be made to the defendant on the basis that she was a member of the deceased's family.

The Court of Appeal held that it could not. In the Court's view, although she was clearly living in the household and was *treated* as a member of the family this was not the same as *being* a member of the family. She had not been legally adopted, nor could it be said that she had been de facto adopted, since she was already an adult when she had moved in with the family.

Support for the distinction between the 'household' and the 'family' is to be found in sociological writings. Leslie defines a household as 'a group of people who share a common dwelling.' It is (he says) often a family group but it need not be: it may be an unrelated group of people who share the customary living arrangements of a family group'.[27] But, equally, social scientists accept that the word 'family' is used in many different senses.[28] In particular, its usage is not confined to categories of kin but may properly be applied to other groups performing analogous social functions.[29]

The legal issue is to determine when the performance of certain social functions justifies the inclusion of an individual in the familial category. It could be argued that the defendant in the *Cairns* case had performed the social role of a sister to the deceased and the role of a daughter to the original tenant and his wife. The difficulty with this is that it may not be possible to ascribe with confidence any distinctive social role to either sisters or daughters. Yet this has not prevented the courts from attempting to do precisely this in relation to unmarried cohabitants. As we have seen, they have been willing to regard a man and woman as living together in the capacity of husband and wife where their relationship has the appearance of permanence and stability and where, in the courts' view, they have behaved towards one another in the way in which a husband and wife might be expected to behave. Significance has been attached to whether they subjectively regarded themselves as spouses and whether this was manifested by public affirmation, for example by the adoption of a common surname.

These criteria were satisfied in *Cairns*. It could hardly be argued that co-residence for almost 50 years lacked permanence or stability and it was clear that the two women regarded themselves as siblings. Presumably they wished to be regarded as such in their dealings with persons outside the household. Nonetheless, the Court of Appeal refused to accept that they could become sisters artificially. The Court did not explain why behaving as sisters is more artificial than behaving as spouses.

Apart from the obvious injustice of exposing this particular lady to eviction, this is an ominous decision for elderly people living together under informal arrangements. It evinces an unwillingness on the part of the courts to accept that a familial relationship can be created where unrelated individuals act as if they are related by performing analogous social functions. It might be objected that, since the concept of 'family' is inherently vague, the courts should not be criticised for failing to arrive at categorical determinations of what is 'familial'. An alternative, and more limited, solution in the present context might be to amend the Housing legislation rather than to appear to be extending the legal meaning of the 'family'. It might, for example, be possible for the purposes of allocating security of tenure, to rely on the concept of the 'household' rather than the 'family' and to grant security to anyone co-residing with the deceased in his 'household' for a specified period up to and including the date of death. Such a solution would, however, be likely to create problems of its own. Unless significant qualifications were incorporated into the household test, the courts might be faced with applications by individuals who enjoyed no meaningful relationship or connection with the deceased at all e.g. lodgers. It is, therefore, suggested, on balance, that the concept of the family is an appropriate one in this context but that it should receive a liberal and sympathetic interpretation in the case of elderly companions.

In relation to public sector tenancies the legislation contains a definition of family membership which, in the case of unrelated individuals, is expressly confined to those living together 'as husband and wife'.[30] It has been held that the expression is not wide enough to embrace a lesbian relationship.[31]

The significance of the decided cases in this area is that unrelated elderly people of the *same* sex are likely to find it impossible to establish the requisite familial connection. Both the courts and, to some extent, the legislature seem fixated on relationships which at least have the appearance of heterosexual unions. This is particularly unfortunate for the elderly since living with a contemporary of the same sex may be a more viable option, especially for women who significantly outnumber men in the older age groups.

The legal position of someone moving in with an elderly home owner may be equally precarious. Since the English courts have no jurisdiction to adjust the property rights of unmarried persons, someone sharing a home in which the legal title is vested solely in another person will have to point to some informally created equitable interest in his favour.[32] The courts have employed a variety of devices in this respect including implied, resulting and constructive trusts, contractual licences and proprietary estoppel.[33]

In order to rely on an interest under a trust it is usually necessary to show a common intention that such an interest should exist. The principal difficulty is that in order to raise this inference the party alleging the interest will generally have to demonstrate that he has incurred expenditure which is referable, directly or indirectly, to the acquisition of the home. Substantial financial contributions to household expenses might suffice for these purposes, but it has been decided that the mere decision to move in with another person cannot *per se* raise the necessary inference.[34] Moreover, the courts have emphasised that what might be termed 'welfare contributions' to family life are also insufficient.[35]

Reliance on a contractual licence to remain in the home is equally problematic. Here it may prove impossible to show that the technical requirements of the law of contract were satisfied in the context of an informal domestic arrangement. The terms of the alleged contract may be too vague or there may be difficulty in showing a mutual intention to create legal relations.[36]

Perhaps the best chance of success lies in the doctrine of estoppel.[37] In order to succeed the home-sharer will need to show that he acted to his detriment in the belief, encouraged by the owner, either that he already possessed an interest in it. The owner will then be estopped from denying the existence of the interest and it will be for the court to determine how the equity is to be satisfied.

In *Pascoe* v *Turner*[38] Mrs. Turner, a widow, moved into the home of Mr. Pascoe, initially as his housekeeper. In reliance on his oral assurance that the house and contents were hers, she spent a quarter of her savings on repairs and improvements. The Court of Appeal ordered Mr. Pascoe to keep his promise by conveying the house outright to her. It was held that she had changed her position for the worse with his acquiescence and encouragement.

Likewise, in *Greasley* v *Cooke*[39] a woman who joined the household of a widower as an unpaid maid succeeded in obtaining a right to remain in the property for life following the death of the last member of the immediate family. She contended that she had stayed on at the request of various members of the family who had assured her that she could remain there for life. The case is important for Lord Denning's general statement that monetary expenditure is not a necessary element in proprietary estoppel. It would seem, for example, that the provision of companionship services and the performance of household tasks could constitute the required detriment and that a claim based on estoppel might succeed where one relying on the existence of a trust might fail.[40]

Estoppel, then, may be apposite where one elderly person relinquishes a secure home to move into the home of another, relying on the informal assurances of that other person that he will be allowed to remain there. The drawback is that it may be difficult to prove that assurances were in fact made or that, if they were, reliance was placed on them. Sharing arrangements may arise solely as a result of kindness or natural affection, or from the mutual recognition of common interests or needs. It may well be that no serious thought is given by those concerned to the legal implications of the arrangement or even to the prospect that it might break down at some future point. In these circumstances, it may be difficult to invoke the doctrine. It is also difficult to predict the future development of estoppel at this point. Recent decisions of the lower courts have been inconsistent in the degree of importance which they have attached to the technicalities of the doctrine.[41] It remains to be seen whether the higher courts will favour a liberal or restrictive approach. In the meantime it is difficult to avoid the impression that the law governing the informal creation of interests in property is something of a lottery in England.

B. Aspects of Financial Security

This section considers two aspects of the law impinging on the financial security of elderly home sharers. The first is the effect of the arrangement on the social security entitlements of one or both of them. The second is the possibility of a claim for financial provision by the survivor where one sharer has died.

Large numbers of the elderly in Britain are dependent to some extent on means-tested social assistance. Until April 1988 this was Supplementary Benefit but this has now been replaced by Income Support.[42] Where two unmarried individuals live together as husband and wife their resources and requirements are aggregated for the purposes of applying the relevant means test.[43] Where an individual currently receiving benefit begins to cohabit this can therefore result in a loss or reduction in benefit. The effect may be to neutralise the financial advantages which the two individuals may have supposed would arise from shared living. Likewise, a woman is liable to lose widow's benefits during any period in which she cohabits with a man.[44] It is, therefore, in this context, of paramount importance that elderly companions should *not* be treated as if they are living together in a quasi-marital union.

Fortunately, both the courts and the Social Security Commissioners have acknowledged that two elderly people may reside in the same household without assuming the character of husband and wife. In the leading decision,[45] the High Court accepted that a male friend who moved into the home of a woman, who had been injured in a road accident, was not cohabiting with her.

The reason for his presence was to offer assistance with daily household tasks which the woman could no longer perform. The Court said that it was not sufficient to show that two people were living in the same household. It was necessary to go on to consider whether there was an explanation for the arrangement. This case was followed by a decision of the Social Security Commissioner that a widow and widower should not be treated as cohabiting where the man's presence in the home arose from consideration of care, companionship and mutual convenience.[46]

These decisions might suggest that elderly sharers who have no intention of forming a marriage-like relationship have nothing to fear. The problem is that the mere fact of their co-residence will raise an issue as to the status of their relationship and may lead to distressing inquiries by the Department of Health and Social Security.[47] Furthermore, the Commissioners have refused to accept the argument that a relationship should necessarily be characterised in accordance with the expressed intentions of the parties. It has been said that intention can only be ascertained from observable conduct.[48] Thus, however adamant two people may be that they are not living as a married couple, they are liable to have this characterisation thrust upon them if their behaviour objectively suggests the adoption of marital roles.

The 'cohabitation rule' can give rise to unfortunate anomalies in the treatment of the elderly.[49] An elderly brother and sister, for example cannot be caught by it. Neither can two people of the same sex. It can therefore discriminate between the elderly on the basis of sex differences even though there may well be no sexual activity in the respective relationships. In relation to social security entitlements it is the single-sex companions who are at an advantage.

The answer to this problem may be the total abolition of the aggregation principle whether applied to married or unmarried partners.[50] This would overcome at a stroke the problem of assumed financial dependence of one sharer on the other, which may or may not be a reality. At the same time, it would preserve equity between those co-residing in marriage and those living together outside marriage. Each claimant would be entitled to be assessed for social security purposes on the basis of his or her own individual needs or resources. Although this solution has always been rejected by governments for reasons of cost, there is no reason in principle why it should not be adopted. It is especially relevant at a time when the 1988 budget recognised the claims which spouses have to financial independence by accepting the principle of separate taxation of husband and wife. Is there any reason (other than cost) why this principle should not also apply in the context of low-income households? Moreover, separate assessment would have the advantage of simplicity since it would avoid the technical difficulties which would be likely to arise from any modification of the cohabitation rule designed to assist the elderly as a social group with particular needs.

Turning to the second issue, English law does not provide for income support rights between unmarried cohabitants. But in certain circumstances maintenance may be sought from the estate of a deceased person by a non-relative who was being maintained by the deceased immediately before the deceased's death.[51] The legislation requires that the deceased should have been making a substantial contribution in money or money's worth to the needs of the applicant otherwise than for valuable consideration.[52] This means that the applicant must have been dependent, at least to some extent, on the deceased. In order to determine whether the required dependency existed at the time of death a balancing exercise must be performed. The financial value of the benefits which each provided for the other must be weighed.[53] The Court of Appeal has conceded that a common sense view of the relationship must be taken and that mathematical precision is not required.[54] Nonetheless, if it emerges that the value of the applicant's contribution either exceeded or was broadly equivalent to that of the deceased, the application must fail since at least a partial financial dependency on the deceased must be demonstrated.

This jurisdiction is particularly unsuited to the provision of relief to someone who has had a relationship of broad equality with the deceased, or where each of them preserved a measure of independence. Where two people share their lives under a reciprocal arrangement, with each contributing financially and to the performance of household tasks and expenses, it may be impossible to find that either was in a dependent position on the other.[55] The test of dependency is also defective in presenting the court with the invidious task of placing a monetary value on such matters as companionship and responsibility for domestic chores. It further produces the paradoxical conclusion that the greater the contribution of the applicant to the welfare of the deceased, the less likely he is to qualify for support.

The requirement of dependency provides a striking illustration of the divergence of law and social policy since it rules out of court those who sought to preserve some independence in their domestic arrangements. Social scientists are telling us that we need to find ways of fostering the independence of elderly people and are emphasising the importance of mutuality in their social relations. The law is telling us that they are out of court unless they can fit the traditional stereotype of dependence of one partner on the other.

Conclusions

This brief review suggests an unwillingness on the part of the English courts and legislature to attach legal significance to living arrangements other than those which fit the traditional familial model, i.e. those founded on formal marriage or those which have 'marriagelike' qualities justifying the description 'cohabitation'. But these are only two of the many states in which people may choose to live together in the same household. The Social Security cases clearly show that 'cohabitation' is an inappropriate characterisation of the relationship of elderly companions. Yet it does not follow that the social needs or expectations of such people are any less worthy of consideration than those of elderly spouses or cohabitants. Elderly people should be entitled to adopt lifestyles which suit their individual circumstances. They should feel able to enter into non-sexual domestic partnerships in the confidence that the law will give effect to their reasonable expectations. The difficulty, of course, is to know what their expectations are. Finding out more about why elderly people enter these arrangements and what they expect from them could usefully be the subject of empirical research.

One general approach could be to encourage elderly people to enter into express contracts. This would have the advantage of putting their expectations into legal form from the outset. Written agreements are a feature of many of the arrangements concluded by housesharing agencies. An example of legislative initiative in this area is the 'Vesper Marriage' law of the Virgin Islands which enables two persons aged over 60 to enter into an enforceable contract to live together as husband and wife without acquiring any interest in the property or income of each other or any right of inheritance.[56] Whether such an agreement would be enforceable in England is still undecided. It is suggested, however, that traditional moral objections should certainly not preclude an agreement between two elderly people for companionship only and which contains no sexual component.

A contractual approach will not however be of much use to those who enter into informal arrangements, with or without assurances from each other. Where social arrangements emanate from existing friendships or altruism it would, it is felt, be unreasonable to expect them to be formalised. Two people may well have come together as a result of life crises faced by one or both of them such as bereavement or ill-health. In these cases, it is contended the legal system should provide the individuals concerned with at least a minimum level of security. It is unlikely that the ordinary principles of law can be relied upon in this respect. The technicalities of trust law and estoppel are such that it is unwise to assume that they can produce a just result in every case. Serious consideration needs to be given to the creation of an adjustive jurisdiction which would enable the courts to give effect to informal assurances in a way which meets the justice of individual circumstances. This type of jurisdiction, confined to informal testamentary promises, was introduced in New Zealand in 1944.[57] Meanwhile, it is suggested that the courts could show greater sensitivity towards the social needs of those who decide to adopt an unconventional lifestyle. It would not have taken more than a modicum of creativity to have found that an elderly woman who had performed the social role of a family member for nearly 50 years had indeed become a member of that family.

In conclusion, the case for shared living among the elderly should not be overstated. It has been estimated that the percentage of older people in the developed countries currently in shared living arrangements with non-relatives may be as low as 1-2%.[58] This may partly be accounted for by the challenge to the traditional values of privacy and personal autonomy which sharing represents and partly by in-built prejudices against forms of unmarried co-residence.

The present generation of elderly people grew up at a time when a considerable social stigma attached to extra-marital cohabitation. But the incidence of elderly partners living together outside marriage should increase substantially in future years given the rise in the divorce rate and the increased social acceptability of informal relationships. If elderly people are to enjoy greater self-determination and freedom of choice, it is important that the legal implications of shared living should be properly addressed. Meanwhile, it is a legal problem in search of a home.

NOTES

* This chapter also appears in *Oxford Journal of Legal Studies volume 9*. I wish to record my thanks to John Eekelaar and Gareth Melles for their comments and assistance. The views presented are mine alone. I also wish to thank New York University for the use of library facilities.

1. See particularly Chris Phillipson and Alan Walker, *Aging and Social Policy*, (1986), Gower.
2. Ibid, chap 14.
3. The expression 'cohabitation' is here used to describe those relationships in which a couple may be characterised as living together 'as husband and wife'.
4. This expression refers to the significantly higher proportion of women than men in the elderly population especially among the very old.
5. E. Shanas, P. Townsend, D. Wedderburn, H. Friis, Milhoj and Stehouver, J,*Old People in Three Industrial Societies*, (1968), Atherton, New York, at p 268.
6. Alfred P. Fengler, Nicholas Danigelis and Virginia C. Little, *Later Life Satisfaction and Household Structure: Living With Others and Living Alone*,(1983) 3 Aging and Society, 357, 371.
7. Ibid, at p 374.
8. Zena Smith Blau, *Aging in a Changing Society*, 2nd Ed (1981), Franklin Watts, New York.
9. Ibid, at p 61.
10. Ibid, at p 64.
11. See the discussion by Alan Walker in *Aging and Social Policy*, Chap 10, op cit n 1.
12. Sheila M. Peace with Charlotte Nusberg, *Shared Living: A Viable Alternative for the Elderly?*, (1984) International Federation on Aging, Washington, D C.
13. Ibid, chap VI.
14. Ibid, chap II.
15. Ibid, at pp 13-14.
16. Age Concern England has produced a 'Companions' factsheet with details of private agencies and the services which they offer entitled 'Companions and Living in Help', September 1986.
17. The author made inquiries in the Social Services Departments of four local authorities in England but was unable to discover any evidence of organised support for private home sharing in those areas.

18. See Robert MacDonald, Hazel Qureshi and Alan Walker, *Sheffield Shows the Way*, Community Care, October 1984 at p 28.
19. For private tenancies the period is 6 months (Para 3, sched 1, Rent Act 1977) and for public tenancies it is 12 months (s 87, Housing Act 1985).
20. [1987] 1 WLR 1433.
21. Supra n 19.
22. *Carega Properties S A* v *Sharratt* [1979] 1W L R 928.
23. *Dyson Holdings Ltd* v *Fox* [1976] Q B 503, *Watson* v *Lucas* [1980] 3 All E R 647.
24. There is no minimum period of cohabitation required and in a recent case two years was held to be sufficient. See *Chios Investment Property Co Ltd* v *Lopez* (1987) Times, 3 November.
25. *Helby* v *Rafferty* [1979] 1W L R 13.
26. (1988) 18 Fam Law 164.
27. Gerald R Leslie, *The Family in Social Context* 5th Ed (1982) at p 20, Oxford University Press.
28. See, for example, C. C. Harris, *The Family* (1970), Chap 3, London, George Allen and Unwin Ltd and Mary Farmer, *The Family* 2nd Ed (1979), Chap 1, Longman Group Ltd.
29. See Harris, ibid at p 82.
30. S 113, Housing Act 1985.
31. *Harrogate Borough Council* v *Simpson* (1986), 16 Fam Law 359.
32. See generally John Eekelaar, *A Woman's Place — A Conflict Between Law and Social Values* [1987] Conv 93.
33. Interests arising under trusts, contractual licences and estoppel are often alleged in the alternative. See, for example, *Layton* v *Martin* (1986) 2 F L R 227.
34. *Grant* v *Edwards* [1986] Ch 638.
35. *Burns* v *Burns* [1984] 1 All E R 224.
36. See, for example, *Coombes* v *Smith* [1986] 1 W L R 808 distinguishing *Tanner* v *Tanner* [1975] 3 All E R 776.
37. This is a view shared by Eekelaar, op cit n 32 at pp 99-101.
38. [1979] 1 W L R 431.
39. [1980] 3 All E R 710.
40. As in *Pascoe* v *Turner*, supra n 38.
41. See *Layton* v *Martin*,*Coombes* v *Smith* (supra) cf. *Re Basham Decd* [1987] 2 F L R 264.
42. The changes were introduced by the implementation of s20, Social Security 1986.
43. Formerly, Sched 1, para 3(1) and s34 Supplementary Benefits Act 1976 as amended. This principle is unaffected by the changes in the 1986 Act.
44. Social Security Act 1975 ss24(2) 25(3) 26(3) as amended.
45. *Butterworth* v *Supplementary Benefits Commission* [1982] 1 All E R 498.
46. *R(SB) 35/85*.
47. This was pointed out by the Commissioner, Mr D G Rice in *R(G) 3/81*.
48. Ibid, at para 8 rejecting the view of Webster J in *Robson* v *Secretary of State for Social Services*(1982) 3 F L R 232.
49. As noted by the Commissioner, Mr I. Edwards-Jones in *R(SB) 35/85* at para 2.
50. For the arguments for and against abolition of the cohabitation rule see Ogus and Barendt, *The Law of Social Security* 2nd Ed (1982) at pp 382-384, Butterworths.
51. S1(1)(e), Inheritance (Provision for Family and Dependants) Act 1975.
52. S1(3).

53. See, for example, *Re Wilkinson* [1978] Fam 22, *Re Beaumont* [1980] Ch. 444.
54. *Jelley* v *Iliffe* [1981] Fam 128.
55. This was essentially the position in *Re Beaumont* (supra).
56. Discussed briefly by Michael S. J. Albano and Donald C. Schiller in *Cohabitation Without Formal Marriage in the USA* (1986) 16 Fam Law 43, 45.
57. For a discussion of the jurisdiction see J G Miller, *The Machinery of Succession*, (1977) at pp 199-201, Professional Books.
58. Peace, op cit n 12 at p 91.

Chapter 29

The Situation of Elderly Cohabitees in Denmark — The Interaction of Family Law, Social Law, Tax Law and the Law of Succession

Ingrid LUND-ANDERSEN and Noe MUNCK
University of Aarhus, Denmark

Introduction

The number of unmarried cohabitees in Denmark has been rising rapidly since the end of the 1960s. Today the group of unmarried cohabitees makes up 19% of all persons living together (married and unmarried).[1] In this statistical report an unmarried cohabitee is defined as a person of 16 years of age or more whose legal marital status is either unmarried, divorced or widow/widower, and who cohabits with a person of the opposite sex in the same household. Thus, not included in these statistics are persons cohabiting with a person of the same sex — another increasing group due to the increased social acceptance of homosexual relationships.[2] However, this chapter is primarily concerned with heterosexual relationships.

Towards the end of the 1960s, living in an unmarried relationship was a phenomenon of youth, a result of the youth rebellion for freedom of the individual and a dissociation from the institutions of the Establishment. The development in Denmark today is moving towards a situation where more and more elderly people are living together without a marriage licence. About one third of the total group of unmarried cohabitees is over 35, and about 5% of all unmarried cohabitees are people living in widowhood. As is the case for young cohabitees the relationships of elderly cohabitees differ widely — i.e., they comprise both relationships on trial and long-term relationships of a more permanent nature.

Probably the primary reason why more elderly people choose to live together without marriage is the fact that due to legal rules the couple is in a better financial position by not marrying. As almost all social groups in

Denmark today accept such relationships without a marriage licence, many people — both young and old — calculate the financial advantages and disadvantages of getting married. However, it is difficult to make an overview of the legal position in this area. What an unmarried couple gains financially in one respect by not marrying they often lose in another. To illustrate the complicated interaction of rules applying to elderly cohabitees, we will consider the most import aspects of Danish family law, social law, administration of estates and the law of succession.

In this connection a number of circumstances characteristic of elderly cohabitees should be emphasized:
1. Elderly cohabitees normally have more capital assets than younger cohabitees, i.e., a house, car, savings. Also, family responsibilities towards children will have ceased.
2. The parties have no joint issue (joint children).
3. Both parties often have grown-up children from a former marriage.
4. Many elderly people are widows/widowers.
5. Elderly people receive more government support, i.e. a pension.
6. The risk of death is great, and for this reason it becomes relevant to secure the position of a cohabitee in the event of a death.

Examples of rules that induce well-off elderly people to choose to cohabit

A. Rules of taxation

Danish property tax is very high compared with other countries: 2.2% of taxable property exceeding DKK 1,329,000 (1988)($204,000). For married couples the property tax is calculated on the basis of the total property of the spouses, whereas unmarried cohabitees are taxed independently.[3] If both possess considerable property at the time of commencing cohabitation there is an evident tax advantage involved in not marrying. Also with regard to the taxation of income in the form of interest, dividends from shares and the like, there may be financial advantages involved in living together without getting married.

In Denmark, tax legislation has moved from joint taxation of spouses towards separate taxation — primarily justified on the ground of equality between the sexes. This leads to the wish to disconnect taxation and marital status. However, the last amendment of the taxation rules in 1986 retained certain joint taxation rules, including the rule on property tax. Since this Bill, however, Parliament seems inclined to remove the "existing discrimination against spouses", as several political parties have expressed it. Therefore, it is to be expected that within a short time there will be a change in the rules for the calculation of property tax so that spouses will be given two tax-free low exemptions of $204,000 each, as is the case for unmarried cohabitees instead of only one low exemption as at present.[4] If this happens, there would be large tax relief for well-off spouses.

B. Rules of Family Law

The main rule of the Ægteskabsloven (the Danish Marriage Act) is that a married couple has community of property (joint ownership). This property arrangement is important when the marriage is dissolved because of separation, or divorce, in which case the total property of the spouses is to be divided equally.[5] However, if the spouses agree, it is possible both before and during the marriage to arrange for the property assets of the parties to be regarded as wholly or partly separate property, so that this part of the property of each party is not to be divided if the marriage is terminated. Only about 5% have agreed on separate property in Denmark.[6]

If there is a substantial difference in the financial situation of each of the partners, there is a clear financial advantage on the part of the financially better off party in not marrying. In such a case this spouse avoids having to lose half his or her property to the other party in case of a later divorce.

For the weaker party in an unmarried cohabitation relationship this will be a corresponding disadvantage, as the person in question is not covered by the protective provisions of the Danish Marriage Act. Women are generally less wealthy than men — and this applies irrespective of the fact that in recent decades the financial situation of women in Denmark has radically improved. About 80% of all women are now employed, but about half work only part time, and the types of jobs selected by women are generally lower paid than those held by men.

Several cases have been decided by the courts where the woman has been cohabiting with a comparatively wealthy man for many years, and has been almost completely without means when the relationship was broken. If the woman is no longer young she will often have difficulty finding employment and will be forced to live on the limited social support from the government. To avoid unreasonable results Danish courts have established a "self-constructed" protection model without the usual support of legislation or other traditionally accepted legal sources. This means that in certain cases the financially weaker party has been awarded a certain compensation from the financially better off party. The courts have based these decisions on two major views:

a. The enrichment view; that is, whether the financially better-off party has gained an unjustified enrichment at the expense of the other party, for example, if the financially worse-off party has contributed financially to enable the richer partner to keep his or her own-eroccupied house where both parties live.
b. The conditional view; that is, the judges have found that the financially worse-off party had a justified expectation not to be left without any means of support when the relationship was terminated. This criterion is particu-

larly important in very special cases where the parties have lived together for many years.

The Danish Committee on Marriage did not wish to leave the matter entirely to the courts, and the committee suggested that a rule of law be introduced to protect the weaker party. The Committee suggested a new rule based on the provisions applicable to marriages with separate property. According to this rule the Probate Court may order one party in a relationship to pay to the other a sum in order to ensure that this party is not left in a clearly unreasonable position, especially in view of the financial circumstances of the parties and the duration of the relationship. Consideration may also be given to the contribution of the person in question to the home of the parties through work, contribution towards the mutual upkeep, privation or otherwise.[7]

C. Rules within the Law of Succession

Under Danish law, the surviving spouse has the possibility of retaining undivided possession of the estate. This means that the estate left by the deceased spouse is not divided among the spouse and the children and other possible beneficiaries, but the surviving spouse keeps all the assets. In this way the spouse avoids having to sell valuable assets in order to pay the inheritance of the children and her own inheritance tax. Furthermore, the spouse has the right "to eat the estate", as it is popularly expressed. The right to retain undivided possession of the estate only applies to community property, but not to separate property.[8] Joint issue (joint children) have a duty to accept the surviving parent's wish to retain undivided possession of the estate. The deceased spouse's children of a former marriage, however, need to consent if the survivor is to retain undivided possession of the estate. About 25% of all estates in Denmark are undivided.

In the case of a new marriage the undivided estate has to be divided.[9] However, cohabitation does not cause such division of the estate. Consequently a widow or widower often chooses to live without a marriage licence with his or her new partner so as to avoid having to pay legal inheritance to the children, which is one third of the joint estate. And at the same time the spouse avoids paying inheritance duty on his or her inheritance from the deceased spouse, as the inheritance is not considered paid when the spouses retain undivided possession of the estate.

The rules on division of an undivided estate in the case of a new marriage thus encourage the surviving spouse to choose cohabitation over marriage. To avoid such "evasion" of the rules on administration of an estate, in 1980 a majority in the Danish Committee on Marriage proposed a rule according to which an heir may demand division of the estate when the surviving spouse has cohabited for two years.[10] The Committee on Marriage is aware that such a rule may give rise to an untimely interference in the personal relations of the surviving spouse on the part of the heirs.

Examples of Rules That Make Elderly People of Limited Means Choose Cohabitation

A. Tax Law

In Danish law, there is a long tradition of particularly lenient taxation of pensioners. Unmarried persons receiving retirement pension (see also section 3.b, below) or an early retirement pension (a social pension paid to persons between 18 and 67 years of age) thus have the right to a particularly high personal income tax allowance — i.e., an allowance on taxable income of DKK 48,400 in 1988 ($7,500), which reduces the tax payable, whereas married pensioners have a lower allowance on taxable personal income of DKK 27,300 in 1988 ($4,200).[11] If two pensioners cohabit, the total personal income tax allowance is DKK 96,800 ($15,000) compared to DKK 54,600 ($8,400) for a married couple. The reason for the high personal allowance for unmarried persons is the assumption that, being single, they have relatively higher living expenses than married persons, particularly for housing, heating and telephone. However, this does not apply to cohabitees. If married persons were to have the same high personal allowance as is granted to unmarried persons this would have cost the government DKK 3.3. millions in 1986.[12]

B. Social Law

Within social law there are considerable advantages to be gained by not marrying. This is due to the fact that spouses have a maintenance liability towards each other, and that the authorities therefore may take the income and property situation of the other spouse into consideration when a person applies for public assistance. However, the general rule for cohabitees is that they are normally granted assistance on the basis of their own financial circumstances. Only if several persons in a household can be said to benefit from such assistance, e.g., contributions towards heating and housing, will the total income situation of the household be taken into account. Of the rules within social law which are relevant for elderly people, the following deserve particular mention:

C. The Rules on Retirement Pension

In Denmark, all persons over 67 are entitled to receive a retirement pension.[13] The pension is awarded according to an individual principle, i.e., irrespective of family relationships. However, the size of the pension differs for married and unmarried persons. Unmarried persons — including cohabitees — receive a higher monthly amount than married persons. On 1 January 1988 unmarried persons were paid DKK 4,002($620) per month, whereas persons married to each other received DKK 3,779($580) each per month. The special rate for married persons is due to the fact that living expenses for a couple are lower than for two single persons.

The rules on retirement pension and the rules on the particularly high personal allowance for unmarried pensioners, mean that the disposable pension after tax for a married couple amounts to about 75% of that of two single pensioners. This difference is so great that it causes many people to live unmarried. And there have been several cases of married pensioners divorcing to improve their financial situation.

In 1986, a committee appointed by the Danish Ministry of Social Affairs published a report (No. 1087/1986) on equality of treatment of relationships within and without marriage in social legislation. The committee concluded that social legislation should not be formulated in such a way that a couple is tempted to consider whether it is financially worthwhile not to marry. The committee considered two models as a possible solution: either that the law should apply a household principle, i.e., that cohabitees are equalised with married persons, or that an individual principle be introduced, under which everyone, irrespective of marital status, would be considered single. The committee stated that the choice of model was a political choice and emphasized that the individual principle would involve considerable additional expense on the part of the state. The additional cost of retirement pensions has been calculated as amounting to DKK 905 million. On 12 February 1987 the Danish Minister of Social Affairs, in principle, supported a gradual introduction of the individual principle within family and social law[14]. However, at the same time the Minister pointed out that it might be necessary to depart from this principle to provide help for groups with a greater need than others,i.e., distributive and socio-political considerations have to be applied. Furthermore, it was mentioned that the household principle should be maintained in the case of assistance from which the entire household benefits, such as contributions towards heating and housing. The Danish Parliament, the "Folketing", accepted the gradual introduction of the individual principle within family and social law on 14 May 1987.

Providing security for the survivor in the case of death of the other party

If one party dies it will normally prove financially disadvantageous for the surviving cohabitee that the couple did not marry. There are a number of rules favourable to a surviving spouse. In particular, the rules of succession and of pensions may be mentioned. A spouse is entitled to one-third of the property of the deceased spouse if the are no children. Futhermore, the surviving spouse has a right to retain undivided possession of the estate without paying inheritance duty and without giving the children their inheritance. The surviving cohabitee has no such right under Danish law.

If the deceased was a civil servant or a member of a pension fund, a spouse will normally be paid a pension (about 60% of the deceased's own pension).[15] However, a surviving cohabitee never receives any pension from his or her deceased partner. Privately employed persons often make private arrangements for pension schemes which, on account of rules of taxation, will only cover a surviving spouse.

When a couple decides not to marry, they should at the same time make provisions to secure the surviving party in the case of the death of the other party. A considerable sum for the surviving cohabitee may be secured by inserting the partner as beneficiary in a life assurance policy. The couple should also draw up mutual wills in which the cohabitee is constituted as heir. If the testator has children, the rules on legitimate portion allow that only half of the property left may be disposed of in a will. If there are no children the cohabitee may inherit the entire property. If there is no will the cohabitee may apply for a sum from the estate by making a compensation claim on the estate of the deceased on the basis of the "enrichment" or "conditional" doctrines (see 2.b. above).

In 1986 the rules on inheritance duty were considerably relaxed. The duty on the inheritance received by a surviving cohabitee is the same low rate as applies to the children of the testator (but not the most favourable rate, which applies only to married couples). It is a condition for this reduced inheritance duty that the couple have been living together for two years[16]. If the surviving cohabitee does not fulfil this condition he or she is to pay inheritance duty at the highest rate.[17]

Official Policy and Reform Considerations

The reform considerations in Denmark are characterized by various viewpoints.

1. *Support of Marriage*. The Committee on Marriage stated in the Report No. 915 on Relationships without Marriage (of 1980) that marriage provides the best framework for family life and the best emotional and financial security for the individual members of the family. Therefore, it concluded that the basis of any reforms should be that no particular advantages should arise on living together without being married. This view is supported by the Report (No. 1084) on Equal Treatment of Relationships within or without Marriage published in 1986 by the committee appointed by the Danish Ministry of Social Affairs. Furthermore, the Committee on Marriage dissociated itself from introducing a complete legal adjustment of relationships without marriage, thereby creating a "second class marriage". This is due to the fact that such legislation would provide a false sense of security for the parties and be likely to discourage them from getting married.

2. There is political support for a gradual introduction of the *individual principle* within family and social law. This principle requires that the individual will only be granted support or achieve rights on the basis of his or her own circumstances. If future legislation departs from this principle, it should only be for a specified reason.

3. *Protective rules* have been introduced for the weaker party in an unmarried relationship in areas where married people are in a particularly strong legal position. However, these rules do not put cohabitees in the same favourable legal position as married couples. We have mentioned the possibility of achieving a reduction in the inheritance duty after two years' cohabitation, the policy of the courts in the case of compensation claims in the case of distribution of property and the proposal on the part of the Committee on Marriage for a general equity rule.

4. Administrative practice has in several cases *equalised* cohabitation with marriage. The Danish Marriage Act provides that maintenance from a former spouse ceases if the person receiving such maintenance remarries. The authorities then administratively introduced a similar rule for cohabitation, as the maintenance amount is reduced to zero if a person receiving such maintenance establishes a cohabitation relationship.[18] (It can also be mentioned that a number of social benefits for children cease if a single parent establishes a cohabitation relationship).

Conclusions

There appear to be mutually conflicting trends within the various spheres of law.

The Committee on Marriage published a policy statement that traditional marriage is to be supported, and it therefore opposes the introduction of a "second class marriage". However, the need for protection of the weaker party within a cohabitation relationship has proved to be so urgent that legislators and courts have in a number of cases been compelled to intervene with protective measures. This is due to the special type of exploitation which can arise from relationships combined with the special obligations which the parties are assumed to have towards each other as a consequence of the relationship. Therefore a set of rules for a "second class marriage" is gradually being constructed, "by underhand means". Side by side with this is a trend within social law for the introduction of an individual principle (supplemented by a household principle in special cases). As a consequence of the present tightening of public spending budgets, the implementation of the individual principle may be expected to be made slowly. For example, if married persons within the large population group who are pensioners were to be given the same financial benefits as unmarried persons, a massive increase in public spending would be required.

It can readily be assumed that the two main principles mentioned within social law will be taken up within other spheres of law where a distinction is presently made between marriage and cohabitation relationships. The need for a revision of the legislation has proved just as urgent for relationships without a marriage licence as for relationships with a marriage licence. One of the key motives in the legislator's wish to "guide couples" into marriage has been the great advantage of the marriage licence as evidence in the allocation of rights. When the individual or household principle is introduced, this justification disappears. Seen in the long term it is likely that the rules on a "second class marriage" will be a transition process on the way to an individual or household principle within all spheres of law.

Notes

1. Statistiske Efterretninger 1987:1 (Statistical Information 1987:1) (Population and Choice) published by the Danmarks Statistik. In Sweden the figure is identical, whereas in the other Nordic countries the number is lower.
2. In 1984 the Danish Minister of Justice appointed a committee to investigate the situation of homosexuals in Danish Society. In 1986 an Act was passed — Act No.339 of 14th June 1986 - according to which the surviving partner in a homosexual relationship is to pay the same low inheritance tax as married spouses. Refer to Report No.1065/1986 re homosexuals and inheritance duty. The committee concluded its work on 25th January 1988 by publishing Report No.1127/1988 on the conditions of homosexuals. A majority of six members were against the introduction of an act on registered partnerships with the same basic legal effect as a marriage. A minority of five members were in favour of such an act. Three political parties who form a majority in the Danish Parliament introduced a Bill for the introduction of registered partnerships on 21st January 1988. In the spring of 1988 a Parliamentary election was called and the Bill is expected to be reintroduced in the new Parliament.
3. Subsection 2 of Section 18 of the Danish Personal Taxation Act.
4. In Bill no. L 251 of 6th April 1988 introduced by the Minister of Inland Revenue there is a proposal for a gradual increase of the low exemption for spouses so that spouses on and after the tax year 1992 have the same low exemption as unmarried cohabitees. See also Notice No. 1136/1988 regarding property tax from April 1988 submitted by a committee appointed by the Minister of Inland Revenue.
5. Cf. Subsection 2 of Section 16 of the Danish Act on the Legal Effects of Marriage.
6. If there are special reasons for this, a spouse may be awarded a sum from the other party's separate property in connection with a separation or divorce decree, cf. Section 56 of the Danish Marriage Act. This provision is applied frequently.
7. See Report No. 915/1980 "Samliv uden ægteskab" (Living together without marriage), pp. 123-24.
8. Section 8 of the Danish Law of Succession.
9. Subsection 2 of Section 17 of the Danish Law of Succession. However, in practice there is a possibility of avoiding such division if the heirs of the deceased spouse

consent to this. Such consent will normally be subject to the establishment of separate property in the new marriage and the existence of an irrevocable will and testament drawn up in favour of the children.

10. Report No.915/1980 "Samliv uden ægteskab", p. 130. In Norway a similar rule has been proposed where the requirement is only one year's cohabitation before the right to retain undivided possession ceases. See NOU 1980:50 "Samliv uten vigsel", pp. 57-60.

11. Subsection 2 of Section 10 of the Danish Personal Taxation Act.

12. See Report on the Equal Treatment of Relationships with and without Marriage within Social Legislation, No. 1087/1986, p. 84.

13. Section 12 of the Danish Act on Social Pension.

14. See the Report from the Danish Folketing 1987, columns 7179-7182.

15. However, the right to receive a pension does not apply if the marriage was contracted after the deceased spouse had achieved a certain age — 60 years (state pension.) or 65 years (rule established by a pension fund).

16. The legal position for cohabitees of opposite sexes is laid down in Circular of 2nd December 1986 of the Danish Taxation Authorities. (Re inheritance duty in the case of homosexual relationships, see note 2).

17. At the highest rate e.g., 40% duty is paid on an estate of DKK 100,000. The duty increases to 90% of amounts exceeding DKK 1 million ($154,000).

18. According to subsection 2 of Section 53 of the Danish Marriage Act the size of the amount may be altered by the authorities when circumstances are in favour thereof.

Chapter 30

Legal Protection of Elderly Consumers in the Philippines

Zenaida S. REYES   University of the Philippines
Law Center, Division of Continuing Legal Education

Concepts and Ideas About Consumer Protection

A. Concept of Consumer Protection in the Philippines

Consumerism, as popularly viewed in the Philippines, is very limited, for it merely involves price comparison and purchasing decisions of consumers. Consumerism is more than this. It is a multi-dimensional phenomenon. To quote a lecturer in "Consumer Initiates", consumerism may be looked at from the psychological perspective as a reaction to powerlessness as well as a sense of right; as an economic revolt and a move to organize action; and in simple management terms, as a critique of bad business practices.[1] Thus, consumerism becomes a movement of consumers seeking redress directed against the inequities and injuries caused by institutions/agencies, whether industrial or governmental, committed through deliberate corporate decision-making or culpable negligence.

Among others, the following causes give rise to consumerism in the Philippines: poor product design, dangerous and toxic substances, insufficient labeling or mislabeling, deceptive packaging, unredeemed guarantees and warranties, failure to service products after sales, irresponsible technology, taking advantage of children's and handicapped persons' ignorance and the gullibility of the elderly and uneducated.

According to one ILO study, "consumer protection" is an apparently new area of public concern. It is of concern to all buyers and users of consumer goods and services — albeit to varying degrees in relation to their economic situation and social environment. To those with a relatively high income who can benefit from a wide variety of choice of high quality goods and services, consumer protection is a rather marginal problem. To those with limited resources, consumer protection is a vital need. The ILO study concluded that in either case, the concept of simple justice demands that consumers should not be exposed to safety and health risks or unfair commercial practices against which they have no defense.[2] For Filipino consumers, including the elderly, consumer protection created high expectations of the improvement in their quality of life. The changes sought for cannot be quantified, as no study has been undertaken in this area. It may be concluded, however, that it will take some time for such improvements to materialize, for the government under the new Philippine President Corazon Aquino is attending to many political and socio-economic problems which they perceive need their immediate attention; thus, consumer protection has been overlooked, as usual.

B. Assumptions and Values Underlying Consumer Protection in the Philippines

Surveys have showed that the average Filipino consumer has a mean annual income of about ₱9,830 or $440.00.[3] On the other hand, the Philippine National Economics and Development Authority has reported that in 1986, people with a monthly income of less than some ₱2,600.00 or $130.00 are living in poverty.

Studies likewise show that Filipino consumers are highly literate. In 1970, 83% of those 10 years old or over, are able to read and write a single message in some language or dialect.[4] This high literacy rate is a reflection of the relatively high educational attainment of the Filipino population. However, this has not modified nor altered the culture of Filipinos as far as family ties are concerned. A consumer advocate wrote in her studies on Filipino families that they usually live with another family including in-laws and cousins. This extended family in one household, especially among the poor consumers, is the family's economic salvation.[5] This extended family concept still continues.

In the Philippines, consumers can be classified by income and by region, there being four regions in the country. If one considers the income of consumers in these regions, there are more consumers living below the poverty line of ₱2,600 or $130/month. These are the consumers who have no motivation to improve their quality of life through consumer protection, for their primary objective is their next meal.

Records of the Bureau of Trade Promotions and Consumer Assistance in the Department of Trade and Industry show that there are only seven consumer groups recognized as legitimate consumer organization.[6] There are some pseudo-consumer organizations with purposes other than protecting the interests and welfare of Filipino consumers, much less the elderly ones. The members of these recognized consumer organizations are generally volunteers who are in the professions. This confirms the prevailing opinion among Filipinos that consumerism is only for the elite or for those who have nothing to do in life. The ordinary Filipino consumer does not have the time or the desire to work for his own protection against hazardous drugs and other products, mislabeling, fraudulent advertisement, and other deceptive trade practices. Consumer protection is left entirely to the few government agencies implementing special consumer laws and to private consumer organizations.

Overview of Consumer Protection

A. The Structure and Main Features of Consumer Protection in the Philippines

In the Philippines there are some government bureaus, offices or agencies designated to implement laws, rules and regulations primarily for the protection of the consumer irrespective of his age. Only the two most important executive departments will be discussed.

Among the important government agencies involved in consumer protection is the Department of Trade and Industry. There are two important bureaus in this department. The Bureau of Trade Promotions and Consumer Assistance, which promotes domestic trade and commerce, monitors the prices of prime commodities, enforces the laws on mislabelling, fraudulent advertisment and monopolies and other combinations in restraint of trade, and attends to consumer education and consumer complaints. There is also the Product Standard Agency, which establishes standards for all agricultural, mineral, industrial and other products to safeguard the life and safety of Filipino consumers.

The other important department is the Department of Health. There is the Bureau of Food and Drugs, which administers the Food, Drug and Cosmetic Act, and analyzes, inspects and establishes standards for food, drugs and cosmetics. There is likewise the Dangerous Drugs Board which, among other things, promulgates rules and regulations on the manner of safekeeping, disposition and condemnation of dangerous drugs, develops educational programs and disseminates information on the hazards of dangerous drugs, as well as conducting scientific, clinical, psychological, physical and biological researches on dangerous drugs.

There is also the Monetary Board of the Central Bank which regulates credit and financing to protect the economic interests of consumers.

Side by side with the government agencies implementing special consumer protection laws are the few non-governmental consumer organizations which undertake steps and adopt measures to reduce the imbalance between suppliers of goods and services on one hand and the consumer on the other hand.

B. General Areas of Concern About Legal Protection of Filipino Consumers

The participants in the First National Consultative Conference of Consumers held in Manila on October 29, 1986 were optimistic about the future of consumer protection because the consumer movement was moving unitedly towards economic nationalism.[7] One speaker at the Conference, however, expressed concern over the existing legal protection of Filipino consumers. One area of concern was that consumers were not receiving correct information since advertising and marketing practices of companies are misinforming consumers.[8] A second was that Filipino consumers have very little purchasing power. They have no power to influence the market and therefore, cannot translate their needs into the demands in the market place.[9]

Another urgent concern of consumers in the Philippines, is the state of implementation of consumer protection laws. Experience shows that there are many cases where there is a large gulf between laws intended to protect the consumer and their implementation, generally leaving consumers with a sense of frustration, diminishing their belief in the legislative process and the sincerity of the executive departments of the government. Failure to enforce laws is frequently due to lack of knowledge, and sometimes due to lack of funds. Additionally, many of these laws are out of date and need to be amended.

Problems and Issues Related to Legal Protection of Elderly Consumers

A. Policy Issues

The International Organization of Consumer Unions and its member organizations have espoused the eight rights of consumers all over the world. These rights are: the right to health and safety, the right to be informed, the right to choose, the right to be heard, the right to be compensated for injuries suffered, the right to consumer education, the right to a clean environment and the right to the basic necessities of life.

While these rights are all equally important, some are more relevant and urgent to elderly Filipino consumers than others. For instance, the enforcement of the following rights given the present socio-economic conditions of the country is imperative for the elderly consumers: the right to health and safety, the right to be informed, the right to choose, the right to be heard, and the right to the basic necessities of life. Elderly consumers, according to a classification made by the Bureau of Census and Statistics are citizens over 65, and these constitute 10% of the population according to a 1980 survey.

Obviously, the members of the Constitutional Commission which drafted the Philippine 1986 Constitution, ratified by the people on 2 February 1987, recognize the rights of elderly consumers. Several specific provisions were included in the Constitution that will protect their interests and welfare. In the area of health, the new Constitution mandates that: "the state shall adopt an integrated and comprehensive approach to health development which shall endeavor to make essential goods, health and other social services available to the people at affordable cost. There shall be priority for the needs of the underprivileged, sick, *elderly*, disabled women and children....".[10]

As regards educational policy the Constitution reads: "provide *adult* citizens, the disabled, and out-of-school youth with training in civics, vocational efficiency, and other skills".[11]

Another constitutional mandate of equal importance is the government's policy on social security for the elderly: "The family has the duty to care for its elderly members but the State may also do so through just programs of social security".[12]

The State's policy on the protection of elderly consumers in the Constitution is not self-executing. The newly elected members of the Philippine Congress must enact laws to implement this policy. At present, specific bills on the subject have yet to be filed in Congress, despite the appointment of a representative of the elderly in Congress by the Philippine President.

B. Inadequacy of Present Structure and Legislation

In recent years, the recognition of the basic rights of the consumer has been the subject of nongovernmental consumer organizations' campaigns. The elderly consumers' interests, however, have not been singled out as a primary concern.

The extended family culture of the Filipinos, wherein the elderly relatives, parents, aunts, uncles and even in-laws, live with and are supported by the younger generation explains the lack of motivation for the elderly to secure better conditions. Likewise, due perhaps to lack of necessary information on the existing State policy of giving priority in health development and social services to the elderly, elderly consumers do not realise the importance of seeking better standards of protection and assistance from the government.

For a small developing country like the Philippines, the 10,000 various pharmaceuticals of different brand names available on the market are too many and too confusing even for younger consumers. It becomes more difficult for the elderly consumer to obtain and understand information regarding the drugs they need, where to obtain them, and how to use them. A study on the use of drugs by the elderly and the nature of the existing special drug labelling for them, if any, has yet to be addressed by the government.

A look at the Capsule Summaries of Health Issues for 1987 prepared by a government agency [13] shows that the health care problems of elderly consumers was not considered as a separate issue. It is simply assumed that the elderly consumer's health is subsumed in all the issues enumerated in the capsules summaries.[14] For elderly consumers, there is something wrong with a health medical system in which they have to go to several hospitals or medical centers for health care problems and at a cost far beyond that which ordinary wage earners can afford. While their everyday needs may be attended to, whether in a satisfactory manner or not, by their immediate kin, their medical care costs, which are very high in the Philippines, should be within their reach and/or free for the very poor.

At present, there are special laws concerning information/warnings about certain products.[15] One law requires information about the brand name, manufacturer's name and complete address, chemical composition of the product, and its net weight and penalizes failure to provide this information.

458 LEGAL PROTECTION OF ELDERLY CONSUMERS IN THE PHILIPPINES

Another requires warnings to be placed in large bold letters on any product containing hazardous substances which will make the product highly irritant, corrosive, inflammable, toxic, or very hazardous to the health and safety of children and elderly consumers.[16] Yet another requires the placing of price tags or labels on all articles/products sold retail and requires that the articles be sold without discrimination to all consumers.[17]

As mentioned above, the elderly are now represented in the Philippine Congress, pursuant to a specific provision of the new Constitution.[18] The President, using the authority given her under this Constitutional provision, has appointed one representative of the elderly or senior citizens[19] to the House of Representatives. Hopefully, this representative will introduce draft legislation which will fully promote the interests and welfare of elderly consumers.

It is not enough simply to pass appropriate laws. Remedies for violations of rights acquired under such laws and regulations are essential. Many impoverished elderly consumers suffer deprivation because of lack of available, speedy, inexpensive and effective remedies. In the absence of any legislation, the only measure available to them when aggrieved is to bring their problems to the concerned government agencies and wait for some assistance, which in many cases takes too long to come. It is unfortunate that nothing concrete has been undertaken in the area of remedies for aggrieved consumers of any age. The infrastructure needed may only become a reality if Congress produces some action/bills on this problem.

The importance of consumer information and education, especially to the elderly and uneducated, cannot be gainsaid. Private consumer organizations are active in this field. It is obvious, however, that their activities can only reach and affect consumers attending their programs which are few and far apart and generally held in urban areas, usually in Manila. Therefore, little positive result can be expected from their information and education programs. Consumer information and education can be better and more efficiently undertaken by government agencies through their regional offices. Moreover, they can categorize their projects or programs into various levels, one of which can be for adult/elderly consumer information and education.

C. Impact of Such Problems and Issues on Individuals and Society

As a result of the inadequate legal structures and measures on consumer protection for the elderly consumers in the Philippines, there is really little protection — institutional or otherwise. In a country with an ailing economy or in any third world country with small resources, for that matter, essential goods and services are unfairly distributed and at prices beyond the reach of most consumers. Elderly consumers, whose primary problems are related to their health and nutrition, medical care, housing and recreation are the worst victims of these circumstances.

To make the situation worse, the Philippines suffers high unemployment. The National Census and Statistics Office announced that as of April 1986, 2.7

million Filipinos were out of work. And the figure will be higher if the underemployed are added. Even the actual need for food cannot be met in Manila. Prices of basic commodities and services remain high while the income of consumers has not risen. Basic social services for consumers, elderly or otherwise, that will make up for low income, are slow to be established by the government. But it is the majority of the elderly who suffer most since their basic needs can hardly be met by their families, due to unemployment or low income.

Further, legal protection for elderly consumers does not work in the abstract. It must relate to the reality of the market in the Philippines. The government must promote competition and prohibit monopolies and other restrictive practices. This will help to lower the prices of basic commodities and may ensure that goods and services are fairly distributed throughout the country, not only in Manila, and at prices within everybody's reach.

Perspectives and Future Possibilities For Better Legal Protection of Elderly Consumers

A. Consumer Protection Reforms in the Philippines

At present, there are several consumer-oriented Bills sponsored by several members of the lower House of Congress as well as in the Senate. They cover the following topics: the declaration of a national drug policy; the creation of a consumer protection administration; requiring the use of general names for drugs, encouraging the purchase of pharmaceuticals in bulk to lower drug prices, regulating the retail prices of drugs; nationalizing the drug industry; regulating advertizing and adopting a Consumer Code of the Philippines.

The primary objective of laws to protect consumers is to establish a policy dealing with relationships between businessmen and their clientele, between the organization man and the individual. Consumers will be better protected if the principles endorsed in the laws enacted for their protection can set the tone of the market place so that businessmen will be more alert to meet consumers' needs, more honest in business deals, disallow fraudulent or deceitful advertizing, and provide legal remedies to aggrieved consumers. In other words, the rule is for laws that will in the long run change the attitude of those who operate business and industry, so that they will deal with their customer in a more humane manner.

Only one or two of the above-mentioned bills now pending in the Philippine Congress may be expected to make legal protection of consumers, elderly or otherwise, more of a reality than an ideal. The proposed Consumer Code of the Philippines being sponsored as a Senate bill and soon to be subjected to a second reading was actually drafted and updated by the auther in 1976 and in 1985, respectively, for the University of the Philippines Law Center and the

Consumers Federated Groups of the Philippines, Inc. The initial draft was submitted for public hearing in the four regions of the country. In 1976, the update of the draft was a corroborative effort of the auther and the heads of agencies implementing consumer protection laws. It is hoped that this proposed Consumer Code has integrated provisions protecting the rights of the elderly consumers in the area of health and safety, economics, legal redress, consumer information and education, and opportunity to be heard.

B. Strategies for Law Reforms

Elderly consumers must organize themselves and work hand in hand with the elderly's representative in Congress towards the adoption of elderly consumer-oriented policies and Bills. Research has to be undertaken to determine the needs of elderly consumers. For instance, what are their needs relative to the laws on labeling and packaging, the pricing of drugs and medical care services, fraudulent and deceptive advertizing and unconscionable and unfair sales practices?

Notes

1. Sheila Harty, "Consumer Initiatives for Public Health, Workers Safety and Product Quality," a lecture series delivered at University College, Cork, Management Department, Faculty of Commerce, Spring 1983.
2. International Labour Office, Geneva, *Study Guide on Consumer Protection: A New Field of International Concern*, E-0091-1:6.
3. The Survey of Households' Family Income and Expenditures of the National Census and Statistics, estimate in 1979.
4. Eduardo L. Roberto, "Profile: The Filipino Consumer," July 1982, *Occasional Papers* No. 4, Asian Institute of Management, Makati, Metro Manila, Philippines.
5. Aida Sevilla Mendoza, *Study on Four Middle-Income Metro Manila Families*.
6. Consumers Federated Groups of the Philippines, Inc., Consumer Movement of the Philippines, Inc., Citizen Alliance for Consumer Protection, Inc., and Church-based Consumer Movement, Consumer Movement of Negros Occidental, Consumer Movement of Davao, United Consumer Association.
7. Dangan — *Consumers Journal*, Vol. VI, No. 1, First Quarter 1987, p.19.
8. Id, *The State of the Filipino Consumers* by Ma. Theresa Diokno, p.7.
9. Id, p.9.
10. 1987 Philippine Constitution, Article XIII, Social Justice and Human Rights, Sec. 11 Health.
11. Id, Article XIV, Education, Science and Technology, Sec. 1 Culture and Sports, Sec. 2, Education, Par. 5.
12. Id, Article XV, The Family, Sec. 4.
13. Department of Health Capsule Summaries of Health Issues and Background Briefing for Legislatures on Health Issues, June 7, June 29, 1987.
14. Issues addressed in the Department of Health's Capsule Summaries of Health

Issues, include: Immunization, Tuberculosis, Malaria, Schistosomiasis, Nutrition Program, Diarrheal diseases, Respiratory Infection, Maternal Care, Family Planning, Leprosy and Cancer.

15. Act. No. 3740, took effect on November 22, 1930 and prohibits and penalizes fraudulent advertizing, mislabeling and misbranding.
16. Presidential Decree No. 881, took effect in January 30, 1976, and empowers the Secretary of Health to regulate the Labeling, Sales and Distribution of Hazardous Substances.
17. Republic Act No. 71, took effect on November 21, 1946.
18. The Philippine 1987 Constitution, Article VI, Legislative Depa;rtment, Sec. 5(2).
19. "Elderly" is classified by the Executive Department as one whose age is 65 years or older.

Chapter 31

The Delivery of Legal Assistance to the Elderly in the United States

Nancy COLEMAN   Director, American Bar Association, Commission on Legal Problems of the Elderly

The Need for Legal Help

There are increasing numbers and percentages of the older people in our society who, by virtue of their age and increasingly failing health, are in need of legal assistance. There are well over 700,000 attorneys in the United States, but few of them are aware of the legal needs of the elderly. In proportion the elderly are the greatest beneficiaries of administrative services and government benefit programs. All of these have different eligibility rules and regulations which are more easily accessed with the help of advocates or lawyers.

Increasingly the elderly are the subject of "diminishing" capacity through their increased frailty. The issues around health care and surrogate decision-making lead to a greater need for help by the legal profession. Planning for incapacity for legal, financial and health care issues has become a way to avoid some of the involuntary court and administrative agency interventions which guardianship and civil commitment might take. Attorneys might be able to help older people plan for incapacity before involuntary actions are necessary.

In 1979 the American Bar Association (ABA) created a special entity within the association to focus on the legal problems of the elderly. This entity is interdisciplinary and draws on the expertise of physicians, social workers, gerontologists, representatives of aging advocacy organizations and attorneys. This group has the responsibility of educating the bar and doing research at the edge of the law and policy. In educating the bar we seek to have the ABA take policy, positions on such issues as non-acquiesence in social security cases, sanctions for enforcement of nursing home regulations, standards for the ways in which guardianship cases should be handled, as well as teaching lawyers about the substance of the law as it affects older persons. We do research, publish our findings, attempt to train the members of the bar and judiciary, and work within the legislative and regulatory arena. As an interdisciplinary group, we bring the best of what both the gerontological community and the legal community have to offer.

The areas of the law in which we work are: 1) Social Security due process: that is the process of assuring access to benefits rather than the political process which increases the benefit levels: 2) age discrimination: 3) guardianship and protective services where we have worked to educate the bar and the judiciary about how the courts can be more sensitive to the needs of the elderly: 4) long-term care where we have developed model legislation for assisted housing, and currently have a project to develop standards to assure the autonomy of frail older people living in their own homes who need home health care: 5) housing: and 6) the development of legal assistance, which is the main topic of this chapter.

American attorneys have served elderly clients in a variety of settings throughout the U.S. However, they have not necessarily addressed the particular problems presented by frail, vulnerable and poor clients. Studies by the Boston Bar Association as early as 1975 and by the Legal Services Corporation in 1979 have found that the poor elderly are a very underserved population. As described earlier, this population has many legal problems and for the most part has not had a history of seeking legal advice. When older people are asked whether they need legal help they often identify problems of income security, health care, or housing as having greater priorities without making the linkage that seeking legal advocacy might assure access to the needed services.

Publicly Funded Legal Programs

A. Federal Programs

1. Legal Services Corporation

The establishment in 1975 of the Legal Services Corporation (LSC) came about because of a concern that the poor in the United States were not being served by the private bar and thus did not have adequate resources to beneficially access the justice system.

The Legal Services Corporation grew out of the War on Poverty Program started by President Lyndon Johnson in the 1960s. LSC is a quasi-governmental entity. It receives an appropriation from Congress annually but has a presidentially appointed Board of Directors who oversee the program. The Board and a central staff monitor and fund local programs throughout the country. In addition they fund twelve national support centers to help with litigation and training. One of the national support centers focuses entirely on the elderly, the National Senior Citizens Law Center, while the others work in areas like healthcare, consumer and welfare law. The LSC programs do not necessarily specialize in serving older clients but do attempt to meet the legal needs of the poor, of which the elderly are a large proportion. Legal services provided by LSC attorneys are given to people based on financial need. Eligibility is based on 125% of the yearly established poverty level. However, as the Legal Services Corporation's own Research Institute pointed out in its 1979 study, the elderly were an underserved population, and special outreach programs were needed to be designed to reach the isolated and vulnerable elderly who did not find their way to the LSC offices. Many elderly who are underserved did not know about LSC nor could others get out of their nursing home beds to go to an attorney.

At its height, before President Reagan cut its budget and tried to abolish it, the legal services program had more than 700 offices throughout the country and was staffed by over 3000 attorneys in addition to paralegals, volunteers and support staff. The predominate method of delivery used by LSC projects is the staff-attorney model. Attorneys are trained in poverty law issues, and provide advocacy to their clients through direct representation. The elderly poor continue to be served by the LSC programs despite the numerous cutbacks. In 1981 President Reagan attempted to abolish the Corporation but only achieved a 25% cutback which, with inflation, in 1988 without any increase in the budget amounts to almost a 40% cut.

LSC attorneys do their primary representation of the elderly in government benefit cases such as Medicare, Social Security, food stamps and public housing. The types of cases in which the LSC might represent the elderly are in housing, consumer issues, such as enforcing home improvement contracts or credit issues, and some health care issues.

2. Older Americans Act

The second federal program funding the delivery of legal assistance to the elderly is the Older Americans Act (OAA). Originally adopted in 1965, a change was made following the 1971 White House Conference on Aging to include legal services during the 1975 reauthorization as a service that could be provided by local providers of legal services.

The structure of the Older Americans Act differs greatly from LSC. Although funded by Congress, an entity that is a sub-unit of a large federal bureaucracy allocates funding to state entities which in turn fund local entities which in turn fund legal services. One of hundreds of services that OAA funds can be used for is legal representation. Competing services are nutrition programs, transportation, health care, recreation and many others. What services are funded at a local level is determined annually by the local political process. Despite the fact that the OAA contains a provision which makes legal representation a required service, no specific dollar amount or percentage has been set aside for this purpose. Those organizations which want to provide legal assistance must apply annually for the funding.

Despite the barriers created by the legislation and the local political process, over 600 legal programs exist throughout the country attempting to meet the legal needs of those elderly who are in the greatest social and economic need.

This targeting of services is needed since the allocation of OAA money to legal services is so small. The theory behind the OAA has been that, despite differing income levels, most older people are isolated, and because of increasing frailty all should be served. There is no means test for programs offered under the Act. Many of the legal programs, perhaps as high as 60%, which receive OAA funding, are the local LSC grantees as well. The remainder are composed of free standing programs or contracts with private attorneys.

OAA funded programs are often different from LSC projects in that the former do a great deal of outreach to the elderly community. OAA funded attorneys often spend as much as 50% of their time speaking at senior centers or nutrition sites and visiting nursing homes or people in their own homes. Programs specialize in government benefits as well as surrogate decision-making (guardianship and protective services) and health care.

Many of the local agencies who fund legal services with OAA monies require programs to do wills and community education. These two areas are good for encouraging local private practitioners to join the program to do *pro bono* work. *Pro bono* projects will be discussed later but I want to indicate here that the political process for determining what a local provider of legal assistance does may determine the extent of law reform or the number of cases which are brought against public agencies in a community. If the funding agency only wants the legal assistance programs to provide wills and community education rather than public benefits, then the elderly will suffer. The current provider may loose interest in these issues and so will not seek a grant the next year. This change in provider may result in a loss of services to the elderly.

The Old Americans Act also requires that each state fund a legal services developer to assure that the legal needs of the elderly are being met. This is an employee of the state aging department or another agency who has a contract with the state agency. In some states the person will act as a general counsel to the state department for the elderly while in others the person may encourage continuing legal education programs or work with the local agencies to ensure that enough funding is being provided for programs to meet the legal needs of the state elderly population. In addition, as in the case of the LSC Act, the OAA requires that national support be provided. The federal agency, the Administration on Aging (AOA) contracts with three entities to provide this support: the National Senior Citizens Law Center (also the LSC national support center): Legal Counsel for the Elderly, a part of the American Association for Retired Persons (the largest older persons organization in the U.S. with 28 million members): and the American Bar Associations' Commission on Legal Problems of the Elderly. AOA also funds other national and local legal assistance demonstration projects.

B. State and Local Support

In some locations throughout the United States, state and local jurisdictions may add funding to projects providing legal assistance. This supplemental funding allows local programs to meet more adequately the legal needs of the elderly. For instance, the California legislature last year considered a supplemental funding allocation which would have provided enough money for California's forty programs which serve the elderly to have at least a minimum level of funding. This did not pass but already has been re-introduced.

1. Filing Fees

Four states have programs which provide funding for legal assistance programs through a mandatory filing fee which is added to all or some specific types of cases whose attorneys seek court jurisdiction. Massachusetts, Ohio, Wisconsin and Oregon supplement the federal funding of legal assistance in this manner. Florida, Georgia, Arizona, and Nevada allow local jurisdictions to add filing fee surcharges for legal services. None of these states however targets specifically the elderly as beneficiaries of this additional funding allocation. Although filing fee programs have a potential to generate income, they do not come near to that of the Interest on Client Trust Funds.

2. Interest on Client Trust Funds

Interest on Client Trust Funds (IOLTA), as a method of collecting funds for the provision of legal assistance, is a rather new concept. Attorneys are required to secure client trust funds but because of their ethical obligations they cannot derive the interest income that accrues from such funds. Because attorneys and law firms have pooled their client trust funds it has been difficult in the past to attribute interest to any given client. With the use of computers this problem is less difficult. However usually banks were the recipients of the income. In the late 1970s the Florida and California bar associations began the processes of establishing administrative entities which could pool the interest and distribute it for charitable purposes. In general IOLTA funds were to be used for providing civil or criminal legal services for the poor and education of the bench and bar. Early law suits to contest the mandatory nature of such confiscation of client interest have been rejected by the courts. (*Cone v State Bar of Florida*, 819 F. 2d. 1002 (11th Circuit 1987)). Not all of the programs have been mandatory as in the Florida case.

Forty-seven states and the District of Columbia have approved programs as of the end of 1987. All but three of these are operational. It is estimated that between $42-45 million was raised last year from such programs. Last years' Legal Services Corporation budget was just over $300 million. So the amount raised by the IOLTA programs can go far to meet the unmet needs.

Each state has its own method for distributing the funds. In California, established programs receive a set percentage of the amount raised each year. New programs can apply for funding and will be considered if additional funding is available.

Many of the IOLTA programs are voluntary. At its February 1988 Meeting, the American Bar Association passed a resolution suggesting that IOLTA programs should be mandatory in order to raise funds for charitable purposes. In voluntary states too much money is spent to recruit and re-recruit volunteers to the program. The ABA argued that the funds could be better used to provide more legal services for the poor. Only the California IOLTA program specifically allocates funds for those programs serving the elderly. This is an area for potential growth in supporting the legal needs of the elderly.

The Private Bar

A. American Bar Association

The American Bar Association is the largest voluntary professional organization in the United States. The ABA's 325,000 members have taken policy positions since the early 1970s to encourage the delivery of legal services to the poor and the elderly through active support of the Legal Services Corporation and the Older Americans Act. Entities within the Association monitor the actions of the LSC and work to support Congressional actions which increase funding to assure that adequate numbers of attorneys are available to meet the legal needs of the poor.

The ABA has many Sections and entities whose substantive law concerns touch the lives of the elderly. The Tax, Real Property, and Probate, Administrative Law, Individual Rights and Responsibilities, Senior Lawyers, Young Lawyers, Tort and Insurance Practice, Judicial Administration Division and Science and Technology Sections all have jurisdictions which address issues affecting the elderly. The Commission, described earlier, attempts to act as an advocate for older persons within the association.

B. Committees of State and Local Bar Associations

There are 35 state and 12 local bar association committees on the elderly. Some of these are free-standing, while others are sub-committees of other state or local bar entities. These entities have largely been established through the staff efforts of the ABA's Commission on Legal Problems of the Elderly. As voluntary activities of the members of such committees, the programs and projects vary as to the initiative and commitment of the leadership. The State Bar of Maine recently established a Section on the Elderly because it considered that a Committee was limited to just a few active members and the problems of the elderly were such a growing issue that as many members of the Maine bar as wanted should be able to participate in activities to benefit older people in their state.

Bar committee membership is usually limited to members of the Bar. In some jurisdictions some committees have followed the structure of the ABA Commission and have an interdisciplinary membership. Some committees have budgets which allow them to travel to meetings (allowing for regular meetings), put on seminars, and/or write and produce monographs. Activities vary from year to year as the leadership changes. Types of projects which might be undertaken are 1) the delivery of legal services: 2) community education: 3) continuing legal education: 4) legislation: and 5) substantive law issues.

1. Delivery of Legal Services

The State or local bar association may initiate programs or be the sponsor of a *pro bono* project or a reduced-fee lawyer referral project. Some committees sponsor specific kinds of *pro bono* programs such as a wills program where attorneys go to Senior Centers on a specific day and do wills. Other programs might designate a number of days where seniors can call for assistance in doing wills. Wills are the most common topic for such projects to specialize in. A few bar committees have done representation in nursing home cases, Social Security disability cases, and representation of the petitioners in guardianship cases. Local bar committees are better suited for this type of representation since they are more accessible to those whom they would seek to serve. The California Bar Committee recently completed a study of the availability of legal assistance which was instrumental in having legislation introduced.

2. Community Education

Bar Committees sponsor a variety of programs for the elderly to educate them about legal issues. The form of such efforts can be pamphlets, videotapes, handbooks, senior fairs, telephone advice lines, law day programs or lectures. These projects are relatively low budget and can give a bar association a great deal of good publicity for doing public service work.

a. Handbooks

The Metropolitan St. Louis Young Lawyers Association developed a handbook for the elderly in the late 1970s which has become the prototype for over twenty-five similar efforts in other states. There are short descriptions of the various government benefit programs, consumer law problems and issues raised about wills and estates. All of the handbooks are done in large print with illustrations and are generally printed in a pamphlet or booklet format. A list of state and local resources is included to help the older residents of that particular jurisdiction find legal as well as social service help.

The work is usually divided between the committee members with each person responsible for one topic. A project such as this should not take very long and can be very useful to seniors. It is easily updated as long as there is some way to finance reprinting. Often local banks, department stores or bar foundations are willing to pay for these costs as a public service.

Pamphlets are just a variation on the handbook. These can be done at a lower cost but are generally limited to one subject.

b. Law Day Programs

May is Senior Citizens Month in the U.S. and is usually designated so by Congress and the President, thus encouraging many activities in the community. Many bar associations have used this effectively with law day programs whether they are on May 1st or just some time during the month. In Dallas, Texas, where the seniors have a fair each year, booths are set up in a shopping mall where service providers hand out literature and discuss local services. The Young Lawyers add their booth and provide legal services. They may set up appointments to see an individual later to provide more legal help but the booth provides access to those who would not otherwise seek out attorneys.

One year another Texas bar association visited all the nursing homes in the area to give talks to the residents about planning for incapacity as a part of a law day program. Last year in California the Young Lawyers made an effort during the first week in May to visit senior centers using 158 attorney volunteers. 920 older people were helped.

c. Telephone Advice Lines

Some bar associations sponsor advice-only telephone hours. These types of programs help the caller to determine whether the problem is a legal one and what course of action should be initiated. Depending on the way such a program is advertised it could just be for certain substantive areas of the law or more general. It could be an on-going program or just a specified evening or week. The Los Angeles barristers designated a week in which they encouraged the elderly to call them on the phone through the bar association. They had a bank of phones and answered several thousand calls.

A variation of this advice-only theme could be a clinic once a month on Tuesday evening or Saturday mornings. In any case, attorneys sign-up for a period of time and provide the requested advice.

d. Lectures

The private bar is well suited to do outreach to the elderly through community education lectures at various senior centers, nutrition sites, elderly housing projects, retiree clubs, church groups or any other type of setting where older persons might congregate. Senior center directors are always looking for guest speakers and participants welcome talks from attorneys. The topics are generally set in cooperation with the speaker and the site director and time is given for questions. There is increased interest in the use of videos and slide/tape presentations to communicate legal issues to the elderly. Bar associations are using local television.

3. Continuing Legal Education

The need to educate the bar about the legal needs of the elderly is an ever-present challenge. The legal issues are complicated by the interaction of traditional estate planning, family law, and public benefits. The use of medical technologies which prolong life contribute to legal interventions which need thoughtful consideration. Continuing legal education (CLE) presented by state accredited programs have concentrated in the traditional disciplines of estate planning and family law. With the development of the Legal Services Corporation in the early 1970s courses in poverty law were given. Those who attended tended to be self-segregating as to the subjects they wished to study. In the late 1970s and early 1980s courses began to develop on law and the elderly. These, however, were sparsely attended generally by practitioners from a variety of backgrounds in the law although predominately from the legal services, or public bar. In the last few years we have seen an increasing number of people from both the public and private bar begin to take courses on "Estate Planning for the Elderly and Disabled" or "Planning for Disability".

Bar committees for the elderly have begun to sponsor continuing legal education seminars which attempt to bring together the traditional estate financial planning with the implications of using public benefits for long-term or nursing home care. With the cost of long-term care so high for client groups such as those with Alzheimers it becomes essential that families should not pauperize themselves in order to care for one member but rather have legal and financial advice as to how to protect the assets of the non-institutionalized spouse while providing adequate care for the disabled spouse. Circumstances such as these present attorneys with specific demands which necessitate preparation through CLE. The Commission has seen more than a dozen such programs sponsored by bar committees during the last couple of years. The desire for such training has been magnified by nationally sponsored courses, and tele-satellite where over 1200 people took the course on one day. However a better model is one which is based on particular state law, given the peculiar nature in the United States of the way in which property and estate laws differ.

There have also been other areas where bar associations have brought the public and private bar together to benefit the elderly. These include the use of Tort law to ensure quality of care in nursing homes, age discrimination in employment, the effects of plant closing or bankruptcies on pension and health care benefits for retired employees; ethical issues in determining who is the client when a family approaches the attorney for help when there might be some diminished capacity; and many more.

Bar association committees for the elderly have limitless possibilities for sponsorship of such programs and can bring many elements of the bar together to foster dialogue to better serve the elderly. The California Bar Committee recently held a seminar at twelve sites throughout the state on "Ethical Issues Raised in Serving Older Clients in Planning for Disability". Different committee members did the training at each site. Over 1500 attended the collective sessions. The Committee members were joined by probate and family attorneys in the local area of each training site.

4. Legislation

Bar committees for the elderly are an excellent place to work on state legislation. Guardianship reform had been a topic of the Florida, New York City Bar, California, Oregon, and the District of Columbia elderly committees during the last year. Through internal studies, education of probate and trust, family law, and judicial sections of bar associations, comprehensive approaches have been made. Legislators, who are often lawyers themselves, look to bar associations for positions and oftentimes for legislative drafting. The impact on legislation can be enormous from this type of effort.

Additional areas where bar committees have been working are in health care surrogate decision-making, living wills, nursing home reform, enforcement of quality of care standards in health care delivery, deceptive sales practices and insurance regulation. The list is limitless.

5. Substantive Law Reform

The Maryland Bar Committee for the Aged recently completed a study of nursing home admission contracts. Originally they had hoped to develop a model contract but found the task overwhelming and ended up suggesting clauses which gave rise to concern, and what the attorney and ultimately the consumer should know about the contracts. A copy of the analysis of what the study found, as well as a consumer pamphlet, are available from the State Bar of Maryland. A similar study done in California by a public interest group had already resulted in changes in state law. The nursing home industry in Maryland asked the bar association not to release the study because of the implications for changes that would have to be made, but the bar has gone forward and distributed the results widely to attorneys and consumers.

In Hennepin County, Minnesota, the bar committee there studied the conduct of attorneys who were representing proposed wards in guardianship cases. As a result of their study a series of recommendations were adopted by both the bench and the bar. Just as in the community and continuing legal education areas, the opportunities for bar associations to make contributions are limitless. The Commission on Legal Problems of the Elderly publishes two periodicals which attempt to encourage efforts of this nature: BIFOCAL, a quarterly and the *State Bar Bulletin*, which is published six times a year.

C. Pro Bono Programs

Since the early 1980s there has been a tremendous growth in the development of large scale *pro bono* programs. This has been fueled by the Legal Services Corporation's requirement that each of their programs spend 12.5% of their funds on private bar involvement and the Older Americans Act requirement that the local entities, area agencies on aging, work with the private bar. In addition the canons of professional responsibility require that each attorney meet an obligation to provide service to the public.

All of the LSC-funded projects have sought a working relationship with state and local bar associations to jointly sponsor *pro bono* programs. The legal service grantee usually trains attorneys, screens clients and acts as a resource for the private attorney about public-benefits law. In return, private attorneys generally take two to four cases a year free, depending on the nature of the cases. The programs and the bar associations work out the type of cases given to *pro bono* attorneys. Some cases may be wills, while others may be litigation seeking law reform. The City Bar of New York has asked that each attorney, whether in a law firm, a corporation or working for the government, spend at least 30 hours each year doing *pro bono* representation. The General Counsel for Exxon and former Secretary of State Cyrus Vance spearheaded the recruitment drive to assure a high level of participation.

One can always tell when a program has become institutionalized; it is when a national association is formed. Around a year ago the national association of *pro bono* coordinators formed an organization and now holds meetings.

The American Bar Association helped to foster the development of *pro bono* by providing technical assistance to bar associations, providing seed grants to programs in their infancy and by providing political clout to the development of such projects. When state or local bar associations might have been skeptical about the idea, or portions of the bar might think that their livelihoods might be in jeopardy, leaders of the ABA would appear on the local level to provide reassurance.

My Commission has just published a piece called PRO BONO SENIORIUM where we describe some of the projects specifically geared to serving the elderly throughout the country. These include a project in Connecticut sponsored by a major insurance company whose attorneys provide services to the elderly using the corporation's library, offices and van to serve clients in Hartford, Connecticut. The success in Hartford led this corporation to develop programs in other parts of the state where they had concentrations of attorneys.

The ABA's Senior Lawyers Section (a relatively new section whose members are over 65) is attempting to develop a cadre of retired administrative law judges to represent older people in Social Security hearings.

Pro Bono programs for the elderly as described in the SENIORIUM can either be a part of a larger *pro bono* program or stand by themselves. None of the *pro bono* programs will do away with the need for staff-based legal services programs. Despite the number of volunteer attorneys, the nature of public benefits law and the need for representation far exceeds the combined capacity of volunteers and staff-based programs to meet the need.

D. Reduced-Fee Programs

There are a great number of lawyer referral programs in the U.S. under which one can receive the names of a few attorneys by calling a bar association. There was an attempt a few years ago to develop sophisticated referral systems which would only refer attorneys who were experienced in very circumscribed areas of the law. The notion was that a person would call a referral number, be screened to determine the nature of the legal problem and then be given the name of lawyers who had also been screened to assure that they knew about the legal issues. This has only been proven to work in very large bar associations where people specialize in specific areas of the law. Attempting then to have an overlay specifically to provide reduced fees for the elderly has been a difficult proposition. The problem of screening fees is impossible unless a fee structure is set up ahead of time to assure that attorneys are simply not reducing the cost of writing a will from $100 to $95, for example.

Legal Counsel for the Elderly (LCE), a program of the American Association of Retired Persons, has put together a legal-help phone service in Pennsylvania and the District of Columbia. Callers reach an attorney who screens the calls for the legal problems and sees if simple telephone advice will suffice. If a referral is to be made the caller is told how much it will cost per hour with an estimate of how much the entire legal bill will be. If the senior goes to the referral lawyer a written contract is signed to let the elderly person know what will be done with the case and what the expected costs will be. The attorneys have agreed ahead of time with LCE as to what the per hour costs will be and the approximate total. LCE has set the rates at a considerable reduction of what the elderly or most others would be able to negotiate in the open market. Attorneys have been willing to participate in the program. The model anticipates that there will be a considerable number of referrals to a relatively small number of attorneys.

In 1980 the lawyer referral models were in a similar state of development to the *pro bono* models. The LSC funding and the support of the ABA have led the development of *pro bono* to far exceed that of reduced-fee lawyer referral. Perhaps the model developed by LCE can inspire reduced-fee programs in other parts of the country.

The Private Practice of Serving the Elderly

Older persons who have financial resources have always had access to the legal profession. Although close to 40% of those in the U.S. die intestate, the majority of the elderly seek out legal representation to write wills. To get one's life in order and to be able to leave one's few possessions is a goal of most older persons. The elderly generally have access to will drafting through LSC or OAA funded attorneys, the wills panels sponsored by bar associations and other private practitioners. Other legal problems may go unmet.

There is another specialized bar which has developed in the U.S. to serve older and disabled individuals with their Social Security problems. Attorneys fees are allowed in Social Security cases and thus a segment of the bar has a primary practice in this area. A national organization exists, the National Association of Social Security Claimants Representatives (NOSSCR), to provide training for attorneys interested in this area. The attorneys' fees paid in this area come from the back-award that a claimant receives. When legal services or *pro bono* attorneys do these cases the client receives the entire back-award. Representation in these cases gives clients a much better chance of any back-award and may continue payments into the future. The cost of losing some of the award by being represented is better than being denied eligibility for any award.

The Academy of Elder Law Specialists

In late 1987 a new group was incorporated known as the Academy of Elder Law Specialists. The purpose of this new organization is to meet the needs of the elderly whose financial resources exceed the services offered by publicly financed legal assistance programs. The hope of the Academy is to become a specialty similar to Matrimonial attorneys, where those who seek services will know that they will be served by experts in the field. There are well over 100 attorneys nationwide who specialize in this type of practice. They predominantly come from either legal services or estate planning backgrounds. An example of the type of work the attorneys do is comprehensive financial, legal, and health care planning with the families of Alzheimer's victims. It is the interplay between government benefit programs and estate planning that brings this specialty its base. However, additional sensitivity to the aging process, knowledge of community services and resources are critical to the success of the elder law specialist. Portions of the Academy membership have met over the last three years to discuss common problems, the economies of the law practice, and the formation of the organization.

Gaps in Services

A. The Middle Class

ABA President-Elect Robert Raven of San Francisco's Morrison & Forrester Law Firm has spoken over the last few months about the lack of access to legal assistance that many Americans have. Despite the LSC, many poor people go unserved. The poor at least have some type of program. The wealthy have access to the bar, but the middle-class cannot afford expensive litigation and do not have alternatives. Recognition of the existence of legal problems, just as for the elderly, is also not something with which most middle-class people have much familiarity. Whether we do it or not, most people recognize that there is a need to see a doctor on a regular basis, if for nothing else than a check-up. Most Americans do not recognize a similar need with respect to attorneys.

The American Bar Association has sponsored programs and demonstration projects to consider alternative means of delivery of legal assistance such as prepaid plans, clinics, lawyer referral programs, and alternative dispute resolution programs. Such programs have not vastly expanded the availability of legal assistance to the middle-class but all have some potential to do so.

B. Isolated and Vulnerable Persons

Frailty may isolate the elderly from society. Many may be great distances from their families, or they may have outlived family members. Outreach to this population is no different for the legal community than for the health care community. The apparent need for social services or health care interventions may be great, but self-evaluation may be lacking in all of the services.

States have begun to become more involved in the lives of isolated and vulnerable by providing interventions known as protective services modeled somewhat after the child abuse and neglect laws. Concern for this population has grown over the last few years and interventions have increased. These interventions might be to remove someone from their home or bring sevices to the client. It is unclear whether these are involuntary or voluntary services.

Social Service agencies may define the services as "good social work" or the civil rights activists might call it a form of non-adjudicated civil commitment. There may be a middle-ground but the intervention strategies need to include a discussion of what the legal consequences of involuntary interventions are and how civil liberties and rights can be maintained and people who may have diminished capacity can be "helped." This, I believe, is a real issue to be worked out between the social work and legal professions in the next few years. This borders on the areas of consent to treatment, civil commitment and guardianship, on all of which there is a great deal of case law.

Conclusion

The delivery of legal assistance to the elderly in the United States is varied and is full of gaps. Just as with most populations, few elderly seek out legal help except in time of crisis. The publicly funded programs are there to serve the economically needy but all the elderly need legal assistance because of their dependence on government benefit (income and health care) programs. The changes in health care technology and surrogate decision-making also increase the need for assistance. The bar, both public and private, is realizing the necessity to prepare for this very large proportion of the population. Hopefully in the near future the potential which is there to meet the legal needs of the elderly will be tapped.

Part Four

Medical Issues and Legal Responses

Introduction

by David PEARL

This part is divided into five sections. *Section One* is devoted to an overview by Dickens (Chapter 32) of all the issues which are developed in this part. He identifies the legal significance of geriatrics, illustrating how physicians and others are under an increasingly rigorous legal duty of care in prescription, explanation and monitoring of drug treatment for the elderly. A major question of course is that of capacity and third party decision making — two topics developed in later chapters in this part. Dickens ends the chapter on a note of caution. Legal rights cannot supply quality of existence. Rather, law and the machinery of law provide a medium to implement social policies. Nevertheless, the role of law is significant in that it can promote priorities and help to attain goals.

Section two is devoted to civil commitment. Hoggett (Chapter 33) examines the response of English common law and English legislation to the legal problems presented by adult incapacity. Compulsory intervention, in her view, should fall within the framework of the "least restrictive alternative," (See also Creyke, Chapter 35). She comments that the present English law is inadequate and she points the way to a new model. Interestingly, she believes that new tests should build upon the concepts developed for the "living will" and "enduring powers of attorney" (See Chapters 40 and 41). Diagnosis is always difficult in this area of civil commitment. Graversen and Pedersen (Chapter 34) in examining the position in Denmark make the point only too clearly. They concentrate on aphasia. This is an impediment of speech and linguistic contacts, but should this necessarily mean that legal capacity be limited? Graversen and Pedersen make the crucial point that civil commitment laws should be flexible. There are, of course, a number of different models. Creyke (Chapter 35) identifies the therapeutic model, the developmental model, and the legalistic model.

Respect for autonomy and self-determination operate in Canada as demonstrated by Shone (Chapter 36). Involuntary hospitalisation is only used in the severest of cases. The problem, of course, is one of identification. As we have seen from Dickens (Chapter 32), diagnosis is often faulty, and Shone wonders, for this and for other reasons, whether special legislation is in any event required.

The other chapters in this section concentrate on guardianship laws. Schulte (Chapter 37) provides an overview of the civil law jurisdictions in Europe.

There are clearly a number of trends which can be identified. First, and perhaps foremost, laws have been developed which emphasise the preventative approach, maximizing individual privacy and autonomy. Secondly, a rights framework has been emphasized by the legislation, and thirdly, there is a general trend towards what Schulte calls a "grades system" of guardianship. The reforms of the guardianship laws in the Federal Republic of Germany serve as an example of what has taken place elsewhere, and these are described in detail by Zenz (Chapter 38). The final chapter of this section by Hughes (Chapter 39) illustrates perhaps one of the more extreme examples of the rights approach, that is in Canada.

Section three opens with two chapters on the Enduring Powers of Attorney and the Living Will. Farrand (Chapter 40) examines the Enduring Powers of Attorney Act 1985 in England, and Rossettenstein (Chapter 41) describes the "state of the art" in the USA in relation to the "living will". As Dickens (Chapter 32) explained, these strategems reflect the fact that elderly people wish to retain maximum control over their personal and medical destiny. But there must always be, as pointed out by Dickens, a degree of caution. A climate must not be created whereby society expects that declarations be made.

Euthanasia and suicide are perhaps the most contentious of all topics in the area of autonomy. The question has been discussed in detail in the Netherlands both by courts and by a State Commission. Rood de Boer (Chapter 42) describes the current debate in that country. Wardle (Chapter 43) provides a detailed study of suicide amongst the elderly. His chapter reminds us of Shakespeare's words in Richard II (Act V scene 1): "*I wasted time, and now doth time waste me..*" It is this sense of isolation and desperation which often brings the elderly to the point where suicide is a viable option. A particularly important point made by Wardle is that in Taiwan and Japan in Asia, increased mobility and rapid economic development, have marked out the elderly in these two countries as vulnerable to suicide. Wardle's chapter and the accompanying tables, should be carefully studied.

The final section of this part, *Section four,* is concerned with the rights of the elderly. Modern science has produced some horrific problems. Some of these are traced by Rubellin-Devichi (Chapter 44). In one sense, this chapter is concerned with the concern of the community to enable the elderly to conceive, if only through artificial means. As she suggests, society is not quite ready to help the elderly in this way. She poses the question, which perhaps will only be answered over the coming decade, whether society should perhaps now be ready to concede this right.

The section ends with two chapters by British authors, one on elder abuse (Freeman, Chapter 45) and the other on the rights of grandparents to be in contact with their grandchildren (Douglas and Lowe, Chapter 46).

Freeman develops the theme identified by Dickens (Chapter 32). He suggests that abuse is in part a product of a failure to give equal respect and concern to the rights of the elderly. He compares elder abuse with child abuse, and hopes that the mistakes made in relation to the latter topic will not be repeated.

Maybe one way of preventing both pathologies would be to develop strategies to interlink the wider family; especially to enable grandchildren greater access to grandparents. This amalgamation of the generations is an important aim, and Douglas and Lowe (Chapter 46), in pointing to shortcomings in English legislation, have a valid message for all who are concerned to provide the elderly with a respected and honoured position within both the family and in society at large.

Section One

Medico-legal Issues

Chapter 32

Medico-Legal Issues Concerning the Elderly — An Overview

Bernard M. DICKENS,   Faculty of Law and
Faculty of Medicine,
University of Toronto, Canada

Introduction

The goal of "health" as perceived by the World Health Organization (W.H.O) is particularly difficult to realize regarding the elderly. The W.H.O. considers health to be not merely the absence of disease and infirmity but a "state of complete physical, mental and social well-being."[1] Health in this sense may be hard to achieve even by persons in the prime of life, but elderly persons are frequently characterized by their liability to illness and impaired physical, mental and social functioning. It must be remembered, however, that a level of performance that may represent pathology in a young person may be a mark of normal or superior capacity in a person of advanced years. Health is not an absolute condition but is assessed by reference to age and other circumstances. A relative scale may therefore be applied to measure whether the elderly's rights to health care are satisfied.

The elderly occupy an uncertain status in international human rights law. The Universal Declaration of Human Rights, adopted and proclaimed by the General Assembly of the United Nations (U.N.) Organization in 1948,[2] provides in Article 2 that:

"Everyone is entitled to all the rights and freedoms set forth in this Declaration, without distinction of any kind, such as race, colour, sex, language, religion, political or other opinion, national or social origin, property, birth or other status."

It may be claimed that, while it is not explicit, an obligation of non-discrimination on grounds of age is implicit in the phrase "birth or other status," but this is a residual category whose content is uncertain. The Preamble of the Universal Declaration observes that:

"... the peoples of the United Nations have in the Charter reaffirmed their faith in fundamental human rights, in the dignity and worth of the human person and in the equal rights of men and women and have determined to promote social progress and better standards of life in larger freedom."

The U.N. Charter itself discloses a narrower perception of human rights than does the Universal Declaration. In determining the Purposes of the U.N., Article 1 (3) of the Charter includes the purpose:

"To achieve international cooperation in slowing international problems of an economic, social, cultural, or humanitarian character, and

in promoting and encouraging respect for human rights and for fundamental freedoms for all without distinction as to race, sex, language, or religion ..."

It may be accepted that the Universal Declaration was intended to give substance to a wider vision of human rights than was the U.N. Charter, including the right to health care, but the two key international conventions that have been achieved to implement the Declaration, namely the International Covenant on Economic, Social, and Cultural Rights[3] and the International Covenant on Civil and Political Rights,[4] fail explicitly to exclude discrimination on grounds of age, or against the elderly. Article 2 (2) of the former Covenant repeats the language of Article 2 of the Universal Declaration. The omission of age from the expressly precluded grounds of discrimination may be understandable in that many and perhaps all of the parties to this Covenant prohibit the young from participation in their national labour forces through paid employment, and have legislation permitting or enforcing involuntary retirement at specified ages. Article 10 (3) of the Economic Covenant positively requires that:

"States should also set age limits before which the paid employment of child labours should be prohibited and punishable by law."

The protective purpose of laws against child labour is worthy, but such purpose in compulsory retirement laws is questionable. Rights to continued employment without regard to age are not protected by the Economic Covenant, although by Article 11 everyone is to be recognized as entitled to an adequate standard of living "for himself and his family," including adequate food, clothing and housing. The indication that this is a right of breadwinners and their families may by inference place at disadvantage those whose families are no longer dependent on their earning capacity. The provision in Article 25 that protects "the inherent right of all peoples to enjoy and utilize fully and freely their natural health and resources" applies to "peoples" rather than "persons"; that is, to collectivities rather than to individuals who may want to market their wealth of experience and resources of skill in paid employment.

Article 2(1) of the Civil and Political Covenant Similarly repeats the language of Article 2 of the Universal Declaration in which protection of the elderly against age discrimination is at best implicit. Sophisticated traditions of constitutional interpretation that have evolved particularly in the jurisprudence of the United States show that enumerated or specified rights are better secured than non-enumerated or unspecified rights, and accordingly it may be speculated that any right to non-discrimination on grounds of advanced age would be less rigorously protected than other specified non-discrimination rights. This would be true concerning, for instance, rights to health care without discrimination on grounds of advanced age, and rights to social welfare benefits. Article 2(3) of the Civil and Political Covenant provides for those claiming a violation of their rights to seek domestic remedies. This right may achieve less than it first appears to offer, because it is available only to "any person whose rights and freedoms are violated." The elderly may be more dependent than others on activists and non-appointed advocates who act on their behalf. Any implicit right the elderly enjoy to legal counsel may not extend to self-appointed, legally unqualified activists. Like other socially-disadvantaged groups, the elderly may find that activists on their behalf are frustrated by legal rules on *locus standi* or standing that obstruct the pursuit of justice through the courts. More detailed provisions will not be presented here to make the argument that the leading international human rights conventions afford the elderly little comfort that their protections against age discrimination have been an international priority or concern.

An obvious contrast exists between the elderly and such traditional victims of discrimination as racial minorities, women and the young. Reinforcing the Universal Declaration of Human Rights are the International Convention on the Elimination of All Forms of Racial Discrimination,[5] which entered into force in 1969, and the Convention on the Elimination of All Forms of Discrimination Against Women,[6] in force since 1981. The Declaration of the Rights of the Child[7] dates back to 1959, the Declaration on the Rights of Mentally Retarded Persons[8] to 1971 and the Declaration on the Rights of Disabled Persons[9] to 1975. Work is actively in hand to develop the Declaration on the Rights of the Child into an operable international convention. The lack of international action on behalf of the elderly, in pursuit of their rights to equitable allocations of health care resources and, for instance, employment opportunities, is striking.

National constitutions and national or regional human rights provisions may go beyond international law to offer guarantees of non-discrimination on grounds of age. In Canada, for instance, Section 15(1) of the Canadian Charter of Rights and Freedoms[10] explicitly governs discrimination "based on race, national or ethnic origin, colour, religion, sex, age or mental or physical disability." These guarantees can be significant where health services are a public responsibility, because elderly persons can complain before tribunals and courts with powers to compel remedies if they are found to have been unfairly treated.[11] Hospital policies such as not to undertake cardiac resuscitation on any patient exceeding a given age, without regard to the patient's clinical prognosis,[12] can be ordered withdrawn. Nevertheless even under such regimes compulsory retirement laws may be upheld, as exceptions, as not constituting discrimination, or as originating in agencies not governed by the anti-discrimination law, such as private-sector agencies.

Individuals often derive much of their self-esteem and status, as well as their economic security, from their employment. Their capacity to maintain employment contributes to their mental and social health, and loss of employment is often associated with a downturn in physical health. Compulsory retirement laws may have been related historically to advances in social security laws, and been perceived, presented and sincerely intended as a source of relief from the perhaps increasingly oppressive scourge of having to earn a living through stressful industrial toil.[13] Improved levels of health maintenance and nutrition, particularly in the developed world, have afforded those aged in their mid-sixties the physical ability to maintain job fitness, however, especially where mechanization has reduced dependency on their physical stamina and prowess. Lowered relative funding of social security and health services in more recent years has aggravated the plight and frustration of those legislated into unemployment and poverty while they have employable skills. This may prejudice their health both immediately and in the wider sense in which the W.H.O. perceives health.

It is increasingly recognized that health is conditioned by an interaction of physical, mental and social conditions and events. Bereavement affects health, for instance, because the social event of death of a loved one induces sadness and depression and a related loss of appetite, energy and immunity to infection. Psychosomatic explanations of causation of illness demonstrate how health and physical welfare respond to a wide range of social and, for instance, economic conditions that affect an individual. Further, explanations analogous to those offered for clinical illness are made at the epidemiological or public health level to explain the state of health of age-groups in a community. Indeed, public health and environmental factors may be shown to influence individuals' health no less than factors internal to the person. External factors and events may trigger individual genetic or other predispositions to illness, in the contexts of both physical and mental health. Accordingly, universal explanations of illness must be treated with considerable caution.

The Legal Significance of Geriatrics

The growth in the medical specialty of geriatrics parallels in some ways the growth of pediatrics. It was once supposed that children were in principle small adults. From early age such as seven they used to be regarded and, for instance, dressed as small-scale grown-ups, and medically treated as adults would be. This period preceded modern pharmacology, and the herbalists of the time addressed disorders of the young much as they treated disorders in those of greater age. With the development of scientific pharmacology and, for instance, neurology, it came to be seen that infancy, childhood and adolescence are distinctive medical conditions, and mark different stages of evolution of human physiology and neurology. Drugs are now customarily prescribed with a separate pediatric dosage range, to accommodate their different effects on the young.

In the same way that the young are no longer treated as adults who are small, the elderly are decreasingly being considered medically simply as adults who have survived a long time. They are recognized to possess distinctive physiological, psychological and, for instance, neurological characteristics that must be medically assessed in their own right. Their tolerance of and reactions to drugs, physical discomfort, noise and, for instance, forms of stimulation are seen to place them in a category different from that of the middle aged; they are coming to be divided *inter se* into the "old" and the "old-old." Pharmacologically, for instance, the elderly's different liability to toxic effects of drugs may soon lead to them having drugs presented with a geriatric dosage scale in contrast to the familiar pediatric dosage scale applicable to the young.

The elderly enjoy a considerable advantage over the young in the testing and development of drug therapies. The young may be disadvantaged because of legal and ethical limits to the types of testing that may be undertaken on them. Younger children cannot volunteer or consent to participate in drug research and parents may be unable to volunteer them for unusual risks, although no more than the level of consent necessary for therapeutic care may be legally required when a test product is proposed as novel therapy or therapeutic innovation;[14] this is undertaken on a therapeutic indication although data of its efficacy and safety will be of secondary interest for purposes of research. The elderly will usually be able, however, to volunteer to participate in research programmes intended to develop effective and safe drug therapies and dosage levels for the geriatric population.[15]

Evolving knowledge of geriatric pharmacology places physicians and other health care professionals under an increasingly rigorous legal duty of care in prescription, explanation and monitoring of drug treatment of the elderly. It has been estimated that up to 20 percent of hospital admissions of geriatric patients in Canada are for adverse drug reactions or errors in drug dosage.[16] Beyond professional errors in prescription of medications are errors in drug compliance or self-administration by the elderly themselves against which they must be warned and perhaps protected. People who are forgetful may omit to take their drugs on time, and then take additional make-up doses later, with the risk of self-inducing toxicity and endangering themselves by over-medication. As against this, those fearful of powerful drugs may reduce the dosage they take for reasons of "safety," and thereby deny themselves effective care. Health professionals dealing with the elderly must be alert and responsive both to their special physiology, particularly where drugs are concerned, and to their predictable personality traits. They risk legal liability, for professional malpractice or negligence in disregarding what they are legally required to know and apply in geriatric care.

Medical and related health care must be adjusted to accommodate the characteristics and problems of advanced age. The elderly should not be measured against or be expected to maintain the behaviour of their earlier lives. It has been seen that reduced capacity to function is not necessarily a measure of sickness in the elderly. Similarly, mental health conditions such as depression and memory-loss may reflect affective traits and cognitive deficits that are symptomatic of normal function in the elderly. Medication and coercive treatments, perhaps administered involuntarily under mental health legislation, may be inappropriate and contraindicated. Approaches may be better pursued through providing social and psychological opportunities rather than through seeking pharmacological pathways to improved mood and functioning. The effects of isolation, perhaps aggravated by declining eyesight and hearing, may explain the medical status of the elderly, which can also be described by reference to reduced levels of interactive behaviour.

Psychosomatic causes of physiological effects in the elderly often have to be considered. A physically disabling feeling of loneliness or isolation, associated perhaps with the generation gap and evolution of a popular or youth culture the elderly find alienating, may be approached by providing suitable companionship. It may be more difficult to redress the elderly's loss of social standing and of utility. In traditional societies the elderly may possess a store of relevant experience that earns respect for their wisdom, but, particularly following rapid technological growth and social change, they may have less relevant experiences. They may seem unworthy of consultation on matters of contemporary significance.

This depressing lack of the esteem of others may be aggravated in widows, whose experiences of life may have been more limited than their husbands' and whose social status may have been dependent on and derived from their husbands' positions. The poverty the elderly commonly experience, particularly women, related in part to the impact of inflation on financial savings put away years before and unemployment with a modest pension following compulsory retirement, may be associated with poor nutrition, poor housing and heating, apprehension about the future, anger and depression. These factors may have a bearing on emotional and physical health that health professionals may be expected to perceive. The specialty of geriatrics is concerned with developing means to identify and cope with the full range of health-related influences on the elderly.

Capacity for Medical Decision-Making

Like other patients, the elderly are entitled in principle to medical autonomy. They may make their own decisions on the acceptance and rejection of recommended medical care.[17] Because elderly people may appear rather more anxious and/or confused than younger people, however, and may require more explanation and clarification of medical information, the question tends to arise more often in their case whether they are legally competent to make medical decisions regarding their health care. It must be remembered, however, that the decision whether or not to have medical treatment is not itself a medical decision. It is a personal decision that the person it most immediately affects must make in awareness not only of material medical information but also of his or her own priorities and aspirations.[18] Elements of personal preferences, beliefs, biases, appetites, fears, fetishes, fantasies and phobias all weigh in the balance. The decision expresses the whole personality of the individual, not simply those aspects of physiology, psychology and, for instance, neurology that are of medical interest.

A physician almost invariably knows more about the prospective patient's medical condition and prognosis than does the patient. As against this, however, the patient knows more about his or her personality, convictions, experiences and preferences than does the physician. In order to consider what medical options may be appropriately offered for the purpose of pursuing the patient's goals of care, the physician must obtain information from the patient about the sort of person the patient is, and about the patient's circumstances. In conducting the discussion from which this information may be obtained, the physician or other person seeking knowledge of the patient may come to question whether the patient is intellectually capable of understanding what has to be discussed. That is, the question may arise of the patient's legal competence to act as the medical decision-maker on his or her own behalf.

It was once supposed that legal competence was an absolute quality that either existed in an individual or was lacking. In more recent times, a distinction has arisen concerning capacity to handle property and commercial transactions, and the ability to exercise health care autonomy and control of one's domestic environment. Distinctions were drawn between cognitive and affective capacities and disorders, the former concerning knowledge of property matters, commercial expectations and, for instance, family structure. The latter concerned temperamental disposition, and was less significant to the individual's capacity to conduct business. The distinction between cognitive and affective capacity remains useful, although it has clear limitations in that what one feels about others is frequently influenced by what one knows or believes about them.

Modern legal and psychiatric analysis has progressed beyond distinguishing between an individual's capacities to manage business affairs and to manage personal health care. It is now recognized that capacity is specific to function; that is, different capacities are required, in legal and psychiatric assessments, for the discharge of specific functions.[19] For instance, legal requirements of capacity to contract a long-term commercial loan are different from, and higher than, those relevant to contracting to purchase routine foods for domestic use. Capacity to make a will is different from capacity to marry. The discharge of the political power to cast an electoral vote, and, for example, to seek or to hold political or public office depends upon possession of capacities specific to each of such functions.

Capacity to make a will, for instance, depends on awareness of the contents of one's estate and of one's family structure and relationships.[20] While legal testamentary capacity requires a relatively high level of cognitive ability, however, a will may legally be revoked by an act such as tearing or crossing through by pen that does not require particular cognitive skills. The revocation may be inspired by an affective state, the testator having to know only that he or she is undoing what was done by the testamentary act.

This analysis presents a medico-legal problem. If capacity to revoke a will does not have to be as high as capacity to make one, there may be different levels of capacity concerning medical care. In particular, capacity to accept medical advice may not be as high as capacity to reject it. Health professionals who find a patient competent when recommended treatment is accepted but who contest the competency of the patient when he or she declines or discontinues recommended care may appear manipulative and self-serving of their own preferred treatment of the patient. On legal analysis, however, their position may be sound. A person may be legally required to have a higher level of awareness and capacity in order to go against medical advice than to accept it.

The influence that this realization gives to medical advice generates a reciprocal responsibility that binds physicians. Their advice must be based not only on an appropriately applied understanding of relevant medical science, but also on an adequately perceptive and attuned understanding of the sort of person the patient is. This is the point at which the teachings of geriatrics and gerontology become important. Physicians treating the elderly must be aware of the psychodynamics of aging and be able to appreciate what factors are material to the choice the competent elderly person is required to make. That is, the physician must be able to adjust disclosures to the elderly patient's informational needs, compatibly with the legal duty of informing that prevails under local jurisprudence.

Informed Consent[21]

The language of "informed consent" is now probably irrevocable in the medical jurisprudence of a number of legal systems, but there are compelling pragmatic and doctrinal reasons not to use it. The expression "informed choice" or "informed decision-making" is much to be preferred. "Informed consent" incorrectly suggests, first, that the purpose of giving information is to obtain or induce consent, whereas its true purpose is to serve the goal of a patient's autonomy, permitting the patient to exercise choice of medical care on an adequately informed basis. Second, the expression is dysfunctional in indicating to physicians that if patients decline proposed treatment, it is because they lack information. Physicians may accordingly give additional information or additionally emphasized information repeatedly, until patients are persuaded to agree with physicians' preferences. This can amount to improper persuasion or even coercion rather than informing. Third, it suggests that patients' refusals of care need not be as informed as their consents to accept treatment. This misconception[22] is based on legal doctrine on the tort or delict of battery, which consists of touching a patient without consent. Consent neutralizes the legal wrong of touching. The legal language of "informed consent" was developed to amplify simple consent, and teach that, to be legally effective and exonerating of health care professionals, consent must be adequately informed. The modern style of legal analysis is to classify the health professional's duty of disclosure by reference to the doctrines not only of battery law but also of negligence law.[23] This latter renders disclosure of appropriate information, discharge of the professional duty of care owed to a patient, and any failure to allow informed choice, whether the choice is to accept or to decline treatment, amounts in law to breach of the duty of care.

The expression "informed consent" suggests in addition that the health professional's function is to give information and a treatment recommendation and that the prospective patient's role is to respond by giving or denying consent. In fact, the health professional may need to know something about the patient, concerning not only the medical history but also the patient's hopes, fears, priorities and ambitions that may be affected by prospective treatments, so that the professional can identify what options may serve the patient's wishes, and the impact that treatment options may have on the patient's preferences for the future. Patients may delegate the function of treatment choice to the physician, but this does not necessarily occur as frequently and very rarely occurs as comprehensively as physicians believe. If a patient says "I'll leave it to you, doctor," the patient is not surrendering his or her entire human destiny to the physician, but delegating only the choice of means to pursue a goal or end the patient believes the physician knows and is willing to serve.

The distinction between medical means and medical ends is of crucial significance. It may not matter to the patient whether, for instance, a surgeon cuts this way or that, or whether a drug has one or another method of pharmacological operation. What does matter is that treatment be considered, assessed and proposed that serves the patient's goals in life to the greatest extent possible, and that the patient be informed of treatment options, benefits and risks in light of such goals. It may be expected that older people have goals and priorities that differ from those of younger people, and that an individual has changed priorities and aspirations that governed earlier years and circumstances. How intimately health care professionals must be informed of patients' preferences is a matter of legal doctrine specific to each country or legal system.

The courts of the United States, for instance, have been most progressive in developing a strongly patient-oriented standard of medical disclosure.[24] In 1980, the Supreme Court of Canada completed a transition of Canadian common law medical jurisprudence from the pre-existing English approach to that developed by U.S. courts.[25] The English courts have declined to change,[26] however, and have retained their historic approach that the Canadian judiciary have rejected on policy grounds. In contemplating the transition, the Supreme

Court of Canada identified three possible standards of giving information to patients. These are:

i) The professional standard of disclosure, which requires a health professional to meet the standards of giving patients information that other like professionals would meet. United States and Canadian courts have found this approach philosophically unsatisfactory in that it appears to preserve professional insularity, elitism and paternalism. They have accepted that in considering what information to give, professionals should take a patient-oriented rather than a professionally-oriented approach. The House of Lords has declined to adopt this approach in England,[27] fearing in part that it might trigger the medical malpractice litigation effect perceived to be harmful in the U.S. This characterization ignores the different dynamics of U.S. litigation practice, and the fact that Canada has seen little of the U.S. experience since adopting a patient-oriented medical jurisprudence.

ii) The subjective patient standard, which requires that information be disclosed that meets the needs of the particular patient-plaintiff. North American courts have rejected this standard of disclosure as being unfair in practice. By definition, plaintiffs are those who complain that they were not told what they needed to know. Courts consider it unfair that the medical defendant should be judged by the plaintiff's answer to the question "Had you known then what you know now (for instance that by accepting the risks of the treatment option you chose you would become paraplegic), would you have accepted that treatment?" Accepting the logistics of litigation, that plaintiffs tend to be people who feel injured, victimized and perhaps betrayed, the courts have held that defendants cannot be at the disposal of their bitter hindsight.

iii) The objective patient standard, which requires that information be given that is material to choice of a reasonable person in the patient's circumstances. North American courts have adopted this as doctrinally sound and practicable. The standard requires not "full" disclosure, but a sensible perception of the type of information that reasonable people require. The Supreme Court of Canada found negligence in the case adopting this standard[28] because a surgeon proposing surgery with a 14 percent risk of triggering an immediate stroke, which the patient suffered, did not consider whether treatment might be postponed until the patient had achieved full insurance protection against lost earning-power due to disability. The patient was an industrial worker supporting a family with several children about to enter college, who was 18 months short of full disability insurance protection, and who would not have moved into a higher category of health risk while waiting 18 months. He was wrongly denied the means to protect his family and his children's future by maintaining his income, which a reasonable person in his circumstances would want to do.

This standard of medical disclosure requires health professionals to give patients means to raise issues of special concern to them that options of health care may affect, and reciprocally requires patients to bring to attention any feature by which they may differ from an ordinary reasonable person in their circumstances. The elderly are not thereby required to bring their age to

B.M. DICKENS   497

medical attention, since their age is one obvious and objective fact of their circumstances. They may be required, however, to present any feature of their lives by which they depart from representative others in their circumstances. For instance, an elderly man for whom prostate surgery is indicated may be expected expressly to mention the fact that he has or anticipates an active sex life, for instance with a relatively young wife.[29] Gerontology teaches that the elderly are not unaffected by sensuality and the instinct to seek sexual satisfaction, however, and a health professional or manager of residential accommodation for the elderly who presumes that elderly patients or residents are asexual may act at his or her legal peril.

The criterion of materiality of risk of harm or of frustration of personal goals in life shows that the degree of invasiveness of medical treatment is significant, decisions about major surgery requiring more disclosure, for instance, than decisions about most non-invasive treatments or relatively minor surgery. Over the years, however, elderly people may have acquired aversions to types of treatment, perhaps by experience or knowledge of the experience of others, that younger patients tend to accept. Older patients' sensitivities have to be anticipated and accommodated, as part of health professionals' discharge of the duty of care according to the legally set standard of care of those in their circumstances. Assessments of risk of damage may also differ between an elderly person and a person of younger age, concerning for instance loss of reproductive capacity, which may affect an older person less, and liability to fracture a limb or a hip, which may affect an older person more.

Underlying the issue of informing patients is their right to autonomy, meaning their right to be treated according to their wishes. Opposing this may be the health professional's presumption that patients be treated according to their health interests, which the health professional is trained to diagnose and assess and is disposed to believe coincides with patients' wishes.[30] Wishes and interests often do coincide because most people wish to be treated in the best interests of their health. Perceptions of best interests may differ, however, particularly when patients make emotional responses to proposed medical treatments, which, of course, they are entitled to do. Competent patients can express their preferences and can usually have them prevail, but the frail or compromised elderly may be incapable of asserting their wishes over their families' or care-givers' different judgments of their best interests. This raises the issues of decision-making by the disadvantaged and decision-making for those unable to make decisions for themselves. The former should be afforded maximum means to be heard and respected, if necessary by legally enforceable procedures. The latter may also be aided by legal analysis of their rights when third parties make decisions about their care.

Third Party Decision-Making

Elderly and other persons who are unable to form or to express personal preferences regarding potential medical treatment may become the charge of family members or of other third-party guardians, but they are not thereby liable to the random disposal of such third parties. Third parties, who are often referred to as substitutes or surrogates, may have the legal power to discharge the responsibilities that they have assumed or that the law has imposed on them, but they cannot be purely arbitrary or primarily self-serving in the use of such powers. Regarding incompetent person's property, third parties who undertake management may be bound by fiduciary duties to act in good faith, and will be liable to equitable accountabilities, for instance through the concept of the constructive trust that will govern their use of benefits they derive from discharge of their assumed or legally-imposed responsibilities. Comparably in medical decision-making, they are not free to advance their own advantage at a cost to their charges. In the *Eve* case,[31] for instance, the Supreme Court of Canada was negatively influenced by the thought that the applicant for the handicapped woman's sterilization, her widowed mother, was apprehensive that she might become liable to rear a child her daughter might bear.

A cardinal principle of third party medical decision-making is that individuals do not lose their right to autonomy simply because they are no longer able to assert it or to invoke it. When they fall under the charge of others, the initial duty of such third parties is to discover and assert the dependent persons' own wishes, expressed when competent.[32] For this reason, a third party decision-maker is usually a family member familiar with the dependent party's preferences and personality. If the task of decision-making was to be discharged on purely medical, objective or interest-based criteria, it could usually be better performed by a physician or public officer such as an official public guardian or public trustee.

When an elderly person remains competent, his or her medical care preferences may evolve and change, so that once-acceptable treatment becomes unacceptable, and treatment once opposed becomes tolerable or welcomed. It should not be supposed that expression of a preference that contradicts an earlier choice is an indication of illness, confusion or incompetence, or that an earlier perhaps more objectively rational view is more authentic as an expression of the person's current true preference. When an elderly person is assessed to have lost medical decision-making competence, however, it cannot be supposed that medical care preferences expressed before such loss are no longer valid. On the contrary, the third party is bound to respect and to implement those views, and where the views were not clear, must conscientiously strive to distill and apply the now dependent party's disposition, preferences, personality and lifestyle to the choice at hand. The fact that the third party finds the resulting conclusion misguided, objectionable, disadvantageous to the dependent party or a violation of the third party's own philosophical or religious convictions is of no consequence. A third party can no more override the expression of the dependent party's wishes than he or she can override that party's last will and testament. The third party's primary responsibility is to make the decision and express the choice the dependent party would have made and expressed in person were he or she competent.

When in good faith a third party decision-maker does not know and cannot discern with reasonable reliability what the dependent person's wishes probably would be, the third party's duty is to make a decision that is in the dependent party's best interests.[33] This objectively-based choice can be made only when a subjectively-based choice specific to the dependent party is impossible to make. The decision should not be made, however, primarily on the subjectively-based choice of the decision-maker. That is, the choice should reflect the dependent party's wishes, or, if not, that party's best interests, but never just the decision-maker's wishes. The third party should where feasible consult relevant sources regarding the interests of a dependent party whose own wishes cannot be discovered. In particular, the views and recommendations of the dependent party's attending physician should be strongly influential, and when they are not known or have not been clearly expressed, they should be actively sought and usually followed. Particular care should be taken to consult appropriately, and perhaps to gain a second, detached opinion, where a choice in the dependent party's interests may also serve or seem to serve the advantage of the decision-maker.

When third parties are confident that they know or have discovered with reasonable reliability their charges' wishes, they may implement them even in ways that will cause risk to or may disadvantage the charges, such as in decisions to withdraw artificial life-sustaining equipment or procedures and let natural death occur.[34] When third parties claim to act in their charges' interests, however, they are more limited. They should seek independent advice on therapeutic care decisions, such as from attending physicians and should be aware that courts are liable to expose their choices to vigorous scrutiny. Courts will be hesitant, for instance, to approve any invasive care when non-invasive treatments of comparable efficacy exist, and will be suspicious of decisions of marginal or unestablished benefit, particularly when they are invasive or coincide with a third party's benefit. Any legislation claimed to authorize nonbeneficial treatment must be very clearly and specifically worded.

Even when third party decisions are legitimately made and are a necessary legal condition of a dependent person's medical treatment, they are not necessarily in themselves a sufficient condition of such treatment. The dependent person who is unable to give legally effective consent may nevertheless be able to give legally effective assent.[35] Further, and more importantly, if a person able to give assent denies it, treatment authorized by a third party's consent may be legally barred. Capacity to assent means capacity to understand that the proposed intervention may occur and what the patient will experience because of it; assent indicates the patient's willingness to allow it to occur. A person who refuses to allow a proposed intervention, by objecting to it in advance or resisting its application at the time it is proposed, cannot be subjected to constraints for purposes of imposition of the treatment, unless perhaps it is immediately necessary to save life or to preserve a limb, vital organ or permanent health.[36] A refusal of assent by a person capable of giving it must in principle be respected.

It has been seen regarding a competent patient that the reverse side of the so-called doctrine of informed consent to care is informed refusal.[37] It may appear that a person incapable of giving informed consent is equally incapable of giving informed refusal, but this does not place such a person under a liability to bear an unacceptable form of treatment on the authorization of a third party. It has been seen above too that information must be pitched at the level of either the reasonable person in the patient's circumstances or of the reasonable health professional, depending on the orientation set by local law.[38] In either case, however, a competent and adequately informed person has no reciprocal duty to make a decision on grounds of reason or rationality. Competent persons may make health care decisions, as they may make other decisions, on irrational grounds such as emotion, sentimentality, superstition, religion or, for instance, past experience or anecdote.[39] Incapable persons have the same right to refuse to assent to a proposed medication, intubation, injection or other form of proposed medical management.

Exceptionally, a refusal of care by an incompetent person may be over-ridden, as it may be in the case of a competent person too, under the legal doctrine of necessity to save life, or to save health against risk of severe injury or harm.[40] This raises the issue of elderly persons' involvement in terminal care decisions.

Terminal Care Decisions

In life-affirming cultures an individual's expression of a wish or preference not to live is often taken as an indication of mental illness. The widespread decriminalization of attempted suicide that placed legal control of suicide under mental health laws has reinforced the view that those who wish to die even a natural but postponable death are to be managed and sustained by interventions authorized by such legislation. Coroners' Juries similarly respond to suicide almost invariably by recording the verdict of "suicide while the balance of the mind was disturbed." The form of verdict is explicable on many other grounds, particularly where willful suicide is considered to be a mortal sin, but it entrenches a view that those who wish no longer to live are mentally disturbed. Mental health laws have tended to evolve through an early stage of permitting involuntary detention and treatment of those whose welfare might thereby be served, through justifying such intervention only on grounds of safety to others or to self, to allowing involuntary intervention on restricted grounds of dangerousness.[41] Many laws that permit persons to be detained and perhaps treated only when they are actually dangerous to others or to themselves include a category of non-violent people who are dangerous to themselves through self-neglect. Such people may include the elderly who forget to eat, or to maintain personal hygiene, or to turn off cooking or heating devices and thereby endanger themselves, and perhaps their neighbours.

Terminal care decisions concern not suicide or accidental death, but natural death. Courts particularly in the United States are becoming increasingly accommodating of elderly or sick persons' preferences to accept death at the time it is ordained by nature rather than be subjected to major bodily invasions and "heroic" efforts to sustain life by artificial means.[42] Palliative care has made significant advances in pain control, so that the pain of terminal conditions and of invasive treatments can frequently be contained, although the benefits of these advances are not universally available. More threatening than pain itself may be suffering[43] due to discomfort, indignity and the pervading sense of desperation in which the patient survives, reinforced perhaps by the feeling of futility. Where health services are not funded by governmental agencies or covered by private insurance, moreover, patients may in addition be apprehensive that the treatment offered will be very costly, and deplete life-savings and the inheritance of spouses and children. The story is apocryphal but telling of the elderly U.S. man who said to his doctor "When I die I want my savings to support my wife and children, not your wife and children, so don't give me expensive treatments and don't send my family the bill."

The incentive to resist natural death lies at the centre of much medical care, and may be the motivation that inspires the young to pursue careers in medicine. A sense of obligation to prolong life may be reinforced in some jurisdictions by the more mundane apprehension that postponable death when a patient was under care will trigger not just an inquest of the medical circumstances and management, but malpractice litigation at the instance of angry grieving relatives of the deceased. Arguments about the quality of life a patient may survive to experience, leading to a possible conclusion that a life of poor or negative quality or of insensate vegetation is not worth living, are resisted by claims of both religious and secular origin regarding the sanctity of life,[44] and that life is the pre-condition of any prospect of a patient's improvement in condition or circumstances. The courts have been prominent in denying that their decisions regarding care of patients such as severely handicapped or compromised newborns and the sick elderly are based on any such criterion, although their actual decisions may be rationalized and understood on such a basis.

Until quite recent times, the right of a patient to refuse proposed life-sustaining care turned on a distinction between ordinary and extraordinary care.[45] Of ethical origin, the distinction was of legal significance in that ordinary care was mandatory to offer, initiate, continue and, on the patient's part, accept, whereas extraordinary care was discretionary. It did not have to be available, offered, initiated, continued or suffered. The distinction arose with development of artificial means of life-support, dependent on mechanical supplementation or replacement of human vital organic functions. Treatments that could be administered at the patient's own bedside or in a rudimentary hospital were ordinary, but sophisticated interventions dependent on scarce and refined machines and integrated skills of highly-trained treatment teams were extraordinary.[46] The ethical language of the ordinary-extraordinary distinction contrasts proportionate and disproportionate care,[47] which is also the language of health economics and cost-effectiveness. The ethical language invokes criteria of macroethics, contrasting potential benefit to a recipient of services and costs borne by other potential beneficiaries denied deployment of the same scarce resources.

The celebrated *Quinlan* case[48] in the U.S. showed that the ordinary-extraordinary distinction was not static, tied to equipment and specialized personnel, but was dynamic, turning on the individual patient's prognosis. For a patient treatment could help to live a life of human experience (what the *Quinlan* court described as a cognitive or sapient life) or to live consciously and free from pain and distress, the treatment was ordinary. For a patient who even with treatment would remain chronically vegetative, or conscious and in unrelievable pain and suffering, use of the same technique or equipment would be extraordinary. Being discretionary, such treatment could be refused by a terminal patient, whose survival would then depend on more passive, ordinary medical care and his or her own natural resources of body, mind and spirit.

A number of U.S. jurisdictions have recently gone beyond this analysis, and have regarded the administration of nutrition and hydration, which is usually undertaken as a nursing rather than a medical service, as extraordinary medical care when applied to a chronically vegetative or sick although not necessarily terminal patient.[49] Courts have respected the wish that food and liquid be withdrawn, and the patient be allowed to die. Further than this, courts have allowed relatives of incompetent patients to show that such patients would so express themselves if they were competent to do so, and, for instance, a wife has been allowed to authorize removal of her non-terminal husband's feeding tube, on the ground that if he were able to speak, he would have said that he wanted it removed.[50] The husband died eight days after removal of the tube.

Startling though this may appear, it conforms to developments in legal doctrine. Once it is accepted that competent terminal patients can compel effective refusal or the removal of treatments that are of no avail to them, and that competent non-terminal patients can decline initiation or continuance of treatments they do not want, as an exercise of autonomy, principles of non-discrimination against the incompetent lead to the conclusion that no-longer competent patients should have the same entitlements, provided that third parties can reliably identify and appropriately express their preferences. As against this, however, it has been seen that when the wishes of incompetent persons cannot be discerned, they are to be treated on the objectively-determined basis of their interests.[51] This applies both to persons who have never reached a stage of developed personality, such as young children and the chronically mentally handicapped, and those who have reached such a stage but whose preferences cannot be credibly determined in good faith. Sustaining of life is not necessarily an imperative in such cases. A U.S. court permitted an elderly chronically retarded man to die of leukemia because he would not understand the reason for chemotherapy that might prolong his life, but would perceive that he was being caused pain and discomfort from the procedure, administered by those on whom he relied for care and comfort.[52]

Much of the above discussion centres on the individual's status as a patient, and on the responsibilities of health professionals triggered by such status. People are not necessarily bound, however, to become or to remain patients. While legal rights of attempted rescue and of necessity to save human life exist, their enforcement against competent people who refuse unwanted rescue or intervention will not necessarily be authorized in advance by courts, or be ratified *ex post facto*. While persons who wish to become or remain patients of hospitals or other health facilities may be obliged to respect the ethic of health care and medical practice that will not suffer professional passivity in the face of postponable death,[53] and will not suffer for instance treatment limited to sedation and comfort measures for patients who choose not to take nutrition or hydration, such patients are free to yield patient status and return to their families or communities, perhaps to die.[54] Where incompetent persons are concerned, they will be treated, as in other cases, according to their wishes formed when they were competent, if these can be adequately determined, or according to their interests if such wishes cannot be credibly determined.

Anticipation of Incompetence — Advanced Directives

Closely related to terminal care decisions, although not limited to them, are concerns particularly elderly persons may have about their medical and associated care, such as nursing home and long-term residential care, should they become legally incompetent to manage their affairs. The increasing incidence of Alzheimer's disease[55] has perhaps concentrated elderly persons' attention on their liability to lose legal competence. Evolving legal doctrines regarding the significance that should be given to clear expressions and demonstrations of their wishes when competent should afford the elderly some assurance that, should they become incompetent they will not fall under the random wishes or whims, or the self-interest, of third parties, including perhaps their nearest of kin. Because such doctrines are not necessarily uniformly applied or clear, however, it is understandable that the elderly should seek some more secure legal means to ensure through advanced directives that their preferences for future medical care formulated when competent should prevail should competence to express them be lost. Three major instruments have been developed for this purpose in Western legal systems, namely:

i)   a "living will,"

    ii)   a Natural Death Act declaration; and

    III) a durable power of attorney.

These instruments may co-exist in some legal systems, such as in the U.S. where some states' Natural Death Acts' declarations are called living wills, and may overlap in practice. If such advanced directives are used at different times, they may indeed contradict each other, when courts will be called on to resolve apparent or actual inconsistencies, perhaps according to legal doctrines already existing for the resolution of conflicting documents or decision-making mechanisms. Further, legislation and/or judicial practice regarding these instruments may be quite detailed in some jurisdictions, and contain a number of refinements and distinguishing points of integration with the surrounding jurisprudence. For description in outline, however, each may be considered in isolation.

    i) *"Living wills."*[56] These somewhat misdescribed documents are declarations, often made through completion of standard forms drafted by or on behalf of a Death With Dignity, Concern for Dying or like-minded society, that usually have no directly binding legal force, although some U.S. states have given them the same force as Natural Death Act declarations (below). Indeed several common forms of living wills expressly provide that they are "binding in honour only" and that they are designed to affect the conscience rather than the legal duties of those at whom they are aimed. They are directed to family members, family physicians and subsequent attending physicians, and state that, if the declarant is not legally competent when medically diagnosed to have entered a terminal condition of life, the declarant does not want any medical means to be used to sustain life, but wants to be permitted to die a natural death. Comfort means may be used but not means that are variously described as artificial, mechanical, extraordinary, invasive, aggressive or heroic. The language chosen can be open to legalistic interpretations, particularly where the courts have elaborated on the significance of particular expressions in general use, living will use or coinciding legislation. The general intention, however, is that patients be allowed to die naturally and comfortably.

    Natural death may be undignified and uncomfortable, especially when precipitated by malignancy, and physicians may not find in such documents guidance about what strategies or medications are intended to be usable and not usable unless they are quite specific. Accordingly, some question exists about what effect these informal documents have in practice, and how satisfactory they are in achieving their professed goal. Concerned associations continue to promote them, however, although many prefer that, where no legislation exists, living wills should gain legal force and definition by local enactment of legislation on natural death. It bears repetition, however, that when local jurisprudence emphasizes that those no longer competent to express themselves should be medically managed according to their earlier expressed preferences, living wills will be legally significant and effective as constituting such expressions regarding terminal care.

    ii) *Natural Death Act declarations.*[57] Many jurisdictions, particularly in the

United States, have enacted legislation by which advanced directives on terminal care, particularly for the rejection of mechanical or similarly described life-sustaining medical means, will be legally effective. Some provide criminal sanctions for willful disregard of a duly made and recorded declaration, but others leave the matter of enforcement to civil remedies and particularly professional discipline, such as charges of professional misconduct presented before professional licensure disciplinary committees.

Legislation has varied definitions of a terminal condition, of how it may be medically diagnosed and of the type of treatment the declarant refuses on entering that condition. Some has an obligatory draft form of declaration a declarant may complete or amend in minor ways in order to invoke the Act, while other legislation permits a declarant to draft an individual declaration that invokes the force and definitions of the Act. Most Acts contain a draft form of declaration, however, so that declarants can simplify or even avoid the use of lawyers. Legislation often considers engagement of lawyers useful, however, both to reduce the chance of ambiguity or ineffectiveness in declarations, and also to reinforce their seriousness to both declarants and those the declarations are intended to bind. Legalistic form may render a statutory declaration unfamiliar or alienating, or financially inaccessible, however, so some Acts seek to find a balance between seriousness of making the declaration and its accessibility to those not accustomed to using lawyers and unable to pay professional fees. Proponents of legislation are aware of the relative simplicity, economy and accessibility of living wills.

When made, declarations are required to be copied to family physicians, and hospital physicians such as attending physicians, if any, and copies may also be given to family lawyers and appropriate relatives. Patterns of distribution cannot ensure, of course, that the declaration will be brought to the attention of a relevant physician at a crucial time, following, for instance, a sudden life-endangering trauma, but particularly in developed countries, computerization of health data can bring the existence of a declaration to relevant attention in many if not most cases of terminal care. Excessive detail in legislation on making and revocation of declarations can be dysfunctional in rendering the mechanism too legalistic and liable to fail for noncompliance with technicalities. Early experience of such legislation has already disclosed a serious dysfunction that subsequent Acts may not have fully eliminated. The belief has arisen in some jurisdictions with such legislation that patients who have not made declarations intend that, when they enter the defined terminal condition and are not competent to express their preferences, they intend that artificial, mechanical or otherwise described medical means should be employed to prolong their lives. That is, their right to natural death can be seriously compromised and frustrated.[58]

iii) *Durable Powers of Attorney.* Based on the legal principle that whatever one can do in person one can do through an attorney, execution of such powers permits principals to discharge a wide range of medico-legal functions through attorneys. Attorneys so appointed can be family members or friends who are not lawyers, although historically lawyers have been so frequently used in commercial practice that in many countries the expression "attorney" is synonymous with "lawyer." Classically, a power of attorney lapsed when the principal lost legal competence, because one could not do through an attorney what one could not do in person. Particularly to accommodate medical decision-making, however, a number of jurisdictions have changed their legislation to permit principals to appoint others with legal powers to act during the principal's anticipated incompetence. This is the sense in which such legislation accommodates a power of attorney that is "durable."

When an individual is confident that his or her medical substitute or surrogate decision-maker knows and will respect his or her wishes, less need may be felt to execute a power of attorney, although this may still be of use to control who the decision-maker will be if the anticipated line of succession should fail for a reason such as prior death or the absence of the expected surrogate. That is, control over alternative attorneys can be exercised through execution of an appropriately designated power. A power of attorney may also be used, however, expressly to displace the normal successor. This may be because that person is not trusted to exercise legal influence in the way the principal finds acceptable, or because the principal does not want to confide his or her preferences to that person. Displacement may also be arranged because the principal wants to spare the natural surrogate, who may be an elderly spouse, responsibility for a burdensome life or death decision affecting the principal that may be a source of regret, remorse, distress or confusion for the remainder of that person's perhaps solitary life.

It is possible to draft a power of attorney so directively that the attorney's choices of decision-making are very limited. That is, a power may be drafted to give the force of private law to a living will. The far more usual exercise of the power, however, is to say not what should be decided when the principal loses medical decision-making capacity, but under whose decision-making power the principal then falls. The principal must then be independently satisfied that the attorney will give effect to the principal's communicated wishes, or trust the judgment the attorney will then exercise without earlier guidance from discussions or other communications with the principal.

The three types of advanced directive, namely the living will, Natural Death Act declaration and durable power of attorney, reflect that elderly people who have been accustomed to exercising a measure of autonomy over their lives want to keep maximum control over their personal and medical destiny to the end of their days. It may be comforting to society to know that the elderly can legally impose their medical treatment preferences on caregivers, and not be subject to family preferences such as, on the one hand, that they die without expensive care, lest children's inheritances may be depleted, and on the other, that they be subjected to every possible intervention lest children may feel guilt in bereavement because they did not do all that was possible. Availability of a living will or Natural Death Act declaration may be a source of less comfort to society, however, if it is feared that elderly persons make them in the belief that their families, physicians or societies expect them to do so, or that the elderly act under the conditioning of an adverse or hostile environment, or in response to an alienated world in which they feel they have no place. They are entitled to respect for their choice, of course, even when it is conditioned by their perceptions that they will have no future social role, utility or respect, but efforts should be made to justify them not having such perceptions, as part of promoting the fullest possible health of the elderly.

Medical Research

The limited but sensitive field of medical research and experimentation raises legal concerns regarding recruitment of the elderly as subjects.[60] Bordering medical research are such related areas as socio-medical, socio-psychological, social welfare and, for instance, purely sociological research. These introduce variants of issues that arise in medical research, and bear on developments in gerontology, but the medical area taken alone offers a relevant focus for discussing in outline some legal issues regarding recruitment of the elderly to participate as subjects of research.[61] Alzheimer's disease is of growing concern, and failure of the medical research community to address it, and of public medical research funding agencies to allocate resources to its study, would constitute discrimination not only against the sick, but particularly against the elderly. Whether and how Alzheimer's disease patients can legally be engaged in its study, however, raises difficult but representative legal questions.

When potential research subjects are legally competent to decide whether to participate in studies, their agreement to do so is not problematic in principle. It may be, however, if they are invited to take part in research by physicians on whom they are dependent for therapeutic care.[62] Their decision to participate may be affected by the fear that, if they frustrate their physicians' research interests by refusal, their therapeutic care may be compromised. In jurisdictions of the common law tradition, it is an equitable presumption that when in unequal relationships a benefit beyond a regular fee passes from the less to the more powerful party, the transaction was affected by the latter's undue influence, and it is voidable. The relationship between physician and patient is unequal in the equitable sense not because the physician willfully exploits an advantage but because of its inherent linking of a person with the power of knowledge and a person depending on that knowledge for his or her well-being. For the patient's consent to be legally effective, the physician-beneficiary must be able to show that the patient took or at least was aware of a means of access to independent advice before accepting his or her physician's invitation to serve as a subject. If someone other than the physician presents the invitation, the physician must similarly be able to show that he or she applied no undue pressure, inducement or influence. Legal fiduciary duties may also bind a physician to make full and frank disclosure to a patient of the professional's interest in the patient's recruitment to run the risks of the study.

When potential research subjects are not competent to exercise choice in medical management, third parties under whose control they fall have very limited legal authority to engage such subjects in medical research. Power probably exists to afford access to their medical files and comparable identifiable records, for retrospective and/or comparative study. Non-invasive studies of a minor nature may also be approved, such as by the fitting of electrodes with minimum shaving of hair, but treatment as invasive as taking a blood sample by venepuncture will be barred unless it can be shown to be beneficial to the potential subject in immediate clinical terms. If the venepuncture is indicated for the subject's medical management as a patient, drawing a small volume of additional blood for use in research is permissible,[63] as is research use of any surplus blood remaining after testing for a diagnostic, therapeutic or monitoring purpose has been satisfied. Nothing as invasive as lumbar puncture or a spinal tap can be authorized by a third party on an incompetent patient, however, for purposes of research alone, even though this may advance knowledge of Alzheimer's disease for the benefit of future sufferers. What otherwise would be a common assault by touching may be neutralized by third party consent, but a breaking of the surface of the skin legally constitutes as wound, and third parties cannot authorize wounding of their charges unless it is for a clearly and immediately beneficial purpose, which medical research is unlikely to be.

Similar limits apply to pharmacological testing of incompetent patients and, for instance, nutritional, climatic or environmental variations that bear greater risks of harmful, distressing or discomforting effects than arise in the management of everyday life events. Only procedures of conservatively assessed benefit to the incompetent person may be legally justified on the basis of third party authorization. This may have the unintended but unavoidable effect of foreclosing their employment in medical research. When competent non-dependent subjects would satisfy the scientific criteria of a research protocol as well as a population of incompetent dependent subjects it is clear that incompetent or dependent persons should not be considered for recruitment. This is more obviously so when equally suitable competent persons have declined to serve as subjects because they find the risks or discomforts of the study unacceptable. In some cases, however, only the incompetent or a population of dependent persons are scientifically appropriate for a study. Investigators then bear the burden of designing a study all of whose incompetent or dependent subjects will benefit in person from their involvement, and the risks of which are justifiable in terms of the therapeutic benefits recruits will receive.

Blood taking may have to be confined, for instance, to occasions when venepuncture will be undertaken for diagnosis or therapy. The law requires physicians to act in good faith in determining what treatments are therapeutically or otherwise indicated when investigators want to use the occasion of treatment to recover some additional blood, tissue or other body substance. More frequent diagnostic testing than is routine will be suspicious, although this and, for instance, more regular or extensive sampling by way of therapeutic monitoring may be properly presented as a benefit the subject receives from the study procedure. Alleged psychological benefit the subject may receive from participating in a study liable to aid comparable sufferers is unlikely to be credible where mentally incompetent patients are concerned.

Competent patients may well find the opportunity for altruism a satisfaction that induces them to join a study. Further, patients who anticipate a future condition of incompetence when investigation of them may yield results of advantage to research may give an advanced directive. An analogy of a living will is of questionable effect because the document itself is not directly legally compelling, and an analogy adapted to submission to research may not justify a third party authorizing more than moderately invasive procedures. It may serve, however, to legitimate venepuncture and comparably low risk interventions for research on an incompetent person. A specifically worded power of attorney may be legally effective to entitle an attorney to authorize such more invasive procedures as spinal tap or lumbar puncture on a now incompetent patient, although particular care will have to be taken to seek any concurring assent the principal is able to give, to respect a withholding of such assent, and to terminate any intervention the principal resists at the time or appears to find distressing or discomforting.

A sometimes contentious area exists between therapy and research often called therapeutic innovation.[64] Therapeutic care of the elderly is clearly lawful and frequently mandatory, but conditions may exist for which no regular therapy is effective. This may be, for instance, because of the particular combination of medical features the patient presents, or because the routine therapy is contraindicated due to some existing treatment, medication or pathology affecting the patient, or because the former therapy has become discredited as ineffective or has been shown to be associated with harmful side-effects. Innovative treatment may then be therapeutically indicated. In that the treatment has not been applied before, the results of its application will be of interest to more than the treating physician, and will be valued by scientific researchers even if the data at first are only anecdotal in character. The secondary use of such data will constitute research. Approval of such documentary research may not require the same high degree of scrutiny or protection of the patient as may physical administration of the treatment itself. Where an incompetent patient is concerned, an appropriately protective third party guardian may be able to authorize release of the data for research use with legal effect.

Elder Abuse

The final medico-legal issue to be considered, elder abuse, is vast in scope, warrants treatment in chapters and books in its own right, and is indeed increasingly the subject of book-length studies.[65] Accordingly, its treatment here will be very superficial, intended only broadly to describe medico-legal aspects of this depressing phenomenon. It is of central concern to health, however, because the incidence of abuse of the elderly goes to the heart of the concept of health offered by the World Health Organization. Abuse of the elderly can be a direct source of their loss of physical, mental and social well-being.

Abuse can be generally classified as either active or passive in nature, and either primarily physical or mental in its impact on health. The border between the active and the passive or neglectful is legally somewhat uncertain, since failure to act to discharge a legal duty is often classified in law as a wrong of commission rather than of omission.[66] The border between the physical and the mental is medically somewhat uncertain, since physical events can trigger psychological and psychiatric consequences or affect neurological functioning with different degrees of directness, and psychosomatic responses can translate emotional states into physiological expressions. Nevertheless, for purposes of description in outline, elder abuse will be classified by reference to these general distinctions.

a) *Active physical abuse,* represented by causing or permitting the elderly to be struck, is an obvious precipitating cause of injury and even death. The distinctive nature of elder abuse, like its analogy of child abuse, is not simply the fact of causing or permitting the assault, however, which itself is a matter for the criminal law, but that the wrong is occasioned within the elderly person's home (including a residential institution) or family, frequently by a person on whom the victim must rely for protection. It is the feature of betrayal that gives such abuse its pathos and bitterness. Abuse may be due to the assailant's violence unrelated to the victim's personality, but may also be due to the assailant's impatience at having to cope with features of the victim's age, such as slowness, forgetfulness or confusion.

b) *Active mental abuse* is often of the same origin as active physical abuse, and may coincide with it. It consists in causing damage to the elderly person's self-image and impairing his or her capacity to function, such as by constant derisive criticism and condemnation of incapacities, often related to age, that sap self-confidence. Castigating an elderly person for forgetfulness, anxiety or, for instance, incontinence, affords the victim no room for correction, and can be corrosive of the individual's personality and capacity for social interaction.

c) *Physical neglect* of an elderly person can be occasioned through a lack of care for the person's nutritional and hygienic status, and for such domestic comforts as cleanliness and heat. Neglected elderly persons, who may be fiercely independent in their insistence on maintaining self-care, may be victims of their families or of social service agencies that undertake to monitor their well-being. Malnutrition, disease and, for instance, hypothermia are frequent manifestations of such neglect, and they may be found among residents of institutional homes that undertake care of the elderly as well as among those who live in their own homes.

d) *Emotional neglect* of the elderly consists in abandoning them to isolation and loneliness. They may at times be difficult companions, and perhaps inconsolable in their chronic grieving for a deceased spouse or child, but some emotional reaching out to them can generate a response, or at least a feeling that they are of relevance to another. It has been observed how a pet animal can reduce feelings of isolation in the elderly, and give some externalized focus to their daily existence, thereby perhaps contributing to their mental, physical and social well-being. Physical isolation may be inescapable in an elderly person's circumstances, especially when the person wants to continue to live in familiar surroundings, but family, social service or voluntary agency visitors may relieve loneliness. In developed countries, furthermore, a telephone may be considered a social service rather than a luxury item, and those who deliver services such as mail or who make house calls in the course of trade may be engaged to make regular contact with the isolated elderly. The role of the law here is less to enforce individual rights of the elderly than to require or authorize public agencies to take relieving initiatives.

This point sets the context of all of the above overview of medico-legal issues concerning the elderly. It has considered medical issues primarily at the clinical or individual level of health care delivery. Legal principles and case-law are applicable at this level of analysis. The contrasting orientation warrants mention in conclusion, however, namely that transcending clinical health care are public health and community health services. Although the health and well-being of elderly persons certainly engage the attention of the medical profession, particularly in the specialty of geriatrics, the general well-being of the elderly is also a function of public health care and of social structures designed to ensure maintenance of at least minimum standards of social care that give the elderly interests in life, a measure of access to companionship, and a sense of belonging and relevance. Legal rights of individuals cannot supply this quality of existence for the elderly. Law provides only a medium to implement social policies whose inspiration is to be found in other institutions of society.

Notes

1. Preamble to the Constitution of the World Health Organization, 2 *Official Records of the W.H.O.* 100 (June 1948).
2. G.A. Res. 216, U.N. Doc. A/810, at 71 (1948).
3. 21 U.N. GAOR Supp. (no. 16) at 49, U.N. Doc. A/6316 (1966).
4. 21 U.N. GAOR Supp. (no. 16) at 52, U.N. Doc. A/6316 (1966).

5. 33 U.N. GAOR Supp. (no. 18) at 108, U.N. Doc. A/33/18 (1978).
6. 34 U.N. G.A. Res. 34/180, 34 GAOR Supp. (no. 46) U.N. Doc. A/39/45 (1979).
7. 14 U.N. G.A. Res. 1386, 14 GAOR Supp. (Item 64), U.N. Doc. A/4354 (1959).
8. 26 U.N. G.A. Res. 2856, U.N. Doc. A/8588 (1971).
9. 30 U.N. G.A. Res. 3447, U.N. Doc. A/10284/add.1 (1975).
10. Being Part I of the Constitution Act,1982, enacted by the Canada Act 1982 (U.K.) c.11.
11. See *id*. s. 24 on enforcement of guaranteed rights and freedoms.
12. See for instance the discussion and proposals in D.Callahan, *Setting Limits: Medical Goals in an Aging Society* (New York: Simon & Schuster, 1987).
13. Middle-class professionals and those in business on their own behalf are rarely subject to such laws. Judges at the highest levels may hold office in many countries without age limit, or up to such an age as 75.
14. R.J. Levine, *Ethics and Regulation of Clinical Research* (Baltimore: Urban & Schwarzenberg, 2nd. ed. 1986).
15. B.H. Stanley *et al.*, "The Elderly Patient and Informed Consent," 252 *J. Amer. Med. Asso.* 1302-1306 (1984).
16. Ontario Ministry of Health estimate; 3 *Centresphere* 6 (1988) (Baycrest Centre for Geriatric Care, Toronto).
17. See B.M. Dickens, "Patients' Interests and Clients' Wishes: Physicians and Lawyers in Discord," 15 *Law, Medicine and Health Care* 110-117 (1987).
18. See. e.g. *Bouvia* v. *Superior Court (Glenchur)*, 225 Cal. Rptr. 297 (Cal. App. 2 Dist. 1986) at 305.
19. See C.M. Culver, "The Clinical Determination of Competence" in M.B. Kapp, H.E. Pies and A.E. Doudera (eds.) *Legal and Ethical Aspects of Health Care for the Elderly*(Ann Arbor: Health Administration Press, 1985) 277 at 297.
20. *Banks* v. *Goodfellow*(1870) L.R. 5 Q.B. 549; see Cockburn, C.J. at 565.
21. See generally B.M. Dickens, "The Doctrine of 'Informed Consent': Informed Choice in Medical Care" in R.S. Abella and M.L. Rothman (eds.), *Justice Beyond Orwell* (Montreal: Les Editions Yvon Blais, 1985) 243-263 (Canadian Institute for the Administration of Justice).
22. See *Truman* v. *Thomas*(1980), 611 P. 2d 902 (Cal. S.C.) and *Chisher* v. *Spak* (1983), 471 N.Y.S. 2d 741 (N.Y.S.C.) for liability when refusals of treatment were inadequately informed.
23. See *Reibl* v. *Hughes* (1980), 114 D.L.R. (3d) 1 (Sup. Ct. Can.), applying *Canterbury* v. *Spence* (1972), 464 F. 2d 772 (U.S.C.A., D.C.) and *Cobbs* v. *Grant* 1972), 502 P. 2d (Cal. S.C.).
24. See *Canterbury* v. *Spence* and *Cobbs* v. *Grant*, *ibid*.
25. *Reibl* v.*Hughes*, note 23 above.
26. *Sidaway* v. *Bethlem Royal Hospital Governors*, [1985] 1 All E.R. 643 (H.L.).
27. *Ibid*.
28. *Reibl* v. *Hughes*, note 23 above.
29. Although it must be noted that people raised before recent times may be conservative about discussing their existing or anticipated sex lives, and reticent to discuss non-marital sexuality.
30. See note 17 above.
31. *Re Eve* (1986), 31 D.L.R. (4th) 1.
32. See [U.S.] President's Commission for the Study of Ethical Problems in Medicine and Biomedical and Behavioral Research, *Making Health Care Decisions: The*

Ethical and Legal Implications of Informed Consent in the Patient-Practitioner Relationship (Washington, D.C.: U.S. Govt. Printing Office, 1982) Vol. 1, ch. 9, Substantive and Procedural Principles of Decisionmaking for Incapacitated Patients, 177-188.

33. *Ibid,* 180-181.
34. See [U.S.] President's Commission for the Study of Ethical Problems in Medicine and Biomedical and Behavioral Research, *Deciding to Forego Life-Sustaining Treatment* (Washington, D.C.: U.S. Govt. Printing Office, 1983) 132-136.
35. For discussion, see R.J. Levine, note 14 above, 265-266.
36. See note 32 above, at 93-94.
37. See note 22 above and accompanying text.
38. See notes 23 and 26 above.
39. See note 21 above, at 251-253.
40. See note 32 above, at 93-94.
41. See W.J. Curran and T.W. Harding, *The Law and Mental Health: Harmonizing Objectives* (Geneva: World Health Organization, 1978).
42. See note 34 above, and Office of Technology Assessment, Congress of the United States, *Life-Sustaining Technologies and the Elderly* (Washington, D.C: U.S. Govt. Printing Office, 1987). ch. 3, Legal Issues, 91-138.
43. See M.A. Somerville, "Pain and Suffering at Interfaces of Law and Medicine" 36 *U.Toronto L.J.* 286-317 (1986).
44. See E.J. Keyserlingk, *Sanctity of Life or Quality of Life* (Ottawa: Law Reform Commission of Canada, Study Paper, 1979).
45. See generally B.M. Dickens, "The Right to Natural Death" 26 *McGill L.J.* 847-879 (1981).
46. See note 34 above, at 82-89.
47. For the Roman Catholic tradition on the distinction, see Sacred Congregation for the Doctrine of the Faith, *Declaration on Euthanasia* (Vatican City, 1980), reprinted in note 34 above, Appendix C. 300-307.
48. *In the Matter of Karen Quinlan* (1976), 355 A. 2d 647 (N.J.S.C.).
49. See e.g. *Barber* v. *Superior Court* (1983), 195 Cal. Rptr. 484 (Cal. C.A.); and *In re Conroy* (1985), 486 A. 2d 1209 (N.J.S.C.).
50. *Brophy* v. *New England Sinai Hospital* (1986), 497 N.E. 2d 626 (Mass, Sup. Jud. Ct.).
51. See note 33 above, and accompanying text.
52. *Superintendent of Belchertown State School* v. *Saikewicz* (1971), 370 N.E. 2d 417 (Mass. Sup. Jud. Ct.).
53. See the discussion *ibid.* at 425 and *Bopuvia* v. *County of Riverside,* No. 159780 (Cal. Super. Ct., Dec. 16, 1983). The subsequent history of the case is discussed in *Life-Sustaining Technologies and the Elderly,* note 42 above, at 100-101.
54. See *Bopuvia, ibid.*
55. See Office of Technology Assessment, Congress of the United States, *Losing a Million Minds: Confronting the Tragedy of Alzheimer's Disease and Other Dementias* (Washington, D.C.: U.S. Govt. Printing Office, 1987).
56. See note 34 above at 139-141 and Office of Technology Assessment, note 42 above, at 121-127.
57. See note 34 above, at 310-387.
58. Attempts to overcome this application of an Act include enactment of a provision, such as in the Washington, D.C. Law, section 6-2429(2), that the legislation " ...

shall create no presumption concerning the intention of an individual who has not executed a declaration to consent to the use or withholding of life-sustaining procedures in the event of a terminal condition"; see note 34 above, at 340.

59. See note 34 above, at 390-437.
60. See note 14 above, at 84-86.
61. "Research" and "experimentation" are taken to be synonymous, although the distinction is occasionally drawn, for instance, that the former is passive and observational whereas the latter is invasive.
62. See World Medical Association Declaration of Helsinki: Recommendations Guiding Medical Doctors in Biomedical Research Involving Human Subjects, principle I. 10, in R.J. Levine, note 14 above, at 122, and Appendix 4, 427-429.
63. Although a cumulative tally should be kept of all blood volumes drawn, lest the patient may be harmed by several low-volume blood drawings over a short time period.
64. See B.M. Dickens, "What Is a Medical Experiment?," 113 *Canadian Med. Assoc.J.* 635-639 (1975).
65. See e.g. B. Schlesinger and R. Schlesinger (eds.), *Abuse of the Elderly: Issues and Annotated Bibliography* (Toronto: University of Toronto Press, 1988).
66. See *The Queen* v. *Instan,* [1893] 1 Q.B. 450 (Ct. for Crown Cases Reserved, England).

Section Two

Guardianship and Civil commitment

Chapter 33

The Elderly Mentally-Ill and Infirm: Procedures for Civil Commitment and Guardianship

Brenda HOGGETT   Law Commission, England

Two principles of the common law often conflict in the case of elderly people. One is the duty to take reasonable care of those who are entrusted to your charge;[1] the other is the right of those same people to decide for themselves what they will do and what may be done to them.[2] How can we reconcile the lawyers' perception that such rights can only be interfered with by due process of law with the professional and family perception that such processes are irrelevant, stigmatizing and authoritarian?

Great Britain, as elsewhere, is experiencing a rapid increase in the numbers of very old people. Those over 75 are expected to rise from 3 million in 1981 to 4 million in 2001, those over 85 from 552,000 to 1,030,000.[3] Around 5% of those over 65 suffer from some degree of dementia but more than 20% of those over 80 are thought to do so.[4] Even so, the great majority of old people, disabled or not, live at home. The rest live in National Health Service hospitals, local authority residential homes, or increasingly in private nursing and residential homes, where the charges are often met by the residents' State welfare benefits. It is no longer an issue whether elderly mentally disabled people should live "in the community."[5] The difficulties, however, are not only more visible but include the impact upon their fellows who are not disabled.

Dementia is not the only mental disorder suffered by the elderly but it is much the most common. Although it leads to loss of capacity which may be compared with mental handicap or the serious mental illnesses, there are some significant differences which make it all the more difficult to find a legal solution. First, unlike congenital mental handicap, dementia involves the loss of previously existing intellectual power. There is a time at which the patient is legally capable and able, therefore, to make decisions about his future. The enduring power of attorney and the "living will" give legal recognition to such decisions: the former is now accepted in English law but the latter is not. But these cannot be a complete solution because a large number of people will never take advantage of them.[6]

Second, dementia usually progresses slowly. Intellectual functions such as concentration and memory gradually recede, while emotional weaknesses such as instability, hyper-sensitivity or fatuity gradually increase. The point at which a person slips from being "confused" or "infirm" to being seriously disabled is difficult to identify. Dementia will always fall within the usual concept of an "illness" as it involves an obvious departure from the sufferer's normal health and, unlike many other mental illnesses, is attributable to known organic causes. Yet in its early stages it will not involve the degree of mental abnormality which would usually be labelled "mental illness" and thought sufficient to justify compulsory measures.

Third, it may be particularly difficult to distinguish between the volitional and the non-volitional patient. A frail and confused elderly person may express and even act upon wishes which those around him believe to be contrary to his own or others' interests, but it may be quite easy for them to distract or dissuade him with little or no force or physical restraint. If a volitional patient refuses to have treatment or insists on leaving home or hospital, then even the professionals would accept that some legal formality will usually be required before his right to self-determination can be interfered with.[7] The incapable or non-volitional patient, however, is unable to express a view one way or the other. How then, it could be said, is there an interference with the right of self-determination if no such determination can take place?

English law provides a variety of possible solutions to these difficulties. None is entirely satisfactory but each can provide us with some pointers to a possible way forward. The issues are already under active discussion, not only in England and Wales,[8] but also in Scotland.[9] There is also extensive discussion in Europe[10] and elsewhere[11] of the legal problems presented by adult incapacity but these have so far tended to focus upon the mentally handicapped rather than the elderly. It is by no means clear that the same solutions are appropriate to both.

Without Formal Process

Recent English law has tended to gloss over the distinction between volitional and non-volitional patients and assume that the non-volitional can be dealt with without formal process. Originally, "voluntary" admission to mental hospitals was reserved for the truly volitional patient who was capable of signing a formal consent form. The Mental Health Act 1959 replaced this with "informal" admission for which no special formalities are required.[12] A major objective was to allow non-volitional patients to be admitted and treated without the stigma of certification and commitment.[13] The great majority of mental hospital admissions are now informal and an even greater proportion of resident patients have informal status.[14] Virtually everyone outside hospital has informal status; a very few people are subject to guardianship or orders under the National Assistance Act 1948, but the use of each is very rare and in some places non-existent; more will be subject to the jurisdiction of the Court of Protection but this is limited to their "property and affairs." Nevertheless the needs of all elderly mentally incapable people are much the same, and it is often a matter of chance where any individual may be living.

The Mental Health Act Commission, a watch dog body set up principally to safeguard the interests of detained patients,[15] is concerned about long stay, incapable, informal patients, many of whom are elderly and some of whom are subject to "*de facto* detention" in locked wards or rooms.[16] Yet the Commission identifies this practice with "a progressive approach (with a resulting reluctance to employ formal detention under the Act even in respect of difficult patients) ....."[17] Although concerned "to ensure that elderly patients receive the protection of the safeguards conferred by the Act on detained patients" the Commission has "no wish to encourage an authoritarian style of management where large numbers of elderly patients would be detained under its provisions."[18] If this is what goes on in practice with the widespread support of the professionals, might the law not do well to recognise and regulate it?

But if this is so, where should the decision-making power lie? On the analogy with minor children, it is tempting to give it to the patient's next of kin or "nearest relative."[19] However, the High Court has recently endorsed the view that relatives have no power to give consent on behalf of incapable patients.[20] This may be just as well. A parent's interest can readily be assumed to lie in bringing up his children to be happy, healthy and productive adults. A child's interest can less readily be assumed to lie in ensuring a long, comfortable and well provisioned old age for his demented or confused parent. The child's own distress at the loss of faculty in one once loved and respected combines with the compassionate wish to spare his parent the pain and distress of degeneration and with less worthy concern to preserve the family patrimony against the costs of improved care and comfort. The more distant the next of kin, the more likely it is that less worthy motives will prevail. The closer the next of kin the less likely this may be, but a spouse (or equivalent[21]) may also be failing to such an extent that it is difficult to know which of them should be labelled the "patient" and which the "nearest relative". Nor are exploitative marriages of elderly people entirely unknown.[22]

The alternative apparently favoured by the Mental Health Act Commission and even by the courts is to trust the professionals. The High Court has recently granted a declaration that it would not be unlawful to perform an abortion and sterilisation upon a severely mentally handicapped women of 19 (over the age of majority) saying:

> "I am content to rely on the principle that in these exceptional circumstances where there is no provision in law for consent to be given and therefore there is none who can give the consent, and where the patient is suffering from such mental abnormality as never to be able to give such consent, a medical adviser is justified in taking such steps as good medical practice "demands" in the sense that I have set it out above and on that basis it is that I have made the

declarations sought."[23]

Earlier the judge had asked:

"What does medical practice demand? I use the word "demand" because I envisage
a situation where based on good medical practice there are really no two views of
what course is for the best."[24]

This decision goes much further than the previously formulated doctrine of
necessity, although it accords with some textbook writers' views.[25]

The practical attractions of this are obvious. Doctors and nursing staff can
get on with their tasks of looking after and treating their patients without
having to spend time and money on formalities which make little difference in
practice. The family can be spared the distress of knowing that a loved one has
been formally committed and that they have agreed to it. The elderly person
can be spared the stigma and distress if he is still in a condition to be aware of
the position. What harm is done to anything or anyone other than the lawyers
and their principles?

Yet that harm is considerable. The doctors' decisions could only be
challenged by later action in the courts, which is unreliable. Doctors often
differ on what good medical practice demands but there is no guarantee that
the decision-maker will seek a second opinion or consult the next of kin. Even
within the National Health Service, personal convenience can often be a factor,
as the restraint practices still found in psycho-geriatric hospitals show.[26] In the
rapidly growing private sector, less worthy motives for cost saving methods of
management and treatment may sometimes prevail. Clearly, good practice
takes time and well-trained staff, costing much more than drugs and mechanical restraints. In any event, the doctrine gives decision-making powers to
doctors but does nothing to help other carers with much more difficult day to
day dilemmas to face.

Nevertheless, it seems that the Mental Health Act Commission (the majority
of whose members are psychiatrists, nurses or psychologists) would like to
combine the continued absence of legal formalities with "good practice"
safeguards akin to those available to detained patients: discussions with
relatives, getting a second consultant opinion, listening to the views of other
professionals, and in exceptional cases consulting the Mental Health Act
Commission.[27]

Non-Judicial Processes

Ironically, the procedures provided by the Mental Health Act 1983 and the
earlier 1959 Act were designed to give patients and professionals the protection
they needed without the delay, stigma and cost of more conventional "due

process" requirements.[28] These provide for admission to hospital for assessment for up to 28 days,[29], admission to hospital for treatment for up to six months[30] and reception into guardianship in the community for up to six months.[31] The latter two are renewable from time to time on medical recommendation. All simply require an application from an approved social worker or the patient's nearest relative,[32] supported by recommendations from two doctors, one an approved specialist.[33] In long-term cases, an objection by the nearest relative can only be overridden by a court.[34] The patient can be discharged by his doctor, in long-term cases his nearest relative,[35] or by a Mental Health Review Tribunal.[36] The Tribunal consists of a lawyer, an independent doctor and another person with relevant experience. The Tribunal usually sits informally and in private. The medical member examines the patient and reports on his condition, but the Tribunal always interviews him as well. In recent years, the patient has also been allowed legal representation and independent medical advice. The Tribunal can recommend leave of absence or transfer from hospital to guardianship but has no power over the patient's care and treatment as such.

The criteria for these procedures say nothing about incapacity. For guardianship and hospital admission for treatment, the patient must be mentally ill.[37] This is clearly a stronger term than "mentally disordered", which is enough for short term admission for assessment. It was meant to be roughly equivalent to madness, lunacy or unsoundness of mind under earlier laws. Unfortunately, as we have already seen, there is no difficulty in characterising the mental infirmity of old age as "mental illness" even if compulsory measures are totally inappropriate. The additional criteria scarcely help. The illness must be of a "nature or degree" which makes hospital treatment "appropriate" or "warrants" guardianship. Compulsory admission for treatment must be necessary for the patient's own health or safety or for the protection of other people while guardianship need simply be necessary in the interests of his welfare.

Guardianship seems the obvious solution for incapable patients but its legal effects are limited. It was intended for community care outside hospital. A guardian may be the local social services authority or a private individual, including the nearest relative, but he has very few powers. (Indeed, as the nearest relative can discharge the patient, it may wrongly have been assumed that he has them already.) He may dictate where the patient lives, where he goes for medical treatment, occupation, education or training, and he may insist that a doctor or other person is allowed to see the patient.[38] There is no express power to "take and convey" the patient to a home or hospital,[39] although there is power to apprehend those who go absent without leave.[40] There is understandable confusion about whether guardianship was ever intended as a means of securing compulsory admission, not only to hospital but also to residential care.[41] There is no power to oblige the patient to accept treatment or to consent to treatment on his behalf.

These limits stem from the entirely laudable desire to keep compulsory intervention to the "least restrictive alternative". In particular, it was thought that compulsory treatment should only be given in hospital where it can more readily be monitored.[42] If a patient is compulsorily admitted to hospital, he can be treated for his psychiatric disorder without his consent[43] but a second opinion is generally required for ECT and long-term drug therapy.[44] Psychosurgery cannot be performed at all without both the patient's consent and a second opinion and is thus illegal for all incapable patients whether informal or compulsory.[45] Under the 1959 Act, the guardian had all the powers of a father over a child under 14, including medical treatment. It was thought that the breadth of these powers was one reason why guardianship was so rarely used. It appears, however, that it is hardly any more popular with the professionals now that the powers are so much more limited.

Substantively, therefore, these procedures suffer from imprecise criteria and effects which are unnecessarily rigid and draw too strict a distinction between hospital and community care. Procedurally, however, apart from the possibility of a subsequent Tribunal hearing, they look very like those that a sensible and conscientious practitioner would operate in any event. Professionals, acting in consultation with the next of kin, arrive at a private consensus as to what should be done. Arguably, this is a much more effective protection for the patient than a judicial process, which in practice is often a rubber stamp unless it is unacceptably elaborate and prolonged. Non-judicial procedures are much less stigmatizing and distressing for patient and family alike. Yet our experience has clearly shown that even these minimal formalities are resisted by caring and conscientious professionals, particularly for their elderly and incapable patients. We still have not achieved the goal of safeguards without stigma.

Judicial Processes

A quite different process for admission to hospital or residential care is provided under the National Assistance Act 1948.[46] This requires the order of a magistrates' court or, in an emergency, a single magistrate. The district community physician and, in an emergency, another doctor must support it and oral evidence is required. Under the full procedure, notice must be given to the patient or someone in charge of him, but in an emergency no notice is required. The patient may be kept for up to three months, or in an emergency three weeks, again extendable by the court from time to time. There is no power to impose medical treatment. The procedure is very little used.[47] It is estimated that up to half the elderly people dealt with under it are mentally disordered.[48] The criteria require that the person *either* has a "grave chronic disease" such as dementia *or* being aged, infirm or physically incapacitated, is living in insanitary conditions; in either event he must be unable to care for himself and uncared for by others; and his removal must be necessary either in his own interests or to prevent injury to the health of or serious nuisance to others.[49]

The power is therefore mainly seen as a public health measure to remedy the appalling conditions of self-neglect into which some old people can fall, as much for the sake of their worried neighbours as for themselves. As with all types of removal from home, it can often and quite rapidly prove fatal.[50] There is always the concern that with better and more sensitive domiciliary services the elderly person could have stayed in his own home. If anything there is even more reluctance to use this procedure than the Mental Health Act.

None of these procedures give any power over the patient's finances. The Court of Protection[51] may take control of these where it is so satisfied on medical evidence that the patient is "incapable, by reason of mental disorder, of managing and administering his property and affairs."[52] This is no longer automatically assumed after compulsory procedures have been operated. The court's powers are extensive but relate solely to administering the patient's affairs[53] and applying the proceeds to maintain him and his family.[54] The court normally appoints a Receiver to do this but may in practice do little to supervise the Receiver's decisions.

The jurisdiction of the Court of Protection is the statutory successor to the Crown's prerogative powers over the person and property of idiots and lunatics[55]. These were irrelevant to the great mass of aged poor, who could be looked after at home or in Poor Law institutions or the asylums which multiplied during the nineteenth century.[56] The elaborate and costly procedures were reserved for the well to do and even they could be admitted to hospital by other means. Hence in practice, jurisdiction over property was separated from questions of care and treatment. When the 1959 Act was passed, there was apparently only a handful of "Chancery lunatics" whose care was committed to an individual by the court. Hence the new statutory powers dealt only with property, leaving care and treatment to be dealt with by the procedures for hospital admission or guardianship discussed earlier. The Royal Prerogative was not expressly abrogated but the Royal Warrant under which its exercise was delegated to the Lord Chancellor and other judges was revoked shortly after the 1959 Act came into force.

The separation of property and care no doubt seemed natural at the time. In the nineteenth century elderly people would either have property which required the court's attention or be paupers in need of public care. Old age pensions and other State welfare benefits were invented in the twentieth century and can be diverted without the court's intervention. Occupational pension schemes and home ownership have only become widespread since the Second World War. Even in 1959 it may have been assumed that people of modest means would be provided for in public hospitals and homes if they could not remain independent or live with their families. The advent of a flourishing private sector relying partly on State payments and partly upon the modest wealth of middle and lower middle class people may not have been contemplated. Yet these developments mean that the strict division between stewardship of property and guardianship of the person no longer makes sense. They also mean that conflicts of interest are much more likely to arise. The elderly grandmother is much more likely to have a "nest egg" which can either be used to provide a better quality of life for her now or be preserved to pass on to the next generation. The person in charge of a home has an even more direct interest. Even the local authority has an interest in securing admission to a private home for which central government pays rather than providing a local authority home or domiciliary services.

Towards a New Model

Our law is clearly inadequate. It provides the multiplicity of procedures with varying criteria and inappropriate effects. It is widely ignored in practice. Yet the dangers are obvious. On what principles might a new model be constructed? The following might be suggested:
  (i)   The procedures should be practical enough to ensure that they are actually used.
  (ii) The criteria should be framed with the needs of the elderly specifically in mind.
  (iii) There should be a "one stop" procedure[57] in which all their needs can be considered and dealt with together.
  (iv) The interventions permitted should be the least restrictive available, and thus tailored to the person's individual needs rather than the same for all.
  (v)   The interventions should reflect the fact that the person concerned once had full legal capacity and may have expressed views over a wide range of issues.
  (vi) The process should recognise that such ideals are meaningless unless linked to a clear entitlement to the services which will preserve as much freedom and human dignity as possible.
  As to (i), any new procedure clearly has to recognise the reluctance of everyone involved to invoke any formal measures at all in the case of elderly people. The Mental Health Act model of a consensus between family and different sorts of professionals should have proved much more attractive than it did. Its failure should make us pessimistic about any potential improvements. Apart from the stigma of being formally committed, the problem may well lie with the *ex post facto* scrutiny of the Mental Health Review Tribunal. Yet any process which was better tailored to the individual needs of the elderly person might require a prior independent decision as to the intervention necessary.[58]
  As to (ii), the test should be specially tailored to the needs and characteristics of the elderly, for otherwise the very real difference between people who become incapable and those who always were so will be obscured. But should it be functional or medical or a combination of the two? A general test of incapacity depends upon predicting the future and tends towards findings of universal incapacity from evidence of difficulty in only a few matters. A general

test of mental illness is difficult to apply to degenerative disorders, nor can it cater for the physically infirm but mentally capable. This limitation may be acceptable to most of us, although the families and neighbours might well protest. Tests depending on diagnostic labels may also be routinely applied and thus automatically stigmatizing, although this has not been our experience. They cannot distinguish between different aspects of incapacity. Both tests are based on the paternalistic assumption that the person concerned is unable or unwilling to behave in the way that others believe to be in his best interests. Might it not be better to begin to build upon the concepts developed for the "living will" or enduring power of attorney?[59] The person's condition may be such that he is no longer able to make decisions in the way that he would have done "but for" his illness. This may either be because he is now unable to make them at all or because his decision-making powers have been distorted by his condition. This test, like one of incapacity, could be applied to specific matters rather than generally.

As to (iii), a one-stop process in which all the person's needs can be considered together and dealt with where necessary would clearly be an advantage. This would mean that a list of interventions should be permitted which are capable of bridging the various rigid divides which we have erected. It should be possible to consent to treatment, to select a home for the elderly person, to protect the patient's own resources and ensure that they are expended for his benefit or that of his family, and in every way to order his life as he might have wished to do.

As to (iv), however, if the intervention powers should be tailored to the individual's needs and in accordance with the principle of the least restrictive alternative, then some prior judicial proceeding may be required to decide which powers are needed. As with the Court of Protection, the proceeding might simply appoint a guardian and select which powers he should have or it might make specific decisions itself. Unfortunately, it is easy to declare that such a proceeding should be informal and inquisitorial, whether along the lines of the English Mental Health Review Tribunals[60] or along the lines of the children's hearings system in Scotland.[61] Nothing can actually ensure that such procedures are invoked where the people actually involved in the person's care and treatment do not wish to do so and the person concerned is in no position to oblige them.

As to (v), if the object of the exercise is to fill in for the capacities which the elderly person has now lost, it seems obvious that any intervention should reflect, not what the interveners consider to be in the person's best interests, but what the person himself would have wished to do had he remained able to do it. In other words, this is the obvious case for the "substituted judgment" over the "best interests" test. If the patient has always said that he would not accept certain sorts of treatment, why should the fact that he has now become incapable of saying one way or the other affect matters? If he was a miser all his life, why should he not continue to suffer discomfort even if it distresses his carers that he should do so? Yet once again, it is easy enough to provide for a substitute decision maker. It is difficult to ensure that the decision maker makes the decisions that his charge would have wished to make, without elaborate procedures for independent scrutiny and control. Nevertheless, guardians of children were expected to respect the parents' wishes in the olden days and appear generally to have done so.

As to (vi), it is a common place that freedom of choice is only available to those who have the means to exercise it. Otherwise we must all take what we are offered on the terms on which it is offered. It is greatly to the credit of those involved in the care and protection of the elderly in Great Britain that they are anxious to ensure that even those who have to accept public services are accorded the same freedom and human dignity as might be expected by those who do not have to do so. It is a short step from that perception to arguing that the elderly should have a legal right to services which will provide the least restrictive alternative, enable them to stay in their homes, if that is what they wish, respect their privacy and dignity in residential homes, and, even more, respect their privacy and dignity in hospital wards. The problem is that ever more sophisticated legal structures with formal safeguards cost money, but they may cost less money than properly funded services for the elderly mentally infirm. The fact that those who are actively concerned in the care of the elderly are as worried about these issues as are the lawyers gives us the best hope for the future.

Notes

1. Hospitals have on occasions been held liable for serious failure to supervise a suicidal patient; see *Selfe* v. *Ilford and District Hospital Management Committee* (1970) 114 S.J. 935; but in *Hyde* v. *Tameside Area Health Authority* [1981] C.L.Y.B. 1854, Lord Denning M.R. said that the policy of the law should discourage such actions; under the Mental Health Act 1983, s.127, it is an offence for hospital staff, guardians, or any one individual who has a mentally disordered patient in his care, to ill-treat or wilfully neglect the patient.
2. Staff could undoubtedly be held liable, or prosecuted, for assault or false imprisonment if a patient or resident is treated or detained against his will and without lawful justification.
3. Family Policy Studies Centre, Fact Sheet 2, *An ageing population* (1984).
4. Age Concern *The Law and Vulnerable Elderly People* (1986), p.15; National Institute for Social Work, *Residential Care - A Positive Choice*, Report of the Independent Review of Residential Care (the Wagner Report) (1988), p.111; see A. Norman, *Mental Illness in Old Age: Meeting the Challenge* (1982); Health Advisory Service, *The Rising Tide — Developing Services for Mental Illness in Old Age* (1982).
5. DHSS Social Services Inspectorate, Inspection of Local Authority Care for Elderly Mentally Disordered People (1985), p.8; c.f. Wagner Report, *op. cit.*, p.112; see also I. Sinclair, "Residential Care for Elderly People", in National Institute for

Social Work, *Residential Care — The Research Reviewed* (1988).

6. Propensity to make a living will may be no greater than propensity to make a conventional one; in England, it is likely that at least one half die intestate.

7. Some steps may be taken under common law doctrines of necessity, defence of self and others, or keeping the peace; see B. Hoggett, *Mental Health Law* (2nd ed. 1984), pp.198-204; P. Fennell, "Detention and Control of Informal Mentally Disordered Patients" [1984] J.S.W.L. 345.

8. A. Norman, *Rights and Risk: A Discussion Document on Civil Liberty in Old Age* (1980); Age Concern (1986), *op. cit.;* a proposal for partial guardianship for adults is now being developed by MIND and other bodies.

9. Scottish Action on Dementia, *Dementia and the Law — The Scottish Experience,* A Discussion Paper prepared by the Rights and Legal Protection Sub-Committee (1987).

10. L. Vogel, *Les Systemes de Protection Juridique des Personnes Handicapées Mentales,* Recherche effectuée pour l'Association Internationale Autism-Europe, Centre de Sociologie du Droit Sociale, University of Brussels (1988); [I am most grateful to Michael Baron, M.B.E., M.A., Solicitor, for this information].

11. E.g. Health Commission of Victoria, Minister's Committee on Rights and Protective Legislation for Intellectually Handicapped Persons, *The Protection of Intellectually Handicapped Persons and the Preservation of their Rights,* A Discussion Paper (1981), Report (1982); see now Guardianship and Administration Board Act 1986.

12. Mental Health Act 1959, s.5(1); see now Mental Health Act 1983, s.131(1).

13. Report of the Royal Commission on the Law relating to Mental Illness and Mental Deficiency 1954-1957 (The Percy Commission) Cmnd. 169 (1957).

14. Compulsory patients are now approximately 6% of the total, compared with 70% of the mentally ill and all of the mentally handicapped in 1955.

15. Mental Health Act 1983, s.121.

16. First Biennial Report of the Mental Health Act Commission 1983-85, H.C. 586 (1985), pp.11 and 24-25; Mental Health Act Commission, Second Biennial Report 1985-87, pp.50-51.

17. First Biennial Report, at p.24.

18. Second Biennial Report, at p.56.

19. Defined for compulsory procedures under the Mental Health Act 1983 by s.26.

20. See *T.* v. *T.* [1988] 2 W.L.R. 189; see also *Re B. (A Minor) (Wardship: Sterilisation)* [1987] 2 W.L.R. 1213; and B. Hoggett, *op. cit.,* at p.203. See also Ref (The Independent) 6 December 1988

21. A cohabitant of six months' standing qualifies as nearest relative if no spouse does so; 1983 Act, s.26(6).

22. E.g. *Re Davey (deceased)* [1981] 1 W.L.R. 164.

23. *T.* v. *T.* [1988] 2 W.L.R. 189, at pp. 203-204.

24. *Ibid.,* at p. 199.

25. L. Gostin, *Mental Health Services Law and Practice* (1986), para. 20.16.1; P. Skegg, *Law, Ethics and Medicine* (1984), p.105.

26. E.g. Health Advisory Service, *Annual Report* (June 1985-June 1986), p.18: "Health Advisory Service teams still report the widespread thoughtless use of restraint in so-called "geriatric" chairs and the automatic use of cot-sides for elderly patients."

27. Mental Health Act Commission, *Consent to Treatment* (1985), section 10.

28. Percy Report, *op. cit.*

29. s.2.
30. s.3.
31. s.7.
32. s.11(1).
33. s.12; for paying patients, both must be independent of the hospital; for N.H.S. patients, only one need be so.
34. ss.11(4) and 29(3)(c).
35. s.23; the nearest relative can be prevented by the doctors from discharging a long-term hospital patient who is dangerous; but he can only be prevented by a court from discharging a patient from guardianship.
36. s.72; except in admissions for treatment, the patient must apply for a review, see ss.66 and 68.
37. The powers also apply to certain types of mental handicap and to treatable psychopathic disorder, but that is another story.
38. s.8(1); c.f. Mental Health Act 1959, s.34(1), which gave the guardian all the powers of a father over a child under 14.
39. c.f. s.6(1) for hospital admission.
40. s.18(3).
41. Mental Health Act Commission, Second Biennial Report, *op. cit.,* p.61; Scottish Action on Dementia, *op. cit.,* para.30. See also G.H. Morris, "The Use of Guardianships to Achieve — or to Avoid — the Least Restrictive Alternative " (1980) 3 I.J.L. and Psych. 97.
42. See L. Gostin, *A Human Condition,* Part I (1975); DHSS *et. al.,* Reform of Mental Health Legislation, Cmnd. 3405 (1981); Review of the Mental Health Act 1959, Cmnd. 7320 (1978).
43. 1983 Act, s.63.
44. s.58.
45. s.57; see s.56(1) and (2).
46. s.47; see National Assistance (Amendment) Act 1951 for the emergency procedure.
47. See M. Grey, "Forcing Old People to Leave Their Homes: The Principle" and C. Harvey, "The Practice", *Community Care,* 8 March 1979, pp. 19 and 20; A.J. Norman, *Rights and Risk: A Discussion Document on Civil Liberty in Old Age* (1980); B.M. Hoggett, *op. cit.,* pp.128-133; Age Concern, *op. cit.,* pp.39-50.
48. Age Concern, *op. cit.* p.40, citing M. Green, Geriatric Medicine, January 1980.
49. s.47(1) and (2).
50. A.J. Norman, *op. cit.;* Age Concern, *op. cit.*
51. See generally Mental Health Act 1983, Part VII; Heywood and Massey, *Court of Protection Practice* (11th ed. 1985 by N.A. Whitehorn).
52. s.94(2).
53. s.96.
54. s.95(1).
55. See further Theobald on *Lunacy* (1924); B. Hoggett, "The Crown's Prerogative in Relation to the Mentally Disordered: Resurrection, Resuscitation, or Rejection?" in M.D.A. Freeman (ed.) *Medicine, Ethics and Law* (1988)
56. K. Jones, *A History of the Mental Health Services* (1972); see also A. Scull, *Museums of Madness: The Social Organisation of Insanity in Nineteenth Century England* (1979), C. Unsworth, *The Politics of Mental Health Legislation* (1987), esp. ch.3.

57. The term is borrowed from Scottish Action on Dementia, *op. cit.*
58. See e.g. the scheme for partial guardianship of adults developed, *inter alia,* by MIND; this draws heavily on the State of Victoria, *Guardianship and Administration Board Act 1986.* See below chapter 35.
59. G.J. Alexander, "Premature Probate. A Different Perspective on Guardianship for the Elderly" (1979) 31 *Stanford L.R.* 1003.
60. Whose composition and procedure are similar to that of the Victorian Board, although their powers are not.
61. As tentatively suggested by Scottish Action on Dementia, *op. cit.*

Chapter 34

Loss of Power of Speech — Does it Mean Loss of Civil Rights? The Law in Denmark

Jorgen GRAVERSEN and Inger Margrete PEDERSEN
Aarhus University, Denmark

Introduction

This chapter deals with elderly citizens in Denmark who are suffering from aphasia, a type of impediment of speech *and* the power of linguistic contact, well known to the medical profession. The complaint is often an after-effect of cerebral hemorrhage. The purpose of this chapter is to study whether aphasia does - directly or indirectly — influence the legal position of the sufferer. We are well aware that elderly people are not the only victims of aphasia, and that elderly people suffer from other impediments of speech than aphasia. But some limitation is necessary when undertaking a brief study. We have chosen aphasia, because a great number of the victims *are* elderly people, and because we think that it is useful to concentrate on a complaint which is well known and has often been described in medical and psychological literature. The most important reason for choosing aphasia as our subject is that aphasia in a great number of cases does not affect the mind of the sufferer in such a way that there is any reason to limit his or her legal capacity because of the complaint. On the other hand, aphasia often causes serious impediment to the sufferer's powers of communication with others — in some cases where aphasia is combined with extensive paralysis, and even complete loss of the ability to communicate.

The purpose of our study is to investigate whether the diminution or loss of the normal channels of communication with others has any legal consequences — in law or in practice. It must be kept in mind that we are dealing with adult persons who are typically struck down without warning — waking up in hospital with a complete loss of memory as to how this happened. They are people who have a long and active life behind them. Some are retired but many still hold down a job. The situation of the patient in relation to his or her ability to provide sufficient financial support has thus, without any previous warning, been drastically changed. The patient (and perhaps also the family) may become dependent on the services offered by public authorities and perhaps also on the financial aid offered by such authorities.

Standard descriptions of aphasia include the following typical symptoms which may not all be combined and which may vary in degree from a slight impediment of speech to the complete loss of ability to communicate with others:

a. The person with aphasia does not understand the speech of others, although he/she has normal hearing (impressive aphasia);

b. The person with aphasia knows what he/she wants to express, but cannot find ("mobilize") the proper words (central aphasia);

c. The power of construction and expression of language may be affected in different ways and for different reasons (expressive aphasia);

In a great number of cases the ability to read, write and do sums is also affected.

Aphasia is frequently combined with paralysis in varying degrees. The person with aphasia is often extremely sensitive and is subject to fits of anger more often than before the illness. He/she tires very quickly. More general confusion of the mind also occurs, sometimes especially when the person feels under stress.

The Initial Stages

Life as an aphasia patient starts in a hospital bed, often with a period of unconsciousness. Retraining is the next stage, which means a rehabilitation hospital, a suitable institution or a geriatric ward.

Fortunately a number of patients recover comparatively well after a retraining period and regain their power of speech so well that they are able to manage their own life again. If they have to retire from their job, apply for a social pension or spend their life in a permanent home for the disabled (e.g. because of paralysis) their situation will not differ fundamentally from that of any other person affected by serious and disabling illness.

During the first period in hospital there may, however, be a need for using the rules in matrimonial law and guardianship law dealing with representation of temporarily disabled persons. A spouse has comparatively wide powers to make such decisions as ought not to be postponed (section 13 of the Matrimonial Property Act). As to unmarried patients it may be necessary to appoint a temporary guardian for special and defined purposes. (Section 59 of the Guardianship Act). We will discuss later whether this section can be utilized when there is a question of sending a person with aphasia to a permanent home for disabled persons.

Lasting Serious Impediment of Speech

A. Guardianship law

The description discussed easlier indicates that the starting point when dealing with persons with aphasia ought to be that they have full legal capacity, although it may be difficult — in extreme cases almost impossible — to ascertain the opinion of an aphasia patient on financial or personal problems.

Do the rules of the Guardianship Act apply in this situation?

Unless there is serious confusion of mind, symptoms like those described above do not justify a Court order declaring the person with aphasia incapable of managing his or her own affairs (Guardianship Act section 2). If the person consents, no. 4 of this section will, however, often apply. This lays down that a person suffering from physical disability, illness or other types of infirmity may be declared incapable with his/her consent.

If the client suffers from confusion of the mind no. 1 of the section will often be applicable. If an order declaring a person legally incapable is made, a guardian is appointed and is then (under due public control) entitled to make decisions concerning financial matters, in principle after consultation with the ward (Guardianship Act section 50). If the ward is married and if the legal regime is community property, the guardian and the spouse administer the ward's community property jointly without any supervision (section 52 of the Matrimonial Property Act).

Although for practical purposes it may be necessary to institute proceedings to obtain a court order, this course of action ought only to be undertaken after careful consideration. The person with aphasia will feel the procedure extremely humiliating, and some of the restrictions placed on persons declared legally incapable may cause considerable inconvenience — quite unnecessarily in families coping in a satisfactory way with the problem. In spite of the fact that a court order declaring a person legally incapable covers financial matters only the ward is deprived from participating in general elections.

Modern methods of psychological and medical treatment stress the importance of supporting the right of disabled persons to preserve their human dignity and personal individuality. This is in accordance with the guidelines followed in private law in which all persons are, in principle, individuals with individual rights. On the other hand, lawyers are well aware that elementary legal safeguards may be necessary to protect our more vulnerable fellow citizens.

In view of this it might be worthwhile to consider reviving the almost defunct institution of "widow's guardianship" mentioned in sections 54-56 of the Guardianship Act. It is not limited to women, and it may be instituted in case of (among other causes) physical disability. A guardian appointed under these sections must act jointly with his ward.

A Court order concerning legal incapacity covers financial matters only, unless there is a special order depriving the ward of his/her capability in personal matters.

If such an order is made, the guardian is entitled to decide that the ward is to become an inmate of an institution for elderly people or disabled persons (see below). The guardian is not entitled to send the ward to a psychiatric hospital or to a permanent home administered by such a hospital, unless the ward consents or the rules of the Insanity Act are observed.

The social subcommittee of the Local Council may, on its own initiative and in certain circumstances, institute proceedings to obtain an order of incapacity (section 36 (2) of the Social Pensions Act). The Subcommittee may also put restrictions on a citizen's right to administer public aid or social pensions, if he/ she is not fit to administer cash unchecked (section 36 of the Social Pensions Act and section 49 of the Social Assistance Act).

B. Staying in your own home

It must be stressed that if a person with aphasia wants to stay in his/her own home he/she is in principle entitled to do so. This right is expressly mentioned in regulation no. 568 of Dec. 21st 1979 (issued by the Ministry of Social Affairs) concerning the application of force (coercion) in institutions for persons with serious physical or mental handicaps. It also conforms with private law, especially with guardianship law.

The life of a person with aphasia is full of hospital wards, training centres and institutions of all types. It is readily understandable that a strong urge to return home and remain there dominates patients. Fortunately many persons will cope well on their own or with the support of family members.

Generally speaking it is also the aim of administrators, doctors, social workers, etc. to make it possible for handicapped and elderly persons to remain in their own home. This is, moreover, the aim of legislators, as was stressed quite recently by Act no. 378 of June 10th 1987 concerning housing for elderly people and disabled persons. This aim is supported by the fact that it is extremely expensive to run communal permanent homes.

Much is therefore done to make it easier for disabled persons to remain in their own home: alteration of home surroundings to make everyday life easier for the clients and/or the relations taking care of them, sending in domestic help employed by the Local Council, establishing day care centres, etc.

These cost money and public budgets are continually being cut down — care of elderly people and other social clients unfortunately, all from a short-term point of view, is in some conflict with the (otherwise laudable) aim of improving the balance of payments as quickly as possible.

A special problem is the housing problem. An old-fashioned flat on the third floor with no toilet in the flat and no lift in the house is not a good solution for an elderly — and perhaps disabled — person.

Cooperation within the family is an important factor. But a spouse may still be holding a job or may be disabled. Grown-up children may be very much taken up by their jobs and by their own families.

In a recent decision of the Superior Social Appeal Board (SM 0-41-87), it was held that a spouse has an extensive duty to nurse her or his spouse. — The husband in this case was very seriously handicapped and needed considerable personal care. The wife took care of the normal household duties, shared the nursing with assistants sent by the local authority, worked four hours a day on the family farm and, moreover, worked as an untrained nurse on night duty for 56 hours every fortnight. During her free fortnights, the local authority cut down on the help she received with the nursing. She left the family home and asked for a judicial separation.

The Ombudsman has asked for comments from the Ministry of Social Affairs. [see his Report 1986 case 17-1.]

C. Leaving your own home permanently?

The circumstances mentioned above often result in the question: Can the client remain in his/her own home, when he/she wants to stay?

Or the problem is: Can a patient in a geriatric ward or in other types of hospital care return to his or her family home?

In cases where the person with aphasia, the relatives, the doctors and the social workers agree that it is no longer practically possible for the client to stay, and where the Local Council can offer satisfactory housing (a good institution, a communal flat) everything usually is satisfactory.

But in many districts — e.g. Copenhagen — there is a considerable shortage of institutions. Patients who cannot remain at home have to "queue" in a geriatric ward, in special wards for queueing patients or in ordinary hospital words.

We are now touching upon a problem which is central to the social policy of any state: How does it treat its senior citizens when they can no longer take care of themselves or be taken care of in their own homes? This subject deserves its own chapter, which would show a very varied picture in different parts of Denmark at least. On the one hand, we find an interested and well-intentioned legislature, Local Councils in the most unexpected places trying out new and constructive ideas, and, by international standards, a high percentage of single rooms in institutions for clients with no psychiatric problems. There is a growing number of doctors, psychologists, administrators and social workers going in for new methods of dealing with the disabled, the frail and the elderly — methods taking as their starting point the needs of the client as an individual with individual rights.

On the other hand we still find paternalistic attitudes — well-meaning, but often completely destructive to the personal dignity of the client.

We also find patients queueing in hospital wards for a right to a personal room in an institution (and not all of them live long enough to see that day). We find psychiatric institutions with a standard far, far below that of institutions for clients with no psychiatric problems. And a number of the most vulnerable elderly patients end their days in these institutions.

But we will return to our subject: How do persons with aphasia fare in this system from a legal point of view? Once more it must be stressed that they are citizens with the same civic rights as other citizens. They cannot be removed to an institution without consent or alternatively without using the normal procedure under the Guardianship Act or the Insanity Act. It happens in practice that consent from a spouse or a grown-up child is considered sufficient. This is based upon a misunderstanding of the law.

Consenting to give up your own home and spending the rest of your life in an institution will, of course, be accompanied by considerable reluctance and resignation, and in some cases with bitterness against relations and/or the social authorities. It is often felt that the removal to an institution might have been avoided, if the authorities/relatives were willing to take more trouble. This is a time when the responsibility of social workers, etc. is especially significant. This problem cannot be solved by legal methods. Consent given with regret and resignation is still valid.

When dealing with clients with aphasia it is, however, a special problem that their normal powers of speech are, typically, especially affected when discusing subjects causing emotional disturbance. A person with aphasia may be able to discuss the nation's trade deficit without any difficulty at one moment, and the next moment be completely unable to convey his/her views on leaving home for an institution. This may make it extremely difficult to assess whether there is consent or dissent — or whether the patient quite simply refuses to make up his mind. In some cases there may also be doubt as to whether he/she has understood the issue. The tendency to quick anger found in many aphasia patients may make it even more difficult to assess the situation. And, of course, many suffer from other complaints, which may also complicate the issue.

In these circumstances it is of the greatest importance to keep in mind that it is, very often, the power of expression only that fails the client. Even if the mind is affected, it may not be to such an extent that legal capability is affected. Very serious impediment of speech does not exclude complete clarity of mind. This is for example shown when persons with language difficulties acquire a new language by mastering a computer. It is also important that those dealing with the client are good and sensitive interpreters.

A head nurse of a rehabilitation hospital has in her recent book *Lend Me Your Power of Speech* lent words to the reactions of an aphasia patient, an academic with very great language difficulties, describing his resentment when one of the other nurses spoke to him as if he were a child. His point of view was that just because he had to be taught to speak all over again, he did not have a mind like a child. It is a not uncommon complaint from speech handicapped clients. Another complaint is that conversations go on in their presence as if the client did not exist. The British Broadcasting Corporation has a radio programme dealing with this problem, called "Does He Take Sugar?".

Medical and nursing staff, as well as social workers and lawyers and family members have to guard against the tendency to identify the lack of power of speech with a lack of power of the mind, and it is especially important in connection with the decision concerning the client's future permanent place of residence.

D. The client refuses consent

What do the medical and social authorities do if there are grounds for serious doubts as to whether the client with aphasia ought to go to an institution or stay in his/her own home and the client will not consent to institutionalization?

As we have said, if the decision is enforced, it will have to be done according to the rules of the Guardianship Law or of the Insanity Act.

But it may be worthwhile to consider whether the wish to send the client to an institution is not based upon a paternalistic view that will not accept somewhat unsatisfactory home conditions for a client who quite clearly prefers independence at this cost.

It is also important to consider the attitude of the family members. If the client is married and if the disability — in our case aphasia — has resulted in matrimonial breakdown (as divorce judges know, a change in the family pattern may cause estrangement) the best way to solve the problem will sometimes be to face a separation or divorce and let the question of the family home (whether rented or owned) be settled by the relevant courts in the usual way. In Court proceedings, it is sometimes proved that the disabled spouse will be able to manage on his/her own in the family home. In that case a rented flat will often be awarded to that spouse and it must be kept in mind that it will be felt as intolerably wounding for a person with aphasia — or any other disability, for that matter — if the fundamental reason for sending him/her to a home for the disabled is disharmony in the marriage.

Even if there is no matrimonial breakdown, the authorities may face rather complicated situations — made additionally complicated the more the person with aphasia is impeded in his/her speech. In theory, family members are the best interpreters because of their intimate knowledge of the person's past history. In practice it may be different. Even well meaning and kindly family members may, when interpreting the expressions of the aphasia patient, be influenced by their own attitudes and wishes. On the other hand the client may make unrealistic demands upon the spouse/relatives.

The authorities will have to ascertain what is the will of the client. The family members have no authority to make decisions on his/her behalf.

A three-sided discussion of the problems between the doctors/social workers, etc., the client and the family ought always to be attempted. An attitude on the part of the authorities stressing that the aphasia patient as well as those that make up a necessary part of his everyday life are individual persons who are expected to make responsible decisions is well in accordance with legal principles, but it will probably also save some tangled situations.

If no solution is found, guardianship law has to be applied. If there is a Court order declaring the client with aphasia financially *and* personally incapable, the guardian may decide that the ward is to go into an institution. If disabled persons have little or no property it has been felt that declaring him/her legally incapable may not be the happiest solution. It will be felt humiliating and there will be little need of a guardian once the question of residence has been settled. In Copenhagen, for example, it has for a number of years been the practice to make use of section 59 of the Guardianship Act (see under (11)), but only if the client does not own property exceeding about a certain sum. Judge S. Danielsen in his book on Guardianship law (1982) p. 324 finds the authority for this solution "thin" It has, however, now been accepted by The Family Directorate of the Ministry of Justice in a circular letter of Nov. 18th 1987.

A number of doctors find the solution unsatisfactory, stressing among other factors that section 59 deals with *temporary* disability. We will discuss this problem in our conclusion.

E. Coercion under the Insanity Act

Some disabled persons are sent to psychiatric hospitals under coercion. The rules are found in the Insanity Act of 1938.

The Act is applicable *if* the patient is insane (in practice: is in a psychotic condition and *if* (a) the person is dangerous to himself and/or others, or (b) the prospects of recovery will be materially diminished if he or she is not treated in a psychiatric hospital.

Aphasia does not in itself constitute a psychotic condition, but of course a person with aphasia may suffer from a psychosis.

The question of consent has special aspects when we are dealing with psychiatric treatment in hospitals. Present practice is described by the Commission on Coercion in Psychiatric Treatment in its final report (no. 1109/1987) on p. 39. It is held that the rules of the Insanity Act of 1938 are not applicable if the patient does not, by word or by other behaviour that cannot be misunderstood, oppose the proposed action. This means that these rules are not applied to the group of patients from whom it is impossible to get an unambiguous answer, whether it is consent or dissent. Elderly confused persons are included in the definition, but so also are many patients suffering from depression or hallucinations or who are in a highly agitated state of mind.

The Commission does not propose any changes in this system, and its proposals in this respect have been upheld in the Bill recently put before Parliament.

These problems were more extensively dealt with in the preliminary report of the Commission (no. 1068/1986) pp. 493-94. It does not deal specifically with the class of patient who will typically become a long-term, perhaps even a lifelong, patient. It is asserted that the law is the same for non-psychiatric hospitals.

A patient with serious impressive and expressive aphasia might find it somewhat difficult to cope with a system like this. A wrong diagnosis may affect his or her future life quite drastically. If psychiatric treatment of the elderly aphasia patient results in his/her recovery from a psychotic condition and return to a fairly acceptable everyday life, the problem would be limited. Indeed taking the trouble to cure acute illnesses of the elderly is in accordance with recent trends in gerontology.

But success in this respect depends on the proper diagnosis being made.

Unfortunately, statistics show that there are no grounds for optimism when an elderly person enters a psychiatric hospital. Until recently, about half of the patients in such hospitals and the permanent homes administered by the hospitals, who have been patients for more than 1 year, were over 65.

The majority of the homes have now been taken over by the social administration of the Regional Councils (County Councils). This will probably affect future statistics and not in a positive direction. This change in the status of the institutions has also affected the status of the patient. The psychiatric hospitals and their permanent homes for psychiatric patients are managed by the same group of doctors. The procedure for decisions to remove the patient from a ward to a permanent home is, therefore, "easy and flexible" (p. 503 in Report no. 1068/1986).

But when a patient has to be removed from a hospital ward to a home managed by the Regional Council the normal procedure for sending people to homes for disabled with psychiatric problems must be followed.

Another problem for the permanent inmate of a psychiatric hospital or one of its permanent homes for the disabled is — as indicated before — that the standard in psychiatric institutions is very different from that of the permanent homes for disabled persons without psychiatric problems. The first group very often have a bed in a room for four persons and a small cupboard. The second group, in contrast, very often have rooms of their own and can bring their own furniture.

There is also, generally speaking, a lower standard as to other facilities, and the psychiatric wards and institutions are often overcrowded. But there is fortunately a trend towards bettering conditions in regionally owned homes.

It is generally admitted that these conditions do not tend to improve the symptoms of psychiatric patients. The tendency, to depression and fits of anger often found in persons with aphasia, may well be aggravated in such circumstances and strengthen the case for letting him/her join the considerable number of elderly people who have no future outside institutions — in spite of the good intentions that politicians have shown in recent legislation.

F. Life in the institutions

It will always be necessary to regulate life in communal institutions to a certain extent. But in principle you do not lose your normal legal rights, because you enter such an institution. An exception of great practical importance is the law concerning social pensioners in institutions and hospitals. They do not pay, but may receive, a certain sum of pocket money instead of their normal pension.

In general discussions, most people would agree that, in principle, regulations ought to be restricted to what is absolutely necessary for the practical organization of the everyday life of the institution and with due regard to the financial rights and personal dignity and integrity of the inmates. We have, however, no public report analysing the question, and as a research subject, the rights of patients and inmates in hospitals and public institutions for disabled and elderly people is still in its initial stages. A Norwegian Parliamentary report on the subject (no. 32/1976-77) does, however, probably in most respects cover the views of Danish lawyers.

In a textbook for staff in permanent homes for the elderly and disabled, the authors (Knud Jensen et al., 1986, p. 25 et seq.) recommend adjusting the everyday life to the habits of the clients as far as possible.

That this is not always done is shown by a circular from one of the central social administrative authorities (Circular Letter no. 696 of 24th July 1980) giving guidelines for permanent homes for clients with serious physical and psychic handicaps. Under (6) it states that suitable organization of the daily work in the institutions has been of great importance to the efforts to avoid forcible or coercive methods in the treatment of the clients. It is stated:

> "In many institutions the organization of the staff's work has been charac-
> terized by unfortunate traditions and routines, e.g. concerning mealtimes,
> hours for getting up and going to bed and especially as to bathing and visiting
> toilets, where the practice often has been to use "fixed times" without regard
> for the inmates' immediate need....
>
> In some institutions conditions have for these reasons often been so
> stressed that a number of inmates became very excited and violent, with the
> result that coercion was used against them....
>
> By changing the organization of work in such a way that unfortunate
> traditions and routines have been replaced by a regard for the need of the
> individual inmates.... it has been possible to avoid many difficult incidents
> during the daytime...."

Recent general regulations issued by central social authorities have given inmates a right to be consulted and/or informed. In Circular no. 153 of Dec. 17th 1986 concerning the abovementioned institutions it is stated that the inmates have the same rights in this respect as inmates in other institutions. If they are, in exceptional circumstances, not able to influence the workings of the institution, relatives etc. will have to represent them.

When it comes to far-reaching decisions, guardianship law applies. This problem has been dealt with in relation to psychiatric hospitals in a recent decision by the Eastern Regional and Appeal Court (3. section 205/1985 — judgment given 15th June 1987). The Court held that a number of psychiatric patients in wards with locked entrance doors might validly consent to a newspaper taking photographs and writing articles about conditions in the wards. Exception was made for two patients only, and for specific reasons. One of them was a young woman who spent 23 hours a day fixed in her bed, but in her case, consent was given by her mother, who was not her guardian, although she was very active in her daughter's affairs. The newspaper cooperated with the doctors, the patients and the mother.

We do not know to what extent the paternalistic attitudes described in the Circular Letter from 1980 still exist. We have, however, several indications that they have not completely disappeared. In view of the importance of the problem, research into that matter might be worthwhile, especially in view of the fact that staff in permanent homes have, in certain districts, complained about the growing number of violent clients.

Some example maybe of interest. In a recent radio programme with interviews it was indicated that it is extremely difficult for clients living at permanent homes for elderly and disabled to be permitted a normal sex life unless they are married. In most homes the staff frowned upon clients developing sexual interests. A research worker said that he had sent questionnaires to a number of institutions, because he wanted to undertake a study of sex problems in homes. He got only one answer — which was very sympathetic, but stated that the Head wanted the consent of the grown up children of the clients before giving them the questionnaires.

Nursing staff have told us that in some geriatric wards and permanent homes there is a tendency to refuse permission to go on holidays and to have weekend visits to persons not approved by the client's family members. We have definite knowledge of one specific case, where it was expressly stated that refusal of permission was not due to medical causes.

In many permanent homes — probably most of them — the clients have to give up their own doctor (unless they are well off) and accept the practitioner appointed by the home. We know of one case, where the clients had to be accompanied by a member of the staff when seeing the doctor, but this case dates back 15 years and would probably not occur now, unless there were specific reasons.

In some hospitals and homes, the recent trend is not to discuss the patient/client with his relatives unless he/she is present. In other institutions and hospitals the disabled person may be kept completely out of the picture (we have well documented examples of both methods).

The legislative trend is to ensure that the elderly and disabled enjoy a life in their own home with a kitchen and toilet and with a right to administer their own finances.

This has resulted in two important Acts in 1987:

a) No. 378 of 10th June 1987 concerning housing for elderly and disabled persons. This Act lays down that only in exceptional cases may housing for the elderly be organised without separate flats and kitchens.

   Clients who live in independent flats for the elderly will automatically preserve their right to administer their own social pension.

b) Act. no. 391 of 10th June 1987 is an amendment of the Public Assistance

Act, making it possible for local authorities to establish pilot projects under which social pensioners living in institutions get their full pension and pay for the services they receive.

Some of the psychiatric permanent homes that have now been taken over by the social administration of the Regional Councils have had permanently locked entrance doors. This system must be abolished by the end of 1988 at the very latest. The general trend is that institutions be abolished as far as possible, and those that remain become homes for individual persons who will have individual personal and financial rights.

How will patients with aphasia fare in this system? A normal life in your own home, or in a good institution for the disabled, where your abilities, your personality and your individual rights are appreciated and respected, is what is advised for aphasia clients. Modern trends will, therefore, if they are carried out in practice, benefit them.

But they are also vulnerable. If they have no one to "lend them a language", if their intellect is weakened, if they become confused and unhappy, then they belong to the groups that may have to pay for the otherwise praiseworthy amendment of the law. In the future, patients who are confused or agitated and who start wandering around "looking for the outer door" may find that the only solution offered to them is a ward in a psychiatric hospital or hospital institution with locked doors.

Conclusion

Although this is a preliminary enquiry, and although it is limited to persons suffering from aphasia, we have, as we were collecting our material, met with an overwhelming number of reactions, confirming our hypothesis: these are problems which must be studied and dealt with if modern society wants to offer the frailer members of the elderly generations acceptable conditions of life.

We have also had confirmed our hypothesis that it is important to deal specifically with speech handicaps, and that this is a subject to which it is necessary and useful to institute close cooperation with a number of other professions: doctors, nursing staff, social scientists and practitioners, administrators, etc. (We are indebted and grateful to many of these, but quite especially to Chief Doctors Jorgen Rosenbeck-Hansen and Nils Chr. Gulmann.)

Research and experiments at all levels — and suitable information about the results — are important. Knowledge of the problems — the more the better — will make all groups, including patients and their relatives, better able to cope with the difficulties. Research concerning the ways in which modern technology — not least computers — may give the patients their language back must have high priority.

Some aims are especially important to achieve:

a. It is necessary to ensure that it is continually kept in mind that persons with an impediment of the power of speech are individuals with individual rights. Any restrictions must be based upon guardianship law or other laws or regulations. This also holds good for social clients and for hospital patients. Good intentions are no excuse.

b. If an elderly client/patient suffers from multiple symptoms it is of extreme importance that aphasia and other speech problems are not overlooked, and especially that they are not mistaken for diminished or vanished mental powers.

Both of us have had the instructive experience of being told by kind but disbelieving doctors that we were mistaken when we thought that we were able to hold meaningful communication with sick relatives.

Curiously enough, the situation is quite different when you have a "conversation" with babies who have not yet learnt to speak! Nobody disbelieves that!

From a lawyer's point of view we think that guardianship law ought to be revised with a view to making it more flexible and more suited to the needs of the growing number of elderly people and the relations who want to give them their best support.

A modernised version of "widows' guardianship" will probably solve a number of problems. It does not deprive the client entirely of his or her powers to act. The support of a guardian with whom you have to act jointly may well be thought an advantage by many, especially those in their "fourth age". The new system ought also to comprise personal affairs, e.g. the decision to go to a permanent home.

The effects of an ordinary incapacity order will, in many cases, be felt as unnecessarily restrictive, both by the ward and by the family or connections. A fairly well-off grandparent ought to be allowed to support a grand-child's studies.

A special study must be made of guardianship rules as they affect the situation where the patient/client must go to a home for the elderly.

Another area that ought to be considered is to create further possibilities for giving the elderly patients/clients the benefit of professional advisers in special situations. One example is the system proposed in the new Insanity Bill (advisers, usually with social training, for patients who go to a psychiatric hospital under coercion).

We concluded, as we legan, with the categorial rejectim of the hypothesis that the loss of the pore of speech should require less of civiltights. A much more sensitive approach to the issue is required.

Chapter 35

Guardianship: Protection and Autonomy — Has the Right Balance Been Achieved?

Robin CREYKE   Australian National University, Canberra, Canada

Introduction

This chapter is about guardianship of elderly people who are incompetent. It does not deal with alternate legal management of their estates. The common law provides a number of mechanisms for substitute decision-making for people who are losing or no longer have legal capacity. Some of these, such as the enduring power of attorney, bank authorisation schemes, joint bank accounts and social security substitute payee schemes can be put in place by the person involved. Others, like guardianship and estate management may only be instituted following incapacity, and the initiative to set them up must be taken by people other than the incompetent person. Devices like bank schemes and the social security substitute payee system (known in Australia as the "nominee" system)[1] are limited in scope. They apply only to financial affairs and are limited to management of the funds in a particular account or from a single source such as a government pension. For people whose income is wholly or substantially of this kind, these financial management systems are quite adequate; for others with more diverse sources of funds or who need assistance with personal affairs, they are not the answer. These people need mechanisms such as the enduring power of attorney and guardianship and estate administration, which are capable of meeting all — or almost all — the social and economic management needs of the person.

Guardianship of the person is the most extensive form of legal control of a ✻ person outside institutional commitment. Over the years, however, limits have been developed or proposed for restricting guardians' authority so as to reduce the loss of civil rights traditionally associated with the imposition of this form of legal control. Some of these — in the form of general restrictive principles — grew out of developments in knowledge of mentally disabling conditions and the civil rights movement in the second half of this century. Others, such as limits on the matters a guardian can control, although rarely articulated, are inherent in the nature of guardians' decision-making. Still others, such as the standards which guardians must attain in their care of people under guardianship have arisen out of the roles which at particular times have been seen as appropriate for guardians or are applied, it is argued for policy reasons, especially in the area of medical treatment. These restrictions are the law's response to the need which has been recognised to define and limit guardians powers.

This chapter examines how many of these limits have been implemented in new guardianship legislation in Victoria (one of the two largest of the Australian States), *The Guardianship and Administration Board Act* 1986.

To point up the undesirable features of older guardianship legislation another Australian example, the Lunacy Act, 1898 (NSW) will be examined. It is a New South Wales Act, since repealed for that State, the guardianship provisions of which, however, remain in force in the Australian Capital Territory ("the ACT" or "the Territory").[2] Finally the question is asked "Are these limitations sufficient to protect the needs — both for the assistance and, where appropriate, for the autonomy — of incapable people, to guide surrogate managers in their tasks and to ensure their accountability?".

Australia — Some Social Issues

In Australia, as with other OECD countries, the number of the aged[3] is growing at a faster rate than the population. Between 1984 and 2021, the general population will increase by 42% while the increase in the aged will be 119%.[4] With the growth in the numbers of the aged the rates of illness, disablement and of chronic mental illnesses such as dementia are also higher.[5]

It is difficult to obtain accurate figures on the break-up of mental illness for the aged. The most recent official Australian survey only looked at two categories of mentally disabling condition: those suffering from forms of intellectual disability;[6] and mental disorders other than intellectual disability. The survey found that the proportion of people in the 65-74 age group suffering from mental disorders other than mental retardation was 41.9 in every 1,000 or 4.2%. The number in the 75 upwards age group was 88 per thousand or 8.8%. This compares with the number in the same age ranges suffering from mental retardation and related disorders of 5.4 and 22.6 per thousand respectively, that is .5% and 2.6%.[7]

What figures there are suggest that dementia is the most prevalent of the mentally incapacitating diseases of the elderly in Australia.[8] The prevalence rate for dementia for the 80-84 age group is 10.5% increasing to 38.6% for the 90-95 age group.[9] It is estimated that the number of elderly people suffering from dementia will increase by up to 75% by the year 2001, and by up to 150% by 2021. At present 108,500 Australians are estimated to have senile dementia. By 2001, the number is likely to be 170,000 or higher, and it may be between

240,000 and 270,000 by the year 2021.[10] Since the effect of moderate to severe, and, at times, even mild dementia is to produce memory loss, loss of social judgment and ability to handle problems and to manage personal care[11], it is apparent that a proportion of dementia sufferers will need assistance with their personal and financial affairs.

In Australia, care of people with chronic illnesses and disability is generally undertaken by spouses and families — eighty percent of the elderly handicapped in Australia are living at home rather than in institutions.[12] Of those in institutions, over half are suffering from dementia,[13] and with the increasing proportion of dementia sufferers in the population, this number is likely to increase. Thus families and those running institutions face the care of a growing number of people suffering a chronic, generally irreversible, mentally disabling condition.

Despite the effects of mentally disabling conditions like dementia, it needs to be recognised that people do not become incompetent overnight. For the majority, there is a pattern of some loss of competence — perhaps triggered by another medical condition — followed by a degree of recovery. In a few cases (generally amongst younger people) dementia and other mentally disabling conditions, may be reversed. In general, however, the competence of people with the disease continues to decline — a process which may occur over some years.[14]

During this period of fluctuating but decreasing competence, the substitute management needs of the person will change — sometimes imperceptibly, sometimes quite suddenly — often from day to day. Prior to or during that period, many older people, from a desire to reduce the potential burden of their incapacity on their children and others, will have made attempts to provide against the time when they are no longer competent, by using one of the devices referred to above. Others, deliberately or inadvertently, will not have done so. Whether they have faced the issue or not, very few people accept impending mental incapacity easily. Psychologically it is difficult to relinquish independence and control. The onset of mentally disabling conditions such as dementia is a difficult period for the sufferer, the carers, and community and government personnel who provide support services. The situation requires considerable tact and sensitivity. Often the least intrusive (and that generally means gradual) removal of control is required. In this context guardianship systems will be considered to see whether they are capable of the flexibility and fine-tuned approach required.

Limits on Guardians' Powers

A. Impetis for Change

In common law countries, limits on guardians' authority are imposed. In the second half of the twentieth century the major development in guardianship law has been a recognition that, in most cases, plenary management is unnecessary, and that less restrictive forms of guardianship should be explored.[15] Impetus for this change has come from a number of sources.

(1) *Changed notions of incapacity.* With better understanding of the causes, prognosis and treatability of mentally disabling conditions, the notion that competence was an "absolute reality" has been exploded.[16] The idea that a person either was competent and able to manage, or incompetent and needed a guardian, has been replaced by an awareness that a person's competence may change over time, may vary with the situation or may depend on whether the person's condition is being controlled by medication.[17] This changed view of incapacity has had most impact in relation to people with intellectual disabilities. However, use of neuroleptic and other drugs to control symptoms of psychiatric illnesses, a recognition that some diseases associated with old age are treatable and that the loss of competence associated with increasing age is generally a gradual process not a sudden event, have all shown this to be true for other mentally disabling conditions.[18] These developments laid the ground for the incorporation into guardianship law of the least restrictive alternative principle and of normalization.

(2) *Least restrictive alternative and normalization.* A further impetus to change has come from the growing international concern to improve the lot of disadvantaged groups in society, including those who are mentally incompetent. In the area of guardianship, this has resulted in declarations in international forums, designed to ensure that substitute management does not mean a total loss of civil rights. The first of these, the *Declaration of General and Special Rights of the Mentally Retarded* made at the San Sebastian Symposium on Guardianship in 1969, stated that where a surrogate manager was appointed for "a mentally retarded person"

> "[t]he procedure used for modification or denial of rights must contain proper legal safeguards against every form of abuse, must be based on an evaluation of the social capability of the mentally retarded person by qualified experts and must be subject to periodic reviews and to the right of appeal to higher authorities."[19]

The statement contains several key elements: procedural safeguards at substitute management proceedings including a right of appeal; assessment of competence in order that the manager is given authority only in those areas where the person cannot manage; and a right of review to ensure that changes in the person's competence[20] are monitored and the authority of the substitute manager adjusted accordingly. It is clear from this statement that the primary focus in guardianship legislation should be on the rights, interests and welfare of the person subject to alternate management. Similar aspirations appear in the UN *Declaration of the Rights of Mentally Retarded Persons* and the UN *Declaration on the Rights of Disabled Persons.*[21] Discernible in these resolutions are the principles of "normalization" and of "the least restrictive alternative" — principles used as criteria on the one hand for encouraging self-reliance and on the other for curtailing the restriction of rights of people with disabilities. These two notions, self-development and respect for autonomy have an important role as standard setters in areas of the law such as guardianship.

Normalization reflects the idea that disabled people should be treated as much as possible like non-disabled people and should be afforded "patterns and conditions of everyday life which are as close as possible to the norms and patterns of the mainstream of society".[22] It is evident, albeit in a qualified form, in Article 1 of the UN *Declaration on the Rights of Mentally Retarded Persons* and Articles 3 and 4 of the UN *Declaration on the Rights of Disabled Persons*, which requires that people with disabilities are to be accorded, where possible, the same rights as non-disabled people.[23] It also emerges from Article 4 of the *Declaration on the Rights of Mentally Retarded Persons*, which states that, where possible, people with intellectual disability should live with their families and be part of the community, and that even where people with such disabilities must live in an institution, the conditions should mirror, as closely as possible, conditions in normal life.[24]

Similarly, the notion of the "least restrictive alternative" (that is, that an individual's freedom should be restricted to the minimum feasible extent)[25] appears in Article 7 of the UN *Declaration on the Rights of Mentally Retarded Persons* (an article which applies to people with any form of disabling condition). It provides that any limitation of the rights of a disabled person should be the least possible and should be imposed only after a proper evaluation of the person's capacity and by a process which safeguards the person's interests[26], words which echo the criteria laid down in the San Sebastian Declaration.

As two Australian writers put it:

> The crux of the issue is that limits (both legal and social) on a retarded person's right to self-determination should be imposed only in those areas and situations in his life where there are no other less restrictive alternatives available; and that in other areas he should be accorded the rights of any other citizen, to come and go as he pleases and make his own decisions about his lifestyle on major and minor matters.[27]

These principles represent two aspects of one idea: as part of the process of achieving the maximum degree of autonomy for people with disabilities, there must be a prohibition on the unnecessary denial of their rights and, at the same time, positive steps must be taken to encourage them to participate in community life to the extent that their disabilities permit.

The adoption in guardianship legislation of these principles - respect for autonomy and self-determination — is capable of making a profound difference in existing laws. As will be apparent from the discussion of the Victorian Act, their impact can be seen at two levels — the general and the specific. At the general level, the requirement that respect for autonomy and encouragement of self determination be standards for determining guardianship applications, is capable of meaning that guardianship is only imposed where there is a real need for a guardian, that even where guardianship is implemented, it is tailored to cover only those aspects of life in which the individual lacks capacity and that plenary guardianship is seen as a last resort. At a more specific level, they ensure the adoption of appointment and review procedures which are designed to prevent unnecessary appointments being made and to reduce to a minimum the extent of guardian's powers and the length of time guardianship is in force.

(3) *Decision-making Standards*

There are two principal measures for decision-making by guardians: the best interests standard and the substituted judgment standard. Although both had originated in English cases decided no later than the early nineteenth century, the more individualistic substituted judgment principle has only recently achieved prominence.

At common law the twin notions of conservative management and benefit to the individual became the principles which governed guardians in their guardianship duties. In time the notions were telescoped into the "best interests" standard for decision-making. During the eighteenth and nineteenth centuries, legislation became the principal source of rules as to substitute management. In the absence of specific criteria in the statutes governing decisions by guardians these common law principles were applied.[28]

B. Three nodels

What is meant by "best interests" today? The answer is illustrated by two models of guardianship which have been identified and, more recently, have been statutorily defined. A third model of guardianship demonstrates the substituted judgment standard for decision-making.

The notion of different models of guardianship owes its origin to North American writers, Frolik in Pittsburgh and McLaughlin in Ontario.[29] Frolik identified three models of guardianship. These have been described as follows:

- a legalistic, or "substituted judgment", model which aims to facilitate only a person's legal functioning in the community;
- a welfare oriented, or therapeutic, model which strives to bring a wider range of benefits to the person; and
- a "parent-child", or developmental, model which aims to promote the development of the individual's functioning in a range of areas.[30]

The first mentioned model will be considered last.

Therapeutic model. Under this model a social welfare agency provides the range of support services needed by an incompetent individual — the "protective services" notion which has, for example, been adopted in a number of American States including California and Ohio[31] — and is applied, in particular, in relation to the elderly. Such services include legal services in order that the agency may (for example), give consent to medical treatment. Hence the agency is also given guardianship powers. Social worker employees of the agency exercise their powers in accordance with their professional judgment as to what is for the benefit or welfare of the individual client — welfare or benefit being gauged according to accepted societal standards. Thus decisions are made according to the social worker-guardian's views of what is best for the client, not what the client would have chosen. It therefore contrasts sharply with the standard generally applied under the legalistic model (see below).

Two famous, and much discussed, empirical studies have been critical of this approach. Professor Levy concluded that in Minnesota, despite the policy of its Public Guardian that services should be available without guardianship and that guardianship should only be imposed in cases of real need, the County Welfare Boards, the delegates of the Public Guardian, ignored his views. It was found that institutionalisation was often the primary reason for guardianship being established, people whose need was doubtful were often subjected to guardianship, and releases from guardianship were infrequent and slow.[32]

This tendency for increased institutionalisation of clients under the social work model was also a finding from another famous study conducted at the Benjamin Rose Franklin Institute, Cleveland, Ohio, a protective service agency for elderly people. The study, which took place over four years, indicated that the control group who were not receiving protective services were better off and had lower mortality rates than those who received protective services — at least if the latter had been placed in institutions. The study concluded that this was principally due to the greater likelihood that the clients receiving agency services would be institutionalised.[33]

A more recent example is found in statements by some members of the British Association of Social Workers which suggested that guardianship might be used for elderly people who, though not exhibiting obvious symptoms of mental disorder, nevertheless behaved in an eccentric and bizarre manner and had a lifestyle which warranted such an appointment — even if only on a temporary basis.[34]

These studies are disturbing, and have not been challenged. They indicate a tendency for coercive — albeit benevolently coercive — decision-making when the best interests standard adopted under this model is applied. The denial of individual preference, the failure to permit what may simply be aberrant behaviour, is one of the main drawbacks of decision-making under this model and has been criticised accordingly. Stone refers to it as "the abusive paternalism of the law-mental health system".[35] The conflict between paternalism and autonomy is illustrated most graphically in relation to the aged. The majority of the aged have managed their affairs for a life-span. They have brought up families, been productive members of the workforce and have contributed to the wider community. Premature loss of their independence, of their right to choose, which may result from the intervention of well-meaning social workers, can be devastating for their self-respect. As Stone has commented, "the mere fact of age, or of some medically-predicated inference of inability to manage properly, should not justify preemptive State intervention. If a man can still hear at 85, who has a better right to walk to a different drummer?"[36]

Developmental model. Just as a child must be guided and protected against harm, so, under this model, must an incompetent adult. It also recognises, however, that as with the familial parent-child relationship, authority should be shared where possible between the guardian and the individual. The notion that a guardian should encourage the development or exercise of power by the person under guardianship and that the guardian's authority may accrue (or decrease) slowly would be advantageous for an elderly person who was gradually losing competence. In practice, to achieve this result would require great sensitivity on the part of the guardian — and it may be difficult for a court or other determining body to adequately monitor the extent of the guardian's authority.

The justification for guardianship under this model is that it is required to protect the incompetent person's interests, and that aspect of the best interests standard is given prominence. This notion that guardianship is in the best interests of the ward has also meant that guardianship hearings under this model tend to be undertaken without stringent procedural safeguards.[37] As a consequence it is inevitable that some people would be subjected to guardianship under this model, in circumstances where less restrictive alternatives would be appropriate.[38]

Another facet of this model which has been identified is that guardians make decisions which will least disturb the *status quo*. As Frolik comments, this conservative attitude means that "[g]uardians are not encouraged to be imaginative or creative."[39] In short, although there are aspects of this model such as the sharing of authority between guardian and person under guardianship which could be beneficial to older people, its lack of procedural safeguards and its inherent paternalism mean that individual preference and self-determination are not likely to be encouraged.

Summary. "Best interests," as expressed in these two models of guardianship emphasises the protective and conservative aspects of a guardian's role, rather than its self-determinative and normalization functions. And although under the developmental model limited recognition, at least in theory, is given to encouraging the individual's exercise of rights, it is doubtful that this concession[40] would permit that degree of autonomy which has been identified as a primary guardianship goal.

Legalistic model. The standard for decision-making adopted under this model is the substituted judgment principle,[41] that is, decision-making is based not on the guardian's judgment of what would be best for the incompetent person but on what the incompetent person would have done, if capable.

The difference between the best interests and the substituted judgment standards is illustrated by the following hypothetical example. Imagine an elderly person with Alzheimer's Disease. The person is living in the family home with a carer spouse. On several occasions during a competent period the disabled spouse has expressed a reluctance to leave home even if incompetent. If the carer spouse seeks guardianship solely for the purpose of placing the disabled spouse in an institution, and the determining body was aware of the person's views, the order appointing the spouse guardian, if made in accordance with the substituted judgment principle, would prohibit institutionalization and require that other home-based services be employed to provide the carer spouse with needed support. The opposite conclusion would be reached if the best interests standard was applied.

There are two significant aspects of the principle. The first is best illustrated in relation to property management (to which it also applies). A guardian or estate manager may use the person's assets to benefit someone other than the person whose affairs are being managed.[42] Hence the conservative standards imposed under the best interests measure (which generally only permit proceeds of the disabled person's estate to be used for the benefit of that person) are modified by this principle. Second, in strict theory the principle is dependant on the expression of opinions by the person subject to the surrogate management.[43] This may not be an issue in cases where the person involved has been competent until the latter stages of a normal lifespan and, during that time, has clearly expressed views on questions with which the guardian or manager must deal. Difficulties arise where either the person has never been competent (for example, a person who suffers from a congenital condition to a severe degree such as intellectual disability) or, while competent, the person never indicated an opinion on the question at issue.

These problems have necessitated some artificial reasoning by the courts when implementing the standard.[44] They have held that where no prior views have been stated or have been formed, a reasonable person standard should be adopted.[45] As Frolik notes of this variation "[i]n essence, the substituted judgment doctrine is but a legalistic rationalization of the imposition of 'rational' societal values upon mental incompetents".[46] In effect the interpretation of the standard in this way amounts to a "best interests" standard at common law.

Nevertheless, despite the problem in formulating the standard in the circumstances posited above, in its optimum sense it does represent the measure which best protects individual autonomy and promotes respect for people's views. It is, therefore, particularly apt for surrogate decision-making for elderly people. Since most older people have had the opportunity to develop and express their ideas about what should happen to them if they lose competence it is the standard which is most easily implemented in relation to this group. It has been enthusiastically endorsed by the US President's Commission in its report, *Deciding to Forego Life-Sustaining Treatment*,[47] and it is consistent with the principle outlined in international covenants.

C. Limits as to Subject Matter

Unlike the position with estate managers whose specific powers and obligations were worked out in the cases and later contained in detailed legislative provisions, the functions of a guardian were never specified. The traditional view of their legal authority was that guardians had all the power of parents of a

young child. This proposition probably owed its origins to the *parens patriae* or
parental jurisdiction of the English Crown. In recent years it has appeared in
legislation or proposed legislation in a number of common law jurisdictions.[48]
This description is, however, not particularly helpful. Although it recognises
that parental powers are extensive, they remain unspecified and conjure up
visions of a paternalism which is out of line with current thinking on the care of
people with disabilities.[49]

D. Guardians' authority to consent to medical treatment

The "parental powers" test certainly authorised guardians to give substitute
consent to medical treatment. This remained unchallenged until quite recently.
It is increasingly being recognised, however, that, as with the decisions
(referred to above) which are "so private, so personal, and so fundamental"[50]
as to be inappropriate for alternate decision-making, so with consent to
medical treatment. The considerations which determine a person's decision to
undergo treatment — a procedure which will affect an individual in the most
intimate fashion — are idiosyncratic and at times unpredictable. Unless there
has been a prior expression of views by a subsequently incompetent person (for
example in a "living will"), it is unsafe for another person to second-guess
decisions as to medical treatment unless they are of the most routine, noncontroversial variety.

This is a complete field of study on its own and in this chapter it is not
intended to do more than mention the issue. Suffice it to say that there are some
writers who argue that third party consent may be ineffective for certain classes
of medical treatment. These are procedures which are not essential for the
preservation of life or health such as non-therapeutic sterilisation, human
tissue transplantation, participation in medical research projects of no direct
benefit to the subject, or blood donation.[51] The authors define "therapeutic" as
"undertaken for the preservation of life or the safeguarding of endangered
health".[52] Where consent cannot be obtained from the person involved, the
solution, they suggest is to seek Supreme Court approval.[53]

This latter suggestion raises a further issue. Are there other ways round the
lack of authority to consent of both the person to be treated and the guardian?
The answer may be that certain kinds of medical treatment should be subjected
to multiple layers of review in order adequately to safeguard the interests of the
individual. Given that, in many cases, guardians would be in a position where
they have financial or moral interests which may interfere with their objectiv-
ity, and given the ethical issues involved in the decisions to consent to some
treatments, the need for a second or third opinion protects them as well as the
people for whom the consent is sought.[54] Thus in the United States, landmark
cases such as *Strunk v Strunk* 1445 SW 2d (Ky 1969) in which the Kentucky
Supreme Court decided that the mother-guardian of a son with intellectual
disability was not permitted, without the concurrence of the Court, to consent
on her son's behalf to the removal of one of the boy's kidneys to donate to his

twin brother, have advocated this restriction on the guardian's powers.[55] An analogy can be seen in the multiple tiered process for obtaining consent by children to the donation of tissue for the purpose of transplantation. In the Australian Capital Territory, for example, consent is required from the child and the child's parents, their consents must be certified by a medical practitioner and final approval must be obtained from a committee comprising a judge, a doctor and a social worker or a psychologist.[56]

E. Limitations on Guardianship — Conclusions

The law's response to the need to limit guardian's powers has been to identify areas of guardianship law in which restrictions must be applied. These are the appointment process, the scope of the subject's life over which guardian's powers are exercisable and the standards by which those powers are to be exercised. It has also formulated general principles — respect for autonomy and self-determination — as benchmarks which can guide the expression of these limitations. It remains to be seen how far these principles are present in the guardianship legislation of the laws which are to be examined.

The Victorian Act

This survey will not attempt to cover every innovative aspect of the legislation. It will deal only with those principles which demonstrate the limitations on guardians' powers. The Victorian government's new guardianship legislation, the *Guardianship and Administration Board Act* 1986, became fully operative on 14 July 1987.[57]

It was the product of a period of intense interest in Australia on matters relating to people with disabilities.[58] There had been a series of State reports on the topic. These were followed by a national report which recommended, amongst other things, that "relevant Commonwealth and State Ministers ... consider the introduction of time limited and partial guardianship provisions under the relevant legislation in all States and Territories."[59] The Victorian Government responded but went further and consciously sought to develop legislation which would incorporate limits on guardians' powers and implement the international obligations outlined above.

Least restrictive alternative and normalization. The least restrictive alternative principle is one of the criteria against which "every function, power, authority, discretion, jurisdiction and duty conferred or imposed by this Act is to be exercised or performed."[60] This provision is of particular significance in view of the Victorian interpretation of legislation which makes it mandatory for all Victorian legislation to be interpreted in accordance with the purposes or objects of the legislation.[61]

The least restrictive alternative or autonomy principle also appears in the provisions which require the Guardianship and Administration Board ("the Board")[62] to assess whether the needs of a person could be met by less restrictive means than guardianship,[63] which only permits the making of a plenary guardianship order where the Board is satisfied that a limited guardianship order would be inadequate,[64] which provides for limited orders,[65] and which requires that the least restrictive form of limited order be made.[66]

It also appears from an examination of the functions given to the Office of the Public Advocate. The Office has been set up to act as a watchdog agency on behalf of persons with a disability,[67] to be the Public Official to act as guardian or administrator of last resort for people for whom no-one else is available,[68] and to be a community educator on issues relating to people with disabilities.[69] Amongst the Public Advocate's roles are the development of services and facilities to enable people with disabilities to act independently; the minimising of restrictions on the rights of such people; and the encouragement of community organisations and individuals to be involved in the management of such services and facilities.[70] Guardians are also required to help the person under guardianship to participate in community life and to be as independent as possible.[71] As the Public Advocate commented in a paper on the new legislation "the main emphasis of the statute is on ensuring that the independence of people with disabilities is, wherever possible, maintained."[72]

The effect of the explicit statement in the legislation of the autonomy and self-determination principles is apparent from public correspondence on the part of its President about the operation of the Victorian Guardianship and Administration Board:

> Unless there is a problem which legal guardianship can solve, there is no need for families ... to have to come before the Guardianship Board. We do not want to, and won't interfere with families who are coping well and sorting out problems themselves.[73]

The use of the least restrictive alternative and normalization principles in the Victorian Act to create a set of specific goals and functions for guardians and the Public Advocate demonstrates how valuable a tool they can be. Even though they are couched in general terms and are not enforced by sanctions (apart from reviews and appeals), there is evidence that the principles *are* exerting an influence. This can only be beneficial for older people for whom preservation of the maximum degree of autonomy while providing assistance with functions which are becoming beyond their capacity should be the goal of surrogate management.

A. Procedural protections.

The least restrictive alternative principle may operate to prevent unnecessary appointments of guardians or to restrict their authority if an appointment is made. That concept, even if stated expressly in legislation (as it has been in

Victoria), operates at a very general level and in the absence of sanctions (and apart from reviews and a right of appeal (see below), none has been provided), whether it is invoked will depend to a large extent on the subjective views of the individual judge or tribunal panel members. A more concrete method of reducing the number of unwarranted appointments or restricting guardian's plenary powers is to introduce specific procedural protections at various stages in the appointment process, and if an appointment is made, to ensure that reviews of the order are undertaken at regular intervals and that the same stringent protections used at the appointment stage apply also to reviews. This approach was advocated in the *Declaration of General and Special Rights of the Mentally Retarded* made at San Sebastian[74] and in Article 7 of the UN *Declaration on the Rights of Mentally Retarded Persons* (see above).[75]

B. Test for and evidence of incapacity.

A pre-requisite for the appointment of a guardian or estate manager is that the person who is the subject of the application is found to be incapable. Most substitute management legislation has a two-fold definition, the so-called "binary approach"[76] of incapacity, namely that the person is suffering from some form of mentally disabling condition and, as a consequence, is incapable of managing personal or business affairs or both. In Victoria the new Act has adopted a three-fold test: disability; functional incapacity; and need for a guardian.[77] The additional requirement should ensure that a guardian will not be appointed unless *de facto* guardianship is unavailable elsewhere and the appointment of a guardian is in the incapable person's best interests.

It is apparent that where disability is one of the qualifying criteria, expert evidence will be required. For many years such evidence was the exclusive preserve of the medical profession. So prevalent was this practice that it has been said of the guardianship hearing that "typically, the only evidence is supplied by a physician or psychiatrist (usually in the form of a written certificate and not oral testimony) who opines that the subject of the petition is mentally incompetent. This conclusion will generally stand unchallenged, making the medical diagnosis determinative of the question of legal incompetency."[78] Not surprisingly in the "protect their civil rights" environment of the 70's, criticism was made of this abdication of the judicial role. Another aspect of the practice at hearings which is out of line with modern guardianship law is the absence of evidence on the second of the qualifying criteria — functional incapacity. This is often a matter best attested to by people who live with, or care for, the subject person. Reform has, therefore, focused on the need to reduce the dependence on medical evidence, to make medical witnesses more effective by insisting that their evidence be open to cross-examination, and by accepting that evidence of para-medical professionals and carers is valuable when determining whether the person is not functioning adequately.

Victoria has taken note of these criticisms. In its legislation no qualifications are specified for witnesses and, following an application, a factual report on any matter relevant to the proceedings may be made by the Office of Public Advocate for presentation to the Board.[79] It is available to the person involved. In addition, the Board may appoint anyone to assist it at a hearing including a medical person, an interpreter, or any other person with appropriate expertise.[80] Furthermore in a paper by the Board's President on the operation of the Board it was noted that "[m]edical, psychological, social work or other health care or professional advice will be relied upon by the Board in establishing the fact of disability".[81] In other words, comprehensive information may be called on to determine the threshhold questions of whether the person is suffering from a disability and of how well the person is coping. This is a very real safeguard for elderly people. Although a doctor can attest to their medical condition, where people live at home (as most do in Australia), evidence of ability to manage their everyday affairs is not within a doctor's competence and, in general, can only be reported on by others.

C. Notice, representation and review.

Notification of intended proceedings is again seen as a means of protecting the individual against arbitrary and unnecessary appointments. The Victorian provisions specify that notice of guardianship proceedings is to be given to at least seven parties.[82] In addition the Board may invite the presence of any other person.[83] More ample notice provisions could not be envisaged. Any people who have an interest in the proceedings may appear and present their views.

There are other procedural protections. In the past, guardianship and estate administration hearings have been critised for failing to ensure the presence of the subject person at hearings. This was almost universally the case — the person's absence being excused on the ground that it would be detrimental to the person's physical or mental welfare.[84] The Victorian Act states specifically that the subject person and the applicant should normally be present in person at the proceedings and both may be represented by a legal practitioner or another person.[85] All other parties to a guardianship application may also be represented with the Board's permission.[86] If the person who is the subject of the proceedings is unrepresented, the Board may appoint a representative.[87]

A review may be held within 12 months of the initial order,[88] and is mandatory within 3 years of the order. Reviews may also be held at any time on request or on the Board's own motion.[89] The initial draft of the legislation contained more generous provisions for reviews[90] but these were obviously curtailed for economic reasons. The list of those entitled to receive notice of the review is similar to the one for an initial application, except that the Public Trustee is not included.[91] There is a right of appeal from Board decisions to an administrative body, the Administrative Appeals Tribunal of Victoria,[92] and the Board may refer issues of law to the Victorian Supreme Court.[93] There is, however, no right of appeal to a judicial body. In summary, the Victorian legislation scores well when measured against human rights criteria of the kinds specified earlier. In fact, as Carney notes, in marked contrast to the ACT

Lunacy Act "it is at the forefront of international initiatives in this area".[94]

The "ACT" Act

A. Least restrictive alternative and normalization

The Lunacy Act, 1898 (as it applies in the ACT) reveals no provisions for limited guardianship orders, much less for an order appointing a guardian[95] made in accordance with any overriding principles such as the least restrictive alternative or normalization. The Act, however, does authorise specific property orders.[96] Given the traditional emphasis in common law guardianship legislation on property matters, it is not surprising to find that this small concession appears in relation to property provisions. The concession is, however, minimal. There is a distinction between specific and limited orders, and the former is no substitute for the latter.

In theory, despite the absence in the Act of specific provision for limited orders, the wide powers of the Supreme Court, in particular in the exercise of its inherent jurisdiction, should permit the making of such orders. It appears, however, that there are no precedents for such a step and it is now unlikely that they will be taken. Although the guardianship provisions in the Act have not been used extensively[97] on occasions where a limited order would have been appropriate, the guardian has, nonetheless, been given plenary powers.[98] This is only one illustration of how out-of-touch this legislation is with current thinking on guardianship.

B. Procedural protections

(a) *Test for and evidence of incapacity.* The ACT Lunacy Act, 1898 adopts the traditional "binary approach."[99] This is unremarkable. What is disturbing is the archaic definition ("... a person is of unsound mind ..." (s102)) which attracts the guardianship provisions of the Act.

It has resulted in guardians only being appointed for those who are mentally ill in the classic sense of that expression — that is, those suffering from psychiatric illness. Specifically senile dementia has been excluded.[100] Thus elderly people suffering from dementia and other disabling conditions such as drug and alcohol related diseases and forms of intellectual disability cannot have the benefit of this form of substitute management.[101]

Mental illness may be determined by a jury[102] or alternatively, if the person is already under involuntary detention in a mental health institution, the Supreme Court may direct its Registrar[103] to examine the person and if there is evidence of need for protection, the Court will appoint a guardian.[104] In its evidentiary requirements, the Act states that its medical witnesses must be cross-examined on their affidavits.[105] There is no specific provision, however, for the evidence of non-medical experts to be given. The definitional problems, however, create significant gaps in the legislation which could be critical for an elderly person whose mentally disabling condition does not amount to mental illness within the meaning attributed to it in the Act.[106]

(b) *Notice, representation and review*. Older legislation like the ACT Lunacy Act, 1898 (NSW) does not provide for reviews — guardianship once instituted remains in force, often for an indeterminate time, or at least until a revocation order[107] is sought from the ACT Supreme Court — and there is no provision for an independent report on the person's competence in borderline cases. A right of appeal is, however, available.[108] As could be expected of 90-year-old legislation, the Lunacy Act, 1898 is out of step with current social values and conditions. If nothing else, its exclusion from guardianship of people with intellectual and other forms of disability not amounting to mental illness justifies new legislation.[109]

Standards for Decision-making — Statutory Expression

The best interests or welfare standard has, in recent times, appeared in guardianship legislation in some jurisdictions.

Victoria alone, however, has attempted to define what is meant by the expression "best interests".

Thus the *Guardianship and Administration Board Act* 1986 states:

Section 28(1) A guardian must act in the best interests of the represented person.

(2) Without limiting sub-section (1), a guardian acts in the best interests of a represented person if the guardian acts as far as possible:

(a) as an advocate for the represented person; and

(b) in such a way as to encourage the represented person to participate as much as possible in the life of the community; and

(c) in such a way as to encourage and assist the represented person to become capable of caring for herself or himself and of making reasonable judgments in respect of matters relating to her or his person; and

(d) in such a way as to protect the represented person from neglect, abuse or exploitation; and

(e) in consultation with the represented person, taking into account, as far as possible, the wishes of the represented person.[111]

Here, for the first time, is an attempt to flesh out the vague and ill-defined notion of best interests. It may be argued that elements of the definition are still expressed broadly, that there are potential contradictions between the protective notion (in paragraph 28(2)(d)) and the need to take into account the wishes of the person (in paragraph 28(2)(e)); and the idea of "reasonable judgments" (in paragraph 28(2)(c)) is notoriously imprecise as well as being a "culturally relative" concept.[112] Nevertheless, the duties are spelt out, are in accordance with international covenants and are specific. Another positive aspect of the definition is that, despite use of the term "best interests", its meaning does not accord with the conservative and paternalistic or protective common law standard of the same name. The focus of decision-making under the Act is to be on the wishes of the individual, rather than the guardians' views of what should be done. In this respect it adopts the substituted judgment principle rather than the orthodox "best interests" standard known to common law — a more appropriate test to encourage guardians to foster the autonomy and self-determination of people under guardianship.

A. Limits as to Subject Matter — Statutory Expression

Again in recent legislation, moves have been made to define guardians' powers with more precision.

Although on the surface a restriction of guardians' powers appears to be in line with self-autonomy principles, the limited range of matters covered in the Act allows too little flexibility. The preferable solution (as has been adopted in Victoria) is to permit the determining body to choose from a wider range of subject areas, the limits in individual cases being imposed in the particular guardianship order.

B. Limits as to Subject Matter — Medical Treatment

The notion that guardians should only have qualified authority to consent to medical treatment has been picked up in the Victorian guardianship legislation. Thus the Act prohibits the guardian's sole consent to "major medical procedures".[113] The guardian or the person under guardianship can apply to the Guardianship and Administration Board for consent to carry out any such procedure. What is meant by "major medical procedures" has not yet been determined but is likely to include at least abortion, sterilisation and non-regenerative tissue transplant.[115]

Some clarification of the extent of the guardian's powers in relation to medical treatment may be forthcoming from another proposed Victorian Act. The common law is not clear as to whether a guardian has power to authorise the turning off of life support systems or the discontinuation of treatment which, again, are matters of prime importance to some elderly people.[116] The Medical Treatment Bill presented to the Victorian Parliament on 1 October 1987 provides that guardians (and agents appointed under enduring powers of attorney), if authorised specifically to do so by the person under guardianship (or the principal),[117] may make decisions about medical treatment including refusal of treatment or further medical treatment.[118]

The proposed Victorian Bill and the existing Victorian Act have gone a considerable way towards clarifying the limits of guardians' powers to consent or refuse to consent to medical treatment. Since this is an area of predominant interest for older people who lack the competence to consent, these moves are welcome.

Conclusion

Modern guardianship law as exemplified, for example, in the recently enacted Victorian statute, has moved a considerable distance from the days when all guardians were given plenary authority and people under guardianship were sentenced to an often indeterminate loss of control over all or most aspects of their lives. People's varying degrees of loss of competence, the need to protect incapable people against unnecessarily encroaching authority and to foster their independence, where possible, are matters which have highlighted the inappropriateness of this form of legal control and led to moves in many jurisdictions to re-shape their guardianship law.

Principles which have been developed to achieve this end — the least restrictive alternative and normalization — aim to promote respect for the autonomy of people with mentally disabling conditions and to encourage them to participate to the maximum extent and for the maximum period in ordinary community life. Translated into concrete terms — these principles have been instrumental in constructing barriers which operate during the appointment process to prevent unnecessary appointments of guardians or their appointment for excessive lengths of time. They have also defined the areas of the life of the incompetent over which the guardian may exercise authority — be it absolute or qualified — and the standards which must be reached in the exercise of that authority.

To the extent that guardianship legislation does not incorporate these legal boundaries, it does not promote the goals of autonomy and normalization for people who suffer some form of mentally disabling condition and is in need of reform. The new Victorian legislation cannot be criticised on this ground. Here, possibly for the first time, is an attempt to fashion guardianship laws which are explicitly based on these goals. The legislation contains the clearest expression of the standards which should govern guardians and which should apply to guardianship proceedings. It is a thoughtful, sensitive and flexible document. In this regard it is a model of all the principles which it has been argued should apply. Will it be successful?

It is too early to provide an answer to that question. The very notion of success may be difficult to measure. That there are likely to be difficulties has, however, already been recognised. An experienced Victorian disability law practitioner has expressed a number of reservations about the new law. He suggested that the objectives of the Act (that guardians perform their functions and duties in a manner that is least restrictive of the person's freedom of decision and action and in the best interests of the person with a disability and, wherever possible, give effect to the wishes of the person) are expressed in terms which are too broad and which are difficult to interpret because unfamiliar. He also noted that the Guardianship and Administration Board's powers are so wide and discretionary, as well as being based upon the imprecise concept of "the need" of the disabled person, that they are likely to be difficult to implement.[119] His concerns can be summed up as follows:

To Lawyers and Accountants who are accustomed to the intricacies of, for example, the *Law of Contract,* the various *Revenue Acts* or the *Crimes Act,* both the language and the philosophy of this Act will be novel and, to many, somewhat troubling. How do Practitioners come to grips with concepts such as "the needs" of "persons with a disability"? How can we deal with a Tribunal which appears to have sweeping powers but few rules?[120]

Although these criticisms have force, they are answerable. As with any new area of practice, practitioners will need to inform themselves of the meanings of unfamiliar concepts. That process will take time, but is not difficult. The psychological climate created by these philosophies in the Act, it is predicted, will inform the thinking of all those involved with guardianship proceedings and shape people's decision-making accordingly. Over time, precedents will be generated which will further elaborate the meaning of novel terms so that more concrete examples are available for guidance.

There are, however, problems of a more fundamental nature. This is an area in which law is operating at the periphery of social control. Whatever rules are devised they do not lessen the practical dilemmas which arise daily in this jurisdiction. For example, even the Victorian definition of best interests contains built-in inconsistencies. Thus it advocates both normalization and protection — ideas which are often in tension. It also requires guardians to take account of the wishes of the incapable person, a practice which, if adhered to, may produce action or decisions which contravene both notions. The very idea of decision-making for someone else has inherent limitations. No one individual can read the mind of another. The subjective element in personal decision-making cannot be eliminated.

It must be accepted, therefore, that neither precedent nor practice will ensure absolute definition in this area of the law. Nor would this be desirable. One of the key elements which will make guardianship legislation work is flexibility. The diversity of disabilities of people for whom guardianship may be sought, the range of functions in which issues of competence may arise, the multi-faceted role of guardians, the variety of values and interests of people involved with a person with a disability create a kaleidescope of matters of which account must be taken. To ensure that each of these factors is given due weight, both guardians and the determination process must be adaptable.

In general the law provides rules in discrete areas of human activity — social security, trade practices, agency. Rarely is it asked to create rules to cover "whole life" decision-making. This is pioneer law-making and the task is not an easy one. The Victorian model for guardianship will be under close scrutiny — particularly in those other Australian jurisdictions like Western Australia, New South Wales and possibly the Australian Capital Territory, which plan to follow its path. In terms of the best and most modern theories of guardianship, the Victorian Act is a model. To live up to its promise and achieve the right balance between promoting individual rights, providing protection and being responsive to the wishes of incapable people will require good-will, sensitivity and commonsense.

Notes

1. In the UK it is called the "appointee" system and in the US the "representative payee" system.
2. An attempt was made to update this Act in 1985 with the presentation of the draft *Guardianship and Management of Property Ordinance* 1985. The draft was recalled following community opposition.
3. Defined for the purposes of this chapter as those 65 and over.
4. Calculations based on: Australian Bureau of Statistics *Projections of the Populations of Australia, States and Territories 1984 to 2021* Canberra, AGPS, 1985, Series A & B.
5. Dr Hal L. Kendig, Dr J. McCallum, *Greying Australia: Future Impacts of Population Aging* Canberra, AGPS, 1986, 45-7, 49.
6. "Mental retardation" was the description adopted in the survey, although the expression "intellectual disability" and "developmental disability" are the terms used most frequently in Australia today.
7. Australian Bureau of Statistics *Handicapped Persons Australia, 1981* (2nd ed) Canberra, AGPS, 1984, 14. The actual numbers of people over 60 with intellectual disability is very low. In Western Australian (population of 1.5m approx) the number is 173; in New South Wales (population of 5.6m approx) it is 371. Figures supplied by AAMR — the National Council on Intellectual Disability, February, 1988.
8. Discussions with Dr A. F. Jorm, National Health and Medical Research Council ("NH & MRC") Social Psychiatry Unit, Australian National University ("ANU"), Canberra, February 1988.
9. A. F. Jorm, A. E. Korten and A. S. Henderson "The prevalence of dementia: A quantitative integration of the literature" Canberra, NH & MRC Social Psychiatry Research Unit, ANU, Canberra, 1987, 8 (a paper to be published in *Acta psychiatrica scanda* in 1988).
10. Mental Health Foundation of Australia and the Australian National Association for Mental Health, Media release 11-87/88 of 5/1/87. The statistics were based on A. F. Jorm and A. E. Korten "A Method for Calculating Projected Increases in the Number of Senile Dementia Sufferers — With Application to Australia and New Zealand" Canberra, NH & MRC Social Psychiatry Unit, ANU, Canberra, 1987 and G. Preston "The Prevalence of Dementia: Estimates and Interpretations in Australia" Melbourne, National Research Institute of Gerontology and Geriatric Medicine, 1984, (unpublished).
11. A. S. Henderson and A. F. Jorm *The Problem of Dementia in Australia* Canberra, AGPS, 1986, 7.
12. Dr Hal L. Kendig, Dr J. McCallum *Greying Australia: Future Impacts of Population Aging* Canberra, AGPS, 1986, 45.
13. *Id* 46.
14. Discussions with Dr A. F. Jorm, NH & MRC, Social Psychiatry Unit, ANU, Canberra, February, 1988.

15. *The President's Panel on Mental Retardation, Report of the Task Force on Law* Washington, US Govt Printing Office, 1963, 25; International League of Societies for the Mentally Handicapped, *Symposium on Guardianship of the Mentally Retarded: Conclusions*, Brussels, ILSMH, 1970, reprinted, New Delhi, Federation for the Welfare of the Mentally Retarded (India), 1977, 11; Samuel J. Brakel *et. al. The Mentally Disabled and the Law* (3rd ed), Chicago, American Bar Foundation, 1985, 5.

16. P. McLaughlin *Guardianship of the Person* Downsview, Ontario, National Institute on Mental Retardation, 1979, 70.

17. *Ibid.*

18. Roger B. Sherman "Guardianship — Time for a Re-assessment" (1980) 49 *Fordham L R* 350, 371-2; Samuel J. Brakel *et. al.* (eds) *The Mentally Disabled and the Law*, Chicago, American Bar Foundation, 1985, 268; M. Kindred *et. al.* (eds)*The Mentally Retarded Citizen and the Law*, New York, The Free Press, 1976, 2, 5; International League of Societies for the Mentally Handicapped, *Symposium on Guardianship of the Mentally Retarded: Conclusions*, Brussels, ILSMH 1970, reprinted, New Delhi, Federation for the Welfare of the Mentally Retarded (India), 1977, 18-19.

19. International League of Societies for the Mentally Handicapped, *Symposium on Guardianship of the Mentally Retarded: Conclusions*, Brussels, ILSMH, 1970, reprinted, New Delhi, Federation for the Welfare of the Mentally Retarded (India), 1977, Appendix A, 31-32, *Declaration of General and Special Rights of the Mentally Retarded*, Art VII.

20. This is especially significant in the case of the elderly and people with intellectual disability. See John J. Regan "Protective services for the elderly: Committment, Guardianship and Alternatives", (1972) 13 *Wm and Mary L R* 569, 608; Susan C. Hayes and Robert Hayes, *Mental Retardation Law, Policy and Administration*, Sydney, Law Book, 1979, 80-85; M. Kindred et. al., *The Mentally Retarded Citizen and the Law*, New York, The Free Press, 1976, 2, 5; Roger B. Sherman "Guardianship — Time for a Re-assessment", (1980) 49 *Fordham L R*, 350, 371-2.

21. UN *Declaration of the Rights of Mentally Retarded Persons,* Arts. 1, 4, 5 and 7. G A Res 2856, 26 UN GAOR Supp (No 29) 93-94, UN Doc A/8429, 1971; UN *Declaration on the Rights of Disabled Persons,* Art 3, 4, 9. G A Res 3447, 30 UN GAOR Supp (No 34) 88, UN Doc A/10034, 1975.

22. Nirje "The Normalization Principle and its Human Management Implications" in R. Kugel and W. Wolfensberger (eds), *President's Committee on Mental Retardation: Changing Patterns in Residential Serviced for the Mentally Retarded*, Washington, US Govt Printing Office, 1979, 181; W. Wolfensberger, *The Principle of Normalization in Human Services*, Toronto, National Institute on Mental Retardation, 1972 (rep 1979).

23. UN *Declaration on the Rights of Mentally Retarded Persons* Art. 1 — "The mentally retarded person has, to the maximum degree of feasibility, the same rights as other human beings." UN *Declaration on the Rights of Disabled Persons* Art. 3 — "Disabled persons have the inherent right to respect for their human dignity. Disabled persons, whatever the origin, nature and seriousness of their handicaps and disabilities, have the same fundamental rights as their fellow-citizens of the same age which implies first and foremost the right to enjoy a decent life, as normal and full as possible." Art. 4 — "Disabled persons have the same civil and political rights as other human beings ... ."

24. UN *Declaration on the Rights of Mentally Retarded Persons* Art 4. "Whenever possible, the mentally retarded person should live with his own family or with foster parents and participate in different forms of community life. The family with which he lives should receive assistance. If care in an institution becomes necessary, it should be provided in surroundings and other circumstances as close as possible to those of normal life."

25. An early statement of the principle was made by the US Supreme Court in *Shelton v Tucker* 364 US 479 (1960):
    In a series of decisions this court has held that, even though governmental purpose be legitimate and substantial, that purpose cannot be pursued by means that broadly stifle fundamental personal liberties when the end can be more narrowly achieved. The breadth of legislative abridgement must be viewed in the light of less drastic means of achieving the same basic purpose.

26. UN *Declaration on the Rights of Mentally Retarded Persons* Art. 7 — "Whenever mentally retarded persons are unable, because of the severity of their handicap, to exercise all their rights in a meaningful way or it should become necessary to restrict or deny some or all of these rights, the procedure used for that restriction or denial of rights must contain proper legal safeguards against every form of abuse. This procedure must be based on an evaluation of the social capability of the mentally retarded person by qualified experts and must be subject to periodic review and to the right of appeal to higher authorities."

27. Susan C. Hayes & Robert Hayes, *Mental Retardation Law, Policy and Administration*, Sydney, Law Book, 1982, 6.

28. *Ex parte Whitbread* (1816) 35 ER 878; *In re Stoer* (1894) 9 PD 120; *In re EDS* (1914) 1 Ch 618.

29. The most influential and frequently quoted of their works on guardianship are: Lawrence A. Frolik, "Plenary Guardianship: an Analysis, a Critique and a Proposal, for Reform", 23 *Ariz L R* 599; Paul McLaughlin, *Guardianship of the Person*, Downsview, Ontario, National Institute on Mental Retardation, 1979.

30. T. Carney and P. Singer, *Ethical and Legal Issues in Guardianship Options for Intellectually Disadvantaged People*, Human Rights Commission Monograph Series No 2, Canberra, AGPS, 1986, 55.

31. E. Helsel "History and Present Status of Protective Services", in W. Wolfensberger and H. Zauha, *Citizen Advocacy and Protective Services for the Impaired and Handicapped*, 131-143; Ohio Rev Code ss 5119, 58-59 (Supp 1973); Donald E. Gelfand and Jody K. Olsen, *The Aging Network Programs and Services*, New York, Springer Publishing, 1980, 106-113; W. Schmidt *et. al., Public Guardianship and the Elderly*, Cambridge, Mass Ballinger Pub. 1981, 10-12.

32. R. J. Levy "Protecting the Mentally Retarded: An Empirical Survey and Evaluation of the Establishment of State Guardianship in Minnesota", (1965) 49 *Minn L Rev* 821.

33. G. Horowitz and C. Estes, *Protective Services for the Aged*, US Department of Health, Education, and Welfare, Office of Human Development, Administration on Aging, Washington, 1971, 36.

34. Age Concern, *The Law and Vulnerable Elderly People*, Mitcham, Surrey, Age Concern England, 1986, 87.

35. A. A. Stone, *Mental Health Law: A System in Transition*, Crime and Delinquency Series, US Department of Health, Education, and Welfare, Rockville, Maryland, National Institute of Mental Health, 1975, reprinted 1976, 174.

36. *Id* 165-6.
37. Lawrence A. Frolik, "Plenary Guardianship: an Analysis, a Critique and Proposal for Reform", (1981) 23 *Ariz L R* 599, 609.
38. T. Carney and P. Singer, *Ethical and Legal Issues in Guardianship Options for Intellectually Disadvantaged People*, Human Rights Commission Monograph Series No 2, Canberra, AGPS, 1986, 68, 70.
39. Lawrence A. Frolik, "Plenary Guardianship: an Analysis, a Critique and a Proposal for Reform", (1981) 23 *Ariz L R* 599, 607.
40. See fn 54.
41. The "substituted judgment principle" came from "the legal doctrine that the court, acting in equity, has the right to substitute its judgment and to act for an incompetent in all matters 'touching the well-being' of the incompetent. The doctrine first arose in the 1816 English case of *Ex parte Whitbread...*". Lawrence A. Frolik, "Plenary Guardianship: an Analysis, a Critique and a Proposal for Reform" (1981) 23 *Ariz L R* 599, 618.
42. *Ex parte Whitbread* (1816) 35 ER 878; *Re Whitaker* (1889) 42 Ch D 119; *Griffin v Union Trustee Co of Australia Ltd* (1947) 48 SR (NSW) 360, 363; *Re DJR and the Mental Health Act, 1958* [1983] 1 NSWLR 557, 564-5.
43. Lawrence A. Frolik, "Plenary Guardianship: an Analysis, a Critique and a Proposal for Reform", (1981) 23 *Ariz L R* 599, 619.
44. The artificiality is demonstrated by the argument in the well known case of *In re Quinlan* 70 NJ 10, 39, 355 A 2d 647, 663 (1976) that the court could consider what Karen would have decided had she been restored to capacity just long enough to comment on whether to disconnect the respirator.
45. *In re Quinlan,* 70 NJ 10, 41, 355 A 2d 647, 664 (1976).
46. Lawrence A. Frolik, "Plenary Guardianship: an Analysis, a Critique and a Proposal for Reform," (1981) 23 *Ariz L R* 599, 622.
47. US President's Commission for the Study of Ethical Problems in Medicine and Biomedical and Behavioral Research, *Deciding to Forego Life-Sustaining Treatment*, Washington, US Govt Printing Office, 1983.
48. e.g. England: Mental Deficiency Act, 1913 (3 & 4 Geo 5 s28) s10(2) now repealed, the Mental Health Act 1959 s34(1) now repealed (where the powers of the guardian were said to be those of a parent of a child under 14); Alberta: *Dependent Adults Act* RSA 1976 c63 s9 (powers of a father in respect of a child under 14); ACT: Draft Guardianship and Management of Property Ordinance 1985 c18(2)(d) (powers of parent of a child under 14); Vic: *Guardianship and Administration Board Act* 1986 s 24(2) (powers of parent of child).
49. For example, the common law powers of a parent include authority to physically punish a child. See also *Reform of Mental Health Legislation*, Cmnd 8405, London, HMSO, 1981, para 43.
50. M Kindred *et. al., The Mentally Retarded Citizen and the Law*, New York, The Free Press, 1976, 76.
51. Susan Hayes and Robert Hayes, "Third-party consent to medical procedures" (1982) *Med J Aust* 2:90-92.
52. *Id* 92.
53. *Ibid*.
54. President's Commission for the Study of Ethical Problems in Medicine and Biomedical and Behavioral Research, *Deciding to Forego Life-Sustaining Treatment*, Washington, US Govt Printing Office, 1983, 128. M. Kindred et. al., *The Mentally*

Retarded Citizen and the Law, New York, The Free Press, 1976, 79-80.

55. *Id* at 149. See also *Eichner v Dillon; In re Storar,* 73 AD 2d 431, 426 NYS 2d 517 (1980).

56. *Transplantation and Anatomy Ordinance*, 1978 (ACT); *Human Tissue Act* 1982 (Vic) Pt 11.

57. *Gazette*, G26, 8/7/87, p 1792.

58. e.g. *New Directions: Report of the Handicapped Programs Review*, Canberra, AGPS, 1985; Victoria: *Report of Minister's Committee on Rights and Protective Legislation for Intellectually Handicapped Persons*, Melbourne, Vic Govt Printer, 1982 (the Cocks Report). See also, SA: *A New Pattern for Services for Intellectually Handicapped People in South Australia*, Vols 1-3, Adelaide, SA Health Commission, 1981 (the Bright Report); NSW: *Inquiry into Health Services for the Psychiatrically Ill and Developmentally Disabled*, Sydney, NSW Dept of Health, 1983 (the Richmond Report).

59. *New Directions: Report of the Handicapped Programs Review*, Canberra, AGPS, 1985, 89.

60. *Guardianship and Administration Board Act* 1986 s4(2). "It is the intention of Parliament that the provisions of this Act be interpreted and that every function, power, authority, discretion, jurisdiction and duty conferred or imposed by this Act is to be exercised or performed so that — (a) the means which is the least restrictive of a person's freedom of decision and action as is possible in the circumstances is adopted ..."

61. *Interpretation of Legislation Act*, 1984 (Vic) s35. In the interpretation of an Act or subordinate instrument — (a) a construction that would promote the purpose or object underlying the Act or subordinate instrument (whether or not that purpose or object is expressly stated in the Act or subordinate instrument) shall be preferred to a construction that would not promote that purpose or object ... .

62. The body which determines whether a person should be placed under guardianship or have business affairs managed, or both of these. *Guardianship and Administration Board Act,* 1986 Pt 2.

63. Sub-section 22(2).

64. Sub-section 22(4).

65. Sub-section 48(2).

66. Sub-section 22(5).

67. Section 15.

68. Sub-section 16(1).

69. Section 15.

70. *Ibid.*

71. Paragraphs 28(2) (b), (c).

72. B. Bodna, "The Role and Responsibilities of the Office of the Public Advocate", a paper presented at a seminar entitled "The Guardianship and Administration Board and the Office of the Public Advocate", Melbourne, Leo Cussen Institute, August 1987.

73. Letter to *The Age,* 22 Oct 1987 from T. Lawson, President of the Guardianship and Administration Board.

74. International League of Societies for the Mentally Handicapped, *Symposium on Guardianship of the Mentally Retarded: Conclusions*, Brussels, ILSMH, 1970, reprinted, New Delhi, Federation for the Welfare of the Mentally Retarded (India), 1977, Appendix A,. 31-32, *Declaration of General and Special Rights of*

the Mentally Retarded, Art VII.

75. See fn. 21, above.

76. Lawrence A. Frolik, "Plenary Guardianship: an Analysis, a Critique and a Proposal for Reform", (1981) 23 *Ariz L R* 599, 616.

77. *Guardianship and Administration Board Act* 1986 ss 22, 46.

78. Annina M. Mitchell, "Involuntary Guardianship for Incompetents: A strategy for Legal Services Advocates", (1978) *Clearinghouse Review,* 451, 454; Samuel J. Brakel *et. al., The Mentally Disabled and the Law*, (3rd ed) Chicago, American Bar Association, 1985, 382.

79. *Guardianship and Administration Board Act* 1986 s 1(2).

80. Sub-section 11(1).

81. Tony Lawson, "Guardianship — New Opportunities for People with Disabilities", paper presented to a seminar in August 1987, Melbourne, Leo Cussen Institute, 1987.

82. *Guardianship and Administration Board Act* 1986 s 21. These are the applicant; the subject person; the nearest relative; the primary carer; the proposed guardian; the Public Advocate; and the property manager or administrator.

83. Section 20.

84. Annina M. Mitchell, "Involuntary Guardianship for Incompetents: A Strategy for Legal Services Advocates, (1978) *Clearinghouse Review* 451, 454.

85. *Guardianship and Administration Board Act* 1986 s 12(1).

86. Section 12.

87. Sub-section 12(3).

88. The President of the Board has stated that "it is likely that the Board will review most orders annually". T. Lawson, "Guardianship — New Opportunities for People with Disabilities", a paper presented at a seminar in August 1987, Melbourne, Leo Cussen Institute, 1987, 7.

89. Section 61.

90. A "fine-tuning" review was to have been held within six months and thereafter reviews were to have been on an annual basis (see Guardianship and Administration Board Bill cll 69, 70. Note also T. Carney, "New civil guardianship laws — another view", (1985) *Law Institute Journal* 956, 959.

91. Section 60.

92. Section 67.

93. Section 64.

94. T. Carney "The Mental Health, Intellectual Disability Services and Guardianship Acts. How Do They Rate? (1986) *Leg Serv Bull* 128, 129.

95. The Act refers to a "committee of the person" or a "committee of the estate". A "committee" is someone to whom an incapable person is "committed".

96. Lunacy Act, 1898 (NSW) s 150. "The Court may by order authorise and direct the committee of the estate of an insane person to do *all or any* of the following things:- ..." (italics supplied).

97. The Registrar estimates that the number of applications made since the ACT Supreme Court was set up in 1933 *(Australian Capital Territory Supreme Court Act* 1933) is less than 20. Information supplied by the Registrar of the Court, 9 February, 1988.

98. For example, in one unreported decision of which the author is aware a guardian was appointed with plenary powers where the sole reason for the application was to provide consent to an operation on a comatose woman.

 99. Lunacy Act, 1898 (NSW) ss 102-3.
100. *RAP v AEP* [1982] 2 NSWLR 508 (Senile dementia not mental illness). See also
     JAH v Medical Superintendent of Rozelle Hospital [1986] ACLD 295; *CN v Medical
     Superintendent of Rozelle Hospital* [1986] ACLD 294 (anorexia nervosa and subst-
     ance abuse not mental illness); *RH v CAH* [1984] 1 NSWLR 694, 696 (mild forms of
     intellectual disability are neither mental illness nor mental incapacity). These cases
     have interpreted the equivalent provisions in the Mental Health Act, 1958 (NSW).
101. Theoretically the inherent or *parens patriae* jurisdiction of the ACT Supreme
     Court should be available for this purpose. (See *Re DJR and Mental Health Act
     1958* [1983] 1 NSWLR 557.) In practice since this jurisdiction has never been
     exercised by the Court, it would now be difficult to invoke.
102. Section 107. To the author's knowledge none has ever been used for this purpose.
103. Section 148 refers to the "Master", that is, the New South Wales Master in Lunacy
     (s3). It would obviously be impracticable for someone from that geographically
     distant office to operate in the Territory so it has been suggested that the ACT
     Registrar is the equivalent of the NSW Master for the purpose. The matter is not,
     however, free of doubt (from discussions with ACT Supreme Court Registrar,
     March 1987).
104. Section 148.
105. Lunacy Act, 1898 (NSW) s 121.
106. Sections 103, 148.
107. Known as a superseding order. Lunacy Act, 1898 (NSW) s 104.
108. Section 114.
109. The Australian Law Reform Commission as part of its Community Law Reform
     program for the ACT is to report on the guardianship needs of the Territory.
110. "Represented person" is the description given in the Act to a person in respect of
     whom either a guardianship or an administration order or both, is in force
     (Guardianship and Administration Board Act 1986 s 3).
111. *Guardianship and Administration Board Act* 1986 s 28.
112. T. Lawson, "Guardianship — New Opportunities for People with Disabilities",
     paper presented at a seminar in August, 1987, Melbourne, Leo Cussen Institute,
     1987, 12.
113. *Guardianship and Administration Board Act* 1986 s 37; see also Disability Services
     and Guardianship Bill 1987 (NSW) cll 36-39.
114. Section 38(2).
115. T. Lawson, "Guardianship — New Opportunities for People with Disabilities" a
     paper given at a seminar in August 1987, published in Melbourne, Leo Cussen
     Institute, 1987, 6. These three procedures were specified in the Guardianship and
     Administration Board Bill (No 2) cll 37-9.
116. M. Kindred, *et. al., The Mentally Retarded Citizen and the Law*, New York, The
     Free Press, 1976, 77-9.
117. Either by a specific provision in a guardianship order, or by a special form of
     enduring powers of attorney. See Medical Treatment Bill 1987 (Vic) cl 9, Schs 2
     and 3.
118. Clauses l(c), 9.
119. L Papaleo *"Guardianship and Administration Board Act, 1986* — The Role of the
     Professional Practitioner" a paper presented at a seminar in August, 1987,
     Melbourne, Leo Cussen Institute, 1987, 2.
120. *Id* 2-3.

Chapter 36

Civil Commitment of the Elderly: Is There a Case for Special Legislation?

Margaret A. SHONE   Institute of Law Research
                    and Reform, Edmonton, Alberta, Canada

Introduction

Over the next three to four decades, mental illness will strike elderly persons in developed countries in numbers that astonish. This foreboding is based, first, on demographic data. The data indicate two trends. One is that developed countries can expect a burgeoning elderly population. The other is that significantly more rapid rises will occur in older age groups — persons 75-84 years and over 85. This population may escalate at a rate of three or more times the rate for persons 65-74 years of age.

The foreboding is based, second, on epidemiological data showing an increasingly higher incidence of mental illness with advancing age, with rates for persons 75 and over being up to five or six times more than those for persons 65-74 years.

A tremendous strain will be placed on mental health resources, resources that even in the best of times are "rarely if ever available in the quantity and quality needed." It is a safe bet that governments the world over are ill prepared for this development.

Several questions come immediately to mind. What are the mental illnesses that affect elderly persons? How do they affect them? How and when do the illnesses occur? What care and treatment is needed? What care and treatment is provided? Do the civil commitment laws apply? Are they adequate?

In this chapter, these questions are examined from the perspective of the operation of civil commitment laws — that is, the laws governing involuntary hospitalization for mental disorder - in the United States, Canada and, to a lesser extent, England. The chapter is divided into seven parts:

I Introduction
II The Population At Risk
III Mental Illnesses of the Elderly
IV Trends in Civil Commitment Law and Social Policy

V   Gaps in Operation of Civil Commitment Law
VI   The Question: Is Special Legislation Needed?
VII Conclusion

An important fact about laws relating to mental illness — or "mental health" laws as they are more often and somewhat euphemistically called — is revealed by the range of questions posed above. It is that they cannot be properly evaluated in isolation from the complex of medical, legal, social, economic, political and other systems of the society in which they operate. As one commentator has stated:

> Mental health law is not to be found exclusively in either the pages of the statute, or the outcomes of mental health hearings, or the decisions of the Supreme Court, or in the professional practices of lawyers and psychiatrists. It is constituted by *all* of these factors, and other (e.g. Government activity — and inactivity — on health issues; institutional work practices). Understanding the current state of mental health law means analyzing the intersection of these factors to see how that law and practice is being continually constituted. I can summarize this point by saying that mental health law should be understood as an ongoing process of implementation.

The truth of these words rings out resoundingly for civil commitment laws applied to elderly persons.

The Population at Risk

Current demographic data describes a trend toward increasing numbers of elderly persons worldwide and particularly in the developed countries. Epidemiological data reveals a higher incidence of mental illness in older age groups.

This information, taken in combination, supports the following three predictions. First, the demand for mental health resources will increase in Canada, the United States and the United Kingdom over the next four decades. Second, the incidence of hospitalization for mental illness will rise. Third, the incidence of civil commitment of mentally ill elderly persons will also increase.

A. Elderly Population Increasing

The absolute numbers of older people is increasing in nations throughout the world. In 1983, 5.8% of the world's population was over age 65. The proportion of elderly persons in developed countries is much higher. In 1980, the elderly constituted 11.1% of the population in developed countries, the proportion of elderly persons in developing countries being only 4%. There is a wide variation between developed countries. In Canada, for example, the proportion of elderly in the population in 1983 was 10%, in the United States in 1982, it was 11.6%, in Japan 9.6%, and in England 15.2%. By the year 2025, the proportion is expected to double in Canada, from 10% to 20%; to increase by almost as much in the United States, from 11.6% to 21.2%; to rise more modestly in Japan, from 9.6% to 23.2%.

The relative proportions of older to younger persons is also increasing in the developed countries. Whereas in the United States at the turn of the century, only 4.1% of the population was 65 and older, by 1985 11.9% were in this age group. By present projections, between the years 2020 and 2030 about 20% or 1 in 5 Americans could be over 65. In Canada, between 1981 and 1991, the population 65 years and over will show an average annual increase in size of 3%, while the entire population will be expanding at a rate barely above 1% per year. The older population is expected to triple in size in the next 45 years.

Because of the decline in mortality rates at the older ages, the older population will itself be aging in the coming decades. Within the older population, rapid growth is expected in the groups with advanced age. In Canada, the population aged 75 and over is expected to grow from approximately 1 million to 3 million in the next 45 years and the group aged 75 and over to increase from 224,000 to nearly 750,000. The 75-plus and 85-plus age groups are also the fastest growing age segments of the population in the United States.

A particularly sharp rise will occur among those aged 75 and over, relative to those 65 and more, over the next 25 years. Whereas the proportion of the population 75 years and over in Canada in 1980 was 3.6%, by 2025 it is expected to more than double to 7.6%. Increases in this age group are also predicted in the USA, from 4.5% in 1980 to 9.5% in 2025, and in the United Kingdom, from 5.6% to 8.6% — a significant but lesser rate of increase. An even more dramatic rise is expected in Japan, from 3.1% to 12.1%.

It is worth noting that the predominance of women increases at successively older ages. In Canada in 1986, for instance, for every 100 men aged 65 to 69 years of age there were 125 women the same age, while for every 100 men aged 80-84 years there were 175 women, and for every 100 men aged 90 years or more there were 267 women. In the United States, for every 100 men over 65 years there are 146 women. In a very concrete sense, civil commitment of the elderly is an issue that predominantly affects women.

B. Incidence of Mental Illness

The belief that decrements in intellectual functioning (e.g. loss of memory, confusion) and emotional functioning (e.g. crumbling into tears, irritability, fits of rage) are synonymous with aging is now regarded to have been a myth.

Where such decrements do occur, they are now recognized as more likely the product of mental illness or a systemic problem that secondarily affects the brain (e.g. toxemia, malnutrition, congestive heart failure, or drug reactions including withdrawal of a drug on which the person has grown dependent).

The extent of mental disorders in old age is considerable. It is currently estimated that up to 20% of the older population need mental health services. It is likely that the true proportion of psychiatric need among older people has not been fully documented.

Mental illnesses escalate over the course of the life cycle. The increase in incidence is marked, decade by decade, with advancing age. Average annual incidence rates of psychosis from the state of Texas for 1951-52 show this clearly. According to the Texas figures, the incidence progresses steadily from 1 in every 10,000 persons under 15 years, to 137 in every 10,000 persons from 65-74 years, to 228 in every 10,000 persons over 75. The rate across total age groups is 73 in every 10,000 persons.

Data produced in Canada and England demonstrate a similar pattern of rising incidence with respect to psychiatric hospitalization. In Canada in 1982-83, the separation rate of hospitalization, in psychiatric hospitals or psychiatric care units of general hospitals, for persons between the ages of 65-74 years was 1,143 per 100,000 population. The separation rate for persons 75 years of age and over was 1,530 per 100,000 population. This compared with 769 for every 100,000 persons of all ages.

In England, in 1985, the separation rate of psychiatric hospital admissions for all ages was much lower, at 425 per 100,000 population. For 65-74 year olds, it was 676 per 100,000 population, or half again the rate for all ages; for 75-84 year olds it was 1,185 per 100,000 population, almost three times the rate for all ages; and for those 75 and over it was 1,598 per 100,000 population or four times the rate for all age groups. The rate for persons 65-74 years is appreciably lower in England than in Canada; the rates appear to coalesce for older age groups.

The statistics for England in 1985 also show an impressive rise in the rate of first admissions in the older ages, from 0.17% of all persons in the population between the ages of 65-74 years, to more than double at 0.38% of all persons between 75-84. The rate of first admission for persons 75 and over is 0.57%, a staggering three times, and more, the rate for persons from 65-74 years. The rate of first admissions for all age groups is 0.11%. The percentage for women in all recorded age groups was, without exception, slightly higher than for men in Canada and England.

Mental Illnesses of the Elderly

Older persons suffering from mental illness fall into two groups. The first group consists of persons who experienced mental illness earlier in life; the second group, of persons who developed mental illness for the first time late in life.

A. Mental Illness Experienced in Early Life

The mental illness suffered by an older person in his younger years may have been mild or severe. It may have occurred in episodes or been chronic in nature. Hospitalization may have been brief, intermittent or prolonged. In the United States it has been estimated that about one third to one half of older patients resident in state and county mental hospitals in 1976 were admitted as younger patients. The remainder were admitted at age 65 or older. Key examples of the illnesses suffered by persons in the first group are the affective disorders and the schizophrenic disorders. The affective disorders include major depression and bipolar disorder. Persons suffering from bipolar disorder experience extremes of mood, vascillating between deep depression and high elation (the manic phase). Bipolar disorder can persist into old age. The first manic episode typically occurs before age 30. In contrast, major depression may begin at any age, including infancy, and the age of onset is fairly evenly distributed throughout adult life.

Schizophrenia is an illness involving multiple psychological processes — disturbance in content of thought, form of thought, perception, affect, sense of self, volition, relationship to the external world and psychomotor behavior. The onset is usually during adolescence or early adulthood, and in any event before age 45. The illness has an incidence of approximately 1 in every 100 persons. Although it can occur in episodes, in a high percentage of cases the illness is chronic, afflicting its victim lifelong. There is mounting evidence that the root of dysfunction is biological.

The manifestations of these mental illnesses in old age do not differ from those in persons of younger years, although the multiple health problems of old age may add layers of complication.

B. Mental Illness Developed in Late Life

1. Organic Brain Disorders

The major illnesses suffered by persons in the second group are the organic brain disorders. These may be senile (age at onset over 65) or presenile (which is much less common). Few cases develop before the age of 49.

Organic brain disorders are primarily responsible for the increased incidence of mental illness in old age. Estimates of prevalence of some form or severity of dementing illness range from 11% to 16% or more. The prevalence for some illnesses increases several-fold in older age groups. According to a Canadian study, the prevalence of primary degenerative disorder of the Alzheimer's type (see below) is 7.8% for persons 65-74 years; doubles to 15% for persons 75-84 years; and soars to 40% for persons over 75. It is the persons in the 85 and over age group who account for much of the startling increase in the rate of psychiatric hospitalization in later years of life. Even mild organic brain disease could interfere markedly with functioning.

The essential feature of the organic brain disorders is a psychological or behavioral disorder associated with structural damage to the brain. An estimated 60-70% of cases of major mental illness (that is, illness likely to lead to hospitalization) are organic in nature. A surprising number of them, perhaps as many as 50%, are reversible. The reversible causes include those aforementioned.

Organic brain disorders are of two main types: (i) primary degenerative dementia (or, in elderly persons, senile dementia of the Alzheimer's type (SDAT)) and (ii) multi-infarct dementia (formerly "cerebral arteriosclerosis").

(1) Primary Degenerative Disorder

Primary degenerative disorder involves a uniform progressive deterioration in mental functioning. The onset is insidious and the disease leads inevitably to death. It is, in fact, one of the main causes of death in old age. The average survival after the onset of symptoms is 5 years, although persons may live 10 years or more.

Approximately 50-60% of older people with dementia are thought to suffer from this disorder. It takes in an estimated 2-4% of the population over the age of 65. The prevalence increases with advancing age, as has been illustrated, particularly after 75.

The disease involves a multi-faceted loss of intellectual ability, the most prominent features of which are memory deficiency, impairment of abstract thinking and impairment of judgement. It also involves disturbances of language and spatial relationships, and changes in personality. As the disease progresses, interference with social or occupational functioning and daily activities becomes more severe. In DSM-III, the progression is described this way:

> In the early stages, memory impairment may be the only apparent cognitive deficit. There may also be subtle personality changes, such as the development of apathy, lack of spontaneity, and a quiet withdrawal from social interactions...With progression to the middle stage of the disease, various cognitive disturbances become quite inherent, and behavior and personality are more obviously affected. By the late stage, the individual may be completely mute and inattentive. At this point he or she is totally incapable of caring for himself or herself.

Eventually, the personality dies or fades away.

A seven-stage progression is described in a recent article. The authors suggest that the impairment is not such as to require intervention in the form of guardianship or other protection until the fourth stage, which corresponds to the middle stage of the DSM-III description.

The disorder is more common in women that in men, probably because of their longer life expectancy. Moreover, significant memory impairment is more frequently found in older women than in older men of the same age.

A genetic factor appears to be involved because first-degree relatives are four times more likely to develop the disease than members of the general population.

(2) Multi-infarct Dementia

Multi-infarct dementia is associated with vascular disease. It is so named because the severity of the disorder appears to be related to repeated infarcts, i.e. multiple minute strokes, of the brain. According to one authority, "82% of all persons over 65 admitted to hospitals for the first time for mental illness suffer from cerebral arteriosclerosis" (i.e. multi-infarct dementia). The average survival of those admitted to a mental hospital has been estimated to be 3-4 years.

The clinical symptoms include "dizziness, headaches, decreased physical and mental vigor and vague physical complaints". In 50% of cases, onset occurs suddenly with an attack of confusion. Other functional deficits are similar to those experienced for primary degenerative dementia; however, the clinical course of multi-infarct dimentia is more erratic, the impairment of memory tends to be spotty, and there is great variation from person to person.

This illness is more common in men.

2. *Other Mental Illnesses in Old Age*

Two other mental illnesses common in old age deserve mention. The first is depression. The second is the paranoid disorders.

(1) Depression

Depression increases in degree and frequency in old age. The features of depression include feelings such as bleakness, hopelessness, despair and pessimism; and physical symptoms such as greatly diminished energy, loss of interest and initiative, insomnia and loss of appetite.

The areas of loss are numerous: death of spouse, relatives and friends; loss of job; loss of status, prestige and participation in society; reduction in income and standard of living; loss of home; loss of health; and loss of liberty. Depression also often accompanies organic disorders.

(2) Paranoid Disorders

Paranoid disorders are also associated with old age, the onset occurring generally in middle or late adult life. They are characterized by persistent persecutory delusions or delusional jealousy that lasts for at least one week. They frequently arise in persons who suffer dementia, depression or some other mental illness. The sense of isolation brought on by hearing loss is a common contributor. The older paranoid person can be dangerous.

Trends in Civil Commitment Laws and Social Policy

Civil commitment is the involuntary hospitalization of a person for mental disorder. It is an extreme form of interference by the state in the life of an individual. For this reason, its use is reserved for the severest of cases.

The laws permitting civil commitment are founded on the rationale that the state has an interest in the well-being of each of its members, including:

(1) the protection of its members from unconscionable harm and harrassment at the instance of other members, and

(2) the provision of adequate and effective treatment to its sick members.

The individual, on the other hand, has an interest in retaining physical freedom and making his or her own choices about personal matters, such as medical care, place of abode and lifestyle. Interference by the state clearly sets the stage for conflict, although it is well accepted that in some circumstances the broader interests of the state take precedence over the wishes of a single individual.

The test to elicit the precisely correct balance between these interests has not yet been devised. The balance perpetually evades both legislators and courts. Civil commitment laws are continually being revised.

Most civil commitment laws contain no restrictions as to age, but the provisions and practice regarding persons in the upper ages vary, as they do at the lower end for children. It should be borne in mind that a goal of civil commitment is to provide the mental health care that is required to assist the return of the patient to the community. This result is regarded as serving the interests of society and of the mentally ill person.

The ensuing discussion is built around the three criterion most commonly named in civil commitment statutes: need for treatment, dangerousness and, more recently, grave disability.

A. Need for Treatment

For the first six decades of this century, the criteria set out in civil commitment laws in England, Canada and the United States were framed in the language of need for treatment of the individual and the safety of others. This language was generously interpreted and civil commitment occurred "whenever well-intentioned people had reasonable grounds to believe that it was in the individual's best interest to be confined."

Few protections existed for the patient. Once hospitalized, the power to make treatment and discharge decisions frequently rested with the hospital medical superintendent. Formal procedures for review of the detention and monitoring of treatment were not a standard part of legislation.

In England major mental health law reform was introduced in mental health legislation enacted in 1959. It became a model for legislation in Canada, the British Commonwealth, and elsewhere. In Canada, it was adopted in Alberta in 1964 and subsequently in some other provinces. It is referred to in the next section, where developments in the United States are also discussed.

B. Dangerousness

In the early 1960's, a number of civil commitment cases were successfully argued in the United States on constitutional grounds. The cases, which placed an extremely high value on human liberty, established dangerousness as a constitutionally required criterion for civil commitment. The dangerousness could be to self or others. Many courts required evidence of a recent overt dangerous act and that the threat of harm be imminent. Before civil commitment will be ordered, the need for confinement must be shown to be truly compelling. Because liberty is in issue, American courts insist on strict procedural protections in commitment decisions. These protections, which continue to the present day, were arrived at by analogy with detention of persons through criminal process. They include: a mandatory hearing prior to hospitalization with a short-term exception for emergencies; the right of the person to be notified of and to be present at the commitment hearing; short time limits on the duration of hospitalization; mandatory review hearings prior to renewal; the right to representation by retained or appointed counsel; application of the rules of evidence; privilege against self-incrimination; and the right to a jury trial. Civil commitment also entails a standard of proof higher than the regular civil "preponderance of the evidence" standard.

The shift to the "dangerousness" criterion and tightening up of procedures in the United States influenced developments in some Canadian provinces. With the constitutional entrenchment of the Canadian Charter of Rights and Freedoms in 1982, (see below chapter 39) commentators and litigators now more than ever before are turning south of the border, for guidance as to its interpretation.

The inclusion of the "dangerousness" criterion notwithstanding, mental health legislation in Canada tends to be based on a medical, rather than judicial, model of admission. This is the model implemented in England in 1959. Under the medical model, the commitment decision is made by physicians (usually two), who issue certificates of admission. After admission, the patient may request a review of the detention at a hearing before a specially-constituted tribunal established by legislation. Procedures not unlike those required in the United States are followed in the proceedings.

C. Grave Disability

A combination of three forces led to large-scale reductions in institutional beds in the mid-1970's. The first, primarily applicable in the United States, was the constitutional decisions affirming the civil rights of civilly committed mentally ill persons. These are referred to above. The second was the emergence of the normalization theory. This theory was introduced in 1970 by writers like Nirje and Wolfensberger. It applies to mentally retarded and mentally ill persons and involves making available to mentally disabled persons "patterns and conditions of every day life which are as close as possible to the norms and patterns of the mainstream of society". The third was the discovery in the early 1950's of the major tranquillizing drugs that had revolutionized mental health care by relieving symptoms and rendering patients manageable.

The "deinstitutionalization" movement, as the trend is called, affected the United States, Canada, and England. It has not been a fully satisfactory experience. Governments are accused of having been motivated by the prospect of fiscal savings, more than by genuine concern for individual benefit. Butler and Lewis have coined the word "transinstitutionalization" to describe the effect of the movement on the mentally ill elderly, many of whom were moved out of mental hospitals into nursing homes at hazard to their health. Mentally ill persons returned to the community typically lack adequate support. In many cases the burden of care shifts by default to families who may be ill-equipped to cope. This fact has spawned the appearance and rapid rise in the mental health field, in the 1980's, of the family movement.

A more disturbing outcome of the deinstitutionalization has been the increase in the 1980's in the numbers of mentally ill persons who are homeless. Elderly persons are included among them.

The failure of the deinstitutionalization experiment has led to the introduction, recently, of a new criterion — "grave disability". This criterion permits the civil commitment of a person who is unable to care for his basic needs which may include mental as well as physical health and safety. Many studies cast doubt on the effectiveness of changes in criteria to produce changes in practice. Not so in the state of Washington. There, the inclusion in the definition of "grave disability", of the inability to care for basic mental health needs caused an overwhelming increase in the number of patients admitted involuntarily to state mental hospitals. Their existing resources were taxed beyond capacity. Patients, who previously had occupied beds voluntarily, were discharged to make room for the influx of involuntary patients. These results are further evidence of the failure of the "dangerousness" criterion, when coupled with the deinstitutionalization policy, to respond adequately to the needs of large numbers of mentally ill persons.

Gaps in Operation of Civil Commitment Law

Three problem areas are discussed in this section. They are diagnosis, the distinction between voluntary and involuntary admissions, and the role of the nursing home. These areas warrant special comment because they reveal gaps in the operation of civil commitment laws and point to legislative need.

A. Faulty Diagnosis

Civil commitment is an intervention that lies at one extreme of the continuum of the mental health law and service delivery systems. Failure to diagnose correctly leads to mishandling of cases, in terms of both treatment and institutional placement, with grave consequences for the individual concerned.

The difficulties in diagnosis are contributed to by a number of factors:

(i)   the operation of the myth that mental functioning deteriorates with age.

(ii) the coincidence of psychiatric and physical illnesses.

The elderly suffer from multiple health problems which may mimic the symptoms of mental illness. Among them are secondary effects attributable to physical diseases (e.g., toxemia, congestive heart disease) and unanticipated systemic reactions to medications. (The problematic reaction may be iatrogenic — i.e. the effects of physician-prescribed medication for other problems. Not only are older people highly sensitive to drugs and other substances, including food, but also the reactions of multiple medications on each other and the body are largely unknown.)

(iii) reticence of the elderly to talk about their problems.

(iv) the co-existence of a non-organic mental illness with an organic brain disorder.

(v)   the coincidence of symptoms. Elderly persons with a major depressive episode may have features that strongly suggest dementia. Conversely, patients with dementia may show emotional, motivational and behavioral abnormalities commonly associated with depression or other disorders.

(vi) the gaps in knowledge about the mental disorders of the elderly.

(vii) the shortage of psychogeriatric medical specialists.

(viii) the lack of centralized comprehensive assessment facilites. Comprehensive examination is required to rule out physical causes and mental conditions which may be treatable in an active treatment unit, or require short-term rather than long-term civil commitment. Even highly debilitating diseases of a chronic nature can be treated and supported to a point.

B. Distinction Between Voluntary and Involuntary Admission

Not all patients in mental hospitals or general hospital psychiatric units are there under civil commitment. Some are admitted voluntarily. Others are admitted on the authority of a guardian named to make decisions for a person who is not capable of deciding personally. Still others are admitted without clear legal authority but in the absence of objection or resistance. Admissions in these other circumstances are accepted as voluntary in a great many jurisdictions. In the latter case, the passive or compliant demeanour of the patient may hide her incompetence, or her dependence on the relative or nursing home worker seeking the hospitalization. Family members may be seeking the hospitalization to gain relief, for a time at least, from the burden of care.

Voluntary admission works satisfactorily for persons who are in fact capable of exerting personal will and exercising personal judgment. It deprives those who are not of the far-reaching procedural safeguards that protect involuntary patients. The voluntary patient has no right to a hearing to assess the need for hospitalization, no time limits are set on the length of hospitalization, no legal services are provided by the state, periodic reassessment is not a requirement, and the right to treatment is not present (although his consent to the treatment that is given is required). In theory, such protections are not needed because the state has not intervened. The voluntary patient is, by definition, a willing patient. If he is not satisfied with the treatment, he is technically free to leave. In actuality, the voluntary patient may be uninformed as to his status, unaware of his rights, and see himself as having no other options. The designation of "voluntary" in such cases is something of a charade.

C. Role of the Nursing Home

Voluntary admission to a psychiatric hospital or general hospital psychiatric unit is one alternative to civil commitment. Another alternative is institutionalization elsewhere, often in a nursing home, although the categories are myriad and include auxiliary hospitals, homes for the aged, extended care homes, foster homes and the like. In this chapter, the expression "nursing home" is used in a generic sense.

In the United States, overall, approximately 5% of the elderly are institutionalized. In Canada, where the trend toward caring for the elderly in long-term care institutions has been increasing for the past two decades, the estimate is 8.4%. The rate for persons 65-74 living in "homes" is 6.7%, comprised of a rate of 4.7% for males and 8.2% for females. For those over age 85, the proportion, 32.5%, is almost five times that of their younger elderly contemporaries. The rate for males in this age group is 24.8% and for females 36.3%. The average age of nursing home residents in the United States is 80 years.

Very high percentages of elderly persons in "homes" suffer from mental illness. The numbers have been variously estimated. In the United States a 1962 report found that 87% of patients showed significant evidence of chronic organic brain syndrome, and that was before the transfer of large numbers of patients out of mental institutions as part of deinstitutionalization. Another estimate is that chronic organic brain syndromes, presumably secondary to senile dementia in most cases, affect 58% of nursing home residents.

One Canadian study found that more than 80% of the institutionalized elderly had dysfunction of memory and orientation, and about a third suffered from moderate to extreme depression. Results of another Canadian survey demonstrate that between one-half and four-fifths of the residents of long-term care institutions in the province of Ontario are not capable of making rational decisions about their lives, let alone demand and effectively defend their rights.

It is obvious from this data that psychiatric hospitalization does not tell the full story of the mentally ill elderly. Much of the literature in North America laments the misuse of nursing homes to provide custodial care but not treatment for elderly persons. Frequently, the nursing home arrangements are made by a family member or guardian in circumstances like those described for technically "voluntary" psychiatric hospitalization. A multitude of other factors also affect placement decisions. They include: the diagnosis of the medical condition; prognosis; the applicable civil commitment criteria (e.g. dangerousness excludes the gravely disabled from civil commitment and many are consequently cared for in nursing homes); ability to pay; government fiscal policies and funding arrangements; available beds; and approaches to care in vogue at the time (e.g. institutionalization or deinstituationalization). Whereas much attention is paid to the rights of patients in psychiatric hospitals, very little is paid to rights in other institutions.

It is questionable whether the principle of the "least restrictive alternative" is met by such placement. The principle of the "least restrictive alternative" was developed by courts in the United States during the civil rights era. It applies in cases of state intervention in private lives to promote a state interest, and is founded in the notion that people should be free to live as they please unless they are harming others. When others in society have a legitimate interest to be met, the state should act through means that curtail individual freedom to no greater extent than is essential for securing the goal. The application of the doctrine in the case of *Lake v. Cameron* was based on the assumption that a nursing home would provide less restrictions for the resident than a psychiatric hospital.

It has been argued that "psychiatric hospitals", by virtue of their more adequate staffing and greater expertise, are in a position to provide a greater degree of freedom than other facilities. Nursing home or other institutional placement of elderly persons, by comparison, may mean foregoing appropriate treatment. A nursing home may or may not provide a less restrictive environment. Doors may be locked, supervision practises restrictive, policies nontherapeutic. Nursing help may be limited, medical and psychiatric treatment marginal, rights unprotected. Residents may be deprived of decision making on their own behalf. At the same time it is evident that psychiatric hospitalization may not be required if needed treatment can be administered in a less restrictive setting.

The Question: Is Special Legislation Needed?

The abolition of civil commitment laws is a goal advocated in some quarters. One route to achieving the goal would be to eliminate mental illness. At the present time, knowledge about the brain and its functioning is advancing at a remarkable rate. This is due largely to major technological advances. The development of sophisticated brain imaging equipment has been a particularly significant contribution. This equipment enables medical researchers to look behind the skull encasing the brain and watch it at work. The discoveries may well assist treatment and lead, eventually, to cures. But none of this is likely to happen overnight.

Another route to achieving the goal would be to provide a wide range of programs, assistance and support to mentally ill persons living in the community. Desirable as this may be, community acceptance is a problem and services of the needed quality are not likely to be supplied in sufficient quantity to meet the requirements of all mentally ill persons. For one thing, governments are not accustomed to spending large sums of money on mental health resources. For another, given the precarious state of the world economy, the money is not likely to be available.

The goal of abolition therefore is not likely to be achieved in the near future. Mentally ill persons will continue to exhibit the behaviours that trigger the operation of civil commitment laws.

These laws serve a useful purpose. They operate in the interests of society and, oft-times, for the benefit of mentally ill persons as well. While there is always room for improvement in the quest for the ideal balance between the interests of the state and the rights of individuals, civil commitment laws, on the whole, provide carefully thought out criteria and procedures upon which to base decisions in individual cases. They respect the right of mentally ill persons to liberty.

This brings the discussion to the question posed in the title: are existing civil commitment laws adequate to meet the needs and circumstances of the mentally ill elderly, or is special legislation needed?

Civil commitment laws in the jurisdictions under study work reasonably well for the persons to whom they apply. However, large numbers of elderly persons living in institutions, in North American at least, are overlooked by the operation of the laws. Many of these persons have, in fact, lost their liberty. Other persons admitted to psychiatric hospitals as voluntary patients are not truly voluntary. Some do not have the ability necessary to make a personal decision. Others succumb to persuasion because of their dependent circumstances (e.g. social, financial).

These cases of avoidance, circumvention or non-application of civil commitment laws cause problems. Legal solutions are required to meet the needs of persons in these circumstances. Solutions are also required to protect the rights of mentally incompetent, frail and dependent mentally ill persons living in the community.

Legal reform could take one or more of a number of paths. For example, "grave disability" could be included in the criteria for civil commitment in jurisdictions now using only "dangerousness". Such an amendment would assist the elderly, as it would younger mentally ill persons who are unable to care for themselves and to meet their own basic needs, health and safety.

Legislation could be enacted to protect the rights of elderly persons in other situations. In North American jurisdictions, legislation of the following sorts has already been enacted:

(i) modern guardianship statutes which are more finely tuned to the individual in question than guardianship laws of the past. (Past laws approached the incompetence on which guardianship is based as an all-or-nothing proposition. The new guardianship laws are intended to preserve autonomy in areas where the individual is capable and protect his best interests where he is not. They provide for decision, by the guardian, about personal as well as property matters.)

(ii) durable power of attorney statutes that permit personal as well as property decision-making.

(iii) elderly protection statutes — comparable to child protection statutes for youth.

(iv) elder ombudsman statutes.

Generally, the application of such legislation is determined by functional ability rather than by age. It would be remiss to enact special civil commitment laws or other legislation for the elderly alone, in that the circumstances of younger mentally ill and disabled adults may be quite similar.

Mental health law reform requires a systematic approach, in recognition that a change in one area will cause changes in other areas. Some examples have been presented in this chapter (e.g. the combined effect of narrow civil commitment criteria and the institutionalization policy). This past experience demonstrates that changes in law lead to changes in pressures on the mental health system, the judicial system, and the private sector. That is to say, a "change in one sector usually shifts a service burden to another sector," often a sector that is not prepared to handle it.

When reform is approached systematically, an almost infinite number of choices opens up. Enactment of the "gravely disabled" standard, for example, is one choice. Improvement of diagnostic processes is another. Meeting the shortage of psychogeriatric specialists is a third. Improving the availability and quality of psychiatric care available in nursing homes is a fourth. And so on.

The goal should be laws that work in close harmony with other systems in which mentally ill persons are caught up. What is needed is a far-reaching, co-ordinated, comprehensive range of care, intervention and legal protection.

Conclusion

The era of the elderly is now dawning. Governments around the world face a major challenge. By 2025, the number of elderly persons will have close to doubled in many developed countries. The prevalence of mental illness will increase dramatically as the proportion of elderly people in older age groups — 75-84 years, 85 and over — also increases. The rate of increase in the age group could be as high as three times the rate of increase for elderly persons in the 65-74 age group.

Existing mental health laws need to be revised, and new laws enacted to adequately protect the legal rights of mentally ill persons. Legal reforms should be undertaken in concert with reforms in other systems having a part to play in society's response to the mentally ill elderly. The time to act is now.

References

Alberta. "Are nursing homes suitable places for Alzheimer's patients?" *Folio,* 19 November 1987, p.4 (University of Alberta.)

Alberta Hospital Association. "Nursing home legislation review" (October 1985) *HospitAlta*14.

Jo Alexander, Debi Berrow, Lisa Dimitrovich, Margarita Donnelly & Cheryl McLean, eds., *Women and Aging: An Anthology by Women,* Calyx Books, Corvallis, Oregon, 1986.

American Psychiatric Association, *Diagnostic and Statistical Manual of Mental Disorders,* Third Edition (DSM-III), Washington, D.C., 1980.

Paul S. Appelbaum, "Special section on APA's model commitment law: an introduction" (1985) 36 *Hospital and Community Psychiatry* 966.

Australia. "The greying of Australia" (1988) Reform 26.

R. Michael Bagby, "The effects of legislative reform on admission rates to psychiatric units of general hospitals" (1987) 10 *Int'l J. of Law and Psychiatry* 383-394.

Margaret Birch, "The elderly and government policy" (1982) 3 *Health Law in Canada* 49-50.

Brian P. Bishop, "The chronically mentally ill — rehabilitation issues", unpublished presentation to the Edmonton Psychiatric Services Planning Committee, October 2, 1986.

Steve Bottomley, "Mental health law reform and psychiatric deinstitutionalization; the issues in New South Wales" (1987) 10 *Int'l J. of Law and Psychiatry* 369-382.

Robert N. Butler and Myrna I. Lewis, *Aging and Mental Health,* A Plume Book, published by The New American Library, New York and Scarborough, Ontario, 1983.

Canada. "Continued slower Population growth", *Canadian Social Trends,* Summer 1987, Special Section.

Canada. Ministry of Health and Welfare, Mental Health Division, "Legal issues in the care of mentally impaired elderly persons: competence, surrogate management, and protection of rights" (1987) 35 *Canada's Mental Health* 6-11. (Prepared by the Working Group on Legal Issues, Committee on Guidelines for Comprehensive Services to Elderly Persons with Psychiatric Disorders.)

James F. Childress, "Ensuring care, respect and fairness for the elderly" (1984) *The Hastings Center Report* 27-31.

Elias S. Cohen, "Autonomy and paternalism: two goals in conflict" (1985) 13 *Law, Medicine & Health Care* 145-150.

Alex Comfort, *A Good Age,* Crown Publishers, Inc., New York, 1976.

Norman Daniels, "Family responsibility initiatives and justice between age groups" (1985) 13 *Law, Medicine & Health Care* 153-159.

Mary Sue Devereaux, "Aging of the Canadian population", *Canadian Social Trends,*

Winter 1987, pp.34-40.

David S. Douglas, David Feinberg, Robin Jacobsohn & Alice B. Stock, "R for the elderly: legal rights (and wrongs) within the health care system" (1985) 20 *Harv. Civil Rights-Civil Liberties Law Rev* 425-483.

M.L. Durham, "Implications of need-for-treatment laws — a study of Washington state's involuntary treatment act" (1985) 36 *Hosp. Commun.* 975.

M.L. Durham & H.D. Carr, "Use of summons in involuntary civil commitment" (1985) 13 *Bull. Am. Acad. Psychiatry Law* 243.

M.L. Durham & J. Q. La Fond, "The empirical consequences and policy implications of broadening the statutory criteria for civil commitment (1985) 3 *Yale Law & Policy Rev.* 395.

England. *Mental Health Statistics for England 1985.* Government Statistical Service, Booklets 1, 5, 11.

William F. Forbes and Jennifer A. Jackson, *Institutionalization of the Elderly in Canada,* Butterworths, Toronto and Vancouver, 1987.

Robert M. Gordon & Simon N. Verdun-Jones, "Privatization and protective services for the elderly: some observations on the economics of the aging process" (1986) 8 *Int'l J. of Law and Psychiatry* 311-325.

Robert M. Gordon & Simon Verdun-Jones, "The implications of the Canadian Charter of Rights and Freedoms for the law relating to guardianship and trusteeship" (1987) 10 *Int'l J. of Law and Psychiatry* 21.

Larry Gostin, "Human rights in mental health: a proposal for five international standards based upon the Japanese experience" (1987) 10 *Int'l J. of Law and Psychiatry* 350-368.

Andrew Grubb & David Pearl, "Medicine, health, the family and the law" (1986) *Family Law* 227-240.

Mary K. Harrison, "The elderly person's right to care: a nursing perspective" (1982) 3 *Health Law in Canada* 55-57. "Housing Alzheimer's patients", *Alberta Heritage Foundation for Medical Research Newsletter,* Jan/Feb. 1988, p.10.

Sandra H. Johnson, "State regulation of long-term care in the legal system" (1985) 13, *Law, Medicine & Health Care* 173-187.

L. Ralph Jones, Richard R. Parlour & Lee W. Badger, "The inappropriate commitment of the aged (1982) 10 *Bulletin of the AAPL* 29-38.

Timothy S. Jost, "Enforcement of quality nursing home care in the legal system" (1985) 13 *Law, Medicine & Health Care* 160-172.

Marshall B. Kapp, "Geriatric medical education: integrating legal and ethical issues" (1985) 4 *Med Law* 401-408.

Joan M. Krauskopf, "New developments in defending commitment of the elderly" (1980-81) 10 *NYU Rev of Law and Social Change* 367.

N.L. Mace et al., *The 36-Hour Day,* Age Concern England, Marketing Dept., 60 Pitcairn Rd., Mitcham, Surrey CR4 3LL.

Donald J. Lange, "Geriatric, psychiatric, and legal aspects of the mental state of the aged" (1979) 2 *Family Law Rev.* 266-279; (1980) 4 *Legal Medical Quarterly* 161.

Betsy MacKenzie, "The decline of stroke mortality", *Canadian Social Trends,* Autumn 1987, pp.34-37.

Susan A. McDaniel, *Canada's Aging Population,* Butterworths, Toronto and Vancouver, 1986.

Mary Ann McLaughlin, "Homelessness in Canada: the report of the national inquiry" (1987) 5 *Social Development Overview* 1-14. (Published by the Canadian Council on

Social Development.)

Barry D. McPherson, *Aging as a Social Process: An Introduction to Individual and Population Aging,* Butterworths, Toronto, 1983.

Mark J. Mills, "Civil commitment of the mentally ill: an overview" (1986) 484 *Annals,* AAPSS (The American Academy of Political and Social Science) 28-41.

Joseph P. Morrissey and Howard H. Goldman, "Care and treatment of the mentally ill in the United States: historical developments and reforms" (1986) 484 *Annals,* AAPSS 12-27.

Sheila Noonan, "Constitutionality of current civil commitment practices: hope for children?" Unpublished paper presented at CALT Conference: Family Law Subsection, April 1985.

Leif Ojesjo, "Law and psychiatry: Scandinavia in the 1980's" (1986) 484 *Annals,* AAPSS 144-154.

Jo-Anne Parliament, "Increased life expectancy, 1921 to 1981," *Canadian Social Trends,* Summer 1987, pp. 15-19.

Brice Pitt, *Psychogeriatrics: An Introduction to the Psychiatry of Old Age* (2nd ed.), Churchill Livingstone, Edinburgh, London, Melbourne and New York, 1982.

John J. Regan, "Process and context: hidden factors in health care decisions for the elderly" (1985) 13 *Law. Medicine & Health Care* 151.

H.F. Reichenfeld, "Elderly psychiatric patients in institutions — implications of the Canadian Charter of Rights and Freedoms" *Health Law in Canada* 83-88.

Arnold J. Rosoff & Gary L. Gottlieb, "Preserving personal autonomy for the elderly: competency, guardianship, and Alzheimer's Disease" (1987) 8 *J. of Legal Medicine* 1-47.

Joel Sadavoy, "Psychiatric aspects of mental competence and protection issues in the elderly" (1983) 4 *Health Law in Canada* 1-5.

Rafael J. Schen, "Misplacement of the elderly in chronic care institutions" (1985) 4 *Springet Vertag.*

Joni Seager and Ann Olson, *Women in the World: An International Atlas,* Pan Books, London and Sydney, 1986.

Leroy O. Stone and Susan Fletcher, *The Seniors Boom: Dramatic Increases in Longevity and Prospects for Better Health,* Statistics Canada, Minister of Supply and Services Canada, 1986.

C.D. Stromberg and A.A. Stone, "A model state law on civil commitment of the mentally ill" (1983) 20 *Harv. Journal on Legislation* 275-396.

Georgann Szala, "Housing alternative for seniors", *Resource News,* February 1988, pp. 7-8. (Published by the Legal Resource Centre, Faculty of Extension, University of Alberta.)

"Protecting nursing-home residents: tort actions are one way" (December 1985) *Trial* 54-61.

M.L. Durham & G.L. Pierce, "Beyond deinstitutionalization: a commitment law in evolution" (1982) 33 *Hosp. Commun.* 216.

M.L. Durham & G.L. Pierce, "Legal intervention in civil commitment: the impact of broadened commitment criteria" (1986) 484 *Annals,* AAPSS (The American Academy of Political and Social Science.) 42-55.

M.L. Durham, H.D. Carr & G.L. Pierce, "Police involvement and influence in involuntary civil commitment (1984) 35 *Hosp. Commun.* 580.

N.L. Mace et al., *The 36-Hour Day,* Age Concern England, Marketing Dept., 60 Pitcairn Rd., Mitcham, Surrey CR4 3LL. (The is a practical guide to caring for

confused elderly people at home. The English edition of the successful US edition has been revised and updated and takes account of legal and social differences in the UK.)
A. Romaniuc, *Current Demographic Analysis. Fertility in Canada: From Baby-boom to Baby-bust,* Statistics Canada, Minister of Supply and Services Canada 1984.

Chapter 37

Reform of Guardianship Laws in Europe — A Comparative and Interdisciplinary Approach

Bernd SCHULTE

Max-Planck Institute, Munich
Federal Republic of Germany

Introduction: United Nations General Assembly-Resolution 2586 (XXVI) adopted 20 December 1971

Declaration on the Rights of Mentally Retarded Persons

"1. The mentally retarded person has, to the maximum degree of feasibility, the same rights as other human beings ...
5. The mentally retarded person has a right to a qualified guardian when this is required to protect his personal well-being and interests. ...
7. Whenever mentally retarded persons are unable, because of the severity of their handicap, to exercise all their rights in a meaningful way or it should become necessary to restrict or deny some or all of these rights, the procedure used for that restriction or denial of rights must contain proper legal safeguards against every form of abuse. This procedure must be based on an evaluation of the social capability of the mentally retarded person by qualified experts and must be subject to periodic review and to the right of appeal to higher authorities." (*Yearbook of the United Nations* 1971, vol. 25, New York 1971, p. 365; *the italics are mine*)

The United Nations Declaration on the Rights of Mentally Retarded Persons, 1971, proclaims that "the mentally retarded person has a right to a qualified guardian when this is required to protect his personal well-being and interests", and calls for "national and international action" to ensure that the Declaration will be used "as a common basis and frame of reference for the protection of these rights". The General Assembly of the United Nations refers thus to the inherent power of the State to protect the disadvantaged members of society (Gunn 1986: 150; Köler 1987: 635).

A right is a legitimate claim to something. When a person has a right to something, there is a corresponding duty on the part of others not to interfere with the person's exercising that right. There may even be a duty on the part of the State to make it possible for the person to exercise his right as in the case of the "right to a qualified guardian". A guardian must therefore be made available to those mentally retarded persons who want it just as such persons have a right to proper medical care, to education, to economic security, to protection from exploitation, to legal procedures, to a life with their own family or with foster parents, and to participation in different forms of community life.

The Declaration thus recognizes the necessity of assisting persons in need of care to develop their abilities in various fields of activity. At the same time it is an example of a new legal approach to the problems which guardianship laws are meant to solve. Legal policy in this area must be considered as a medium of reform in order to adapt law to social change as well as to initiate desirable social change by law.

A. The Case for Reform

Legal capacity, as an inalienable right, is generally understood to be an attribute of every human being without exception and beginning at the time of birth. The capacity to act is the power to acquire entitlements, to assume duties, and to incur liabilities through one's own acts. The normal capacity to do business is generally acquired on reaching the age of majority.

The formal distinction between the normally competent and the incompetent has long, perhaps too long, been relevant to the legal treatment of a variety of groups, notably children, the mentally ill, handicapped and retarded, as well as elderly people suffering from what is called senility. The legal status of these groups continues to be characterized by legal incapacities, regulated dependencies and exclusions from various kinds of legal, economic, political and social activities.

The reforms which have been undertaken or which are envisaged in Western European countries — e.g. Austria, France, the Federal Republic of Germany (see ch.38) and the Netherlands — may therefore be considered as challenges to the inferior status of these groups. A shift "from status to contract" (Minow 1987: 144) has been made possible by a variety of factors which appear in medicine, mental health care, law and social welfare.

The bill which led to the French reform of guardianship in 1968 was presented to parliament as follows:

> "La psychiatrie moderne recommande au droit civil d'éviter l'idée d'une incapacité générale, enveloppant toute la personne, ce qui a pour effect de la mettre en état de ségrégation par rapport au reste de la société" (Foyer, J.O., Débat. Ass. Nat. 10.4.1966; quote. In Delpérée 1987: 37).

(1) Changes in *medical* knowledge about the origins and the treatment of mental illnesses contribute to the reexamination of public policies towards the

above-mentioned groups. New drug treatments offer a medical basis for managing certain aspects of mental illness outside institutional settings. These and other changes need to be viewed in the wider perspective of demographic and social transition. With respect to the demographic evolution of Western societies, a sharp decline of birth rates has been observed in nearly all countries of Europe since the mid-60's. Though the starting levels and the speed of the decline showed differences, the trend is comparable and seems to remain at a level below reproduction. The demographic change is likely to raise demands for health services and old age pensions and it constitutes therefore a challenge to the Welfare State, too. The falling birth-rate, the aging of the population and the rising numbers of non-family households are accompanied by social and cultural trends which are of significance for mental health and the care for the elderly such as a decline in family and neighborhood support systems. Up to now, increased life expectancy and the increasing frequency of chronic illness have resulted in an hitherto unheard-of increase in the number of old people in need of care, who are looked after in the family by (mostly non-working female) relatives, by home nursing or in residential institutions. Home nursing makes it possible for the patient to remain in his own home and social environments, thus making life more tolerable.

(2) The situation of the mentally ill and handicapped and of the elderly in need of care became a subject of public concern in Western Europe in the 60's. As regards mental health care, there have been significant changes on the psychiatric scene in Western Europe marked by a transition from an essentially custodial approach to one based firmly on therapy and rehabilitation.

The number of beds in mental hospitals has declined, the number of psychiatric units in general hospitals has increased, and the length of hospital stay has decreased in most Western European countries. The number of psychiatrists and of other professions active in the care of the mentally ill (e.g. psychologists, social workers) has become larger in absolute terms as well as in relation to other medical disciplines. New forms of psychiatric services have emerged. Changes in the organisation of services include decentralisation and increasing reliance on various forms of self-help movements. Standards of care have generally been improved. There is, however, less evidence that the attitudes of the population towards the mentally ill have improved or that better care of the mentally ill and disabled is given sufficient priority by decision makers (Sartorius 1987: 4).

In a recent article 'The Direction of Change in Western European Mental Health Care' Breemer ter Stege/Gittelman (1987: 22) describe the common back ground of mental health care in Western Europe as follows:

"However diverse they may be, the mental health care systems of the Western European nations also offer us much similarity. Almost all, for example, share the asylum past, a past in which the mentally ill, though often inadequately treated even in terms of then-current knowledge of their condition, at least had shelter and a modicum of care. These countries all experienced the 'medicalization' of psychiatry and — much later — the advent of the welfare state. Common to all as well is the financially troubled present, the economic crisis ... ."

(3) Characteristic of new and pending *mental health legislation* is an emphasis on *patient rights:* These include;

(a) stricter specification of who may be hospitalized involuntarily;

(b) provision of care with no more restriction of liberty than is inevitable;

(c) protection of patient rights in general (e.g. appeal and review procedures);

(d) the setting of limits on established psychiatric measures relating, e.g. to compulsory admission and treatment (especially to hazardous measures even when taken with the consent of the patient);

(e) primary focus on the right to treatment, and less on control;

(f) growing respect of the right to self-determination by psychiatric patients as regards the treatment they should receive (the principles of competency and consent justifying legal interference in the therapeutic relationship);

(g) the guarantee of the basic rights and of civil status of the consumers of psychiatric services and of their human dignity ('right to life', 'right to corporeal integrity and to the unhampered development of the personality', 'equality before the law', 'right to hearing in the courts' etc.).

Another aim of the new legislation is the development of new patterns of facilities through the regulation of the structure, the organization and the financing of care. A new role has been developing in law which can and should be used as a strategy in the provision of services and according to which the access to health and social services should be based on enforceable statutory rights instead of charitable or professional discretion (Gostin 1983: 23-30).

(4) The provision of psychiatric care and social services for the elderly is largely controlled by the social welfare system. Almost the entire population in Western European countries is covered by health services retirement pension schemes. The dominant perceptions of the Welfare State may be summarized as follows. A state that:

a) provides economic security and social services for certain categories (or all) of its citizens,

b) takes care of a substantial redistribution of resources from the wealthy to the poor,

c) has instituted social rights as part of citizenship,

d) aims at security for and equality among its citizens,

e) is assumed to be explicitly responsible for the well-being of all of its members (Kaufmann 1985: 45).

Social rights are therefore essential correlates of state activities (see definition c).

Critics of the Welfare State emphasize five points (Kaufmann 1985: 50):

– juridication, e.g. the fact that human miseries and their treatments are regulated and then altered by the forms of law (see Juridication... 1987);

– bureaucratization and centralization, i.e. the tendencies towards more

influence of the central state and more interorganizational controls leading to more rigid standard setting, towards loss of initiative and of
individual attention, etc.;
- economization, i.e. the tendency to consider social services under the
  aspect of costs alone and not of their utility;
- professionalization, i.e. the fact that social services are administered more
  and more by professionals cultivating their particular vision of life and
  social problems.

The principles underlying the concept of community care are related to these
five points of criticism:
- a preference for home life over institutional care;
- the pursuit of the ideal of normalization and integration, and avoidance so
  far as possible of separate provision, segregation and restriction (i.e. the
  concept of the 'least restricted alternative');
- a preference for small over large;
- a preference for local services over distant ones (cf. Ayer/Alascewski
  1984: 257-258).

The promotion of community care as an element in social welfare policy has
a fairly long history. There has been however, in recent years an emphasis upon
the value and responsibility of the family as the locus of care (which is coupled
with a more general emphasis upon limitation of the growth in statutory
provision of welfare). 'Privatisation' is not just about the involvement of the
commercial sector in welfare provision but may also be seen as a more general
policy of returning welfare functions to the private — as opposed to statutory/
public — domaine. In this broader conception the family, friends, neighbours
and the 'informal sector' play a key role. For there is evidence that old people
with families are far less likely to be admitted to institutions than those without,
and those with small families are more likely to be admitted than those with
larger ones.

Such a 'remaking of the welfare map' (Leat/Gay 1987: 2) seems to be,
however, rather illusory, because there is a lot of evidence on demographic and
other social trends which suggests that the 'informal sector', in particular the
family, which currently provides indeed significant quantities of care (cf. (2)),
does not have the capacity to continue doing so and will not have the capacity to
cope with any additional responsibilities.

B. Guardianship Laws and Legal Reform in Western Europe

The linkage of the above-mentioned medical, legal, welfare, etc. aspects to
guardianship can be illustrated very clearly by a consideration of the Federal
Republic of Germany in the mid-70's.

The provision of care for the mentally ill and mentally handicapped in the
Federal Republic of Germany was scrutinized by an independent Expert
Commission. The report given by this commission to the Parliament (Bundes-
tag) stated that the current situation was characterized by serious deficiencies

in the provision of all forms of care. These deficiencies called for a reorganization of the care of the mentally ill and handicapped, designed to achieve the
following objectives:
  – that mental illnesses and handicaps should be subject to early recognition
    and intervention, so that serious impediments can be averted as far as
    possible;
  – that where treatment is required, the need for hospital admission should
    be reduced by means of out-patient and related facilities;
  – that the segregation of the mentally ill and handicapped from their normal
    social environment should be avoided;
  – that psychiatric hospitals should be put in a position, in terms of personnel,
    buildings, and administration, to offer real prospects of cure or relief for
    mental illness and handicap (Deutscher Bundestag 1975 a: 12).
  As regards the legal problems in the care of the mentally ill and handicapped,
the Expert Commission made a series of recommendations:
  In all regulations governing social welfare and rehabilitation, mentally
handicapped and mentally retarded persons should be awarded equal rights
with the physically ill;
  – the greatest possible use should be made of existing legal possibilities for
    improving out-patient care;
  – with regard to the necessary division of work between medical and non-
    medical personnel in treating the sick, the legislators should define clear
    areas of activity and responsibility for non-medical professions, e.g.
    psychologists;
  – the laws governing compulsory admission in the federal Länder should be
    revised; in particular, a generally stronger emphasis on the welfare aspects
    of admission — for example, by inclusion of preventive and follow-up
    supportive measures — should be taken into consideration;
They agreed that a general reform of the guardianship laws was necessary in
the interest of improvement of the care of the mentally ill and handicapped:

> "What is needed is the development of a graded system of care, instead of
> or as a supplement to the existing guardianship system, with inclusion of
> welfare admissions, as well as replacement of testamentory incapacity by
> ascertainment of "need for care" and simultaneous appointment of a "care-
> giver" with definition of his area of responsibility (Deutscher Bundestag
> 1976: 28-29; the italics are mine. See also Cooper/Bauer 1987: 79-80).

  In December 1987 a draft bill ('Diskussions-Teilentwurf Gesetz Über die
Betreuung Volljähriger (Betreuungsgesetz — BtG')) was published (Bundes-
minister der Justiz 1987; cf. Zenz, 'The End of Guardianship for the Aged?
Facts and Goals in the Discussion of a Legal Reform Project in the Federal
Republic of Germany' Chapter 38).
  In Austria, the deficiencies in the provision of care for the mentally ill and
handicapped became a subject of public concern and scientific interest in the

mid-70's. The Ministry of Justice then took steps towards amendment of the existing legislation. This initiative led to the adoption of a new guardianship law in 1983 ('Gesetz über die Sachwalterschaft für behinderte Personen vom 2. Feber 1983) (Ent/Hopf 1983; Forster et al. 1985; Forster 1987; Hopf 1986; Kremzow 1984; Maurer 1984; Pelikan 1984 a; 1984 b; Recht und Psychiatrie 1985; Schulte 1986, 1988 a, 1988 b, Zierl 1986; Trompisch 1986).

The old legal provisions which dated from 1916 and which were very similar to the provisions of the German civil code ('Bügerliches Gesetzbuch v. 18 August 1896'; cf. Zenz), stood in urgent need of improvement. The situation was characterized by deficiencies as follows:

– The legal status of a person received under guardianship because of mental illness and retardation, prodigality, excessive drinking or drug addiction was analogous to that either of an infant of less than seven years ('Vollentmündigung') or to that of a minor ('beschränkte Entmündigung'). The person affected lost totally, or for the greater part, his competence to enter into legal transactions, i.e. to dispose of his person, affairs and property.
– If the court decided to place a person under guardianship it appointed simultaneously a legal representative (guardian) ('Kurator' or 'Beistand') who represented the person under guardianship and looked after his interests both personal and material.
– A person who had been declared incapable because of mental illness was totally incompetent to enter into legal transactions. A person who had been placed under guardianship because of feeblemindedness or habitual drunkenness was, with respect to competency to enter into legal transactions, in the position of a minor who has completed his seventh year of age, and required for legal transactions the consent of his legal representative (cf. *Zenz* for the analoguous situation in the F.R.G.).
– These general limitations upon capacity were frequently unnecessarily imposed or upheld by court. No legal representation was provided for during the proceedings leading to the imposition of such limitations. Many guardians were not sufficiently competent. The judicial control of guardians was usually limited to questions of property and in many cases there was no control at all. The limitation of capacity was in practice most often a lifelong measure.
– Guardians were often not fully aware of the problems of the persons received under guardianship or of the facilities and services they could use. Their activities were often ineffective. Guardians (among them many lawyers) often lacked experience and skill in dealing with disabled and elderly persons. Therefore an urgent need was felt for a more qualified representation of people who needed a guardian.

The new legislation ('Sachwaltergesetz' brought into force July 1, 1984) provides for less restrictive forms of guardianship, reinforces the position of those affected by such measures in relation to that of the guardians, clarifies and reduces the powers of the guardian, and prescribes tighter judicial control of the guardian as well as of the necessity to maintain the guardianship in certain cases of improvement. A new, independently organized and state-subsidised institution ("Sachwalterverein") which is predominantly staffed with legally trained professional social workers, ensures competent advocacy and support in cases where no suitable relative or other such person is available.

Nearly four years after the enactment of this new legislation, first experiences have been evaluated. Implementation of the new legislation has caused problems. The expectation was that these changes would lead to a significant decrease in the use of guardianship. That would, however, not appear to be the case. Surprisingly there are now more new guardianships per year than compared to the number of legal limitations ("Entmündigungen") before. The reasons for this need to be examined. First, it can be suggested that there had been an element of inertia involved in the failure to use the former type of guardianship ('Entmündigung' and 'Vormundschaft'). Possibly, positive experience with the new guardians leads to the inclusion of a wider range of problems and to a more frequent use of guardians. The total number of affected persons, however, has decreased because of the abolition of unnecessary or unjustified guardianships.

Courts are reluctant to make use of the new and more complicated rules of procedure, especially with regard to the differentiation of the extent of limitations of capacity. The courts are also slow in reviewing existing guardianships. These shortcomings are accounted for by a lack of time and resources (especially in personnel), inflexible organizational structures, lack of psychosocial competence and the persistence of traditional professional identities.

The expansion of state-subsidised guardianship ("Sachwalterschaft") is rather slow, too. At present, only about 1/4 of the final staffing — about 140 professional guardians all over Austria (entire population: 6.5 million) — has been reached. This slow implementation of the "Sachwaltergesetz" is mainly due to the fact that there is no legal commitment of the state with regard to the financing of the "Sachwaltervereine" and to financial subsidies, in general. The experiences with the new legislation, are however, positive as regards the legal position of the mentally ill and handicapped.

The new legislation may, however, have been introduced by Parliament too fast, and its substance may be based on too little consultation with the medical and legal professionals involved.

In France, guardianship is included in chapter XI of Book 1 of the Civil Code. The relevant provisions were placed on a new legislative basis in 1968 ('Loi du 3.1.1968 portant réforme du droit des incapables majeurs'). Whereas the former law ('De la majorité, de l'interdiction, et du conseil judiciaire') was rather similar to the provisions of the German (cf. Zenz) and Austrian (cf. above) legislation, the new law ('De la majorité et des majeurs protégés par la loi') has introduced a more differentiated and individualized system which is applicable 'ratione personae' to a wider range of persons (including physically disabled persons who cannot express their will) who are unable to look after

their affairs. There is now a graded system:
- 'Sauvegarde de justice' (Art. 491 et sv. C. civ.),
- 'Tutelle' ('tutelle complète', 'administration légale', 'tutelle en gérance', 'tutelle d'Etat') (Art. 492 et sv. C. civ.),
- 'Curatelle' (Art. 508 et. sv. C. civ.)
- 'Tutelle aux prestations sociales' (Décret du 25.4.1969 C. Séc. soc.)

The accommodation, i.e. the home of the person in question, especially that of elderly people is particularly protected because of its importance for the psychological well-being of these persons:

"Aussi longtemps qu'il est possible" (i.e. as long as a return home may be reasonably expected) 'le logement de la personne protégée doit être conservé à sa disposition" (Art. 490-2 C. civ.). Any measure taken in this field requires a medical certificate.

The protection of the rights of the persons in question is provided by the Court ('Juge de tutelle'), the medical doctor and the family. The last normally plays an important role in the placement under guardianship and in the administration of guardianship (for details cf. Delpérée 1987: pp. 20).

In Switzerland there is discussion on a reform of guardianship laws. (cf. Schuller 1985).

The present system:
- 'Beistandschaft' ('curatelle')
- 'Beiratschaft' ('conseil légal')
- 'Vormundschaft' ('tutelle')
is thought to be too rigid and too restrictive.

In Luxemburg legislation was introduced in 1982 ('De la majorité et des majeurs qui sont protégés par la loi') which follows the French law of 1968 (cf. for details Delpérée 1987: 55-57). In Belgium reform is envisaged which follow the French example (cf. Délpée 1987: 59-69).

In the Netherlands a person can be placed under guardianship ('Curatele') according to Chapter XVI of Book 1 of the Civil Code ('Burgerlijk Wetboek') by the civil court on account of:
- a mental disorder, because of which the disordered person is, permanently or intermittantly, unable or impeded in looking properly after his own interests,
- prodigality,
- the habit of excessive drinking because of which he does not look properly after his interests, repeatedly causes scandal in public or endangers himself or others (art. 378 B.W.).

The guardianship can be requested by the person in question, his spouse or nearest relatives, or the public prosecutor. If the court decides to place a person under guardianship it appoints a guardian simultaneously. The latter represents the person in question and looks after his interests. The legal status of a person received under guardianship because of mental disorder is analogous to that of an infant, i.e. the person in question is legally incompetent. A person received under guardianship on account of prodigality or excessive drinking remains competent to perform certain legal acts (e.g. marriage and last will).

In September, 1982, the so-called 'beschermingsbewind' (enactment of May 15, 1981) came into force. According to official estimates, this legal instrument will affect about 10,000 persons per year (Jansen 1983: 11). The law is a less restrictive alternative to the 'curatele' because it does not lead to total, but only to partial legal incompetence in the running of the (economic) affairs of the person in question.

Since this new scheme came into force there exists a graded system of care as a supplement to traditional guardianship ('curatele').

In July 1987 a draft bill ('Mentorschap ten behoeve van meerderjarigen (voorontwerp van wet)') was published by the Ministry of Justice and the Ministry of Social Affairs ('Ministerie van Welzijn, Volksgezondheid en Cultuur'). This bill is to introduce a Chapter 20 into Book 1 of the Civil Code. A special guardianship for adults ('mentorschap ten behoeve van meerderjarigen') who, because of their mental state, are unable to look after their personal affairs is to supplement the 'beschermingsbewind'.

Common Trends

The impetus to reform guardianship laws in Western Europe came about as a result of a change in attitudes towards the relationship of the State to society and to the individual. The new and pending legislation has emerged as a response to contemporary problems and is not limited to civil law or law in general, but envisages a reform of social welfare as well.

In many cases, an elderly person will only need assistance without any restrictions of his capacity to act being required. There are, however, circumstances in which a person may be denied the capacity to make his own decisions, either in general or in a particular case. This can only happen, however, where it seems necessary to protect the person in question and where there is a legal power of control. The mentally disordered person must be protected against the risk of exploitation and abuse as well as against the unjustified removal of his right to look after his own affairs.

Different actors; the courts, the administration, the medical profession, social workers, the family and voluntary helpers are encouraged to establish a working relationship which will benefit the person in question. People in need of care, especially old people, equally should be encouraged to face up to life in spite of their debilities. In recent years, public and private organizations have been increasingly active in the area of policy for the aged. Programmes were developed which provide housing, out-patient care and aid services in the form of counselling, activities, etc. as well as old people's nursing homes. This policy emphasizes the preventive approach. Individual privacy and autonomy need to be maximized. The aged should be helped to take up activities, to find companionship or to make contact with those close to them, especially with their family. Individuality and independence are expressed through choice. A person cannot live a full life if all choice and responsibility is removed from him. Above all, old people need to be able to preserve the right to make their own choices and their own decisions whenever possible. When placed under guardianship they should retain an active part in the running of their own household and affairs and they should be involved as much as possible in decisions bearing on their lives.

Lawyers have a new view of the liberty and of the rights of the subject before the law. They have created a rights framework which translates needs, objections and hopes of people into claims of right and they have initiated legislative efforts to implement these rights. People in need of care should be informed of their rights and obtain assistance in the exercise of their rights.

Legally the placement under guardianship should be the least restrictive alternative. The necessity of the measure should be periodically reviewed and a time limit should be set.

Welfare agencies are often large bureaucracies which tend to be slow, impersonal and insensitive to the needs of individual clients. Instead of bureaucratic and professional interventions, there is a call for self-help and mutual help of non-professionals, for the reactivation of families and neighbourhoods as some kind of new solidarity. The caring capacity of the community should be enhanced.

On the basis of available information, there is a general trend towards a more graded system of guardianship. Credit for this trend must be shared by many: legal and medical professionals, social workers, families of the mentally ill and the patients themselves.

At the same time, there is a growing awareness of the need for legal control through the courts. The quality of court hearings should be improved. Strict procedural guarantees afforded to clients cannot improve sufficiently the accuracy of the decision-making process. The client will benefit from a hearing only if the decisions taken by the court are based upon complete information about the medical and social aspects of the case. Judges should be trained not only to utilize appropriate legal procedures but also to examine medical opinion in order to ensure that it is based both upon empirical evidence and on sound medical and social reports. They should also explore the availability of housing, care or treatment in the family, the neighbourhood and the community.

The court should be obliged to order an investigation by medical experts. These experts should take into consideration not only medical, but also psychological and social factors. Competent social workers may provide a unique social dimension to understanding and intervening appropriately in the problems of the person in question. Therefore there should be a specific provision in the procedure for an assessment of the patient's social competence.

The court should be obliged to hear the person whose guardianship has been requested. This hearing should take place (with the consent of the person) in his home. The person in question should be informed in writing or, if necessary, orally about all decisions which relate to his guardianship.

Appeal against such decisions should be possible. A person received under guardianship should remain competent to request the termination of his guardianship.

The court should not grant the same powers to all guardians in each case, but the decision should depend upon the individual need of the person in question, the guideline for the court being 'the best interests of the patient'.

There should be a clear distinction between the management and care of the individual's person and the management of his property and affairs though the dividing line will not always be easy to draw.

The home of the person in question should be specifically protected by law and by the court.

There is an element of advocacy embodied in the concept of guardianship. The guardian has to represent, as far as possible, the views of the person received under guardianship from the latter's perspective. He has "to side with" his client. The role of the guardian will therefore be similar to that adopted by a patient advocate (cf. Legemaate 1985), the latter, however, being invited to mediate disputes, e.g. between patient and the hospital, and not being authorized to take decisions.

Guardians should have to undergo intensive training with the purpose of acquiring knowledge of the medical/social/legal aspects of guardianship.

There is evidence in all countries that in the future, not all people in need of guardianship will get the necessary support without having to rely on professionals. There seems to be, however, a common belief that priority should be given to the family and other relatives of the person in question, to neighbours, friends and other 'ordinary people' as voluntary helpers. Professionals, e.g. social workers should play a subsidiary role especially in difficult cases, i.e. when professional help is needed. The role of the legal professionals in guardianship should be similarly limited. Information and advice regarding the problems, statutory rights and duties as well as benefits and services for the persons received under guardianship should be readily available and be conveyed to relatives, voluntary helpers, etc. by professionals and/or community agencies.

Such agencies should be responsible for the recruitment of guardians and for the delivery of guardianship.

Placement under guardianship should be subsidiary to alternative arrangements, e.g. activities arranged by voluntary agencies, local authority social activities, support from specialist services (home help services, 'day care' programmes). Welfare provision is, on the other hand, often fragmented and uncoordinated. There is especially a major shortage in services for the elderly. Therefore there will often be a need for someone who acts permanently for an elderly person with special needs, i.e. for a guardian.

The guardian, however, should not usurp the functions of the caring professions.

The powers of the guardian should be clarified and emphasis should be placed on the person in need of care and not on the concerns of third parties, e.g. relatives or society. Once this principle is accepted, it follows that help should be provided as a right according to the needs of the person and not at the discretion of the guardian. Consent should be the operative factor and not what others feel would be in his best interest.

Guardianship does have financial implications for the competent state authorities either in acting as guardians, in employing public guardians or in fulfilling oversight functions over private guardians. In any case, the State must ensure that enough staff are employed to act as guardians. It must check the suitability of potential guardians, organize the training of guardians, supervise guardians and, possibly, pay guardians. The nature and the level of such payments need to be discussed. In times of tight financial constraints in social policy (the payments often being conceived of as a savings policy), this means that innovations will not easily be achieved.

In closing this chapter, I should like to quote once more a French author on the new French legislation in this area:

"Il faut se garder d'un droit rigide, oú tout ce qui n'est pas expressément permis oú prévu par la loi est présumé interdit, et s'orienter vers un droit instrument de prévu changement social, flexible et innovateur" (Cohen-Tanugi; quot. Delpérée 1987: 40).

References

Ayer, S./Alaszewski, A. (1984), *Community Care and the Mentally Handicapped*, London: Croom Helm.
Beiträge zur Reform des Vormundschafts- und Pflegschaftsrechts fur Menschen mit geistiger Behinderung. Referate und Diskussionsergebnisse zur Fachtagung im März 1986 in Marburg/Lahn (ed.: U. Hellmann) (1986), Marburg: Bundesvereinigung Lebenshilfe fur Geistig Behinderte.
Blankman, K. (1982), De geestelijke gehandicapte en de curatele, in: *Tijdschrift voor Familie- en Jeugdrecht*, pp. 125 — 137.
Blankman, K. (1985), Curatele, en dan?, Den Haag: Vuga-Uitgeverij.
Blankman, K. et al. (1987), De persoon van de geestelijke gestoorde en gehandicapte, Zwolle: Tjeenk Willink.
Blankman, K. et al. (1987), Studiedag over de persoon van de geestelijke gestoorde en gehandicapte, in: *Tijdschrift voor Familie- en Jeugdrecht*, pp. 203 — 224.
Booth, T. (1985), *Home Truths. Old People's Homes and the Outcome of Care* Aldershot: Gower.
Breemer Ter Stege, C./Gittelman, M. (1987), The Direction of Change in Western European Mental Health Care, *Int. J. Ment. Health*, vol. 16, pp. 6 — 20.
Bru, V. (1981), Les problémes juridiques relatifs aux nouvelles méthodes de traitement des maladies mentales, in: *Rev. dr. sanit.*, pp. 167 — 210.
Bundesminister der Justiz (ed.) (1985), Gutachten zu einer Neuordnung des Entmündi-

gungs-, des Vormundschafts- und des Pflegschaftsrechts, Koln: Bundesanzeiger-Verlag.

Bundesminister der Justiz (ed.)(1987), Diskussions-Teilentwurf Gesetz über die Betreuung Volljähriger (Betreuungsgesetz — BtG), köln: Bundesanzeiger-Verlag.

Bundesministerium für Justiz (ed.) (1979), Reform der Entmündigungsordnung — Enquête 1987 -, Wien: Bundesministerium für Justiz.

Bundesministerium für Justiz (ed.)(1982), Rechtliche Vorsorge für geistig und psychisch Behinderte. Tagung der Österreichischen Juristenkommission in Weißenbach/Attersee, Wien: Bundesministerium für Justiz.

Bundesministerium für Justiz (ed.) (1983), Justiz und Zeitgeschichte. Symposion "Schutz der Persönlichkeitsrechte am Beispiel der Behandlung von Geisteskranken 1780 — 1982, Wien: Bundesministerium für Justiz.

Bundesministerium für Justiz (ed.)(1984), Rechtsfürsorge für psychisch Kranke und geistig Behinderte, Wien: Bundesministerium für Justiz.

Bundesregierung (der Bundesrepublik Deutschland) (1987). Antwort auf die Große Anfrage der Fraktion der SPD im Deutschen Bundestag zur rechtlichen Situation der geistig Behinderten und psychisch Kranken, BT-Drucks. 10/5970, Bonn.

Butler, T. (1985), *Mental Health, Social Policy and the Law*, London: Macmillan.

Canaris, V. (1987), "Verstöße gegen das verfassungsrechtliche Übermaßverbot im Recht der Geschäftsfähigkeit und im Schadensersatzrecht", in: *JZ*, pp. 993 — 999.

Cooper, B./Bauer, M. (1987), "Developments in Mental Health Care and Services in the Federal Republic of Germany", in: *Int. J. Ment, Health*, vol. 16, pp. 78 — 93.

Cordier, B., et al. (1981), *Aspects législatifs et administratifs de la psychiatrie*, Paris: Maloine.

Council of Europe/Conseil de l'Europe (1983), Legal Protection of Persons Suffering from Mental Disorder Placed as Involuntary Patients. Recommendation No. R (83) 2 adopted by the Committee of Ministers of the Council of Europe on 22 February 1983 and Explanatory Memorandum, Strasbourg: Council of Europe.

Damrau, J. (1984), "Das österreichische Gesetz über die Sachwalterschaft für behinderte Personen", in: *FamRZ* 1984, 236 — 239.

Dekker, G. (1979), "Mental Health Legislation in the Netherlands: Civil and Administrative Law", in: *International Journal of Law and Psychiatry*, vol. 2, pp. 469 — 484.

Delpérée, N. (1987), Protection juridique des personnes âgées présentant des troubles du comportement (Mémoire), Toulouse: Université Paul Sabatier.

Deutscher Bundestag (1975). Bericht über die Lage der Psychiatrie in der Bundesrepublik Deutschland, BT-Drucks. 7/4200 (mit Anlageband BT-Drucks. 7/4201), Bonn: Hegner (cf. Mental Health Care in the Federal Republic of Germany. Summary of the report given by an Expert Commission to the Parliament (Bundestag) (1976), Bonn: AKTION PSYCHISCH KRANKE)

Ent, H./Hopf, G. (1983), Das Sachwalterrecht für Behinderte, Wien: Manz.

Forster, R. (1984), Entmündigt. Ein Rückblick auf Anwendungen und Auswirkungen eines Rechtsinstituts anhand von Fallderstellungen, Wien: Ludwig-Boltzmann-Institut.

Forster, R. (1985), Die Entmündigung — ein Ruckblick anhand sozialwissenschaftlicher Forschungsergebnisse, in: Österreichische Richterzeitung, pp. 241 — 246.

Forster, R. et al. (1985), Entwicklungskonzept für die Vereinssachwalterschaft, Wien: Ludwig-Boltzmann-Institut.

Forster, R. (1987), "Trends in Mental Health Care in Austria in the Past 25 Years", in: *Int. J. Ment. Health*, vol. 16, pp. 21 — 41.

Fuchs, W. (1985), "Entmündigung und Zwangseinwelsung — rechtliche Situation in der Schweiz", in: *Recht und Psychiatrie* (note), pp. 237 — 248.

Gostin, L. (1983 a), "The Ideology of entitlement: the application of contemporary legal approaches to psychiatry," in: *Mental Illness: Changes and Trends*, Chichester: John Wiley, pp. 27 — 54.

Gostin, L. (1983 b), A Practical Guide to Mental Health Law. The Mental Health Act 1983 and Related Legislation, London: MIND.

Gunn. M. (1986), "Mental Health Act Guardianship: Where Now?," in: *J.S.W.L.* 1986, pp. 144 — 152.

Heldrich, A. (1985), Die Betreuung behinderter Volljähriger durch Bestellung eines Repräsentanten oder Beistands in Frankreich, Belgien, der Schweiz und England, Stand: 28. Oktober 1976; Ergänzung vom Dezember 1981, in: Bundesminister der Justiz (ed.), Gutachten (note), pp. 51 — 114.

Hellmann, U. (1986), "Gesetzliche Regelungen des Rechtsschutzes geistig behinderter Menschen in der DDR, den Niederlanden, Frankreich und England," in: *Beiträge zur Reform des Vormundschafts- und Pflegschaftsrechts* (note), pp. 53 — 68.

Hoggett, B. (1984), *Mental Health Law*, 2nd. ed., London: Sweet & Maxwell.

Hopf, G. (1986), "Das Österreichische Sachwalterrecht," in: *Beiträge zur Reform des Vormundschafts- und Pflegschaftsrechts* (note), pp. 26 — 45.

Jansen, I. (1983 a), Beschermingsbewind, Den Haag: Vuga-Uitgeverij.

Jansen, I. (1983 b), Rechtspositie van geestelijk gehandicapten, Den Haag: Federatie van Ouderverenigingen voor gesstelijk gehandicapten.

Jones, K. (1980), "The Limitations of the Legal Approach to Mental Health," in: *International Journal of Law and Psychiatry*, vol. 3, pp. 1 — 15.

Jones, K. (1987), Trends in the Organisation of Mental Health Services in Great Britain in the Past 25 Years, in: *Int. J. Ment. Health*, vol. 16, pp. 94 — 107.

Jones, R. (1982), The Mental Health Act 1983, London: Sweet & Maxwell.

Juridification of Social Spheres (ed. G. Teubner) (1987), Berlin: de Gruyter.

Kaufmann, F.-X., "Major Problems and Dimensions of the Welfare State," in: Eisenstadt. S./Ahimeir, O. (ed.), *The Welfare State and Its Aftermath*, Beckenham: Croom Helm.

Kohler, P. (1987), *Sozialpolitische und sozialrechtliche Aktivitäten der Vereinten Nationen*, Baden-Baden: Nomos.

Kremzow, F. (1984), Österreichisches Sachwalterrecht. Eine kommentierte Darstellung, Eisenstadt: Prugg-Verlag.

Krul-Steketee, J. (1978), *De psychiatrische patient en de recht*, Zwolle: Tjeenk Willink.

Leat, D./Gay, P. (1987), *Paying for Care*, London: Policy Studies Institute.

Legemaate, J. (1985), "Patients' Rights Advocacy: The Dutch Model" (paper presented at the WFNH/MIND "Mental Health 2000" Congress, Brighton, 18 July 1985), Utrecht.

Ludwig Boltzmann-Institut (ed.) (1986), Materialien zur Vereinssachwalterschaft 1985/86, Wien: Ludwig Boltzmann-Institut.

Massip, J. (1971), *La réforme du droit des incapables majeurs*, 2nd. ed., Paris: Defrénois.

Maurer, E. (1984), *Sachwalterrecht in der Praxis*, Wien: Juridica-Verlag.

Max-Planck-Institut für ausländisches und internationales Privatrecht (1985), "Die Vormundschaft und Pflegschaft im niederländischen Recht," in: Bundesminister der Justiz (ed.), Gutachten (note), pp. 115 — 183.

Mende, W. (1985), "Psychiatrische Implikationen zur Vorbereitung einer Neuordnung des Rechts der Entmündigung, der Vormundschaft und Pflegschaft für geistig Behinderte sowie der Unterbringung nach Bürgerlichem Recht," in: Bundesminister der Justiz (ed.), Gutachten (note), pp. 7-49.

Mental Illness: Changes and Trends (ed.: P. Bean) (1983), Chichester: John Wiley.

Ministerie van Justitie (ed.) (1983), Onderbewindstelling ter Bescherming van Meer-derjarigen, Den Haag: Ministerie van Justitie.

Minow, M. (1987), "Where difference has its home: group homes for the mentally retarded, equal protection and equal treatment of difference," in: *Harvard Civil Rights Civil Liberties Law Review* 22, pp. 111-189.

Morris, G. (1980), "The Use of Guardianships to Achieve — Or to Avoid — the Least Restrictive Alternative," in: *International Journal of Law and Psychiatry*, vol 3, pp. 97-115.

Pelikan, J. (1984 a), "Zur Initiierung der Vereinssachwalterschaft," in: Bundesminis-terium der Justiz (ed.), Rechtsfürsorge (note), pp. 1-42.

Pelikan, J. (1984 b), "Besonderer Rechts- und Persönlichkeitsschutz für psychiat-rische Patienten — Eine Konsequenz des Doppelcharakters der Psychiatrie." in: *Grenzen der Behandlung* (ed.: I. Eisenbach-Stangl/W. Stangle), Opladen: West-deutscher Verlag.

Pennings, F./Wolff, D. (1987), "Verbetering van de rechtsbescherming in het beis-tandsrecht?," in: *Social Recht* 1987, pp. 9-13.

Posch, M./Lingelbach, P. (1985), "Regelung der rechtlichen fursorge für geistig Behinderte und die Einweisung psychisch kranker in der Deutschen Demokratis-chen Republik," in: *Recht und Psychiatrie* (note), pp. 224-236.

Recht und Pscyhiatrie. Neuere Tendenzen des Persönlichkeitsschutzes und der Rechtsfursorge — das österreichische Modell (ed.: R. Forster/J. Pelikan) (1985), Kriminalsoziologische Bibliographie (Wien), vol. 12, No. 47/48 Special.

Saldeen, A./Westmann, P. (1985), "Grundzüge und Probleme des schwedischen Vormundschaftsrechts," in: Bundesminister der Justiz (ed.), Gutachten (note), pp. 185-210.

Sartorius, N. (1987), "Preface," in: *Int. J. Ment. Health* 16, pp. 3 - 5.

Sauvaine, R. (1978), *Le malade mental et les pouvoirs publics*, 2nd. ed., Paris: Editions de Scarabée.

Sauer, O. (1974), *Die Neugestaltung des Entmündigungsrechts in materieller und formeller Hinsicht unter Berücksichtigung der Regelungen der DDR, Österreichs, der Schweiz und Frankreichs*, Marburg: Jur. Diss.

Schnyder, B. (19l75), "Zur Revision des Vormundschaftsrechtes," in: *Zeitschrift für Vormundschaftswesen*, vol. 30, pp. 41-54.

Schuller, S. (1982), Zur Revision des Vormundschaftsrechts, in: *Schweizerische Juristen-Zeitung*, vol. 82, pp. 156-159.

Schulte, B. (1981), "Probleme Zwischen Recht und Psychiatrie — Dialog mit Juristen —" in: *Güterloher Fortbildungswoche* 1980, Münster: Landschaftsverband West-falen-Lippe.

Schulte, B. (1983), "Entmündigung — wohin?," in: Die "Unheilbaren". 85. Güter-loher Fortbildungswoche 1983, Rehburg-Loccum, pp. 87-106.

Schulte, B. (1985), "Schutz- und Hilfsmaßnahmen für psychisch Kranke und Behin-derte — Zur Situation in der BRD," in: *Recht und Psychiatrie* (note), pp. 185-223.

Schulte, B, (1986), "Reformvorstellungen unter besonderer Berücksichtigung der aus ländischen Regelungen und Erfahrungen," in: *Beitrage zur Reform des Vormundschafts- und Pflegschaftsrechts* (note), pp. 97-131.

Schulte, B. (1986 a), "Anmerkungen zur Reform des Entmündigungs-, Vormundschafts- und Pflegschaftsrechts," in: *Zeitschrift für Rechtspolitik*, vol. 19, pp. 249-254.

Schulte, B. (1987), "Juristische Überlegungen zu den rechtlichen Grundlagen für Entmündigung, Vormundschaft und Pflegschaft," in: *Das öffentliche Gesundheitswesen*, pp. 309-315.

Schulte, B. (1987 a), "Rechtsgrundlagen der Rehabilitation in der Psychiatrie — Internationale Perspektiven," in: *ZfSH/SGB*, vol.26, pp. 561-576.

Schulte, B. (1988 a), "Erste Erfahrungen mit dem österreichischen Sachwalterrecht — Lehren für die Reformdiskussion hierzulande?," in: *Deutscher Verein für öffentliche und private Fürsorge*. Dokumentation einer Fachtagung, Frankfurt/M.: Eigenverlag des Deutschen Vereins (forthcoming).

Schulte, B. (1988 b), "Das Österreichisch Bundesgesetz über die Sachwalterschaft für behinderte Personen — Die Reform des Entmündigungs-, Vormundschafts- und Pflegschaftsrechts für Volljährige in Öusterreich," in: *Archiv für Theorie und Prais der sozialen Arbeit* (forthcoming)

Spitzer, G. (1977/1978), "Die Revision des Vormundschaftsrechtes," in: *Zeitschrift für Vormundschaftswesen*, vol. 32 (1977), pp. 1-18, vol. 33 (1978), pp. 140-150.

Stefanis, C. (1987), "The Challenge of Current Developments in Psychiatry," in: *J. Ment. Health*, vol. 16, pp. 236-243.

Tercier, p. (1976), "Vers une revision du droit de la tutelle," in: *Zeitschrift für Vormundschaftswesen*, vol. 31, pp. 121-135.

Trompisch, H. (1982), Die Verankerung und Absicherung der Grundrechte von Österreichern mit geistiger Behinderung, VIII. Weltkongress der Internationalen Liga von Vereinigungen für Menschen mit geistiger Behinderung, Nairobi (Kenya); Ms.

Trompisch, H. (1986), "Praxisbericht über erste Erfahrungen mit dem neuen Sachwalterrecht," in: *Beiträge zur Reform des Vormundschafts- und Pflegschaftsrechts* (note), pp. 46-52.

Zenz, G./von Eicken, B./Ernst, E./Hofmann, C. (1987), Vormundschaft und Pflegschaft für Volljährige. Eine Untersuchung zur Praxis und Kritik des geltenden Rechts (ed.: Bundesministerium der Justiz), Köln: Bundesanzeiger-Verlag.

Zenz, G. (1987 a), "Die persönliche Freiheit im Vormundschafts-und Pflegschaftsrecht," in: *Das öffentliche Gesundheitswesen*, vol. 49, pp. 486-489.

Zierl, H. (1986), *Sachwalterschaft und Verwaltung*, Wien: Juridica.

Abbreviations

art.	article
Assoc. Nat.	Assemblée Nationale
BT-Drucks.	Druckasache des Deutschen Bundestages (Parliament of the FRG)
B.W.	Burgerlijk Wetboek
C. civ.	Code civil
C. séc. soc.	Code de la Sécurite sociale
Diss.	Dissertation
ed.	edition; editor(s)

FamRZ	Zeitschrift für das gesamte Familienrecht
Int. J. Ment. Health	International Journal of Mental Health
J.O.	Journal Officiel
J.S.W.L.	Journal of Social Welfare Law
JZ	Juristen-Zeitung
nc.	number/Number
p., pp.	page(s)
Rev. sanit. soc.	Revue du droit sanitaire et social
sv.	suivant(s)
ZfSH/SGB	Zeitschrift für Sozialhilfe und Sozialgesetzbuch
vol(s)	volume(s)

Chapter 38

The End of Guardianship for the Elderly? Facts and Objectives in Current Discussions on the Proposed Reform Legislation in the Federal Republic of Germany

Gisela ZENZ
University of Frankfurt
Federal Republic of Germany

Legal Policy

The reform of guardianship and tutelage laws in the Federal Republic of Germany is currently in preparation. The existing legislation, which is part of the German Civil Code, has been in force for nearly 100 years, and has remained virtually unchanged in all that time. Of course it was criticized from very early on. Calls for specific reforms of the law have been made since the 1970s by theoreticians and practitioners alike,[1] and advocated with increasing urgency by private welfare organizations as well as political parties. In response to these efforts, the Federal Ministry of Justice commissioned comparative legal and psychiatric expert opinions[2] as well as an investigation into the practical application of the legislation in the courts.[3] In 1986 it began, in collaboration with a group of advisors comprised of legal experts and psychiatrists, to lay the groundwork for a reform law. A "Partial Draft for Discussion of a Care and Assistance Law" (Betreunngsgesetz)[4] was proposed at the beginning of 1988 which is intended to replace the incompetency, guardianship and tutelage legislation which has been in effect heretofore. Many aspects of this draft were inspired by the reform legislation which was brought into fore in Austria in 1984, although the specific provisions of the German proposal are quite different.

The basic idea of an "enduring power of attorney" as it has been brought into the German discussion by Muller-Freienfels in 1982[5] has been very important for the development of the new concept. This would mean, that the "normal case" of care and assistance — as provided for in the new draft — comes very close to this model and may even be combined with it.

In other words, there is a widespread consensus on the need for reform, as well as the basic orientation and key issues which the reform should involve: it not only takes into consideration the altered social situation of people who are in need of care and assistance, but also allows for the potential improvements in their state of mind or body now afforded by therapeutic treatment, as well as changed legal views. In particular, the personal freedom of the person in need of care and assistance is also to be protected and strengthened to a greater degree than it has in the past. However, there are differences of opinion on specific aspects of the reform. In any event, considerable difficulties are expected to arise in the application and financing of the reform.

Guardianship and tutelage as legal institutions of the German Civil Code

Even for the legislators who drafted the German Civil Code around 1900, the personal freedom of the individual was an important legal-political value on a par with the interests of the family and commerce. Their concern at the time, however, was almost exclusively focused on the "legally competent citizen's" freedom to act. The suspension or restriction of this right by legally declaring a person to be "incompetent" was only held to be legitimate if extreme mental or moral incompetence posed a recognizable, serious danger to the individual, his/her family or society as a whole. According to Section 6 of the German Civil Code, a person can be declared incompetent if
  – he is unable to take care of his affairs as a result of mental illness or feeblemindedness,
  – he places himself or his family's welfare in extreme jeopardy through squandering,
  – he is unable, owing to alcohol or drug addiction, to take care of his affairs or places the welfare of his family in extreme jeopardy or endangers the safety of others.
    Mental illness and feeblemindedness are to be understood as legal terms, which serve to distinguish, respectively, between the more severe limitations and the milder forms of incapacitation. This differentiation is significant in terms of the consequences of a declared incompetency, which are regulated in Section 104 of the German Civil Code. According to this provision, a person being legally declared to be incompetent because of mental illness renders that person incompetent to contract, i.e. the incompetent can no longer effectively take part in legal business. On the other hand, when a person is declared incompetent on grounds of feeblemindedness, squandering, alcoholism or drug addition, this results in a restriction of his competence to contract: the incompetent is considered the equivalent of a child over seven years of age. This means that he can take part in legally binding affairs, but requires the approval of his legal representative for all transactions which do not only afford

him a legal benefit.

In order to safeguard the impartiality of incompetency decisions against abuse by third-party interests, responsibility was placed in the hands of the (civil) courts and tied to strict procedural rules in the German Civil Court Procedure. In particular, they require that the alleged incompetent be given a hearing and a medical expert opinion be obtained.

At the same time, however, the incompetency procedure was soon circumvented owing to its severe consequences, the "red tape" involved, and the related stigmatizing effects, and instead replaced by the assignment of "tutelages" (*Pflegschaften*). The frailty tutelage was designed by the Civil Code legislators as a means of support for people who "as a result of mental or physical frailties are unable to take care of certain matters or a specific kind of matter" (Section 109 German Civil Code). It does not restrict the frail person's competence to contract, and may, on principle only, be initiated and executed with the person's consent — that is, unless "it is not possible to make oneself understood to that person" (Section 1910, Para. 3 German Civil Code). This "compulsory tutelage" (*Zwangspflegschaft*) which was originally intended to serve as an exceptional arrangement, has in recent years now come to be applied with increasing frequency to custody of the person's property as a whole and the authority to determine where the person will live. It thus became a virtual substitute for incompetency rulings, but without being subject to the strict procedural rules of the incompetency procedure.

However, regardless of whether a person is declared incompetent or assigned a compulsory tutelary, the Civil Code legislation no longer recognizes any "rights" for the ward in these cases, but only "interests" which another, namely, the guardian or tutelary, is now responsible for pursuing in that person's place. The appointment of a legal guardian or tutelary by the guardianship court was supposed to take the matter, so to speak, out of the delicately balanced relationship between the private citizen and the state, and return it to the private domain of civil society, whose autonomy, especially in the family domain and in family-related affairs, the state had to respect. And guardianship was by all means patterned after the model of the family — which is to say, according to paternal authority as it was understood around 1900. This means it was and has remained up to the present day a patriarchal-authoritarian form of custody which leaves the ward no rights of his own, but only interests which the guardian for the most part has to preserve at his own discretion.

Custody of the person (*Personensorge*) is limited to that "which is necessary in the framework of the guardianship"; the guardian must obtain court approval if his/her ward is to be committed. No other regulations with regard to custody of the person are provided for in the German Civil Code — unlike parental custody of the person, for example, which was newly revised in 1980; in important respects it now defines the growing child's right to have a say in his affairs as well as the parents' duties to take the child's rights into account. Custody of the ward's property (*Vermögenssorge*), on the other hand, is more precisely regulated in the German Civil Code. The guardian must prepare a list of the property for the guardianship court in charge of monitoring the guardianship, and he has to submit annual accounts and obtain prior approval from the guardianship court before various kinds of decisions can be made. At the time, it was anticipated that abuses would occur above all from economic motives — thus the interests of under-age children were also protected by the German Civil Code in particular in the domain of proprietary rights.

The basic prerequisite for such a patriarchal concept of guardianship and tutelage was the German Civil Code legislators' notions with regard to the person of the guardian or tutelary: as a rule this was supposed to be an individual — guardianship is conceived of as a civil honour. The legislators had relatives, friends of the family, or respected members of the community in mind; a private welfare organization or public agency was only to be appointed if there was no individual available to fulfil this task. In other words, it was assumed that guardianship would be based on a personal relationship between the guardian and the ward.

Application of the law and practical consequences to date

There is very little information, (and this is not representative), and some statistical data[6] available on the factual effects of guardianship law and its application by the courts.

In 1986, incompetency was declared in 41.2% of the cases filed on grounds of mental illness, 50.6% for feeblemindedness, and 7.7% because of alcoholism. Squandering and drug addiction are hardly ever cited any longer as exclusive grounds for these decisions.

Declarations of incompetency in most cases remain in effect for the person's lifetime or at least for a very prolonged period of time. The incompetency ruling is only suspended in approximately 10% of all cases.

The total number of guardianships as of December 31, 1986 was estimated to be 66,360, with the total number of frailty tutelages at 176,709 (of which about 80% are compulsory tutelages) for adults. The number of legally declared incompetents and thus also of guardianships has steadily declined in recent years, whereas the number of tutelages is increasing at a higher rate than the decrease in incompetency declarations.

There is an above-average percentage of elderly among the group of incompetents or persons subject to compulsory tutelage. This percentage is growing steadily in relation to other groups — the mentally ill and mentally retarded — namely, in the same proportion as ever more elderly people today are reaching an age which obliges them to experience the deterioration of their intellectual and emotional capabilities.

An individual person is still usually appointed as the guardian or tutelary, but in only little more than half the cases does this involve relatives or a person close to the ward; rather, more and more frequently the guardians or tutelaries are attorneys who, in some cases, are responsible for as many as 250 guardianships and tutelages at a time. These are case figures which, needless to say, do not permit any form of personal care. Moreover, a relatively small number of guardianships are in the hands of private welfare organizations and some are exercised with a considerable amount of personal commitment. The bulk of very severe cases is ultimately handled by the authorities in the form of public guardianships or tutelages. In these cases, the excessively high number of cases (100-200) as well as the lack of adequate funds, resources and support for the agencies' staff thwart the willingness to make a personal commitment.

With regard to procedure, it must be pointed out that contrary to the requirements of the highest court rulings in a large number of tutelage cases, the potential wards are not given a personal hearing. It is equally significant that detailed psychiatric expert opinions are nearly always only obtained in incompetency procedures, whereas in many cases all that is required for the appointment of a compulsory tutelary is a three-sentence affidavit from the hospital or nursing home physician which contains little more than a very general medical diagnosis ("cerebral sclerosis").

Criticism and demands for reform

Criticism of the existing legislation is focused primarily on the following aspects:

(1) The discriminatory and counter-therapeutic effect of incompetency declarations which reduce the ward, as a whole and in most cases irreversibly, to the level of a child, without regard for the person's individual capabilities and abilities or for changes in the person's state of mind or body which may result from therapeutic measures. This is not warranted in the large majority of cases, neither for the individual's protection nor the family's protection nor for that of the legally transacted affairs involved. Consequently, this violates the constitutional principle of reasonableness (*Grundsatz der Verhältnismäßigkeit*). The automatic linking of a supportive measure (appointment of the guardian or tutelary) with the loss or restriction of the competence to contract is not justified in many cases.

(2) Over-emphasis of property interests as opposed to the ward's existential, personal interests (living conditions, privacy, health, social contacts).

(3) The extended scope of uncontrolled authority exercised by the guardian and/or tutelary within the internal relationship between the two parties.

(4) Inadequate safeguards for the due-process rights of the affected person and the unsatisfactory quality of medical expert opinions.

(5) Faulty organization of the manner in which the guardian has to perform

the tasks involved, which in a large number of cases renders any personal care impossible, and consequently allows the individual to become a mere case of administration.

The Partial Draft for Discussion prepared by the Federal Ministry of Justice in 1987

The current draft for a care and assistance law (*Betreuungsgesetz*) is a "partial draft" in that it is limited to a re-definition of the substantial rights and due-process rights, but leaves the question of reorganizing the guardianship system open for the time being. Only the main features of the draft can be presented here.

The draft no longer provides for incompetency declarations, i.e. no constitutive declaration of the incapacity to transact legal business. In place of guardianship and tutelage, "care and assistance" (*Betreuung*) is to be a uniform legal institution which permits a flexible combination of support and intervention in the capacity to transact legal business, depending on the requirements of the individual case.

A "caretaker" (Betreuer) in the new legal sense is appointed by the court either at the person's request or without it if, owing to mental illness or a physical or mental handicap, the person is unable to take care of some or all of his affairs (Section 1896). The court determines the tasks of the caretaker, who represents the assisted person both in court and outside of court. If the person in need of care and assistance requests that a certain person be appointed, the court has to appoint this person. If there is no proposal, the court has to look for an apt person, taking into account familial and other personal relationships of the affected person. These regulations are obviously shaped according to the basic idea of an (enduring) power of attorney. The care and assistance arrangement is subsidiary: it cannot be ordered by the court if the affected person can be helped just as easily by other means which do not involve the appointment of a legal representative.

Whether or not a restriction of the capacity to transact legal business is necessary, is something which has to be especially examined in each case by the court: "To the extent that such is necessary, the guardianship court orders that the assisted person require the consent of the caretaker for any legal business which affects the caretaker's tasks" (section 1903).

The draft in Section 1901 seeks to preserve the dignity of the assisted person and protect his civil rights and liberties as an individual within the internal relationship to the caretaker as follows: "The caretaker shall tend to the assisted person's affairs in such a way that it is for the latter's best interest. The assisted person's best interest also includes the possibility of shaping his life according to his own desires and ideas to the extent that his capabilities allow him to do so". (Para. 1). "The caretaker shall act in accordance with the assisted person's wishes, to the extent that this does not conflict with the latter's best interest and does not place undue demands on the caretaker. Before the caretaker takes care of important matters, he shall discuss these with the assisted person, unless this would conflict with the latter's best interest" (Para. 2). The caretaker has to assist the affected person particularly in making use of health care and rehabilitative measures that could enable him to get along without the help of a caretaker.

Certain decisions made by the caretaker which have a particularly severe effect on the assisted person's freedom to shape his own life and on his basic constitutional rights as an individual (medical treatment, sterilization, confinement/institutionalization, and giving up an apartment) are subject to specific regulations in the draft. In addition to substantive legal criteria applying to these decisions, the reform legislation is also planned to include safeguards for procedural rights, especially the obligatory involvement of the guardianship court. All of these case situations not only raise difficult questions in terms of legal technicalities, but also complex moral and political issues which are the subject of much debate.

Legally ordered care and assistance will not to affect the person's ability to marry or prepare a will in any way. The question of voting rights is still open for the time being — this, too, promises to be a controversial issue.

The legal status of the affected person in the procedure for ordering a care and assistance arrangement is to be strengthened and also defined more precisely by comparison to the procedure that has applied to incompetency in the past. The new regulations focus on expanding the role of the personal hearing, the obligatory appointment of a procedural representative in certain cases, and afford the person an opportunity to enlist the support of someone he trusts. The court's investigations are to be supported by a special agency knowledgeable in the field. The obligatory expert opinion has to cover not only the medical, but also the psychological and social aspects of the need for a legal caretaking arrangement. Care and assistance may be ordered only for a limited period of time — a maximum of five years — after which it is again subject to the same process of legal investigation and court decision as in the original proceedings.

Although the draft does not govern the practical application of the new requirements for care and assistance, it does set up certain provisions. Thus, for example, only a natural person may be appointed as a caretaker in the new legal sense, and not an organization or agency; the latter may, in turn, only become involved in support of the individual caretaker who is personally responsible to the guardianship court (Sect. 1898 German Civil Code). This is designed to ensure that the relationship between the caretaker and the person in need of assistance is personal in nature: the assignment of caseworkers by a private welfare organization or public agency would jeopardize the personal nature of a relationship, in that they may be arbitarily replaced or interchanged. Sect. 1898 also provides for the following: "Whoever has a dependent relationship or other close ties to an institution, home or other facility in which the adult is accommodated or lives may not be appointed as a caretaker." This is intended as a precaution against conflicts of interest on the caretaker's part; an issue which has repeatedly come under attack in the past.

There is also a consensus that it should no longer be permissible under the new caretaking arrangement for lawyers or even overworked agency employees to perform the related tasks on the side. However, it is still not clear how to provide for the increasing number of needed caretakers and the quality of their work. There will certainly be a need for "volunteers" as well as for "professional" or "trained" people. Questions are raised about how to ensure that the caretakers are qualified, have access to counselling and assistance, and are also subject to controls; but it is also a question of providing for the financial security of both volunteer and professional caretakers taking into consideration the risk of liability as well as the provision for necessary expenses and possibly also financial compensation for the time involved. The considerations in this regard are now in the process of being further developed in cooperation with the private welfare organizations and public agencies already active in the field.

Notes

1. Bericht über die Lage der Psychiatrie in der Bundesrepublik Deutschland, Bundestagsdrucksache 7/4200 and 7/4201, Bonn, 1975; Hellmann, Ulrich (ed.), Beiträge zur Reform des Vormundschafts- und Pflegschaftsrechts für Menschen mit geistiger Behinderung (especially the articles by Werner Bienwald and Bernd Schulte).
2. Werner Mende, Psychiatrische Implikationen zur Vorbereitung einer Neuordnung des Rechts der Entmündigung, der Vormundschaft und Pflegschaft; Andreas Heldrich, Die Betreuung behinderter Volljähriger durch Bestellung eines Repräsentanten oder Beistands in Frankreich, Belgien, der Schweiz und England; Max-Planck-Institut für ausländisches und internationales Privatrecht, Die Vormundschaft und Pflegschaft im niederländischen Recht; Ake Seldeen, Per Westmann, Peter Dopffel, Grundzüge und Probleme des schwedischen Vormundschaftsrechts, in: Gutachten zu einer Neuordnung des Entimündigungs-, des Vormundschafts- und des Pflegschaftsrechts, published by the Federal Ministry of Justice, Bonn 1986.
3. Gisela Zenz, Barbara von Eicken, Ellen Ernst, Cornelia Hofmann, Vormundschaft und Pflegschaft für Volljährige. Eine Untersuchung zur Praxis und Kritik des geltenden Rechts. Published in the series 'Rechtstatsachenforschung', Federal Ministry of Justice, Bonn 1987.
4. Diskussions-Teilentwurf Gesetz über die Betreuung Volljähriger (Betreuungsgesetz-BtG), published by the Federal Ministry of Justice, 1982.
5. Wolfram Müller-Freienfels, Die Altersvorsorge — Vollmacht, in: Festschrift für Coing 1982, 395.
6. The following statistical data are taken from the introduction to the draft of the care and assistance law (footnote 4); all other information is drawn from the investigation of guardianship legislation in practice (footnote 3).
7. For a detailed discussion, see Zenz, op. cit. (footnote 3), pp. 31 ff.

Chapter 39

Personal Guardianship and the Elderly in the Canadian Common Law Provinces: An Overview of the Law and Charter Implications

Margaret E. HUGHES   Faculty of Law,
The University of Calgary, Canada

Introduction

Canadian law presumes the right of an individual to manage her[1] own personal and financial affairs and it presumes that a person is competent to handle those affairs until sufficient evidence of incompetency or incapacity is adduced to prove otherwise. When incapacity is alleged, Canadian law broadly distinguishes between the incapacity to handle personal care decisions (such as where to live, how to dress, what to eat, and whether to consent to medical treatment) and the incapacity to handle property and financial affairs. A person found to be incompetent to make personal care decisions will be provided with a guardian or committee of the person to make such decisions on the incompetent person's behalf, while a person found to be incompetent to make financial management decisions will be provided with a guardian, trustee or committee of the estate.

This chapter provides an overview of the law in the common law provinces in Canada regarding the appointment by a court of a guardian on behalf of a person who is incapable of making decisions relating to her personal welfare and who therefore may be in need of care and protection. It also deals briefly with adult protection legislation which authorizes intervention on an emergency basis. This is in contrast to the guardianship situation, where there is usually no emergency, but rather a perceived, long-term need for assistance in decision-making to allow the elderly individual to manage some or all of her personal care.

Concept of Guardianship of the Person and its Increasing Importance in Canadian Society

a Guardianship of the Person

The concept of guardianship is not clearly defined. It is essentially a legal device by which one specified individual with legal capacity (the guardian) is given legal authority to make decisions on behalf of another person (the ward or dependent adult) who, because of some significant degree of judicially verified mental disability, is considered to lack the legal capacity to exercise some or all of the rights that adults have in the country in which she is a citizen.[2] The guardian is a substitute decision-maker for the ward and is legally charged with protecting the ward and her interests, and for exercising essential rights on her behalf.[3] Guardianship has been described as one of the most intrusive encroachments on personal liberty that a democratic society can impose.[4]

Historically, Canadian guardianship law has been primarily, if not almost exclusively, concerned with the appointment of a guardian to manage and protect the property and financial interests of the incapacitated person.[5] The guardianship legislation in all of the common law provinces except Alberta reflects its medieval English law origins. It is property-oriented and provides few guidelines for guardianship of the person. It is even an open question whether the legislation of several Canadian jurisdictions permits the appointment of a guardian on behalf of someone who has no property[6] or whether the court in some provinces can appoint a personal guardian without also appointing a guardian of the estate.[7] Canada has an increasingly aging population. This fact, combined with enhanced medical knowledge of the aging process, is focusing attention on the adequacy of the Canadian legal framework for personal guardianship.

b Demographic Aging and Changing Economic and Social Policies

Canada's population has been aging gradually for over a century. This is primarily due to changing patterns of fertility and immigration rather than simply because of increased longevity and decreased mortality resulting from better medical care.[8] Statistics show that both the number of individuals and the proportion of the population over 65 years of age are steadily increasing. In 1901, 5% of the population was 65 or over. In 1961, 7.6% of the population was 65 or over; this had increased to 8.1% by 1971 and to 9.7% by 1981.[9] It is projected that the proportion of the population 65 years and over by 2001 will be between 12 and 14%.[10] Furthermore, if the age group over 65 is subdivided to more accurately reflect the changing age structure within the older population, it is clear that the oldest age group, aged 85 and older, is growing faster than the "young-old" (65 to 74) and the "middle-old" (75 to 84) groups of elderly.[11] The problem of providing guardianship assistance to the elderly will become increasingly important if the projected growth of Canadians aged 65 and over proves accurate.

The acceleration of population aging exacerbates problems in the health care system. The elderly often do not have the personal assets or family support necessary to sustain and care for them. Thus, there is an increasing demand for more health care and social welfare services for the elderly such as housing and home care, and pensions and other income security measures. This increased demand is occurring when governmental economic and social policies are emphasizing fiscal restraint in public sector funding and non-institutionaliza-tion, de-institutionalization and privatization as the preferred methods of providing care and treatment. Aging is increasingly viewed as a three-stage process corresponding to a need for very little supplemental care and protec-tion, then increasing community-based services and eventually some form of institutionalization for the very old.[12]

There also appears to be an increased demand for the appointment of personal guardians. This may be because more elderly are in community care facilities, and the caretakers, administrators, nurses and doctors in these facilities want legal protection particularly in regard to securing the valid consent to treatment required before medical care or treatment can be administered or provided. Mental competency is one of the elements required for a valid consent to medical treatment.[13] If there are doubts regarding the competency of the adult patient, the health care professional may refuse to treat on the basis of that individual's consent and instead require a personal guardian to provide a substitute consent. This problem apparently arose less frequently when institutionalization was the norm because treatment was permitted without consent when a person was placed in a mental health facility.[14]

Canadian Models of Personal Guardianship

All Canadian common law provinces, except Newfoundland, have legislation permitting a court to hear applications from interested persons who believe that an adult person is incompetent and in need of a guardian.[15] The physical presence of the alleged incompetent person within the territorial jurisdiction of the court is thought to be the sole basis of jurisdiction.[16] As the guardianship law in Canada is provincial and is primarily statutory, the details vary signific-antly across the provinces.[17] However, there are basically two approaches or models of personal guardianship in the common law provinces. One exists in Alberta, while the other is used in the remaining provinces.

a Common Law Provinces other than Alberta — The All or Nothing Approach

Historically, Canadian guardianship laws have viewed mental incompetency as an absolute. The laws have not recognized degrees of incapacity or that incapacity can change over time or depending on the situation or environment. Persons either are found to be mentally competent and hence not in need of a guardian for anything, or mentally incompetent and in need of a guardian for everything. Thus, once the court determines that a person is mentally incompetent, that adult may be considered to have a blanket disability that prevents the exercise of any civil rights.[18]

The appointment of a personal guardian attempts to ensure that the ward will receive the care and protection necessary by placing a duty on the guardian to act in the best interests of the ward and by granting the guardian the powers and authority necessary to discharge that duty.[19] However, the powers and responsibilities of a personal guardian are not specified in most Canadian legislation or in most court orders of guardianship, so the legal scope of a personal guardian's authority to make decisions on behalf of a ward is uncertain.

The Ontario legislation will be used to illustrate the prevalent Canadian model of personal guardianship. A declaration of mental incompetency is a prerequisite for the appointment of a personal guardian in Ontario. Under the Mental Incompetency Act,[20] the court, upon application, may declare that an individual is a "mentally incompetent person" if the court is satisfied that the evidence establishes beyond reasonable doubt that that is so.[21] A "mentally incompetent person" means a person,

(i) in whom there is such a condition of arrested or incomplete development of mind, whether arising from inherent causes or induced by disease or injury, or

(ii) who is suffering from such a disorder of the mind, that he requires care, supervision and control for his protection and the protection of his property...[22]

If the court is not satisfied beyond a reasonable doubt that a person is mentally incompetent, or if for any other reason it considers it expedient to do so, the court may direct a trial of the issue of alleged mental incompetency.[23] The inquiry is then restricted to the question whether the person at the time of the inquiry is "a mentally incompetent person and incapable of managing himself or his affairs."[24]

There is no requirement in the Mental Incompetency Act that notice be served on the alleged mentally incompetent person or on anyone else. However, to the extent that an incompetency application is treated as any other form of civil litigation, basic rights are granted by virtue of the Ontario Rules of Civil Procedure. Notice of application must be served on the alleged mentally incompetent person in Ontario at least ten days prior to the hearing date,[25] and the practice and procedure for the trial of the issue is the same as for any other directed issue.[26] Provision is also made for a jury trial in certain situations at the demand of the alleged mentally incompetent person.[27]

Once an order has been made declaring an individual a mentally incompetent person, the court must appoint a guardian of the person or the estate or both.[28] There is no express provision in the Ontario legislation for the court to order partial or limited guardianship or to restrict a guardian's powers when the ward does not require the assistance of a guardian in all aspects of her personal life. However, it has been argued that a court could either: (1) use its *parens patriae* jurisdiction over mentally incompetent persons to fill in any gaps in the legislation, thereby giving the court the power to restrict the guardian's authority if this were considered to be in the ward's best interests; or (2) utilize its general power to impose conditions and restrictions to restrict the guardian's authority when making a guardianship order.[29]

Because the proceedings for a declaration or an adjudication of mentally incompetent person (or mentally disordered person in other provinces) are cumbersome, expensive and highly stigmatic,[30] the legislation provides an alternative route for protective intervention when a person is, through mental infirmity arising from disease, age or other cause, or by reason of habitual drunkenness or the use of drugs, incapable of managing her affairs.[31] The standard of proof required appears to be the civil standard of a balance of probabilities. While the legislation provides that the court shall appoint a guardian of the person or the estate or both, of a person declared incapable of managing her affairs through mental infirmity, the caselaw suggests that the court can only appoint a guardian of an estate and not a personal guardian for those declared incapacitated rather than mentally incompetent.[32] Presumably then, the court cannot appoint a personal guardian for an individual who is incapable of managing her affairs by reason of severe physical disability if the person is mentally competent.[33]

Ontario's legislation, like that of most provinces, does not specify the powers and responsibilities of a personal guardian. While there are a number of situations in which commentators believe that a personal guardian clearly can act on behalf of a ward, such as deciding where the ward will reside and consenting to medical treatment that is not life-threatening and is in the interests of the ward, and others in which it is equally clear that a guardian cannot act on behalf of the ward, such as writing the ward's will, there is a vast gray area in between.[34] It is also questionable under Ontario's all-or-nothing approach to mental incompetency and guardianship whether the ward can retain any control or decision-making power relating to her personal care and welfare, such as the right to consent to or refuse medical treatment when she understands the nature and consequences of the proposed treatment. One can argue that the personal guardian always has the final say in Ontario unless overruled by a court and the court will not likely override the guardian's decision unless it is clearly wrong and contrary to the best interests of the ward.[35]

There is no requirement for time-limited orders or mandatory periodic review or accountability of the guardian. However, there are provisions for appealing both a declaration of mental incompetency following a hearing of an application and a declaration following a trial.[36] Furthermore, provision is made for applying, when the appeal periods have expired, for a review of the order and the issuing of a new order superseding, vacating or setting aside the declaration of mental incompetency.[37]

The inflexibility of the guardianship laws in all provinces but Alberta, and their failure to allow the courts to adapt the order to the specific demonstrated incapacities of the ward, have been severely criticized.[38] Current medical knowledge of the aging process makes simple distinctions between mentally competent and incompetent adults obsolete, and the notion that a person must be mentally incompetent before a personal guardian can be appointed is no longer useful.[39] As McLaughlin states:

> There are gradations of capacity, ranging from full capacity through degrees of impairment of capacity... to substantial impairments of capacity. Furthermore, determinations of mental capacity cannot be abstracted from the demands of particular situations. A person might be capable of giving consent to medical treatment if the proposed treatment is minor and is presented to him in comfortable, non-threatening surroundings; the same person might be quite incapable of consenting to major surgery when suffering from pain, under the influence of drugs, or overwhelmed by the authority of medical professionals and the depersonalization of a hospital.

Mental capacity also varies over time. Thus, diminished capacity may more properly require that, for persons who are unable to take care of themselves, a personal guardian be appointed with partial or limited decision-making power over the ward's life and behavior and for a limited period of time only before automatically terminating, unless renewed by the court on a review application.

Part of the uncertainty over the legal scope of a guardian's authority could be eliminated if the guardianship laws were amended to reflect the principle of the right of the ward to the least restrictive of interventions or the least restrictive of alternative courses of care or treatment. The all-or-nothing approach to mental incompetency of all common law provinces but Alberta authorizes maximum rather than minimum intervention upon a ward's right to self-determination and to mental and physical integrity. The principle of the least restrictive alternative recognizes the intrusive nature of guardianship and emphasizes the importance of personal liberty in our society. It attempts to balance the state's duty to intervene and protect the health and welfare needs of the ward with the ward's right to privacy and self-determination. Adoption of this principle would mean that a court ought not to appoint a guardian if there exists a less restrictive means of ensuring that the individual receives the care and protection she requires and, if a guardian is appointed, that guardian should be required to exercise her power and authority in the least intrusive manner, thus minimizing as much as possible the infringement of the rights of the ward.[41]

b Alberta — Limited or Partial Guardianship

The Dependent Adults Act[42] of Alberta was proclaimed in force in 1978 and represented an attempt by government to rethink the basic principles of guardianship and to respond to criticisms of the inadequacy of Canadian laws given advances in medical knowledge of the process of aging. The Act is based on the philosophy that an individual should be allowed to retain as much authority as possible to make daily living decisions and that the state should interfere in the least restrictive way to assist the individual and only when it is absolutely necessary to do so. A relatively simple procedure is provided for any interested person to bring application for a limited or partial guardianship order in respect of an adult person or for a plenary or total order, where a limited order is inappropriate given the needs of the dependent adult.[43] Evidence of the specific incapacity alleged must be set out and proven in court before the court can appoint a guardian to assist in the specific area(s) of a person's life where there is incapacity. The person is left with the control and freedom to make choices in all other areas of her life.

Before a guardianship order can be made under the Alberta legislation, the court must be satisfied that the person named in the application is an adult and is repeatedly or continuously unable to care for herself and to make reasonable judgments in respect of matters relating to her person.[44] An inability to care for oneself may result from any number of reasons including either physical or mental infirmity. Therefore, unlike in Ontario, mental incompetency is not a prerequisite for the appointment of a guardian. Furthermore, the court cannot make an order appointing a guardian unless it is satisfied that such an order would be in the best interests of, and would result in substantial benefit to, the person in respect of whom the application is made.[45] While there is no express requirement in the Act that the judge be satisfied that there is no less restrictive alternative available before appointing a guardian, it is the likely result of the application of the best interests and substantial benefit requirements.

There is little reported case law to clarify the meaning of "unable to care for herself," "reasonable judgments," "in the best interest of the person," or "substantial benefit" and subjective value judgments about how other people are supposed to live are inherent in these vague criteria. For example, is the test an inability to personally care for oneself *at all* or to care for oneself *very well?* Also, the inquiries overlap and may in fact turn out to be the same question since a person's inability to care for herself may arise from her inability to make reasonable judgments in relation to matters affecting her person. One might also ask at what point a refusal to care for oneself is transformed into an inability to care for oneself and how does the court measure the reasonableness of another person's judgments in matters of personal affairs? Also, could a guardianship order be in the best interests of the dependent adult if it did not result in a substantial benefit to that person?

The Office of the Public Guardian of Alberta has issued internal policy directives on how the term "substantial benefit" to the dependent adult is to be interpreted and applied in guardianship applications and reviews in an attempt, in the absence of case law, to achieve uniformity throughout the province.[46] Substantial benefit will vary depending upon the conditions and circumstances of the individual, her known values and beliefs and her service needs and, therefore, specific details of these factors must be included in the application.[47]

The test of substantial benefit resulting to the dependent adult must be applied to each area of guardianship requested because guardianship is "a last resort" to be sought when all means, legal and other, will not protect the person's rights or ensure that appropriate decisions are made.[48] Furthermore, the test can only be applied after the court is satisfied that the other conditions have been met; that is, the individual repeatedly or continually cannot care for herself and make reasonable judgments regarding matters of her personal care and it would be in her best interests to have a guardian appointed.[49]

It must also be noted that by defining a dependent adult as an adult who is repeatedly or continuously unable to care for herself and make reasonable judgments in respect of matters relating to her person, the Act has substantially broadened the range of individuals who might be subject to a guardianship order as contrasted to the narrower scope of application of the Ontario criteria. For example, certain alcoholic and drug addicted persons could be designated as dependent adults in Alberta.[50]

The Act does not specify whether the standard of proof to be applied is the civil standard of a balance of probabilities or whether the evidence must establish the incapacity and other criteria beyond a reasonable doubt, although the case law suggests it is the civil standard.[51] The Act specifies that, when the court has any doubt as to whether a guardian should be appointed the court may appoint a person to prepare a report on the allegedly dependent adult with respect to any or all of her present and future physical, mental, social, vocational, residential, educational or other needs, and on her ability generally to care for herself and make reasonable judgments regarding matters relating to her welfare.[52]

A copy of the guardianship application and the required accompanying report of a physician or psychologist must be served on the alleged dependent adult, among others, at least ten days before the hearing date.[53] However, the court may, if it considers it appropriate, shorten the time for service or dispense with service on the alleged dependent adult altogether, provided the Public Guardian consents and the court is satisfied that it is in the best interests of the alleged dependent adult to do so.[54] The alleged dependent person may appear and make representations.[55]

If a guardian is appointed, the court is to grant to the guardian the minimum amount of authority over the dependent adult's behavior and lifestyle that is required to meet the dependent adult's needs. The Act specifies powers and requires the court to grant only those powers listed that are necessary for the guardian to make or assist in making reasonable judgments regarding the person of the dependent adult.[56] The court can restrict, modify or add to any of the powers listed and can impose any restrictions or conditions on the guardian's authority that it considers necessary.[57] Presumably, the guardian cannot be given powers over issues in which the dependent adult has the capacity to make reasonable judgments. Before appointing an adult person as a guardian, the court must be satisfied that the person will act in the best interests of the dependent person.[58] The Act also specifies that a guardian shall exercise her power in the best interests of the dependent adult and in the least restrictive manner possible and in such a way as to encourage the dependent adult to become capable of caring for herself and making reasonable personal judgments.[59]

Unlike the other provinces, Alberta provides for an automatic periodic review of all guardianship orders. When the court makes or reviews a guardianship order, it must specify: the time within which the order must be reviewed by the court, which cannot be later than six years; the person required to apply for the review; and any requirements that the guardian is to comply with in respect of a review of the dependent adult's circumstances.[60] However, there are no provisions for the automatic termination of the order or for sanctions that can be imposed if it is not reviewed as required. Also, the dependent adult, or any interested person acting on her behalf, may apply to the court for a review of the order at any time.[61] Upon hearing an application for review, the court must consider whether the conditions required originally for a guardianship order are still applicable and whether the guardian has exercised her powers correctly. The court may amend, vary, cancel, terminate or replace the order subject to any conditions it considers necessary.[62] There is also provision for an appeal by a dependent adult or any interested person on her behalf.[63]

Canadian provinces other than Alberta need new personal guardianship legislation as it is recognized that mere "tinkering" with the existing legislation will only provide an inadequate response to the need for law reform.[64] The Alberta model of personal guardianship has been extensively and favorably reviewed by several Canadian provinces and is likely to be the approach adopted in future Canadian law reform.[65]

Adult Protection Legislation

Three Maritime provinces, Newfoundland,[66] New Brunswick[67] and Nova Scotia[68] have legislation providing an alternative to guardianship proceedings in the case of adults who are abused, neglected or otherwise in need of care or protection by reason of physical disability or mental infirmity and who are unable or unwilling to extricate themselves from the situation. Although the three statutes use different terminology and criteria, they are similar to child welfare legislation in philosophy and approach and provide a method for government intervention to protect adults from abuse or neglect at their own hands or at the hands of others. Two of the statutes even impose a mandatory reporting duty, similar to that imposed under child welfare legislation, on any person who has information, whether or not the information is confidential or privileged, that an adult is in need of protection.[69] These adult protection statutes are thought to provide for quicker intervention in emergency or crisis situations than do the court proceedings necessary for obtaining a guardianship order.

The statutes grant sweeping powers of investigation to certain social or community service officials, such as the right to have a medical practitioner examine the adult. If, following the investigation, the officials are satisfied that there are reasonable and probable grounds to believe that a person is an adult who is neglected, abused or otherwise in need of protection, they may apply to the court for an order so declaring. If the court is satisfied on a balance of probabilities that the person is an adult in need of protection, it then decides, based on a consideration of the adult's best interests, what type of order to issue.[70] For example, the court might order that the adult be placed in the care and custody of a responsible adult or be committed to the care and custody of the Department of Social Services, which may place the adult in a home or institution. The court may also make an order for hospitalization and treatment and it may order a person who is a source of danger to the adult to cease to reside in the same premises, to refrain from or limit contact with the adult in need of protection, and to pay maintenance for that adult.[71] None of the statutes require the court to order the least intrusive or restrictive option. In New Brunswick[72] and Nova Scotia[73] the protection order expires after six months unless it is renewed by the court, while in Newfoundland there is no time limit. There is a right to apply for a variation of the order and a right to appeal in all three provinces.[74]

Adult protection legislation is intended for emergency intervention and not to provide long-term care and assistance or long-term substitute decision-making as guardianship legislation does. Once the affected adult's situation has been rectified, she is encouraged to seek medical and social services on a voluntary basis although if the affected adult's situation does not improve, an application for guardianship may eventually result.

Adult protection legislation in Canada has been criticized for paternalistic over-reach[75] and for failing to effectively balance state protective intervention and the right of the adult to self-determination and due process. Critics have argued that the legislators, in enacting adult welfare legislation, have failed to recognize the medical and psychological differences between children and the elderly, as well as the legal implications of the difference between intervening in the lives of children versus those of adults, who by law possess fundamental rights and freedoms.[76] The self-neglecting elderly reclusive living in unsanitary and dangerous conditions is often used as an example to illustrate that the adult protection legislation contains value judgments embodied in vague terms and grants wide powers and discretion to professionals to transform a neglected adult's right to receive care and protective services into an obligation to receive the offered assistance regardless of its form or duration. The proclamation of the Canadian Charter of Rights and Freedoms has intensified the criticism.

The Canadian Charter of Rights and Freedoms

The Charter of Rights and Freedoms[77] came into force in 1982 as part of the patriation and entrenchment of Canada's Constitution, although section 15, the so-called equality rights or anti-discrimination section, only came into force in April 1985. The purpose of the delay was to allow the provincial and federal governments a three-year period to scrutinize their legislation and amend or repeal provisions that might offend the equality rights section. The Charter applies to the federal Parliament and provincial governments and is increasingly shaping Canadian law, both through judicial decisions and legislative reform.

The Charter deals with fundamental rights and discrimination in law. Therefore, a federal or provincial statute or regulation, or the common law[78] must be alleged to be inconsistent with the Charter. It is important to note that the rights and freedoms entrenched in the Charter are by no means absolute. They are subject under section 1 to "such reasonable limits prescribed by law as can be demonstrably justified in a free and democratic society."[79] The onus of establishing that an infringement of a right, otherwise guaranteed by the Charter, is allowed by section 1 is a very substantial onus and is borne by the party seeking to uphold the limitation.[80] The standard of proof under section 1 is the civil standard, namely, proof by a preponderance of probabilities, but the probability test must be applied rigorously.[81] Furthermore, section 33 permits Parliament and provincial legislatures to override the Charter rights by expressly legislating that the legislation will operate notwithstanding the Charter. However, political reality will curtail the use by legislators of the notwithstanding clause.

a Applicability to Personal Guardianship Proceedings and Orders

To date, there has been little litigation under the Charter in the area of guardianship or non-criminal mental health law. However, there are a number of Charter provisions that may love an impact upon Canadian personal guardianship legislation. These provisions are particularly sections 8-14 dealing with legal rights, section 7 dealing with the protection of life, liberty and security of the person, section 15 dealing with equality rights, and section 24 dealing with remedies for breach of the Charter provisions. The rights and freedoms guaranteed by these sections apply to "everyone" or to "every individual" and the right to apply to a court of competent jurisdiction for a remedy under section 24 (1) is given to "anyone"; consequently the ward should be protected by these Charter provisions.

Section 7 of the Charter provides that "everyone has the right to life, liberty and security of the person and the right not to be deprived thereof except in accordance with the principles of fundamental justice," while section 15 declares every individual's right to equality before and under the law and the right to equal protection and equal benefit of the law without discrimination on the basis of, among other grounds, age or mental or physical disability.

According to the Supreme Court, the application of section 7 involves three issues: first, whether a right set out in the "rights" component of section 7 has been infringed; secondly, whether the infringement violates principles of fundamental justice; and thirdly, whether section 1 excuses the violation.[82] Furthermore, "life, liberty and security of the person" are independent interests, each of which must be given independent significance by the court.[83] Therefore, it is possible to treat only one aspect of the rights clause before proceeding to determine whether the infringement of that interest accords with the principles of fundamental justice.[84]

Liberty involves letting citizens live as they choose, without interference, as long as they do not break the law or endanger others. In *Morgentaler*, Wilson J. advances the "personal autonomy" concept of liberty holding that the term grants the individual a degree of autonomy in making decisions of fundamental personal importance and, while liberty in a free and democratic society does not require the state to approve the personal decisions made by citizens, it does require the state to respect them.[85] Furthermore, while there may be disagreement as to whether the term "security of the person" encompasses health and threats to psychological security in the non-criminal law areas[86], the term clearly covers the concept of physical control and threats to physical security. Thus, the appointment of a personal guardian, even under a limited or partial guardianship order, infringes on the ward's right to liberty and security of her person. To take specific examples, the power of a guardian to decide where the ward is to live infringes upon the ward's liberty, while the guardian's power to give substitute consent to medical care and treatment of the ward infringes upon the ward's right to security of the person. At issue is whether the infringement conforms with the principles of fundamental justice.

The Supreme Court has held that the "principles of fundamental justice" are not synonymous with natural justice and while many of the principles of fundamental justice are procedural in nature, the phrase extends to substantive law.[87] Whether any given principle may be said to be a principle of fundamental justice within the meaning of section 7 is said to rest upon an analysis of the nature, sources, rationale and essential role of that principle within the judicial process and in our legal system as it evolves.[88] Thus, the court has held that the phrase "principles of natural justice" cannot be given any exhaustive content or simple enumerative definition and will take on concrete meaning as the court addresses alleged violations of section 7.[89]

Due to the serious loss of freedom and stigmatization flowing from a guardianship of the person order, there should be considerable procedural protection available to the alleged dependent adult. While procedural fairness may demand different things in different contexts, at a minimum, it requires some kind of fair hearing before an impartial tribunal, upon proper notice to the person affected, and an opportunity provided to the person affected to adequately state her case.[90]

The personal guardianship legislation appears to meet the procedural standards of fundamental justice insofar as it requires notice and judicial proceedings before a personal guardian can be appointed and it provides a right to appeal the court's decision. However, some Canadian experts have argued that the right to procedural fairness probably dictates that current statutory procedures and practices be enhanced by the inclusion of specific rights such as the right to legal representation, the right to review any documents submitted to the court, the right to secure an adjournment of the proceedings and the right to be informed of the outcome and the reasons for the decisions.[91]

In the recent *Morgentaler*[92] decision, the Supreme Court held that section 7 imposes upon courts the duty to review the substance of legislation once it has been determined that the legislation infringes upon an individual's right to "life, liberty and security of the person" although the courts should avoid adjudication of the merits of public policy.[93] It can be argued that fundamental justice requires that there be a compelling reason to justify a deprivation of liberty and security.[94] The societal values reflected in section 7 are that Canadian citizens have the right to physical freedom and to self-determination and they should be free from unnecessary intervention, whether by government or well-meaning relatives. It may be argued that a guardianship order that is otherwise procedurally sound is inconsistent with the principles of fundamental justice if the mentally incompetent person is capable of making some personal care and medical treatment decisions but has had this liberty and security completely removed by the all-or-nothing inflexible approach to guardianship that exists in provinces such as Ontario. This argument would not be valid in Alberta, where limited or partial guardianship orders are made and the court is required to limit the authority and powers of a guardian to the specific demonstrated incapacities of the dependent adult, and the guardian is required to exercise her power in the best interests of the ward and in the least restrictive manner possible.

b Applicability to Activities of Personal Guardians

While the Charter applies to both the federal and provincial governments, it is questionable whether it applies to private sector activities and ordinary citizens. At least one constitutional law expert[95] has argued that the Charter should apply to the private as well as the public sector but the Supreme Court of Canada has recently held[96] that the Charter did not apply to private litigation between purely private parties in the absence of any exercise of, or relevance to, governmental action that would invoke the Charter. This will be an important issue if the Charter is to be used to provide a remedy to a mentally incompetent or dependent adult in situations where the personal guardian's conduct is alleged to offend the ward's Charter rights. This includes not only the rights guaranteed by section 7 but also rights such as those provided in sections 8, 9 and 12, which protect an individual from unreasonable search and seizure, from being arbitrarily detained or imprisoned and from cruel and unusual treatment. If the Charter applies only to governmental activities and undertakings, then the issue will be how broadly the term "government" will be defined[97] and whether it will extend to cover the conduct of a personal guardian who is not a government employee but a private citizen appointed by a court under the authority of provincial legislation.

Conclusion

The personal guardianship laws of all provinces but Alberta should be repealed and replaced with legislation that reflects current medical knowledge of the physiological process of aging and the letter and spirit of the Canadian Charter of Rights and Freedoms. As adults, the elderly are presumed legally competent to make decisions for themselves, however indecisive, confused or wrong they may appear, and their independence is not to be interfered with without due process of law, no matter how well-motivated the interference. While there will undoubtedly be situations where the state must intervene to provide care and protection for an incapacitated adult, each of these individuals has unique needs. Some will require total guardianship, while others will require only some degree of assistance in their personal life and perhaps only for a limited period of time.

The laws of personal guardianship must better balance the civil rights and freedoms of elderly citizens to self-determination, privacy, and mental and physical security with the state's duty to care for the elderly who are no longer able to care for themselves or who represent a danger to others. The enactment of guardianship laws that recognize varying degrees of incapacity and adopt the principle of freedom from unnecessary intervention, combined with the principle of the accountability of personal guardians, will more properly balance the state's duty to care for the incapacitated elderly with its duty to protect the elderly's civil rights and freedoms.

Notes

1. "Her" will be used throughout the chapter rather than the more cumbersome his/her description.
2. International League of Societies for the Mentally Handicapped, *Symposium* on *Guardianship of the Mentally Retarded: Conclusions* (Brussels: ILSMH, 1969).
3. P. McLaughlin, *Guardianship of the Person*, (Downsview, Ont.: National Institute on Mental Retardation, 1979) at 54; McLaughlin draws upon the definitions of the International League of Societies for the Mentally Handicapped (ILSMH), supra, note 2.
4. A. Borovoy, "Guardianship and Civil Liberties" (1982) 3 *Health L. Can.* 51.
5. This has been emphasized by many commentators. See for example McLaughlin, supra, note 3 at 35.

6. Mental Health Act, R.S.P.E.I. 1974, c.M-9, s.30.
7. Mental Health Act, R.S.P.E.I. 1974, c.M-9, s.30.11; The Incompetent Persons Act, R.S.N.S. 1974, c.135, s.2(2); G.B. Robertson, *Mental Disability and the Law in Canada* (Toronto: Carswell, 1987) at 114-15.
8. S.A. McDaniel, *Canada's Aging Population* (Toronto: Butterworths, 1986) at 5-8.
9. Statistics Canada, *The Elderly in Canada*, (Catalogue No. 99-932) (Ottawa: Minister of Supply and Services, 1984); McDaniel, supra, note 8 at 3.
10. McDaniel, supra, note 8 at 106.
11. McDaniel, supra, note 8 at 11.
12. Law Reform Commission of Saskatchewan, *Tentative Proposals for a Guardianship Act,* Part 1: Personal Guardianship (Saskatoon, Sask., 1981) at 2.
13. For a valid consent, the patient, besides being mentally competent, must be fully informed about the nature and consequences of the procedure to be performed and must give her consent freely and voluntarily in relation to it.
14. R.M. Gordon, S.N. Verdun-Jones & D.J. MacDougall, *Standing in Their Shoes: Guardianship, Trusteeship and the Elderly Canadian*, A Report to the Social Sciences and Humanities Research Council of Canada [unpublished, 1987 at 532].
15. Dependent Adults Act, R.S.A. 1980, c.D-32 (as amended); Patients Property Act, R.S.B.C. 1979, c.313; Mental Health Act, R.S.M. 1970, c.M-110; Infirm Persons Act, R.S.N.B. 1973, c.I-8; Incompetent Persons Act, R.S.N.S. 1967, c.135; Mental Incompetency Act, R.S.O. 1980, c.264; Mental Health Act, R.S.P.E.I. 1974, c.M-9; Mentally Disordered Persons Act, R.S.S. 1978, c.M-14; Mentally Incompetent Person's Estate Act, R.S.N. 1970, c.234 authorizes only the appointment of a guardian of a person's estate.
16. Robertson, supra, note 7 at 27-28, 106.
17. For an exhaustive review of the guardianship legislation of each province, see the seminal works by Gordon, Verdun-Jones & MacDougall, supra, note 14 and by Robertson, supra, note 7.
18. P. McLaughlin, *Guardianship of the Person*, (Downsview, Ont.: National Institute on Mental Retardation, 1979) at 71.
19. G.B. Robertson, *Mental Disability and the Law in Canada* (Toronto: Carswell, 1987) at 100.
20. Mental Incompetency Act, R.S.O. 1980, c.264.
21. Ibid., s.7(1). The legislative terminology in Ontario is "committee" (not guardian) of the person but "guardian" will be used throughout this paper for uniformity.
22. Ibid., s.1(e).
23. Ibid., s.8(1).
24. Ibid., s.8(5).
25. Rule 38.07 (1) and (3). Where the notice is served outside Ontario, it must be served at least 20 days before the hearing date. For relevant case law, see R.M. Gordon, S.N. Verdun-Jones & D.J. MacDougall, *Standing in Their Shoes: Guardianship, Trusteeship and the Elderly Canadian,* A Report to the Social Sciences and Humanities Research Council of Canada [unpublished, 1987 at 268].
26. Mental Incompetency Act, R.S.O. 1980, c.264, s.8(6).
27. Ibid., s.9.
28. Ibid., s.12(1).
29. Robertson, supra, note 18 at 146 & 102.
30. Law Reform Commission of Saskatchewan, *Tentative Proposals for a Guardianship Act,* Part 1: Personal Guardianship (Saskatoon, Sask., 1981) at 8.

31. Mental Incompetency Act., R.S.O. 1980, c.264, s.39(1).
32. *Re Burton,* [1965] 1 O.R. 125 (H.C.)
33. *Clark* v *Clark* (1982), 40 R.R. (2d) 383 (Co.Ct.). For an analysis see J. Staub, "Mental Incompetency and Civil Rights: Issues Raised by the Justin Clark and Martyn Humm Cases" (1985) 6 *Health L. Can* 3, and G.B. Robertson, *Mental Disability and the Law in Canada* (Toronto: Carswell, 1987) at 110-13.
34. P. McLaughlin, *Guardianship of the Person*, (Downsview, Ont.: National Institute on Mental Retardation, 1979) at 55-56.
35. For a detailed discussion, see Robertson, supra, note 32 at 133-42.
36. Mental Incompetency Act., R.S.O. 1980, c.264, ss 7(3)(4), 8(7).
37.Ibid., s.11(5).
38. For example, see McLaughlin, supra, note 33 at 70; R.M. Gordon, S.N. Verdun-Jones & D.J. MacDougall, *Standing in Their Shoes: Guardianship, Trusteeship and the Elderly Canadian,* A Report to the Social Sciences and Humanities Research Council of Canada [unpublished, 1987] at 75.
39. Law Reform Commission of Saskatchewan, supra, note 29 at 9.
40. McLaughlin, supra, note 33 at 71-72.
41. Gordon, Verdun-Jones & MacDougall, supra, note 37 at 124-28.
42. R.S.A. 1980, c.D-32.
43.The 1978 legislation (Dependent Adults Act, S.A. 1976, c.63) used the terms "plenary" and "partial" guardians. These labels were removed by amending legislation in 1985 (1985, c.21, s.7) but the concepts remain.
44. Dependent Adults Act, R.S.A. 1980, c.D-32, s.6(1) [S.A. 1985, c.21, s.7].
45. Ibid., s.4(1) [S.A. 1985, c.21, s.6].
46. Policy Directives of the Public Guardian (1985), Amendments to the Dependent Adults Act, Legal Education Society of Alberta, (Edmonton, Alberta, 1985) 32 at 33. The definitions provided are:
    Substantial: Having substance as opposed to form, important, essential, considerable in content, value or worth. A right materially affecting those interests which one is entitled to have preserved and protected by law.
    Benefit: Helpful, advantageous and conducive to well-being. That which guards, aids or promotes well-being particularly health or social well-being.
47. Ibid, at 34.
48. Ibid.
49. Ibid.
50. P. McLaughlin, *Guardianship of the Person*, (Downsview, Ont.: National Institute on Mental Retardation, 1979) at 68.
51. *Re Johannasen* (1984), 48 A.L.R. 15 (Surr.Ct.).
52. Dependent Adults Act, supra, note 43, s.4(2).
53. Dependent Adults Act, R.S.A. 1980, c.D-32, s.3(2).
54. Ibid., s.3(3).
55. Ibid., s.5.
56. Ibid., s.10(a) [re-en. 1985, c.21, s.11(1). Under s.10(1), amended 1985, c.21, s.11(2), the court can modify or add to any of the itemized powers.]
57. Ibid., s.10(3) [amended 1985, c.21, s.11].
58. Ibid., s.7(1)(a).
59. Ibid., s.11[amended R.S.A. 1980, c.6 (Supp.) s.11].
60. Ibid., s.8 [amended S.A. 1985, c.21, s.9].
61. Ibid., s.15(1).

62. Ibid., s.16(1).

63. Ibid., ss.67, 68.

64. P. McLaughlin, *Guardianship of the Person*, (Downsview, Ont.: National Institute on Mental Retardation, 1979) at 49; Law Reform Commission of Saskatchewan, *Tentative Proposals for a Guardianship Act*, Part 1: Personal Guardianship (Saskatoon, Sask., 1981) at 12.

65. For example, see Law Reform Commission of Saskatchewan, *Proposals for a Guardianship Act*, Part 1: Personal Guardianship (Saskatoon, Sask., 1983); Quebec Civil Code, ss 280-282 (Bill 20 passed but not proclaimed).

66. Neglected Adults Welfare Act, S.N. 1973, No. 81.

67. Family Services Act, S.N.B. 1980, c.C-2.1, ss 34-42 [title amended 1983, c.16, s.1].

68. Adult Protection Act, S.N.S. 1985, c.2.

69. Neglected Adults Welfare Act, S.N. 1973, No. 81, s.4; Adult Protection Act, S.N.S. 1985, c.2, s.5.

70. *Nova Scotia* (Minister of Social Services) v. *J.G.* (1986), 73 N.S.R. (2d) 204 (Fam. Ct).

71. Neglected Adults Welfare Act, S.N. 1973, No. 81, s.6(4); Family Services Act, S.N.B. 1980, c.C-2.1, s.39(1); Adult Protection Act, S.N.S. 1985, c.2, s.9(3).

72. Family Services Act, S.N.B. 1980, c.C-2.1, s.39(4).

73. Adult Protection Act, S.N.S. 1985, c.2, ss 9(5), 9(6), 9(8).

74. Neglected Adults Welfare Act, S.N. 1973, No. 81, ss 9, 16 (as amended 1974, c.57, s.38(264)(x)); 2979, c.34, Sch.; 1979, c.38, s.7; 1986, c.42 Sch. B, item s 9; Family Services Act, S.N.B. 1980, c.C-2.1, ss 39(5), 41; Adult Protection Act, S.N.S. 1985, c.2, ss 9(6), 9(10).

75. R.M. Gordon, S.N. Verdun-Jones & D.J. MacDougall, *Standing in Their Shoes; Guardianship, Trusteeship and the Elderly Canadian*, A Report to the Social Sciences and Humanities Research Council of Canada [unpublished, 1987] at 57.

76. Ibid., at 55.

77. Part I of the Constitution Act, 1982, being Schedule B of the Canada Act 1982 (U.K.), 1982, c.11.

78. In *Retail, Wholesale and Department Store Union, Local 580 et al.* v. *Dolphin Delivery Ltd.* (1986), 33 D.L.R. (4th) 174 (S.C.C.), the Supreme Court held that the Charter applies to the common law. To adopt a construction of section 52(1) (which provides that "any law that is inconsistent with the provisions of the Constitution is, to the extent of the inconsistency, of no force or effect") which would exclude from Charter application the whole body of the common law which in great part governs the rights and obligations of individuals in society, would be unrealistic and contrary to the clear language employed in section 52(1). See pp. 190-191.

79. "Prescribed by law" need not be an explicit limitation of a particular right or freedom. In *R* v. *Therens*, [1985] 1 S.C.R. 613 at 645 the Supreme Court held that a limit was "prescribed by law" within the meaning of section 1 of the Charter where it was "expressly provided" by statute or regulation; or results by "necessary implication" from the terms of a statute or regulation; or from the "operating requirements" of a statute or regulation.

80. *R.* v. *Oakes*, [1986] 1 S.C.R. 103 at 137.

81. Ibid. at 137-138. The Supreme Court held that proof beyond a reasonable doubt would be unduly onerous on the party seeking to limit the Charter right because concepts such as "reasonableness", "justifiability", and "free and democratic

society" are not amenable to such a standard.

82. *Re Singh and Minister of Employment and Immigration*, [1985] 1 S.C.R. 177 at 204 and *R.* v. *Morgentaler* [1988] 1 S.C.R. 30 per Dickson, C.J.C. at 52.

83. Reference re Section 94(2) of the Motor Vehicle Act, [1985] 2 S.C.R. 486 at 500, adopted by Dickson, C.J. in *R.* v. *Morgentaler,* [1988] 1 S.C.R. 30 at 52.

84. *R.* v. *Morgentaler,* [1988] 1 S.C.R. 30 at 52 per Dickson, C.J.C.

85. Ibid., at 166-167.

86. Supra, note 84. Contrast the reasoning of Wilson, J. with Dickson, C.J.C. and Beetz, J.

87. Reference Re Section 94(2) Motor Vehicle Act (B.C.), [1985] 2 S.C.R. 486 at 501, per Lamer, J.

88. Ibid., at 513.

89. Ibid.

90. *R.* v. *Ontario Racing Commission, ex parte Taylor* (1970), 13 D.L.R. (3d) 405 (Ont. H.C.), rev'd (1970) 15 D.L.R. (3d) 430 (Ont. C.A.).

91. Gordon, Verdun-Jones & MacDougall, supra, note 70 at 567.

92. *R.* v. *Morgentaler* [1988] 1 S.C.R. 30 at 53 per Dickson, C.J.C.

93. Ibid.

94. C. McKague, "The Charter of Rights and Freedoms" (1986) 4 *Just Cause* 3 at 4.

95. D. Gibson, *The Law of the Charter: General Principles* (Toronto: Carswell, 1986) at 2, 110-18.

96. *Retail, Wholesale and Department Store Union, Local 580 et al.* v. *Dolphin Delivery Ltd.* (1986), 33 D.L.R. (4th) 174 (S.C.C.).

97. Gibson, supra note 95 at 89.

Section Three

Miscellaneous Issues

Chapter 40

Enduring Powers of Attorney

Julian T. FARRAND   Law Commission, England

The seemingly esoteric subject of powers of attorney has so far twice been specifically referred to the Law Commission by the Lord Chancellor. The first reference was in 1966 when "we"[1] were asked to undertake a comprehensive review of the statutory provisions applicable when one person (i.e. a principal or donor) appoints another (i.e. the agent, attorney or donee) by a formal document (i.e. a power of attorney) to act for him or her in one specific transaction or, more commonly, in a series of transactions or to manage his affairs generally.[2] The review led comparatively quickly and almost entirely directly to the enactment of the Powers of Attorney Act 1971. This statute certainly replaced existing provisions with a considerably more rational and reliable scheme, clarifying the law and providing a short standard form of power. In particular, the protection against revocation of the power afforded to persons dealing with the attorney as well as to the attorney himself (often a solicitor) was usefully strengthened by the Act.

In the consultation paper which constituted an essential feature of the Law Commission's review of powers of attorney there appeared the following paragraph:

> **"Incapacity of Donor**
>
> There is little doubt that it would be highly convenient if it were possible to grant a power of attorney under which the donee would be entitled to continue to handle the affairs of the donor, notwithstanding the latter's incapacity, resulting, for example, from mental illness. Indeed, it often seems to be assumed that so long as a power of attorney has been obtained before the donor becomes mentally incapable, the donee can safely continue to operate; readers of the history of the Times newspaper will remember the efforts made to obtain a power of attorney from the mentally ailing Lord Northcliffe. It is felt, however, that it would go too far to provide for this facility since it would drive a coach and horses through the safeguards provided by the Court of Protection. It might, however, be possible and valuable to attempt some clarification of the exact circumstances in which temporary incapacity operates to revoke the power. It presumably cannot be the law that the donee is not entitled to act merely because, at the moment when he acts, the donor is incapable of doing so because, for example, he is

asleep, under an anaesthetic or in a coma. All this, however, seems to be a
facet of the general law of agency, a clarification of which would have to await
codification of that branch of the law."[3]

It emerged, however, that this paragraph aroused considerably more interest and response than had been anticipated. Indeed, far from being left to wait,
the Commission's attempt to find a solution was actually blamed for the delay
in reporting.[4] But in the end the Commission remained satisfied that "without a
more far-reaching review of the arrangements for the administration of the
property of persons of unsound mind, no solution can be found which would
satisfy both the desires of the people concerned and the safe-guards which the
Court of Protection regards as essential."[5] So there the matter was left to wait.

It waited until 1973 when a second reference was received from the Lord
Chancellor, not seeking any very wide review but merely:

> "To consider the law and practice governing powers of attorney and other
> forms of agency in relation to the mental incapacity of the principal, and to
> make recommendations."[6]

A consultation accordingly commenced on the basis that the authority
conferred on an attorney or any other agent would, as a rule of law, be revoked
by the supervening mental incapacity of the principal.[7] The paper proceeded to
identify at the outset the main points of difficulty seen as flowing from that rule
of law as follows:[8]

" (a) There is uncertainty as to the exact circumstances in which mental
      incapacity revokes a power, and it is particularly difficult for the
      attorney of an elderly person whose faculties are failing to decide if and
      when the power has been revoked by mental incapacity.
  (b) There are probably many attorneys who continue to act when in strict
      law the power has been revoked. Most of these act honestly and in the
      best interests of their principals, but in doing so they put themselves at
      risk with regard to third parties or their principals. A further result is
      that the law is being ignored on a large scale, which is an undesirable
      situation.
  (c) The average layman would probably be very surprised to learn that a
      power of attorney is revoked just at the point when he would regard it as
      being most needed.
  (d) Whilst accepting that the Court of Protection exists to look after the
      property and affairs of those who, by reason of mental disorder, are
      unable to do so themselves, the procedure is, it is said, inevitably
      cumbersome, time-consuming and expensive. Also there is reluctance
      to resort to it by relatives of people whose inability to manage their
      affairs is the result of old age or brain damage caused by a stroke or
      accident, or other disabilities which are not mental disorders in the
      narrower sense."[8]

It was also recognised that the scale of the difficulties was likely to increase with the growing ability of medical science to keep people alive after many of their faculties have become dulled.

The rule of law blamed as the root of all these difficulties might itself have been questioned: it seems more assumed than established. The rule stems not from any Act of Parliament but from one case in the Court of Appeal.[9] The decision is undoubtedly of long-standing — over a century old — but for present purposes it appears at first sight pretty nearly irrelevant. Indeed, in the case, despite the supervening mental incapacity of a principal, an agent's authority effectively continued.[10] The rule rests on *dicta* which, if not strictly *obiter*,[11] are definitely not decisive. To begin with, Brett LJ did plainly say "insanity of this kind does put an end to the agent's authority."[12]

But then Bramwell LJ said "it has been assumed by Brett LJ, that the insanity of the defendant was such as to amount to a revocation of his wife's authority. I doubt whether partial mental derangement would have that effect. I think that in order to annul the authority of an agent, insanity must amount to dementia."[13] And the other member of the Court, Cotton LJ, simply sent a message that "he does not wish to decide whether the authority of the defendant's wife was terminated, or whether the liability of a contractor lasts until a committee has been appointed."[14] After which Brett LJ further remarked that "... from the mere fact of mental derangement it ought not to be assumed that a person is incompetent to contract; mere weakness of mind or partial derangement is insufficient to exempt a person from responsibility upon the engagements into which he has entered."[15] Apart from this evidently inconclusive case, the only other decision ever cited is one where it was simply accepted without argument as a fact (not law) that a firm of solicitors' authority to act had ceased by reason of the unsoundness of mind of their client.[16] The solicitors were, exceptionally, held liable for breach of warranty of authority for taking steps in legal proceedings despite being unaware that their client had been certified of unsound mind: they had merely been informed that he "was suffering from a nervous breakdown, and was in a home and unable to attend to any business"[17] — insufficient, it seems, to revoke their authority![17a]

Thus the rule of law causing all the difficulties may understandably be thought not soundly grounded even though it is generally accepted as established.[18] In addition, there are certain significant exceptions to note:- *First*, an attorney who acts under a power that has been revoked without knowing of the revocation does not thereby incur liability to either the donor or anyone else.[19] *Secondly*, where an attorney acts under a revoked power, anyone with whom he deals who is himself unaware of the revocation may rely on the attorney's ostensible authority and the transaction will be binding on the donor.[20] *Thirdly*, where a power has been given to the attorney to secure a proprietary interest of the attorney or the performance of an obligation owed to him; such powers are often given by mortgagors to mortgagees to facilitate the power of sale by the latter should this prove necessary and are irrevocable.[21] *Fourthly*, where "necessaries" are supplied for a mentally incapacitated principal, he must pay a reasonable price for them, which may be paid on his behalf and recovered from him.[22]

Although these exceptions, especially the fourth, seem to cover much of what may be needed when mental incapacity supervenes, they have not been thought sufficient. In particular, they do not directly meet the desire of many people, in substance, to choose a personal representative to administer their estate on mental incapacity as on death.

It was also pointed out that —

"... applying the existing law puts on honest and conscientious attorneys the difficult burden of deciding when the donor of a power of attorney, who gradually becomes more and more senile, has reached the stage of incapacity when the power is in law revoked. The attorney may incur risk if he continues to act after evidence of his principal's mental incapacity has come to his notice. Although the attorney may continue to supply his principal with necessaries or to see that he is so supplied by others, transactions such as selling his house or buying him an annuity (which may well be desirable and necessary transactions in the case of an old person) may involve risk to the attorney.

It should be recognised that, while the law may be clear that money spent on necessaries for an incapable person may be recovered, this involves difficulties in practice. Apart from the decision as to what are necessaries in a particular case, and what is a reasonable price, there is the problem of how they are to be paid for in the first instance. A mentally incapable person can no longer draw on his own bank account, and any authority he may have given to another person to draw on it will have been revoked by the incapacity."[23]

Considerable support for this point of view was found amongst (honest and conscientous) practising solicitors.[24]

There were arguments against, including the telling reminder that the Court of Protection will usually and easily grant receivership to a suitable attorney already acting.[25] As to this aspect, the Law Commission, after fairly full consideration, observed —

"The underlying complaint is not that the Court of Protection is unapproachable or unnecessarily slow or inflexible. It is none of those things. Inevitably, however, it has procedures, and procedures always involve time and expense. For example, before making a receivership order the Court always requires production of *medical evidence* because it has to be satisfied that the proposed patient is indeed a "patient".

"The originating application must usually be accompanied by a substantial *affidavit* to enable the Court to judge the suitability of the proposed receiver and (looking to the future) to assist the Court to give directions on questions relating to the administration of the patient's estate. Furthermore, the receiver may as a condition of his appointment be required to provide *security*. He will also usually be required to render annual *accounts* to the Court and he may have to attend Court to have these passed. Finally, in order to finance the Court's activities, *fees* are payable by the patient's estate. At the outset each originating application bears a commencement fee of £50. Additionally, there are fairly substantial fees charged annually on the patient's clear annual income as well as "transaction" fees for some individual dealings with the patient's estate (including the making of a statutory will)."[26]

In other words, perhaps, the Court of Protection does things properly but paternalistically and at a price.

In the result, the Law Commission eventually recommended as most convenient, the solution of a special statutory power of attorney which would continue in force notwithstanding the principal's mental incapacity.[27]

"While the convenience would be by no means confined to cases where the mental incapacity arises through senility, such cases provide perhaps the most obvious examples. We can, indeed, go further and say that the convenience is likely to be most marked in cases of senility: firstly, because of the special difficulty in reaching a decision as to whether a person's mental faculties have deteriorated simply through age to such an extent that he has become incapable in law of acting for himself: and secondly, because the problem in such cases is often expected to be relatively short-term and the family may rightly doubt whether the making of more formal arrangements would be worthwhile."[28]

The difficulties may have been felt initially as arising out of the practical need to protect attorneys, whether relatives or solicitors, and the persons dealing with them from potential liabilities through continuing to act on behalf of persons becoming mentally incapable. Nevertheless, the real need to facilitate the continued management of the property and affairs of mentally incapacitated persons in their own best interests was also recognised. Accordingly, the simplistic solution of legalising current practice by abolishing the (supposed) rule that a principal's incapacity revokes an attorney's authority was rejected, most importantly because there would be no safeguards for the principal once he had become incapable.[29]

The non-simplistic solution of creating a novel device with built-in safeguards, which was done by the Enduring Powers of Attorney Act 1985, had received overwhelming support on consultation. However there was no general consensus as to how to reconcile two conflicting objectives: to provide an easily usable and inexpensive scheme whilst also protecting the principal and his property from exploitation.[30]

An examination was undertaken of schemes operating in other common law jurisdictions.[31] These schemes were apparently popular[32] but revealed no standard model.[33] Nevertheless, three basic safeguards could be extracted from most schemes:

(a) a requirement that the EPA instrument contain a statement by the donor showing his intention that the power should be able to survive his mental incapacity;

(b) a requirement that the donor's signature be witnessed by someone other than the attorney;

(c) machinery whereby the EPA could be terminated (or at least controlled) by the intervention of the court or some other official body.[34]

However, the Law Commission did not regard these basic safeguards as offering sufficient protection for the elderly and highly suggestible people of England and Wales.[35] Therefore, whilst still ostensibly trying to strike a balance between safeguards and simplicity, additional rules and regulations were recommended and adopted by Parliament.

Primarily the Enduring Power of Attorney Act 1985[36] requires the use of an instrument in a prescribed form with a prescribed execution plus especially prescribed explanatory information — like a Government Health Warning on cigarette packets.

The prescribing has now been done — or rather redone: 1987 Regulations[37] replaced an earlier form much criticized for incomprehensibility to laymen as well as for technical inaccuracies.[38] [For a reproduction of what must be used see the Appendix to this Chapter.]

Once granted, an enduring power of attorney will operate in effect as an ordinary power of attorney unless and until the principal's mental incapacity supervenes when the power is not revoked but suspended until registered by the Court of Protection.[39] However, the attorney and third persons will still be protected by the Powers of Attorney Act 1971.[40] After applying for registration, the attorney make take action to maintain the principal or other persons (including himself) or to prevent loss to the principal's estate.[41] The attorney is under a duty to apply for registration as soon as practicable if he "has reason to believe that the [principal] is or is becoming mentally incapable."[42] Notices must first be given not only to certain of the closest relatives but also to the principal himself.[43] The obvious reason for such notices is to enable objections to registration by the Court to be made on one or more of the following grounds:

(a) that the power purported to have been created by the instrument was not valid as an enduring power of attorney;

(b) that the power created by the instrument no longer subsists;

(c) that the application is premature because the donor is not yet becoming mentally incapable;

(d) that fraud or undue pressure was used to induce the donor to create the power;

(d) that, having regard to all the circumstances and in particular the attorney's relationship to or connection with the donor, the attorney is unsuitable to be the donor's attorney.[44]

The potential impact of such notices, asserting the onset of mental incapacity, upon the various recipients does not seem to have been contemplated by the Law Commission.[45]

The attorney cannot validly disclaim the power "unless and until [he] gives notice of it to the court"[46] but then it seems his disclaimer cannot be declined.

After registration, the donor cannot revoke (or extend or restrict) the power, even whilst not mentally incapable, without confirmation from the Court of Protection.[47] The Court has various supervisory functions in respect of registered powers which include cancellation of the registration in specified circumstances.[48]

Protection for attorneys and third persons where a registered power is, unknown to them, invalid or revoked is provided.[49] There is also, in favour of purchasers, a conclusive presumption of the validity of a transaction by an attorney with a third person if either it occurred within twelve months of registration or an appropriate statutory declaration is obtained from the third person.[50]

The authority conferred on the attorney may be general or subject to express conditions or restrictions.[51] Also the Act authorises certain beneficial actions as follows:[52]

(a) he may so act in relation to himself or in relation to any other person if the donor might be expected to provide for his or that person's needs respectively: and

(b) he may do whatever the donor might be expected to do to meet those needs.

In addition, certain gifts are authorised as follows:[53]

(a) he may make gifts of a seasonal nature or at a time, or on an anniversary, of a birth or a marriage, to persons (including himself) who are related to or connected with the donor; and

(b) he may make gifts to any charity to whom the donor made or might be expected to make gifts provided that the value of each gift is not unreasonable having regard to all the circumstances and in particular the size of the donor's estate.

The prescribed form warns potential principals: "Don't sign this form unless you understand what it means". But the statute does not stipulate the mental capacity necessary to create a valid enduring power of attorney. However, it has recently been held that such a power can be validly created if the principal understands the nature and effect of the power itself even though not then capable of managing his own property and affairs.[54] In other words, despite the fact that the principal's mental incapacity is such that an ordinary power or authority would be revoked, the donor may still be capable of granting an enduring power.[55]

The distinctions are nice and the consequences significant so some extra explanation should surely be welcomed:

"Finally I should say something about what is meant by understanding the nature and effect of the power. What degree of understanding is involved? Plainly one cannot expect that the donor should have been able to pass an examination on the provisions of the 1985 Act. At the other extreme, I do not think that it would be sufficient if he realised only that it gave cousin William power to look after his property. Counsel as *amicus curiae* helpfully summar-

ised the matters which the donor should have understood in order that he can
be said to have understood the nature and effect of the power: first, if such be
the terms of the power, that the attorney will be able to assume complete
authority over the donor's affairs; second, if such be the terms of the power,
that the attorney will in general be able to do anything with the donor's
property which the donor could have done; third, that the authority will
continue if the donor should be or become mentally incapable; fourth, that if
he should be or become mentally incapable, the power will be irrevocable
without confirmation by the court. I do not wish to prescribe another form of
words in competition with the explanatory notes prescribed by the Lord
Chancellor, but I accept the summary of counsel as *amicus curiae* as a
statement of the matters which should ordinarily be explained to the donor
whatever the precise language which may be used and which the evidence
should show he has understood."[56]

Do the scales seem to be tipping against the simple and inexpensive?
The Act contains its own slightly curious definition:

"mentally incapable' or 'mental incapacity', *except where it refers to revocation at common law,* means, in relation to any person, that he is incapable by
reason of mental disorder of managing and administering his property and
affairs and "mentally capable" and "mental capacity" shall be construed
accordingly;.[57]

The Law Commission realised that common law incapacity and statutory
incapacity might not necessarily mean the same thing but were content to let
the uncertainty stand.[58] A measure of resignation may, however, be perceived
in the observation:

"A particular difficulty in this area is the identification of incapacity. A
donor's failure to manage his affairs properly may be as easily attributable to
lack of inclination as to positive lack of mental capacity. He may have "good"
as well as "bad" days. Applying any definition of "incapacity" inevitably
involves taking a subjective rather than an objective view. The donor's doctor
may consider that he is incapable while his wife may attribute his behaviour to
eccentricity. Our recommendations reflect the uncertainties prevalent in this
area."[59]

Enduring powers have apparently proved popular with the elderly but a
number of inherent difficulties persist: What measure of mental capacity is
required for the creation of a valid enduring power? What measure of mental
*in*capacity suffices to bring an enduring power into operation? Is the position in
between, when there will be a general power, satisfactory? Can abuse of their
powers by attorneys be sufficiently checked (particularly where elderly principals lack close relatives)? The English and Welsh rules also suffer several
technical complexities, especially as to co-owners (e.g. spouses) who are

themselves trustees of property (e.g. the matrimonial home).[60] Yet what better solution can there be?[61]

A better solution may lie, not in any different device, but in a more imaginative use by practitioners of enduring powers of attorney themselves.[62] The scope of the authority which may be conferred by the principal is spelled out rather widely in the statute: the attorney may act "in relation to all or a specified part of the property *and affairs* of the donor"; authority may be given "to do *specified things*" or "*anything* which the donor can lawfully do by an attorney."[63] All of this may effectively be made subject "to any conditions or restrictions contained in the instrument." From the statutory wording, the use of enduring powers of attorney is by no means necessarily confined to managing property but can, on the face of it, extend to any of the affairs or things, whether business or personal, of the principal.[64] It follows that the principal's wishes as to the decisions which should be taken in the future on the occasion of a range of hypothetical circumstances might be written into the power. Whether this could effectively extend to the giving or withholding of consents to medical treatment is obviously problematical. Nevertheless, it appears reasonably clear that the attorney could be given effective instructions about paying or not paying for certain forms of treatment.

Beyond wishes, the form of enduring power of attorney could well be used to impose duties. In other words, the attorney need not just be authorised to act, he could be required to act. The statute, no doubt for explicable reasons, does not impose any duties on the attorney, except as to registering the power.[65] It does provide that, after application and before registration, "the attorney *may* take action — to maintain the donor or prevent loss to his estate."[66] But, extraordinarily, taking such action is never made a duty. Surely it would be reasonable and sensible for obligations to act in the best interests of the principal to be written in.[67] These best interests could be left to be judged objectively or by the attorney alone as he sees fit or, better, in accordance with the view taken (and expressed) by the principal before he was incapacitated.

In short, it ought not to take much at all to turn an ordinary enduring power of attorney into a fully fledged "living will". This development therefore may easily be seen as the best solution by all concerned not least the potentially incapacitated.

Notes

1. i.e. the present Commissioners' best known predecessors, the famous five initially appointed under the Law Commissions Act 1969 - as they then were, Messrs Justice Scarman OBE, LCB Gower MBE, Neil Lawson QC, NS Marsh QC and Andrew Martin QC.
2. See para 1 of Report on Powers of Attorney Law Com No. 30 (1970), also acknowledging that a suggestion from the Holborn Law Society was the source of

the reference.
3. Working Paper No. 11 (1967) para 21.
4. Law Com No. 30 para 1; both The Law Society and the Holborn Law Society submitted detailed proposals for special types of powers of attorney: see ibid para 27. The Report was published in 1970.
5. ibid para 1; see also the recommendation in para 41(c).
6. Report on the Incapacitated Principal Law Com. No. 122 (1983) para 1.3.
7. Working Paper No. 69 (1976) para 1.
8. Ibid para 2.
9. *Drew v Nunn* (1878-79) 4 QBD 661.
10. The short headnote reads:
   "The plaintiff was a tradesman, and the defendant had given his wife authority to deal with the plaintiff, and had held her out as his agent and as entitled to pledge his credit. Afterwards, the defendant became insane, and whilst his malady lasted, his wife ordered goods from the plaintiff, who accordingly supplied them. At the time of supplying the goods the plaintiff was unaware that the defendant had become insane. The defendant afterwards recovered his reason, and then refused to pay for the goods supplied to his wife by the plaintiff:-
   Held, that the defendant was liable for the price of the goods."
   In other words, he had to pay for his boots and shoes supplied whilst he was confined in a lunatic asylum.
11. The *ratio decidendi* turned on the absence of notice of revocation.
12. Ibid. ps 665-6 where he equated bankruptcy, death and the marriage of females so as to deduce as the satisfactory principle to adopt that "where such a change occurs as to the principal that he can no longer act for himself, the agent whom he has appointed can no longer act for him".
13. Ibid p. 669, adding: "If a man becomes so far insane as to have no mind, perhaps he ought to be deemed dead for the purpose of contracting."
14. Ibid p. 669, to which was added: "He bases his decision simply upon the ground that the defendant, by holding out his wife as agent, entered into a contract with the plaintiff that she had authority to act upon his behalf, and that until the plaintiff had notice that this authority was revoked he was entitled to act upon the defendant's representations."
15. Ibid ps. 669-670.
16. *Yonge v Toynbee* [1910]1KB 215, see per Buckley LJ at p. 228 but see also Vaughan Williams LJ at p. 235 "*If* the authority was determined by the lunacy ..." (doubting emphasis supplied.)
17. See ibid p. 216.
17a. i.e. it was the unknown certification which was taken as effecting a revocation.
18. See e.g. per Hoffman J in *Re K* [1988]1 All ER 358 at p. 360.
19. Power of Attorney Act 1971 s. 5(1). This has the effect, so far as powers of attorney are concerned, of reversing the decision in *Yonge v Toynbee* [1910]1 KB 215.
20. Powers of Attorney Act 1971 s. 5(2). Sect. 5(4) provides means whereby it may (for the benefit of a subsequent purchaser) be conclusively presumed that the person with whom the attorney dealt was not aware of the revocation of the power.
21. See generally s. 4 of the Powers of Attorney Act 1971.
22. See *Re Beaven* [1912]1 Ch 196; also Sale of Goods Act 1979 s. 3 where "necessaries" means goods "suitable to the condition in life of [the mentally incapacitated person] and to his actual requirements at the time of the sale and delivery.

23. Working Paper No. 69 para. 37.
24. Ibid. para. 39.
25. See ibid. para. 42.
26. Report on the Incapacitated Principal. Law Com No. 122 (1983) para 2.27; cp. "The Court of Protection" by Larry Gostin; also 1983, a MIND Special Report taking a critical look at the Court.
27. Report on the Incapacitated Principal. Law Com No. 122 (1983).
28. Ibid para 1.1.
29. Ibid para 3.7.
30. Ibid para 3.9. For example, The Law Society had, *inter alia,* predictably proposed: "In order to ensure the reliability of attorneys under special powers and to protect those who may be unfitted for the responsibilities from being pressed to undertake them, there should be not less than two joint attorneys, at least one of whom is not a member of the donor's family, and at least one of whom must be, and remain, a member of a professional body or an organisation which is, for practical purposes, in a position to guarantee his honesty. The latter requirement would be satisfied by a solicitor holding a practising certificate or a trust corporation."
See Working Paper 69 Appendix.
31. Northern Territory of Australia, Victoria, British Columbia, Ontario, Manitoba, and some 3/4 of the USA: ibid para 3.14.
32. Ibid para 3.15.
33. Ibid para 3.16.
34. Ibid para 3.17.
35. Ibid para 3.21.
36. s. 2(1).
37. SI No. 1612.
38. cp. 1986 SI No. 126.
39. 1985 Act ss. 1(1) and 13(1).
40. Ibid. s. 1(2)
41. s. 1(2); see also s. 5 as to Court directions prior to registration.
42. s. 4(1) (2).
43. s. 4(3) and Sched. 1.
44. s. 6(4).
45. Practical problems are amusingly anticipated by Richard Simon in an article in *Law Society's Gazette* (1986) vol. 83, p 2079 which concludes:
"I think the difficulties are well illustrated by King Lear. Suppose he had given an enduring power of attorney to the Fool. Regan and Gonerial already expressed doubts about his mental capacity in Act I, when he was actively managing his own affairs. When should the power be registered? Clearly this is overdue by the storm scene, and the fool's authority would have been suspended well before the weather turned nasty. Registration during Act II would have been highly provocative, and caused all sorts of trouble with the old boy at a time when the Fool was doing his best to calm him down. No point asking the court to dispense with notice to the King: Regan and Goneril are out for what they can get and would be bound to object to registration so it would all come out. Cordelia is abroad, marrying the King of France ('super wedding, daddy'). The only other person with Lear's interests at heart is Kent, who is masquerading as a servant but is meant to be in exile and is not entitled to notice anyway. There would also be problems in the sub-plot, where Gloucester has given and revoked enduring powers to Edgar and Edmund as his

affections shift to and fro, and then suffers suicidal neurosis following the loss of his eyes. Edgar has disappeared, feigning madness, and Edmund (who would be entitled to notice, though illegitimate) is a plausible villain capable of any form of deceit.

I will leave it to the reader to consider how to advise Rosencranz and Guildenstern in relation to an enduring power given by Hamlet."

46. s. 4(6) also s. 7(1)(b).
47. s. 7.
48. s. 8; see also the Court of Protection (Enduring Powers of Attorney) Rules 1986 (SI No. 127)).
49. s. 9.
50. s. 9(4).
51. s. 3(1) and (2).
52. s. 3(4).
53. s. 3(5).
54. *Re K* [1988] 1 All ER 358.
55. The case also concerned a Mrs F:
    "She was a lady of 75 suffering from presenile dementia. Although she was at times lucid and capable of making decisions with full understanding of what she was doing, at other times she would become confused and suffer loss of memory. The medical evidence was that when she executed the power she fully understood its nature and effect, but that on account of her recurrent disability she could not in general terms be said to be capable of managing and administering her property." per Hoffman J at p. 361.
56. per Hoffman J at p. 363.
57. s. 13(1) emphasis supplied.
58. See Law Com No. 122 para 3.3 fn. 58.
59. *loc cit.*
60. As to trustees, the Enduring Powers of Attorney Act 1985 seems somewhat confused (and the Prescribed Form Regulations 1987 now ignore this aspect). It is first provided, for obvious reasons (i.e. limited duration), that a power of attorney under s. 25 of the Trustee Act 1925 cannot be an enduring power (s. 2(8)). This would, in effect, mean that trustees could never give enduring powers of attorney. Then it is provided that (s. 3(3)):
    "subject to any conditions or restrictions contained in the instrument, an attorney under an enduring power, whether general or limited may (without obtaining any consent) execute or exercise all or any of the trusts, powers or discretions vested in the donor as trustee and may (without the concurrence of "any other person") give a valid receipt for capital or other money paid."
    Intended simply to enable beneficial co-owners to give enduring powers to each other despite being strictly trustees (cp. *Walia v Michael Naughton Ltd* [1985] 1 WLR 1115) this subsection is not so limited. One commentator has said:
    "It does in fact apply to trusts of all kinds and, in doing so, it drives a coach and horses through fundamental principles of trust law which have hitherto been regarded as essential to the protection of trust beneficiaries."
    (R T Oerton, Trustees and the Enduring Powers of Attorney Act 1985: a Legislative Blunder (1986) *Solicitor's Journal*, vol 130, p. 24). He explained as follows (ibid pp 24-25):
    "First it delegates the donor's trustee functions whether he intends it to or not ...

Secondly this result endures whether the EPA is general or limited ...

Thirdly it enables the attorney to exercise the trustee functions 'without obtaining any consent ...'

Fourthly ... it contains no prohibition on the appointement as attorney of an individual who is the donor's only co-trustee ...

Fifthly it enables a trustee 'without the concurrence of any other person' to 'give a valid receipt for capital or other money paid' ...

Sixthly there is no limit to the duration of the power ...

Seventhly there is no requirement ... for notice to be given to the other trustees, who may remain in complete ignorance of the power ..."

6l. In this connection, it may be worth noticing that the Scottish Law Commission proposes, as soon as other commitments permit, discussing options and consulting in pursuance of two separate references received from the Law Society of Scotland. One is:

"To consider the law relating to the administration of the property of persons who are incapable of managing their own affairs, and the law relating to judicial factors and their supervision by the Accountant of Court, with a view to proposing appropriate reform of the law where that may appear to be necessary."

And the other is:

"To consider the law relating to powers of attorney with a view to proposing appropriate reform of the law where that may appear to be necessary."

(See Scot Law Com No. 109, Twenty-Second Annual Report 1986-87 paras. 2.46-2.48.)

62. So far solicitors seem only to have tried inserting charging clauses into the prescribed form which appears to be acceptable to the Court of Protection although not expressly authorised— indeed it might actually be thought inconsistent with the explicit provision as to gifts, seasonal and anniversary, which may be made under section 3(5) of the 1985 Act.

63. Enduring Powers of Attorney Act 1985 section 3(1) and (2), emphasis supplied.

63. Ibid.

64. The Act provides no definition of "affairs" or "things".

65. The Enduring Powers of Attorney Act 1985 section 7.

66. Ibid, section 1(2)(a) [emphasis supplied].

67. Solicitor–attorneys might not welcome the risks of liability for inaction but should think of their charging clause as a *quid pro quo* and remember the lack of a monopoly here.

APPENDIX [Extract from Regulations]

Part B: To be completed by the 'donor' (the person appointing the attorney(s))
Don't sign this form unless you understand what it means

Please read the notes in the margin	
Donor's name and address	I _____
	of _____
Donor's date of birth	born on _____
Attorney(s) name(s) and address(es)	appoint _____
see note 1 on the front of this form. if you are appointing only one attorney you should cross out everything between the square brackets	of _____ • [and _____ of _____
Cross out the one which does not apply (see note 1 on the front of this form)	1. • jointly • jointly and severally] to be my attorney(s) for the purpose of the Enduring Powers of Attorney Act 1985
Cross out the one which does not apply (see note 2 on the front of this form)	• with general authority to act on my behalf • with authority to do the following on my behalf:
If you don't want the attorney(s) to have general power, you must give details here of what authority you are giving the attorney(s)	

Cross out the one which does not apply	in relation to
	   • all my property and affairs
	   • the following property and affairs:

Part B:continued

Please read the notes in
the margin

2 ● subject to the following restrictions and conditions:

If there are restrictions or
conditions, insert them
here; if not, cross out
these words (See note 3
on the front of this form)

I intend that this power shall continue even if I become
mentally incapable.

I have read or have had read to me the notes in Part A which
are part of, and explain, this form.

Your signature   Signed, sealed and
                                  delivered by me   _____

Date   on _____
someone must witness
your signature
Signature of witness   In the presence of _____

Your attorney(s) cannot   Full name of witness _____
be your witness. If you are
married it is not advisable
for your husband or wife   Address of witness _____
to be your witness
                                  _____

                                  _____

                                  _____

Part C: To be completed by the attorney(s)
- This form may be adapted to provide for sealing by a corporation with its common seal
- If there are more than two attorneys attach an additional Part C

Don't sign this form before the donor has signed Part B	I understand that I have a duty to apply to the Court for the registration of this form under the Enduring Powers of Attorney Act 1985 when the donor is becoming or has become mentally incapable. I also understand my limited power to use the donor's property to benefit persons other than the donor. I am not a minor
Signature of attorney	Signed, sealed and delivered by me _____
Date	on _____
Signature of witness	in the presence of _____
Each attorney must sign the form and each signature must be witnessed. The donor may not be the witness and one attorney may not witness the signature of the other	Full name of witness _____ Address of witness _____ _____ _____
To be completed only if there is a second attorney	I understand that I have a duty to apply to the Court for the registration of this form under the Enduring Powers of Attorney Act 1985 when the donor is becoming or has become mentally incapable. I also understand my limited power to use the donor's property to benefit persons other than the donor. I am not a minor
Signature of attorney	Signed, sealed and delivered by me _____
Date	on _____
Signature of witness	in the presence of _____
Each attorney must sign the form and each signature must be witnessed. The donor may not be the witness and one attorney may not witness the signature of the other	Full name of witness_____ Address of witness _____ _____ _____

Chapter 41

Living Wills in the United States: The Role of the Family

David S. ROSETTENSTEIN   University of Bridgeport,
                                                            USA

Introduction

Scientific and technological developments in the medical field have made it possible to maintain many of the vital functions of the human body notwithstanding the irreversible failure of, or damage to, other of the body's significant functions.[1] Apart from the fundamental question of when death has occurred,[2] these developments have raised the spectre of the "tyranny of technology"[3] — an artificially maintained life which substantively is not worth living.[4]

For nearly two decades, the law in the United States has grappled with the issues of whether, when, and how an individual might terminate or refuse life support treatment. The complex interaction of law, technology and ethics has now raised a new spectre, that of the tyranny of terminology.[5] The solution of problems in this field has become particularly pressing as the population has aged,[6] health care costs have risen,[7] and as degenerative diseases have replaced communicable diseases as the leading cause of death.[8] Although the resolution of the issues in this area is normally difficult, it becomes infinitely more so in the context of a patient who is comatose, or one whose mental competency is open to question.[9]

A cornerstone of the legal response in this area is provided by what is popularly and sometimes technically known as a living will — a directive executed by an individual when competent, indicating what medical treatment that individual does not wish to receive (or might wish to receive) should the receipt or continuance of that treatment be considered at a stage when the individual is not competent. In 1976 California became the first state to give statutory sanction to living wills.[10] Since that time, legislation in nearly forty jurisdictions has recognized some form of living will.[11]

This chapter starts by locating the concept of the living will in a broader legal context. Thereafter, some of the common prerequisites for the recognition and enforcement of living wills are looked at, along with a number of problems that the legislation has raised. Finally, other legal processes which are emerging to deal with the inadequacies of living will legislation are considered. Since the concern is with a patient who is in one sense or another incompetent, in many circumstances there will be a need for a surrogate decision-maker. Frequently, but not inevitably, the surrogate will be a member of the patient's family. A significant portion of this chapter focuses on the identity and role of that surrogate.

The Broader Legal Context

The concept of a living will was introduced into the legal literature by Kutner in 1969.[12] This took place in the context of an attempt to revive interest in euthanasia.[13] This environment might have led to the demise of the concept[14] were it not for the fact that constitutional law developments together with the analysis in the celebrated *Quinlan case*[15] provided a means of refocusing on the issue. In particular, in some instances, it became possible to consider the withholding of treatment not as something that was being done to the patient, but rather as something which the patient was choosing to do to himself or herself. However, it is necessary to backtrack for a moment, and in so doing, to observe that normally the extent to which a *competent* patient can control his or her medical care is regulated by the doctrines of common law tort[16] or constitutional law.

A. Common Law

Tort law recognizes that each individual is entitled to preserve his or her bodily integrity. Treatment violating that integrity is a basis for exposure to common law tort actions in the nature of battery[17] and the like. Since consent is a defense to these actions,[18] a line of analysis almost inevitably revolves around whether such consent was given. This raises the question of whether the patient was sufficiently well informed to give his or her consent.[19] Thus evolved the doctrine of informed consent. In due course, this doctrine came to occupy centre stage, with the doctor's failure to obtain the informed consent of the patient becoming actionable in its own right.[20]

The doctrine of informed consent, as outlined above, would seem to require that the patient agree to any proposed course of treatment[21] — at least for the doctor to be legally protected. This in turn suggests that a patient may prevent treatment by refusing to give his or her consent.[22] Thus, for a competent patient, faced with the prospect of a lingering technology-supported life, the solution seems to be to rely on this apparent right of refusal. However, the ability to do so depends upon whether state law, giving effect to its public policy concerns, is prepared to recognize an absolute right of refusal.[23] Here constitutional law comes into play — a topic that will be dealt with shortly. For the moment it should simply be noted that the legal development proceeds on the basis that it is the patient's autonomy which ought to be safeguarded.[24]

Of immediate interest to us, is the question of the patient's autonomy where the patient is incompetent[25] and thus unable to personally exercise such right of consent or refusal as may be available. The standard example of this is the medical emergency.[26] Here the law usually implies the patient's consent on the basis that a reasonable patient would so consent[27] — an objective reference standard. In such contexts, doctors try to obtain the consent of members of the patient's family. However, at common law, consent from a family member normally may have no legal significance so far as the patient's own right to consent is concerned. The family member's consent probably does no more than indicate the doctor's good faith and prevent consenting family members from successfully suing the doctor.[28] The ability of a mere family member, let alone a close friend, to exercise control in these situations becomes even more problematic when the issue is the refusal to allow treatment, or to compel the withdrawal of treatment. This aspect will be dealt with later on.

Our present concern involves a search for a legal vehicle by means of which an individual, *while competent,* might exercise the apparent right to choose or refuse treatment, so that that decision would be effective *even after the individual ceased to be competent.* The concept of a living will — an advance directive as to the individual's wishes — appeared to provide such a legal vehicle.

The common law efficacy of a living will is highly problematic. For example, does the doctrine of informed consent, which is the conceptual foundation for living wills, envisage the possibility of advance consent? After all, the doctrine is premised on the patient knowing his or her actual circumstances and the impact of treatment on them, in order to properly exercise the rights involved.[29] Does the advance directive actually cover the proposed treatment? To what extent does the patient's subsequent incompetency operate to revoke or prevent the revocation of the directive — an issue that it is necessary to deal with, if one envisages the possibility of the patient changing his or her mind? Finally, does a state's public policy, reflected in common law or statute, permit the recognition of such an advance directive, where the goal of the instrument in most instances is to facilitate the patient's death? Constitutional law developments brought some focus to the discussion of this last question, and it is to these developments that we now turn.

B. Constitutional Law

During the 1970's, the United States Supreme Court developed the fundamental right of privacy from within the interstices of the federal constitution. This court has never expressly acknowledged that the right of privacy protects an individual's ability to forego treatment. Nevertheless, numerous commentators and a number of state courts have accepted this to be the case.[30]

However, the acceptance that the regulation of treatment falls within the umbrella of the fundamental right of privacy, does not endow the individual with absolute control of his or her treatment. Rather, the legal significance is that to limit the patient's choice in this area, it is necessary for a state to advance important, substantial, or compelling reasons.[31]

Courts have come to recognize four interests which the state may seek to advance. These are the preservation of life, the protection of the interests of innocent third parties, the prevention of suicide, and the maintenance of the ethical integrity of the medical profession.[32] While in abstract these interests might appear compelling, their application in the context of certain specific fact patterns will require these interests to be balanced against the patient's asserted right of privacy.[33] In this balancing process, the state's actual interest may emerge as having little significance.[34] Thus, where the patient will die shortly anyway, the state interest in the preservation of life is generally of little import. By contrast, with a view to protecting the financial and emotional interests of a child of a patient, a state may make a cogent case, say, for compelling the blood transfusion of that patient, if the patient would recover as a result.[35]

One final aspect of the constitutional law needs to be looked at. Our primary concern is with patients who are incompetent. These individuals, for example, might be retarded, deranged, or permanently comatose. As was touched on above, the patient's physical state may have an impact on the interest balancing process. Thus, by way of example, a permanently comatose patient is unlikely to be able to affect the financial well-being of a child, except in a negative sense. But, beyond this type of issue, lies a more fundamental question: to what extent is it appropriate to consider a patient in, say, a chronic vegetative state, as having a right of privacy? A consensus seems to have emerged that these rights persist, notwithstanding the patient's condition.[36] But, how may these rights, vested in an incompetent person, be asserted? Like those rights arising from the common law doctrine of informed consent, the concept of a living will also appears to provide a suitable vehicle for the assertion of constitutional rights. However, the many problems associated with the common law and constitutional doctrines applicable to this area of law made the need for legislation compelling. This legislation will be considered now.

Living Will Statutes

A. Introduction

Nearly forty states have enacted legislation sanctioning living wills.[37] Although there is a significant divergence between the states in their treatment of the issues raised by the concept of a living will, generally speaking they all had to deal with the same concerns and, to some extent, a number of standard approaches have emerged.[38] Because of space considerations, this chapter will focus on only some of the aspects and problems of this legislation.

Before proceeding, it is useful to remember that what the legislation is seeking to identify and render enforceable, is a declaration or directive by a competent individual in which that individual indicates the circumstances — generally involving the individual's incompetency — in which he or she does not wish to receive (or might wish to receive) particular forms of medical treatment. We will now look at how the legislative schemes go about this process.

B. Form and Execution

Proof of the existence and content of a living will directive is a matter of critical importance. To this end, all living will statutes make provision for a written directive. In addition, a few states allow a directive to be issued in oral or other form.[39] Most statutes contain a standard form which may, but need not necessarily, be used for the directive.[40] Some statutes reserve to the patient the right to give individualized instructions in his or her living will.[41] But, some states require that any declaration must "substantially" comply — probably as to form and substance — with a specimen directive in the statute.[42]

Standard form facilitates the achievement of certainty in the scope and interpretation of the instrument. It also provides a means by which the nature and significance of the instrument may be communicated to the person executing it.[43] But the requirement of "substantial" compliance with a standard form has been criticized as possibly leading to a reluctance to follow a declaration which deviates from the sanctioned form,[44] especially since any care-provider's statutory legal immunity is usually premised on the existence of a facially valid declaration.[45]

Regardless of whether they insist on the use of a standard form declaration, states have tried to avoid doubts as to technical compliance with the act by enacting presumptions relating to such matters as the validity of the instrument[46] and the competency[47] of the patient at the time of execution. In addition, compliance with the declaration is encouraged by making defenses available to the health-care-provider. These defenses are premised on the provider's good faith,[48] compliance with reasonable medical standards,[49] or the absence of actual notice.[50] Some statutes specifically articulate a continuing liability for negligence.[51]

Virtually all states have significant requirements relating to the witnessing of the living will declaration. Two or more witnesses are usually required to establish the authenticity of the instrument.[52] To ensure that the witnesses are independent and that the execution of the instrument was uncoerced, states often prohibit a person related to the patient by blood, marriage, or adoption, from acting as a witness.[53] Such a provision tends to assist a patient to execute a declaration over the objections of family members who for psychological reasons would be opposed to the termination of treatment.[54] The elimination of family members as eligible witnesses also helps to minimize the risk that a patient is executing the instrument out of a sense of guilt towards family members.[55] Additionally, this type of provision is a means of protecting the patient from those who would usually stand to gain if the patient's assets are not consumed by the cost of medical care.[56] Some states have addressed this issue directly by prohibiting any person who stands to gain financially from the death of the declarant — even simply as a creditor of the declarant — from acting as a witness.[57]

Also suspect as a class of witnesses are those who are factually or financially responsible for the patient's health care.[58] Depending on the circumstances, these individuals, or the institutions which employ them, will see an increase or decrease in the factual or financial burden or benefit in the event of the patient's death. But there is also a suspicion that the dependency relationship between these potential witnesses and the patient is such that the patient's will may be overborne.[59] Accordingly, some states require that when a living will is executed in a hospital or nursing home, one of the formal participants in the process must be a patient's ombudsman or advocate.[60] To help ensure that the declaration is freely executed, a number of states specify that no doctor or health care facility can make it a condition of treatment that the patient has or has not executed a living will.[61]

Normally, it is envisioned that the patient will sign the declaration, but some states allow another person to sign on the patient's behalf.[62] In some states these substitutes may not provide health care to the patient nor be an individual who stands to gain financially from the patient's death.[63] A person may also be prohibited from acting as both witness and substitute declarant.[64]

The last aspect of the execution of a living will to be looked at is the capacity and competency of the individual executing the instrument. Normally, a person must be at least eighteen years old to execute a living will.[65] In addition, virtually all states require the individual to be competent or of sound mind.[66]

Many statutes use the term "competent", but virtually none explain it. At best, a state may attempt to mitigate the term's inherent obscurity by a tangential treatment. Thus statutes may create a presumption that the individual was of sound mind at the time of execution,[67] or specify that age should not be a factor in the determination of competency.[68] A significant number of states have legislated that the mere fact that the individual executed a living will should not be taken as an indication of incompetency.[69] Finally, some states impose essentially the same demands for execution of a living will as they require for the execution of a testamentary will.[70] Whatever the state's legislative treatment is, it would seem that its goal should be, and probably is, to ensure that the individual understands the nature and effect of the instrument being executed.[71]

"Competency" may require a technical analysis in other contexts as well. Statutes usually require the person executing the living will to be "competent" and envisage that the instrument will then become operative once the individual becomes unable to make decisions regarding health care procedures.[72] Although statutes generally do not emphasize the distinction, it would seem important to accept that being unable to make health care decisions does not *necessarily* mean that the individual is not "competent" to execute a living will.[73] For some individuals, this distinction keeps open the possibility of executing the instrument after the onset of the illness or injury.

There is a converse aspect to this analysis as well. Many statutes spell out that the patient's own decisions as to treatment will override the living will as long as the patient is able to make these decisions.[74] However, statutes generally also provide that a living will may be revoked, often without regard to the patient's mental state or competency,[75] and often with a minimum of formality.[76] What is usually required in such situations is the manifestation of an intent to revoke.[77] Obviously, because the situation may be irreversible once the instructions are implemented, legislatures have felt it desirable to err on the side of caution and thus make living wills readily revocable.[78] However, given that a living will would not even be relevant were it not for the fact that there were doubts about the patient's ability to supervise his or her own treatment, what the patient really intended to communicate regarding treatment and/or revocation may be problematic.[79] But as in the case of execution of the instrument, there probably is a class of patient who can formulate the intention to revoke the living will although unable to make treatment decisions. In any event, there is always going to be a potential tension in this area. On the one hand, the goal of living will legislation is to provide a means by which an individual's instructions can be made effective beyond the time when that individual is competent to issue those instructions.[80] But, on the other hand, it is desirable to keep the door to revocation open as wide as possible even where the patient's competency and intentions are doubtful.[81]

C. The Triggering Event

A major difficulty for people drafting legislation is to describe the circumstances in which a living will becomes operative. A variety of competing concerns are at work. First, there is the need to protect the patient's life. This would suggest that the will should only operate in narrowly defined circumstances. This concern would be reinforced by a general social concern with the sanctity of life and a traditional reluctance to support conduct having the appearance of euthanasia or suicide.[82] Against these concerns stand the common law and constitutional perspectives which suggest that a patient's rights should allow the patient to control the course of the treatment — or lack thereof. This view would require the operative circumstances to be defined as broadly as possible. Moreover, excessive constraints would increase the risk that the patient would be subjected to the very pain, suffering and indignity which the recognition of living wills was intended to avoid, for example where the statute's substantive or procedural requirements only permit treatment withholding at a very late stage or after a long delay.[83]

With these considerations in mind, recent legislation tends to demand that the patient be suffering from an illness, disease or injury from which he or she cannot recover,[84] or as some statutes put it, which is "incurable or irreversible".[85] To dispel notions that the statute supports euthanasia, legislation often requires that without the administration of the so-called "life-sustaining" treatment the patient's condition would result in the patient's death.[86] In the same vein, many states do not want to be seen to be permitting conduct which accelerates death. They require that in the absence of the relevant treatment, death would be "imminent" or occur in a "short" or "relatively short" time.[87] In principle, the more proximate death must be before treatment is withheld, the greater is the likelihood that the patient's suffering will be extended.

A requirement that death be proximate, or that the condition cause death produces other problems. A significant source of difficulty is the patient in a persistent vegetative state. This state, or whatever caused it, need not, in and of itself, result in death.[88] As a consequence, it may not be possible to activate a living will. Very few states have made a specific effort to address this problem.[89] In the absence of such an effort, individuals like those in a vegetative state may have to seek their relief through a different legal vehicle. We shall return to this topic later. For the moment, we must consider yet another set of restrictions tending to limit the efficacy of living will legislation, namely, those provisions dealing with the nature of the treatment which may be withheld.

D. Treatment To be Withheld

The provisions regulating the treatment which may be withheld also seek to indicate that the law does not sanction suicide or euthanasia. Accordingly, in most states it is only treatment which serves to "prolong the dying process" that may be covered by a living will.[90] Since, in one sense, the dying process begins at the moment of birth, legislators have long wrestled with how to describe the relevant procedures. Much of the early literature in the field characterized the procedures as "heroic" or "extraordinary". But, given the pace of development, today's "heroic" is tomorrow's "passé".[91] Accordingly, some legislation sought comfort in highlighting the artificiality of the procedure involved.[92] It might rely on a "technical or electronic device", or "mechanical or other artificial means" which assisted or replaced a "vital" "organ" or "function".[93] However, depending on one's viewpoint, this type of terminology tends to be seen as too broad, or not broad enough, as technology continues to push medicine and the law to the outer limits of ethical comfort. This is most obvious when efforts are made to deal with the consequences of artificial feeding.[94]

In many common medical procedures intravenous feeding or hydration is employed. Obviously, such techniques can readily be described as a "mechanical" or "artificial" means used to assist or replace a "vital" function. This means that it is necessary to decide if there is any jurisprudential basis for distinguishing these techniques from, say, the use of a nasogastric or a jejeunostomy tube which feed and hydrate through the nose or the intestine.[95] These latter techniques are often the major reason why a patient in a persistent vegetative state remains alive.[96]

Some states have realized that a technical description of the treatment which may be withheld is often both irrational and inefficient. Accordingly they restrict living wills to covering treatment which only "prolongs the dying process" and at the same time, indicate procedures which may *not* be withheld.[97] In relation to artificial feeding (which clearly is capable of prolonging the dying process), this approach forces a state to face the hard question of when, if at all, it is acceptable to allow a patient to die through starvation or dehydration.[98] A significant number of statutes prohibit the withholding of food and water when implementing the instructions in a living will.[99] However, unless the state can demonstrate a compelling legitimate interest for the continuation of artificial feeding, given the patient's underlying constitutional rights, these restrictions may be invalid.[100] Conversely, some states specifically permit the withdrawal of artificial feeding generally,[101] while others do so in limited circumstances.[102] Finally, many statutes indicate that life sustaining treatment may not be withdrawn pursuant to a living will directive if the treatment is necessary for patient comfort or the relief of pain.[103] Again, for constitutional reasons, this prohibition may also be invalid.

E. Shortcomings

Although living will legislation appears to meet a crying need for relief, in some ways it raises as many problems as it solves. Indeed, in the eyes of its harshest critics, living will legislation does more harm than good.[104] Certainly, the technicality of the statutes raises the spectre of uncertainty as to the validity of execution, whether there is substantial compliance with a mandatory form, whether the conditions to trigger the will's operation have been met, and whether the treatment to be withheld falls within the scope of the act.[105] It is argued that because of these types of uncertainties, medical care providers will be more reluctant to withhold treatment than they previously were when the issue was regulated by common law principles and the dictates of medical ethics and sound practice.[106]

The fact that most states have now enacted some form of legislation covering living wills, coupled with the mobility of the American population,[107] has added a further wrinkle to what is already a complex legal situation. The technical scope and underlying policy concerns of the various statutes often diverge. Yet very few legislatures have tackled the conflicts of laws analysis applicable to a living will executed in another state.[108] The few efforts made have sought to render enforceable a living will if it is valid in the state in which it was executed.[109]

Beyond the technical complexity of living will legislation, ignorance and inertia may be the greatest stumbling blocks to assisting a patient to regulate his or her terminal care.[110] The vast majority of individuals have not executed a living will and probably would not do so even if they were aware of the possibility.[111] In such circumstances, to regulate their treatment, patients have to fall back on whatever other legal rights they may possess. This too is the fate of those who never were competent to execute a living will. Fortunately, the majority of recent living will legislation has made it clear that the rights generated by the legislation do not impair such other legal rights to have treatment withdrawn as may exist.[112] It is in the exercise of the patient's rights which exist outside of living will legislation that the role of the family really comes to the fore.

The Role Of The Family

A. As Recognized by Living Will Statutes

By way of transition it should be noted that there are areas where some living will statutes themselves identify a role for family members and in a few statutes the nature of the family's role is very dramatic indeed.

First, as to the less dramatic aspects of the legislation, a physician may be required to advise family members of his or her intention to implement a living will directive so that they will have an opportunity to challenge this decision.[113] Similarly, before carrying out the directive, the physician may be required to obtain the consent of the "next of kin".[114] Also, if the treating physician is unable to implement the directive in a living will because of reasons of conscience, the family may be able to compel the transfer of the patient to another physician.[115]

In some states the family's role may be characterized as dramatic because the statute may permit family members to themselves execute a living will on behalf of the patient. The basis on which this is to be done is not always clear. It may be that in some versions the statute's authority extends no further than to the technical execution of the instrument pursuant to the patient's actual directions.[116] However, in some statutes, treatment may be withheld where the patient is not competent to direct his own care and has not executed a living will, if the written or perhaps oral consent of a member of the patient's family is obtained.[117] The statute may give no indication as to what considerations should regulate the family member's decision. This approach should be contrasted with that of at least one living will statute which enables a family member and the physician to decide to withdraw treatment based upon what the patient would have desired — if known.[118] Although the statutory language is not clear, it suggests that even if the patient's desires are not known, the decision to withhold treatment may be made on the basis of what the patient might have desired. This is known as the "substituted judgment" approach.[119] It reflects what appears to be an emerging judicial viewpoint based upon the interaction of common law and constitutional principles. We shall return to this topic later.

It is interesting to note that in many of the instances just outlined, where the statute authorizes or requires a family member's consent, the family member is just one of a number of alternative individuals who may consent; that there is commonly a priority among the alternatives; that the family member is often not ranked highest in the order; and that even between family members there may be a priority. Typically, the patient's spouse will be preferred over adult children, parents, siblings and near relatives — in that order. Legal guardians or individuals designated by the patient usually take priority over any members of the group just mentioned.[120] However, often the legal guardian or designated individual will be a member of this group. It seems logical to accord the highest priority to the patient's choice, or to the court's preference after a guardianship inquiry. Beyond that, the ranking scheme is somewhat arbitrary, but presumably it is premised on the legislature's view as to who is more likely to be familiar with the patient's wishes and have the patient's interests at heart.[121]

B. Outside of Living Will Legislation

While there are thus a few statutory schemes which expressly accord family members the authority to participate in a decision to withhold treatment from an incompetent patient who has not executed a living will, most states have no such scheme. Nor is it too surprising that legislatures have declined to set foot in the value-laden bramble-bush thicket that this area of law represents, despite frantic pleas for assistance from the courts.[122]

One statutory avenue may enable a patient to help himself or herself. All states have legislation making it possible to generate what is called a durable power of attorney.[123] Under these schemes, the attorney's authority to act persists after the patient ceases to be competent, notwithstanding the normal common law rule of agency to the contrary.[124] This statutory device was developed as a cheaper and more efficient alternative to guardianship proceedings to provide a substitute decision-maker for an individual unable to manage his or her affairs.[125]

Unfortunately, only a handful of states have clearly indicated that a durable power may be used to give the attorney-in-fact (as the incompetent's designee is known) the authority to make medical decisions for the incompetent.[126] There is some doubt that the attorney-in-fact's authority extends to the area of medical treatment, partly because the statutory schemes were originally formulated with a view to protecting the incompetent's estate, and partly because it is suggested that the nature of the decisions required are too personal to be delegable.[127] However, some state courts have accepted that the durable power legislation may be applied to medical decision-making.[128] In these contexts, the patient might designate a family member as attorney-in-fact, but would not be obligated to do so.

The recognition of durable powers in this area of law would help to protect the patient's autonomy, if not as to the actual decision, then at least as to the decision-maker. This procedural option is likely to become of greater significance, because, in the absence of a living will or other legislation, there appears to be a slowly emerging trend for state courts to develop common law procedures by which treatment-withholding decisions may be made.[129] Furthermore, there seems to be a strong inclination to disengage the courts from this decision-making process, and to deposit responsibility with the medical community and members of the patient's family.[130]

In this regard, in the absence of a compelling indication to the contrary, for example by the patient executing a durable power naming a non-family member as attorney-in-fact,[131] courts presume to look to members of the patient's traditional family as people who are likely to know the patient's subjective preferences and who are likely to act out of a concern for the patient.[132] Unfortunately, as individuals become older, and in the context of relatively smaller families and a mobile society, there is a real risk that the patient may have no surviving relatives who have close contact with the patient.[133] This contact is surely a prerequisite for the knowledge and concern which the court assumes when endowing these family members with decision-making authority. Further, in any event, the community of interest which courts assume to exist between patient and family may actually be absent.[134]

To patients without family or close family ties, a living will or a durable power of attorney would appear to be preferred methods of asserting control over decisions to withhold treatment. Unfortunately both of these techniques require affirmative acts. Thus, it is likely that for the forseeable future most patients will become subject to statutory or court-devised common law schemes for substituted decision-making.

As to the latter, probably no state's courts have gone further than those of New Jersey[135] in developing common law procedures by which a decision to withhold treatment may be made.[136] Starting with a premise of a patient's right to self-determination reflected in the common law and constitutional law,[137] New Jersey courts have sought to develop a set of procedures involving a series of checks and balances.[138] As a result, when a patient becomes incompetent, while interested parties are able to participate in the decision-making process, these parties' own interests are not allowed to operate to the detriment of the patient's wishes as far as they are known or assumed to exist. New Jersey law has accepted that, once a patient becomes incompetent, his or her rights may be asserted by a surrogate decision-maker.[139] Three different substituted decision-making approaches[140] have been described by the courts.

The purely "subjective" approach[141] seeks to give effect to the patient's own wishes. Because it is the patient's actual wishes that are to be followed, this procedure has fewer safeguards once the wishes have been identified. However, special care is required to establish that they are the patient's wishes. The proof required is such as would satisfy a "clever and convincing" evidentiary standard.[142] Such proof might be provided, for example, by a "living will" (even though New Jersey has no living will legislation), or by a durable power of attorney to make medical decisions, coupled with strong evidence as to what the patient's wishes were.[143]

The court-developed procedures involve a medical evaluation by the patient's physician and an independent medical evaluation.[144] If the patient is elderly (over sixty), the state's Ombudsman for the Institutionalized Elderly, an official charged with protecting elderly patients from abuse,[145] must be notified.[146] If the standards of the "subjective" approach are satisfied and if the patient designated a family member or close friend to make medical decisions, the court requires the ombudsman to defer to that person.[147] If the patient made no such designation, the ombudsman is to defer to a close, caring, family member — normally a spouse, parent, adult child or sibling.[148] If there is no family member or no appropriate family member, a guardian has to be appointed,[149] *even if* it is possible to identify a close friend as the person who most cares about the patient.[150] The court's structural preference for family members arises because of a perception that the family "has an intimate understanding of the patient's medical attitudes and general world view", and that they are most likely to be concerned about the patient's "comfort, care and best interests."[151]

Where there is no clear and convincing evidence as to the patient's subjective wishes, two other lines of analysis have developed. Under the "limited-objective" approach, the ombudsman must defer to the surrogate decision-maker's decision to withhold or terminate treatment, if there is "trustworthy" (as distinct from clear) evidence that the patient would have declined the treatment and the burdens to the patient, in terms of pain and suffering, markedly outweigh the benefits in terms of physical pleasure, emotional enjoyment, or intellectual satisfaction.[152] Finally, under the so-called "objective" approach, to be used if there is no evidence or less than trustworthy evidence of the patient's wishes, the ombudsman must defer to the surrogate's decision, if the pain and suffering of the patient's life clearly and markedly outweigh the benefit, and the patient is suffering from so much pain that prolonging his or her life would be inhumane.[153]

Where the patient is in a persistent vegetative state, the tests balancing benefits and burdens are abandoned (as is the subjective-objective distinction) in favour of a simple analysis as to whether there is a reasonable possibility of a return to a cognitive sapient state. If the attending physician and the independent medical evaluation answers this in the negative, the ombudsman must defer to the guardian and the family if they agree that the patient would have wanted the treatment terminated.[154] In this regard, they need only exercise their "best judgment" which need not be supported by clear and convincing evidence of the patient's intentions.[155]

The procedures developed by the New Jersey courts reflect that they have essentially withdrawn from the decision-making arena, at least absent a conflict between the parties to whom responsibility is left.[156] One reason for this withdrawal may be that in some scenarios the decision-making process involves an evaluation of the quality of the patient's remaining life. Concern for the patient's autonomy should require this evaluation to be conducted from the subjective perspective of the patient. However, if performed by the court, there is a real risk of the decision taking on objective overtones and being transformed from one of the patient's view as to the quality of his or her life, to a decision about the value of life in general and of this patient's life to society in particular.[157] While New Jersey courts shy away from such involvement, other jurisdictions have been less diffident. They require that the court lend its *imprimatur* to the decision to withhold treatment.[158]

Relatively few jurisdictions have conclusively resolved the question of the role of the courts in the decision to withhold treatment.[159] But, the demands of judicial economy, coupled with an appreciation that a cumbersome judicial process may effectively frustrate the rights sought to be protected, and given the difficult nature of the underlying decisions which are probably inappropriate for a public forum in any event, it seems likely that, in time, most states will adopt the New Jersey approach and commit the decision-making to the care of the medical profession and the family.[160]

Conclusion

United States constitutional and common law recognizes that a patient has the right to refuse treatment. A living will appears to be an ideal legal vehicle by means of which an individual could assert this right, should the need to do so arise at a time when he or she is no longer competent to exercise personal control of health care decisions. However, statutes significantly limit the circumstances in which a living will may be employed — with reference both to the patient's condition and the treatment which may be withheld. Moreover, the execution of a living will requires an affirmative act by the patient as well as compliance with specified statutory formalities. As a result, it is likely that at the critical moment, relatively few patients will have the benefit of an operative living will.

In the absence of a living will, the patient might be able to exercise indirect control by having executed a durable power of attorney authorizing another person to make treatment decisions on the patient's behalf. While only some living will statutes provide a role for the patient's family, it would seem likely that the person appointed as attorney-in-fact under a durable power would often be a family member. However, again, the durable power requires an advance affirmative act. Accordingly, unless a relevant statutory scheme exists, it is likely that most patients will be left with no more than whatever common law procedures may be available to assert a right to have treatment withheld in the face of a lingering death at the hands of a tyrannical technology. In this context, it seems likely that most courts will allow the patient's physicians and family to decide whether treatment should be withheld. This seems appropriate, since generally the family is more likely than others to know the patient's views as to the character of a meaningful life, and indeed, as to the value of life itself, the issues which, after all, are at the heart of the decision to withhold treatment.

Notes

1. For some examples, see *Hearings on Death with Dignity Before the Senate Special Comm. on Aging,* 92d Cong., 2d Sess. 79 (1972) [hereinafter cited as *Hearings on Death*].
2. See President's Comm'n for the Study of Ethical Problems in Medicine and Biomedical and Behavioral Research, *Deciding to forego Life-Sustaining Treatment* 172-173 (1983) [hereinafter cited as *Deciding to Forego*].
3. Johnson, "Sequential Domination, Autonomy and Living Wills," 9 *Western New England L. Rev.* 113, 118 (1987); Note, "Rejection of Extraordinary Medical Care by a Terminal Patient: A Proposed Living Will Statute, 64 *Iowa L. Rev.* 573, 577 (1979) [hereinafter cited as *Rejection of Extraordinary Medical Care*].
4. See *Leach v. Akron Gen. Medical Center,* No. C 10-10-20 (Ohio Common Pleas Court, 1980), quote in "In Re Storar: The Right to Die and Incompetent Patients," 43 *U. Pitt. L. Rev.* 1087, 1107 (1982).
5. See Burt, "Withholding Nutrition and Mistrusting Nurturance: The Vocabulary of *In re Conroy,*" 2 *Issues in L. and Med.* 317 (1987); Horan and Marzen, "Death With Dignity and the "Living Will"; A Commentary on Legislative Developments," 5 *J. of Legis.* 81 (1978).
6. Martyn and Jacobs, "Legislating Advance Directives for the Terminally Ill: The Living Will and Durable Power of Attorney," 63 *Neb. L. Rev.* 779, 785 n.34 (1984); Bureau of Census, U.S. Dept of Commerce, *Statistical Abstract of the United States* 1987, 14, Table 13, *Total Population by Age and Sex] 1960 to 1985.*
7. *Deciding to Forego,* supra n. 2, 95-100, 243-244; Cantor, *Legal Frontiers of Death and Dying* 83-84 (1987); Martyn and Jacobs, supra n.6., 785; Bureau of Census, supra n.6, 85, Table 126, *National Health Expenditures by Type: 1970 to 1985.*
8. *Deciding to Forego,* supra n.2, 16.
9. Ibid., at 171 et seq. and 121 et seq.
10. Natural Death Act, Cal. Health and Safety Code Section §§7185-7195)West Supp. 1987). The legal efficacy of a living will not sanctioned by a statute is unknown; see infra, text associated with n.29.
11. For a comprehensive list together with citations, see Society for the Right to Die, *Handbook of Living Will Laws,* 1987 edition, 28-29 (1987).
12. Kutner, "Due Process of Euthanasia: The Living Will, A Proposal," 44 *Indiana L.J.* 539 (1969).
13. Ibid.; Williams, *The Sanctity of Life and the Criminal Law* (1957).
14. Kamisar," Some Non-religious Views Against Proposed "Mercy-Killing" Legislation," 42 *Minn. L. Rev.* 969 (1958).
15. *Matter of Quinlan,* 70 N.J. 10, 355 A. 2d 647 (1976).
16. The issue might be regulated by contract law. But, patient ignorance, practitioner reluctance, and an absence of foresight or a stable relationship between doctor and patient, has meant that there is little established law; see Shultz, "From Informed Consent to Patient Choice: A New Protected Interest," 95 *Yale L.J.* 219, 264-265 (1985).
17. *Schloendorff v. Society of N.Y. Hosp.,* 211 N.Y. 125, 129, 105 N.E. 92, 93 (1914); *Matter of Conroy,* 98 N.J. 321, 346, 486 A. 2d 1209, 1222 (1985).
18. *Matter of Storar,* 52 N.Y. 2d 363, 376, 420 N.E. 2d 64, 70 (1981).

19. For example, *Estate of Leach v. Shapiro,* 13 Ohio App. 3d 393, 395, 469 N.E. 2d 1047, 1052 (Ohio App. 1984).

20. Shultz, supra n.16, 226-227.

21. *Matter of Conroy,* supra n.17, 346, 486 A. 2d at 1222.

22. Ibid., 347, 486 A. 2d at 1222; *Bouvia v. Superior Court,* 179 Cal. App. 3d 1127, 1138, 225 Cal. Rptr. 297, 301 (Cal. App. 2 Dist. 1986).

23. *Matter of Welfare of Colyer,* 99 Wash. 2d 114, 121, 660 P. 2d 738, 743 (1983); *Bouvia,* supra n.22, 1142-1147, 225 Cal. Rptr. at 304-307.

24. *Matter of Conroy,* supra n.17, 348, 486 A. 2d at 1223. This is somewhat fictional, since informed consent is tested on the basis of what an ordinary competent doctor would have done or on the basis of what a reasonable patient would have desired to know, see Shultz, supra n.16, at 227.

25. As in *Matter of Conroy,* supra n.17.

26. For example see *Estate of Leach,* supra n.19, 395, 469 N.E. 2d at 1052.

27. Note, "The "Living Will": The Right to Death with Dignity," 26 *Case W. Res, L. Rev.* 485, 494 (1976).

28. Note, Appointing an Agent to Make Medical Treatment Choices, 84 Colum. L. Rev. 985, 994 (1984). But see, *In Matter of Spring,* 8 Mass. App. 831, 836, 399 N.E. 2d 493, 497, n.5 (1979).

29. Schulz, supra n.16, 227.

30. For example, see Martyn and Jacobs, supra n.6, 784-785 and cases cited in n.31. But see, "Maine's Living Will Act and the Termination of Life-Sustaining Medical Procedures," 39 *Me. L. Rev.* 83, 115 (1987).

31. For example, see *Matter of Welfare of Colyer,* supra n.23, 123, 660 P.2d at 744.

32. For example, see *Superintendent of Belchertown State Sch. v. Saikewicz,* 373 Mass. 728, 741, 370 N.E. 2D 417, 425 (1977).

33. For example, see *Bartling v. Superior Court,* 163 Cal. App. 3d 186, 195, 209 Cal. Rptr. 220, 225 (Cal. App. 2 Dist. 1984).

34. For example, see *Matter of Conroy,* supra n.17, 349-353, 486 A. 2d at 1223-1225.

35. See *Application of the President and Directors of Georgetown College, Inc.,* 331 F. 2d 1000, 1008 (D.C. Cir. 1964); *Matter of Conroy,* supra n.17, 353, 486 A. 2d at 1225. By contrast see *Matter of Farrell,* 108 N.J. 335, 352, 529 A. 2d 404, 413 (1987).

36. *Matter of Quinlan,* supra n.15, 41, 355 A. 2d at 644; "Note, Equality for the Elderly Incompetent: A Proposal for Dignified Death," 39 *Stanford L. Rev.* 689, 705 (1987).

37. Supra n.11. These statutes are often called "Natural Death" statutes, probably because of the original California statute, supra n.10.

38. In 1985 the National Conference of Commissioners on Uniform State Laws adopted the Uniform Rights of the Terminally Ill Act, Section 1-18, 9B U.L.A. 609 (1985). Six states have adopted at least some of the Uniform Act's provisions.

39. For example, Tex. Rev. Civ. Stat. Ann. art. 4590h, Section 3(b) (Vernon supp. 1987).

40. For examp;le, N.H. Rev. Stat. Ann. Section 137-H:3 (Supp. 1986).

41. For example, Tex. Rev. Civ. Stat. Ann. art. 4590h, Section 3(e) (Vernon Supp. 1987).

42. For example, Md. Health-Gen. Code Ann. Section 5-602(c) (1) (Supp. 1986).

43. For example, S.C. Code Ann. Section 44-77-50 (Law. Co-op. Supp. 1986).

44. Horan and Marzen, supra n.5, 85-86.

45. For example see, Note, "The California Natural Death Act: An Empirical Study of Physicians' Practices," 31 *Stanford L. Rev.* 913, 923 n.54 (hereinafter cited as *The California Natural Death Act)*. The California statute requires the physician to investigate the validity of the direcive.
46. For example, Haw. Rev. Stat. Section 327D-5(a) (Supp. 1986).
47. For example, Ariz. Rev. Stat. Ann. Section 36-3205(B) (1986).
48. For example, Ariz. Rev. Stat. Ann. Section 36-3205(C) (1986).
49. For example, Iowa Code Ann. Section 144 A.9(2) (West Supp. 1986).
50. For example, S.C. Code Ann. Section 44-77-90 (Law. Co-op. Supp. 1986).
51. For example, Okla. Stat. Ann. Tit. 63, Section 3106 (West Supp. 1987).
52. Even indeed if the declaration is oral. See Tex. Rev. Civ. Stat. Ann. art. 4590h, Section 3(b) (Vernon Supp. 1987).
53. For example, Haw. Rev. Stat. Sections 327D-3(b), 327D-4 (Supp. 1986).
54. The family's emotional and rational responses may be in conflict. See *Hearings on Death,* supra n.1, 89.
55. *Rejection of Extraordinary Medical Care,* supra n.3, 578.
56. See Cantor, supra n.7, 87-91.
57. For example, Md. Health-Gen. Code Ann. Section 5-602(a) (4) (Supp. 1986).
58. Ibid.
59. *Deciding to Forego,* supra N.2, 49-50, 143-144.
60. For example, S.C. Code Ann. Section 44-77-60 (Law. Co-op. Supp. 1986).
61. For example, N.H. Rev. Stat. Ann. Section 137-H:11 (Supp. 1986). The health care provider's attitude will presumably reflect the provider's ethical position or the patient's financial resources.
62. For example, Mo. Ann. Stat. Section 459.015 1(2) (Vernon Supp. 1987).
63. For example, Colo. Rev. Stat. Section 15-18-105 (Supp. 1986).
64. For example, Mo. Ann. Stat. Section 459.015 (4) (Vernon Supp. 1987).
65. For example, Alaska Stat. Section 18.12.010(a) (1986); but see Okla. Stat. Ann. tit. 63, Section 3102(5) (West Supp. 1987).
66. For example, Alaska, supra; Ind. Code Ann. Section 16-8-11-11(a) (Burns Supp. 1987).
67. For example, Haw. Rev. Stat. Section 327D-5(b) (Supp. 1986).
68. Ibid., Section 327D-5(c).
69. Ibid., See also *Hearings on Death,* supra. n.1., 83.
70. For example, Ill. Ann. Stat. ch. 110 1/2, para. 703 (Smith-Hurd Supp. 1987); N.M. Stat. Ann. Section 24-7-3 (1986); Nev. Rev. Stat. Section 449.600 (1985).
71. See *Deciding to Forego,* supra n.2, 44-45, 149. This work sees the critical issue as whether the patient is able to understand the choices involved in the decision.
72. For example, Colo. Rev. Stat. Section 15-18-104(1) (Supp. 1986).
73. See *Matter of Conroy,* supra n.17, 382-383, 486 A. 2d at 1241, where the converse situation is discussed.
74. For example, Alaska Stat. Section 18.12.040(a) (1986).
75. For example, Me. Rev. State. Ann. tit. 22, Section 2923(1) (Supp. 1986).
76. Ibid.
77. Ibid.
78. See *Matter of Conroy,* supra n.17, 368, 486 A. 2d at 1233.
79. The law may have to deal with a conflict between the apparent wishes of the patient and the instructions of a designated proxy: see *Deciding to Forego,* supra n2, 152.
80. *Deciding to Forego,* supra n.2, 142-143.

81. Shultz, supra n.16, 292.
82. For example, see Me. Rev. Stat. Ann. tit. 22, Section 2929(6) (Supp. 1986).
83. *Deciding to Forego*, supra n.2, 142-143, see also comment, "Changing Attitudes in Florida's 'Right to Die' Law," XIV *Stetson L. Rev.* 375, 393 (1985).
84. For example, S.C. Code Ann. Section 44-77-20(d) (Law. Co-op. Supp. 1986).
85. For example, Haw. Rev. Stat. Section 327D-2 (Supp. 1986).
86. For example, Ark. Stat. Ann. Sections 82-3801(4) and 82-3801(9) (Supp. 1987).
87. For example, Md. Health-Gen. Code Ann. Section 5-601(g) (Supp. 1986); Mo. Ann Stat. Section 459.010(3) (Vernon Supp. 1987); Alaska Stat. Section 18.12.100(7) (1986). A few states like Arizona do not require that death must be anticipated within a specified time; Rev. Stat. Ann. Section 36-3201(6) (1986).
88. *Deciding to Forego*, supra n.2, 171-181; *Matter of Jobes,* 108 N.J. 394, 403-407, 529 A. 2d 434, 438-440.
89. For example, Arkansas allows treatment to be withdrawn if the treatment serves to maintain the patient in a condition of permanent unconsciousness; Ark. Stat. Ann. Section 82-3801(4) (Supp. 1987).
90. For example, Ind. Code Ann. Section 16-8-ll-4(2) (Burns Supp. 1987).
91. Gelfand, "Euthanasia and the Terminally Ill Patient," 63 *Neb. L. Rev.* 741, 754, 563 (1984); *Moral, Ethical, and Legal Questions of Extraordinary Health Care, 1975,* Hearings before the Subcomm. on Health of the Senate Comm. on Labor and Public Welfare, November 6, 1975, 21-22. Because it is difficult to give substance to a distinction between "ordinary" and "extraordinary" procedures, the President's Commission suggested that the focus should be on the burdens imposed on the patient versus the utility of the treatment: *Deciding to Forego*, supra n.2., 88. See too Cantor, supra n.7, 35-38, *Matter of Conroy*, supra n.17, 371, 486 A. 2d at 1234-1235.
92. See *Moral, Ethical and Legal Questions of Extraordinary Health Care, 1975*, supra n.91, 18.
93. For example, see Conn. Gen Stat. Ann. Section 19(a)-570(1) (West Supp. 1987); Ind. Code Ann. Section 16-8-11-4(1) (Burns Supp. 1987).
94. Cantor, supra n.7, 38-45.
95. Ibid., 39-40.
96. See for example, *Barber v. Superior Court,* 147 Cal. App 3d 1006, 1010-1011, 195 Cal. Rptr. 484, 486 (Cal. App. 2 Dist. 1983).
97. For example, Colo. Rev. Stat. Section 15-18-103(7) (Supp. 1986).
98. Tennessee allows the withholding of artificial or forced feeding, but will not allow "the withholding of simple nourishment or fluids so as to condone death by starvation or dehydration.": Tenn. Code Ann. Section 32-11-103(5) (Supp. 1987). See also, Cantor, supra n.7, 39-40.
99. For example Colorado, supra n.97.
100. *Bouvia,* supra n.22, 1142-1147, 225 Cal. Rptr. at 304-307;. see also *Corbett v. D'Alessandro,* 487 So. 2d 368 (Fla. Dist. Ct. App. 1986).
101. For example, see the Declaration in Alaska Stat. Section 18.12.010(c) (1986).
102. Supra, n.98.
103. For example Colorado, supra n.97. Many statutes prohibit the withholding of treatment if the patient is pregnant: for example see Alaska Stat. Section 18.12.040(c) (1986). These provisions give rise to significant constitutional law difficulties.
104. Horan and Marzen, supra n.5, 82-83.

105. See for example, *The California Natural Death Act,* supra n.45, 932-933.
106. See for example, *Deciding to Forego*, supra, n.2, 144-145. There is some empirical support for this position: see *The California Natural Death Act,* supra n.45, 939. It is argued that rigid common law rules are equally undesirable: see Burt, supra, n.5, 329.
107. Approximately 9% of the total population changed state between 1980 and 1985: Bureau of Census, supra n.6, 25, Table 29, *Mobility Status of the Population by Selected Characteristics- 1980-1985.*
108. Only three states of the nineteen that have enacted or amended living will legislation in the last two years have attempted to do so.
109. Ark. Stat. Ann. Section 82-3812 (Supp. 1987); Me. Rev. Stat. Ann. tit. 22, Section 2930 (Supp. 1986); Mont. Code Ann. Section 50-9-111 (1987).
110. For example see, Barber, supra n.96, 1014-1015, 195 Cal. Rptr. at 489.
111. Thus, while sanctioned by legislation, no living will had been executed in *Matter of Welfare of Colyer,* supra n.23. In *Matter of Jobes,* supra n.88, 409-410, 529 A. 2d at 442, although New Jersey has no legislation sanctioning a living will, the patient had actually gone as far as to acquire a standard form card declaring her wishes, but it could not be found.
112. For example, Iowa Code Ann. Section 144A. 11(5) (West Supp. 1986). Courts have come to the same conclusion: see for example, *Matter of Welfare of Colyer*, supra n.23, 118, 660 P. 2d at 741.
113. For example, Colo. Rev. Stat. Section 15-18-107 (Supp. 1986).
114. For example, Conn. Gen. Stat. Ann. Section 19(a)-571 (West Supp. 1987).
115. For example, Tenn. Code Ann. Section 32-11-108 (Supp. 1987).
116. See Utah Code Ann. Section 75-2-ll04(2) (b) (Supp. 1987); but contrast Ark. Stat. Ann. Section 82-3814 (Supp. 1987).
117. Utah Code Ann. Section 75-2-1107 (Supp. 1987); Conn. Gen. Stat. Ann. Section 19(a)-571 (West Supp. 1987).
118. Contrast Utah, supra n.117, with Tex. Rev. Civ. Stat. Ann. art. 4590h, Section 4C(b).
119. See for example, *Appointing an Agent to Make Medical Treatment Choices,* supra n.28, 1003-1004; *Maine's Living Will Act and the Termination of Life-Sustaining Medical Procedures,* supra n.30, 83. The expression is somewhat confusing since the basis for the decision may range from the patient's known wishes to objective considerations such as a balancing of the treatment's benefits and burdens to the patient or simply the patient's prognosis. Objective considerations are sometimes said to trigger a "best interests" approach rather than a "substituted judgment" approach: ibid. In an attempt to avoid the confusion, this chapter uses the expression "substituted decision-making" as reflecting the procedure rather than the standards (infra, text associated with n.140 et seq.).
120. See for example, Iowa Code Ann. Section 144A.7(1) (West Supp. 1986); Texas Rev. Civ. Stat. Ann. art. 4590h, Section 4C (Vernon Supp. 1987); Utah Code Ann. Section 75-2-1105(2)(6) (Supp. 1987).
121. See *Deciding to Forego*, supra n.2, 128. Ideally, there should be some formal or informal screening process: See Cantor, supra n.7, 109. The influence of medical professionals should not be overlooked: id., 108-109.
122. For example, see *Severns v. Wilmington Medical Center, Inc.,* 421 A. 2d 1334, 1346 (Del. 1980).
123. The statutes vary considerably: see *Appointing an Agent to Make Medical*

Treatment Choices, supra n.28, 1012 n.175.

124. Ibid., 1014.
125. Ibid.
126. See Martyn and Jacobs, supra n.6,. 787.
127. *Matter of Storar,* supra, n.18, 378, 420 N.E. 2d at 71.
128. *Matter of Peter by Johanning,* 108 N.J. 365, 378-379, 529 A. 2d 419, 426 (1987).
129. Note, "The "Terminal Condition" Condition in Virginia's Natural Death Act," 73 *Va. L. Rev.* 749, 769 et seq. (1987).
130. *Matter of Peter by Johanning,* supra n.128, 385, 529 A. 2d at 430.
131. See ibid., 384, 529 A. 2d at 429.
132. *Matter of Jobes,* supra n.88, 414-420, 529 A. 2d at 444-447.
133. *Deciding to Forego,* supra n.2, 46 fn.10.
134. But see *Matter of Jobes,* supra n.88, 420, 529 A. 2d at 447.
135. For a contrast to the approach of other states see Comment, "The Role of the Family in Medical Decision-making for Incompetent Adult Patients: A Historical Perspective and Case Analysis," 48 *U. Pitt. L. Rev.* 539 (1987).
136. In recent years, New Jersey Courts have tended to emphasize "procedures" and to some extent downplay "standards". This may be because of an appreciation that general policy reflected in "standards" may not be sufficiently subtle to deal with individual cases. Suitable procedures are however needed to protect individual interests. See *Deciding to Forego,* supra n.2, 27-28.
137. *Matter of Quinlan,* supra n.15, 41, 355 A.2d at 664; *Matter of Conroy,* supra n.17, 359-360, 486A. 2d at 1229.
138. Infra, text associated with nn.142-155.
139. For example, *Matter of Quinlan,* supra n.15, 41-42, 355 A. 2d at 664.
140. See supra n.119 and associated text.
141. *Matter of Conroy,* supra n.17, 359-364, 486 A. 2d at 1229-1231.
142. *Matter of Peter by Johanning,* supra n.128, 377, 529 A. 2d at 425.
143. Ibid., supra n.128, 378, 529 A. 2d at 426. *Matter of Conroy,* supra n.17, 361, 486 A. 2d at 1229-1230.
144. If the "subjective" approach is being employed, it appears that the medical evidence need only deal with the patient's competency — as to the patient's ability to control treatment (see *Matter of Farrell,* supra n.35, 356, 529 A. 2d at 415) — and whether the triggering circumstances specified by the patient for the withholding of treatment have been met. This is because once the patient's wishes are known, the treatment is to be withheld regardless of the patient's medical condition or competency: *Matter of Peter by Johanning,* supra n.142. With the "limited-objective" or "objective" approaches (infra, text associated with n.152 et seq.) the medical evidence must establish that the patient is incompetent with severe and permanent mental and physical impairment and that the patient has a life expectancy of no more than a year. The surrogate decision-maker must be provided with as much medical information as the patient would have had if competent: *Matter of Conroy,* supra n.17, 363, 486 A. 2d at 1231. If the medical evidence is that the patient is in a persistent vegetative state, there is no requirement that the patient have a life expectancy of less than a year: *Matter of Peter by Johanning,* supra n.128, 374, 529 A. at 424.
145. N.J. Stat. Ann. Section 52:27G — 1 et seq. (West 1986).
146. *Matter of Conroy,* supra n.17, 383-384, 486 A. 2d at 1241.
147. *Matter of Peter by Johanning,* supra n.128, 384, 529 A. 2d at 429.

148. Ibid.
149. *Matter of Jobes,* supra n.88, 420, 529 A. 2d at 447.
150. *Matter of Peter by Johanning,* supra n.128, 384, 529 A. 2d at 429.
151. *Matter of Jobes,* supra n.88, 415-416, 529 A. 2d at 445.
152. *Matter of Conroy,* supra n.17, 365-366, 486 A. 2d at 1232; *Matter of Peter by Johanning,* supra n.128, 374, 529 A. 2d at 423.
153. *Matter of Conroy,* supra n.17, 366-367, 486 A. 2d at 1232; *Matter of Peter by Johanning,* supra n.128, 374, 529 A. 2d at 423.
154. *Matter of Peter by Johanning,* supra n.128, 376-377, 529 A. 2d at 424-425.
155. Ibid. *Matter of Jobes,* supra n.88, 420-422, 529 A. 2d at 447-448. To avoid the confusion, supra n.119, generated by the umbrella expressions "substituted judgment" and "best interests" in the context of the decision-making process, it is important primarily to focus on what the triggering conditions and procedures of each approach are, rather than the expressions themselves.
156. See, for example, *Matter of Jobes,* supra n.88, 420, 529 A. 2d at 447.
157. See *Matter of Conroy,* supra n.17, 367, 486 A. 2d at 1232-1233. The New Jersey Supreme Court has suggested, ibid., that it has not delegated these types of decisions to others. This is debateable. A better view would seem to be that the Court's delegates, namely family and physicians, are generally just more suitable repositories of the decision-making authority. See too Cantor, supra n.7, 53-57, 74, 117 et seq..
158. *Deciding to Forego*, supra n.7, 115.
159. Cantor, supra n.7, 115.
160. Ibid., 113-117.

Chapter 42

The Problem of Euthanasia in the Netherlands

Matzy Rood DE-BOER

Tilburg University,
The Netherlands

Introduction

In the non-Dutch media the solution to the problem of euthanasia in the Netherlands has not been accurately depicted. The purpose of this chapter is to provide correct information and then place the issues into a legal framework. Euthanasia is not only relevant to elderly people. It is a legal medical and ethical problem concerning very sick persons of all ages. But it is an established fact that most of those asking for euthanasia are older than 55 years of age. I will confine myself to this age group.

In the Netherlands we operate a registration system known as Continuous Morbidity Registration (CMR),[1] originally initiated by the Ministry of Health, and which is based on the practice of general practitioners. A national network of so called "gauging stations" (peilstations (p.s.)) covers 1% of the Dutch population. The participating family doctors report weekly certain medical occurrences and actions, for instance how many times the physician has received a request by one of his patients for euthanasia.

Total population of the Netherlands 14.500.000.
Requests for euthanasia reported to the p.s.

| Year | Age group | | Total |
	−55	+55	
1976	2	13	15
1977	2	7	9
1978	3	7	10
1979	3	25	28
1980	2	20	22
1981	8	22	30
1982	–	26	26
1983	3	30	33
1984	5	35	40
1985	8	31	39
1986	7	21	28

Remark 1: These numbers cannot be extrapolated to the whole population, because this registration only relates to persons who are really terminally ill.
Remark 2: The data mentioned above are based on the CMR of general practitioners. Up to now we do not have an official registration of euthanasia requests in hospitals or pensions and homes for the elderly.
Remark 3: The CMR marks the request; not how many times it was granted.
Some scholars and journalists tend to think that the Dutch have solved the problem of euthanasia[2]. On the contrary, and sadly, the problem is more complicated than ever.

Should Euthanasia be a Crime?

This question has been discussed in my country for more than 15 years. There have been heated discussions, first on the desirability of new legislation, *i.e.* amending the criminal code 1886 and making euthanasia "more of a crime", or in contrast de-criminalizing euthanasia by taking it out of the criminal code.

In our legal terminology we only speak of euthanasia or mercy killing in those cases where there is an explicit and most serious request by the terminally ill patient to put an end to his life.

The termination of lifesaving treatment, based on a well-informed decision by a *compos mentis* patient, does not really raise legal problems in the present situation. Such a decision is regarded as a part of and an interpretation of the constitutional right to self-determination (Const. 1983, art. 10 and 11). Of course the physician has to inform the patient about the consequences of his refusal of treatment or therapy, but if the patient so wishes, if he wants to leave the hospital to die at home, so be it. This is not so much a case of euthanasia as a kind of suicide, an example of an "informed choice".

But if the patient asks for action which world deliberately shorten his life, the physician who agrees to do so could be in danger of committing a crime. In the Netherlands, as in all Western-European countries, active euthanasia is a crime (Crim. Code art. 292). It bears a maximum punishment of twelve years in prison.

However, since 1973, the courts have been lenient in applying the law, usually finding some justification for acquitting the accused physician[3]. A very influential legal writer, Ch. J. Enschedé, has said again and again that it was not at all necessary to change the law in one way or another, because the judge cannot punish a physician who has acted according to professional medical ethics, and in fact the physician should not even be prosecuted. Enschedé's opinion has been of great influence[4].

Guidelines

The Dutch Medical Association (15,000 members *i.e.* nearly all Dutch physicians) published in 1984[5] definitive standards for all physicians who were requested to commit euthanasia. They amount to the following:
- only a physician is allowed to mercifully "help" the patient;
- the patient has to make his/her own decision, well-informed and the request must be explicit and serious;
- the patient must be suffering unbearably without possibiliy of a change for the better;
- no other measures are available to improve the patient's situation;
- the physician has to act with the utmost care;
- the physician must consult at least one other independent physician.

This last standard was meant especially for the general practitioner. Most hospitals had already installed a medical/ethical committee to give advice on difficult problems like euthanasia.

Of course these guidelines could only be accepted in a social and cultural climate where a certain practice and many publications[6] more or less had paved the way to loosen the rigid rules of the Criminal Code of 1886.

Report of an Official Commission

A State Commission on Euthanasia was established in 1982 under the chairmanship of H. Jeukens, a former professor of administrative and constitutional law at Tilburg University, now the Catholic University Brabant, and a member of the Supreme Court. The report[7] advises modification of the Criminal Code so that a physician committing euthanasia according to medical/ethical rules when a patient finds himself in an emergency situation without any prospect at all made will not be prosecuted or punished. The recommendation was of a return to health on a majority of 13 votes. A small minority of 2 persons disagreed on religious grounds. Because the Report of the State Commission was not unanimous, discussion goes on about possible law reform.

Bills

At the time of winting, two bills concerning euthanasia are before Parliament. They are completely contradictory. The first one is a so-called "initiative bill" of a group of liberal politicians. This bill (1985) had almost passed the legislative process when the second bill was introduced (1987) by the christian democrats. Probably the bills will be discussed together and no one knows what the outcome will be. But because the Council of State has advised observing a certain waiting period and because the issue is so very sensitive, there is likely to be no progress for some time.

Most physicians are opposed to legislation. I agree with them. Enschedé's opinion has many followers in the Netherlands. Even an old and obsolete law can be interpreted extensively by a judiciary willing to extend the rules. That would be far more difficult to do with a new piece of legislation.

The legislators will have to deal with two more legal obstacles *i.e.* the question of whether a national statute to legalize (more or less) euthanasia is in accordance with art. 2 ECHR[8] and with a 1976 recommendation of the Council of Europe[9].

Justifications for Physicians

"The public prosecutors have sent only a small number of cases to the courts." ... they usually ended in ... a more or less symbolic sentence ..." [10]. The lower courts especially have been lenient in cases of euthanasia by physicians. In the relatively small number of published cases, four defences have been used:
 - the lack of material unlawfulness;
 - the so-called medical exception;
 - *force majeure* because of coercion of conscience;
 - *force majeure* because of an emergency situation.

The last construction is described in legal literature[11] as the defense that at this moment is most used in euthanasia cases. It means that the emergency situation is, for the physician, the result of a conflict of different loyalties. The Supreme Court is of the opinion[12] that the physician can rely on such an emergency situation when he has carefully weighed duties and interests against one another and has made a justified and balanced choice, according to medical/ethical criteria. The lower courts and also the Supreme Court have been reacting in a manner rather similar to public opinion on this issue. According to recent opinion polls, people tend to tolerate mercy killing under certain conditions and especially if the terminally ill person is old or very old. I must add however that some religious (minority) groups are putting up a stubborn resistance; and certainly tolerance has limits.

A Physician's Dilemma? [13]

One might get the impression that the euthanasia problem has found a solution in the Netherlands, not through legislation but in the courts. But the problem is more or less like mountain climbing. As soon as you reach one mountaintop you will observe another, higher mountain looming behind. The climb has to start all over again.

How does one react, for instance, to those persons close to the dying terminally-ill man or woman, who want to fulfill the patient's last wish to "have it over", to put this life to an end, but who cannot find a physician to accomplish the task? Are they, relatives or friends not being practitioners themselves, allowed to administer the lethal medicine or injection? Why should only the physician be granted a justification for mercy killing and why not the lifelong partner or friend? Up to now such cases have been prosecuted and the "offenders" have been convicted, though mostly with suspended sentences.

In March 1988 an important case was decided by the Amsterdam Court. Four nurses committed euthanasia on three irreversibly ill coma patients. The nurses were prosecuted for murder. They said in court that the head of the neurosurgery ward where the patients were being cared for was a surgeon with whom it was impossible to discuss any form of euthanasia. They contended that they acted justifiably because of *force majeure* by coercion of conscience. But the public prosecutor said they committed murder! The court convicted the nurses, but they only received suspended sentences. Whatever one may think about the outcome of this case, the question remains undecided whether euthanasia is a "doctor's problem" only.

Other Dilemmas

As long as the patient can make his own informed decision, his wishes about dying are obvious. And when he has made a so-called "living will" his wishes are obvious too.

But most people never make a living will and never make distinct arrangements with their physicians. What does one do for instance with the requests of children to put an end to a father's life because they cannot stand his suffering anymore?

To give this problem a more juridical setting: can we accept as "legal representatives" children or partners of the dying coma patient, or the relatives of the mentally handicapped person who is in the same hopeless situation? Do they have "enduring powers of attorney" because they are blood relatives? The legal guardianship or administratorship of those who are incapable to act for themselves has bearing only on property and pensions.

Is the physician to make his own responsible decision in difficult cases like this without an urgent and explicit request by the patient himself? Probably the patient will die some weeks later, suffering and losing more and more dignity if the physician refuses to act.

At this moment, the physician has to act carefully so as not to be prosecuted for a criminal offence nor be involved in disciplinary measures. And some practitioners will be wary of liability suits. In the Netherlands up to now the phenomenon of suing for damages in euthanasia cases has not been experienced but it could arise in the future.

Death Certificates

Recently the Supreme Court delivered a decision[14] with rather a narrow interpretation, relating to the signing of a death certificate without mention of a mercy killing. The Supreme Court ruled that the physician acting according to his professional standards is not allowed to put on the certificate that such a patient has died of a natural cause. This would be forgery.

The decision seems very clearcut, but again, it has complicated matters. Since then, according to the Dutch Medical Association, most physicians have decided not to report euthanasia on death certificates because of the risks[15]. It must not be underestimated how difficult it is first of all for a physician to be more open about euthanasia, secondly to comply with the patients' wishes and then to report this act on the death certificate! In the end he probably will not be prosecuted and even if he is, he will not be convicted, but he has to live through a period of great uncertainty.

The Legal Framework

What has happened legally speaking to the problem of euthanasia in the Netherlands?
  A. As far as *legislation* is concerned, nothing has been decided yet. The two bills before parliament are contradictory;
  B. but *euthanasia* is slowly slipping out of the criminal context; it is being decriminalised.
  C. This is happening because the *judiciary* is giving an extensive interpretation of the old law.
  D. The patient and his physician make arrangements together. We could say they have a *private law contract* to act under certain conditions and in certain circumstances.
  E. Is such a contract not *against public order and good morals?* My answer would be: no,
      1. the patient has no *constitutional right* to self determination.
      2. the physician has a duty to act according to his *professional standards.*
  F. The registration decision of the Supreme Court has put an *administrative law* emphasis on the whole problem.
  G. Some practitioners who do not want to put "euthanasia" on the death certificate as the cause of death promise their patients to supply them with a bottle of lethal medicine which they can use themselves when they

think they cannot stand it anymore. This is another civil law contract with the purpose of supplying the terminally ill patient with means *to commit suicide*. That is still a crime, but a minor one and up to now, hardly ever prosecuted.

Notes

1. Published yearly by the Dutch Research Institute on First Line Health Care (NIVEL)–Utrecht.
2. *Newsweek*, March 14, 1988 p.46-53 "A Right to Die?"
3. "Legal developments concerning active euthanasia on request in the Netherlands" J.K.M. Gevers, *Bioethics* 1987, p.156-162
4. "De dokter en de dood. Over sterven en het recht" (The doctor and death. On Dying and the Law). Kluwer-Deventer, 1985.
5. "Standpunt inzake euthanasie" (Stand on euthanasia) KNMG, Medisch Contact 3.8.1984
6. To name a few:
   - Rapport van de advieskommissie inzake wetgeving betreffende toelaatbare euthanasie (Report on eventual regulation of permitted euthanasia), 1978. Chairman Prof. dr. P. Muntendam. Publ. of the Dutch Assoc. for Voluntary Euthanasia.
   - "Verantwoorde euthanasie. Handleiding voor artsen" (Justified euthanasia. Instruction booklet for physicians) 1980 by Dr P V Admiraal. Publ. of the Dutch Assoc. for Vol. Euth.
   - "Het leven verlaten" (Leave Life Behind), 1984 by Dr E G H Kenter. De Toorts. A doctor tells about his own experiences with cases of passive and active euthanasia.
7. See a (non-official) English summary of the report (1985) in *Bioethics* 1987, p. 163-174.
8. European Convention on Human Rights 1950, on the right to life.
9. Recommendation 779, 1976, on the rights of the sick and dying.
10. Enschedé, 1985, (see note 4) p. 15.
11. "Euthanasie en noodtoestand" *NJB* 1987 J.H.P.J. Willems, p.694.
12. HR 27.11.1984, NJ 1986 106.
13. "Een toeschouwersperspectief op de euthanasiediskussie" *NJB* 1987, J Griffiths, P. 690. (A view from the bridge on the euthanasia discussion).
14. HR 15.12.1987, publ. 15.1.1988 Medisch Contact '88 p. 43.
15. "Euthanasie en verklaring van overlijden" H.R.G. Feber, M.C. 15.1.1988 p. 41-43.

Chapter 43

Suicide Among the Elderly: A Family Perspective[1]

Lynn D. WARDLE   Reuben Clark Law School
Brigham Young University, U.S.A.

World Suicide Rates and Distribution.

Behold, I will send you Elijah the prophet before the coming of the great and dreadful day of the Lord:
And he shall turn the heart of the fathers to the children, and the heart of the children to their fathers, lest I come and smite the earth with a curse.
— Malachi 4:5,6 (King James Vcision)

Statistinal Trends

The population of the world is increasing. As Appendix 1 shows, world population has grown from 2.5 billion in 1950 to over 5 billion today, and by the year 2025 the population of the world is expected to be 8.2 billion.

The world population is also getting older. The median age of world population actually declined between 1950 and 1970, from 22.9 years to 21.4 years, and in 1980 the median age was still only 22.4 years.[2] But for the next forty years, at least, the median age of the world's inhabitants is expected to increase. In the year 2025, the median age for the world is expected to be 31.0 years — nearly ten years older than the median age in 1970.[3]

"At the same time the populations as a whole are aging, the elderly population itself is growing older."[4] As Appendices 4 and 5 graphically illustrate, the proportion of the world's population 60 years old and over is rapidly rising and in the twenty-first century will escalate even faster as post World War II "baby boomers" age. Between 1950 and 2025, the total number of persons aged sixty-plus will increase from 214,000,000 (8.5% of the total population) to 1,121,000,000 (13.7%).[5] As Appendix 1 shows, the percentage of world population aged 65 and over will increase during the same period from 5.3% to 9.5%. In other words, in less than forty years, approximately one out of every seven inhabitants of the world will be 60 years of age or older; one out of every ten will be 65 or over.

The distribution and proportionate impact of the world's elderly population also is changing. As Appendix 3 shows, in 1950, developed and less developed regions of the world contained 44% and 56% respectively of the total world population aged 60 and over. But by the 2025 nearly three-fourths of the world's population age 60 and over will reside in less developed regions. Ironically, however, it is in the developed regions of the world where the impact of the increase in numbers of aged persons will be felt most acutely. Because of dramatic reductions in the birth rates in developed countries since World War II, the proportion of elderly-to-younger population has risen sharply, and will continue to rise dramatically, especially in the first quarter of the twenty-first century. For instance, in Europe persons age 65 or over presently constitute 12.4% of the total population; in 2025 they will constitute 18.4% of the population. In North America, by 2025 persons in this age group will grow from 11.3 to 17.3% of the population. By contrast, in Africa, persons age 65 and over will only constitute 3.8% of the population in 2025.[6] The elderly are also becoming urbanized. In 1980, 53% of the world's elderly lived in rural areas. By the year 2000, 55% of them will be living in urban areas.[7]

These population trends are important for many reasons. For the purposes of this chapter, they are important because the rate of suicide among the elderly generally is much higher than for younger persons, and both the number and proportion of elderly persons at risk of committing suicide are likely to increase substantially during the next four decades. Thus, the social ramifications of suicide among the elderly are of increasing world significance because of the demographic shift that is occurring.

World Suicide Rates and Distribution.

Suicide is among the ten most common causes of death in industrialized nations; worldwide, more than 1,000 persons kill themselves every day.[8]

International comparisons of suicide rates are difficult. Suicides clearly are underreported, for cultural as well as technical reasons.[9] In some regions, the discrepancies are extraordinary.[10] Nevertheless, even accounting for substantial differences in underreporting "[t]the range of variation of adjusted suicide rates between countries is striking. . ."[11]

Two patterns of suicide, however, appear to remain consistent in most cultures of the world. As shown by appendix 7, the elderly are more likely to commit suicide than younger persons, and males commit suicide more often than females. "[G]enerally, suicide rates increase with progressing age . . . ."[12] For instance, a 1980 study of the suicide rates of 45 nations, including very traditional and modern economies and cultures, demonstrated a direct, statistically significant relationship between the age of the population and the rate of suicide: countries with older populations had higher rates of suicide.[13] In almost all countries, the rate of suicide among males steadily rises with age, and the rate of suicide among women rises until middle age (menopause) and then drops.[14] Ruzicka identified four different patterns of suicide among the age population of various countries. As shown in Appendix 8, the patterns are strikingly differently. But they all show definite (if distinctive) age correlation to an increase in the suicide rate. Also, the elderly are much more serious about suicide: they make fewer token attempts, communicate their attempt to commit suicide less frequently, use more lethal methods, and are successful much more often than the average suicide-attempter population.[15]

Males, particularly white males, commit suicide at a higher rate than females. "In all societies for which data were available, suicide rates have been found to be higher for males than females (although the opposite is true for attempted suicides . . .)."[16]

During the past twenty years much of the research regarding suicide among the elderly has reported optimistic data. Suicide rates among the elderly were dropping, national economics were strengthening, programs for the health and security of older persons were increasing, and at first glance the prospects for lowering the rate of suicide among the elderly in the future seemed encouraging. But closer examination of the data, and more recent research, provides cause for grave concern that, within the next forty years, suicide among the elderly may increase to crisis proportions globally.

First, the rates of suicide among the elderly have stopped falling, and have started to rise again. Suicide data for elderly white males in the United States, at five-year age intervals from 1940, plotted in Appendix 9, emphasize the upturn in suicide rates for the elderly during the past ten or fifteen years. Appendices 10-A through 10-S graph the suicide rates for the elderly in 18 nations during the past forty years.[17] They show that the suicide rates among the elderly worldwide generally declined during the 1950's and 1960's but during the past five-to-fifteen years have stopped declining, and have started to rise. The upturn in suicide rates is discernible earliest and most definitely in the oldest age group, persons 75 and older; it moves next to the mid-elderly, persons 65-74, and reaches the young elderly, aged 55-64, last.

Second, as Appendix 10-S illustrates, the gap between the rate of suicide of elderly men and women is narrowing; women are closing the gap by increasing their rates of suicide.[18] To the extent that this is related to significant changes in social expectations of women, particularly their participation in the paid work force, the rates for elderly female suicides can be expected to rise.

Third, recent cohort analyses of suicide rates shed an ominous light on the future of suicide among the elderly. A birth cohort consists of all individuals born during the same time period (usually a five year period). Cohort analysis tracks the suicide rate of each particular cohort as they age, comparing their suicide rates at each stage of aging with the suicide rates of earlier and later birth cohorts. The general finding of cohort analysis of recent suicide rates, as stated by Murphy and Wetzel on the basis of their study of suicide in the United States, is that since about 1955 "[n]ot only does each successive birth cohort start with a higher suicide rate, [but] at each successive five-year interval it has a higher rate than the preceding cohort had at that age."[19] Appendices 11 and 12 illustrate the cohort phenomenon.[20] Similar findings reflecting increasing cohort-specific suicide rates have been made in many other countries including Canada,[21] Japan,[22] Taiwan,[23] Australia,[24] the Federal Republic of Germany,[25] and Switzerland[26] A study in Great Britain disputes the cohort phenomenon.[27] And a brief cohort analysis for Sweden showed no correlation.[28]

Murphy and Wetzel note that their data "most strongly imply an early and lasting influence, possibly one of steadily increasing strength."[29] If this thesis is valid, it "suggests that the problem of suicide among older people will take on increasing significance" as the post-war "baby boom" birth cohorts age, "bringing with them the problems inherent to large birth cohorts, including high rates of suicide."[30] The consequences can be demonstrated statistically. For example, two researchers have predicted a dramatic increase in suicides among the elderly in the United States in the coming decades.[31]

A fourth source of major concern about suicide among the elderly in the future comes from analysis of "dependency ratios."[32] Pyramid bar graphs in Appendix 5 graphically demonstrate the changing age-composition of world population between 1950 and 2025. Because of declining birth rates, the childhood age dependency ratio is expected to fall for the entire world from 60.8 in 1980 to 37.5 in the year 2025, as Appendix 14 shows. However, the old age dependency will rise from 9.8 to 14.4 worldwide. In some countries, the rise will be substantially greater. For instance, in North America the rate will rise from 16.7 to 27.6. In Europe it will rise from 20.1 to 29.2. In other words, only three to four workers in Europe and North America in the year 2025 will be supporting each person 65 or older. As Appendix 13 illustrates, although the birth rate will decline substantially in Europe, the total dependency ratio will increase substantially because of the marked increase in the old age dependency ratio. And as Appendix 15 shows, the effects of this change will be felt most intensively in the more developed regions of the world. In 1950, the number of persons 15-59 to the number of persons of 60 or over was about 7.5:1. By the year 2025 it will drop to about 5.5:1. But in the more developed parts of the world, the ratio in 1950 was 5.5:1, and by 2025 it will drop to 2.5:1 — meaning that less than forty years from now there will be only two-and-a-half worker-aged persons for every retirement-aged person in developed countries.

The economic implications of this are staggering. Since old age dependents are generally much more expensive to care for than childhood dependents, the ramifications of this demographic development are very foreboding. And since financial and medical concerns are among those which most immediately

precipitate suicide among the elderly, the effect of this demographic development on suicide among the elderly could be dramatic.

The economic pressures resulting from the massive demographic changes
now in progress may cause some countries to restrict or deny medical care to
the aged, and indirectly or directly encourage them to commit suicide for the
good of the (younger) society. Already there is talk about this in the United
States.[33] Some believe this is what the practice of euthanasia in the Netherlands
is all about.[34]

A fifth cause for concern about suicide among the elderly comes from the
first national study of suicide among residents of long-term care facilities
(nursing homes, homes for the aged, etc.) in the United States.[35] The study
revealed that the completed suicide rate in long-term care facilities was 94.9 per
100,000 population (more than four times the overall national rate, and double
the elderly suicide age-rate); one percent of the patients in such facilities
engaged in suicidal behavior.[36] One of the risks of institutionalization of the
elderly is that institutionalization involves the loss of autonomy, privacy,
control and choice, leading to "learned dependency," culminating frequently
in self-destructive behavior.[37] Indirect suicidal behavior (refusing to eat,
refusing to take necessary medication) is a direct result of the loss of control
and learned helplessness in institutions. As the numbers of elderly living in
institutions increase,[38] the Osgood data suggests that the rate of suicide among
the elderly may be expected to increase.

Sixth, there is a trend worldwide, at least in developed countries, toward
loosening the legal restraints against suicide and assisted suicide.[39] Literature
espousing a legal "right to die" — that is, the right of persons to commit
"rational suicide" by ending their own lives, has proliferated recently.[40] In the
Netherlands, active euthanasia has become openly and widely practiced during
the past fifteen years.[41] Official death registry figures reportedly show that
3,000 Dutch patients each year are being killed by Dutch doctors.[42] But the
actual number of medically-assisted euthanasia deaths in the Netherlands
probably is higher because of under-reporting by doctors who are still worried
about possible prosecutions. Survey extrapolations estimate that there are at
least 5,000 Dutch patients killed annually by doctors (not including those in
hospitals) and other estimates range from 6,000 to 20,000 euthanasia killings
per year.[43] The most reliable estimates are in the 5-10,000 range. In 1986 there
were 125,000 reported deaths in the Netherlands,[44] so apparently between four
and eight percent of all of the persons who die in the Netherlands are being put
to death by Dutch physicians.

The discussion of a "right to die" and the practice of it have not been confined
to persons suffering with terminal illness. Rather, the elderly and persons with
disabilities often have been lumped together with the terminally ill and persons
in persistent vegetative conditions in a way that may be viewed as threatening.
The National Task Force on Suicide in Canada noted:

Give the steady increase in the proportion of elderly in Canadian society, the younger generation is beginning to perceive its existence as an increasing burden. As a result within the last few years there has been a noticeable shift in the attitude towards suicide among the elderly. Sakinofsky describes the prevailing attitude: "If a young person commits suicide, it is regarded as a tragedy; but in the old, it can be regarded as an acceptable solution ... It is frequently condoned and described as 'rational', 'self-determined' or 'voluntary euthanasia'. These attitudes reflect a lack of respect and appreciation of the elderly, which too often leads to a lack of self-respect in the elderly individual ..."[45]

American historian Paul Longmore concurs.

This advocacy of assisted suicide gives society an excuse for offering elderly people and people with disabilities only the alternatives of deprivation or death. By rationalizing suicide among those oppressed groups, it helps foster a climate that will promote it. Indeed, such a climate already exists. Worldwide suicide rates among persons over sixty, notes the Austrian authority, Dr. Erwin Ringel, "are high and steadily increasing." "This may be no surprise," he continues "if we look at the behavior of many people toward the old and even toward the merely aging, we may begin to wonder just how sincere the wish of the community is to keep its older people alive."[46]

Thus, it is not surprising to learn that one survey of elderly residents living in homes for the aged and living independently in the Netherlands reported that 95% of the nursing home residents and 66% of the aged living independently opposed making euthanasia legal, and that one-fourth of the elderly who are living independently and 60% of the elderly living in nursing homes were fearful that their own lives may be involuntarily terminated.[47]

The "right to die" as applied to the elderly in general may imply a "duty to die."[48] In some nations, the risk to the lives of the elderly might be even more direct; there is the precedent of coercive programs to curtail childbearing that have been enforced by some governments.[49] Just as severely restrictive birth control programs have stimulated the practice of infanticide in some societies,[50] severely restrictive food, housing, medical or other social policies may promote neglect of and encourage suicide among the elderly.

Thus, there are many good reasons for concern that suicide among the elderly may reach crisis proportions worldwide during the next forty years. Demographic changes, economic pressures, changing social attitudes toward and diminishing legal protections for the elderly may produce unprecedented rates of suicide among the aged. That is a tragic prospect; it would entail a wasted human resource of inestimable value to all nations, cultures and peoples.

Family Factors Associated With Suicide Among the Elderly

In considering what can be done to reduce the causes of suicide among the elderly, much attention has been focused on economic,[51] medical,[52] and cultural factors.[53] The influence of such variables is undeniable, and efforts to diminish the pressures that produce suicidal behavior must address these subjects. But there is one category of factors associated with suicide that often is overlooked when approaches to preventing suicide among the elderly are considered. I refer to the family.

The importance of the family in protecting individuals against, or creating or exacerbating the stresses and pressures that lead to, suicide cannot be overstated. Almost every stage of suicidal behavior may be influenced profoundly, positively or negatively, by family relations.

Suicide is a result of many interrelated factors.[54] Suicide among the elderly appears to be influenced by a multitude of complex variables including isolation, bereavement, serious physical illness, depression, organic brain disease, and poverty.[55] In his pioneering sociological analysis of suicide, Emile Durkheim found that social forces, especially social integration, heavily influence suicide rates. He described three types of suicidal behavior. "Egoistic" suicides result when the individual has an excessive ego, inadequate integration into society, and is detached from meaningful associations. "Altruistic" suicides involve an excess of integration of an individual into a unit of society — e.g., wives following their husbands to death, etc. "Anomic" suicides result from major disturbances of the equilibrium of society as a whole, massive social upheaval, such as the Great Depression, etc.[56] A few years later Sigmund Freud provided psychological analysis of suicide. Thoughts about suicide arise in the unconscious mind from a natural impulse toward self-destruction. Suicide may be murder in reverse. People commit suicide when they turn inward the hostility they feel towards a rejecting loved one; when an indispensable object is deemed threatened. They commit suicide to achieve peace, harmony and to rescue the object/relationship by self-destruction.[57] Perhaps the best model of suicidal behavior among the elderly has been prepared by Kenneth Shulman.[58] A copy of this model is provided in Appendix 16. "Depression is a major determinant of suicide; indeed Shulman has argued that it provides the final common pathway for all of the various antecedent factors that predispose to suicide, at least in the elderly."[59] Isolation also is a primary cause of suicide among the elderly.[60]

Family factors are associated with suicide in at least seven ways. First, marriage tends to insulate individuals, especially men, to some extent from suicidal behavior. Durkheim found that persons who are deeply and intimately involved with others have little risk of suicide, while those who are isolated, unattached, and unintegrated in meaningful relationships are at greater risk of committing suicide. Consequently, he found that suicide rates were highest among the unmarried.[61] Since then numerous suicide researchers have confirmed this hypothesis.[62] "Marriage, it is argued, not only integrates the individual into a close and meaningful association but also regulates him by requiring him to take the other person into account in many, perhaps the most significant, of his activities."[63] But the importance of marriage as a suicide preventative is not absolute. Durkheim surmised that marriage, alone, was substantially less beneficial to women than men,[64] and later studies have confirmed this.[65] While marriage may give significant protection against suicide, it must be reinforced by other social bonds if the suicide rate of married persons is to be significantly reduced.[66]

Second, marriage may be an indirect cause of suicide, or increased risk of suicide, if the parties become bonded too tightly to each other, to the exclusion of other associations. "Marriage increases the social cohesiveness among the nuclear family members but increases their isolation and despair in relation to the greater society."[67] Persons who have never been married appear to be less vulnerable to certain types of suicide that arise from the disruption of intimate personal relations. The widowed, especially widowed men, have a higher rate of suicide.[68] One study of suicide among the elderly found that the rate of suicide among widowers was more then seven times as high as the rate of suicide among widows.[69] Increased risk of suicide exists during the first four years after death of a spouse, and is especially high in the first year following the death.[70] It appears that women are more active in maintaining other relationships, and more successful in doing so during their marriage than are men, so the effect of the death of a spouse upon them is not as drastic and does not cause as much isolation as it does for men. When dependent spouses are faced with the loss of the other, it may lead to a suicide pact and "Van Dusen"–type dual suicide.[71]

Third, marital and other family problems are among major causes of suicide among the elderly worldwide.[72] In particular, divorce is frequently associated with suicide.[73] Although the degree to which divorce enhances the risk of suicide has been dropping in western countries as the stigma of divorce is diminishing, the divorced population is still at greater risk of suicide than the married, the never married, and the widowed.[74] Durkheim surmised that the suicide rate varies inversely with the degree of normative regulation. Thus, while liberalization of divorce laws have had the positive effect of reducing the stigma of divorce, they appear to have had a negative effect upon suicide rates generally. As Appendix 17 demonstrates, using data from the United States, there appears to be some parallel between the rate of divorce and the suicide rate in the population group in which there is the highest rate of divorce, and in suicide among children, who are often the victims of divorce.

Fourth, while excessively nonrestrictive divorce laws produce an increase in suicide rates, overly restrictive divorce laws are also associated with suicide:

> Many attempted and completed suicides are women's protests against
> unwanted marriages. In Arabic countries such a protest is often manifested

by a woman's burning herself to death ... A large number of female self-poisonings are based on marital problems, infidelity of the husband, abuse, quarrels over the interference from the extended family, ...

Divorces may be obtained by women in Arabic countries, but most commonly women are divorced by their husbands. Although divorced women find themselves in an unenviable position, both social and financially, many of them ... prefer to remain in that status rather than remarry. No doubt a large proportion of Muslim women are deterred from divorce not only by law but by lack of alternatives for the future ... Muslim religious law is a compelling disadvantageous factor for women who are unhappy in marriage, often leading them to attempt suicide.

Divorces in Southeast Asia and Central Asia are difficult for women, who face serious financial problems, especially if they are allowed to keep the children. Divorced women are also socially disadvantaged ... Asian women who choose not to incur the disadvantages of divorce or who feel unable to leave a painful ... situation may see suicide as the only avenue of escape.[75]

Fifth, the number of children in a family is inversely related to the rate of suicide; persons with children are less likely to commit suicide than persons without children, and persons with more children are less likely than with persons with fewer children.[76] Most of the research to date has focused on the effects of having children upon younger parents, but the potential significance of the relationship between adult children and their elderly parents is apparent. Suicide among the elderly is associated with isolation. When adult children do not maintain adequate contact with their elderly parents the elderly parents become isolated.[77] The elderly, particularly those living in nursing homes, are distressed by infrequent contact with their children, desire increased contact with their children, and that loneliness is a major source of depression for them.[78]

Integration of the elderly into the family, allowing the elderly to live with their adult children and perform functions, and occupy respected roles within the family system, may be why, in many Asian countries, suicide rates among the elderly decline for some period. That may explain why the suicide rates among the elderly in Japan and Taiwan are so much higher than they are in many other Asian countries: the rapid economic development of these countries has produced a mobility in society which may separate adult children from their elderly parents, increasing the isolation of the elderly and making them more vulnerable to suicide. The correlation between suicide and Home Help for the Aged in Japan, which is a government substitute for family integration and support of the aged, suggests that there is validity in this hypothesis.[80]

A sixth family factor associated with suicide is a family history of suicide. Suicidal behavior, like depression, can be learned.[81] Studies of families of suicide attempters and completers reveal more suicidal behavior among the parents and relatives than in families of non-suicidal psychiatric patients; one recent investigation reported that almost half of the 243 psychiatric patients studied, with a family history of suicide, attempted suicide themselves.[82]

A seventh family factor relating to suicide that must be mentioned is abuse of the elderly. Seventy-five percent of the victims of elderly abuse lived with their abusers; eighty percent of their abusers were their own relatives.[83]

Conclusion: Turning the Heart of the Children to Their Fathers

Suicide is a complex, multi-faceted behavior, and effective social responses to the problem must occur at many levels. Because suicide is so complex, it would be foolish to ignore the family dimensions of the behavior. As the fundamental social unit in all cultures, the family is the principal mediating structure through which external influences pass to effect most individuals; and the family is the intimate setting in which most individuals respond to the crises in their lives. As Justice Lewis Powell of the United States Supreme Court noted in a case recognizing extended family association as a fundamental liberty protected by the U.S. Constitution:

> Ours is by no means a tradition limited to respect for the bonds uniting the members of the nuclear family. ... The tradition of ... especially grandparents sharing a household along with parents and children has roots equally venerable and equally deserving of constitutional recognition. ... Out of choice, necessity, or a sense of family responsibility, it has been common for close relatives to draw together and participate in the duties and the satisfactions of a common home. ... Especially in times of adversity, such as the death of a spouse or economic need, the broader family has tended to come together for mutual sustenance and to maintain or rebuild a secure home life.[84]

Even in the United States "the amount of social care that families provide for their elderly and handicapped members far exceeds the amount of social care provided by the state."[85]

Aging is not a cause of suicide; most aged individuals and demographic groups do not commit suicide when they get old. But age increases the vulnerability of persons to the pressures that push some people into committing suicide: isolation, depression, poverty, chronic pain and insignificance. Because these factors are precipitators of suicide among the elderly, the lifesaving potential of family approaches to preventing suicide among the elderly cannot be ignored.

Let me conclude this chapter with four recommendations. These are personal and strongly held views. First, public policies should encourage and strengthen extended family relations. Social programs that facilitate and reward family fragmentation, however well-intentioned, can be expected to have deadly consequences for the elderly. Second, direct or indirect coercion of the elderly to commit suicide, including age discrimination in the public provision of or eligibility for the necessities of life must be forbidden. Denial of necessary food, housing and medical treatment for the elderly or their families must be recognized as inhumane, primitive policy. Third, encouragement of and assistance for suicide among the elderly must be criminally prohibited. The "action of ... assisted suicide for the elderly would offer them little practical help and would serve as a threatening symbol of devaluation of old age."[86] It is naive to believe that depressed, isolated elderly truly volunteer to end their lives. Consensual or rational suicide among the elderly usually is tragic fiction, and always is a message of despair to the aged. Finally, the family dimensions of suicide among the elderly merit further serious attention by legal scholars, sociologists, and policy makers throughout the world. We may discover that the ultimate solution to the curse of human self-destruction lies, as Malachi prophesied, in turning the heart of parents to their children, and of children to the parents.

Notes

1. The author acknowledges his indebtedness to Mr. Randall Richards for his timely assistance with research and preparing the graphs, and to Susan Laufenberg, and Cheryl Long for their patient persistence in typing the paper.
2. Dept. Int'l. Econ. & Assoc. Affairs, Population Studies, No. 93, World Population Trends, Population and Development Interrelations and Population Policies, 1983 Monitoring Report at 31 (U.N. 1985) (hereinafter cited as "DIESA, Population Studies, No. 93").
3. There is considerable variance in the median ages of the various nations and regions of the world. European countries have the highest median ages — averaging 33.0 years in 1980 (FRG had 36.6) whereas Africa, at 17.3 years, had the lowest median ages in 1980 (Kenya was 14.2). *Ibid.* at 31.
4. Dept. of Int'l Econ. & Soc. Affairs, The World Aging Situation: Strategies and Policies at 39 (U.N. 1985) (hereinafter cited as "DIESA, The World Aging Situation").
5. *Ibid.* at 13. *See also* Appendix 3.
6. *See* Appendix 1.
7. DIESA, World Aging Situation at 31, 33. The percentage of elderly living in urban areas will be even greater for developed nations and for women. *Ibid.*
8. National Institute of Mental Health, Useful Information on Suicide 1 (U.S. Dep't of Health and Human Services 1986) (hereinafter cited as "NIMH"). In the United States the elderly constitute about 10% of the population, but account for nearly 25% of the suicides. Suicide and Suicide Prevention: A Briefing by the Subcomm. on Human Services of the Select Comm. on Aging, H. Rep., 98th Cong., 2d Sess., Comm. Publ. No. 98-497 (Nov. 1, 1984) at 26; *see also* Bock, Aging and Suicide: The Significance of Marital, Kinship, and Alternative Relations, 21 Fam. Coord. 71 (1972).

9. Ruzicka, *Suicide, 1950 to 1971,* 29 World H. Statistics. Rep. 396, 397 (1976).
10. Suicide in Asia and the Near East 356 (L. Headley and N. Farberow eds. 1984) (hereinafter cited as "Suicide in Asia"). The number of attempted suicides by poisoning alone in Teheran was 70-108 times as large as the average number of suicide deaths reported for the same period; the number of suicide cases treated at one Cairo hospital in one month was higher than the total number of suicides deaths reported for the entire country for the entire year. *Ibid.*)
11. Ruzicka, *supra* note 9 at 399.
12. Ruzicka, *supra* note 9 at 400.
13. Stack, *The Effect of Age Composition on Suicide in Traditional and Industrial Societies,* 111 J. Soc. Psych. 143 (1980).
14. Ruzicka, *supra* note 9, at 398; N. Osgood & J. McIntosh, Suicide and the Elderly, An Annotated Bibliography and Review 106 (1986) (hereinafter cited as "Osgood & McIntosh")(abstract of Jedlicka, *Suicide and Adaptation to Aging in More Developed Countries,* paper presented for the 11th International Congress of Gerontology, Tokyo, Japan); Atchley, *Aging and Suicide: Reflections of the Quality of Life* in Second Conference on the Epidemiology of Aging 141, 150 (S. Haynes & M. Feinleib eds. 1980).
15. Bock, *supra* note 8, at 77; Osgood & McIntosh, *supra* note 14, at 116 (abstract of Lonnqvist & Achte, *Follow up Study of the Attempted Suicides Among the Elderly in Helsinki in 1973-79,* 6 Crisis: Int'l. J. of Suicide and Crisis-Studies 10 (1985)); Shulman, *Suicide and Parasuicide in Old Age: A Review,* 7 Age and Ageing 201 (1978).
16. Ruzicka, *supra* note 9, at 398. Atchley, *supra* note 14, at 150. In the United States, male suicide rates by age ranges from two to seven times the female suicide rate for comparable ages. Frederick, *Current Trends in Suicidal Behavior in the United States,* 32 Am. J. Psychotherapy 172, 176 (1968).
17. In doing my research I was disappointed to find no recent multi-national data showing the rate of suicide among the elderly over time. So I went to the raw data reported by the World Health Organization and I compiled the data on suicide rates among the elderly for fourteen nations from 1955 to 1985 at approximately five year intervals, and for four other nations from 1970 to 1985. Then I plotted the data on line graphs for each nation separately, and one graph for the composite data. Appendices 10-A through 10-S.
18. Burvelle, *Recent Decreased Ratio of Male-female Suicide Rates: Analysis of Rates in Selected Countries Specific for Age and Sex,* 18 Int'l J. Soc. Psychiatry 137 (1972); Hellon & Solomon, *Suicide and Aging Alberta, Canada, 1951 to 1977, The Changing Profile,* 37 Arch. Gen. Psychiatry 505 (1980); Kruijt, *The Suicide Rate in the Western World Since World War II,* 13 The Netherlands J. Sociology 55 (1977).
19. Murphy & Wetzel, *Suicide Risk by Birth Cohort in the United States, 1949 to 1974,* 37 Arch. Gen. Psychiatry 519 (1980). "Owing to the relative lateness of the effect being studied (i.e., commencing about 1955) data are incomplete for later ages for those cohorts." *Ibid.* at 522. *See also* Lester, *Suicide Risk by Birth Cohort,* 14 Suicide and Life-Threatening Behavior 132 (1984).
20. Appendix 11, an enhanced and updated copy of a table made by Murphy & Wetzel, graphically demonstrates the cohort effect on suicides of white males in the United States. Following the diagonal lines you can see that the suicide rate for a given cohort increases as that cohort grows older (at five year intervals). Reading horizontally you can see that the suicide rate for succeeding birth cohorts at each

age level is higher than it was for the preceding birth cohort. Appendix 12 graphically illustrates this cohort effect using data from the United States beginning with the year 1955 and ending in 1984 (covering six different five-year cohorts). Although there are isolated exceptions to the upward trend, the overall continuous nature of the increase in suicide rates, both within cohorts and for succeeding cohorts, is disturbing.

21. One of the earliest studies to document this effect was based in Alberta, Canada. Solomon & Hellon, *Suicide and Age in Alberta, Canada, 1951-1977, A Cohort Analysis,* 37 Arch. Gen. Psychiatry 511 (1980). A 1985 study replicated Solomon's Alberta study throughout Canada and validated its general conclusions. Reed, Camus & Last, *Suicide in Canada: Birth Cohort Analysis,* 76 Canada J. Pub. H. 43(1985) as abstracted in Osgood & McIntosh at 133. *See also* Health and Welfare Canada, Suicide in Canada 9 (1987).

22. Wen, *Secular Suicidal Trends in Postwar Japan and Taiwan, an Examination of Hypothesis,* 20 Int'l J. Soc. Psychiatry 8 (1974) (This may be the earliest cohort analysis of suicide rates).

23. *Ibid.*

24. Goldney & Katsikitis, *Cohort Analysis of Suicide Rates in Australia,* 40 Arch. Gen. Psychiatry 71 (1983).

25. Hafner & Schmidtke, *Do Cohort Effects Influence Suicide Rates,* 42 Arch. Gen. Psychiatry 26 (1985) (letter).

26. *Ibid.*

27. Murphy, Lindesay, & Grundy, *60 Years of Suicide in England and Wales,* 43 Arch. Gen. Psychiatry 969 (1986) (finding no discernable trend among the younger cohorts, a fall in suicide rates of successive older cohorts, prolonged effect of generational events, such as war, detoxification of domestic gas but admitting that there is evidence of a recent upturn in suicide among the younger age groups, which appears to have been sustained as they have gotten older). Because there was no sharp increase in suicides among the young in Britain until recently, this study may simply mean that it was done too early to discern a cohort effect in Great Britain.

28. Hafner & Schmidtke, *supra* note 25, at 927.

29. Murphy & Wetzel *supra* note 19, at 522.

30. Haas & Hendin, *Suicide Among Older People: Projections for the Future* 13 Suicide and Life-Threatening Behavior 147, 152, 153 (1983).

31. "[A]lmost 11,000 white males over the age of 55 will commit suicide in 2020 and about 14,500 in about 2040 ..." *Ibid.* at 152, 153.

32. The dependency ratio consists of the number of persons that are generally deemed too young or too old to work to the total population of the world. The childhood dependency ratio is defined as the ratio of population age 0-14 to those aged 15-64, and the old age dependency ratio is defined as the population of 65 or over to those aged 15-64, multiplied by 100.

33. Daniel Callaghan, has recently proposed cutting off aggressive medical treatment for all persons above a certain age limit as an unavoidable and natural step toward medical cost containment. D. Callaghan, Setting Limits: Medical Goals in an Aging Society (1987). Historically, the provision of scarce medical resources has discriminated against those deemed to be of minor social worth, including the aged. Minow, *Foreword: Justice Engendered,* 101 Harv. L. Rev. 10, 11 (1987).

34. *See infra* notes 41 through 47 and accompanying text.

35. Osgood, *Suicide Behavior in Long-Term Care Facilities,* Newslink, American

Association of Suicidology (February 1988) (abstract).

36. *Ibid.* (The completed suicide rate included both overt suicide and indirect suicidal behavior — intentional life-threatening behavior — such as refusing to eat, refusing to take necessary medication, etc.)

37. Mercer, *Consequences of Institutionalization of the Aged* in Abuse and Maltreatment of the Elderly, Causes and Intervention 84, 90-96 (J. Kosberg ed. 1983). *Ibid.* at 99. In the institutional setting, "a sense of control can make the difference between living and dying." *Ibid.* at 98. *See also* Note, *Criminal Liability for Assisting Suicide,* 86 Colum. L. Rev. 348, 355 (1986).

38. In the U.S. the number of nursing home residents is predicted to rise more than 35% between 1985 and 2000. D. Callaghan, *supra* note 33, at 151.

39. For example, in 1976 the first International Conference on Euthenasia was held in Tokyo; only six organizations were represented. In April 1988, a sequel to that conference was held in San Francisco; 32 organizations from around the world were represented. [Telephone interview with Derek Humphry, President, Hemlock Society, Feb. 25, 1988].

40. D. Humphry & A. Wickett, The Right to Die: Understanding Euthanasia (1986); P. Riga, Right Die or Right to Live: Legal Aspects of Dying and Death (1981); Davenport, *The Right to Die: Sources of Information,* 5 Legal Ref. Serv. Q. 47 (Spring 1985) (30 pages listing American books and articles dealing with the subject); Williams, *The Right to Die,* 134 New L. J. 73 (1984); Helm, *Voluntary Euthanasia — An International Perspective,* 17 Law/Tech. 3 (3rd Quarter 1984); Marzen, O'Dowd, Crone & Balch, *Suicide: A Constitutional Right?,* 24 Duq. L. Rev. 1 (1986) (summarizing civil, criminal, statutory, constitutional and common laws of all American states); *The Right to Live or Die* 105 F.R.D. 389 (Proceedings of the 45th Jud. Conf. of the D.C. Cir.); Oddi, *The Tort of Interference with the Right to Die,* 75 Geo. L.J. 625 (1985).

41. See chapter 42. Although active euthanasia is a crime in the Netherlands under Article 293 of the Criminal Code, a series of judicial decisions over the past 15 years have established that no punishment will be imposed upon a doctor who administers a lethal injection to a person under medically established, judicially endorsed guidelines. Essentially active euthanasia is permitted if a patient personally requests it (or has requested it in a living will before becoming comatose or incompetent), the request has been made when the patient is conscious and rational, the request is repeated over time, the patient is deemed to be a position of "unbearable" distress or suffering, the prospects for improvement are nil, and a second doctor approves. *See* Otten, *Fateful Decision in the Netherlands, the Very Ill have Option to Euthanasia,* Wall. J., Aug. 21, 1987, at 1, col. 1; Clines, *Dutch are Quietly Taking the Lead in Euthanasia,* N.Y. Times, Oct. 31, 1986, sec. 1, at 4, col. 3; Cody, *Dutch Way of Legalizing the Use of Euthanasia,* Washington Post, Mar. 16, 1987, at Al, Col. 3; *Euthanasia and the Law in the Netherlands* in A Matter of Life and Death (1986) (English translation); Guidelines of the Royal Netherlands Association for the Promotion of Medicine and the Association of Nurses Relating to Euthanasia (March 1987) (English translation); P. Schepens, *Euthanasia: Our Future* (English translation); J.K.M. Gevers, "Legal Developments Concerning Active Euthanasia on Request in the Netherlands," vol. 1, *Bioethics* (1987),p.156

42. P. Schepens, *supra* note 41.

43. *Ibid. See also* Dessaur & Rutenfrans, *The Present-date Practice of Euthanasia* in May the Doctor Kill (1986)(criminologists at the University of Nijmegen report

varying estimates from 3-4,000 per year to 10-12,000 per year, and other specula-
tions up to 18,000 per year); P. Schepens, *supra* note 41. (estimates range up to
20,000).
44. P. Schepens, *supra* note 41.
45. Suicide in Canada *supra* note 21, at 32.
46. Longmore, Elizabeth Bouvia, *Assisted Suicide and Social Prejudice,* 3 Issues in L. &
Med. 141, 161 (1988).
47. Segers, Elderly Persons on the Subject of Euthanasia (Feb. 1987) (English translation). While there appears to be broad support for euthanasia in the Dutch public
opinion polls, there has been concern raised recently that the opinions of the elderly
persons living in the Netherlands have been overlooked. *Most Elderly People
Afraid of Euthanasia* in De Telegraf, Mar. 13, 1987 (English translation).
48. A few years ago, a prominent American politician opined that elderly Americans
had "a duty to die." Otten, *Ethesis Draws Fire with Proposal for Limiting Health
Care to Aged,* Wall St. J., Jan. 22, 1988 at 23 (quoting Colorado Gov. Richard
Lamm).
49. For descriptions of China's forced abortion policy *see* S. Mosher, Broken Earth:
The Rural Chinese (1983); S. Mosher, Journey to Forbidden China (1985);
Weiskopf, *Abortion Policy Tears at China's Society,* Wash. Post, Jan. 7, 1986, at Al,
col. 1.
50. *See* Weiskopf, *China's Birth Control Policy Drives Some to Kill Baby Girls,* Wash.
Post, Jan 8, 1986, at Al, col. 1.
51. "Economic depression seems to lead to increased suicide rates, during the war as a
specific decline has been observed." Ruzicka, *supra* note 9, at 398. For many
nations the peak in the suicide rate of the century occurred during the great
depression. *See generally* Frederick, *Current Trends in Suicide Behavior in the
United States,* 32 Int'l. J. Psychotheraphy 172, 173 (1978); Suicide in Canada *supra*
note 21, at 12-16. "[T]he rapid rise in the level of prosperity has been of decisive
importance for the post-war drop in the suicide rate among 65-74 year old males in
the western world." Kruijt, *supra* note 18, at 61. (However, Kruijt notes that at the
same time the suicide rate of males over 74, and the suicide rates of young adult
males and women over 45 continue to rise during a period of prosperity. *Ibid.* at 62.)
The relationship between unemployment and suicide is not clear. There is a
statistical correlation between unemployment and suicide in some countries, but an
inverse relationship or no statistically significant correlation in other countries.
Baudry, *New and Old Factors in Suicide* in Suicide and The Right to Die 6 (J.
Pohiers & D. Mieth eds. 1985); Suicide in Canada, *supra* note 21, at 23; Suicide in
Asia *supra* note 10, at 358; M. Iga, The Thorn in the Chrysanthemum 44 (1986); but
see Wen, *supra* note 22, at 11 (no correlation between unemployment and suicide in
Japan). In societies where there is greater acceptance of unemployment and
poverty, unemployment does not appear to be related to suicide because "the
familiar stigma is absent." *Ibid.* at 23 (explaining lack of correlation between
unemployment and suicide in the Maritimes). One recent British study concluded
that there is no significant correlation between retirement and suicide, though the
age at which older people stop all work was associated with suicide. Shephard and
Barraclough, *Work and Suicide: An Empirical Investigation,* 136 Brit. J. Psychiatry
469 (1980), abstracted in Osgood & McIntosh, *supra* note 14, at 139.
52. Physical health and pain are among the most often mentioned causes in elderly
suicides. Suicide and Suicide Prevention, *supra* note 8, at 27. Bock, *supra* note 8, at

74. One study reported that suicide victims had active illnesses at the time of their suicide in 70% of the cases, and 50% of the suicides (three-fourths of those with active illnesses) were considered to have been affected by the illness. Dorpat, Anderson & Ripley, *The Relationship of Physical Illness to Suicide* in Suicide Behaviors: Diagnosis and Management 209 (Resnik ed. 1968), as abstracted in Osgood & McIntosh *supra* note 14, at 98. Between 70 and 90 percent of elderly individuals who commit suicide see their family physicians within three months of their deaths, "typically displaying hypochondriacal concerns and physical symptoms of depression ..." Suicide in Canada, *supra* note 21, at 53. Analysis of World Health Organization data from twenty countries regarding ten chronic diseases showed no significant correlation between suicide rates for persons below the age of 65 and those diseases, but above age 65 those diseases proved to be powerful predicter of the suicide rates. Atchley, *supra* note 14, at 148.

53. "Societies with hierarchical systems which are based on unalterable factors such as sex and age ... exert strong pressure [for suicide.] ... The stricter and more rigid the authoritative controlling system, the more suicide attempts will be made ..." Suicide in Asia, *supra* note 10, at 355. The pattern of suicides in Asian and European nations provide clear cultural contrasts. For one thing, the incidence of suicide generally *declines* with age, especially after age 35. *Ibid.* at 350 (except Japan, Taiwan and Sri Lanka). Moreover, the difference between the male suicide rate and female suicide rate is much smaller in Asia than it is in most western nations; in fact, in some countries for some age groups the rate of suicide among females is even higher than it is for males. *Ibid.* at 353; Wen, *supra* note 22, at 10; Yap, *Aged and Mental Health in Hong Kong* in II, Processes of Aging: Social and Psychological Perspectives 176-91 (R. Williams, C. Tibbits & W. Donahue eds. 1963) as abstracted in Osgood and McIntosh, *supra* note 14, at 149; Lester, *The Distribution of Sex and Age Among Completed Suicides: A Cross-National Study,* 28 Int'l J. Soc. Psychiatry 256 (1982). *See also* M. Iga, *supra* note 51, at 48-68. In Japan, unlike European nations, rural residence is associated with greater risk of suicide among males than urban residence. Araki & Muratea, *Social Life Factors Affecting Suicide in Japanese Men and Women,* 116 Suicide & Life-Threatening Behavior 458, 464 (1986). And while the notion of "honorable suicide" in Japan has been distorted in some western writing, *see* Palmore, *The Status and Integration of the Aged in Japanese Society,* 30 J. Gerontology 199, 208 (1975), the romantic concepts associated with suicide and ritual suicide in Japan illustrate the importance and complexity of cultural variables. See Iga, *supra* note 51, at 148-160; Wen, *supra* note 22, at 10-12. See further Appendix 10-J (the confused pattern of suicide in Israel); Shichor & Bergman, *Patterns of Suicide Among the Elderly in Israel,* 19 Gerontologist 248 (1979) (suicide patterns based on country of origin).

54. Ruzicka, supra note 9, at 398; Kruijt, supra note 18, at 62-64; Suicide in Asia, supra note 10, at 350-59; Iraki & Murata, *Social Life Factors Affecting Suicide in Japanese Men and Women,* 16 Suicide and Life-Threatening Behavior 458 (1986).

55. Atchley, *supra* note 8, at 141; Lyons, *Observable and Subjective Factors Associated With Attempted Suicide in Later Life,* 15 Suicide and Life-Threatening Behavior 168 (1985). *See generally,* M. Miller, Suicide After Sixty: The Final Alternative (1979); N. Osgood, Suicide and the Elderly (1985); Kirsling, *Review of Suicide Among Elderly Persons,* 59 Psychological Rep. 359 (1986).

56. E. Durkheim, Suicide: A Study in Sociology (1951) (originally published in 1897 in French). *See generally* Baudry, *The Sociological Approach to Suicide, From Dirk-*

heim to the Present Day in Suicide and the Right to Die 12-26 (J. Pohier & D. Mieth, eds. 1985).

57. Henseler, *The Psychology of Suicide,* in Suicide and the Right to Die, *supra* note 51, at 21-26; NIMH *supra* note 8, at 10.

58. Shulman, *supra* note 15, at 206. Shulman identifies the major factors in suicide among the aged to be depression, hypochondria, bereavement, social isolation, and physical illness. *Ibid.* at 205.

59. Murphy, Lindesay & Grunt, *Sixty Years of Suicide in England and Wales,* 43 Arch. Gen. Psychiatry 969, 976 (1986) (citing Shulman, supra note 15). One study found that 90% of suicides are committed by persons suffering from neurotic disturbance. Henseler, *The Psychology of Suicide* in Suicide and the Right to Die, supra note 51, at 22. *See also* Brown, Henteleff, Barakat & Rowe, *Is It Normal for Terminally Ill Patients to Desire Death?,* 143 Am. J. Psychiatry 208 (1986) (all of the terminally ill patients who had considered suicide, or wished their lives to be ended, "were judged to be suffering from clinical depressive illness.").

60. *See* Bock, *supra* note 9, at 77; Shulman, *supra* note 15.

61. E. Durkheim, *supra* note 56.

62. Ruzicka, *supra* note 9, at 398; Suicide in Canada, *supra* note 21, at 22; NIMH, *supra* note 8, at 1, 10, 11; Osgood & McIntosh, *supra* note 14, *passim* (abstracting numerous studies).

63. Bock, *supra* note 8, at 72.

64. "In itself conjugal society is harmful to the woman and agravates her tendency to suicide ... In general, the wife profits less from family life than the husband." E. Duirkheim, *supra* note 56, at 188; see also ibid at 275.

65. See generally Suicide in Canada at 22; Bock, *supra* note 8, at 75; Rico-Velasco & Mynko, *Suicide in Marital Status: A Changing Relationship,* 35 J. Marr. & Fam. 239 (1973).

66. Bock, *supra* note 8, at 77.

67. P. Slater, The Pursuit of Loneliness (1970) cited in Rico-Valasco & Mynko, *supra* note 65, at 244.

68. Bock, *supra* note 8, at 75.

69. Bock & Webber, *Suicide Among the Elderly: Isolating Widowhood and Mitigating Alternatives,* 34 J. Marr & Fam. 24 (1972) abstracted in Osgood & McIntosh, *supra* note 14, at 90.

70. MacMahon & Pugh, *Suicide in Widowhood,* 81 Am. J. Epidemiology 23 (1965) summarized in Osgood and McIntosh, *supra* note 14, at 119.

71. Berdes, *Social Services for the Aged, Dying and Bereaved in International Perspective* 26-41 (1978) abstracted in Osgood & McIntosh, *supra* note 14, at 42; Note, 86 Colum. L. Rev., *supra* note 38, at 357.

72. See generally Suicide in Asia, supra note 10, at 358; Simon & Lumry, *Suicide of the Spouse as a Divorce Substitute,* 31, Diseases of the Nervous System 608 (1970) abstracted in Osgood & McIntosh, *supra* note 14, at 140 (60% of the persons who commited suicide had serious marital discord); Richman, *Pyschotherapy and Family Therapy with the Suicidal Elderly* in Proceedings of the 15th Annual Meeting of the American Association of Suicidology 84-86 (1984) abstracted in Osgood & McIntosh *supra* note 14, at 60 (family dissention was a major factor in the great majority of suicide attempts of the old and the young).

73. See generallySuicide in Canada, *supra* note 21, at 22: Suicide in Asia, *supra* note 10, at 354-58.

74. Megenhagen, Lee & Gove, *Till Death Do Us Part: Recent Changes in the Relation-ship Between Marital Status and Mortality,* 70 Sociology and Social Race 53, 56 (2985). See Rico-Valasco & Mynko, *supra* note 65, at 239.
75. Suicide in Asia, *supra* note 10, at 354; *see also* Wen, *supra* note 22, at 12-14, M. Iga, *supra* note 51, at 48-68, 181-83.
76. Suicide in Canada, *supra* note 21, at 22; Rico-Velasco & Mynko, *supra* note 65, at 240-44; Wenz, *Family Constaliation Factors, Depression and Parent Suicide Poten-tial,* 49 Am. J. Orthopsychiatry, 164 (1979); Osgood & McIntosh, *supra* note 14, at 146 (survey of 245 families validates thesis that the greater the family size the greater the protection against suicide) Veevers, *Parenthood and Suicide: An Examination of a Neglected Variable,* 7 Social Science and Medicine, 135 (1973) reviews and confirms that in Great Britain childless married women have higher rates of suicide than those with children; Ruzicka, *supra* note 9, at 398; NIMH *supra* note 8, at 1, 3.
77. The suicide rate of widowers who had relatives living nearby and/or belonged to other organizations was less than half the rate of those who had no social ties. MacMahon & Pugh, *supra* note 70, at 76.
78. Segers, *supra* note 47, at 11-30.
79. *See generally* Suicide in Asia, *supra* note 10, at 352; Palmore, *supra* note 53, at 201-08; Bock, *supra* note 8, at 73; Lester, *supra* note 53 (the distribution of sex and age) at 256.
80. Araki & Murata, *supra* note 51, at 464, 65; *see also* Wen, *supra* note 22, at 10-14.
81. NIMH, *supra* note 8, at 1-10.
82. NIMH, *supra* note 10, at 11; Batchler & Napier, *Attempted Suicide in Old Age,* 2 Brit. Med. J. 1186 (1953), Osgood & McIntosh, *supra* note 14, at 88; Lester & Beck, *Age Differences in Patterns in Attempted Suicide* 5 Omega: J. Death and Dying 317 (1974) Osgood & McIntosh, *supra* note 14, at 114.
83. Steinmetz, *Dependency, Stress and Violence Between Middle-aged Care Givers and Their Elderly Parents* in Abuse and Maltreatment of the Elderly, *supra* note 33, at 134, 137.
84. *Moore* v. *City of East Cleveland,* 431 U.S. 494, 505-05 (1977) (plurality opinion) (upholding the right of a grandmother to have two of her grandchildren live with her notwithstanding a city zoning restriction against it).
85. Zimmerman, *Reassessing the Effect of Public Policy on Family Functioning,* 59 Soc. Casework 451, 452 (1978). *See generally* Hafen, *The Constitutional Status of Marriage, Kinship and Sexual Privacy — Balancing the Individual and Social Interests,* 81 Mich. L. Rev. 463, 479-84 (1983).
86. D. Callaghan, *supra* note 33, at 194.

APPENDIX 1

Table 9. Aging Population, Growth Rate And Percentage Aged 65 Years Or Over In Tot
World And Major Regions, 1950-2000   (Population in thousands)

	1950	1960	1970	1980	1985	1990	2000
World (Total Pop.)	2,504 000	3,014 000	3,683 000	4,453 000	4,482 000	5,248 000	6,127 000
Population aged 60+	203 181	233 915	297 361	370 849	415 570	471 851	595 301
Population aged 65+	132 165		192 304	255 939	277 388	312 612	404966
Growth rate. ages 65+	—	1.3	2.5	2.7	1.7	2.4	2.4
Percentage aged 65+	5.3	5.1	5.2	5.7	5.7	6.0	6.6
More developed regions (Total Pop.)	NA	945 000	1,047 000	1,136 000	1,173 000	1,209 000	1,276 000
Population aged 60+	94 558	118 559	149 624	172 733	185 199	202 966	233 681
Population aged 65+	63 517	80 260	101 746	129 791	130 627	141 102	168 313
Growth rate, ages 65+	—	2.2	2.3	2.2	0.2	1.5	1.4
Percentage aged 65+	7.6	8.5	9.7	11.4	11.1	11.7	13.2
Less developed regions (Total Pop.)	NA	2,069 000	2,636 000	3,317 000	3,669 000	4,040 000	4,851 000
Population aged 60+	108 623	115 356	147 737	198 116	230 371	268 885	361 619
Population aged 65+	68 648	73 196	90 558	126 148	146 761	171 509	236 653
Growth rate. ages 65+	—	0.3	2.7	3.3	3.0	3.1	3.2
Percentage aged 65+	7.6	8.5	9.7	11.4	11.1	11.7	13.2
Africa (Total Pop.)	222 000	278 000	357 000	476 000	553 000	645 000	877 000
Population aged 60 +	12 849	14 402	18 107	23 237	26 600	30 825	41 822
Population aged 65+	68 648	73 196	90 558	126 148	146 761	171 509	236 653
Growth rate. ages 65+	—	2.2	2.3	2.2	0.2	1.5	1.4
Percentage aged 65+	4.1	3.5	3.4	3.8	4.0	4.2	4.9
Americas							
Latin America (Total Pop.)	165 000	217 000	284 000	362 000	406 000	453 000	550 000
Population aged 60+	8 896	12 260	17 087	23 312	27 149	31 577	41 768
Population aged 65+	5 524	7 678	11 029	15 507	17 948	21 026	28 396
Growth rate. ages 65+	—	3.4	3.6	3.5	2.9	3.2	2.9
Percentage aged 65+	3.3	3.5	3.9	4.3	4.4	4.6	5.2
Northern America (Total Pop.)	166 000	199 000	227 000	252 000	263 000	275 000	298 000
Population aged 60+	20 062	25 756	31 228	38 941	41 882	44 212	46 804
Population ages 65+	13 454	18 029	21 799	27 873	29 752	32 286	34 934
Growth rate. ages 65+	—	2.7	1.8	2.5	1.3	1.7	0.5
Percentage aged 65+	8.1	9.1	9.6	11.1	11.3	11.7	11.7
Asia							
East Asia (Total Pop.)	671 000	801 000	984 000	1,183 000	1,252 000	1,317 000	1,470 000
Population aged 60+	39 329	48 115	67 093	91 843	106 448	123 595	162 122
Population aged 65+	23 976	28 981	41 326	60 112	69 964	81 245	110 215
Growth rate. ages 65+	—	1.7	4.1	3.5	3.0	3.0	3.0
Percentage aged 65+	3.6	3.6	4.2	5.1	5.6	6.2	7.5
South Asia (Total Pop.)	695 000	864 000	1,111 000	1,408 000	1,572 000	1,740 000	2,074 000
Population aged 60+	53 832	48 763	56 365	74 478	87 110	102 881	142 036
Population aged 65+	35 070	32 909	34 175	46 371	53 843	63 402	90 092
Growth rate. ages 65+	—	-1.3	1.1	3.2	3.0	3.3	3.5
Percentage aged 65+	5.0	3.8	3.1	3.3	3.4	3.6	4.3
Europe (Total Pop.)	392 000	425 000	459 000	484 000	492 000	499 000	513 000
Population aged 60+	50 554	61 347	76 490	81 684	86 805	91 877	101 705
Population aged 65+	34 114	41 272	52 414	63 043	61 175	65 526	74 606
Growth rate. ages 65+	—	1.7	2.5	1.5	-0.6	1.3	1.1
Percentage aged 65+	8.7	9.7	11.4	13.0	12.4	13.1	14.5
Oceania (Total Pop.)	126 000	16 000	19 000	23 000	25 000	27 000	30 000
Population aged 60+	1 428	1 708	2 085	2 644	2 997	3 323	3 836
Population aged 65+	943	1 174	1 408	1 825	2 040	2 324	2 756
Growth rate. ages 65+	—	1.9	1.8	2.8	2.2	2.6	1.4
Percentage aged 65+	7.5	7.4	7.3	7.9	8.2	8.7	9.1
Union of Soviet Republics (T.P.)	180 000	214 000	242 000	265 000	278 000	291 000	315 000
Population aged 60+	16 231	21 564	28 905	34 711	36 579	43 560	55 148
Population aged 65+	10 974	14 484	18 875	26 654	25 983	27 506	37 325
Growth rate. aged 65+	—	2.6	2.1	3.2	-0.1	1.3	1.9
Percentage aged 65+	6.1	6.8	7.8	10.0	9.3	9.4	11.9

NOTE: Growth rate refers to the average annual rate of increase for each five-year period since the preceding date.

SOURCES: Dept. Int'l. Econ, & Soc. Affairs, Population studies, No. 9 world Population Trends, Population and Development Interrelations
and Population Policies (U.N. 1985) (hereinafter ""DIESA, Population Studies No. 93") at 34 (Table enhanced with data from
Tables 1 & 2 and from Demographic Yearbook: 1984 (U.N. 1986) at 143.

APPENDIX 2

Table 7. Sex Ratio And Median Age, Medium Variant, World And Major Regions, 1950-2025

	Sex ratio				Median age			
	1950	1980	2000	2025	1950	1980	2000	2025
World	98.9	100.6	101.2	100.6	22.9	22.4	26.4	31.0
Africa	97.2	98.3	99.3	99.5	18.9	17.3	17.3	21.8
Americas								
Latin America	101.0	100.0	99.7	99.0	19.7	19.8	23.7	29.8
Northern America	99.6	95.3	95.8	95.5	30.0	29.9	35.7	38.0
Asia								
East Asia	102.0	103.4	102.5	100.5	22.4	22.6	30.6	38.4
South Asia	105.8	104.8	104.9	104.1	19.7	19.3	23.5	31.2
Europe	92.5	95.2	96.5	96.4	30.5	33.0	37.2	40.6
Oceania	103.7	102.2	101.2	99.7	27.9	26.4	30.1	33.7
Union of Soviet Socialist Republics	78.3	87.8	93.4	95.8	24.7	29.4	33.7	35.6

Source: Results of the United Nations demographic estimates and projections as assessed in 1982. DIESA, Populations Studies No. 93

APPENDIX 3

Table 3. Number of elderly persons by age and percentage distribution in the world and in the more developed and less developed regions, 1950-2025

Area	Age group	1950	1975	2000	2025
A. Number (In millions)					
World	60 years and over	214	346	590	1 12
	60–69	133	208	338	65
	70–79	65	106	193	37
	80+	15	32	60	11
More developed regions	60 years and over	95	166	230	31
	60–69	56	93	119	16
	70–79	31	53	81	10
	80+	8	19	30	4
Less developed regions	60 years and over	119	180	360	80
	60–69	78	115	219	49
	70–79	35	53	111	24
	80+	7	13	29	6
B. Percentage of population 60 years of age and over					
World		100	100	100	10
More developed regions		44	48	39	2
Less developed regions		56	52	61	7

DIESA, The World Aging Situation: at Strategies and Policies (U.N. 1985)

PERCENTAGE

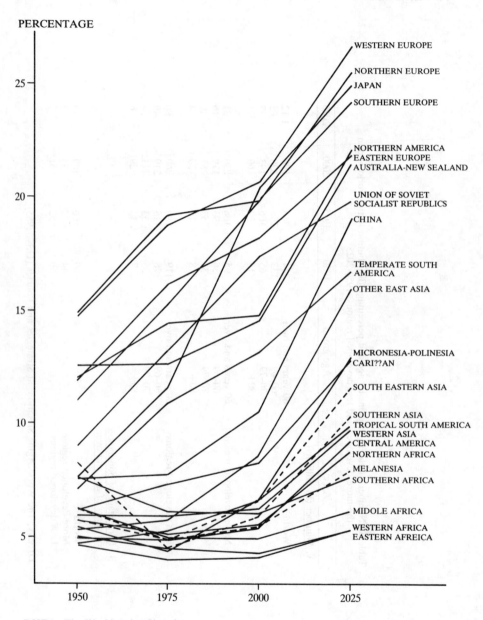

DISEA, The World Aging Situation

Population, 1950, 1980 and 2025

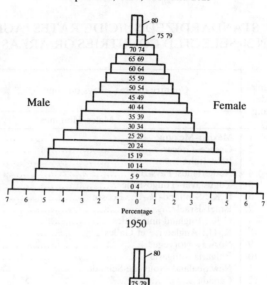

Male   Female

7 6 5 4 3 2 1 0 1 2 3 4 5 6 7
Percentage
1950

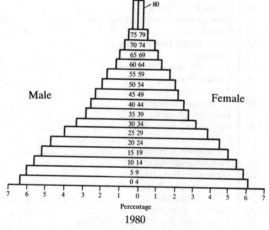

Male   Female

7 6 5 4 3 2 1 0 1 2 3 4 5 6 7
Percentage
1980

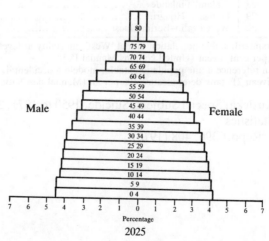

Male   Female

7 6 5 4 3 2 1 0 1 2 3 4 5 6 7
Percentage
2025

DIESA, Population Studies No. 93 at 31

TABLE 4. STANDARDIZED SUICIDE RATES (AGES 15 AND OVER) IN 30 SELECTED COUNTRIES OR AREAS, 1965-1969

Rank order Rang	Country or area - Pays ou zone	Suicides per (pour) 100 000
	Males–Hommes	
1	Mexico–Mexique	4.44
2	Greece–Grèce	6.38
3	Italy–Italie	10.19
4	Netherlands–Pays-Bas	11.78
5	Yugoslavia–Yougoslavie	11.97
6	U.K.: Scotiand–R.-U.: Ecosse	12.00
7	Israel–Israel	12.74
8	U.K.: England and Wales R.-U.: Angleterre et Galles	14.71
9	Norway–Norvege	14.75
10	Bulgaria–Buigarie	18.32
11	New Sealand–Nouvelle-Selande	19.11
12	Canada	20.63
13	Hong Kong–Hong-kong	21.40
14	Portugal	22.44
15	United States–Etats-Units	22.98
16	Poland–Pologne	24.51
17	Japan–Japon	24.71
18	Australia–Australie	25.43
19	Belgium–Belgique	25.43
20	Singapore–singapour	27.50
21	France	30.20
22	Denmark–Denmark	31.84
23	Wsitzerland–Suisse	34.69
24	Germany, Fed. Rep. of– Allemagne, Rep. féad. d'	35.64
25	Sweden–Suégde	36.81
26	Austria–Autriche	41.48
27	Czechoslovakia–Tchéacoslovaquie	45.18
28	Finland–Finlande	47.98
29	Hungary–Hongrie	58.46
30	West Berlin–Berlin Ouest	63.90

* Standard: stable population model 'West', mortallty at level 21, rate of growth 1 per cent a year (United Nations Manual IV).
En référence à une population stable, modele à occidentai, mortailte au niveau 21, taux de croissance 1% per an (Manual des Nations U

Ruzicka, Special Subject, Suicide, 1950 to 1971, 29 World Health Statistics
Report 396, 408 (1976)

CHART 1. TYPES OF AGE-SPECIFIC INCICENCE OF SUICIDE (MALES)
GRAPHIQUE 1. TYPES D'INCIDENCE DU SUICIDE PA AGE (HOMMES)

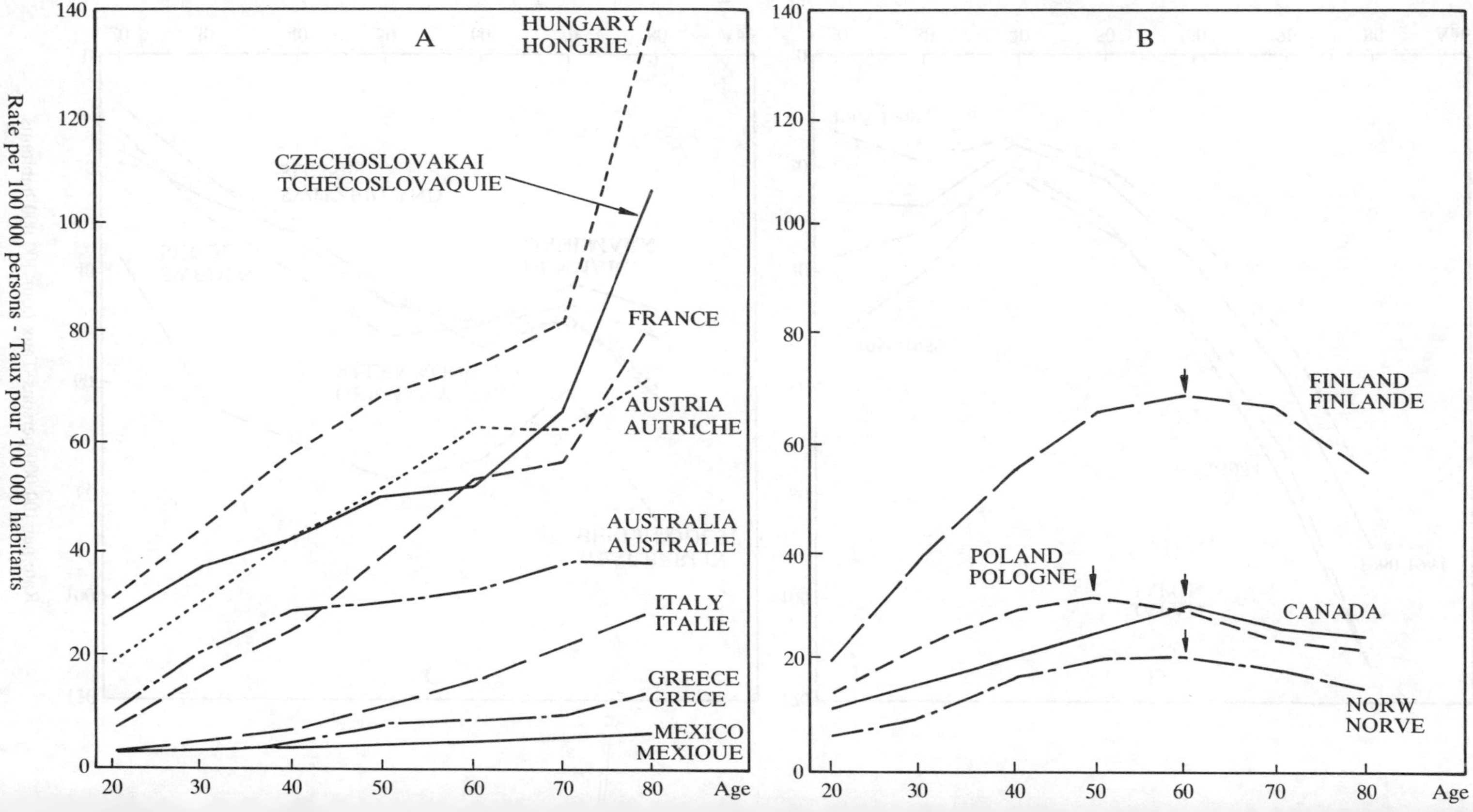
A
B
HUNGARY
HONGRIE
CZECHOSLOVAKAI
TCHECOSLOVAQUIE
FRANCE
AUSTRIA
AUTRICHE
AUSTRALIA
AUSTRALIE
ITALY
ITALIE
GREECE
GRECE
MEXICO
MEXIOUE
FINLAND
FINLANDE
POLAND
POLOGNE
CANADA
NORW
NORVE
140
120
100
80
60
40
20
0
20
30
40
50
60
70
80
Age
Rate per 100 000 persons - Taux pour 100 000 habitants

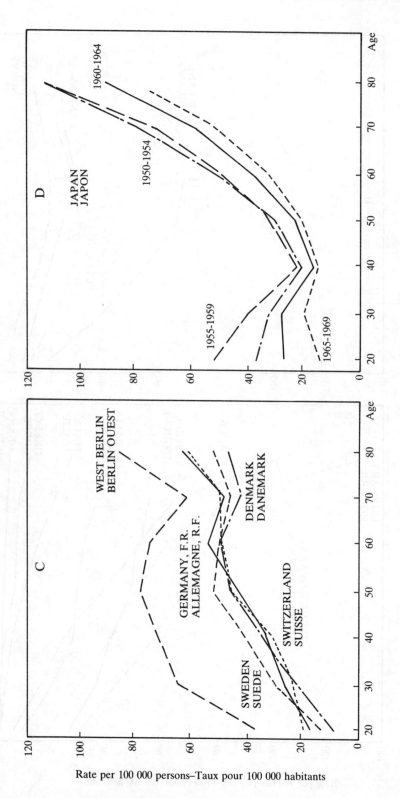

Rrzica. Special Report, Suicide. 1950 to 1971. 29 World Health Statistics Report 396. 40 (1976).

Rate per 100 000 persons–Taux pour 100 000 habitants

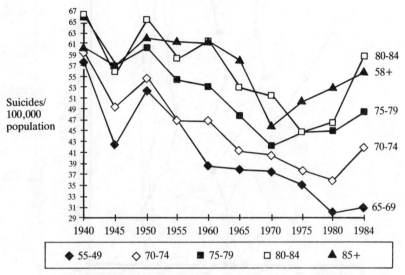

WHITE MALE SUICIDE RATES AMONG ELDERLY IN USA

37 GEN. ARCH. PSYCHIATRY &vital Statistics of the United Staces.
1980 & 1984. Table 1-8   (compiled from data)

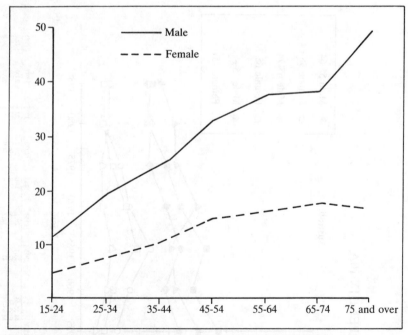

Mean Suicide rate, by age and sex, for 20 selected countries, 1963-66.

Atchley, Aging and Reflection on the Quality of Life in
Second Conference on the Epidemiology of Aging 141,
146 (S. Haynes & M. Feinbeib eds. 1980)

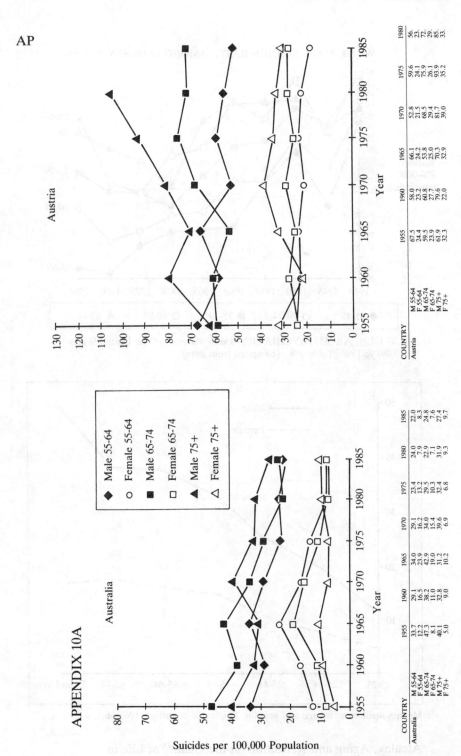

APPENDIX 10A

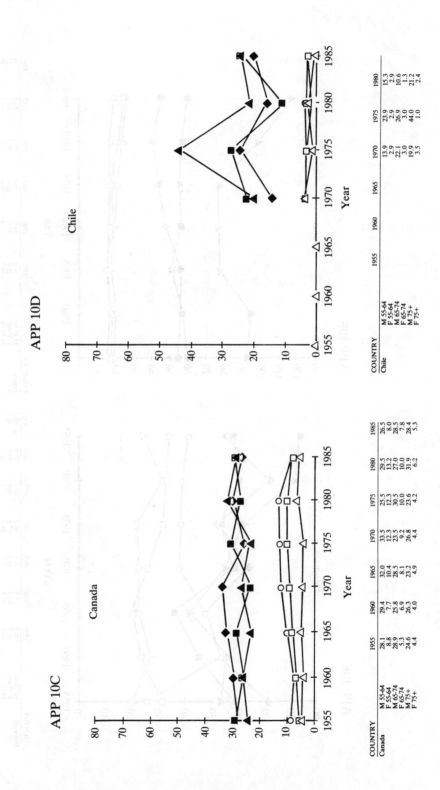

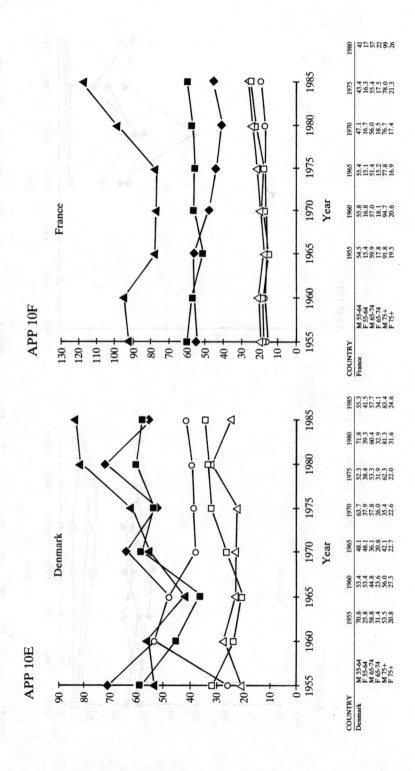

APP 10E

Denmark

COUNTRY		1955	1960	1965	1970	1975	1980	1985
Denmark	M 55-64	70.8	53.4	48.1	63.7	52.3	71.8	55.3
	F 55-64	25.8	53.4	48.1	37.9	38.4	39.3	41.5
	M 65-74	58.8	44.8	36.1	57.8	53.3	60.4	57.7
	F 65-74	31.4	23.6	20.8	26.0	31.9	32.9	34.1
	M 75+	53.5	56.0	42.1	35.4	62.3	81.3	83.4
	F 75+	20.8	27.5	22.7	22.6	22.0	31.6	24.6

APP 10F

France

COUNTRY		1955	1960	1965	1970	1975	1980
France	M 55-64	54.5	55.8	55.1	47.1	43.4	41
	F 55-64	15.4	16.8	15.1	16.7	16.3	17
	M 65-74	59.9	57.0	51.4	56.0	55.4	57
	F 65-74	17.8	18.1	15.2	18.5	17.5	22
	M 75+	91.8	94.7	77.8	76.7	78.0	99
	F 75+	19.5	20.6	16.9	17.4	21.3	26

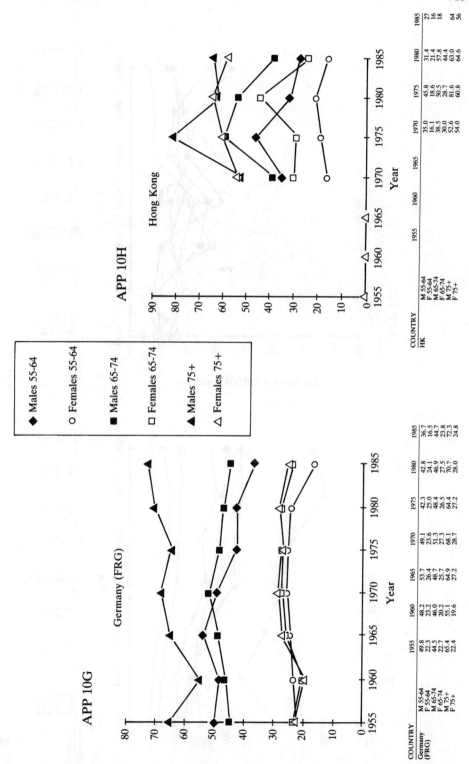

APP 10H

Hong Kong

Year

APP 10G

Germany (FRG)

Year

- ◆ Males 55-64
- ○ Females 55-64
- ■ Males 65-74
- □ Females 65-74
- ▲ Males 75+
- △ Females 75+

COUNTRY		1955	1960	1965	1970	1975	1980	1985
HK	M 55-64				35.0	45.8	31.4	27
	F 55-64				16.1	18.6	21.4	16
	M 65-74				38.5	50.5	57.8	18
	M 75+				30.0	28.7	44.4	64
	F 75+				52.6	81.6	63.0	56
					54.0	60.8	64.6	

COUNTRY		1955	1960	1965	1970	1975	1980	1985
Germany (FRG)	M 55-64	49.8	48.2	53.7	49.1	42.3	42.8	36.7
	F 55-64	22.3	23.2	26.4	23.6	25.0	24.1	16.5
	M 65-74	44.5	46.0	48.7	51.3	48.4	46.9	44.7
	M 75+	22.7	20.2	25.7	27.3	26.5	27.5	23.8
	F 75+	65.4	55.1	64.9	68.1	64.4	70.7	72.3
		22.4	19.6	27.2	28.7	27.2	28.0	24.8

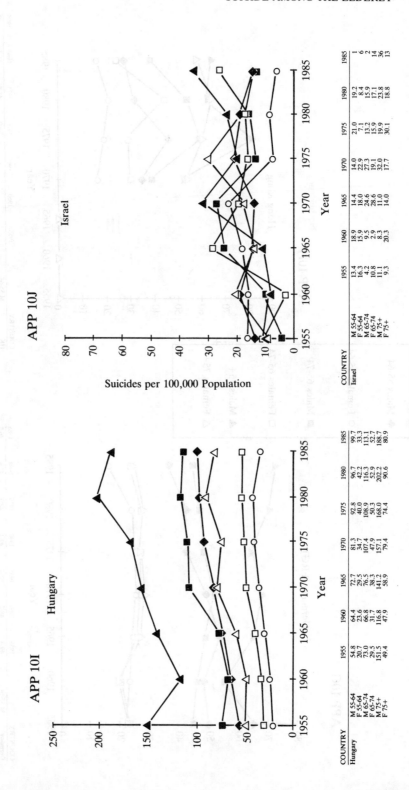

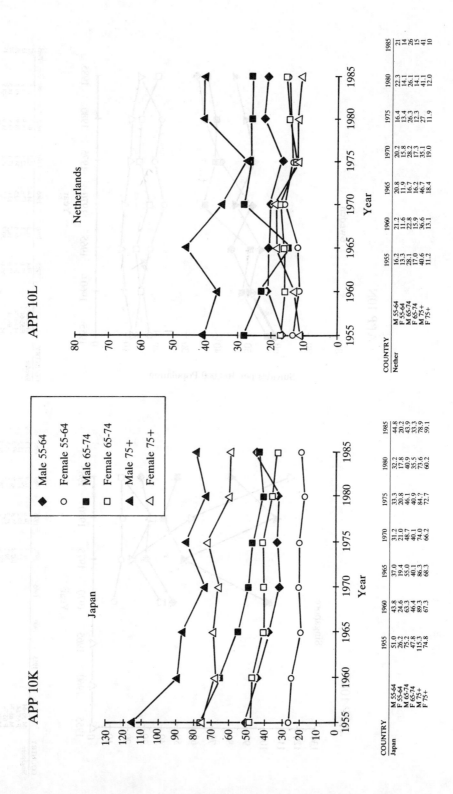

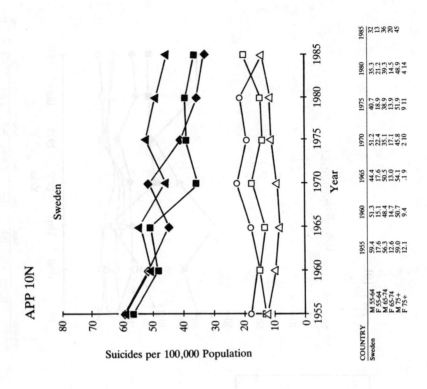

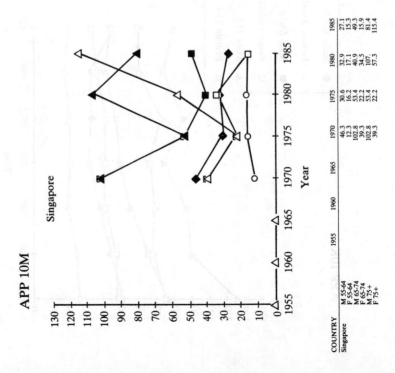

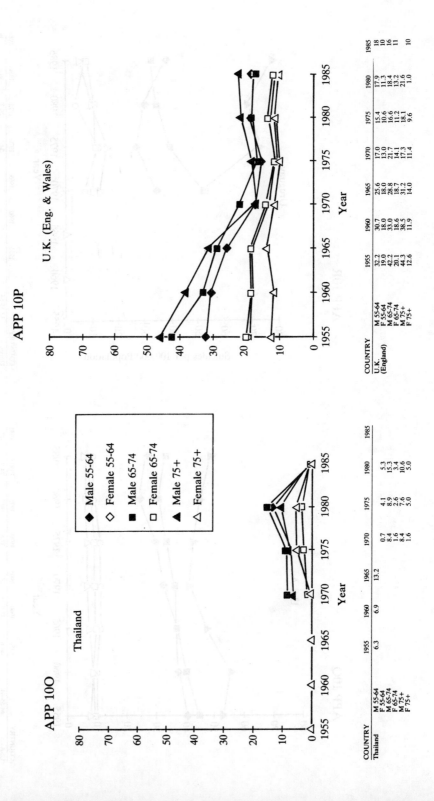

APP 10P

U.K. (Eng. & Wales)

COUNTRY		1955	1960	1965	1970	1975	1980	1985
U.K.	M 55-64	32.2	30.7	25.6	17.0	15.4	17.9	18
(England)	F 55-64	19.0	18.0	18.0	13.0	10.6	11.3	10
	M 65-74	42.2	33.0	28.8	21.7	16.6	18.4	16
	F 65-74	20.1	18.6	28.7	14.1	11.2	13.2	11
	M 75+	44.3	38.5	31.2	17.3	18.1	21.6	
	F 75+	12.6	11.9	14.0	11.4	9.6	1.0	10

APP 10O

Thailand

Legend:
- ◆ Male 55-64
- ◇ Female 55-64
- ■ Male 65-74
- □ Female 65-74
- ▲ Male 75+
- △ Female 75+

COUNTRY		1955	1960	1965	1970	1975	1980	1985
Thailand	M 55-64					0.7	4.1	5.3
	F 55-64	6.3	6.9	13.2		8.4	8.9	15.3
	M 65-74					1.6	2.6	5.4
	F 65-74					8.4	7.6	10.6
	M 75+					1.6	5.0	5.0
	F 75+							

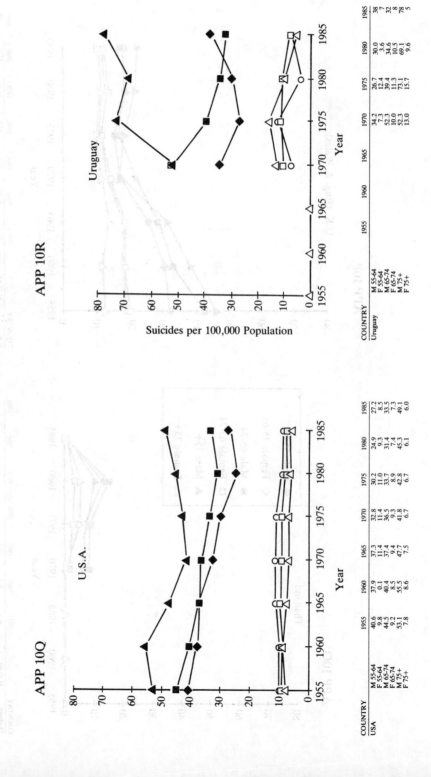

APP 10R

Uruguay

Suicides per 100,000 Population

Year

COUNTRY		1955	1960	1965	1970	1975	1980	1985
Uruguay	M 55-64				34.2	26.7	30.0	38
	F 55-64				7.3	12.4	3.6	7
	M 65-74				52.3	39.4	34.6	32
	F 65-74				10.0	11.3	10.5	8
	M 75+				52.3	73.1	69.1	78
	F 75+				13.0	15.7	9.6	5

APP 10Q

U.S.A.

Year

COUNTRY		1955	1960	1965	1970	1975	1980	1985
USA	M 55-64	40.6	37.9	37.3	32.8	30.2	24.9	27.2
	F 55-64	9.8	0.1	11.4	11.4	11.0	9.3	8.5
	M 65-74	44.5	40.4	9.4	36.5	33.7	31.4	33.5
	F 65-74	9.2	8.5	9.4	9.3	8.9	7.4	7.3
	M 75+	53.1	55.5	47.7	41.8	42.8	45.3	49.1
	F 75+	7.8	8.6	7.5	6.7	6.7	6.1	6.0

APP 10S

Suicides Among the Elderly: composite Multinational Trends

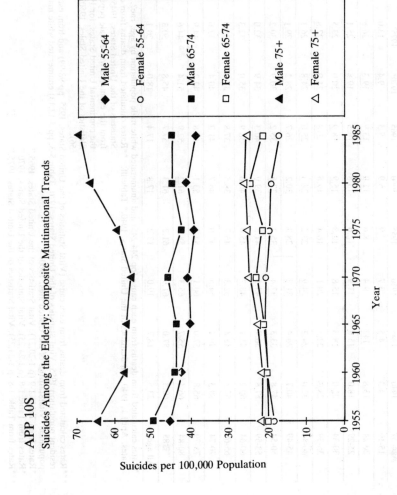

APPENDIX 11

Table 6. –Age-Specific White Male Suicide Rates per 100,000 Population by year in five-Year Intervals

A Mailed Age. yr	1940	1945	1950	1955 b 1935-Year	1960 b 1940-45-	1965 b 1945-50	1970* b 1950 55	1975** b 1955-60	1980 b.1960-65
15-19	4.3	4.5	3.7	3.9	5.9	5.3	9.4	13.0	15.0
20-24	13.8	142	9.4	8.6	11.9	13.9	19.3	26.8	27.8
25-29	18.0	15.8	11.9	12.6	13.8	16.5	19.8	25.1	27.5
30-34	22.0	18.3	15.8	12.8	15.9	18.9	20.0	23.5	23.5
35-39	28.3	22.3	20.1	16.4	19.6	218	21.9	22.8	24.0
40-44	32.0	24.2	24.9	23.2	24.3	25.0	24.8	26.1	23.0
45-49	40.7	26.4	31.2	28.3	30.2	26.7	28.2	29.1	23.2
50-54	47.8	33.3	37.4	35.7	37.6	35.2	30.9	30.2	25.3
55-59	57.8	36.7	43.5	41.5	39.9	40.3	34.9	32.0	26.2
60-64	60.2	41.1	48.7	45.0	40.6	38.9	35.0	32.3	25.4
65-69	57.5	42.4	52.3	46.7	38.5	37.8	37.4	35.0	30.0
70-74	59.3	49.4	54.5	47.0	46.7	41.2	40.4	37.6	35.9
75-79	65.8	57.0	60.1	54.2	53.1	47.8	42.2	44.9	44.9
80-84	66.4	55.7	65.3	58.2	61.2	52.9	51.4	44.6	46.5
≧85	60.3	57.0	61.9	61.2	61.3	57.7	45.8	50.3	52.8
All ages	23.5	18.7	19.0	17.2	17.8	17.4	18.0	20.1	19.9

Rates caiculated from deaths from each cause (pp 244-245) and anumerated white male population by age. rac?. and sex, United States. April 1, 1940. ital Statistics of the United States. 1940. Table III. **Rates calculated from deaths from each cause (Vital Statistics of the United States. 1945. pp 92-93) and from the estimated white male population ?siding in the continental United States, for 1945(Vital Slatistics of the United Stales. 1950. Table 2.21, p 56).

***Rates calculated from deaths from each cause (Vital Statistics of the United States. 1955, pp 98-99) and from estimated white male resident population 1955. Vital Slatistics of the United States. 1970. Table 5-3. pp 5-12.13) enumerated white male resident population, VitalStatistics of the United ates. 1960."

*Rates from Table 1-9 (p 1-20,21). Vital Statlstics of the United States. 1965."
**Rates from Table 1-8 (p 1-24,25). Vital Statistics of the United States. 1970."
***Rates from Table 1-8 (p 1-24,25), Vital Statistics of the United States. 1975."

APPENDIX 12

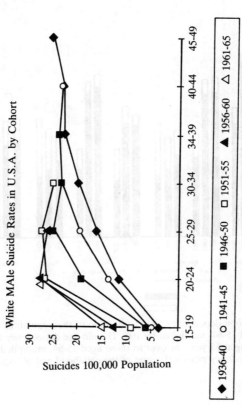

White MAle Suicide Rates in U.S.A. by Cohort

Suicides 100,000 Population

◆ 1936-40   ○ 1941-45   ■ 1946-50   □ 1951-55   ▲ 1956-60   △ 1961-65

Compiled from data in 37 GEN. ARCH. PSYCHIATRY & Vital Statistics of the United States. 1980 & 1984. Table 1-8.

DIESAL, Populations Studies No. 93 at 36,35

Figure IV. Childhood, old-age and total dependency ratios, medium 1950. 1980 and 2025

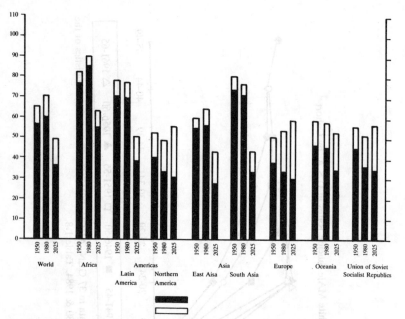

NOTE: The childhood dependency ratio is the ratio of the population aged 0-14 years to those aged 15-64. multiplied by 100. The old-age dependency ratio is the ratio of those aged 65 years or over to those aged 15-64. multiplied by 100. The total age dependency ratio is the sum of the childhood and old-age dependeny ratios.

APPENDIX 14

TABLE 10. CHILDHOOD, OLD-AGE AND TOTAL DEPENDENCY RATIOS, MEDIUM VARIANT, WORLD AND MAJOR REGIONS, 1950-2025

	Childhood age dependency ratio a				Old-age dependency ratio b				Total age dependency ratio c			
	1950	1980	2000	2025	1950	1980	2000	2025	1950	1980	2000	2025
World	59.0	60.8	48.2	37.5	8.9	9.8	10.5	14.4	67.9	70.6	58.7	51.9
Africa	77.9	87.5	87.3	58.6	6.7	5.9	5.9	6.3	84.7	93.4	93.1	63.9
Americas												
Lain America	72.1	69.9	54.3	39.7	6.0	7.6	8.4	12.4	78.1	77.5	62.7	52.1
Northern America	41.9	34.0	32.3	32.2	12.5	16.7	17.6	27.6	54.4	50.7	49.9	59.8
Asia												
East Asia	58.0	59.6	34.3	27.0	5.9	8.5	10.9	19.4	63.9	68.2	45.2	46.4
South Asia	73.4	72.9	53.2	34.7	9.2	5.9	7.0	0.8	82.6	78.8	60.2	35.5
Europe	38.5	34.5	29.2	29.3	13.2	20.1	22.0	29.2	51.7	54.6	51.2	58.5
Oceania	47.4	47.2	40.4	35.5	11.9	12.7	14.0	19.2	59.2	59.9	54.4	54.7
Union of Soviet Socialist Republics ...	47.1	37.1	36.6	34.9	9.5	15.3	18.4	23.6	56.7	52.4	55.0	58.7

Source: Results of the United Nations demographic estimates and projections as assessed in 1982.

a Childhood dependency ratio is defined as the ratio of the population aged 0-14 years to those aged 15-64, multiplied by 100.

b Old-age dependency ratio is defined as the ratio of the population aged 65 years or over to those aged 15-64, multiplied by 100.

c Total age dependency ratio is defined as the sum of the childhood and old-age dependency ratios.

APPENDIX 15

Table 11. Differential growth of various age groups
(Percentage)

Age group	Proportion of age group in total population in 1950	Interperiod growth			Proportion of age group in total population in 2025
		1950-1975	1975-2000	2000-2025	
A. Less developed regions					
0-4	15.03	78.52	25.52	5.00	8.78
5-14	23.19	94.20	36.46	13.31	17.29
15-59	54.73	70.30	82.30	47.22	62.10
60+	7.03	50.69	100.07	123.96	11.03
Total	100.00	75.69	62.96	40.62	100.00
B. More developed regions					
0-4	10.23	1.70	2.11	4.61	6.72
5-14	17.55	26.25	-3.20	2.00	13.22
15-59	60.85	29.45	18.26	1.54	57.16
60+	11.37	75.54	38.76	36.89	22.90
Total	100.00	31.29	16.47	8.22	100.00
C. World					
0-4	13.44	59.26	21.77	4.94	8.43
5-14	21.32	75.78	28.74	11.66	16.60
15-59	56.76	55.87	63.50	37.52	61.29
60+	8.48	61.65	70.69	89.99	13.68
Total	100.00	61.02	50.47	33.92	100.00

Source: Demographic Indicators of Countries ...

Note: Percentages do not necessarily add to total, because of rounding.

APPENDIX 16

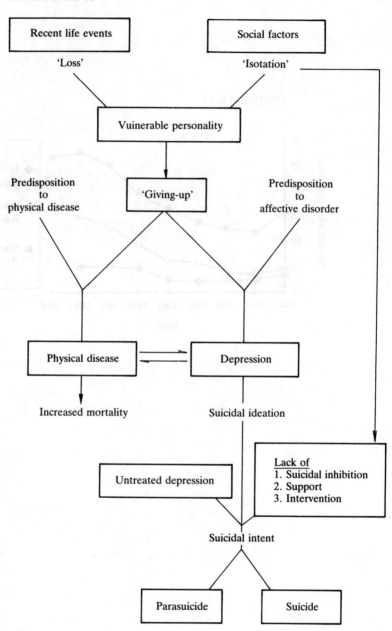

Shulman, Suicide and Parasuicide in Old Age: A Review, 7 AGE AND AGEING 201. 06 (1978)

APPENDIX 17

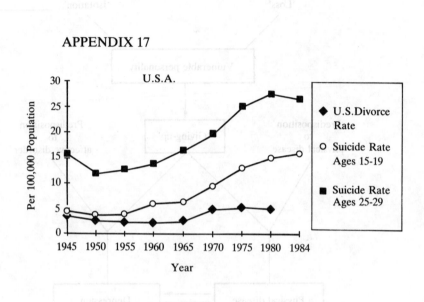

Section Four

Rights of the Elderly

Chapter 44

Elderly People and Assisted Conception

Jacqueline RUBELLIN-DEVICHI   Université Jean Moulin
Centre de droit de la famille
Lyon, France

Introduction

The birth of John the Baptist is described in the Bible thus: as an angel is announcing to Zacharia that "his prayer has been answered, and his wife Elizabeth will give him a son", Zacharia replies: "I am an old man, and my wife is old too". Zacharia is struck dumb because he has doubted the word of the angel. He recovers his speech only when his son is born.[1] Another passage, this time in the Old Testament[2] shows how the Hebrews faced the problem of sterility; this is the text usually referred to the world over when one comes to speak of assisted conception: Sarah had been unable to give a child to Abraham; so she sent her husband to her servant Hagar, who gave Abraham a son.[3]

This chapter provides me with the opportunity to recall that Sarah and Abraham, when they were elderly (Sarah was 90 and Abraham 100),[4] together produced a son whom they called Isaac.[5] It was not surprising to see a man conceiving a child in his old age: in the Bible, the Patriarchs commonly have children after they are 100; but it always causes surprise to hear about a woman who conceives when she is elderly. And this is true even today.

It is necessary to remind ourselves of the effects of biological progress and improvements in the standards of living; in modern societies, people die much later. In France, expectation of life is now 82.4 years for women and 74.8 for men.[7] We may suppose that by 2020, in France (a country where the fecundity index seems to be a bit higher than in some other European countries), people over 60 will be more numerous than people under 20 (a little more than 15 millions and a little more than 13 millions); very old people (more than 85), who today number 700,000, will be more than one million.[8]. The Government has announced it intends to introduce measures to help the elderly;[9] to help to keep some of them in their homes, help to find others a family to stay with; they even think of a "charter of rights and liberties for the Elderly."

But one of the happy consequences of such a state of affairs is that persons become old much later than heretofore: people get married (or live together), have children, often get divorced at a time when their children are still very young,[10] find a new partner (and get married or cohabit). In this new family, children will be brought up; children will be those of the new couple and, more often than we think[11] children from former relationships. This, of course, is a new source of problems.

Today women want to give birth when they are almost old enough (or even old enough) to be grandmothers; Professor Minkowsky, whilst working with the High Council for Population and Family, has even said to women in their forties: "Don't be afraid to have children", for he has noticed[12] that these women were very anxious to be mothers.[13] Researchers have been to try to postpone the menopause process. This is probably related to working elderly women wanting to become mothers, which, until now, has occurred rather seldom.

Using assisted conception methods can certainly be a help when sterility is caused by the age of one of the partners. We will describe the different technical possibilities offered by assisted conception before we consider the legal problems these methods have caused.

Different techniques of assisted conception

Some couples have to face only a relative sterility, for they are sterile only when they are together. Most of the time, age has nothing to do with this problem. It needs only to be mentioned that very new techniques (even injecting spermatozoa inside the ovum) have been used to fight this type of sterility: two persons who have been unable to have a child could, as they grow old, try this as a last chance. But in order to explain how it is possible for elderly people to conceive a child by using assisted conception, it is necessary first to distinguish, successively, deficiencies relating to the male and deficiencies relating to the female partner.

A. Deficiencies relating to the male partner

Deficiencies relating to the male partner may first be solved by using *in vitro* fertilization or "GIFT";[14] If the sperm is hypofertile, defects such as spermatozoa being not sufficiently numerous or movable, one can use *in vitro* fertilization or GIFT to good effect. If male deficiencies are accompanied by deficiencies in the female partner, one can also use a donated embryo or seek a surrogate mother. But the most commonly used process (and also the easiest to control) is artificial insemination by a donor.

Artificial insemination can be practised with fresh sperm — it is the rule in Sweden for instance or, in France, when a patient sees a private gynaecologist if he does not wish to resort to CECOS[15] but in France, the doctor usually uses frozen sperm. With frozen sperm, it is easier to select the semen in cases of artificial insemination by donor (AID). In cases of artificial insemination with the husband's sperm (AIH), the man has his sperm frozen in order to store it and thus delay the insemination.

(1) Artificial insemination by donor

In France, the doctor will employ AID when the male partner is completely sterile, or when he is a possible carrier of genetic defects.[16] The CECOS do not permit the use of AID just to suit such people as lonely women or homosexual couples. However they would probably not dare to refuse an elderly couple (whether married or not).[17]

(2) Artificial insemination with the husband's, or the male partner's sperm

Of course, AIH implies the use of frozen sperm (the sperm has been first stored by CECOS). AIH is used in two different cases: first when a man is hypofertile, and must have his sperm treated to become of better quality; secondly, when he may become unable to have children because he has cancer and must be treated by chemotherapy. CECOS would not accept the storing of sperm merely for the convenience of people, as seems to have been accepted for quite some time in the U.S.A.[18] When the courts examined the possibility of allowing a widow to be inseminated with the stored sperm of her dead husband, they decided to refuse to sanction this action.[19]

(3) When a man cannot have children and must ask for AID, and his wife is sterile

The couple may choose between 3 solutions: First, the couple may ask for a donated embryo; this is not very common in France. The "Comité Consultatif National d'Ethique pour les Sciences de la Vie et de la Santé" has cautioned against it (notice dated 1986, Dec. 15).[20] Some French hospital teams have used this method, however, for they have taken into account the aim of both husband and wife to be treated equally (when the woman is unable to have a child).

Second, they can look for a surrogate mother — that is to say, a woman who agrees to be inseminated with the sperm of another man (of course not the husband), and, when the child is born, to give away the baby she herself has conceived and borne.

Third, they could give up the idea of any type of assisted conception and try to adopt a child. This is a last resort.[21]

B. Deficiencies relating to the female partner

It is totally different to speak of assisted conception when the female partner happens to be sterile. Whereas a man can have children during almost his whole life, a woman's period of fertility is limited, unless she has been treated to delay the menopause.[22] More over, being a mother means two different phases (conception and pregnancy) and deficiencies may be related to either one. The concept of being a father is unique (at least from a biological point of view); but motherhood may be divided into two phases, or "split into two,"[23] as Professor Daniele Huet-Weiller has put it in a very acute way. It is already possible to solve these two different problems, since we know how to fertilize an ovum *in vitro* and then how to freeze the fertilized ovum. But it is easier, and more common, to look for a surrogate mother.

(1) In vitro fertilization and transfer of embryos

In vitro fertilization followed by transfer of the embryo is not the only response to female sterility (at least when there is no problem with the Fallopian tubes).[24] In France, GIFT (gamete inter-fallopian transfer) is also very common.[25] This new process was discovered in 1983 by an American. One must collect the ova, as for an *in vitro* fertilization, and then replace the ova and spermatozoids inside the Fallopian tubes: conception thus takes place naturally. People are advised to use this method in case of unexplained sterility or in some cases of males deficiences.[26] In France, 220 cases had been reported in 1987 (June), at a time when 12,000 experiments on IVF had been reported (Tours Congress).

As we have already seen, IVF is used in cases of male hypofertility; it is also used when a woman has had her Fallopian tubes seriously damaged and has as a result become sterile. If a doctor tries to determine the cause of sterility and discovers the Fallopian tubes have been damaged, he must choose between surgery and IVF. If the woman is over 35, IVF is the only course open. Until now, IVF has been the only safe way to regulate the sex of an embryo[27] — which can be highly important in cases of hereditary diseases related to one sex only.[28] This problem has very little to do with elderly people; but it must be observed that research has been so rapid that some couples who could not choose to have children when they were young enough, are now in a position to be parents and be certain that their baby will be free from the genetic disease in question.

(2) In vitro fertilization and frozen embryos

Freezing ova still seems to be difficult to achieve,[29] and people are very cautious, for apparently there is a high rate of chromosomic defects; by contrast an embryo can be frozen with complete success.

Let us not speak of the terrifying problem of "supernumerary embryos" (that is to say, those which are neglected because one does not know what to do with them when the aim — birth of one or several children — is reached). Because we can freeze embryos, it has become possible to collect ova to fertilize them with the husband's sperm, to freeze the embryos afterwards, and wait for the right moment before placing one embryo inside the mother.[30] This is very useful when a woman naturally produces very few ova,[31] or when a couple must know for certain if the woman is expecting a girl or a boy. In addition, it is possible to use such a technique for a woman who would wish to conceive a child while she is young enough, but then bring it up when she is older, when she would not be working and therefore have more time at her disposal. In France, this can be imagined, but cannot happen because no IVF centre would treat such a woman, and in all probability very few women would wish to take the risk of a late pregnancy just for that reason.

It is possible also to collect ova, to fertilize them, to freeze the embryos and then to place them in the body of another woman. This technique allows a woman to receive donated ova. This technique is useful for women who have no ovaries, or who are affected by "Turner Syndrome", or even after an operation or a chemotherapy.[32] This could also prove useful for a woman who does not produce ova any longer, but who would still be able to be pregnant — for example, where menopause has occurred very early in life. But French doctors would advise any elderly woman from doing such a thing, because it is always risky to be pregnant, and it becomes more and more risky as one grows older.

(3) Looking for surrogate mothers

If a woman is unable either to produce ova or to be pregnant, which means she is, or she has become, completely sterile, she is likely to look for a surrogate mother, that is to say a woman who agrees to be inseminated with the husband's sperm and to surrender the child after the birth.

(4) Two other solutions

Two other solutions must be mentioned here, because couples use them more often than one would think. One is totally illegal: buying a child who has been abandoned when he was born; this of course involves the falsification of numerous records in order to register the child. The other method is legal: adopting a child. But adoption is difficult for an elderly couple, because in France, the courts would never authorise an adoption unless it is in the child's best interest.

Although data is scant,[33] it would seem that when couples are "too old" to start a family, they usually prefer a surrogate mother instead of medical treatment for their deficiencies (especially deficiencies related to the female partner). The reason why they do so seems to be related to the moral code of biologists and practitioners.

Legal and moral problems relating to assisted conception

When elderly people (or when one out of the two partners is elderly) ask for assisted conception, this raises specific problems. We would be deceiving ourselves not to notice that using such techniques always raises problems.

A. Elderly people asking for assisted conception

In modern law the concept of the "paterfamilias" has totally disappeared[34] and has given way to today's idea of both parents undertaking moral and material responsibility for their family.

People are rather reluctant to admit the use of assisted conception by elderly people: there is a tendency to think that it is risky to fight against nature. All of us are now very conscious of the necessity for a child to have both of his parents and we fear that the child of an elderly couple may become an early orphan. On the other hand, since sterility is a great misfortune, many doctors think it would be cruel to forebear from using any of the new techniques with couples who could have become parents earlier if only scientific progress had occurred earlier. But the reactions, and the problems, are very different depending on whether it is a case of a man, or a woman being too old to become a parent.

(1) A man wishing to have a child when he is old

In France, an old man cannot be accepted as a sperm donor by CECOS.[35] The centres where IVF is practiced would take his age into account, and would decide to use IVF and embryo-transfer to his wife only if she is young enough.

If the man is sterile, whatever his age, the CECOS will never refuse a couple requesting AID; the decision will again depend on the age of the woman.

In contrast, if a man wished to have his sperm stored in order to use it later, or even after his death, he could not do so in France, where it is not permitted to use AIH for that kind of personal convenience. There is a general legal principle that forbids a man satisfying his desire for immortality; a desire which would be granted by the power to procreate after death. Besides, as far as the child is concerned, other problems would be created: for example in France, where the parental link gives a right to inherit, such a child would be linked only to his mother and would not be legally related to a man who was no longer living at the time of conception. The child would not as a result be able to inherit.[36]

(2) If an elderly woman wishes to become a mother, she probably finds it very difficult to get help

First, considering that it is risky for an elderly woman to be pregnant, a lot of CECOS refuse to treat women over 40. But the waiting period for an IVF may be extremely long and couples have sometimes asked for an IVF as they were not too old to use it.

The situation of a woman having an IVF and then freezing the embryo, planning to bear the child later is, so far as France is concerned, only hypothetical. The Centres for IVF will not cater to personal convenience. In such a case, though, the parental link (with the mother, at least) would not be a problem.

The same applies and for the same reasons, in the case of a woman being too old to ovulate but young enough to be pregnant with a donated ovum (fertilized by her husband). French practitioners have used such a technique for women who have no ovaries (because they were born so or because they had an accident, or an operation later). But they would certainly be very reluctant to consider this alternative for an elderly woman who wished to become pregnant. The story of the South African "surrogate grandmother" (a woman aged 48 years who became pregnant with an embryo given by her daughter and son-in-law who could not have a second child) certainly could not happen in France.[37] Turning to the case of a woman being pregnant with a donated ovum (fertilized *in vitro* with her husband's semen), or through a "leasing womb" (we often speak of a second-type of surrogate mother), we see no problem regarding the maternal link, for in French law, as in the law many countries, the mother is the woman giving birth to the baby. In the first example, this solution perfectly suits the desire of the couple; in the second case the surrogate mother is legally considered the mother, and in order to escape from this motherhood, the South African grandmother should have her child adopted ... by her own daughter.[38]

(3) Looking for a surrogate mother

This commonly happens in France in two different types of cases the Firstly, it will arise when a young woman is sterile because she had a hysterectomy after a first pregnancy, and she and her husband want another child and prefer to have "half their own" baby. It needs to be added that finding a child to adopt is so difficult that such an attitude is readily encouraged.

Second, when an elderly woman is sterile (sometimes she has had children herself when she was younger), the couple will often try to find a surrogate mother. The "customers" of one of the best-known French surrogate mother were a husband and wife who had been married for more than 20 years and had lost their only son in a car accident. We have been told, too, about a Greek man aged 50: because he could not leave France with his child who was not mentioned on his passport, he had to go back to a French association which had provided him with a surrogate mother. Another case concerned a couple who conceived a child in order to surrender it to a couple of friends, and then changed their minds. The case came to court. The man was 60 and the woman 53.[39]

It is easy to understand why, in France, elderly people prefer to find a surrogate mother: if the woman is considered to be old, she is not allowed treatment at IVF Centres, or any CECOS; and if both parents are too old, they have no right whatsoever to ask for an adopted child. The only ways remaining are surrogacy or the buying of a child. It is precisely for such a case that the Health and Family Ministry has declared that any organisation which arranges meetings between sterile couples and surrogate mothers is not legal. A young girl became pregnant and decided to surrender the baby to one of these associations; but when the child was born, she changed her mind, and the matter was referred to Court.[40] Such associations have been considered contrary to public policy, for a human body (or a baby) cannot be bought or sold. Besides, the French law punishes incitement to abandon a born or expected child. Contrary to what happens in some of the American States, in France one cannot think of a contract between the couple and the woman who expects the child and has to surrender it after the birth: the mother remains free and may refuse to surrender the baby.[41] However, the mother generally carries out her contract and gives birth anonymously; the male partner of the commissioning couple, who has given the sperm, becomes the legal father and his wife adopts the child. People generally don't like this way of doing things; but even so, it is not possible to think of eliminating the use of surrogate mothers. Even if surrogacy is punished (But how? Prison? Taking away the baby?), it will go on, as abortion went on before it was legalized. And the fact that it is illicit may even encourage the practice, as in the case with dangerous drugs.

Using one's descendants in assisted conception.

As assisted conception has become common, it has meant a traumatic change for grandparents: their grandchildren may now be heirs who cannot be totally disinherited even if their parents die, and they have no parental link with "their" grandparents. In 1966, it was decided that an adopted child should have the same rights as a biological one — but no one thought of asking the grandparents what they thought about the adoption; at that time, people were dubious about how those grandparents would react. But it seems that they are quite satisfied to see their children solving their sterility problem in this way. There is the same tendency with assisted conception, but the "blood" parental link appears to be overvalued at the same time. After an inquiry in the IVF centres, it appeared that the parents of a sterile couple (who were potential grandparents) tried to help morally and materially as well as they could.

There was, too, the case of a young woman who became sterile after she had had a first child: she wanted to look for a surrogate mother, and her own mother helped her in the search and finally signed the contract. In all the cases, the reason why these grandparents were so helpful was not their own desire to become grandparents, for all of them already had grandchildren.[44]

But people are sometimes very much bound to the idea of "blood" parental links: when a couple uses AID, they have to fear their parents' reaction; men may be dubious about how their parents will react when they learn that their own child is sterile, and when they hear that he intends to have a child who will have no biological link with him. Besides, the CECOS and the IVF centres have had several examples of people asking to be allowed to store the sperm of a son just killed in a car accident, or even a father-in-law who wished to give his sperm to his son's wife because his son was dead or sterile: people want so eagerly to see their son (or their blood) alive again, that they do not even consider what kind of problems such an attitude (mixing of generations) can cause, or if it would be easy for a child to live after being conceived in such circumstances. For inevitably one must think of incest.

Today, in France, public opinion seems to agree with the use of assisted conception when it is a matter of helping a sterile couple young enough to have children, especially if it is possible to conceive a child with the parents' own gamete. But people become very reluctant when assisted conception implies a change of natural order, and most strongly when one wishes to allow an elderly couple to have children, that is to say, if the couple is older than is normally the case when people decide to become parents.

Notes

1. New Testament, Gospel according to Saint Luke, chapter 1, verses 5 to 25. In the same passage, one can notice that it is assumed that sterility always comes from the female partner: "They had no children, for Elizabeth was sterile and both of them were elderly" (verse 7). One can see, too, that sterility is considered a great disease and source of dishonour. When Elizabeth is pregnant, she says: "This is by the grace of the Lord who has looked at me and delivered me from shame."
2. Gen. 16, 3.
3. This is the reason why the French association for sterile women who wish to use assisted conception has been called "Saint Sarah."
4. Gen. 21, 5; 17, 17.
5. Gen. 21.3. People usually forget that Sarah does not forgive her servant: when Hagar became pregnant, Sarah was so enraged that Hagar was forced to escape (Gen. 16, 6) and later, when she saw the two boys playing together, Sarah said to Abraham: "Put this servant and her son away, the son of a servant should not be your heir with my son Isaac." (Gen 21, 10).
7. "Population et société," 1988, Feb.
8. "Le Monde," 1987, Oct. 30.
9. "Le Monde", 1988, Feb. 19.
10. In France, almost one million children whose parents have divorced are under 17. See J.L. Rallu, Du divorce et des enfants, INED, cahier no. 111.
11. See "Les beaux-enfants. Remariages et recompositions familiales", Revue Dialogue, 3 ème tr. 1987, prepared by M.N. Mathias and I. Théry.
12. See "Enfants", 1986, Aug.: in the interview he gave to this newspaper, Professor Minkowsky said that in 1985, there had been 120,000 children born from women in their forties. As there were only 30,000 in 1950 (mostly children born to unmarried women), which shows rather clearly that French society has accepted new patterns

of family life.

13. See "Marie-Claire", 1988, Jan.: "Pregnant at 50".
14. See infra.
15. Centre for Studying and Storing Human Sperm (CECOS): we have about twenty of them in France, gathered into a federation. All of them have the same rules: free, anonymous gift by a married man (or a man living with a woman) who is already a father.
16. CECOS examine difficult cases. A recent problem is the case of couples asking for AID because the male partner is HIV Sero-positive.
17. In France, partners who are manifestly living together are treated as married people.
18. See Jean Bernard, "L'homme changé par l'homme". In France, the Sperm Bank for Nobel prize winners still causes surprise and even indignation.
19. In a famous case, though (See trib. gr. inst. Creteil, 1.8. 1984, Rev. trim. dr. civ. 1984 p. 703 obs. Rubellin-Devichi and ref. Quot.), the court decided differently. The insemination was performed by a private doctor who does not belong to any CECOS, and failed. The widow has since married again, and become a mother.
20. See Rubellin-Devichi, "Procréations assistées. Etat des questions", Rev. trim. dr. civ. 1987, No. 3.
21. In France, there were 100,000 orphans (children without any known parents, or any relatives) in 1950; 10,400 in 1985; about 7,000 in 1987. Those children usually find it difficult to be adopted: they are too old, are coloured, or are physically or mentally handicapped; they are "peculiar" children, and the Social Services are very cautious in letting them be adopted. There is about 1 child for 20 to 30 couples asking for an adopted child; old people wishing to adopt have particular difficulty.
22. Complications may occur more often with elderly women. In France, a pregnant woman after 38 may legally have a free amniosynthesis.
23. See D. Huet-Weiller, "Le droit de la filiation face aux nouveaux modes de procreation", Revue de metaphysique et de morale, 1987, p. 331.
24. In vitro fertilization still remains the only possibility of being pregnant for women with no Fallopian tubes or with severely damaged Fallopian tubes.
25. Maybe too common, as some seem to think that people use GIFT when the female partner is not sterile, which could explain the high rate of success.
26. Two new methods are now also available in France: FIP (intrapeutoneum Fecoudation); and civete (Intravaginal Culture and Embryo Transfert) [liquid containing ovum and sperm is introduced into the mother's womb].
27. Separating the chromosomes was achieved in 1984 at Keio University in Tokyo, but the method still does not give 100% success.
28. Hemophilia or myopathy for instance only occurs in boys; Turner syndrome only occurs in girls.
29. It has been a success at least once, in Australia: See Chen, "Pregnancy after human avocyte cryopreservation", Lancet 1986, p. 884-886.
30. In France, most of the doctors choose to replace three, sometimes four (maximum) ova.
31. One can try again several times if the first attempt fails.
32. But it has been tried (with success) to place an ovary into a woman's arm in order to keep the ovary safe at the commencement of treatment including chemotherapy.
33. See, mostly, the Report by the Legal Sociology Laboratory of Paris 2 and the Centre for the family rights in 1988, March.

34. In Roman Law, the "paterfamilias" retained full rights over his wife and children (even when children were married grown-ups and had their own children). This idea of the father, has been partially transmitted and can still be recognized in the "Civil Code" and elsewhere.
35. Another reason why French people don't like the American Nobel Sperm Bank. But centres where the semen of sportsmen is stored are not popular either ...
36. It would be different for a child conceived before his father's death, but born after it. Twins were born through an IVF, when their father (a rather famous racing-car driver) was dead, but the replacing of the embryos had occured while their father was still living.
37. More than that: some research seems to show that it is easier to have a young woman bearing the embryo of an elderly woman that the other way round. The uterus of an elderly woman is not good enough and may prevent the child's growing.
38. In fact, the two parents' (the grandmother and her son-in-law) should reach an agreement and the son-in-law would remain the legal father.
39. The judge did not interfere: the child could not be brought up by the couple who had given birth. To take the child away from his "commissioning" parents would have meant taking him into care.
40. The Parisian Court, (directed by M. Peigné) has recently pronounced a very interesting and humane judgement.
41. Contrary to the 'Baby M' case in New Jersey, a French court would not decide to give the child to the couple asking for it. But they would decide that the father has the parental authority if they think it is better for the child.
42. The South African grandmother surrogate also has a first grandchild.

Chapter 45

The Abuse of the Elderly — Legal Responses in England.

Michael D. A. FREEMAN   University College London,
England

When I published my monograph *Violence in the Home*; *A Socio-Legal Study* in 1979,[1] abuse of the elderly was barely recognised as a social problem. Yet it is clearly no more a new phenomenon than child abuse or domestic violence. Ten years ago I devoted barely two pages to the problem,[2] which I called, quite inaccurately I now concede, 'granny bashing'. The expression is emotive and incorrect, it is sexist and (to use a concept of the 1980s) ageist. Our knowledge and understanding of elder abuse is greater now than it was 10 years ago. Writing then, I could note that a leading text on social and medical problems of the elderly could attribute falls in the elderly to seven causes and ignore assault by a relative[3] and that Howells, the author of a passionate account of the *Colwell* affair,[4] nowhere included any reference to the problems of abuse and neglect of the elderly in his *Modern Perspectives in the Psychiatry of Old Age,* a book of over 600 pages.[5] We've seen it all before: what attention was given to child abuse 25 years ago (to their sexual abuse even 5 years ago)? How did we respond to violence against women in the home 15 years ago?[6] In Britain, it was a music hall joke — as elder abuse largely still is.[7] Elder abuse can no longer be ignored. Nevertheless, our knowledge of it remains sketchy and imperfect and managerial and legal responses are, in Britain at least, little more than amateur. This chapter accordingly offers an account of the problem, its aetiology and assesses possible responses to it.

Elder Abuse: Towards A Definition

There is no agreed definition of elder abuse. It may be defined as the systematic, serious and continuous abuse of an elderly person by a carer, usually, but not always, a relative, on whom that elderly person is dependent.[8] This definition hinges on several concepts, all of which need further amplification. First, 'abuse' itself must be grasped. As with child abuse, definitions are variegated and depend on the purpose for which the definition is sought. The lawyer's definition may emphasise intention or *mens rea*: that of the manager, or the sociologist or psychologist may look to different factors. Elder abuse can be defined narrowly (it can be confined to violence) or widely and diffusively (anything which interferes with the optimal life chances of an elderly person could be considered to be abuse). Many who define elder abuse do so by listing that which they consider to be encompassed by it. For example Mervyn Eastman argues it includes (i) physical assault including pushing, pinching, punching, slapping, forced feeding and forced medication; (ii) threats of physical assault; (iii) neglect, including locking a dependent person in a bedroom, refusing to supply meals or to give various kinds of necessary support; (iv) abandonment, either to residential or hospital care; (v) exploitation, including appropriation of finance and property; (vi) sexual abuse by carers or their family; (vii) psychological abuse, including shouting, screaming, and threats to deprive.[9] Chen *et al* define abuse as 'abusive action inflicted by abusers on adults sixty years of age or older'[10] and categorise abuse into four categories of physical abuse (non-accidental, wilful infliction of physical pain and injury, physical neglect, deprivation of nutrition); psychological abuse (emotional harm, mental anguish, unreasonable confinement, emotional neglect); sexual abuse (deprivation of human services; involuntary isolation, financial abuse). Others emphasise neglect. For example, Hickey and Douglass[11] define elder abuse in terms of physical neglect (leaving the elderly person alone, isolated or forgotten), active neglect (including the withholding of items necessary for daily living such as food, medicine, companionship and bathroom assistance) as well as verbal, emotional and physical abuse. In Sengstock and Liang's study[12] five types of abuse were identified (i) physical abuse; (ii) physical neglect; (iii) financial abuse; (iv) psychological neglect; and (v) psychological abuse. It was psychological abuse which they found to be most prevalent, occurring in 58% of their cases. They believed its incidence to be high because it often accompanies other forms of abuse. Financial abuse was also common (55% of cases). Physical abuse, by contrast, occurred in only 20% of cases, physical neglect in 23% and psychological neglect in 23%. However, it should be stressed that, although physical abuse and neglect were found to be the least common types, it was these manifestations of abuse that were likely to produce greatest pain and suffering for the victims.

It is not just 'abuse' which has to be understood. Also crucial to an understanding of elder abuse is the concept of dependency. This should not surprise for there is little doubt that everywhere violence is found in a domestic setting, the victims are likely to be found to be dependent (either in fact or at least in terms of cultural construct). Tied to the notion of dependency are subordination and powerlessness. To be subordinate is to be the legitimate victim of abuse.[13] Part of that badge of inferiority is to be susceptible to corporal chastisement. At least the elderly are spared this. Eastman points out that 'changes in dependency needs, both physical and emotional, unbalance the equilibrium on which relationships are based.'[14]

The definition posited of elder abuse has indicted the carer and indicated that this is usually a relative. But abuse is not confined to the domestic setting. Indeed, in Britain there have been numerous recent revelations of abuse of elderly people in residential institutions by paid care-givers.[15] *Sans Everything*,[16] edited by Barbara Robb, is an indictment of the unbelievable brutality of some institutions, in particular mental hospitals. It was published over 20 years ago and, though de-institutionalisation has proceeded apace since, with a great emphasis in Britain on 'community care' (a euphemism for care in families invariably by women), there have been numerous reports since, many within the last year, of unacceptable conditions prevailing in the remaining old-age homes and several enquiries have been held. It is notable that we are prepared to consider abuse in residential settings despite our reluctance to believe it can exist in that 'haven in a heartless world',[17] the privatised family.[18] This is not the place to investigate the origins or power of that defensive myth.

Causes of Elder Abuse

We must put mythology aside and ask whether we have any understanding as to why abuse of the elderly occurs. We do not, of course, know why children are abused or why women are battered. Those who have sought causes of those phenomenon have helped us to construct three models. There is the psycho-pathological model which imputes some 'sickness' to the abuser. There is something wrong with him/her. This model individualises abuse: it gives us 'sick people'.[19] There is, secondly, the socio-environmental model of abuse. This directs us to material and social factors. Instead of 'sick people' we get a 'sick society',[20] one in which poverty is rife. Abuse is linked to poverty and to its multi-faceted correlates, including bad housing and homelessness, unemployment, racial discrimination and, particularly in the context of child abuse, absence of alternative child care facilities. This leads to stress and through this (and sanctioned violence) comes abuse. A third view of abuse is cultural. It tries to understand abuse by examining cultural norms and expectations.[21] If children are property rather than persons, or social problems, if women were chattels, if both were and children still are denied rights, then abuse is to be expected. In these terms abuse is not abnormal and can be expected to continue until there is a redefinition of status attendant upon a cultural revolution.

It would be fair to say that the first of these models long held sway. Indeed, its influence is still profound, as will be all too evident to readers of the seminal document *A Child in Trust*,[22] published in 1985.[23] However, the claims of the second model are, I think, now more generally accepted, even if its implications have not been taken on board. Poverty could be eliminated if we had the political will. The third view as yet has few supporters, though in my view it is the key to an understanding of the problem.

When we turn our attention to elder abuse, we find striking similarities, though knowledge about the causes of abuse remains largely underdeveloped.[24] Much of the research is based on a limited number of reported incidents. Janice Davidson[25] suggests the causes include the following:

(i)   Economic and population changes which affect the caretaking abilities of adult children.[26] For example, higher costs of living create greater demands for women to work. A growing number of elderly people increases the demand for alternative living arrangements.[27]

(ii)   Changes in the elderly parent's life. For example, the comfort and freedom he (she) anticipated may not be attained as they have increasing physical and mental impairment.[28]

(iii)   Changes in the carer's lifestyle. The carer may be close to retirement age and looking forward to a more relaxed lifestyle only to face the unwelcomed problem of caring for a dependent person.

(iv)   Family relationships, in particular where the caring role falls to only one adult child, who comes to see the parent as a burden without relief. The carer may find herself caught between the demands of the parent and those of a husband and children. The carer herself may be 'elderly and senile' and not be aware of the consequences of her behaviour. Unresolved conflicts between the dependent and carer may create power struggles which can, in extreme cases, lead to a mother and daughter being bound together in a hostile dependent relationship.[29]

Sengstock and Liang identify a number of family situations as conducive to abuse. They point to (i) substance abuse, that is alcohol and drugs; (ii) the presence of mental and emotional illness; (iii) a generally abusive situation in the family; (iv) financial need or greed; (v) taking strangers or near strangers into the home; and occasionally (vi) victim precipitation.[30]

Explaining abuse is complex because there is no single cause.[31] But, as with child abuse and violence against women, the suggested causes of elder abuse can be constructed into a number of models or perspectives. Thus, Hickey and Douglass suggest that there are three approaches.[32] First, there is a psychopathological framework which explains abuse and neglect in terms of pathological problems inherent in the abuser. Secondly, there is an environmental or social structural perspective which explains abuse in terms of situational conflicts and crises, and long-term environmental conditions, largely those associated with poverty such as crowded housing and insufficient income and resources. The third model they posit (the developmental) explains abuse in terms of a latent developmental disorder which renders some individuals incapable of sustaining personal relationships in the inter-dependent context of the family. In particular, it suggests that children of dysfunctional parents are unlikely to develop integrated relationships.

The problem is clearly multi-faceted and requires a multi-dimensional explanation. None of these explanations is sufficient in itself and all may go some way towards increasing our understanding of the problem. The parallels with explanations of child and woman abuse are too close to need emphasising. But what is missing, as compared with explanations of abuse of children and women, is any attempt to situate elder abuse within a cultural or socio-economic context. In coming to understand this we should look at old age rather more critically than we have conventionally done. One of the most perceptive of writers on old age is Simone de Beauvoir.[33] She shows that as people moved from the countryside to the burgeoning towns of the Industrial Revolution, the old were among those most victimised and neglected by their families. Families had to work unceasingly for pitifully low rewards and were barely able to feed themselves. Were they to feed their children, on whom they might be subsequently dependent, or their elderly dependents? Children were hardly treated well, as we all know,[34] but elderly people fared worse: they were starved at best and not infrequently killed off by families. As Eastman comments: 'the seeds of productivity linked to social status were sown and later the stereotyped elderly were reaped'.[35] We know all too little of attitudes towards the elderly: compared to childhood the concept of old age has been but little investigated. Indeed, only recently has 'ageism' entered our vocabulary. But, as we become aware of discrimination against the elderly, we will surely recognise that our attitudes towards old age in part explain why abuse of the elderly takes place.[36]

Legal Responses

A. Some Principles for Decision-Making

There can be little doubt that elderly abuse is a significant social problem.[37] Our challenge must be to find ways of reducing it and of helping both the carers and their elderly dependents. The only experience on which we can draw is child abuse. Procedures developed to tackle this offer, if nothing more, a starting point. We have made, and continue to make, errors in tackling child abuse: it may be that we can learn from these errors. If so, we may at the least have a framework for practice.[38]

There are a number of principles which should govern intervention in cases of elderly abuse. The American researchers, Edwin Villmoare and Jane Bergman have usefully set these out.[39] Most important is the client's right to determine for him/herself whether to accept intervention and help.[40] It is easy to pay lip-service to self-determination. But failure to recognise fundamental liberties is itself a form of abuse. Admission procedures to homes, in particular where compulsory removal[41] is involved, must be sensitised to this need.

A second principle is the importance of keeping the family together. Evidence from case histories in the United States show clearly that many families have learnt to cope and deal with stress leading to abuse because separation is not offered to them as the only solution. The work of Levin[42] shows that most families are motivated to keep their elderly dependent within the family network. Obviously, as with child abuse, much must depend on the degree and amount of abuse or neglect. Where it is extreme, removal to an alternative environment may be essential, for both protection and medical treatment.

A third principle follows from this. If separation is to be avoided, then whenever possible the emphasis should be on community-based services rather than old people's homes.[43] If removal to residential homes is essential, what must be avoided at all costs is the sort of complacency which holds that once in a home the old person is immune to abuse. Rather as abused children are sometimes abused further in alternative care arrangements, so we know from ample evidence that the old do sometimes suffer abuse from the hands of residential staff. Both physical and emotional abuse can occur. Indeed, one recent report in England found that exploitation and degradation of old people at private rest houses (and there are of 70,000 old people in such homes) was 'the norm and not the exception'.[44] Whether this is so or not, there is considerable disquiet in Britain about the standard of care in residential homes and removal of an old person to such an establishment can be no guarantee that abuse or neglect does not continue.[45]

This leads to a fourth principle: adequate or inappropriate intervention may be worse than none at all. This applies both to intervention which leads to the removal of the old people to a 'place of safety',[46] and also to supportive measures to keep the elderly within the family setting. Promises of unrealistic support can harm relationships and too much 'help' can, as with child abuse, become part of the caring family's nightmare and aggravate the situation. Intervention must always be balanced and sensitive.

There is perhaps a fifth principle. I leave it to last since it is rather more tentative. The relationship between the caring abuser and the elderly victim is interlaced with pain, guilt and tension. It is therefore necessary that the professional confronting the problematic home should, wherever possible, avoid blame. It is easy, as elsewhere, to blame the victim: it is equally tempting to blame the abuser.[47] Neither response is satisfactory. Neither will pacify and neither will ensure that abuse comes to an end.

B. Responses of Agencies

The victim of elder abuse is often mentally or physically very frail and dependent. It is unlikely that such people will report abuse, either because of continuing dependence, or a wish to keep family stress private, or a fear of being put in an institution. The police are only likely to get involved in extreme cases, for example where death results. As with abuse of women they are reluctant to take control measures in the absence of complainant's wishes and willing testimony.[48] In 1982 the Home Secretary was asked if he would issue guidelines to police forces on dealing with problems of abuse of elderly people by their relatives. This induced an unhelpful and complacent response. When allegations of criminal activity were reported to the police, 'appropriate action will be taken'.[49] But, said the Under-Secretary, 'We have no evidence to suggest that the issue of guidance to chief officers on this subject is called for'. It will take a scandal, such as we have become used to in child abuse cases, to disturb this complacency. What the guidance then issued should be remains a matter for debate. The criminal law in this area, as in child abuse, is likely to be a blunt instrument but this should not rule out a role for sensitive policing.

Few elderly people have direct contact with social services. Only 3 per cent receive meals on wheels and 10 per cent only have home helps.[50] If a complaint is made to a social services department, there are no systematic procedures or uniform national guidelines to apply. In cases where children are involved, social services departments have a duty to intervene and investigate complaints. There is no mandatory reporting of child abuse in Britain,[51] as there is in the USA.[52] A recent enquiry report toyed with the idea, but ultimately rejected it. The British Association of Social Workers produced quite recently guidelines for use in cases of suspected child abuse.[53] There has been no similar initiative as regards elder abuse. Social workers have no right of access to the home of an elderly person or any power in law to summon the parties concerned to a case conference, the primary diagnostic measure undertaken with child abuse. There are no powers to remove an elderly person from home to a place of safety, other than through the rather draconian s. 47 of the National Assistance Act 1948 (to which reference will be made later in this chapter), or through the Mental Health Act 1983, where this is appropriate, as it rarely will be.[54] There are no powers, either, to arrange for an assessment.

Health visitors concentrate their attention on mothers and young children. Their emphasis is squarely on preventive work. Few see the elderly as within their field of concern. Even if they do they have no statutory right of access to the home.

The brunt of help is thus likely to fall upon the shoulders of the social work profession. But what is good social work practice in this area? It is difficult to identify this when so much of the profession is oblivious to the problem. Is elder abuse ever considered in social work education courses? Do social workers in practice get any training in it at all? It is natural that when the problem erupts, a social worker should model her response on the action she has learnt to take when dealing with child abuse. The case conference will thus be central to her thinking.

C. Legal Resources

There are many differences between child and elder abuse. The one that concerns us here is the legal resources available in each context. The differences are profound. There is a whole panoply of protective measures that social workers can call upon when they think it necessary to protect an abused child or one 'at risk'.[55] But little can be done to protect vulnerable old people unless they explicitly ask for such protection, or unless they can be brought within the terms of the Mental Health Act 1983. However, there are many old people who are vulnerable through chronic disability or mental or physical infirmity who do not come within the purview of mental health legislation.

One procedure through which the old (and mentally competent) can be forcibly removed without consent is contained in s. 47 of the National Assistance Act 1948.[56] It is estimated that the powers contained in this are used some 200 times a year in England. The power is draconian, often criticised and can itself amount to a form of abuse.[57] It has origins in the Poor Law and in Public Health measures concerned with facilitating slum clearance.[58] It is estimated that up to 50 per cent of elderly people proceeded against under Section 47 are in fact mentally disordered and thus would come within the terms of the mental health legislation.[59] On the other hand it follows that half of those dealt with under s. 47 are not mentally disordered, so that the suggestion frequently made that s. 47 could be repealed and its clientele brought within the Mental Health Act would result in a hundred or so elderly persons a year being diagnosed as mentally disordered when they are not.

Under s. 47 (as amended in 1951)[60] adults can be forcibly placed in institutional care to 'secure the necessary care and attention' if they;

(i)   are suffering from grave chronic disease or being aged, infirm, or physically incapacitated, are living in unsanitary conditions, and

(ii)   are unable to devote to themselves and are not receiving from other persons proper care and attention.

Section 47 is commonly applied in two different situations: one when the person has put him/herself 'at risk' through self-neglect over a lengthy period and a crisis has arisen; the other when a person has become seriously ill and is refusing hospital admission. The procedure is set in motion by the community physician who certifies to the local authority that a person should be put into institutional care 'in the interests of any such person.....or not preventing injury to the health of or serious nuisance to other persons'. The local authority may then apply to a magistrates' court for an order committing that person to institutional care. The maximum period for such an order is 3 months but it is renewable. Only after 6 weeks have elapsed from the making of an order can an application be made by, or on behalf of, the person subject to it for its revocation.

Section 47 has been heavily criticised.[61] It uses vague concepts like 'insanitary conditions' (as, of course, does child care legislation).[62] It constitutes potentially a gross infringement of civil liberties. Its use is geographically patchy and uneven. The decision-making process leaves much to be desired, for example the quality of evidence used and the values employed by professionals. Few persons removed under s. 47 ever return to their own homes (15 per cent is a common estimate)[63] and the average survival rate is about 2 years.

We can look at this power in two ways. It can be used to protect a few of the elderly against abuse, though it rarely is, unless 'abuse' is more widely defined than in existing literature. It certainly was not designed with abuse in mind and does not obviously cover it. It can also be seen, from a civil libertarian perspective, as a form of abuse in itself. The temptation to use it to protect the elderly is there partly because of the inadequacy of alternative legal resources. At the very least s. 47 should be reformed. More safeguards could be built into it. It is troubling that at the moment no legal aid is available, by way of representation in court, to people who wish to oppose an application that they be 'taken into care' under s. 47. No admission should be permitted without the opportunity of legal representation (and legal aid, for few old persons in these circumstances are likely to be able to afford legal fees). Additionally, thought ought to be given to establishing an institution, rather like the 'visitor' under the Mental Health Act for those whose affairs are managed by the Court of Protection, the primary responsibility of which would be to represent the interests of anyone for whom s. 47 is being considered or who is in care under that section.[64]

Another possibility would be to amend s. 47 to make it clear that it did cover elderly people abused by relatives. At one level this seems an obvious step to take. Yet it makes use, indeed extends the use, of a justly-criticised and potentially destructive provision. Should we countenance the extension of a provision that others would wish to remove altogether? If consideration is given to extending s. 47 to cover abuse, a narrow definition of abuse, probably extending no further than 'non-accidental injury' would have to be adopted.

This raises the question as to what sort of statutory and managerial framework needs to be created to assist the process of protecting the elderly from abuse. Having rejected mandatory reporting of child abuse, such an obligation in the care of the elderly must be considered a non-starter. But there is no reason why a duty should not be imposed on local authorities to consider and assess the needs of elderly persons considered to be vulnerable. The request could come from the elderly, a carer or possibly another relative or neighbour. It is, however, important to recognise and respect the autonomy of the elderly person and his or her right accordingly to remain in the household if determined to do so. It is a difficult balancing act to weigh the right of a 'consenting' victim to self-determination against the paternalistic initiative to protect the vulnerable against their own, possibly destructive, wishes.[65] Intervention can take a number of forms and it is vital that powers to help, including the provision of resources to prevent crises occurring, be actively considered. It is here that the principles already delineated assume greatest importance.

D. Abuse in Institutions

Abuse also takes place in institutions. Again this is nothing new. The revelations of today mirror those of Robb in the 1960s.[66] The catalogue of misery and ill-treatment in *Sans Everything* is matched by recent reports. Thus, there are allegations that old people in South London may have been deliberately 'helped' to die by workers who exposed them to the cold.[67] A report in the West Midlands claims to have uncovered a pattern of over-charging residents, overcrowding, poor food, dangerous medication practices, inhuman treatment, inadequate fire standards, regimentation, under-staffing, exploitation of trainees, and atrocious working conditions.[68] A number of deliberate acts of cruelty were also observed. There are high profits in running homes and too many owners have no desire to care for old people.

The scandal need not be documented further. What answers are there? It is clear that resources must be put into establishing an efficient and independent inspectorate. In addition better complaints procedures need to be set up.[70] The old need organisations with legal and social work personnel to assist them when making allegations against a home. Further, staff working in residential homes need to be encouraged to report incidents of suspected ill-treatment. It remains far too easy to open a home, and the proper training of those who wish to do so should be made a pre-condition of the registration of a home.

Conclusion

As with child abuse, there are no easy answers. In Britain we do not even know the magnitude of the problem. In the United States the estimate is that 4 per cent of the nation's elderly are victims of abuse each year. If that figure is replicated in Britain, and there seems to be no reason why it should not be, about one quarter of a million elderly British persons will suffer some form of abuse each year.[71] It could be even more. One problem with child abuse is that much of it remains hidden; this problem is accentuated in the case of elder abuse.

Old age abuse must be further investigated. Its dimensions must be uncovered, its causes better understood before we can grapple with it. It is a problem that must be sensitively policed: intervention into the abusive household can itself abuse, and removal to a home is no panacea, as the discussion of residential abuse reveals. Above all else the old person's autonomy must be respected wherever possible. Abuse is in part a product of a failure to give equal respect and concern to the rights of the elderly. We have made many errors in attempting to conquer child abuse: it is to be hoped that fewer will be encountered as we tackle, what few deny will be, a major social problem of the 1990s, and the next century.

Notes

1. Saxon House and subsequently Gower.
2. I discuss it at pages 237-239.
3. J.Hazell, *Social and Medical Problems of the Elderly,* Hutchinson, 3rd ed., 1973, pp.240-241.
4. *Remember Maria,* Butterworths, 1974.
5. Published by Churchill Livingston, 1975.
6. Though the physical abuse of children and violence against women were perceived as social problems at earlier periods. A good American account is E. Pleck,

Domestic Tragedy, Oxford U.P., 1987. On England see M. May in (ed) J. P. Martin, *Violence and the Family,* Wiley, 1978, pp.135-167.

7. The first English media article I can trace which took it seriously appeared in *The Guardian,* 15 May 1976 entitled "Granny bashing incidents go up." This followed A. A. Baker "Granny Battering" in *Modern Geriatrics,* August 1975.

8. This is close to that suggested by Mervyn Eastman in *Old Age Abuse,* Age Concern, 1984, p.23.

9. See "Granny Battering: A Hidden Problem", *She,* February 1983. The list is not intended to be, and is not, exhaustive.

10. N. Chen *et al,* "Elderly Abuse in Domestic Settings: A Pilot Study", *Journal of Gerontological Social Work,* vol.4 (1), Autumn 1981.

11. T. Hickey and R. L. Douglass "Neglect and Abuse of Older Family Members: Professionals' Perspectives and Case Experience", *Gerontologist,* vol.21 (2), April 1981, pp.171-176.

12. Mary C. Sengstock and Jersey Liang, *Identifying and Characterising Elder Abuse,* Institute of Gerontology, Wayne State University, Michigan, 1982.

13. This is very much the theme of my *Violence In The Home, op.cit.,* note 1, and *The Rights and Wrongs of Children,* Frances Pinter, 1983.

14. *Op.Cit.,* note 8, p.15.

15. Examples are the report by the National Union of Public Employees and West Midlands County Council entitled *Realities of Home Life,* published by Trade Union Resource Centre, Birmingham, 1986 (see *The Guardian,* 29 April 1986) and the revelations about the Nye Bevan home in South London, widely reported in July 1987, most fully in *The Independent,* 22 July 1987. There are also two useful articles by Anne Smith in *The Guardian,* 12 and 19 November 1986, but see the critical comments in "Second Opinion", 3 December 1986.

16. *Sans Everything — A Case to Answer,* Nelson, 1967.

17. The expression is Christopher Lasch's in his book of the same title, published by Basic Books, 1977.

18. Why is violence in the family a subject for family lawyers, rather than criminal lawyers?

19. See R.Gelles, "Child Abuse as Psychopathology: A Sociological Critique and Reformulation", *American Journal of Orthopsychiatry,* 43, pp.611-21 (1973); D. Gil, *Violence Against Children,* Harvard U.P., 1970; N.Parton, *The Politics of Child Abuse,* Macmillan, 1985.

20. C. McGrath, "The Crisis of Domestic Order", *Socialist Review,* 45, pp.11-30 (1979).

21. See my *Violence in the Home, op.cit.,* note 1, pp/31-32, 141-148; *The Rights and Wrongs of Children, op.cit.,* note 13, pp.123-124. See also, in relation to women, R. Dobash and R. Dobash, *Violence Against Wives,* Open Books, 1980.

22. This was the report of an enquiry into the death of a child, Jasmine Beckford, who was in the care of Brent Social Services. The report was published in December 1985 by the London Borough of Brent. The Chairman was Louis Blom-Cooper Q.C.

23. The report was influenced greatly by the work of Professor Cyril Greenland, whose *Preventing CAN deaths,* Tavistock, 1988, has recently been published. A useful critique of the Beckford report from the perspective of its underlying ideological position is N. Parton, "The Beckford Report: A Critical Appraisal", *British Journal of Social Work,* 16, pp. 511-530 (1986).

24. C. Cloke, *Old Age Abuse in the Domestic Setting — A Review*, Age Concern, 1983; *Elder Abuse: The Hidden Problem*, prepared for the House Select Committee on Aging, 96 Cons:1st Session (Comm. Print 1979); Rosalie Wolf *et al*, *Elder Abuse and Neglect: Final Report from Three Medical Projects*, University of Massachusetts, 1984.

25. "Elder Abuse" in (eds) Marilyn R. Block and Jan D. Sinnott, *The Battered Elder Syndrome, An Explanatory Study*, Center on Aging, University of Maryland, 1979, p.49 at pp.53-55.

26. See S. K. Steinmetz, "Battered Parents", *Society* 15 (15), 1978, pp.54-55.

27. G. R. Burston, "Granny Battering", *British Medical Journal*, 6 September 1975, 3 (5983), p 592, views battering as a natural consequence of inadequate services to families who need support in caring for older family members.

28. There is also an attitude of "worthlessness and hopelessness" among the aged (see C. Strow and R. Mackreth, "Family Group Meetings — Strengthening a Partnership", *Journal of Gerontological Nursing*, 3 (1), 30-35, at p.31 [1977]).

29. See, further, M. Blenker, "Social Work and Family Relationships in Later Life: Some Thoughts on Filial Maturity" in E. Sharnas and G. Streib (eds), *Social Structure and the Family: Generational Relations*, Prentice Hall, 1965.

30. *Op.cit.*, note 12.

31. Jordan I. Kosberg, *Abuse and Maltreatment of the Elderly: Causes and Interventions*, John Wright, 1983.

32. *Op.cit.*, note 11. See also R.L.Douglass and T.Hickey, "Domestic Neglect and Abuse of the Elderly: Research Findings and a Systems Perspective for Service Delivery Planning" in (ed) J. J. Kosberg, *op.cit.*, note 31, pp.115-135, at pp.124-128.

33. *Old Age*, Weidenfeld and Nicolson, 1972.

34. Though Linda Pollock, among others, have attempted some revision of this orthodox opinion: see, for example, her *Forgotten Children*, Cambridge U.P., 1983.

35. *Op.cit.*, note 8, p.12.

36. See, further, Anthea Tinker, *The Elderly in Modern Society*, Longman, 1984, 2nd edition and C.Phillipson, *Capitalism and the Construction of Old Age*, Macmillan, 1982.

37. I make no attempt in this chapter to assess its quantum. At this stage, it would be unrealistic to try to attain statistics with any meaningful accuracy. M. Sutton and M. Eastman, however, estimate 500,000 elderly persons in the U.K. are at risk of abuse and this is the figure widely quoted (see "Granny Battering" in *Geriatric Medicine* November 1982). The figure should be approached with caution: it is based on an extrapolation of American studies and statistics, on the problems of which see C.Cloke, *op.cit.*, note 24, paras 3.4 — 4.4.

38. And see T. Philpot's Editorial "An Old Age Problem" in *Community Care*, 25 August 1983.The editorial was provoked by Cloke's survey (*op.cit*, note 24) and Hugh Geach's attack on child abuse procedures in (eds) H. Geach and E. Szwed, *Providing Civil Justice for Children*, Arnold, 1983 published at the same time.

39. "Elder Abuse and Neglect: a Guide for Practitioners and Policy-Makers" in *Hearing Before the Subcommittee on Retirement Income and Employment* (Appendix 1), 9th Congress (1st Session), USA, 3 April 1981, pp.79-134.

40. Emphasised in the Wagner Report, *Residential Care: A Positive Choice*, 1988.

41. This is possible in England under legislation, now the National Assistance Act 1948

s.47 (see below).

42. Reference to by M. Eastman, *op.cit.*, note 8, p.71.

43. See R.Clough, *Old Age Homes,* Allen and Unwin, 1981.

44. *Realities of Home Life, op.cit.,* note 15.

45. There is a new code of practice contained in the report of a Working Party sponsored by the DHSS and convened by the Centre for Policy on Aging under the Chairmanship of Lady Avebury. See *Home Life,* Centre for Policy on Ageing, 1984. The publication in 1988 of two reports, the Wagner report (*op.cit,* note 40) and Griffith's report may ultimately improve practices, procedures and conditions of residential homes.

46. Under the National Assistance Act 1948 s.47.

47. See, in other contexts, W. Ryan, *Blaming the Victorian,* Vintage Books, revised edition, 1976.

48. But there are some changes here: see Sandra Horley, "A Pioneering Police Plan to Help Battered Women", *Social Work Today,* 19(29), p.24, (24 March 1988).

49. H.C. *Hansard,* 24 November 1982, col. 495.

50. See *General Household Survey,* 1980, H.M.S.O.

51. See S. Maidment (1978) *Current Legal Problems,* 31, 149-176.

52. A mandatory reporting law has been suggested (for the elderly) in the USA. See Marilyn R. Block and Janice L. Davidson, "Proposed Mandatory Reporting Law" in (eds) M. R. Block and J. D. Sinnott, *op.cit.,* note 25, pp.97-107. Would this overcome the difficulties the elderly encounter in getting access to the law? As to which see L. G. Forer, "Protection from and Prevention of Physical Abuse: The Need for New Legal Procedures", in (ed) R. L. Sadoff, *Violence and Responsibility,* SP Medical and Scientific Books, 1978.

53. *The Management of Child Abuse,* November 1985.

54. To do so it is necessary to prove that it is of "urgent necessity" that the person be admitted to hospital and that compliance with the full procedure for admission for assessment under s.2 would involve "undesirable delay" (s.4 of the Mental Health Act 1983). Two other alternatives (less commonly used) are detention by police (s.136 of the 1983 Act) and detention under warrant (s.135 of the 1983 Act).

55. These range from, "voluntary" reception into care (see s.2 of Child Care Act 1980) to compulsory measures of care (the use of care orders in particular). The ability to use wardship also exists.

56. See, further, Age Concern, *The Law and Vulnerable Elderly People,* Age Concern, 1986, ch.2.

57. A good discussion of the civil liberties issues is Alison Norman, *Rights and Risks,* Centre for Policy on Ageing, 1980, ch.2. See also J. Muir Gray, "The Ethics of Compulsory Removal" in (ed) M. Lockwood, *Moral Discussions in Modern Medicine,* Oxford U.P., 1986. See more generally, John J. Regan "Protective Services for the Elderly: Benefit or Threat?", in J. I. Kosbert (ed), *op.cit.,* note 31, pp.279-291.

58. See J. Muir Gray, "Forcing Old People to Leave their Homes", *Community Care,* 8 March 1979, pp.19-20.

59. See M. Green, *Geriatric Medicine,* January 1980.

60. By the National Assistance (Amendment) Act 1951.

61. See Sally Greengross, "Protection or Compulsion", *Journal of the Royal Society of Health,* 1982; Elaine Murphy, "Section 47 — Protection or Compulsion", *New Age,* Autumn 1983.

62. This uses different vague and value-laden concepts such as "in moral danger", "of such habits or mode of life as to be unfit to have the care of a child", etc.
63. See D. P. Forster and P. Tiplady, *British Medical Journal,* 8 March 1980.
64. The British Geriatric Society and British Association of Social Workers have drawn up guidelines for the criteria to be used in the definition of suitable persons and procedures. See BASW, *Services for Elderly People.*
65. The classic source is John Stuart Mill, *On Liberty,* first published in 1859.
66. See above before.
67. *Op.cit.,* note 16.
68. See *The Independent,* 22 July 1987, p.5.
69. *Realities of Home Life, op.cit.,* note 15.
70. *Home Life, op.cit.,* note 45, suggests residents should complain to local authority inspectors. For the National Health Service, the National Association of Health Authorities has issued guidelines for handling staff complaints through the hospital administrator or health service commissioner (see NAHA, *Protecting Patients,* 1985).
71. See S. K. Steinmetz, "Elder Abuse", *Ageing:* 315-316 (January — February, 1981), pp.6-10.

Chapter 46

The Grandparent-Grandchild Relationship in English Law*

Nigel LOWE
Gillian DOUGLAS

University of Bristol, England

Introduction

In many families it is taken as read that there should be regular grandparental contact with their grandchildren. It is not unusual for grandparents to play an active role in bringing up the children, looking after them, for example, where the parents are both out at work. Many parents no doubt turn to their own parents for help and advice in bringing up their children. What is the position, however, where there is disagreement about the role that grandparents should play? How common are legal disputes involving grandparents and what rights of legal redress are there?

The legal position of grandparents in establishing and maintaining contact with their grandchildren has hitherto received relatively little attention from English family lawyers. Yet over the last ten years English law has begun to make specific provision for grandparents to apply for access to their grandchildren and to become parties in proceedings brought by the local authority to remove the children from the family. The aim of this chapter is to examine the current legal position. We first consider the legal remedies available to grandparents who seek to safeguard or strengthen their position vis-a-vis their grandchildren. We then examine how often they resort to such remedies. Finally, we consider what legal reforms, if any, might reasonably be needed. In order to help answer some of the above questions we have conducted a small pilot study and we report the results in this chapter.

The Current Position in English Law[1]

A. Express recognition of grandparents

English law accords grandparents no automatic rights in respect of the care or upbringing of their grandchildren.[2] This means that, like any other non-parent, grandparents have to obtain a court order in their favour before they can acquire any formal legal rights over their grandchildren. For a long time, beyond classifying grandparents as "relatives", English law made no specific provision for such persons to apply for legal authority over their grandchildren. Indeed before 1978 there had been few express statutory provisions referring to grandparents.[3] It is not surprising that little or no recognition was given to grandparents by assignment of any rights over the child, given the heavy emphasis English law initially placed on parents', particularly fathers' rights. After all, it was not until the implementation of the Guardianship Act 1973 that *mothers* had equal rights with those of fathers in respect of legitimate children!

The Domestic Proceedings and Magistrates' Courts Act 1978, however, brought about the first significant change in the position of grandparents by giving them express rights to apply for access in certain defined circumstances. The 1978 legislation had been prompted by a Private Member's Bill, following the discovery of a number of cases in which grandparents had been denied access following their child's divorce or death.[4] The discovery of a further pool of aggrieved grandparents[5] led another MP to make specific provision for them in his Private Member's Bill which became the Children and Young Persons (Amendment) Act 1986. Under this Act certain grandparents can apply to become parties in care proceedings (in which a local authority commonly seeks to remove children from their parents).

B. What rights do grandparents have under English law?

(1) Rights of Action Contingent on Other Proceedings having Been Taken.

Like other interested persons[6] grandparents can seek leave to intervene in divorce, nullity or judicial separation proceedings involving their child. Upon being granted leave, they can seek custody or access to their grandchildren. In deciding what order to make, the court will be guided solely by the welfare principle, that is, it must treat the child's welfare as the first and paramount consideration.[7]

Although in custody proceedings brought under the Domestic Proceedings and Magistrates' Courts Act 1978 and the Guardianship of Minors Act 1971 the court does have power to grant custodianship to third parties, including therefore grandparents,[8] there appears to be no procedure entitling third parties to intervene in such proceedings and seek orders for themselves. However, as a result of the 1978 legislation, grandparents have been given special rights to apply for *access,* namely:

(a) on the making of a legal custody order under the 1978 Act or at any time while such a custody order remains in force.[9]
(b) on the making of a legal custody order under the 1971 Act or at any time while such a custody order remains in force.[10]
(c) following the death of the parent of the child in question, this right being conferred only upon the parent of the deceased parent of the child.[11]
(d) The 1978 Act also amended previous legislation so that access may be ordered on the making of a custodianship order or at any time while such an order is in force.[12]

Who ranks as a grandparent for these purposes? Under the 1978 Act s.14(6) expressly states that the court can grant access to a grandparent of a child "notwithstanding that the child is illegitimate". The term "grandparent", however, is not defined. It would seem that in the case of a child who is a "child of the family" but who is not the biological child of both the spouses,[13] the parent of a spouse who is not the parent of the child cannot be considered a "grandparent" for the purpose of applying for access. Furthermore, upon the basis that unmarried fathers are not regarded as "parents"[14], it would seem that if the *parent* of the child is illegitimate, only the *mother* of that person can rank as a "grandparent".

A not dissimilar position obtains under s.14A (6) of the 1971 Act but when the Family Law Reform Act 1987 is fully implemented all parents of a parent of a child will rank as "grandparents" for the purposes of this act regardless of whether the grandparents or the parents have been married.[15]

In the case of applying for access to a grandchild who is the subject of a custodianship order it would seem that all parents of a parent of such a child already rank as "grandparents" since for these purposes they are classified as "relatives"[16] i.e. "a grandparent, brother, sister, uncle or aunt, whether of the full blood or half-blood or by affinity and includes, where the child is illegitimate, the father of the child and any person who would be a relative within the meaning of this definition if the child were the legitimate child of his mother and father.."

(2) Rights to Initiate Proceedings

The above actions are essentially reactive in that they are either dependent upon proceedings being brought by someone else or upon one of the parents dying. Grandparents do, however, have proactive rights to bring certain proceedings. In this respect, however, they are not given any greater rights than any other relatives. These actions are as follows:

(i) If they have provided a "home" for the child for at least 13 weeks prior to the hearing they, like other relatives, can apply to adopt the grandchild.[17] An adoption order transfers all the parental rights from the parents to the adopters, so that, if successful, the grandparents will in law become the child's parents.[18] Like other relatives, grandparents are not subject to the requirement that the child must be placed by an adoption agency so that informal placements with them by the mother are perfectly lawful.[19]

(ii) Again, as for other relatives, provided the grandparents have provided a "home" for the child for the requisite period, they are entitled to apply for a custodianship order. The requisite period depends upon whether a person with legal custody consents to the application. If there is consent, the home requirement is three months, if not, the period is three years.[20] A custodianship order vests legal custody in the applicant(s) and suspends any other person's rights to legal custody.[21] Legal custody vests all the parental rights over the person of the child in the applicants[22] and essentially entitles the "custodian(s)" to bring up the child.

Although the above actions are dependent upon the applicant providing a home for the child, grandparents who have not done so are not remedyless. Under the Guardianship of Minors Act 1971, ss.3 and 5, if either or both the parents are dead and there are no guardians or, if there are, they are unwilling to act as such, then any interested person may apply to the court to become a guardian. However, it is generally thought that such an action is not very appropriate in cases of dispute because of the inadequate enforcement powers that the court has.[23] In such cases the preferable option is wardship.

The wardship jurisdiction has a wide application. Any interested person can make a child a ward of court, the effect of which is to vest legal control of the child in the court.[24] The court has the widest possible powers and inter alia can grant care and control and/or access to the ward to any person it considers appropriate. From the grandparents' point of view the great advantage of wardship is that it is an action that they can initiate and it is not dependent upon technical requirements such as having to have looked after the child. The great drawback is that proceedings have to be brought in the High Court[25] which can be both expensive and time-consuming. Furthermore the child will remain subject to the overall control of the court.

(3) The position vis-a-vis local authorities

Another area of grandparent involvement is in connection with local authority intervention. Under English law, local authorities are empowered to bring proceedings to remove children from their family and to vest in the authority parental rights and duties. Once in their care, local authorities have wide powers to look after the child including making arrangements for the child's long-term upbringing which may include planning for the child's adoption.

Grandparents are in a weak position as against local authorities. They have no automatic right to take part in care proceedings in which the local authority seeks the care of the child. As a result of the Children and Young Persons (Amendment) Act 1987, they can now apply for leave to become parties[26], but only in cases where the court has made a separate representation order and the grandparent has had a substantial involvement in the infant upbringing at any time during the infant's lifetime.[27] The term "grandparent" is not defined but on the normal canons of construction[28] would appear to include only the maternal grandparents of an illegitimate child, and only the grandmother if the parent of the child is illegitimate. Even if a grandparent has successfully become a party, somewhat curiously, the 1986 Act gives that person no right of appeal.

Once the child is in care, the grandparent's position is even weaker, for although local authorities are expressly enjoined by the Code of Practice on *Access to Children in Care* issued by the Department of Health & Social Security, to take into account the child's family when considering access,[29] there is no effective mechanism for grandparents (or other relatives) to take the issue to court. In particular, local authorities are under no obligation to serve notice of termination or refusal of access upon grandparents. Consequently, grandparents, unlike parents, have no statutory right to challenge a denial of access to a child in care.[30] It has also been held by the House of Lords in *Re W (A Minor)(Wardship: Jurisdiction)*[31] that grandparents cannot look to the wardship jurisdiction as a means of challenging a local authority decision, for example, to place the child with foster parents, to deny or restrict access to grandparents or to apply to free the child for adoption. Instead, application should be made to have the decision quashed by means of judicial review. This is an unsatisfactory action, however, since the court has no power to investigate the merits of the case (as it would have under the wardship jurisdiction) but is solely concerned with procedural impropriety or irrationality in reaching the decision in question. Even if successful, the case will be sent back to the local authority for reconsideration and there is no guarantee that the authority will look upon the grandparents any more favourably.[32]

An attempt was made to improve grandparents' rights to apply for access inter alia to children in care in a recent Private Member's Bill, namely, the Grandparents (Adoption of Children) Bill. Though the Bill failed, the Government undertook to incorporate such a right in its forthcoming revision of child care legislation.[33]

Use Made of Legal Proceedings

The Judicial Statistics and other sources of data indicate very low take-up of these opportunities for legal redress. The Law Commission[34] found that, in 1985, divorce county courts made only 400 orders giving *custody* after divorce to third parties, which represented 0.5% of all custody orders made. (Figures are not kept on the number of *access* orders made in favour of grandparents on divorce.) This figure does not relate solely to grandparents — other relatives and probably parents who were not parties to the marriage being dissolved, are also included. Nevertheless grandparents are the most common group of interveners[35]. The Law Commission also carried out a survey of wardship cases in the Principal Registry of the Family Division which revealed that, leaving aside applications from local authorities, only 14.6% of all cases were initiated by a non-parent, of which grandparents made up by far the largest category —

forming 61.2% of the non-parent cases (but only 8.9% of the whole sample of 705 cases). We understand from research currently being undertaken at Bristol University[36] into the use made of custodianship, that a significant proportion of applicants are grandparents. As to the specific legal provisions addressed to grandparents seeking access after there has been a custody order made under the Guardianship of Minors Act 1971 or Domestic Proceedings and Magistrates' Courts Act 1978, only 51 orders for access were made in magistrates' courts and only 21 orders in county courts in 1986.

A. Our Survey

To try to find out why such minimal use is apparently made by grandparents of these various legal options, we undertook a small survey of three different groups, namely, solicitors having significant family law practices; social workers dealing with children in care and grandparents themselves. We had initially thought that we would be able to scrutinise court records for some indication of the outcome of applications from grandparents, but because of the difficulty of finding a sample of even 20 court cases, we decided to look outside the courts for the bulk of our information.

(1) Solicitors

Given the low number of cases initiated in courts by grandparents, we decided that practitioners belonging to the Solicitors Family Law Association[37] were more likely than a more general sample to have had experience of dealing with such cases, and so we sent questionnaires to all the members of the Bristol branch — 71 members. We also gave questionnaires to 30 solicitors attending a continuing education course on family law held at Bristol University. 41 Solicitors replied. 26 had dealt with cases involving children in the last 12 months where the grandparents had been in some way involved, and 19 had actually advised grandparents concerning their grandchildren in that time. But no respondent had advised grandparents in more than 5 cases during that year. Where advice had been given, applications in legal proceedings were made as follows:

to adopt the grandchild	— 4
to seek a custodianship order	— 2
to become a guardian	— 1
to obtain access under GMA/DPMCA	— 11
to make the child a ward of court	
in order to obtain care and control	— 1
in order to obtain access	— 2
to intervene in matrimonial proceedings	
to obtain custody	— 2
to intervene in matrimonial proceedings	
to obtain access	— 8

Although one must be wary of drawing too much from such a small sample it is of interest that even those practitioners who see themselves as family specialists deal with very few grandparents in the course of a year.[38] Secondly, it is clear that grandparents are most likely to seek access to their grandchildren, and relatively few are hoping to take over the day-to-day care of their grandchildren.[39] No doubt, in many cases, grandparents would regard themselves as too old to contemplate this even if they wanted it. We asked the solicitors their views about whether they considered that grandparents are accorded sufficient legal recognition. There was no common view as to this, although 4 thought that grandparents were insufficiently aware of their legal position. Some considered that there was adequate legal provision made, and that grandparents should not be encouraged to think in terms of having "rights" over their grandchildren, any more than parents should.

> "It seems to me that to accord such [additional legal recognition] moves counter to the trend away from viewing children as possessions in respect of whom others can have rights rather than duties."

Some respondents noted that grandparents could be both benign and disruptive influences, and that adding extra legal procedures for them to take could prove counter-productive for the children caught in the middle. On the other hand, the view was expressed that

> "the extended family should continue to be involved with children after parents separate. Realistically, that involvement is not worth much without parents' co-operation. Legal status assists in changing social attitudes so that further involvement is more readily accepted. Also, lawyers can put more pressure on parents! How far to the extended family should it go, bearing in mind public policy aspects over legal costs and getting some definitive end to legal proceedings? Certainly to grandparents."

No mention was made of how the attitudes of the local judiciary might have affected their advice to grandparents, either to proceed with or to give up the idea of legal action. Priest and Whybrow found that solicitors in their sample considered that courts (and welfare reports) are not inclined to go against a custodial parent's wishes and are reluctant to overload a case with orders".[40] Most of the magistrates they interviewed stated that, in theory, they would take a favourable attitude towards grandparents' access applications, "because of their view that children need all the help and support they can get from the extended family. Nevertheless, two felt that they would view applications with caution and suspicion, and the general view was that a formal order would be a last resort and that much would depend on the nature of the parental objection to access".[41] From our own examination of the case-law, we could not discern any dominant attitude to grandparents or particular policy towards them.

Perhaps the lack of a particular approach accurately reflects the fact that

grandparents have a diversity of roles and individual grandparents play different parts in individual families. It clearly would be undesirable for the courts to
take too sweeping and generalised a view of what grandparents can and cannot
do for their grandchildren.

(2) Grandparents and Local Authorities

In their study *Long-Term Foster Care*[42], Rowe *et al* found that "children
fostered by relatives seemed to be doing better in virtually all respects than
those fostered by others". Of 55 children being fostered within their extended
family, 39 were fostered by grandparents — the largest category by far. 22% of
this group were full or half orphans, a higher proportion than for fostered
children generally, and the children were older than children placed with non-
family foster-parents. As one would expect, children saw more of the parent
who was the child of the grandparents fostering them than the other parent.
Some parents felt that the grandparents had 'taken over' the child from them,
often when a young mother had returned home with a baby, a view shared by
some of the social workers whom we interviewed in our study. Overall, the
findings confirmed that placement with relatives was beneficial for the child,
and operated generally smoothly for both social worker and foster-parent. Yet,
in a survey of fostering practice,[43] Rowe noted "the small but steady decline in
the number of children who are formally boarded out with relatives. Between
1978 and 1980 when …. overall numbers of foster placements were increasing,
the numbers of placements with relatives dropped by 6 per cent …. With the
increase of children coming into care following their parents' divorce, placement with relatives would appear to be an option that deserves fuller exploration than it often receives." Another important study by Milham et al[44] which
examined how children may lose contact with their families once in care (and
did not focus on the role of relatives), found that, in a sample of 450 children
who went into care, one-third had been seeing a grandparent at least once a
week before going into care. Since nearly three-quarters of the sample were
then found to experience barriers to maintaining contact with their parents and
wider family; it would seem that this link with grandparents will have been lost
in a significant number of cases. This is in spite of the recommendation by the
DHSS to local authorities in the Code of Practice *Access to Children in Care*[45]
that consideration of access should take into account the child's wider family.

   We carried out a small survey in two local authorities of similar type, having
large rural areas and two or three sizeable urban centres. Because Authority B
covers a wide geographical area, and its social work department is organised on
a different basis from that in Authority A, our returns for this authority derive
from the largest urban centre within its boundaries. National statistics relating
to Children in Care[46] showed that 18% of children in care were placed with
relatives or at home in 1982. Unfortunately, this figure is not broken down
further. Our findings were as follows:

	Auth. A	*Auth. B*
Number of children in care	166	84
Of these,		
(a) number home on trial with grandparents	1	1
(b) number boarded out with grandparents	16	1
(c) number having regular access with grandparents	33	28

From these figures, it will be seen that in Authority A, just under a third of children in care (50 out of 166) have some significant contact with grandparents, while in Authority B, the proportion is just over one-third (30 out of 84). But the type of contact appears to be different in the two authorities. Eight times as many children in care were boarded with grandparents[47] in Authority A as in Authority B, reflecting Rowe's finding of wide variations in placement with relatives in the five authorities she studied in her survey. Since the social workers in both authorities told us that neither has any particular policy regarding the use of grandparents for placements, this disparity may be due to demographic differences in the two areas (e.g. it may be that, because Authority B covers an area where a high number of Armed Services families live, there are fewer grandparents nearby with whom the children could be placed). Alternatively, the social workers responsible for placing the children may take a less favourable view towards grandparents, and may prefer to place with other relatives or outside the family altogether, but our survey did not establish this. As regards access, there appears to be a significant difference between the two authorities, with one-fifth of children in Authority A, as compared with one-third of children in Authority B, enjoying regular access. This difference may be due, at least in part, to the different use made of boarding-out with grandparents.

In Authority A, we had replies from 29 field social workers, and in Authority B, from 17. We asked them if they had any views on the role of grandparents in child care cases. In Authority A, 17 made comments, and in Authority B, 12 expressed views. As one would expect, views ranged widely in both authorities. For example one respondent said:

"I believe the potential use of grandparents to be valuable to a child, at a time when the child is experiencing great upheaval and disruption. Grandparents can often give a child a sense of security, commitment and continuity."

Another said that, in his/her experience, in

"many cases, natural parents have prevented grandparents' involvement and the department has tended to accept parental views. I am beginning to feel that in the child's interests, the parents' views should not be accepted, but the natural extended family involved."

On the other hand, it was said that many grandparents could themselves be "the instigators of the care problems", perhaps by undermining parents' competence in looking after their children. Views differed as to whether inadequate parenting could be due to the inadequacy of the grandparents, thus ruling them out of caring for the grandchild. Some workers *did* feel this was a relevant consideration, while others attached no credence to such a theory. Interestingly, we were able to interview solicitors responsible for the conduct of care proceedings in one of the authorities, and they did subscribe to this view quite strongly, and took a generally negative approach to grandparents, considering them usually to be little involved with the grandchildren and unlikely to wish to become more so.

The most common view expressed was the understandable one that grandparents can be both positive and negative influences. It was suggested that grandparents' involvement in care cases reflects their relationship with the child's parents.

> "If the relationship is strained, grandparents tend to adopt a monitoring role, reporting incidents [to the department], generally unwilling to take over care particularly of teenagers. Where relationships are good and grandparents are willing to care for grandchildren, the family is unlikely to come to the notice of the [department]".

The age and circumstances of grandparents must obviously be a significant factor, since elderly grandparents may be unable to take over care, and younger grandparents may be working and unable to give care either. The age of the *social worker* could also be a factor. One respondent suggested that the older social worker will more readily have grandparents in mind. An interesting view expressed by workers in both authorities was that grandparents' involvement can be difficult for social workers to cope with, given their confusion as to the legal position of grandparents vis-a-vis the children and the parents.

These local authorities do not appear to have a general policy concerning grandparents. Unless grandparents are actively on the scene, social workers may not always consider them in their overall plan for the child. In this latter sense they may arguably be acting in breach of the spirit of the Code of Practice.

(3) The Grandparents

In unpublished research carried out by Murch and others at Bristol University (kindly made available to us) a sample of divorcing parents was asked about the extent of contact between their children and any of the grandparents prior to the parents' separation. 62% of wives with care of the children reported that the children had seen their grandparents frequently (117 out of 190). Where the husband had care, 44% said there had been frequent contact (16 out of 36). When asked if the amount of contact the children had with their grandparents had altered since the marriage broke down, 60% of wives with care reported no change, while only 7% said there was less contact. Of the husbands with care, 42% said there was no change, while 14% reported less contact. Finally, the parents were asked how big a part grandparents played in their children's lives. 73% of wives with care considered that grandparents played some or a major part, while 45% of husbands with care felt this. It is interesting that husbands consistently reported less of a role for grandparents than wives did. Unfortunately, the research does not distinguish between maternal and paternal grandparents. Our own research, which centred on *grandparents,* not parents, did seek to investigate this.

Our contact derived first from media publicity given to our research, as a result of which a number of grandparents wrote to us, and secondly, through the good offices of the Family Rights Group who arranged for our questionnaire to be circulated among members of their Grandparents' Federation. In all we received 87 questionnaire returns. We cannot claim that they are a representative sample and, in any event, they are distorted by the replies solicited through the Grandparents' Federation, which organisation is almost exclusively concerned with cases involving local authorities. For this latter reason we have divided our findings between those cases involving local authorities and those which do not. Of the 87 replies, 52 involved local authorities and 35 were private law disputes. Before analysing the returns in detail, we have selected two replies illustrating the type of distressing problems that grandparents can face.

The first concerned the consequences after the child's mother died, and illustrates the dilemma of how to respond when contact with the grandchild has been denied.

> "My only daughter died in 1979 from cancer, she was 31 and Lee then was four and a half years old... Both grannies rallied around to keep the family together, I had Lee every weekend, and his other gran was very good. The trouble started five and a half years ago when a young girl moved in [with son-in-law]... Lee was immediately cut off from both grannies and families, though things are alright for [paternal grandmother] now.
>
> No way would I have expected to have Lee every weekend, as his happiness was all I wished for, but my son-in-law would not concede I had any rights.
>
> After about 9 months, I consulted a lawyer, and he tried for almost two years to find a friendly solution — but my son-in-law just ignored us. The lawyer, in his dealings, felt for my grandson's sake, if we could all manage a happy outcome, it would be best, as his Dad is not the sort to be told even by law who his son could visit. However, we eventually had to admit defeat, but by that time Lee would have said he didn't want to see me. So in retrospect, I regret not going to court in the first place, but it was all done to guard my grandson.
>
> Our family still keeps in touch, with cards at every occasion, all of which are returned."

The second extract illustrates a case concerning a local authority taking the grandchild into care, and shows how contact between the grandparent and grandchild can be lost following local authority intervention in response to inadequate parenting.

> "Scott was made a ward of court while in the hospital and taken into care at about six weeks due to drug problems and instability of father — my daughter had displayed nothing but deep love and concern for her son and had the makings of a devoted mother but because of her husband, found herself in a quagmire of emotions — at one point when her husband deserted her and went back to live with his mother she asked her lawyer to start divorce proceedings but was dissuaded.....as it would "rock the boat"... my daughter was anxious after the lawyer's reluctance over any divorce to make a go of things — both she and her husband were coming off valium and ativan....
>
> [Scott] was placed with a foster-mother after his discharge from hospital — the Magistrate granted an order for his return to the parents but my son-in-law physically attacked the social worker when he was actually bringing Scott back ... so he was immediately handed over to a second foster mother. [The foster parents applied to adopt Scott.]
>
> My daughter by that time was on the verge of a nervous breakdown and had to make the decision of agreeing to Scott's adoption while under the most appalling pressure — it was strongly against her wishes but she considered Scott's welfare — the foster parents' situation was ideal.... I feel I have been torn apart from what has happened regarding Scott."

Table A. The Grandparents: 80 returns

	LA cases n = 52	Private Law cases n = 35
1) *Age of grandparents*		
average age	58	60
youngest	36	39
eldest	81	77
2) *Grandparents' partners*		
alive	40	25
dead	9	8
divorced	2	1
no answer	1	1
3) *Maternal or paternal*		
maternal	44	15
paternal	7	20
no answer	1	–

From the above Table it can be seen that in terms of the age of the grandparents there seemed to be little distinction between the local authority cases and the private law cases. There was also remarkable similarity in the position concerning the grandparents' partners. In most cases (65 out of

87) the respondent's spouse was still alive (and in these 65, all but one actively supported their partner's dispute); 16 spouses were dead and few were divorced (3 out of 87).

A most interesting finding is in relation to whether the disputants were the maternal or paternal grandparents. In this respect there is a marked discrepancy between the local authority cases, where the overwhelming number (44 out of 52) were maternal grandparents, and the private law cases, where 15 were maternal, but 20 were the paternal grandparents. It seems that where the whole family is under threat, i.e. where the local authority removes the child from the family then this is much more likely to be challenged by the maternal rather than the paternal grandparents.

We were able to analyse the private law cases more closely:

*Table B. Maternal/Paternal division in the disputes following divorce,
            separation or death of parent(s)*

	Total	Maternal	Paternal
Following divorce or separation	18	5	13
Following death	10	7	3

From the above Table, it can be seen that paternal grandparents are more commonly involved following the divorce or separation of their son, when presumably their daughter-in-law has custody of their grandchild. This finding seems contrary to the finding in America by Colleen Johnson[48] that "conflict between paternal grandparents and their son's former wives was less common than between maternal grandparents and former sons-in-law."

According to our findings the maternal grandparents are more likely to be involved following the death of a parent. This is presumably because in the case of a mother's death the father might unexpectedly have custody. It might be noted that in one of our 10 cases, the dispute followed the death of the daughter in law[49], so that the paternal grandparents had no remedy under the provisions of the Guardianship of Minors Act 1971.[50]

Table C. The Grandchildren

	LA Cases	Private Law Cases
Total number of grandchildren	71	46
Age of grandchildren		
0 — 5	44	22
6 — 10	17	17
11 — 15	6	6
16 — 18	4	1

It will be seen from the above Table that of the 117 children included in our survey, most were aged 10 or under (100 in all) and over half were under 5 (66 in all). Though there was relatively little distinction between the cases involving local authorities and the private law cases, the grandchildren in the former cases were slightly younger. It should perhaps be added that many of the disputes included in our survey were long-running and some gave the ages of the children at the beginning of the dispute and others as they are currently.

Table D. Cause of private law disputes

	Number
Following divorce	13
Following separation	5
Following death	10
Following "family feuds"	6
Not specified	1

Table E. Remedy sought in the Private Law cases

Child to live with grandparents	4
Access	31

That the major cause of disputes was the parents' divorce or separation is not surprising, but the relatively high proportion of disputes following the death of a parent did surprise us, although our sample is too small to draw any firm conclusions. Whatever the cause of dispute the overwhelming desire of our respondents was to have access to rather than to look after their grandchildren.

Table F. Action Taken

	LA Cases n = 52		Private Law Cases n = 35	
	Yes	No	Yes	No
1) Consulted a solicitor?	45	7	31	4
2) Did solicitor advise legal action?	31	13	15	14
	(N/A 1)		(N/A 2)	
3) If yes, did you take action?	22	9	12	3
4) Were the proceedings successful?	5	9	4	4
Outcome still pending	6	–	4	–

It will be seen that in the vast majority of all the cases (76 out of 87) the grandparents consulted a solicitor (where they did not, finances seemed to be the main reason); but the advice that they received about taking legal action differed significantly for, whereas in nearly half the private law cases no legal action was advised (14 out of 31) this was so in less than one third of the local authority cases (13 out of 45). These findings are a little surprising. First the high consultation rate seems contrary to our findings in our survey of solicitors; it may be that our grandparents are particularly enterprising. Secondly, we would not have anticipated so many grandparents being advised to take legal action in the local authority context, given their general lack of rights. Some of these cases, however, seemed to be last ditch attempts to oppose adoption, and some were in support of the parents.

Among the reasons advanced for the advice not to take legal action in cases involving the local authority were that the grandparents had no rights, or that the case was not worth pursuing against the authority. One respondent was told that it would "damage the child" and one did not know why they had been advised not to take action. In the private law context, a few were advised that they had no rights but another important reason for the advice not to go to court was that legal action was not worth it as it would only antagonise the parent and that it might be better simply to wait and hope that "things would improve".

It should also be noticed that a number of those advised to take legal proceedings did not in fact do so (in all 12 out of 46). The reasons for not taking legal action seemed to be first, the inability to obtain legal aid coupled with a reluctance or inability to meet the high legal costs and secondly, the wish to avoid making things worse and suffering "more heartache".

Our grandparent respondents generally favoured being given automatic rights to have access to their grandchildren — "We would like the law extended to provide for a right of access by the grandparent even if the parents are still living together". One respondent felt this should be so, provided the grandparent "had previously shown interest in the child". Others would go further, suggesting that grandparents should "have the same rights from the start as a parent" and the right "to take part in the child's upbringing". Those who were in dispute with the local authority were, not surprisingly, strongly critical of the social workers in the case, feeling that they regarded the grandparents as "interferers" and "nuisances". Our respondents also frequently took a negative view of the utility of going to court. They had found it a "considerable strain", some had felt humiliated and rudely treated. Some doubted the effectiveness of the court's order anyway — "It is so easy for the parent to agree in court, then make access impossible."

Overall, the grandparents felt that they are "an important part of family life. The law should be changed to recognise this." There was a "failure of those in authority to recognise the extended family — a lack of true understanding of the importance of family ties/roots to children." While some of their suggestions for legal reform might be impracticable and too sweeping, there is no denying the deep distress and frequent bitterness which these grandparents felt. The law has clearly failed them.

Conclusion

Our grandparent respondents considered that they were in a special position regarding their grandchildren, which should be recognised by the law vesting automatic rights in grandparents to have access to and to seek care of grandchildren. Such automatic rights do not seem to us the right way to meet the concerns of grandparents anxious to retain contact and to do the best for their grandchildren. English law has moved away from the language of parental rights, towards parental responsibilities, and it would hardly be appropriate to reintroduce the concept of rights into this area.

Indeed, one may query whether English law has not gone too far in placing grandparents in a special position over and above that enjoyed by other relatives, by giving, for example, the right to seek access after a custody order has been made. These legal provisions have emerged in haphazard fashion as a result of private members' initiatives rather than from a coherent policy of either Government or the Law Commission. The fact that they are seldom used and rarely successful suggests that giving rights to initiate legal action may not be the best method of promoting the claims of grandparents or of the child. On the other hand, grandparents *do* form the largest category of relative-litigants, suggesting that they are more prepared than other relatives to take action. To cut out this possibility would clearly deprive a number of grandparents of a potential means of redress they feel is important and worth pursuing.

Two alternative approaches may be suggested as offering a better answer. The first would be to enable grandparents (and indeed any interested person) to initiate legal proceedings, for access or care, without the necessity of a prior custody order between the parents (as is currently a requirement under the 1971 and 1978 Acts), but only with the leave of the court. Such a procedure would allow other members of the extended family to seek legal redress, and not single out grandparents for special treatment. There seems no good reason to prevent uncles and aunts, or even great-grandparents, for example, from obtaining the same remedies as grandparents, even if they were less likely to take advantage of the possibility.[51] Further, it would obviate the need, where there was no prior dispute between the parents, for the grandparent to take wardship proceedings in the High Court. Such a procedure is surely too drastic, too expensive, and unlikely to restore family harmony.[52]

A more low-key action, in perhaps the County Court or the magistrates court, *might* downplay this problem. The Law Commission has proposed a similar scheme[53] in relation to applicants seeking care and control, and has suggested that applications could be made *ex parte* "to avoid causing needless anxiety to parents or children in cases where there was no reasonable prospect of success."[54] We would suggest that such an approach may be apt not just for care and control but for access also, and where the dispute concerns the style of upbringing of the child.

The second approach may be to *require* courts dealing with children to consider the wider family and the possible need for access orders, etc. in their favour. This method mirrors the recommendations in the Code of Practice on Access to Children in Care, and can be regarded as encouraging good practice on the part of the judges. If the wider family is regarded as important in the local authority context, it is arguably equally important in "private law" situations. If the onus was on the court to consider grandparents, they would avoid the expense and difficulty of taking proceedings themselves, and parents might be more willing to co-operate with orders emanating from the court's initiative rather than that of the grandparents. Such a solution would not help the "family feud" situation, however, where there are no proceedings between the parents, but simply disagreement between grandparents and parents. As of now, the only remedy for such a problem under this approach would be to make the child a ward of the court — an unsatisfactory remedy, as already indicated.

Perhaps a combination of these approaches is therefore required. We should note that in the local authority context, the Children and Young Persons (Amendment) Act 1986 enables grandparents to apply to be joined as parties in care proceedings. Will grandparents be encouraged to do this? Will local authorities have to think more carefully about grandparents as a result? It seems unlikely that significant numbers of grandparents will take advantage of the change, given their generally low level of take-up of legal procedures, and that they tend to seek access to, rather than care of, their grandchildren. The Government's White Paper (55) proposals to enable grandparents (and others) to challenge local authority access decisions may prove more attractive to them. It is arguable that the automatic consideration approach is more appropriate in this context than in the private law cases. Where the dispute is between the parents themselves, the court's primary task is to consider which parent is better able to meet the child's needs, and only if neither is suitable should the court turn its attention elsewhere. But where the issue is whether to take the child away from his or her home, and inevitably to reduce overall contact with the rest of the family, perhaps the court should be required to give greater weight to what the members of that family can continue to offer the child.

Implicit in our discussion is the view that the welfare of the child must remain the paramount consideration, and that the "rights" of others must be subordinate to safeguarding that welfare.[56] Realistically, this means that in many, if not most cases, if parents will not co-operate with grandparents *without* a court order, they are unlikely to do so with one. Hence, whatever their formal legal remedies, grandparents will continue to lose court actions if the court feels that compliance is unlikely to be forthcoming or will be grudgingly offered.[57] From this point of view, grandparents are in precisely the same situation as absent parents struggling to maintain links with their children. However, grandparents face a further problem in that they are generally uncertain about their legal position, and unable to obtain clear advice, even from solicitors, as to what they can do. It is difficult to suggest how this problem can be overcome, although the simplified procedures and legal provisions we have suggested might enable legal advisers to offer more comprehensible advice.

Until there is greater awareness throughout society of the needs of children to keep contact with many family members, grandparents as others will continue to be frustrated and devastated when things go wrong between them and the child's parents.

Notes

* This chapter was written prior to the introduction of the Children Bill (1988) into Parliament
1. See J. Priest *In Place of a Parent* (1986) Jordans.
2. This comes as a surprise and disappointment to many of the grandparents that we have contacted.
3. One example is the Administration of Justice Act 1925, s.46 under which grandparents are given specific rights of succession (ranking behind parents and siblings) upon their grandchild's intestacy. See also the Non-Contentious Probate Rules 1987, r 22.
4. See Hansard, HC Debs 1977 Vol 935 Cols 225-227 and R. Rhodes James M.P., *Access rights for grandparents* (1978) 1 Adoption and Fostering 37.
5. See Hansard, HC Debs 1986 Vol 90 Col 1199, and see *Re W (a minor) (Wardship: Jurisdiction)* [1985] AC 791.
6. Save guardians, step-parents and those with a custody order already in their favour, who do not have to seek prior leave to intervene: Matrimonial Causes Rules 1977 r 92 (3). Applications for leave are made before a registrar: Matrimonial Causes Rules 1977 r 122 (1). It should be noted that the court may make an order in favour of third parties even without their intervention.
7. Pursuant to the Guardianship of Minors Act 1971 s 1. For a discussion of the welfare principle see e.g. Bromley's *Family Law* (7th Edn by Bromley and Lowe) pp 311 — 318. For an example of custody being granted to grandparents see *Cahill v Cahill* (1974) 5 Fam Law 16.
8. See respectively the Domestic Proceedings and Magistrates' Courts Act 1978, s 8 (3) and the Children Act 1975 s 37 (3). Custodianship orders are discussed below.
9. S 14 of the Domestic Proceedings and Magistrates' Courts Act 1978.
10. S 14A (1) of the Guardianship of Minors Act 1971.
11. S 14A (2) of the 1971 Act. The restriction of the right to parents of the deceased parent of the child rested upon the belief that it is only in that situation that conflict between the grandparent and the surviving parent arises. In our experience conflicts also arise between the surviving parent and his or her own parent.
12. S 34 (1) of the Children Act 1975 as substituted by s 64 of the 1978 Act.
13. I.e. a child, not being a local authority foster child, who has been treated by both spouses as a child of the family — s 88 (1) of the 1978 Act.
14. Cf. *Re M (An Infant)* [1955] 2 QB 479.
15. Pursuant to s 2 of the 1987 Act, under which the 1971 Act is to be interpreted in accordance with s 1 of the 1987 Act.
16. Children Act 1975, s 107 and Adoption Act 1976 s 72 (1).

17. Adoption Act 1976 s 13.
18. It is this distortion of the natural relationship which is sometimes said to be a reason for not granting the order, see the discussion in Bromley op.,cit. p.390.
19. Cf. Adoption Act 1976 s 11. It might be noted that the controls imposed by the Foster Care Act 1980 on private fostering (i.e. having to notify the local authority) do not apply to grandparents or other relatives.
20. Children Act 1975 ss 33 (3)(a)(c) It will be noted that only one person with legal custody need consent and that if the child is in "permanent" care of a local authority, that authority can consent.
21. Children Act 1975 ss 33 (1) and 44 (1).
22. Children Act 1975 s 86.
23. See *Re N (Minors)(Parental Rights)* [1974] Fam 40 (dispute between grandparent and putative father) and see also *Re H (an infant)* [1959] 3 All ER 746. Discussed inter alia in Bromley at pp 354 and 355.
24. For a short account of the wardship jurisdiction see inter alia Bromley ch 13 and for a detailed account see Lowe and White: *Wards of Court* (2nd Edn, Barry Rose/ Kluwer).
25. Once initiated, proceedings can be transferred to the county court under s 38 of the Matrimonial and Family Proceedings Act 1984.
26. Without party status, they cannot directly ask the court to consider their position.
27. Children and Young Persons (Amendment) Act 1986 s.3(2) and Magistrates' Courts (Children and Young Persons) Rules 1988 r. 17. The court must also be satisfied that making a grandparent a party is likely to be in the interests of the welfare of the relevant infant — see r. 17 (1)(b).
28. See the discussion above.
29. As para 8 of the Code states: "..access arrangements should include relatives — siblings, grandparents, putative fathers, for example — with whom contact should be preserved. In some cases it may be appropriate to identify relatives ..... with whom contact has lapsed and to follow up the prospects of re-establishing contact."
30. I.e. they have no rights under the Child Care Act 1980 ss 12A — E.
31. [1985] AC 791, sub nom *W v Hertfordshire County Council* [1985] 2 WLR 892, [1985] 2 All ER 301.
32. There are further possible remedies of complaining to the "local ombudsman" (who can only make recommendations after finding 'maladministration' and cannot investigate the merits of a local authority's decision), or to the European Commission and European Court of Human Rights. The Latter two have recognised that grandparents may have a right to respect for their family life under Article 8 in respect of their grandchildren; see *Marckx,* Judgement Series A, Vol.31, and application No.8924/80, 24 D & R, 183.
33. See Hansard 1988 H.C. Debs. The children Bill (1988) is now reswing of Portamentary debate.
34. Working Paper No.96 *Review of Child Law: Custody* para.5.38
35. See *Custody Law in Practice in the Divorce and Domestic Courts,* by Priest and Whybrow, Supplement to Working Paper No.96, para. 7.4
36. By E. Malos and E. Bullard.
37. A body which acts as a loose interest group for family practitioners.
38. A view confirmed by interviews with specialist practictioners in other parts of the country.
39. A similar picture emerged from our grandparents survey (see Table E).

40. Loc.cit.para. 6.8 and see our own findings in Table F(4)
41. Ibid. para. 6.9
42. Rowe J. et al. *Long Term Foster Care* (1984), Batsford, London.
43. Rowe J. *Fostering in the Eighties* (1983). BAAF, London.
44. Milham S. et al. *Lost in Care* (1986) Gower. Aldershot.
45. Loc.cit. at para.8
46. DHSS (1982) London
47. The reason why boarding out is preferred to sending a child "home on trial" is because if the child is officially "boarded out", an allowance can be paid to the foster-parent.
48. In V. Bengtson and J. Robertson, *Grandparenthood* (1985) Sage, California.
49. The father remarried and the dispute was generated by his new partner.
50. See the discussion above.
51. Cf. the position in Scotland, where "any person claiming interest may make an application to the court for an order relating to parental rights...." s.3(1) Law Reform (Parent and Child) (Scotland) Act 1986. See J. Thomson, *Family Law in Scotland* (1987) Butterworths, London.
52. An important concern for a number of our grandparent respondents, see above.
53. See *Custody* Working Paper, para. 7.33 to 7.36
54. Loc, cit. at para, 7.33.
55. *The Law on Child Care and Family Services* Cm. 62 (1987)
56. A view taken by the House of Lords in *Re K D* (A Minor) (Ward: Termination of Access) [1988] 2 WLR 398.
57. A view strongly expressed to us by the National Association of Grandparents, a self-help group concerned with disputes arising out of divorce. A further group, "POPETS" (Parents of Parents Eternal Triance) also represents and provides support for such grandparents.

Part Five

Inheritance And Pensions

Introduction

by John EEKELAAR

The demographic changes described in Part One have implications for the institution of inheritance which have as yet been little appreciated. *Section One* of this part deals with issues of inheritance. *Section Two* takes a closer look at problems relating to pension provision which, in new and subtle ways, may now be related to issues of inheritance.

Danielsen (Chapter 47) describes the current position in the laws of the Scandinavian countries regarding succession to matrimonial property. (The position of cohabitees has been discussed, for Denmark, by Lund-Andersen and Munck in Chapter 29). It is noted that, as parents are living much longer, children are coming into their inheritance at correspondingly older ages as well, usually when they have established themselves financially, so their needs for capital assistance are usually less than those of a surviving elderly parent. Such changes have been taken into account in the Scandinavian systems.

But have the implications of these demographic changes been sufficiently appreciated? In Britain it is becoming apparent that a significant new source of wealth has been accruing to people, often in their forties, who already enjoy good incomes and, more importantly, high property status. It is coming from the inflated estates of their deceased parents. (See *New Society* 22 April 1988). But here lies the dilemma. While such large inheritances may constitute a windfall to the children, the property they represent may have been of little use to the parents, whose needs in their last years will have been for income (whether to sustain them while they lived at home or in institutional care),not capital. But to sell the property would deprive the children of their inheritance; something which, as Dobris (Chapter 48) observes, a parent is loath to do. Yet is the state, if it makes provision for a parent, to ignore the potential wealth tied up in the property? If it does, then we may encounter the phenomenon described by Dobris of the parents divesting themselves of property in order to qualify for assistance.

Clearly there are a number of values in conflict here. It might be argued that, in view of the demographic changes, expectations of inheritance have become anachronistic. Where old people have the capital resources, these should be converted into sources of support for their last years. This could be done by disposing of them in the market in return for an annuity, or by the state taking a lien over property in return for its support for the elderly owner. Can the "rights" of the middle-classes to their inheritance, proclaimed by Dobris, be challenged in this way? Where such schemes are operated, by what means are the interests of the elderly protected against possible exploitation?

It is for reasons such as these that Chapter 49 by Verschraegen assumes much interest. It deals mainly with institutions of Austrian, German and Swiss law, which seem at first sight to be remote from contemporary concerns, for they deal with inheritances to farmlands. Nevertheless, the principles may be worth consideration. They involve a kind of "anticipated succession" whereby the property passes to the heir when the farmer is no longer able to work the land. But the transferor retains the right to live in the property and, indeed, the transaction may also involve an obligation to support the farmer in cash or kind. Such an arrangement ensures that the heir receives the inheritance, but links this with the needs of the parents. Of course, it might be observed that legal institutions elsewhere may be utilised to achieve these purposes. Verschraegen notes that the Austrian institution is open to contractual variation. Yet such a development would benefit from a framework, into which standard forms could be built, and, if considered desirable, linked to fiscal incentives. This is a matter where legal inventiveness could make an important contribution to one aspect of old-age policy.

The role of the resources of the elderly in pension policy may not be insignificant. As Holtzmann (Chapter 50) points out, at the beginning of *Section Two*, the OECD countries are faced with a potential crisis in their public pension schemes: demographic change alone will require doubling contribution rates or halving benefits if present coverage is to be maintained, but the problem is aggravated by the effects of system maturation. The income of the elderly could be boosted by increasing the component drawn from labor (postponing retirement) or enhancing income from private sources, either capital savings, or private (and occupational) pensions.

Nielsen and Vindelov (Chapter 51) re-iterate many of these concerns in their examination of Danish pension policy. In addition to the fundamental problem of meeting the pension burden, they draw attention to the question of distribution of pension benefits. The proliferation of schemes and fragmentary nature of their take-up will in due course be reflected in greatly differing levels of retirement income being received by those due to retire in the medium-term future. (A disparity between men and women is particularly marked). Yet if the national pension burden is to be reduced by significant introduction of private resources (moving, as Nielsen and Vindelov put it, from the "pay-as-you-go" strategy of distributing income *between* persons to a strategy of distributing the receipt by each individual of his or her income over his or her lifetime) then it is inevitable that the outcome will reflect the differing wealth between individuals. But Nielsen and Vindelov, understandably, are reluctant to see distribution of income among pensioners becoming more unequal than it is amongst employees. The best solution envisaged is to maintain a basic state pension at an acceptable level and to allow provisions of family law to provide for participation by certain family members in the supplementary pensions of others.

This last issue is taken up by Pask (Chapter 52) and by Frank (Chapter 53)

Pask accepts that certain groups of elderly are better-off now than they were before retirement (reverting to a theme raised in Part Three) but recognizes, too, that many elderly groups, in which women are strongly represented, are on very low incomes. The position of women is a direct consequence of their unfavorable position in the labor market vis-a-vis men, and this follows from their exercise of family roles. Where they have remained married, they can take the benefit of their husband's retirement income, and will benefit from survivorship rights on his death. Pask illustrates the ways in which Canadian provisions have extended these benefits to a survivor of a non-marital cohabitation. Further problems arise on divorce: or separation, if the couple did not marry. In principle, pension rights can be divided on divorce as being a species of matrimonial property. Yet this usually results in the non-member having to rely on the member passing over the correct share of the benefit regularly, as it is paid, since mechanisms for establishing direct payment by pension administrators are difficult to construct. Although some improvements have been achieved, problems of valuation of the benefit to be divided remain. Pension-splitting is generally not available for cohabitees (except under the federal pension plan). Of course the pension position of women can be improved by extending their opportunities to qualify for substantial pensions in their own right. Frank (Chapter 53) explains how in Germany the pensions of people on lower incomes (mostly women) were boosted by an alteration in their mode of calculation. Instead of using the individual's *actual* income as a base of calculation, an *assumed* base equivalent to 75 per cent of the earnings of all insured persons is used. Also, credit is given for time spent bringing up children (one year credit for every child). This is rather a meager addition, but is compelled by financial considerations. Yet it concedes the principle of recognition of such activities for pension purposes, and this may be of future importance. Yet, as Frank observes, considerations of cost require that any improvement in the position of the housekeeping spouse can only be achieved either by increasing contributions (already heavy) or reducing other benefits. He considers various proposals of this nature.

Westerhäll (Chapter 55) discusses recent trends in Swedish pension policy. These center around a policy of encouraging early retirement. This is partly in order to take people already long unemployed off unemployment benefit and into the pension system. But it also applies to people who, in the years immediately before official retirement (in itself reduced from age 67 to 65) confront difficulties in employment or finding new employment (as in the case of their redundancy) and is administered generously. Westerhäll also refers to the flexible retirement policy, which also allows early retirement and receipt of pension in conjunction with continuation of work on a part-time basis. Such schemes underline the relationship between retirement/pension policy and employment policy. The tendency to push people into the pension system at earlier ages increases the burden on pension funds and could be said to hasten retired peoples' isolation from society. Yet the combination of part-time work and partial retirement, perhaps extending for some considerable time *after* "official" retirement age, could be an important option, especially if, as may be happening, at least in some occupations in some countries, present retirement requirements pose the threat of a serious reduction of the skilled and experienced workforce. [This is discussed further in M-T Meulders-Klein and J. Eekelaar (eds), *Family, State and Individual Economic Security* (Story Scientia, 1988) vol.2, especially chapter 44]. But great though all these problems are in the industrialized world, the problems confronting pension schemes and similar mechanisms in developing countries are greater, as, at the risk of ending this work on a depressing note, Wanitzek makes clear in Chapter 51. Yet perhaps there is a lesson for everyone here. Too great a readiness to rely simply on cash resources to confront the evolving requirements in the life cycle might lead to disaster. Social justice cannot simply be "bought". On the other hand, our societies need to examine more closely the extent of their fundamental commitment to wealth distribution. For a community's attitude to *all* its less well-off members will be reflected also in its treatment of the vulnerable and disadvantaged elderly.

Section One

Inheritance

Chapter 47

The Surviving Spouse: Inheritance and Undivided Matrimonial Property in Scandinavian Law

Svend DANIELSEN
Judge of the High Court, Holte, Denmark

Among the elderly, married couples constitute a large group. One of the spouses will go through the turmoil of losing her or his lifelong companion. This means not only a great loss, a sorrow and a feeling of loneliness, but also a fear for the future. In most cases the surviving spouse will be the wife. While her husband was alive, she will often have had little knowledge of the economy of the family. She will in many cases be in doubt as to the possibility of being able to keep the family home intact. Many decisions have to be made within a short period of time. To get an insight into the economic situation of the widow or the widower, it is of course important to look at the surviving spouse's income from public old age pension schemes, from pensions from the former employer of the deceased spouse and perhaps also from his or her own former employment, and from insurance to be paid as a result of the death. These questions will not be a topic of this chapter. Rather, we shall describe what will happen to the property the couple had at the time of the death.

The solutions that have been chosen in Denmark, Norway and Sweden will first be described, and figures will be given. The statistical background to the provisions are mentioned and some policy considerations behind the rules are explained. We follow this by a description of the matrimonial property regimes and their consequences in case of death, the rules of testate and intestate succession and an examination of the special Scandinavian solutions to retain undivided possession of the estate after the death during the life time of the surviving spouse. Finally some numbers are given to describe what actually happens in these cases.

The statistical background

To get a better knowledge of the situation of the surviving spouse in order to evaluate the considerations for the heirs, especially the children, it may be of value to examine the statistical information.

Last year a Danish professor wrote in his textbook on inheritance law:

> "People, who live to the age where they have children, will on an average die when they are 70-80 years old. Because children in general are born when their parents are between 20 and 35, they normally will have reached the age of from around 35 till about 60, when their parents die."

It would be helpful when evaluating the condition of the widow and the widower to look into the number of estates of deceased spouses. Surveys are not available from Denmark, but the Norwegian Inheritance Law Reform Committee conducted a survey in 1955, and the Swedish Marriage Law Committee conducted a similar investigation in 1947. In the Norwegian study, for a period of a year all the estates where the deceased left a spouse were examined. The number was 10,922 consisting of around 30% of all estates in that year. The Swedish survey totaled 5,700 cases — all the estates with a surviving spouse in a two months' period.

According to the Norwegian figures the average age of the surviving spouse was 65, and the corresponding age of the children 34. Official statistics show a different perspective. They illustrate that if a marriage took place in the middle of the century the man would then be around 29 years old and the woman about 26. They would as an average have 2.4 children. The husband would die after about 46 years of marriage at the age of about 75. The children would then, as the average, be 41 years old. The wife would die 51 years after the marriage at the age of 77 after having been a widow for five years.

The Swedish survey showed that in 70% of the cases the husband was the first spouse to die. On average the husbands were 71.7 years old at the time of death and the wives 70. Only a small percent of married people died before reaching the age of 30. In 86% of the marriages in the study there were one or more children. The number of cases where children, at the time of death of the first of their parents, were below the age of 20, was only 10%. There were stepchildren in 5% of the estates, but the figure is not exact. In 85% of the estates the deceased left children and in 1% grandchildren. In 11% the only surviving family apart from the spouse were parents, brothers and sisters or their children. In 45% the only surviving relative was the spouse.

Danish statistics show that on average, people get older now than before. Around the turn of the century men died at the age of 50 on average. In 1934-35 men as an average lived to be 62 and women to be 63.8 years old. The figures from 1985 show that men are now an average of 71.6 years old at the time of death and women 77.5.

Policy considerations

A Danish Inheritance Law Reform Committee had in its report of 1941 the following thoughts about the policy on division of the matrimonial property after the death of a spouse:

> "The rules should be the result of different considerations. On the one hand they shall secure the surviving spouse, but on the other it must be considered to what extent the rights of the widow or widower shall be more important than regard for the family, whether they are heirs, perhaps children from another relationship, or parents and other relatives."

In a Swedish government proposal from last year for a new marriage code there were the following policy considerations:

> "As regards the rules on inheritance it should be taken into account that the general development in society, especially in the economic fields, has had the result that children are less dependent on their inheritance from their deceased parent for their maintenance than before. At the same time it is appropriate to strengthen the protection of the surviving spouse against a break up of the family home, when the other spouse has died."

1. The most important policy consideration in the Scandinavian countries is the *protection* of *the surviving spouse*, typically a widow. She has, often during a long marriage, played a part in creating the wealth the married couple possesses at the time of the death. It might be by the aid of the earnings from her work outside the family home; it could also be by the aid she has rendered her husband in his business, whether it is a farm, a shop or the office in his firm. Also she may have contributed with her work at home and her upbringing of their children. The effort of the couple makes it natural and fair that the surviving spouse should be able to keep the assets undivided and to continue to enjoy them. After all, these assets have provided the framework for the life of the family. It is important for the widow to know whether it will be possible for her to maintain the standard of living to which she is accustomed, or how much she must lower it. It will often be her wish to remain in the home in which she has lived with her husband surrounded by well-known furniture and other belongings. Another important consideration will be for her to be able to finance life in her old age without being dependent on economic support from others.

2. It is important for the *Community* at large that the elderly have satisfactory economic means to take care of themselves. If the law forces the surviving spouse to transfer property to the other heirs it might give the surviving spouse less chance of avoiding public support.

3. The *position* of *the children* of the marriage is very important when the

law of inheritance is considered. Society has an interest that the property the parents have accumulated should pass to the younger generation at a time when they most need it. The fact that people now live longer means that this is not a realistic approach. The statistics mentioned earlier illustrate that children may well be as old as forty or more when the first of their parents dies. At that age they have long finished their education, have reached the position at work they may expect and have a well established family themselves. Their own children are already teenagers or older, and have often moved away from home. To make it law that children shall inherit when the first of their parents dies, will therefore not fulfil any needs that it may be thought important to protect. Scandinavian children feel it natural that they should wait until the last of their parents dies before they inherit from them. Another fact is that the amount each child would inherit in general is so small that it would not create any significant rise of living standards.

4. In the Scandinavian welfare societies, people who need support will most likely obtain it from the state. Thus *the social function* of the inheritance law — to secure the economic circumstances of the children — has *lessened*. This point is strengthened by the legal relationship between the generations. Children have no legal obligation to support their parents, not even if the parents need economic assistance, and generally are not thought to be morally obliged to do so. It is no longer the norm that a mother, after having become a widow, will move in with one of the children.

5. *Stepchildren* are of growing importance and their special situation should be taken into account. More people marry twice. In 1985 about a fourth of all Danish marriages were contracted when one party was a divorcee. Often there will be children of the first marriage, which means that the widow or widower will compete with stepchildren for the estate. The mutual feelings between them are not as deep, as the stepchildren have often not been living in the family and the surviving spouse may barely know them.

6. Finally, there is a relatively small number of cases where the deceased did not have any children. Here the question arises whether *the parents* or *brothers* and *sisters* of the deceased should be heirs together with the surviving spouse.

The division of the matrimonial property

The first question is what will happen, according to the matrimonial property laws, to the property the couple has accumulated?

A. The Scandinavian system is known as a *deferred matrimonial property regime*. Each spouse during the marriage has a large degree of independence in economic matters, but on the other hand at the end of the marriage the property is divided into equal shares. The rules are the same both after divorce and after the death of one partner. There are no legal exceptions as regards property owned before the marriage, inherited property or gifts. The details of the rules of division are almost the same in case of divorce and death.

The division of the matrimonial property into *equal shares* has been the main rule in Scandinavian law for a long time. Marriage law reform committees in all the three countries have had the occasion within the last decade of reconsidering the rules, and the result has been a wish to keep the status quo. Exceptions have been made when a divorce takes place after a short marriage. In its decision to propose to continue a division in equal shares as the main rule, the Danish Marriage Law Reform Committee was especially aware of the position of married women. Although they work away from their homes in growing numbers even when the children are small, to a large extent such work is part-time. The statistics show that the average income of women with full-time employment is below that of men. The conclusion of the committee was that it will take many years before married women will be economically equal to their husbands.

B. In all three countries it is possible for married couples to *agree* on a system of *separate property* which is exempt from the division. The same is true if there is a decision relating to inheritance by will and property received by way of gift. In Denmark spouses are only allowed to make a general agreement covering the situation which could arise on divorce and in the case of death. In Norway, it is possible to make an agreement so that a division shall not take place in the case of divorce, whilst the general rule of partition in equal shares should be applied in the event of death. A similar system has been proposed in Denmark but has not yet been made law.

C. In the Swedish Marriage Code a new principle has been introduced. Independently of the fundamental rule of division of the matrimonial property into equal shares after the death of one of a married couple, the surviving spouse can declare that no division shall take place. The result will be that he or she keeps his or her own belongings, and the heirs of the deceased share the rest.

The inheritance rights of the surviving spouse

A. The legal rules

During the last few decades, committees in all three Scandinavian countries have discussed changes in the position of the surviving spouse, and new provisions have become law.

The result of the discussions in Denmark is The Inheritance Act, whereby the surviving spouse inherits 1/3 of the estate of the deceased when children are alive. This means that the widow or widower apart from the half which is acquired as a result of the matrimonial property division described above inherits 1/3 of the half that is the deceased spouse's estate, or altogether takes over 2/3 of the married couple's assets. The share was raised from 1/4 to 1/3. If the deceased dies without surviving children, the surviving spouse is the sole heir in competition with the parents, sisters or brothers. When the surviving spouse dies, the fortune is distributed in equal proportions to each of the spouse's heirs. Among the reasons for the change was a survey in 1956-58, showing that in 70% of all cases, where there was a conflict between a surviving spouse and the parents, sisters and brothers of the deceased, he or she had made a will making the spouse the sole heir.

In Norway it was decided in The Inheritance Act to keep the rules that were similar to those previously in force in Denmark. The surviving spouse inherits 1/4 in competition with children and 1/2, if she or he inherits together with parents, sisters and brothers.

In Sweden new provisions in The Inheritance Act did not change the position of the surviving spouse, who is not an heir when there are children of the marriage or stepchildren.

B. Wills

Another question is whether a spouse can by testamentary succession over-throw the entitlement of the other spouse or of the children. According to Danish and Swedish law this is only possible as regards half of the estate, and in Norway the possibility to dispose of the belongings by will is limited to a third. In Norway and Sweden only the children are compulsory heirs, in Norway limited to a certain amount, and the surviving spouse is not protected against testamentary dispositions. Recent Swedish proposals to abolish the heir's indispensable rights did not materialize.

It may be of interest to examine to what extent married couples in practice made wills and what they contain. In Denmark it is not possible to answer the first question. However, a small survey of Danish wills made by married testators showed that almost one half diminished the inheritance rights of the children, especially the testator's own, in favour of the other spouse. In a Swedish study, wills were made in 7% of all the estates in the sample. In 2/3 of the estates of married persons there were wills in favour of the surviving spouse, which is probably due to the fact that the position of the widow or widower is weaker in Sweden than in the other countries.

The undivided matrimonial property

In Danish-Norwegian law it has through centuries been an important feature of the marriage and inheritance provisions that the rules of division described above are not necessarily applied when the first of a married couple dies. It is fundamental that the surviving spouse has a right to retain undivided posses-sion of the estate.

The system implies that the division of the matrimonial property is post-poned if the surviving spouse declares that she or he does not wish at that moment to share the property with the children. The right does not exist if the married couple have made an agreement that the matrimonial property division shall not be applied. It is also possible in a will to decide that the property affected by the will shall be immediately parceled out to the heirs. The children of the marriage cannot influence the choice of the surviving spouse. She or he must administer the estate in the interest of the children, and they have certain rights in case of misuse of the property. In most cases, the property remains undivided until the death of the last spouse, and the whole estate is then distributed equally amongst the heirs of each spouse. The surviving spouse is free to decide on a division of the property at any time and has, in case of remarriage, a duty to divide the estate. In these cases the surviving spouse takes over two-thirds of the estate as her part of the matrimonial property and as an heir.

In Sweden the arrangement to retain undivided possession of the estate after death is not known. In 1987 rules were introduced that, to a large extent, have the same effect as the Danish and Norwegian laws and place the surviving spouse in a similarly favorable position. If there are children of the marriage, the widow or widower is free to retain the property of the deceased in an undivided form, and the children have no right to receive their shares until both parents have died. The right is independent of the matrimonial property arrangement.

In all three countries special provisions exist as regards *stepchildren*. As mentioned above they often do not have a close relationship with their stepmother or stepfather. These heirs have a right to claim their share at once. If they or their guardian do not consent, the surviving spouse cannot retain undivided possession of the estate.

The rules have particular safeguards in relation to *small estates*. The surviving spouse has a right to take out an amount which in Denmark and Norway is around 8,000 dollars and in Sweden perhaps double that amount. This means that the widow or widower can take over the whole matrimonial property if it does not exceed these figures. The right is independent of whether there were special agreements on the matrimonial property, if there are stepchildren of the marriage, and if there are testamentary dispositions of the deceased. Furthermore, the surviving spouse has an unrestricted right to dispose of the property and is not required to share the property with the children in case of remarriage.

Statistics

Finally, what really happens after a death in a marriage will be examined.

In between a fourth and a third of all cases no property is left, or so little that it only meets the expenses of the funeral. The rules of division are not applied.

Danish statistics from around 1980 illustrate that there were 20,600 estates

with a surviving spouse. Of those, 14,700 were passed on undivided to the
widow or widower and 2,600 were covered by the rules of small estates. Only in
3,300 cases, or less than 15%, was the estate divided amongst the heirs. In a
portion of those cases the estate was taken over by the surviving spouse as sole
heir, as the deceased did not leave any children. In Norway the system of the
undivided matrimonial property after death is so popular, that the surviving
spouse decides on this in 92.6% of all the cases.

References

Legal provisions:
Denmark: the Inheritance Act of 1963 as amended and last published as No. 584 in
1986, especially chapter 2 and 3. The Matrimonial Property Act of 1925 as amended and
last published as No. 628 in 1986.
Norway: The Inheritance Act of March 3, 1972, especially chapters II and III. The
Matrimonial Property Act Of May the 20th 1927.
Sweden: The Inheritance Act of 1926 as published 1981:359 with later changes
1987:231, especially chapter 3. The Marriage Act 1987:230, especially chapter 9.
Literature:
Denmark: Finn Taksøe-Jensen:: Arveretten, 1986, p. 16-26 and 64-123. Torben
Svenne Schmidt (ed.), Jørgen Graversen, Jørgen Nørgaard og Peter Vesterdorf:Ar-
veret, 1985, p. 25-69, and Svend Danielsen: Arveloven med Kommentarer, 3.ed., 1982.
Norway: Carl Jacob Arnholm: Arveretten, 7. ed., 1984, p. 123-47, and Per Augdahl
and Peter E. Hambro: Arveloven med kommentarer, 1985, p. 46-124.
Sweden: Anders Agell: Aktenskaps- och samboenderatt enligt 1987 ars lagstiftning,
2. ed., 1987, p. 131-49.
Committee reports and government proposals:
Denmark: Report on inheritance provisions (No.291/61) and Report No. 3 from the
Marriage Law Reform Committee of 1968 on the matrimonial property system (No.719/
74).
Norway: Report from the Inheritance Law Reform Committee, 1962 and Ot.prp.
No.36(1968-69).
Sweden: Report from the Marriage Law Reform Committee SOU 1981:85 and Prop.
1986/87:1.
Statistics:
Denmark: Befolkningens Bevægelser, 1984, tabel 32, Report from the Inheritance
Taxation Committee (No.1014/84) p. 285 and Taksøe-Jensen: Arveretten p. 134-37.
Norway: Report from the Inheritance Law Reform Committee 1962 p. 25-27.
Sweden: SOU 1981:35 p. 533-61.

Chapter 48

Divestment of Assets to Qualify for Medicaid: Artificial Pauperization to Qualify for Nursing Home and Home Care Benefits

Joel C. DOBRIS   School of Law,
                          University of California, Davis, USA

This chapter is about a phenomenon that is quite fascinating: old people in America giving away their property to qualify for government nursing home benefits. Simply put it goes like this.[2]

As of 1987, 12% of the U.S. population was over 65.[3] The proportion of older people in the United States population has increased steadily since 1900 and is expected to continue to grow for the next forty years. This comes from declines in both the birth rate and the mortality rate.[4] A falling birth rate means a decrease in the number of young people in the population, and declining mortality increases longevity. Declining mortality is a function of improved healthcare and advances in life style.[5]

Today, of that population over 65, 1.3 million are in nursing homes[6] Using 1984-85 figures, that means essentially 5% of the over 65 population is in nursing homes.[7] Forty-nine percent of those age 65-69 today will spend some time in a nursing home, and 25% of the people over 85 now live in nursing homes.[8] Seventy-five percent of that nursing home population is female[9]. Indeed, the problems of aging in the United States are very much women's problems. This is a world-wide phenomenon. People over 80 are likely to be women,[10] which is to say that within the elderly population the number of women is increasing disproportionately.[11] And, most of those women are likely to be widows.[12]

When one looks at a married couple and observes one spouse going into a nursing home, it is likely to be the husband who has to go in the home and it is likely to be the wife who remains on the outside, on a reduced income.[13] Furthermore, care inside the family is likely to come from a female relative and outside the family from a female worker.[14]

In 1986, the average annual nursing home cost was $30,000 in California and New York and the national average was $22,000.[15] And a luxury home can cost $60,000. In 1985, $35 billion dollars was spent on nursing home care.[16] Old people are scared. So are their middle-aged children. What is to be done? If one is poor, there is Medicaid.[17] The rich take care of themselves.[18] Rich for these purposes is probably $500,000 in investment assets, or the equivalent in income, per senior citizen.[19] It is the people in the middle who have the problem.[20]

To better understand the problem, it is useful to consider what goals old people have in this context.

First and foremost, independence. Most want to stay out of the nursing home as long as possible, ideally forever. If they have to go in, they want it to be as pleasant as possible and that takes money. If they are married, they want to keep the so-called community[21] spouse afloat after one has to go into a home. They want to keep the family house and its contents, especially if they are women. The house symbolizes, for many middle-class women who are now elderly, much of their adult lives.[22] They want to live in the house as long as possible and they want to pass it on to the next generation, especially if there is even a hope of it being used by a family member. If possible, they want to pass an inheritance on to their children and grandchildren.[23] They also want to keep their good names. They do not want to cheat and they do not want to go on "welfare".[24]

What do the children want?[25] They want good lives and good care for their parents. They want their parents spared the indignities of poverty. They do not want to act as nurses and orderlies if planning can generate the money to get help. They would like not to contribute money to parental care if they can help it. And, children want their inheritances.[26] Especially in this world where things seem to be getting harder for the middle class and the pie seems to be shrinking, a modest, middle-class inheritance can look awfully good.[27] Simplifying, whether the middle-class, middle-aged children of America will inherit anything is ultimately a function of whether their parents stay out of the nursing home or engage in so-called divestment planning to qualify for Medicaid nursing home benefits. That is quite a surprise. In the United States, we keep seeing different items anointed as the true middle-class estate planning concern.[28] Nursing home costs may well be the real concern. It certainly is the latest candidate. It seems fair to say the same pot of money is being asked to do several jobs — cushion the nursing home blow, support the community spouse if there is one and provide an inheritance.[29] There is an obvious conflict and people are coming up short.

Somehow, people want as much assurance as they can get that if someone has to go into the nursing home it is not going to bankrupt the family.[30]

The private sector is responding in several ways, including planning of the sort discussed here;[31] nursing home insurance;[32] and real estate development aimed at seniors.[33]

It is fascinating that the real estate developers of America are going to solve all these social problems. As a capitalist society we have turned over this vexing problem to our ultimate entrepreneurs. Remarkably, it appears at the moment that they may be solving the problem for prosperous, middle-class people.[34]

Not a week goes by that these matters are not discussed in the paper, and usually in the real estate[35] or business[36] sections.[37]

Currently, there is only one government program that that provides long-term nursing home care and that is Medicaid.[38] Medicare[39] does not provide any meaningful coverage. In a sentence, Medicare is hospital and medical insurance for people over sixty-five, but not nursing home insurance.[40] Private *health* insurance does not provide any meaningful coverage either.[41]

Medicaid[42] is a joint state and federal program designed to provide health care for the poor of all ages.[43] The ticket for admission is that an applicant has to be poor, as defined in the program.[44] There's poor and there's poor. Half the people in nursing homes on Medicaid started out paying their own bills.[45] The figure is two-thirds in New York.[46] One can have some meaningful assets and still qualify.[47] And one can have a spouse with some assets and still qualify.[48] So, there is some planning to be done.[49]

What are the planning tools? Specific detail is beyond the scope of this chapter for a variety of reasons, including the complexity of the topic, the multiple variables, and the need for field experience to speak with authority. An academic in this area needs practice exposure to have the clearest view possible.[50] Practice experience may well be of geographically limited value. There are important variations in this planning practice from state to state[51] and there are likely variations from county to county.[52]

This almost feudal division of the Medicaid landscape is quite interesting. It is reminiscent of the variations among counties in both probate court rules and land use planning.[53] When local government is given discretion and the duty to interpret and when there is money at stake, then, as was said in the American musical comedy, *The Music Man*, you gotta know the territory.[54]

Simplifying, the planning tools include the following:

(a) Giving away assets more than two years before one needs to go into a nursing home;[55]
(b) Holding assets in exempt form so they do not "count"[56] when the social welfare authorities are trying to determine eligibility, the classic exempt asset being the family house;[57]
and (c) rearranging assets held by husband and wife so that assets attributed to the healthy spouse are protected to the extent possible.[58] This often involves splitting the assets of husband and wife and considering a gift of the unhealthy spouse's half of the family house to the healthier spouse.[59]

Perhaps the reader is beginning to see one of the things that is so fascinating about this topic. This is, in some sense, familiar territory for American estate planners — gifts in contemplation of Medicaid! That sounds a lot like the old estate tax doctrine of gifts in contemplation of death.[60] American estates lawyers are not strangers to rearranging assets between husband and wife to take advantage of government rules.[61] Like so much tax planning, what looks tainted from the outside to the casual observer, is in fact proper. None of this is fraud, although regulators like to say things like that to reporters[62]. Perhaps they do that in the hope of reducing the number of applicants. No doubt there is fraud in this area, but that is not the topic of this chapter.[63]

What this chapter is about is a rather remarkable use by the middle class, under particular circumstances, of a social welfare program initially intended only for the poor.[64] Simply put, members of the middle class are asserting their "right" to some of these Great Society poverty funds.[65]

And, they are often doing it through lawyers.[66] Why lawyers? First, there is a lot of money at stake. When there is a lot of money at stake Americans turn to lawyers.[67] Second, there is a serious problem here, and when there is a problem in America, lawyers get called in to help.[68] Third, this is a classic situation where people will pay a lawyer and so it makes sense for lawyers to establish a speciality practice.[69] And, fourth, the surplus of lawyers in the United States helps assure people of representation.[70]

The glue that holds it together is the feeling on the part of applicants, and their children, that they are entitled to these benefits, that it is some kind of insurance, and that somehow it is an extension of Social Security[71] and Medicare which cover almost all elderly people.[72] People assume that Medicare and Social Security have put a safety net under the elderly and they have formed the expectation[73] that nursing home coverage is included. And frankly, people are not terribly interested in hearing that there is no such coverage. When they choose to, they are taking it without a twinge of conscience.

It seems fair to say that the elderly change their minds about the propriety and desirability of this kind of planning. As to propriety, a great deal depends on how it is categorized. If it is welfare,[74] nobody wants it. If it is seen, however, as an extension of Medicare, or an entitlement, or insurance, then the curse is off it. An earned benefit, transferred at life's end from a grateful state, is a lot easier to take than a handout.[75]

As to desirability, it seems fair to say that the likeliest candidates for this kind of planning are husbands and wives who are looking at the imminent institutionalization of a spouse. Then the needs of the spouse who will remain in the community are likely to suggest qualifying the institutionalized spouse for Medicaid as quickly as possible while preserving assets for the spouse who stays in the community.[76] The healthier spouse's future needs require getting the frail spouse on Medicaid, even though private care may be better.[77]

If the older person has no spouse, then it may well be a mistake to make transfers to qualify for Medicaid, although people are doing it every day. The single older person is probably better advised to hold on to her assets. There is no spouse to worry about and the older person's well-being is more important than an inheritance for her children, especially in an era when access to Medicaid may be lessening. Of course, not all children will agree.

While parents may change their minds about the propriety of this planning, it seems fair to say that the middle-aged children have much less concern about propriety than their parents.[78] The funds are there, at least for the moment, the planning is legal and the stakes are high. And the chances are the children do not care what people think, especially when the children do not live in the same community as the parents.[79] In other words, the social sanction is gone.

Are people entitled to do this? Yes. A just America should not bankrupt her senior citizens as the ticket for admission to the nursing home. It is bad national policy to face the middle class, the backbone of this country, with a financially impossible task — saving enough to pay for nursing home costs. To fathom the impossibility of the task, imagine a middle-aged husband and wife, with both of their parents alive, contemplating the possibility of four parents in the nursing home.[80] It is bad social policy to arrange things so that if one is unlucky a whole lifetime of work will be swept away.[81]

Several theoretical risks exist for American society in the current system —
(1) demoralization of the citizenry[82]
(2) less saving by older folks because it seems futile,[83] and/or
(3) more hidden savings.[84]

Anything that discourages savings is obviously bad.[85] The great strength of the Japanese economy is proof enough of that for today.[86] Anything that encourages hiding assets is unwise in a nation that relies on voluntary payment of income taxes.[87] We do not want people mad at the government or getting a taste for hiding their assets if we are counting on them to voluntarily pay their taxes. The person who would not bother to cheat on his income taxes to save a few tax dollars may well be willing to cheat to save many thousands of inheritance dollars, and he is likely to seriously consider cheating on his taxes thereafter.[88] He has already taken the first step, lured by the hope of great gain. The rest is easy. Anything that encourages consumption[89] is subject to question. Presumably there is some consumption encouraged by despair at ever being able to save enough for a nursing home, and it may well be unwholesome. Of course, uncertainty about the future may also encourage genuine gifts as well. There is an old saying that shrouds have no pockets. Neither do nursing home gowns.

The expectations of both generations about there being an inheritance are entitled to be vindicated.[90] The elderly middle class expect to be able to provide something for their children, and the children have come to have a settled expectation of an inheritance. The desire to provide an inheritance is part of the essential definition of personhood for many middle-class people.[91] To take away this essential property "right" is a serious matter.[92] As Holmes said, expectations about property take "root in your being and cannot be torn away without your resenting the act".[93]

It is fair to say American politicians have been listening to all of this. The Medicare Catastrophic Protection Bill,[94] which seems certain of enactment, allows married applicants to make certain transfers between themselves and to keep some property for the community spouse and still qualify for Medicaid.[95] And the California legislature has recognized the propriety of husband and wife asset-splitting.[96] And, if the reader remains unconvinced, one can only say that Englishmen and Americans have been legally planning to beat the government since at least the 13th century.

The long-term solution seems to be compulsory, government insurance. However, the Reagan administration is against compulsory insurance. They prefer voluntary private insurance, tax credits or tax-deferred savings accounts. Coverage has to be compulsory because very few people want to buy nursing home insurance until they need it.[97] Currently only about 400,000 policies are in force.[98] People will not even buy disability insurance which they need more than nursing home insurance.[99] At the moment it is hard to get excited about the insurance products being offered, but things are changing almost daily. And, long-term care insurance may become a popular employee benefit, so long as it is cheap or free.[100]

In the meantime, where is the money to come from? The short answer is, one does not know. To the extent that the money is to come from the Medicaid budget, there is a problem. Obviously, the Medicaid budget is finite.[101]

This means divestment planning constitutes transfers from poor Medicaid recipients to middle-class Medicaid recipients. Thus it is a transfer from those who do not vote to those who do.[102]

To further complicate things, the Medicaid budget is a major source of funding for AIDS patients, because many AIDS patients are on Medicaid.[103] So, in the future, there may well be a tragic tug of war for Medicaid funds, and nursing home beds in some large cities, between the elderly and the dying young. Short-term, there has to be a nursing home bed shortage in some metropolitan areas if the AIDS crisis worsens before new nursing homes are built.[104]

It seems there is going to be a race between those who want the government to provide funding and those who want the private sector to provide funding. Once enough middle class people are covered by private insurance or the like, the political pressure on the government will be diminished.

Surely, this divestment/bankruptcy system is a terrible way to distribute any social welfare benefit. It places an inappropriate premium on lawyers and on being aggressive. It is a mistake to ration the social benefit of nursing home aid through the intermediation of lawyers who specialize in Medicaid planning and through the use of a legal, fictional poverty.[105] One ends up thinking of this system as a "tax" on the unlucky, the meek,[106] and the lawyer averse.[107] That is surely unjust, but one must wonder if there is an economic explanation for allowing the system to exist. Perhaps there is a rational selection or rationing process at work here. Only those who want the money enough will fight to keep it. And only those who are clever enough will succeed in keeping the inheritance. Perhaps they are better suited than the government to use the money saved. Perhaps they will use it more productively, and as to the rest, let the devil take the hindmost. Perhaps there is a social imperative to drive the unlucky out of the middle class. Improbable as it is, it is something to think about.

The ability to leave an inheritance is one of the key elements of a capitalist society.[108] It is ironic that the failure to provide a benefit that used to be called socialized medicine may wipe out a meaningful number of middle-class inheritances in American society.

Obviously, there is a terrible waste of assets on the bureaucracy that distributes Medicaid. More preferable would be a lower cost bureaucracy passing out vouchers that could be redeemed for home care or nursing home care, funded by compulsory insurance and combined with a decent minimum of property that can be saved for inheritance. The key problem with funding home care is the concern on the part of everyone that the vouchers will be used to pay family members for home care they have been providing for free.[109]

One can conclude with a striking passage from a William Faulkner novel, a bit of dialog spoken by an old man. He says, "We are old; you cannot understand...that nothing is worth anything but peace, peace, peace. I cannot help it. I want peace now. I don't want equity or justice. I don't want happiness; I just want peace".[110]

Although we are concerned with equity and justice we are denying old people the peace they crave, and they seem to be taking the matter into their own hands.

Notes

1. Copyright (c) Joel C. Dobris 1988. The author would like to thank the American Council of Learned Societies, the John D. and Catherine T. MacArthur Foundation, The National Endowment   for the Humanities, the convenor of the conference, Professor Shimazu, and the University of California for the travel grants that made the presentation of this article in Tokyo possible.
2. For further discussion of the topic see Levy, "Supporting the Aged: The Problem of Family Responsibility," in this volume.
3. See Wall St. J., Apr. 24, 1987, at 33D, col. 1 (w.ed.)
4. See Aaron, When is a Burden Not a Burden? The Elderly in America, *The Brookings Rev.* 17 (Summer 1986).
5. See E. Crimmins & R. Easterlin, *The Graying of America*, The 1988 World Book Year Book 103.
6. See *N.Y. Times*, Mar. 30, 1988, section 1, at 9, col. 1. (nat'l ed.) (quoting from Nat'l Center for Health United States 1987). 106,000 over 65 people are in nursing homes in New York State. See Brainard, No Cheap Answers, *Knickerbocker News*, Mar. 16, 1988.
7. See C. Taeuber, *America in Transition: An Aging Society* 17 (Current Population Reports Series P-23, No. 128, Sept. 1983 Bureau of the Census, U.S. Dep't of Commerce).
8. See *N.Y. Times*, Mar. 30, 1988, section 1, at 9, col. 1.(nat'l ed.) (quoting from Nat'l Center for Health Statistics, Dep't of Health and Human Services, Health United States 1987)
9. See Older Women's League, *The Picture of Health* 8 (1987) (quoting Census Bureau, PC 80-2-4d (1984).
10. See K. Davis & D. Rowland, *Medicare Policy* 9 (1986).
11. See K. Davis & D. Rowland, *Medicare Policy 12* (1986).

12. See Langbein, The Twentieth-Century Revolution in Family Wealth Transmis-
    sion, 88 *Mich. L. Rev.* 726 (1988). Widows live an average of 18.5 years beyond the
    death of their husbands. See P. Doress & D. Siegal, *Ourselves Growing Older* 183
    (1987).
13. See A Rivlin & J. Wiener, *Caring for the Disabled Elderly*, 273 n.17 (1988).
14. See T. Sommers & L. Shields, *Women Take Care* 21, 106 (1987). As the male
    reader can see, this has little to do with him. He will be dead.
15. See J. Crichton, *The Age Care Sourcebook* 211(1987).
16. "Older people and their families pay nearly half (48%) of the nation's annual
    nursing home bill, which totaled $27 billion in 1982. Medicaid pays just about the
    same percentage (49%). With its coverage limited, Medicare funds only 2% of
    total nursing home expenditures, and private insurance pays the balance (less than
    1%)." J. Crichton, 211,212 (1987).
17. 42 U.S.C. section 1396 (1982 & Supp. III 1985).
18. There are riches besides money. Seventy-five percent of nursing home residents
    have no spouse to care for them at home. See J. Crichton, 207 (1987). And, fewer
    than ten percent of the skilled nursing facility residents have a child with an income
    over $20,000 per year. See K. Davis & D. Rowland, *Medicare Policy* 62 (1986).
19. See Freedman, Guide to Medicaid Eligibility, in Representing the Elderly and
    Incapacitated Client and His or Her Family 3, 7 (NYSBA 1987).
20. See generally *Not Only the Poor* (R. Goodin & J. Le Grand ed. 1987) For
    discussions of the problems of the middle-class elderly, see Aaron, When is a
    Burden Not a Burden? The Elderly in America, *The Brookings Rev.* 17 (Summer
    1986). See also Langbein, The Twentieth-Century Revolution in Family Wealth
    Transmission, 88 *Mich. L. Rev.* 726 (1988).
21. The spouse who does not go into the nursing home is called the "community"
    spouse. See, e.g., Collins, *Issues and Options: Potential Legislation for the
    Prevention of Spousal Impoverishment in Medicaid Cases*, Inst. on Law and Rights
    of Older Adults, Brookdale Center on Aging of Hunter College (1983).
22. Some readers of this chapter in draft form have concluded that this is a human
    reaction, not necessarily gender specific. Fine. For many of the women of the
    author's mother's generation, husband, house, offspring and the ability to drive a
    car, describe the four corners of a full life. As today's young woman finds freedom
    in a law degree, yesterday's found it in a driver's license. For a discussion of the
    house as a special asset, in the context of will contests, see Schoenblum, Will
    Contests: An Empirical Study, 22 *Real Property, Probate and Trusts Journal* 607,
    642 (1987)
23. For a current discussion of the true nature of the middle-class inheritance see
    Langbein, The Twentieth-Century Revolution in Family Wealth Transmission, 88
    Mich. L. Rev. 726 (1988).
24. See L. Jarvik & G. Small, *Parentcare* 53-54 (1988).
25. See L. Jarvik & G. Small, id 1-10 (1988).
26. Children of the middle class have come to expect an inheritance even though in the
    United States (except for Louisiana) children are not protected from disinheri-
    tance. For a discussion of so-called pretermitted heir statutes which, simplifying,
    provided typically that a child who is not mentioned or provided for in a parent's
    will is entitled to an intestate share see Haskell, Restraints Upon the Disinheri-
    tance of Family Members, in *Death, Taxes and Family Property* 105, 110 (E.
    Halbach ed. 1977).

27. See generally *Not Only the Poor* (R. Goodin & J. Le Grand ed. 1987); Aaron, When is a Burden Not a Burden? The Elderly in America, *The Brookings Rev.* 17 (Summer 1986); Langbein, The Twentieth-Century Revolution in Family Wealth Transmission, 88 *Mich. L. Rev.* 726 (1988).

28. For discussions of middle-class estate planning concerns see Solomon, Modifying the Wealth Transmission Process for the Modestly Affluent, 120 *Tr. & Est.* 27 (1981); Solomon, Planning Estates for the Forgotten Middle Class, 18 *Inst. on Est. Pl.* section 1300 (1982). See also Langbein, The Twentieth-Century Revolution in Family Wealth Transmission, 88 *Mich. L. Rev.* 726 (1988).

29. For a discussion of the importance of inheritance in our society see Friedman, The Law of Succession in Social Perspective, in *Death, Taxes, and Family Property* 9 (E. Halbach ed. 1977).

30. See generally J. Crichton, *The Age Care Sourcebook* 23-46 (1987); P. Doress & D. Siegal, *Ourselves Growing Older* 185-97 (1987); L. Jarvik & G. Small, *Parentcare* 39-54 (1988).

31. For a discussion of the various factors to be considered when undertaking divestment planning for the elderly, see e.g. Hankin, Estate Planning for the Disabled or Incompetent: How to Plan for and Manage the Twilight Zone in Estate Planning 1987, *UCLA-CEB Est. Pl. Inst.* at sections 5.1-.62.

32. Human Resources Division, U.S. General Accounting Office, *Long-term Care Insurance* (1987).

33. Langdon, Housing an Aging Nation, *Atlantic*, April 1988, at 67.

34. The catalog of real estate based solutions includes apartments with a variety of useful services promised for increasing amounts of money. Services often include food, cleaning, and both short-term and long-term convalescent care. Some of the arrangements seem to be variants on the age-old promise, "Give me all your money and I'll solve all your problems." Most of the arrangements strike the author as ways for the developer to borrow money from the tenants for the developer's other projects. This alone is a rational explanation for why developers are so attracted to the business. Typical cost information is as follows. A one bedroom apartment in a median-price life care development in 1988 would cost $55,000 plus $740 per month. Top of the line prices start at about $78,000 for a one bedroom apartment with a monthly charge beginning at about $1,700. See Langdon, Housing an Aging Nation, *Atlantic*, April 1988, at 67. One must distinguish between the business of running nursing homes and the business of running apartments with some care and with a nursing home attached, or available nearby.
Obviously, one has to wonder whether the promises made by the developer to apartment occupants will be kept. Less obviously, one might wonder if those promises are ones that "run with the land" as covenants or equitable servitudes. As to such see French, Toward a Modern Law of Servitudes: Reweaving the Ancient Strands, 55 S. Cal. L Rev. 1261 (1982).

35. See Merkel, The Old School Lures Retirees, Dec. 6, 1987, section 8, page 21, col. 3.

36. See Hummel, 30-Acre Project For the Elderly, *N.Y. Times*, Mar. 6, 1988 section 10, page 21, col. 3.

37. For a discussion of the entrepreneurial side of real estate development aimed at the elderly, see Cook, New Ideas in Housing the Aged, *N.Y. Times*, Jul. 26, 1987, at 1, col. 1 (real estate section, nat'l ed.)

38. 42 U.S.C. section 1396 (1982 & Supp. III 1985).
39. 42 U.S.C. section 1395 (1982 & Supp. III 1985).
40. See J. Regan, *Tax, Estate & Financial Planning for the Elderly,* sections 9.09-9.13, 9.15-.16 (1988 rev.).
41. Nor does what is called Medigap insurance. Medigap insurance is private insurance designed to cover Medicare deductibles. See J. Regan, *Tax, Estate & Financial Planning for the Elderly,* section 9.19 (1988 rev.).
42. See 42 U.S.C. section 1396 (1982 & Supp. III 1985); K. Davis & D. Rowland, *Medicare Policy* 50 (1986).
43. See 42 C.F.R. section 435.1 (1986).
44. See J. Regan, id. sections 10.03 -.06 (1988 rev.).
45. "Nearly one-half of residents [in nursing homes] are impoverished and qualify for Medicaid assistance to pay their nursing home bills. For the most part, these people were not poor when they entered the nursing home; they became impoverished and eligible for Medicaid when the cost of care in the nursing home exhausted their personal resources." K. Davis & D. Rowland, *Medicare Policy* 29 (1986).
46. Brainard, No Cheap Answers, *Knickerbocker News,* Mar. 16, 1988.
47. See generally Freedman, Guide to Medicaid Eligibility, in *Representing the Elderly and Incapacitated Client and His or Her Family* 3 (NYSBA 1987).
48. See Hankin, Estate Planning for the Disabled or Incompetent: How to Plan for and Manage the Twilight Zone in Estate Planning 1987, *UCLA-CEB Est. Pl. Inst.* at section 5.2.
49. See generally Hankin, Estate Planning for the Disabled or Incompetent: How to Plan for and Manage the Twilight Zone in Estate Planning 1987, *UCLA-CEB Est. Pl. Inst.* at section 5.1.
50. Similarly, American estate planning professors concluded they had to get practical experience to understand that field..
51. One can see the differences from state to state in a different context. In Alabama, a family of four with an adjusted income of $1,764 a year earns too much to qualify for AFDC (Aid to Families with Dependent Children) and Medicaid. In California, the same family could have an adjusted income of $8,808 per year and qualify for Medicaid. See Woodside, Health Care for the Poor: How to Pay for It, *Wall St. J.,* May 29, 1987. For a comprehensive table on the characteristics of state Medicaid programs in 1980, see T. Grannemann & M. Pauly, *Controlling Medicaid Costs* 109 (1983).
52. It is the counties that ultimately distribute the benefit. See 42 C.F.R. section 431.50 (1987).
53. As to probate variation see, e.g., Cal. Continuing Educ. of the B., California Local Probate Rules (1988) which is more than two inches thick.
54. "...[H]e doesn't know the territory." Salesman 2 speaking of Professor Harold Hill. M. Wilson,*The Music Man* 21 (1958). Divestment is a dangerous game. Situations can change. Regions differ. One needs to know the territory.
55. See J. Regan, id. section 15.04 (1988 rev.).
56. See 42 C.F.R. section 435.732 (1986).
57. For a discussion of typically exempt assets, see Talis, Medicaid as an Estate Planning Tool for the Elderly, 66 *Mass. L. Rev.* 89 (1981).
58. See Hankin, Estate Planning for the Disabled or Incompetent: How to Plan for and Manage the Twilight Zone in Estate Planning 1987, *UCLA-CEB Est.Pl. Inst.*

at section 5.2

59. See Prensky, Healthy Legal Advice, 5 *Cal. Law.* Nov. 1985 at 12. However, in the aftermath of the Catastrophic Health Care bill, it may well be that this technique will be of less value in the future.

60. For a discussion of gifts in contemplation of death see D. Westfall, *Estate Planning Law and Taxation* section 7.02 (1983).

61. See Dobris, Marital Deduction Estate Planning: Variations on a Classic Theme, 20 *San Diego L. Rev.* 801 (1983). For a comparison of divestment planning to estate planning see Gilfix, Advising Aging Clients, 6 *Cal. Law.* 53 (Sept. 1986).

62. For a regulator's perspective, see Pear, Curbs On Medicaid Being Considered, *N.Y.Times*, Jul. 13, 1986, section 1, page 8, col. 1 (nat'l ed.). That article discusses the need to delay or deny Medicaid benefits to make people spend more of their own money, a concept promoted by the Reagan administration.

    At least one judge was offended, as well, by divestment. In dissent he indicated that anyone who transfers assets for less than full value and then applies for Medicaid lacks even a "modicum of decency" and has sunk to "immoral depths." *Randall V. Lukhard*, 729 F. 2d 966, 969 (4th Cir. 1984).

    For allegations of fraud on the part of service providers, see Spiegel & Hurst, Medi-cal Rules Abet Poor Care, *L.A Times*. Apr. 8, 1988, section 1, page 1, col.1.

63. For a discussion of Medicaid fraud in different contexts see McDowell, The Medicare-Medicaid Anti-fraud and Abuse Amendments: Their Impact on the Present Health Care System, 36 *Emory L. J.* 691 (1987); Fox, Attachment by State Agency Upheld, Medicaid Fraud Defendants Lose Appeal to Protect Assets, 199 *N.Y.L.J.*, Feb. 3, 1988, at 1, col. 3; Kohn, 16 Accused of Medicaid Fraud in Federal-State Investigation, 196 N.Y.L.J., Sept. 4, 1985, at 1, col. 3.

64. For an extensive analysis of this development in the use of social welfare programs see *Not Only the Poor* (R. Gookin & J. Le Grand ed. 1987).

65. The Great Society Program was the popular name for the welfare programs of President Lyndon Johnson. It was an effort to eliminate poverty in the United States. The Antipoverty Act, P.L. 88-452, was the keystone of his program. The balance of the program can be found in 42 U.S.C. sections 2991, 2992, 2996 (1982 & Supp. III 1985).

66. See Protecting Family Assets: A New Breed of Medicaid Counselor Steps In, *N.Y.Times*, Nov. 26, 1987, section B, page 12, col. 1 (nat'l ed.).

67. See Coffey, Preserving the Homestead in the Age of Medicaid and Nursing Homes, *N.Y.St. B.J.*, Feb. 1988, at 18.

68. Calabresi, Law and Medicine in Confrontation (unpublished speech, Dec. 9, 1985, copy in author's files).

69. See Gilfix & Strauss, New Age Estate Planning: The Emergence of Elder Law. *Tr. & Est.*, Apr. 1988 at 14.

70. Calabresi, Law and Medicine in Confrontation (unpublished speech, Dec. 9, 1985, copy in author's files).

71. 42 U.S.C. sections 301-433 (1982 & Supp III 1985).

72. For a discussion of the role of the middle class in the maintenance of the welfare system and the basis of the middle-class feeling of entitlement to social services in Britain, see Le Grand & Winter, The Middle Classes and the Defence of the British Welfare State, in *Not Only the Poor* 151-55 (R. Goodin & J. Le Grand ed. 1987).

73. For one of many expositions of the thought that property consists of vindicated

expectations see J. Bentham, *Theory of Legislation* 111-13 (4th ed. 1882).

74. See Hanson, The Expansion and Contraction of the American Welfare State, in *Not Only the Poor* 169-70 (R. Goodin & J. Le Grand ed. 1987).

75. For a discussion of the "deserving" poor in a pre-Social Security context see D. DiNitto & T. Dye, *Social Welfare Politics and Public Policy* 79 (1983).

76. See The Special Committee On Legal Problems of the Aging, Six Issues Critical To Older Americans: A Checklist of Topics That Should Be Discussed By Lawyers With Their Older Clients, 7 *The Record of the A. of the B. of the City of N.Y.* 792 (1986).

77. Common sense suggests private pay nursing home care is better than government paid nursing home care. The answer, however, apparently varies from situation to situation, from state to state and even from nursing home to nursing home.

78. The author believes that virtually all older middle-class people at least consider giving property away and that many of them do it to one degree or another.

79. For a discussion of the Poor Law of 1601 and enforcement of parental support duties see, Thomson, 'I'm not my father's keeper': Families and the Elderly in Nineteenth Century England, 2 *Law & Hist. Rev.* 265.

80. "The average annual cost of a year's stay in a nursing home is now about $22,000, but the cost rises to as much as $45,000 in metropolitan areas such as New York City." Who Can Afford a Nursing Home? 1988 *Consumer Rep.* 300.

81. See Who Can Afford a Nursing Home? 1988 *Consumer Rep.* 300.

82. Waiting to see if one is wiped out and watching the irrational distribution of the nursing home component of Medicaid is surely demoralizing. Anything that demoralizes the middle class is obviously politically unsound.

83. For a discussion of incentives on saving behavior, see, Jatscher, The Aims of Death Taxation, in *Death, Taxes and Family Property* 40, 41-44 (E. Halbach ed. 1977).

84. See generally, Song & Yarbrough, Tax Ethics and Taxpayer Attitudes: A Survey, 38 *Pub Admin. Rev.* 442.

85. For a discussion of a life-cycle savings model see H. Aaron & G. Burtless, *Retirement and Economic Behavior* 18 (1984).

86. See Sheppard, Is the U.S. a Spendthrift Nation? 36 *Tax Notes* 939.

87. See Birnbaum, Showdown at Gucci Gulch, 40 *Nat'l Tax J.* 357, 359 (1987).

88. See Mason & Calvin, Public Confidence and Admitted Tax Evasion, 37 *Nat'l Tax J.* 489 (1984).

89. See Sheppard, Is the U.S. a Spendthrift Nation? 36 *Tax Notes* 939.

90. For a discussion of the psychological importance of will making see Shaffer, "Death Property and Ideals" in *Death, Taxes, and Family Property* 26, 29 (E.Halbach ed. 1977).

91. See C. Shammas, M. Salmon & M. Dahlin, 'Inheritance' in *America From Colonial Times to the Present* 3 (1987). As to the interrelationship of person and property in another context see Radin, Property and Personhood, 34 *Stan. L. Rev.* 957 (1982).

92. As to the essential nature of the right to pass property at death see Friedman, The Law of Succession in Social Perspective, in *Death, Taxes, and Family Property* 9 (E. Halbach ed. 1977).

93. Holmes, The Path of the Law, 10 *Harv. L. Rev.* 456, at 477 (1897). See J. Bentham, *Theory of Legislation* 111-13 (4th ed. 1882).

94. H.R. Rep. No. 105, 100th Cong., 1st Sess., pt.2 (1987).

95. H.R. Rep. No. 105, 100th Cong., 1st Sess., pt.2 at 44 (1987). The Medicare Catastrophic Protection Bill caps the amount of money the community spouse may retain when the institutionalized spouse qualifies for Medicaid. The result is that in some jurisdictions the congressional recognition of Medicaid asset planning may be worse for the family than the old system.

96. See *Cal. Welf. & Inst. Code*. section 14006.2 (West 1988). In a different context, the California legislature has also approved welfare-oriented planning for trust beneficiaries in the probate code. See Prob. Code section 15306. Indeed, in a context somewhat similar to the one discussed, a whole world of trust planning for disabled adults who receive state welfare benefits has sprung up. And Bruce Babbitt, one of the vanquished candidates for the Democratic nomination for President, called for an increase in the amount of property people may keep and still get Medicaid. See *N.Y. Times*, Nov. 15, 1987, section 1, at 15, col. 3 (nat'l ed.) Babbit dropped out of the campaign on February 18, 1988. See Dowd, Babbitt Won't 'Overstay Welcome,' *N.Y. Times*, Feb. 18, 1988, section 1, at 10, col. 3 (nat'l ed.).

97. Compulsory insurance strikes the author as a rational response to the problem of extended life expectancies, the increased need for care, and the failure of most people to purchase insurance as individuals.

98. See Who Can Afford a Nursing Home? 1988 *Consumer Rep*. 300.

99. One assumes that 80 year old new applicants for insurance do not spell big profits for insurance companies if the premiums are reasonable. Who Can Afford a Nursing Home? 1988 *Consumer Rep*. 300.

100. One has to wonder whether corporations will cheerfully provide long-term care insurance given the unexpected rise in the cost of retiree health costs. See Bennett, Firms Stunned by Retiree Health Costs, *Wall St. J*. May 24, 1988, at 37, col 3.

101. See T. Grannemann & Pauly, *Controlling Medicaid costs: Federalism, Competition, and Choice* 27 (1983).

102. See Edsall, The Return of Inequality, *Atlantic*, June 1988, 86 at 94 ("The single most effective mechanism available in this country to advance broad economic interests is the voting booth, particularly for those who lack wealth, power, and access to the people making political decisions.")

103. In 1986 40% of the AIDS population was on Medicaid. Medicaid reimbursed $200 million in AIDS-related expenses. That figure is predicted to be $600 million by 1991. In January, 1986, 16, 138 people had AIDS. In 1988, a study indicated that the typical AIDS claim presented to health insurers fell in the $50,000 to $150,000 range. See Kramon, A Few Medical Costs Are Focus of Campaign, *N.Y. Times*, Feb. 18, 1988, section 1, at 14, col. 1 (nat'l ed.). in the Spring of 1988, 31,420 persons were said to have died from AIDS . See *L.A. Times*, Metro Section, April 7, 1988, L. Becklund, Quilt Stitches Together Shared Sorrow of AIDS, page 1, col. 1, at page 4, col. 4. See also, Chase, AIDS Treatments in 1991 May Cost About $4.5 Billion, *Wall St. J.,* May 26, 1988 section 1, page 2, col. 2.

104. See Nursing Homes Face Pressures That Imperil Care for Elderly, *N.Y. Times*, May 28, 1988, section 1, at 1, col. 1 (nat'l ed.). Bed availability, like access to Medicaid benefits, is very much a local question.

105. The use of fictions in our legal system is a relic.

106. We may consider several years in a nursing home the equivalent of a 100% death tax, a tax assessed essentially against the middle class.

107. See *Barry v. American Sec. & Trust Co.* 135 F. 2d 470, 473 (D.C.Cir. 1943). For a

discussion of why the elderly are legally underserved see Commission on Legal Problems of the Elderly, Young Lawyers' Division, Committee on Delivery of Legal Services to the Elderly, A.B.A., *Legal Services for the Elderly: Where the Nation Stands* 5 (3d ed. 1984).
108. Halbach, Succession — Its Past, Future and Justification, in *Death, Taxes, and Family Property* 5 (E. Halbach ed. 1977).
109. Older Women's League, *Mother's Day Report* 1986 at 7 (1986).
110. W. Faulkner, *Pylon* 315 (1935).

Chapter 49

Non-State Contributions From Third Parties or Spouses to the Family Unit - The Provisions of the Austrian, German and Swiss Civil Codes

Bea VERSCHRAEGEN   Institute of Comparative Law, University of Vienna, Austria; Swiss Institute of Comparative Law, Lausanne, Switzerland

"Non-State" contributions to the family can take various forms. Maintenance as a support payment on a regular basis is only one example. I will not deal with these contributions, however, as they do not exclusively concern the elderly. I will also exclude questions relating to welfare and social insurance systems. These contributions most probably have the most important role in the practice of the countries under consideration in this chapter, but they are of a public nature and were developed beyond the (scope of application of the) Civil Codes. They assume an (albeit limited) responsibility of the State for certain persons or groups of persons in need of public help, accorded nation-wide, because (as the policy is usually justified, and an all-embracing state-control assured) mere private means do not suffice. Whether the rationale is convincing or not, state resources are shrinking and finding new ways of securing "old-age support" has become a primary task.

As a great number of regulations of the Civil Codes of Austria, Germany and Switzerland expressly or implicitly provide some kind of "support" for the elderly, it seemed useful to take a closer look at and to assess their present practical value.

An Austrian institution is the so-called "usufruct in case of death" ("Advitalitätsrecht", artt. 1255-1258 ABGB[2]). Its contents are defined by the Code: One spouse grants to the other the usufruct of his (or her) property in the case of survival by the other (art. 1255 leg. cit.). The "usufruct" will be granted through the "marriage contract" ("Ehevertrag"). This contract can be concluded at any time, but must be drawn up between the spouses before a notary; or at least there must be a condition that the contracting parties will marry. Within the Austrian legal system, the "usufruct in case of death" can be regarded as a "testamentary contract", i.e. an agreement of inheritance

("Erbvertrang"). As such, its validity also depends on compliance with the legal provisions applying to written wills (artt. 578 et seq. leg. cit.).

The "usufruct" can cover any property (movables as well as immovables), in toto or only in part. If "funded property", i.e. full ownership of capital ("Kapital") was promised, this is a marriage settlement in form of a "jointure" (art. 1230 leg. cit., infra). If, in contrast, "annuities", a maintenance pension or some other kind of support on a regular basis ("Renten") had been stipulated, it is assumed that the parties agreed upon a marriage settlement in the form of a "widow's allowance" (art. 1242 leg. cit., infra).[3] These distinctions have some practical import. Both a testamentary contract and a marriage settlement must be drawn up before a notary, but only the former must, in addition, conform to the rules on written testaments.

The "usufruct in case of death" is an agreement which is mutually applicable: both spouses can mutually assign the usufruct to each other, i.e. for the benefit of the surviving spouse. If the surviving spouse remarries or wishes to assign the usufruct to another person, the children of the deceased spouse have the right to demand that the usufruct be delivered to them upon payment of a suitable annuity (art. 1257 leg. cit.). It should be noted here that only the children can claim the usufruct; in return, they are obliged to pay adequate annuities; a simple lump sum will not do.[4]

According to some authors,[5] this contract originated in Poland and is therefore unknown in Germany and Switzerland; according to others, however, the "usufruct in case of death" was influenced by the German "Leibgedinge", an old-age annuity that used to be a dowry, but became a legal form of support of the surviving spouse in the Late Middle Ages.[6]

However, the Austrian legislators incorporated this contract within the chapter of "marriage settlements" ("Ehepakte"). For historical reasons, such as the unification of the law and the consideration of distinct regional provisions and laws relating to different classes, a considerable number of different kinds of "marriage settlements" were in fact introduced, such as the "dowry" "Heiratsgut", art. 1218 leg. cit.), the "jointure" ("Widerlage", art. 1230 et seq leg. cit.), the "gift on the morning after the nuptial day" ("Morgengabe", art. 1232 leg. cit.), the "community of property" ("Gütergemeinschaft", artt. 1233 et seq leg. cit.) and the "mutual testaments" ("wechselseitiges Ehegatten-testament", art. 1248 leg. cit.).

Most of these agreements are designed to ease the financial burden of the spouse. However, for various reasons the practical impact of these agreements can be ignored. Today, within the frame of the Civil Codes, the support of the surviving spouse is secured, among other things, by succession rights of the spouses. The surviving spouse has a legal right to a "statutory reserve" ("Pflichtteil") and a legal share of the inheritance, rights that were gradually introduced and increased. The same is true of the spouse's maintenance rights that he/her can claim from the heirs, if the maintenance right does not exceed the value of the deceased spouse's estate and as long as the surviving spouse does not remarry. The shift from "(old-age) support" on a *contractual basis* (the provisions on "marriage settlements" still provide an impressive illustration of those different contractual forms) to an "(old-age) support" *guaranteed by the law* (of inheritance) is one of the reasons why the agreements mentioned earlier have become much less important. The difference between rural and urban customs, the easing of divorce, making "(old-age) support" on a contractual basis obviously a somewhat "premature" settlement, the overall emphasis on the last will of the testator, i.e. the freedom to bequeath the property to anybody with due observance of the statutory reserves provided by the law and finally the fact that many couples who are without means marry are additional reasons for the lack of practical value of the "agreements". The "jointure" ("Widerlage") for example, is only due, if a "dowry" ("Heiratsgut") was stipulated, which itself is very seldom the case, but still more often in rural than in urban areas. In fact, the legislator of 1811 who was part of the university nobility,[7] introduced a matrimonial property regime which was already more or less outdated.[8] Meanwhile, the "dowry" and its legal counterpart, the "jointure", were entirely replaced by the right of both son and daughter to claim adequate material provision from their parents (or other ascendants respectively, the so-called "Ausstattungsanspruch", art. 1220, 1231 leg. cit.), when they get married and if the claiming child needs it.[9] These (nonrecurring) contributions have the purpose of giving the children a start in their marriage and can not be considered an "(old-age) support" or a functional equivalent thereof.[10] As far as the "community of property" is concerned, it is practically out of use. Although it *could* function as an old-age support, spouses simply do not wish to tie their property to one another. In addition, the statutory regime is characterized by the separation of goods; however, the spouses are free to opt out and to agree upon some other regime, which they rarely do. The "widow's allowance" ("Witwengehalt", art. 1242 leg. cit.) has no practical importance either. It is stipulated in a "marriage settlement" and probably for that reason, is unpopular. But, more important, the surviving spouse has a statutory right to maintenance that she can claim from the heirs (art. 796 leg. cit.), as already mentioned above.[11] Therefore, the "widow's allowance" has in effect become redundant.

Hence the question arises, whether there are any other means provided by the Austrian Civil Code or developed by Austrian case-law by which the support of the elderly is guaranteed. In fact, there are. The so-called "Ausgedinge" or "Altenteil" constitutes a share of property reserved by a farmer on his retirement and is a typical form of "old-age support". Evidently, only a limited number of persons will have the benefit from this rural contract of transfer of property from the farmer to another person, i.e. "farm-transfer", whereby the farmer, his relatives or occasionally third parties are supported for life. The "Ausgedinge" is created by contract, testamentary provision, marriage settlement or by the law.[12] When he wishes to transfer his farm, the transferor will agree upon a simple contract, which is usually considered a sales contract; if he wants to create an "old age support" for his surviving wife, a marriage settlement, being a special kind of agreement (as indicated above), is the correct legal form. In fact, much depends on the person who will be the benefitting transferee. He/she may be an heir, but need not necessarily be so, and may not even be a member of the family at all.

The transfer can be agreed upon independently of any retirement of the transferor.[13] In practice, however, the transfer of property coincides with the retirement of the transferor, not only because it is then that he wants to benefit from the "share of property" reserved by him, but also because the law (i.e. pension retirement plans) requires a minimum number of years during which the farmer has regularly contributed to his (future) pension. Usually, he will only be able to afford such payments as long as he is working, i.e. before the farm-transfer. There is even an increasing tendency among farmers to continue to work and, hence, to postpone the farm-transfer, either because they have not yet reached retirement age or because no descendants are willing to take over the farm. The latter look for other jobs very early (e.g. as a tourist guide or ski instructor in mountain regions, or as an industrial worker in others) either because the farm-transfer lies in the distant future or because they are not interested in farm work and think of contributing towards their own pension years as well as the difficult employment situation. Very often the cumulation of two different incomes has tax disadvantages.

In most cases, the "Ausgedinge" is agreed upon in rural areas, between a farmer, i.e. the transferor, and the transferee. The latter is obliged to pay an allowance in kind, and/or in cash and/or in the form of labour, depending on what the contracting parties stipulated. Usually, it will be the right to remain in the house or a part thereof for life, i.e. the right of habitation. It could also be the right to use the (piece of) land and the usufruct thereof (such as income from sale of fruit,), board and lodging or simply food and care, pocket money, services (e.g. medical care, fare to the doctor or to church etc.), a decent burial or eventually the support of the surviving spouse.[14]

The legal nature of this "old age support" is still disputed. It has aspects of a right to claim a servitude and recurrent charges on real estate, depending on what is agreed. It is not generally known that the contract "Ausgedinge" need not be linked with a farm-transfer or rural property at all. The "Ausgedinge" can perfectly well be accorded in other contexts, such as a house without a farm connected to it.[15]

The purpose of these contracts invariably is to provide "old-age support", and so all resulting disputes have to be settled in the light of this contractual aim. Hence, if dispute arises between the transferee and the retired farmer, the "Ausgedinge" will be cancelled and replaced by an allowance if the relationship between the parties is seriously ruptured. In other words a simple conflict will not be an occasion for cancelling the agreement. It is assumed that any payment in cash is too heavy a burden on the real estate. Some case law has been developed with regard to these problems. One of the questions the courts have had to decide was whether the old farmer can be prevented from living with his cohabitee as husband and wife. If he needs nursing and the cohabitee is able to provide it, no objections will probably be raised against the cohabitation, even though the purpose of the "Ausgedinge" continues to be "old-age support". Another problem is the defective performance of the contract: if the old farmer is not given sufficient food, or is not permitted access to the bathroom, etc. In the former case, the transferee will be liable to pay damages; in the latter, the farmer can start execution proceedings in order to enforce his claim against the transferee. These misunderstandings are considered to be "everyday conflicts"; according to the courts they are neither deep nor intolerable enough to justify the cancellation of the "Ausgedinge-agreement".

This kind of "old-age support" is expressly stipulated in the Austrian "law on the principal heirship" (art. 14 I "Anerbengesetz"),[16] providing a principal, i.e. sole, heir to the real estate, by whom the other heirs are automatically excluded, and introducing *ex lege* an "Ausgedinge" for the benefit of the surviving spouse, if he/she is not the "Anerbe", i.e. the sole heir to the real estate. The heirs who were excluded from the property (defined by the law) have the right to claim compensation.

The "Ausgedinge" is (or at least has been) generally regarded as an *"anticipated succession".*[17] The notion comprehends all situations in which a succession is anticipated by transfer of property during the life of the testator; the successor thereby receives at an earlier time what he would have received upon the death of the testator; at the same time, his position as future heir has generally been taken into consideration. Technical, yet interesting questions that arise mainly concern the diminishing resort to the succession law and the increasing importance of the provisions relating to contracts.[18]

Examples of "anticipated succession" can be found not only in rural areas (e.g. contracts of property transfer combined with the "Ausgedinge" for the benefit of [usually] one heir and compensation of the others); they also occur in nonrural areas in form of the "anticipated property transfer", for example with regard to industrial enterprises. In return, annuities are due as consideration (e.g. heirs are offered an interest in a corporate enterprise or the children [of the testator] become partners of a non-trading company).[19] Consequently, all contributions from the transferor to the transferee and to heirs standing aside in favour of the latter are *ex lege* treated as an "anticipated succession".

In the framework of the regulations applying to matrimonial property,[20] the contracting parties are completely free to depart from the types of contract presented in the Code, which are only examples of contracts then in use. Thus, the parties are free to create new forms of contracts. This is in line with the general policy of Austrian legislation favouring contractual autonomy.[21]

As to the "law on principal heirship", i.e. the law of succession to an undivided farm estate and related issues, such as the "old-age support" referred to above, one can say that these questions are usually defined as problems of "agricultural law" in a broad sense of the word.[22] This is very rarely made the subject of comparative legal studies. Since most aspects of this distinct, albeit rather neglected, branch of law, are considered to be part of "public law", "old-age support" as a non-state contribution from third parties (a parent, an uncle, or a spouse) seems to be a legal instrument developed by case law in line with the principles of private law. Yet the public law elements relating to the ownership and exploitation of agricultural land outnumber the private law aspects, and are extensively linked to problems of regional or rural planning, company law, social welfare and the economy in general which go beyond the scope of any Civil Code.

A general analysis of the Swiss and German Civil Codes shows different approaches to similar problems. In fact, interesting conclusions can be drawn from the "Introductory Act to the German Civil Code".[23] Art. 96 of the Act[24] acknowledges the parties' *contractual autonomy* with regard to the so-called "Altenteil" (i.e. "Ausgedinge"), the "old-age support" as a share of property (usually) reserved by a farmer on his retirement. State intervention is permitted insofar as it sets up additional provisions relating to the farmer's "old-age support" contract.[25] Again, these problems are part of "agricultural law" in the broadest sense of the word. According to leading experts, we are dealing with its traditional branch, "Landwirtschaft".[26] The same applies, of course, to the "law on principal heirship" ("Anerbenrecht") mentioned in art. 64 of the Introductory Act to the German Civil Code, because it represents the equivalent to the Austrian "Anerbengesetz" referred to earlier.[27] The right of the testator to make a testamentary disposition of the piece of land which is subject to the right of principal (i.e. sole) heirship may not be restricted by state laws;[28] it is therefore a provision of mere historical significance.[29] Both countries, Germany as well Austria, have regional provisions relating to the "law on principal heirship", introducing either a mandatory or only an optional right of principal heirship, implying, of course, an "Ausgedinge" or "Altenteil" respectively.

This form of "successio anticipata" did not and still does not exist in Switzerland. The Swiss legislature introduced what is known as the so-called "Zuweisungsverfahren", i.e. a procedure by which one of the heirs who appears capable of managing the farm takes it over in its entirety after the farmer's death. The "ratio legislatoris" was primarily designed to prevent further fragmentation and overindebtedness of the farm.[30] In this respect there are remarkable parallels to the (facultative) law of principal heirship.[31] Yet recently Swiss marriage and succession law were subject to (rather complicated) amendments,[32] the result of which may turn out to the disadvantage of the farmer's surviving spouse. If one of the heirs is prepared to take over the farm it will be allotted to him according to its value as based on its annual return, not (as in other countries), according to its market value (art. 617 leg. cit.). In other words, the surviving spouse of a farmer will be at less of a disadvantage economically the larger the portion of the farmer's estate he/she is allotted (which is indeed possible according to art. 481 I leg. cit.[33]) or, if he/she eventually succeeds in having the value assessed at the allotment of the agricultural enterprise increased. This is possible under extraordinary circumstances, such as the requirements for his/her maintenance.[34] The testator can instead also leave to the surviving spouse the "usufruct in the whole of the share of the inheritance devolving on their common descendants, the non-common descendants begotten during the time of their marriage and their descendants" (art. 473 I leg. cit.); i. e. the surviving spouse has in such a case "the right to possession, use and enjoyment of the res fructuaria", as well as the mangement thereof (art. 755 leg. cit.). At first sight, it might seem that the usufruct provides an effective form of "old-age support", but in practice, an heir claiming to take over the farm who appears capable of managing it (art. 620 I leg. cit.), will have priority according to the law. The surviving spouse, i.e. the usufructuary, will only be given a share in the profits.[35]

Hence, the general trend seems to underline the policy already referred to of preventing fragmentation and overindebtedness of the farm-land. An additional aspect may well be the general interest in keeping the farm in the same family.[36] The surviving spouse (farmers as well as non-farmers) will (under certain conditions and depending on the matrimonial regime)[37] be granted the right of residence and the ownership of personal chattels.[38] Art. 612a leg. cit.[39] expressly provides that where the house or the apartment in which the spouses lived or the household effects are part of the inheritance, he/she can demand that they become his/her property on payment of compensation.[40] Since payment is necessary for these benefits, they cannot be compared with the Austrian "Ausgedinge". If the chance of continuing in one's present life-style can be considered a form of "old-age support" in a broad interpretation of the expression then it probably qualifies as such. The possibilities of "old-age support" in the Civil Code are, however, more of a *contributory* nature. The right of residence ("Wohnrecht", artt. 776 et seq. leg. cit.) is a servitude, not necessarily linked with a farm, although it can be. The allocation of the farm to the heir according to art. 620 leg. cit. will in principle not reduce the right of residence.[41] An "old-age support" comparable with the "Ausgedinge" (or "Altenteil") can therefore be created by testamentary disposition, but again, the heir taking over the farm will have priority, and in case of doubt, the person benefitting from the right of residence will be accorded a share in the profits.[42]

As already mentioned, no testamentary disposition can generally prevent a capable heir from taking over the farm, if he wishes to do so.[43] Contrary to the laws on principal heirship as they are known in Germany and Austria, Swiss law merely provides an "allocation procedure", but no specific heir ("Anerbe", e.g. the eldest or youngest son), who will take over the farm.[44] However, an heir can be specified as the new owner of the entire farm by testamentary disposition, if there are several heirs who seem to be capable and would like to take over (art. 621 bis III ZGB).

Swiss law also does not regard a "dowry" or other means of transferring property by the deceased as form of "old-age support", as the heirs have to bring all such gifts into hotchpot, unless of course, the contrary was stated in the will (artt. 626 et seq. leg. cit.). In principle, however, we are dealing with an "anticipated succession".[45]

Surely the Swiss provisions relating to the agricultural law of succession which provide a procedure according to which one of the heirs willing to and capable of managing the farm takes it over, have some similarities with the

German and Austrian "law on principal heirship", at least with regard to its *function*: in all three countries the provisions serve or can serve as an "old-age support", although the legislative approach and historical background are quite different.[46]

In Austria, unless stipulated otherwise by special regional laws, the farm with its assets is allotted together and ex officio, where as according to Swiss law, the allotment of the movables must be demanded expressly. The price calculation differs too. In Switzerland, the valuation of the farm is based on its annual return and of the assets on their use value, whereas in Austria, the price is fixed on the basis of equity. Which of these solutions ought to prevail naturally depends on several factors: social considerations, public interest, principles of constitutional law, such as equality between heirs or perhaps husband and wife.[47] These questions are very often interrelated and to make a cost-benefit analysis would be difficult.

Furthers aspects should be mentioned. The Swiss Civil Code provides different forms of settlement of family property for the benefit of the family: first there is the "family foundation" ("Familienstiftung", art. 335 I ZGB), the "Community of property" ("Gemeinderschaft", art 336 leg. cit.), the "homestead" ("Heimstätte", art. 337 leg. cit.) and, at least indirectly, the so-called "perpetual trust for the benefit of a family" ("Familienfideikommisse, art. 335 II leg. cit.).

How far do these provisions constitute a form of "old-age support"? The "family foundation" has a very limited purpose: property is settled on a family to provide for the cost of education or maintenance of the members of the family or for similar purposes where this need has arisen in cases of emergency, even if it extends for years, but not simply used for the maintenance of a family in general. The contribution must be needed; therefore the donation of a castle for official or social purposes will not be allowed.[48]

By contrast, a "perpetual trust" is property that is usually passed on by testamentary disposition to specific members of the family according to an invariable plan. In fact, in addition to preserving the family and stressing the role of the family property, the perpetual trust aims at protecting the family from misery and poverty. But, in addition and in contrast to the basic purpose of the trust, the expenditure for renovation and repair frequently outweighs the actual income. Moreover, the trustee usually lacks full freedom of action thus preventing economic planning.[49] According to the law, the "perpetual trust for the benefit of the family" was prohibited after 1912. This means that the law does not permit new trusts to be created, yet the existing ones were not abolished. In several cantons such trusts are still valid.[50]

From a practical point of view, the "family foundation" is quite interesting. In industrialized societies, such foundations in general seem to be a better solution for the "support of family members" (and also for "old-age support") than, for example, the "perpetual trust". It is interesting to note that in Germany, new "perpetual trusts" could be founded until 1919. They were abolished in 1938, but a partial conversion into "family foundations" was encouraged.[51] The disadvantage of the German and the Austrian law in comparison to the Swiss provisions with regard to the "family foundation" is that, according to the former, foundations can be created, but are subject to the ordinary rules for "foundations" in general, without introducing any advantages for "family foundations".[52]

The "community of property" according to the meaning of art. 336 ZGB is created by agreeing to leave the whole or a portion of an inheritance accrued to the members of the family as their common undivided property, or by bringing their property into the common stock. It should not be regarded as a form of "old-age support", not even indirectly. Economic difficulties or the marriage of one of the parties will lead to the redemption of the share.

Another form of community property is the so-called "homestead" (artt. 349 et seq. leg. cit.). Its constitution can be authorized by the cantons, subject to the provisions of federal Civil law. The "homestead" in Swiss law has its parallel in German law.[53] Only small farms or dwellings no larger than is necessary to support or house one family are covered. Certain protective measures were introduced over these properties, such as some restrictions on alienation. According to art. 335 of the Swiss Civil Code, an owner can be compelled to admit into the "homestead" certain relatives, if their circumstances urgently require it and they are not unworthy of it. Of course, the "homestead" is nowadays regarded as a far-reaching restriction of property rights, rather than as a possible form of "old-age support". Its origin can be found in North-America, where it provided accommodation for colonists and protection against their creditors. The rationale of the "homestead" is to tie the property to the family in such a way that it can always fall back upon it if board and lodging are required; it should protect against crises and risks of modern economic life.[54] Up to now, not a single "homestead" has been introduced in Switzerland.[55] Notwithstanding the total lack of success of the "homestead" legislation, which could have been adapted to the needs of each canton, as implementation of legislation is within their competence, it could have functioned as "(old-age) support", of which an important aspect is the need for "board and lodging", which is exactly what the "homestead" could offer.

The discussion of these legal forms which provide certain kinds of family or even "old-age support" seems outdated at first glance. Today there are the general law of inheritance, which usually takes into account certain ascendants. Family law often imposes maintenance obligations towards towards a close elderly family member. The whole system of social security is designed to meet the needs of different groups of people. What can legal forms of special succession rights or family property and marriage settlements offer to the elderly today?

This primarily depends on the economic situation of the family and the social structure. If there is neither real estate nor any other financial resources, "old-age support" necessarily becomes a problem of social welfare. In addition, we are also faced with (the awareness of) the responsibility for elderly family members or of the family unit as such, because lack of public resources always has repercussions in the private sphere.

The legal response to financial problems of the elderly can take the form of the promotion and support of family firms and foundations by the State. So-called "anticipated successions" may prevent owners of family property carrying on with small or medium-sized undertakings that could be run much better by their successor(s). Whether the "old-age support" as it is known in rural areas, where the old farmer can claim support for life ("Altenteil" or "Ausgedinge") can actually and effectively be extended beyond its present field of application, seems to be a legitimate question: "Shared-Housing" is a possible solution. However, the general trend today is rather towards small family units, its underlying philosophy one of "individualism". In my view, neither the trend nor its consequences are absolutely compelling. Even if the legal forms for providing "old-age support" discussed here have their roots in an earlier age, that is no argument against them.

Notes

The text of the report presented at the VIth World Conference of the International Society on Family Law was slightly changed and adapted. I am most grateful to Hofrat Univ. -Doz. Dr. E. Lang, Amt der Tiroler Landesregierung, Innsbruck, for useful information; to Dr. Dopffel, Max-Planck-Institut, Hamburg and to J. Eekelaar, Pembroke College, Oxford for their critical remarks.

1. English terminology and translation of the Austrian provisions according to P. *Baeck*, The General Civil Code of Austria, 1972.
2. ABGB, i.e. Allgemeines Bürgerliches Gesetz-Buch, Austrian Civil Code 1812.
3. For the "widow's allowance" see W. *Brauneder*, Freiheit des Vertragsinhalts und Typenbildung im Ehegüterrecht, Zeitschrift fur Rechtsvergleichung (ZfRZ) 1974, l; E. *Weiss*, in Klang V, 707 et seq.; A. & A. *Ehrenzweig/Fr.Schwind*, System des österreichischen allgemeinen Privatrechts, Das Familienrecht, 1984, 101 et seq., 106 et seq.
4. See i.a. H. *Krasnopolski*/Br.*Kafka* Oesterreichisches Familienrecht, 1911, 206 et seq.; *Ehrenzweig/Schwind*(3) 97 et seq., 106; H. *Klang*, in Klang II 624 et seq.
5. *Krasnopolski/Kafka* (4) ibidem.
6. See W. *Brauneder*, Die Entwicklung des Ehegüterrechts in Oesterreich, 1973, 83 et seq., 335 et seq.
7. W. *Brauneder*, Zur Auslegung und Reform des 28. Hauptstückes des ABGB "Von den Ehepakten", Oesterreichische Notariats-Zeitung (NZ) 1978, 69 et seq.
8. *Brauneder* (6) 389.
9. R.*Ostheim*, Familienrechtsreform und Ausstattungsanspruch, Oesterreichische Juristen-Zeitung (OEJZ) 1978, 505 et seq.
10. They are contracts between the parents and the child, not between the spouses, and do not influence the spouse's statutory or contractual regime. See i.a. H.*Koziol*/R. *Welser*, Grundriss des bürgerlichen Rechts, II, 7th ed., 1985, 188.
11. The "mutual testaments" (art. 1248 leg. cit.) are mentioned in the 28th chapter of the Code, entitled "marriage settlements"; they are not considered such agree-

ments in the strict sense of the term, but must be interpreted according to the provisions of the law of succession.

12. A typical example was introduced by the Austrian) "law of succession to an undivided farm estate", i.e "law on principal heirship" (art. 14 I "Anerbengesetz").

13. Special laws provide different mandatory retirement ages, depending on the profession (farmer, employee, civil servant, etc.). An early retirement will have repercussions on the determination of the pension.

14. For details see Fr. *Petrasch*, in Rummel, ABGB, no. 5 ad §530 with case law; J. *Piegler*, Rechtsfragen um Grtsübergabe und Ausgedinge, OEJZ 1956, 561(563 et seq.); also H. *Klang*, in Klang II 624 et seq.; *Krehan*, Das Ausgedinge im österreichischen Recht, Notariats-Zeitung (NZ) 1969, 117; *Koziol/Welser* (10) 150 et seq.; Fr. *Gschnitzer/*Chr. *Faistenberger/*H. *Barta/*G. *Call/*B. *Eccher*, Oesterreichisches Sachenrecht, 1985, 183 et seq.

15. For a case concerning a house, see OGH, 31.3.1954, 3 Ob 688/53, EvBl 1954/189.

16. Bundesgesetz vom 21. Mai 1958 über besondere Vorschriften für die bäuerliche Erbteilung ("Anerbengesetz")/Federal Law on Special Provisions concerning the Rural Division of the Estate, the Law on the Principal Heirship, BGBl 1958/106. These provisions are not in force in Carinthia, Tyrol and Vorarlberg (see art. 21 leg. cit.). The States Tyrol and Carinthia have their own provisions: Tiroler Höfegesetz, LGBl 1900/47; Kärntner Erbhöfegestz, LGBl 1903/33. See e.g. H. *Zemen* Die gestzliche Erbfolge nach der Familienrechtsreform, 1981, 209. Vorarlberg refused any restrictions at that time.

17. See B. *Eccher*, Antizipierte Erbfolge, 1979, 12.

18. See e.g. *Eccher* (17) 2, 12.

19. For details see *Eccher* (17) 13 et seq.

20. Cf. in general M. *Rheinstein/*M.A.*Glendon, International Encyclopedia of Comparative Law*, Vol. IV Persons and Family, Chapter 4, Interspousal Relations, 1980, 47 et seq., 124 et seq., 148 et seq.

21. See *Braunder* (3) 1; *Koziol/Welser* (10) 188.

22. M. *Welan*, Oesterreichischer Landesbericht, in K.F. Kreuzer (ed.), Agrarrecht in Europa/Droit agraire en Europe/Agricultural Law in Europe. Stand und Perspektiven in Forschung und Lehre, Konstanzer Symposium 29.9. — 2.10.1982,1983, 289(290).

23. Translation according to S. *Goren/*I.S.*Forrester*, Introductory Act to the German Civil Code and Marriage Law of the Federal Republic of Germany, 1976.

24. "The provisions of the state laws, which concern contracts for old age annuities, life annuities, old age support or annuity charges on estates relating to the transfer of a piece of land in so far as they regulate the contractual obligation resulting from the contract in the event that no special agreements are to be made, remain unaffected."

25. More details by P. *Bassenge*, in Palandt, Bürgerliches Gesetzbuch, Beck'sche Kurz-Kommentare, 47th ed., 1988, ad art. 96 of the Introductory Act.

26. See e.g. *Kroeschell*, Deutscher Landesbericht, in Kreuzer (22) 57 (59).

27. Art. 64 of the Introductory Act: "(1) The provisions of the state laws concerning the right of principal heirship with respect to agricultural or forest land and the accessories thereof remain unaffected. (2) The state laws may not restrict the right of the testator to make a testamentary disposition of the piece of land which is subject to the right of principal heirship."

28. See W. *Edenhofer*, in Palandt (25) and art. 64 of the Introductory Act.

29. K.F. *Kroeschell*, Landwirtschaftsrecht, 2nd. ed. 1966, 71 et seq.
30. Cf. i.a. A. *Pikalo*, Das landwirtschaftliche Zuweisungsverfahren, Neue Juristische Wochenschrift (NJW) 1955, 1174 (1175).
    It is interesting to note that *Swiss* law provided an example for the Finnish legislator who introduced a "Zuweisungsverfahren" in 1977 which is similar to the Swiss system. See P. *Dopffel* who analyzed the former and current law(s) of succession of Sweden and Finland, in 'Entwicklung des Erbrechts in Schweden und Finnland,' in: Das schwedische Reichsgesetzbuch (Sveriges Rikes Lag) von 1734. Beiträge zur Entstehungs- und Entwicklungsgeschichte einer vollständigen Kodifikation (W. Wagner, ed.), Ius Commune, Sonderhefte, 29, 1986, 185 (261 et seq.).
31. See i.a. I. *Krüger*, Das schweizerische und französische Zuweisungsrecht-Eine Rechtsvergleichung, 1967, 18 et seq.
32. Cf. in this context the Federal statute of Oct. 5, 1984, in force since Jan. 1, 1988 (BBl 1979 II 1191).
33. Art 481 I Swiss Civil Code: "(1) A testator can by will or pact dispose of the whole or a part of the divisible portion of his estate."
34. See e.g. H. *Etter-Strebel*, Die Interessenlagen von Ehefrau und Kind im bäuerlichen Bodenrecht, 1987, 172, 175, 275 et seq.
35. Arg. art. 621bis: "An heir who desires to manage the farm in person and who seems to be qualified for this task can be deprived of this right neither through testamentary disposition nor through a testamentary pact; according to a decision of the Swiss Federal Court, BGE 108 II 177 et seq. For details cf. *Etter-Strebel* (34) 177 et seq.
36. See e.g. W. *Neukomm*/A. *Czettler*, Das bäuerliche Erbrecht, 1982, 19; *Pikalo*(30) 1175 n. 22.
37. Under the system of participation of acquisitions ("Errungenschaftsbeteiligung", artt. 181 et seq. leg. cit.) according to art. 219: "(1) To enable the surviving spouse to continue the style of life he or she is granted at his or her instance, against compensation, the usufruct of, or the right of residence in, the house or the apartment in which the spouses have lived and which belonged to the deceased spouse; provisions are made for another arrangement by a marriage covenant. (2)In the same circumstances he or she can demand the ownership of the personal chattels. (3)Where the circumstances justify it, at the instance of the surviving spouse or the other legal heirs of the deceased spouse, the usufruct or the right of residence can be replaced by the ownership of the house or the apartment. (4)The surviving spouse cannot claim these rights to the rooms where the deceased spouse exercised a trade or a profession if a descendant of the deceased spouse requires these rooms for the continuation of the exercise of this trade or profession; provisions are made for the operation of the laws of inheritance to agricultural estates."
38. Under the system of community of property, according to art. 244: "(1) Where the house or the apartment in which the spouses lived or the household equipment belonged to the common property, the surviving spouse can demand that the ownership thereof is allotted to him or her against compensation. (2) Where the circumstances justify it, the surviving spouse or the other legal heirs of the deceased can demand that in place of ownership the usufruct of the house or apartment or a right of residence is granted. (3) Where the community of property is not dissolved by a spouse's death, each spouse can make these petitions, provided this spouse proves that he or she has a preponderant interest."

39. Under other systems such as separation of goods.
40. See i.a.*Etter-Strebel* (34) 154 et seq. For the allocation of flats, for example, in Swedish law see the interesting developments scrutinized by *Dopffel* (30) 229, 245 et seq.
41. *Neukomm/Czettler* (36) 106.
42. The Swiss "Zuweisungsverfahren" is laid down by law in the following way: If the farm forms an economic entity, it must be allotted to him in its entirety; the valuation of the farm taken over by the heir will be based on its annual return; the farmer can also demand the allotment of movables (e.g. the farming implements, supplies and livestock serving the farm). (Artt. 620 and 620bis ZGB[Swiss Civil Code]. Translation of these provisions by S. *Wyler*/B. *Wyler*, The Swiss Civil Code, Vol I, Preliminary Chapter, Part I: Law of Persons; Part II: Family Law, 1987; see also R. *Gmür*, Das Schweizerische Zivilgesetzbuch verglichen mit dem deutschen Bürgerlichen Gesetz-Buch, 1963, 106 et seq.) Competent authorities decide the case if the allotment to a particular heir is contested. If an heir wishes to take over the farm in its entirety, he should be capable of doing so. In order to argue the case, the qualification of the heir's spouse may well be a decisive consideration. In case several heirs qualified for the work wish to take over the farm, and if the size and the nature of the farm permit the partition without unduly charging the farm, the parcelling into several viable farms is permitted(art. 621quater leg. cit.). The sole owner of the farm can demand postponement of the partition: then, the co-heirs need not accept the community of profits, but can claim the assignment of their share in the form of a money sum secured by an encumbrance on the common property. Alternatively, if the common property is burdened beyond three-quarters of its assessed value, the heir in possession of the farm is, as regards the excess, and according to art. 624 leg. cit., only bound to give an estate charge note-the so-called "Erbengült" — terminable at the end of ten years at the earliest and bearing no higher rate of interest than that allowed in the case of other land charges. The "Erbengült" (estate charge note) and the "Gült" (land charge note resp. negotiable land charge) (art. 842 et seq.) are special kinds of mortgage on real estate, characteristic of Swiss law. We are here dealing with a typical Swiss form of negotiable securities. The general trend seems to be the money payment to those persons advancing a legitimate claim. Cf. i.a.art. 631 II Swiss Civil Code stating, that "children who at the death of the deceased had not yet completed their education or training or are subject to some infirmity must be allowed at partition to receive a fair amount in advance". Beneficiaries are children, not the elderly. Similar claims exist of course in other countries, e.g. in Germany art. 1371 BGB.
43. Artt. 621 and 621bis ZGB; exceptions to the rule ibidem. See P. *Liver*, Die Aenderungen am bäuerlichen Erbrecht des Zivilgesetzbuches durch das Bundesgesetz Über die Entschuldung landwirtschaftlicher Heimwesen, in Festschrift zum 70. Geburtstag von Prof. Dr. Peter Tuor — Zum Schweizerischen Erbrecht, 1946, 49 (51).
44. *Neukomm/Czettler*(36) 3, 7.
45. See also the exceptions to the rule, e.g. art. 631 I ZGB according to which the ordinary costs of education are exempt from the hotchpot; or art. 632 ZGB stating that customary presents need not be brought into hotchpot.
46. Cf. *Kroeschell* (29) 70 et seq. for a comparison of Swiss and French law; M. *Welan*, Landwirtschaftliches Sondererbrecht in der Schweiz, in Frankreich und in Oesterreich, in Festschrift Wilburg zum 70. Geburtstag, 1975, 423 for a comparison of

French, Swiss and Austrian law.

47. Concerning problems of constitutional nature see i.a. A. *Pikalo*, Anerbenrecht und Verfassungsrecht, NJW 1959, 1609 et seq.

48. See BGE 93 II 449 (451), cited in P. *Tuor/B. Schnyder*, Das Schweizerische Zivilgesetzbuch, 9th ed., 1979, 314.

49. See E. *Steiger*, Die Familienfideikommisse in der Schweiz, 1986, 83 et seq.

50. For details see *Steiger* (49) 39 et seq.

51. Details in *Gmür* (42) 95; but see also *Dopffel* (30) 240 et seq. on the problem in general as well as on historical developments in Swedish and Finnish law. He provides an analysis of the historical background, i.e. the political ties between Sweden and France that were a legitimate reason to prevent new "perpetual trusts" from being founded in 1810: the principles of equality and freedom had also been the main impetus to abolish the "perpetual trust" in France in 1792. A Swedish law of 1963 determined that "perpetual trusts" should provide for a conversion into joint-stock companies. For details see *Dopffel*, op. cit., 243 et seq.

52. See artt. 80-88 German BGB and the Austrian Bundes-Stiftungs- und Fonds-Gesetz, 1974, BGBl 1975/11.

53. Here, the "homestead" is rather of public than of a private law nature. Reichsheim-stättengesetz, 25.11.1937, BGBl III 2 Nr. 2332-1 with Avo, 19.7.1940, BGBl III 2 Nr. 2332-1-1. See H. *Westermann*,Sachenrecht, 4th ed., 1960, § 333 et seg.

54. Detailed *Tuor/Schnyder* (48) 318.

55. For details see *Tuor/Schnyder* (48) 317 et seq.

Section Two

Retirement and Pensions

Chapter 50

Pension Policies in the OECD Countries: Background and Trends

Robert HOLTZMANN*   Public Finance and
            Economic Policy, University of Vienna, Austria,
                          International Monetary Fund,
                          Fiscal Affairs Dept., Washington

Introduction[1]

Concerns about restructuring old-age income provisions, and especially about reforming public pension schemes, are an OECD-wide phenomenon not restricted to just a few countries. There are essentially two reasons why all OECD member countries are considering implementing or have already implemented reforms of their public retirement schemes. First, the social and economic framework in which retirement schemes operate has changed substantially in recent decades and these developments have led to consideration of reform as a reaction. In a prominent place in the reform consideration are rising budgetary constraints at the level of both social security schemes and the general public budget. Second, the anticipation of future developments, mainly of a demographic nature, has created additional pressure for reform.

In most countries of the OECD, political perceptions of the need for reform have so far been mainly of the reactive type. Future developments, especially the projected aging of the population, serve more as a justification than a cause of intended or implemented reforms. This political behavior pattern is hardly surprising: short-term reactions are characteristic of voter-oriented Western democracies.

The tendency for economic, social, and demographic developments in Western industrialized countries to move in the same direction means that there is strong similarity in the discussions about reform and in the trends in old-age income provisions. This common pattern is stronger than the differences in the systems might lead one to believe. Notable differences do, of course, remain. However, this chapter will concentrate more on the shared features than on the divergences in past developments and current tendencies.

The structure of the chapter is as follows. Section II highlights the background and the various causes of the reform debate. The pressures for reform in three broad areas — budgetary, economic, and social — are summarized. By doing so, this section offers a better understanding of the current trends and prospects of retirement income provisions. Section III presents the major directions of reform and future prospects for social security schemes. Since the trends for reform in the OECD countries are strikingly similar and the purpose of the chapter is to present broad developments, the various reform directions are summarized under broad headings. Some tentative conclusions are drawn in Section IV.

Background and Pressure for Adjustment

Although the reasons for a reorientation of old-age income support, especially within social security systems, are seemingly quite diverse across the OECD area, their main determinants are practically identical in all countries.

The changes in the socioeconomic framework and hence the creation of pressures for reform can be summarized under three broad headings: budgetary, economic, and social.

A. Budgetary dimension

The budgetary dimension can be discerned from the increase in public expenditures for retirement income (old-age, disability, and survivors). Across the OECD area, the share of these expenditures as a percentage of GDP was 4.4 percent in 1960 and has more doubled since, reaching almost 9 percent in 1985. The most dynamic growth was experienced in Japan, whose share quadrupled from a low level of 1.3 percent in 1960 to 5.2 percent in 1985. The highest absolute increase was experienced in Italy, where public expenditures for pensions rose from 4.9 percent of GDP in 1960 to 14.2 percent in 1985. This value is at present the highest among OECD countries. The average expenditure shares in the seven smaller and larger OECD countries differ little in magnitude and trend; the shares of the latter are presented in Chart 1.

For most countries the rise was more pronounced after the first oil shock, reflecting the endogenous response of pension schemes to the large number of beneficiaries and lower real growth rates. The more recent changes vary widely and show a tendency for flattening or even a reduction of the trend in the expenditure share in some OECD countries. This leveling-off can largely be related to three factors: first, the reforms and adjustments of public schemes that took place during the 1980s in the OECD countries; second, a short-term improvement in the demographic structure due to the entering of smaller post-World War I birth cohorts into retirement age; and third, the recent upswing in the economic performance that raised the denominator of the expenditure share (GDP) more strongly at a time when the numerator (expenditure) was

Chart 1. *Public Pension Expenditure Share*
(Seven major OECD countries)

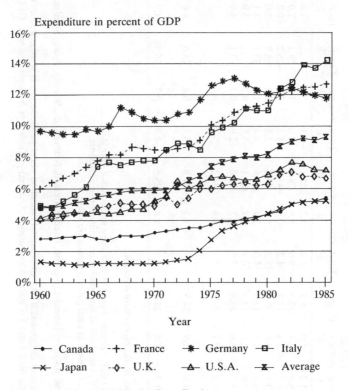

Expenditure in percent of GDP

Year

—•— Canada   –+– France   –*– Germany   –□– Italy

–×– Japan   –◇– U.K.   –△– U.S.A.   –×– Average

Source: OECD, Social Policy Data Bank

relatively more stable.

Nevertheless, the global trend in expenditure and the implied dramatic change in the resources that are transfered via public means from the working to the retired population have several consequences for the public budget:

(1) In purely arithmetic terms, the rise in public pension expenditure has contributed significantly to the growth of the relative share of the public sector, i.e., total public expenditure as a percentage of GDP. Across the OECD, the average contribution of public pension schemes to the increase in the public sector share was one-fourth over the last 25 years; in Italy it was more than one-third. In some countries, and especially after the two oil-price shocks, the contribution was 50 percent and more (Table 1).

Table 1. *Contribution of Public Pension Expenditure to Total Public Sector Growth in OECD Countries, 1960-85*

	1960–85			1960–75			1975–85			1975–79			1979–85		
	Total 1/	Pension 2/	Contr. 3/	Total 1/	Pension 2/	Contr. 3/	Total 1/	Pension 2/	Contr. 3/	Total 1/	Pension 2/	Contr. 3/	Total 1/	Pension 2/	Contr. 3/
Canada	17.8	2.6	14.8	11.2	1.0	8.7	6.6	1.7	25.1	-1.1	0.4	...	7.8	1.2	15.7
France	17.9	6.7	37.2	8.9	4.1	45.5	9.0	2.6	28.8	2.0	1.2	59.1	7.0	1.4	20.3
Germany	15.0	2.2	14.6	16.5	2.9	17.7	-1.5	-0.7	-41.6	-1.3	-0.3	-26.2	-0.2	-0.4	...
Italy	28.3	10.2	36.9	13.1	4.9	37.6	15.2	5.2	34.4	2.2	1.3	58.9	3.0	3.9	30.2
Japan (1965-86)	14.0	4.2	30.0	8.5	1.5	13.5	5.5	2.7	49.6	4.4	1.4	33.1	1.1	1.3	114.2
United Kingdom	15.4	2.8	17.9	15.0	2.0	13.6	0.4	0.7	182.1	-3.5	0.2	...	3.9	0.5	14.0
United States	9.6	3.1	32.2	7.2	2.6	33.6	2.0	0.5	26.0	-2.9	-0.1	-3.1	4.9	0.6	12.5
Average of above countries 4/	16.8	4.5	26.9	11.5	2.7	23.5	5.3	1.8	34.2	—	0.6	...	5.3	1.2	23.1
Average of smaller OECD countries 5/	17.3	4.6	26.4	11.8	2.9	24.9	7.9	1.7	21.8	3.4	0.8	24.8	4.6	0.9	0.2
OECD average 4/	17.1	4.5	26.6	11.7	2.8	24.1	6.9	1.8	25.5	2.7	0.7	35.9	4.9	1.0	21.1

Source: OECD, *National Accounts* and Social Policy Data Bank, expenditure segment.

1/ Change in total public expenditure as a percentage of GDP, calculated as final year share minus initial year share.
2/ Change in pension expenditure as a percentage of GDP, calculated as final year share minus initial year share.
3/ Change in pension expenditure share as a percentage of change in total public expenditure share.
4/ Unweighted average.
5/ Countries contained in this table are Australia, Austria, Belgium, Denmark, Finland, Greece, Ireland, Netherlands, Norway, Spain, Sweden, and Switzerland.

Notes: Total public expenditures essentially consist of current disbursement plus gross capital formation of the public sector. It is measured by the sum of lines 38 (Income and Outlay Account), 9, 10, 13, 14 and 15 less lines 2 and 3 (Capital Accumulation Account) in Table 6 of *National Accounts*, OECD, Volume II, Detailed Tables.

(2) The financing of public pension schemes is closely related to the financing needs of public budgets: directly, as in the case of basic schemes financed from general revenues or the budgetary transfers required by contributory schemes; and indirectly, since higher contribution rates compete with other public levies.

(3)There is seemingly a strong relationship between the growth of expenditures for public pensions and the explosion of national debt in almost all OECD countries (OECD 1986).

The relationship between public pensions and the general budget on one hand, and the pressure for budgetary consolidation on the other makes it inevitable that ministers of finance, anxious to control budgetary expenditure, will also turn to their retirement schemes during this critical review. Some observers even suggest that the financial consolidation of pension schemes is a necessary condition for budgetary control in most OECD countries.

B. The economic impact

The economic pressures for restructuring retirement systems are based on their assumed negative impact on economic performance. The goals of public pension schemes and their implementation have been pursued by social policy-makers for a long time, largely independently from economic policy. However, since the 1970s and the lagging performance of OECD economies, critical voices are becoming stronger. In particular, the impact on two markets — the labor market and the financial market — is being called into question. Many economists and politicians argue that the rising social security contribution rates are partly to blame for the current labor market problems; others consider the benefit structure responsible for the decreasing labor force participation of the elderly. Furthermore, sluggish capital formation and low economic growth in OECD countries are said to be linked to the influence of public schemes, financed on a pay-as-you-go basis, on the private savings rate. Although firm evidence of both alleged(negative) effects is still lacking, these arguments are increasingly being picked up in economic debate.[2]

This shift in the discussion goes along with changes in the paradigm(s) of economic policy. Until the 1970s economic policy was dominated by Keynesian views, emphasizing the positive aspects of public retirement provisions: their multiplier and automatic stabilization effects, or their positive distributional impact. However, economic events and the apparently decreasing effectiveness of traditional demand-side policy shifted the emphasis to supply-side economics, i.e., considerations that also take account of individual reactions to changes in the socio-economic setting. Public pension schemes, with their mandatory membership, certainly exert a strong influence.

A further economic pressure for rearranging total retirement provisions is exerted by the changing price of public pension schemes. Their price has increased because the internal rate of return of these schemes is decreasing and will continue to fall. This implicit interest rate, which brings past contributions into equilibrium with future benefit streams, was very high for the starting generation of pension schemes financed on a pay-as-you-go basis. As the systems mature, this rate decreases and — with a negative population growth outweighing productivity growth — may even become negative in the next decades in a number of countries. Chart 2 shows estimated real internal rates of return(RIRR) for selected pension-cohorts in the Austrian employees' social security scheme between 1961 and 2051 (Holzmann 1988b). The values and trends of these RIRRs are likely to be similar in other OECD countries with an insurance system (see e.g., Leimer-Petri 1981 or Hudges 1985), and they point to two important policy consequences: first, with positive rates of return on financial investments (also in the long run, since in each country they are increasingly determined by the world financial market (Fukao-Hanazaki, 1987)) but decreasing RIRR for social security contributions, portfolio theory predicts substantial changes in the retirement asset composition (assuming constant variance-covariance relations between public and private sector rates). The implied change in the optimal retirement portfolio should have important consequences for the societal demand for social security provisions. Second, the important differences in the RIRR that prevail between different groups suggest considerable problems in achieving a social consensus for reform, since the current system regulations will be advantageous for some groups, even if contribution rates increase drastically.

Chart 2. Real Rates of Return in Social Security
(Austrian General Pension Scheme)

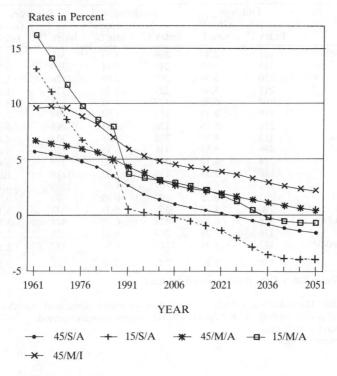

45/M/A:Contribution years/Married-Single
/Average-Increasing income Profile
Source: Holzmann(1988b)

The discussion about reforming old-age income provisions is also influenced
by the improved economic position of the elderly in society. Available evidence suggests that poverty among the elderly has dramatically decreased over
recent decades so that in many countries their risk of poverty is today below
that of the population on average (OECD 1988a). This is largely the result of
increased eligibility and rising real benefits per capita, the latter often exceeding the income growth of the active population. Moreover, comparing gross
pension benefits with gross earnings largely underestimates the relative income
position of beneficiaries since they pay little or no social security contributions,
are less exposed to income tax progressivity and may enjoy preferential tax
treatment. In contrast, the working population is subject to a high and
increasing tax burden. Thus, it is argued, the income position reached by the
elderly should permit reforms of public pension schemes, especially since new
"problem" groups in society are emerging (e.g., single parent families) and the
tax burden of the active population is still rising.

Table 2. Changes in Real Benefit Positions of Public Pensioners, 1960-85

	Old Age		Invalidity		Survivors	
	Index 1/	Growth rate 2/	Index 1/	Growth rate 2/	Index 1/	Growth rate 2/
Australia (1961-85)	181	2.40	269	4.03	315	4.69
Austria	335	4.96	249	3.71	360	5.26
Canada	230	3.38	205	2.91	76	−1.11
Denmark	211	3.04	225	3.29	136	1.23
Finland	469	6.38	327	4.85	233	3.44
Germany	180	2.38	158	1.84	194	2.69
Ireland	351	5.15	226	3.31	295	4.42
Italy	313	4.67	328	4.86	324	4.82
Japan(1961-84)	498	6.63	446	6.16	756	8.43
Netherlands	274	4.12	205	2.92	233	3.44
New Zealand	188	2.55	139	1.32	129	1.01
Norway	301	4.51	301	4.50	169	2.12
Portugal(1960-84)	83	−0.75	102	0.09	79	−0.94
Sweden(1960-84)	290	4.35	369	5.36	347	5.10
Switzerland(1960-84)	529	6.89	439	6.10	417	5.88
United Kingdom	176	2.28	267	4.01	228	3.36
United States(1960-84)	182	2.43	147	1.54	187	2.53
Average 3/	256	3.83	240	3.56	225	3.29

Source: OECD, Social Policy Data Bank, pension segment.

1/ Index 1960 = 100. The index was calculated on the basis of annual compound growth rates and for the total period 1960-85 even if the growth rate covers a smaller period.
2/ Annual compound growth rate.
3/ Unweighted geometric mean.

C. Social change

This last statement leads to consideration of changes in the social framework pressing for adjustment in pension regulations. First, changes in the family structure can be cited. The creation of public pension schemes was a (late) reaction to the break-up of an extended family structure that included all generations, and to the formation of smaller families. Most pension schemes are oriented toward the model of a nuclear family, consisting of a working husband and a housekeeping wife who cares for a number of children. However, the situation has changed again and if current trends continue this model-type family soon will not be representative: For women, the risk of divorce is nowadays higher than the risk of being widowed; labor market participation of women is increasing and approaches that of men for some age-groups and in a few countries. Hence, the current forms of survivor's pension and other regulations are becoming obsolete.

In addition, a number of pension experts point to changes in the socio-economic setting that could constitute an objective justification for less public and more private retirement provisions (Kessler 1986). Given the evidence of a decreasing dispersion of mortality rates and thus a reduction in the uncertainty of life duration, a lower probability of adverse selection may be concluded. Some studies indicate shifts in the population from myopic individuals, with a very short planning horizon (à la Keynes-Tobin) to life-cyclers (à la Modigliani). Finally, it is argued that a decrease in risk aversion on the part of individuals can be stated (owing to rising income levels).

However, the current reform discussion is not only determined by the pressures of, and reactions to, past changes in the socio-economic framework and the current financial situation of public schemes. Increasingly, future and anticipated developments are taken into account. The most important influence is exerted by the projected shift in the age structure and the aging of populations.

D. Aging populations

Population aging is not a new phenomenon for the OECD area, where on average the share of those aged 65 and over in the population increased from 8.5 percent in 1950 to 12.5 percent in 1985. Nevertheless, an increase of almost 50 percent in the proportion of elderly people during the period contributed little to the growth of pension expenditure; this growth was largely determined by wider eligibility and higher real benefits (OECD 1985, Holzmann 1987a).

On the basis of current demographic projections — national and international — all OECD countries can expect a significant shift in the age distribution between now and the second quarter of the next century. The most recent projection by the OECD Secretariat (OECD 1988b) up to 2050 suggests for most countries a moderate growth in the proportion of elderly people (65 and over) between 1985 and 2010 followed by a considerable acceleration and a peak around 2040 (12.5 percent, 15.3 percent, and 21.9 percent in 1985, 2010, and 2040.

This aging of the population has three main components: (1) "aging from above", since life-expectancy will continue to rise in the coming decades; (2) "aging from below", as in all OECD-countries fertility rates have been falling since the 1960s and are now well below replacement level in most countries; and (3) the march of the baby-boom generation through the age structure. Since for most countries this last effect is of crucial importance, even a rapid return of the fertility rate to replacement level or above could not prevent a significant aging of population in the decades to come.[3]

Such a projected shift in the age structure is particularly alarming for public pension schemes, which are nowadays financed on a pay-as-you-go basis. (The substantial social security funds in Canada, Japan, and Sweden are no exception). The financial consequences of the demographic shift can be explored through the use of a simple model (OECD 1988a). Under the assumption of constant replacement rates (i.e., benefits as a percentage of labor earnings), constant labor force participation rates, etc., public pension expenditures as a percentage of GDP are expected to double across the OECD area between

1985 and 2040.

Chart 3 illustrates projections of the impact of population aging on the pension expenditure share for the seven larger OECD countries. The general trend of expenditures is much the same in all countries, but the levels differ substantially, reflecting differences in the initial expenditure level and in the projected demographic change. Since base year conditions are assumed throughout the projection period, the demographic component essentially reflects alternative developments in the old age dependency ratio (i.e., the ratio of people 65 and over to the working-age population, aged 15 to 64).

Chart 3. Population Aging and Public Pension Expenditure

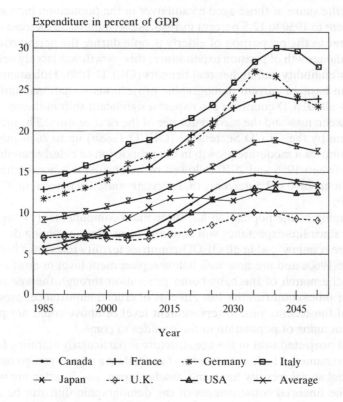

Source: OECD, Social Policy Data Bank;
Author's calculations

E. System maturation

To cope with this demographically induced expenditure growth of public retirement schemes, either a doubling of the contribution rates or a halving of benefits per retiree would be necessary. However, in many OECD countries this expenditure growth due to aging is likely to be reinforced as systems mature. The restructuring of social security schemes in the 1950s and 1960s as well as various improvements during the golden years of high economic growth and low unemployment have had long-term effects in coverage and benefit levels that will reach far into the next century. In the Japanese pension scheme, before the 1985 reform, the estimated impact of system maturation on expenditure growth was greater than the demographic effect, the latter already being considerable compared with many other countries. For many European OECD countries, a statement in a recent report by the French government may be representative: "The doubling of the pension burden from now until 2025 is almost equally split between demographic changes and system maturation; until 2005 system maturation is the main determinant, as population is relatively stable; afterwards, the population aging is decisive" (Ruellan 1986).

The presentation of the various pressures for reform — if only the most essential ones — should have made it clear that current financial problems and future demographic shifts are only two among many other pressures to reorganize total old-age income provisions when reforming social security systems. The multiplicity of motives is one of the main reasons for the difficulties encountered in the reform process, and explains the major directions taken by reform proposals.

Trends in the Restructuring of Old-Age Income Provisions

To indicate trends in retirement policy is, in principle, a delicate and problematic task. To restrict such a presentation to already implemented reforms would not be very revealing of the future, as current reform proposals are not included. However, taking account of the total scope of reform discussions would also be misleading, since a number of proposals — and not only from the academic world — are unlikely to receive political backing. The following selection and presentation of trends is situated somewhere in the middle and aims to be representative of the state of (political) reform considerations in the member countries of the OECD.

Surveying the numerous steps toward reforms undertaken and current intentions, their trends can be summarized and discussed in four broad areas:

(1) There is no move to abolish current public pension systems, but only a desire for reforms within the existing approach.

(2) There is a tendency to give greater importance to basic income support for the elderly.

(3) The approaches to reform are largely characterized by a double strategy: emphasizing social adequacy and individual equity.
(4) The reform considerations aim at a redistribution of the sources of old-age income, namely labor earnings, transfers, and capital income.

A. Reform, not revolution

None of the recent changes in public pension systems in OECD member countries constitutes a revolution, nor is such an attempt currently envisaged. Some countries have substantially adjusted their retirement programs in recent reforms, but these adjustments always took place within the existing philosophy.

A question frequently asked is why are retirement schemes so hard to reform? It has been argued that a necessary prerequisite for reform is a substantial political consensus about: (a) the deficiencies of the current system structure and the need for change; and (b) the particular alternatives that would be superior. Some of the main arguments can be repeated here (see Thompson 1983; Holzmann 1988c):

(i) Not all groups in a country are convinced that a restructuring of retirement provisions is necessary. Some believe that a slight streamlining would be sufficient for the time being, a conviction often held by groups who fear the potential loss of their own favorable status.

(ii) Attitudes as to what constitutes an equitable distribution of the costs and benefits of a public retirement system are ultimately based on value judgments, since neither theory nor empirical evidence are likely to provide objective criteria.

(iii) There is little agreement about the effects of the current systems on economic variables such as labor supply and savings, and hence on economic performance. But even if these effects were undesirable and detrimental to the employment situation or to economic growth, it is often unclear that the proposed alternatives would be less harmful.

(iv) Public retirement systems serve more than one objective, so that even if there were agreement that a particular purpose would be better served in some other way, the adoption of a reform may involve an unacceptable sacrifice of other objectives.

(v) Social programs are interdependent, even if for historical, administrative, and other reasons the main contingencies in most countries are covered under separate programs. Reforms in one program may conflict with the structure and objectives of other programs that derive their political and social support from groups that are different in age, occupational, or ethnic composition.

(vi) Even if consensus for a new or largely restructured system can be obtained, there are existing entitlements that cannot easily be changed and new entitlements that are being created. This creates important technical problems of transition, social problems of equal treatment between generations, and political trade-offs between long-term advantages and short-term costs.

These, and numerous other restrictions, led to "reforms" within the established approach, which nevertheless have been substantial in a few countries. This was the case in the United States in 1983, in Japan in 1985/86, and in the United Kingdom in 1986.

The U.S. reform was a multi-instrument approach, comprising, *inter alia*, adjustments in the benefit formula, the inclusion of (newly hired) civil servants in the general public pension scheme (OASDI), a scheduled increase in contribution rates above current expenditure requirements to build up a substantial social fund to cope with future demographic changes, a planned increase in the retirement age, and partial taxation of hitherto untaxed benefits.

The Japanese reform also had the goal of harmonization of pension schemes, but mainly involved a cut in future benefit levels (by fixing the current replacement rates) and the introduction of basic income support for the elderly (OECD 1988c).

The reform in the United Kingdom reduced future replacement rates in the SERPS (State Earnings-Related Pension Scheme) from 25 percent to 20 percent, decreased the benefit level for survivors, and extended the assessment period for benefit calculation. In addition, contracting out from SERPS (i.e., the supply of earnings-related supplementary public benefits via occupational pensions in exchange for reduced contribution rates) was extended to personal pensions.

How is it that a few countries have succeeded in a substantial reform of their public pension schemes and received the necessary political support? Insofar as the small size of the sample permits a generalization, the following explanations are suggested.

In the case of Japan and the United Kingdom, the systems had been introduced fairly recently and an entitlement to full benefits was not yet established. The largely immature state of the schemes made it possible in both cases to reduce future benefit levels without changing current benefits.

In the United States, the Social Security Act requires projections of the financial situation of the (public) old-age, survivors' and disability insurance (OASDI) over a period of 75 years. The Annual Report of the Board of Trustees of the OASDI-Trust Funds represents a political as well as legal obligation for politicians to act with a view to the long-term and provides the general public with a comprehensive insight into the future financial prospects of the scheme.

Furthermore, in all three countries private retirement provisions — via occupational and personal arrangements — are important. Hence, adjustments in public benefits are softened in their effects on the total income of retirees, and in addition are politically eased, since these cuts are partly compensated for by special provisions from low-income groups, and by tax concessions for private provisions, from which mostly higher income groups profit. Hence, the conclusion can be drawn that a reform of public schemes is the more difficult, the greater is their importance for the income position of the individual.

B. Extension of basic provisions

Although there has been little attempt at drastic reform in public retirement provisions in the OECD countries, some basic provisions for the elderly, independent of earlier contributions, are being introduced in social insurance schemes in some countries and are under discussion in others. The emphasis on basic income support can be seen to arise from socio-economic changes as the next step in the evolution of the welfare state. In this stylized model of historical evolution, the first stage was paternalism, when private charity and public assistance were provided to the less fortunate. The second stage was social insurance, when compulsory programs were developed to cover increasing numbers of occupations and contingencies. The third stage emphasized the ideas of prevention and universality. In the process of transition from paternalism through social insurance to concern with maintaining the quality of life, the basic income schemes for the elderly (and other population groups) are expected to play an increasing role.

In addition to these largely qualitative arguments, which are linked with general income levels in post-industrial societies, there are technical, economic, and political arguments in support of the introduction of basic provisions.

(i) Basic income support can be seen as a useful device to cope with changes in household structure and the problems connected with divorced women and other disadvantaged groups in society. These arguments led to the recent introduction of basic provisions in Japan.

(ii) The introduction of basic flat-rate provisions into social insurance schemes is also favored by those who would like a clearer distinction between the transfer and the insurance annuity elements of social insurance programs. This separation of social insurance policy and assistance policy should increase the effectiveness of the systems as it makes it possible, within limits, to separate considerations of equity and efficiency.

(iii) An extension of the private retirement provisions is undoubtedly viewed as favoring higher income groups and persons with longer working records. Thus, it might be necessary to reinforce the basic provisions on social and political grounds, if a move toward private provisions is intended.

At present about half of the 24 OECD member countries have basic provisions. Japan recently joined the group of countries that provide basic as well as earnings-related public pensions; this group includes the Scandinavian countries and to some extent the United Kingdom and Ireland. Countries that provide basic provisions only are Australia, New Zealand, and Iceland. In the third group, countries with (pure) social insurance schemes (e.g., Switzerland and the Netherlands) have almost universal basic coverage, and in a number of other countries elements of basic provisions were introduced in the 1960s and 1970s (e.g., Pensione Soziale in Italy, or Supplementary Security Income in the

United States). Whether the current discussion in many other countries will eventually lead to basic income support for all elderly is not yet decided, though it is likely in some countries.

C. Social adequacy and individual equity

The last contention can be supported by other indications that characterize the third general tendency, namely the double strategy of social adequacy and individual equity in the adjustment process of public pension schemes. Budgetary constraints and the limited scope of reform options within the existing philosophy determine this approach.

This leads to measures that concentrate available but scarce financial resources on the most needy among the retired population. This tendency is particularly visible in countries with basic income support only: Australia recently reintroduced an asset-test alongside the income-test for granting basic benefits, and New Zealand, with its universal basic scheme without retirement test, recently introduced a tax surcharge which absorbs all payments received from the "National Superannuation Scheme" for the highest income group.

A stronger emphasis on social adequacy is also detectible in countries with earnings-related public pension schemes. The afore-mentioned partial taxation of benefits in the United States can be classified under this tendency, as well as various adjustments in favor of low-income groups in a number of other OECD countries. In countries with earnings-related benefits a second tendency is visible, namely to strengthen (again) the links between benefits and contributions. The political logic behind this approach is the restricted options that are available in an approach to reform that essentially stays within the given system. To moderate current and future expenditure growth, the only options available are a reduction in eligibility and/or a decrease in the benefit levels, either by reduced replacement rate or lower indexation. However, these "adjustments" require additional justification other than financial and budgetary considerations. That justification is found in the underlying insurance principle and the implied individual equity concept, relating individual contributions to benefits.

This strengthening of the insurance principle in social insurance schemes can be seen in the lengthening of the assessment period for benefit calculation, e.g., in Austria from the last five to the last ten years, in Spain from the last two to the last eight years, and in the United Kingdom from the best 15 years of contribution base (i.e., earnings below ceiling) to lifetime earnings. This tendency to base the benefit calculation not on the last earnings, or best earnings during a number of years, but on lifetime earnings can be noted in almost all countries. A second indication of efforts to tie the benefit structure more closely to earnings is the attempt to reduce non-contributory periods (such as education, unemployment, etc.). The abolition or reduction of multiple public pension benefits (especially in the case of own and survivors' benefits) that takes place in a number of OECD countries is also seen as a means to foster social adequacy and individual equity (beside the main objective of reducing spending). Finally, in a number of countries, reductions and credits for earlier or later withdrawal from the labor market are adjusted toward a more actuarial structure. This restructuring also has the goal of making the impact of social security schemes on labor supply and retirement decisions more neutral.

In recent years most OECD countries also modified their indexation procedures to slow down pension growth. The techniques applied ranged from index switch, index modification, and changes in the review period of the index, to capping and temporarily suspending periodic indexation (see Wartonick-Packard 1983, Fuery 1985, and OECD 1988a). These adjustments were mainly an ad hoc answer to financing pressures, with severe drawbacks and an unanswered central policy question, namely; should reduced benefit levels be achieved primarily via reduced new benefits or reduced indexation? Even if both modifications lead to the same present value of benefits, they are likely to have different effects on the individual. Currently, most countries apply both policy options with varying weights, and a discussion about their social and economic consequences is only starting.

D. Redistributing the sources of old-age income

The reform of public pensions will lead to a redistribution of income sources in old age — not merely as a result, but quite often as an objective in itself. The main income sources are: labor earnings, transfer income, and capital income.

The past trends in these three income sources for selected OECD countries show strong similarities but also differences in their relative importance for the elderly (Tables 3 to 7). For all countries, the decreasing importance of labor earnings in elderly households over the past decades can be noted, reflecting the decreasing labor market participation of the elderly. In some countries this reduction was totally compensated by increased transfer income; the relative importance of capital income or personal old-age saving remained low and largely constant. In some other countries, in particular the United States, Canada, and Finland, transfer income increased, but the share of capital income rose even more. The United States, for example, experienced a reduction of the labor-earnings share from 29 to 16 percent between 1962 and 1984; during the same period the share of transfer income rose only slightly, form 43 to 46 percent, but the share of capital income grew from 19 to 34 percent.

The current and anticipated financial crises of public pension schemes as well as other considerations have stimulated discussion about a redistribution between these shares.

A first approach is an increase in the legal or actual retirement age. Until now, only the United States under the 1983 reform foresees an increase in the standard retirement age from 65 at present to 67 by 2000-2027. The recent reform of the Japanese Employees Pension Schemes allows only for an

Table 3. Composition and Trend of Gross Income for Elderly Households[1]
in Canada, 1965-82
(As percent of total)

	1965	1971	1975	1982
Employment income	44	35	30	21
Investment income	14	18	17	25
Retirement pensions	36	44	48	48
of which:				
OAS/GIS	28	32	33	29
CPP/QPP		1	4	8
Private	8	11	11	11
Other income	6	3	5	6
Total income = 100				
In current prices Can$1,000	2.774	4.426	6.505	16.259

Source: C. Goodman, "Changing Structures of Retirement Income in Canada," in
    Conjugating Public and Private: The Case of Pensions, ISSA Studies and Research
    No. 24, Geneva, 1987.
[1] Census households with head 65 and older; all units.

Table 4. Composition and Trend of Gross Income of Old-Age Pension
Recipients in Finland, 1974-83
(As percent of total)

	Males		Females	
	1974	1983	1974	1983
Earnings	9.8	4.3	3.6	1.8
Private income	5.0	2.2	3.8	1.7
Income from self-employment	14.0	7.9	2.7	3.0
Retirement pensions	70.8	84.8	89.6	92.5
Of which:				
National pensions	29.4	26.6	58.3	47.3
employment pensions	41.4	58.2	31.3	45.2
Other income	0.4	0.8	0.3	1.0
Total income = 100				
In 1984 prices Fmk1,000	35.5	44.2	20.3	27.1

Source: E. Karlimo, and P. Siren, "Trends in the Composition and Levels of Retirement
    Income in Finland," in *Conjugating Public and Private: The Case of Pensions*, ISSA
    Studies and Research No. 24, Geneva, 1987.

Table 5. *Composition and Trend of Gross Income of Elderly Households[1]*
in Japan, 1975-84
(As percent of total)

	1975	1977	1979	1981	1983	1984
Earnings	56.0	42.8	44.1	43.6	35.0	34.5
Property income	9.6	10.4	11.3	8.1	6.9	8.7
Social security pensions	26.2	34.1	37.3	43.2	50.4	51.4
Other social security benefits	—	2.7	3.2	2.0	2.4	2.1
Other income[2]	8.1	10.1	4.0	3.0	5.3	3.4
Total income = 100 In ¥ 1,000	1,147	1,534	1,824	2,174	2,108	2,146

Source: Japanese Ministry of Health and Welfare.
[1] Elderly households are defined as households where the male head is 66 and over and the wife 61 and over, or the male head is 68 and over with children in the household 15 and below, or the single female head is 63 and over.
[2] Comprises payments from occupational pension schemes. However, in the past, payments were normally made on a lump-sum basis.

Table 6. *Composition and Trend of Gross Income of Pensioners[1] in the*
United Kingdom, 1951-85
(As percent of total)

	1951	1961	1971	1981-82	1984-85[2]
Earnings	27	22	18	10	9
Investment income	15	15	13	10	9
Occupational pensions	15	16	21	21	22
Total public transfers	42	48	48	59	60
Of which:					
National insurance retirement pension	35	41	40	47	49
Other social security benefits[3]	8	6	7	12	11
Total	100	100	100	100	100

Source: *Social Trends*, Vol. 16, 1986 Edition.
[1] Adjusted for differences in size and composition of household.
[2] Projections.
[3] Mainly supplementary and housing benefits. Growth in the 1970s was largely due to housing and disability benefits.

Table 7. Composition and Trend of Gross Income of Aged Persons in the
United States, 1962-84
(As percent of total)

	1962	1967	1976	1980	1984
Earnings	29	29	23	19	16
Asset income	16	15	18	22	28
Retirement pensions	40	46	53	54	51
Social security	31	34	40	40	38
Private	3	5	7	7	6
Government employee	6	7	6	7	7
Public assistance	6	4	2	1	1
Other income	9	6	4	4	4
Total	100	100	100	100	100

Source: M. Upp, "Relative Importance of Various Income Sources of the Aged, 1980,"
Social Security Bulletin, current population surveys, March 1985.

increase in standard retirement age for women from 55 at present to 60 before
the year 2000. In all other OECD countries, an increase in the retirement
age(s) is part of the reform discussion and will probably be implemented in the
future, especially since this option could lead to a substantial moderation in the
expenditure growth (Halter-Hemming 1987). Hence, increasing the retirement age would lead to a reduction in transfer income and probably also to an
increase in labor earnings among the income sources in old age.

A second and complementary approach is to replace future reduced public
retirement provisions by private income support for old age. A shift in the
responsibility between transfer and savings support has various dimensions:

(i) In economic terms the pay-as-you-go component of income support
would be reduced, to be replaced by greater reliance on funded provisions,
with various requirements and implications at the macro- and microeconomic
levels.

(ii) In political terms the question arises whether pensions should be public
or private; this distinction has become ideologically charged and its usefulness
has been questioned. Yet in practical terms it covers the size and degree of
public intervention, the issue of public provision versus public regulation, and
the scope for individual choice.

(iii) In institutional terms a distinction must be made between the supplier
and the kind of old-age income support: the government via public pensions,
the employer via occupational pensions, and the financial institutions via
personal pensions.

The issues involved in a reexamination and redistribution of old-age income
responsibilities are numerous and interrelated. They concern the analysis of
alleged advantages resulting from a redistribution of responsibilities, the
design of alternative methods of old-age income support, the identification of

requirements for redistribution in economic, social, and institutional terms, and the investigation of the likely consequences of redistribution on the economy and society (Holzmann 1987b).

Although firm empirical evidence cannot be given for any of these issues and information at both the international and national levels is still lacking, in most OECD countries some consideration is being given to redistribution "at the margin" (EBRI 1987).

In France, for instance, the Government has recently made some efforts to imitate the U.S. Individual Retirement Accounts; in Austria a similar approach is under discussion within the planned tax reform; and in Italy there are several serious attempts to follow the U.S. example of occupational provisions (see e.g., Gabrielli-Fano 1986). And in other countries, where public, occupational,and personal pensions are already providing income to the elderly, a number of adjustments have been made, e.g., in the United Kingdom, the extension of "contracting out" from public to occupational, and now to personal, provisions. In Canada, in 1986, a substantial change in the framework of occupational and personal provisions has also taken place. In Switzerland, minimum occupational pensions were made mandatory since 1985. Finally, in Australia a similar approach is under discussion, or at least a stronger emphasis and regulation of the "Occupational Superannuation" has been suggested.

Tentative Conclusions

This chapter has tried to present the broad trends in old-age income provisions in the OECD countries by analyzing the background and pressures for reform and its major tendencies. Emphasis was given throughout to public or social security schemes, but since they cannot be viewed in isolation, references to other old-age income programs had to be made as well. In view of the complexity of the subject, and limitations of time and space, numerous questions must remain unanswered, *inter alia*,

(i)   Are the current attempts at reform sufficient to cope with economic constraints, social changes and demographic developments?

(ii)   In what direction should the retirement systems in industrialized countries move? Toward the Swiss model, consisting of universal public, mandatory occupational and voluntary personal provisions? What should be the distribution between these programs?

(iii) How should retirement programs be coordinated with the tax system in order to achieve certain social goals, while preventing negative allocative effects?

No satisfactory answer can yet be given to these and many other questions. The reasons are many. First, answers involve issues of social consensus and a solution through political debate is tedious and time-consuming. Second, too little information is at present available at the national and international levels to give sufficient support in tackling many crucial questions. And third, the economic situation in future decades, and hence the required degree of reform, is not known.

Nevertheless, the current discussion of reform of public schemes and the OECD-wide tendency to give more responsibility for old-age income to the private sector may give cause for some optimism about adequate income for the elderly in the future, and about a reasonable burden on the future working population. In turn, enhanced private provisions may also ease the process of reform in public pension schemes. But to prevent unrealistic optimism or unwarranted pessimism it is desirable to evaluate more clearly the areas where a redistribution can be advantageous, and to identify precisely the necessary conditions in economic, regulatory, and social terms (OECD,1987).

Notes

* The views expressed are those of the author alone.
1. Numerous studies and reform proposals for public pension schemes exist at a national level in every OECD member country. For issues at the international level see the references, although the list is by no means exhaustive.
2. There is a growing body of academic literature on this subject. For a survey, see, e.g., Danziger-Haveman-Plotnick (1981), Aarron (1982), Burtless-Aaron (1984), Wise (1985), and Holzmann (1988a).
3. The assumptions of the OECD medium-variant projection — although similar to the UN demographic projections — can be considered rather optimistic, since they assume a moderate growth in life expectancy, negligible migration flows, and the return of the fertility rate to replacement level in the long term. Lower fertility rates and higher life expectancy at retirement age, however, would considerably exacerbate the aging of the population, especially if linked with an increase in the mortality rates of the working population. The latter could be a consequence of AIDS, if current trends in the spread of the disease continue.
4. In most other OECD-countries the required projection period is 5 to 15 years, if projections requirements exist at all. The contention is that long-term projection by an official, but independent institution (similar to the U.S. Board of Trustees) would substantially change the attitude toward reform in other countries as well.

References

Aaron, H., *Economic Effects of Social Security* (Washington: The Brookings Institution, 1982).

Burtless, G., and H. Aaron, eds., *Retirement and Economic Behavior,* (Washington:

The Brookings Institution, 1984).

Council of Europe, *The Protection of the Very Old* (Strasbourg, 1984).

Danziger, S., R. Haveman, and R. Plotnick, "How Income Transfer Programmes Affect Work, Savings and the Income Distribution: A Critical Review," *Journal of Economic Literature* Vol. 19 (September 1981).

Dument, J.-P., *L'impact de la crise économique sur les systèmes de protection sociale*, Etude réalisé pour le Bureau International de Travail (Paris: 1987).

EBRI(Employee Benefit Research Institute), "International Trends in Corporate and Individual Retirement Plans", *EBRI Issue Brief*, August 1987, No. 69.

Fuery M., "Indexing Pension — Pension Adjustment Procedures in Ten OECD Countries," Social Security Journal (June, 1985).

Fukao, M., and M. Hanazaki, Internationalization of Financial Markets and the Allocation of Capital, *"OECD Economic Studies* (No. 8, Spring 1987).

Gabrielli, G. and D. Fano, eds., *The Challenge of Private Pension Funds-Present Trends and Future Prospects in Industrialised Countries*, Special Report No. 1058 (London, 1986).

Halter, W.,and R. Hemming, "The Impact of Demographic Change on Social Security Financing," *Staff Papers* (Washington), Vol. 34, (No 3, September 1987).

Heller, P.S., R. Hemming, R. and P. Kohnert, "Aging and Social Expenditure in the Major Industrialized Countries, 1980-2025," Occasional Paper, No. 47 (Washington: International Monetary Fund, 1986).

Holzmann, R. (1987a), "Ageing and Social Security Costs," *European Journal of Population/Revue Européene de Démographie*, Vol. 3.

(1987b), "Redistribution of the Responsibilities for Old-Age Income Support — What Are the Issues? OECD Meeting of invited experts on the interaction of public, occupational, and personal retirement provisions (Paris, November), restricted.

(1988a), ed., *Oekonomische Analyse der Sozialversicherung* (Vienna)

(1988b), "Zu oekonomischen Effekten der oesterreichischen Sozialversicherung: Einkommensersatz, Ruhestandsentscheidung und interne Ertragsraten, in: *Oekonomische Analyse der Sozialversicherung*, op.cit.

(1988c), "Issues in the Development of Pension Schemes: International and Historical Perspectives," in OECD (1988c).

Hudges, C., *Payroll Tax Incidence, the Direct Tax Burden and the Rate of Return on State Pensions Contributions in Ireland*(Dublin, 1985).

ILO, *Into the Twenty-first Century: The Development of Social Security*, (Geneva, 1984).

Kessler, D., *On the Microfoundations of Social Security and Pension Expenditures*, OECD Meeting of invited experts on the interaction of public, occupational, and personal retirement provisions (Paris, November 1986), restricted.

Leimer, D.R., and P.A. Petri, "Cohort-Specific Effects of Social Security Policy," *National Tax Journal*, Vol. XXXIV (March 1981).

Economic Outlook (March, 1986).

Report on the Meeting of Invited Experts on the Interaction of Public, Occupational and Personal Retirement Provisions, WP-Document, March 1987, restricted.

(1988a), *Reforming Public Pensions: Background, Pressures and Options*(Paris).

(1988b), *The Social Policy Implications of Aging Populations* (Paris).

(1988c), *Health and Pension Policies in the Context of Demographic Evolution and Economic Constraint* (Paris); Japanese edition: Tokyo 1986.

Rosa, J.J., ed., *The World Crisis in Social Security*, Institute of Contemporary Studies-

California/Fondation National d'Economie Politique, Paris (1984).

Ruellan Rapport, Groupe Technique sur l'Avenir des Régimes de Retraite, Commissariat Général Plan (Paris, March 1986).

Thompson L., "The Social Security Reform Debate," *Journal of Economic Literature*, Vol. 21, December 1983, pp. 1425-67.

Wartonick, D., and M. Packard, "Slowing Down Pension Indexing: The Foreign Experience," *Social Security Bulletin*, June 1983.

Wise, D.A., *Pension, Labor, and Individual Choice*, Chicago and London,

Chapter 51

Support of the Elderly in Denmark: The Pension System — Its Problems and Challenges

Linda NIELSEN and Vibeke VINDELØV,
University of Copenhagen, Denmark

The Support System

As in all of Scandinavia the support of elderly citizens is part of Danish welfare policy. Every citizen over 67 is granted a basic pension by the State. In addition, elderly citizens may also receive a supplementary pension if that is provided by a specific pension arrangement.

A. Pension from the State (Basic pension)

Independently of his or her previous income, sex and marital status, any citizen over 67 is entitled to a pension from the State — *the national pension scheme*. The scheme covers the whole Danish population. Entitlement to a pension is thus not conditional on payment of contributions nor on periods of completed employment. The regulations on social pensions are laid down in Act No. 217 of May 16, 1984 and in consequential orders and directions ("Folkepensionloven").

The national pension is regarded as a right; it is financed by the Central Government from income raised by direct and indirect taxation. In Denmark the burden of taxation is considered very heavy; OECD has estimated it to be approximately 52% on average.

The national pension scheme consists of a basic sum with a supplement depending on income. The basic sum is about 3.400 D.kr. a month, and the supplement 900 D. kr. a month. The average monthly salary is about 15.000 D. kr. The pension is sufficient to cover all living expenses, at a modest level. Retired persons in need may also be granted supplementary payments, such as for heating.

Both the basic benefit and the pension supplement taper off in proportion to earned income which exceeds a certain minimum — the basic benefit though only for persons between 67 and 70. The basic amount is also reduced when each spouse receives the national pension.

A so-called *pre-age pension* may be paid to citizens between 50 and 67 where earning capacity is reduced by at least 50% due to ill health, or a combination of medical and social factors. If the applicant and his or her spouse, however, have an income exceeding a modest limit, no pension will be granted. The pre-age pension can be of importance for widows who are in need. The conditions under which persons working at home, in effect housewives, may obtain pre-age pension are stricter than for other applicants, as it is assumed that housekeeping demands less of the applicant than the labour market does.

The national pension scheme is supplemented by other *socially indicated benefits*. Thus the legislation on taxation provides for an increased personal allowance, which is especially advantageous for single pensioners. Another example is a special housing allowance according to which pensioners need pay only 15% of their income on housing expenses. The rest will be covered (within certain limits) by the State. A third example is the cheap transport offered by public transport.

To this it must be added that Denmark provides various services free of charge which are of importance to pensioners, such as medical care, nursing services and home-help.

In effect the various grants to pensioners exceed the nominal amount of the national pension. The Danish Association of Savings Banks has shown that a non-pensioner must earn 7.000 — 10.000 D.kr. a month to reach a consumption ability equal to that of a single pensioner who has a national pension with supplements and other grants.

A special arrangement for retired employees between 60 and 67 - *voluntary early retirement pension* ("Efterløn") — lies on the borderline between the national pension and private pensions. An employee may apply for early retirement pension between the age of 60 and 67, on condition that he has contributed to the unemployment insurance for a certain period. This arrangement has come about in order to increase the opportunities of young people to obtain work. The amount paid as early retirement pension is considerably higher than the national pension. It may amount to 9.000 D.kr a month, although it is reduced during the period of early retirement pension. On the other hand, the receiver of an early retirement pension cannot obtain the special grants available to pensioners.

Finally a new *Partial Pension* ("Delpension") has been introduced for employees, self- employed business people and others who are between 60 and 67, if they reduce their usual working hours. The purpose is to achieve a smoother transition from an active working life to retirement. The applicant must have been in employment previously for a long period, and must reduce activity by at least 25%. The rate of a partial pension usually equals that of the early retirement pension, when the reduced working hours are taken into account. Partial Pensions have not as yet been used very much.

B. Supplementary Pensions

Only about half of the 4 million Danes who are over 16 are covered by some form of supplementary pension or insurance scheme. 400.000 people are members only of group life-insurance schemes, that is, they have secured their dependents on their death, but they have not acquired an old-age pension for themselves on a private basis. About one-third of persons employed — that is 700.000 persons — have a pension arrangement (occupational pension) as part of their terms of employment; some 800.000 participate in private pension schemes so that in all about 1.5 million persons have a supplementary pension arrangement for their old-age.

Occupational Pensions

The most general form of occupational pension — (*Additional Pension from the Labour Market*) — ("Arbejdsmarkedets Tillægspension" — "ATP") is available for all employees except the self-employed and people working only in the home. The arrangement is obligatory, financed by contributions from employers and employees in the ratio 2:1 respectively. The pension, currently paid from the pensioner's 67th year, is very modest. In certain cases a surviving spouse may obtain a very small pension on the death of the pensioner.

The Pension for Public Servants is another general occupational pension available for persons employed by the Government, municipalities and public offices. About 220.000 persons are covered by this pension scheme, which is currently paid from such time as the public servant may choose to retire between the ages 60-69, or when he reaches 70, when retirement is compulsory. The pension for public servants is mandatory, earned through years in service, and is proportional to the duration of employment and the size of final salary. This pension is large. A recipient of the Pension for public servants suffers reduction in the national social pension, a situation much criticized at present. A surviving spouse will receive a widow(er)'s pension on the death of the public servant.

Several *other occupational pensions* contribute much to present old age arrangements. They often form part of mandatory, collective pension schemes, when employer and employee contribute to the premium. The typical share for the employee amounts to 10, 12 or 15% of income, paid to a pension fund, a life assurance company, or a financial institution. Also several occupational pension schemes are established on the initiative of the employee himself and paid by him only. The pension may be in the form of income; but a special Danish phenomenon is that some occupational pensions are paid as capital sums, allowing the pensioner to receive an amount once and for all, when he has reached a certain age, typically 60, 65 or 67.

With regard to pensions payable as income, the surviving spouse of a deceased pensioner will often be entitled to a pension after the death, but not always. In the case of capital pension schemes, if the pensioner dies before the sum has been paid, the pension benefit will normally granted be to the beneficiary, who is usually the spouse.

Private Pensions

Some individuals enter pension schemes on their own initiative. Encouraged by fiscal advantages, some take out life insurance, capital insurance and so on; others participate in capital pension schemes with financial institutions. These especially concern independent business people but also persons who are entitled to an occupational pension and at the same time wish to enter into private pension schemes as a supplement in old age. However, people who are outside the labour market very rarely enter life insurance and pension schemes, which may result in their having a low basic income when they become pensioners.

The private pension schemes payable as income may be supplemented by a survivorship annuity payable to the surviving spouses. Typically capital pension schemes are established so that the surviving spouse is the beneficiary and may receive a pension on the death of the pensioner.

Problems of the Pension System

The Danish pension system presents difficulties, especially in consequence of its growing financial burden. In addition it lacks clarity and pension funds are poorly distributed.

A. The growing Pension Burden.

The national pension scheme is financed by the State one pay-as-you-go basis. There is no provision for accumulating funds, and the present working generation has to finance the pension payments through taxes. This is very problematic as the birth rate has been dropping since 1975, and a further drop is probable from the beginning of the next century. At the same time a great increase in the number of citizens over 67 is anticipated (See Table 1 and 2).

Table 1. Percentage of Population, by age

	1984	2010	2025
0-17 years	24	18	16
18-66 years	63	68	65
67 and over	13	14	19

Table 2 Percentage of pensioners (by age) to persons employed

Age of retirement	1984	2010	2025
60	36	42	54
63	29	32	42
67	20	21	30

Thus the *burden of supporting* pensioners will *increase* considerably, and a continuation of the present tendency towards lower retirement ages would be serious. The economic burden of support will depend on the productivity and the expenses generated by each pensioner. The public cost of older and younger persons[2] has been calculated at the following percentage rates proportional to the gross national product (on the basis of retirement at 63 and at 63 now and 60 after the year 2000 respectively).

Table 3 Percentage cost of older and younger population to GNP

Age of retirement	1982	2010	2025
63 years	22^3	21	25
63/60 years	22^4	27	31

B. Maldistribution of Pension Funds.

The pension system may seem confusing, and at times, inconsistent. For an individual choosing a pension scheme and a retirement date, it is very difficult to calculate all the advantages and disadvantages involved. In addition, the number of persons with supplementary pension schemes is increasing rapidly. This increase especially involves occupational pensions, which have become common over the past 20-30 years, and entitle the individual to a comparatively large pension. This is especially so for persons in public service. The bulk of contributing families is found among those aged between 30 and 60, but with a tendency that private, individual pension schemes are established later than the occupational pension schemes and are usually more modest. Typically pension contributions increase with age, in line with an increase in income.[5] Men generally make larger contributions towards pension schemes than women.[6] This applies especially to married men, largely on account of the sex-divided labour market and the different conditions for men and women trying to make a career.

It has been calculated,[7] that of those retiring at the beginning of the 21st century, about one-quarter can expect a pension at an adequate level; about one-half will receive a pension a little higher than the basic national pension. However, the rest will have no supplementary pension. Neither skilled nor unskilled workers are generally covered. This applies to the unemployed and homeworking housewives as well as to persons who have been outside the labour market for several years or have been in part-time work and will receive a smaller pension than others. This will mostly affect women.[8]

When certain groups do not contribute to pension schemes, it is probably due to the availability of special grants from the national pension scheme depending on income. As a supplementary pension will mean that those grants are not obtained, low-income groups have little interest in contributing to supplementary pensions schemes (the so-called problem of interplay). For many women the low level is connected with the expectation of being with their husbands in old age and thus sharing his pension with him. If the spouse dies, this expectation fails, though provision may have been made for a widow's pension, insurance or savings. In the case of divorce the expectation usually fails the divorcee obtaining an essential share of the husband's pension privileges.

Distribution of the supplementary pension schemes will result in considerable maladjustments of pension coverage in the future. Although to a certain degree this inequality reflects the general income inequality of the employed, the discrepancy may be unreasonable towards some pensioners and may cause tensions relating to distribution policy, threatening the functioning of the pension system.

Challenges — Pension Policy Goals.

The question is how to arrange the pension system today to adapt to the situation tomorrow. Thus the pension system ought to include contingency plans enabling it to bear the increasing economic burden of pensions and at the same time minimize the absurdities and social tensions which may be caused by future differences in the income of pensioners.

A. Pension Policy Goals

As stressed above, a growing pension burden may be expected at the beginning of the 21st century. For this reason the goal of pension policy should be *to* encourage the accumulation of pension funds to meet the future burden of *support*. Furthermore, it has been mentioned above that the pension system lacks clarity and consistency. So a second goal of pension policy should be *that the pension system be arranged so that it is clear and coherent.*

For nearly a hundred years it has been an established principle in Denmark that every individual should be secured a certain minimum income in old age regardless of previous occupational earnings. It is a characteristic of the Danish pension system that the national pension scheme is allotted to people who have not earned an occupational income. Thus a third basic goal of pension policy should be *that all Danish citizens be secured a certain minimum income in their old age.*

Finally it may be widely accepted that the pension system as a whole should not aggravate inequalities of pension payments between pensioners. As income amongst employees is notably unequal, probably a fourth goal of pension policy should be formulated moderately: *that the pension system should not cause the distribution of income amongst pensioners to be essentially more maladjusted than it is amongst employees.*

C. Challenges and Possibilities

Whilst some of the goals of pension policy are compatible, others give rise to certain contradictions.

1. In what way is accumulation of pension funds encouraged?

The question is whether politico-economic arrangements are possible which will lessen the burden of support in the future. These questions concern the interplay between pension policy, economic development, and general economic policy. The wish to encourage accumulation of funds may call for the introduction of a general supplementary pension scheme. In this way the burden of support for the next generation may be lessened to some degree, the financing being moved from "pay-as-you-go" to an insurance scheme with accumulation. In other words, the goal of the distribution policy will be moved from a distribution of income *between* persons to a distribution of income of each *individual over a lifetime*. Furthermore, the goal of accumulation of funds suggests an obligatory arrangement. This has the drawback that it may be contrary to an individual's wishes to have a pension at all. This danger will be diminished to the extent that the supplementary pension is on a relatively low level. However, a low level may lead to groups in the lower income bracket benefitting from the arrangement to a smaller extent, because they would lose those supplements granted to recipients of the national pension.

2. In what way is the pension system made more easily understood?

A general supplementary pension scheme can contribute towards making a pension system clearer. Moreover, consideration should be given to abolishing special rules for pensioners in other areas, such as taxes and housing subsidies. Also regulations might be introduced for the clarification and simplification of pension offers from assurance companies and financial institutions.

3. Who shall receive a social pension-and how much?

The introduction of a general supplementary occupational pension would affect the national pension scheme, thereby creating a basis for a reduction or regulation of income from the national pension scheme.

A reduction should be avoided, since the national pension will still be the sole source of income for many citizens. Therefore, it must be accepted that the public basic pension should remain on a level which makes it possible to maintain an acceptable existence with no other income than the national pension. Otherwise one of the main features of the welfare state would disappear.

But stricter regulation of income may become necessary in view of the future burden of support. However, it may mean that the national pension scheme might be reserved for a badly-off, non-homogeneous group of elderly, for whom it would be difficult to create political sympathy justifying an increase in the tax burden, when the majority apparently saves towards their own retirement. Income regulation, therefore, should retain the principle of the national pension scheme as a citizen's right as far as possible, so that it avoids the stigma of charity.

4. What connection should there be between pension and previous income?

A general supplementary pension scheme will maintain the inequality in income existing between employees to the extent to which pension contributions are related to salary. This may be critical, as the solidarity with the less fortunate and lower income groups will be abandoned to a certain extent. Problems of interplay may continue to be considerable in the lower income groups. Also, there will be groups of pensioners who do not accumulate a supplementary pension at all, thus remaining dependent on the national pension scheme. This will be so for the unemployed and homeworking housewives. This might seem unfair towards a spouse who contributed towards the conditions making it possible for a supplementary pension to be earned. This often applies to a wife whose work at home (or part-time employment) and care for the children made it possible for the husband to accumulate a pension. Here, probably, solidarity between family members ought to lead to the spouse being allowed a share of the accumulated pension when the pensioner dies; also that the accumulated pension be shared between the spouses in case of divorce. This is a problem of family law, which, however, is relevant to the political aspects of pension policy.

Final Remarks.

All these matters, especially the increasing economic burden of support, have led to negotiations in Denmark regarding an introduction of a general supplementary occupational pension. It is being debated, for instance, whether it should be carried through by law or by agreement between employees and employers. However, at present it is not possible to outline more specifically what the content of an eventual reform might be.

NOTES

1. Cf. a paper on pension policy from May 1986, "Hvordan munde mættes og goder og glæder deles. Et pensions-politisk debatoplæg." p. 16.
2. This includes the cost of the national pension scheme, early retirement pension, nursing homes, home assistance, hospital costs, housing subsidiaries, etc. for the elderly and of day-nurseries, schools, children allowances, hospital costs, etc. for children. See also the Danish Association of Savings Banks' paper on pension policy, mentioned in note 1.
3. The expenditure on the elderly constitutes 13% of the 22%; see calculations made in the paper on pension policy mentioned in note 1.
4. See note 3.
5. Cf. statement from the legislative secretariat of the Ministry of Economic Affairs (1985) on economic conditions of the pensioner: "De Økonomiske vilkår for pensionister".
6. Cf. Jan Peter Henriksen, Per Kampmann and Jørgen Rasmussen: "Fordelingen af private pensioner" (1988), espec. p. 160 and 257.
7. Cf. note 6, p. 251.
8. While the "omnibus research", developed by the Danish Statistical Department used the individual to map pension rights, the legislative secretariat uses "the family" as a unit.

Chapter 52

The Effect of Family Breakdown on Retirement Planning

E. Diane PASK* Associate Professor,
Faculty of Law,
University of Calgary, Alberta, Canada

Introduction

Pension plans, whether employer or government-sponsored, are an increasingly important component of personal income security arrangements for Canada's aging population. While many older persons have adequate retirement income security, elderly women living alone constitute the group most likely to be in poverty. Those women who have forfeited job skills and career development during their working years in favour of childbearing and homemaking find, should their marriages break down, that access to pension benefits accumulated throughout the marriage is of increasing importance to them. However, division of accumulated pension benefits between spouses is subject to difficulties.

This chapter outlines recent legislative changes affecting this division: it is now more likely for "cohabitors" to share pension benefits or credits; the mechanisms of dividing the pension benefit value and enforcing that division are, in some jurisdictions, placed in the hands of plan administrators. Both of these charges may be intended to benefit female retirees. However, they appear to be accompanied by methodologies which reduce the value of the share assigned to the non-member spouse (usually the woman) and by limitations on the contractual arrangements available to spouses who wish to settle their affairs outside of court.

These legislative changes reflect underlying social policy choices which have implicitly weighed administrative cost and convenience against fairness to the non-member spouse; governmental interest in uniformity of result against the individuals' right to contract; and, to some extent, priorities between married persons and cohabitors. It is not clear that the cumulative implications are recognized notwithstanding that the decisions are often to the disadvantage of the spouse least equipped to deal with their effects.

Demographic Trends in Canada

Recent demographic studies have indicated that Canada has a declining birth rate and an increasingly aging population. Between 1961 and 1984, the average number of children born to ever-married women aged 25-34, declined from 2.5 to 1.6 while the proportion of childless women in that age group increased from 11.5% to 21.9%. The average number of births per woman decreased from 3.8 in 1961 to 1.7 in 1981, and remained at 1.7 in 1984.[1]

In October, 1986, 2.7 million of Canada's population consisted of persons aged 65 years or over.[2] This population is rapidly increasing: it is expected to reach 6 million by 2021 and 7.5 million by 2031.[3] That means that by 2031, or within 43 years, the older population will have tripled in size.

By 2031, the number of those aged 75 and over is expected to triple in size, from approximately 1 million in 1986 to an expected 3 million or over in 2031.[4] The number over 85 years is also increasing: it is expected to more than triple by 2031, increasing from 224,000 in 1986 to nearly 750,000, almost 3.5 times its 1986 population. This population projection represents an average annual growth rate of 4% or more for those aged 85 and over for the years between 1991-2001. By way of comparison, the average annual growth rate for Canada's total population for that decade will be just over 1%.[5] Thus, it is apparent that the older population will be larger. It will probably also be subdivided into "older" and "very old", and we may also expect to find the older group, i.e. those approximately 65-75 years old caring for the very old, those over 85 years.[6]

This scenario of a future "aged" society has raised concerns that our pension system will constitute an enormous tax burden on future citizens. This concern is of particular relevance in light of the recent decline in the birth rate and the obvious impact this will have on the size of the younger population.[7] It has been estimated that if the contribution rate for the Canada Pension Plan (CPP) is maintained at its current level of 3.6%, the C.P.P. account will be exhausted by 2004.[8] Furthermore, business interests have warned government to reduce or stabilize the public pension commitment and to be sensitive to expectations concerning the future level of public pensions.[9]

Income Security and the Elderly

It is often asserted that the elderly are faced with serious economic hardship. Recent statistics, however, suggest that this image of the impoverished retired pensioner is not always accurate. For example, a recent survey in Japan found that people over 60 years had more financial assets than any other age group. It has also been reported that the disposable income in Britain of the average pensioner has risen from approximately 40% of that of non-pensioners in 1951 to almost 70% of that in 1986 and married couples in the United States aged over 65 years have a higher real income than they did as young workers in 1950.[10] This apparent financial security may result from the lack of mortgage or rent obligations, since most homes are fully purchased by retirement, and from the recent increase in the number of plans which provide for a survivor's pension. As women generally live longer than men, this provision may operate largely to the benefit of widows. Thus, married persons and some widows may be reasonably well-off during their retirement years.

Despite the security of certain groups, however, it is true that others experience significant financial difficulty in their later years. As a group, women are more likely to be impoverished in their later years than men: they are less likely to have retirement security and, as they live longer, and retirement income they do have must cover a longer period of time.

The ratio of women to men in all the older age categories has greatly increased since the 1950s.[11] Although this rise in the ratio of women to men appears to have stabilized as men have also experienced a major decline in their mortality rate, women will continue to outnumber men in all over-65 categories.[12] This will be particularly noticeable in the group surviving into their 90s.[13] Of women aged 80 in 1971, 20% could expect to live to 92 years and 12% to live to 94 years after which their survival chances rapidly diminish. Men in this group had only a 15% chance of reaching age 90 and their survival chances diminish rapidly after age 92.[14] Over 70% of women surviving to 80-84 years in 2021 are projected to live to be 85-89 years of age in 2026 whereas only 51% of such men are expected to survive to be 85-89 in 2026.[15]

During these elderly years, the economic situation of women is cause for concern. The National Council on Welfare has reported that 25% of aged Canadians live below the poverty line, that the unattached elderly are five times more likely to be poor than the elderly living in families and that most of these unattached elderly are women.[16] Although this figure has improved, falling from 62.2% in 1981, so that by 1985 just over 50% of elderly unattached women were of low income, this figure is still substantially above that of most other major socio-economic groups.[17]

There are two major related reasons for the poor economic situation of many elderly women who were employed during their working years: the low income levels of women during their earning years and their low levels of participation in pension plans. Female workers are statistically unlikely to have access to a pension plan or to be earning enough to make personal arrangements for future income security, even assuming full-time employment. Labour Canada reported that in 1984, 59.5% of working women were employed in clerical, sales and services occupations, a slight decrease from 62.1% in 1982; 7.5% of working women were represented in management and administration, up from 5.6% in 1982.[18] Women's average earned income was consistently below men's in every occupational category in 1982-83. Even in the managerial category, women averaged only 62.1% of men's salaries.[19] Overall, women employed full-time earned an average of 64.0% of men's wages in 1982. These occupational and income statistics suggest that, compared with men, women employed full-time lack the funds required to ensure retirement income security.

As a group, women are also less likely than men to receive a pension. In 1984, the paid labour force numbered 9,334,000; of this group 38.7% women and 54.0% men participated in an employer-sponsored pension plan in December, 1984.[20] Of these 4,397,000 private pension plan members, only 36.8% were women. If full-time employees only are considered, 58.4% of men and 48.1% of women participated in a pension plan.[21] However, women represent only 35.2% of all full-time paid workers who are members of employer-sponsored pension plans.[22]

When part-time paid workers are considered, only 160,000 of the total of 1,538,000 part-time workers are members of a employer-sponsored pension plan.[23] Most of those members or 81.3%, are women.[24] This is still a small number i.e. 130,000, of those women who are part-time paid workers, i.e. 1,091,000. This small number reflects eligibility requirements for pension plan membership which are a function of income levels and hours of employment. The eligibility requirements in Alberta, which are similar to those in most provinces, require annual earnings of 35% of the Year's Maximum Pensionable Earnings (Y.M.P.E. as established under the Canada Pension Plan) and 2 consecutive years of employment.[25] In 1986 eligibility required annual earnings of no less than $9,030.[26] In fact, the average annual earning for a part-time worker is $5,627.96.

It should be noted that minimum wage earners could also fall below the 35% YMPE, even if they work full-time.[27] As more women than men are found in the lower income categories,[28] one may expect more women full-time workers to fail to meet the salary requirement in order to establish eligibility for plan membership.

An examination of the recipients of the Canada Pension Plan reveals that women are less likely to receive these benefits at all or to receive benefits of $200 per month or more. In 1984 women constituted 35.9% of all C.P.P. recipients.[29] C.P.P. monthly benefits of $200 or more were received by 56.2% of all 1984 recipients but only 36.8% of women recipients were in this category as compared to 67% of male recipients.[30]

The women who are most likely to encounter particularly difficult financial problems in old age are those whose marriages have ended by divorce at 40-45 years of age or older. Where those women (and those in cohabitational relationships, as well) have forfeited job skills and career development in favour of child-rearing and homemaking, they will have no personal employment-based pension, either public or private, and little chance of acquiring one. As a result of divorce, these women lose their right to any survivor's benefit arising under a pension plan of which their spouse is a member; a similar result applies to any such rights available to a cohabitor.[31] Thus, for many women, the acquisition of pension assets during the division of spousal property may be particularly important. In the case of married women, this division is governed by provincial matrimonial property statutes. Single women and men may be eligible to share pension credits where the legislation or the plan itself provides for the availability of benefits to cohabiting "spouses". It is of major concern, therefore, to observe that many women fail to recognize the value of the pension benefit accrued during marriage, taking it into account either inadequately or not at all on marriage breakdown.[32]

The Canadian Pension Benefits System

Canada's pensions system consists of plans sponsored by government and by employers. Governmentally-sponsored pension plans are the Canada and Quebec Pension Plans; employer-sponsored plans consist of both public and private plans. In the context of this chapter 1, private pension plans are defined as those funded according to legislation requiring the employer to either pay the necessary sum into a trust fund or to purchase insurance to cover it. Funding ensures that the employees have security of benefits notwithstanding financial insufficiency on the part of the employer. Public pension plans, on the other hand, are exempt from any such legislative funding requirement since the pension benefits under these plans are guaranteed by the government.

Concern that the declining numbers of young working people will be unable to support pension benefits in the future may lead to increased emphasis on private retirement security arrangements and decreased reliance on governmental pensions. Employers and governments may also look towards reduction of their obligations. Such a movement will probably be manifested in labour-management negotiations in both public and private sectors as in, for example, a shift from defined benefit plans to defined contribution plans, a re-examination of indexing and increases in contributor requirements. Thus, required contributions to the Canada Pension Plan are expected to approximately double by 2004, with no increase in benefits.[33]

Rights As Between Cohabitors and Married Spouses

Cohabitation, as distinct from statutory marriage, may entitle the "cohabitors" or "common-law spouses" to certain rights and remedies vis-a-vis each other. The rights and remedies available are determined by the applicable law. Prior to recent reform a cohabitor was legally entitled to little in terms of his or her partner's employment and pension benefits. Thus if a pension plan made no provision for spousal eligibility for a survivors' benefit other than for a statutorily married spouse, a cohabitor received no benefits.

It was perceived as unfair that these benefits were denied to cohabitors in lengthy relationships, whether because of the terms of the particular plan or because of a plan member's actions. Therefore, recent legislative reform has extended survivorship benefits to cover cohabitors in certain circumstances. Priority for survivorship benefits depends on meeting the legislative requirements.

A second aspect of such reform concerns the sharing of pension benefits or pension plan credits between spouses, which in certain circumstances may include cohabitors. These reforms hinge on the broadening of the definition of "spouse" to include cohabitors where specific conditions are met. These reforms have occurred at the federal and provincial levels. They interact with provincial matrimonial property legislation to determine how benefits are dealt with in the context of a statutory marriage upon marriage breakdown, disability or death.

A. Treatment of Survivors' Benefits

The requirements which a cohabitor must meet in order to be eligible for survivors' benefits vary from province to province and between private and public plans within a province; the provincial requirements also differ from those applicable to federal public plans or to the mandatory governmental plans i.e. the Canada Pension Plan and the Quebec Pension Plan. The only consistent requirement for eligibility is that the cohabitees be of opposite sexes. These eligibility requirements focus on such factors as the length of time the cohabitors have lived together, the presence of children or the nature of the relationship, as seen by the couple themselves or as represented to the public.

By way of example, most of Alberta's public pension plans legislation (covering academics, provincial politicians, civil servants, local authorities, police) provide that priority in coverage goes:[34] firstly, to a married spouse living with the plan member at the relevant time or to a married, separated but dependent spouse; secondly, if no such married spouse exists, to a person of the opposite sex, where the couple has, immediately preceding the relevant time, lived together for five years or for two years if they have had a child and the "spouse" has been held out to the community as the consort of the member; thirdly and in last priority, to a married but separated spouse who was not dependent on the member.

Under Alberta private plans, benefits go firstly to a married spouse living with the member at the relevant time.[35] Second priority is accorded to a person of the opposite sex who has lived with the plan member for an immediately preceding three-year period where the spouse has been held out to the community as the consort of the member.

At the federal level, priority for survivors' benefits is first given to a person cohabiting with the member in a conjugal relationship at the time of death, having so cohabited for a continuous period of one year.[36] Second priority goes to a person who is married to the member at the relevant time. Thus, a person married to the member and living with the member at the relevant time would expect first priority.

The difference between the provincial and federal provisions outlined above is that at the provincial level the nature of the non-married relationship is identified solely on the basis of the member's conduct or intention in representing the claimant to the community. This approach formerly existed under other legislation which required that there be "public representation as spouse" by the member of the claimant.[37] This requirement led to two major problems: firstly, where the member, in fact, was married but was cohabiting with the claimant at the time of death and the fact of the existing marriage was known in the community, the cohabitor could not succeed in a claim for survivors' benefits. This resulted regardless of the length of time over which the relationship had prevailed, even were it a 20 year relationship.

The second problem concerned the effect of a claimant's personal or business independence on evidence of public representation by the member. If a woman did not adopt the contributor's surname or parties maintained separate bank accounts, or the live-in spouse was only sometimes referred to as the "wife", the public representation requirement was held not to be met.[38] In many cases, an attempt was made to compare the facts of the case with various indices of "marital life". The difficulty is that many married couples no longer adhere to the types of behaviours expected, under the legislation, of cohabitors. To put it another way, nowadays married couples act like unmarried couples. It is not uncommon for married persons to maintain separate bank accounts and for women to retain their maiden names after marriage. Admittedly, there must be some reliable and consistent means to determine when a relationship takes on a colour of "coupleness" rather than mere shared residency. Yet, it is out of step with current society to expect people who are not married to pretend to be otherwise and to base eligibility for benefits on such a test.

The current federal approach represents a movement away from a situation in which couples living together outside of marriage were essentially required to misrepresent their status to the community for the purpose of obtaining benefits. Legislation which requires a consideration of the relationship as a whole, in which the key issues are cohabitation and conjugality, provides a more honest basis from which to make decisions concerning entitlements to pension benefits.

A further issue concerns the alternative time periods required to establish eligibility for survivors' benefits: two years where there is a child vs. five years where there is not under Alberta's public plans; three years under Alberta's public plans; three years under Alberta's private plans; and, one year under federal legislation. The figures do not appear to have been set according to any criteria. Further, in a society where it is no longer uncommon for people to have a number of semi-permanent live-in partners for varying periods of time, it may be argued that the one-year requirement is too short. Previous case law has made it clear that fairness and equity are irrelevant when determining which party is entitled to receive spousal benefits under the Plan; instead, it is the statutory requirements that determine entitlement. Thus, there are concerns that a short-term cohabiting partner could defeat a claim for survivor benefits made by a long-term married spouse.[39]

These recent changes in federal and provincial pension legislation have made it more likely that cohabitors will share in survivors' benefits. Married persons must be aware of this as one possible result of a lengthy separation. It is yet another effect of marriage breakdown to be taken into account in resolving the marital estate, which should include the need to ensure the equality of the retirement security positions of the parties.

B. Pension Credit-Splitting Between Cohabitors

The value of pension benefits accumulated during the marriage is, as a general rule, subject to division between married persons throughout common law Canada. This occurs either because these benefits constitute matrimonial property persuant to provincial statute or judicial decision or because loss of an interest in the pension, while itself not held to be matrimonial property, is seen as inequitable and to be compensated. However, as yet no provincial matrimonial property statute divides pensions between cohabiting persons.

However, at the federal level in 1986, the Canada Pension Plan was amended to permit the splitting between cohabitors of unadjusted pensionable earnings (or credits) accumulated during the cohabitation based on the same definition of "spouse" as for survivors benefit.[40] This right had been available as between married persons since 1978.

Under the amendments, married or non-married spouses must have cohabited for a continuous period of only one year before they are eligible for a division. In general, in the case of non-married spouses and spouses who have been living separate and apart for one year followed by death, division is subject to Ministerial discretion. This is not required in the case of spouses who divorce or have their marriage annulled.[41]

The most dramatic effect of division of pension credits occurs where one former spouse was a contributor and the other was not and where the marriage lasted over *half* of the total contributory period of the member. In that case a division will radically lower benefits earned by the member.

The amendments may increase the liklihood that cohabitors will share in pension credits accumulated under the Canada Pension Plan during the relationship. The basis upon which Ministerial approval for a division will be granted or withheld is not indicated in the legislation but almost certainly will include a consideration of the facts upon which the application, as a "spouse", is based.

Mechanisms of Valuation & Division: Cost and Convenience vs. Fairness

A major problem with division of pension benefits under the authority of provincial matrimonial property statutes concerns the enforcement of that division. The spouse holding the pension i.e. the member spouse, does not always have sufficient other assets to satisfy the share of the pension to which the non-member spouse is entitled after division. This is particularly likely where the marriage has been lengthy and pension benefits have been accumulating throughout that time.

Until recently, Canadian courts have had little alternative in that circumstance but to issue an order dividing the pension proceeds if and when they are received by the member spouse.[42] Orders of that type tie the parties together in the sense that the non-member spouse is dependent upon the member spouse forwarding to her the correct share of the monthly pension cheque. The non-member spouse must hope that the member spouse choses to pay the correct share as opposed to playing global hide and seek in order to avoid enforcement of the order.[43]

This situation arises because most provincial pension benefits are governed by legislation which renders them immune to attachment, garnishment and other enforcement mechanisms.[44] Pension plan administrators claim to have no legislative responsibility for dividing the benefit and operating a mechanism which would ensure that the non-member spouse receives his or her rightful share of the benefit once it is in pay. The court order or agreement determining the share is of little effect in ensuring actual receipt of the award.

The establishment of such mechanisms has been rejected by plan administrators on the basis that the costs involved are too high as is the inconvenience to the system. However, there is no consensus among administrators as to the costs involved. Nor is it clear why the mere existence of costs is a major hurdle. Perhaps these costs could be borne by the spouses themselves; the expense appears likely to be much less than that resulting from litigation or legal enforcement procedures. Nor is it clear why the inconvenience to plan administrators is so important a consideration as to outweigh the fairness to the spouses most in need of such a system.

Several Canadian provinces and the federal government have enacted legislation going some way towards reducing the problem.[45] This legislation specifies the circumstances in which plan administrators are required to divide the value of the pension benefit, for example, as of the date of a court order or agreement requiring the division. The non-member spouse is generally given some options as to the form in which to take the divided benefit; for example, by directing the fund into a Registered Retirement Savings Fund or by having a retirement annuity purchased with the amount of the benefit. This mechanism represents an improvement over the situation previously described by providing a means of division which separates the spousal interests and avoids the problems of enforcement.

However, these improvements are being accompanied by a substantial reduction in the value of the share assigned to the non-member spouse. This occurs because the regulations provide that the value of the share is to be calculated by the "termination method" of valuation, under which the member is assumed to have terminated employment on the date of valuation of the pension benefit. The termination method of valuation works very well for a particular type of pension plan, the defined contribution type, in which contributions to the benefit are regularly assigned to accounts established for the plan members. The total amount of contributions plus interest in the member's account represents the value of the pension and can be accurately determined at any time.

The termination method of valuation does not work well in regard to a common type of plan, the defined benefit plan. This type of plan is extremely common in Canada among public employees, teachers, university professors, management, legislators and the judiciary. The benefit is defined by a formula which, most commonly, is based on the member's average salary over a specified number of his or her final or best earning years. These years usually are the years immediately prior to retirement. The formula, therefore, ensures that the member begins retirement with a pension which is level with inflation, since a certain component of most salary increases relates to inflation. This (or a hybrid of this type of plan) is the only type of plan providing protection from inflation in the plan structure or formula.

When the termination method of valuation is applied to this type of plan, value is calculated on the salary level the member is then receiving as if the member had terminated employment. In most cases employment is not, in fact, terminated. Thus, the termination method of valuation makes no allowance for the protective aspect of the plan. As has been judicially pointed out, in a plan of this type the early years of employment and contribution establish the base upon which the ultimate value of the benefit rests.[46] Courts ordering a distribution of the proceeds of the pension if and when received have often based the distribution on the actual salary at the time of retirement, rather than at the time of the breakdown of the marriage or of trial.[47]

Use of the termination method of valuation under the new legislative mechanism for dividing pensions will result in a much lower benefit being received by the non-member spouse. This occurs because the benefit in a defined benefit plan increases sharply over the years immediately prior to retirement: a couple divorcing at age 55 could share a much lower pension, were the benefit to be calculated at that time, than if it were calculated at actual retirement at age 65.

An additional problem with the termination method of valuation is that there are different ways of calculating it. The Canadian Institute of Actuaries has recommended a method which would "reflect the employee's full benefit entitlement... at date of termination".[48] This calculation of a termination value would include the value of death benefits and of the value of indexation of the benefit during its life, where those benefits were a part of the benefit contract.

A number of Canadian cases, on the other hand, have calculated termination value by deducting the value of those benefits before calculating the shareable value of the pension benefit. This, again, results in a substantially lowered share of the value of the benefit being provided to the non-member spouse. The member spouse retains for the benefit of his or her estate the value of the death benefit, enjoys the anti-inflationary effect of indexing and, upon retirement, the value of his share of the full benefit built up over the marriage.

In the result, there is a danger that improvements in the method of distribution between spouses of the divided pension will be accompanied by valuation methods that substantially reduce the amount of pension received by the non-member spouse. While the termination method of valuation is being legislatively adopted, it is not clear which method of calculation will be utilized by plan administrators. If they adopt the method which excludes benefits contained in the plan, in fact, the non-member spouse will have been unfairly dealt with at every step of the process. This deletes much of the benefit anticipated from a division of pensions as marital property.

Contracting Out of Pension Division

All provinces permit spouses to contract with each other regarding a division of marital property. This permits a spouse to give up any interest in a pension benefit to which the other spouse is entitled in most of Canada.

The exception to this, at the provincial level, arises in the province of Manitoba and, at the federal level, in the Canada Pension Plan. Manitoba makes an equal division of a pension benefit credit or payment mandatory as between the spouses or parties to a common-law relationship, where the family assets are to be divided by court order or agreement.[49] This reform, however, affects Manitoba residents only and only those plans administered under the Manitoba Act. The Canada Pension Plan, while purporting to permit spouses and cohabitors to waive a division, also appears designed to prevent any such waiver in fact. This less-than-candid policy decision is significant for the millions of spouses and cohabitors across Canada (including those in Manitoba) who are C.P.P. members.

A. The Issue

There are two conflicting policies affecting the contracting-out of pension splitting. On the one hand, there is the principle that competent adults are at liberty to make their own arrangements and that such arrangements, subject to the law of contracts, are enforceable. This argument would permit pension rights to be traded in the context of spousal agreements, as for example, for an immediately available asset. On the other hand, there is the concern that pensions are acquired during a marriage to provide income security for retirement. When pension benefits are given up they are not easily replaced, resulting in the loss of retirement income security for the person who relinquished those rights.

Prior to 1983, under the Canada Pension Plan, where parties had agreed to waive a division of unadjusted pensionable earnings and where, notwithstanding the agreement, one party subsequently applied for the division, departmental officials took the position that the waiver was invalid. In 1983, the matter was settled when the Pension Appeal Board held that a waiver of all present and future rights as between the parties was effective to prevent any division of pension rights.[50] That result was based on a Supreme Court of Canada decision holding that the right to contract is a fundamental principle which can only be affected by express legislation. As there was then no express intention in the Canada Pension Plan to prevent such domestic agreements, a specific agreement expressing the parties' intention to make no further claims on each other would operate to waive division of C.P.P. rights.

Public comment suggested that many of the general waivers of rights were entered without consideration of their effect on the division of rights under the Canada Pension Plan. When the Plan came up for amendment in 1986, the Debate and Committee discussions[51] indicated concern that mandatory division of C.P.P. rights be ensured, with little or no opportunity for waiver of those rights:

> For example, in the case of a marriage breakdown, there are an awful lot of sharp lawyers out there with sharp pencils who attempt to make the pension credit a part of the divorce settlement by offering the woman a lump sum payment rather than the credit. Very often because of the circumstances of the marriage breakdown, the lump sum seems to be attractive at that time. However, when the woman reaches age 65 and discovers how much pension she is about receive, she then questions if it was indeed wise to accept the lump sum payment.[52]

B. The Legislative Response

The C.P.P. amendments at issue arise in ss. 53.3 and 53.4, beginning with 53.3(1) and (1)(a), which provide that a "division of unadjusted pensionable earnings shall take place... following the issuance of a decree absolute, a divorce judgment under the Divorce Act, 1985 and a judgment of nullity." The section also provides for such a division in the context of separation, death and in circumstances affecting cohabitors. For the purposes of division, ss. 53.3(3) and (4) provide that spouses must have cohabited for a continuous period of at least one year and that the period upon which division is calculated encompasses only the months of cohabitation.

There are only two exceptions to this division: the Minister may disallow a division if he is satisfied that the division would be to the detriment of *both* spouses or former spouses (this would seem to be an extremely narrow exception) or where there is a spousal agreement which is binding on the Minister. Court orders or spousal agreements made on or after June 4, 1986, are not binding on the Minister, except as provided in ss. 53.4(3). Since that subsection makes no reference whatever to court orders, it is clear that court orders are ineffective in preventing the division of unadjusted pensionable earnings.

Spousal agreements are defined in section 53.4(1) as agreements made between spouses (including cohabitors) by way of a pre-marriage agreement, a separation agreement or any other agreement, as long as the agreement is entered into before an application for division is made or, where applicable, before the issuance of a decree absolute of divorce, divorce judgment or judgment of nullity.

The only effective spousal agreements are those in compliance with section 53.4(3), which provides as follows:

(3) Where

(a) a spousal agreement entered into on or after June 4, 1986 contains a provision that expressly mentions this Act and indicates the intention of the spouses or former spouses that there be no division of unadjusted pensionable earnings under section 53.2 or 53.3,

(b) provision of the spousal agreement is expressly permitted under the provincial law that governs the spousal agreement, and

(c) that provision of the spousal agreement has not been invalidated by a court order, the Minister shall not make a division under section 53.2 and 53.3.

Compliance with (3)(a) requires only a specific reference to the Canada Pension Plan and the requisite intention; although the specific wording of the section should certainly be adopted, the requirement itself is straight forward. The requirements of (3)(c), that the provision of the spousal agreement has not been invalidated by court order, is equally clear.

The legal issue relates to the meaning of ss. (3)(b). It is at this point that the expressed legislative intention to permit spouses to waive or contract away their C.P.P. rights begins to look less than candid. Is it sufficient if the provincial law referred to is one which permits spousal agreements dealing with property? Such spousal agreements, if formally and essentially valid and in compliance with statutory requirements, are effective in all provinces to waive rights.

However, it is argued that the true meaning of the section is to require provincial law to contain a provision expressly permitting spouses to agree that there is to be no division of unadjusted pensionable earnings under the C.P.P. or its successor. This interpretation would have the factual result of denying the effectiveness of any spousal agreements because no province has yet passed such a provision: therefore, at present, it is impossible for a spousal agreement to meet the requirements of the section. Only one province has introduced a bill containing such a provision.[53] It is considered unlikely that many provincial governments will open up their matrimonial property legislation in order to insert such an amendment because those statutes are seen as politically sensitive.[54]

Some might see the true issue as paternalism arrayed in concern for retirement income security. Those persons concerned for the poverty level of many elderly women stressed the need to ensure that the pressures of marriage breakdown and the little-understood reality of the irreplaceable lost pension benefits, were not working against the party in the weakest bargaining position.[55] Others felt that many other women were losing an element of choice in arranging their affairs. Thus, legislation resulted which purports to address both policies with a foot in each camp.

Conclusion

This chapter has outlined a number of developments in the context of the division between spouses of pension, pension benefits or credits. These developments primarily impinge on the retirement planning of spouses whose marriages are breaking up. The soon-to-be former spouse most seriously affected is the spouse who has chosen the traditional role, exchanging the development of work skills, job seniority, pension and employment benefits for children and homemaking. Where this spouse begins a career after many years of marriage, the lost pension benefits, in particular, will never be recovered. Yet, division of ordinary marital assets does not compensate for this loss and maintenance awards are few in number and low in quantum. Accordingly, in order to avoid a poverty-striken old age, it is particularly important for these women to ensure that a fair share of the pension benefit built up during the marriage is received.

However, most of the developments in the area of pension division seem to operate against that result. On the one hand, cohabitors are being granted access to pension division; the mechanisms of dividing the pension and enforcing that division are slowly being placed in the hands of administrators. These are improvements in the present Canadian system which, in general, will work to benefit the group of poverty-stricken elderly women. On the other hand, these improvements are being accompanied by a reduction in the value of the share assigned to the non-member spouse, again, a disadvantage to this group.

Overall, limitations are being placed on the contractual arrangements permitted those spouses who wish to settle their affairs outside of court. This development has been applauded by some women, criticized by others.

Although there is a lack of consistency among the policy choices being made, it would seem that the interest of the administrator in pursuing efficiency, economy and uniformity is in the ascendency. Arguments on the basis of fairness are receiving less attention.

At the same time, governmental concern over the projected tax burden of an aging population is increasing . This concern may be expected to develop into an emphasis on the accumulation of private resources for retirement security. It will be interesting to see whether that concern translates into a recognition of the need to develop more equitable methods of sharing the existing private retirement resources. At the least, perhaps this increased emphasis will result in an increased awareness among homemakers of the problem; perhaps greater consideration will be give by them to retirement planning in the context of marital separation.

* This paper is based on research supported by the Alberta Law Foundation and by the Women's Division of Labour Canada, Government of Canada.

NOTES

1. S.T. Wargon, "Canada's Families in the 1980s: Crisis or Challenge?"(1987), 17 *Transition*, 10.
2. Statistics Canada, *The Seniors Boom* by Stone L.O. and Fletcher, S. (Hull, Que.: Supply and Services Canada, 1986) at 1.1.
3. *Ibid.*
4. *Supra*, Statistics Canada, n.2 at Chart 1.1.
5. *Ibid.* at Chart 1.2.
6. Wargon, *supra*, note 1.
7. It has been estimated that at present in Canada there are 8.3 workers per retired person whereas by the 1st or 2nd decade of the next century there will be only 3.8 workers.
8. "A Report to the Minister of National Health and Welfare from the Canada Pension Plan Advisory Committee on the Funding of the Canada Pension Plan", tabled in Parliament on March 12, 1985 and reported at C.E.B. & P.G.R. 5532 (hereinafter *Report.*)
9. *The Economist*, reprinted in the *Globe and Mail*, January 26, 1987 at A7.
10. *Ibid.*, *The Economist*.
11. Statistics Canada, *supra*, n.2. at Chart 2.6.3.: in 1956 the ratio of women to men was 125:100 in the 75 and older group whereas in 1981 the ratio was 195:100.
12. Statistics Canada, *ibid.*
13. Statistics Canada, *ibid.*, at 3.4. The effective human life span, once thought to be fixed, may now be on the rise: "the effective human life span is the age to which the hardiest one-tenth of one percent (1 in 1000) of a birth cohort will survive and may well be between 95 and 100 years of age."
14. Statistics Canada, *ibid.*
15. Statistics Canada, *ibid.*, at 3.5.
16. National Council on Welfare, "Sixty-five and Older" (1984). Reported in C.E.B. & P.G.R. 5511.

17. Methot, Suzanne, "Low Income in Canada", *Canadian Social Trends*, Spring, 1987, at 6.
18. Labour Canada, *Women In the Labour Force* (1985-86) at XXV.
19. *Ibid.*, Table II-4 at 46.
20. *Ibid.*, at Table IV-5 at 81. These figures relate to plans sponsored by both public and private sector employers and exclude the self-employed.
21. *Ibid.*, at Table IV-6 at 82.
22. *Ibid.*, Table IV-6.
23. *Ibid.*, Table IV-7 at 83.
24. *Ibid.*
25. *Employment Pension Plans Act* S.A. s.22; 350 hours of employment for each of two consecutive plan years applies to multi-employer pension plans in lieu of the requirement of two years of employment.
26. This figure is calculated on the average 15.8 hours/week worked by part-time workers in 1984 and the average salary of $5627.96, as reported in 1986 by Statistics Canada.
27. At Alberta's minimum wage rate of $3.80/hour, a person working a 40-hour work week would have annual earnings calculated at $7,904.
28. Labour Canada, *Women in the Labour Force* 1986-87 ed. (Supply and Services, Canada), Table II-8 at 50: the categories are under $5000, $5000-$9999, $10,000 to $14,999, $15,000 to $19,999.
29. Labour Canada, *ibid.*, Table IV-4 at 92, showing 381,691 women recipients: 682,893 men recipients.
30. Labour Canada, *ibid.*, Table IV-5 at 93; in 1985 only 40.1% of female recipients were in this category compared to 71.2% of male recipients.
31. As a result of recent legislative reform, cohabitors who qualify as spouses and whose relationship has not terminated may be eligible in some circumstances for a survivor's benefit.
32. Pask, E. Diane, "Pension Plans and Employee Contributions: *Tutiah* v. *Tutiah*" (1986), XXXIV *Alta. L. Rev.* 530.
33. Report, *supra*, note 8 at 5534.
34. *Universities Academic Pension Plan Act*, S.A. 1985, c. U-6.1, s.1(u); *Local Authorities Pension Plan Act*, S.A. 1985, c. L-28.1, s.1(t); *Members of the Legislative Assembly Pension Plan Act*, S.A.1985, c. M-12.5, s.1(1)(u);*Public Service Management Pension Plan Act*, S.A.1984, c. P-34.1, s.1(1)(s); *Special Forces Pension Plan Act*, S.A. 1985, c. S-21.1, S. 1(1)(v). This provision is not found in the *Teachers Retirement Fund Act*, R.S.A. 1980, c. T-2 or the pension scheme approved by Cabinet under the *Alberta Government Telephones Act*, R.S.A. 1980, c. A-23.
35. Plans sponsored by private employers are governed by the *Employment Pension Plans Act*, S.A. 1986, C.E-10.05, s.1(1)(hh).
36. *Canada Pension Plan*, R.S.C. 1970, c. C-5, s. 2(1) as amended by *An Act to Amend the Canada Pension Plan and the Federal Court Act* S.C. 1986, c.38, s.2(1) applicable in s.56; *Pension Benefits Standards Act*, *1985*, s.c. 1986, c.40, s. 2(1).
37. *Canada Pension Plan* , R.S.C. 1970, c. C-5, s. 63(2).
38. *E.g., Minister of National Health and Welfare* v. *Akiko Szekeley et al.*(1983), C.E.B. & P.G.R. #8915 (P.A.B.); *Minister of National Health and Welfare* v. *Patricia Kresnick et al.* (1985), C.E.B. & P.G.R. #8960 (P.A.B.); *Minister of National Health and Welfare* v. *Helen P. Green et al.*(1986), C.E.B. & P.G.R. #8969 (P.A.B.); but see, *contra, Minister of National Health and Welfare* v.

Jacqueline E. Brodie (1985), C.E.B. & P.G.R. #8959 (P.A.B.).

39. Canada Pension Plan, R.S.C. 1970, c. C-5, s.2(1) as amended. The rights of the married spouse are not clear although an application for division of the pension credits earned during the marriage might leave the cohabitor to obtain a survivors' benefit calculated on only the one-half of the credits belonging to the deceased member spouse.

40. Canada Pension Plan, R.S.C. 1970, c. C-5, s.2(1) and s. 53.3, as amended.

41. *Canada Pension Plan, ibid.*, the section defines living separate and apart in language similar to that found in the *Divorce Act, 1985*.

42. *Rutherford* v. *Rutherford* [1981] 6 W.W.R. 485 (B.C.C.A.); additional reasons [1983] (1981) 44 B.C.L.R. 279 (B.C.C.A.); *McAlister* v. *McAlister* [1983] 2 W.W.R. 8 (Alta. Q.B.) app'd in *Herchuk* v. *Herchuk* (1984) 38 R.F.L. (2d) 240 (Alta. C.A.). It is noted that by that time the member will be a "former-spouse", since a divorce will have been completed.

43. Some protection for the non-member's interest can be provided through use of a bond or life insurance policy but these techniques have their own drawbacks.

44. Legislation permitting the garnishment of pensions in pay in order to satisfy maintenance orders does not assist when the order is made under the jurisdiction of an order for division of marital property.

45. *Pension Benefits Act* R.S.M. 1987, c. P32; *Pension Benefits Act*, S.N.B. 1987, c. P-5.1, to come into force upon proclamation; *Pension Benefits Act*, S.N.S. 1987, c. 11; *Pension Benefits Act, 1987*, S.O. 1987, c. 35; *Pension Benefits Standards Act*, 1985, S.C. 1986, c.40.

46. *George* v. *George* (1983) 35 R.F.L. (2d) 225 (Man. C.A.).

47. *E.g.Herchuk* vs. *Herchuk* (1983) 35 R.F.L. (2d) 327 (Alta. C.A.).

48. Report of the Council of the Canadian Institute of Actuaries (Toronto, 1987) setting out standards for the calculation of a minimum transfer value which is, essentially, a termination value.

49. *An Act to Amend the Pension Benefits Act* c.79, S.M. 1982-83-84, P.32, s.27(2) assented to Aug. 18, 1983, now the *Pension Benefits Act* R.S.M. 1987, c. P-32, s. 31(2). S. 1(2) provides that "parties to a common-law relationship" are those who file a declaration to that effect with the pension plan administrator; the *Pension Benefits Act Regulation* Man. Reg. 188/87R, gazetted June 6, 1987 and effective May 25, 1987 provides that a division for the purposes of ss. 27(2) (now s.31(2)) of the Act shall be equal and shall apply only to credits and payments accrued from the date the marriage or common-law relationship began.

50. *Minister of National Health and Welfare* v. *Preece* (1983) C.E.B. & P.G.R. #8914.

51. Canada, *House of Commons Debates*, 1st Session, 33rd Parliament, Vol. 10 at 14251 (11 June 1986) and 14877 (26 June 1986) Canada House of Commons; *Minutes of the Proceedings and Evidence of the Standing Committee on National Health and Welfare* at 6:5-6:34 (13 June 1986).

52. H.C., *ibid.* at 14259.

53. A bill has been introduced in Saskatchewan which may be intended to address this problem: Bill 92, *An Act to Amend the Matrimonial Property Act*, 1st Session, 21st Leg. Sask., 1987 (first reading October 1987). The relevant section provides as follows:

    4(1) Without limiting the generality of subsection (4), an interspousal contract entered into on or after June 4, 1986 may provide that, notwithstanding the *Canada Pension Plan*, as amended from time to time, there may be less than an equal division or no division between the parties of unadjusted pensionable earnings pursuant to that Act.

54. There is also an interpretation which would argue that the express provision, required in provincial law, need only refer to pensions and not to the C.P.P. As a few provinces would qualify, some waivers would be effective.

55. Standing Committee, *supra*, note 51 at 6:6.

Chapter 53

Providing for the surviving spouse under the German law of social security

Rainer FRANK

Institute für ausländisches v.
Internationales Privatrecht der
Universität Freiburg, West Germany

Providing for the surviving spouse under German Private Law

In the vast majority of cases the wife survives her husband. Therefore, the question of providing for the surviving spouse is primarily a question of providing for the widow. Historically, this matter was regulated by private law. Children and other relatives took care of aged people who did not have sufficient income of their own. Even today private law continues to play a subordinate role in regulating provision for the aged in general and the surviving spouse in particular.

Firstly, under the *law of inheritance* the surviving spouse receives a share of the deceased's estate. Like children, the spouse as an heir-at-law is entitled to one-quarter of the estate. Furthermore, it is not uncommon for spouses to name each other as sole heir in their wills.

Over and above this, under the *law of property* the survivor is, as a rule, entitled to a share of the wealth acquired by the spouse during the marriage. The statutory status of property in community of accrued gain provides for the division at the end of marriage of any gain which accrues during the marriage to either the husband or the wife into two equal halves. If the marriage is ended by death, under the provisions of the law of property the statutory share of the inheritance of the surviving spouse is increased by one-quarter. The surviving spouse thus receives, apart from the quarter under the law of inheritance mentioned above, another quarter under the law of property, i.e. in total one-half of the estate.

However, neither the law of inheritance nor the law of property makes any provision for the maintenace of the surviving spouse when the deceased leaves little or no property.

This raises the question of whether in private law the widow or widower has a *claim to maintenance* against relations, in particular against sons and daughters. This is indeed the case. The German Civil Code of 1900 not only establishes a parental duty to maintain children but, conversely, also a filial duty towards parents. However, this duty lapses when the sons and daughters need their available means to maintain their own families at a reasonable standard of living. For spouses and relations in the descending line have a stronger claim to maintenance than relations in the ascending line. Besides, a parent's claim to maintenance presupposes need, and persons are not in need when a national pension scheme puts them in a position reasonably to maintain themselves. Therefore, the following considerations will concentrate on how the German pensions system provides for the surviving spouse.

The basis of the German law of social security

Notwithstanding criticism within the Federal Republic itself, in the rest of the world the German social security system is regarded as comprehensive and functional. It is primarily *financed by contributions*. The Federal government subsidizes the pension fund to the equivalent of about 16% of pension expenditure.[1]

a) As in other industrialized countries, the German pension system was introduced towards the end of the last century, as the first industrial revolution approached its peak and in the process the extended family network gradually broke down.[2] Every wage-earner automatically became a member of the newly created statutory pension fund. Most members were male. In accordance with the statutory provisions of the time, women had to keep house and take care of the children. Even among the working class only about 25% of women were wage-earners.

Only those who themselves had earned their living as workers or salaried employees were entitled to an old-age pension; usually it was the husband. As long as he lived, worked or later drew an old-age or disability pension he had to maintain his wife with the means at his disposal. When he died, his widow was left without any insurance. Regardless of her age and the number of dependent children, she was now suddenly forced to find employment.

The first step towards alleviating this situation was taken in 1912, when *widows of salaried employees* were granted a pension equal to 40% of that of the husband to compensate for maintenance lost through the husband's death. Initially, *widows of workers* were granted a similar pension on condition that they themselves were incapable of gainful employment. Only in 1949 was an unconditional pension introduced for this class of widow. Henceforth, the law of social security effectively guaranteed the wife's right to maintenance, as anchored in the Civil Code, for the rest of her life. Today, widows of workers and salaried employees receive a pension equal to 60% of that of their husband. We shall return to this point below.

b) Although the system of old age insurance has been largely standardized in the course of its history, it still appears confusing on account of the *variety of statutory sources* and a mass of regulations governing detail. The reasons for this confusing variety of statutory regulations are chiefly historical. The introduction of and improvements to obligatory insurance for employees was a complicated process which differed in time and speed from occupation to occupation. Even today there are still different statutory regulations for the old-age pensions of civil servants, workers, salaried employees, miners, and so on.

The keystone of the old age pension system in the Federal Republic is the statutory *national pension scheme for workers and salaried employees.* It encompasses nearly all of the more than 20 million workers and salaried employees, and thus about 80% of the economically active population. Only a few persons with high incomes may be exempted from obligatory membership at their own request. For the sake of simplicity, the following will refer only to the statutory national pension scheme for workers and salaried employees.

Apart from the national pension scheme for workers and salaried employees, there are also company pension schemes, state civil service pension funds and pension schemes of the various trades and professions.[3]

Company pension schemes have a considerably longer tradition than statutory social security. Today they play only a supplementary role, filling gaps where the statutory national pension scheme provides inadequate compensation for income earned while economically active. Company pension schemes are financed by voluntary contributions from employers. About half of all employees in the private sector enjoy such benefits.

The *state civil service pension funds* provide old age pensions for more than two million civil servants as well as supplementary old-age benefits for a part of those government employees without full civil servant status whose pension is paid by the national pension fund.

The *pension schemes of the trades and professions* guarantee the pensions of professional people. Medical doctors and pharmacists, for instance, have to contribute to the security fund of their respective associations. Certain states in the Federal Republic have recently introduced a similar requirement for lawyers. Artists are now also liable to pension contributions as well. Farmers, artisans and miners now also have their own pension schemes. However, compulsory old age insurance in the latter occupations is conceived of as the basis for a minimum pension, which needs to be supplemented by individual pension arrangements.

Nowadays, only about 3-4% of the retired population in the Federal Republic lives off largely private means (life insurance, savings, rents, leases, etc.).

The gainfully employed spouse's pension in his own right

Every spouse in gainful employment acquires a right to his or her own pension. If both spouses work, each acquires a right to his or her own pension. The death of one spouse in no way affects the continuance of the survivor's pension in his own right.

The old age pension should enable the insured person to maintain a reasonable standard of living after retirement. A person's standard of living during employment depends on the individual's current income. The person's pension is oriented to this: the function of the pension is to *compensate earnings,* not to provide a general minimum basic security in old age.[4] In accordance with this compensatory function, the individual's contribution to the pension fund is income-related, namely a percentage of income. This percentage is the same for all insured persons. In the case of employees, the employer and the employee each pay half of the contribution, i.e. at present 9.6% respectively.

The size of the pension does not depend only on the level of earnings but also on the *length of the credit period,* i.e. the number of years prior to retirement for which contributions have been paid. An individual participates through contributions in the the communal solidarity of all insured persons. This participation may be adversely affected by events for which the individual is not or is only partly responsible, but which render him unable to meet his contributions in full or part for a period of time. Under certain conditions, such as military service or temporary disability due to accident or illness, such periods are credited in full towards the person's pension rights. The condition for an old age pension is a minimum credit period of fifteen years.

Finally, the size of the pension is also determined by an annual adjustment to changes in the general level of income *('indexed' or 'dynamic pension').* Thus, old age pensions are increased not only to compensate for inflation but also when the average income of the economically active population grows with general economic development. After forty years of pension contributions, an insured person who has always earned an average income can draw a pension equal to about 60% of current average earnings. Hence, the annual pension adjustment protects the living standards of pensioners, which would otherwise fall relatively as prices and incomes rise.

Hence, under German law, it would appear that providing for the surviving spouse does not create any problems, provided that both spouses are or were economically active. But this is not always the case. Pension statistics show that the *average pension of women* is *considerably lower* than that of men. In 1987, for instance, the average male pensioner drew DM 1,572 but the average female pensioner only DM 547.[5] What are the reasons for this difference?

The first lies in the number of paid-up years, one decisive determinant of the size of a person's pension. Married women in general pay contributions for considerably fewer years than men. For women often give up work temporarily or permanently to bring up children and, thus, work just long enough to fulfil the requirements for a minimum pension.[6]

The second reason lies in the level of monthly income, the other decisive determinant of the size of a person's pension. The average monthly income of women is lower than that of men for various reasons. Many women prefer part-time work. In addition, a proportion of women are in lower-paid jobs, both because many, in particular older women, are less educated and because the period of leave to bring up children makes it difficult to find an equally or better paying job later. Over and above these, the cumulative effects of earlier wage-discrimination against women still depresses the size of their pensions.

Despite lengthy credit periods, many pensions, especially those of women, are often even lower than welfare benefits. To help redress this situation, in 1973 the legislator compensated disadvantages arising from wage-discrimination by the so-called pension for minimum income.[7] This is not a minimum pension. To improve the position of these pensioners (mostly, but not exclusively women) the basis for calculating pensions was amended. Instead of calculating pensions on the basis of the individual's average actual annual wage-income of all years for which obligatory social insurance contributions were paid, calculations were henceforth based on an average minimum annual income equal to 75% of the average earnings of all insured persons.

The pensions of working women were further improved by the *Pension Reform of 1986*, which recognizes periods spent on bringing up children as counting towards pension rights.[8] Women's pension credit periods are generally shorter than men's because bringing up children prevents them from working away from home. But in respect of the national pension scheme there is a direct relationship between bringing up children and the system of social security in old age. For each successive generation bears the burden of providing for the older generation retiring from gainful employment. Accordingly, bringing up children is similar in function to contributing financially to the national pension scheme. Admittedly, the 1986 reform has only marginally improved the position of wives and mothers who bring up children: their pension rights are credited with 1 year for every child they bring up. In terms of its effects on pension qualifications and improvements this *contribution-free child-care-year* is equivalent to any other year credited on the basis of some other activity requiring obligatory insurance.

The child-care periods are included in pension calculations on the basis of 75% of the average earnings of all insured persons. At present this corresponds to a monthly pension increase of about DM 25 per child. Both fathers and mothers are equally entitled to claim this so-called baby year. If they take care of the child together the right accrues to the mother unless the couple make a declaration to the contrary.

Recognizing child-care periods as a basis for pension rights within the statutory national pension system appears to be a suitable step towards the frequently proclaimed *goal of independent social security for women*. However, all efforts to improve the position of women keeping house and bringing up children will not produce the desired equality between men and women in the German national pension scheme so long as those activities are not credited in full as qualifications for pension rights.[9] But at present a special pension for housewives cannot be financed. The obligation to pay pension contributions for the housekeeping spouse would be an unbearable burden for the family because the contributions would have to be paid by the single breadwinner. The contribution for the gainfully employed spouse's own pension is already 19.2% of his income, compared to 10% in 1949. All indications are that this rate will rise in the coming years. If one considers that this contribution would have to be doubled to finance an additional pension for the housekeeping spouse, it is easy to see that this would be beyond the means of the average family.

If the housekeeping wife cannot acquire her won pension, this raises the question of whether, through her husband, she can acquire rights to a widow's pension which adequately provides for her old age.

The derived pension for surviving spouses prior to the reform of 1986

A. Widow's pension

The widows of gainfully employed workers and salaried employees receive a pension *equal to 60% of the pension of the deceased husband*. This so-called "derived widow's pension" is based on the gainful employment of the husband and is quite independent of any additional pension to which the widow may be entitled on the basis of her own gainful employment. Thus, *numerous widows receive two pensions*.

Surviving spouses receive a pension only if the deceased was already entitled to a social security pension at the time of his death, or if he had a credit period through contributions, or equivalent substitutes, of five years.[10] The length of the marriage is immaterial. Even marriages validly contracted on the death bed create a right to the full widow's pension.

During the first three months after the death of the spouse the widow receives the full pension of the deceased. The reduction from 100% to 60% takes place after this three-month period. Once the three-month mourning period is passed, German law distinguishes between *a full and a reduced widow's pension*.[11] The full widow's pension is the rule. It is equal to *60% of the full pension* of the deceased, i.e. 60% of the pension that the deceased actually received after reaching the age of retirement, or which he would have received had he been prematurely disabled. The widow is entitled to the full widow's pension provided that she is at least 45 or though younger, has to bring up at least one child under the age of 18, or is herself disabled or incapable of earning a living. If the widow is younger than 45, is neither disabled nor incapable of earning a living, nor has to bring up young children, she receives only the reduced widow's pension. The reduced widow's pension is also equal to *60%* of her deceased husband's pension; but it is calculated on the basis *of a much reduced part-pension* and is therefore smaller than the full widow's pension. The reform of 1986 has not affected the distinction between the full and the reduced widow's pension. In 1987, the average full-widow's pension was DM 922, the average reduced-widow's pension DM 319.

B. Widower's pension

Whereas before the pension reform of 1986 every married woman received a widow's pension equal to 60% of the pension her husband was or would have been entitled to, the widower of a gainfully employed woman was entitled to a pension only if his insured wife had been *largely responsible for maintaining the family*.[12] Accordingly, until 1986, widows received 99.8% of the pensions paid out to surviving spouses, and widowers only 0.2%.

The *differences in conditions governing the pension rights of widows and widowers* were rooted in the law of maintenance as conceived of in the German Civil Code. Under the law of equality of 1957, the spouses had a duty to maintain each other. However, as a rule, the wife had to fulfil her duty by keeping house, the husband, by contrast, through gainful employment. The intention of widows' and widowers' pensions respectively was to compensate for economic loss incurred by one spouse through the death of the other. Although housework and gainful employment were formally recognized as equal, because of the statutory separation of roles, economic loss was typically incurred by women. In the case of husbands, the lost 'maintenance benefits' of a personal nature resulting from the death of the wife were, as a rule, offset by cessation of maintenance payments for the deceased. On the other hand, the wife's housewifely benefits which her husband had enjoyed now became economicaly irrelevant through his death, and could not be economically realized elsewhere. The cessation of her housewifely benefits did not offset her economic loss of the husband's monetary benefits. Accordingly, the death of the spouse incurred an economic loss for women alone. At any rate, this was the justification for judgments of the Constitutional Court in cases dealing with the differences in conditions governing the rights of surviving spouses in the 1950s and again in 1963.

However, by the 1970s this view of married women as housewives—upon which the distinction between widows' and widowers' pensions was based—no longer reflected reality nor, later, the legal position. Already by 1975, 40% of all married German women were gainfully employed. The 1976 reform of marriage and family law finally abandoned the view of married women as housewives: henceforth, in terms of the German Civil Code, the spouses settled the running of the household by mutual agreement, and in principle both had the right to gainful employment.

Thus, it is not surprising that reservations about the constitutional validity of differences in conditions governing widows' and widowers' pensions increased. Finally, in an action brought by a man in 1975, the Constitutional Court had to examine whether the above-mentioned legal position on pensions was prejudiced against men because wives were always entitled to a pension on the death of the gainfully employed husband, whereas husbands were only so entitled when the wife had been largely responsible for the maintenance of the family.[13]

C. The mandate for reform from the Constitutional Court

Although the Constitutional Court did not render the existing legal provision void, it gave the legislator a mandate to reform the law on surviving spouses by the end of 1984 in a way that removed any unequal treatment whatsoever of the persons affected. At the same time such a reform should facilitate independent social insurance for women. Although married women, especially if gainfully employed, were legally in a better position than men — for as surviving spouses they always derived pension rights from their husbands and under certain circumstances received a pension in their own right as well — the value of their claims were on average considerably lower than those of men. Widows who were not entitled to a pension in their own right received only a widow's pension equal to 60% of that of the deceased husband, whereas after the death of his wife a man continued to draw 100% of his pension. In the meantime, more than one-third of all women drawing a widow's pension under the national pension scheme were also drawing a pension in their own right. But the total pension income of even these women with two pensions was on average lower than that of men because their pensions in their own right were so low that even together with their widow's pension equal to 60% of that of their husband's they did not receive as much as the husband's full pension of 100%. Statistics from the mid-1970s show that the total income from pensions of widows drawing both a widow's pension and a pension in their own right was on average 10% lower than the pensions of widowers, who received only the pension in their own right.[14]

Hence, a large percentage of widows had to rely on welfare benefits. In the Federal Republic of Germany, any person who is unable to earn enough to cover his basic needs has a right to welfare benefits.[15] At present the maximum level of these benefits is DM 410 per month for single persons. Persons over the age of 65 receive an additional 20%, i.e. a maximum amount of just under DM 500. In addition, the cost of accommodation is borne by the social welfare department. Although welfare benefits are intended to enable the recipients to preserve their self-esteem, they are widely criticized as inadequate. In practice, a person has to apply for welfare benefits, and, in keeping with the principle of secondary liability, they are granted only after relatives liable to maintain the applicant have proved that they are unable to provide support. It is estimated that the combined effect of both these facts discourages about half the persons entitled to welfare benefits from applying for them. The consequence is widespread poverty among widows in old age. Hence the 1986 reform of the law on surviving spouses aimed not only at creating a social security system for surviving spouses which conformed to the principle of equality, but also at facilitating independent social security for women.

Providing for the surviving spouse after the 1986 reform

The pension reform of 1986 removed the *inequalities in the treatment of widows and widowers*. Henceforth, just as widows had been entitled to a pension of 60% on the death of the husband, so widowers are similarly entitled to a pension of 60% on the death of the wife without having to satisfy additional conditions.

Had this provision become law without any other corrections, the pension rights of widows would not have changed at all, whereas those of widowers would have been considerably improved. The costs incurred would have placed a considerable additional burden on the national pension fund, whose reserves have been causing concern for a number of years. Although the provisions of the reform establish that widows and widowers derive the right to a pension under the same conditions after the death of the spouse, to avoid additional costs a provision was introduced in terms of which an individual's own income — thus including a pension in one's own right beyond a certain level — is taken into account in calculating the pension of the surviving spouse.[16] This is new. Previously, a pension in one's own right and a derived pension were granted absolutely independently and without any deductions on account of each other.

The details of the new provision are as follows:

If a person's pension in his or her own right or any other income lies below a limit of, at present, DM 900 per month — plus, in the event of children, an additional allowance of about DM 190 per child — there are no deductions. 40% of all income above this limit is deducted from the widow's or widower's pension.

Example: A widow draws a pension in her own right of DM 500 and a derived widow's pension of DM 1000.

As her pension in her own right lies below the free allowance of DM 900, there are no deductions. Thus, the widow receives DM 1000 + DM 500 = DM 1,500 per month.

Example: A widow draws a pension in her own right of DM 1000 and a derived widow's pension of DM 1000 as well.

Here her pension in her own right exceeds the free allowance of DM 900. 40% of the amount exceeding the limit of DM 900, i.e. 40% of DM 100 = DM 40, is deducted from her widow's pension. Thus, the widow receives her own pension of DM 1000 and a widow's pension of DM 1000 − DM 40 = DM 960, i.e. together DM 1,960.

In both examples it is immaterial whether the surviving spouse is a widow or a widower.

All in all, the 1986 reform has improved the position of widowers, as henceforth it is easier for them to drive a pension from the gainful employment of their wives.[17] In actual fact, though, the husbands' pensions in their own right are usually so large that, under the new system of deduction, they receive precious little of their derived widower's pension.

The 1986 reform has worsened the financial situation of a portion of widows. Whereas previously there was no restriction on widows drawing both a pension in their own right and a surviving spouse's pension, henceforth they have to reckon with deductions from their derived pension equal to 40% of the amount by which their pension in their own right exceeds DM 900 (plus DM 190 per child). However, this provision only affects female pensioners who have a relatively high income in their own right.

This development to the prejudice of widows has been partially alleviated by the above-mentioned recognition of the so-called baby year in calculating widows' pensions in their own right. The results of the 1986 reform can be broadly summarized in two sentences. The unequal treatment of widows' and widowers' statutory pension rights has been redressed. *Yet the provision for widows has not been improved*, and to this extent the Constitutional Court's 1976 mandate for reform has not been fulfilled.

Thoughts on improving the provision for housekeeping spouses

Civil law recognizes the *equality of housekeeping and gainful employment*. This is particularly apparent in the law relating to property between husband and wife. The statutory *status of property in community of accrued gain* is based on the general consideration that both partners are responsible in equal parts for accrued gain and loss of assets during marriage — irrespective of which partner is gainfully employed and which not. Accordingly, when the marriage ends, accrued gain and loss are halved. The *equalization of pension rights* is based on a similar consideration. But it is practised only in the event of divorce. Retirement pension expectancies accruing during marriage to one or both partners are also halved in the event of divorce. Thus, each partner is later entitled to a pension of equal size relative to the duration of the marriage. However, in the absence of divorce the housekeeping spouse derives only a right to a pension of 60% after the death of the spouse, whereas the gainfully employed spouse draws his or her full pension both before as well as after the death of the spouse. Because, as a rule, the wife keeps house, this provision of the existing law on social security works primarily to the prejudice of widows. It is *incompatible with the principle of equality between housekeeping and gainful employment*.

It is generally recognized that the German national pension scheme is in need of reform. However, any attempt to improve the pension rights of the housekeeping spouse raises almost insuperable financial problems. The national pension scheme has no leeway at present. On the contrary: since 1977 the discussion on reform of the national pension scheme has centred on the fund's *financial difficulties*. The roots of these financial difficulties are obvious. The Federal Republic of Germany has one of the lowest birth rates in the world. The number of births per annum has declined from 812,835 in 1950 to 625,963 in 1986. The average life expectancy, on the other hand, has risen from 64.56 years in 1950 to 77.79 in 1984. As a result of this change in the demographic structure, every two economically active persons are supporting one pensioner. In 1957 this ratio was was 3:1. Projections for 2035 give a ratio of 1:1. The high unemployment rate (almost 10% in 1987) adds a further burden to the national pension scheme since unemployed persons do not pay any social security contributions whatsoever.

Under present conditions, any reform of the national pension scheme must be *'financially neutral'*. That is, any improvement in the pensions of housekeeping spouses should not further burden the pension fund as a whole. There are two conceivable solutions to the dilemma:

1. Contributions are raised to cover the additional costs. This possibility is generally rejected because the current burden of old-age pension contributions is already very high for families and will have to be increased in coming years in any case.

2. The only solution which remains is the *model of a more equitable redistribution of the benefits* which the national pension scheme is currently in a position to offer. Any improvement in the pension of the housekeeping spouse — and one must be frank about this — can only be made at the expense of the pension of the gainfully employed spouse.

With this in mind, the federal government appointed a *commission of experts* to consider the matter in 1979. It submitted the following *proposal*:

As long as both spouses are still alive, the present provisions of the law should continue to hold; viz only the gainfully employed should receive a pension in their own right. As long as a marriage exists this provision is acceptable, because the right to maintenance in private law ensures an equitable distribution of all the available means within the family.

After the death of one spouse, the retirement pension expectancies accruing to both spouses during the marriage should be consolidated into a single retirement pension equal to 70 or 75%. Thus, the surviving spouse should 'participate' in the consolidated pension rights accruing from the marriage (the so-called *'participatory pension'*).[18]

Example: The husband has acquired a retirement pension expectancy of DM 2000. The wife was never gainfully employed.

After the death of the husband, the wife would have a pension in her own right of 70 or 75% (= DM 1400 or 1500). Similarly, after the death of the wife the pension of the husband would be reduced to DM 1400 or 1500.

Note that the consolidated retirement pension is based only on those retirement pension expectancies which accrued during the marriage. Retirement pension expectancies which accrued before marriage would remain the right of the spouse to whom they had accrued.

Example: The husband had worked for 10 years before he married. In this period he acquired a retirement pension expectancy of DM 400 per month. During the same period the woman he subsequently married had also worked and acquired a retirement pension expectancy of DM 300 per month.

The consolidated retirement pension for the husband or the wife is based only on the retirement pension expectancies acquired during the marriage. The antenuptial retirement pension expectancy of DM 400 accrues only to the husband, that of DM 300 only to the wife.

The advantage of this model is that the housekeeping spouse is not at a disadvantage compared with the gainfully employed spouse. He acquires a pension in his own right for keeping house, possibly in combination with his own gainful employment.

The disadvantage of this solution, however, is that the situation of the housekeeping spouse is improved at the expense of the gainfully employed. For, at the death of the housekeeping spouse the formerly gainfully employed husband no longer receives — as at present — the full pension but only a reduced pension of 70 or 75% and is thus worse off than a person who has never married and in consequence retains his full pension until the end of his life. Furthermore, this model may also be to the disadvantage of the housekeeping spouse himself, who, under existing law, always receives 60% of the full pension of the deceased spouse. In the individual case, 60% of the full pension (based on gainful employment before *and* during the marriage) may exceed 75% of the retirement pension expectancy acquired during the marriage.

Example: If the widow has no retirement pension expectancy, but the deceased husband one of DM 1000, under existing law the woman would receive a pension for surviving spouses of 60% of DM 1000 = DM 600. Should the man have accrued DM 400 of his expectancy before and DM 600 during the marriage, then 75% of the DM 600 expectancy accrued during marriage would be only DM 450 (as compared with DM 600 under existing law).

The commission of experts developed several alternative solutions to reduce these disadvantages, none of which, however, was financially neutral. Ultimately, the planned reform foundered for this reason.

Because of the general financial situation it is unlikely that a comprehensive reform of the national pension scheme will be tackled in the near future. Nonetheless, there is widespread consensus on the long-term objective: it should make no difference to the old-age pension of the surviving spouse whether he kept house or was gainfully employed.

Notes

1. For the financing of the national pension scheme in general see *Pelikan*, Rentenversicherung, 6th ed., 1986, pp. 68ff.; for Federal subsidies, p. 71.
2. On the history of old age insurance see *Köhler/Zacher*, Ein Jahrhundert Sozialversicherung in der Bundesrepublik Deutschland, Frankreich, Großbritannien, Osterreich und der Schweiz, 1981.
3. Cf. *Hilfer*, Das System sozialer Alterssicherung in der Bundesrepublik Deutschland, 1982, pp. 55ff.
4. On the basic concepts of pension calculation see *Hilfer*, op. cit., pp. 23ff.
5. Survey of pensions in Verband Deutscher Rentenversicherungsträger, Statistik Rentenbestand am 1. Januar 1987, Übersicht.
6. For an analysis of the causes of lower pensions for women see Sachverständigenkommission für die soziale Sicherung der Frau und der Hinterbliebenen, Vorschläge zur sozialen Sicherung der Frau und der Hinterbliebenen, Gutachten der Sachverständigenkommission, pp. 20ff.
7. *Pelikan*, op. cit., pp. 449ff.
8. See *Kaltenbach/Clausing*, Das neue Rentenrecht 1986, 1985.
9. On the model of obligatory insurance for the housekeeping spouse see Sachverständigenkommission für die soziale Sicherung der Frau und der Hinterbliebenen, op. cit., pp. 44f.
10. On the conditions necessary to claim a surviving dependant's pension see *Pelikan*, op. cit., pp. 314ff.
11. *Pelikan*, op. cit., pp. 315ff.
12. On the widow's pension under the old law see *Pelikan*, op. cit., pp. 351ff.
13. BVerfGE 39, 169.
14. Sachverständigenkommission für die soziale Sicherung der Frau und der Hinterbliebenen, op. cit., p. 28.
15. *Hilfer*, op. cit., pp. 96ff.
16. *Kaltenbach/Clausing*, op. cit., pp. 12ff.
17. On the distributive effects of the reform see *Michaelis*, Renten für Witwen und Witwer, 1985, pp. 13f.
18. Sachverständigenkommission für die soziale Sicherung der Frau und der Hinterbliebenen, op. cit., pp. 47ff.

Chapter 54

Disability Pensioning and the Elderly: An Analysis of Legal Rules and Their Application in Sweden with Regard to Early Retirement

Lotta Westerhäll   University of Uppsala, Sweden

Background

The 1970's witnessed the introduction of significant reforms regarding the right of elderly people to receive pensions. These reforms involved the granting of old-age pensions as well as disability pensions. In order to provide a general background, and an appropriate context in which to view the rules on disability pensions, it seems expedient to begin by making a few introductory remarks on the old-age pension and partial-pension schemes.

The general retirement age used to be 67. It was possible to start drawing your pension prematurely from age 63; pension withdrawal could also be deferred beyond 67. On 1 July 1976, the retirement age was lowered to 65 as a result of proposals made by the Retirement Age Committee in its Report, SOU 74:15 (Bill 74:129). At the same time, proposals made by the same Committee in the Report entitled SOU 75:10 (Bill 75:97) led to the establishment of greater opportunities for flexible retirement, the new 65-year limit serving as a point of departure. It is now possible to receive old-age pension prematurely — which involves a reduction of the amount received — as from the month when the insured person reaches 60. An increase of the pension amount due to deferred withdrawal takes place up to, and including, the month during which the insured person turns 70.

The flexible-retirement-age system which was introduced on 1 July 1976, contained a component amounting to a new insurance scheme for employees where partial pensioning was combined with part-time work. The pertinent regulations were contained in the Partial Pension Insurance Act (*lagen om delpensionsförsäkring*, 75:380). This insurance is an independent scheme, although it is, in certain respects, coordinated with the general pension system under the General Insurance Act (*lagen om allmän försäkring*, the AFL).

From 1 January 1980, the partial-pension scheme was extended to include self-employed people and persons working on temporary assignments. In consequence, this legislation was altered, and the previous Act was replaced by a new Partial Insurance Act (79:84). According to this Act, partial pensions may be paid to gainfully employed persons aged 60 to 64 who reduce their working hours in preparation for retirement on old-age pensions.

Eligibility for early retirement/disability pension — some general remarks

The following regulations are found in Section 7, subsection 1 of the AFL:

> "An insured person over sixteen who does not receive an old-age pension in accordance with this Act, is entitled to a basic pension in the form of a disability pension for a period of time before he is 65, if his capacity for work is reduced by at least half due to illness or some other diminution of his physical or mental capability and this reduction is believed to be permanent.
>
> A right to early-retirement/disability pension also exists in the case of an insured person aged 60 or over, who has, as a result of unemployment, received benefits from an approved unemployment fund for the maximum period during which such benefits may be paid, or who has received cash labour-market assistance according to the Cash Labour Market Assistance Act (*lagen om kontant arbetsmarknadsstöd*, 1973:371) for four hundred and fifty days, provided that his ability to secure continued income by means of such employment as he has previously had, or by some other appropriate occupation accessible to him, is reduced by at least half and that reduction may be regarded as permanent. An insured person who has not received cash labour-market assistance for the full four hundred and fifty days is still entitled to an early retirement/disability pension according to the rules contained herein, if he has exhausted the right to that assistance at an earlier point in time.
>
> If the diminution in a person's capacity for work is not regarded as permanent, but may be assumed to remain for a considerable period of time, the insured person is entitled to a basic pension in the form of invalidity benefit. Such a benefit is limited to a certain period. The regulations concerning early retirement/disability pension that are contained in subsection 1 shall apply to invalidity benefit as well." (SFS 74:784)

The basic aim of the disability-pension scheme is to ensure the financial security of citizens whose capacity to work is prematurely lost or diminished. The pension is not intended to be an indemnification for invalidity, but to serve as compensation for the consequences that are brought about by illness or injury with regard to a person's ability to support himself/herself financially. The nature of these consequences varies greatly from case to case due to a multitude of differing circumstances. Also, they can, to a greater or lesser extent, be affected by various measures undertaken with a view to increasing an insured person's capacity for work, or to making it possible for him/her to utilise the remainder of his/her capacity for full or partial work.

A fundamental condition for the right to disability pension is that there must be a reduction of the capacity to work due to medical causes. This medical factor can be physical or mental illness, or a consequence of illness. Congenital defects are included.

Some alterations in the Act took effect on 1 July 1972 (Bill 72:55). They entailed the right on the part of elderly unemployed people to receive a disability pension purely on the basis of labour-market considerations — that is to say, without having had their capacity for work diminished by any medical circumstance. Following a proposal made in Bill 73:46, a fixed lower age limit, 60, was established in respect of the right to obtain a disability pension for labour-market reasons; the provision came into force on 1 January 1974. This basis for granting disability pensions will be further discussed below.

The AFL contains the following regulations in Section 7, subsection 3:

> "When the extent to which an insured person's capacity for work is reduced is to be assessed, consideration shall be given to his ability to obtain an income from work despite the relevant diminution of his capability, the work concerned being of a kind that corresponds to his strength and skills and that can reasonably be demanded of him in view of his training and previous activity as well as his age, domicile, and comparable circumstances. The assessment shall be made on the same grounds irrespective of the nature of the diminution of the person's capability. In the case of an elderly insured person, the assessment will primarily focus on his ability and opportunity to secure a continuous income by means of such work as he has previously carried out, or by other suitable employment which is open to him. The value of domestic work in the household will be held to correspond to "income from work" to a reasonable degree. If the insured person is subjected to such measures as are stated in Chapter 2, Section 11, his capacity for work shall be considered to be reduced while the measure is being implemented, if and to the extent that the insured person is prevented from pursuing gainful employment due to the measure concerned." (SFS 70:279 and 1013)

This section contains more detailed regulations regarding the assessment of disability in disability-pension/early-retirement cases. The disability concept applied in the field of disability pension/early retirement may be designated as disablement which affects the ability to work and is based on medical factors. If the insured person is to be entitled to a pension, he/she must be suffering from illness or some other reduction of his/her capability which affects his/her ability to support himself/herself. Furthermore, there must be a causal connexion between the medical factors and the reduction of the insured person's capacity for work. Hence, people who voluntarily refrain from gainful occupation cannot claim disability pensions.

In every case, the starting-point when assessing a person's right to a disability pension is that anyone who is healthy should expect to be offered employment and to receive unemployment benefit, or some other compensation, if no suitable employment can be secured for him/her. This basic principle means that people who find it difficult to obtain gainful employment for reasons other than illness, or some other reduction of their physical or mental capabilities, are not entitled to disability pension on such grounds.

The assessment of disability shall proceed from the insured person's personal qualifications and social situation. This applies when estimating the importance of the medical factors, too. Every case calls for an individual assessment, where the importance of medical factors shall be considered in relation to the insured person's age, profession, training, and social environment. With regard to people who used to do physically strenuous industrial work, and whose chances of finding an alternative occupation elsewhere are limited, a medical impairment of sufficient importance to justify a pension could thus be held to exist in the case of a handicap which might not be regarded as sufficient to affect a salaried employee's capacity for work. Where insured persons in the older age groups are concerned, the medical-reduction requirement is considerably lower than for young and middle-aged people.

In order to qualify for disability pension, it is not necessary to show a medical disablement amounting to 50 per cent or more. A medical disablement of below 50 per cent may constitute the basis for an insured person's being granted a disability pension, if the disablement in question has a severe effect on the insured person's capacity for work. On the other hand, the mere presence of a physical or mental defect which is considerable from a medical point of view does not constitute sufficient grounds for a right to disability pension. The defect must also entail significant consequences for the insured person's ability to support himself/herself by means of his/her own work and must be impossible to neutralise by rehabilitative measures. The application of the disability, or disablement, concept calls for a joint consideration of medical and financial criteria, since the first subsection of the pertinent legal section contains certain directives to be taken into account when assessing the extent to which the insured person's capacity for work is diminished. In accordance with these directives, consideration must be given to the person's ability to secure, despite the reduction of capability, an income by performing work which corresponds to his strength and skills and which can reasonably be demanded of him in view of his training and previous activities as well as his age, residence, and similar circumstances.

Finally, it should be pointed out that a disability-pension case is usually begun either as a result of the insured person's own initiative (application cases, AFL 6:1, subsection 1) *or*, when sickness allowance or compensation for hospital care is being paid, in consequence of action taken by the Local Social Insurance Office (AFL 6:1, subsection 2).

Statistics

The number of people with disability pensions has increased markedly over the past ten years. The sharp rise in the early 1970s may be explained by, among other things, legal changes made for the benefit of elderly members of the labour force. The increase in the number of people with disability pensions is mainly accounted for by persons aged 50 to 64 years. With regard to the age group 16-29, the number of disability pensioners remained much the same during this period of time. At present, the number of people with disability pensions is slightly over 300,000, and the insurance expenditure is assessed at approximately SEK 13 billion for the year 1985. Clearly, disability pensioning is a matter of considerable proportion.

Granting disability pensions to elderly people due to labour-market considerations

Provided the conditions referred to above have been met, an insured person aged 60 or over may be granted a disability pension on purely labour-market-orientated grounds (AFL 7:1, subsection 2). These cases do not come up for medical assessment and are not processed by a pension delegation. A person who wishes to receive a disability pension on labour-market grounds must have made the greatest possible use of unemployment -benefit-society payments and cash labour-market assistance. These are the formal requirements; they are associated with the condition that the individual's capacity for obtaining an income either from gainful employment of a kind he/she used to perform previously, or from some other suitable occupation accessible to him/her, is permanently reduced by at least half. Maximum utilisation of unemployment benefit makes it clear that long-term unemployment has already been experienced, and when this condition is satisfied, it comprises a forecast according to which future unemployment of at least two years' duration ("permanent") is expected. A brief presentation of the conditions that have to be fulfilled for a person to be entitled to compensation from unemployment insurance and cash labour-market assistance is supplied below.

Unemployment insurance is voluntary. It is administered by State-supported unemployment benefit societies under State supervision. In principle, anyone aged 15 or over, who is working within the professional field described in the statutes of the respective society, is entitled to membership in one of the authorised unemployment societies. Membership ceases on reaching 65. A member who becomes unemployed will, if certain conditions are fulfilled, receive compensation from the society after a waiting period. There are some general requirements that must be met for a right to compensation to exist. The unemployed member must be capable of working, and he/she must not be prevented from accepting work due to any other circumstances. Also, he/she must be prepared to accept suitable employment when offered. Furthermore, the person concerned has to be registered as an applicant for employment with the public Labour Exchange, and he/she must be unable to obtain a suitable position. Employment offered will, by and large, be held to be suitable if reasonable consideration has been given to the member's professional experience and fitness for work from other points of view, as well as to his/her personal circumstances. From a qualitative point of view, the benefits supplied by the proposed employment must match those contained in collective agreements; if there are no collective agreements to refer to, they must be found to be reasonable in comparison with the benefits received by people performing similar jobs for comparable employers. In addition, compensation can only be paid if a so-called "membership condition" is fulfilled; also, the so-called "working requirement" must have been met. This means that the unemployed member must have been gainfully employed to a certain extent for at least five months for the period of twelve months before the beginning of the unemployment period. The compensation from the unemployment insurance is paid in the form of a daily benefit which is taxable and qualifies the recipient for contributions from the National Supplementary Pensions scheme. The daily benefit is paid for a limited period of time, called the compensation period. The compensation period comprises 300 days after the waiting period has expired. For a member 55 or over, the compensation period is 450 days. The right to compensation ceases at the expiration of the month before the member reaches 65. In accordance with Section 21 of the 73:370 Act, a person's daily benefit is in certain ways co-ordinated with his/her old-age pension.

A person who is unemployed, and is not a member of an authorised unemployment society, may receive cash labour-market assistance (KAS). It can also be paid to a member who has not yet fulfilled the membership requirement, or who is not entitled to compensation because the compensation period has expired after he/she has become 60, or more, and who satisfies certain general requirements as well as a working requirement or a special qualification requirement following the completion of training. Compensation is paid after the expiration of a waiting period which is the same as the period prescribed in connexion with compensation from the unemployment insurance scheme. The general conditions which obtain in respect of unemployment insurance apply to KAS, too. Consequently, no compensation is paid unless the unemployed person is capable of working. This means that he/she must be able to perform according to normal standards in a job suitable for him/her. Anyone who cannot carry out work due to illness, disability, or advanced age is hence not entitled to KAS. Other people excluded from the right to KAS are those who receive a full disability pension or a full invalidity benefit.

When an assessment is made of the suitability of a certain job for a certain applicant, consideration must be given to personal circumstances, such as the applicant's professional experience; but the supply of job opportunities must impose limits on the extent to which such consideration can apply. The applicant must not refuse offered employment merely because he/she has previously been working in a certain professional field. A person who is, for various reasons, prevented from accepting employment in another area may be granted a right to act as a local applicant only. This, however, does not mean that he/she may restrict his/her availability for employment to jobs in the actual town/city where he/she is resident. It is not possible to establish any definite age limits which could serve as a reason for turning down an offered job. With regard to an elderly applicant, though, his/her previous employment usually allows for certain conclusions in this respect. If an applicant quotes medical reasons for refusing offered employment, and it is not immediately clear that such reasons prevail, a physician's certificate must be presented before the refusal can be accepted.

Where cash labour-market assistance is concerned, there is a working requirement corresponding (by and large) to that which obtains in the field of unemployment insurance.

KAS is paid as a certain fixed amount per day for a maximum of five days a week. A person who is only unemployed for part of a week, or who applies for part-time employment, receives assistance according to an established conversion table. KAS is not related to income. The assistance is taxable and qualifies for contributions from the National Supplementary Pensions scheme. The right to KAS expires at the age of 65 or when, before that time, full invalidity benefit, full disability pension, or full old-age pension according to AFL begins to be paid (Section 14, subsection 3 of the 73: 371 Act; see above).

In view of the current situation on the Swedish labour market, it should be fairly easy to conclude that a permanent incapacity for work obtains in the case of a person over 60 who has exhausted the various possibilities in the way of unemployment benefits. In most cases, such a person's chances of securing suitable employment are slight indeed. Hence, it often seems that the person's chances of obtaining an income from such employment are reduced by at least half. In practice, Labour Exchanges have ceased to suggest a person aged 60 or over, who has been unemployed for a long time, seek a job. Instead, the job is passed on to a younger unemployed person; it is felt that higher demands can be made of such a prospective employee where performance and hiring options are concerned. In other words, the rules regarding the right to disability pension/early retirement on labour-market-orientated grounds lead to very few chances of employment being offered to the elderly unemployed.

Early retirement on medical grounds in the older age groups

Some elderly people who cannot be granted disability pensions on purely labour-market-orientated grounds are still, according to AFL 7:3, subject to certain special rules regarding the assessment of their capacity for work. The most important aspect of reduced work capacity relates to the insured person's ability and opportunity to secure a continued income from work of a kind he/she has done before, or from some other suitable employment accessible to him/her. In consequence, the claim of reduction of capacity for work due to medical reasons is less stringent, and greater consideration is given to the difficulties involved in obtaining suitable employment in this category on the labour market. The preliminary material pertaining to the Act says that the nature of the relevant employment may be taken into account when making the assessment — for instance, whether it is physically strenuous, mentally exhausting, rigorously scheduled, or stressful. Two typical cases are quoted: the person who can longer cope with the exigencies of his/her job, and the person who loses his/her job due to the closure of a business. There are no demands for rehabilitation where this group is concerned. The importance of the medical basis for the reduced capacity has been greatly diminished. The actual legal text does not set any lower age limit regarding the application of extended disability pensioning for the elderly; according to the preliminary material, however, 60 years of age should serve as such a limit.

Judicial practice shows that a number of Local Social Insurance Offices tend to apply the regulations for the elderly to people under 60 too. The reason for this is said to be found in the situation on the labour market.

The application of the special regulations concerning disability pensioning for the elderly to people aged less than 60 is, in all likelihood, due to the fact that Labour Exchanges, as well as other labour-market bodies, do not feel that there is much point in trying to train and obtain employment for people whose capacity for work is reduced, and who are approaching 60. The difficulties involved in securing jobs for people aged 55-60, after retraining, are considerable. It is even harder to effect a transfer to another occupation without supplementary training. Hence, a return to work does not seem possible for many people in this age group. Even so, the regulations for the elderly were not intended to be applied to this group. According to the main rule that governs disability-pension assessments, however, the insured person's strength and skills, training, and previous activity must be taken into consideration in every case, as well as his/her age, domicile, and comparable circumstances.

The chances of being able to obtain, and retain, a job decrease as people grow older. Poor education, experience of one field of work only, or close ties to one particular town or area also cause edlerly people greater difficulties when it comes to finding a new job. When an assessment is made, circumstances which militate against the person being retrained or advised to move elsewhere are taken into account to a varying extent. In this context, advanced age is a strongly negative factor. A significant number of people whose capacity for work is diminished, and who are between 55 and 60, therefore fulfill the conditions for receiving disability pensions without needing to have the regulations for the elderly applied to them.

As matters stand at present, then, Labour Exchanges are disinclined to make much of an effort on behalf of people aged 55 to 60. Also, to a certain extent, extended pensioning for elderly people is applied as soon as a medical defect of any kind is present. The number of refusals is very low, and in some Local Social Insurance Offices, refusals only seem to be considered in cases where it really seems doubtful whether any medical impairment of any description, exists at all.

The legal application also shows that Local Social Insurance Offices have different ideas as to how great the reduction of capacity for medical reasons should be before the regulations for the elderly can be put into operation. The concept of "slightness" must be related to the duties that the person concerned is expected to carry out in his/her job. For the medical defect to be taken into account in this context, it must affect the person's performance at work.

Pensioning cases initiated by the Local Social Insurance Office

According to AFL 16:1, subsection 2, the Local Social Insurance Office is obliged to ensure that a pension assessment takes place even if the insured person does not apply for it himself/herself. Judicial practice shows that Offices wait for the so-called "one-year limit" to pass before dealing with the pension issue, even if the capacity for work may be held before that time to be permanently reduced. In many cases of sickness — especially among working people in the older age groups — it may be argued that the Office should, in view of the diagnosis, be able to establish whether there is a permanent reduction in the person's capacity for work at an early stage of a sickness case. Still, the Office delays the pension assessment, allowing the insured person to receive a sickness allowance for a year. The reasons for this policy have, in part, been said to be of a financial nature, as it is usually more advantageous for the individual to receive a sickness allowance than a disability pension.

In point of fact, the right to a sickness allowance could probably be called in question in several of the so-called "elderly cases". Where the right to disability pension was concerned, less stringent demands were made with regard to the reduction of the capacity for work on medical grounds as soon as elderly people were involved; these more lenient terms do not, however, apply to the right to sickness allowance. In consequence of the one-year limit, the Local Social

Insurance Office frequently does not, if the insured person is over 60, take steps to obtain medical statements or records at an early stage of the illness. Instead, the Office allows sickness allowance to be paid up to the time when a pension assessment is due. Hence, the right to a sickness allowance is not always put to an actual test.

This one-year limit may entail a measure of inertia when cases of sickness are dealt with. In some cases, the relevant medical documents are not acquired until the Office intends to decide whether a sickness allowance should be replaced by a pension. As a result of poor medical documentation, no factual assessment of the right to a sickness allowance is made, and chances of rehabilitation, if any, may be ruined as a result of medical records being called for too late.

One vital point may, however, be made in favour of the one-year limit. In cases where the sickness allowance amounts to a considerably higher sum than the pension, it is surely reasonable that the insured person is not in any danger of involuntarily having his/her sickness allowance replaced by a pension too soon after reporting sick.

Comparisons with Finnish law

Finnish law contains rules corresponding to the Swedish rules regarding disability pensions/early retirement for elderly insured persons. The National Basic Pension Act prescribes that the national pension scheme should pay old-age pensions to insured persons aged 65 plus, disability pensions to insured persons who are incapable of working and are not yet 65, (or disability pension in the form of an early-retirement pension to an insured person who is 55 or over, but not 65), and unemployment pensions to insured persons who have been unemployed for a long time and have reached 60 but are not yet 65.

Among these different kinds of pensions the most interesting, for the purposes of this chapter, seem to be the disability pension in the form of an individual early-retirement pension and the unemployment pension, since they affect the age groups 55-65 and 60-65.

Section 22a of the National Basic Pension Act prescribes that an insured person aged 55 plus is entitled to a disability pension in the form of an individual early-retirement pension, if his/her capacity for work has been reduced to such a degree that the person concerned cannot reasonably be expected to continue in gainful employment, consideration being given to any illness, handicap or injury, factors associated with advancing age, long-term service in one profession, duties entailing severe strain and exhaustion to the person concerned and conditions at work.

An additional requirement for the granting of a pension is that the insured person has either ceased to be gainfully employed, or has an income from work which can be estimated to be below a monthly average of FIM 689.58. The employment must have ceased, or the income have dropped, no earlier than one year before the beginning of the individual early-retirement pension. When this one-year period is calculated, days on which the insured person had time-off for study in accordance with the Leave of Absence for Purposes of Study Act (273/79) shall not be included; nor shall those days on which the insured person received daily benefits in accordance with the Subsistence Protection for Unemployed Persons Act (620/84). In the latter case, however, the number of days must not exceed the maximum number of days for which daily benefit, calculated on the basis of the person's earnings, may be paid according to Section 26 of the Subsistence Protection for Unemployed Persons Act. This rule corresponds to the above-mentioned possibility of granting disability pensions to elderly people (according to the preliminary material, people aged 60 plus, but in practice persons between 55 and 60 years of age as well) on medical grounds, which means that even a slight medical disorder may, in conjunction with the insured person's psycho-social status and his/her labour-market situations, lead to early retirement.

The prescription which corresponds to disability pensioning/early retirement on labour-market-orientated grounds is set down in Section 22c of the National Basic Pension Act. According to that regulation, a person who "has been unemployed for a long time" is an insured person who is able to present a certificate, made out by a labour-market authority, stating that he/she is a job applicant registered with the labour bureau, and that he/she cannot be directed to employment of a kind which he/she cannot refuse to accept without losing his/her right to daily unemployment benefit in accordance with the Subsistence Protection for Unemployed Persons Act (620/84). Another requirement that has to be met before an unemployment pension can be granted is that the insured person produce a further certificate, issued by the National Pension Office or by an unemployment benefit society. This certificate should state that the person concerned has, in the course of the last 60 weeks, received the kind of daily unemployment benefit that is referred to in the Subsistence Protection for Unemployed Persons Act for no less than 200 days altogether, counted from a day no earlier than a month before the issuing of the labour-market-authority certificate mentioned above — or, alternatively, that he/she, in accordance with Section 26, subsections 1 and 3, of the Subsistence Protection for Unemployed Persons Act, is no longer entitled to daily unemployment benefit calculated on the basis of his/her earnings.

Conclusion

The regulations concerning elderly persons in Swedish and Finnish law express that dual message with regard to the right to security and the right to employment which is disseminated by the Welfare State. If no work can be offered, basic social security must be provided instead — a kind of security

whose effects are not always welcome in the eyes of the individual. Society's
resources in respect of rehabilitation, retraining, and active labour deployment
are not utilised for the benefit of older people. The basic social security that was
created by the disability-pension/early-retirement scheme is offered instead.
The fact that the individual himself/herself is often unwilling to be pensioned
off prematurely is clear from the large number of early-retirement cases that
have been initiated by Local Social Insurance Offices. A prematurely retired
person no longer enjoys employment protection, and the compensation he/she
receives is not related to income from gainful employment. When you receive
an early-retirement pension, you no longer belong to the "labour market". In
actual fact, then, the retirement age limit has been moved down from 65 to 60
years — or even to 55 years. In my view, a society which cannot integrate the
older population in its working life and its productive efforts is not moving in an
altogether healthy direction.

Chapter 55

State Provisions for Old-Age Security in Tanzania

Ulrike Wanitzek

University of Bayreuth,
Federal Republic of Germany

Introduction

State provision of old-age security in Tanzania,[1] as in most other African states, was initiated by the colonial government. It should be seen partly as a method of coping with the effects of economic and social change and partly as an inevitable package accompanying wage-employment.[2] Among the first measures taken by the colonial state to provide for the old-age security of employees was the enactment of several Pensions and Provident Fund Ordinances, all of which provided for old-age benefits to those employed in public service.[3] After Independence, the National Provident Fund was established in 1964 to provide for those persons employed in the private sector.[4] And in 1978, the Parastatal Pension Fund was also established to secure the employees of parastatal organisations.[5]

After a short statistical overview, this chapter first discusses the legal provisions governing the aforementioned schemes of old-age security.[6] It is then shown that the amount of social security provided under these schemes is often insufficient for the retired to base their living on, particularly because of the low benefit amounts which are further eroded by the ever-rising inflation rate. There are also practical problems in the administration of these schemes, which often cause delay in securing the benefits when they are due. The chapter concludes with some suggestions for a possible improvement of the situation of pensioners.

Some Statistical Data

Only a minority of the population, i.e. those who are employed in the formal sector, benefit from the state-provided old-age security schemes. The majority are not covered by the state-provided social security schemes and are completely dependent on other sources of old-age security. As Fuchs notes, this is due to the labour-centred social security concepts to be found in Third World countries (1986: 2, 7).

According to the 1978 Population Census, Tanzania-mainland had a population of 17,036,498 in 1978. 7,851,330 (=46.14%) were below the age of 15; 7,781,167 (=45.73%) were between 15 and 54; and 1,383,301 (=8.13%) were 55 and above.[7]

A survey made in 1979/80 shows that 599,827 persons were formally employed in 1979.[8] This is 7.71% of the population group aged 15-54 which represents the main labour force of the country.[9] Another survey based on the estimated number of those insured under an old-age insurance scheme shows similar figures and proportions. Of an estimated total population of 13,270,000 in 1976, about 500,000 were insured,[10] which is less than 10% of the economically active population.[11] Self-employed, casual, unpaid and family workers and the rural population on a whole, fall outside these schemes.[12]

Despite the low percentage of the population benefitting from state-provided old-age security schemes, it is still important to find out whether they provide a satisfactory basis for supporting old age. In the following paragraphs the three existing types of old-age security schemes in Tanzania are therefore examined.

The Public Pension Scheme

A. General

Social security systems for civil servants are the oldest schemes of old-age security in Tanzania, as is the case with many other African countries (Mouton 1975: 3). The public pension scheme under the Pensions Ordinance, Cap. 371 (PO), being the most important of these schemes, will be discussed below in detail.[13] Other schemes include those for the teaching service, the defence forces, the political leaders, and the specified state leaders.[14]

The Public Pension Scheme is administered by the State. It is a non-contributory scheme for certain categories of persons in the public service, which provides benefits to those who have retired or terminated their employment prematurely under certain circumstances. The pensions, gratuities and other allowances under this Scheme are paid out of a consolidated Fund and are financed wholly out of general taxation (Mbunda 1986: 10; Mongi 1986: 12).[15]

B. Qualification for Pension Benefits

The Pensions Ordinance (PO) applies to every officer in the service of Tanganyika (s. 22(1)(a) PO).[16] Under ss. 2(1), 3(1) PO, an office may be declared by the President, by order published in the Gazette, to be a pensionable office. This has been done in a number of such orders which enlist in detail all pensionable offices.[17]

The minimum period of qualifying service is ten years (Pensions Regulation (Reg.) 4[18]). The qualifying service excludes periods of probation, unless confirmed later, and periods of employment of an officer below 18 years.[19]

Pensions, etc. under the PO are granted only on retirement of an officer from the public service a) on or after attaining the age of 50 years;[20] b) on medical grounds, i.e. on medical evidence of the officer's physical or mental incapacity, likely to be permanent, to further discharge hie duties of office; c) on involuntary termination of service in the public interest or due to the abolition or re-organisation of the office; d) if the officer retires with the consent of the President; and e) in the case of a female officer, by reason of her marriage (s. 8 PO, as amended by Act 4/78).

Upon the attainment of the age of 50, or, in the case of a female officer, upon marriage, the officer can elect to retire, or the appropriate authority can require him/her to do so (s. 10(1) PO; see the exceptions as indicated there). [21] In general, no officer may continue to serve after he/she attains the age of 55 (s. 10(2) PO); and where an officer continues to serve beyond this age for reasons of public interest, the final age limit is 60 (s. 10(3) PO).

C. Benefits

There is no absolute right to pensions, gratuities or other allowances (s. 6(1) PO). The State may dismiss any officer at any time without compensation. If it is established to the satisfaction of the appropriate authority[22] that an officer has been guilty of negligence, irregularity or misconduct, the pension, gratuity or other allowance may be reduced or altogether withheld (s. 6(2) PO). Pensions etc. may cease, under the Bankruptcy Ordinance, where a petitioner is adjudicated bankrupt or declared insolvent by judgement of a competent court; or where a pensioner is sentenced for a term of imprisonment by a competent court for any offence (ss. 16, 17, 18 PO).[23] A relieving provision to the principle of disqualification is contained in s. 17(4) PO. Pensions, gratuities and other allowances are not assignable or transferrable except for purposes of satisfying a debt due to the Government, for the purposes of this section.

The law provides for two options: the granting of a reduced annual pension together with a gratuity in the form of a lump sum, or of an unreduced annual pension. Whereas before 1978 the unreduced pension was granted automatically, and the reduced pension plus gratuity was granted only when it was opted for after Act 4/78 the unreduced pension must be opted for in writing if it is preferred and this decision is irrevocable (Reg. 23(1), (3), in the amended version of Act 15/81).

1) Unreduced Annual Pension

The unreduced annual pension is computed as follows:
annual pension = 1/600 × annual salary × number of months
                 (1)   (2)   (3)

(1) The pension factor is 1/600 (Reg. 4). [24]

(2) The annual salary, or "pensionable emoluments" (Reg. 4), includes the salary, overseas allowance, personal allowance and house allowance (in certain cases). In respect of service outside Tanzania, "pensionable emoluments mean emoluments which count for pension under the law of the country of such service" (s. 2(1) PO). The final annual salary immediately before retirement is relevant if the pensionable office was held at least for three years (Reg. 18(1)(a); for details, where this was not the case, see Reg. 18).

(3) The third factor is the number of months of pensionable service. "Pensionable service" means service which may be taken into account in computing pensions, gratuities or other allowances under the Pensions Regulations (Reg. 2(1), 4); and this means the period of holding a "pensionable office" (see above).

2) Reduced Annual Pension and Gratuity

While until 1981 the annual pension could be reduced by one-quarter only, Act 15/81 amended the relevant Reg. 23 to the effect that it is now reduced by one-half. The reduced annual pension is computed as follows:

annual pension = 1/2 × (1/600 × annual salary × number of months)
                         (1)   (2)   (3)

The commuted pension gratuity, paid as a lump sum, is calculated as follows:

lump sum = 12.5 × 1/2 × (1/600 × annual salary × number of months)
                          (1)   (2)   (3)

The advantage of this lump sum is that it is tax-free, while the annual pension is considered as income in the sense of the Income Tax Act 1973 and is therefore taxed (ss. 3(2)(c), 8(5) Income Tax Act). [25]

A maximum pension is fixed at two-thirds of the highest pensionable emoluments drawn at any time in the course of the officer's service in Tanzania (s. 11(1) PO). [26] A minimum pension, meaning a specified amount of money to be declared from time to time by the President by order published in the Gazette, is provided for pensioners who are citizens ordinarily resident in the United Republic of Tanzania (s. 11 A PO, as amended by Acts Nos. 29/80 and 15/81).

3) Other Benefits

Where the length of service has been less than ten years and therefore does not qualify for a pension, but where an officer is otherwise qualified for a pension, he may be granted a gratuity on retirement, the maximum amount of which is computed as follows (Reg. 5):

maximum gratuity = 5 × (1/600 × annual salary × number of months)

$$(1) \qquad\qquad (2) \qquad\qquad (3)$$

A gratuity due upon marriage is provided for, with several options. Reg. 6. S. 19 PO provides for death gratuities, granted to an officer's legal personal representative, if the officer dies in service, or after retirement before receiving his pension. Survivors' benefits for dependants may be granted, in addition to the death gratuities. The distribution of survivors' benefits as between the dependants must be made in accordance with the intestate succession law of the community to which the officer belonged (s. 20 A (3) PO). The payment ceases after three years, or, in the case of a widow, upon remarriage, or, in the case of a dependent child, when he/she attains the age of 18 (s. 20 A (4) PO). S. 20 PO provides for pensions to dependants when an officer dies of injuries sustained while on duty.

D. Overview

The Public Pension Scheme differs basically from the two other schemes discussed below insofar as it is a non-contributory scheme. This means that benefits are not paid on the basis of the employee's contributions, but for his services and that the benefits are not financed by contributions but by general tax revenues. As is usual with non-contributory schemes, the principle of disqualification applies, and members have no absolute right to benefits. Broad powers are conferred on the government in deciding on the granting of benefits. The Public Pension Scheme has been criticised because it therefore cannot be relied upon with confidence (Mbunda 1986: 16). Problems connected with the often low amounts of the pension benefits, the inexpedient use of lump sums and organisational difficulties which pensioners face when they try to get the pension benefits to which they are entitled, are discussed in the general assessment below, as these problems concern also the other old-age security schemes.

However, with regard to the pension factor and other criteria relevant for the computation of the amount of benefits, there is a considerable advantage for those receiving benefits under the Public Pension Scheme, compared to the Parastatal Pension Scheme and the National Provident Fund (below). On the whole, the Public Pension Scheme gives more effective protection than the other schemes (Bossert 1986: 13), which can also be observed in many other African countries (Mouton 1975: 11).

The Parastatal Pension Fund

A. General

Before the enactment of the Parastatal Pensions Act of 1978 (PPA)[27] various parastatal organisations in Tanzania had differing pension schemes, and some of them had no schemes at all. One of the goals of the Parastatal Pensions Act was to introduce some uniformity and certainty in the conditions for award of a pension and other related benefits to employees of parastatal organisations (Mattaka 1986:2). The National Insurance Corporation manages the Fund on behalf of a Board of Trustees.[28]

According to s. 2(1) of the PPA, a parastatal organisation is a company registered under the Companies Ordinance, in which the government or another parastatal organisation owns not less than 50% of its share capital.[29] The employees of parastatal organisations are provided with a special pension Scheme which manifests considerable differences from the Public Pensions Scheme (available primarily for employees of private employers, described below) on the other hand.

B. Qualification for Benefits

1) Membership in the Scheme

All employees of a parastatal organisation who are confirmed in a pensionable office in the service become members of the Scheme from the date of employment or from the date of commencement of the Scheme, whichever is later (s. 5 PPA). Membership is compulsory and the Act does not provide for cases of voluntary membership, as is the case with the National Provident Fund (see below).

An employee within the definition of the Act is a person who is, on a full-time basis, permanently employed by a parastatal organisation in a pensionable office. Not included are those employees who are employed on contract terms or on a temporary, daily-paid or casual basis (s. 2(1) PPA). 'Pensionable office' means an office in a parastatal organisation which is approved by its management to be pensionable (s. 2(1) PPA).

Membership is limited, however, on the basis of age, to those who are below 40 at the date of their first employment with a parastatal organisation (s. 5(a) PPA). An employee, who has reached 40 at the commencement of the Scheme, is also excluded from membership, except for the case where he/she has to his/her credit a period of qualifying service[30] which, when aggregated with the period which he/she would serve as an employee until he/she reaches the retirement age of 50 would be not less than ten years (s. 5(b) PPA).

2) Contributions to the Fund

Contributions are compulsory for members as well as for the employing parastatal organisations(s. 8 PPA). The employee has to contribute 5% of his/ her salary. If at the time of becoming a member of the Fund he/she was contributing to any other employees' terminal benefit Scheme, his/her contribution is to be determined by the Board, in consultation with the Minister, to be not more than what he would have contributed to this Scheme, had it continued to be operative (s. 8(1) PPA). The employer has to contribute "Such amount as will be necessary to meet the Board's obligation in respect of the member under this Act, and as will be determined by the Board in consultation with the minister (s. 8 (1) PPA). According to Bossert, this is actually 8% of the employee's salary (1985: 112); and it may be more in the case of s. 8(1), Proviso, PPA, as mentioned above. The employer remits both his and the employee's contribution (which is deducted monthly from his/her salary) to the National Insurance Corporation (NIC) which administers the Fund (ss. 8(2), 2(1) PPA).

An employer, who fails to remit contributions within the period prescribed by the Act,[31] is liable to pay a penalty of 5-10% of the amount due, together with the principal sum ("additional contributions", s. 9 PPA). However, this penalty is rather low, and the only sanction provided for persistent failure to remit contributions is a report by the NIC to the Minister. According to Mattaka (1986: 4), there has been no action on the part of the Minister against reported defaulting employers, and the absence of legal enforcement may have grave consequences for the employee, since the period of contributions, which is relevant for the computation of benefits (see below), may thus be reduced by the employer's failure to remit contributions, even when deducted from the employee's salary.

3) Qualification for Benefits

A minimum of ten years service is a precondition for the granting of full pensions and gratuities under s. 28 of the PPA. The rate of the pension or gratuity awarded depends on the period of qualifying service. This excludes periods of probation, unless confirmed later, and of leave without pay, unless the leave was granted on grounds of public policy and the employer pays both his and the employee's contributions during this leave. It further excludes periods of employment where the employee is below the age of 18 (s. 27 PPA). On the other hand, the period of qualifying service includes, apart from the pensionable service, prior periods of service for another parastatal organisation or within the public service (s. 2(1) PPA).

Pensions and gratuities may be awarded to a member of the Parastatal Pension Scheme on or after attaining the age of 50: on medical evidence of his permanent physical or mental incapability to discharge his duties of office; on compulsory retirement for certain reasons concerning the organisation of the parastatal; in the case of transfer to public service, if he is permitted by the relevant law to retire on pension or gratuity; in the case of removal from service in the public interest as provided in this Act; on retirement with the consent or at the direction of the President; and, in the case of a woman employee, when she retires for her marriage (s. 26 PPA).

On reaching 50, the employee may retire, or his employer may require him to do so. The same is the case when a female employee gets married. No employee can continue to serve after reaching 55 unless the appropriate authority considers it to be in the public interest and the employee consents in writing (s. 24(1) PPA). At 60, service on pensionable terms is excluded without any exception (s. 24(2) PPA).

C. Benefits

The Scheme provides for old-age benefits (pensions), gratuities, survivors' benefits[32] and withdrawal benefits.[33] There is no absolute right to these benefits (s. 25(1) PPA), with the exception of withdrawal benefits which are not mentioned in s. 25(1) PPA.[34] The benefits may be reduced or totally withheld if a member has been guilty of negligence, irregularity or misconduct (s. 25(2) PPA). If a member receiving a pension or gratuity is sentenced to a term of imprisonment or is detained, the pension ceases on the date of imprisonment or detention (s. 32(1) PPA).[35] The fact that the employee is thus indirectly deprived even of his own contributions, and that this may be on the basis of a conviction or detention not necessarily related to the public office he holds, is heavily criticised (Mattaka 1986: 5).

There are two alternative forms of benefits for members who have served for the total period of ten years of qualifying service. The normal case is the granting of a reduced annual pension in combination with a commuted pension gratuity in the form of a lump sum. The alternative option, which must be exercised by the employee in writing, is an unreduced annual pension (s. 28 (1) PPA).

1) Unreduced Annual Pension

The unreduced annual pension, which is called a "specified amount" in the PPA, is computed as follows (s. 28(2) PPA):

$$\text{annual pension} = \underset{(1)}{1/960} \times \underset{(2)}{\text{annual salary}} \times \underset{(3)}{\text{number of months}}$$

(1) The pension factor is 1/960 (s. 28 (2) PPA).[36]
(2) S. 28(2) PPA uses the term "annual pensionable emoluments". This is interpreted in s. 2(1) PPA as the "annual salary" which means the basic salary excluding bonus, commission, cost of living allowance, incentive allowance, over-time payment, director's fees and any other additional emoluments.

(3) The third factor is the number of months of pensionable service. "Pensionable service" means any period of continuous service with one or several parastatal organisations rendered by a member of the Scheme, or rendered prior to his/her becoming a member of the scheme, if she-he was covered by any employee's terminal benefits Scheme providing for the payment of pension. This includes periods of absence from duty on leave with not less than half the salary.

2) Reduced Annual Pension and Gratuity

Whereas the unreduced annual pension is the exception which can be opted for in writing, the common form of pension consists of a combination of a reduced annual pension of three-fourths of the full pension, and a commuted pension gratuity, in the form of a lump sum. The reduced annual pension is therefore computed as follows:

$$\text{annual pension} = \underset{(1)}{3/4} \times (\underset{(2)}{1/960} \times \text{annual salary} \times \underset{(3)}{\text{number of months}})$$

The commuted pension gratuity is calculated as follows:

$$\text{lump sum} = \underset{(1)}{12.5} \times 1/4 \times (\underset{(2)}{1/960} \times \text{annual salary} \times \underset{(3)}{\text{number of months}})$$

This means that one-quarter of the amount of unreduced annual pension (i.e. the "specified amount") can be commuted into a lump sum payment of 12.5 times this one-quarter of the specified amount. The commutation percentage of 25% is rather low, compared to the other pension schemes, where it is 50%.[37]

The Act does not provide for a minimum pension (Mattaka 1986:7). But it provides for a maximum pension not exceeding two-thirds of the highest pensionable emoluments drawn by the member in the course of his service (s. 29(1) PPA).

3) Other Benefits

Where the length of service does not qualify for pension, i.e. is below ten years, but a member is otherwise qualified for a pension, he/she may be awarded, on retirement, a gratuity not exceeding five times the "specified amount", and not less than the aggregate of the member's own contributions and the interest of 5% p.a. (s. 34 PPA):

$$\text{maximum gratuity} = \underset{(1)}{5} \times (\underset{(2)}{1/960} \times \text{annual salary} \times \underset{(3)}{\text{number of months}})$$

D. Overview

When the benefits under the Parastatal Pension Scheme are compared with the other pension schemes, a number of disadvantages which parastatal employees face becomes evident. The pension factor is 1/960 and therefore worse than the factor of the other schemes which is 1/600. The Parastatal Pension Scheme is the only pension scheme which does not provide for a minimum pension. The commutation percentage is only 25%, compared to 50% under the other schemes. This is of importance with regard to tax, since under the Income Tax Act, an amount of up to 50% of commuted pension, payable as a lump sum, is exempt from tax. Parastatal employees thus can make use of this possibility only partially. Beyond this, it has been suggested that all pension payments shoud be made completely tax-free (Mattaka 1986: 11).[38]

Unlike the other pension schemes, the Parastatal Pension Scheme is contributory. In order to remove this inequity, it is suggested that it should either be made it non-contributory like all the other pension schemes, or that the latter should be made contributory instead (Mattaka 1986: 9 f.).[39] A further disadvantage of the Parastatal Pension Scheme is that the principle of disqualification applies, even though this is a contributory scheme.

The National Provident Fund

A. General

The National Provident Fund was established in 1964 under the National Provident Fund Act (NPFA), Cap. 564.[40] It is not an instrument of social security in the narrow sense, but a mere compulsory saving system, under which the contributions remitted to the Fund, including the accrued interest, are later paid out to the members of the Fund.[41] The advantage for the State lies in the fact that the Provident Fund is financed by employers and employees. The government thus is not forced to transfer resouces from the national budget to supplement the payment of benefits and the administration of the scheme (Mulozi 1983: 580). The National Provident Fund was established in addition to several pre-existing Provident Funds for non-pensionable government employees, employees of local authorities etc.[42] In 1975, a Board of Trustees of the National Provident Fund was established to manage and administer the Fund in accordance with the provisions of the NPFA and the Board of Trustees of National Provident Fund (Establishment) Act, 1975. [43] Under s. 48 of the NPFA, regulations have been made with respect to certain procedural questions.[44]

B. Membership in the Fund and Contributing Employers[45]

1) Who Can Be a Member?

In general, only 'employees' are registerable as members of the Fund.[46] 'Employee' means a person above the apparent age of 15[47] (or above 18, where he is receiving full-time education or training for which he is not paid), who is employed in Tanganyika under a contract of service or apprenticeship with an employer (s. 2(1) NPFA).[48] This definition is not affected by the type of work done under the contract,[49] the method of payment, or the amount of remuneration paid.[50]

Excluded from membership are 'exempt employees' and 'temporary employees' (s. 11(1)(a), (b) NPFA). The term 'exempt employee' is defined in s. 2 and the 2nd Schedule of the NPFA and includes those public and parastatal employees who are exempt from the National Provident Fund because they are covered by other schemes of social security.[51] The term 'temporary employee' is defined in s. 2 of the NPFA as an employee engaged on a daily contract of service who has not been employed by that employer for a continuous period of three months.[52] In principle, temporary employees are not registrable as members of the Fund. However, exceptions are possible where the Minister declares by order in the Gazette that temporary employees in general, or those of a certain category, are registrable as members (s. 11(1)(b) NPFA).[53]

2) Compulsory Membership

S. 8(1) of the NPFA empowers the Minister of Labour to declare, by order in the Gazette, any employees or category of employees to be registrable as members of the Fund; and to declare any employer or category of employers to be contributing employers. Such an order was made in 1964[54] declaring all private employers of ten or more employees to be contributing employers,[55] and their employees to be registrable as members of the National Provident Fund, as well as the employees of the Government, the Common Services Organization, the Local Government Service or a Municipal Council, as far as they are not exempt or temporary employees or members of the crew of a shop. By a later order, the number of employees was reduced to four instead of ten.[56] However, as Fuchs (1985: 165) notes with respect to Kenya, the lack of a sufficient administrative infrastructure often causes difficulties in registering all those who are liable to contribute to the Fund.

3) Voluntary Membership

Where the Minister of Labour has made an order under s. 8(1) of the NPFA declaring categories of employees or of contributing employers by reference to the numbers of employees in the service of an employer, and where an employer has in his service fewer employees than the minimum number and does not make contributions in their behalf, membership of the National Provident Fund is possible under two conditions, i.e. if the majority of employees consent in writing to the membership, and if the Board of Trustees of the National Provident Fund approves the application[57] for membership (s. 9(1) NPFA). In this case, the present as well as the future employees of the applicant can be registered as members of the Fund.[58]

C. Contributions and Payments to the Fund

The Act distinguishes between a) statutory and b) special contributions by the employer and c) payments by the employee.

1) Statutory Contributions

The statutory contribution (s. 15 NPFA) is determined by s. 2 and the third Schedule of the NPFA, as amended by Act 26/78, as a sum of "ten cents for every complete shilling of wages", i.e. 10% of the wages, notwithstanding whether the contribution period is one month, one fortnight or one week. Statutory contributions are obligatory and are due immediately when a person is employed. They must be paid by the employer to the Fund within a certain period (s. 15(2) NPFA).

The contribution, which amounts to 10% of the wages as defined above, is to be paid by the employer, but half of it, i.e. 5% of the wages, is deductible from the employee's wages (ss. 16, 2, 3rd Schedule of the NPFA).[59] This may be done either at the end of the contribution period, i.e. of one month, one fortnight or one week, or within six months after the end of the contribution period. In the latter case, the deduction is to be made in not less than four approximately equal installments, unless the employee agrees to have it deducted in fewer installments or in one lump sum. Other arrangements for deduction are not permitted (s. 16(1) NPFA).[60] If the employer has deducted the employee's share of a statutory contribution from his wages, but has not paid the statutory contribution or the employee's share of it to the Fund, the Board of Trustees may nevertheless credit the amount of the employee's share to his account in the Fund. This does not depend upon whether this amount can be received from the employer (s. 16(3) NFPA). This provision provides a certain protection to employees who would otherwise be prejudiced by negligent employers and the lack of sufficient supervision of them by the authorities.[61]

2) Special Contributions

With respect to temporary employees — unless they have been declared in an order made by the Minister under s. 11 of the NPFA to be registrable as members of the Fund — every contributing employer has to make a special contribution of "five cents for every full shilling of the total wages paid to all the temporary employees for the relevant contribution period" (s. 17(5) NPFA).

The employee does not have to contribute in this case and the money is not allocated to his account, but is paid into the Reserve Account of the Fund (s. 17(3) NPFA). The purpose of this provision is to prevent employers' evading a contribution to the Fund by employing on a temporary basis. However, it has been reported that even this provision has been evaded by some employers (Mbunda 1986:7).[62]

3) Payments by Employees

Payment by employees instead of employers is possible under s. 18 of the NPFA, if the employee who is a member of the Fund is not employed by a contributing employer liable to make statutory contribution.

4) Failure to Make Contributions

Persons who try to evade payment of contributions are, under certain conditions, guilty of an offence and liable on conviction to a fine of up to 2,000 TShs and/or to imprisonment for a term of up to six months (s. 38(1) NPFA). The court before which such person is convicted of an offence of this kind may, without prejudice to any civil remedy, order him/her to pay to the Board the unpaid contributions (s. 38(2) NPFA). Criminal proceedings under s. 38 NPFA, as well as civil proceedings for the recovery of contributions, may be instituted by certain representatives of the Board (s. 40 NPFA). All magistrates' courts other than Primary Courts have jurisdiction for matters arising under the NPFA (s. 38(4) NPFA).

5) Inalienability of Contributions

The Board of Trustees of the National Provident Fund establishes and maintains for each member of the Fund an account to which all statutory contributions (under s. 15 NPFA), all payments made by a member (under s. 18 NPFA), and all interest (credited under s. 36 NPFA) are credited. To this account are charged, on the other hand, all benefits granted or refunds made regarding a member (s. 14 NPFA).

The contributions, payments and interest are inalienable. They are not assets for the benefit of creditors in the event of bankruptcy or insolvency of a member, nor are they liable to attachment for a member's debts. Any security, pledge or assignment given, which purports to include any such contribution, payment or interest, shall to that extent be void (s. 21(1) NPFA). The only exception to this important protection of the member's position lies in the possibility, under s. 21(3) of the NPFA, of having to compensate the employer from the member's account for financial loss suffered as a result of an offence involving dishonesty of which the member has been convicted. The amount of this compensation must not exceed the aggregate of statutory contributions made by the employer.[63]

D. Benefits

Members are entitled to a benefit equivalent to the balance of their account with the Fund at the date of payment, including contributions and accrued interest, after having deducted any subsidiary benefits drawn (Fourth Schedule of the NPFA). The principle of disqualification does not apply.[65] The rate of interest may be fixed, from time to time, by the Minister of Labour, with the concurrence of the Minister of Finance and after consultation with the Board (s. 36(1) NPFA). It is limited by the net income of the Fund (s. 36(2) NPFA).

The Act provides for three classes of benefits, i.e. a) main benefits payable on account of age, survivorship and disability, b) subsidiary benefits payable in case of sickness exceeding three months, and c) withdrawal benefits payable on withdrawal from the Fund, emigration, and marriage or maternity (s. 22(1) NPFA). s. 30 NPFA provides for restriction on double benefits.

1) Main Benefits

Main benefits may be paid either in one lump sum or, with the approval of the Board, may be converted into and paid as an annuity (s. 22(2) NPFA).[66] Age benefits are payable to a member who has attained the retirement age of 55[67] and has retired from regular employment (s. 23 NPFA). Disability benefits are payable to a member who, due to physical or mental disability, is unemployable.[68] Survivors' benefits which are due on the member's death in favour of dependants of the deceased are payable primarily to the widow of the deceased for her own maintenance and the maintenance of the deceased's minor or disabled children, including stepchildren, illegitimate children and adopted children (ss. 24, 2(1) NPFA). If there is no widow, the benefits are payable to a guardian of the deceased's minor children, or to any disabled children, or to any other dependent.[69]

2) Subsidiary Benefits

Sickness benefits are payable if the person who has been a member of the Fund for not less than one year has been sick and therefore incapable of working for more than three months (s. 26 NPFA). The benefits are payable after three months of illness, excluding a number of cases in which the employee receives other payments, e.g. for maternity leave, under the Workmen's Compensation Act, or where the employer pays for sick leave (s. 27 NPFA). As was mentioned above, the payment of sickness benefits reduces the sum of money payable for old-age benefits. The maximum amount of sickness benefits per working day is extremely low (TShs 3.50, Fourth Schedule, (b), of the NPFA).

3) Withdrawal Benefits

Withdrawal benefits are payable to a female member of the Fund who has permanently given up wage labour for reasons of her marriage or maternity (s. 28 NPFA). Withdrawal benefits are further payable in cases of emigration to a foreign country with which no reciprocal agreement pursuant to s. 50 of the NPFA has been concluded (s. 29(1)8a) NPFA); and they are payable where a member of the Fund has reached 55 has not been employed by an employer required to make a statutory contribution in his behalf for at least six months immediately preceding the application (s. 29(1)(b) NPFA). Where such a person has not yet reached 55, the benefits are payable in installments (s. 29(2) NPFA). Because they do not depend on age requirements, the withdrawal benefits are payable where a person has retired from employment for the purpose of permanently residing in a village in Tanganyika and this has been certified by the Minister (s. 29(1)(c) NPFA).

E. Overview

The fact that the National Provident Fund is not an insurance model has various obvious disadvantage. Only after very long periods of contributions can a sufficient amount be expected at retirement age. However, because of the unstable labour market and other reasons, such sufficiency is often not achieved (Fuchs 1985: 28). The possibility of receiving withdrawal benefits without a social contingency can be easily misused by members of the Fund, which reduces the amounts available at retirement(Bossert 1986: 13). But even if benefits are drawn, for instance in case of sickness, this has the same effect since all benefits ever received are deducted from the member's account.

The lump sum often is not invested or otherwise used to secure a long-term financial basis for the retired, but is spent within a short time. In such cases the National Provident Fund does not provide proper long-term protection for old people (Fuchs 1986: 4; 1985: 169). All these obvious shortcomings weigh heavier than the purported advantages of the system, which lie in its simplicity, understandability and easy administration (Fuchs 1985: 27; Mouton 1975: 24). Discussions have been held in various countries on the conversion of National Provident Fund schemes into pension schemes; but the governments appear not to show much enthusiasm to do so (Kenya: Fuchs 1985: 172; 1986: 15; Ghana: Mouton 1975: 24).

An Assessment

A. Problems of State-Provided Old-Age Security Schemes

A central problem, which all the schemes of old-age security described above have in common, is that the benefits are usually insufficient to provide a living for the retired. It has been noted that "benefits from the government-regulated pension schemes are inadequate and do not meet the basic needs of the recipient for shelter, food and clothing" (Mongi 1986: 1). This problem is continuously aggravated by the high inflation rate (Mattaka 1986: 10; Bossert 1985: 135 ff., 1986: 13).

The pension amounts are particularly inadequate if the working period was not very long which may be due to instabilities of the labour market (see Mattaka 1986: 9, with some examples; Fuchs 1986: 4). But even if an employee has been working for the usual maximum working period of 35 or 40 years, the pension would be less than one half of the final basic salary in the case of a parastatal employee (pension factor 1/960), and still less than two-thirds in the case of a civil servant (pension factor 1/600). Since the full salaries themselves are much too low to live on, it is obvious that these pension benefits do not guarantee decent living circumstances in old age.

It has been suggested, therefore, that either the pension factor be increased, particularly in the case of the parastatal pension scheme; or the pension benefits be linked to price indices; or a general minimum pension be fixed, for instance at two-thirds of the salary after a minimum of 20 years of service (Mattaka 1986: 15). The problem of lump sum benefits not being efficient and reliable instruments for long-term old-age security has been mentioned above (see also Bossert 1985: 133 f.).

Another problem which has been discussed in this context is the pension age. It is noted that at the age of 55, or even at a lower retirement age, an employee usually has not yet finalised his financial commitments (Mattaka 1986: 10). The question also arises whether a developing country can afford to retire its trained manpower at an age when many employees have acquired good experience and are most productive (Mongi 1986: 4). As the situation is now, at the time of retirement, because of the insufficiency of the pension benefits. people usually start or continue working in their own private business or become engaged in agricultural activities in their home village. This continuation of working life at another level is seen by many as normal (Fuchs 1985: 172, on Kenya). It has been suggested, therefore, that certain elements of the pension laws should be re-examined (Mongi 1986: 23).

Retirement benefits received under any of the schemes described above constitute an "income" for the purpose of taxation and are therefore taxed (ss. 3(2)(c), 8(4) of the Income Tax Act (ITA).[71] Only commuted pensions in the form of lump sums (see above) of up to 50% of the total pension entitlement are tax-free (s. 8(5) ITA).[72] For those insured under the contributory schemes, this results in double taxation, because the employees' contributions to the Fund are not exempt from taxation.[73] The situation is similar for those self-employed persons and non-insured employees,[74] who have annuity contracts, etc. with the NIC. They do not enjoy any tax relief for their premiums either, and when they receive their annuities, these are taxed in the same way as the pensions (Luoga 1986: 6). Luoga reports that in practice, however, the Income Tax Department allows a deduction of an amount which represents an employee's own contribution to his pension, before assessing his tax (1986: 5).[75]

Further problems in the context of taxation of old-age benefits are that taxes should be capable of motivating people to increase their productivity; and that they should not impair the saving capacity of the tax-payer. Neither goal is furthered by the present tax law (Luoga 1986: 9).

On the whole, there are therefore a number of reasons for re-examining tax law with regard to retirement benefits and for the introduction of some tax relief. However, it is also obvious that the state needs these payments to finance the whole, rather costly, machinery for the administration of retirement benefits. It has been suggested, therefore, that these costs could be reduced by entrusting the administration of retirement benefits solely to the NIC, which has already an infrastructure and the necessary experience.

A further major problem which is common to all the schemes, seems to be inefficient management (Bossert 1985: 138 ff.). Employers fail to pay their contributions into the Fund and yet escape serious consequences. The NIC, for instance, which manages the Parastatal Pension Fund, could not always assure the flow of contributions and returns from the parastatal organisations (Mongi 1986: 10). The lack of an administrative infrastructure in the country, like the absence of reliable civil registers, problems with the postal system, and the lack of sufficiently qualified personnel, also causes inefficiency. It has been reported that files have been incomplete or even lost, that people have to travel in vain to distant towns, thus incurring much expense, before payments (if any) could be effected.[76] So ever the little money to which they are entitled often is not recovered.

B. Some Possible Solutions to the Dilemma of Pensioners

The foregoing points make it necessary to examine other modes of securing old age than the state-provided old-age security schemes. A number of suggestions have been made to this effect. The National Insurance Corporation offers group pension schemes, annuity policies, life assurance or endowment assurance policies under private arrangements. These may be made either in addition to existing entitlements under the state-provided schemes; or by persons who are not insured under these schemes (Luoga 1986: 2; Mattaka 1986). However, this may be a problem for many people who cannot afford the rather high contributions. Mongi suggests, in this context, re-introducing tax concessions on self-employed pension funds (i.e. those pension funds which are established by individuals, other than the occupational pension funds established by employers on behalf of their employees), as an incentive for the re-establishment of self-employed pension schemes. He further suggests that NIC could include "loanback" privileges under self-employed schemes, which means that self-employed persons could obtain loans for business expansion, etc., on the security of any assets in their possession (1986: 6, 8, 23).

The use of loans for housing with the housing bank, and the general use of the banking system are suggested as further options which can be used as a complement to the existing pension schemes. For instance, post office deposit and saving accounts can be used by rural people with small incomes to save their returns on the sale of cotton, coffee, etc., for a while and then they could use the deposits for various investments, rather than spend the money immediately.

However, the high inflation rate is an ubiquitous obstacle to many of these devices. Moreover, such shemes require a certain financial basis. If this does not exist to a sufficient degree, the only remaining options are the extended family, mutual help associations, and similar groups which may provide some kind of informal social security. The functioning of this social network in contemporary African societies, and its combination with state-provided measures, has been examined by a number of authors and has been assessed in quite contradictory ways.[77] It is not possible within this chapter to discuss these various findings, but it is important to be aware that "whatever role the extended family still pays in providing for the aged, this role has undergone radical transformation" (See Rwezaura, chapter 7 of this work).

For the time being, one can only note that State measures do not sufficiently meet the actual needs for old-age security. People therefore tend to use both the formal and informal systems of social security simultaneously, trying to draw the most out of each.[78] It is suggested that, in the current situation, only the mobilisation, encouragement and support of informal mutual help, in addition to and in combination with the state-run system, can fill the gap which currently exists.

* I would like to express my gratitude to Professor B.A. Rwezaura Ms. Eva-Maria Hohnerlein and Professor Anne Adams for their advice and to Ms. Antje Diwisch for her efficient and patient assistance with the manuscript preparation.

Notes

1. The term Tanzania is used in this paper to include only mainland-Tanzania but not Zanzibar, which must be looked at separately.
2. Fuchs 1986: 1 f. For the development and conditions of permanent wage labour during the colonial period see Shivji 1986: 106 ff. The working class struggles, which took place between 1939 and 1950, had among their goals also the provision of old-age security for workers, Shivji 1986: 155 ff., 169 f. On the developments in Kenya during the colonial period, see Fuchs 1985: 86 ff.
3. These date from the European Officers Pensions Ordinance, Cap. 47, 1.4.1927 to the Posts and Telegraphs Amalgamated Department (Asiatic Officers' Widows' and Orphans' Pensions) Ordinance, Cap. 91, 9.6.1939.
4. Act 36/1964, Cap. 564.
5. Act 14/1978.

6. On the historical development of formal social security in Tanzania and for an overview of the existing schemes, see Bossert 1985: 101 ff. An overview of all African countries is given by Mouton 1975: 4 ff.

7. 1978 Population Census, Bureau of Statistics, Ministry of Planning and Economic Affairs, Vol. 7 "Basic Demographic and Socio-Economic Characteristics", Dar es Salaam, 1982, Table 1, p. 1.

8. Survey of Employment and Earnings, 1979-80, Bureau of Statistics, Ministry of Planning and Economic Affairs, Dar es Salaam 1983, as quoted by Mongi 1986: 4.

9. Since 55 is the normal retirement age in Tanzania, 55, and not 60 or 65, is used to determine this group of the population. See for instance Fuchs 1985: 169, who refers to the 15- to 64-year age-group in the case of Kenya.

10. Fuchs 1985: 35, who refers to an ISSA source of 1980, and Mouton 1975: 13, who, however, notes that these figures are highly approximate.

11. In the cases of some other African countries, the estimated figures show the following proportions: Kenya: 500,000 insured of a total of 11,690,000; Ghana: 500,000 insured of a total of 8,640,000; Zambia: 350,000 insured of a total of 4,150,000. Thus, while in many countries, including Tanzania and Kenya, the proportion of insured persons in relation to the economically active population appears to be below 10%, in others like Ghana and Zambia, it may be slightly or even considerably higher, which may be due, in the case of Zambia, to a higher degree of urbanisation (see Mouton 1975: 13, Tribe 1976: 185).

12. According to the 1978 Census (see above note 7), these were 86.75% of the total population in 1979. See Kludze 1986: 4 f., on the situation of the Ghanaian rural population.

13. Similar schemes exist, e.g., in Kenya: Pensions Act, Cap. 189, see Fuchs 1985: 172 ff.; and in Ghana, see Pensions Ordinance, Cap. 30.

14. Political Leaders' Pensions Act, 14/1981; Specified State Leaders' Pensions Act 2/ 1986.

15. This is different, e.g., in Zambia. While before independence, the pension scheme was non-contributory, this was changed in 1961 and the rates of contributions are 6% or 7.25% of the salary. The government as the employer pays an equal amount into the Fund (Mulozi 1983: 582).

16. For further cases see s. 22(1)(b), (c),(2) PO.

17. G.Ns. 166/63, 239/63, 100/64, 452/65, 439/65, 440/65, 80/66, 123/67, 190/68, 22/70, 124/70, 186/70.

18. Regulations for the Granting of Pensions, Gratuities and other Allowances to Officers (Pensions Regulations), Schedule to the PO Cap. 371.

19. Leave without salary is not excluded, as is the case under the Parastatal Pensions Act, see below.

20. The retirement age was reduced in 1978 from 55 to 50 years. For police officers it is 40 years, for prison officers 45 years, s. 8(a), Proviso (i), (ii), PO, as amended by Act 4/78. Kenya: 45 or 50 years, s. 6 Pensions Act, Cap. 189. Ghana: 45 years, with a final age limit of 60 years, since 1982, Public Officers (Pensions) Law, P.N.D.C.L. 23.

21. It would be interesting to find out how far married women are affected by this provision in practice.

22. I.e. the Principal Secretary of the Treasury.

23. Mbunda (1986: 12) explains the rationale behind the principle of disqualification as valid in the non-contributory pension schemes, different from most contributory

schemes.
24. The pension factor is the same in Ghana, s. 1 Pensions (Amd.) Decree 1972, N.R.C.D. 74. In Kenya, it is 1/500, see Reg. 4, 1st Sched., Pensions Act, Cap. 189. Some authors use a pension factor of 1/50 and multiply it with the annual salary and the number of years (instead of months), e.g. Mattaka 1986, Mongi 1986. The result, however, is the same.
25. This is not the case in Ghana where pensions are exempt from income tax; s. 3 Public Officers (Pensions) Law 1982, P.N.D.C.L. 23.
26. The same is the case in Kenya, s. 10 Pensions Act. In Ghana, the maximum pension was fixed more generously, in s. 1 Pensions (Amd.) Decree 1978, S.M.C.D. 166, as "the final pensionable emoluments drawn by (the officer) at the time of his retirement".
27. Act 14/78.
28. See Mongi's suggestions to provide for appointment of Trustees by each parastatal organisation to assist in the administration of the scheme (1986: 23).
29. For further forms of parastatal organisations, see s. 2(1) of the PPA.
30. Definition of this term in s. 2(1) PPA.
31. I.e. within 30 days after the end of the month to which the contributions relate, s. 8(2) PPA.
32. See ss. 38 ff. PPA.
33. See s. 44 PPA; Mattaka (1986: 5, 12) criticises the fact that withdrawal benefits do not include the employer's contributions, which are not refunded to the employer either.
34. See also Mattaka 1986: 4.
35. See also s. 32(2)-(5) PPA.
36. For an alternative mode of computation see note 16 above; this would result in a pension factor of 1/80 in this case (Mattaka 1986, Mongi 1986).
37. This is the case for the civil service, political leaders, teachers' service and defence forces, Act 15/81, Mattaka 1986: 9.
38. Actually, only benefits under the political leaders' and the specified state leaders' schemes seem to be tax-free, see Mattaka 1986: 9.
39. This solution was chose in Zambia: "All social security schemes are contributory ones, thereby confining the burden of contributions to those who are direct benefactors of the scheme instead of deriving funds from the general revenue" (Mulozi 1983: 584).
40. Act 36/64, in operation since 1st October 1964.
41. A similar system was established in 1965 in Kenya under the National Social Security Fund Act 1965, Cap. 258 of the Laws of Kenya. See Fuchs 1985: 163 ff. Provident Funds have also been set up in Nigeria (1961), Ghana (Social Security Act 1965, Act 279; Social Security Decree 1972, N.R.C.D. 127), Zambia (1965), Uganda (1967)(Mouton 1975: 9) and Swaziland (Mulozi 1983: 579).
42. Provident Fund (Government Employees) Ordinance, Cap. 51; see also the amending Act 52/65 and the Provident Fund (Government Employees) Regulations, G.N. 388/42, 453/42, 66/44, 66/45; Provident Fund (Local Authorities) Ordinance, Cap. 53.
43. Act 2/75, ss. 4 ff. Before 1975, the National Provident Fund was headed by a director under the direction of the Minister of Labour.
44. National Provident Fund (General) Regulations, G.N. 582/64.
45. For details of registration of members and contributing employers, see ss. 4 ff. of

the National Provident Fund (General) Regulations, G.N.582/64.

46. See ss. 8 and 9 of the NPFA. In addition, also clergymen may be registrable as members of the Fund under s. 10 NPFA.This is the case also in other Anglophone countries (Mouton 1975: 12).

47. In Zambia, membership of the Fund is restricted to persons 18 and above (Mulozi 1983: 580).

48. A crew member of a ship is an 'employee' in the sense of this Act only where he is permanently resident in Tanganyika and the owners of the ship have a place of business or agents in East Africa. Somebody who is employed outside of Tanganyika is an 'employee' in this sense only if he/she is permanently resident in Tanganyika and if the employer by whom he/she is paid is in Tanganyika (s. 2(1) NPFA).

49. While Zambia's Provident Fund Scheme had originally excluded domestic household workers, these are covered by the Fund since an amendment of 1973, (Mulozi 1983: 581).

50. Mouton (1975: 11), reports that in Uganda workers earning less than a certain amount are excluded from the Provident Fund.

51. For details see the 2nd Schedule of the NPFA. But see also s. 47 NPFA.

52. Continuity is given, for the purposes of this definition, even if there is an interruption of up to 14 working days during a period of three months.

53. This author is not aware of the existence of any such order.

54. G.N. 566/64.

55. The same number is reported by Mouton (1975: 11), with regard to Nigeria.

56. Bossert 1985: 110 f. In Kenya, since 1975 compulsory membership no longer depends on a minimum number of employees, see Fuchs 1985: 163. The same is the case in Zambia since 1968, while before, membership was restricted to enterprises with five or more employees (Mulozi 1983: 580). Ghana requires five or more employees; see s. 23 (1) Social Security Decree 1972.

57. Which is to be made by the employer.

58. A special provision exists providing for voluntary membership of clergymen, see s. 10 NPFA. In Ghana, the law contains similar provisions on voluntary membership. Moreover, it provides for the voluntary insurance of non-wage employees, s. 25 Social Security Decree 1972. Mouton notes that no use appears to be made of the latter provision (1975: 12).

59. For this and other deductions from employees' wages see also s. 64(1)(i) of the Employment Ordinance and Shivji 1986: 122 f. In Ghana, the contribution is 12.5% of the employee's salary; 5% is deducted from the salary and 7.5% is contributed by the employer, s. 27 Social Security Decree 1972.

60. For further details see s. 16(2), (3) NPFA.

61. See Fuchs 1985: 165, with respect to Kenya.

62. This author is not sure, however, whether this provision has already come into operation, see s. 17(1) NPFA.

63. There are similar provisions for the government provident funds mentioned above. Similar provisions exist also in Ghana; but there is an additional "protection" of the employer: loans and advances granted by him to the employee may be recovered in full from the total benefit payable to the employee, s. 37 Social Security Decree 1972.

64. In the case of survivors' benefits, estate duty, if due, may be deducted before payment.

65. This principle usually does not apply for contributory schemes. But it applies in the case of the Parastatal Pension Fund, see above and Mbunda 1986: 8.
66. Also in Zambia, part of the contributions can be converted into an annuity, (Mulozi 1983: 581).
67. For the qualifying age in some other countries, see Mouton 1975: 25. Ghana: 50 or 55 for men, 45 or 50 for women, s. 45 Social Security Decree 1972.
68. Exceptions may be sanctioned by the Minister. See also s. 25(2) NPFA if claims under the Workmen's Compensation Ordinance arise.
69. For further details, see s. 24 NFPA.
70. At the present exchange rate this is less than DM 0.10 per working day.
71. Act 33/73. For details of the tax rates, see s. 8(4) ITA in the case of residents; s. 34(1)(f), para 5 (f) of the 3^d Sched. of the ITA for non-residents; Luoga 1986: 4 ff.
72. For two other minor exceptions see Luoga 1986: 5.
73. The employers' contributions, however, are, within certain limits, deductable expenses for the purposes of taxation, ss. 16(2)(n), (o), 17(1)(d), (e), 25 ITA.
74. I.e. those whose employers do not run such schemes, or who are not covered by their employers' schemes.
75. In Ghana, old age benefits are generally exempt from tax, s. 38 (1) Social Security Decree 1972, s. 3 Public Officers (Pensions) Law 1982.
76. *Sunday News*, Dar es Salaam, 15.12.85, annex to the paper presented by A. Bakari at the Symposium on Formal and Informal Social Security, Tutzing, FRG, 2nd-6th June, 1988.
77. See for instance the papers presented at the Symposium on Formal and Informal Social Security at Tutzing, FRG, 2nd-6th June, 1986 (von Benda-Beckmann et al. (eds.) 1988.
78. See Bossert 1985.

Bibliography

BAKARI, A.H., 1986
 'The Law of Provident Fund Schemes,' Paper, presented at the Seminar on the Law Relating to Pensions and Other Retirement Benefits (Social Security Laws), Department of Economic Law, Faculty of Law, University of Dar es Salaam, 15th-19th September 1986.
BENDA-BECKMANN, F. von, et al. (eds.), 1988
 Between Kinship and the State: Social Security Law in the   Developing Countries, Dordrecht, Foris.
BOSSERT, A., 1986
 'Formal and Informal Social Security — A Case Study of Tanzania,' Paper, presented at the Symposium on Formal and Informal Social Security, Commission on Folk Law and Legal Pluralism and Max-Planck-Institute of Foreign and International Security Law, Tutzing, 2nd-6th June 1986.
—, 1985
 Traditionelle und moderne Formen sozialer Sicherung in Tansania. Eine Untersuchung ihrer Entwicklungsbedingungen. Berlin, Duncker & Humblot.
FUCHS, M., 1986
 'Formal Social Security in Third World Countries: History, Legal Framework and

Reform Perspectives; Paper, presented at the Symposium on Formal and Informal Social Security, Commission on Folk Law and Legal Pluralism and Max-Planck-Institute of Foreign and International Social Security Law, Tutzing, 2nd-6th June 1986.
—, 1985
Soziale Sicherheit in der Dritten Welt — Zugleich eine Fallstudie Kenia. Baden-Baden, Nomos.
KLUDZE, A.K.P., 1986
'Formal and Informal Social Security in Ghana'; Paper, presented at the Symposium on Formal and Informal Social Security, Commission on Folk Law and Legal Pluralism and Max-Planck-Institute of Foreign and International Social Security Law, Tutzing, 2nd-6th June 1986.
LUOGA, F.D.A.M., 1986
'The Taxation of Retirement Benefits under the Income Tax Laws of Tanzania'; Paper, presented at the Seminar on the Law Relating to Pensions and Other Retirement Benefits (Social Security Laws), Department of Economic Law, Faculty of Law, University of Dar es Salaam, 15th-19th September 1986.
MATTAKA, D., 1986
'Parastatal Pension Scheme: Salient Features and Issues at Stake'; Paper, presented at the Seminar on the Law Relating to Pensions and Other Retirement Benefits (Social Security Laws), Department of Economic Law, Faculty of Law, University of Dar es Salaam, 15th-19th September 1986.
MBUNDA, L.X.C. 1986
'Principles Relating to Social Security Schemes in Tanzania', Paper, presented at the Seminar on the Law Relating to Pensions and Other Retirement Benefits (Social Security Laws), Department of Economic Law, Faculty of Law, University of Dar es Salaam, 15th-19th September 1986.
MONGI, R., 1986
'Theoretical and Practical Aspects of Group Pension and Assurance Schemes; Paper, presented at the Seminar on the Law Relating to Pensions and Other Retirement Benefits (Social Security Laws), Department of Economic Law, Faculty of Law, University of Dar es Salaam, 15th-19th September 1986.
MOUTON, P, 1975
Social Security in Africa. Trends, Problems and Perspectives. Geneva, International Labour Office.
MULOZI, S.L., 1983
'The Role of Social Insurance in Developing Countries. An Example from Africa (Zambia)', in: P.A. Köhler/H.F. Zacher (eds.), *Beiträge zu Geschichte und aktueller Situation der Sozialversicherung*. Berlin, Duncker & Humblot, 579-585.
SHIVJI, I.G., 1986
Law, State and the Working Class in Tanzania, c. 1920-1964. London: James Currey, Portsmouth: Heinemann, Dar es Salaam: Tanzania Publishing House.
TRIBE, M.A., 1976
'The Household Economy and Social Security Policy. With Particular Reference to Africa South of the Sahara', *International Journal of Social Economics* 3, 179-197.
WAMALI, M.K.B., 1986
'The Principles, Policies and Interpretation of Social Security Legislation'; Paper, presented at the Seminar on the Law Relating to Pensions and Other Retirement Benefits (Social Security Laws), Department of Economic Law, Faculty of Law, University of Dar es Salaam, 15th-19th September 1986.